ENCYCLOPEDIA OF APPLIED ETHICS

VOLUME 1

A–D

ENCYCLOPEDIA OF APPLIED ETHICS

VOLUME 1

A–D

ACADEMIC PRESS

SAN DIEGO　LONDON　BOSTON　NEW YORK　SYDNEY　TOKYO　TORONTO

Academic Press
a division of Harcourt Brace & Company
525 B Street, Suite 1900, San Diego, California 92101-4495, USA
http://www.apnet.com

Academic Press Limited
24-28 Oval Road, London NW1 7DX, UK
http://www.hbuk.co.uk/ap/

Library of Congress Card Catalog Number: 97-074395

International Standard Book Number: 0-12-227065-7 (set)
International Standard Book Number: 0-12-227066-5 (v. 1)
International Standard Book Number: 0-12-227067-3 (v. 2)
International Standard Book Number: 0-12-227068-1 (v. 3)
International Standard Book Number: 0-12-227069-X (v. 4)

PRINTED IN THE UNITED STATES OF AMERICA
98 99 00 01 02 03 MM 9 8 7 6 5 4 3 2

CONTENTS

CONTENTS OF OTHER VOLUMES

CONTENTS OF VOLUME 3

CONTENTS OF VOLUME 4

CONTENTS BY SUBJECT AREA

THEORIES OF ETHICS

APPLIED ETHICS, CHALLENGES TO

APPLIED ETHICS, OVERVIEW

ARISTOTELIAN ETHICS

AUTONOMY

BUDDHISM

CASUISTRY

CHRISTIAN ETHICS, PROTESTANT

CHRISTIAN ETHICS, ROMAN CATHOLIC

CODES OF ETHICS

CONFUCIANISM

CONSEQUENTIALISM AND DEONTOLOGY

CONTRACTARIAN ETHICS

DISCOURSE ETHICS

DISTRIBUTIVE JUSTICE, THEORIES OF

EGOISM AND ALTRUISM

EPICUREANISM

EVOLUTIONARY PERSPECTIVES ON ETHICS

EXISTENTIALISM

FEMINIST ETHICS

FREUDIANISM

GREEK ETHICS, OVERVIEW

HEDONISM

HINDUISM

HUMAN NATURE, VIEWS OF

HUMANISM

ISLAM

JUDAISM

KANTIANISM

MARX AND ETHICS

NATIVE AMERICAN CULTURES

PACIFISM

PERFECTIONISM

PLATONISM

RELIGION AND ETHICS

RIGHTS THEORY

SIKHISM

STOICISM

TAOISM

THEORIES OF ETHICS, OVERVIEW

THEORIES OF JUSTICE: HUMAN NEEDS

THEORIES OF JUSTICE: RAWLS

THOMISM

UTILITARIANISM

VIRTUE ETHICS

ETHICAL CONCEPTS

DISCRIMINATION, CONCEPT OF

GAME THEORY

LIFE, CONCEPT OF

MERCY AND FORGIVENESS

MORAL DEVELOPMENT

MORAL RELATIVISM

NATURE VERSUS NURTURE

PAINISM

PATERNALISM

LEGAL ETHICS

ETHICS IN EDUCATION

ETHICS AND POLITICS

CONTRIBUTORS

G. JOHN M. ABBARNO
HOMELESSNESS
    D'Youville College
    Buffalo, New York

FRANCIS J. AGUILAR
CORPORATIONS, ETHICS IN
    Harvard University
    Cambridge, Massachusetts

WILLIAM AIKEN
CHILDREN'S RIGHTS
    Chatham College
    Chatham, New York

TIMO AIRAKSINEN
PROFESSIONAL ETHICS
    University of Helsinki
    Helsinki, Finland

LARRY ALEXANDER
FREEDOM OF SPEECH
    University of San Diego
    San Diego, California

ANDREW ALEXANDRA
EXECUTIVE COMPENSATION
    Charles Sturt University
    Bathurst, New South Wales, Australia

GARLAND E. ALLEN
GENETICS AND BEHAVIOR
NATURE VERSUS NURTURE
    Washington University
    St. Louis, Missouri

JONATHAN ALDRED
WILDLIFE CONSERVATION
    Cambridge University
    Cambridge, England, UK

DAVID ARCHARD
CHILD ABUSE
    University of St. Andrews
    Fife, Scotland, UK

MARY BETH ARMSTRONG
CONFIDENTIALITY, GENERAL ISSUES OF
    California Polytechnic Institute
    San Luis Obispo, California

RICHARD J. ARNESON
EQUALITY AND EGALITARIANISM
    University of California, San Diego
    San Diego, California

ROBERT L. ARRINGTON
ADVERTISING
    Georgia State University
    Atlanta, Georgia

RICHARD ASHCROFT
HUMAN RESEARCH SUBJECTS, SELECTION OF
    University of Bristol
    Bristol, England, UK

SUE ASHFORD
TERRORISM
    University of Western Australia and Murdoch
    University
    Medina, Western Australia

ROBIN ATTFIELD
ENVIRONMENTAL ETHICS, OVERVIEW
    University of Wales, Cardiff
    Cardiff, Wales, UK

ROBERT D. BAIRD
HINDUISM
    School of Religion, University of Iowa
    Iowa City, Iowa

DOUGLAS BAKER
LAND USE ISSUES
    University of Northern British Columbia
    Prince George, British Columbia

NORMAN BARRY
WELFARE POLICIES
    University of Buckingham
    Buckingham, England, UK

BERNARD BAUMRIN
DIVORCE
City University of New York
New York, New York

JOHN D. BECKER
NATIONAL SECURITY ISSUES
WARFARE, STRATEGIES AND TACTICS
United States Air Force Academy
Colorado Springs, Colorado

HUGO ADAM BEDAU
CAPITAL PUNISHMENT
CIVIL DISOBEDIENCE
Tufts University
Medford, Massachusetts

RON L. P. BERGHMANS
COERCIVE TREATMENT IN PSYCHIATRY
Institute for Bioethics
Maastricht, The Netherlands

ROBERT H. BLANK
FETAL RESEARCH
University of Canterbury
Canterbury, England, UK

PAULA BODDINGTON
SELF-DECEPTION
Australian National University
Canberra, Australia

ANNIE BOOTH
LAND USE ISSUES
University of Northern British Columbia
Prince George, British Columbia

STEPHEN St. C. BOSTOCK
ZOOS AND ZOOLOGICAL PARKS
Glasgow Zoo and University of Glasgow
Glasgow, Scotland, UK

ANDREW BRENNAN
GAIA HYPOTHESIS
The University of Western Australia
Nedlands, Western Australia

ANDREW BRIEN
JURY CONDUCT
MERCY AND FORGIVENESS
Australian National University
Canberra, Australia

ROGER L. BURRITT
ENVIRONMENTAL COMPLIANCE BY INDUSTRY
Australian National University
Canberra, Australia

EDMUND F. BYRNE
PRIVACY
Indiana University
Indianapolis, Indiana

JOAN C. CALLAHAN
BIRTH-CONTROL ETHICS
University of Kentucky
Lexington, Kentucky

EAMONN CALLAN
PLURALISM IN EDUCATION
University of Alberta
Edmonton, Alberta

ARTHUR L. CAPLAN
INFORMED CONSENT
University of Pennsylvania
Philadelphia, Pennsylvania

ALEXANDER MORGAN CAPRON
DEATH, DEFINITION OF
University of Southern California
Los Angeles, California

ALAN CARLING
EXPLOITATION
University of Bradford
Bradford, England, UK

STANLEY R. CARPENTER
SUSTAINABILITY
Georgia Institute of Technology
Atlanta, Georgia

RUTH CHADWICK
GENETIC SCREENING
ORGAN TRANSPLANTS AND DONORS
Centre for Professional Ethics
University of Central Lancashire
Preston, England, UK

TIMOTHY CHAPPELL
PLATONISM
THEORIES OF ETHICS, OVERVIEW
University of Manchester
Manchester, England, UK

VICHAI CHOKEVIVAT
AIDS IN THE DEVELOPING WORLD
Thai Department of Health and Human Welfare

JOHN CHRISTMAN
PROPERTY RIGHTS
Virginia Polytechnic Institute and State University
Blacksburg, Virginia

JOHN P. CLARK
POLITICAL ECOLOGY
Loyola University
New Orleans, Louisiana

ANGUS CLARKE
GENETIC COUNSELING
University of Wales College of Medicine
Cardiff, Wales, UK

MARGARET COFFEY
BROADCAST JOURNALISM
Australian Broadcasting Corporation
Malvern, Australia

DAVID CONWAY
LIBERALISM
Middlesex University
London, England, UK

LINDSEY COOMBES
MENTAL HEALTH
  Oxford Brookes University
  Oxford, England, UK

WILLIAM COONEY
RIGHTS THEORY
  Briar Cliff College
  Sioux City, Iowa

PRESTON K. COVEY
GUN CONTROL
  Center for the Advancement of Applied Ethics
  Carnegie Mellon University
  Pittsburgh, Pennsylvania

CHRISTOPHER J. COWTON
SOCIALLY RESPONSIBLE INVESTMENT
  University of Huddersfield
  Queensgate, Huddersfield, England, UK

CHARLES CRITCHER
MEDIA DEPICTION OF ETHNIC MINORITIES
  Sheffield Hallam University
  Sheffield, England, UK

THOMAS CLOUGH DAFFERN
NATIVE AMERICAN CULTURES
  University of London
  London, England, UK

TIM DARE
APPLIED ETHICS, CHALLENGES TO
  The University of Auckland
  Auckland, New Zealand

MICHAEL DAVIS
CONFLICT OF INTEREST
  Illinois Institute of Technology
  Chicago, Illinois

ANGUS DAWSON
PSYCHOPHARMACOLOGY
  University of Liverpool
  Liverpool, England, UK

JUDITH WAGNER DECEW
WARFARE, CODES OF
  Clark University
  West Newton, Massachusetts

C. A. DEFANTI
BRAIN DEATH
  United Hospitals of Bergamo
  Bergamo, Italy

CARLOS DEL RIO
AIDS IN THE DEVELOPING WORLD
  Emory University

PHILIP E. DEVINE
HOMICIDE, CRIMINAL VERSUS JUSTIFIABLE
PUBLISH-OR-PERISH SYNDROME
  Providence College
  Providence, Rhode Island

BERNARD DICKENS
PATIENTS' RIGHTS
  University of Toronto Law School
  Toronto, Ontario

SUSAN DIMOCK
CRIME AND SOCIETY
JUVENILE CRIME
  York University
  North York, Ontario

SUSAN DODDS
SEX EQUALITY
  University of Wollongong
  Wollongong, Australia

STRACHAN DONNELLEY
HUMAN NATURE, VIEWS OF
  The Hastings Center
  Briarcliff Manor, New York

JUDE P. DOUGHERTY
THOMISM
  Catholic University of America
  Washington, DC

NIGEL DOWER
DEVELOPMENT ETHICS
DEVELOPMENT ISSUES, ENVIRONMENTAL
WORLD ETHICS
  University of Aberdeen
  Aberdeen, Scotland, UK

HEATHER DRAPER
EUTHANASIA
  University of Birmingham
  Birmingham, England, UK

DENIS DUTTON
PLAGIARISM AND FORGERY
  University of Canterbury
  Christchurch, New Zealand

SUSAN EASTON
PORNOGRAPHY
  Brunel University
  Uxbridge, England, UK

ANDREW EDGAR
QUALITY OF LIFE INDICATORS
SPORTS, ETHICS OF
  University of Wales
  Cardiff, Wales, UK

BENGT ERIK ERIKSSON
PREVENTIVE MEDICINE
  University of Linköping
  Linköping, Sweden

GAVIN FAIRBAIRN
SUICIDE
  North East Wales Institute of Higher Education
  Wrexham, Wales, UK

JOHN FENDER
ALTRUISM AND ECONOMICS
University of Birmingham
Birmingham, England, UK

DAVID E. W. FENNER
ARTS, THE
University of North Florida
Jacksonville, Florida

J. CARL FICARROTTA
MORAL RELATIVISM
United States Air Force Academy
Colorado Springs, Colorado

BETH A. FISCHER
SCIENTIFIC PUBLISHING
University of Pittsburgh
Pittsburgh, Pennsylvania

ANTHONY FISHER
CHRISTIAN ETHICS, ROMAN CATHOLIC
Australian Catholic University
Ascot Vale, Australia

CHARLES J. FOMBRUN
REPUTATION MANAGEMENT BY CORPORATIONS
New York University
New York, New York

NORMAN FORD
FETUS
Caroline Chisholm Centre for Health Ethics
East Melbourne, Australia

CLAIRE FOSTER
RESEARCH ETHICS COMMITTEES
King's College
London, England, UK

LESLIE PICKERING FRANCIS
RAPE
University of Utah
Salt Lake City, Utah

LUCY FRITH
REPRODUCTIVE TECHNOLOGIES
University of Liverpool and University of Oxford
England, UK

K. W. M. FULFORD
MENTAL ILLNESS, CONCEPT OF
University of Warwick
Coventry, England, UK

SUSANNE GIBSON
ABORTION
ACTS AND OMISSIONS
University College of St. Martin
Lancaster, England, UK

CHRISTOPHER GILL
GREEK ETHICS, OVERVIEW
University of Exeter
Exeter, England, UK

RAANAN GILLON
BIOETHICS, OVERVIEW
Imperial College
London University
London, England, UK

ANDREW GILMAN
PERSONAL RELATIONSHIPS
Andover Newton Theological School
Stratham, New Hampshire

DONALD A. GRAFT
SPECIESISM
Software Engineer Manager
Pondicherry, India

WILLIAM GREY
PLAYING GOD
University of Queensland
Queensland, Australia

MATTHEW W. HALLGARTH
CONSEQUENTIALISM AND DEONTOLOGY
United States Air Force Academy
Colorado Springs, Colorado

JOCELYN Y. HATTAB
PSYCHIATRIC ETHICS
Eitanim Mental Health Center
Hebrew University
Jerusalem, Israel

HETA HÄYRY
GENETIC ENGINEERING
PATERNALISM
University of Helsinki
Helsinki, Finland

MATTI HÄYRY
GENETIC ENGINEERING
University of Helsinki
Helsinki, Finland

TIM HAYWARD
ANTHROPOCENTRISM
University of Edinburgh
Edinburgh, Scotland, UK

ADAM M. HEDGECOE
GENE THERAPY
GENOME ANALYSIS
Centre for Professional Ethics
University of Central Lancashire
Preston, England, UK

ERIC HEINZE
VICTIMLESS CRIMES
University of London
London, England, UK

SIRKKU HELLSTEN
DISTRIBUTIVE JUSTICE, THEORIES OF
University of Helsinki
Helsinki, Finland

ALAN HOLLAND
ECOLOGICAL BALANCE
    Lancaster University
    Lancaster, England, UK

SØREN HOLM
AUTONOMY
EMBRYOLOGY, ETHICS OF
    University of Copenhagen
    Copenhagen, Denmark

TERRY HOPTON
POLITICAL OBLIGATION
    University of Central Lancashire
    Preston, England, UK

J. STUART HORNER
MEDICAL ETHICS, HISTORY OF
    University of Central Lancashire
    Preston, England, UK

GILLIAN HOWIE
GENDER ROLES
    University of Liverpool
    Liverpool, England, UK

RICHARD HUGMAN
ETHICS AND SOCIAL SERVICES, OVERVIEW
    Curtin University of Technology
    Perth, Australia

GEOFFREY HUNT
WHISTLE-BLOWING
    European Centre for Professional Ethics
    University of London
    London, England, UK

DOUGLAS N. HUSAK
DRUGS: MORAL AND LEGAL ISSUES
    Rutgers University
    New Brunswick, New Jersey

JENNIFER JACKSON
BUSINESS ETHICS, OVERVIEW
    University of Leeds
    Leeds, England, UK

MARJA JÄRVELÄ
ENVIRONMENTAL IMPACT ASSESSMENT
    The University of Jyväskylä
    Jyväskylä, Finland

MARGOT JEFFREYS
AGED PEOPLE, SOCIETAL ATTITUDES TOWARD
    Centre of Medical Law and Ethics
    King's College
    London, England, UK

MARIANNE M. JENNINGS
ELECTION STRATEGIES
    Arizona State University
    Tempe, Arizona

EDWARD JOHNSON
INTELLIGENCE TESTING
MEDIA OWNERSHIP
POLITICAL CORRECTNESS
    University of New Orleans
    New Orleans, Louisiana

JEFFERY L. JOHNSON
NUCLEAR DETERRENCE
    Eastern Oregon State College
    LaGrande, Oregon

PAULINE JOHNSON
SEXISM
    Macquarie University
    Sydney, Australia

TREVOR JONES
POLICE AND RACE RELATIONS
    Policy Studies Institute
    London, England, UK

RABINDRA N. KANUNGO
LEADERSHIP, ETHICS OF
    McGill University
    Montreal, Quebec

HELMUT F. KAPLAN
VEGETARIANISM
    University of Salzburg
    Salzburg, Austria

PAUL KELLY
CONTRACTARIAN ETHICS
    London School of Economics
    London, England, UK

DAMIEN KEOWN
BUDDHISM
    Goldsmiths College, University of London
    London, England, UK

JACINTA KERIN
SEXUAL ORIENTATION
    Monash University
    Toronto, Ontario

EDWARD W. KEYSERLINGK
MEDICAL CODES AND OATHS
    McGill University
    Montreal, Quebec

JUKKA KILPI
MERGERS AND ACQUISITIONS
    University of Helsinki
    Helsinki, Finland and Monash University
    Clayton, Victoria, Australia

DAHLIAN KIRBY
TRANSSEXUALISM
    University of Wales
    Cardiff, Wales, UK

STEPHEN KLAIDMAN
FREEDOM OF THE PRESS IN THE USA
Georgetown University
Washington, DC

JAMES W. KNIGHT
BIRTH-CONTROL TECHNOLOGY
Virginia Polytechnic Institute and State University
Blacksburg, Virginia

LORETTA M. KOPELMAN
FEMALE CIRCUMCISION AND GENITAL MUTILATION
MEDICAL FUTILITY
East Carolina University School of Medicine
Greenville, North Carolina

MARK KUCZEWSKI
CASUISTRY
Medical College of Wisconsin
Madison, Wisconsin

PAUL ALFRED KURZMAN
WORKPLACE ETHICS: ISSUES FOR HUMAN SERVICE
PROFESSIONALS
Hunter College, City University of New York
New York, New York

KRISTIINA KUVAJA-PUUMALAINEN
ENVIRONMENTAL IMPACT ASSESSMENT
Jyvaskyla University
Jyvaskyla, Finland

WILL KYMLICKA
ETHNOCULTURAL MINORITY GROUPS, STATUS AND TREATMENT OF
University of Ottawa
Ottawa, Ontario

OLLI LAGERSPETZ
TRUST
Abo Academy
Abo, Finland
and The University of Wales at Swansea

DAVID LAMB
DEATH, MEDICAL ASPECTS OF
University of Birmingham
Birmingham, England, UK

HAROLD Q. LANGENDERFER
ACCOUNTING AND BUSINESS ETHICS
University of North Carolina
Chapel Hill, North Carolina

DUNCAN LANGFORD
INTERNET PROTOCOL
University of Kent
Canterbury, England, UK

ROBERT LARMER
IMPROPER PAYMENTS AND GIFTS
University of New Brunswick
Fredericton, New Brunswick

OLIVER LEAMAN
JUDAISM
Liverpool John Moores University
Liverpool, England, UK

GRANT S. LEE
TAOISM
Colorado State University
Fort Collins, Colorado

KEEKOK LEE
BIODIVERSITY
The University of Manchester
Manchester, England, UK

STEVEN LEE
NUCLEAR TESTING
Hobart and William Smith Colleges
Geneva, New York

BURTON M. LEISER
CORPORAL PUNISHMENT
SLAVERY
Pace University
Briarcliff Manor, New York

A. CARL LEOPOLD
STEWARDSHIP
Boyce Thompson Institute for Plant Research
Cornell University
Ithaca, New York

HARRY LESSER
AGEISM
University of Manchester
Manchester, England, UK

CAROL LEVINE
CUSTODY OF CHILDREN
The Orphan Project
New York, New York

MAIRI LEVITT
RELIGION IN SCHOOLS
University of Central Lancashire
Preston, England, UK

XIAORONG LI
WOMEN'S RIGHTS
University of Maryland
College Park, Maryland

JUDITH LICHTENBERG
OBJECTIVITY IN REPORTING
University of Maryland
College Park, Maryland

C. DAVID LISMAN
ETHICS EDUCATION IN SCHOOLS
Community College of Aurora
Aurora, Colorado

ANDROS LOIZOU
THEORIES OF JUSTICE: RAWLS
University of Central Lancashire
Preston, England, UK

VALERIE C. LORENZ
GAMBLING
  Compulsive Gambling Center, Inc.
  Baltimore, Maryland

ROBERT B. LOUDEN
VIRTUE ETHICS
  Westfalische WIlhelms-Universitat
  Munster, Germany

JOHN LYDEN
CHRISTIAN ETHICS, PROTESTANT
  Dana College
  Omaha, Nebraska

CHRIS MACDONALD
EVOLUTIONARY PERSPECTIVES ON ETHICS
  University of British Columbia
  Vancouver, British Columbia

CARLOS MAGIS
AIDS IN THE DEVELOPING WORLD
  Conasida, Mexico

THOMAS MAGNELL
EPICUREANISM
  Drew University
  Madison, New Jersey

RUDOLPH J. MARCUS
GOVERNMENT FUNDING OF RESEARCH
  Ethics Consultant
  Sonoma, California

IAN MARKHAM
RELIGION AND ETHICS
  Liverpool Hope University College
  Liverpool, England, UK

GARY T. MARX
ELECTRONIC SURVEILLANCE
UNDERCOVER INVESTIGATIONS, ETHICS OF
  Center for Advanced Study in the Behavioral
  Sciences
  Stanford, California

RICHARD O. MASON
GENETIC RESEARCH
INFORMATION MANAGEMENT
  Southern Methodist University
  Dallas, Texas

TODD MAY
POSTSTRUCTURALISM
  Clemson University
  Clemson, South Carolina

MARY ANN MCCLURE
INFERTILITY
  John Jay College of Criminal Justice
  New York, New York

PATRICIA E. MCCREIGHT
ENVIRONMENTAL COMPLIANCE BY INDUSTRY
  Australian National University
  Canberra, Australia

TONY MCGLEENAN
GENETIC TECHNOLOGY, LEGAL REGULATION OF
  The Queen's University of Belfast
  Belfast, Northern Ireland, UK

C. B. MEGONE
ARISTOTELIAN ETHICS
  University of Leeds
  Leeds, England, UK

GREGORY MELLEMA
COLLECTIVE GUILT
  Calvin College
  Grand Rapids, Michigan

MANUEL MENDONCA
LEADERSHIP, ETHICS OF
  McGill University
  Montreal, Quebec

MICHAEL A. MENLOWE
SAFETY LAWS
  University of Edinburgh
  Edinburgh, Scotland, UK

BEN MEPHAM
AGRICULTURAL ETHICS
  University of Nottingham
  Loughborough, England, UK

SEUMAS MILLER
TABLOID JOURNALISM
  Charles Sturt University
  Wagga Wagga, Australia

JEAN-NOËL MISSA
PSYCHOSURGERY AND PHYSICAL BRAIN MANIPULATION
  Free University of Brussels
  Brussels, Belgium

DARRELL MOELLENDORF
IMPERIALISM
  University of Witwatersrand
  Johannesburg, South Africa

PETER MOIZER
AUDITING PRACTICES
  University of Leeds
  Leeds, England, UK

DAVID WENDELL MOLLER
DEATH, SOCIETAL ATTITUDES TOWARD
  Indiana University
  Indianapolis, Indiana

J. DONALD MOON
COMMUNITARIANISM
  Wesleyan University
  Middletown, Connecticut

EMILIO MORDINI
SUGGESTION, ETHICS OF
  Psychoanalytic Institute for Social Research
  Rome, Italy

JONATHAN D. MORENO
INFORMED CONSENT
  SUNY Health Science Center at Brooklyn
  Brooklyn, New York

MAURIZIO MORI
LIFE, CONCEPT OF
  Center for Research in Politics and Ethics
  Milan, Italy

STEPHEN J. MORSE
INSANITY, LEGAL CONCEPT OF
  University of Pennsylvania Law School
  Philadelphia, Pennsylvania

PETER MUNZ
DARWINISM
  Victoria University of Wellington
  Wellington, New Zealand

TIMOTHY F. MURPHY
AIDS
  University of Illinois College of Medicine
  Chicago, Illinois

CHARLES R. MYERS
MILITARY CODES OF BEHAVIOR
  United States Air Force Academy
  Colorado Springs, Colorado

JAN NARVESON
CONSUMER RIGHTS
EGOISM AND ALTRUISM
STOICISM
  University of Waterloo
  Waterloo, Ontario

DEMETRIO NERI
EUGENICS
  University of Messina
  Messina, Italy

NINA NIKKU
PREVENTIVE MEDICINE
  University of Linköping
  Linköping, Sweden

RICHARD NORMAN
PACIFISM
  University of Kent
  Canterbury, England, UK

DAVID NOVITZ
LITERATURE AND ETHICS
  University of Canterbury, New Zealand
  Christchurch, New Zealand

KATHERINE O'DONOVAN
FEMINIST JURISPRUDENCE
  Queen Mary's Westfield College
  University of London
  London, England, UK

JOHN O'NEILL
TRUTH TELLING AS CONSTITUTIVE OF JOURNALISM
  Lancaster University
  Lancaster, England, UK

GERALD M. OPPENHEIMER
HEALTH CARE FINANCING
  Brooklyn College, City University of New York
  Brooklyn, New York

WILLIAM OUTHWAITE
DISCOURSE ETHICS
  University of Sussex
  Sussex, England, UK

GUILLERMO OWEN
GAME THEORY
  Naval Postgraduate School
  Monterey, California

ROBERT A. PADGUG
HEALTH CARE FINANCING
  Brooklyn College, City University of New York
  Brooklyn, New York

GABRIEL PALMER-FERNÁNDEZ
CIVILIAN POPULATIONS IN WAR, TARGETING OF
  Youngstown State University
  Youngstown, Ohio

MARK PARASCANDOLA
ANIMAL RESEARCH
  Smithsonian Fellow
  Washington, D.C.

JENNETH PARKER
PRECAUTIONARY PRINCIPLE
  Lecturer
  Hastings, England, UK

MICHAEL PARKER
MORAL DEVELOPMENT
  The Open University
  Milton Keynes, England, UK

ELLEN FRANKEL PAUL
AFFIRMATIVE ACTION
SEXUAL HARASSMENT
  Bowling Green State University
  Bowling Green, Ohio

MICHEL PETHERAM
CONFIDENTIALITY OF SOURCES
  The Open University
  Milton Keynes, England, UK

JON PIKE
STRIKES
  Glasgow University
  Glasgow, Scotland, UK

EVELYN PLUHAR
ANIMAL RIGHTS
  The Pennsylvania State University, Fayette Campus
  Uniontown, Pennsylvania

GAYNOR POLLARD
RELIGION IN SCHOOLS
   University College Chester
   Chester, England, UK

NELSON POTTER
KANTIANISM
   University of Nebraska-Lincoln
   Lincoln, Nebraska

IGOR PRIMORATZ
PROSTITUTION
   Hebrew University
   Jerusalem, Israel

JANE PRITCHARD
CODES OF ETHICS
   Centre for Professional Ethics
   University of Central Lancashire
   Preston, England, UK

ROBERT PROSSER
TOURISM
   University of Birmingham
   Birmingham, England, UK

LAURA M. PURDY
CHILDREN'S RIGHTS
   Wells College
   Aurora, New York

K. ANNE PYBURN
ARCHAEOLOGICAL ETHICS
   Indiana University
   Indianapolis, Indiana

MAUREEN RAMSAY
MACHIAVELLIANISM
   University of Leeds
   Leeds, England, UK

DOUGLAS B. RASMUSSEN
PERFECTIONISM
   St. John's University
   Jamaica, Queens, New York

KATE RAWLES
BIOCENTRISM
   Lancaster University
   Lancaster, England, UK

RUPERT READ
COURTROOM PROCEEDINGS, REPORTING OF
   University of Manchester
   Manchester, England, UK

FREDERIC G. REAMER
SOCIAL WORK
   Rhode Island College
   Providence, Rhode Island

MICHAEL REISS
BIOTECHNOLOGY
   Homerton College, Cambridge
   Cambridge, England, UK

TONY RILEY
HOMOSEXUALITY, SOCIETAL ATTITUDES TOWARD
   Yale University School of Medicine
   New Haven, Connecticut

SIMON ROGERSON
COMPUTER AND INFORMATION ETHICS
   De Montfort University
   Leicester, England, UK

BERNARD E. ROLLIN
VETERINARY ETHICS
   Colorado State University
   Fort Collins, Colorado

RICHARD D. RYDER
PAINISM
   Tulane University
   New Orleans, Louisiana

MARK SAGOFF
ENVIRONMENTAL ECONOMICS
   University of Maryland
   College Park, Maryland

HANS-MARTIN SASS
ADVANCE DIRECTIVES
   Kennedy Institute of Ethics
   Georgetown University
   Washington, DC

GEOFFREY SCARRE
UTILITARIANISM
   University of Durham
   Durham, England, UK

UDO SCHÜKLENK
AIDS IN THE DEVELOPING WORLD
HOMOSEXUALITY, SOCIETAL ATTITUDES TOWARD
ORGAN TRANSPLANTS AND DONORS
SEXUAL ORIENTATION
   Centre for Professional Ethics
   University of Central Lancashire
   Preston, England, UK

ADINA SCHWARTZ
PUBLIC DEFENDERS
   John Jay College of Criminal Justice
   City University of New York
   New York, New York

ANNE SELLER
PACIFISM
   University of Kent
   Canterbury, England, UK

JOHN J. SHEPHERD
ISLAM
   University College of St. Martin
   Lancaster, England, UK

RUBEN SHER
AIDS TREATMENT AND BIOETHICS IN SOUTH AFRICA
   National AIDS Training and Outreach Program
   Johannesburg, South Africa

DARREN SHICKLE
PRIVACY VERSUS PUBLIC RIGHT TO KNOW
RESOURCE ALLOCATION
University of Sheffield
Sheffield, England, UK

KRISTIN SHRADER-FRECHETTE
HAZARDOUS AND TOXIC SUBSTANCES
NUCLEAR POWER
University of South Florida
Tampa, Florida

DEBORAH H. SIEGEL
ADOPTION
School of Social Work
Rhode Island College
Providence, Rhode Island

ANITA SILVERS
DISABILITY RIGHTS
San Francisco State University
San Francisco, California

NIKKY-GUNINDER KAUR SINGH
SIKHISM
Colby College
Waterville, Maine

ANTHONY J. SKILLEN
RACISM
University of Kent
Canterbury, England, UK

JOHN SNAPPER
TRADE SECRETS AND PROPRIETARY INFORMATION
Illinois Institute of Technology
Chicago, Illinois

EUGENE SPAFFORD
COMPUTER SECURITY
Purdue University
West Lafayette, Indiana

CLIVE L. SPASH
WILDLIFE CONSERVATION
Cambridge University
Cambridge, England, UK

PAUL SPICKER
POVERTY
SOCIAL SECURITY
SOCIAL WELFARE: PROVISION AND FINANCE
University of Dundee
Dundee, Scotland, UK

R. E. SPIER
SCIENCE AND ENGINEERING ETHICS, OVERVIEW
University of Surrey
Guildford, England, UK

DEAN A. STEELE
HONOR CODES
United States Air Force Academy
Colorado Springs, Colorado

ELIZA STEELWATER
HUMANISM
University of Illinois
Champaign, Illinois

EDWARD STEIN
SEXUAL ORIENTATION
Yale University
New Haven, Connecticut

JON STEWART
EXISTENTIALISM
Søren Kierkegaard Research Center
University of Copenhagen
Copenhagen, Denmark

TADEUSZ SZUBKA
FREUDIANISM
University of Queensland
Brisbane, Australia

WIN TADD
NURSES' ETHICS
University of Wales
Cardiff, Wales, UK

CARL TALBOT
DEEP ECOLOGY
ENVIRONMENTAL JUSTICE
University of Wales, Cardiff
Cardiff, Wales, UK

JULIA PO-WAH LAI TAO
CONFUCIANISM
City University of Hong Kong
Kowloon, Hong Kong

LAURENCE THOMAS
FRIENDSHIP
Syracuse University
Syracuse, New York

JOHN J. TILLEY
HEDONISM
Indiana University/Purdue University
Indianapolis, Indiana

G. E. TOMLINSON
GENETIC RESEARCH
University of Texas
Dallas, Texas

ROSEMARIE TONG
FEMINIST ETHICS
Davidson College
Davidson, North Carolina

MAX TRAVERS
COURTROOM PROCEEDINGS, REPORTING OF
Buckinghamshire College

JOHN C. TULLOCH
VIOLENCE IN FILMS AND TELEVISION
Charles Sturt University
Bathurst, Australia

MARIAN I. TULLOCH
VIOLENCE IN FILMS AND TELEVISION
Charles Sturt University
Bathurst, Australia

RICHARD H. S. TUR
LEGAL ETHICS, OVERVIEW
Oriel College
Oxford, England, UK

ROBERT TWYCROSS
PALLIATIVE CARE
Oxford University and Churchill Hospital
Oxford, England, UK

CAROLE ULANOWSKY
FAMILY, THE
The Open University
Milton Keynes, England, UK

GREGORY UNGAR
ELECTRONIC SURVEILLANCE
University of Colorado
Boulder, Colorado

JORGE M. VALADEZ
INDIGENOUS RIGHTS
Marquette University
Milwaukee, Wisconsin

JOHANNES J. M. VAN DELDEN
DO-NOT-RESUSCITATE DECISIONS
Center for Bioethics and Health Law
Utrecht University
Utrecht, The Netherlands

WIBREN VAN DER BURG
SLIPPERY SLOPE ARGUMENTS
Tilburg University
Tilburg, The Netherlands

PAUL VIMINITZ
NUCLEAR WARFARE
University of Waterloo
Waterloo, Ontario

ANDREW VINCENT
MARX AND ETHICS
University of Wales, Cardiff
Cardiff, Wales, UK

ROBERT WACHBROIT
HEALTH AND DISEASE, CONCEPTS OF
Institute for Philosophy and Public Policy
University of Maryland
College Park, Maryland

NEIL WALKER
POLICE ACCOUNTABILITY
University of Aberdeen
Aberdeen, Scotland, UK

DANIEL WARNER
CITIZENSHIP
Graduate Institute of International Studies
Geneva, Switzerland

DAVID WASSERMAN
DISCRIMINATION, CONCEPT OF
Institute for Philosophy and Public Policy
University of Maryland
College Park, Maryland

JOHN WECKERT
SEXUAL CONTENT IN FILMS AND TELEVISION
Charles Sturt University
Bathurst, New South Wales, Australia

CHARLES WEIJER
RESEARCH METHODS AND POLICIES
Joint Centre for Bioethics
University of Toronto/Mount Sinai Hospital
Toronto, Ontario

D. DON WELCH
SOCIAL ETHICS, OVERVIEW
Vanderbilt University School of Law
Nashville, Tennessee

JOS V. M. WELIE
PLACEBO TREATMENT
Creighton University
Omaha, Nebraska

CELIA WELLS
CORPORATE RESPONSIBILITY
Cardiff Law School
University of Wales
Cardiff, Wales, UK

CAROLINE WHITBECK
RESEARCH ETHICS
Case Western Reserve University
Cleveland, Ohio

MARGARET WHITELEGG
ALTERNATIVE MEDICINE
University of Central Lancashire
Preston, England, UK

URBAN WIESING
MEDICAL ETHICS, USE OF HISTORICAL EVIDENCE IN
University of Münster
Münster, Germany

JOHN R. WILCOX
HIGHER EDUCATION, ETHICS OF
Manhattan College
Riverdale, Bronx, New York

RICHARD R. WILK
ARCHAEOLOGICAL ETHICS
Indiana University
Indianapolis, Indiana

BERNARD WILLIAMS
CENSORSHIP
University of California, Berkeley

CHRISTOPHER WINCH
AUTHORITY IN EDUCATION
>   Nene College
>   Northhampton, England, UK

EARL R. WINKLER
APPLIED ETHICS, OVERVIEW
>   University of British Columbia
>   Vancouver, British Columbia

CLARK WOLF
THEORIES OF JUSTICE: HUMAN NEEDS
>   University of Colorado
>   Boulder, Colorado

PAUL ROOT WOLPE
INFORMED CONSENT
>   University of Pennsylvania
>   Philadelphia, Pennsylvania

MICHAEL WREEN
PATENTS
>   Marquette University
>   Milwaukee, Wisconsin

MICHAEL J. ZIGMOND
SCIENTIFIC PUBLISHING
>   University of Pittsburgh
>   Pittsburgh, Pennsylvania

A GUIDE TO THE ENCYCLOPEDIA

The *Encyclopedia of Applied Ethics* is a complete source of information contained within the covers of a single unified work. It is the first reference book that addresses the relatively new discipline of applied ethics in a comprehensive manner; thus in effect it will provide the first general description of the components and boundaries of this challenging field.

The Encyclopedia consists of four volumes and includes 281 separate full-length articles on the whole range of applied ethics. It includes not only entries on the leading theories and concepts of ethics, but also a vast selection of entries on practical issues ranging from medical, scientific, and environmental ethics to the ethics of social relationships and social services. Each article provides a detailed overview of the selected topic to inform a broad spectrum of readers, from research professionals to students to the interested general public.

In order that you, the reader, will derive maximum benefit from your use of the *Encyclopedia of Applied Ethics,* we have provided this Guide. It explains how the Encyclopedia is organized and how the information within it can be located.

ORGANIZATION

The *Encyclopedia of Applied Ethics* is organized to provide the maximum ease of use for its readers. All of the articles are arranged in a single alphabetical sequence by title. Articles whose titles begin with the letters A to D are in Volume 1, articles with titles from E to I are in Volume 2, and those from J to R are in Volume 3. Volume 4 contains the articles from S to Z and also the Index.

So that they can be easily located, article titles generally begin with the key word or phrase indicating the topic, with any descriptive terms following. For example, "Distributive Justice, Theories of" is the article title

rather than "Theories of Distributive Justice" because the specific phrase *distributive justice* is the key term rather than the more general term *theories*. Similarly "Sports, Ethics of" is the article title rather than "Ethics of Sports" and "Human Nature, Views of" is the title rather than "Views of Human Nature."

TABLE OF CONTENTS

A complete alphabetical table of contents for the *Encyclopedia of Applied Ethics* appears at the front of each volume of the set, beginning on page v of the Introduction. This list includes not only the articles that appear in that particular volume but also those in the other three volumes.

The list of article titles represents topics that have been carefully selected by the Editor-in-Chief, Prof. Ruth Chadwick, Head of the Centre for Professional Ethics, University of Central Lancashire, UK, in collaboration with the members of the Editorial Board.

In addition to the alphabetical table of contents, the Encyclopedia also provides a second table of contents at the front of each volume, one that lists all the articles according to their subject area. The Encyclopedia provides coverage of 12 specific subject areas within the overall field of applied ethics, as indicated below:

- **Theories of Ethics**
- **Ethical Concepts**
- **Medical Ethics**
- **Scientific Ethics**
- **Environmental Ethics**
- **Legal Ethics**
- **Ethics in Education**
- **Ethics and Politics**
- **Business and Economic Ethics**
- **Media Ethics**
- **Ethics and Social Services**
- **Social Ethics**

ARTICLE FORMAT

Articles in the *Encyclopedia of Applied Ethics* are arranged in a single alphabetical list by title. Each new article begins at the top of a right-hand page, so that it may be quickly located. The author's name and affiliation are displayed at the beginning of the article. The article is organized according to a standard format, as follows:

- **Title and Author**
- **Outline**
- **Glossary**
- **Defining Statement**
- **Main Body of the Article**
- **Cross-References**
- **Bibliography**

OUTLINE

Each article in the Encyclopedia begins with an Outline that indicates the general content of the article. This outline serves two functions. First, it provides a brief preview of the article, so that the reader can get a sense of what is contained there without having to leaf through the pages. Second, it serves to highlight important subtopics that are discussed within the article. For example, the article "Genome Analysis" includes the subtopic "The Human Genome Project."

The Outline is intended as an overview and thus it lists only the major headings of the article. In addition, extensive second-level and third-level headings will be found within the article.

GLOSSARY

The Glossary contains terms that are important to an understanding of the article and that may be unfamiliar to the reader. Each term is defined in the context of the particular article in which it is used. Thus the same term may appear as a Glossary entry in two or more articles, with the details of the definition varying slightly from one article to another. The Encyclopedia includes more than 1,000 glossary entries.

The following example is a glossary entry that appears with the article "Precautionary Principle."

indicator species A particular species whose presence (or absence) is regarded as characteristic of a given environment, and whose ability or failure to thrive there is thus thought to be indicative of the overall ecological status of this environment.

DEFINING STATEMENT

The text of each article in the Encyclopedia begins with a single introductory paragraph that defines the topic under discussion and summarizes the content of the article. For example, the article "Biotechnology" begins with the following statement:

BIOTECHNOLOGY is the application of biology for human ends. It involves using organisms to provide humans with food, clothes, medicines, and other products.

CROSS-REFERENCES

Nearly all of the articles in the Encyclopedia have cross-references to other articles. These cross-references appear at the end of the article, following the conclusion of the text. They indicate related articles that can be consulted for further information on the same topic, or for other information on a related topic. For example, the article "Biotechnology" contains cross-references to the articles "Agricultural Ethics," "Animal Research," "Eugenics," "Genetic Counseling," and "Genetic Engineering."

BIBLIOGRAPHY

The Bibliography appears as the last element in an article. It lists recent secondary sources to aid the reader in locating more detailed or technical information. Review articles and research papers that are important to an understanding of the topic are also listed.

The bibliographies in this Encyclopedia are for the benefit of the reader, to provide references for further reading or research on the given topic. Thus they typically consist of no more than ten to twelve entries. They are not intended to represent a complete listing of all the materials consulted by the author in preparing the article, as would be the case, for example, with a journal article.

INDEX

The Subject Index in Volume 4 contains more than 5000 entries. The entries are listed alphabetically and indicate the volume and page number where information on this topic will be found. Within the entry for a given topic, references to the coverage of the topic also appear alphabetically. The Index serves, along with the alphabetical Table of Contents, as the starting point for information on a subject of interest.

PREFACE

Applied Ethics has come to prominence as a field of study in the last 25 to 30 years, after a period in which the prevailing view among philosophers, at least, was that Philosophy could not usefully be applied to practical problems. The importance of Applied Ethics became obvious first in the medical context, where in the aftermath of World War II and the expanding interest in human rights, developments in technology gave rise to challenging ethical issues such as the use of transplant technology and the allocation of scarce resources such as kidney dialysis. Questions such as the extent to which health care professionals should intervene to extend life became extensively debated. Medical Ethics as a defined area became established, with principles such as autonomy being given central importance. In more recent times contested topics have included assisted reproduction and the advances in and implications of human genome analysis. The latter have led to controversy not only about the options concerning the applications of the technology in medical practice, but also about their wider social uses and even their implications for the meaning of what it is to be human.

Applied Ethics is, however, by no means confined to the medical context and to the social implications of technologies that have been developed for medical purposes or have clear medical applications. Ethical issues arise in any area of life where the interests of individuals or groups conflict, including the interests of different species. In compiling the Encyclopedia we became increasingly aware of the enormity of the task—the list of topics covered could have been expanded indefinitely. We chose to concentrate, however, on areas we regarded as central in contemporary society such as issues concerning the environment, law, politics, the media, science and engineering, education, economics, the family and personal relationships, mental health, social work, policing and punishment, minority rights.

In addition to these areas in which particular issues arise, it is essential for those engaged in Applied Ethics to reflect on what, if anything, is being applied. We therefore included a number of entries on ethical and philosophical approaches, both historical and contemporary, religious and secular. There are different models concerning what is involved in Applied Ethics—for example, whether it is a matter of "applying" a particular theory to a specific ethical dilemma; or whether phenomena, specific developments, particular cases, can affect the development of appropriate theory; whether there is room for a ëbottom-upí rather than a ëtop-downí approach. Some would argue that a central task of Applied Ethics, and one that is prior to the application of theory, is the very identification of the moral dimensions of a situation. Thus we have also included entries on Applied Ethics itself and on challenges to it.

Several disciplines may be involved in Applied Ethics; one branch of Applied Ethics, for example, Bioethics, is commonly explicated in terms of ethical, legal and social issues. In this Encyclopedia by no means all the entries are written by philosophers: some are written by practitioners in the particular field in question; other disciplines represented include law and economics. The Encyclopedia will be a reference work for use by a number of readerships, working in a variety of specialisms; but particularly for students in higher education studying on Applied Ethics courses, for which there is increasing demand. It also has much to offer the general reader interested in the ethical issues arising in contemporary social life.

The number of people who have enabled this enterprise to come to fruition is very large. I should like to thank, first, the members of the Editorial Board and Advisory Council, for participating in the project and for their expert advice on and help with the selection and reviewing of material; the reviewers of the articles, for their time in making the assessments of individual submissions; the University of Central Lancashire, for providing research assistance in the Centre for Professional Ethics—first Jane Pritchard and then Adam Hedgecoe, without whom I cannot imagine how the task would have been completed; and of course Academic Press, especially Scott Bentley and Naomi Henning, for their unfailing support throughout, but also their colleagues in the San Diego office who looked after me extremely well on my visit in 1996. All of my colleagues in the Centre for Professional Ethics have given their support to the project—some by writing entries themselves. Finally, the authors of the articles deserve a very large thank you, for contributing their expertise in their field and for working to very tight deadlines to produce the 281 entries in this Encyclopedia.

RUTH CHADWICK

ABORTION

Susanne Gibson
University College of St. Martin

GLOSSARY

Human Fertilisation and Embryology Act 1990 The most recent legislation on infertility treatment, embryo experimentation, and abortion in the United Kingdom.

in vitro **fertilization (IVF)** A method of infertility treatment. The sperm and egg are mixed together in a glass dish and the resulting embryo is then transferred to the woman's body.

Roe v. Wade The landmark case in which the U.S. Supreme Court ruled that the abortion law of Texas, which prohibited abortion performed for any reason other than to save the mother's life, was unconstitutional.

trimester A term used to denote the different stages of pregnancy. A pregnancy consists of three trimesters of roughly 3 months each.

ABORTION is the termination of a pregnancy at any point between conception and birth, resulting in the death of the fetus (the term "fetus" is used inclusively to cover all stages of prenatal development). A distinction is sometimes made between spontaneous abortion, also known as miscarriage, and induced abortion. Ethicists are typically concerned with induced abortion. That is, it is asked whether the deliberate termination of a pregnancy that, it is assumed, would otherwise have resulted in a live birth is ever morally permissible, and if so, in what circumstances.

There are a number of methods of abortion, including suction evacuation, prostaglandin termination, and salt poisoning. More recently, an "abortion pill" has been manufactured and launched in France. RU486, or mifepristone, dislodges or prevents implantation of the fertilized ovum without the need for surgery or anesthetic. However, for political and legal reasons it is not currently widely available (D. Morgan and R. G. Lee, 1991. *Blackstone's Guide to the Human Fertilisation and Embryology Act 1990,* p. 60. Blackstone, London).

In general, there has been a liberalization of abortion legislation in the United States and in the United Kingdom in the last few decades. However, abortion remains a passionately contested issue in bioethics and, indeed, in the public and political arenas.

I. THE STATUS OF THE FETUS

Much of the debate has focused on the question of the moral status of the fetus. That is, it is asked whether the fetus is morally significant, and if so, whether its significance is equal to that of other interested parties, in particular the mother (the term "mother" is used here to denote the woman who is carrying the fetus whose future development is in question).

Hursthouse discerns five positions on the moral status of the fetus:

1. The conservative view. According to the conservative view the fetus has more or less the same moral standing as an adult human being from the moment of conception. Hence this view yields a conservative or restrictive position on the permissibility of abortion. It is not permissible to do to the fetus what it would not be permissible to do to an adult human being. Therefore it would not normally be permissible to kill the fetus, although exceptions may be made, for example, where the mother's life is at stake. In the Western world, the conservative position is most often associated with the teaching of the Catholic Church.

2. The extreme liberal view. The extreme liberal view is diametrically opposed to the conservative view. It is not denied that the fetus is in some sense human. However, according to this view, the fetus is compared not to the adult of the species, but is held to be more like a piece of human tissue. Hence the fetus is accorded very little, if any, moral significance, and an extreme liberal stance on abortion is yielded whereby it is permissible at any stage of pregnancy, for any reason.

I will consider some extreme liberal positions below. The following two positions are both moderately liberal in that they accord the fetus some moral significance, but not full moral standing.

3. The animal view. The fetus is compared to an animal as regards its moral status. Thus, just as most people regard animals as morally significant, but not as morally significant as human beings, the fetus is regarded as morally significant, but not as significant as a child or an adult. There are different versions of the animal view, depending on what kind of animal the proponent takes the fetus to resemble. In general the view is that the fetus, like many animals, is sentient but not self-conscious (although there is controversy over precisely when the fetus develops the capacity to feel pain). In any case, there is so much controversy over the moral standing of animals, it is not clear how

helpful this position is in clearing up the controversy over abortion.

4. The mixed strategy. The mixed strategy bestows the fetus with a varying moral status, according to its stage of development:

> Initially it is, in most morally relevant respects, like a bit of tissue or an organ of the body. As it develops it gradually becomes, in most morally relevant respects, like a lower animal, then like a higher one, and in the later stages of its development it is, in most if not all morally relevant respects, like a baby, and hence on a par with fully-developed, normal, adult human being. (R. Hursthouse, 1987. *Beginning Lives,* p. 65. Basil Blackwell, Oxford).

This mixed strategy, also referred to as the "gradualist" or "moderate" position, is implicitly if not explicitly reflected in abortion legislation in the United States and the United Kingdom and appears to be in accord with many people's intuitions on abortion. The philosopher's endeavor becomes one of determining what it is that makes the different stages morally distinct, and where abouts in its the development the fetus moves from one stage to the next.

5. The potentiality view. Finally, it is argued that, although the fetus is not an actual human being, it is a potential human being, and in that respect, is morally unique. This position, although a popular one, is less determinate than the other four (apart from perhaps the animal strategy) in yielding a conclusion regarding abortion, since although it might be agreed that there is a sense in which the fetus has the potential to become a human being, it is not clear what follows from this. Does a potential human being have the same moral status as an actual human being—in which case abortion would seem to be impermissible—or only the potential for the moral status of a human being—in which case it is not obvious that abortion is impermissible?

Although there are a variety of views on the status of the fetus, much of the debate in the philosophical literature has been between those who adopt one of the first two positions. This debate has often been framed in terms of whether or not the fetus has a right to life.

II. PERSONS, NONPERSONS, AND THE RIGHT TO LIFE

Judith Jarvis Thomson sets out the conservative position as follows:

Every person has a right to life. So the foetus has a right to life. No doubt the mother has a right to decide what shall happen in and to her body; everyone would grant that. But surely a person's right to life is stronger and more stringent than the mother's right to decide what happens in and to her body, and so outweighs it. So the foetus may not be killed; an abortion may not be performed. (1977. In *The Philosophy of Law*. (R. M. Dworkin, Ed.), p. 113. Oxford Univ. Press, Oxford).

The argument may be put as follows: (a) Every person has a right to life (which is stronger than the right to decide what happens in and to one's body). (b) The fetus is a person. (c) Therefore, the fetus has a right to life (which is stronger than the mother's right to decide what happens in and to her body). (d) Therefore abortion is impermissible.

The argument is clearly valid: disagreement arises over whether or not it is sound; that is, over whether or not the premises are true. In particular, the claim that the fetus is a person is disputed (although it will be seen below that Thomson calls into question the first rather than the second premise). Although both sides generally agree that the fetus is human—that is, it is a member of the species *homo sapiens*—they disagree over whether being human is synonymous with being a person. Conservatives tend to equate "being human" with "being a person," whereas liberals contend that an entity can be human without necessarily being a person.

Mary Anne Warren, for example, distinguishes the "morally relevant" or "*moral* sense" of the term "human" from the "*genetic* sense" (Warren, 1984, 110). To be human in the moral sense is to be a member of the moral community and to be in possession of the corresponding moral rights. However, although all of and only those who are members of the species *homo sapiens* are human in the genetic sense, species membership is neither necessary nor sufficient for humanness in the moral sense: the two groups may overlap, but cannot be assumed to be the same—it is possible to be human in either sense without being human in the other.

According to Warren, the argument that states that it is wrong to kill innocent human beings, and that since fetuses are innocent human beings it is wrong to kill fetuses, confuses the two different senses of the term "human." The fetus is clearly human in the genetic sense, but in order for the argument to work, it must be shown that the fetus is also human in the moral sense, or in other words, that it is a member of the moral community. So, what sorts of things are members of the moral community with full moral rights, includ-

ing the right to life? Here Warren introduces the distinction between being human and being a person: the moral community is held to consist exclusively of persons, who may or may not be human.

Of course, what is needed is some account of what it is to be a person. Warren suggests a number of characteristics that fit broadly within the wider philosophical tradition on personhood; that is, personhood requires such attributes as consciousness, reason, communication, self-awareness, and so on. The important point is that, since the fetus possesses none of these capacities, it is not a person, and therefore is not human in the sense that would allow it a right to life.

One other view worth considering here is that of Michael Tooley. Tooley has written extensively on the ethics of abortion, consistently maintaining an extreme liberal position. Like Warren, Tooley claims that only persons can have a right to life. However, instead of drawing on the philosophical tradition to give an account of what it is to be a person, Tooley addresses much more directly the question of what kind of thing can be said to have rights, and in particular, the right to life.

For Tooley, having a right involves having a desire. Tooley appeals to Feinberg's "interest principle," according to which a thing can only have rights if it has or can have interests, and it can only have interests if it has or can have desires. Thus something that cannot have desires—for example, a newspaper or a chair—cannot be said to have either interests or rights.

In applying the interest principle to the issue of abortion, Tooley further refines the principle, suggesting that although it is true that a thing must be capable of having at least some interest in order for it to have any rights at all, there are more specific connections to be found between particular interests and particular rights. Hence, the "particular-interests principle" states that "an entity cannot have a particular right, R, unless it is at least capable of having some interest, I, which is furthered by its having right R" (M. Tooley, 1984. In *The Problem of Abortion* (J. Feinberg, Ed.), 2nd ed., p. 125. Wadsworth, Belmont, CA).

So, what particular interests or desires must an entity possess in order for it to have a right to life, and what kind of entity can be said to have those interests or desires? Tooley claims that a right to life can belong to something if and only if "its continued existence can be in its interest" (Tooley, 1984, 127). However, it is argued that human fetuses are not sufficiently developed to possess a concept of a continuing self, and therefore cannot be said to have an interest in or desire for their own continued existence and therefore cannot be said to have a right to life. Further, Tooley denies that the fetus can be granted interests and therefore rights on the grounds of the desires and interests that it will come to have if it is allowed to develop. Here he appeals to a conception of personal identity, claiming that the fetus and the person that the fetus will become enjoy physical but not personal identity: an individual physical organism need not be an individual subject of consciousness. In this way, Tooley is able to claim that although I may, at this point in time, be glad that the fetus who became me was not aborted, it does not follow that that fetus had an interest in continuing to exist or that it was in its interests to continue to exist.

It has been argued that any defense of abortion based on an appeal to the fetus's lack of personhood is question-begging. William Cooney takes issues with Warren for defining personhood by providing a list of criteria and then stating that an entity which satisfies none of these criteria cannot be a person. For Warren, to deny that a fetus cannot be a person is to misunderstand what is meant by the term, or to confuse the concept of personhood with the concept of genetic humanity. However, Cooney points out that it is this distinction between personhood and genetic humanity that Warren's list is supposed to establish. Thus Warren's premise—that an entity that satisfies none of the five criteria is not a person—assumes the truth of the conclusion—that there is a morally relevant distinction to be made between genetic humanity and moral humanity, or personhood. For those who hold that genetic humanity is either a sufficient or necessary condition for personhood, the list of criteria is incomplete. Further, it is contended that Tooley's argument suffers from the same circularity as Warren's: one has to accept Tooley's criteria for personhood before one can accept his conclusion that the fetus is not a person, or accept his account of what it is to have a right to life before one can accept that the fetus does not have such a right.

It is contended, then, that the liberals do not have absolute jurisdiction over the correct use of the term "person." Thus although liberal arguments for abortion based on the notion of personhood do draw on a particular philosophical tradition, from Aristotle through Locke and Kant, it is pointed out that the term person is used in a variety of ways, not just by philosophers but also in the fields of theology and law, and in ordinary usage. Further, even if the traditional philosophical account of personhood is accepted—that is, the account based on rationality, self-consciousness, and so on—it is suggested that membership of a species of typically rational or self-conscious beings may be a sufficient condition for classification as a person, or for full moral standing. Teichman points out that in

considering the term "mammalian," it is clear that an individual animal may be termed a mammal, even if it does not itself have the ability to suckle its young since "it needs only to belong to a species some members of which—the adult females—are able, if normal, to suckle the young" (Teichman, 1985, 181). This response appears to allow that fetuses are persons, without thereby falling afoul of the standard charge of speciesism: it is not simply because they are members of the human species that they count, it is because they are members of a species of persons. However, some account still needs to be given of the precise moral standing accorded to an entity on the basis of its membership of a species of persons. Does it, for example, have the same moral standing as a fully fledged member of the same species, or as a fully fledged member of a different species of persons?

In considering some of the complexities of the debate between those who claim that the fetus has a right to life (or more generally, full moral standing) and those who deny this claim, it becomes apparent how difficult it is to decide the issue. One of the problems here is that both positions have counterintuitive implications. On the one hand, giving full moral standing to the fetus results in it being unclear as to whether the mother's interests or rights can ever be given priority over those of the fetus, for example, where the mother's life is at stake. On the other hand, to deny the fetus any moral standing on the grounds that it is not a person not only offends those who think that the fetus must be given some status, if only in the later stages of pregnancy, it also implies that other nonpersons, including newborn infants, also lack moral standing. Some liberals, for example, Tooley, are comfortable with this implication. Others are not, and have attempted to provide arguments against infanticide while maintaining the core of the argument for abortion.

It is unlikely that there will ever be agreement regarding the moral status of the fetus, since any account must draw on prior moral convictions. As Hursthouse points out, whether the possession of certain characteristics rather than others is held to be important will probably be decided at least in part on the basis of one's prior convictions about abortion and infanticide. Although certain factual, empirically verifiable considerations will be relevant—for example, whether or not and at what stage the fetus can feel pain—it is clear that the question of the moral status of the fetus cannot be decided entirely in these terms. As one influential report into the ethical issues surrounding human reproduction and embryology has stated, "[a]lthough the questions of when life or personhood begin appear to be questions of fact susceptible of straightforward answers ... the answers to such questions in fact are complex amalgams of factual and moral judgements" (M. Warnock, 1985. *A Question of Life,* p. 60. Basil Blackwell, Oxford).

Perhaps because of these difficulties, some have attempted to sidestep the question of the moral status of the fetus altogether. A notable example of this approach is found in the work of Judith Jarvis Thomson.

III. THOMSON ON ABORTION

Through a series of examples, Thomson attempts to show that, even allowing the conservatives their assumption that the fetus is a person with a right to life, abortion is morally permissible in some cases. For Thomson, the permissibility of abortion hinges on what having a right to life entails. Importantly, it is argued that it does not entail an absolute right to whatever is necessary to maintain one's life. Thus it cannot be assumed without argument that the fetus's right to life entails a right to the use of its mother's body.

Thomson's most memorable example is that of the violinist. The reader is asked to suppose that she wakes up one morning and finds that she has been kidnapped and a famous violinist's circulatory system has been plugged into her own so that he can use her kidneys. If she unplugs herself, or is unplugged, the violinist will die. However, if she remains attached to him for nine months, then the violinist will recover and they can go their separate ways.

What this analogy is meant to illustrate is the implausibility of the claim that one person's right to life always outweighs another's right to decide what happens in and to her own body. Although the violinist, as a person, has a right to life and will die without the use of the woman's body, he does not thereby have a right to the use of her body. He does not have that right, because she has not given it to him. Thus, according to Thomson, a fetus only has the right to the use of its mother's body if the woman has given it that right, and at least in some cases of pregnancy—for example, those that are the result of rape or failed contraception—it is not clear that the woman has given it that right. Thomson distinguishes between just and unjust killing, and claims that where the woman has not invited the fetus to use her body, then killing the fetus is not unjust, and therefore not a violation of its rights.

Thomson's argument allows for abortion in a limited number of cases: where the mother's life is at stake (here the mother is claimed to have a property right in her own body, which tips the balance in her favor), where the pregnancy is a result of rape, where a reasonable effort has been made to avoid pregnancy (e.g., failed contraception), or where it is the result of ignorance. However, abortion remains impermissible in those cases where the woman can be said to have given the fetus the right to the use of her body and where, therefore, killing the fetus would be unjust. Thus it is not permissible for a woman who has conceived deliberately and is now 7 months pregnant to abort just because she wants to go on a foreign holiday and the pregnancy is inconvenient.

There have been a number of responses to Thomson's paper which take issue with a variety of different points in her argument. Some, for example, object to her fairly narrow interpretation of what it is to have a right to life. Others criticize her emphasis on property rights. However, as one of the earliest and subsequently most referenced contributions to the contemporary debate, Thomson's paper has been described as a "landmark" in its field.

IV. FEMINIST APPROACHES TO ABORTION

In arguing for abortion on the basis of a woman's right to control what happens in and to her own body, Thomson, like Warren, is firmly within the feminist tradition. On the whole, feminists have been vocal in their support for permissive abortion legislation. Indeed, in the United Kingdom, one of the Women's Liberation Movement's four original demands was for "free abortion on demand." However, although to begin with feminists were happy to couch their arguments in the language of rights, in the last decade or so there has been mounting dissatisfaction with this approach with regard to the ethics of pregnancy and abortion and more generally. Hence, feminist writers have begun to develop more sophisticated accounts of abortion, and further, it has been recognized that feminism is not necessarily incompatible with an antiabortion stance.

It is claimed that by pitting the rights of the fetus against the rights of the mother, the nature of the relationship between the mother and the child is misrepresented. The paradigm of individual rights is appropriate in contexts where the relevant relationships are freely entered into by separate and self-interested individuals. However, it is clear that in the case of pregnancy and abortion, even if the woman enters freely into the relationship, the fetus does not. Therefore, it is argued that insofar as writers such as Thomson rest their case for abortion on the woman's right to control her own body, or on the right to choose whether or not to contract to its use by another, they cannot hope to give an adequate account of the morality of abortion: hence the counterintuitive implications of some such arguments.

The alternatives to rights-based arguments that have been offered are varied. Hursthouse puts forward a virtue-based account. Other more explicitly feminist writers have appealed to the ethics of care—a branch of feminist philosophy that has had some influence in the field of applied ethics and particularly bioethics in recent years. The ethics of care is contrasted with rights-based approaches insofar as it begins with the individual as related to others, enmeshed in a network of often unchosen and unequal attachments, out of which certain responsibilities arise. Interestingly, this approach has been used to argue for both a prochoice and an antiabortion stance. The question becomes one of making a decision regarding whether or not to continue a pregnancy based not only on one's responsibilities to the fetus, but also to the particular others to whom one is connected as well as to oneself. Once again, however, disagreement arises over what those responsibilities are. Similarly, the virtue theorists disagree over whether or not and in what circumstances the virtuous person (or rather, woman) would choose abortion.

In general, one of the central problems faced by feminists has been to give an account of abortion which is compatible with the goal of ending women's oppression, and which recognizes the importance of reproductive freedom in reaching this goal, but which does not at the same time perpetuate other forms of oppression, including the oppression of the fetus. The fact that women are oppressed, it is said, does not provide any justification for disregarding the question of the moral status of the fetus: "Being disadvantaged does not remove from individuals or groups moral responsibilities to care about and protect other beings" (K. Jenni, 1994. *Social Theory Practice* **20**(1), 59–83).

V. UTILITARIANISM

There is of course an approach that is widely appealed to in applied ethics that has very little use for the idea of individual rights, namely, utilitarianism. As with other areas of applied ethics, the utilitarian tends not to take an absolute position on abortion. In general, abortion is permissible in those cases in which it would maximize utility and impermissible in cases where it would not.

As far as policy recommendations are concerned, differences in opinion arise out of different assessments of the overall effect of a restrictive or permissive policy on the balance of utility, although of course disagreement will also arise where there are differing accounts of what utility consists of.

In any case, those who take a broadly utilitarian approach have not been silent on the subject of abortion. Again the question of the status of the fetus is seen to be important here, although it is more a question of who is to count in the utilitarian calculation than who is in possession of particular rights. However, like those who focus on rights, several utilitarian writers have appealed to the fetus's alleged lack of personhood to justify abortion. John Harris, for example, argues for a principle of utility that states that we should seek to maximize valuable lives: therefore, valuable lives should not be ended. However, not all lives are valuable in the morally relevant sense. In particular, the entity whose life is in question must have the capacity to value its own life. That is, it must have the capacities that are necessary for personhood, in the sense of the philosophical tradition referred to previously. The fetus, of course, is not a person in this sense, and "therefore cannot be wronged if its life is ended prematurely," although it can be wronged in other ways, or for other reasons, for example, if it is sentient and is caused pain (J. Harris, 1985. *The Value of Life: An Introduction to Medical Ethics*, p. 159. Routledge, London).

It was already seen that there are counterintuitive implications to this kind of approach. Anne Maclean has offered a detailed criticism of some of those who combine arguments for the fetus's lack of personhood with a utilitarian stance. However, even without appeals to personhood, the utilitarian has a problem in applying the principle of utility to abortion. That is, whether or not the utilitarian wishes to argue for a permissive or a restrictive stance on abortion, in appealing to the principle of maximization, the utilitarian may be unable to distinguish between abortion on the one hand and celibacy and contraception on the other in a way that is morally convincing and that fits in with ordinary and widely shared intuitions. The problem is that if abortion is seen as the taking of a life, and if this is seen as a reduction of utility, and therefore as a *prima facie* wrong, then insofar as preventing a life from coming into being is also a reduction of utility, this too might be seen as equally wrong. Therefore it seems that whatever is wrong with abortion is also wrong with contraception and celibacy.

VI. ABORTION AND THE NEW REPRODUCTIVE TECHNOLOGIES

In some respects, the abortion debate has taken a back seat to the debates about the ethics of the new reproductive technologies in recent years. However, advancements in reproductive and childbirth technologies have themselves had an impact on the abortion debate.

This impact is also reflected in changes that have been made in abortion legislation in the United Kingdom. Following the Abortion Act 1967, abortion became legally available in the United Kingdom under certain conditions and up to the 28th week of pregnancy on the grounds that this was roughly the point at which the fetus was capable of being born alive. However, the Human Fertilisation and Embryology Act 1990 included an amendment to the 1967 Abortion Act which reduced the time limit to 24 weeks, a reduction which, it has been claimed, was made partly on the grounds that developments in medical technology have meant that it is possible to maintain the lives of severely premature neonates at a much younger age than was previously the case. Hence it is said that the fetus is now capable of being born alive, or is "viable," at 24 rather than 28 weeks, and that therefore the availability of abortion ought to be severely restricted after this point.

VII. VIABILITY

In light of the previous section, it is worth saying something more about viability as a relevant factor in the abortion debate. The idea that the fetus gains moral status, or more specifically, a right to life, at the point at which it becomes viable is appealing insofar as it gives some grounding to the "mixed strategy" outlined above, and like the mixed strategy, is also reflected in abortion legislation. In *Roe v. Wade* (1973) the United States Supreme Court legalized abortion in the first and second trimesters, stating that "with respect to the State's important and legitimate interest in potential life, the "compelling" point is viability" (D. Callahan, Feb. 1986. *Hastings Center Rep.*, 33–42). However, there are a number of problems in appealing to the notion of viability as the decisive point at which abortion becomes impermissible. To begin with, it has to be asked precisely what is meant by the term viability: does it require independent survival without technological assistance or with technological assistance? To define viability in terms of the ability to survive without external assistance would appear to render not only all fetuses unviable, but also many other human beings, from the newborn to the elderly. However, if viability does include some place for technological assistance, then it becomes a very unstable reference point in the abortion debate, altering with developments in technology. Indeed, were ectogenesis, or the use of an artificial womb, ever to become a possibility, then abortion might become impermissible altogether. Thus many of those who want to give some consideration to interests other than those of the fetus are wary about relying too heavily on viability as the cutoff point for abortion.

Another issue that arises out of developing childbirth technology is the question of what the woman's right to abort—if there is such a right—entails. That is, if it becomes routinely possible to remove a fetus from the woman's body without ending the fetus's life, does the woman then have the right to demand that the fetus is killed? Some have argued that the right to abortion is only the right to fetal evacuation and not fetal death (Thomson, 1977). However, others have argued that in order for women to have true reproductive autonomy, a woman must have a right to end the fetus's life as well as the right to remove the fetus from her body.

VIII. EMBRYO EXPERIMENTATION

There have also been developments in technology as applied to the beginnings of pregnancy, in particular with regard to *in vitro* fertilization (IVF) and embryo experimentation, or embryology. These have thrown up a number of moral problems in their own right. However, with regard to abortion, it has been pointed out that there are contradictions in attitudes toward the IVF embryo and a developing fetus. In the United Kingdom, for example, although abortion is allowed up until the 24th week of pregnancy, embryo experimentation is not allowed beyond 14 days of development. The advent of IVF and embryology has also introduced a new term into the debate over the moral standing of the fetus. The term "preembryo" has been introduced to refer to the first 14 days of development, during which time it is not clear whether the fertilized ovum will develop into one or more embryos, or will develop into an embryo at all. However, insofar as this term is used to deny the "preembryo" moral status, the introduction of the term has been described as verbal maneuvering.

IX. THE USE OF FETAL TISSUE IN THERAPY AND RESEARCH

Finally, advances in medical technology have led to the possibility of aborted fetal tissue being used in research and therapy, including infertility treatment. Thus the debate over abortion has become a debate not just over whether or not a fetus can be aborted, but over what can be done with the fetus once it has been removed from the woman's body. Those who wish to prevent abortion, or at least to minimize its incidence, tend to view the use of fetal tissue as condoning abortion, and therefore view the practice as undesirable. Others argue that if abortion is permissible, then so too is the use of fetal tissue, particularly where its use results in some good for individuals or for society. Others still have raised concerns over the place of informed consent in the procedures: clearly the fetus cannot consent, but is the mother's consent either necessary or sufficient for its use, or should the father, for example, also be involved?

X. CONCLUSION

The ferocity of the debate surrounding abortion shows no sign of abating. Given the variety of the different parties' convictions, and the strength with which they are held, it is unlikely that there will ever be agreement on this issue. However, philosophers have done much to help to clarify the moral and philosophical aspects of the debate, and show every sign of continuing to do so as they engage in one of the most important moral arguments of the 20th century.

Also See the Following Articles

BIRTH-CONTROL TECHNOLOGY • EMBRYOLOGY, ETHICS OF • FETAL RESEARCH • FETUS • LIFE, CONCEPT OF

Bibliography

Cooney, W. (1991). The fallacy of all person-denying arguments for abortion. *Journal of Applied Philosophy,* 8(2), 161–165.

Dworkin, R. (1995). Life's Dominion: An Argument about Abortion and Euthanasia. HarperCollins, London.

English, J. (1984). Abortion and the concept of a person. In "The Problem of Abortion" (J. Feinberg, Ed.), 2nd ed. Wadsworth, Belmont, CA.

Fost, N., Chudwin, D., and Wikler, D. (1980). The limited moral significance of "fetal viability." *Hastings Center Rep.* December, 10–13.

Gatens-Robinson, E. (1992). A defense of women's choice: Abortion and the ethics of care. *The Southern Journal of Philosophy,* 15(3), 29–66.

Holland, A. (1990). A fortnight of my life is missing: A discussion of the status of the human "pre-embryo." *Journal of Applied Philosophy,* 7(1), 25–38.

Hutchinson, D. (1982). Utilitarianism and children. *Canadian Journal of Philosophy,* 12(1), 61–73.

Jenni, K. (1994). Dilemmas in social philosophy: Abortion and animal rights. *Social Theory and Practice* 20(1), 59–83.

Lovenduski, J., and Randall, V. (1993). "Contemporary Feminist Politics: Women and Power in Britain." Oxford Univ. Press, Oxford.

Mackenzie, C. (1992). Abortion and embodiement. *Australian Journal of Philosophy,* 70(2), 136–155.

Maclean, A. (1993). "The Elimination of Morality: Reflections on Utilitarianism and Bioethics." Routledge, London.

Noonan, J. T. (1984). An almost absolute value in history. In "The Problem of Abortion" (J. Feinberg, Ed.), 2nd ed. Wadsworth, Belmont, CA.

Overall, C. (1985). New reproductive technology: Some implications for the abortion issue. *The Journal of Value Inquiry* 19, 279–292.

Singer, P. (1995). "Rethinking Life and Death: The Collapse of Our Traditional Ethics." Oxford Univ. Press, Oxford.

Sumner, L. W. (1984). A third way. In "The Problem of Abortion" (J. Feinberg, Ed.), 2nd ed. Wadsworth, Belmont, CA.

Teichman, J. (1985). The definition of person. *Philosophy* 60, 175–185.

Warren, M. A. (1992). The moral significance of birth. In "Feminist Perspectives in Medical Ethics" (H. B. Holmes and L. M. Purdy, Eds.). Indiana Univ. Press, Bloomington/Indianapolis.

Wolfe-Devine, C. (1989). Abortion and the feminine voice. *Public Affairs Quarterly,* 3(3), 81–97.

ACCOUNTING AND BUSINESS ETHICS

Harold Q. Langenderfer
University of North Carolina at Chapel Hill

GLOSSARY

accountant One who keeps, audits, or inspects accounting records for individuals or businesses and prepares financial reports or tax returns.

certified public accountant (CPA) An accountant who performs accounting services for the public and who has passed the CPA exam and has met other state standards for public service.

codes of ethics The rules or standards governing the conduct of employees of a company or members of a profession.

external auditor A CPA who is hired by a client company to inspect its financial records and render an opinion as to whether the company's financial statements were prepared in accordance with generally accepted accounting principles.

internal auditor One who oversees the accounting records within a company or other organization. An internal auditor is often a member of the Institute of Internal Auditors (see Section IIA).

management accountant An accountant who performs accounting services in the form of recordkeeping or systems analysis for his or her employer. The employer could be an individual, a company, or some other organization. A management accountant often possesses a CPA certificate or a CMA certificate (Certified Management Accountant).

securities and exchange commission (SEC) A U.S. government agency that supervises the sale or exchange of securities so as to protect investors against malpractice.

whistleblower A person who reports an unethical act to a third party who can take action to protect external stakeholders.

ACCOUNTING AND BUSINESS ETHICS can be defined as a level of professional and business performance that is appropriate societal behavior in performing obligated duties to protect the users of financial information who are making significant investment and other business decisions. Assigned professional and business performances are expected to adhere to (1) the legal rules, (2) professional ethics codes, (3) the ethics of the culture, and (4) what is morally right on a global basis. These four levels of ethical performance are significant because the more levels that are affected by an ethics issue, the larger the number of stakeholders involved, leading to more complexity in resolving the ethics issue. Because accountants perform accounting services for individuals and for a variety of business and social organizations, accounting ethics and business ethics are universally intertwined. Often, the accountant's client or his company is performing an unethical or illegal act that, when discovered, forces the accountant to decide who should deal with the situation and how it should be resolved, including whether the unethical act should be reported, and if so, to whom.

I. LEVELS OF EXPECTED PROFESSIONAL BEHAVIOR IN AN ETHICAL HIERARCHY

Accounting ethics can be viewed as a level of expected professional behavior within a hierarchy of ethics levels that apply to involved parties in specific situations. These ethical levels can be diagrammed in the form of a triangle. The triangle of ethics levels suggests that a highly ethical person or group is expected to evolve their ethical practices up to the level that is appropriate for the participants' obligated duties and the stakeholders affected by an unethical act.

A. Legal Laws and Rules

In this hierarchy, the legal rules, that is, the law of the designated jurisdiction, are considered to be the minimum acceptable form of behavior. The law is viewed as the lowest form because it applies to everyone within a designated jurisdiction, which suggests that laws are not passed until there is significant consensus among all of the parties in the jurisdiction. In effect, everyone within a jurisdiction is expected to obey the law that has been officially promulgated as one that is in the best interests of all parties in that jurisdiction.

B. Professional and Organizational Codes

When groups of individuals organize to perform specific types of services, certain behavioral expectations are needed to reflect a minimum level of satisfaction for the participants who benefit from the services performed, such as customers, creditors, shareholders, employees, and management. The minimum expected level of satisfaction is reflected in the organization's code of ethics. For example, more than 95% of Fortune 500 companies now have codes of ethics.

If an organization or an individual performs services for others that are professional rather than commercial, the standards of behavior are higher for a professional activity. Thus, professional codes exist for doctors, lawyers, and accountants, for example, who are expected to serve their clients in a highly professional and ethical manner than transcends the expected level of service by a commercial organization to its customers. Accordingly, accounting groups have codes of ethics that specify the minimum quality of acceptable behavior for their clients.

C. Ethics of the Culture

An ethics culture reflects a set of customs of a given society, class, or social group that regulate relationships and prescribe modes of behavior to enhance the group's survival. Cultural ethics is often germane to specific geographic regions, especially countries. What might be acceptable behavior in one country or region may not be acceptable in another country or region.

D. Moral Right and Wrong

This level of ethics should apply to all human beings regardless of what country they live in, for what organization they work, or what their local laws and rules are. What is morally right and wrong constitutes the highest level of ethical behavior because it applies in principle to all humans on earth.

E. Observations Regarding These Ethics Levels

It should be carefully noted that these four levels of ethical performance are especially significant when resolving ethics issues. The more levels affected by an ethics issue, the larger the number of stakeholders involved, which leads to more complexity in resolving the issue! Such complications help to explain why accounting ethics cannot be extensively explored without tying it to business ethics. Accountants perform accounting services for individuals, unincorporated businesses, corporations, and other organizations. Often it is the accountant's client who is performing the unethical or illegal act. The accountant who learns of such acts must decide who should handle them, including if or to whom the acts should be reported. The next section describes the roles of various types of accountants, in business specifically and in society more generally, to help explain the ethical interactions between accounting and business.

II. THE ROLES OF VARIOUS TYPES OF ACCOUNTANTS IN BUSINESS AND SOCIETY

The roles and functions of five types of accountants are described below: external auditors, internal auditors, management accountants, income tax preparers, and accounting educators.

A. External Auditors

An external auditor is an accountant who examines the financial records of corporations and other types of organizations in order to render an opinion as to whether the organization's financial statements fairly present the financial status and the designated period's operating results in conformity with generally accepted accounting principles. In most states in the United States, the accountant must be a certified public accountant (CPA) in order to render an opinion on financial statements. A CPA must pass a national CPA exam, which is offered twice a year in each state. After the exam is passed, the CPA registers with his state's board of CPAs and becomes responsible for following the ethics code and rules of that state in performing accounting services. Most states require up to 40 hours of continuing professional education each year in order to maintain an active CPA certificate. Many if not most CPAs also become members of both their state CPA society and the national society, the American Institute of Certified Public Accountants (AICPA). The state CPA board, the state CPA society, and the AICPA have codes of ethics that practicing CPAs who are members are expected to follow in their accounting practices.

B. Internal Auditors

Internal auditors are employees of corporations or other organizations. As internal auditors they perform independent appraisal activities within their organization by monitoring the accounting, financial, and other operations as a basis for protective and objective service to management. The professional organization for internal auditors is the Institute of Internal Auditors (IAA), which was formed in 1941 and issued its first code of ethics in 1968. The IIA Code views the employer–auditor relationship as being one of *trust* on the part of the employer and *loyalty* on the part of the internal auditors.

C. Management Accountants

Management accountants are employees of corporations or other organizations. These accountants establish and operate internal accounting systems, oversee financial records, and prepare the firm's financial statements. A management accountant often is a CPA or a CMA. The CPA will usually be a member of the state society of CPAs and often will also be a member of the American Institute of CPAs (AICPA). The CMA must pass the certified management accountants' exam and is then a member of the Institute of Management Accountants (IMA), which also has a code of ethics. The CMA is a private sector award and is not a credential recognized by state boards of accountancy.

D. Income Tax Preparers

A tax preparer is any person who prepares, for compensation, all or a substantial portion of an income tax return or a claim for an income tax refund. A tax preparer can be an employer, an employee, or a self-employed person. Tax return preparation includes activities in addition to the physical completion of a tax return. Tax advisers, tax planners, software designers, and consultants are all considered to be tax preparers if they prepare, review, or give the taxpayer advice about a tax return. Any person who furnishes a taxpayer or other preparer with enough information and advice so that completion of the return is largely a mechanical matter is considered to be a tax preparer.

The Internal Revenue Service has in effect preparer disclosure penalties, preparer conduct civil penalties, and preparer criminal conduct penalties. The American Institute of CPAs has a code of conduct and standards regarding practices a CPA should follow in recommending tax return positions and in preparing and signing tax returns, including fees to be charged and claims for refunds.

E. Accounting Educators

An accounting educator is a person who teaches accounting courses in a college or a university. Accounting educators are often CPAs and/or CMAs and therefore are subject to the codes of ethics of the American Institute of CPAs and/or the Institute of Management Accountants. Accounting educators also may be members of their state CPA society and/or the Institute of Internal Auditors and they may be subject to their codes of ethics.

III. THE PSYCHOLOGICAL BASIS OF ETHICAL DILEMMAS FOR ACCOUNTANTS

One theory of moral development is that morality is primarily constructed by the individual based on principles learned in the home, at school, or from church participation. On the other hand, socialization theories maintain that morality is acquired more generally from society as a whole. Some studies have suggested that accountants in general have not progressed to the same level of moral development as other college graduates. If accountants have not progressed to a high level of moral development, and this fact is coupled with strong evidence of the existence of ethical socialization, then accountants are likely to be prone to such unethical behavior as questionable independence judgments, underreporting of audit time, and the avoidance of whistle-blowing. In addition, firm socialization studies indicate that management is more likely to promote individuals who share common views of the organization and its people. Furthermore, other studies within the accounting profession have shown that individuals who remain in a profession tend to assimilate the ethical culture of the profession. Another study found that the moral reasoning level of auditors is inversely related to the position level of the auditors. Moral reasoning levels tend to increase from a staff position to a senior position and then these moral reasoning levels tend to decrease, and become more homogenous, at the manager and partner levels. Because these moral reasoning levels tend to be recognized in the promotion process, those individuals who have been promoted tend to have ethical reasoning levels similar to those of management. These tendencies support the belief that an individual's

promotability may be constrained by the ethical culture of the accounting firm or corporation they work for.

Other studies generally show that accountants examine information more completely and evaluate it more carefully when they expect to be held accountable for their decisions. This concept is especially relevant in the area of auditing. Because auditors expect their work to be reviewed by their superiors to whom they are held accountable, auditors generally develop a good understanding of the inherent level of accountability in the profession. Several studies on accountability indicate that the concept of accountability affects auditors' judgments by increasing consensus and insights. Auditors who have a strong sense of accountability are more likely to issue qualified opinions. In effect, the source of the accountability pressure and the strength of the pressure are related to the quality of the audit decision made. In essence, the level of moral reasoning, the effects of cultural socialization, and the degree of accountability pressure are the determining factors that affect an accountant's ethically sensitive decisions. These factors should be kept in mind as subsequent topics in this article explore how the ethical culture in business and industry affects accountants generally and to what extent the codes of ethics of accountants reinforce the effects of cultural socialization and the degree of accountability pressure.

IV. THE NATURE OF ACCOUNTING ETHICS CODES AND THEIR STATUS

In this section attention will be directed to an analysis of the ethical codes of three groups: (1) management accountants in industry (CMA), (2) internal auditors (CIA), and (3) management accountants who are CPAs. The role of independent CPAs who audit financial statements in relation to their codes of ethics will be discussed later in this article.

A. Management Accountants in Industry (CMAs)

The Institute of Management Accountants (IMA) is the name of what was, originally, the National Association of Cost Accountants (NACA), and later the National Association of the Accountants (NAA). The NAA's code of ethics was established in 1983 with brief revisions made later in the 1980s. The code has been continued under the auspices of the Institute of Management

Accountants (IMA) since the early 1990s. The code covers four standards of ethical conduct (competence, confidentiality, integrity, and objectivity). In addition the code provides guidelines for the "resolution of ethical conflict." The introductory statement describes to whom management accountants are obligated: "Management accountants have an obligation to the organizations they serve, their profession, the public, and themselves to maintain the highest standards of ethical conduct." This language implies that management accountants have a first obligation to the organizations they serve in case there is a conflict between the organization, the accounting profession, the public, and themselves. This obligation to the organization is reinforced under the standard of confidentiality, which states, "Management accountants have a responsibility to (1) refrain from disclosing confidential information acquired in the course of their work except when authorized, unless legally obligated to do so, and (2) refrain from using or appearing to use confidential information acquired in the course of their work for unethical or illegal advantage either personally or through third parties."

These provisions of the standard on confidentiality suggest at least two conflicts for the management accountant who becomes aware of illegal or unethical practices within his or her organization. First, no distinction is made between confidential information that is legal and that which is illegal or unethical. Confidential information that is illegal or unethical cannot be discussed outside of the company without authorization unless it is legally obligated, which is not likely without exposure outside the company. Secondly, even though CMAs have obligations to their profession, the public, and themselves to maintain the highest standards of ethical conduct, they are precluded from being a "whistle-blower" outside of the company without authorization from the company. In essence, CMAs are expected to be loyal to their organizations by not revealing confidential information, even though, as professionals, there may be professional obligations to third parties, such as the Securities and Exchange Commission (SEC), shareholders, creditors, and other external stakeholders.

As to that portion of the IMA standards on ethical conduct that describe how to resolve ethical conflict, the management accountant must (1) "discuss the problem with the immediate superior, unless it appears that the superior is involved, in which case the problem should be presented initially to the next higher managerial level. Contact with levels above the immediate superior should be initiated only with the superior's knowledge,

assuming the superior is not involved." Then the management accountant with the ethical problems should "clarify relevant concepts with an objective adviser to obtain an understanding of possible courses of action." (3) "If the ethical conflict still exists after exhausting all levels of internal review, the management accountant may have no other recourse on significant matters than to resign from the organization and submit an informative memorandum to an appropriate representative of the organization." Finally, the IMA code states that "except where legally prescribed, communication of such problems to authorities or individuals not employed or engaged by the organization is not considered appropriate."

1. Commentary on These IMA Standards

These procedures for resolving ethical conflicts raise several questions: (1) If the ethical conflict still exists after exhausting all levels of internal review, to which representative is it appropriate to submit an informative memorandum? (2) Are the external auditors for the company considered "engaged by the organization" so that an informative memorandum to the external auditors would be acceptable without violating the confidentiality rule described above that requires no external disclosure of confidential information except when authorized or legally obligated to do so? In effect, when the management accountant, as a CMA, has no support within the company with respect to an illegal or an unethical problem, then the accountant's integrity and job are at risk. The management accountant might not receive help from the company or the accounting profession because the IMA code does not suggest the existence of any professional responsibilities to external stakeholders, such as shareholders, creditors, and regulators.

B. Internal Auditors in Corporations or Private Businesses

The code of ethics of the Institute of Internal Auditors (IIA) was originally issued in 1968 (27 years after the IIA was created in 1941). The IIA codes has not been revised since 1976, and then only for the purpose of recasting the language in the plural rather than the singular. The code received little attention until 1972 when the certified internal auditor program was established and the code became important in preparing for the certified internal auditor (CIA) examination.

The fundamental nature of the IIA code is embodied in Articles II, V, and VI, which are cited here. Article II: "Members, in holding the trust of their employers, shall exhibit loyalty in all matters pertaining to the affairs of the employer or to whomever they may be rendering a service. However, members shall not knowingly be a party to any illegal or improper activity." Article V: Members shall be prudent in the use of information acquired in the course of their duties. They shall not use confidential information for any personal gain nor in a manner which would be detrimental to the welfare of their employer." Article VI: "... in their reporting members shall reveal such material facts which, if not revealed, could either distort the report of the results of operations under review or conceal unlawful practice."

1. Commentary

As one author suggested, the IIA views the employer–auditor relationship as a very special one that is comprised of trust on the part of the employer and loyalty on the part of the internal auditor. This expected loyalty is based on the premise that internal auditors have access to privileged information to somewhat the same degree as do many members of management. Thus, employers would not be willing to grant internal auditors access to information about facilities, records, personnel, and financial data unless they were assured of the loyalty of their internal auditors. Based on this sense of loyalty, internal auditors are expected to report employee fraud and unethical and unlawful practices to their employers. Furthermore, there are no provisions in the IIA code that even remotely suggest that internal auditors should, independently, report employee fraud to external agencies, such as law enforcement, regulatory agencies, or to the general public. If, however, management and the directors decline to take action on significant internal matters, internal auditors may need to evaluate their position in the firm and may have no choice except to resign from the company if continued association with the employer would violate their legal responsibilities or jeopardize their sense of honor and loyalty. It also should be carefully noted that if the internal auditor does resign, their code would require that they not violate the employer's expectation of confidentiality. In effect, the internal auditor who resigns is not legally protected by the code if he or she blows the whistle externally. Furthermore, the IIA code does not suggest that the internal auditor has any professional responsibility to external stakeholders, such as shareholders, creditors, and regulators.

C. Internal Management Accountants Who Are CPAs

In 1993 the American Institute of CPAs (AICPA) adopted an ethics code specifically applicable to CPAs who are employed as management accountants. The following portions of the AICPA code are applicable to CPAs who are management accountants.

Section 102.3: Obligation of a Member to His or Her Employer's External Accountant: "... A member must be candid and not knowingly misrepresent the facts or knowingly fail to disclose material factors, i.e., such as responding to specific inquiries for which his or her employer's external accountant requests written representation."

Section 102.4: Subordination of Judgment by a Member. "If a member and his or her supervisor have a disagreement or dispute relating to the preparation of financial statements or the recording of transactions, the member should take the following steps to ensure that the situation does not constitute a subordination of judgment: (1) ... if after appropriate research and consultation, the member concludes that the matter has authoritative support and/or does not result in a material misrepresentation, the member need do nothing further. (2) If the member concludes that the financial statements or records could be materially misstated, the member should make his or her concerns known to the appropriate higher levels in the organization and consider documenting his or her understanding of the facts, the accounting principles involved, the application of those principles to the facts, and the parties with whom these matters were discussed. (3) If, after disclosing his or her concerns with the appropriate persons in the organization, the member concludes that appropriate action was not taken, he or she should consider his or her continuing relationship with the employer ... and should also consider a responsibility to third parties, such as regulatory authorities, and the employer's (former employer's) external accountants. In this connection, the member may wish to consult with his or her legal counsel."

1. Commentary

This AICPA code for CPAs in industry implies that the internal CPA may have a professional responsibility to third party stakeholders, but is not definitive with respect to that responsibility. In essence, this code goes minimally beyond the concept of employer loyalty that is reflected in the IIA and IMA codes, but stops short of a definitive requirement to report materially misstated financial statements to appropriate third parties. If the external auditor does not make specific inquiries in the form of a written representation, the internal CPA's action to deal with such material misrepresentation on financial statements will depend on the CPA's integrity and personal responsibility and not on any specific obligation specified in their code of ethics. Thus, the burden of responsibility is squarely on the internal CPA to suffer the consequences if he or she chooses to be a whistleblower. Because of the unstated concept of employee loyalty to the employer, the internal CPA does not appear to have the same obligation to report illegal acts as does the independent public accountant, as described later in this paper.

D. General Commentary on Management Accountants

The loyalty provisions of the IMA code, the IIA code, and the AICPA code for CPAs who are management accountants are all consistent with federal and state common laws governing the actions of agents. Employees of companies are considered to be agents of their employer, who is generally described as the principal. Two provisions of agency law, duty of loyalty and duty of obedience, are applicable to this discussion.

Duty of Loyalty (Section 395): "Unless otherwise agreed, an agent, i.e. employee, is subject to a duty to the principal, i.e. employer, not to use or communicate confidential information ... but an agent is privileged to reveal information confidentially acquired by him in the course of the agency in the protection of himself or of a third person. Thus, if the confidential information is to the effect that the principal is committing ... a crime, the agent is under no duty not to reveal it."

Duty of Obedience (Section 385): "Unless otherwise agreed, an agent has a duty to obey all reasonable directions ... but in no event does an agent have a duty to perform acts which, although otherwise within the scope of his duties, are illegal or unethical ..."

The basic problem with the accountants' ethics codes and the rules of agency is that accountants who are aware of unethical or illegal acts receive no protection of their job or their financial future if they choose to take the professional course of action and reveal company transgressions to external stakeholders. In effect, internal auditors and management accountants are not referees for the "games" of business as they are played out, and if they "blow the whistle" on illegal or unethical acts, the probability is that they will be punished through job loss, demotion, or ostricization instead of seeing the basic business transgressions corrected. This pattern of business behavior might be tolerated if one could be certain that, on the whole, the culture in the business world was one of highly ethical behavior. Unfortunately, this is not the case here late in the twentieth century as will be indicated below in the discussion of the ethical culture of business and industry.

V. THE ETHICAL CULTURE IN BUSINESS AND INDUSTRY AND ITS EFFECTS ON ACCOUNTANTS

The source of the information for this section is an article entitled "Business Ethics: A View from the Trenches" (*California Management Review,* January, 1995). The article is based principally on in-depth interviews with 30 recent graduates of the Harvard University MBA program who now hold jobs in a variety of companies. Here is a list of some of the experiences of these young managers, which reveal several disturbing patterns:

A. Many received explicit instructions from middle managers to do things that were unethical or illegal: (1) make up data to support a new product introduction, (2) falsify calculations of rates of return for a new investment so that it surpasses the hurdle rate, (3) overlook kickback schemes, (4) overlook safety defects in products, including Navy F-18 fighters and in weapons systems, (5) ship products that do not meet customer specifications, (6) find ways to fire employees, and (7) acquiesce in cover-ups involving sexual harassment.

B. Corporate ethics programs, codes of conduct, mission statements, and hot lines make little or no difference: (1) programs fail to address issues faced by young managers; (2) programs are ignored; (3) programs are inconsistent with what the company is all about; (4) only one manager in a corporate setting actually tried to make use of a code of conduct or any other corporate ethics device.

C. Senior managers forget what life in the trenches is all about. They are detached from day-to-day ethical issues and become jaded as their careers advance.

D. A number of conclusions were drawn as to what is wrong with today's baseline business ethics process: (1) Ethical vulnerabilities are not well understood; (2) the costs of a poor ethical climate are not well understood; (3) programs are not targeted to vulnerabilities; (4) there are pitfalls in the use of hotlines in fostering open communication; (5) there is an absence of recognition and rewards for doing the right thing; (6) there is an absence of ongoing monitoring and measurement of ethics process performance; and (7) managers are not held accountable for managing the ethical climate within their departments on an ongoing basis.

1. Commentary

It is estimated that the cost to the North American economy is $100 billion per year (1) to investigate fraud and wrongdoing, (2) to solve the problems, and (3) to ensure no recurrence. Other costs include layoffs, litigation, plant closings, business failures, missed opportunities, mass exodus of talent, and lost corporate pride and reputation. Another loss that is related to the focus of this paper is the cost to the accounting profession in the form of inaccurate financial statements, lack of professionalism in not supporting the positions of external stakeholders, and a degree of general malaise that is consistent with the extent of unethical practices described above occurring in the business world.

VI. PRACTICING PUBLIC ACCOUNTING IN AN UNLICENSED, UNREGULATED ENVIRONMENT

The effects described above about the ethical culture of the business world and its effects on socialization and the degree of accountability results in another major issue for some users of CPA services. Recent opportunities have surfaced to allow unlicensed business organizations, such as American Express, to provide professional accounting services now offered only by CPA firms. Even though the general public views the CPA designation as a hallmark of quality, there is an important distinction between ethics in a business firm and ethics in a professional services firm. CPAs who offer professional services as employees of a non-CPA firm can face serious ethical conflicts between their professional responsibilities and their organizational responsibilities to their employers. CPAs working in business firms are expected to follow the rules of the accounting profession, but these responsibilities may be obscured by competing demands placed on them by the company's management, customers, and shareholders. The ethical tone of business firms are significantly different from the tone of professional firms because there are significant economic and social incentives that could confuse the CPA's professional role and responsibility.

A key issue, then, is whether the accounting profession should allow licensed CPAs to practice public accounting while they are employees of a nonprofessional business organization (*The CPA Journal*, August 1996).

VII. THE NATURE OF ETHICS EDUCATION AS AN INTEGRAL COMPONENT OF ACCOUNTING EDUCATION

In the 1980s, a commission was created that was known as the Treadway Commission after the chairman's name. The focus of the commission was to explore the problems of fraudulent financial reporting in the United States. The commission was made up of representatives from a variety of accounting and business organizations. Its final report pointed out that fraudulent financial reporting was the responsibility of four groups: (1) the companies that do it, (2) the auditors who do not detect it, (3) the regulators who provide inadequate oversight, and (4) the accounting educators who do not teach ethics in accounting programs. Among other actions, this report challenged educators to initiate a program to incorporate ethics education into the accounting curriculum. Bill Beaver, a Stanford University professor who was president of the American Accounting Association (AAA) at the time, worked out an arrangement with the then-Big Eight accounting firms to each contribute $10,000 to help the AAA to finance an ethics education program. Seven of the accounting firms contributed the money and the eighth, Arthur Andersen, made its contribution in the form of developing a series of videos depicting ethics scenarios in accounting, finance, and management, and providing facilities for an ethics conference. A newly created AAA ethics committee set to work to collect ethics cases and encourage university accounting faculty to introduce ethics education into their accounting courses. At the present time there is an AAA ethics casebook of 50 ethics cases, each with a teaching note edited by an ethicist. A variety of ethics seminars have been conducted by the AAA and by individual universities on an annual basis in various geographic locations. It is not certain how many universities actually offer ethics courses or introduce ethics discussions in individual accounting courses. Clearly, there is room for growth because it appears that only 2% of accounting academics listed in a national directory indicated that ethics is one of their teaching and research specialties. A significant development in accounting education has been the introduction of a number of ethics decision models that students and practicing accountants can learn to use to resolve an ethics issue. In theory, the use of a decision model should help a person involved in an ethical dilemma to analyze the situation in a logical manner and, it is hoped, make a rational decision instead of an emotional one. The model in the appendix that follows this article is just one version of several decision models that are in use.

Another educational development that is gradually being initiated by state CPA societies is a requirement for new CPAs and CPAs who transfer into the state through reciprocity to take an 8-hour ethics course or to pass an ethics examination before receiving their initial CPA certificate in that state. North Carolina is one example of the few states that offer an 8-hour ethics course for new CPAs about 15 times per year in various locations around the state. CPAs with current certificates in effect also are eligible to take the course for CPE credit. Other states require the successful completion of a written examination. It is conceivable that, in the near future, some states may require all practicing CPAs to take an ethics course every 3 years or so as part of their CPE requirements. Such a requirement would be one of many steps needed to improve the ethical climate of the business world. Other initiatives related to improving the ethical climate of business are described below.

VIII. CHANGES NEEDED TO IMPROVE THE ETHICAL CLIMATE IN SOCIETY

Based on the nature of the ethical culture of the business community and the vagueness of the language of corporate and accounting codes of ethics, new initiatives are being developed to help improve the ethical climate of U.S. society. These initiatives include (1) changing the primary purpose of the external audit; (2) identifying the responsibilities of public accountants who audit financial statements; (3) improving the business ethics process; and (4) focusing on the professional responsibilities of management accountants and internal auditors.

A. Changing the Primary Purpose of the External Audit

Until the 1930s, the external audit function emphasized the detection of fraud as the primary purpose of the audit. Perhaps as a result of the depression of the 1930s, the accounting profession by 1939 came to the conclu-

sion that the detection of fraud was prohibitively costly. By the early 1960s, it was decided that an audit could not be relied on to discover fraud. In 1977 the auditor was viewed as having the responsibility within the inherent limitations of the audit process to focus his examination on the search for material errors and irregularities. By 1988 an AICPA draft of audit standards on fraud detection stipulated that the auditor should design the audit to provide reasonable assurance of detecting material errors and irregularities. In the early 1990s, the philosophy shifted to a more in-depth assessment of the existence and effective use of the best ethical practices by companies being audited. The need for an in-depth assessment has been reinforced by the Private Securities Litigation Reform Act of 1995 (described below), which stipulates that the auditor is protected as a whistleblower to the SEC under specified conditions. These developments focus attention on developing an effective business-ethics process that will have significant benefits for companies and at the same time provide more assurance to auditors that the financial statements are fairly presented. The Private Securities Litigation Reform Act is described next, followed by a discussion of a risk-assessment process for the purpose of improving the ethical culture of business and industry.

B. The Responsibilites of Public Accountants Who Audit Financial Statements

Audit Requirements: The Private Securities Litigation Reform Act of 1995 imposed a significant set of obligations upon independent public accountants who audit financial statements required by the 1934 Act. The Reform Act authorizes the SEC to adopt rules that modify or supplement the practices and procedures followed by auditors in the conduct of an audit. Moreover, the act requires auditors to establish procedures capable of detecting material illegal acts, identifying material-related party transactions, and evaluating whether there is a substantial doubt about the issuer's ability to continue as a going concern during the next fiscal year.

"If the auditor becomes aware of information indicating an illegal act, it must determine whether an illegal act occurred and the illegal act's possible effect on the issuer's financial statements. Then the auditor must inform the issuer's management about any illegal activity and assure itself that the audit committee or the board of directors is adequately informed. If the auditor concludes that (1) the illegal act has a material effect on the issuer's financial statements, (2) neither the senior management nor the board has taken timely and appropriate remedial actions, and (3) the failure to take remedial action is reasonably expected to warrant departure from a standard auditor report or warrant resignation from the auditor's engagement, then the auditor must promptly report its conclusions to the issuer's board. Within one day of receiving such report, the issuer must notify the SEC and furnish the auditor with a copy of that notice. If the auditor does not receive such notice, then the auditor must either resign or furnish the SEC with its report to the board. If the auditor resigns, it must furnish the SEC with a copy of its report."

"The Reform Act provides that an auditor shall not be held liable in a private action for any finding, conclusion, or statement expressed in the report which the act requires the auditor to make to the SEC. The SEC can impose civil penalties against an auditor who willfully violates the Reform Act by failing to resign or to furnish a report to the SEC."

1. Commentary

Because the *Private Securities Litigation Reform Act of 1995* has only been in force for a short time there is little information available as to how effective this requirement will be. In essense, the Act puts specific requirements on the external auditor rather than on individual CPAs. Whether other actions will eventually put pressure on accounting organizations that regulate the actions of management accountants, such as CMAs, IIAs, or CPAs, to modify their codes of ethics to place more specific responsibilities on internal professional management accountants to report illegal acts to the external accountants remains to be seen. In the meantime the move toward the development of a business ethics process within a company or other organization to improve its ethical culture may trigger a review of the codes of ethics of management accountants.

C. An Initiative to Improve the Business Ethics Process

The baseline business ethics process during the early 1990s consisted of three initiatives: (1) A corporate code of ethics; (2) ethics training and awareness programs; and (3) ethics hotlines. Although these initiatives were based on good intentions, they have not prevented the types of illegal and unethical practices described earlier. For instance, although 95% of Fortune 500 companies have codes of ethics, a recent survey suggested that only 25% have an ethical culture consistent with the code (ethical management). Furthermore, ethics training programs often are perfunctory and often do not target ethical vulnerabilities. Hotlines often tend to dampen the communication process because of efforts to find and punish the person who reported the ethical transgression rather than focusing on solving the underlying problem. These weaknesses in the current business ethics process has stimulated some accounting firms to develop a more advanced business ethics process. A process initiated by KPMG Peat Marwick as a consulting service to companies and other organizations will be described here briefly to develop and help explain the components and benefits of such processes.

The purpose of an effective business ethics process is to make it easier for an organization's management and employees to comply with all applicable laws and regulations and to base their business decisions and daily work actions primarily on ethical values. The KPMG approach to building an effective business ethics process involves six functions: (1) Identify and prioritize the ethical and legal risks; (2) target messages in the company's ethics code, values statement, and mission statement to high priority risks; (4) develop innovative ways to motivate and monitor ethical performance; (5) do a periodic external monitoring of ethical performance; and (6) make every effort to continuously improve the business ethics process.

The fundamental purpose of building an effective business ethics process is to shift the focus from a control mindset to an empowerment mindset. A control mindset focuses on regulatory compliance strategy, reports of misconduct, compliance standards and audits, employee hotlines, and aggressive investigation. With a new focus, the emphasis is on empowerment, educational and consultative strategy, training and education to build awareness, individual and management consultancy, and the transfer of learning through active employee communications. In effect, the focus of an effective business ethics program is to change the company culture from a boss–employee orientation to a leaders-and-teams orientation. The following benefits are perceived to be achieved through an effective business ethics process: (1) A better business reputation; (2) a workplace culture that fosters pride and a sense of purpose and value; (3) improved employee morale and productivity; (4) better communications and organizational learning; (5) prevention of fraud and organizational wrongdoing; (6) development of strong relationships built on trust; and (7) reduced litigation risk.

Another significant benefit of this risk assessment

process is that it provides support for internal and external professional accountants and auditors (CMAs, IIAs, and CPAs) in carrying out their professional duties without facing the personal risks of being whistle-blowers to external parties on matters not protected by their codes of ethics. The relationship of the professional responsibilities of accountants and the specifications of accountants' codes of ethics are briefly discussed next.

D. The Professional Responsibilities of Management Accountants (CPA, CMA) and Internal Auditors (IIA)

Accounting is considered a *profession* because to earn the designation requires advanced education and training and involves intellectual skills. An accountant is considered a *professional* because of great skill and experience in fields such as financial reporting, taxation, and auditing. Accountants are expected to exhibit professionalism in their work because of their professional status, which means that they perform their services *in the public interest* using appropriate methods, character, and standards. Within this level of responsibility accountants are expected or obligated to account to designated parties on various financial matters. As a professional, an accountant is accountable for his or her behavior in the form of legal and moral obligations to answer to someone sitting in judgment. In effect, the accountant is legally and ethically accountable for the welfare of others, which involves personal accountability and the ability to act without guidance or superior authority. The accountant is expected to be capable of making moral or rational decisions on one's own and therefore to be answerable for one's behavior.

These qualifications seem to imply that an accountant has a minimum duty to apply generally accepted accounting principles within the framework of the accounting organization's code of ethics. If the code of ethics is not definitive in handling a particular ethical or legal issue, the accountant, as a professional, would normally be expected to take a moral high ground to answer to those stakeholders materially affected by the decision of those who are sitting in judgment. Unfortunately, because the codes of ethics of management accountants and internal auditors emphasize loyalty to their employer, external stakeholders are not protected from unethical or illegal practices if the management accountant's organization insists on internal loyalty for "cooked" financial statements, and so on. For example, the language of the AICPA code of ethics for management accountants who are CPAs states: "If, after dis-

cussing his or her concerns with the appropriate persons of the organization, the member concludes that appropriate actions was not taken, he or she should consider his or her continuing relationship with the employer ... and should also consider a responsibility to third parties, such as regulatory authorities and the employee's (former employee's) external accountants. In this connection the member may wish to consult his or her legal counsel."

This language in the AICPA code suggests that professionalism is being sacrificed for the protection of the employer. In such a case, it seems clear that the culture of the organization is one of a boss–employee mindset that results in punishment of the whistleblower instead of correcting the illegal or unethical act, to the detriment of external stakeholders such as shareholders, creditors, and new investors. This situation points to a crucial question: is the existing language in codes of ethics of management accountants that places loyalty to the employer as a priority over external stakeholders (such as creditors and shareholders) a justifiable position for organizations that should be fostering a sense of professionalism and responsibility for its members and protecting them at the same time?

IX. CURRENT AND FUTURE ISSUES IN ACCOUNTING AND BUSINESS ETHICS

To this point the thrust of this article has been to explain the nature of the accounting function and to describe the development of the ethical culture within the accounting profession and in industry. There is considerable evidence that the culture of the business community is less ethical than what our capital markets should expect with respect to the integrity of our system of financial reporting. This lack of an ethical posture in the business community puts a heavy burden on the profession of accounting, not only to detect unethical practices that effect financial reporting, but also because there is pressure on accountants to rationalize certain unethical behaviors and to accept improper financial positions. One example of such a situation was noted in a speech by Walter Scheutze, chief accountant of the SEC, who chided the external auditors for being "cheerleaders" for their clients. Unfortunately, the accounting profession did not support those charges and exerted enough pressure on Scheutze that he chose to resign his position as chief accountant of the SEC. In any case, in order to move the business community and the accounting profession to an acceptable level of ethical behavior, it is important to understand what factors have contributed to the frequent existence of lower levels of ethical responses than what is desired in a viable economic system.

A. The Concepts of Morality and Socialization

As discussed in Section III, psychological research suggests that morality is either developed by the individual or is acquired through the ethical socialization of the culture. Based on these theories, we must ask which theory, moral reasoning or socialization, explains an accountant's approach to ethical dilemmas? Studies that have investigated the influence of an individual's level of moral development on accounting-related decisions suggest that the individual with lower reasoning levels is more prone to make questionable independent judgments, underreport audit time, and avoid whistleblowing. If management of an audit firm is more likely to promote individuals who have values common to the organization and its people, then moral reasoning levels are likely to be more homogeneous at the manager and partner ranks. Thus, an audit firm's socialization level is likely to be related to the individual auditor's level of moral reasoning, with an individual's promotability tied to the ethical culture of the accounting firm.

In addition to the potential conflict between their moral level of reasoning and the effects of a socialization culture, an accountant must also deal with the fact that their ethical domain consists of at least four groups: the client who pays for the services rendered, the professional accounting firm that employs the accountant, the accounting profession, and the users of the financial statement information. Thus, accountants' ethically sensitive decisions are affected by their moral level of reasoning, the effects of socialization in their work environment, and the accountability pressures that may tend to alter an ethically sensitive decision.

B. The Need for Definitive Guidance on Ethics Issues

The conflicting pressures that both external auditors and internal management accountants face would suggest the need for definitive guidance by the accounting organizations (AICPA, IMA, and IIA) to help external and internal accountants make intelligent, ethically acceptable decisions on complicated issues. There seems to be little support for the use of ethics decision models (see the example in the Appendix), and the codes of

ethics of each of these accounting organizations tend to supply loyalty to the employer rather than responsibility to at least the direct stakeholders who are materially affected by an unethical decision.

Several steps might be initiated to support morally correct decisions by external and internal accountants. These initiatives might include (1) broadening the definition of what it means to be professional; (2) using more definitive wording in the codes of ethics of accountants to support concrete actions to solve the ethical dilemma without penalizing the reporting accountant; (3) more support by accounting organizations for regulators, such as the SEC, instead of a willingness to take the low road to satisfy the socialization mindset of their members; and (4) a strong message to the corporate world to build an effective business ethics process within their organizations to shift the organizational culture from a control mindset to an empowerment mindset described earlier in this article.

APPENDIX: DECISION MODEL FOR RESOLVING ETHICAL ISSUES

I. Describe the unethical opportunity that existed in the case or is being proposed (what, where, when, how).

II. Who are the stakeholders? (Persons or groups directly or indirectly affected by the actions. Examples: your boss, financial vice president, president, directors, IRS, the community, creditors, owners, regulators, families, employees, labor union, accounting profession.)

III. What are the pressures driving the motivations of the key stakeholders?

To be unethical	To be ethical
Desire to keep a client	Confidentiality rules
Job security	Personal integrity
Loyalty to superior or firm	Professional responsibilities
Personal benefit	Compliance with the law
Loyalty to company priorities	Loyalty to company policies
Short-term family welfare	Long-term family welfare
Has authority and avoids responsibility	Rights of others
	Improve product quality
Rationalization	Likely to be held accountable

IV. Identify alternative courses of action.
   A. Rationalize unethical stance (malicious obedience);
   B. Exit the problem: transfer to another division or quit the company;

C. Voice your concern by standing up for the ethical alternative.

V. Assess the probable consequences of each alternative.

   A. Rationalization: Keep job, compromise integrity, loyalty to company priorities, short-term family welfare, keep the client, are not contributing to changing the ethical culture of the company, minimal objective reasoning as to the consequences, ignoring the code of ethics of your profession;

   B. Exit the situation: Keep job or get a new job, no contribution to changing the ethical culture, avoiding responsibility;

   C. Voice concern: Maintain integrity and professional responsibility, likely treated as a whistleblower: demoted, fired, or ostracized.

VI. Make a decision: Select alternative supporting the most important stakeholders, supports your integrity and professional responsibilities.

Also See the Following Articles

AUDITING PRACTICES • BUSINESS ETHICS, OVERVIEW • CORPORATE RESPONSIBILITY • WHISTLE-BLOWING

Bibliography

Axline, L. L. (1990, December). The bottom line of ethics: A fresh perspective on a worthwhile subject. *Journal of Accountancy.*

Badaracco, J. L. & Webb, A. Jr. (1995, January). Business ethics: A view from the trenches. *California Management Review.*

Boisjoly, R. M. (1993, March). Personal integrity and accountability. *Accounting Horizons.*

Bruns, W. J., Jr., & Merchant, K. A. (1990, August). The dangerous morality of managing earnings. *Management Accounting.*

Courtemanche, Gil (1988, February). The ethics of whistleblowing. *Internal Auditor.*

Ghosh, D., & Crain, T. (1996). Experimental investigation of ethical standards and perceived probability of audit on intentional noncompliance, behavioral research in accounting (1996 Supplement). American Acct. Assn.

Hanson, K. (1987, September). What Good Are Ethics Courses? Stanford University, Across the Board Commentary.

Lane, M. R. (1991, February). Improving American business ethics in three steps. *The CPA Journal.*

Loeb, S. E. (1990, Fall). Whistleblowing and accounting education. *Accounting Education.*

Mednick, R. (1990, January). Independence: Let's get back to basics. *Journal of Accountancy.*

Mihalek, P. H., Rich, A. J., & Smith, C. S. (1987). Ethics and Management Accountants.

Naj, A. K. (1992, July 22). Internal suspicions: GE's drive to purge fraud is hampered by workers' distrust. *Wall Street Journal.*

Ponemon, L. A. (1996). Practicing Public Accounting in an Unlicensed, Unregulated Environment.

Poynter, H., & Thomas, C. (1994, January). Review: Can ethics be taught? *Management Accounting.*

Rigdon, J. E. (1992, August 27). Tipsters telephoning ethics hot lines can end up sabotaging their own jobs. *Wall Street Journal.*

Silas, C. J., "P." (1994, December) The moral dimension of competitiveness. *Management Accounting.*

Wallace, D., & White, J. B. (1988, Summer). Building integrity in organizations. *New Management.*

ACTS AND OMISSIONS

Susanne Gibson
University College of St. Martin

GLOSSARY

active euthanasia Bringing about the death of another, for his or her own good, by means of a positive act, for example, administering a lethal injection.

consequentialism The view that the only morally relevant feature of an action is its consequences. Utilitarianism is the most well-known form of consequentialism.

deontology The view that morality is based on doing whatever it is one's duty to do. Acting morally consists of acting in accordance with duty, or as some have put it, acting for the sake of duty.

passive euthanasia Bringing about the death of another, for his or her own good, by means of an omission, for example, failing to administer life-saving medication.

rights theory The view that morality is based on rights. Acting morally becomes a matter of not infringing on the moral rights of others, which may entail both duties of noninterference and duties of positive assistance.

virtue theory The view that morality is a matter of discerning and developing the moral virtues. The emphasis is on developing a moral character, and the answer to the question, "What should I do?" becomes, "Do what is virtuous, or what the virtuous person would do."

THE DOCTRINE OF ACTS AND OMISSIONS (DAO) states roughly that there is, or is sometimes, a morally relevant difference between an act and an omission, where the consequences of the act and the omission are identical. As Jonathan Glover puts it, "the 'acts and omissions doctrine' says that, in certain contexts, failure to perform an act, with certain foreseen bad consequences of that failure, is morally less bad than to perform a different act which has the identical foreseen bad consequences" (J. Glover, 1977. *Causing Death and Saving Lives*, p. 92. Penguin, Harmondsworth, UK). The doctrine is founded on a more general claim that there is more to morality than the weighing of consequences.

I. DEBATE OVER THE STANDING OF THE DOCTRINE

There has been extensive debate over the standing of the DAO. At a theoretical level, the debate is often situated within the wider disagreement between virtue theorists and deontologists, who tend to have some sympathy for the DAO, and consequentialists, who tend to reject its validity. This wider disagreement also often encompasses the debate over the principle of double effect (PDE). What both the DAO and the PDE have in common is that they imply or assume that it is not just the consequences of an action that count when assessing its moral worth or the moral worth of the actor.

At a practical level, the DAO has been invoked by those who claim that there is a difference between "killing" and "letting die," which more or less corresponds to the morally relevant difference between active and passive euthanasia. At the same time, the rejection of the doctrine has led some to reject the idea that there is a morally relevant distinction between active and passive euthanasia. Thus the intelligibility of the doctrine has important repercussions for one of the most controversial issues in contemporary applied ethics, although it has been suggested that the question of whether the claim that passive but not active euthanasia is permissible can be maintained does not hinge on the standing of the DAO, or on the moral relevance of the distinction between killing and letting die.

Even at a theoretical level, however, the debate is firmly rooted in practical examples, insofar as the formulation of the doctrine often begins with the intuitive appeal of cases in which there do appear to be morally relevant differences between an act and an omission with identical consequences:

1. Although it is morally wrong to allow people in underdeveloped countries to die of starvation, to do so is not as wrong as sending them poisoned food.
2. Although it might be morally permissible to leave one injured person to die by the roadside when hurrying to the rescue of several, it would be outrageous to drive over a recumbent person in order to reach the others in time.

However, opponents of the doctrine are quick to point to cases in which it would generally be agreed that an omission is at least as bad as an act:

1. If a man who will inherit a fortune when his father dies omits to give him the medicine necessary for keeping him alive, this is as bad as actively killing him.
2. Smith and Jones both stand to gain a large inheritance if their 6-year-old cousins die. Smith drowns the child while she is taking a bath and arranges things to make it look like an accident. Jones enters the bathroom while his cousin is taking a bath, also intending to drown the child. However, as he does so, he sees the child slip, hit her head, and fall face down in the bath. Jones watches and does nothing as the child drowns.

However, the debate does not, and cannot, proceed simply in terms of which side can provide the most, or the most convincing, illustrations. Indeed, those who support the doctrine accept that there are many cases in which the distinction does not apply, and those who oppose it accept that there are cases in which it does. The disagreement arises over whether, where there does appear to be a difference, that difference can be explained and justified in terms of the mere fact that one case is an act and the other an omission.

II. THE CONCEPTUAL DISTINCTION

A. Drawing the Distinction

Before the standing of the DAO can be assessed, some work has to be done by way of clarifying the conceptual distinction between an act and an omission. Some opponents argue that there simply is not a clear distinction, since some "events" can be described equally well either as an act or as an omission. For example, in the case cited already in which a man omits to give his father the medicine necessary for keeping him alive, it is suggested that the man's culpability for his father's death is such that it may be fitting to describe what happens not as an omission but as "a positive act of withholding the medicine" (Glover, 1977, 95). Similarly, it is suggested that when a signalman fails to pull the lever necessary to prevent the train from crashing, we are naturally inclined to think of and describe his omission as something that he does.

This is not, however, simply a point about the vicissitudes of language. The problem that proponents of the DAO face is the difficulty of formulating an account of the conceptual difference between an act and an omission that does not beg the question in favor of the doctrine. As Glover points out, to draw the distinction on the basis of an agent's culpability, such that an act is taken to be anything which we consider the agent to be morally responsible for, would make the doctrine an empty analytic truth: an agent is morally responsible for her acts, and an act is anything for which the agent is morally responsible.

B. Some Alternatives

1. Doing and Allowing

The distinction is often put in terms of "doing" and "allowing": an act is something that one does, and an omission is something that one merely allows to happen. The first thing to note, however, is that there are different kinds of "allowing," not all of which can be correlated with an omission. Foot points to the difference between allowing in the sense of "forbearing to prevent" and allowing in the sense of enabling something to happen. In the first sense we are to think of a sequence of events as already begun, where the agent could intervene to prevent something from happening, but does not. For example, he could mend the dripping tap, but allows it to go on leaking. In the second sense, the agent allows something to happen by removing an obstacle. For example, she removes a plug and allows the water to drain away. According to Foot, it is only in the first sense that allowing requires an omission, or is equivalent to an omission. In the second sense, we are more likely to talk of commission.

Second, it is clear that "allowing" is often held to be just as bad as "doing." For example, allowing one's dog to die of neglect is just as bad as, if not worse, than feeding it poison. In this case, of course, it might be said that to neglect one's dog is to initiate a sequence of events such that the dog will die, and therefore might be thought of as a commission. However, suppose that the neglected animal finds its way into the agent's home. The agent is not thereby permitted to feed it poison, but neither is it clear that he is permitted to ignore the situation, that is, to fail to intervene in a sequence of events that are already underway. There must be more to the distinction, then, than simply the difference between "doing" and "allowing."

2. Positive and Negative Duties

Although it is important to be clear about what we intend by the difference between an act and an omission, it is apparent that proponents of the doctrine cannot get very far by means of clarification of the terms alone. At some point it becomes necessary to appeal to moral concepts in order to explain and justify the distinction. Foot, for example, in one of her early treatments of the topic, draws on the concept of duty, and appeals to the distinction between positive and negative duties, or between "what we owe people in the form of aid and what we owe them in the way of non-interference" (P. Foot, 1967. The problem of abortion and the doctrine of double effect. *The Oxford Review*, pp. 5–13).

For Foot, the duty of noninterference, or the duty to refrain from injuring another person, is stronger than the duty to give aid, or to help another person. Hence it is sometimes less wrong to fail to help someone (to fail to fulfill a positive duty) than it is to injure them (to fail to fulfill a negative duty).

3. Individual Rights

Similarly, Judith Jarvis Thomson argues that the difference between doing and allowing, or more specifically, between killing and letting die, can be explained in terms of individual rights. Thomson approaches the problem by asking why it is sometimes permissible to kill one instead of killing five, but not, it seems, permissible to kill one in order to prevent the deaths of five. It is suggested that it cannot just be that killing is worse than letting die, or that an act is worse than an omission, since there are some cases in which the agent is permitted to kill one in order to save five. Thomson explains the fact that it is often considered worse to kill than it is to allow to die by appealing to the notion of a right to life: killing usually infringes the right to life, whereas letting die does not. However, it is argued that since killing does not always infringe the right to life, and since there is more to morality than rights, we cannot make a clear-cut distinction between killing on the one hand and letting die on the other. It might seem then that Thomson does not in fact accept the validity of the DAO. However, she can be aligned with authors such as Foot insofar as she clearly does believe that there is more to morality than consequences or outcomes, and that there is sometimes a morally relevant difference between an act and an omission.

4. Causal Responsibility

Another way to approach the question is to ask when, if ever, an agent is causally responsible for failing to prevent something. Since most if not all proponents of the DAO will accept that we are sometimes just as responsible for the harm we fail to prevent as for the harm we bring about, an account needs to be given of the circumstances in which we are or are not culpable for what we allow to happen. In a more recent paper, Foot puts the distinction in terms of "allowing something to happen and being the agent to whom the happening can be ascribed" (1985, 24), where allowing is again understood as not intervening in a train of events that are already underway, and where agency is ascribed on the grounds that a sequence of events is initiated by the agent, and where a train of events can be initiated by refraining from doing something as well as by a positive act. However, as Foot admits, it is not always easy to draw this distinction in practice, since it is not always possible to determine exactly where one sequence of events ends and another begins.

Following Jeremy Bentham, John Harris refers to those omissions that can be thought of as the cause of an occurrence, and for which the agent is therefore responsible, as "negative actions." Harris considers a number of accounts which attempt to limit our negative actions to those failures to act in a way that it is our duty to act, or in a way that we might be expected to act, or when not acting constitutes a departure from what normally happens. However, Harris argues that insofar as all these accounts appeal in some way to expectation, we need some explanation of what those expectations are grounded in. For Harris our expectations are or ought to be grounded in a principle of harm: we have a duty to prevent harm and therefore we expect moral agents to minimize harm. This means, however, that the expectation that the agent will act so as to prevent harm arises out of the duty to do so, and not the other way around. Since a failure to prevent harm is just as likely to arise out of an omission as it is out of an act, there is no clear distinction between the two.

The dispute between Harris and those with whom he takes issue can best be understood in the context of the much bigger dispute over the standing of competing moral theories, or competing approaches to moral practice.

III. CONSEQUENTIALISM, VIRTUE THEORY, AND DEONTOLOGY

It was already pointed out that many of those who object to the DAO are consequentialists. It is not difficult to see why this should be the case. A consequentialist judges outcomes rather than the process by which an outcome is reached: it is ends that matter, not the means to the end. Where two outcomes are identical, then it cannot make any difference whether they are the result of an act or an omission. Harris, in focusing on the idea of harm, claims that a bad state of affairs is, *prima facie,* one in which harm occurs which might not have occurred, had those involved behaved differently. However, Harris argues,

> [t]here are two ways in which we inflict harm on our fellows. ... One way of inflicting harm on others is to do something which results in their being harmed; the other is to fail to do something

the consequence of which is that they are harmed, in short, to fail to prevent harm. (Harris, 1980, 1)

Further, Harris holds that we are just as responsible for the harm that we fail to prevent as we are for the harm that we inflict as a result of something that we do. Thus for Harris, there is no morally significant difference between an act and an omission.

It is not so much that consequentialists refuse to accept that there can sometimes be a difference between an act and an omission where they appear to have the same consequences. Rather, it is suggested that where there is an apparent difference between an act and an omission with the same consequences, this difference can be explained without reference to the DAO. One suggestion is that where there appears to be a difference, this is not because a harmful act is intrinsically worse than a harmful omission; rather, the difference is held to lie in the different side effects. That is, it is suggested that once all the consequences of the act are taken into account, it can be seen that the act and the omission do not have identical consequences after all. For example, the difference between killing and letting die might be explained in terms of the feelings of horror or of guilt that a killing produces, or in terms of the undermining of security. However, if the difference does lie in the different side effects, then it is clear that the DAO no longer applies: since side effects are also consequences, then it is no longer the case that the act and the omission have the same outcome overall.

Nevertheless, in spite of the appeal of the idea that we are responsible for the harm that we fail to prevent a well as the harm that we actively bring about, and in spite of the consequentialists' attempts to explain away the fact that many do still feel that there is some difference between acts and omissions, it remains the case that the DAO is deeply embedded in what might be called "ordinary morality." That is, it fits with some ordinary intuitions about the limits of moral responsibility, and with the intuition that it is not just the consequences of an action (or omission) that matter, but sometimes also how those consequences come about. The appeal of the DAO, then, lies in the way in which it offers at least a partial explanation of why morality is not simply a question of "the size of the evil" (Foot, 1967, 14).

It is fitting here to consider the dispute between the consequentialist on the one hand and the virtue theorist, deontologist, or rights theorist on the other. Since the virtue theorist is concerned with how the agent acts, and not just with the outcome of the action, then how a set of consequences come about is as important as the nature of the consequences themselves. For the virtue theorist, morality is not just a matter of comparing different states of affairs: considerations of character and motive are also important. Similarly, for the deontologist and the rights theorist, there are things that must not be done, whatever the consequences.

If consequentialism is the only acceptable moral theory, then the DAO is false. However, it can be argued that whether or not consequentialism is an acceptable moral theory depends at least in part on how far it can account for our ordinary intuitions about moral responsibility and moral obligation. Therefore, the debate over the standing of the DAO must be seen as part of the debate over the standing of consequentialism, and not just as dependent on the outcome of that debate. The problem for proponents of the doctrine, on the other hand, is in finding an account of the distinction that does not collapse into the kind of circularity that says that we are only morally responsible for those omissions for which we are morally responsible.

IV. EUTHANASIA: KILLING AND LETTING DIE

Despite the disagreement over the DAO, it is clear that the principle has been put into practice in legal contexts. Most notably, as previously mentioned, it has been applied in the case of euthanasia. Thus the distinction between killing and letting die, or between active euthanasia and passive euthanasia, is not only felt to be a moral difference, it is also enshrined in law in most parts of the Western world. When, for example, in the United Kingdom in 1993 the decision was made to allow Tony Bland, a victim of the Hillsborough soccer tragedy, to die by withdrawing artificial feeding, Lord Goff of Chievely pointed out that

the law draws a crucial distinction between cases in which a doctor decides not to provide, or to continue to provide, for his patient treatment or care which could or might prolong his life, and those in which he decides, for example by administering a lethal drug, actively to bring his patient's life to an end. (In P. Singer, 1994. *Rethinking Life and Death*, p. 76. Oxford Univ. Press, Oxford)

Not surprisingly, however, the moral standing of the distinction between active and passive euthanasia is controversial, and it is worth pointing to the ways in which this controversy mirrors the debate over the more general distinction between an act and an omission. To begin with, just as there are difficulties in drawing the distinction between an act and an omission, so too are there difficulties in drawing a clear distinction between active and passive euthanasia. Again, the Tony Bland case is a case in point: is the removing of a feeding tube a positive act of killing, or a case of allowing to die? The confusion here is again reflected in the legal deliberations:

[Removing the tube] is undoubtedly a positive act, similar to switching off a ventilator in the case of a patient whose life is being sustained by artificial ventilation. But in my judgment in neither case should the act be classified as positive. ... [E]ssentially what is being done is to omit to feed or to ventilate; the removal of the nasogastric tube or the switching off of a ventilator are merely incidents of that omission. (Lord Browne-Wilkinson in Singer, 1994, 77)

Further, and perhaps more importantly, there is disagreement over the moral relevance of the distinction between active and passive euthanasia. It has been argued by a number of authors that if the purpose of passive euthanasia is to relieve suffering, and if it can be justified on the grounds of the prevention of suffering, then active euthanasia can also be justified in this way. Indeed, some argue that active euthanasia is preferable to passive euthanasia in some cases, since it provides a swifter and more effective means of ending a life. Nevertheless, some feel very strongly that it ought not to be part of a health professional's remit actively to end a life. Indeed, this is reflected in professional guidelines and codes of conduct. In health care ethics as in other areas of ethics, it is not so much, or not only, a question of preventing the most amount of harm possible, but of what it is permissible for one person to do to another.

Also See the Following Articles

CONSEQUENTIALISM AND DEONTOLOGY • EUTHANASIA • RIGHTS THEORY • VIRTUE ETHICS

Bibliography

Bennett, J. (1995). "The Act Itself." Clarendon Press, Oxford.
Foot, P. (1985). Morality, action and outcome. In "Morality and Objectivity" (T. Honderich, Ed.). Routledge & Kegan Paul, London.

Harris, J. (1985). "The Value of Life: An Introduction to Medical Ethics." Routledge, London.

Harris, J. (1980). "Violence and Responsibility." Routledge & Kegan Paul, London.

Nesbitt, W. (1993). Euthanasia and the distinction between acts and omissions. *Journal of Applied Philosophy,* **10**(2), 253–255.

Quinn, W. S. (1989). Actions, intentions, and consequences: The doctrine of doing and allowing. *The Philosophical Review,* **98**(3), 287–312.

Rachels, J. (1986). "The End of Life: Euthanasia and Morality." Oxford Univ. Press, Oxford.

Thomson, J. J. (1993). The trolley problem. In "Rights, Restitution and Risk." Harvard Univ. Press, Cambridge, MA.

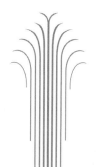

ADOPTION

Deborah H. Siegel
Rhode Island College

I. Historical Context of Today's Ethical Debates
II. Overview of Ethical Issues in Adoption
III. Conclusions

GLOSSARY

adoptee A person who has been adopted.

adoption The act of transferring legal parental rights from one parent to another.

birthparent The biological mother or father; the mother or father who has a genetic connection to the adoptee.

confidential adoption Adoption in which all identifying information about the birthparents is sealed in agency and court records; also referred to as closed adoption or traditional adoption.

open adoption Adoption in which there is contact and exchange of identifying information between birth and adoptive families.

special needs adoption Adoption of a child who is over age 3, of color, in a sibling group, or has a behavioral, emotional, or physical disability or developmental delay.

THERE ARE TWO TYPES OF ADOPTION—related and nonrelated. In related adoptions a child is adopted by a stepparent, grandparent, aunt, uncle, or other relative of the birthparent. In nonrelated adoptions, all legal ties to the child's biological family are severed and the child legally enters a family with whom she or he shares no known genetic links. There are more adoptions in the United States than in any other country. According to statistics published in 1996 by the National Adoption Information Clearinghouse, in 1992 in the United States about 127,441 adoptions were finalized; 42% of these were stepparent or relative adoptions, 15.5% were adoptions of children from the foster care system, 5% were of children from other countries, and 37.5% were either private agency or independent adoptions of children from the United States.

Adoptions are arranged under different auspices. Public agencies, usually in the form of government-funded child welfare departments, tend to focus their adoption efforts on seeking families for children who have special needs, because these youngsters tend to come to their attention through child protective services. Private agencies, both nonprofit and for profit, too sometimes serve children who have special needs, funding those services under governmental grants. Private agencies also have programs geared to finding homes for healthy infants who are available for adoption. Adoptions can, in addition, occur without agency involvement; lawyers and private individuals (sometimes called adoption facilitators) perform this service. "Identified adoption" is the term used for situations that combine elements of agency and independent adoption; in these situations, prospective adoptive parents and birthparents who want to make an adoption plan locate each other without an agency's help, and then seek out an agency for pre- and postplacement services. International adoptions, in which prospective adoptive parents in one country adopt a child from another country, also happen under this array of auspices.

Changing societal norms, values, and demographic trends are reshaping long-held beliefs and practices regarding adoption. The emergence of the birth control pill, legal access to abortion, and growing acceptance of single parenthood have drastically decreased the number of babies available for adoption and increased the stigma attached to a birthparent choosing adoption instead of choosing to parent her or his child (although this stigma applies more to birthmothers than birthfathers). As the number of babies available for adoption fell, the postwar baby boom generation reached its family building years, so the number of infertile people seeking children to adopt increased. Hence, forces of supply and demand have generated an adoption industry in which private agencies, lawyers, and adoption facilitators charge fees. At the same time, new human rights movements emerged (e.g., calling for civil rights, women's rights, welfare rights, prisoners' rights); an adoption rights movement was born in this climate. Many birthparents and adoptees, spurred by an evolving sense of their rights, now proclaim a need for knowledge of and contact with each other, and decry laws that seal adoptees' original birth certificates and adoption records forever. All of these changes have generated new ethical issues.

I. HISTORICAL CONTEXT OF TODAY'S ETHICAL DEBATES

Adoption has been a part of human history since ancient times; for example, in the Bible, the pharaoh's daughter adopted Moses. The notion of nonrelative adults providing a home for a child in need has intuitive moral appeal in many, although not all, cultures.

In most communities today's laws require sealed records that preclude contact between birth and adoptive families, but this has not always been the case. In ancient Hawaiian culture, for instance, birthparents physically handed their children to the adoptive parents, giving them explicit personal permission to become the child's parents and maintaining frequent contact with them. The idea that birthparents and adoptees should have their relationship severed legally and completely became codified in the United States in 1851 in a Massachusetts law that served as a model for many

subsequent laws. Sealed adoption records became standard as an effort to protect adoptees from the stigma of illegitimacy and birthmothers from the stigma of out-of-wedlock pregnancy. Generally, society held the view that the least a wayward unwed mother could do for her illegitimate child was place the child in an adoptive two-parent family. This advice may have reflected views that any woman who had sexual intercourse outside of marriage was morally tainted and deserved to lose her child, and any knowledge about that child, forever.

The 1960s spawned new questions about old values, including beliefs about adoption. Many people began to argue that openness and honesty are preferable to secrecy in adoption. Whereas at one time adoptive parents were advised to keep the fact of adoption from their child, the new advice was to tell children that they were adopted. Some birthmothers emerged from their shadow of shame to describe the lifelong grief they endured over their loss and to assert their right to have a voice in deciding on a family for the children they placed for adoption and their need for occasional updates about their children's well-being. Some adult adoptees formed an adoption rights movement, declaring that adoption laws deprived them of a basic human right to knowledge of their genetic heritage, causing them emotional anguish. Today in the United States, organizations such as the American Adoption Congress, Concerned United Birth Parents, and the Council for Equal Rights in Adoption challenge laws requiring sealed adoption records and frustrating adoptees' and birthparents' efforts to find one another. These efforts are countered by the National Committee for Adoption which advocates traditional confidential adoption practices.

Underlying many debates about adoption issues are questions about whether adoption should primarily serve children's needs, or should primarily, or equally, serve birthparents' or adoptive parents' interests. Today most adoption professionals maintain that adoption's primary purpose is to meet the needs of children. However, many others claim that attention to children's needs in adoption must be balanced with birthparents' and adoptive parents' perceptions of their own needs and presumed "rights" as well. One's position on this issue profoundly shapes one's stance on many ethical issues in adoption.

Clearly, adoption is a deeply value-laden arena, permeated by competing "truths" that spawn a panoply of ethical, legal, interpersonal, and emotional issues. The ethical issues involve questions regarding the right to privacy, confidentiality, truth telling, deception, self-determination and autonomy, paternalism, exploitation, distributive justice, the duty to aid, and questions about fundamental human rights. These ethical questions exist in an historical and cultural context, and infuse the categories of adoption controversies that follow.

II. OVERVIEW OF ETHICAL ISSUES IN ADOPTION

A. Adoption as an Option

Adoption is viewed differently in different societies. For instance, the Islamic world has no word for adoption; legal termination of parental rights does not exist. In Sweden most adoptions are of children from other countries, not from within Sweden itself; this reflects the widely accepted view in Sweden that every biological family can be helped to nurture its children adequately, and biological parents' rights should not be terminated. In France, Italy, and Japan there is very little adoption since adoption is generally not regarded as a suitable way to build a family.

Some voices in the adoption rights movement question whether adoption should be allowed at all. Even in the most extreme cases of child abuse and neglect, they maintain, given the necessary resources and support, a birthparent or birthfamily members can provide adequately for a child. Some who question whether adoption should exist assert that every child, even the newborn, is primally wounded by permanent separation from the birthparent(s). They believe that adult adoptees who say they have no need to search for their birthparents are in denial, captives of a society that has brainwashed them into believing the lie that the adoptee acquires the adoptive family's bloodline. Those who question the existence of adoption further maintain that birthparents are also irreparably wounded by adoption—that birthparents do not ever willingly choose adoption, but instead succumb at a time of intense vulnerability to pressure from social workers, lawyers, and other people in authority who profit from skillfully manipulating birthparents into providing children for a more economically and socially privileged class.

Proponents of adoption, on the other hand, assert that all biological parents have a right to choose adoption, some biological families are unable to care adequately for children even when assisted by extensive social services, and all children deserve a safe and loving permanent family regardless of whether that family is the child's through birth or adoption.

B. Confidentiality and Secrecy

Earlier in this century, folk wisdom was that because a child might feel hurt by the knowledge that she or he was adopted, it was best to keep that information from the child. Even today, adults in their thirties, forties, sixties, and older sometimes learn for the very first time, in going through a deceased parent's papers, that they were adopted.

Current thinking is that children ought to know they were adopted, but controversy characterizes discussions of the age at which the child should be told, the language one ought to use in the telling, and how much information one ought to share with the child about the reasons for the adoption and about the birthparents' lives and circumstances. Controversy also pervades discussions of whether one ought to wait for children to ask specific questions about their adoptions before volunteering any information, or should instead expect that all children who are adopted feel curious about such matters and may feel hesitant to ask, so parents should initiate discussions. All participants in these debates claim that their approach best protects adoptees' psychological health.

These are ethical as well as psychological issues. These issues involve questions about whether human beings have a right to know the truth about how they entered their families; whether it is right to let people assume that they were born to their parents, when in fact they were born to someone else; and whether there is a moral obligation for parents to tell their children that they adopted them, to answer questions about the adoption, and to volunteer information about the adoption when questions are not asked.

It is also not uncommon for some third party, other than the adoptive parents, to disclose to an adoptee that she or he was adopted. Extended family members, friends, and even agency personnel have at times appropriated that responsibility. When, if ever, is this ethically justifiable? In one case, for example, an adult adoptee sent away for a copy of his original birth certificate; a state clerk told him that he had none, and referred him for further information to a social service agency noted in his file. The social service agency worker told the bewildered man that the original birth certificate had been sealed. When the man, who obviously had no idea that he had been adopted, asked why, the worker decided to tell him, stating that he had a right to know. The man sued the agency, claiming that he had no need to know and that the knowledge had hurt him.

Laws regarding confidentiality in adoption have engendered conflicts among competing values. Should adoption records be sealed forever, in light of the large numbers of adult adoptees who claim a need and right to know from whence they came? If records are to be opened, at what age and in what circumstances? How can a sealed record be justifiably opened when birthparents were promised confidentiality in perpetuity? Are such promises of confidentiality relevant when they may have been made to birthparents who did not want to be severed forever from their offspring? Do adoptees, birthparents, and adoptive parents have rights to privacy from each other? Are there any limitations to this right?

For example, in some cases, courts have ordered a record to be opened and a birthparent contacted via an intermediary in order to obtain medical information deemed necessary for adequately treating an adoptee's medical condition. Controversy fills discussions of whose needs should be taken into account and held primary in making such a decision—the birthparents', the adoptee's, or the adoptive parents'. In one case, a court order led an agency to contact a birthmother with the information that the daughter she had placed for adoption 17 years before had recently been hospitalized for suicidal depression. The agency worker told the birthmother that the child's psychiatrist and adoptive parents wanted to know if there was any mental illness in the birthfamily. This incident left the birthmother deeply distraught, since the agency worker would not answer her questions about the child's well-being. The birthmother felt that the information obtained from her via the court order was not worth the anguish that opening the record caused her. When the various parties' needs and interests clash irreconcilably in this way, whose should be held paramount?

It has been argued that the most powerless, vulnerable player in the adoption circle is the young adoptee, since that person has the least voice in the adoption decision. Hence, some argue, that person's interests should supersede the birthparents' and adoptive parents'. Others ask if this holds true when the birthparent is mentally impaired or herself a youthful victim of incest, sexual or emotional abuse, or rape. Others maintain that if the adoptive parents feel that their ability to provide adequate emotional care to their child is comprised by the opening of records, that is sufficient grounds to override the adoptee's need to know.

Many adoptees have implored policy makers to understand that adoptees are unfairly denied information about themselves that is by law everyone else's birthright. These adoptees feel punished for some "crime" they never committed. Similarly, many birthparents feel

that sealed records are punishment for choosing adoption, not a protection of privacy and self-determination rights.

Many adoptees, upon reaching adolescence or adulthood, search for their birthparents. Many birthparents begin their own search, usually (but not always) waiting until the children they placed for adoption are adults. Clearly, such searches open a morass of ethical conundrums. These include whether a minor or adult adoptee has the right to seek out a birthparent who might not want to be found; if a birthparent has the right to seek out a minor or adult child, regardless of the child's feelings about that prospect; if adoptive parents have any say in this, and if so, whether they should have the legal power to interfere in the adoptee's search once the adoptee is over age 21; if once the sought for person's location has been identified, how contact should be made (should one use an intermediary, write a letter, make a phone call, or simply show up unannounced); and if the sought for person wants no contact, whether she or he has the right to decline it.

Many governments now have adoption registries created to help biological relatives, separated by adoption, find each other. There are two forms of adoption registries. In a passive registry, people seeking a biological relative simply place their names on a list and wait. If the sought for person also signs up with the same registry, a match is made. Otherwise, nothing happens. In an active registry, once one places one's name on the list, a registry employee begins a search for the sought party. Once that party is found, an invitation to receive information about or have contact with the searcher is offered.

Obviously, the ethical issues embedded in each type of registry differ. For example, some claim that a passive registry can be virtually useless, only providing an illusion of self-determination, since a birthparent who gave birth in one locale may have no idea that the baby she placed for adoption went to a family in a community far away. Similarly, her child may put his name on a list in his home community, never knowing that his birthmother would not know to put her name on that community's list. With an active registry, on the other hand, privacy rights may be violated; it may be profoundly disturbing to someone to be contacted by an intermediary, even though the sought for person has the right to reject contact by the biological relative. And it is possible that an adoptee contacted by an active registry does not even know that she or he was adopted.

Generally, use of registries is available only to adult adoptees. This leaves unanswered the question of what right minor adoptees have to access to genealogical and medical information and contact with birth relatives. Also, at least one government allows adoptive parents of adult adoptees to forbid their adult adopted child to sign on to a passive registry. This law reflects a view that the adoptive parent has a right to control this aspect of the adult adoptee's behavior.

Often adoptees, adoptive parents, and birthparents who are searching seek help from the agency that facilitated the adoption. Agencies often are bound by law to protect the confidentiality of their adoption records. Some agency workers, however, have chosen to engage in a form of civil disobedience, circumventing agency policy and law through practices such as purposefully placing a record on a desk and leaving the room, leaving the searcher alone with the file. Clearly, these workers see the searcher's need and right to know as more ethically compelling than the law.

C. Open Adoption

Given the well-documented struggles generated by secrecy and sealed records, various ways of handling issues of privacy, confidentiality, and disclosure of information have emerged in the past 15 years. Some agencies, upon placing a child in an adoptive home, give adoptive parents lengthy forms full of medical and social information about the birthparents. Some governments, such as Israel's, allow adoptees, upon age of majority, access to their sealed adoption records. New Zealand law requires that all adoptions be open.

Open adoption advocates go further, maintaining that there is a fundamental human right not only to information about one's genetic heritage, but also to ongoing contact among birthfamily members. The jury is still out on the open adoption debate, with some arguing that open adoptions are a long overdue innovation, and others maintaining that open adoption is a grave mistake that jeopardizes the adoptee's emotional development and physical safety, compromises the adoptive parents' ability to bond with and nurture their child effectively, and impairs the birthparents' grieving process.

The long-range effects of open adoptions are not yet known, since large numbers of children of open adoption have not reached adulthood. Controversies about open adoptions are numerous. For example, people argue about whether agencies should forbid, discourage, promote, or require some form of openness in adoption. There is disagreement about whose role it ought to be to make these decisions—the law, agency policy, a particular adoption facilitator (such as an attorney, social worker, or other intermediary), the birthparent, or birth and adoptive parents together.

There are many forms of openness in adoptions. Sometimes, birth and adoptive parents meet, but do not exchange any identifying information. Perhaps they exchange photographs and letters via an intermediary; sometimes they correspond directly. Sometimes they visit in each other's homes. There is a virtually infinite array of kinds and amounts of contact. Who should decide what contact will consist of?

People who agree that birthparents and adoptees have a right to have contact with each other during the adoptee's childhood sometimes disagree about whether there should be any limitations to this right. Most open adoption advocates maintain that the child's needs are primary, so birthparents who pose a physical or emotional threat to the child's well-being should be denied access to the child. Not everyone agrees, since contact can be supervised.

Some open adoption advocates have retracted their promotion of open adoption as standard practice because under the guise of openness, some prospective adoptive parents have falsely lured birthparents into terminating parental rights and making adoption plans in the belief that the adopting family would honor promises regarding ongoing contact, only to disappear once the adoption has been finalized. Adoptive parents may excuse these lies and deceptions with statements such as, "We are good parents." "The birthmother has poor judgment." "This is better for the baby." "At first we thought we were comfortable with open adoption, but now that we have the baby we feel differently," and so on. As a result of this sort of reneging on open adoption agreements, some open adoption advocates now argue that the agreements should be legally enforceable.

In the scramble to find a prospective birthmother, some would-be adoptive parents may engage in deception about their circumstances. Research on open adoption has disclosed that while prospective adoptive parents want full, honest information from birthparents, they sometimes withhold or distort information about themselves (e.g., their own alcoholism, marital distress, mental illness, and financial security).

Open adoption has also created opportunities for prospective birthparents to deceive and exploit infertile individuals and couples desperate for children. There are stories of destitute pregnant women and their partners claiming to make an adoption plan, and acquiring large sums of prenatal support money from prospective adoptive parents, while planning all along to disappear before or when the baby is born.

In open adoptions, adoptive parents typically have access to detailed, specific information about their child's genetic background and biological relatives. The openness in the adoption often suggests to people outside the immediate adoptive family that it is appropriate to ask highly personal questions about the child. This raises unique issues for adoptive parents regarding their children's right to privacy and to control the kinds and amounts of information shared about them with interested curious others.

D. International Adoption

Ethical controversy often characterizes the international adoption arena as well. Those who support international adoption note that typically a child moves from impoverished to affluent circumstances, avoiding a life of deprivation and despair. Opponents counter that children adopted internationally face many, often unrecognized, losses in addition to their loss of birthfamily—loss of country, culture, language, food, music, and religion. These children often physically look very different from the families that adopt them, so experience racism due to their minority status. Typically, the children are seen in their adoptive country as lucky to have been saved from the deprivation of their origins; this denial of the children's losses can exacerbate their isolation and pain.

International adoption is neither right nor fair, say some. These critics argue that children are better off being cared for in their countries of origin. International adoption is another form of imperialism, of the rich exploiting the poor and self-indulgently harvesting a precious resource of the developing world.

Further, some critics assert that too many adoptive parents choose international adoption for reasons other than a desire to become a bicultural family. For example, prospective adoptive parents may pursue an international adoption because they see it as more affordable, easier, and quicker to accomplish than domestic adoption, or they feel there is less possibility of their child from abroad ever successfully contacting the birthparents. Adoptive parents who rely on these reasons may be unprepared to cope effectively with the unique issues of loss and ethnicity that families formed through international adoption often face. As a result, their children suffer.

Finally, critics assert that justice would be better served if the large sums of money spent on the typical international adoption went instead to international economic development programs so that children in impoverished countries could be parented adequately in their homelands.

International adoption proponents counter that individual children ought not be sacrificed in service of an ideal that the world is far from attaining—that it is better to have a safe, caring family in another country than to languish as a malnourished, diseased, preyed upon juvenile street beggar or in an orphanage in one's country of origin.

In response to some of the critics' concerns, most adoption professionals today advise parents who adopt children from abroad to incorporate into their family's life the foods, language, art, music, and culture of their child's land of origin, and to join support groups of other adoptive families whose children come from the same country. These efforts to honor rather than deny the child's heritage, to recognize rather than belittle the child's losses, are also efforts to respond in part to ethical questions about international adoption.

E. Transracial Adoption

Similar intense debate characterizes the world of transracial adoption, both domestic and international. Most transracial adoptions in the United States consist of white families adopting children of color. Some claim that this is at least in part because agency workers use culturally biased criteria that disqualify otherwise eligible families of color seeking a child to adopt. Often children of color who are available for adoption endure long waits in foster or institutional care while an adoptive family for them is sought. Those who support transracial adoption may recognize that same-race placements are desirable, but they assert that it is more hurtful for a child to languish in emotional limbo in temporary care with no permanent family than to grow up in an adoptive family of a different race.

Different policymaking bodies have adopted different stances on this issue. In 1994 the National Association of Black Social Workers (NABSW) in the United States asserted in a position paper that "transracial adoption should be considered only after documented evidence of unsuccessful same race placement efforts have been reviewed and supported by appropriate representatives of the African American community." Amendments passed in 1996 to the Howard Metzenbaum Multiethnic Placement Act of 1994 (PL 103-382, 108 SP, Stat. 4056, Section 553 ammended) in the United States now forbid strict racial matching when children of color are awaiting adoption and adoptive families of a different race (usually white) are available.

Many opponents of transracial adoption argue that

in allowing transracial adoption, society abrogates its responsibility to recruit, train, and support same-race adoptive families for children of color. They maintain that transracial adoption enables agencies to relax efforts to find same-race homes for children, further limiting the availability of such placements. Families of color are better prepared to help children of color learn how to cope with racism and to feel secure in and good about their racial and cultural identities. Transracial adoption is seen as an unrecognized form of cultural genocide and child abuse. Children adopted transracially are destined to be seen as interlopers in the white world and aliens in the community of their race.

Interestingly, in the United States federal proscriptions against racial matching do not apply to children of Native American descent. A compelling example of the controversies regarding transracial adoption in the United States involves the Indian Child Welfare Act (ICWA) of 1978 (P.L. 95-608, 92 Stat. 3069), which gives Native American tribes control over adoption decisions for children who have a portion of Native American blood. The act requires that the tribe, not the birthparents, choose the adoptive placement. Critics claim that this law makes tribal survival more important than children's safety or birthparent rights. They question whether it is right, particularly in circumstances when neither birthparent identifies with a Native American heritage, that the tribe has final say over where a child is placed. To some, this law is a form of racism and an obstacle to self-determination; to others, it is an effort to avert centuries of racist policies that have exploited, abused, and partially annihilated Native American peoples.

Ethical issues have also emerged about when a child's Native American heritage must be disclosed. When birthparents sign a statement that they are not subject to the ICWA, and subsequently an adoption is finalized with a non-Native American family, and then the birthparents reveal that they do, in fact, have Native American blood, there are competing perspectives about whether or not the child should remain in the original adoptive home.

F. Adoption of Children Who Have Special Needs

Children who are over age 3; are of color; need a family that will adopt them as part of a sibling group; are the survivors of abuse or neglect at the hands of their birthfamilies or of the child welfare system; or have learning disabilities, behavior disorders, or physical disabilities were once called "hard to place." That term is now eschewed in favor of "children who have special needs" in order to avoid stigmatizing or blaming the child.

Often, finding homes for these children is a challenge. Lawmakers argue over the extent to which society is responsible to fund efforts to promptly secure a safe, loving, permanent home for children who have special needs. Monies to recruit, train, and provide the necessary lifelong support services for families who adopt children who have special needs are profoundly inadequate to the task. The 1980 Adoption Assistance and Child Welfare Act (P.L. 96-272, 94 Stat. 500) in the United States is designed to provide subsidies to any adoptive family of a child who has special needs identified before the adoption takes place, but many factors continue to impede provision of adequate funds.

Issues of deception and the duty to disclose are many in the arena of special needs adoptions. Naturally, in the struggle to find adoptive homes, agencies face powerful incentives to describe available children in the most positive terms. This can lead to agencies withholding, minimizing, distorting, or failing to discover information about a child's special needs and previous traumatic experiences. Sometimes, prospective parents are left to read between the lines; for example, an agency might use the phrase "he is extremely active" to describe a youngster instead of the more clinically precise and revealing phrase, "he has attention deficit hyperactivity disorder." Recent successful lawsuits by adoptive parents who learn only after an adoption has been finalized that the agency withheld crucial information from them will undoubtedly affect such agency practices in the future.

There are numerous kinds of active and passive manipulations of information about children's special needs. An agency may tell prospective adoptive parents that a child was, for example, sexually abused, but may not inform those parents that it is possible the child may, as a result, engage in behaviors such as fire setting, sexually molesting other children, masturbating in public, torturing animals, highly sexualized snuggling with adults, and so forth. Agency workers may fail to educate prospective adoptive parents about the possibility that love and clear, consistent, firm discipline may not be enough to overcome or cope with the effects of early, severe, prolonged deprivation and abuse prior to adoption.

Agencies may also not fully disclose statistical data on the disruption and dissolution rates of adoptions of children who have certain kinds of special needs, out of concern that the numbers may discourage prospective families from adopting a child with those special needs.

In addition, agency personnel may reassure prospective adoptive parents that adoption subsidy payments to defray costs of special educational, medical, and counseling services are available. But personnel may neglect to inform parents that they must first pay such fees out of pocket, wait lengthy periods for reimbursement, and sometimes have requests for full reimbursement denied.

Limited adoption subsidy monies and large caseloads of children awaiting adoptive families are both incentives for agencies to conduct an unassertive, incomplete assessment of a child's special needs. Thus, the burden is sometimes on the prospective adoptive parent to probe for a child's abuse history.

Most adoption experts argue that ethical adoption practice requires that agencies fully inform prospective adoptive families of the full range of risks they may face in adopting children with or without special needs. Postadoption support services to preserve adoptive placements are also ethically obligatory, although often unavailable. Practices and policies that promote placements but do not sustain them victimize both children and parents.

Finally, some question the common practice of advertising specific children (in newspapers and magazines, and on TV and the internet) who are available for adoption. Adoption parties or picnics, where dozens of prospective adoptive parents gather with dozens of children who have special needs and are available for adoption, are also controversial. Some argue that the adoptive placements derived from advertisements and parties are not worth the emotional upheaval they cause to the waiting children on display; others see these practices as creative ways of recruiting adoptive families and matching children with parents.

G. Routes to Adoption

Some governments allow, and some forbid, adoption advertisements; in these ads, usually placed in newspapers and other periodicals, prospective adoptive parents announce their desire to adopt and invite pregnant women to call them or their intermediary to make an adoption plan. Clearly, some people believe it is wrong to advertise for a baby; others have no moral qualms about this.

Some families, wishing to adopt, become foster parents with the hope that they may be able to adopt a child who enters their family as a foster child. This too is a controversial practice. On the one hand, this sort of continuity in a child's life is highly desirable, minimizing the trauma of multiple placements. On the other

hand, the foster parents who hope to adopt the child in their care may consciously or unwittingly sabotage the birthfamily's efforts to regain custody before termination of parental rights occurs.

Some governments require that all adoptions go through a licensed social service agency. This is an effort to forestall "baby selling" that sometimes occurs in the independent adoption field and to ensure that both birthparents and adoptive parents receive adequate pre- and postadoption counseling and services. Opponents of such laws argue that these requirements are paternalistic and serve mainly to advance the self-interests of agencies, which, given a monopoly over adoption, can charge large fees for their services. Opponents also argue that birthparents and adoptive parents, like anyone else, should be free to choose or reject counseling as they choose, and that agencies often dictate arrangements regarding confidentiality and openness in an adoption, rather than empowering birthparents and adoptive parents to make these decisions for themselves. The underlying ethical questions here are (1) whether social service agency involvement should be mandatory and (2) whether agencies should be charged with protecting birthparents and adoptive parents from themselves. An underlying practical question is whether agency involvement provides protection or simply increases the cost of adoption and introduces another morass of ethical problems.

H. Ethical Issues in Agency Policies

Agency policies shape adoptions. Intermediaries who facilitate adoptions—be they agency workers, attorneys, physicians, or family friends—often control much of the process of how biological parental rights are terminated, who is allowed to adopt, and the kinds of openness and confidentiality in an adoption. This control entails multiple ethical issues.

Issues of distributive justice abound. How does an agency decide whom they will permit to adopt a child, who gets which child, and within what time frame? Numerous criteria can be used to make these kinds of choices, such as how long a prospective parent has been on the agency's waiting list, how many attempts at adoption have fallen through for that person, the agency worker's personal or professional assessment of the person's parenting skills, a lottery, or some other guideline or rule. Examples of criteria used in some agencies include the birthparent's meeting several prospective adoptive parents through the agency and then choosing the family who will adopt the child; only childless parents are permitted to adopt; once the agency has placed a child in a family, that family is promised a second child through the agency; families who have been on the agency's waiting list longer than a prescribed length of time are given first priority. The guidelines agencies use reflect either an implicit or explicit judgment regarding distributive justice.

Agency policies also direct decisions about who is to be allowed to adopt, and these decisions may stem from values, beliefs, and biases as much as they do from an ethical calculus. For example, agencies in the United States typically exclude single parents unless the single person is interested in adopting a child who has special needs. From an ethical point of view, this is interesting. Undoubtedly, the bias against single parents adopting stems from the notion that children are better off in two-parent households. Yet the children who are likely to be the most needy and demanding to care for are allowed to be adopted by the people who are seen as least likely to have a daily in-home other adult to assist them. In crass terms, it appears as if the "least desirable" children are given the "least desirable" parents. The rationale may be that a child who has special needs is better off with at least one adoptive parent, rather than none.

Some agencies exclude gay or lesbian prospective adoptive parents, despite the lack of data indicating that homosexual couples are less skilled parents than heterosexual ones, or that growing up in a gay or lesbian family deleteriously affects a child's development. Other agencies take the position that placement in a family headed by lesbian or gay parents is fine as long as the birthparent consents to that.

Some agencies also have rules that preclude prospective adoptive parents with physical or emotional disabilities from adopting, regardless of the extent to which those disabilities actually interfere in the person's prospects for parenting effectively.

Money is another major criterion that screens out many would-be adoptive parents. Private agencies, for example, often require large sums of money up front in order to begin the homestudy and adoption processes.

Agencies also control information available to birthparents and adoptive parents alike. Some agencies do not inform clients about other adoption options that exist, because the agency views those options as inferior, or because if the client goes elsewhere the agency will lose the fees to be generated by that case. For example, an agency may believe that confidentiality and closed records are best, so may simply not inform a birthparent that various forms of open adoption can be considered. In some instances, birthparents have learned only after terminating their parental rights that

had they gone to another agency they would not have had to say good-bye to their child forever, but could have arranged an adoption that allowed them occasional photographs of, or even visits with, their child.

In numerous ways, agencies may either intentionally or unwittingly mislead birthparents, adoptive parents, and children. Workers may assure a birthparent that through adoption they can provide the child a happy upbringing in a good family. But, like all families, adoptive families can fall prey to prolonged unemployment, divorce, disability, untimely death of a parent, alcoholism, incest, and so on. A favorable homestudy is no guarantee of a family's current or future fitness. Or an agency may allow adoptive parents to embark upon adoptive parenthood unprepared because the agency fails adequately to educate prospective adoptive parents about the lifelong grief issues many adoptees face.

Agency policies also differ regarding prospective adoptive parents' rights to turn down a particular child offered to them. A child may become available for adoption at a time that does not feel right to a prospective parent, or when actually faced, for example, with adopting a specific child of a different race, a prospective parent may rethink her or his initial willingness to become an interracial family. Some agencies permanently remove this would-be parent from their waiting list or move that person to the bottom of the waiting list. Other agencies take the position that adoptive parents need to feel that they are a good match with a particular child, so turning down a referral is a right to be respected without punitive consequences. Differences among agencies regarding this issue reflect different views of adoptive parents' rights.

Agencies have different views of what an ethical approach is in counseling birthparents. Some have a biological family preservation focus, try to dissuade birthparents from making an adoption plan, and assertively seek services to keep the child in the family of origin. These agencies see adoption as a birthparent's option of last resort. Other agencies tell birthparents that choosing adoption for their child is simply another option on par with choosing to parent that child. These different approaches to counseling can powerfully influence a birthparent's final decision about whether to parent the child or carry out an adoption plan.

Agencies also have differing views about what their role ought to be in providing preadoption education and lifelong postadoption services. Some see their role as ending with the creation of the adoptive family. Others believe they have an ethical obligation to handle adoption, not as an event, but as a lifelong process which people tackle more effectively with education and episodic professional guidance. Thus, agencies differ in the extent to which they provide preadoption education and postadoption services.

Similarly, agencies have different views of their role in controlling, supervising, or monitoring contact between birth and adoptive families. Some agencies promote self-determination and allow the families direct access to each other to work out agreements about contact; other agencies are more paternalistic and require that any contact occur by letters, which are screened by an agency worker who removes all identifying information before forwarding the correspondence.

Agency practices regarding birthfathers vary as well. Some workers may view birthfathers as interferences or potential adversaries, and unenthusiastically include them in service delivery; others hold birthfathers' needs and rights in high regard and vigorously and assertively reach out to them to include them in the adoption planning process.

I. Financial Considerations

Adoption is an industry, a business that occurs in a marketplace. Especially in adoptions of children who have no special needs, and in private agency, independent, or identified adoptions, adoptive parents pay legal, medical, agency, and other fees, and sometimes prospective birthparents' living expenses as well. Hence, there are powerful financial incentives for private agencies, lawyers, adoption facilitators, physicians, and others to promote adoption. Some question whether this is morally justifiable. They wonder if adoption fees are a sophisticated indirect form of baby selling and buying.

In many instances, law allows prospective adoptive parents to pay for a prospective birthparent's living expenses. Critics of this practice argue that these payments may exert subtle pressure on prospective birthparents to follow through with an adoption plan because of a sense that, having taken the money, they now owe someone the baby.

Given the law of supply and demand, in many cultures it costs more to adopt a healthy white infant than to adopt a healthy baby of color or a child who has other special needs. Some question the ethics involved in prospective white adoptive families agreeing to adopt a child of color because that is what they can afford, not because they enthusiastically and knowledgeably embrace the prospect of becoming an interracial family and facing racism in their daily lives. Some argue that agencies should charge a flat fee for all adoptions, re-

gardless of the child's race or disability. Others counter that doing so would further limit the number of families available to adopt children who have special needs.

Some agencies charge homestudy and adoption placement fees that exceed the actual cost of those services. Thus, adoptive parents subsidize other, less profitable, agency programs. Many argue that infertile people, who have no access to parenthood other than adoption, should not be put in the position of paying for programs that have nothing to do with adoption. They assert that these practices are unethical, exploit the vulnerable, and are not justifiable on utilitarian grounds.

Further, some agencies allow or encourage prospective adoptive parents who are awaiting a child to participate in fund raising efforts on behalf of the agency. Other agencies forbid this practice, out of concern that parents may feel, either rightly or mistakenly, that the more money they generate for the agency, the faster the agency will find them a child.

Many agencies in the business of placing healthy white infants turn away requests that they find homes for children who have special needs, saying that they are not equipped to perform that service. Finding babies for infertile couples is profitable, while finding homes for all children in need is not. Is there a duty to aid the children most in need? What are the limits to such a duty?

There is debate also about whether agencies should disclose their financial health to prospective clients. In recent years, the number of adoption agencies has grown, while simultaneously the number of people in the baby boom generation seeking to build families through adoption has diminished because of advancing age. This has meant that private adoption agencies are competing more fiercely for prospective adoptive parents who can pay fees. As a result, some agencies have suddenly closed their doors, unable to reimburse prospective adoptive parents for fees paid in anticipation of services to come. This has left many prospective adoptive parents with no money to pursue adoption through other avenues. These agency closings also breach the agency's promise to be available to facilitate contact between birth and adoptive families formed through that agency.

J. Terminating Birthparent Rights

Ethical issues surrounding termination of parental rights are among the most divisive, explosive, and emotional. Debates rage over whose rights are primary—the child's right to safety, or the biological parents' right to parent. People argue irreconcilably over the extent to which society is responsible for providing therapeutic, financial, and supportive services to keep biological families intact so that adoption is not needed.

Different views of whose rights are primary are also reflected in the wide array of laws regarding the length of time that must pass before birthparents may voluntarily terminate their parental rights following a baby's birth. Some governments permit voluntary termination of parental rights 24 hr after birth in an effort to facilitate the child's speedy placement in an adoptive family; other governments, in an effort to protect birthparent rights, require that 6 months or more must pass.

The notorious Baby Richard case in Illinois highlights troubling ethical issues regarding termination of parental rights. Baby Richard's birthmother's uncle lied to the birthfather, telling him that the baby died. The birthmother then finalized an adoption. When the birthfather learned of the lie, he asserted his right to parent. When the trial court, and subsequently the court of appeals, ruled that Baby Richard stay in the adoptive family, the birthfather appealed the case to the Illinois Supreme Court. By this time Baby Richard was 4 years old. The state Supreme Court maintained that the birthfather's rights superseded the child's right to remain in the only family he had ever known and the adoptive parents' right to be protected by following the law. Public outcry following this case led the Illinois legislature, within just 2 weeks of the Supreme Court decision, to change Illinois adoption law so as to keep Baby Richard in his adoptive family. The Illinois Supreme Court then ruled that the new law could not be applied retroactively to Baby Richard.

There are numerous other ethical issues surrounding birthfathers. Laws regarding birthfathers' rights and obligations vary. According to law in some communities, a man is responsible for finding out if he has impregnated a woman. Law in other locales holds the woman responsible to seek out the man to tell him. One state, Indiana, has a putative father registry through which a man who has had sexual intercourse with any particular woman can indicate his wish to be notified by the state if that woman makes an adoption plan. In some communities a man abrogates his parental rights when he offers no support to a woman during her pregnancy. In other communities a man's parental rights are unaffected by his failure to provide for a woman pregnant with his child. When the birthfather or his whereabouts are unknown, generally the legal protocol is to advertise for him in newspapers. Many question whether this is a fair and adequate practice or a futile and meaningless exercise.

K. The Ethics of Adoption Language

The language used to describe adoption experiences and issues has embedded within it perspectives that shape public policies and private lives. Some argue that certain terms used to describe adoption are less judgmental and pejorative and are, thus, more ethically justifiable. For example, often birthparents are called the "natural" or "real" parent, suggesting that adoptive parents are unnatural or unreal. Most discussions of birthparents focus on the birthmother, excluding mention of birthfathers. This may perpetuate sexist policies and practices. Instead of saying that a birthmother "made an adoption plan," a phrase that implies a responsible proactive choice made out of caring and concern for the child, typically one hears the phrase, "she put her baby up for adoption," or "she gave her baby away," phrases that imply a lack of love or desire for her child. Some assert that there is an obligation, at least among professionals in the world of adoption, to use more neutral or positive language in discussing adoption as a way of slowly and gently undoing some of the negative images associated with adoption that emotionally burden people touched by adoption.

L. Advanced Reproductive Technology and Adoption

Advanced reproductive technology now makes possible live births using donor egg, donor sperm, surrogate mothers, and other people's frozen embryos. All these are forms of adoption, since at least one person who ends up as the child's parent is not biologically related to that child. As in traditional confidential adoption, often few people other than the adoptive parents, health care personnel, and attorneys know the circumstances surrounding the child's birth and entry into the family. All the issues of secrecy, confidentiality, and privacy discussed earlier apply.

III. CONCLUSIONS

Debates over whether adoption exists to serve primarily the needs of children or adults, and over issues of truth telling, active and passive deceit, paternalism, self-determination, fundamental human rights, social justice, distributive justice, exploitation, the duty to aid, confidentiality and privacy, lexical ordering of values, and application of concepts used in ethical decision making (e.g., utilitarianism, deontology, and teleology), are inextricably woven throughout discussions of adoption law, agency practices, and counseling of people whose lives are touched by adoption. This article introduces the range of these issues and illustrates the complexity of disagreement about them.

Also See the Following Articles

CHILDREN'S RIGHTS • CONFIDENTIALITY, GENERAL ISSUES OF • DISTRIBUTIVE JUSTICE

Bibliography

Baran, A., Sorosky, A., and Pannor, R. (1989). "The Adoption Triangle." Corona, San Antonio, TX.

Barth, R. P. (1995). Adoption. In "Encyclopedia of Social Work," pp. 48–59. National Association of Social Workers, Washington, DC.

Bartholet, E. (1993). "Family Bonds: Adoption and the Politics of Parenting." Houghton Mifflin, Boston.

Kadushin, A., and Martin, J. A. (1988). "Child Welfare Services," 4th ed., pp. 533–668. Macmillan, New York.

Lee, R., and Hull, R. K. (1983). Legal, casework and ethical issues in "risk adoption." *Child Welfare* 62(5), 450–454.

Lifton, B. J. (1994). "Journey of the Adopted Self: A Quest for Wholeness." Basic Books, New York.

Lifton, B. J., and Baran, A. (1995). Adoption. In "Encyclopedia of Bioethics," 2nd ed. Macmillan, Indianapolis, IN.

McRoy, R. G. (1989). An organizational dilemma: The case of transracial adoptions. *J. Appl. Behav. Sci.* 25, 145–160.

Post, S. G. (1996). Reflections on adoption ethics. *Cambridge Quart. Healthcare Ethics* 5(3), 430.

Siegel, D. H. (1993). Open adoption of infants. *Social Work* 38(1), 15–25.

Smith, J. F. (1996). Analyzing ethical conflict in the transracial adoption debate: Three conflicts involving community. *Hypatia* 11(2), 1–33.

Wiltse, K. T. (1985). Ethical issues in permanency planning. *Children Youth Services Rev.* 7(2–3), 259–266.

ADVANCE DIRECTIVES

Hans-Martin Sass
Ruhr Universitaet Bochum, Kennedy Institute of Ethics

I. Normative Issues
II. Forms of Advance Care Documents
III. Legal and Attitudinal Issues
IV. Implementational Issues

GLOSSARY

advance directive A written or oral directive given by a competent person in order to govern and to control medical decision making for future situations of incapacity.

durable power of attorney for health care A written statement designating a trusted person as health care representative.

living will An instructional advance directive refusing or requesting specific types of medical intervention in the event of future incapacity.

palliative care Medical treatment to reduce or alleviate pain and symptoms of mental or physical stress, such as restlessness, angst, depression, cramps, spasms, and respiratory distress. Palliative treatments may cause side effects such as sleepiness, reduction of mental and intellectual alertness, euphoria, or drug dependency, or they may have the unintended double effect of shortening life.

values history Value anamnesis. Information given by the patient or prospective patient on personal values, visions, wishes, and attitudes that should govern medical treatment in case of future incapacity in decision making. Information can be given by using value-and-wish checklists, narrative methods, or comments on selected critical care scenarios.

AN ADVANCE DIRECTIVE is usually a written, although sometimes oral, statement intended to govern health care decision making for its author in case of future situations where there exists a mental incapacity to make such decisions, as well as to govern or join in clinical decision making. Advance directives can be in form of a living will containing more or less detailed and flexible instructions for medical interventions, a durable power of attorney appointing a surrogate decision maker with full or partial authority to make or to share in clinical decisions, or a values history providing information on personal values, wishes, visions, hopes, fears, and attitudes which together with clinical and laboratory information must be implemented into differential diagnosis, prognosis, and treatment decisions.

Advance directives are an essential and indispensible part of modern medicine, particularly in the care for the mentally incapacitated, the dying, and those in palliative care, for at least three reasons: (a) Progress in medicine, in particular in extending the life span of patients suffering from progressive chronic and multimorbid diseases and in intensive care treatment, allows for a rich variety of options for treating or modifying treatment, not all of which might be in the patient's best interest; some might actually violate the *salus aegroti,* the beneficence principle, since the determination of what is for the "good of the patient" and the definition of "futility" are difficult to define without the patient's communication and cooperation in decision making. (b) The multicultural forces of postmodern pluralistic societies which place the autonomy, self-determination, and self-responsibility of the individual over established paternalistic and professional codes of conduct and paternalistic benevolence do not allow physicians to treat individual patients on the basis of general procedures or rules alone or using the physician's own personal preferences and attitudes. (c) The execution, recognition, and review of advance directives might improve the patient–physician "partnership-in-trust" and help overcome differences in lay and expert cultures and attitudes toward health care decision making, in particular in the treatment of incapacitated patients and end-of-life treatment decisions.

I. NORMATIVE ISSUES

Many controversies in academic bioethics and societal and cultural clashes over values are based in unsuccessful, and often unnecessary and unwarranted, attempts to provide objective solutions for what basically are not objective, but rather personal and private, issues. Many clinical challenges associated with the beginnings and ends of human life seem to warrant individual, rather than general, conflict solutions. Where consensus in content cannot and must not be achieved, consensus over how to deal with dissensus and how to protect obligations and rights in individual value-based decision making becomes the preferred means of protecting individual health literacy and responsibility and trust-based provider–client interaction in the professional setting, and for reducing societal conflict. Four normative issues addressed by advance directives are more appropriately resolved on an individual rather than an objective level: (1) the definition of criteria for the salus aegroti maxim; (2) the discussion of risks and benefits of advance health care planning and of giving instructional directives in advance; (3) the authorization of a trusted surrogate decision maker; and (4) the acceptance of risk associated with definite directives for situations not yet fully understood or experienced.

A. Defining the Salus Aegroti

By emphasizing the principle of patients *autonomy*, contemporary American bioethics has identified the principle of self-determination as the prime reason for introducing model legislation supportive of advance directives. Such a reference to autonomy was strongly made by the Patient Self-Determination Act (1991) of the U.S. Congress. But there is another line of argument which is not based primarily on patients' autonomy and is more likely to be accepted by the traditional, paternalistic physician's ethics of *benevolence*: given the postmodern diversity in values and visions of a pluralistic society, a benevolent physician cannot define the "good of the patient" or "futility of intervention" based on the physician's own values, but rather needs information on the patient's values, visions, and wishes in order to incorporate the patient's criteria for "good" into differential diagnosis, prognosis, and intervention.

Therefore advance health care planning by the patient or prospective patient, including the execution of advance directives, must be regarded as indispensable for good clinical practice, as it alone will provide definite necessary and vital information to define the salus aegroti, the "good of the patient." The need to have advance directives for medical care is based not only on the principle of autonomy, but also on the principle of benevolence—respect for patients as persons is a prime moral principle in the health care provider's ethics and does not allow diagnoses and interventions to be based on medical–technical criteria alone, but requires the introduction of patients' individual values, wishes, and visions into individualized treatment decisions.

B. Benefits and Risks of Advance Medical Directives

There is a hazard associated with making predictions prior to fully understanding the parameters and the internal and external forces governing future situations, in particular when (a) the patient has no prior experience with those situations, (b) a layperson does not fully understand decisions made in a highly technical and professional setting, and (c) future technical or other developments are beyond the patient's control or are not foreseeable. All three risks influence advance medical directives by laypersons: Laypeople rarely have prior personal and existential experience with situations of death and dying, dementia, severe suffering, or coma, and they do not understand the complex technical risks and uncertainties associated with medical procedures. And no one, lay or expert, can fully address the nonmedical circumstances of future situations they have to issue distinct directives for, nor can they take into account future professional and technical advances which may result from further clinical research, or the lack thereof, or changes in health care financing. In regard to advance health care directives, it is well known that medical experts, physicians and nurses, are quite reluctant to give very specific and inflexible directives which in a future situation might not be in their best interest, and might actually be counterproductive to their "good."

C. Risks Associated with Surrogate Decision Making

These risks are well known in all areas of personal and professional life. To reduce them, personal prudence, experience-based trust, and a competent and trustworthy trustee are needed. Also to be considered is the exclusion of conflict of interest as much as possible, as well as legal, regulatory, or administrative protection against abuse. These protective measures, however, carry their own risks and uncertainties. An additional challenge for proxy decisions by laypersons in health care matters is that clinical decisions and their risk parameters, uncertainties, and consequences quite often are technically difficult to understand and require not only trust between the designator, the designee, and the professional team, but also competence to understand the consequences of clinical intervention or the refusal thereof. On the other hand, the proxy decision maker will have insight into the details of future situations as they arise, and is best equipped to translate the designator's wishes, hopes, and fears most adequately into the situational decision-making process.

D. The "Old" and the "New" Person

There is an extended bioethical debate over whether previous directives should be honored or whether the "presumed actual will" of the patient at the time of intervention should guide medical decisions. This normative conflict can be illustrated by a German example where a Chamber of Physicians guideline for the care of the dying requests that previous oral or written directives only be taken as a clue to determine the presumed actual will of the patient, while a Supreme Court decision holds that previous directives are binding and that so-called objective criteria of "futility" or best interest" may only be used as a default position in the clear absence of the expression of individual preference.

A conflict between previous and "current" wishes is possible, but the controversy seems to be somewhat artificial and will have to be discussed using different scenarios. (a) As long as competent persons have not changed oral or written statements and directives, those statements should be taken as their true position and others should act accordingly—it is the right and obligation of competent persons who change their views and preferences to let others know, and if they do not do so they carry the risk of being misunderstood and mistreated. (b) If someone falls into a nonresponsive state, i.e., they are incapable of expressing wishes or values, such as in a deep and prolonged coma, this person will have no new experiences on which a change of values and wishes could be based and therefore should be treated according to wishes and values previously expressed. (c) Patients suffering from chronic and progressive illnesses and persons suddenly confronted with physical disabilities may or may not adapt to new and quite different quality of life parameters. Clinicians are very aware that many chronically ill patients and those suddenly in a situation which they might have thought previously would not be worth living in do adjust to new challenges over and over again. As long as these patients are competent, they have ample opportunity to accept or reject treatment; for these patients the use of advance directives is not indicated, and if they choose to do so, they may adjust their previously stated preferences according to their new experiences and visions of life. (d) a severely demented patient who does not know who they are or where they are, and is unable to recognize friends and loved ones, but who while fully competent executed advance directives refusing or requesting certain interventions for future situations, should be honored as the persons they were and those decisions which they then felt would be the most appropriate expression of their visions and values should be used. (e) More difficult cases are those in which patients are semicompetent, patients are in psychiatric confusion, or incompetent patients request forms of comfort care which would contradict previous instructions. These are situations full of ambiguity, and often the care as presently expressed by the patient probably should be honored over previous statements. Whatever the additional problems are in cases of reduced or partial competence, a discussion of values and visions, and subsequently of preferences, wishes, and rejections of certain treatments, is the only, sometimes uneven way to determine what is best for the patient.

II. FORMS OF ADVANCE CARE DOCUMENTS

Given the normative challenges in preparing, executing, and reviewing advance care documents, there cannot be one single best model or form. Quite a variety of *advance directive* forms have been developed; they range from legalistic forms; to value statements, questionnaires, and checklists; and to narrative models of value anamnesis. A terse, comprehensive form has not yet been developed that could provide sufficient and adequate information and be flexible enough to address all unforeseeable future events. Also, no form has been developed that persuasively solves the epistemological and prognostic problem of applying delicate values and wishes to unknown situations, a problem not unfamiliar in most fields of long-term planning and risk reduction. Basically, there are three different approaches: (1) the rejectionist legal approach, which forbids the physician to perform certain interventions under general or certain conditions; (2) the proxy approach, or the designating of a trusted person to speak for the patient and to request or reject certain procedures when the time has come and the situation is less uncertain; and (3) the value history approach, in which the patient provides information about his or her values and wishes that can later be included in the medical history and might provide the necessary information on which prognosis and intervention decisions can be based for individualized treatment. A fourth alternative is a combination of different forms and variations on the above approaches. All models have their own specific and distinct advantages and disadvantages.

A. Rejectionist Legal Directives

This type of advance directive, characterized as a legalistic and rejectionist document, is widely distributed in the United States, uses language provided by state law, and is difficult to translate into clinical reality. Nevertheless, the documents are useful in that they give loved ones and caregivers a sense of direction (see Box 1, a draft of a living will written in religious language which gives directives for a small number of specific end-of-life scenarios and makes reference to religious beliefs). For instance, such a document might indicate that a patient does not want intensive care at the end of life or painful prolongation of life, even if the exact circumstances are either not clearly defined (e.g., if vague terminology such as "no extraordinary means" is used) or too narrowly fixed (e.g., if extended lists of rejected procedures for specific situations are presented). Research has shown that physicians are reluctant to follow or to even recognize detailed rejectionist requests. Some physicians might argue that the directives are too vague or do not address the actual situation and therefore are not applicable and do not represent the actual presumed

---

Box 1

An Instructional Advance Directive Based on Religious Values

In order to protect my life, a gift from GOD, it is my wish that all prudent medical treatment be provided to me with the aim of effecting my recovery or reducing the effects of chronic illnesses or disorders. Should that be deemed impossible, I request compassionate nursing care and the alleviation of suffering to the extent of all appropriate measures only. If interventions necessary to provide comfort care and the alleviation of suffering cause harm to my body or shorten my life, then let it be, as this may be GOD's way to take from me what HE has given. In no circumstances, however, do I want to be intentionally killed, nor do I ask that my life, a gift from GOD, be taken on the basis of my presumed consent or request.

Should I be in unrelenting and unrelievable suffering or pain, then I request that I be allowed to die and let the LORD take what HE has given. If such a situation occurs, I request all possible comfort care and the medical alleviation of suffering associated with my condition as death approaches. If I fall into prolonged coma or if physicians diagnose that my life continues in what is called a persistent vegetative state only, then I request comfort care only. If I become mentally incapacitated so that I do not know who I am and where I am and do not recognize loved ones and friends anymore, then I want/do not want that my life be prolonged by extraordinary means such as major diagnostic or therapeutic interventions.

As I know that may life is in GOD's hands, I request that "extraordinary means" such as technical ventilation or artificial nutrition or hydration be withheld or withdrawn in situations of unrelenting and relieveable pain (yes/no), prolonged coma or persistent vegetative state (yes/no), or the severest forms of dementia (yes/no). I ask for your prayers and for religious support in all situations of weakness, incompetence, suffering, and dying. If possible, I would like to die in surroundings familiar to me (yes/no).

Regarding preexisting medical conditions, I request/suggest. . . .

[signature]

will of the patient. Those rejectionist living wills that are written in legal language are difficult to translate into clinical practice and therefore may not be in the patient's best interests.

B. Designation of a Proxy Decision Maker

The designation of a proxy decision maker is part of many living wills. But even apart from a will, such a designation is a valid and flexible instrument which can prevent the harm that an overly specific living will, drafted long before the specific situation arises, is capable of. However, if the proxy fails to understand and to represent the patient's values adequately, it can be a very risky instrument. The proxy model can be used to nominate additional advisers or decision makers to assist the main proxy decision maker (see Box 2). When used in combination with a durable power of attorney for health care, rejectionist documents can become more flexible and easily adaptable to specific situations. And, on the other hand, the designation of a proxy together with personal statements on values and wishes also reduces the risk of proxy decisions which are not in the designator's best interest. If a proxy is nominated without further instructions or requests, this represents a paternalistic model of decision making by the will of the designator. If the proxy designation is associated with value-and-wish statements, the model resembles a model of weak paternalism. If proxy designations and instructions are interconnected, it must be clearly

articulated in the document which voice shall have precedence in the event that conflicts arise between the physician and the care team, the surrogate, or the value-and-wish statements.

C. Belief-and-Value Status Forms

The values history document uses checklists of general values, wishes, and preferences, in particular those associated with medical care for the terminally ill or the comatose (see Box 3). A value anamnesis or values history is an instrument that establishes a person's value

---

Box 2

Designating a Proxy Decision Maker for Health Care

If I in a future situation will no longer be capable of expressing my values and wishes, I designate [name] to be my legal and health care representative.

I recommend/request that my representative seeks and follows the advice of [name] in religious and value matters, of [name] in medical matters, and of [name] in legal or financial matters.

If a conflict arises among my representative, those other trusted persons I have named, and/or the medical team or the physician with primary responsibility, or if their interpretations of my values and wishes differ, I hereby declare that final authority shall rest with my representative/physician [name] . . . .

[signature]

Box 3

Values History Questionnaire

In this questionnaire I express personal values and wishes which shall govern my medical treatment in situations where I might be incapacitated to make decisions or to give consent.

(1) I want to live as long as possible: as long as I am in good health/if I am ill but overall recovery is expected/even if I am permanently unconscious/even if I am mentally incompetent/even if I am terminally ill.

(2) I want to be without pain: yes/no/even if clear thinking is compromised by pain medication/even if medication makes me drowsy or sleepy.

(3) When my time has come I prefer to: die at home/die in the hospital/die with loving people around/be left alone.

(4) I want a comfortable dying process: yes/not important/even at the cost of heavy sedation/even at the cost of shortening life/even if it means active euthanasia or physician-assisted suicide.

(5) If my prognosis is terminal: I want full disclosure/I do not want to be informed/my proxy must be told/my family physician must be told/[name] must be told.

(6) When I become incapacitated I do not want to be a burden: to my family/to the financial resources of my family/to health care professionals/to society.

(7) I want health care professionals to honor the values and wishes expressed above: fully/as a recommendation only/depending on the situation/depending on their own judgment/depending on the wishes of my family/at the advice of my designated proxy.

[signature]

profile, which can then (a) be used by the patient to establish a more explicit directive, (b) be attached to a formal living will as an instrument for its interpretation, and (c) be used by the surrogate decision maker as a guidance tool. Checklists or questionnaires have been developed in conjunction with formal advance care instruments. These questionnaires address suffering and end-of-life issues, thereby helping to overcome the denial of a topic that is considered taboo. They are good instruments with which to generate discussions within the family and between the patient and the prospective surrogate or the health care provider. But questionnaires can only replace other forms of advance directives if they are treatment-specific and precise, and address conditions for which the value-and-wish statements are not too vague.

Physicians and nurses do not need to be told by laypersons what to do in a specific future situation, but they need to know about their patient's visions, values, wishes, and concerns; otherwise they cannot provide for individualized treatment and the patient's good.

D. Combination Forms

Given the complexities of projecting one's values and wishes into a yet to be determined future situation, probably the best method for identifying, promoting, and protecting one's own values and wishes is to invest time in the process of communicating with loved ones, trusted physicians, and friends, and drafting a combination form that is not too inflexible but provides adequately precise insight into one's own value reasoning. These forms should then be validated with a physician, routinely reassessed, and eventually readjusted based on additional experiences and changes in value priorities. Just as a Last Will might improve when drafted and reviewed by a legal expert, so might a Living Will benefit from consultation and review by a medical expert.

An informative, directive, and still flexible Living Will has to contain four segments in its anatomical structure: (1) information on personal values, hopes, and fears; (2) a small list of medical directives or instructions; (3) designation of one or more proxies; and (4) validation issues.

1. The most important information for clinical decision making is information on the potential patient's *value-and-wish status*. Values and wishes can be stated in religious or secular terminology. Values can be stated in different ways: narratively, by checklists, or by description. The more informative the document is, the better it can be used in clinical hermeneutics to intro-

duce bioethical information with biomedical information into differential diagnosis, prognosis, and the determination of individualized and patient-oriented treatment decision and review.

2. As far as *instructional medical directives* are concerned, it is advisable to keep instructions brief and clear, and allow for flexibility. Scenarios to be addressed are: (a) preterminal and terminal stages with irreversible and often painful underlying diseases and various forms of multimorbidity, (b) prolonged coma and persistent vegetative state, and (c) severe dementia. Issues to be addressed include: (a) palliative care, (b) withholding of withdrawing of interventions, (c) acceptance of the "double effect" of pain-controlling or other medication which unintentionally might allow for or hasten death, (d) withdrawal of basic life-sustaining support such as ventilation, nutrition, and hydration, and (e) wishes regarding the social and living environment.

The administering of the best palliative care available, the double effect which certain medications might have, and the respect for patient's wishes regarding the environment they prefer to live and to die in are fully accepted by a wide majority of religious and secular bioethicists and physicians. Withholding of technically possible intervention at the request of the patient or her proxy is easier to accept than the active termination or withdrawal of already initiated intervention as there is an emotional as well an ethical difference between passive "acceptance" and active "doing."

The clinical administration of nutrition and hydration can be understood either as medical intervention or as basic care and an act of basic human solidarity; the latter position creates ethical problems when withholding medically administered life support, in particular hydration. But recent clinical studies have reversed the traditional idea that dehydration at the end of life is associated with additional painful suffering. As these studies suggest that dehydration results in a euphoric rather than a painful state, they may increase the number of clinicians and bioethicists who honor clearly expressed wishes to withhold even hydration and to allow for a naturally occurring death without medical intervention.

It is understood that even in situations of withholding possible medical treatments, *comfort care*, such as the moistening of lips and mouth, must continue and be given full attention, as comfort care will be the last and only avenue left for care, support, and compassion.

As future medical scenarios are impossible to predict, some argue that it is not reasonable and not in the patient's best interest to be too detailed in giving medical instructions for yet to be determined clinical situations. Others, including the states of Missouri, Minnesota, New York, and Delaware in the United States, request clear and convincing detailed instructions and preferences. Patients expecting predictable developments of preexisting conditions should address those situations, thus alleviating loved ones from making hard choices later on; e.g., patients suffering from amyotrophic lateral sclerosis might express the wish not to ever start ventilation support. Also, atypical treatment preferences or rejections, such as those based on religious beliefs, should be clearly outlined and the reasons behind them be given clearly and without hesitation. But the longer the lists of medical intervention rejections, the more likely that they might be counterproductive and not in the reasonable interest of the patient since the risk of inflexibility is too high.

3. *Surrogates* are much more flexible than written instructions for guiding clinical decision making. Surrogates are of particular importance when patients slip into or are already in dementia. As the nomination of surrogates is the designator's personal choice, the proxy instrument replaces the traditional paternalistic model of physician's beneficence with a model of weak or strong paternlism. Sometimes such a decision is overshadowd by cultural or familial preferences, such as in Asian cultures where the family is the natural surrogate. The argument has been made that surrogates other than immediate family members would reduce the burden on the family. Others would leave it up to the family to choose the speaker for the patient (and the family). Probable conflict of interest, lack of expertise in decision making, and no or minimal medical understanding are other arguments voiced against the nomination of family members as proxies.

4. The issue of *validating* Living Wills by reference to and a review by a trusted physician who has explained terminology, options, and consequences of refusal and who witnesses in regard to the sound state of mind of the person executing the Living Will has been neglected. Laypersons need medical terms and options to be explained as well as information on the consequences in clinical treatment of the withholding of certain forms of treatment based on the patient's instructions and directives. Validation is especially desirable where the patient has or has had a history of mental disorder or shown a lack of understanding of basic medical information and options or of the capacity for prudent decision making.

Whatever form is used, advance directives seem to be indispensable for providing the best possible care for those who cannot express their treatment preferences anymore. Advance directives should inform the health care professional and other surrogate decision makers primarily about values and wishes that shall govern treatment, should nominate proxy decision makers, and should refrain from detailed medical instructions, except where existing and progressing disorders or the decisional capacity of the patient allows for definite instructions.

III. LEGAL AND ATTITUDINAL ISSUES

The legal parameters surrounding the recognition and use of advance directives are necessarily different from country to country; also, national medical associations have different self-regulating guidelines or recommendations governing recognition and authority of patients' advance directives or durable power of attorney. In the United States the Patient Self-Determination Act (PSDA) requires hospitals and nursing homes to inform patients at the time of admittance about the availability of advance directive forms, but the real impact of the PSDA on patients' and physicians' attitudes and on the prevalence of advance directives is uncertain, and there is abundant evidence that advance care documents are sometimes ignored or not fully recognized.

Traditional settings of paternalistic physician–patient interaction, such as in Japanese and Chinese clinics, rarely recognize preferences of competent adult patients—even less so statements written in advance and probably expressing distrust toward the medical establishment and the individual physician, which would be understood as offensive toward the physician as well as unethical since the patient would not be displaying culturally expected compliance and trust. The Japanese language has no technical term for advance directives.

Guidelines by the German Chamber of Physicians request that physicians act on the basis of the presumed will of the patient at the time of intervention and do not recognize previously expressed written or oral statements as adequate evidence of the presumed actual will. However, a Supreme Court decision in 1994 ruled that subjective criteria expressed in written or oral form by the patient are to be given priority over objective criteria, and over what others might feel to be "normal" or "prudent."

As far as advance directives request physician-assisted suicide or mercy killing by physicians, the vast majority of medical associations and individual physicians reject those requests as contrary to physicians' ethics and the ethos of healing and the protecting life. In the Netherlands, however, a social and ethical experiment is underway, accepting voluntary active euthanasia and physician-assisted suicide. As many as 9000 patients require physician-assisted suicide or to be killed, and about one-third of those requests are honored by physicians annually. In the United States some federal courts of appeal have ruled that it is not unconstitutional for patients to request and for physicians to honor those voluntary requests, based on the constitutional right of self-determination. One court, the Third U.S. Court of Appeals, in *Compassion in Dying v. State of Washington,* compared the right to request physician's assisted suicide to the right to abortion and the U.S. Supreme Court ruling in *Roe v. Wade.*

But, whatever the national laws, rules, or regulations governing the recognition and use of advance directives are, there seems to be limited authority of legal or regulatory instruments over the traditional *attitudes* of physicians not to recognize patients' directives and patients' involvement in complex clinical decision making. But many jurisdictions and state laws contain legal sanctions against health care practitioners who fail to comply with patients' wishes or who provide treatment without proper informed consent. On the other hand, prospective patients are reluctant to execute advance directives, to insist on their recognition, and to make them realistically and practically available. The reasons for the limited use of advance care planning and for the recognition of advance directives seem to be primarily attitudinal rather than legal. Denmark is the only country where a central registry is available for registering a living will and where physicians and hospitals are requested to check for one in specific situations.

There is widespread *denial* of issues such as suffering, dependence, weakness, death, and dying, particularly, in societies and cultures with heavy emphasis on success, power, and quality of life. People find it difficult to discuss death and dying even with close friends and family. Such issues are routinely avoided in physician–patient interactions. Health care professionals may choose to let technology dictate the final outcome of a certain intervention and not ask whether such an intervention was in the patient's best interest or whether the patient would have refused it if asked prior to the crisis. Denial by both sides, health care professionals and laypersons, and compliance by the patient and professional beneficence based on the ethos of protecting (prolonging) life can lead to the indirect acceptance of prolonged suffering and an agonizing death. National membership societies promoting "death with dignity" call for better palliative care and the recognition of patient's preferences, including the wish to be killed or assisted in suicide. These societies, such as the Hemlock Society in the United States, are not uncontroversial.

IV. IMPLEMENTATIONAL ISSUES

Cultural and attitudinal rather than legal and administrative issues challenge the use and recognition of advance care documents. Therefore legal and regulatory intervention will be of limited success in promoting instruments which would serve a more individualized treatment of the comatose, the demented, and those suffering in preterminal and terminal stages of life. Promotion of specialized educational programs for health care professionals and laypersons, routine discussions of advance care issues in nonacute situations of primary care medicine, and the reimbursement of physicians for advance directive counseling and review seem to be the instruments of choice for changing the situation. The literature suggests that even if advance directives do not yet play an essential role in clinical decision making at the end of life or for the demented, in many situations they already serve as catalysts for improving discussions between patients and providers, within the family, and among health care professionals, and for helping individuals in addressing emotionally, conceptually, and decisionally complex issues.

Physicians must come to be recognized as the experts of choice for individuals who want to direct future medical interventions. Health care experts have to accept this new role, which has been made possible and necessary as a result of progress in intensive life-extending care and the diversification of values in a postmodern society. They also need to be reimbursed for counseling and review. Structured processes of implementation and of promotion of validated forms and models of advance directives should be developed. Much still has to be done to understand the role of good palliative care and what effects the expectation of such care will have on patients' preferences. Much work is also needed on how communication on death-and-dying issues between health care provider and patient affect mutual trust and cooperation in decision making.

Given the attitudinal, psychological, and cognitive problems in addressing issues of end-of-life medical care among the layperson and the experts, the implementation of advance directives in the institutional setting will encounter certain difficulties. But some institutional approaches, such as the introduction of hospices and the development of new institutional ethics in hospice care, have been successful. This success suggests that more efforts should be made to provide for a greater variety of delivery systems of health care, in particular for the demented, those in pain and suffering, and end-of-life situations.

Advance directives, whether written in secular or in

religious language, must express the person's values and wishes, designate proxies, and direct from a layperson's perspective and understanding the preferred medical interventions in a state of incompetence or in a preterminal or terminal phase of life. They should be informative and instructive enough to provide guidance, but not be too inflexible so as to allow for compassionate clinical decision making for the "good of the patient," as it is expressed in the patient's advance directive.

Also See the Following Articles

DO-NOT-RESUSCITATE DECISIONS • INFORMED CONSENT • PATIENTS' RIGHTS

Bibliography

Bundesärztekammer (1993). Richtlinien für die ärztliche Sterbebegleitung. *Deutsches Ärzteblatt* 90(37), C1628–1629.

Bundesgerichtshof (1994). Urteil vom 13. September 1994. *BGH-1 StR 357/94-LG Kempten*. BGH, Karlsruhe.

Cantor, N. L. (1993). "Advance Directives and the Pursuit of Death with Dignity." Indiana Univ. Press, Bloomington.

Doukas, D. J., and McCullough, L. B. (1991). The values history. The evaluation of the patient's values and advance directives. *Journal of Family Practice* 32(2), 145–153.

Doukas, D. J., and Reichel, W. (1993). "Planning for Uncertainty. A Guide to Living Wills and Other Advance Directives for Health Care." John Hopkins Univ. Press, Baltimore.

Emanuel, L. L. (1993). Advance directives: What have we learned so far? *Journal of Clinical Ethics* 4(1), 8–16.

Eser, A., and Koch, H. G. (1991). "Materialien zur Sterbehilfe." Max Planck Institut für ausländisches und internationales Strafrecht (an international collection of Advance Directive forms and legal documents), Freiburg.

Kielstein, R. and Sass, H. M. (1993). Using stories to assess values and establish medical directives. *Kennedy Institute of Ethics Journal* 3, 303–325.

King, N. M. P. (1991). "Making Sense of Advance Directives." Kluwer, Dordrecht.

Miles, S. H., Koepp, R., and Weber, E. P. (1996). Advance end-of-life treatment planning. *Archives of Internal Medicine* 156, 1062–1068.

Olick, R. S. (1991). Approximating informed consent and fostering communication: The anatomy of an advance directive. *Journal of Clinical Ethics* 2(3), 181–189.

Pearlman, R. A., Cain, K. C., Patrick, D. L., *et al.* (1993). Insights pertaining to patients' assessment of states worse than death. *Journal of Clinical Ethics* 4(1) 33–41.

Sass, H. M., Bonkovsky, F. O., Akabayashi, A., Kielstein, R., and Olick, R. S. (1996). Advance health care documents in multicultural perspectives. *Jahrbuch für Recht und Ethik/Annual Review of Law and Ethics* 4, 465–508.

SUPPORT Investigators (1995). A controlled clinical trial to improve care for the seriously ill hospitalized patients. *Journal of the American Medical Association* 274, 1591–1598.

Teno, J. M., Nelson, H. L., and Lynn, J. (1994). Advance care planning: Priorities for ethical and empirical research. *Hastings Center Report.* 24(6), S32–S36.

Thurber, (1996). Public awareness of the nature of CPR: A case for values-centered advance directives. *Journal of Clinical Ethics* 7(1), 55–59.

U.S. State Court of Appeals for the Ninth Circuit (1996). Compassion in Dying vs. State of Washington. *U.S. State Court of Appeals, No. 94-35534. D.C. No. CV-94-119-BJR Opinion,* 3109ff, 3161ff, 3219ff.

ADVERTISING

Robert L. Arrington
Georgia State University

GLOSSARY

control The power to bring about in an unavoidable manner the attitudes, beliefs, or actions of a person or group of people.

deception The act or practice of intentionally causing a person or group of people to have false beliefs.

dependence effect The process by which advertisers create new desires in consumers for the products they then supply.

manipulation The process of taking advantage of the desires or wishes of a person in order to bring about an action which otherwise would not occur and which benefits the manipulator.

materialism A value orientation that stresses the importance of material goods, financial success, and acquisitiveness.

persuasion The process of changing another person's beliefs, attitudes, or preferences by rational or emotional means.

puffery A term for the practice in advertising of making exaggerated or fanciful claims about a product.

ADVERTISING is a significant part of contemporary business practice. It is viewed by many members of the business world as an ethically innocuous means of informing the public of goods for sale. Critics, in contrast, see it as a practice having the potential for numerous ethical misdeeds, ranging from the promotion of a materialistic form of life to the manipulation and deception of consumers.

I. ADVERTISING AND CONTEMPORARY SOCIETY

Like it or not, advertising is a large and ever-expanding part of our lives. In the United States,

> every day, 12 billion display and 184 billion classified advertising messages pour forth from 1,710 daily newspapers, billions of others from 7,600 weekly newspapers, and 6 billion more each day from 430 general magazines and 10,500 other periodicals. There are 4,658 AM and 3,367 FM radio stations broadcasting an average of 2,600,000 commercials a day; and 844 television stations broadcast 330,000 commercials a day, redisseminated by 5,000 cable systems. Every day, millions of people are confronted with over 500,000 outdoor billboards and painted bulletins, with 1.5 million car cards and posters in buses, subways, and commuter trains, with 40 million

direct mail pieces and leaflets, and with billions of display and promotion items. (Bogart, L., 1990. "Strategy in Advertising," 2nd ed., pp. 1–2. Lincolnwood, IL: NTC Business Books. Reprinted with permission.)

It has been said that each one of us, on average, sees 1600 ads each day. Such depressing or—as you choose to look at them—gratifying statistics reveal not only the amount of advertising, but also its diversity. The amount gets larger every year: "Just between 1967 and 1986, the number of TV, radio, magazine, and newspaper advertisements disseminated in the United States increased by 133%. The number of TV messages alone increased by 257%...." (Bogart, xxvi). We are simply inundated with advertisements. But we do not seem to mind, since many of us have ourselves become walking advertisements, e.g., T-shirts with the Nike (or Reebok, Wilson, Brooks Brothers, etc.) logo emblazoned across the front or back.

Advertising is big business. According to one source, $133 billion was spent on advertising in the United States in 1990, "more than the gross national product of all but a handful of nations" (Bogart, xvii). At about that time, the ninth largest advertising agency in the country had billings of $1.79 billion! In spite of the fact that no one has been able to give an accurate measure of the impact advertising has on sales, it remains the case that industries, corporations, retail businesses, and "mom and pop" stores avail themselves of ads in order to bring their products to the attention of the buying public—and, hopefully, increase sales.

Big as it is, and as involved as we members of the general public are in it, advertising is one of the most morally questionable and ambiguous practices in contemporary society. More often than not, scholars and intellectuals condemn this practice, while apologists for advertising create ads defending it, some of those published by the American Association of Advertising Agencies having the appearance of *scholarly* attempts to refute, point by point, the "lies" and falsehoods told by advertising's opponents. Advertising has been called "a very powerful aggression" by Marshall McLuhan and "an instrument of moral, as well as intellectual, miseducation [which prepares people] for submitting to a totalitarian regime" by Arnold Toynbee (cited by Bogart, p. 4). Turning the tables, its apologists have labeled its opponents as "misinformed," "ideologically controlled," and worse. No less a personage than Winston Churchill defended

the practice of advertising in, as one would expect, bold terms:

> Advertising nourishes the consuming power of men. It creates wants for a better standard of living. It sets up before a man the goal of a better home, better clothing, better food for himself and his family. It spurs individual exertion and greater production. (Rotzoll, K., Haefner, J., and Standage, C., 1986. "Advertising in Contemporary Society." Cincinnati, OH: Southwestern Publishing. Reprinted with permission.)

The general public cannot seem to make up its mind about the moral character of advertising. Public opinion polls always show a divided mind in the populace at large; some, indeed most, of the polls reveal that the majority of people think advertising is "dishonest," "misleading," "socially damaging," or culpable in other ways, and other polls indicate that the majority of people think the advertising business is morally okay "for the most part."

Defenders of advertising usually portray it as a vital cog in the free market system. Its functions are to bring a product to the attention of the buying public and thereby to increase sales. It is a coordinating link between supply and demand. Free market advocates are generally committed to high ideals of political liberty, and they see the rights of advertisers as nothing less than an expression of citizens' rights to freedom of speech. But critics of advertising need not be left-wing revolutionaries. Many accept the basic principles of the free market system but see advertising as violating the moral norms presupposed by this very system (e.g., the rights of the informed consumer), or they view advertising as having disutility within the system (in effect, a waste of money).

In what follows, we shall concern ourselves with the philosophical, ethical arguments that have been developed pro and con the practice of advertising and only indirectly allude to economic and political considerations. Most of the philosophical arguments in defense have been made in response to attacks on the advertising practice. Thus we shall begin with criticisms and in each case follow these with rejoinders.

Criticisms of advertising fall into three groups: (a) claims that advertising has pernicious social consequences; (b) claims that it involves manipulation or, worse than that, control over members of the buying public; and (c) claims that it is often misleading and deceptive. We begin with (a).

II. THE SOCIAL CONSEQUENCES OF ADVERTISING

A. Criticisms

The relationship between society and any one of its constituent institutions or practices like advertising is difficult to decipher. Basically we confront a "chicken and egg" dilemma. Is advertising simply a reflection of the social norms and values of society, or is advertising responsible in large part for making our society what it is? It has been said that the advertisements we are exposed to "constitute a cultural bombardment with an ideology of acquisitiveness" (Waide, J., 1987. The making of self and world in advertising. *Journal of Business Ethics, 6,* 76. Reprinted with permission from Kluwer Academic Publishers.). Certainly ads encourage us to buy, and to buy more and more, and more and more often. They often celebrate the person who owns lots of consumer products. Frequently (for example, in ads for luxury automobiles) they stress "good American values" like individuality and achievement and go on to correlate the attainment of these values with one's ability to purchase expensive consumer goods. In a Lexus, for instance, one can "take the road less traveled," which means that one's level of success will exceed that of most other people, who cannot afford such an expensive automobile. We are told that we fulfill ourselves by acquiring things and that true individuality is being able to buy things others cannot have.

But what here is cause, and what is effect? Is advertising responsible for the acquisitiveness we encounter almost everywhere in our society? Here is a contrary view:

> One may build a compelling case that American culture is—beyond redemption—money mad, hedonistic, superficial, rushing heedlessly down a railroad track called Progress. De Tocqueville and other observers of the young republic describe America in these terms in the early 1800s, decades before the development of national advertising. (Fox, Stephen, 1984. *The Mirror Makers,* William Morrow and Co, New York, p. 381; cited by Rotzoll, Haefner, and Sandage, 1986)

Do not blame advertising, the apologists cry out, for what is not its fault. Advertising is simply an extension of the cultural values that already exist, and ads do nothing more than express these socially sanctioned goals. One can back away, however, from the excessive claim that advertising is *responsible* for the hedonism and superficiality of contemporary society and still charge that this practice heavily *reinforces* these attributes. It sustains them and, arguably, intensifies them. To the extent that we oppose excessive concern with money, consumer goods, and economic progress, we can certainly point a finger at advertising as a contributing cause.

Acquisitiveness is wrapped up with a materialistic view of life, one that stresses the importance of material possessions, financial success, and sensations of pleasure and sensual activities. A large proportion of the ads seen in the public media focus on the delights of sex. These ads work by drawing an associative connection between the recommended product and the enhancement of one's sexual powers or prospects. Seldom if ever do ads celebrate the life of modesty and restraint; seldom do they offer for sale products designed to enhance moderation; seldom do they praise self-sacrifice. With the advertising world's almost exclusive focus on individual success, the virtues of social solidarity, compassion, and kindness are seldom expressed or reinforced—except, perhaps, in those highly cynical examples of advertising that show a child offering a soft drink to a hardworking, enormously wealthy, successful, and famous professional athlete. Ads prompt us to be more materialistic—and they gladly show us how to bring it off.

Inevitably a practice motivated by a materialistic ethos will project stereotypes that instantiate the defining values of this ethos. The rich corporate executive (who celebrates his "independence" by buying a Cadillac with the Northstar system), the hardworking athlete (who gives it his all, suffers great pain, and comes out, invariably, on top—wearing his Nikes), and the cutely bumbling charmer (who gets his girl, but only because of his American Express card), these are the "ideal types" of American advertising. Women usually do not figure among these ideal types—more often than not they play roles in ads for hemorrhoids, laxatives, sanitary napkins, cleansing detergents, and the like, roles that define them in terms of their suffering and their secondary, supporting position in American life. Watching ads on television is excellent instruction in the personality types and life styles that contemporary Westerners value and to which they aspire.

These stereotypes and ideal types throw into relief the failures of our society: someone who cannot afford the Cadillac (almost all of us), or someone who works hard but does not play on the winning team (almost all of us). As the ideal types are celebrated by advertising, the failures are derided—we are told, as it were, not to be or become like *that,* and the solution to our problems is always the product on display. Such a success–failure dichotomy, one can confidently assert, is unhealthy. It can induce severe psychological insecurities: what if one cannot jump high enough to win, in spite of great effort? What if one cannot afford the luxury car, in spite of working 16 hours a day? In the cultural environment shaped by advertising's values, it becomes increasingly difficult not to see oneself as a failure if one does not obtain these values. Yet common sense tells us that obtaining them is not always, or even often, just a matter of working hard, wearing the right shoes, or even having an American Express card. Thus the contemporary cultural world reinforced by advertising condemns many of its members to the ignominy of failure and defeat. If we "ask what kinds of lives are sustained, made possible, or fostered" (Waide) by advertising, we may conclude that in promoting cultural absolutes that are difficult to obtain, and implying negative evaluations of the lives most of us actually lead, advertising does a disservice to the members of society.

The finger can also be pointed at the deplorable standards of aesthetic taste set by advertising. The simple jingle, not a complex form of varied meter and rhythm, sets the standard. To be effective, an ad must be memorable, and the simpler it is, the more memorable. At their best, ads are "cute" and amusing, but such ads often promote an "airhead's" idea of humor. Often they are ridiculous and repulsive—after all, these two traits correlate well with memorability. On aesthetic grounds, ads in general must be given a low score.

The simplicity and idiocy of many commercials seem aimed primarily at the "brain dead" among us, and something like a self-fulfilling prophecy seems to be at work: if you treat people as idiots long enough, they soon become idiots. It is hard to claim that advertising fosters critical thinking, analysis, reflectiveness, or imagination. On the contrary, it often appears to promote a "knee-jerk" response, gullibility, and simplemindedness. A daily dose of television commercials can make one think in clichés and exercise imagination by means of overly simple, often sentimental, images. One's affective capacities are also impacted, often in a very unfortunate manner. After the inescapable violence on television has dulled one's sensitivity, thereby making it difficult to have an emotional response to events not rising to the level of excitement shown on the little screen, the ensuing commercials wreck havoc with other normal sentiments. We may, for instance, find it difficult to develop a sexual or romantic interest in people whose natural attractions do not measure up to the standard set by the stars of commercials. And the value of individual pleasure and success drummed into our heads by most ads can make it increasingly difficult to enjoy the more gregarious sentiments and to appreciate other individuals as valuable in themselves.

Special mention should be made of the effects of advertising on children. Not only are children easy prey for persuasive advertising, as we shall discuss, they quickly assimilate the social messages conveyed by advertisements. One writer reports how, as a young girl, she learned to walk "correctly" by watching television commercials (Moog, C., 1990. *Are they selling her lips?: Advertising and identity* (p. 13). New York: William Morrow.) Children also quickly imbibe the materialism and acquisitiveness permeating the ads they view. On a more pernicious level, they become conditioned early on, through many of the toys on display, to a culture in which acts of violence are everyday occurrences.

Such are some of the undesirable social consequences that critics find advertising to have. The problems can be posed in terms of explicitly ethical categories: advertising fosters false ideals of self-fulfillment; advertising projects values that rank low in terms of emotional, social, and spiritual richness; advertising is socially divisive; and advertising celebrates the individual over society and the community. Utilitarians (who seek the greatest good for the greatest number), Kantians (who stress the importance of duty, reason, and the dignity of persons), self-realizationists (who urge the most complete development of human nature), and virtue ethicists (who encourage the development of individual virtues like moderation and social ones like kindness) can join hands in decrying the social consequences of advertising.

B. Rejoinders

The main defense against these social criticisms is to reiterate the claim that the values embodied in ads and commercials simply reflect the preexisting values of the buying public. An argument can be given that if the public did not already value personal independence, "winning," sexual prowess, and the like, associating these features with a product would not enhance the marketability of the product. If the public did not find the "simpleminded" commercials amusing, these ads would not receive such high audience approval ratings. In effect, blaming advertising for the social consequences discussed above is simply "shooting the messenger."

Advertising can also be defended against the above charges by pointing out that no one is being forced by ads to buy a product or to buy into the ethos in which it cloaks itself. "Let the buyer beware" still has some applicability in the marketplace, and advertisers retain the rights of all citizens to express and promote their values, whether or not others agree with them. But the question of whether or not advertising is coercive or simply an individual or corporate expression of values leads to the second set of criticisms of this practice.

III. ADVERTISING, MANIPULATION, AND PERSUASION

A. Criticisms

These criticisms embody the claim that in one way or another, and to one degree or another, advertising is a manipulative practice. In order to come to grips with this claim, we need to have in mind a clear conception of manipulation. First, what we might call *simple manipulation* occurs when one party takes advantage of the beliefs or desires of a second party so as to get this person to act in ways that are in the interests of the first party. Manipulation of this sort usually ignores the interests of the second party, the person manipulated. An older brother, for instance, might manipulate a younger sibling into doing something the brother wants by offering the sibling lots of candy, paying no heed to the fact that the candy is not good for the younger person. In a case of simple manipulation, the manipulating agent uses the subject's own motivational structure to secure a result that would otherwise not be forthcoming. Second, more complex and morally problematic practices embody *deep manipulation*. In such cases, the manipulating agent actually creates in another person the beliefs or desires that then work to the advantage of the manipulator. The classic case of deep manipulation is brainwashing, in which a manipulator puts thoughts, beliefs, or desires into the mind of a subject and then uses these implanted contents to the manipulator's advantage (and usually to the subject's disadvantage). Instances of both simple and deep manipulation raise the question of *control*. When manipulation occurs, it can appear that our very freedom or autonomy is taken away from us—although to different degrees in different cases.

1. Simple Manipulation

A clear and extreme example of simple manipulation is blackmail. The blackmailer manipulates his victim by, say, agreeing to withhold information that would ruin the victim's much valued or desired career—in exchange, of course, for a large financial payoff. The blackmailer appeals to what the victim *wants*—a particular career. Given this want or desire and its level of intensity, the disvalue of what is threatened exceeds the disvalue of the payoff, and the victim accedes to the blackmailer's demands. A far less serious case of simple manipulation would occur if a person manipulated a friend by getting her to agree to join him at a concert (which, as he knows, she would prefer not to attend) simply by appeal to their friendship. This act of manipulation takes advantage of the friend's feelings and leads her to act in a way contrary to her immediate wishes. Although not nearly as morally contemptible as blackmail or bribery, such manipulation is still troubling.

In cases of simple manipulation there is a common pattern. The person manipulated agrees to undertake a course of action. In one sense, this individual "wants" to do what she in fact does; the act is an expression of her overall, hierarchical set of desires (the blackmailed party's desire for a career is stronger than her aversion to the payoff; a person's feelings of friendship are stronger than her aversion to going to the concert). In another sense, the manipulated person does not want to do what she does; she would not have done it had she not been manipulated into doing so. Manipulation thus involves a violation (however minor and however subtle) of one's autonomy, one's right to do as one pleases.

Do we find instances of simple manipulation in advertising? Certainly not all ads are guilty of it. Consider a "classified ad" in which only factual information about the advertised product is provided. A person may read the ad, like what she finds out about the product, and offer to buy it at the advertised price. Here we have a case of one party providing factual information to another about a product that the potential buyer antecedently wants and, presumably, can afford. There is nothing morally problematic about such a transaction, at least not in any obvious way. No manipulation has occurred.

But consider a common type of television commercial, one, say, that commends the purchase of a luxury automobile. A young woman new to the workforce may bring to the viewing of this commercial an interest in a new car and a need for one. Given her entry-level salary, what she needs is safe, reliable, relatively inexpensive transportation. But the female model driving the car in the ad is stunning in appearance, and at the end of the commercial she is met by an equally stunning man. The ad suggests to our viewer that owning this car will make one attractive and lead to amorous results. The young woman runs out to the agency and buys the car in question, signing up for loan payments she can ill afford.

In defense of the ad, it might be said that it appeals to the viewer's actual interests (the woman does want to look more attractive and to meet a handsome man). But given her meager means, her need is for an inexpensive vehicle. The car she buys as a result of the commercial will not satisfy this need—and, of course, may not and probably will not satisfy her desire for glamour and romance! The ad takes advantage of this latter desire and induces her to buy something contrary to her real interests. This is a case of simple manipulation.

Manipulation of the above sort is ethically questionable because of its disutility with regard to the customer's well-being or happiness. It can also be argued that such advertising is unethical because it infringes on the autonomy of the purchaser. (See Crisp, R., 1987. Persuasive advertising, autonomy, and the creation of desire, *Journal of Business Ethics, 6,* 413–18.) By appealing to the young woman's strong desire for glamour and romance, the advertisement activates feelings in her that often are beyond rational control. Her purchase of the car is not the result of a rational process in which she weighs reasons for buying it against reasons for not doing so. In leading her to bypass the process of rational choice and decision making, the ad violates her autonomy as a person who can, and should, rationally make up her mind about her purchases.

2. Deep Manipulation

Let us now consider a case of deep manipulation in advertising. As we have seen, simple manipulation utilizes feelings and desires that exist prior to the ad. In the case of deep manipulation, advertisements *create* the desires that motivate one to purchase a product. John Kenneth Galbraith is well known for bringing this possibility to our attention (1958, *The affluent society,* Boston, MA: Houghton Mifflin Co.). He calls it the "Dependence Effect." Galbraith claims that the chief function of advertising is to create the very desires that the advertised product aims at satisfying. As an example, let us take the case of ads promoting suntan lotion and skin bronzing cream. We know that desires for a particular mode of skin coloration vary widely from age to age; in the not-too-distant past, a white, pale complexion was considered desirable for women. But ads for suntan lotions and bronzing creams have created in many contemporary Westerners a desire for a dark, sun-tanned appearance. Here the advertising

audience has been manipulated into wanting a quality that the advertised products will supply. Without the ads, the desire for this appearance would likely not have existed.

What is ethically wrong about this scenario? After all, we *do* want a good tan, and so, given the information provided in the ad for a bronzing cream, we voluntarily buy it. But the appearance of individual consumer autonomy is superficial. The problem resides in the deep way in which the consumer's autonomy has been violated. Advertisements have *molded* us into potential consumers with certain desires. Unbeknown to us, the magic of advertising has shaped our desire structure. We are no better than puppets controlled by a puppet master, otherwise known as the advertising agency and the company sponsoring the ad. Hence our autonomy, our right to decide for ourselves what we want and what we pursue, has been eroded. And if we add to our scenario regarding suntan lotion the well-known fact that tanning is hazardous to one's health, we can also object to ads utilizing the dependence effect in that they often lead us to act in ways detrimental to our well being.

3. Control

Do cases of simple and deep manipulation amount to *control*? It has been claimed by many that this is the case. In his popular book *The Hidden Persuaders,* Vance Packard points to the burgeoning industry of motivational research and notes the belief that many people have in psychology's ability to control human behavior (1958, Pocket Books, New York). B. F. Skinner, the well-known behaviorist, subscribed to such a view (see his *Walden Two,* 1948 and 1976, Macmillan, New York; and his *Beyond Freedom and Dignity,* 1971, Knopf). He argued on many occasions that behavioristic psychology is a science of human behavior capable of identifying the laws governing all forms of behavior. And he explicitly noted how advertising makes use of such knowledge in controling the purchasing patterns of human beings. Skinner's conclusion was that advertising practices demonstrate that human freedom is a myth: "The concept of freedom that has emerged as part of the cultural practice of our group makes little or no provision for recognizing or dealing with these kinds of control" (Reprinted with permission from B. F. Skinner, 1956, Some issues concerning the control of human behavior: A symposium. *Science, 124,* 1058. Copyright 1956, American Association for the Advancement of Science). Advertising reveals how patterns of stimuli generated in accord with the laws of behavior can shape our actions even when we (falsely) think we make purchases as a result of our own voluntary decisions. Far from being free and responsible agents, the argument has it, we are under the control of the advertiser.

One particular and highly controversial form of manipulation and control should be mentioned before we leave this area of criticism. This is the case of subliminal control (see Key, W., 1973. *Subliminal seduction*. New York: New American Library; and Key, W., 1976. *Media sexploitation*. Englewood Cliffs, N.J.: Prentice–Hall). In this practice an advertiser supposedly sends out signals that boast of the benefits of a product but which cannot be consciously processed by the receiver of the signals. These signals go into the subconscious or unconscious mind and play on the motivations found in this subterranean realm. Thus it has been said that movie theaters sometimes broadcast subliminal messages advertising their refreshments, and that department stores encode subliminal signals into their Muzak offerings touting, say, their irresistible cashmere sweaters. Totally without realizing why, the story goes, we run out and buy popcorn and candy, or without realizing what prompts us to do so, we buy a cashmere sweater. Those who believe that subliminal control is found in advertising usually point to unconscious sexual stimulation as the mechanism employed. Print ads are claimed to have embedded in them sexual innuendos or suggestions about the positive sexual effects of the product advertised. Thus it is not, say, our conscious desire for a warm coat that leads us to buy the parka advertised, it is the suggestion coded into the ad that this parka will improve our sex lives that does the trick. The purchase is out of our hands—out of the conscious decision maker's reach—and in the hands of drives and desires we have little if any control over. That is to say, control is exercised here by bypassing the rational, conscious, reflective aspects of the mind. Insofar as autonomous agents are those who make up their minds on the basis of available information processed rationally, subliminal control overwhelms our autonomy. As one writer has put it, in such cases people act "automatonously" rather than autonomously. If subliminal control exists, it is to be ethically condemned.

4. Persuasion

The issues we have considered under the rubric of manipulation can also be expressed using the idea of persuasion (see Santelli, P. C., 1983. The informative and persuasive functions of advertising: A moral appraisal. *Journal of Business Ethics, 2*, 27–33). To persuade is to convince someone to do or believe something. Often this is a matter of changing someone's mind or leading a person from a position of indifference to one of inter-

est or commitment to the issue at hand. A person may be persuaded simply on the basis of factual information and logical argument, but as every student of elementary logic knows, people may also be persuaded by invalid forms of argumentation, particularly appeals to emotion. Persuasion can be deemed rational if it limits itself to true claims and valid arguments; if it appeals directly to emotion or feeling, it may well be irrational. To be sure, a physician may use emotional strategies to persuade a person to have an operation, but such emotional persuasion is justified in light of the patient's real need for the operation. If the emotional appeal is not grounded in real need, or if it is not designed to be processed rationally, it is unjustified. Thus advertisements can be divided into (a) those that limit themselves to factual information and valid arguments; (b) those that make emotional appeals based on the real needs of the individuals at whom the ads are directed; and (c) those that make emotional appeals that are not grounded in the real needs of the target audience. The first two forms of advertising constitute morally legitimate kinds of persuasion, but the third is morally illegitimate. Classified ads for the most part fall into the first category; many public service ads and some ads for commercial products (e.g., smoke detectors) fall into the second. A very large number of mass media ads and commercials seem to fall squarely into the third. Inasmuch as most mass media ads are aimed at the public at large, no assessment of the needs of the members of this public will usually have taken place. Thus the emotive appeals these ads often contain, not being based on the needs of most members of the audience, fall into the morally questionable category.

Once again, the advertising of children's products merits special attention. Because the cognitive abilities of children are still underdeveloped, ads aimed at children are by their very nature emotionally persuasive, many, if not most, of them in an objectionable way. Perhaps all interactions with children appeal to their easily aroused emotions and desires, but some are aimed at improving the children (and developing their rational abilities). Ads for children's toys and the like seem for the most part aimed only at the improvement of the advertiser's profits. And many of the ads are for products that are straightforwardly dangerous for children.

B. Rejoinders

Defenders of advertising categorically deny that ads and commercials manipulate and control people. As one manifesto of the American Association of Advertising Agencies puts it:

[W]hen was the last time you returned home from the local shopping mall with a bag full of things you had absolutely no use for? The truth is, nothing short of a pointed gun can get *anybody* to spend money on something he or she doesn't want. (Rotzoll *et al.*, 24)

The truth is, so the defense goes, advertising works when, and *only* when, it appeals to desires and preferences people have. Many products fail in the marketplace in spite of massive advertising, simply because the buying public did not want the product or did not find it appealing (witness the "New Coca-Cola" debacle). To purchase something one wants or finds attractive is a classic instance of *voluntary* behavior. One is forced to do something against one's will only when one is coerced into doing what one does not want to do. According to advertising's defenders, this seldom if ever happens in advertising.

It is possible to develop a more philosophical formulation of the above defense (see Arrington, R. L., 1982. Advertising and behavior control. *Journal of Business Ethics, 1*, 3–12). Coercion or control by advertising, it can be said, occurs if a purchaser acts on an advertising-induced desire she does not want to have. This state of affairs needs to be understood in the following way. In addition to our first-order desires (for particular objects) and first-order feelings (for particular persons or things), we have any number of second-order desires: desires or feelings *about* first-order desires and feelings. For instance, a person may wish that she did not have a desire to smoke. If, nevertheless, she continues to smoke, she is acting against her own will, being "in the grip" of an uncontrollable first-order desire. If a person does not disapprove of her desire to smoke, she is not acting against her will in doing so. Inasmuch as most of us want the products we purchase (as a result of advertisements) and most of us have second-order desires approving of these first-order wants, our response to advertising is perfectly voluntary. To claim that behavior is controlled is to deny that it is voluntary. But an agent acts voluntarily when she acts on the basis of motives approved by her own second-order desires. In such cases—which include most purchasing activities influenced by advertising—no control exists.

With regard to subliminal advertising, it suffices perhaps to say that the reality of this type of control is very much in doubt. In fact, the very idea of unconscious desires is not one that currently commands widespread respect in the field of psychology, as it once did in the heyday of Freudianism.

Advertising apologists have also denied that deep manipulation occurs in advertising. Galbraith is simply wrong, they claim, in thinking that advertising creates desires.

Of course, people didn't desire the automobile before it was invented. However, they did desire mobility, and once the automobile was invented many thought it was a good means to mobility.... Men couldn't have desired Aramis before that scent was concocted, but they desired to attract women, and when Aramis became available many thought Aramis was a good means to attract women.... In general, then, advertising does not create desires; given a certain desire, the advertiser brings to the consumer's attention a product that may satisfy that desire. (Collins, C., 1992. In defense of advertising. In *Business Ethics* (M. Snoeyenbos, J. Humber, and R. Almeder, Eds.), rev. ed., p. 425. Buffalo, NY: Prometheus. Reprinted with permission.)

We have preexistent *general* desires (for mobility, comfort, sexual attractiveness, etc.), and advertising at most generates desires for particular products thought to satisfy these general desires. Accordingly, the rejoinder has it, there is no deep manipulation going on here.

What about simple manipulation? Does not advertising sometimes lead us to purchase products we do not need? Defenders of the practice may argue that it is unfair to draw an analogy between manipulating a small child by giving her candy and influencing an adult to purchase a car she does not need. The child is unable to reach a decision based on a consideration of relevant facts (the effects of eating candy). The young woman in our previous example can be presumed to know the relevant facts about her financial status and to be aware that she cannot afford a luxury automobile (unless, perhaps, she cuts back on other expenses, or gets a loan from her parents, or pursues any of a number of other options that may be available to her). Thus being an adult she can be presumed responsible for her own decisions. If her desire for glamour is great and if she is aware of this desire and has no second-order aversion to it, she is hardly being manipulated. If in purchasing the luxury car she does something foolish, she, not the advertising agency, has to take responsibility for this.

Furthermore, how do we know that advertising leads people to purchase things inconsistent with their needs? It is possible to ascertain needs only when it is possible to make a clear distinction between subjective and objective opinions about the matter at hand. We adults can pronounce on the needs of children in ways that may conflict with their preferences; a physician can pronounce on our medical needs in ways that may conflict with our desires. In both cases we distinguish the objective point of view from the subjective one. But can anyone pronounce on the social and emotional needs of the adult woman and proclaim that what she needs is different from what she wants? Does anyone have a more objective point of view of her life than she does? Although some psychotherapists may pretend to occupy this superior perspective, a degree of skepticism is in order.

IV. ADVERTISING AND DECEPTION

A. Criticisms

1. Puffery

Let us turn now to the third set of criticisms aimed at advertising, the charge that many advertisements are deceptive. One thing is certain: ads often do not stick to the cold, unvarnished facts. When an ad for an automobile says, "Everybody's talking about the new Starfire," it is obvious to any reasonably informed person that this simply is not true. Likewise, the ad for women's underwear which states, "A woman in *Distinctive Foundations* is so beautiful that all other women want to kill her," is clearly overstating the facts. So if truth be our measure, much advertising falls short of the mark. But before we reach the hasty conclusion that ads such as the two just cited are deceptive and morally suspect, we need to recognize them for exactly what they are. They are not intended to be taken literally, and almost no one would take them that way. Even the advertiser, who may *hope* that they will be taken literally, does not actually anticipate that they will be. The ads above are examples of what in the advertising business is called puffery. Puffery is the practice of making exaggerated, highly fanciful, or suggestive claims about a product or service with the intent of conveying the impression that the product or service is highly desired and/or highly desirable. While most adults realize that not everybody is talking about the Starfire, the ad does leave one with the believable impression that lots of people are talking about it, that is, find it desirable. Is this true or false? It's hard to say, but given the flexibility of "lots," it may well be true. And *some* women may entertain murderous impulses toward those wearing Distinctive Foundations. So once we identify the intentions behind instances of puffery, it is more difficult to claim that such forms of advertising are intrinsically deceptive. Puffery is a matter of

bragging, and bragging is not something inherently wrong from a moral point of view. Although what the braggart says is not literally true, we usually do not accuse this person of lying or deliberately disseminating false information. Bragging is not that kind of speech act; neither is puffery.

2. Half-Truths

But putting puffery aside, there are other advertising techniques that more legitimately arouse moral suspicion. An example is the case of half-truths. Advertisements always emphasize the positive, valuable characteristics of a product; never are the negative characteristics identified. In omitting the negatives, an ad expresses a half-truth. The most egregious instances of this fault occur in ads for products that are well known to have deleterious effects on one's health or safety. Ads for cigarettes stress the enjoyment one receives from smoking and the social status it (allegedly) conveys; until required by the government, none of the statistics about its harmful effects were revealed in the manufacturers' ads. Automobile designs have been known by the manufacturer to have mechanical problems, but these are not identified in the literature or sales talk. Assuming that the manufacturers are aware of these negative features (something they always deny), telling only part of the story irresponsibly conveys a dangerously incomplete picture of the product. In presenting a half-truth, a manufacturer does not lie about its product or make a false claim, but it is nevertheless morally culpable for concealing its harmful features. The advertising industry sees itself as providing *information* about products. If this information is to create informed consumers, the information needs to be as complete as possible, particularly with respect to harmful or negative product features.

3. Misleading Images

In addition to purveying half-truths, the advertising industry not infrequently engages in other misleading forms of promotion. Instances of recent Volvo ads are notorious for an alleged form of deception involving misleading images. One ad showed a Volvo holding up a 6-ton truck that had been lowered onto it, testifying, supposedly, to the tremendous strength of the car's tires and suspension. In fact, the car was held up by jacks hidden behind the tires. Volvo claimed the ads were intended to show the strength of the roof and body of the car, not that of the tires and suspension. Nevertheless, the ad can be seen as conveying the misleading impression that the tires and suspension would hold up the car under these conditions. In cases such as this, no outright statements are being made: Volvo does not say that the tires and suspension hold up the car. Thus again the ads do not constitute outright lies. But the images used in them may convey very definite impressions to the normal viewer that are incorrect. In using such misleading forms of communication, advertisers, it is claimed, are guilty of deception.

The precise kind of moral culpability in a case like this depends on the intentions of the advertiser. If a company intends to give a misleading impression of its product's nature, it is guilty of deliberately deceiving the buying public. If it does not intend to do this but nevertheless conveys false information about its product, it may still be liable, in accordance with provisions of so-called strict liability, if any damage is done as a result of this misleading information. Cases of deliberate deception are more serious morally and legally than cases of strict liability, but both are morally, and sometimes legally, culpable.

4. Deception

What exactly is deception? Carson, Wokutch, and Cox have proposed the following definition: "x deceives y if and only if : x causes y to have certain false beliefs (b) and x intends or expects his actions to cause y to believe b" (Carson, T., Wokutch, R., and Cox, J., Jr., 1985. An ethical analysis of deception in advertising. *J. Bus. Ethics* 4, 98. Reprinted with permission from Kluwer Academic Publishers.). The virtues of this definition, according to its authors, are that (1) it indicates that an ad "must [itself] be the cause of one's misinformation or lack of reasonable knowledge," (2) it allows for deceptive ads aimed at children, since it does not require that an ad must mislead "a reasonable man" in order to be deceptive, and (3) it stresses the intent to deceive as a necessary condition of deception. Carson, Wokutch, and Cox grant that additional standards may be needed in order to pass legal and moral judgment on advertisements. Some would argue that among these additional standards (at least for advertising aimed at adults) is the "reasonable man" standard: an ad is deceptive not if it misleads just anyone (an ignorant person, say) but only if it misleads a person who has a reasonable amount of knowledge sufficient to discriminate obvious examples of false claims. Thus a person knowledgeable of automobiles might still be misled by the Volvo ads, because arguably it would take more than the knowledge of the reasonable adult to identify the false claims suggested by these ads.

Carson, Wokutch, and Cox point out that the American Federal Trade Commission has recently enacted standards for deception that require that for an ad to be found deceptive, it must not only have a capacity to mislead but also cause harm to the reasonable consumer. This regulatory edict raises the question of what exactly constitutes harm. From some ethical points of view, misleading a person—through lies, false promises, half-truths, or suggestive images—is itself a form of harm, a failure to recognize the consumer as a person of value in herself (accompanied by an interpretation of the consumer simply as a means to the end of the advertiser). Other ethical systems might require that an ad cause a person physical or psychological pain as a condition for harming that person. And there are intermediate positions which would recognize as harm the undermining of a general atmosphere of trust, even when no specific individual suffers as a result of this undermining. Clearly, these different ethical systems will evaluate differently the moral status of misleading advertisements.

B. Rejoinders

Defenders of advertising point out that it is illegal to lie or make false claims in advertisements, and they note that very few if any ads actually do so. They also urge us to reflect on the likelihood that in a highly competitive market, false claims on the part of an advertiser will immediately be identified by a competitor (but Alan Goldman has pointed out that there have been high-visibility cases in which this did not occur). And they argue that the "reasonable man" standard for truth in advertising allows for half-truths: any reasonable person, they claim, will realize that an advertiser only focuses on positive attributes of its product. The reasonable person must be presumed to have the responsibility to investigate any negative features the product may have. No one, however, defends a manufacturer's deliberate attempt to ignore features of a product known to be dangerous. But legislation and the mechanics of the marketplace are sufficient, the argument goes, to reduce incidents of this type to a minimum.

These, then, are some of the ethical arguments pro and con advertising. If we put them all together and sum up the results, what do we get? Is advertising "the single most value-destroying activity of a business civilization" (Heilbroner, R. L., 1985. Advertising as agitprop, *Harper's* (January), 71–76. Reprinted with permission.)? Or is it simply a free market practice whose "goal is the dispensing of information important to all consumers" (Brooks, F., 1985. Departing LEAP praises program, *The 4A's Washington Newsletter* (April), American Association of Advertising Agencies, Washington, DC, p. 8)? The reader must decide.

Also See the Following Articles

CONSUMER RIGHTS • CORPORATE RESPONSIBILITY • REPUTATION MANAGEMENT BY CORPORATIONS

Bibliography

De George, R. T., and Pichler, J. A. (Eds.) (1978). *Ethics, free enterprise, and public policy.* New York: Oxford University Press.

Donaldson, T., and Werhane, P. H. (Eds.) (1996). *Ethical issues in business,* 5th ed., Upper Saddle River, NJ: Prentice–Hall.

Goldman, A. (1984). Ethical issues in advertising. In T. Regan (Ed.) *Just business* (pp. 235–270). New York: Random House.

Iannone, P. A. (Ed.) (1989). *Contemporary moral controversies in business.* Oxford: Oxford University Press.

Kirkpatrick, J. (1994). *In defense of advertising: Arguments from reason, ethical egoism, and laissez-faire capitalism,* Westport, CT/London: Quorum Books.

Regan, T. (Ed.) (1984). *Just business.* New York: Random House.

Schudson, M. (1984). *Advertising, the uneasy persuasion: Its dubious impact on american society.* New York: Basic Books.

Snoeyenbos, M., Humber, J., and Almeder, R. (Eds.) (1992). *Business ethics,* rev. ed. Buffalo, NY: Prometheus.

AFFIRMATIVE ACTION

Ellen Frankel Paul
Bowling Green State University

GLOSSARY

affirmative action A term with various interpretations; it signifies policies intended to promote the interests and welfare of individuals from racial and ethnic minorities, and women, in order to redress the lingering effects of past discrimination.

affirmative action plan A yearly plan required of all but minor federal contractors (including companies and higher educational institutions) establishing specific goals for the hiring or admission of individuals from underrepresented minorities or women. These plans may also result from a court order, a consent decree ending a lawsuit, or as a voluntary effort to assist members of groups that have been discriminated against.

Black Codes Laws that were passed immediately after the Civil War by southern White landowners to make the new freedmen's economic condition as nearly like slavery as possible. Rights to land ownership and free movement were curtailed, and many Blacks were faced with the choice of signing disadvanta-geous yearly employment contracts with their former masters, or going to jail.

Civil Rights Act of 1964 The most significant civil rights act since Reconstruction; the act banned discrimination in employment, in public accommodations, and in programs receiving federal funds.

compensatory (backward-looking) arguments The principle that in formulating social policy, rectificatory justice requires that the past be taken into account, and that past injustices be recompensed.

consent decrees and court orders Devices utilized by the government through the courts to get employers and government agencies (such as police divisions or fire departments) to adopt and implement affirmative action plans. A consent decree is an agreement reached between the government and an accused discriminatory employer to cease discriminating and to implement an affirmative action plan. A consent decree is reviewed by the presiding judge. A court order accomplishes the same objective through a direct order by a judge upon motion of the government.

consequentialist (forward-looking) arguments The principle that in formulating social policy, distributive justice involves examining the likely future benefits and costs of adopting a policy.

EEOC Equal Employment Opportunity Commission, the federal regulatory agency created by the Civil Rights Act of 1964 to receive complaints of employment discrimination from workers throughout the United States, to assess the merits of such claims, and to facilitate a conciliation agreement to resolve the matter amicably, or (after 1972) to file a lawsuit on the complainant's behalf.

goals and timetables The key elements of an affirmative action plan that establish the number of new hires from protected groups that will need to be employed within a designated time period.

Jim Crow Although the provenance of this term is unclear, it came to stand for the segregation of Blacks in the South, their ostracism to inferior accommodations on railroads, steamboats, parks, schools, lunch counters, lavatories, housing, and other public places, and the denial to them of the franchise. Segregation was written into the law books in southern states during the last 20 years of the nineteenth century and in the first decade of the twentieth century.

merit A term often used by opponents of affirmative action to contrast their ideal of selection by individual achievement, with selection by preferences for protected-group members.

OFCCP Office of Federal Contract Compliance Programs, the unit within the United States Labor Department that oversees the letting of federal contracts and ensures that all contractors abide by affirmative action guidelines in their employment practices and meet the "goals and timetables" in their affirmative action plans.

pattern or practice cases An enforcement mechanism based on the Civil Rights Act of 1964 which gave the Attorney General the right to file suits against employers who appeared to practice systematic employment discrimination. This power was aimed at extirpating discrimination in large companies and giving public visibility to the antidiscrimination cause. Amendments to the act passed in 1972 gave this enforcement power to the EEOC, which originally had only informal powers of conciliation.

preferences In its weaker form, preferences under affirmative action plans mean that when two applicants for employment or college admissions are both highly and equally qualified, the person from the discriminated-against group ought to be selected. In its stronger version, a qualified protected-group member should be chosen over a more qualified applicant from a non-protected group.

protected group The language of the Civil Rights Act of 1964 prohibited discrimination against all people, but the principal purpose of the act was to remove impediments to the advancement and civil liberties of African Americans. Over the years several other distinct groups have come to enjoy special protection under the act because of their legacy of discrimina-

tory treatment. The list of protected groups usually includes African Americans, Hispanics, Asians and Pacific Islanders, and Native Americans. Discrimination on the basis of sex was also banned in the act, and women also became a protected group.

quotas A disputed term, in that where advocates of affirmative action see benign "goals and timetables" to advance the prospects of members of disadvantaged groups, opponents see malign quotas that limit the opportunities of other individuals and that divide the population into hostile and competing factions.

reverse discrimination A charge frequently made by opponents of affirmative action who argue that employment, college selection, and government contracting policies that favor Blacks, other minorities, and women are themselves discriminatory because they treat unfairly young White men who themselves are not responsible for the injustices of the past.

segregation See Jim Crow.

Title VII The section of the Civil Rights Act of 1964 that bans discrimination in employment based on a person's race, color, religion, sex, or national origin.

underrepresented or underutilized In a company, an underrepresented group is one in which the number of people employed from that group is less than their proportion in the surrounding labor market (or in a particular profession). In university admissions, correspondingly, an underrepresented group is any protected group that has been excluded or that has suffered discrimination in admissions in the past.

AFFIRMATIVE ACTION is an attempt by society to accelerate the advancement of members of racial, ethnic, and gender groups that have suffered extreme forms of discrimination in the past. In the United States, affirmative action programs began in the late 1960s and came to play a prominent role in most hiring, promotion, and firing decisions and in college admissions by the following decade. Affirmative action officers are employed by virtually all federal and state government agencies, by institutions of higher education, and by large corporations. Their role is to ensure that employers implement affirmative action plans and make all major employment decisions in conformity with federal and state guidelines against discrimination.

Although our discussion will be confined mostly to the United States, policies similar to affirmative action have been utilized by other countries to facilitate the betterment of groups victimized by discrimination or economic disadvantages. In countries as disparate as

Sri Lanka, Malaysia, Fiji, India, and Nigeria, group preferences in education or employment are practiced. While minority groups are the usual beneficiaries of group preferences, in Sri Lanka and Malaysia, majority populations receive preferences in order to overcome the economic dominance of a highly successful minority group.

I. THE CONTROVERSY

In its original understanding, affirmative action programs would open up employment opportunities to all without regard to race, color, or sex. Artificial barriers to advancement—such as classified advertisements in newspapers that distinguished female from male jobs, and union and employer practices that excluded African Americans from all but the lowest job categories—would be eradicated. Jobs would be widely advertised, especially in outlets likely to be received by women and minorities, and employers would aggressively seek out qualified applicants from disadvantaged groups.

Shortly after its inception, affirmative action took on a more expansive connotation. Opening jobs and college admissions to all on a color-blind, equal basis, would not solve the problem of racism and sexism quickly enough, many influential social thinkers and government officials argued, because the victims of discrimination were hampered at the starting gate as the result of opportunities denied in the past. Affirmative action, if it were to be successful, would have to grant preferences to those handicapped by discrimination. In addition, there would have to be written affirmative action plans with hiring and promotion "goals and timetables" for employers to attain. These plans would also facilitate the monitoring of progress by courts and government antidiscrimination agencies.

The initial rationale for affirmative action was to ameliorate the lingering effects of slavery and the discrimination that followed emancipation. Racial animus toward Blacks since the Civil War has taken many guises. The Black Codes tried to reduce the manumitted slaves to an economic condition akin to the slavery they had just left. Radical Reconstruction, imposed by northern Republicans in Congress, repealed these early attempts at re-subjugation. However, when the armies of the North finally departed from the last two formerly Confederate states, South Carolina and Louisiana, in April of 1877, the South reimposed restrictions on the intermingling of the races by segregating them in public places, and confining Blacks to the least desirable accommodations. This regime of segregation became known as Jim Crow.

After Blacks in the 1960s received affirmative action benefits, other minority groups pleaded their cases for inclusion in these programs as "protected groups." They cited their own legacies of discrimination, and today many groups, including Asians, Hispanics, Native Americans, Eskimos, and Aleuts, are beneficiaries of various affirmative action programs. Women, too, enjoy the protection of these programs. The case for affirmative action, however, has always been strongest when the descendants of the southern bondsmen are its beneficiaries.

Affirmative action, in its stronger, preferential form, has been a highly controversial tool, and its critics have not relented over the ensuing decades. If preferences are given in college admissions, hiring, and promotion to minorities and women, and if opportunities for advancement are not infinitely expansible, then some group must lose out if others are granted preferences. This latter group is comprised mostly of younger White males in the early stages of their working lives. The critics contend that this is unfair, because those who pay the cost are largely blameless for the injustices of the past when they were not yet living. Scholars who criticize affirmative action view it as tantamount to reverse discrimination. Discrimination is discrimination whether it is practiced for benign or malevolent reasons, they contend. These critics do not see how committing a second wrong, this time against young White males, can vindicate the original injustice against Blacks.

Proponents of affirmative action are no less persistent. For them, any adverse impact on White males is considered to be the unfortunate byproduct of finally dealing with America's racist and sexist past. If younger White males suffer setbacks to their careers when minorities or women are hired or promoted ahead of them, these setbacks are viewed as merely temporary and incidental. White males unjustly enriched themselves for centuries in America at the expense of African Americans, women, and other aggrieved minorities. Young White males today are the spiritual heirs of those that perpetrated injustice, and it is only fitting that they should cede some of their undeserved social and economic advantages, the advocates argue.

Thus, the debate over affirmative action both in the country at large and among moral philosophers is fundamentally over justice. Is society justified in rectifying past injustices by granting preferential treatment to the descendants of those unjustly treated? How much ought majority-group members sacrifice today in order to recompense the descendants of African slaves and other minorities? How extensive and how long must preferences be retained before injustice has been vanquished? Injustice and how to eradicate its effects will be discussed from a moral perspective in Section IV, but first, let us see how affirmative action developed as a social policy.

II. AFFIRMATIVE ACTION AS PUBLIC POLICY

A. The Civil Rights Act of 1964

The Civil Rights Act of 1964 was the culmination of an extraordinary effort by civil rights groups to pass the first truly significant national legislation to ameliorate the legacy of slavery in the United States in nearly a century. Legislation and constitutional amendments (the Thirteenth, Fourteenth, and Fifteenth) enacted in the decade following the Civil War (1865–1875) had ostensibly guaranteed freedom and equal rights of citizenship to the emancipated freedmen. These well-intentioned devices, often undermined by the Supreme Court, had largely failed to stem the abuses of legality and the social opprobrium that a century later still attached to being Black, especially in the southern states.

Passed by Congress in the wake of riots and protests in the South and the assassination of President Kennedy, the Civil Rights Act of 1964 would have far-reaching effects in transforming race relations, if not always improving them to the extent anticipated by its drafters. The act sought to end the infamous Jim Crow practices in the South that excluded African Americans from White public schools, from exercising their franchise, from intermingling with Whites in public places such as hotels, restaurants, and railroad cars, and even from using the same public lavatories and drinking fountains.

Various sections of the Civil Rights Act addressed the most egregious inequities. Title I struck at barriers to Blacks' voting in federal elections in the South, barriers that had been erected in the late nineteenth and early twentieth centuries to solidify the Democratic Party's dominance by eliminating the Black, predominantly Republican vote. Henceforth, literacy tests, unless required of everyone, would be prohibited. The subsequent Voting Rights Act of 1965 would further enlarge federal oversight of elections in the South. Title II banned discrimination in places of public accommodation—such as hotels, restaurants, theaters, movie houses, and sports arenas—thus eliminating Jim Crow's most visible and humiliating badges of inferiority. Title IV aimed at implementing the famous *Brown v. Board of Education* (1954) Supreme Court decision outlawing segregation in the public schools that, despite the passage of 10 years, had barely produced any integration in the South. In Title VI discrimination was also prohibited in all programs receiving federal assistance in the form of loans, grants, or contracts. Title VII as originally crafted proscribed discrimination on the basis of race, color, religion, sex, or national origin by all employers with 25 or more workers (reduced to 15 by amendment in 1972), employment agencies, and labor unions. Amendments to the original act enacted in subsequent years extended Title VII's protection to employees of state and local governments, and to most federal workers. Antidiscrimination laws proliferated over the years since the enactment of the 1964 Act. In addition to race, sex, color, religion, and national origin—categories covered in 1964—protection against employment discrimination is now provided for those over the age of 40 (enacted in 1967), for pregnant women (1978), and for the disabled (1973 for federal employees and 1990 for the private sector and state and local governments).

Over the years, Title VII has generated a tidal wave of complaints of discriminatory labor practices to the Equal Employment Opportunity Commission (EEOC, the agency established by the Civil Rights Act to receive and investigate such complaints) and its sister agencies in the states. During the 1990s, in particular, the EEOC has struggled with huge backlogs of complaints waiting to be investigated. Employment discrimination cases in the courts have also proliferated, with no letup in sight after more than three decades.

B. The Emergence of Affirmative Action

The conception of justice held by the supporters of the Civil Rights Act of 1964 embraced equality before the law, equal rights of citizenship, and equal treatment in the public domains of daily life, principally the schools, stores, restaurants, hotels, and all forms of transport. From the congressional floor leaders who guided the act through Congress, to the northern Democratic and Republican congressman and senators who voted for it, and to the civil rights groups that worked so tirelessly for its enactment, justice as equality of rights before the law was the common understanding. The overriding conviction was that people should be treated on the basis of their own individual merit, regardless of irrelevant qualities of skin color or heritage. This conception was deeply individualistic, for it regarded people as individuals rather than as representatives of discrete groups without common bonds of understanding. In banning employment discrimination the wording of the act's Title VII is individualistic: "It shall be an unlawful employment practice for an employer to fail or refuse to hire or to discharge *any individual* ... because of such individual's race, color, religion, sex, or national origin ..." (emphasis added). Such individualistic language is mirrored in other sections of the act. The Supreme Court revisited the hostile environment sexual harassment issue again in 1993, in *Harris v. Forklift Systems, Inc.* (510 U.S. 17). The Court tried to illuminate its "severe or pervasive" criteria, first articulated in *Meritor v. Vison.* While the victim need not prove psychological harm from the alleged harassment, psychological effect should be one factor that courts consider in assessing sexual harassment. Other factors, the Court suggested, could include the frequency of the conduct, severity, whether it is threatening of humiliating, or merely offensive, and whether it unreasonably interferes with work performance. In addition to the victim's perception that the environment was abusive, the Court blended an objective test: that a reasonable person would consider the environment abusive, as well.

Within the first few years after the passage of this seminal act, however, this consensus on the ultimate goal of achieving a color-blind society quickly eroded. If progress in ending employment discrimination needed to be quantified, then employers would have to identify their workers by race and sex. Civil rights groups, so long opposed to employment applications that required photographs or other devices for identifying one's race in order to discriminate against Blacks, and with a resounding victory just in hand, found themselves acquiescing to counting by race in the workplace. Quotas for university admissions and employment—so detested by those denied admission for discriminatory reasons and despite sterling records—became acceptable in the form of numerical "goals" to benefit members of groups formerly proscribed.

The Republican Senate minority leader, Everett Dirksen, had tried to forestall this course by proposing a friendly amendment to Title VII that was intended to prevent the government from requiring employers to:

grant preferential treatment to any individual or to any group because of the race, color, religion, sex, or national origin of such individual or group, on account of an imbalance which may exist with respect to the total number or percentage of any

race, color ... in comparison with the total number or percentage of persons of such race, color ... in any community or in the available work force in any community....

Although the bill's principal supporters in the Senate agreed to the amendment, they thought it unnecessary, and assured their colleagues that no one intended to impose quotas or demand preferential treatment. History would soon prove Senator Dirksen's prescience.

Executive agencies, the president, and the courts, all frustrated by the obduracy of discrimination, sought more effective means of guaranteeing entry to the outcasts. They felt that the individual rights to nondiscrimination, guaranteed by Title VII, were not effective enough, and certainly not quick enough to quench their thirst for justice, still a century late in coming. Preferences and goals might succeed with greater rapidity than the individualized focus on the discriminatory employer that the Civil Rights Act targeted. For many who found the act's enforcement provisions too nebulous, because too focused on errant employers, remedying societal discrimination with a more effective instrument seemed to be a necessity. Although the act's sponsors had insisted that they did not wish to hold particular employers responsible for the societal discrimination that had denied Blacks the education and job opportunities that would make them truly competitive with Whites, many civil rights advocates soon recognized that such an approach might be ineffective, and certainly would be slow to achieve results. Perhaps, the strongest argument for some form of affirmative action at the time was the substantial gap between White and Black test scores, a gap that handicapped Blacks in competition for college admissions as well as in pursuit of many types of employment where tests were employed to judge candidates. The intractability of this gap, and its persistence even after several decades of affirmative action programs, is still a deep concern to those desirous of remedying the injustices of the past.

C. The Role of Federal Enforcement Agencies

Very shortly after its creation, in the summer of 1965, the Equal Employment Opportunity Commission determined that more aggressive measures needed to be taken than the Civil Rights Act seemingly anticipated. President Lyndon Johnson, who as Vice President had been in charge of a civil rights committee set up by President Kennedy, but without enforcement powers or congressional approval, understood the ineffectiveness of past presidential antidiscrimination efforts dating back to the administration of Franklin D. Roosevelt. He too wished to engage in more aggressive enforcement.

1. Executive Order 11246

Executive Order 11246, issued by President Johnson in 1965, marked the true beginning of "affirmative action" as a national imperative, although the term itself can be found, bearing a different connotation, in the Civil Rights Acts and in an earlier Executive Order of President Kennedy's. Johnson's order, as amended over the years, charges the Secretary of Labor with ensuring nondiscriminatory employment practices and affirmative action by all federal contractors who do more than $50,000 in business annually with the federal government. The Office of Federal Contract Compliance Programs (OFCCP), within the Labor Department, is in charge of implementation.

2. The Philadelphia Plan

The defining moment for affirmative action in federal contracting came in the Nixon Administration, when in 1969 the Secretary of Labor resuscitated a plan for overcoming barriers to the employment of Blacks in some of the construction trades in Philadelphia. The plan had been floated 2 years earlier by President Johnson's labor department as the Philadelphia Plan, an attempt to implement Executive Order 11246, but the plan had been declared illegal by the Comptroller General, whose function it was to oversee federal expenditures. The revised plan, slightly reconfigured to overcome the bidding irregularity first flagged by the Comptroller, required would-be contractors to agree to an affirmative action plan that initially set goals for minority hiring at 4–6%, increasing to 20% over 4 years. Contractors who failed to meet their goals would have to demonstrate a "good faith effort" to comply. The plan prohibited contractors from discriminating against anyone in pursuit of these goals.

Not surprisingly, the Philadelphia Plan evoked considerable controversy. Critics saw it as nothing more than quotas, which could only be met by preferential treatment, precisely the mechanisms that Dirksen's addition to the Civil Rights Act was designed to forestall. The Comptroller again found the plan defective. Contractors would necessarily have to hire by race to meet their obligations under the plan, he argued, and this is precluded by Title VII's call for nondiscrimination in hiring and its ban on quotas and preferences. This time his objection proved to no avail, as Nixon's Attorney

General, John Mitchell, declared the plan permissible. The Attorney General offered an argument that would be repeated many times in the coming years: that the plan did not violate the Civil Rights Act because it only required a broadening of the recruitment pool, not impermissible quotas or preferences. An attempt in the Senate to block the plan and uphold the Comptroller's position failed.

3. The Office of Federal Contract Compliance Programs

Since 1971, OFCCP has enforced essentially the same affirmative action rules. Federal contractors must file an annual utilization analysis. If underutilization of protected minorities or women is found, according to a complicated eight-factor analysis that basically compares the composition of the surrounding workforce to the employer's workforce, contractors must establish "goals and timetables" to remedy any disparities. (In the wake of a 1995 Supreme Court decision that tightened standards for preferences in federal contracting, OFCCP indicated that the eight-factor test may be revised to include fewer factors.) Those contractors who fail to comply can lose their contracts and can be barred from bidding on future contracts, although these penalties have been rarely levied.

4. The Equal Employment Opportunity Commission

While OFCCP is limited to combating discrimination by federal contractors, who employ roughly 21% of the United States' workforce, the Equal Employment Opportunity Commission has a wider purview. Federal agencies and all but the smallest employers (or those filing with OFCCP) must file annual reports that divide their employees by race and sex. When complaints are received by the agency against an employer, the agency investigates, and then attempts to reach a conciliation agreement with the employer, and if that fails legal action can be taken by the agency or the worker can file a suit. Conciliation agreements may include "goals and timetables" or they may be imposed against refractory businesses by court order or consent decree.

5. The Justice Department's Civil Rights Division

The Civil Rights Division of the Justice Department is the third major enforcement agency for combating employment discrimination. The division pursued many "pattern or practice" cases, suing employers who exhibited systematic discrimination in their employment practices. Many successful suits were brought against police agencies, fire departments, state universities, local and state governments, and other recipients of federal aid. These suits resulted in consent decrees or court orders that established affirmative action hiring and promotion goals as the remedy for past discrimination. The high-visibility cases litigated by the division sent a message to employers everywhere that the federal government would actively pursue violators of the anti-discrimination laws.

D. Affirmative Action in the Courts

The courts of the United States, and most influentially, the Supreme Court, were instrumental in validating affirmative action, for the courts heard the charges brought by the various enforcement agencies, accepted their interpretations of the civil rights laws for the most part, and approved their affirmative action remedies. This approval, especially in the Supreme Court, came at a steep price in controversy, for these affirmative action cases as a group were the most contentious and fractious that the Court would ever decide. In society at large, by the mid-1970s, affirmative action aroused passionate dispute, and the Court mirrored that division, sometimes in acrimonious dissents.

From the first affirmative action case that it heard in 1978 to the cases of the 1990s, it is the rare case that has elicited anything approaching clearly drawn majority and minority opinions. Rather, the norm is for numerous opinions for the majority, for the minority, and for fractured voting, because justices often cannot bring themselves to share more than a few sections of their colleagues' opinions. Without clear judicial guidance from the high Court, the lower courts have cobbled together decisions that often conflict with each other from circuit to circuit. Fluctuating membership on the Supreme Court and some justices who seem of two minds from case to case, only add to the confusion.

Regents of the University of California v. Bakke (438 U.S. 265 (1978)), the first affirmative action case that reached the Supreme Court, set the pattern. The justices penned six separate opinions, and two shifting majorities agreed to different parts of the leading opinion. This opinion, drafted by Justice Powell, is hardly a model of clarity, easily avoiding the hobgoblin of consistency. In fact, Justice Powell was the only justice who assented to his workmanship in its entirety.

The case arose from a complaint by a rejected White-male applicant to the Medical School at the University of California at Davis. Despite two attempts (in 1973 and 1974) and a strong record of achievement, Allan Bakke was spurned for one of the 100 slots in the entering class. His benchmark scores (a combination based upon undergraduate grade point average, score on the Medical College Admissions Test, letters of recommendation, interview, and other factors) of 468 out of 500 the first year and 549 out of 600 the second, were just a sliver below the cutoff for the general admissions program. What irked Bakke was the operation of a special admissions committee, with 16 slots reserved for economically or educationally disadvantaged students and minorities. This special committee admitted students with credentials much weaker than his. Although the special dispensation was in theory open to nonminority applicants, and many applied, only minority-group members had won admission through this special committee. In contrast, 44 minority students over a 4-year period had attained admission through the regular admissions process.

Bakke sued the Medical School, charging that the admissions process violated (1) the U.S. Constitution's Fourteenth Amendment Equal Protection Clause, a vital portion of one of the post-Civil War amendments that guarantees to all persons equality before the law, (2) a similar provision in the California Constitution, and (3) Title VI of the Civil Rights Act of 1964, which mandates nondiscrimination in all programs receiving federal funds.

Bakke received favorable hearings in two California courts. The trial court agreed with him on all three grounds, but denied him admission, nevertheless, because he could not prove that he would have been admitted had the special admissions policy not existed. The California Supreme Court, basing its decision on the Equal Protection Clause, found that the special admissions program was not the least intrusive means to achieve the legitimate end of increasing minority doctors. That court ordered Bakke's admission.

The United States Supreme Court, in the person of Powell and his first, cobbled-together conservative majority, agreed with the California Supreme Court that Bakke should be admitted, but his second, liberal majority, refused to prohibit race as a factor in admissions decisions. The liberals agreed with Powell's assessment that racial classifications, although inherently suspect, may be used to overcome chronic minority underrepresentation. They declared invalid the Medical School's special admissions program because, Powell argued, it smacked of a quota by designating 16 positions for minorities, and by selecting minority admittees in a separate pool that sheltered them from competition with other applicants.

Emerging from the maze of convoluted opinions—partial concurrences and partial dissents—that *Bakke* elicited from the Supreme Court, is one overriding teaching: that it is permissible to take race into account in university admissions if the selection mechanism does not set aside a fixed number of slots for minorities, and if race is considered as a "plus factor." In the words of Justice Blackmun, words destined to be repeated often in subsequent cases and by legal commentators, "In order to get beyond racism, we must first take account of race. There is no other way. And in order to treat some persons equally, we must treat them differently."

In the years that followed, the Supreme Court would hear many affirmative action cases, and the disputed elements of the *Bakke* decision would never be resolved. First, what level of scrutiny should benign racial classifications receive from the courts? The more conservative justices favor a "strict scrutiny" standard that would have courts apply microscopic examination to any racial classification as a potential violation of the Equal Protection Clause. Liberals, in contrast, are willing to apply a heightened scrutiny, but one less searching than strict scrutiny. Liberals suspect that the conservatives' "strict scrutiny" would be "strict in theory, and fatal in fact." Second, what is the appropriate "interest" that a government agency must meet in order to justify classifying people by race? For the liberals, an "important" government interest is sufficient for their "intermediate scrutiny." Their test is satisfied by a claim to be remedying an underrepresentation of minorities that derives from societal discrimination in general or by an employer's desire to promote diversity. For the conservatives' tougher test, a university or employer must explicitly seek to remedy its own past discrimination. Neither camp, however, favors using the weakest standard of judicial review—the reasonable relationship test. This test is the one that the Court employed for decades in cases challenging economic regulation; it is a test that shows great deference to legislators and involves minimal judicial scrutiny.

After *Bakke,* universities continued to apply racial classifications to applicants, counting race as a "plus factor," and admitting minority students with significantly lower qualifications over White applicants with better grades and test scores. Sometimes they did so in a process very similar to the one invalidated in *Bakke,* by considering minority candidates in a separate pool, by a separate committee, and on relaxed standards.

For affirmative action beyond the university, another reverse discrimination case that the Supreme Court decided the year after *Bakke* set the pattern. In *United Steelworkers v. Weber* (443 U.S. 193 (1979)), the justices upheld a "voluntary" affirmative action program established by Kaiser Aluminum and the United Steelworkers Union to set aside 50% of all openings in a training program for craft positions for Blacks, until the number of Blacks in such positions reflected their proportion of the local population. Over the objection of a displaced White worker, the Court upheld the plan as a legitimate means to remedy Kaiser's own past discrimination, as evidenced by the paucity of Blacks among its craft workers, and the more general history of racial discrimination in the craft unions. From the disparity between a local population that was 39% Black and the plant's skilled employees who were only 2% Black, the Court inferred that discrimination must have been a factor.

Weber objected to the affirmative action plan on the grounds of discrimination by race, as interdicted by Title VII of the Civil Rights Act of 1964. Unlike *Bakke,* this case was not decided on constitutional grounds, because Weber's employer was in the private sector and not subject, as the Davis Medical School had been, to the Equal Protection Clause. Writing for the majority, Justice Brennan, a liberal jurist, finessed the Dirksen Amendment, aimed at preventing the use of preferences or quotas, by contending that Congress merely banned "requiring" companies to utilize racial preferences, but did not, although it easily could have, prohibit "permitting" the use of preferences. *Weber* would stand for the proposition that an affirmative action plan must remedy past discrimination (but whether societal or specific would remain unsettled), that the remedy must not completely exclude Whites, and that the plan must expire at such time as the effects of past discrimination have been overcome.

Following these two precedent-setting cases, the Court's subsequent decisions would vacillate between the two main antagonistic positions of the conservatives and liberals, depending in large part on the composition of the Court. For example, in *Fullilove v. Klutznick* (448 U.S. 448 (1980)) the Court deferred to Congress's intent to remedy past discrimination by establishing "set-aside" programs or preferences for minorities in federal contracting. With the conservatives on the ascendancy in a 1989 case, *Richmond v. J. A. Croson* (488 U.S. 469 (1989)), the Court overturned the City of Richmond's set-aside scheme for minorities, by arguing that state and local governments, under the Fourteenth Amendment, did not have the same latitude as the federal government in remedying past discrimination. With the swing vote deserting the conservatives the following year, the Court's liberals struck back with *Metro Broadcasting Inc. v. Federal Communications Commission* (497 U.S. 547 (1990)), upholding a regulatory policy of the FCC granting preferential treatment to minorities in the granting of broadcast licenses. The conservatives marshaled their forces 5 years later, in *Adarand v. Pena* (115 S. Ct. 2097 (1995)), and came full circle by in effect nullifying *Fullilove* and applying the same "strict scrutiny" standard from *Croson* to federal set-aside programs.

The *Adarand* decision applying "strict scrutiny" to federal contracting by racial preference had an immediate impact. President Clinton ordered his Justice Department to determine which federal contracting programs would fall afoul of the newly imposed "strict scrutiny" standard, just as *Croson* had sent state and local governments scurrying to complete disparity studies to demonstrate the two elements of the "strict scrutiny" test: that they had discriminated in the past; and that their set-aside programs were "narrowly tailored" to remedy their own past discrimination.

Beyond the issue of set-asides, *Adarand* sent a wider signal that several appeals courts quickly interpreted to mean that affirmative action in general ought to be subjected to a more searching examination, and perhaps found wanting. A quick check of *Adarand*'s potential impact can be discerned in a case denying admission to several nonminority applicants to the University of Texas Law School, a case challenging an affirmative action admissions scheme much like the one that had been supposedly forbidden in *Bakke*. The law school set goals of 5% for admission of Black students and 10% for Mexican-Americans; it screened minority applicants through a separate selection committee; and it offered admission to minority students with significantly lower qualifications than rejected White students. Race looked like something more than just a "plus factor."

It is worth noting, since the data on comparative academic records of White and minority students at competitive universities has been so tightly held by admissions committees, that the disparities revealed at the University of Texas Law School are substantial, and of the same scope as at other elite universities whose practices have become known, always reluctantly. All applicants received a Texas Index score which reflected their grades and test scores on the Law School Admission Test. Nonpreferred applicants were placed in a "presumptive admit" category with a score of 199 or above, while those below 192 fell into the "presumptive deny" category. In contrast, Blacks and Mexican-Americans were placed in the "presumptive admit" category with a score of 189 and above and in "presumptive

deny" at 179. Those falling between the two extremes for both minority and nonminority groups of applicants received the closest examination, and some were admitted and some not. The effect of this program was that minority students were placed in "presumptive admit" at scores lower than ones that disqualified the nonpreferred White and Asian applicants.

The Fifth Circuit Court of Appeals, in *Hopwood, et al. v. State of Texas, et al.* (78 F. 3d 932 (1996)), hinged its decision on the Supreme Court's reasoning in *Adarand*. Reaching a far harsher verdict on the law school's admissions policy than had the original, pre-*Adarand* district court (the court that had originally tried the case), the appeals court found the scheme objectionable in its entirety. The judges engaged in exactly the sort of searching analysis called for by the conservative majority in *Croson* (the set-aside case decided in 1989) and *Adarand*, in which the Supreme Court endorsed a strict scrutiny standard for "benign" racial classifications. The appeals court discerned no compelling justification on Fourteenth Amendment, Equal Protection Clause grounds for "elevat[ing] some races over others, even for the wholesome purpose of correcting perceived racial imbalance in the student body." The court, likewise, found unacceptable the diversity rationale for affirmative action, concluding that only remedying an organization's own prior history of discrimination with present effects could justify a remedy that takes race into account. The judges seemed genuinely disconcerted by a presumption that they found implicit in the diversity argument, that is, that "a certain individual possessed characteristics [or viewpoints] by virtue of being a member of a certain racial group." While allowing consideration of social and economic disadvantage on an individual basis, the court spurned "any consideration of race or ethnicity by the law school for the purpose of achieving a diverse student body."

More ominously yet for affirmative action's supporters was the court's reasoning on the law school's argument that its program sought to remedy the present effects of past discrimination throughout the Texas public education system. Parsing every detail, as strict scrutiny requires, the court could find no compelling state interest in such a broad mission. The law school would have had to present a justification relying solely on its own past history of discrimination, the court opined. Because many of the successful minority applicants had come from states other than Texas or from private schools, any vestiges of discrimination in the Texas educational system were deemed irrelevant. For good measure, the court added that even a narrowly framed rationale based on the law school trying to remedy its own prior discrimination would be deficient, because the law school had been actively recruiting minority students under various affirmative action programs since the late 1960s.

Perhaps another court, parsing Texas's history of maintaining segregated public schools, universities, and professional schools, might have reached a different conclusion, even on *Adarand's* strict scrutiny standard. Indeed, the law school's affirmative action plan had not been adopted voluntarily, but rather after years of protracted litigation attacking its remaining vestiges of discrimination against Blacks and Hispanics. In fact, the Office of Civil Rights (OCR, then a part of the U.S. Department of Health, Education, and Welfare and now a unit of the Department of Education) had been ordered in 1977 by the District Court for the District of Columbia to investigate Texas's admissions policies in its institutions of higher education. In 1980, the OCR concluded that the system was still in violation of Title VI of the Civil Rights Act of 1964. It took several more years for the Texas system to present a plan that the OCR found acceptable for remedying this legacy. In 1983, after a threat from the district court to order enforcement proceedings, the OCR approved a revised "Texas Plan," one that agreed to instruct all state professional schools to "admit black and Hispanic students who demonstrate potential for success but who do not necessarily meet all the traditional admission requirements." In 1988, when the plan was scheduled to expire, the OCR agreed with Texas that a new "Plan II" would replace the first one, because the state had not yet been certified by the Department of Education as having achieved compliance with Title VI. The new "Plan II" employed a more rigorous quantitative technique for judging applicants, and allowed for considerably less subjectivity in assessing minority applicants than the plan it replaced. By 1994, 2 years after Hopwood and her fellow disappointed applicants had been denied admission, Texas was still under OCR supervision. Thus, even for a post-*Adarand* court applying strict scrutiny, there was much past history that could have led to a different result.

This court, however, saw matters quite differently. Employing unusually harsh language, the judges seemed offended by what they called the "segregated" mechanisms employed in the law school's admissions procedures—separate color-coding of applications by race, a separate committee to review and admit minority students, and "segregated" waiting lists. Such exclusionary selection mechanisms treated people as members of groups, rather than as individuals, and this greatly disturbed the judges. On their reading, the Equal Protection Clause implies an individualism incompatible with the group entitlement implications that they drew from the law school's scheme.

It is too early for any definitive conclusions about the scope of permissible affirmative action on campus. In the wake of *Adarand, Hopwood,* and a pre-*Adarand* decision by the Fourth Circuit that invalidated race-based scholarships at the University of Maryland (*Podberesky v. Kirwan,* 38 F. 3d 147 (1994)), the viability of affirmative action programs similar to the one at Texas is doubtful. The Supreme Court declined to hear an appeal in *Hopwood* (116 S.Ct. 2581 (1996)), thus leaving this harsh condemnation of affirmative action standing as precedent in the Fifth Circuit, and possibly influential in other circuits as well. Since most universities' affirmative action programs share much in common with the one invalidated in *Hopwood,* only time will tell how influential this blast at "racial social engineering" will prove to be.

E. Summary: Affirmative Action as Public Policy

Affirmative action first emerged in the late 1960s as an unforeseen outgrowth of the Civil Rights Act of 1964. Frustrated by the subsequent, slower-than-anticipated pace of integration throughout the society, executive branch and judicial officials sought a more aggressive approach. Taking race into account in order to overcome racism became the regnant social policy, enforced by government agencies and courts, and embraced by universities and large corporations. First seriously challenged in the Reagan Administration, affirmative action received renewed inspiration from the Civil Rights Act of 1991. This act overturned several conservative Supreme Court decisions in the late 1980s that had chipped away at affirmative action's legal underpinnings and made Title VII employment discrimination cases harder for workers to win. With renewed vigor, the conservative position reasserted itself in the mid-1990s, as the high Court imposed a strict scrutiny test on programs employing racial preferences. In this unsettled environment, universities and employers are likely to find themselves defending against many more reverse discrimination suits that will be more difficult to vanquish under the microscopic analysis demanded by strict scrutiny. At the same time, they will still in all likelihood be pressured by regulatory agencies to abide by affirmative action requirements.

III. AFFIRMATIVE ACTION ABROAD

Spurred by equal opportunity efforts in the United States dating back to the Roosevelt Administration, by the passage of the Civil Rights Act of 1964, and by the subsequent emergence of affirmative action, countries of the European Community, Canada, and Australia, to differing extents, modeled new laws on American practice. The United Nations's adoption in 1948 of the Universal Declaration of Human Rights and similar declarations over the years by the UN and its agencies, were also influential in enshrining in Western law recognition of the "inherent dignity and of the equal and inalienable rights of all members of the human family...." Equal employment opportunity law and affirmative action in Australia make that country a particularly interesting one to discuss alongside American practices, and the two countries share many similarities in background and social tensions.

Australia has been particularly energetic in fashioning equal employment opportunity laws, consciously modeled after efforts in the United States. The heterogeneity of Australia's population, and the presence of the Aborigines, explains part of Australia's vigilance. Australia's highly structured labor markets, in which labor contracts are negotiated before national labor boards, is another reason why the country proved amenable to the sorts of interferences in the labor market that vigorous equal employment enforcement requires. Dating back to the turn of the century, Australia has set wage rates for almost all occupations by federal and state wage tribunals, with employers and workers left free to negotiate overawards through a modified collective bargaining process. It was only in the period between 1969 and 1975 that the Commonwealth Conciliation and Arbitration Commission—the federal wage tribunal—handed down two decisions that ended the long-standing practice of a two-tier wage structure for men and women. Prior to World War II, women's wages for each occupation were set at 54% of men's wages; after the war, the figure rose to 75%. Australia's labor market continues to be highly segmented by sex.

Australia has five major Commonwealth Government (federal) laws, each enacted in response to the country's signing of an international human rights declaration, and its states and territories (with the single exception of Tasmania) have also passed civil rights measures of even greater scope. Because Australia's federal constitution is one of delegated powers, and none was given to enact antidiscrimination laws, the Parliament hinged its equal opportunity legislation on its power to enact laws affecting "external affairs," hence the connection to international declarations. The first act, the Racial Discrimination Act of 1975 (tied to the country's signing of the UN's International Convention on the Elimination of all Forms of Racial Discrimination), makes discrimination on the basis of race, color, or national and ethnic origin illegal. This act has broad sweep, declaring that:

> It is unlawful for a person to do any act involving a distinction, exclusion, restriction or preference based on race, colour, descent or national or ethnic origin which has the purpose or effect of nullifying or impairing the recognition, enjoyment or exercise, on an equal footing, of any human right or fundamental freedom in the political, economic, social, cultural or any other field of public life.

The act covers "access to places and facilities" open to the public (including means of travel), estates or other interests in land, housing, provision of goods and services, membership in trade unions, employment, advertisements, and incitement to acts prohibited by the law. To enforce the act, a position of commissioner was established to investigate and conciliate complaints of breaches of the act. Recourse to the civil courts, should conciliation fail, was also provided, with much leeway for judges to fashion remedies to restore the aggrieved person to the position that he or she would have been in had no discrimination occurred, to void discriminatory contracts, and to provide monetary damages.

Another fundamental act extended protection to women and, also, enhanced enforcement mechanisms. The Sex Discrimination Act of 1984, passed after Australia signed the UN's International Convention on the Elimination of All Forms of Discrimination Against Women, banned discrimination based on sex, marital status, dismissal from a job for caring for family members, pregnancy or potential pregnancy, and made sexual harassment unlawful. It, too, covered a wide scope of human interactions, including employment, employment agencies, education, goods, services and facilities, accommodations, land, clubs (but single-sex clubs are permitted), partnerships of over six people, and the administration of Commonwealth laws and programs. The act permits "special measures" to promote the interests of women and their quest for equal opportunity. Numerous exceptions—for household workers, employees who take care of children, combat soldiers, thespians, competitive athletes, the sale of insurance policies based on actuarial or statistic data that varies by sex, the ordination of religious leaders, selection of staff members of denominational schools, and so on—make this a very lengthy, intricate, and cumbersome law. Thus, it is a law highly dependent on those who do the interpreting: commissioners and judges.

Three major Commonwealth acts have been added to this structure over the ensuing years, each covering approximately the same range of human activities as the earlier legislation. These acts include: (1) The Human Rights and Equal Opportunity Commission Act of 1986, which established a Human Rights and Equal Opportunity Commission to enforce all of the antidiscrimination acts and made it illegal to retaliate against anyone filing a complaint (termed "victimisation"); (2) The Disability Discrimination Act of 1992 prohibits discrimination on the basis of physical, intellectual, psychiatric, sensory, and neurological disabilities, as well as infectious diseases such as being a carrier of the HIV virus that causes AIDS. This act also bans harassment of the disabled. Employers are permitted to argue in their defense that a disabled employee could not perform the "inherent requirements" of the job, or that in order to carry out these duties, the disabled person would require services or facilities not required by others and that the provision of these supplements would "impose an unjustifiable hardship on the employer." Similar defenses are permitted for those operating educational institutions, public facilities, and so on. Numerous exceptions make this another very cumbersome, lengthy, and interpretable act. "Victimization" of someone for contemplating or filing a complaint is punishable by imprisonment for 6 months. The act permits "special measures" to help the disabled achieve equal opportunity, just as the Sex Discrimination Act permitted such measures to benefit women. (3) The Affirmative Action (Equal Employment Opportunity for Women) Act of 1986 made women the only group of Australians (with the exception of some categories of federal employees) specifically entitled by Commonwealth legislation to affirmative action. Educational institutions and employers of over 100 workers must implement programs to advance the careers of women and break down barriers to their advancement, and they must file an annual report. Statistical comparisons of the employment of men and women in various occupations within a company lead to the setting of "objectives" and "forward estimates" for the employment of women. "Objective" is defined as a "qualitative measure or aim, expressed as a general principle" that can "reasonably be implemented by the relevant employer within a specified time." "Forward estimate" is a "quantitative measure or aim, which may be expressed in numerical terms," designed to achieve equality of opportunity for women within a "specified time." An employer who fails to provide reports to the director of affirmative action, a member of the Human Rights and Equal Employment Commission, can be reported to the Minister with oversight authority, named in Parliament, and denied government contracts.

Although Australian enforcement authorities are inclined to distinguish their affirmative action practices from the "quotas" that they perceive in American affirmative action programs, their "objectives" and "forward estimates" seem indistinguishable from the "goals and timetables" of America's Office of Federal Contract Compliance Programs.

As a result of reforms in the Public Service Act in 1984, all government agencies must develop affirmative action plans, and they include "objectives" for the hiring not only of women but also of Aborigines and Torres Strait Islanders (another native population), people with disabilities, and people of non-English speaking background. The most recent plan, launched in 1993, sets objectives for increasing government employment of these groups through the year 2000, and each department must report its progress and the strategies it has employed toward these objectives each year. Year 2000 goals are set at 2% for Aborigines/Torres Strait Islanders, 5% for people with disabilities, 20% for women and 28% for women in senior officers grades, and 15% for people of non-English speaking background. As of the 1994–1995 report, these objectives were nearly achieved or, in the case of Aborigines/Torres Strait Islanders, already fulfilled. The only objective still wide of its mark is for employment of senior-grade women, which stood at 23.38%. Public service agencies are also legally obligated to institute measures to combat sexual harassment.

Australia's equal employment opportunity regime seems more aggressive than that in the United States, with laws that are written in a more cumbersome and expansive style than in the States, and with Australian states and territories seeming to exceed the federal government in solicitude. Some states even forbid discrimination on political and religious grounds, and newspapers can be brought before tribunals to answer for such things as refusing to publish letters to the editor based on grounds of alleged political discrimination. As is evident from the statistics reported by government agencies—percentages carried to the hundredth place—"objectives" can easily become indistinguishable from quotas, a quandary shared by the United States's OFCCP. While Australia has been influenced greatly by American practices, it seems to be an instance of the student exceeding the teacher in enthusiasm and assiduity.

IV. PHILOSOPHICAL ARGUMENTS

Affirmative action from its inception has been bathed in controversy. Political disputation centered upon the logical inconsistency of seeking to eradicate racial discrimination by means of racial discrimination. Just as the Supreme Court struggled with itself in a futile attempt at reconciling this conflict, society at large engaged in vigorous debate throughout the 1970s. Periodic echoes of that public debate erupted in the 1980s during the Reagan Administration, and again in the 1990s with salvos from the Court and grass-roots opposition in the form of an antiaffirmative action referendum placed on the 1996 California ballot. Philosophers, too, proved no slouches in producing vigorous arguments on both sides of the issue, although their interest flagged during the 1980s when it seemed that every conceivable argument, pro and con, that could be made had been made already in the 1970s. Renewed public debate in the 1990s, spurred by the California Civil Rights Initiative to end affirmative action in that state, also rekindled the interest of moral philosophers in reexamining this issue. During both rounds of the philosophical debate, justifications for affirmative action have fallen within two main types—compensatory and consequentialist—although much variety can be found in the details.

A. The Proponents' Arguments

1. The Compensatory Argument

Compensatory arguments are backward-looking and justify affirmative action as a remedy for slavery and its continuing present-day legacy, segregation and its lingering effects, and ongoing racism in defiance of the spirit of *Brown v. Board of Education* and the 1964 Civil Rights Act. In order to attain a just society, compensation in some form must be paid to those who are racism's most visible victims. Just as Germany was forced by the Allies to make recompense to the surviving victims of Nazi extermination camps, their children, Jewish organizations, and (after 1948) the newly created Israeli state, African Americans ought to receive reparations in some manner for the injustices inflicted on their ancestors and themselves by a slave-holding and segregationist society.

Backward-looking arguments are most compelling when they identify African Americans as the victimized group deserving of recompense, because the outrage of capture and forced transport, followed by generations of servitude is so repugnant to modern ideals of justice.

Yet, persuasive arguments have been made for extending the compensatory argument to other aggrieved groups. Women deserve inclusion because of a denial of the suffrage until 1920, much like the disfranchisement of Blacks during the last 2 decades of the nineteenth century. Bound to the home by social custom—or, some more radically feminist thinkers argue, male oppression—women were barred from an active role in social life and were denied admission to exclusive male institutions of power: the university, the corporate world, and the political realm. Legal disabilities of various sorts prevented women from entering certain professions, laboring as long as men, or exercising control over marital property. These artificial barriers liken women to Blacks, many argue, and warrant their inclusion in any argument for the rectification of historical injustice. In similar fashion, arguments are made based on historical victimization for the inclusion of Asians, Hispanics, Native Americans, Eskimos, and occasionally other groups.

Gertrude Ezorsky, a philosophy professor, makes a typical compensatory argument for preferences in her book *Racism and Justice: The Case for Affirmative Action* (1991, Cornell University Press, Ithaca and London). Racism against African Americans in America has been and continues to be "so pervasive that none, regardless of wealth or position, has managed to escape its impact." Enslavement followed by a century of legalized discrimination marks all Blacks, and none are required to prove their individual injuries in order to justify compensation. Perhaps, if emancipation had ended the impediments placed in the path of Blacks' advancement, the argument from historical injustice would have been attenuated over the years, but such was not the case. Racism never ended and still persists today. Thus Ezorsky finds preferential policies necessary as a remedy for historical wrongs, especially against Blacks, because their suffering was of a different kind than that endured by other disfavored groups.

Sensitive to charges by critics of affirmative action that the price of compensation falls whimsically on the few, young, and White males, Ezorsky hopes to blunt this charge by diffusing the costs over a larger group. For example, layoffs disproportionately affect Blacks because they usually have the least seniority—last hired, first fired. Instead of layoffs, Ezorsky suggests that employers consider alternatives that would spread the burden more widely: early retirement incentives, payless holidays, or work-sharing. If none of these were feasible, she suggests laying off the same percentage of the least senior Blacks and Whites. Thus, 10% of Blacks and 10% of Whites might be handed their pink slips, and some of the Blacks retained would likely have less seniority than some of the discarded Whites. The federal government might have a program, funded by progressive taxation, to compensate displaced Whites by augmenting their unemployment insurance, she suggests, thus spreading the burden of compensating Blacks for past injustice over all of society. Similarly, Whites denied promotions in favor of less qualified Blacks could receive monetary compensation from the government.

2. The Consequentialist Argument

The second category of arguments supporting affirmative action is based on a forward-looking, consequentialist approach. Consequentialist arguments look ahead, rather than backward, to the good things that will happen once racial discrimination is eviscerated and society can take advantage of the talents of all. Forward-looking arguments have been represented in the debate over affirmative action from its inception, and they have enjoyed renewed interest in the latest round of the discussion. Backward-looking arguments have become less compelling after a quarter century of compensatory affirmative action programs, and after the withering critiques made by early opponents. Thus, forward-looking arguments dominate debate in the 1990s, just as backward-looking rationales had in the 1970s.

Consequentialist arguments typically take one of these forms: (1) that diversity of students or workers by race, ethnicity, and sex will provide a more stimulating campus or work environment that will redound to the benefit of all, White males included; (2) that inclusiveness in the workplace will become even more of a necessity for business survival in the future as the United States workforce becomes increasingly darker-complected and female; (3) that a multicultural curriculum in our educational institutions at all levels will broaden everyone's understanding and enrich us all; and (4) that the beneficiaries of preferences and "goals and timetables" will become the role models for their groups as they become visible and successful members of their chosen professions.

Most forward-looking arguments for affirmative action are based on a conception of distributive justice—the aspect of justice that deals with the distribution of rewards, benefits, and other good things in society. Equal opportunity is the anticipated result. Equal opportunity can mean just that all "positions" in society are open to all in an unbiased competition, with the best candidate prevailing. More typically, though, a liberal understanding of equal opportunity involves some attempt to make people more equal at the starting line

of life's competitions. Affirmative action, in the form of preferences for the victims of discrimination, will make the race fairer at the outset, liberals contend, and will produce a more just society as the great game of life is played out.

Legal philosopher Ronald Dworkin makes a typical, liberal argument for preferences (1977, *Taking Rights Seriously,* Harvard University Press, Cambridge, MA). For Dworkin, all people deserve equal respect, and that is the basis for acknowledging their right to be treated as equals. Treating people unequally, however, may be necessary in order to achieve the ideal state of affairs in which people can be treated equally. Just as a parent might treat a sick child and a well child with respect, yet devote more resources to making the sick one well, society may grant preferences to the victims of discrimination, yet still respect all individuals equally.

Philosopher Thomas Nagel, in his essay "Equal Treatment and Compensatory Justice" (1977, *Equality and Social Justice,* Cohen, Nagel, and Scanlon, eds., Princeton University Press, Princeton, NJ), makes a more radical, egalitarian, forward-looking argument than Dworkin's. Preferential policies are not "seriously unjust" and ought to be implemented, but Nagel does not think that they will solve the basic societal problem of injustice. Even if affirmative action were completely successful in removing and remedying racial and gender impediments, individuals would still receive unequal and undeserved rewards as the result of unequal and undeserved talents. The injustice caused by racial and sexual discrimination, for Nagel, can only be completely surmounted by a radical reorganization of society along egalitarian lines.

Although compensatory and consequentialist arguments are separable, the consequentialist arguments, to a great extent, depend upon the moral imperative derived from the historical, rectificatory arguments. Consequentialist justifications for affirmative action, absent a litany of historical outrages, would not be nearly as compelling.

B. The Arguments of Affirmative Action's Critics

1. Defects in the Compensatory Argument

During the 1970s, affirmative action's critics were no less industrious than its proponents. The critics targeted defects in the proponents' compensatory argument, the linchpin of their case for preferences. While agreeing with the proponents that historical outrages had been perpetrated against Blacks—slavery and segregation the most egregious—the critics found the proponents' remedy counterproductive. Rather than compensating individuals for past discrimination against them in particular, affirmative action attempts to compensate groups.

Present-day special entitlements, or "group rights," the critics opined, cannot rectify atrocities of the distant past. With the passage of time, the compensatory argument becomes attenuated, with those who suffered the worst outrages long dead. Their descendants have a much weaker claim to recompense from American society, composed as it is of the sons and daughters, grandchildren, and great grandchildren of immigrants, many of whom fled discrimination of varying sorts in their countries of origin. Tracing historical victimhood, they argue, is a convoluted, disputatious enterprise, and one likely to erode social solidarity by Balkanizing people into groups of bitter rivals. Even if historical atrocities could be fairly attributed, the critics fail to see how a group right to preferences for the victims' descendants can ever compensate the aggrieved forebearers. Furthermore, if compensation can only be made to people who share the same skin color, race, sex, or national origin as the victims, and not to their actual descendants, then the critics find the rectificatory argument even less compelling.

Proponents employ group-rights arguments to claim preferences for current members of minority groups or women because of historical injustices that members of these groups suffered. Opponents reply that compensatory racial preferences create new groups of victims from the people who must pay the price of recompense in educational and professional opportunities denied. They view this as "reverse discrimination," benign in intent but ultimately of the same nature as the racial discrimination that led to slavery and segregation. Critics, in effect, deny that discrimination of any type can be benign, faulting reasoning such as Justice Blackmun's that sometimes race must be taken into account in order to overcome racism. Reverse discrimination just creates new groups of victims. Justice Scalia, in a concurring opinion in *Adarand,* succinctly framed the critique:

To pursue the concept of racial entitlement— even for the most admirable and benign of purposes—is to reinforce and preserve for future mischief the way of thinking that produced race slavery, race privilege and race hatred. In the eyes of government, we are just one race here. It is American.

2. Defects in the Consequentialist Argument

Critics also target the various forward-looking arguments for diversity, multiculturalism, inclusion, and role models. Rather than achieving a more just and egalitarian society, with opportunities open to all regardless of race, ethnicity, or gender, affirmative action in the form of group rights, preferences, and reverse discrimination will only serve to stigmatize their recipients as the undeserving beneficiaries of unfair advantage. While proponents of preferences view them as stepping-stones to overcoming negative stereotypes about minorities and women, opponents see them as solidifying stereotypes by implying that the recipients of preferences are not capable of achievement by their own devices.

Diversity and inclusiveness, if bought at the price of undeserved advantages and merit denied, will not further social amity, the opponents believe. Individuals deserve to be treated on their own merits, and if the violation of this principle is enshrined in law and practice, as affirmative action has been, artificial promotion of minorities will lead Whites to make invidious comparisons. In addition, the value of successful minorities as role models will be tarnished by the perception that but for preferential policies—from college admissions, to graduate and professional school admissions, to hiring and promotion—they would not have attained their positions. Not only will they be stigmatized in the eyes of others by preferential treatment, but they may come to question their own competence. Could I really have competed with my fellow students or colleagues if I had not been granted a special dispensation, will be a concern that undermines the recipient's self-esteem.

In English professor Shelby Steele's *The Content of Our Character: A New Vision of Race in America* (1990, St. Martin's, New York), the effect of preferences on self-esteem is an overriding concern. Accepting racial preferences for the children of the Black middle class, who have not been hindered in their ambitions by discrimination although they may have experienced racial slights, is for Steele something of a "Faustian bargain." He perceives one result as "a kind of demoralization, or put another way, an enlargement of self-doubt. Under affirmative action the quality that earns us preferential treatment is an implied inferiority." He cites the contrast between the 18 Black students who comprised his freshman class at college in 1964 (before racial preferences), who all graduated, with the failure rate of 72% for a much larger number of Blacks at the university at which he taught, San Jose State University in California. This high failure rate occurred despite numerous university programs to assist Black students, none of which existed in the sixties: academic support programs, counseling, an Afro-American studies department, the presence of Black faculty, a mentor program, and other aids. Steele would like affirmative action to mean what it did originally: enforcing equal opportunity by punishing those who actually discriminate; and helping to develop the abilities of the educationally and economically disadvantaged of all races.

Economist and social commentator Thomas Sowell (like Steele, an African American) has repeatedly made the point, echoed by Steele, that some Black students recruited for affirmative action goals at elite universities will be unprepared for rigorous intellectual competition with better prepared White students, and will come to doubt themselves, and often fail. Such failures are unnecessary, Sowell contends, because these very same Black students could have been successful at slightly less exclusive colleges. Sowell sees affirmative action as producing a ratcheting-up effect in which minorities throughout the spectrum from elite to nonselective universities are systematically mismatched—set-up for failure.

Other critics suggest that we reexamine the 1964 Civil Rights Act's reach, perhaps limiting its application to government agencies and permitting private companies to make their own decisions. Such a revised affirmative action regime would allow employers to adopt a variety of measures of their choice—or presumably, none at all—to achieve a diverse workforce. Voluntary plans, they argue, would offer the advantage of experimentation, and allow employers to better tailor their practices to the nature of their businesses. The result, they feel, might be a more vibrant labor market, and one in which we could better assess what interventions work and what do not.

C. The Advocates' Response

Over the years, defenders of affirmative action have heard these criticisms innumerable times. They respond by refuting the various charges, reformulating their original arguments to take the objections into account, or fashioning novel defenses. The rebuttal arguments of the proponents include the following: to the critics' argument that affirmative action compensates the wrong people by aiding those least affected by discrimination, they respond that racism is endemic, and thus all Blacks are its victims; to the argument that selection for scarce positions ought to be meritocratic, they respond that colleges admit legacies and academically

impaired athletes, and that job preferences for veterans are well accepted; to the argument that racial preferences foster loss of self-esteem, self-doubt, and failure, they point to those same effects but attribute them to continuing White racism; to the argument that group rights and claims of entitlement undermine social cohesion, they argue that Whites never objected when such perquisites were the preserve of Whites to the detriment of Blacks held in servitude or prevented by segregation from competing for desirable jobs; to the argument that affirmative action is tantamount to reverse discrimination, they counter that their racial classifications grant everyone equal respect, while the old racial categories were born of malevolence.

Three of the newer defenses for affirmative action deserve mention. The first attempt was to salvage such programs, despite renewed attack in the political arena and the courts in the 1990s, by generalizing preferential programs to allow all of the disadvantaged to receive benefits, not just Blacks, women, and the other traditional beneficiaries. Recognizing that they will likely have to accept some retrenchment in these programs, because of public weariness or effective opposition, proponents hope to salvage as much of affirmative action as they can. These arguments for preference by class, instead of by race, do not seem to be any advocate's truly favored course, but a weak second best.

Curiously, class-based affirmative action may even play a role in the tactics of the opponents of racial and gender preferences. For example, the California Board of Regents, in their 1995 vote to end affirmative action in university admissions in that state, left open the possibility that economic and social disadvantages, but not race, could be taken into account in admissions.

A second strategy is to try to undermine the critics' meritocratic argument by insisting that a candidate for admissions or employment who brings diversity to the community is meritorious on this ground. In other words, race or sex provides an additional qualification for a minority or female candidate. Advocates contend that: minorities and women share life experiences that cannot be understood or communicated by White male professors; that members of these maligned groups share a common consciousness; and that the dominant White male society ought to hear their grievances and learn from them.

Dorit Bar-On proposes a third strategy in defense of affirmative action. Writing in the journal *Public Affairs Quarterly* ("Discrimination, Individual Justice and Preferential Treatment," Vol. 4, No. 2, 1990, 111–137), Bar-On's novel defense is based upon a notion of counterfactual justice. Bar-On's objective is to redeploy the merit argument—so beloved by the critics—into a support for affirmative action. A qualified Black candidate for a job may not be the most qualified, but the evaluation should not end there. Employers should try to exclude from consideration the deficiencies that are probably the result of discrimination. Preferential treatment, then, would aim at "picking out candidates who would be deserving of the positions on grounds of competence, were it not for the present effects of past injustice." Philosopher Robert L. Simon, in his essay "Affirmative Action and the University: Faculty Appointment and Preferential Treatment" (in *Affirmative Action and the University: A Philosophical Inquiry,* ed. Steven M. Cahn, 1993, Temple University Press, Philadelphia), criticized this selection process as unworkable. How can employers and admissions committees judge nonexistent qualifications from the perspective of a perfectly just world that none of us can know, Simon wonders.

Arguments, no doubt, will continue to proliferate on both sides of this contentious issue, but it is unlikely that a truly innovative one will sprout after a quarter century of debate. Proponents will fashion compensatory and consequentialist justifications that differ little from their predecessors, and the critics' rejoinders will be mutations at best. This is well-worn territory for philosophers, but the two camps seem as unreconciled as ever. Charles Lockhart (Winter 1994, "Socially Constructed Conceptions of Distributive Justice: The Case of Affirmative Action," *Review of Politics,* Vol. 56), offers an explanation for the intractability of the debate, arguing that the two sides are formed by people of antagonistic temperaments. Egalitarians support affirmative action because they identify with groups and interpret equal opportunity as necessitating the eradication of great disparities in wealth and advantage between different groups in society. Individualists oppose affirmative action because they shy away from group entanglements, tend to be loners, and view equal opportunity as requiring only the eradication of government regulation of the marketplace. These "socially embedded preferences" that egalitarians and individualists hold result in rival ways of life that make the differences between the two camps on this issue "not resolvable in any deep sense."

V. CONCLUSION: FUTURE PROSPECTS

Affirmative action developed piecemeal through regulatory agency activism, judicial acquiescence, and presidential prodding. With its rapid transformation in

meaning from simply opening up opportunities into the principle that victims of discrimination ought to receive racial preferences, affirmative action became highly contentious. While the battle lines in the later years of the debate have tended to be sharply drawn, many people empathize with elements of each side's arguments. America has a strong legal and moral tradition of individualism and meritocracy, and affirmative action challenges these principles, yet many feel the tug of past injustices unremedied.

Public debate in the 1990s intensified as the decade began with revelations that the federal government had been race-norming its standard employment tests. This test, given to millions of job applicants and reported to potential private sector employers, had been graded by race, comparing White applicants only to each other and Black applicants only to each other. Thus, the percentile ranking reported to a potential employer might be the same for two applicants of different races, yet represent a significantly higher objective score for the White applicant. Under intensive public criticism, the Bush Administration was forced to rescind the policy.

Political discord over affirmative action accelerated with several developments in California. The Civil Rights Initiative, proposed by two college professors, and entered on the 1996 ballot as a referendum issue, called for an end to affirmative action in state agencies, the universities included. What its drafters envisioned is a return to the original meaning of Title VII, that is, protecting individuals (rather than groups) from employment discrimination. California's governor, Pete Wilson, as part of his ultimately futile presidential bid, issued an executive order (June 1, 1995) banning preferences in state operations not mandated by law. In July 1995 the regents of the University of California system voted to end racial and gender preferences in admissions and hiring. Vocal public protests, by students, faculty, and activist groups, failed to persuade the regents to repudiate their vote. Senator Robert Dole, likewise in the early days of his presidential quest, introduced (with a House Republican colleague) the Equal Opportunity Act of 1995, which if passed would have ended all preferential programs in the federal government. The California Civil Rights Initiative fared better than Senator Dole in the November 1996 elections, prevailing by a solid majority. Acts of civil disobedience, calls for tying up the initiative in court battles, and grumbling by city and university officials called into question how effective the initiative will be in securing its objectives.

This political ferment, combined with the judicial shift toward a heightened standard for evaluating racial classifications and preferences, suggests that affirmative action will continue to be in great flux. Courts have always said that affirmative action is a temporary expediency, and a questionable necessity, to remedy extraordinary historical discrimination. Whether affirmative action in the form of racial preferences survives many years into the next millennium is for the first time since its inception truly in doubt. Political ferment, as reflected in the Supreme Court's heightened vigilance and by the passage of the California Civil Rights Initiative, may result in the gradual phasing out of affirmative action in the form of preferences and "goals and timetables." However, political sentiments can mutate quite rapidly, and new appointees to the Supreme Court may shift the tide back in affirmative action's favor. One is on more solid ground in predicting the future of the philosophical debate than in the outcome of political cross-currents, and for philosophical disputation it seems safe to prognosticate that the future will not likely generate truly novel arguments either for or against.

Also See the Following Articles

DISCRIMINATION, CONCEPT OF • PLURALISM IN EDUCATION

Bibliography

Belz, H. (1984). *Affirmative action from Kennedy to Reagan: Redefining American equality*. Washington, DC: Washington Legal Foundation.

Bergmann, B. R. (1996). *In defense of affirmative action*. New York: Basic Books.

Bolick, C. (1996). *The affirmative action fraud: Can we restore the American civil rights vision?* Washington, DC: Cato Institute.

Boxill, B. R. (1992). *Blacks and social justice*. (Rev. Ed.) Lanham, U.K.: Rowman & Littlefield.

Cahn, S. M. (Ed.) (1993). *Affirmative action and the university: A philosophical inquiry*. Philadelphia: Temple University Press.

Carter, S. L. (1991). *Confessions of an affirmative action baby*. New York: Basic Books.

Epstein, R. A. (1992). *Forbidden grounds: The case against employment discrimination laws*. Cambridge, MA and London: Harvard University Press.

Ezorsky, G. (1991). *Racism and justice: The case for affirmative action*. Ithaca, NY: Cornell University Press.

Graham, H. D. (1990). *The civil rights era*. Oxford: Oxford University Press.

Koppelman, A. (1996). *Antidiscrimination law and social equality*. New Haven and London: Yale University Press.

Skrentny, J. D. (1996). *The ironies of affirmative action: Politics, culture, and justice in America*. Chicago and London: University of Chicago Press.

Sowell, T. (1994). *Race and culture: A world view*. New York: Basic Books.

AGED PEOPLE, SOCIETAL ATTITUDES TOWARD

Margot Jefferys
University of London

GLOSSARY

ageism Discriminatory attitudes expressed about, or behavior exercised with respect to, individuals entirely on account of their age.

birth cohort Individuals born during the same historical period (usually a 5-year band).

elder abuse Physical violence or mental torture of older persons whether by related kin or by others with the power to inflict such treatment.

longevity The chronological age which half the members of a group of individuals born at the same period are expected to reach, given current mortality rates.

sexism Discriminatory attitudes expressed about, or behavior exercised with respect to, individuals solely on account of their sex.

SOCIETAL ATTITUDES TOWARD AGED PEOPLE are subject to many different influences. These not only include the intrinsic shared values of a society, which are reinforced by religious and moral precepts about the duties owed to older and possibly frailer members and which may or may not be formally recognized in a country's legal system, they also reflect the part which people of different ages play in the economic life of their community as producers and consumers and as decision makers or dependents in family and kinship networks.

Therefore it is not surprising that, since all these influences vary from society to society and are themselves subject to historical change, societal attitudes to aged persons are always contingent and never absolute.

It is further inevitable that when social change occurs very rapidly and a society cannot rely on historical precedent to guide it—the case at the beginning of the new millennium—attitudes toward older people and their own self-perceptions should be in a state of flux. Conflicts of values and objectives are the norm.

It is the contention of this entry that societies everywhere are now trying to come to terms with a demographic transition. This is transforming populations from predominantly youthful aggregations with a small scattering of old survivors into ones where those aged 60 and over are as or more numerous than those under 15. For this reason, we begin with the contemporary phenomenon of population aging.

I. POPULATION AGING

A. The Historical Record

1. The Developed World

The 20th century has witnessed an unprecedented increase in world population. In the rapidly industrializing countries of Europe and North America the increase was already under way at the beginning of the 20th century and, although varying in pace from country to country for cultural and economic reasons, has been steady throughout.

The causes of the increase are multiple and complex, but the major reason has been a decline in mortality during infancy, childhood, and early adult life as infectious killer diseases in one way or another have been brought under control. As a result, a greater proportion of each successive birth cohort of females reached healthy sexual maturity and reproduced. With better nutrition and more knowledge of how to reduce the hazards of child bearing, as well as of how to control fertility, the reductions in mortality among adult women were particularly marked from the mid-century onward, and were greater than the rates for men.

The differential gender mortality rates at early ages—already apparent at the start of the 20th century and variously attributed to systematic differences in life styles and/or innate biological characteristics—mean that there are, typically, substantially more women than men survivors into extreme old age. Attitudes toward the value of masculinity and femininity differ and are undergoing considerable contemporary change. Attitudes toward aged people also differ according to gender (see Section IV).

2. The Developing World

Population aging in many of the countries of Asia, South America, and Africa, which have arrived later on the scene of industrialization and urbanization, is now spectacular. In a matter of a few decades rather than a century, for example, Japanese life prospects have been transformed. Longevity is now greater there than in any other country of the world. Between 1960 and 1990 Brazil saw an increase in life expectancy at birth from 52 to 66 years of age (World Bank, 1993. *World Development Report 1993. Investing in Health,* p. 200. Oxford Univ. Press, London).

The causes of population aging as well as its rate in these societies—as well as in countries like India where increasing survival into old age is at an even earlier stage–are rather different from those of the West. Coming at a later stage, the decline in infant and childhood mortality owes rather more to the application of effective medical knowledge and rather less to a voluntary limitation of family size—although this too is occurring—than was the case in the countries with a preponderance of people of European descent.

As a result, particularly in countries at a low level of economic prosperity, the potential conflict in meeting the needs of both old and young from meager finite resources is more apparent. Because many such societies, while purporting to venerate age *per se,* nevertheless value male life over female life, older widowed or never-married women are at greater risk of rejection or abuse by younger kin when they can no longer contribute to the economic life of their families.

II. RELIGIOUS AND MORAL TENETS

A. The Judeo-Christian Ethic

In the Western world, the dominant form of religious expression has been Christianity. It in turn had its origins in Judaism, with which it shares many basic moral precepts. Included in the Ten Commandments, which set out rules to govern everyday conduct accepted by adherents of both faiths, is one which requires them to "honor thy father and thy mother." Christ's own teaching further called for benevolence to the poor and needy and love for neighbors, even at the expense of self. The Talmud too contains many references to the need to support the frail and old.

There is of course much evidence both historically and contemporaneously that this commandment as well as others is often honored in the breach rather than in its observance by practicing christians and Jews. But there is no doubt that religious precepts, as expressed in the Commandments, have served to reinforce the legitimacy of measures taken by secular authorities to induce younger kin to take responsibility for aging relatives if and when they become frail and in need of care.

B. Other Major Religions

Economic development in the 20th century has resulted in the large-scale migration to the Western world of peoples from Eastern countries where other forms of religion are practiced and other religious beliefs prevail. While this has resulted in an awareness of some differences in basic codes of ethical behavior, the major religions, with greater or less emphasis, endorse views held by Christians and Jews on the need to honor parents and continue to respect them as they become more and more dependent.

Islam in the Koran calls on its followers to "show kindness" to parents, indicating that it is part of the Divine Will as revealed in Mohammed's teaching. *Buddhism* is both a philosophy of life and a practical discipline. The sanctity of every kind of life is an inviolable principle and may well serve as a safeguard against discrimination on grounds of age or infirmity. The way to salvation for individuals lies in *karma,* whereby good acts are rewarded by higher levels of existence in subsequent reincarnations. Full-blown *Confucianism,* as practiced in Japan, although now under threat as a result of a recent economic development, stresses filial piety and respect for the elderly.

Hinduism, the predominant religious movement in India, also calls for reciprocal intergenerational obligations throughout life. In theory, at least, parental authority over offspring only comes to an end with the death of the male head of family. Thereafter, the fate of a surviving widow is less certain. She may choose or be encouraged by others to commit suttee, self-immolation on her husband's funeral pyre. This is now much less likely to occur, but her fate as a surviving widow is not secure. It is likely to depend on the resources of the family and on the affection she has generated earlier as much as on any strict adherence to religious obligation.

C. Ancestor Worship and Other Types of Religious Belief

The paradigm most commonly considered as representing the emphasis on veneration of the aged is Chinese culture. But it is by no means unique. Elsewhere in many Asian and African countries local custom and beliefs about the nature of the cosmos see older people as requiring honor and piety because they are the custodians of the wisdom of the ancestors whom they are destined to join in the near future. Cherishing them ensures the continuity and welfare of the society.

In the 20th century, aggressive Western culture, which has spread throughout the world and permeated continents with very different traditions, places emphasis on the value of youth. Predominant images of the aged appear to those elsewhere to be ones of decrepitude and social irrelevance, if not of burden on the young. Not surprisingly, many people in developing societies feel that such attitudes undermine their own conventional culturally bound tenets.

III. THE EFFECT OF TECHNOLOGICAL CHANGE

A. Older People in the Productive Process

In modern technologically advanced societies, in contrast to older ones based unashamedly on social hierarchies of power and status, democratic ideals demand that equal value should attach to individuals whatever their age or social position. In practice, this ideal may not be realized. Almost universally, for example, those who are excluded from participation in the society's productive processes as a result of physical or mental frailty are accorded less social standing than those who are not.

In societies where the family household was the main unit of production, older members were not systematically excluded from its work as they aged. In the absence of technological innovation their wisdom and experience were welcome, and they would continue to make a valued if diminishing contribution until failing health or strength took its toll. Then they could expect still to be valued as a member of the kinship network.

With the advancing pace of technological change, which has largely eliminated the household as the productive unit, a variety of new pressures undermined the position of the old. Competition for work by landless and propertyless young adults led their representatives to try to exclude older individuals from the labor market.

In richer countries, this has been achieved through a variety of strategies. In particular, the gradual social acceptance of "retirement" bolstered by pensions as a legitimate and desirable life stage for everyone has proved a socially acceptable way of compensating older men, theoretically without loss of face, while at the same time reducing their interest in competing for jobs with younger workers. Many poorer countries have not been able to afford this solution and still lack an infrastructure of effective regulations providing dignified financial support for veterans. Hence, the latter are as dependent on the goodwill and capacity of their descendants' household units to provide for them as they were when such units were producing as well as consuming economic units.

An accompanying trend in industrial societies has been to undermine the confidence of older people in the value of their contribution to the productive process. Psychological research showing that speed and flexibility in many work processes decline with increasing age has been used to justify wholesale dismissal of older workers. When physical strength or resilience is also a job requirement, the older person may well accept that his or her contribution is of lesser value than that of younger workers. He may not be told or reminded that other research has shown that increasing age brings assets such as reliability and job commitment which can more than compensate for any loss of speed.

B. Substituting Technological for Gerontocratic Authority

When societies experienced comparatively little change in productive processes over decades, it was possible to establish generally accepted rules about the transfer of power from one generation to the next. The most senior society members were likely to retain their authority until they either died or were demonstrably incapable of consistent thought.

In the past century, however, country after country has introduced radical changes in its productive methods so that the accumulated knowledge of the older generation has been constantly devalued and contrasted unfavorably with the innovatory enthusiasms of more youthful members. Ideas of respect due to seniors persist, however, and are reinforced when, as is often the case among the most powerful classes of a society, they are property owners or have substantial influence in its political institutions. Nevertheless, generally, the legitimacy of the authority invested in elders is increasingly challenged.

Some technological innovations themselves assist the challenge. The mass media is mostly controlled by younger adults and has helped to disseminate and legitimize dissenting ideas about the value of age *per se,* while at the same time emphasizing with various positive images the attractiveness and advantages of youth.

C. Older People as Consumers and as Recipients of Service

A minority of old people worldwide possess substantial wealth which enables them to exercise considerable choice in their purchases and the life styles they adopt. Such individuals are likely to be treated deferentially by those who seek to serve them or expect to benefit from their wealth when they die.

Nevertheless, the visible affluence of some aged people in Western societies—who may be receiving occupational retirement pensions or have income from inherited or acquired property—may cause resentment among younger people, particularly if it is felt that it is at their expense when, simultaneously, they also have to support dependent children. Typically, however, the numbers of aged people living in real luxury are often exaggerated while the relative impoverishment of the majority is forgotten.

As the numbers surviving into extreme old age increase, so too does the cost to society of providing them with medical and social support. Elder abuse, which is perhaps more common than the few cases which receive publicity would indicate, and which can occur within private households as well as in institutional settings, may reflect the stress and resentment caused by the obligation to sustain failing life in straitened social and economic circumstances when primary affectional ties between helper and helped are absent.

IV. GENDERED AGING

A. The Gendered Life Course

At one time, writers observing differences in the everyday life and experiences of adult men and women were apt to attribute them to their fundamental biological roles in the reproduction of the species. These too were held responsible for differences in their health and in the causes and age of dying. In so far as their life styles and habits were demonstrably different, it was considered due primarily to these biologically determined roles.

Dramatic but rather different changes in the past century in the health of both women and men, in their mortality patterns, and in the position of women in the economy of advanced Western societies as well greater knowledge and interest in the different social roles played by both sexes in less advanced societies have combined to give more authority to the work of social scientists who have sought to prove that gender roles and experiences are largely socially constructed rather than biologically determined.

A succession of feminist writers from the 1960s to the present, moreover, have claimed that the gender divisions are dictated by the desire of male hierarchies to sustain their dominance and the subordination of females. Some have argued, furthermore, that for this reason women and men are socially valued for different reasons. While a man's value depends upon the power which he can exercise over others as a result of his physical prowess, the economic strength of his institutional position, or his superior intellect, a woman's is solely based on her physical attractiveness.

The result is that advancing age affects differently the value attached to being female or being male. Aging men can well be more highly valued as their wealth or institutional power increases with age. This may more than compensate for any diminution in their physical looks or performance. Women, on the other hand, because their value resides above all in their potential as sexual partners and as bearers or rearers of children, are likely to be progressively devalued as they age.

The images of the world created or displayed by the contemporary mass media do much to confirm these academic propositions. The epithets regularly employed to depict older women emphasize and even caricature some of the negative features of aging—wrinkles, bent backs, slow gait, and confusion when faced with technology. Older men, on the other hand, are more often treated with indulgence as eccentric individualists with endearing qualities. However, men of any age can be insulted effectively by describing them as "old women," until recently a socially acceptable term of abuse.

On the other hand, not all the cultural messages are uniformly negative or sexist. Some of them recognize that older women, as a result of their earlier life experiences as nurturing mothers and carers of adult dependents, are usually more able to perform socially valuable roles in the domestic economies of family and neighborhood than older men, whose earlier lives have been shaped by their primary function of income generators.

V. ETHICAL CONSIDERATIONS

Population aging, transformation in the health and life styles of older as well as younger people, increasing secularism now modified by a recrudescence of intolerant religious fundamentalism manifest on a worldwide scale, an accelerating rate of technological innovations, and reshaped relationships between social groups and among rich and poor countries have together affected and confused longstanding assumptions about the value of the aging process for individuals and of aged people as a section of society.

Presently, societal attitudes throughout the world to aging and to survivors as a group are consequently characterized by ambivalence. Humanitarian as well as religious precepts call on the young to respect older men and women and ensure that they obtain the share of the community's wealth which will provide them with as dignified an existence until death as modern technological knowledge and community resources can produce. These moral precepts are reinforced by emotional bonds between young and old forged in families where the once young have appreciated the nurturing they received from their parents and other significant older figures.

Yet considerable concern is felt that, instead of aged persons benefiting unreservedly from the success which reductions in mortality at early ages has occasioned, they may fare less well today than those who survived into old age at earlier periods. The continued presence of so many older people, many of whom may suffer from advanced dementias or physical limitations and whose positive contribution to the community is essentially in the past rather than the present, calls on younger people to give services in money, time, or emotional compassion which they may consider sacrifices depriving them of opportunities for alternative allocation of their resources. Previous generations were not faced with so many individuals experiencing a long drawn-out period of frailty and dependency.

It is not altogether surprising that in such circumstances the least contemplative and most socially vulnerable should express resentment if they attribute their own difficulties to older people, individually or collectively. Here are the seeds of elder abuse. But, even when there is no question of ill treatment or neglect, more thoughtful people may consider that there is a case for restricting medical procedures which prolong life in extreme old age, particularly if in doing so younger people may profit from health care.

It is in this context too that the increase in the numbers of older people themselves who, through the mechanism of living wills or some such demonstration of future intentions, ask for the withholding or withdrawal of life sustaining procedures in otherwise terminal illness or even for physician-assisted suicide must be seen.

The ethical implications of meeting such requests when their validity may be questionable are manifest. Many moral philosophers and lawyers as well as religious leaders and laypeople point out that institutional acceptance of the legitimacy of these practices without safeguards for the vulnerable could undermine the basic belief in the sanctity of individual human life, however handicapped or disadvantaged it may be. How much is a request a demonstration of the autonomy of judgment which, in theory, is considered the right of every sentient, mentally competent human adult? Could it be a recognition by an aged person, anticipating increasing unacceptable pain or dependency, of the socially appropriate time to disengage? Could it stem from the unscrupulous pressure of relatives or other potential beneficiaries from a death?

No man or woman is an island. Attitudes of aged people themselves as well as the meaning and value they attach to their own lives, past, present, and future, are constructed from the messages they have received over a lifetime from others close to them, their professional careers, and the wider society. It would be misleading to convey great consistency or persistence in attitudes at a time of unprecedented global change.

Also See the Following Articles

CHILDREN'S RIGHTS • FEMINIST ETHICS • RELIGION AND ETHICS

Bibliography

Achenbaum, A., Jakobi, P., and Kastenbaum, R. (Eds.) (1993). "Voices and Visions. Towards a Critical Gerontology." Springer, New York.

Achebaum, W. A., and Schale, K. W. (1993). "Aging and Social Structures. Historical Perspectives." Springer, New York.

Arber, S., and Ginn, J. (1991). "Gender and Later Life." Sage, London.

Binstock, R. H., and George, L. K. (Eds.) (1990). "Handbook of Aging and the Social Sciences." Academic Press, San Diego.

Blakemore, K., and Boneham, M. (1994). "Age, Race and Ethnicity. A Comparative Approach." Open Univ. Press, Philadelphia.

Bond, J., Coleman, P., and Peace, S. (Eds.) (1993). "Ageing & Society. An Introduction to Social Gerontology," 2nd ed. Sage, London.

Cole, T. R. (1992). "The Journey of Life: A Cultural History of Aging in America." Cambridge Univ. Press, London/New York.

Featherstone, M., and Wernick, A. (Eds.) (1995). "Images of Aging: Cultural Representations of Late Life." Routledge, London/New York.

Friedan, B. (1993). "The Fountain of Age." Vintage, London/New York.

Minkler, M., and Estes, C. L. (Eds.) (1991). "Critical Perspectives on Aging. The Political and Moral Economy of Growing Old." Baywood, Amityville, NY.

Riley, M. W., Kahn, R. L., and Foner, A. (Eds.) (1994). "Age and Structured Lag." Wiley, New York.

Spencer, P. (Ed.) (1990). "Anthropology and the Riddle of the Sphinx. Paradoxes of Change in the Life Course." Routledge, London.

Woodward, K. (1991). "Aging and Its Discontents: Freud and Other Fictions." Indiana Univ. Press, Bloomington.

World Bank (1993). "World Development Report 1993. Investing in Health," p. 200. Oxford Univ. Press, Oxford/New York.

AGEISM

Harry Lesser
University of Manchester

GLOSSARY

age cohort The group of people born over a particular period, such as a period of 5 or 10 years.

ageism Treating a person less favorably than others because of his or her chronological age.

fair innings argument The argument that those who have not yet reached normal life expectancy have a stronger claim on medical resources than those who have.

QALY An acronym for quality-adjusted life year, used as a measure for calculating the likely benefit of a particular medical treatment in terms of the years added to people's lives and the likely level of quality of life in those extra years.

triage A method of selecting those who need treatment most urgently, using as criteria the likelihood of the treatment succeeding and the likelihood of the patient failing to recover without it; i.e., highest priority is given to those who will recover with treatment as opposed to those who will recover without it or those who will not recover even with treatment.

AGEISM, a recent coinage on the model of "racism" and "sexism," may be defined as wrongful or unjustifiable adverse discrimination on the grounds of age. As such, the term can be applied either to discrimination against the old or to discrimination against the young. Both of these will be discussed in this entry, but in practice "ageism" refers more often to discrimination against the old, partly because this is probably more common in contemporary Western society, and partly because the issue of which kinds of discrimination are unjustified and which (if any) are defensible is, with regard to the old, both more complex and more disputed. Whether we are dealing with the old or the young, three kinds of ageism can be distinguished: (1) using the mere fact of chronological age as grounds for adverse discrimination; (2) attributing to the members of a particular age group a characteristic they do not in fact possess, and using it as a ground for adverse discrimination; and (3) attributing to the members of a particular age group a characteristic possessed by only some of them, and using it as a ground for adverse discrimination.

I. CHILDREN AND AGEISM

In all societies there are activities permitted to all, or at least some, adults, but forbidden to those below a certain age, the age varying with the society and the activity—voting, driving, and sexual activity are obvious examples. In general, this is considered reasonable, though there is much argument about what the appropriate age should be. It is considered reasonable because most people believe that those below these ages lack the competence, whether physical, mental, or emotional, or all three, to take part in or perform these activities without harming themselves or others. There are, however, those who believe this to be "ageist," though they may not use the word, on one of three grounds.

First, they may hold that all children have sufficient competence to be granted the same rights as adults. It is argued that some activities, such as voting, are ones in which anyone with an interest in their result is entitled to take part, so that competence is the wrong criterion; with others, such as sexual activity, children only lack competence because they are deliberately and needlessly kept in a state of ignorance; and with others, such as managing one's own property, those incapable of performing them (e.g., children in arms) are also incapable of wanting to perform them, so that they can be given the right to do them without the rights actually being taken up—this would apply, as an additional point, also to some activities of the first two sorts.

However, all of these arguments are open to objection. To the first it may be objected that if one is seriously concerned with a person's real interests, one must for that very reason protect them from making incompetent choices which they will regret. To the second, one may point out that competence requires emotional maturity as well as factual knowledge, so that, for example, improved sexual education and knowledge would not be enough to equip children with the ability to protect themselves from exploitation and the responsibility to deal with the consequences of their actions that are needed before a person ought to be sexually active. And the third is simply and obviously false: children do want to do many things, e.g., to try alcohol or to drive a car, at an age when to allow them to act in this way would be disastrous. If these arguments are correct, we should continue to regard it as necessary to prevent young children from taking part in those activities for which they lack the competence.

But there are two other arguments for "children's rights." One is that, even though what has been said above is true of young children, we continue to place restrictions on them well beyond the age at which they are necessary, so that it is not just a matter of modifying the minimum ages for voting, etc., but of radically lowering them. The objection to this is the same as that to the second point above: if what is required is some level of emotional maturity and stability, in addition to such things as knowledge, cleverness, or physical agility, which can be acquired relatively early, then there are obvious limits on any feasible reduction of these minimum ages, though some such reduction might be justified.

This, however, invites a reply which is also the third and strongest argument that our present practices are ageist. It is that, if emotional maturity is what is crucial, it is clear that people mature at very different rates. To set minimum ages, unless they are very low, and to treat all those of the same chronological age in the same way, is thus inherently unjust: a minimum voting age of 18, for example, excludes some people who are perfectly competent to vote and includes some who really are not. Similarly, it might be argued, any minimum age for legal sexual experience, unless it were set absurdly low, excludes some people who are sexually mature (emotionally as well as physically) and allows sexual activity for some people who are not. Hence our laws are ageist in the third sense distinguished in the definition: they treat all people under a certain age as incompetent when in fact some (perhaps the majority) are, but many are not. And this is inherent in any setting of age limits, given how much individuals vary.

This argument, I think, shows that our practices are to some extent ageist. There is, though, a question of whether any attempt to remove this ageism would not be a cure worse than the disease. The only alternative to an age test is presumably a competence test, or set of tests, and this would raise several problems. Some activities, such as driving, already require a test; a prior test of a person's suitability for being instructed seems a bizarre complication. Some of the necessary qualities cannot in any obvious way be tested for, but show up only in practice—how on earth would one test for emotional sexual maturity? (Moreover, qualities such as emotional maturity are needed not only in personal relationships but also in such skills as driving.) In general any use of competence tests would be enormously, perhaps prohibitively, complicated and time consuming, and, however just in principle, very unlikely to be administered fairly in practice both because of difficulties in deciding whether or not a person is competent and because of the likelihood of corruption—it was competence tests, unjustly administered, that kept many Black Americans disfranchised.

One final reply might be made—if a practice is unjust, such pragmatic arguments are not enough to justify keeping it, and since these arguments are not allowed, by most people, to justify racism or sexism, they should not justify ageism. But ageism is not quite like racism or sexism. People are Black or White, or female or male, normally all their lives with no possibility of change: any racial or sexual discrimination, unless corrected, works against a person for good. But with age we are all, if we are lucky, young, middle-aged, and old in turn: a discrimination against the young is temporary and shared by all sections of the community. Hence, though our practices are ageist and do discriminate against those who mature early, there is a strong argument for retaining them. Whether it is conclusive is a matter for the reader and for further investigation.

This all refers to ageism in the second and third senses outlined in the definition. But there has also been a pervasive attitude toward children and young adults, probably not fully conscious, which could be seen as being ageist in the first sense. It is the attitude that those who have lived longer are in that respect superior and entitled to more respect and privilege than are those who are younger. It was sarcastically alluded to in the 18th century by British Prime Minister Pitt (the elder) when he declared, "The heinous crime of being a young man I will endeavour neither to palliate nor to deny." It is, fairly clearly, less pervasive now than in the past, and coexists with a reverse prejudice against the old. But it clearly still exists, though it would take a lot of sociological investigation to work out exactly where and how it exists, and what practices in effect assume it—whether, for example, there are still schools that give privileges to senior pupils beyond what greater maturity and responsibility might reasonably entitle them to. In so far as such attitudes and practices do still exist, can they be justified?

One might suggest that, though age itself cannot be a just ground for increased "worth" or privilege, there are a number of situations in which other things are involved. There are situations in which older people are responsible for looking after younger ones, and this extends from the parent–child relation to older and younger siblings, or older and younger pupils in a school. Here, as has been pointed out at least since the time of John Locke, the duty of the older person means that they have the right to what is necessary to carry out that duty: since they cannot look after the child unless the child obeys them, they have a right to obedience (not total obedience but appropriate obedience). There are also situations in which the fairest way of distributing a particular benefit is seniority, because it means that everyone will get it in turn and after the same waiting period—this is not always just, because it ignores merit, but merit is not always the appropriate criterion. In contrast, there are situations where it seems just that the benefit should be earned, and therefore should be withheld from those too young to have done sufficient work to have earned it. Finally, there are situations where it may be felt, simply, that to give people too much too soon works against their long-term happiness, so that certain privileges should be withheld from the young for this reason (this argument

requires empirical support, but if supported by suitable evidence it would be a fair argument).

What all this suggests is that there can be other reasons besides lack of competence for validly "discriminating" against children and even young adults. But the reasons always relate to something more than age itself—the need to ensure that everyone gets the benefit, the moral requirement that the benefit be earned, or the supposed advantages of having to wait for it. It would seem to remain true that if age is being used as the only criterion, then the discrimination will always be unjust.

The appropriate conclusion would seem to be that the claim of the advocates of children's rights that there is institutionalized ageism against the young has not been supported—at least, such is this author's opinion, but others, after studying the arguments, may reach a different conclusion. However, there are grounds for recognizing that particular attitudes or practices can be unjustified or ageist, and hence should always be open to review: while there has to be an official age of competence, which must not be too low, it also must not be excessively high. The concept of ageism against the young can be misused, but it is a legitimate and sometimes appropriate ethical concept.

II. DISCRIMINATION AGAINST THE ELDERLY

A. Compulsory Retirement

With regard to ageism at the other end of life, the main issues concern provision of resources, particularly health resources. But there is also an issue that parallels the one concerning young people—whether compulsory retirement ages constitute unjustifiable discrimination. Three reasons can be given in favor of compulsory retirement. One is that the ability to do a job competently is lost with age; even if the mental capacity remains, the energy and adaptability eventually go. This is in one way true. Just as we are born without the competencies that most of us acquire with age, so, if we live long enough (which is often not the case), many of them are lost—though, it is important to note, not all: the basic ability to perceive and reason need never disappear. Nevertheless, the argument from loss of competence is clearly an ageist argument. Competence is lost, if at all, by different people at different ages, and to assume it is lost by a particular age by everybody is a false and ageist assumption. The only reply that might be made is the one I suggested could be made with regard to minimum age limits: that to test for competence in each case would be both time consuming and invidious. This *may* be a sufficient answer, but it should be noted (a) that given the high proportion of people who eventually want to retire, this might not be so time consuming or even so invidious as it looks, and (b) that, whereas in general minimum ages could not be lowered without real risk, retirement ages in many jobs could be appreciably raised without any serious risk of letting in the incompetent and inefficient, and this is becoming more true as people not only live longer but stay healthy longer.

Secondly, there is an argument, or set of arguments, from what is to be required if a job is to be done efficiently. The strength of these arguments varies with the nature of the work. In general, perhaps the weakest is the argument that to run efficient insurance schemes requires that most people retire at around the same age. There does not seem to be anything to rule out flexibility. A stronger argument is the suggestion that it is often desirable for a workplace, or even a profession as a whole, to have its members spread fairly evenly over the various age groups, so that there is a steady but limited change of personnel, avoiding the problems of lack of experience (if the age profile is "bottom heavy") and lack of initiative (if it is "top heavy" and there are too many older people). There is also the argument, connected with this last point, that the work suffers if the same people remain in senior positions too long, even if they are doing a reasonable job. Probably none of these arguments would hold across the board, but all could, and do, have force in particular contexts. The question remains, though, of whether this gain in efficiency is at the expense of an injustice done to those who are compulsorily retired.

This brings us to the third argument, that there is an injustice to the young if the old remain in work, particularly in senior positions, too long. This argument could take three slightly different forms. One is that different age cohorts should have, as far as is practicable, equal opportunities to find work and to obtain promotion. Obviously this depends partly on personal ability, partly on luck, and partly on changes in technology and the economic system that are beyond anyone's control. Nevertheless it might be argued that we ought not to make the situation worse by allowing some cohorts to remain in work so long that many of those after them can obtain a job and then promotion only at a time of life when it has lost much of its value. The second form of the argument, if justifiable, would be even stronger. It would be the argument that people are entitled, when this is possible, to the opportunity to work and to strive for promotion at an age when these things are most beneficial to them (and perhaps to others). It is of course only the *opportunity* they could have a claim to, and even this may not always be possible. But to set the retiring age too high, or to have none at all, could be seen as an unwarranted restriction of the opportunity. The third form of the argument would be the claim that the relatively young have, *in general,* a greater need for work than the relatively old, both because they tend to need more money, in order to support their families, and because, given the structure and attitudes of most (maybe all) societies, they suffer more psychologically from the lack of a recognized and worthwhile occupation.

One may conclude from this, I think, that with regard to employment, ageism is not quite like racism or sexism. It is clear that sex and race ought to be simply irrelevant to work opportunities. There are some strong arguments for positive discrimination but they justify it (if at all) only as a temporary expedient to help society progress toward genuine equality of opportunity. In contrast, age restrictions, whether maximum or minimum, even though they discriminate against certain people regardless of their suitability for the work, may nevertheless be seen as a necessary part of a fair and just employment structure. Once again, the weighing of a number of different and complex arguments is a matter for the reader.

Before we leave this section, two other kinds of general ageism should be considered. The first concerns equality of treatment. It would be generally agreed that standards of politeness, providing information, and concern for a person's comfort ought not to vary with age. But in hospitals and elsewhere, even though this would be agreed, there is too often a failure to realize that to implement this may require *different* treatment for the elderly—special but not more favorable treatment. For example, customs change over time. Whereas younger people may find being addressed by their first names a friendly practice, older people in the past, and perhaps still, have found it unduly familiar. Again, even those elderly people who are perfectly able to understand their situation and are by no means incompetent may still need to have things explained to them in terms they can understand, and perhaps with more repetitions. A person may be by no means mentally ill and still require to be reminded that they are in hospital and what they are there for. Again, what old people need in order to be comfortable is not always what younger people need. The general point is that fair treatment requires not only the same treatment, as appropriate, but also different treatment, as appropriate, in accordance with the particular needs of particular people. Although these range from person to person, there are, to some extent, needs commonly found in particular age groups. It can well be argued that there has been much too little done to identify the particular needs of the elderly, and that this constitutes, as it were, ageism by default. (A similar point can be made about children. More work has been done on trying to identify children's needs, but with limited success, partly because people have assumed they know what is needed without being prepared to "look and find out.")

Secondly, there is still too great a readiness to treat the old as being unable to understand their situation or decide what they want. Certainly, some elderly people, for physical or other reasons, become mentally disturbed, and some are clearly not capable of making decisions for themselves. But it is equally certain that sometimes the opportunity is denied them, either because they are presumed, with insufficient evidence, to be incompetent or because, though competent, they are not given the necessary information sufficiently slowly and carefully for them to assimilate it and make use of it. What one has here, consciously or unconsciously, is the blanket assumption that everyone above a certain age is mentally incompetent. This is ageism in sense (3) above. It is not as common as it was, but is by no means extinct.

We may summarize this section by saying that with regard to the elderly there are three general issues concerning ageism:

1. Whether a system of employment based on equality of opportunity does or does not require compulsory retiring ages.
2. What special needs are in general possessed by the elderly that have to be taken into account if they are to be treated with as much politeness and consideration as other age groups.
3. What ageist assumptions still influence our institutions and attitudes, and need to be detected and changed.

B. Triage

We now come to what is perhaps the most important current philosophical issue concerning ageism, which will extend over the next three subsections of this entry. This is whether, particularly in the provision of health care, of which the elderly, who form a growing proportion of the population, are the main "consumers," there is any justification for discrimination against those above a certain age. Three arguments will be considered

in these three subsections—the argument from the principle of triage, the argument from assessment by quality-adjusted life years (QALYs), and the "fair innings" argument. But before discussing triage, we need to dispose of two certainly invalid arguments for discrimination against the elderly in health care.

The first is the argument that it is natural to grow old and die, and wrong to interfere with this process. The short answer is that all medicine is an interference with natural processes, and this in itself is morally neutral. It is, in the opinion of many, inhumane and unjust to keep an elderly person alive artificially at the cost of much suffering to that person and against his or her will. However, to restore them, even artificially, to what they find a worthwhile existence is neither inhumane nor unjust. The distinction between right and wrong, or justified and unjustified, cannot rest on whether a thing is natural or artificial, even supposing that the distinction between natural and artificial can be made, particularly in a species for whom the use of artifacts is natural.

The second invalid argument is the argument that the elderly consume more than their "fair share" of health care resources. In the first place, "the elderly" are a changing group, so that this supposed advantage is in fact possessed by most people when their turn comes. Age distribution differs importantly from distribution according to sex or race in this respect. Secondly, it is entirely fair that health care resources go to those who need them, and it is the elderly who are most often ill. In a sense, to say the elderly consume more than their fair share of health care is like saying that women consume more than their fair share of maternity benefits! If the elderly are most in need, they should, in justice, have the most. The problems are (a) whether, as the argument from triage suggests, the needs of the elderly are not as great as we think, and (b) whether, as the QALYs and "fair innings" arguments suggest, the needs of the young can have a claim that overrides the needs of the old.

We may begin with the argument from triage. The principle of triage, as a way of deciding which cases for treatment should have priority, was devised on the battlefield. It requires the doctor, or other medical practitioner, to put those presenting for treatment into three groups: those who will probably recover, even if untreated; those who will probably die, even if treated; and those for whom treatment will probably make the difference between life and death (or something similar, such as disability and "normality"). Top priority is then given to the third group, with the first and second being attended to in whatever time is left.

This principle seems both to be just, since it puts those in the greatest need at the top of the list (we will assume the justice of distributing health care according to need), and to lead to the most efficient use of scarce resources. It may then be argued that, since resources are always scarce and there are always more demands for treatment than can be immediately met, triage should be used as a general principle for the distribution of health care. But if this is done, those who will die soon anyway, such as the very old, have for that reason less of a claim to health care than younger people. Hence some discrimination against the very old is fair and reasonable.

To this argument, three replies may be given. The first is that being close to death never correlates exactly with any chronological age. In every age group there will be some people in this position and some not. The percentage, minute but above zero in the younger age groups, will of course increase with age, but there is no point at which one could say, "everyone over this age is bound to die very soon." It may well be right not to waste resources on those who are going to die anyway, and instead to concentrate on making their end as easy and comfortable as possible, but this group, though it is predominantly elderly, excludes some of the very old and includes some of the very young. Triage thus lends no support for discrimination based on age.

Secondly, the principle of triage may be held to apply only when death is really imminent. There is a problem in deciding how limited a period we should be concerned with, but, given that withholding treatment is a very serious matter, it is plainly right to use a pretty tight definition of "going to die soon"—from one standpoint we are all going to die soon! Presumably, we should be considering only people who will probably die within days or perhaps weeks—months are already a different matter. Hence this principle should not in any way be used to exclude those people who do not, admittedly, have very long to live, but still have months or years.

Thirdly, one may argue that, though it is just to apply triage in a situation of emergency, or with regard to the distribution of a very specific and scarce resource, it is not just to apply it "across the board." An example may make this clear. It would presumably be right for a doctor about to treat a patient with, say, an uncomfortable but in no way dangerous skin complaint, who was then suddenly told that there was an accident victim in danger of bleeding to death outside, to ask the patient to wait and deal with the emergency. But it would not be right or just for the doctor to refuse to ever treat skin complaints on the ground (in itself true) that there

were always more urgent cases to attend to, or for a public health system to be set up in such a way that because of the pressure of urgent cases the nonurgent ones were simply denied access altogether. This seems to show that triage, though just as a principle for dealing with emergencies, is not a fair principle for deciding how to organize a health service as a whole or for doctors to use in deciding how to allocate their time—it is one thing to give precedence to the most urgent cases and another to concentrate on them alone. If one accepts this point and the other two arguments, one would conclude that the triage principle provides no justification for treating the elderly, *qua* elderly, in any way differently from anyone else needing health care.

C. Quality-Adjusted Life Years

In the literature of medical ethics there has been much discussion of QALYs as a means for deciding the best use of medical resources. The idea is this. It is assumed that the right use of resources is the one that will do the most good. It is then argued that in principle the amount of good likely to result from any particular use of resources is quantifiable by considering (a) the number of people benefited, (b) the extra years of life each person may expect as a result of the treatment, and (c) the improvement in the quality of life produced by the treatment (reduction in pain, freedom from disability, etc.). This might be applied at the macro level, to decide what kinds of treatment a public health service should offer, or at the micro level, to decide which patients, within the system, should be given priority. In either case, the use of QALYs will tend to favor the young over the old, although strictly speaking it favors treating those who may expect to live longer rather than those who have a shorter life expectation, which, as we saw in the last section, does not always correlate with age. Nevertheless, since the use of QALYs as a principle is more radical than the use of triage, because it requires us to consider in general how long a person may expect to live and not merely whether or not they will die very soon, it will certainly tend in practice to work against the elderly.

The first objection to QALYs is that only in the fantasy worlds of (some) health economists is any precise quantification possible. In the real world this could be done only in a very crude and approximate way. But, one might reply, in a crude way it can be done. It *could*, for example, be decided that medical research and resources should be concentrated on conditions which attack the relatively young (such as AIDS) rather than those which much more often attack the more elderly (such as cancer), or that patients below a certain age (unless likely to die relatively soon anyway) should be given preferential access to life-saving treatment. The question, however, is whether it would be right, even if it were possible. Many people have argued that, even if this is the most efficient use of resources, it is inherently unjust, especially, though not only, to the old.

If the argument of the preceding section on triage is correct, then it follows that a total application of QALYs would be unjust. Essentially, the argument is that everyone who needs medical treatment has some claim to it. Since needs vary in strength and urgency, some claims are stronger than others. This could justify a choice of whom to treat in an emergency, as triage does, or it could justify putting more resources into one area than another, but it could not justify totally withholding resources from a particular area or totally excluding particular people, such as those over a certain age, from being eligible for treatment.

In other words, the principle of QALYs *may* provide a stronger argument than the principle of triage for saying that there can be legitimate discrimination against the elderly in health care. It *could* be right to give more resources to the treatment of conditions that affect younger rather than older people (though very few diseases and conditions affect only the old). It *could* also be right, in an emergency, to give priority to younger over older people. But many people would argue that to do more than this is clearly unjust, because it would involve treating people with at least *some* claim to resources as if they had no claim at all. Even the more limited claim has not yet been shown to be legitimate. To see whether or not it is justified, we have to consider whether there is any argument from justice, rather than from efficiency and welfare, for discrimination against the old, since it is often argued that considerations of justice should take priority. This leads us to the "fair innings" argument.

D. The "Fair Innings" Argument

The expression "fair innings argument" is a metaphor taken from the game of cricket, but no knowledge of the game is required to understand the argument itself, which in any case is in no way confined to the cricket-playing world. The idea is that anyone who has reached the normal span of human life—currently somewhere between 70 and 80 years old—has for that reason less claim on resources than someone who still has some time to go, and therefore it is positively just, when necessary, to favor younger people over those who have "had their life." It is worth noting that this argument, unlike the preceding two, comes from ordinary moral experience. QALYs were invented by economists and philosophers, and triage was devised by medical practitioners (though it does fit ordinary moral ideas of justice), but the "fair innings" argument expresses what in general people, old as well as young, often feel to be just. And, as was said above, it is often held that only by an argument from justice can discrimination be legitimized.

However, the argument is limited in scope and also open to objection. First, it applies only to those who have reached normal life expectancy, and not in general to older rather than younger people. It will be noted that this article has so far not attempted to define "old" or "elderly"; this argument is the first one which is based on a particular definition, and it is quite a restricted one—perhaps 75 and over. Secondly, if the arguments given in the two previous sections are correct, it could justify only two things. One is giving priority to a younger person in an emergency; the other is to give some limited preference in the allocation of medical resources to dealing with conditions particularly affecting the young. Moreover, with regard to the second of these, it is arguable that already geriatric medicine receives less rather than more of its fair share of resources. Hence, even though the argument fits many people's sense of justice, there are grounds for thinking that there is not a great deal which it justifies in actual practice.

Also, there are considerations of justice which constitute objections to the argument itself. Some have argued that all people who wish to live, whether old or young, have an equal claim to have their wishes met, and therefore, if they cannot all be saved, it would be more just to take people at random, or on a "first come, first served" basis, than to pretend that some have a stronger claim. It can also be argued that the old have earned a right to treatment in a way the young have not as yet, either through their work or because they have contributed, through British National Insurance contributions, for example, to the welfare of the generation above theirs and are now entitled to the same treatment from the generation below. It could also be argued that *some* of the elderly who lived hard lives when young may have had much less of the enjoyable part of their lives than some younger people, and could claim in a real sense that they have not yet "had their life." The "fair innings" argument thus stands as one principle of justice among several. Even though the old as well as the young often accept it, it is not yet clear when, if ever, it is the principle that ought to be followed, and there are also arguments for holding that its practical application should be limited (see, e.g., Harris "More and better justice" in Bell and Mendus (1988)).

III. SUMMARY

Issues of ageism arise, as we have seen, in a number of areas. These can involve either the young or the old and include age restrictions on a range of activities; access to employment; general attitudes; and the distribution of resources, particularly, but not only, medical resources, between the old and the young. It is hoped that the brief discussions of these issues have given the reader some indication of the problems. Ageism is a particularly complex area because of the difficulties (a) in determining when a piece of discrimination is based on age; (b) in deciding whether a piece of "discrimination" (e.g., a minimum age restriction) is adverse to someone's real advantage; and (c) in deciding when discrimination based on age is justified and therefore not ageist. Thus with regard to age limits the issue is essentially whether it is right to treat everyone under or over a certain age in the same way, even though they are not all the same in the relevant respects. With regard to general attitudes the issue is what constitutes equal respect for people with different needs and requirements. With regard to employment and to resources the issue is what system is the most fair, or the least unfair, to all age groups. All these are difficult questions. So far, they have not had a great deal of philosophical attention, but it is to be hoped that this will change.

This is to be hoped for both theoretical and practical reasons: the issues are theoretically difficult and in some ways more so than issues of racism and sexism, and the practical need for them to be discussed is urgent. In order to both make the distribution of resources and opportunities more just and give more people their proper level of respect and consideration, ageism needs to be raised as a philosophical, political, and human issue. In particular, our existing practices and attitudes, toward both the old and the young, need to be carefully examined, and those that are found to be ageist altered accordingly.

Also See the Following Articles

AGED PEOPLE, SOCIETAL ATTITUDES TOWARD • CHILDREN'S RIGHTS • DISCRIMINATION, CONCEPT OF • HEALTH CARE FINANCING • RESOURCE ALLOCATION

Bibliography

Archard, D. (1993). "Children: Rights and Childhood." Routledge, London/New York.

Bell, J. M., and Mendus, S. (Ed.) (1988). "Philosophy and Medical Welfare." Cambridge Univ. Press, Cambridge.

Cohen, L. M. (Ed.) (1993). "Justice across Generations: What Does It Mean?" American Association of Retired Persons, Washington, DC.

Daniels, N. (1988). "Am I My Parents' Keeper? An Essay on Justice between the Young and the Old." Oxford Univ. Press, New York.

Johnson, P., Conrad, C., and Thomson, D. (1989). "Workers versus Pensioners: Intergenerational Justice in an Ageing World." Manchester Univ. Press, Manchester.

Thornton, J. E., and Winkler, E. R. (1988). "Ethics and Ageing." Univ. of British Columbia Press, Vancouver.

AGRICULTURAL ETHICS

Ben Mepham
University of Nottingham

I. The Nature of Agriculture and Its Ethical Dimensions
II. Ethical Theory and the Formulation of Agricultural Policy
III. Applications of Ethical Theory: Socioeconomic Issues
IV. Agricultural Bioethics
V. Agriculture and the Environment
VI. Ethics and Agricultural Research
VII. Conclusions

GLOSSARY

agrarianism A social or political movement, and its associated philosophical theories, that seeks to maintain the values and economic status of family farmers.

biotechnology Application of the understanding of living organisms (animals, plants, and microbes) to create industrial products and processes; exemplified by transgenesis, in which genes from one species are stably incorporated into the genome of another species causing it, for example, to produce novel products or grow more rapidly.

distributive justice The standards of fair distribution in democratic societies that determine the extent of individual liberties, political rights, opportunities, and ownership of property. Failure to implement this principle is most evident in the persistence of global hunger.

social contract An unwritten agreement between members of a society, serving as the basis for social cooperation, legal provision, and governance.

sustainability A concept open to several definitions, all of which address the perceived need for agricultural systems to sustain Earth's growing human population by maintaining the ecological viability of the biosphere.

AGRICULTURAL ETHICS is an emerging discipline that is principally concerned with ethical issues relevant to public policy. Features of agriculture that distinguish it from other types of industrial activity are the universal requirement for its major product, food, its dependence on the nature of the global physical environment, and its foundational importance for national economies. Consequently, agriculture encompasses a broad range of ethical issues, such as the mismatch between global food supplies and human nutritional needs, the impact of agribusiness on rural employment, the consequences of modern agricultural biotechnologies for human and animal welfare, and the effects of intensive production systems on the sustainability of the global environment. Different ethical traditions, such as utilitarianism and deontology, contribute in distinctive ways to the consideration of ethical issues in this field. The aim of agricultural ethics is to devise a coherent and unified ethical framework, which is relevant to the formulation of public policy within the context of a social contract.

Encyclopedia of Applied Ethics, Volume 1

I. THE NATURE OF AGRICULTURE AND ITS ETHICAL DIMENSIONS

A. The Nature of Agriculture

The current structure of agriculture is a product of its history. Hence, it is important to consider briefly the historical development of agriculture before reviewing its economic and biological dimensions relating to agricultural ethics.

1. Historical Dimensions

In discussing the development through history in agricultural systems, it is conventional to refer to several "agricultural revolutions." Settled agriculture, involving planting of crops and the domestication of wild animals, was adopted, perhaps 12,000 years ago, in place of hunter-gathering practices; and over the succeeding millennia numerous developments, employing, for example, primitive tools and crop rotation, increased productive efficiency. By the Middle Ages, there had been substantial developments in agricultural technology (for example, in relation to irrigation and harvesting) and later the growth of international trade meant both that crop and animal species crossed continental barriers (e.g., the Americas provided Europe with potatoes and turkeys) and that produce from some countries was imported into others, as in the cases of sugar and spices. Much of this trade was inextricably entangled with a concomitant trade in slaves and a subjugation of indigenous agriculture to the requirements of colonial masters.

Many changes were dependent on social evolution. The Reformation in Europe altered the power relations between church and state, disturbing land ownership patterns; and pressures from landowners for capital in response to the changing economic climate led to demands for increased incomes and hence for improved productivity from the land. In the Agricultural Revolution of the eighteenth and nineteenth centuries, increased efficiency was achieved by a combination of privatization of land (enclosure of fields); more effective crop rotations; selective breeding of crops and animals; and exploitation of fossil fuels for mechanization, fertilizers, and pesticides. Many developments were responses to the exigencies of war, urbanization, and the intensified competition in international trade that followed technological advances such as refrigeration, canning, and steam-powered transport. In developed countries, increased standards of living, of which the improved supply of cheaper, safer, and more nutritious food was an important element, greatly improved public health and increased life expectancy. In less developed countries such changes have been slower and less marked, but Thomas Malthus' prediction, in the eighteenth century, that population would soon outstrip food supply, has not been realized.

Following the Second World War, new social and economic pressures led to increasing intensification in agriculture. In the United Kingdom (U.K.), for example, the 1947 Agriculture Act aimed to increase production and improve farmers' incomes. Monoculture of arable crops, involving large fields, application of artificial fertilizers and pesticides, and mechanization of plowing, drilling, and harvesting became the norm; as did confinement of laying poultry in battery cages, and breeding sows in stalls. The Green Revolution, in which yields of wheat and rice were improved by conventional selective breeding, greatly increased productivity, but like other technologies had both beneficial and detrimental outcomes, socially and environmentally. The incipient Biotechnological Revolution, employing techniques such as genetic engineering, has the potential to transform agriculture by designing, to order, highly prolific varieties of crops and animals for use as food and as materials for medical and industrial purposes. The impact of such developments will be realized within the new economic order defined by the General Agreement on Tariffs and Trade (GATT), which aims to liberalize world trade, but which also has the capability of exacerbating existing differences between richer and poorer countries.

The historical development of agriculture illustrates trends that underpin many of the ethical issues currently faced. Life of the human (or any other) population depends on consumption of components of the surrounding environment, and as the population has grown so have its demands on natural resources. Advantages for certain nations and sections of society have been gained by appropriation of a greater share of the available global resources, as a consequence of good fortune (e.g., inheritance), skills (e.g., in the form of technology) or military success (often unrelated to justice). The fundamental significance of agriculture to national economies means that many less developed countries are currently as profoundly disadvantaged by the need to compete with highly intensified, subsidized, and protected agricultures of developed countries as they were in the colonial era: and much land that could be producing food for home consumption is instead devoted to cash crops, such as tea and tobacco, for Western markets. Yet the high standards of living in westernized countries depend on an intensified agriculture that consumes a disproportionate amount of resources and has significant adverse impacts on the social and physical environment.

2. Economic Dimensions

The structure of agriculture in any particular economic environment reflects the use made of its three basic factors: land, labor, and capital. In market economies, these factors can, to a degree, be substituted for each other. When, for example, labor is more expensive than capital, it is profitable to employ fewer people and more machinery. Where land is abundant, extensive production systems with low inputs of labor and capital are indicated. But while in market economies agriculture is a business enterprise, and food a commodity, in less developed countries, subsistence farming is the only conceivable way of life for many millions. Consequently, in industrialized countries very few people are directly engaged in agriculture (e.g., approximately 2% in the U.K.), whereas the vast majority are so engaged in many less developed countries.

However, the principles of laissez-faire economics have long been abandoned in developed countries and state intervention is extensive. The rationale is the need to ensure food security. Left to the vagaries of the market, food security is threatened by factors such as the "persistent low-income problem" (the tendency for farmers' financial returns to decline as a percentage of national economic activity—leading to closure of farming businesses and to rural depopulation) and extreme fluctuations in food supply (as a result, for example, of climatic variation).

For example, in the European Union (EU), the Common Agricultural Policy (Treaty of Rome, 1958) aims to improve food security, maintain employment, and stabilize markets. These objectives have been achieved by various policies, involving price guarantees to farmers, import levies, and import quotas. However, such protectionism has penalized less developed countries who face severe competition on global markets. Market prices have been stabilized by intervention, that is, placing surplus commodity in store when prices fall below a target value, thus producing the infamous "butter mountains" and "milk lakes." Moreover, because targets have been set too high, such policies have encouraged intensification, with its associated environmental and animal welfare problems ("externalities" that do not feature in conventional accounting). When surplus stocks are released onto the global market, world commodity prices are depressed, again penalizing less developed countries. More recently, in the EU production has been curbed by the imposition of quotas and the enforcement of "set aside," in which farmers receive payment for not cultivating their land.

On a global scale, traders (i.e., importers, exporters, merchants, and brokers) are responsible for the majority of agricultural trade. In 1991, the total value of trade in agricultural and fishery products amounted to $367 billion. For many commodities, only about six companies dominate world trade: they account for 90% of the trade in pineapples, 90% of cocoa beans, 85% of wheat, 85% of tea, 85% of coffee, 85% of corn, 70% of rice, 65% of bananas, and 60% of sugar. The power of international traders resides in: the scale of their resources, the integration of their operations (from growers through to consumers), their access to finance, their ability to manipulate the market, and the ease with which they are able to switch their operations from one source to another, according to price and conditions. The major trading companies rely on extensive global information networks, permitting trading with the most up-to-date knowledge of markets and climatic conditions worldwide. Inevitably, primary producers, particularly those in less developed countries whose incomes often depend crucially on cash crops, are vulnerable to volatile demands for their produce.

3. The Biological Basis of Agriculture

Agriculture consists of the application of rational methods to the cultivation of crops and animals and to the harvesting of their products. In its totality, it is characterized by the adoption of several practices that seek to optimize the utility of species advantageous to humans for the production of food and industrial raw materials (such as, rubber, oil, wood, wool, and pharmaceuticals). These practices include:

- modification of crop/animal genotypes by selective breeding or by modern biotechnological techniques;
- enhancement of their productivity by optimizing nutrient supplies (e.g., water, fertilizer, and scientifically formulated animal feeds);
- increasing their prolificacy (e.g., by stimulating multiple ovulation in cattle);
- protecting them from pests and diseases (e.g., by using pesticides, herbicides) and environmental stresses (e.g., by use of glasshouses);
- improving their utility (e.g., the nutritional and microbiological qualities of food);
- improving the efficiency and working conditions of agricultural workers (e.g., by mechanization).

However, to regard agriculture as simply another manufacturing industry, furnishing products in response to consumer demand, is to overlook its most distinctive features. These are:

- food is vital to human survival, in a way in which cars and washing machines are not;
- food production is an organic process, which depends on the exploitation of living resources;
- sustainable food supply necessitates ecological and environmental stability and depends on the recycling of essential nutrients, for example, in the carbon and nitrogen cycles;
- the ultimate dependence of agricultural productivity on capture of the energy of solar radiation in plants necessitates uses of extensive land area, which has implications for the competing claims of social amenity;
- farming is a way of life that contributes to cultural norms to an extent disproportionate to the numbers actively engaged in agriculture: it also safeguards skills which might prove of inestimable value in the event of military or environmental crisis.

In short, to a greater degree than most other industrial activities, agriculture's impact permeates our physical, social, and cultural environment and is likely to do so for the foreseeable future.

B. Ethical Issues in Agriculture

It is clear that ethical issues are implicit in every aspect of agricultural practice. They arise in relation to land ownership, to the exploitation of land, and the resulting effects on its continuing fertility. In Western societies, they have become prominent in relation both to intensive animal production systems in which high productivity is achieved by excessive confinement, which is alleged to severely reduce animal welfare, and to arable farming, which relies on high applications of fertilizers, pesticides, and nonrenewable energy, which are deemed to threaten human safety and the survival of many species of wild plants and animals. But ethical concerns are perhaps most pressing in relation to the welfare of the human population, of whom many go hungry through an inability to afford adequate food, while others suffer from a surfeit of food.

II. ETHICAL THEORY AND THE FORMULATION OF AGRICULTURAL POLICY

A. Agriculture and the Social Contract

Ethics is commonly taken to refer to personal behavior, in terms such as honesty, duty, and tolerance; and while such ethical norms impact on agriculturalists as on others, the essential focus of agricultural ethics relates to public policy. This stems from the fact that many of the most important decisions in agriculture are those where government policy limits personal choice. So universal is the need for food, so pervasive the ramifications of the modern "food chain," and so interdependent the social and environmental consequences of global agriculture, that individual farmers are necessarily constrained by regulations as to what is required, prohibited, or subject to control. Agricultural ethics seeks to inform such policy making by articulating its ethical dimensions.

While other forms might exist, the assumption made here is that agricultural ethics is a feature of democratic societies, in which its deliberations pertain to the social contract. However, while the focus is on public policy made by governments, many of the issues also directly concern private corporations, who have great influence in shaping agriculture on a global scale. In Western societies, at least, major retailers are increasingly aware of public interest in "ethical consumerism," that is, purchasing choices determined by concern for issues such as animal welfare and environmental conservation.

A social contract with respect to agriculture is essential in a democratic society for several reasons. Society needs to ensure a supply of safe, nutritious food at prices the poorest can afford: other circumstances are inconsistent with the harmony and equity upon which a viable democracy depends. The contract also needs to take account of public sensibilities to the treatment of animals, impacts on the countryside as a social amenity, the working conditions of farm workers, and the national economy. Decisions need to be made as to what is to be enforced or prohibited by law, what is to be encouraged or discouraged (e.g., by fiscal policy or by public education) and whether and how much provision is to be made for dissenters from the social contract (e.g., as in special exemptions for animal slaughter practices by religious groups).

However, because the normal outcome of the exercise of human reason within democratic societies is "a plurality of reasonable yet incompatible doctrines" (Rawls, 1993), consensus on a moral orthodoxy is an unrealistic scenario, and, probably, a dangerous objective. Rather, the task is to devise a social contract that benefits from social cooperation despite the differences of opinion between the contractors. Thus, the role of ethical theory in this process is not to determine *the right* policies but to act as a means of assessing whether specific proposed policies are ethically acceptable.

Moreover, ethical theory, while frequently invoked prominently in political rhetoric, is by no means the only factor determining policy decisions. Economic and political circumstances often constrain action such that ethically sound policies are perceived as too disruptive to the status quo to be feasible: we are not obligated to do what we *cannot* do. On the other hand, windows of opportunity may arise that facilitate implementation of ethically desirable policies that were previously considered impracticable.

B. Ethical Theories and the Social Contract

Ethical theories relevant to the social contract fall into two broad categories:

1. Procedural theories, which concern the rules governing how decisions are to be made, irrespective of what the decisions are. They define, for example, the constituency charged with the role of decision making (e.g., a parliamentary division or membership of a farming union) and the manner in which decisions should be made (e.g., by a simple majority vote or a two-thirds majority)
2. Substantive theories, which deal with the substance of policies. These can be further divided into:
   a. Utilitarian theories, which embody the notion that actions are deemed ethical or not in consequence of their effects, and that those policies are best that are likely to confer the greatest benefits and least harm on society as a whole. These consequentialist theories can be further subdivided into:
      i. rule utilitarianism, which justifies judgments about actions by appeal to rules, which are in turn justified by the principle of utility, and
      ii. act utilitarianism, which seeks to consider the consequences of each particular act, a process which may necessitate disregarding rules in the interests of maximising utility.
   b. Deontological theories, which appeal to the

rights of individuals and the duties of others to respect those rights, irrespective of consequences. Such theories, which owe much to Kant, can be further subdivided, for example, into:
   i. libertarian theory, which regards the duties of government as minimal (confined e.g., to protection of life and property, and from interference by others), individuals being otherwise responsible for their own destinies, and
   ii. egalitarian theories, which assert government's role in ensuring equality of opportunity as well as the protection afforded by libertarian theories. Common examples of egalitarian theory are *welfare* and *communitarian* theories.

It is certain that few people, if any, act exclusively in accordance with one type of ethical theory. Instead, rational deliberation interacts with intuitive inclination and experiential evidence to achieve a condition of "reflective equilibrium." Appeal to ethical theory thus serves as a means of promoting individual moral growth and as a basis for the evolution of policies conducive to a just and humane social order.

C. The Application of Ethical Theory to Agricultural Policy

As all aspects of agriculture are closely integrated, in considering its ethical dimensions one is confronted by a seamless web. However, it is possible to identify three major strands, consideration of each of which in turn facilitates examination of the salient features of the discipline. These are: the socioeconomic strand, dealing for example with issues of distributive justice; the bioethical strand, concerned primarily with issues arising from the application of new biotechnologies, which is predicated on a dialectical relationship between biological understanding and ethical theory; and the agroenvironmental strand, addressing the impacts of agriculture on physical and social environments. The following discussion employs these distinctions. However, within the confines of a short article, certain issues that are discussed only in one context are, in fact, applicable more widely: and some important issues have had to be omitted altogether.

Public policy changes over time in response to changing circumstances. There may be quantifiable physical or economic changes (such as population growth, increasing rates of unemployment, or increased levels of environmental pollution) or attitudinal changes (for example, increasing concerns over the welfare of farm animals or a growing demand for assurances over food safety). At a threshold level of social concern over such changes, the need becomes apparent for the formulation or reformulation of policy.

While it is possible to identify numerous steps in the genesis of a new policy, ethical theory impacts on the process most evidently in respect of the *structure* of the policy and in respect of its (anticipated) *performance*. Ethical evaluation of the structure of a policy addresses the question of whether, for example, it satisfies notions of rights and duties whereas evaluation of performance addresses the question of how effectively a given policy achieves its (ethical) objectives. Hence in evaluating prospective or existing policies, two types of approach can be adopted: structure focused (which emphasises deontological theories) and performance focused (primarily concerned with the utility of the consequences).

III. APPLICATIONS OF ETHICAL THEORY: SOCIOECONOMIC ISSUES

The distinctive impacts of structure-focused and performance-focused theories are here illustrated by appeal to four examples. While there are overlaps with the types of issue discussed in subsequent sections, the main focus of the analysis here is on socioeconomic dimensions. Moreover, it should be appreciated that for each of the examples cited, the ethical issues raised in practice are by no means limited to those identified for each particular example.

A. Appeal to Deontological and Utilitarian Theories: Pesticide Use

Modern intensive systems of arable farming, which are encouraged by current agricultural support programs in Western societies, rely on application of pesticides to ensure high crop yields. According to a libertarian ethic, society should respect the industry of farmers whose efforts secure high yields by effectively exploiting available resources to provide essential products like food: they have a right to higher financial returns than, say, their neighbors who work to less productive effect. Unfortunately, there are disadvantages to pesticide use: for example, their toxicity threatens human health by polluting rivers and waterways. Thus, according to the

U.S. Office of Technology Assessment, in the United States of America up to 90% of cancers (accounting for a quarter of all deaths) are considered due to "theoretically preventable" environmental factors, to which agricultural pesticides make a significant contribution. Moreover, globally, 40,000 deaths and a million cases of illness annually are attributed to pesticide misuse.

While a structure-focused approach to regulating use of a new pesticide might favor little regulation, in the interests of protecting farmers' rights to make living, a performance-focused approach would need to concentrate on weighing the benefits of increased productivity against the environmental and public health costs. Were all the costs to be born by the farmer, it could be argued that provided she or he were aware of the problems, the law would have no reason to interfere. But the situation becomes more complex when the benefits accrue to one party and the costs are born by another. For example, an employee has a right to be warned of the nature of a toxic material handled in the course of pursuing his or her duties and to be given adequate protection from its adverse effects. More generally, the benefits of pesticide use accrue largely to the individual farmer using the pesticide (by increasing crop yield), whereas the costs are inflicted indiscriminately on others as environmental pollution.

This is a clear case in which a performance-focused (utilitarian) approach to government policy on use of the pesticide would need careful consideration. Typically, this would take the form of a cost/benefit analysis (CBA). However, CBA is not without significant difficulties. Two basic types of CBA can be defined, depending on whether and how the costs and benefits are measured. *Quantitative* CBA is expressed in terms of quantifiable units, such as hectares of land or monetary units (in which case the CBA is monetized), while *informal* CBA provides a systematic analysis of the issues but neither quantifies nor monetizes them. Thus, one problem with CBA is the incommensurability of the terms in which it might be expressed.

Another significant problem is the scope of the analysis. For example, how wide should the remit of the CBA be? Should it include costs to the health service of caring for patients affected by pesticide use? Should it take account of impacts on trade, if warnings have to be issued to consumers of the need to wash food thoroughly or discard parts of it (as happened recently in the U.K. in relation to pesticide residues on carrots); or even, of intangible concerns, such as the negative effects of public scepticism over government assurances of food safety? Over how long a period should costs and benefits be aggregated? And to what extent should alternative means of controlling pests, such as integrated pest management, be included in the analysis?

Public policy aimed at maximizing the efficient use of resources at a government's disposal (which are inevitably limited), might satisfy this aim in respect of certain criteria but fail to do so for others. This implies that evaluation procedures need to take account of *allocative efficiency*, that is, the notion that free exchanges between individuals will maximize the social utility for all participants in the economy. This free-choice position might be said to provide a link between structure-focused and performance-focused approaches to policy. Policy makers thus need some means of assessing the efficiency of allocative efficiency, and it is here that resort is often made to *marginal utility analysis*. By this means, allocative efficiency is achieved by ensuring (with reference to the example of pesticides) that the marginal social benefit of restrictions on pesticide use is not outweighed by the marginal social cost due to loss of crops to pests.

B. Private Goods and the Public Good: Animal Welfare

This example illustrates further features of the use of ethical theory in policy formulation. Particularly since the Second World War, animal production systems in westernized societies have become increasingly intensified. By confining animals to controlled environments, feeding them scientifically formulated diets to maximize productivity and controlling infection by prophylactic use of antibiotics, the output of meat, milk, and eggs has been increased greatly. Typically, 30,000 laying poultry are confined to a single building, where they are caged with up to 5 others, allowing a floor area of 315 cm^2 per bird in the United States and 450 cm^2 per bird in the EU, for the whole of their productive lives. Breeding sows and veal calves are also closely confined on many farms. The justification advanced for such systems is essentially performance focused: it allows the farmer to produce large amounts of animal products, by economically efficient procedures, ensuring both low cost food for consumers and acceptable incomes for producers.

In recent years, public attitudes to animal use have undergone substantial change, notably in the United Kingdom and some other northern European countries. For example, in England in 1995 there was a vociferous campaign against the export of veal calves to mainland Europe, where they were destined to spend the remainder of their short lives in veal crates (which had been banned in the U.K.). Against this background, U.K.

policy makers were encouraged to attempt to improve legislation on the welfare of farm animals throughout the EU.

Structure-focused approaches address the question of the competing rights of humans and animals, or indeed whether animals can be said to have "rights" if they do not exercise responsibilities. Animal rightists stress the requirement of civilized societies to respect the rights of farm animals, in the same way that this respect has been extended in recent history to other hitherto repressed groups, such as women, ethnic minorities, and the disabled. It is unlikely that many people regard animal rights as equivalent to human rights, yet the notion of rights captures concerns about the moral status of nonhuman animals which are not solely of a utilitarian nature.

Performance-focused approaches concentrate on the extent to which it is ethically acceptable to infringe animal welfare (that is, the extent to which pain or distress is caused), as distinct from animal rights, in pursuit of human ends. Such disputes illustrate the fact that utilitarian theory "cuts both ways," since it can form the basis of the arguments used to justify intensification, on the one hand, and vegetarianism, on the other. What is essentially at stake is the scope of the analysis: and there has been a growing tendency for farm animals to be considered as ethically relevant agents, whose well-being is a significant element of the CBA. There are several ways in which welfare can be assessed (involving behavioral and physiological indices) but the crucial missing criterion is knowledge of what it feels like to be pig, chicken, or calf. Inevitably, then, animal welfare considerations are left to human judgment, and we need to consider how such concerns might be expressed.

One perspective suggests that animal welfare is a subset of human welfare, perceived animal cruelty being seen as an affront to human sensibilities. However, there are certain to be cultural differences in these sensibilities, depending on what different people (races, religions, individuals) consider (un)acceptable and (un)necessary. From the public policy perspective, a decision has to be made as to the minimum permissible standards of welfare. But some consumers might wish to purchase only those animal products raised under higher welfare standards, and for them to be able to exercise that judgment (and indeed to decide whether to purchase animal products at all) demands that adequate information about the welfare status of the animals be provided.

This brief discussion highlights the ethical debate over whether animal welfare is to be regarded as a public good, so that all consumers (however poor) are ensured by legal provisions that high animal welfare standards are observed, or as (above a certain threshold level) a private good, in which consumers wishing to promote higher welfare standards can pay a premium, for example, for "free-range eggs" or "outdoor-raised pigs." In the United Kingdom, certain retailers sell "Freedom Foods," products from animals raised under specified welfare standards, which are monitored by the Royal Society for the Prevention of Cruelty to Animals (RSPCA).

C. Risk and Consent: Food Safety

In common with almost all human activity, food production entails hazards, which become especially significant in modern agricultural practice because of the "distance" (socially and geographically) between producer and consumer and the latter's unique relationship with the product (that is, veritable "consumption"). Consequently, concerns over the perceived purity and safety of food have for many acquired a fastidiousness unparalleled in other spheres.

Hazards in food arise from a number of sources, not all of which are attributable to the production process. Some hazards are natural toxins (such as oxalic acid in rhubarb leaves) or chemical additives employed at the processing stage to give flavor, improved appearance, or extended shelf-life, while others arise after the purchase of the food (such as those due to inadequate cooking). Those attributable to agricultural practice are principally: chemicals used in crop and animal production, such as pesticides and antibiotics, respectively, and contagious diseases that result from animal production systems. A recent EU funded study in the United Kingdom showed that 60% of fresh chickens on sale were contaminated with salmonella and/or campylobacter, two types of bacteria responsible for the growing incidence of food poisoning. Poultry reared in close confinement in intensive systems are susceptible to such infections, and the automated procedures used for slaughter promote cross contamination of carcasses.

A notable example of the impact of animal feeding practice on food safety came to light with the U.K. government's announcement in March 1996 of a presumed link between the incidence of bovine spongiform encephalopathy (BSE or "mad cow disease"), which had been present in the nation's dairy herd since 1985, and cases of Creutzfeldt-Jakob Disease (CJD) in the human population, through consumption of infected beef. The incidence of BSE was believed to be due to feeding cattle with sheep remains infected with scrapie (a similar disease afflicting sheep), in the interests of economic utilization of resources. However, the resulting loss of consumer confidence led to the EU imposing a world-wide ban on the export of British beef, which threatened the economic viability of the whole beef industry in the United Kingdom and further afield.

Food hazards have a number of dimensions, which translate into risks of varying significance. Relevant factors are the frequency of occurrence, the severity of the effect (e.g., from a mild headache, at one extreme, to death, at the other), the duration of the effect, and whether it affects some (such as pregnant women or children) more than others, and the reversibility of the effect (that is, the extent to which recovery is complete).

Structure-focused approaches to food safety policy emphasize the need for consumers to be informed of potential hazards in their food (e.g., by labeling) and the need to ensure that food sold for human consumption is "safe," according to the normal definition of the word. Performance-focused approaches concentrate on how food safety might best be ensured, consistent with the need to satisfy peoples' nutritional needs and at the same time provide a measure of choice, irrespective of "the right to know." Moreover, respect for the latter principle frequently leads to "food scares," which often have negative economic consequences for the food industry out of all proportion to the low level of risks to which consumers are exposed.

However, performance-structured CBA is by no means unproblematical. Frequently, it is not so much quantifiable costs that are considered but calculated risks—and risk analysis is not simply a matter of scientific assessment. Typically, chemical toxicity tests are performed on rodents, which may differ physiologically to an extent that renders invalid any extrapolation of results to humans. Moreover, many toxicity tests exhibit no threshold level below which effects are absent, so that deciding on safety levels is a matter of judgment. Scientists' evaluations of the safety, quality, and efficacy of the chemical agent employed (the three criteria customarily assessed by scientific advisory committees) are, in themselves, inadequate to the task of deciding what levels of risk are acceptable and how to respect the rights of people to pursue a livelihood even though that might incur some risk or offense to others.

Additional difficulties arise with the importation of foods from other countries where food safety policies might differ substantially from that in the importing country, a problem likely to be exacerbated by the liberalization of trade following implementation of the GATT agreement.

In recent years, food safety issues have come to encompass the concept of the "healthy diet." There is much evidence that some diseases, such as coronary heart disease and certain forms of cancer, are related to diet, such that certain people consuming, for example foods rich in saturated fats, are at greater risk of suffering a heart attack. Structure- and performance-focused approaches to public policy might here coincide in seeking ways of reducing risks to public health, yet for a government to be interventionist in this matter might be regarded as undermining individual liberties, particularly when such diets are part of the traditional fare. Radical solutions to such problems could lie in the encouragement of farming practices that produce healthier food, for example, meat with a higher lean/fat ratio—as was the case before animals were raised under intensive conditions.

In the United Kingdom, the Food Safety Act 1990 gave the government a wide range of powers to ensure maintenance of safety standards, although in 1994 the food hygiene regulations were replaced by less restrictive rules in line with the EC Food Hygiene Directive. However, a continuing source of controversy in the United Kingdom surrounds the alleged conflict of interest that arises from the dual responsibilities of the Ministry of Agriculture, Fisheries and Food (MAFF) for both food producers and consumers. Many people consider that food safety issues would be best assured by the setting up of a separate Ministry of Food, responsible for consumer interests, analogous to the Food and Drugs Administration in the United States.

D. Distributive Justice: Global Hunger

Agriculture is concerned with many outputs but there is more than one sense in which its most vital product is food. If agriculture is, above all, about providing sustenance for the world's population, it must be said to have failed dismally. Thus, a recent FAO (United Nations Food and Agriculture Organization) conference predicted that by the year 2010 chronic malnutrition in the 93 developing countries would continue to afflict 637 million people. Yet adequate food is currently produced to satisfy the world's population (predicted to be 6 billion in the year 2000). The immediate problem for the starving is that they have insufficient money to purchase food in adequate amounts.

Ethical assessments of the problem of global hunger must start with theories of obligation. An uncompromising economic libertarian would deny the duty to help alleviate others' ills, and beyond constraints on behavior ensuring that we do not directly cause harm, assert that we all have freedom to pursue our own interests unfettered by guilt. In contrast are several theories, based in deontology and utilitarianism, which suggest that the well-fed have obligations to the hungry.

A modern Kantian approach regards hunger and poverty as undermining the proper development and exercise of rational agency, so that relief of hunger is necessary to restore people's autonomy. Singer's utilitarian theory addresses the issue in the following terms: "If it is in our power to prevent something bad from happening without thereby sacrificing anything of comparable moral importance, we ought, morally, to do it". Human rights theory holds that there are three basic rights—to subsistence, security, and liberty—implying corresponding obligations on those who possess them to provide for those who lack them. While, according to the contractarian theory elaborated by Rawls, a fair distribution of resources entails that only those differences in wealth can be justified which enable the least well off to be better off than under any other arrangements.

However, even if there is a consensus on the duty to alleviate hunger, performance-focused evaluations of appropriate policies are presented with significant problems. Thus, aid—providing a gift of food to starving people—might appear more worthy than trade in food: in practice, the distinction is less clear. Aid is often provided by richer countries for political reasons (e.g., to build up export markets or to dispose of a surplus commodity), while its impact might be to undermine the markets of producers in the recipient country. On the other hand, trade, while capable of encouraging development and alleviating hunger and poverty from "the ground up," is prone to numerous imperfections, from exploitation to coercion (for example, when food trade is use as a "weapon").

It seems clear that the solution to hunger is not to be found in simply moving food supplies around the world. Increased productivity would seem to be necessary in many countries to ensure food security, regenerate national economics, and improve public health—objectives usually encompassed by the term "development." However, while improvements are evident in some countries, many people within those countries continue to starve. Notably, in Africa, food produced per capita has declined markedly over the last decade. Ethical evaluations of the appropriate ways to alleviate hunger thus require far more than good intents.

IV. AGRICULTURAL BIOETHICS

A. Definition

The subdiscipline of agricultural bioethics concerns issues the ethical dimensions of which are grounded in biology. Principally, these arise from the (prospective) application of modern biotechnologies, such as reproductive technologies in farm animals and genetic engineering of animals, plants, and microbes; and they concern a raft of issues relating to animal and human welfare, environmental implications and the perceived challenge that implementation of such technologies makes to the concept of the "natural." Such is the technical nature of many of these issues that ethical theory needs to interact with biological understanding in a dialectical manner; that is, ethical theory needs to address the complex issues as they unfold in any discussion of biotechnological practice, its consequences, and alternative solutions to perceived problems.

B. Reproductive Technologies in Farm Animals

These include technologies such as artificial insemination (AI) and multiple ovulation embryo-transfer (MOET), which are aimed at the achievement of rapid and sustained genetic improvements in farm animal productivity. For example, AI has been the single most effective technique for genetic enhancement of milk yield in cattle, enabling spermatozoa from one highly selected bull to inseminate thousands of cows (up to 50,000 annually) and facilitating wide distribution of valuable genes. In MOET, cows are superovulated by injection of hormones, and then subjected to AI and later to embryo flushing. The flushed embryos are transferred, after hormonal treatment, to recipient cows that deliver the calves at term.

In some cases with cattle and pigs, and usually with other species such as sheep, surgical procedures are involved at various stages of the process. In cattle, the most significant welfare problem relates to the mismatch between the embryo and the recipient cow, leading sometimes to development of large double-muscled fetuses (of beef animals) that either cause dystocia (difficult delivery) or are too large for normal delivery and necessitate resort to cesarean section.

Performance-focused critiques of such technologies concentrate on CBA relating economic advantages of breeding highly prolific animals to the reduced welfare of animals subjected to repeated hormonal stimulation and surgical procedures. Some benefits for farmers are not entirely financial, for example, the ability to dispense with keeping a (dangerous) bull and the convenience of manipulating breeding programs to a planned schedule. However, in the United Kingdom there is concern among veterinarians that recent legislation permits nonveterinarians to collect embryos and administer anesthesia.

Structure-focused analyses highlight the instrumentalist assumptions the technologies make concerning the relationship of humans to the animals in their care (that is, the tendency evident in some scientific publications to regard sentient beings merely as biological material), and the resulting medicalization of animal agriculture. To submit animals to surgery, not in their own interests, but for economic gain offends many people's concept of the natural order. To deny animals expression of natural patterns of sexual behavior, by repetitively teasing bulls prior to stimulating them to ejaculate, or by inducing them to do so in some cases by electrical stimulation, may be seen as violations of respect for their intrinsic value as sentient beings.

C. Transgenesis

AI and MOET have recently been exploited more fully by combination with techniques of genetic engineering to produce transgenic farm animals. Such animals contain genes (in the form of the DNA, which codes for a particular protein) derived from other animals (or from humans), which are incorporated into the transgenic animal's genome. There are numerous objectives. One application results in the transgenic animals secreting pharmaceutical proteins in their milk, such as a blood clotting factor needed by human patients suffering from hemophilia. Another application, in which the novel protein produced is growth hormone, which enters the animal's own bloodstream, is aimed at producing faster-growing, leaner animals.

As with AI and MOET, structured-focused evaluation of transgenic animal applications is chiefly concerned with the deontological principles of respect for the animals' autonomy and intrinsic value. Such concerns are said to embody *intrinsic objections* to genetic engineering of animals. Regardless of the consequences, some people consider scientists' attempts to "play God" by crossing species barriers in this way to be ethically unacceptable. The view is sometimes expressed in religious terms, where transgenesis is seen as an attempt to undermine a natural order created by God, but objections are not confined to those subscribing to explicit theological doctrines. Moreover, animal transgenesis might be regarded as the first step to ultimate application in humans: and it is true that virtually all medical technologies applied to humans were first performed in animals.

Performance-focused evaluations of farm animal transgenesis depend on CBA. Frequently, perceived benefits are monetized, comparing, for example, the economic saving involved in producing a pharmaceutical from a so-called animal *bioreactor* with production in alternative systems. However, monetized CBA fails to take account of significant, but less easily quantified, intangible costs such as animal suffering, which may result from the procedures. Thus, transgenesis in farm animals involves microinjection of several hundred copies of the cloned prospective transgene into a pronucleus of an early embryo, often recovered from a superovulated animal. The efficiency of the process is very low, with frequently less than 1% of the injected embryos becoming transgenic offspring. Transgene incorporation into the genome is a random process and multiple copies of the gene are often incorporated as tandem repeats at a single insertion site. Because many genes have widespread effects, the offspring may suffer unpredictable and adverse mutational effects if the transgene becomes incorporated within an endogenous gene, or as a result of inaccurate repair of genes broken in the microinjection process. The result is that fetuses are often aborted: alternatively, some of those which go to term may be born deformed or suffer subsequent disabilities. Certain applications of farm animal transgenesis have a very poor welfare record. Thus, pigs and sheep with additional growth hormone genes suffer from lameness and arthritis, impaired fertility and thermoregulatory capacities, and increased susceptibility to pneumonia.

The report of a committee appointed by the U.K. Ministry of Agriculture, Fisheries and Food (1995) suggested that new technologies in farm animal breeding should be assessed from an ethical perspective according to the application of three principles:

- harms of a certain degree and kind ought under no circumstances to be inflicted on an animal;
- any harm to an animal, even if it is not absolutely impermissible, nonetheless requires justification and must be outweighed by the good that is realistically sought in so treating it;
- any harm that is justified by the second principle ought, however, to be minimized as far as is reasonably possible.

Clearly, the recommendations encompass both deontological and utilitarian criteria. What is more contentious is the order in which the principles are listed, giving precedence to deontology. Indeed, the authors of the report claim that: "... as a moral philosophy consequentialism [of which utilitarianism is a form] has been subject to some very severe and sustained philosophical criticism—so much so that it can hardly be regarded as a sound or acceptable basis on which

to advance recommendations of public policy." The U.K. government accepted the general tenor of the report's recommendations, although it is uncertain how decisions as to the first principle would be implemented in any particular case.

D. Animal Productivity Promotants

By inserting transgenes into bacteria, bovine growth hormone (also called bovine somatotrophin or BST) is produced on a commercial scale for injection into dairy cattle, thereby stimulating their milk yields. Although licensed for use in several countries, including the United States (since 1994), BST use is currently banned in the EU. The product achieved prominence as the first product of genetic engineering to be used in animal agriculture, and it continues to be the subject of considerable debate, much of it with an ethical dimension.

Concerns have tended to center on performance-focused criteria, with advocates claiming that BST use improves productive efficiency with little cost to the animals, while opponents highlight animal welfare concerns (illustrated by the 21 adverse side effects admitted by manufacturers to be associated with BST use), possible health effects on consumers, and socioeconomic consequences for smaller farmers of introducing a yield enhancing technology in a time of milk surplus.

E. Transgenic Crops

Transgenesis in crops is more advanced than in farm animals. Claimed potential benefits include production of plant varieties with: enhanced yields; improved taste and nutritional value; longer shelf life; reduced dependence on fertilizers and pesticides; and the ability to provide fuels, biodegradable plastics, and medicines.

Presumably in consequence of their perceived lack of sentience, genetic modification of plants has encountered fewer intrinsic objections than in the case of animals. Ethical evaluations thus tend to be performance focused and criticism concentrates on the likely costs, tangible and intangible, which might be involved. An important difference between application of genetic engineering to plants and animals is the relative lack of control over environmental impacts in the former case (although this also applies to transgenic fish).

The latter point is illustrated by reference to one of the most common applications, production of transgenic crops with herbicide resistance, the aim of which is to reduce damage to the crop from herbicide application. However, there are several potential risks: herbicide resistance might be transferred to other species and if these were weeds, a superweed might be produced which was difficult to eradicate; or herbicide resistance in the target crop might encourage a more extensive use of chemical herbicides, to the detriment of the environment. In general, modern plant biotechnology leads to an increasing dependence on fewer and fewer varieties, with the attendant risks associated with disease epidemics, as occurred in nineteenth-century Ireland with potato blight. (The same types of risk are associated with the narrowing of the gene pool in farm animals.)

Another risk, which has been considered negligible, but which may assume greater significance as transgenic crops multiply, is the use of antibiotic resistance genes as "markers" in the process of producing the crops. As bacterial species progressively acquire antibiotic resistance (a process exacerbated by the use of antibiotics as growth promotants in intensive animal production systems), there may be adverse effects on human health: already there is medical concern over the increasing number of multiresistant strains of bacteria.

Many Western governments have established advisory committees to oversee safety issues concerning foods produced by the techniques of genetic engineering. For example, in the United Kingdom the Advisory Committee on Novel Foods and Processes reports to MAFF.

F. Patenting of Transgenic Species

Patenting raises both deontological and utilitarian concerns. Patents provide legal protection for inventions that are new, inventive, and useful. They are a form of intellectual property, giving the owner exclusive rights over the exploitation of the invention for up to 20 years, and it is claimed that they are necessary for recovery of costs entailed in research and development. If patents were not granted on "genetic inventions," it is argued, there would be little incentive to invest time, money, and effort, and progress in biotechnology would be hindered. Thus, both from the viewpoint of "fairness" to the inventor and in terms of social benefit, patenting can be ethically justified.

Contrary arguments deploy the ethical theories differently. Thus, it is claimed the granting of patents for life-forms fails to respect living beings, seeing them rather as a mere collection of chemicals. Patents will, according to this view, concentrate power in the hands of a few multinational companies to the detriment of smaller companies and consumers. For example, 14 companies own nearly 80% of all genetically engineered plant patents. In particular, products derived from the gene pool of less developed countries will be sold back to them at prices inflated by the royalty charge, aggravating their existing debt burdens.

V. AGRICULTURE AND THE ENVIRONMENT

A. Introduction

Agriculture differs from many other industries in its necessity to consider the long term: a truth encapsulated with typical Victorian piety by the nineteenth-century English motto: "Live as if you are going to die tomorrow, but farm as if you are going to live for ever." It is a caveat that was largely overlooked in the postwar years of increasing agricultural intensification, but latterly it has been resurrected in the form of the concept of sustainability. Philosophically, the concerns here are with the issue identified above as the agro-environmental strand of agricultural ethics, that is, exploration of the relationship between the demands for sustenance of the current and future human population through agricultural activity and the requirements (and perhaps rights) of the biosphere as a whole.

B. The Challenge to the Productionist Paradigm

Thompson has pointed out that, traditionally, the drive for increased productivity from the land has been pursued in accordance with deep-seated metaphysical beliefs, such as "the doctrine of grace" (that prolificacy is a sign of God's blessing) and the "myth of the Garden" (which placed on humans a moral obligation to tame and cultivate "wild" nature for human benefit). Latterly, however, this simplistic, but seemingly ethically endorsed, productionist paradigm has been found wanting. It has resulted in intensive agricultural practices which have led to:

- environmental contamination (by pesticides, fertilizers, animal wastes, etc.);
- habitat destruction (e.g., deforestation, draining of wetlands);
- resource depletion (e.g., reduced biodiversity; use of nonrenewable fossil fuels; soil erosion; water depletion);
- the loss of many small farms and the reduced independence of many that remain as they are required to submit to corporate demands.

As a consequence, the future capability of Earth's surface to support the growing human population is seriously threatened. Agricultural practice is, of course, not alone in adversely affecting the environment, nor will agricultural production be the only victim. Yet the impacts on agriculture are likely to be among the most significant, both because of its fundamental dependence on land and climate as substrates for its activity and because life and health are ultimately limited by food supply.

C. Sustainability

A commonly held solution to such problems is the pursuit of sustainability: but what is sustainability? There is no generally agreed definition. Philosophical theories of sustainability tend to conform either to an ecocentric worldview, which takes account of the ethical relevance of nonhuman members of the biosphere, or to an anthropocentric view, considering sustainable practices as in human interests, if not now then certainly in the future. Between the two poles is a position best characterized as *stewardship,* which sees legitimate human aspirations as tempered by respect for other forms of life; and interwoven with these deontological and utilitarian theories are those that stress the fundamental social significance of humanity maintaining a close and sympathetic relationship with the earth, as provider of sustenance.

However, many regard sustainability in much more pragmatic terms. In the United Kingdom, the National Farmers Union considers sustainability to be about how current use of "natural resources will affect their availability and use tomorrow, and the action necessary to protect natural resources for future generations." More surprisingly, the U.S. government's definition of sustainability suggests that it should "make the most efficient use of nonrenewable resources." But, while commonly perceived in terms of the physical environment, sustainability is equally concerned with social relationships and with the future role of agriculturalists, and there is merit in regarding it as a multidimensional concept in which agronomic, ecological, and social dimensions are viewed as elements of a continuum.

It is, however, questionable whether sustainability represents a sound ethical principle on which to judge future developments in agriculture. Clearly, mere persistence over time (as in the case of deserts) is an inadequate criterion, while certain activities that have long endured (such as slavery) would hardly qualify for inclusion in an ethically sound definition. If a sustainable system were only to be achieved by means that infringed

human rights, in what sense would it be preferable to a socially just but less sustainable system? Despite such objections, there is perhaps a pragmatic argument for regarding sustainable agriculture as an important means to the achievement of a just, healthy, and democratic global society, and thus shorn of its sententious overtones it may play a useful role in a structure-focused evaluation of forward-looking agricultural policies.

D. Performance-Focused Dimensions of Agro-environmental Policy

If the major threats to the physical and social environment posed by intensive agriculture are overreliance on chemical inputs, monocultural practices, support energy, and fewer, capital-intensive producers, then a performance-focused evaluation of policy must necessarily consider alternatives. The highly complex interaction between physical and biological components of the environment, in its widest sense, implies the need for holistic strategies in achieving sustainable systems. A prominent approach of this type is designated *organic farming,* although there are several varieties of this, for example, *ecofarming* and *permaculture.* Some consider that the ideological commitments of the organic movement, by setting excessively stringent standards, foreclose adoption of practices that stand a greater prospect of success in achieving shared goals. The latter practices might fall within the definition of *alternative agriculture,* which can be said to aim inter alia at:

- improved conservation of biological resources, energy, soil, and water;
- incorporation of natural processes into the productive cycle, by, for example, integrated pest management, nitrogen fixation, reduced use of off-farm inputs;
- use of low-intensity systems of animal production, avoiding growth-promoting and reproductive technologies.

A serious constraint on the implementation of appropriate policies for sustainable agriculture is the dearth of knowledge about how successful such alternative systems might be. There is thus an urgent need for more extensive research: for example, in the United Kingdom, the MAFF spends less than 1% of its £130 million annual research budget on organic farming systems.

But traditional agricultural practices do not necessarily provide the best strategies for achieving sustained and universal food security in the face of a rapidly growing global population. A generic term for the type of holistic programs that may be required is *systems approaches,* which entail the interaction of specialists (such as agriculturalists, biologists, economists, sociologists, and ethicists) in formulating appropriate questions, proposing, conducting, and appraising relevant research and integrating the results. Advocates of this approach generally see no prima facie reason for excluding biotechnology, information technology, and robotic systems, provided they are employed sensitively within a holistic program.

Thus, in contrast to issues discussed in other contexts, where ethical evaluation was brought to bear on existing, well-defined options, the ethical questions concerning agriculture and the environment relate to choices between existing unsatisfactory practices and ill-defined alternatives. Necessarily, this implies an ethical evaluation of research programs directed to humane, sustainable systems, coupled with expeditious promotion of appropriate existing alternative practices. Among proposals for the latter are promotion of *regionality,* according to which producers exploit local inputs and products to full effect, and *full cost accounting,* which requires costs to reflect deleterious impacts on the environment, for example, in terms of silage effluents.

E. Agrarianism

As noted above, agribusiness has tended to dominate agriculture in developed and, increasingly, in less developed countries. The productionist paradigm, grounded in a utilitarian ethic, fosters high input, intensive systems, which tend to force small farmers out of business. In the United Kingdom, for example, the numbers engaged in agriculture declined from 639,000 in 1980–1982 to 552,000 in 1991. Moreover, those who remain in business are increasingly obliged to tread a technological treadmill: as each new productivity-enhancing technology is introduced, there is pressure to adopt it to stay in business, although the resulting fall in prices tends to benefit the consumer rather than the producer.

Traditionally, governments in the West have subsidized agriculture in the interests of sustaining both food supplies and rural communities, but often subsidies have benefitted large-scale, capital-intensive farmers to the detriment of small farmers (e.g., in the EU where farmers receive "set-aside" payments for not cultivating land). A criticism of the utilitarian CBA that generally influences public policy is that it relies excessively on short-term economic criteria, whereas sustainable agri-

culture is a long-term enterprise that depends on hard-won skills, on sensitive stewardship of physical resources (e.g., in conserving soil structure) and biological resources (e.g., in maintaining earthworm populations and hedgerows, as well as tending to agricultural animals and crops), and on an uncommon degree of personal commitment from its practitioners. Hence, utilitarian agrarian theories reject simplistic, short-term, monetized CBA as an appropriate means of evaluating the worth of farmers' activities. They point to the need to aggregate costs and benefits over a longer time scale than is usual (emphasizing the incorporation of sustainability indices), but also stress the value of indirect and intangible costs and benefits, such as those affecting aesthetic criteria (the beauty of the countryside) and appreciation of "heritage," at both national and regional levels.

However, current agricultural support policies in Western countries are subject to criticism even in terms of monetized utilitarian indices. Thus, it has been demonstrated that the "parity ratio" (prices received divided by prices paid by farmers) is inversely related to farm size, so that although larger enterprises make bigger profits they do so with progressively declining financial efficiency. In the United States the parity ratio fell by 40% between 1950 and 1976, and the trend has continued since then. This highlights the important distinction between "production" (gross output), on the one hand, and "productivity" (output per unit of input), on the other. Clearly, where more complex analyses of costs and benefits are performed (taking account, for example, of the environmental pollution resulting from pesticide use or the transportation of animal feeds around the world) simple CBA may be misleading.

Another significant cost, which often eludes actuarial calculation, is the effect of farm closures on rural communities. For example, it is a common occurrence in the United Kingdom that, as farms have closed and farm workers have moved to urban employment, the villages that formerly supported a range of services (school, shops, post office) have become transformed into "dormitories" for middle-class urban executives or retired people, whose social life is focused on the neighboring large city (accessible only by private transport). Not only does village life become bereft of a sense of community but the "gentrification" and urbanization process forces up house prices such that young people from farming families are unable either to find employment or to afford to live where they have grown up. Thus, an important aspect of national culture is threatened.

But the ethical case for treating agriculture as a special form of industry does not only rest on utilitarian arguments. In the eighteenth century, Thomas Jefferson famously described the farming community in America as especially chosen to receive God's blessing, and the notion has persisted, if only symbolically, that farmers embody the virtues of industry, independence, and dependability through which nations endure and prosper. Accordingly, the public has a particular duty to protect and preserve its farming communities.

Deontological theory impacts on agrarianism in two forms, as "populism" and as "traditionalism." Agrarian populists stress the importance of the "right to farm" as a fundamental opportunity right (enshrined, for example, in Jeffersonian philosophy). They assert that economic liberty for the poorer sections of society demands preservation of this right so that they will not have to rely on low wage employment to ensure solvency. According to this view, the health of a democracy depends on its maintaining this entrepreneurial opportunity for all members of society.

Agrarian traditionalism is less easy to accommodate within the social contract theory that, in this article, has been presumed to inform public policy. Its philosophical roots accord more closely to a form of "virtue theory," perhaps first described by Aristotle, which emphasizes "character," respect for the natural order, loyalty to the community, and the value of work as essential to the traditional agrarian lifestyle.

Whatever the ethical theory, agrarianism asserts the need for public policy to take account of the special features and values of farmers, their families, and the rural community. But it must be admitted that such protectionist policies are now severely threatened by the increasingly competitive world economic order signaled by the General Agreement on Tariffs and Trade. A major challenge to the implementation of ethically sensitive public policy is to combine respect for agrarianism with respect for international and intergenerational justice.

VI. ETHICS AND AGRICULTURAL RESEARCH

It is evident that over the last 50 years agriculture has been totally transformed by the application of science. Characteristically, small numbers of scientists, through a combination of industry, skill, and ingenuity have devised technologies that have profoundly affected society, the physical environment, and international trade. While the effects in increasing the yields of crops and animal products have been generally welcomed, these benefits have been bought at a cost to the livelihood of many farmers and the welfare of agricultural animals, and have caused degradation and pollution of the physical environment. Agricultural research has been the engine of that productionist drive, and as such must be held responsible for the costs as well as for the benefits.

The dynamic nature of the relationship between aggregate human needs (as global population expands) and the earth's capacity to meet them (as international trade and global climate change, and nonrenewable resources become exhausted) implies the necessity for the urgent formulation of policies for agriculture at the international level that are not simply determined by free market economics. Among these, the institution of agricultural research programs to secure global and sustainable food security must lay claim to a high priority. A framework for such research already exists in the Consultative Group on International Agricultural Research (CGIAR) which supports a network of 17 international research centers throughout the world, although there would be merit in greater input than at present from research centers in developed counties. Whatever programs are devised for meeting the growing nutritional, environmental, and social challenges of the twenty-first century, it is clearly of the greatest importance that they are evaluated within an appropriate ethical framework.

VII. CONCLUSIONS

Agricultural ethics is concerned with the management of Earth's biological resources for the production of food and other industrial products in ways that are prudent, fair, and humane. Most effectively, ethical theory is applied in the context of the formulation of public policy, by providing a framework for evaluation of the ethical acceptability of proposed policies.

Effective deliberation on ethical theory requires inputs from practitioners of a range of disciplines, such as agriculturalists, agricultural scientists, biotechnologists, economists, ecologists, and ethicists. Many of the ethical issues that agriculture faces can be attributed, at least in part, to adoption in the past of an excessively reductionist approach, which has paid insufficient attention both to the rights of people and animals and to the wider ecological consequences of agricultural practices. An authentic theory of agricultural ethics would integrate the separate socioeconomic, biological, and environmental strands discussed above within the framework of a broadly acceptable social contract.

Also See the Following Articles

ANIMAL RIGHTS • BIOTECHNOLOGY • GENETIC
ENGINEERING • HAZARDOUS AND TOXIC
SUBSTANCES • REPRODUCTIVE
TECHNOLOGIES • SUSTAINABILITY

Bibliography

Blatz, C. V. (Ed.) (1991). *Ethics and agriculture.* Moscow: University of Idaho Press.

Mepham, T. B. (Ed.) (1996). *Food ethics.* London: Routledge.

Mepham T. B., Tucker, G. A., & Wiseman, J. (Eds.) (1995). *Issues in agricultural bioethics.* Nottingham: Nottingham University Press.

Rawls, J. (1993). *Political liberalism.* New York: Columbia University Press.

Singer, P. (1979). *Practical ethics.* London: Cambridge University Press.

Tansey, G., & Worsley, T. (1995). *The food system: A guide.* London: Earthscan.

Thompson, P. B., & Stout, B. A. (Eds.) (1991). *Beyond the large farm: Ethics and research goals for agriculture.* Boulder: Westview Press.

Thompson, P. B., Matthews, R. J., & van Ravenswaay, E. O. (1994). *Ethics, public policy and agriculture.* New York: Macmillan.

UK Ministry of Agriculture, Fisheries and Food. (1995). *Report of the committee to consider the ethical implications of emerging technologies in animal breeding.* London: HMSO.

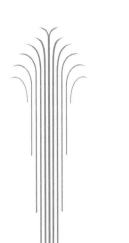

AIDS

Timothy F. Murphy
University of Illinois College of Medicine

GLOSSARY

AIDS Acquired Immune Deficiency Syndrome, an array of disorders caused by infection with HIV.
autonomy A condition of being able to make free choices; also, a moral concept that human beings should be respected in their free choices.
duty An obligation based in moral or legal principles.
epidemic A significant upward variation in the occurrence and distribution of a disorder compared to its normal rate.
HIV The family of human immunodeficiency viruses; the presumptive cause of AIDS.
self-incurred Describing a condition brought on by one's own actions.
supererogation The act or fact of doing more than duty requires.

AIDS is the widely used acronym for the Acquired Immunodeficiency Syndrome, a pathological syndrome caused by infection with the human immunodeficiency viruses (HIV). Infection with HIV suppresses the immune system and makes people susceptible to a wide array of lethal disorders, including bacterial and fungal infections and cancers. First formally identified in the early 1980s, AIDS has struck millions of people worldwide. Simply because it involves a communicable, deadly, and widespread condition, the epidemic would have raised many urgent moral questions. The fact that, in developed countries, the syndrome affects primarily homosexual men and intravenous drug users has added further moral interest to the epidemic. This article will first describe the medical background of AIDS. It will then discuss the moral significance of the epidemic, starting with an analysis of religious and moral meanings attributed to AIDS. It will then consider the impact of AIDS on health care relationships in key areas: (a) the duty to treat people with HIV, (b) the right to know about HIV infection in health care providers, (c) HIV testing policies, (d) experimental treatments, (e) the financing of AIDS costs, and (f) the allocation of funds for research and treatment. The article will then consider select moral and legal issues: (a) entitlement to medical privacy in employment, (b) legal duties to disclose and warn about diagnoses of HIV/AIDS, and (c) the regulation of bathhouses and injecting needles. In closing, this article will consider how personal choices frame many of the most poignant questions raised by the epidemic activism: fidelity to the sick and reproductive choices among them.

I. FEATURES OF THE EPIDEMIC

A. AIDS Defined

AIDS refers to an array of disorders and diseases related to an infectious agent, HIV, which incapacitates the immune system. According to the U.S. Centers for Disease Control, there have been more than a half-million cases of AIDS in the United States. By some World Health Organization estimates there are as many as 17.5 million cases of HIV infection worldwide. Estimates for the year 2000 range between 38 and 108 million cases of HIV infection. This is all the more astonishing given that prior to the early 1980s, AIDS was unknown to biomedical science. Some of the more common disorders associated with AIDS are *Pneumocystis carinii* pneumonia (a virulent bacterial infection of the lungs), *candidiasis* (a yeast infection common in the esophagus and mouth), herpes ulcerations, Kaposi's sarcoma (a cancer of the capillary linings), dementia, and a wasting syndrome that thwarts efforts to maintain body weight.

B. How AIDS Is Contracted

HIV infection can be contracted through blood exposure to bodily fluids—blood and semen most notably—that contain sufficient quantities of HIV. Such exposure can occur in, for example, anal or vaginal intercourse and blood transfusions. Sharing needles during drug injections is also an efficient mechanism of infection. Needle-stick accidents in hospitals can induce infection if infected blood is present on the needle. Infection can also be passed from pregnant women to their fetuses. Tissue and organ transplantation can also be a source of infection. The likelihood of infection by other methods, oral sex, for example, is a matter of continuing investigation. There is no evidence that HIV infection can be contracted by inhaling viral particles or by other casual means.

C. Who Gets AIDS?

Worldwide, most people with AIDS (PWAs) have contracted HIV through heterosexual sex. In the United States and some other countries, most PWAs have been men who have sex with other men, followed by those who share needles during drug use. The greatest number of people with HIV infection are adult men, though large numbers of women and children are also infected. Most PWAs live in the Third World. It is now manifestly clear that anyone can contract AIDS, although this does not mean that all persons are equally at risk. Risk re-

mains highest for those having unprotected sex or sharing drug needles with someone who is infected. Children are also at significant risk of HIV infection if born to infected mothers.

D. Treatment and Prevention

There are at present no vaccines that can produce immunity to HIV infection. For many people, treatment for AIDS consists of treatment for the particular disorders involved. For example, someone with AIDS may be treated for *Pneumocystis* pneumonia and fungal infections even if they are not treated for the underlying infection that permits those conditions to develop. Some people do receive treatment, though, for HIV infection properly speaking, and there is considerable research underway to identify treatments that would neutralize HIV infection by, for example, blocking the life cycle of the virus. Because it is impossible to predict experimental outcomes, fully effective treatments may be a long way off, especially ones that preserve acceptable quality of life. Because of the limited capacity of biomedicine to respond to AIDS, health officials stress the importance of educating people to avoid HIV infection.

II. THE MORAL MEANING OF DISEASE

The word pain derives from the Greek word for punishment, and some commentators have described AIDS as punishment for sinful or immoral behavior. In fact, AIDS is merely the latest instance of associating health with morality and ill health with immorality. Other commentators reject these interpretations of AIDS because, they say, that judgment is inconsistently applied and because it works against an open and honest confrontation with the disease.

A. Religious and Moral Interpretations of AIDS

This view that AIDS is punishment for evil behavior is hard to maintain consistently for it is unclear why some sins or immoralities are subject to divine punishment in ways that others are not. If AIDS is a punishment from God for illicit sex and drug use, it is unclear why that punishment affects only a tiny fraction of the people involved in these behaviors. It is, after all, only a minority of gay men, drug users, adulterers, fornicators, and other sinners who have ever contracted an HIV infection. If wrongful behavior is punished sometimes but not always, human beings do not have a rational basis in theology or ethics for making a decision about whether to engage in this behavior—so far as risk of punishment is concerned. Moreover, it is also unclear why homosexuality, drug use, and prostitution should be punished and other wrongdoings should go altogether unpunished. Even if one were to concede that the behaviors in question are sinful, it is unclear why they deserve a punishment as severe as AIDS. Homosexual behavior, for example, ordinarily involves consenting adults and would appear to be far less serious than other wrongdoing such as murder or involuntary sex, which are not punished by disease. If there are answers to these questions, they have not been well developed by those interpreting AIDS as punishment.

Other religious commentators have focused not on the origins of AIDS but on the social response to AIDS. Pointing to long theological traditions of compassion, these commentators typically urge sympathy for the ill. They note the importance of drawing a distinction between the sinner and the sin so that the human needs of the ill are not eclipsed by objections to particular sins. Noting that all people are fallible, these religious commentators have often been important allies in helping PWAs receive compassionate health care.

Some commentators see AIDS not as the punishment of God but as the moral consequence of violations of nature. In such a view homosexuality is said to be a violation of the reproductive purposes of nature and drug use is a violation of the physical integrity toward which nature strives. Beyond agreement that homosexuality and drug use occur as events in the world, however, there is little agreement about what nature is or means for the choices of human beings. One can hardly, for example, simply refer questions about the morality of human choices to descriptions of the behavior of other animals, for human beings are fundamentally unlike other animals. Some philosophical traditions, like Natural Law, try to describe human morality in terms of the goods toward which human beings are inclined by nature: reproduction and physical integrity among them. But it is unclear whether these descriptions in fact disclose fundamental essences of human nature or represent idealized visions of human life. Claims that homosexuality is contrary to nature seem to be interpretations of nature rather than the disclosure of the "facts" of nature properly speaking. It may be, therefore, that judgments that AIDS represents violations of nature are better understood as interpretations rather than as literal claims.

B. Self-Incurred Disease

Self-incurred disorders are those that one "brings on one's self" through one's own choices and in awareness of risks. For example, despite well-confirmed and well-publicized links between tobacco, lung cancer, and emphysema, people continue to smoke. Whether disorders are self-incurred in these ways has moral relevance. For example, some analysts have argued that society has no responsibility in the provision of health care in cases where people get ill after ignoring known risks. According to this view, public health care resources should go first to people who face disorders through no choice of their own (for example, genetic illness) or because of social injustice (for example, exposure to toxic substances).

Can AIDS be described as self-incurred and therefore without entitlement to socially supported health care? This view is controversial for a number of reasons. Those who first developed AIDS did so at a time when there was no knowledge whatsoever about the existence or risks of the syndrome. At the present time, although the existence of AIDS is widely known, it is unclear that the constituencies most at risk for AIDS receive the assistance that helps them avoid risk across the entirety of their lives. Limited access to sterile needles, for example, may hamper the efforts of drug users to protect themselves against HIV. Controversies about the propriety of sex education in high schools, and specifically education about homosexuality, may hamper the abilities of teenagers to protect themselves against HIV. It is therefore important to be sure that the notion of self-incurred disease is not applied selectively. A great deal of heart disease, for example, may be described as self-incurred in the sense that it follows a lifetime of choices about diet and exercise. Yet there are no calls for eliminating insurance or government support for the treatment of heart disease. Even if AIDS is self-incurred, so is a great deal of other disease, and it would be prejudicial to cut off public support for AIDS but not other similar conditions.

III. HEALTH CARE RELATIONSHIPS

A. Duty to Treat

One of the first moral questions raised about the epidemic by health-care workers was whether they had a right to refuse treatment for people with AIDS/HIV. Some insisted that they did and invoked two main reasons. First, they asserted that they did not have a responsibility to accept the level of risk posed by caring for patients with AIDS/HIV. Second, they argued that there was nothing in their professional ethics that required them to serve any and all patients, let alone those who might pose risks of HIV infection. For example, there is nothing in the Hippocratic Oath that requires physicians to accept each and every patient who might need help. Even today, the American Medical Association (AMA) asserts in its *Principles of Medical Ethics* (1996–1997 edition) that except in emergencies physicians should be free to choose their patients. It would make for bad medicine if physicians and other health workers were forced to accept patients they did not want to treat.

Other medical practitioners argue that there is a duty to treat PWAs. In this view, the profession of medicine has voluntarily assumed responsibilities in healing and the relief of suffering and, therefore, duties not imposed on the average citizen. In any case, it is said, the risks of HIV infection are not so great as to justify refusing to treat all PWAs. The duty to treat, it is further argued, is implicit in the purposes and goals of medicine. For reasons like this, the AMA did itself adopt the judgment that it is unethical to deny treatment to people simply because they are HIV-infected. Philosopher Normal Daniels has also pointed out that if some professionals do treat patients with AIDS while most do not, the former professionals face higher risks of infection. That heightened risk is unfair, he argues, because it distributes risks of infection unequally across the profession, with some practitioners accepting no risk at all.

While there are arguments to be made on each side of this ethical disagreement, there may be practical ways to dissolve the dilemma. For example, if a hospital accepts a patient with AIDS into its care, it must have personnel who are competent and willing to treating that person. If it does not, it faces serious liability. Consequently, it is in the best interests of institutions to educate their staffs in ways to take care of PWAs while at the same time protecting themselves from infection. As the risks of HIV infection are identifiable risks, they may be avoidable through vigilant safety measures involving needles and exposure to bodily fluids, which measures should work to reduce anxiety about treating PWAs. Some jurisdictions have adopted legislation that specifically forbids discrimination by health workers against PWAs. These laws prove another incentive to find creative ways of identifying and minimizing risks feared by health care workers. AIDS/HIV will remain a permanent feature of human suffering for the foreseeable future. Rather than debate whether health care professionals have the duty to treat PWAs,

health care education and institutions should prepare professionals for the kinds of patients they will have, and many have already gone a long way toward doing exactly that.

B. Right to Know

Unfortunately, there have been a few of instances in which health care professionals with AIDS have infected their patients. One of the most well known of these cases involved a U.S. dentist who apparently infected 5 of his patients during the 1980s, although it is far from certain how this infection occurred. Even though this kind of transmission is the least significant means of infection in the epidemic, some patients and their advocates have asserted that patients have the right to know whether their doctor or nurse has an HIV infection. This right is said to be grounded in the traditional respect for informed consent (the right to information about medical risks) and patient autonomy (voluntary agreement to receive health care).

While it is true that many people would like to know whether their health workers have an HIV infection, the relevant moral question is whether that information belongs in the category of information that should be disclosed. After all, health care workers do not have the duty to disclose any and all information a patient might want to know. One way to protect patient interests and health workers at the same time is to focus the question of the right to know on treatment methods. HIV infection will not be a risk for a great many medical treatments, including, for example, most diagnostic procedures and interactions that do not involve blood exposure. For such routine interactions, it does not appear that there can be a convincing case that a patient has the right to know whether a nurse, for example, has an asymptomatic HIV infection. There are, however, medical interventions that do expose patients to risks of infection, for example, surgical treatments in which a physician might accidentally cut his or her hand and bleed into a patient's abdominal cavity. In these instances, it would appear that a physician has the duty to disclose the risks of HIV infection and to identify what measures might be taken to prevent an accident. If the patient found these measures insufficient, he or she could decline the services of that physician. From a legal point of view, some courts have held that health care workers have a duty of disclosure, though the extent of this duty is not yet fully explored under the law.

Framing the question of HIV risks to individual patients and practitioners in terms of their rights and duties might offer only a tenuous solution to safety in health care relationships. Patients are often ill situated to make inquiries about the risks they face in medical treatment, and it may be in the interest of physicians to conceal their own HIV diagnoses in order to protect their employment and professional standing. Consequently, while the exact extent of the right to know and the duty to disclose can be debated, a more satisfying solution will probably be found in finding inventive ways to protect all health care interactions from HIV risks, whether it is the patient or the health worker who might have an HIV infection.

C. HIV Testing Policies

Under what conditions should people be tested for HIV? Many commentators see widespread testing as highly beneficial. They argue that widespread testing is important both for accurate data about the incidence and prevalence of HIV infection and for the health care of infected people. While no one disputes these claims, there is debate about how testing should go forward and whether some testing should in fact be involuntary.

The case against involuntary testing rests on the doctrine of autonomy, the right to choose or decline any medical service. If for example, a hospital were to test all patients for HIV without their consent as a matter of general policy, patients would forfeit their right to be tested elsewhere at, for example, test sites that preserve their anonymity. Those opposed to involuntary testing also point out that involuntary testing can forfeit opportunities for education that occur in the process of obtaining consent for the test. On the other side of the argument, commentators point out that physicians initiate many tests for which they do not seek specific informed consent. HIV is merely part of the background information that they should routinely gather and not necessarily after checking with the patient. For this reason, some countries routinely test all newborns for HIV infection, although results are not always returned to mothers even when they reveal an infection. In the mid-1990s, furthermore, the U.S. Centers for Disease Control urged doctors to test all pregnant women for HIV as a matter of routine policy. They urged this policy in order to identify women with HIV who might otherwise go undetected and to help prevent HIV infections in fetuses, such as this is possible. This proposal is not exactly mandatory testing, as women retain the right to refuse, but they can only refuse if specifically advised that testing will occur, and some critics worry that the process of informed consent will not be observed with these women.

Widespread testing is also attractive outside health care settings. The U.S. military, for example, is entitled by law to test recruits and/or draftees for HIV and exclude them from services if they are infected. The military argues that this exclusion is necessary in order to protect against accidental infections in the course of emergency battlefield transfusions. Other groups, such as religious orders, also have an interest in learning about their members' health. Insurance companies and employers also have an interest in widespread HIV testing. In order to contain health care costs, there are economic incentives to exclude people with HIV infection from insurance coverage (see Section I.E below). Some HIV testing is put to the use of determining eligibility for employment, travel, and immigration (see Section II.A below). HIV screening has also been debated in regard to prisoners and newborns, although these issues will not be treated here. In the main, those who propose involuntary testing bear the burden of proof relative to the conditions philosopher James Childress has laid out: whether the involuntary testing is (a) effective, (b) proportional to the infringement imposed, (c) necessary in the sense of being the only pathway to the desired information, (d) as little intrusive as possible, and (e) disclosed to the parties involved.

D. Experimental Research

Even two decades into the AIDS epidemic there are more questions than answers about effective treatment. That many PWAs are often desperate for treatment leads them to both unorthodox and orthodox medical practitioners. PWAs have sought all manner of unorthodox treatments, including exotic plant extracts, herbal therapies, organic and inorganic compounds, and every manner of spiritual therapy. AIDS quackery is a sometimes thriving business because unproven treatments hold out hope where orthodox medicine has nothing to offer. In more orthodox contexts, there is considerable government and private investment in producing useful treatments. While orthodox medicine has certainly improved its treatments since the beginning of the epidemic, it is often as ultimately powerless as unorthodox medicine in preventing AIDS deaths.

Compared to unorthodox medicine, orthodox medicine has the benefit that it makes active efforts to measure the value of its treatments. Whereas unorthodox medicine often relies on anecdotal evidence, orthodox medicine attempts to reduce the distorting influence of anecdotes by subjecting its efforts to rigorous study. In order to achieve this scientific goal and to protect people from unsafe treatments, there is considerable government regulation of medical experimentation. These regulations require demonstration that proposed treatments are safe, efficacious, and clinically beneficial before they can go on the market. Scientific methodology also requires limitations on the persons who enter the experiments; they must be "eligible" by reason of a particular condition. Moreover, some trials require the use of a control group which receives only a sham treatment, in order to measure the actual effects of the experimental treatment. A control group is sometimes necessary to counteract the placebo effect (people who believe that they are receiving a useful treatment may in fact show signs of improvement) and to provide an objective standard for measuring effects of the treatment. While these measures are all to the scientific good, they can make experimentation a long and laborious process. Given that many PWAs face imminent death, there have been many demands that the process be streamlined and made more attentive to their needs.

PWAs have demanded, for example, that control groups be eliminated or reduced in order to extend the benefits of experimentation to as many people as possible. They have also sought access to data as soon as possible, so that people in the trials could move from the control group into the study group if there were positive effects of the experiment. They have also sought to make trials more accessible to a greater number and variety of people, including fertile women (who were sometimes excluded because of worries about fetal damage if they became pregnant) and minorities (who were underrepresented in the trials compared to their total number as PWAs). Expectations of this kind often involve a rejection of paternalism on the part of government and orthodox medicine about what risks people may accept to choose. They also invoke at least one issue of social justice, namely that the benefits of biomedical research be distributed justly among those affected by AIDS.

While these moral concerns can be appreciated, they are not universally accepted. Some commentators, for example, note that the very desperation of PWAs makes them poor judges of what is in their best interest. To make this point, they note that if there is only one treatment alternative, that limitation can be itself an impediment to autonomy. These commentators therefore argue that some degree of paternalism is required as a matter of protecting the medical consumer from choices made in desperation. While it can be granted that there are good moral reasons to give PWAs access to experimental medicine, it should also be noted that experimental therapy is not necessarily a benefit. In

fact, it can be risky in the extreme. Consequently, it is prejudicial to describe access to experimentation as if it were entirely beneficial. Unregulated access to experimental treatments might ultimately prove harmful to PWAs if they rush from one treatment to the next. So long as AIDS remains the chronic, lethal condition that it is, there will be tensions between activists and researchers about rights of access and duties of paternalism in experimental research.

E. Financing AIDS Costs

At the beginning of the epidemic there were dire predictions about the costs of AIDS. In fact, AIDS costs are comparable to the lifetime costs of treating cancer and heart disease. Nevertheless, AIDS costs are considerable, and a person with AIDS may incur costs in tens of thousands of dollars for a single round of treatment. Given that there are millions of people world-wide with AIDS/HIV, serious questions follow about financing the cost of their health care.

Health care is financed in four main ways: (a) direct payment by an individual patient, in an arrangement known as fee-for-service, (b) group purchase of coverage that is the basis of all insurance, with individuals or employers contributing payments to a pool from which claims are paid in the event of actual illness, (c) government-sponsored programs that entitle people to health care simply because they are citizens or because they are of a certain age, have a disability, are poor, or are military veterans, and (d) charitable health care that is provided free of charge by individuals or groups. The costs of AIDS have in many ways aggravated weaknesses in whatever mechanisms prevail in a nation's health care system, leading to moral critique of the design of those systems.

Most people with AIDS/HIV find it impossible to find an insurer willing to sell them individual health coverage because insurers know these people are likely to incur significant costs. While some states have tried to prohibit insurers from requiring information about HIV from applicants, most insurers reject individuals known to have AIDS/HIV. The backbone of health insurance in the United States is not individual coverage but group coverage paid for by employers. While people who have group insurance may not have to disclose their AIDS/HIV status, and thus not be excluded from coverage on that basis, insurers have other mechanisms for limiting expenditures related to AIDS/HIV. They can, for example, cap the amount they are obligated to expend for a person with AIDS. U.S. courts have in fact upheld the right of certain employers to limit health care for PWAs. Under these circumstances, even employed people with insurance may not be able to meet the costs of their health care. Because of the disabling conditions of AIDS, people may also lose their jobs; if they do, they lose their health insurance too. Most insurance programs require some form of payment by the patient for services and medications; these can be significant burdens to PWAs. It is also worth noting that insurers almost never pay for experimental treatments. Many people with AIDS/HIV are not able, therefore, to afford desired experimental treatments.

Most governments do provide some degree of health care, and the health care system in the United States is often compared unfavorably to nations that provide health care as a matter of national policy and do not tie its benefits to employment. This option seems attractive when one considers that the United States has tens of millions of citizens who have no health insurance. In fact, a great deal of health care is already provided by the U.S. government in the form of programs for the poor, the disabled, the aged, veterans, and government employees. The moral question is whether this kind of coverage should be extended generally to all citizens. It does not automatically follow, however, that government-sponsored health care is the best health care, and for certain individuals there may be advantages in the current system. For example, some critics of national health services point out that treatments may not be as immediately available as they are in the United States—for those able to afford them. Certainly, it does not follow that simply because government provides health care that it will provide optimal care. Because there are other priorities to which the government must attend, health care can be limited even in a state-sponsored system. In any case, whether health insurance will be uncoupled from employment in the United States is not only a moral question, it is also a political one. While religion, morality, and a political philosophy based on equality offer many reasons to care for the sick, there are also economic and political forces working to keep the U.S. system as it is. It cannot be denied, however, that the current system does work to the disadvantage of many people with AIDS/HIV.

F. Resource Allocation

Where should AIDS stand in national priorities of funding research and treatment? Certainly there is a strong case to be made that AIDS deserves significant priority by reason of its prevalence, its communicability, its

costs in health care, and its damage to social productivity. By contrast, some critics have said that AIDS research has been funded for mistaken reasons, ungrounded fear of infection among them. Journalist Michael Fumento, for example, contends that the damages of AIDS have been exaggerated and that other diseases have been neglected as a result. While the exact figures that ought to be accorded to AIDS research and treatment can always be debated, there is a moral consideration that suggests that insofar as the epidemic affects people unjustly treated, society does owe a certain amount of economic investment in research and treatment.

Philosophers Richard D. Mohr and Patricia Illingworth have argued that society owes gay men and/or drug users compensation when they are diagnosed with AIDS. These arguments suggest that gay men and drug users are treated unjustly because society wrongly (a) obstructs them from forming the sorts of relations that are necessary to take care of their sick and (b) increases risks of HIV infection by not promoting the behavior and policies that would reduce infection. For example, if gay men were encouraged to form monogamous relationships and were permitted to marry, they would be better positioned to withstand the burdens of ill health. Social failure to acknowledge and educate gay men on their own terms also channels them into making poor decisions against HIV risk. Society fails to protect drug users, the argument goes forward, by failing to make available the treatment they need to halt drug use. Consequently, it is held, society has a duty to expend research and treatment funds on behalf of AIDS as compensation for its ethical lapses. These are plausible moral arguments, but it is unclear to what extent they should prevail. There are many failures that may be laid at the door of social injustice. For example, disease related to environmental toxins may be equally the fault of society. It would require considerable analysis to make a determination about where AIDS stood in line of priority if social policy were to be guided by this kind of argument.

Because of the numbers of people AIDS affects and because of who those people are, it does seem eminently reasonable to say that AIDS should remain a high priority in biomedical research and treatment. That AIDS is a profoundly disabling condition would, additionally, lend it priority to the extent funding recognizes the need to help the least advantaged of a society. Should advances in research produce effective treatments of AIDS (but not an outright cure), its claim to priority in research funding would likely diminish compared to other diseases that had no treatments available whatever.

IV. LEGAL ASPECTS

A. Privacy and Employment

Medical ethics has long recognized the importance of confidentiality in health care. Confidentiality is valuable not only for its own sake but also for its consequences. It protects people in vulnerable states and encourages patients to be entirely candid about their injuries and disorders. Without the expectation of confidentiality, patients may withhold crucial information and adversely affect treatment decisions. The law also recognizes the importance of confidentiality, although it usually discusses that issue in terms of a right to privacy. Because of the fear of discrimination against PWAs, some jurisdictions adopted specific legislation governing access to and confidentiality of diagnoses of AIDS/HIV. The traditions of confidentiality in ethics and privacy in the law merge in the assumption that medical diagnoses should ordinarily be disclosed only with the consent of the patient, unless there are compelling reasons to the contrary.

It is the question of exceptions that drives continuing debate about the proper limits of privacy. Some legal jurisdictions permit state officials to learn, for example, whether an individual accused of a specific sexual crime has an HIV infection. Health workers who have been exposed to the blood of a particular patient are also sometimes given the right to learn whether the patient has an HIV infection. More globally relevant perhaps is the question of whether employers have the right to learn whether job candidates have HIV/AIDS. The U.S. military tests all candidates and bars the entry of every infected person. Should other employers have the right to do the same?

Existing understandings of social justice do not permit employers to test all job candidates for AIDS/HIV on the assumption that a confirmed diagnosis makes them unfit for employment. In the first place, a diagnosis of AIDS/HIV may be benign with regard to worker fitness: a person with HIV may be asymptomatic for years, or a person with AIDS may experience one bout of pneumonia without any lingering ill effects. AIDS/HIV diagnoses are not necessarily indicators of unfitness to work. Social policy in many countries has, moreover, come to the conclusion that it is better as a matter of social ethics to favor access to jobs rather than to permit employers to test according to their perceptions of who

will and will not make a fit employee. For this reason, there are many laws protecting the disabled and handicapped from discrimination in employment. These laws have been supported by court decisions that include PWAs under antidiscrimination statutes so long as their disability would not meaningfully interfere with their expected tasks. This is not to say that employers must hire job candidates with AIDS/HIV, but it is to say that they cannot refuse to do so simply because someone has AIDS/HIV. Neither is this to say that people with AIDS/HIV cannot be fired if they cannot do their jobs. To be sure, there are many jurisdictions around the world that do not recognize these sorts of antidiscrimination policies. The relevant moral question is whether coupling employability to fitness should prevail as the relevant hiring issue, no matter where one is.

In the United States, the interest in testing for HIV is strongly influenced by the goal of minimizing health insurance costs paid for by the employer. Even the costs of replacing PWAs who must be let go from work are of interest to employers, as is the loss of time involved. In instances like this, there are direct conflicts between the economic interests of a given employer and social interests in protecting groups of people. There are important issues of social and moral philosophy at stake here. The protection of people with HIV/AIDS seems to be, however, enough reason that social policy regarding access to jobs should take precedence over the immediate economic interests of employers. The question of health insurance returns here once again. In protecting access to jobs, in countries where employers pay the bulk of health insurance costs, society is protecting access of people with AIDS/HIV to insurance. If that health care could be protected in other ways, HIV testing at employment would decrease in significance as a moral question.

B. Duty to Warn

Some physicians and other health professionals find themselves faced with a situation in which they believe a patient's undisclosed diagnosis of AIDS/HIV endangers another person. For example, a physician may learn that a male patient with asymptomatic HIV infection has not disclosed his condition to the woman with whom he has lived and had sex for many years. This woman may be known to the physician because she visits her hospitalized companion. Alternately, that physician may learn that a male patient with an asymptomatic HIV infection works as a prostitute and has sex with two and sometimes three men a day. These men are entirely unknown and unidentifiable to the physician.

One possible moral view of these examples is that physicians should never breach medical confidentiality because they would divide their loyalty to the patient if they did so. Courts, however, have not accepted a blanket policy of confidentiality. For example, U.S. courts have recognized a duty of physicians to warn endangered parties under certain circumstances. The 1976 case *Tarasoff v. Board of Regents* held that a health professional has a duty to warn if there is a strong likelihood of imminent danger to an identified person. While these matters are not well litigated in the case of AIDS, courts could uphold a duty to warn in the case of the female partner mentioned above. Whether or not they would do so will depend on the facts of the case at issue and the way in which the matter is treated in court. It does not appear, however, that a physician would have a duty to try and identify potential sex partners of the prostitute described above. There is no moral duty to pursue a course of action beyond one's means, in this case, identifying all past and potential clients of the prostitute.

Apart from the courts, there may be other social mechanisms to implement a duty to warn. Many countries around the world have some form of contact tracing programs. These programs try to locate and inform any and all persons who might have been exposed to HIV risk. In jurisdictions with these programs, physicians may have a duty to identify to these agencies those persons whom they believe are putting others at risk of infection. The agencies then assume the responsibility of locating and warning people that they may have been exposed to HIV, though they need not identify the specific person responsible for that exposure. As these programs are not well studied, it is unclear whether they have a significant effect on the overall incidence and prevalence of HIV.

What may be said in regard to duties of people with AIDS/HIV themselves? Because AIDS can open one to real and perceived risks of discrimination, there are often hesitations about disclosing diagnoses to others. Given that sex practices and drug use figure as mechanisms of personal identity and validation, it is often hard to make disclosures that would disrupt existing sexual behavior and drug use. Some people are therefore extremely reluctant to disclose an HIV infection in the course of sex or needle use. They might believe, moreover, that they have no duty to disclose when all others should be taking measures to protect themselves against infection. To the extent they do not, they have assumed any and all risk of HIV infection. More dramatically, in isolated instances, people have tried to use their HIV infection as a

mechanism of revenge against others and purposefully withheld their diagnoses.

U.S. law has in fact recognized the duty of people with HIV infection to disclose their infectious states under some circumstances. For example, some PWAs have been successfully charged with attempted murder and various kinds of criminal endangerment because they have failed to disclose their diagnoses prior to sexual relations, for example. The same logic has been sustained in civil suits. The most famous U.S. case of this kind involved the movie star Rock Hudson, whose estate was successfully sued by Marc Christian on the grounds that Hudson lied about his condition, thereby preventing Christian from taking measures to protect himself during sex. The law certainly does not, however, require blanket disclosures, but it does seem to require disclosure in specific instances where infection might occur. This legal entitlement may be of limited value. Because of legal complexity and cost, redress in court or successful criminal prosecutions are available only to some of the people who are deceived and thereby exposed to HIV infection. Legal protections are, moreover, available only after the fact—when infection may have already occurred. For this reason, it is wise to assume that sexual and drug-using partners may be infected with HIV. This assumption does not however absolve people with AIDS/HIV from moral and legal responsibilities to disclose their diagnoses when failing to do so can endanger others.

C. Bathhouses and Needle Use

The dangers of AIDS were often grafted onto preexisting assumptions about the dangers of homosexuality and drug use. It was tempting to confront the AIDS epidemic, therefore, by constraining homosexuality and drug use through, respectively, the closure of bathhouses and declining to make sterile needles available to drug users.

Bathhouses have a long history not only as places for washing but also for socializing. Even as widely available domestic plumbing reduced the importance of bathhouses for washing, they retained their importance for socializing, especially for gay men whose emergence as a social class in the post-World War II era took the form of a brotherhood unbashedly devoted to sexual adventure. In this culture, bathhouses were the proving grounds of gay affirmation. Ironically, they also proved efficient in facilitating HIV infection. Public health analysts therefore called for their outright closure, and bathhouses were closed in several major cities, although not in all. These closures were defended paternalistically, that is, as protecting people from dangers they were incapable of resisting. Commentators noted that because bathhouses were money-making ventures, they were ill-suited to take measures to protect the health of their patrons. Some gay critics found it hard to distinguish efforts to close bathhouses from a culture of sexual repression and antigay attitudes. They saw closures as part of a backlash against gay people. More sophisticated criticism pointed out that, under liberalism, people have the right to consensual sex, and that the state may not interfere with that right even if it means that some people will get an HIV infection. In this view, the state may encourage and educate people about ways to avoid HIV infection, but it cannot require that they do so or take measures to force them to protect themselves. The debate about bathhouses is likely to revisit these arguments many times, although it is clear that bathhouse sex is entirely compatible with sex practices that minimize HIV risk; if so, paternalistic arguments for closure are far from convincing.

By law, injecting needles are available only by prescription in most of the United States. In part, this regulation is intended to inhibit drug injection. In practice, injecting needles are available to drug users through black markets. Their relative scarcity, however, fosters sharing and reuse, which in turn fosters HIV infection. Some analysts have suggested, therefore, that health agencies make sterile needles available to drug users through exchange programs (one used needle for a new one) or outright distribution. There is also an urgency to needle programs because drug use incapacitates people, it is said, and the state therefore has a paternalistic responsibility to help protect them from their poor judgment. Other analysts, by contrast, argue that giving out needles inappropriately condones wrongful drug use. For them, the relevant moral question is whether needle programs condone behavior that is objectionable in the first place. Like the closure of bathhouses, moral arguments about drug use turn on questions about the extent of personal autonomy and the limits of social paternalism. Because drug use is a morally controversial topic, the debate over needle programs is likely to remain split between public health advocates committed to pragmatic measures of reducing HIV infection and others who want to frame public policy with moral opposition to drug use as the solution to HIV infection.

V. PERSONAL CHOICES

Many of the questions involved in the epidemic do involve questions of public policy, but many more are best understood in terms of the choices individual persons must make on their own apart from questions of public policy.

A. Fidelity to the Sick

Appropriate standards of confidentiality and protection from wrongful social discrimination can encourage people to disclose HIV infection, but no law can mandate the continuation of relationships. Many PWAs face questions about their relationship with intimates, family, and friends, and AIDS has proved both the breaking point and the test of those relationships. For example, some partners and family members have been unwilling to assume the responsibility for caring for a chronically ill spouse, child, relative, or friend. On the other hand, the quiet heroism of friends, family, and health care workers has supported PWAs at their times of great need. Indeed, many of the needs of PWAs can only be met through supererogation, that is, through efforts beyond those specifically required as a matter of moral duty. For this reason, it is important to note that moral philosophy should not be conceived entirely as a matter of rights and duties. Moral analyses of the epidemic must also take into account virtues such as courage and fidelity. There is no reason to think that AIDS will ever disappear from the catalogue of human suffering. For that reason alone, it is important to foster the virtues that will enable people to support one another in the epidemic, whether they have AIDS or not.

B. Activism

The AIDS epidemic fell on people unprepared for it and without regard to their ability to cope with it. In many ways, it therefore fell to the first PWAs and their allies to be AIDS activists, to draw social attention to the syndrome and to shape policies favorable to the people affected by it. In his 1987 history of the epidemic's early years, *And the Band Played On,* Randy Shilts argued that the social perception of AIDS as a disease confined to gay men and drug users slowed appropriate social response. AIDS activists therefore rose to challenge this social indifference. A thin line separated the pursuit of health care by PWAs and activism to improve health care and society in general. These efforts sometimes led to clashes with government agencies and politicians and involved acts of civil disobedience, including the obstruction of traffic, building entrances, and telephone lines. In keeping with the tenets of civil disobedience, activists carrying out these obstructions were prepared to accept arrest and conviction. In practice, though, many of these charges were dropped for one reason or another. The heyday of confrontational AIDS activism seems to be over, partly because of the successes of the earliest activism: social institutions now attend to AIDS. The challenges that remain ahead may be of a different order, namely how to advocate the causes important to PWAs when the epidemic has become "normalized," when news media have come to see AIDS stories as routine, when it appears that there can be no quick fixes for the epidemic and that biomedical research will yield results only slowly. For these reasons, AIDS activism may need to modify its methods and adopt conventional lobbying practices rather than revisit the confrontational rhetoric and disruptions that were the common coin of early AIDS activism.

C. Reproductive Decisions

Most children with AIDS were born to HIV-infected mothers. While data vary from study to study, not all children born to women with HIV infections are themselves infected, and drug treatment appears to play a role in reducing transmission like this. Because of this uncertainty, some women go forward with pregnancy in the hope that their children will not be affected; they are often confounded in that hope. Some parents have abandoned children with AIDS because they are unable and/or unwilling to care for them. These children ordinarily become wards of the state. Women who do keep their children often face significant challenges trying to provide appropriate care, especially because many women with AIDS are economically disadvantaged. Knowing that they will die, unable to raise their children, some parents with AIDS face wrenching questions about the placement and care of the children who will survive them.

When women have an HIV infection, is it ethical for them to get pregnant and to have children? It should be immediately noted that some women do not know they have an HIV infection when they become pregnant. For these women, there is no question of moral culpability. Even when women know they have an HIV infection, some will take the risk of pregnancy. This choice is not altogether unreasonable given how important motherhood is to many women as a cornerstone of their identity and because not all children are affected. Because prenatal testing cannot reveal whether a particular fetus is affected by HIV, women who are prepared to abort do not have that option available to them. Even if prenatal testing were revealing, other women reject abortion as a worse evil than having a child affected with AIDS, so that option would not be morally available to them either. There are also many social impediments to the use of contraceptives by HIV-infected women,

such as their relative powerlessness and prevailing views that condom use indicates promiscuity. These impediments make it implausible to argue that an HIV-infected woman has necessarily acted immorally if she becomes pregnant and bears a child with an HIV infection.

Under ideal circumstances, no parents should have children without some capacity to serve the interests of those children. It appears that if a woman has one child affected with HIV, subsequent children are likely to be infected as well. This sort of knowledge should be incorporated in choices about having additional children, as should capacities to provide support for a child. It is far from ideal that some women become pregnant facing a high likelihood that their children will be infected with AIDS and that these women have no options for the care of those children except to abandon them to the care of the state. By the same token, it is hardly ideal either if society does not help women avoid pregnancies likely to end this way. The moral responsibilities for children with HIV may not belong, that is, to individual women alone but may also involve the ways in which society helps women avoid pregnancies likely to end with the birth of an HIV-infected child.

VI. CONCLUSIONS

Some commentators were quick to note that AIDS did not raise any new kind of moral question. While that may be true, it is also uninterestingly true. While the global issues raised here may be familiar in other contexts, it is important not to lose sight of the specific circumstances that make the experience of AIDS unique. That it is often gay men, drug users, their sexual partners, and children who get AIDS, and that the largest number of PWAs live in the Third World makes the epidemic morally interesting in its own right. For people with AIDS/HIV, many of the most pressing ethical issues will involve planning for the future, balancing competing demands on time and health, examining religious beliefs, and making judgments about how to value the world and the people in it. These questions are not without parallel in other diseases, but the social context of AIDS confers on them a meaning all their own.

Because ethical views can differ and because human beings are fallible, there will be differences in judgments about ethical conduct in both the public and the personal domain. In all instances, however, it should be remembered that PWAs will have more needs than can be met by relying on the notion of duty alone. Notions of personal virtue must therefore take their own prominent place in answers to moral questions about AIDS.

Bibliography

Burris, S., & the Yale AIDS Law Project (Eds.). (1993). *AIDS law today.* New Haven, CT: Yale University Press.

Cameron, M. (1993). *Living with AIDS: Experiencing ethical problems.* Newbury Park, CA: Sage.

Daniels, N. (1995). *Seeking fair treatment: From the AIDS epidemic to national health care reform.* New York: Oxford University Press.

Faden, R. R., Kass, N. E. (Eds.). (1996). *HIV, AIDS, and childbearing: Public policy, private lives.* New York: Oxford University Press.

Gray, J. N., Lyons, P. M. Jr., Melton G. B. (1995). *Ethical and legal issues in AIDS research.* Baltimore, MD: Johns Hopkins University Press.

Mann, J., Tarantola, D. J. M., Netter T. W. (Eds.). (1992). *AIDS in the world.* Cambridge: Harvard University Press.

Murphy, T. F. (1994). *Ethics in an epidemic: AIDS, morality, and culture.* Berkeley: University of California Press.

Reamer, F. G. (Ed.). (1991). *AIDS and ethics.* New York: Columbia University Press.

Schoub, B. D. (1994). *AIDS & HIV in perspective: A guide to understanding the virus and its consequences.* Cambridge: Cambridge University Press.

Watney, S. (1994). *Practices of freedom: Selected writings on HIV/ AIDS.* Durham, NC: Duke University Press.

AIDS IN THE DEVELOPING WORLD

Udo Schüklenk,* Carlos del Rio,† Carlos Magis,‡
and Vichai Chokevivat‖
*University of Central Lancashire, †Emory University, ‡CONASIDA, Mexico,
‖Thai Department of Health and Human Welfare

GLOSSARY

clinical research Trials conducted primarily in order to enhance knowledge and to help future patient generations.

confidentiality The principle that information gathered by a doctor from a patient will not be provided to third parties without the patient's approval.

informed consent The principle that physicians and researchers must obtain the permission of their patients who have been fully informed of any risks before they agree to medical intervention or research.

resource allocation The distribution of available means to reach certain ends

sex education In a health educational context, information about implications of sexual behaviour is provided in order to support public health goals

THE AIDS EPIDEMIC in developing countries has led to a variety of reactions. Most responses were character-ized as an epidemic of anxiety, religiously motivated moralizing, and stigmatization. In Mexico, as well as in much of Latin America, AIDS is perceived as a predominantly "gay disease," afflicting mostly gay men. Thus, the "risk of AIDS" has been used as a pretext to discriminate against this "risk group." The result has been that people with AIDS are seen as the cause of the epidemic rather than victims of it. Attempts have also been made to limit the civil rights of gay men as well as other risk groups, such as sex workers, by using "public health" as an excuse to do so.

The AIDS problem in developing countries is characterized by a number of factors, most notably that in many developing countries there is a higher prevalence of AIDS cases, there are limited resources for prevention and patient care, there is a greater influence of traditional religious values that may impede public health educational efforts, and, finally, there are the ethical implications of clinical research undertaken by Western researchers with subjects from such countries.

I. CLINICAL RESEARCH

A. Clinical Research and Informed Consent

Preventive vaccine trials are currently underway in a number of developing countries chosen by the World Health Organization (WHO). These countries have been chosen mostly for epidemiological reasons: a higher rate of infections is likely to lead to faster results from preventive vaccine trials. In this article we will focus on preventive vaccine trials because of the enormous scale of the epidemic in a number of non-Western societies, such as Uganda and Thailand. For economic reasons a therapeutic vaccine would probably prove inaccessible for most of those who are infected in these parts of the world. Utilitarian reasons, too, would suggest that it is good idea to conduct clinical research in developing countries, because the impact of the disease is quite high and because there are no realistic alternative modes of action available.

U.S. bioethicist Nicholas A. Christakis suggested that first-person informed consent should not be a *conditio sine qua non* in clinical trials in Africa because in many African countries individuals often perceive themselves as extensions of their family or their community rather than as individuals in their own right. He argued that consent of the community leader may be the only alternative to individual consent (Christakis, N. A. (1988). The ethical design of an AIDS vaccine trial in Africa. *Hastings Center Report* 18(3), 31–37). This has been resoundingly rejected as a naive interpretation of African culture, based on outdated anthropological literature of the 1960s. (Ijsselmuiden, C. B., and Faden, R. R. (1992). Research and Informed Consent in Africa, *New England Journal of Medicine* 326, pp. 830–834). The Nigerian Ebun Ekunwe argues that first-person informed consent is ethically required in all trials that carry risks greater than standard procedures (Ekunwe, E. O. (1984). Informed consent in the developing world, p. 23. *Hastings Center Report* 14(3)). This seems all the more important as many African governments are little more than dictatorships with no legitimate claim to represent their citizens. They often rule with disregard for the lives of their individual citizens. To leave the decision about which of their citizens should participate in clinical trials to such "community leaders" is incompatible with virtually all medical ethics principles whether these are of consequentialist, deontological, or of other theoretical backgrounds.

Ethical concerns have been raised about preventive vaccine clinical trials in developing countries. They have to do with the gathering of informed consent from prospective participants in research clinical trials. The institutions sponsoring such trials must ensure that patients are able to give voluntary first-person informed consent as required by the WHO and the Council for International Organizations of Medical Sciences in its International Ethical Guidelines for Biomedical Research Involving Human Subjects (CIOMS). This requires that people *know* what they are consenting to. Empirical data suggest that not only in the Western world but also in developing countries such as Brazil many trial participants have a therapeutic misconception and they believe that the experimental agent they have been given is actually a successfully working drug. (Queiroz de Fonseca Filho, O., and Lie, R. K. (1995). Informed consent to preventive AIDS vaccine trials in Brazil, *AIDS and Public Policy Journal* 10, pp. 22–26). Peter Lamptey, a native of Ghana and the head of an AIDS research institution, is aware of a number of trials where, if asked, the research subjects would not have understood what they have consented to (Nowak, R. (1995). Staging ethical AIDS trials in Africa, *Science* 269, pp. 1332–1335). This poses a particular ethical problem in preventive vaccine trials because these vaccines are tested on HIV-negative human subjects who need to have unsafe sex in order to test the vaccine. The UN has set up its own body, UNAIDS, that deals with the world-wide AIDS problem. The organization propagates safer sex to people at risk of contracting HIV but at the same time it needs a least some of the trial participants to practice unsafe sex. The ethical problem clearly lies in a potential institutional conflict of interest under such circumstances. Kirby has suggested that informed consent procedures must not only involve first-person voluntary informed consent but must also be improved up to the stage where patients have a sufficient understanding of the procedure they are giving consent to (Kirby, M. (1983). Informed consent: what does it mean. *Journal of Medical Ethics,* 9, 69–75).

B. Clinical Research and Access to Newly Developed Drugs

Another concern has to do with a sensible ethics requirement mentioned in the WHO/CIOMS ethics guidelines. It requires that if drugs are successfully tested by Western researchers in developing countries the people in those countries must subsequently have access to the drug. This ethical demand is also reflected in a number of ethics codes that are in operation in developing countries. Thailand, for instance, in its National Plan for HIV/AIDS Vaccine Development and Evaluation requires that "there must be written assurance that, if the study vaccine proves to be effective and appropriate for large scale public use, the vaccine manufacturer will supply the vaccine to Thailand at special and affordable prices within an appropriate time frame." Knowing that pharmaceutical companies are usually not sensitive toward demands from developing countries for affordable drugs it seems only just to suggest that they should offer these drugs to people in those countries where clinical trials have made the development of the drug possible in the first place. Unfortunately, this requirement has not been met by UNAIDS in regard to AIDS preventive vaccine trials. It is interesting to note that a UN organization disregards international WHO/CIOMS ethics guidelines that pertain directly to its own work. Merck, one of the manufacturers of a promising new class of drugs, the so-called protease inhibitors, has undertaken clinical trials of this drug in Brazil. The company subsequently has not provided access to protease inhibitors to Brazilians with HIV and AIDS.

Ndinya-Achola has suggested that developing countries should demand that vaccines be tested in the country where they are manufactured first before large-scale trials occur in developing countries (J. O. Ndinya-Achjola (1991). A review of ethical issues in AIDS Research. *East African Medical Journal* 68, 735–740). We tend to agree that this is a reasonable demand except in situations that clearly demand a different mode of action. One such exception could be that of a candidate subtype E vaccine, which is currently being tested in phase I and phase II trials in Thai subjects. This is because the virus it is supposed to deal with is highly prevalent in Thailand and is virtually unknown in developed countries. For technical reasons it would therefore be impossible to test this drug in the country where it is manufactured, and also because the country where it is manufactured is not considered a target market by the manufacturer.

On a more general level the 1948 UN Declaration of Human Rights declares that "everyone has a right to a standard of living adequate for the health and well-being of himself and his family, including [. . .] medical care." Clearly, there is a huge gap between the ideal explicated in this ground-breaking UN human rights document and the reality of access to drugs and health care in developing countries. It is all the more disturbing that in cases where there is significant risk to the citizens of developing countries in the development of new drugs, which are then patented by international pharmaceutical companies, these people are not guaranteed access to these drugs once their efficacy and safety is established.

II. SEX EDUCATION

AIDS awareness programs in developing countries are generally under fire from religious institutions because of their opposition to sex education. Health educational programs in The Sudan have been halted because of religiously motivated objections. Islamic religious leaders insist that "Allah can cure AIDS," and they have forced the government to outlaw sex education altogether. The importation of condoms has also been re-

stricted. In a number of developing countries representatives of the Roman Catholic Church have gone to great lengths in their attempts to frustrate governmental and nongovernmental health education that informs the public about safe sex. Religiously motivated resistance to public health education promoting the use of condoms was particularly fierce in predominantly Catholic countries such as the Philippines and in Uganda.

Because of pressure from religious organizations and other conservative lobby groups, Latin American governments have been hesitant to develop effective preventive campaigns. Instead, they designed lukewarm campaigns so as not to offend or enrage the powerful religious sector of society. Health promotion campaigns that recommend the use of condoms were attacked as "permissive and conducive to promiscuity." The Mexican government was singled out for criticism by Catholic lobbyists who requested a return to "traditional sexual behavior." In Kenya, Catholic bishops and teenagers from Catholic schools held public marches at which they burned condoms and health educational booklets.

The ethical conflict lies in the question of whether adhering to moral teachings of major religions is of greater importance than saving human lives through adequate sex education. Christian ethicists, for instance, have argued that no lives would be endangered by not using condoms as long as people adhere to religious teachings about correct sexual behavior. The question, however, is whether this prevention strategy can reasonably be expected to succeed as a viable means of health promotion for entire societies. This seems quite doubtful. Therefore, the ethical problem has to do with the issue of whether it is better to adhere to religious teachings in health promotion materials or whether realistic practices for the prevention of AIDS, such as the use of condoms, should be addressed explicitly. The answer seems to follow from the issue of what the legitimate function of a state is. If the primary function of the state is to further the welfare of its citizens, it seems clear that AIDS prevention is of greater importance than is upholding religious moral values. However, if one believes that the function of the state is primarily to uphold religious values, no matter at what cost, one could argue that the government of the Sudan is ethically justified in withholding vital AIDS prevention information from its citizens. It is doubtful that such views would be supported by many people other than religious fundamentalists. Indeed, the view that the primary function of the state is to improve the quality of life of its citizens is widely shared among governments and is undoubtedly in the best interest of those affected by governmental policies. Usually, religious beliefs are considered a private matter and the state is not seen to be responsible for implementing such beliefs for all its citizens. This is particularly true for those citizens who do not subscribe to the beliefs of the religion in question.

III. RESOURCE ALLOCATION

The just allocation of scarce health care resources is already a problem in many developed countries where costs for high-tech medical interventions as well as costs for newly developed drugs have skyrocketed over recent decades. Given the limited resources of many developing countries these problems have much greater urgency than is the case in the developed world. In situations where only about 2% of the GNP is devoted to public health care, it is difficult to see how disease can be dealt with effectively. In Latin America the ethical debate has centered on the issue of the high cost of available treatments and the denial of care to victims of discrimination.

Countries such as Laos or Myanmar are still unable to provide a safe blood supply because screening all units before transfusion is not economically sustainable. The crucial ethical question concerns the microallocation of resources within overall spending for health care. In Thailand, for instance, 75% is devoted to medical care for people with AIDS, while 25% of the 1997 AIDS-related budget is spent on AIDS prevention.

The price of antiretroviral medications varies widely worldwide and has no relation to a country's income, its GNP, or the number of HIV/AIDS patients that it has. Only Zidovudine (AZT) is manufactured by more than one laboratory (Glaxo-Wellcome, as well as several generics) and thus the price varies widely. In Mexico Retrovir (a brand name of AZT) costs the equivalent of about $200 per month, while generic AZT is available for under $100 per month. Of the protease inhibitors, data on price for comparison is available only for Indinavir. In Mexico, the third country in the world to approve Indinavir, the price is lower than in other countries such as the the United States, Argentina, Chile, Brazil, and Venezuela. Despite this, the use of a combination of AZT, 3TC, and Indinavir in Mexico costs around $783 per month ($681 if generic AZT is used), which is more than either times the minimum wage in the country. If the minimum wage is related to the price of drugs it becomes obvious that in developing countries the cost of antiretroviral medications is, comparatively, 80% more than it is in developed countries.

Analysis of indirect costs as well as direct pricing of drugs provides a better indicator of the need for such "expensive drugs," even in developing nations. It has been calculated that each year of life gained for an AIDS patient in a developing country costs about $6000, which compares quite favorably with other health interventions, such as dialysis ($32,000 per year), which are now routine in many countries that are still debating whether to subsidize anti-retroviral drugs.

Unfortunately, the funds available for AIDS treatment are insufficient to care for all those who have already developed AIDS illnesses. Because of these problems it is clear that, worldwide, only a few lucky and wealthy AIDS patients will be able to pay for the expensive combination of effective anti-retroviral treatments. This increases the pressure to find an effective vaccine or adequate educational interventions. The argument to invest in preventing new cases rather than spending all the available money to help those already sick is based on a utilitarian weighing of costs and benefits. Usually, disease prevention is cheaper than treatment of illnesses that have already occurred. If the funds one has are limited it may be prudent to prevent further increases in cost through greater numbers of patients by investing in the prevention of new infections.

Some have argued that Western countries have a moral obligation to provide resources and know-how in order to fight the AIDS epidemic in developing countries. Welfarist theories of distributive justice would support this course of action. However, there is some reason to assume that the problem is caused to a large degree by a situation where Western governments allow markets to determine the price of new drugs. Nonmarket solutions utilized to determine a just price might be an ethically justifiable alternative to the current status quo and this has the potential to solve some of the resource allocation problems that occur in developing countries.

IV. CONFIDENTIALITY

It is often difficult to maintain confidentiality in hospitals where people with AIDS are separated from other patients. Many ethics textbooks mention that it is unjustifiably discriminatory to treat people with AIDS differently than other patients. They should be treated like every other patient in order to avoid stigmatization. However, ethical conflicts may also occur if people with AIDS, who have already severely compromised immune functions were exposed to the wide variety of pathogens that characterize hospitals everywhere. Hence, special treatments might be considered for AIDS cases in developing countries in order to limit risks to other patients. This benevolent course of action could then lead to a breakdown of confidentiality.

In Mexico many cases of AIDS are not reported because of fears of confidentiality breakdown. AIDS cases are often reported using identifiers such as name, address, and so on, to prevent repeated case reporting. A consequence of this confidentiality breakdown is often the "epidemiological persecution" of those affected. Candidates for many jobs are tested for HIV even though this is prohibited by law. People also lose their jobs because they are HIV positive, even though this is illegal. Because health insurance in Mexico is provided through the workplace, people with AIDS lose their coverage the moment they lose their jobs.

V. CONCLUSION

The AIDS situation in developing countries is not fundamentally different from that in developed nations. Indeed the ethical analysis is not different in any meaningful way. The factors that have an impact on AIDS in these parts of the world are different than they are elsewhere, as we saw in the discussion of the resource allocation problems and the issue of religious values. This does not mean that a new method of ethical analysis is warranted; the existing instruments are sufficient for this issue. However, there is some evidence for that Western bioethicists writing about the AIDS issue in developing countries lack sufficient knowledge of the actual problems at stake. It is important, in particular in regard to AIDS, to carefully distinguish fact from fiction.

Also See the Following Articles

CONFIDENTIALITY, GENERAL ISSUES OF • INFORMED CONSENT • PATIENTS' RIGHTS • RESOURCE ALLOCATION

Bibliography

CIOMS/WHO. (1993). *International ethical guidelines for biomedical research involving human subjects.* Geneva: CIOMS.

Faden, R. R., & Beauchamp, T. L. (1986). *A history and theory of informed consent.* New York: Oxford University Press.

Grady, C. (1995). *The search for an AIDS vaccine: Ethical issues in the development and testing of a preventive AIDS vaccine.* Bloomington: Indiana University Press.

Green, E. C. (1994). *AIDS and STDs in Africa: Bridging the gap between traditional healing and modern medicine.* Boulder, CO: Westview Press.

Miller, N., & Rockwell, R. C. (1988). *AIDS in Africa: The social and policy impact.* Lewiston, NY: Edwin Mellen Press.

AIDS TREATMENT AND BIOETHICS IN SOUTH AFRICA

Ruben Sher
National AIDS Training and Outreach Program, South Africa

GLOSSARY

informed consent The concept that a patient, before undergoing medical treatment, has been aware of the procedures involved, the possible risks and expected benefits, the likely consequence of avoiding treatment, and the nature of alternative treatments that may be substituted for this treatment.

orthodox medicine A term for medical practices adhering to Western or First World standards; i.e., the methods and codes of physicians and other health care workers trained or certified by medical schools and other such formalized medical facilities.

siyavuma makosi Literally, "we agree." The counterpart of informed consent in traditional medicine, an agreement by the family of an afflicted person that

the diagnosis of the traditional healer is acceptable to the patient and his family.

traditional African healer (TAH) A person who practices the traditional medicine of sub-Saharan Africa.

traditional medicine In the context of sub-Saharan Africa, a term for medical practices in the indigenous tradition; i.e., the ancient methods and codes of healers passed down orally from previous generations of healers.

Umthakathi Literally, a person who does bad things; a so-called witch doctor who practices traditional medicine in a harmful manner.

witch doctor A derogatory term for a person practicing nonorthodox medicine in Africa. Sometimes regarded as a synonym for traditional healer, but more correctly a description of an untrained, self-styled healer.

AIDS TREATMENT IN SOUTH AFRICA is particularly affected by the presence of two contrasting types of medical practice, one conforming to formal Western-style procedures and the other following traditional African methods.

I. INTRODUCTION

South Africa lies at the southern-most end of the African continent. The total population of geographical South

Africa in 1995 was 41,244,000, comprising four different racial groups: 31,461,000 blacks, 5,224,000 whites, 3,508,000 mixed races (colored); and 1,051,000 asians.

The diversity of the population groups is compounded by many different languages and sociocultural attitudes, traditions, and sexual mores. Two distinct and different medical care facilities coexist. Firstly there is orthodox (First World or Western type) medicine, and secondly there is black traditional medicine (African type), each with its own code of bioethics. Whereas the ethics of orthodox medicine is a written code accepted by constitutional bodies and the judiciary, there is no written code in traditional medicine; rather it has been handed down orally from healer to healer over many centuries. Although the bioethical practices of traditional healers are not officially recognized, currently they are respected by millions of black people. South Africa represents a microcosm of the rest of sub-Saharan Africa in respect of the presence of both orthodox and traditional healers. Although certain ethnic differences may prevail in various countries, the basic concepts of traditional healing are universal. To appreciate and understand the various ethical practices of traditional African healers (TAHs) vis-à-vis HIV/AIDS in Africa, a description of the selection, training, regulation, and practices of TAHs in South Africa is presented.

II. SELECTION OF TRAINEE HEALERS

Medical schools and selection criteria for entry to these medical facilities, based mainly on academic merit, do not exist in the training of TAHs.

The selection of candidates for training and practice of TAHs is based on a calling from the ancestors to a particular person in the community to become a healer. A grandmother or grandfather who was a healer would choose one of the family, such as a daughter or granddaughter, or a sister's or brother's child, to become a healer. According to African folklore, when one dies it is only the body that dies, and the spirit lives on in a special place. The spirit of the ancestor enters the body of a chosen candidate and informs that person to become a healer. If the chosen one refuses to comply, he or she could become very ill or suffer injury. The nature of this illness may be difficult for orthodox doctors to diagnose. A candidate is chosen after the onset of sexual maturity; e.g., after menstruation in women. The person cannot practice as long as an older person in the family is still a practicing healer. She or he could, however, become an assistant to the older healer. Certain criteria

exist for the suitability of candidates: (1) they should be able to feel pain for another person (empathy); (2) they should always be willing to help another person (altruism); (3) they must not be greedy, which is exhibited by the sharing of possessions; and (4) they should practice honesty.

III. TRAINING OF HEALERS

Candidate healers become "apprenticed" to a healer, usually one that is not a member of the family. Training will last for 2–6 years and varies from person to person and area to area. No qualifying examinations are held and certification does not occur. Registration with a statutory body is not required. There is therefore no ethical or legal guidelines or constraints on African traditional healer practice. This is illustrated by following:

1. The use of herbs or drugs that do not require any prior research or ethical approval.
2. The death of a patient under a healer's care is usually not apportioned to the healer, as the family and the healer agreed previously that he should continue treatment of the patient. Provided no negligence has occurred, such as the administration of an enema to a weak patient, death is usually accepted by the healer and family with the understanding that the patient's time was up and that it was the will of the ancestors.

Candidates are taught the following by their tutor healers: (1) appropriate professional behavior; (2) how to throw bones and their interpretations; (3) how to communicate with the ancestors; and (4) how to recognize, gather, and mix herbs. The bones, comprising those of animals such as the leopard, lion, and goat, and sea shells are used for communication with the ancestors. The ancestors play a central role in the practice of a TAH. They are the guardians and judges of traditional medicine. No formal or statutory body exists to standarize training, certification, treatment, or ethical practices.

IV. CLASSIFICATION OF TRADITIONAL AFRICAN HEALERS

A number of different classes of healers, based mainly on their mode of diagnosis and healing, are recognized. These are described in Table I. Strict compartmentalization may not occur in certain areas, and overlap is seen.

TABLE I

Inyanga (Traditional Healers)

	Types[a]			
	Zanusi[b]	Sangoma[c]	Ixhwele	Umthandazi
English terminology	Senior healer, diviner	Generalist practitioner	Herbalist, pharmacist	Spiritual healer
Functions	Diagnosis and treatment. Divining.	Diagnosis and treatment.	Collection, preparation, and storage of medicines from plants and animals.	Diagnosis and treatment.
Medium of healing	Throwing bones. Communicating with and appealing to the ancestors.	Throwing bones. Communicating with and appealing to the ancestors through singing and dancing, use of drums, burning incense, and smoking snuff	Sells products to Inyangas for dispensing to patients.	Prayer. Use of holy water. Lighting of a candle and using the flame for diagnosis and treatment.

[a] These divisions are not strictly adhered to and overlap as practices may occur.
[b] Previously a Zanusi would not treat but refer a patient to a Sangoma; however, in current practice Zanusi do treat.
[c] Whereas Sangomas are usually females, Zanusi are usually males.

First World countries often use the term *witch doctor* synonymously and interchangeably with traditional healer. This practice is insulting to genuine traditional healers and should be avoided. TAHs do not recognize or support in any way so-called witch doctors. The Umthakathi, or witch doctors, are seen as untrained, self-styled healers whose function is to reverse the work that has been done by other healers. They use evil spirits and magic as their medium of treatment. The use of human tissues by witch doctors for the preparation of *muti* (medicine) has been reported. "Umthakathi" literally means a person who does bad things. In this article witch doctors and their practices will not be discussed since they fall outside the definitions of TAHs.

V. ASPECTS OF TRADITIONAL HEALERS PRACTICE

When a person becomes sick it becomes the concern of the parents, siblings, aunts and uncles, and other relatives who take over the care of the sick person. They decide to seek the help of a TAH and also decide which healer to consult. Usually a number of relatives will accompany the patient to a healer. This ensures that all the facts and instructions from the healer are known, understood, and pursued.

The patient does not inform the healer about his complaint; rather the healer by "throwing the bones" informs the patient what is the matter. History taking, physical examination, and laboratory investigations are not part of the healer's practice. Bones, which should not exceed 12, are thrown three times on a mat placed on the floor. After a diagnosis has been put forward to the patient and his attending family, the patient is entitled to respond. He may reject or accept the diagnosis or visit another healer for a second opinion and then decide which healer to go to. If the family is in agreement (siyavuma makosi), there are two options the healer can take. Either he can dispense various remedies to the patient, who will then be cared for at home by the family, or the patient can be admitted to the clinic managed by the healer. The clinic is known as the "traditional ancestral hut" and is recognizable by its roof, which is made of grass and not corrugated zinc. Patients with communicable diseases are not permitted to occupy the same hut as other patients. The admission of patients is mainly to observe the complaints of the person. Visitation by the family is only allowed when the patient is better. When the patient has been treated, scarification with a blade or skin puncture with a porcupine quill is performed. These practices are regarded as a form of immunization against future evil spirits, enemies, and general diseases.

Payment to a healer is usually made in the following way: a deposit is made at the initial visit, prior to the healer talking, and has been referred to as the "mouth opener." The balance is paid after treatment is completed.

Healers are very protective of their herbs and roots. They do not disclose or share these with other healers or patients as a precaution against misuse. Healing powers are a gift from the ancestors and what may work for one healer may not work for another. Furthermore a healer will not disclose to another healer his diagnosis and treatment. Healing is thus very individualistic, protective, and nonstandardized.

Epidemiological data indicate that the majority of HIV/AIDS patients are occurring in the heterosexual black community, and many of these patients will at some stage during their illness consult and be cared for by TAHs.

VI. ETHICS IN HIV/AIDS MANAGEMENT

The common denominator in both traditional and orthodox healing is welfare of the patient. First World ethical codes are based on two criteria: fundamental obligations and derivative obligations. Respect for autonomy, nonmaleficence, beneficence, and justice compose the fundamental obligations, and veracity, confidentiality, privacy, and fidelity are the derivative obligations. AIDS has rekindled and stressed, as no previous disease has, the absolute need for the recognition and adherence to just bioethics. Violations of ethical codes have and are occurring during the HIV/AIDS pandemic. The reasons for this are thought to be ignorance, fear, and prejudice. The adherence to ethical codes of medical practice will ensure that HIV/AIDS patients will continue to receive proper and humane health care as other patients do, without discrimination and prejudice. AIDS has brought TAHs and orthodox doctors closer together, and if we are to deliver the best treatment to our patients, mutual respect, understanding, and working together are a sine qua non. The intent of this article is to discuss the various bioethics relevant to the AIDS epidemic from both a First and a Third World perspective, concerning doctor–patient relationships.

VII. OBLIGATIONS OF HEALTH CARE PROVIDERS

Physicians have been confronted with a number of profound ethical dilemmas, such as obligations to treat, confidentiality, informed consent, serological testing, the HIV-infected doctor, drug and vaccine trials and research, and individual patients' rights versus the rights of the community.

A. The Obligation to Treat

The physician's primary obligation is to treat the sick without discrimination. This duty is firmly grounded in the nature of medical knowledge and the covenant physicians enter into with society when they accept a medical education and take an oath of commitment to the care of the sick. Medical knowledge has been assigned for the purpose of healing and helping the sick. This knowledge is acquired by the invasion of the privacy of sick people. Knowledge thus acquired should be used for the benefit of the sick and not for the physician's benefit. The physician's knowledge, therefore, is not individually owned and ought not to be used primarily for personal gain, prestige, and power. Rather the profession holds this knowledge in trust for the good of the sick. Although the risks of becoming infected with the HIV while treating patients is remote, it has been accepted that an element of risk exists for doctors. The public expect doctors to take a measure of risk in caring for HIV-infected patients just as they expect a policeman to take risks in upholding the law and apprehending the criminal. The same may be said of the soldier or the firefighter. Are we not servants of the public, or is medicine a commodity to be sold on a "free market" basis? The basis for the treatment of patients by physicians is set out in the Declaration of Geneva as amended in Sydney in 1968: "The health of my patient will be my first consideration."

Refusal of treatment, irrespective of the ailment, does not occur in traditional medicine. The term "refuse" is seldom used. This is facilitated by the fact that TAHs do not accept the "germ theory" of disease; hence the risk of contagion is irrelevant. Diseases are thought to be caused by the wrath of the ancestors or spells cast by one's enemies. A healer can only refuse to treat patients if he cannot cure them. The healer informs the patient that the ancestors have told him that he should seek treatment from an orthodox physician or another TAH, most likely a senior healer.

B. Confidentially

The HIV epidemic has brought into conflict confidentiality and public safety. Since Hippocratic times the physician has been bound to safeguard what she knows about her patient. Because of discrimination and victimization of HIV-infected people it is even more urgent that confidentiality be strictly adhered to; however, the duty to respect confidentiality is not absolute. Permissible breaches of confidentiality follow.

1. When the Patient Gives Permission

This usually follows after a consultation with the physician when it is advisable for the patient to inform either a sexual partner or a health care provider who may be directly involved with the care of the patient, and the knowledge of the patient's status will be beneficial to his or her health.

2. The Doctor in Society

The doctor's overriding duty to society represents what is arguably the most controversial permissible exception to confidentiality. The right to inform sexual partners (spouses and nonspouses) and health care providers involved in the patient's care is controversial. However, most medical bodies agree that the requirements to protect sexual partners and health care providers from becoming infected with HIV override patient confidentiality. The physician has an ethical duty to protect other members of the community, and personal rights may have to be relinquished in order to maximize public safety.

TAHs generally observe strict confidentiality. They never discuss their patients with other healers and are not obligated to inform other healers of the diagnosis. When a third party, such as a wife or husband, is at risk of acquiring an infection, the patient is encouraged to inform the spouse, but if he refuses then the healer deals with the impasse as follows: He refuses to give the patient any treatment (roots/plants), and when the patient returns home empty handed, the spouse becomes suspicious and enquires as to what has gone wrong and returns to the healer with the patient, whereupon the information will be divulged.

Traditionally sickness is a family concern and responsibility. As the family members live with the person and care for him or her, they need to understand what the problem is—what the disease is. This is claimed to be essential for optimizing care, feeling the pain the patient feels, and empathizing with the patient. Prevention of suicide may be obviated when the family is cognizant of the patient's HIV status. If a patient is known to be HIV positive and is seen with a partner, the healer will call the patient and inform him or her to bring the partner to his surgery. The Sangoma will indirectly tell the patient's partner that the patient is HIV positive by asking them if they use condoms and informing them that they should both be tested. There is no resource to legal enquiry or punishment in this regard.

3. For the Purpose of Medical Research

For vaccine and experimental drug trials, confidentiality may be broken.

4. Legal Requirements

Breaches of confidentiality occur when information is required by due legal process. There is no professional immunity in South African courts. In conclusion, the physician must always be able to justify his breach of confidentiality. Human dignity and confidentiality must be balanced against the health and welfare of the community.

VIII. INFORMED CONSENT AND SEROLOGICAL TESTING

The taking of blood is required as an invasive procedure and as such requires informed consent. When testing is done, the physician has a strong obligation not only to observe confidentiality, but also to provide counseling necessary to help the patient overcome the severe implications of a positive test. Informed consent for the carrying out of certain procedures requires mental competence. In the absence of such competence, which may be a common event in HIV infection, certainly terminal infections, physicians should discuss these problems with patients while they are mentally competent, permitting them to exercise their autonomy. Involuntary testing of patients provides yet another ethical dilemma. In the donation of human tissue or blood, involuntary testing for HIV is morally justifiable; however, involuntary testing prior to surgery because of the danger to health professionals is controversial.

Because of the current low risk of infection in the workplace and the use of universal precautions, there is no scientific justification in involuntary testing prior to surgery. As TAHs do not take blood from patients, informed consent does not play a significant role in diagnostic traditional medical practice. However, therapeutic procedures such as scarification do not require informed consent, as it is part of the treatment to which the family and patient have agreed to. The patient, however, has the right to refuse any treatment, and also to establish the capabilities of the healer.

IX. DRUG AND VACCINE TRIALS AND THE RESEARCHER

All biomedical research should be based on the guidelines as laid down in the Declaration of Helsinki of 1964 and the Nuremberg Code of 1974 involving human subjects. One of the most contentious ethical dilemmas is that of placebo-controlled trials in people with fatal disease. Accepted drug evaluation research trials require the use of the placebo to accurately evaluate the efficacy of a drug and its correct dosage. People with AIDS claim that to use placebos and deprive patients of a therapeutic measure that could prolong or improve quality of life is unethical. Their claim that they will act as their own controls is difficult to oppose and may be morally correct. Less rigorous criteria for drug evaluations seem justifiable in patients with clinical AIDS.

South Africa is a multicultural society, and therefore the basic ethical principles that guide human investigation need to be interpreted and applied within different cultural settings. All investigations need to be culturally sensitive, and research ethics need to be made culturally relevant. TAHs are not allowed to prescribe any medicine that they themselves have not tried. They should drink the medicine in front of patients. If a healer makes an incision on a patient, he has to make it on himself first.

X. THE PHYSICIAN AND LIFE-SUSTAINING TREATMENT

AIDS raises ethical dilemmas about when to provide and when to withdraw life-sustaining treatments such as mechanical ventilation and cardiopulmonary resuscitation. The decision is complicated by the fact that many patients become mentally incompetent and are unable to participate in decision making. Ethical consideration about intensive care should apply equally to people with HIV infection as it applies to other life-threatening diseases. The nature of the disease is not the important consideration, but rather the prognosis. Caregivers have no ethical or medical obligation to provide futile care. The problem is to decide what treatments are futile. Decisions for competent patients should be made jointly by physicians and the informed patients themselves. Decisions for incompetent patients should be made by the physicians and patient surrogates in accordance with previous competent wishes of the patient. Doctors should encourage patients to express their wishes about life-sustaining treatment in advance while they are still competent.

XI. THE PHYSICIAN AND EUTHANASIA

Euthanasia creates a moral crisis, and AIDS has exacerbated the need to examine the question of the right to choose the timing of one's own death. The physician is neither morally empowered nor qualified to make decisions about the quality of life of another person. The patient's moral right to autonomy does not extend to assisted suicide. Clinicians have a moral obligation based on nonmaleficence, beneficence, and autonomy to relieve the patient's pain in accord with his or her wishes and interests; however, it is important to preserve the distinction between the intention to relieve pain at the risk of hastening death and the intention to kill in order to relieve pain. Passive euthanasia remains controversial and may be influenced by religious, cultural, and social norms. In traditional medicine, a healer is generally not allowed to help people die. In terminally ill patients, she can administer medication to relieve pain but nothing to help a person die. There are, however, three exceptions to this ethical rule, which deals mainly with active euthanasia.

1. If a child is born defective or ill, and it is judged that the child will not survive as a human being, then the parents and healers in consultation will decide whether the child should be killed. It is the mother's duty to kill the child, as she brought the child into the world, and therefore she must take it away. This practice is controversial with modern-day healers and not often practiced.

2. In extreme old age, associated with the inability to eat or drink and the presence of sores on the buttocks (bed sores), active euthanasia can be exercised as follows: the patient is given "knock-out" medicine and covered by the skin of a white cow, and a herd of cattle is driven over the person, resulting in death.

3. The last example of morally permitted active euthanasia is during periods of extreme drought, resulting in hunger and wasting. A patient so afflicted is taken to a "donga" (ravine or wide ditch) and instructed to hold up the walls, and wild animals are allowed to eat the person. Passive euthanasia often, double-effect euthanasia sometimes, and active euthanasia rarely have become present-day morally acceptable practices.

XII. HIV-POSITIVE PHYSICIANS

The AIDS pandemic has created a rather unique ethical dilemma in the HIV-infected health care provider and her right to practice medicine. The reason for this is the possible transmission of the HIV from an infected physician to a patient during a surgical procedure. Although six people have become infected from a single dentist, most likely through dental surgery, these are the only known cases of such transmission. The possibility of physician-to-patient transmission is remote, and it would, therefore, seem unethical to impose restrictions on the nature of medical practice by HIV-infected physicians. Theoretically, the highest-risk disciplines are surgeons, obstetricians, and gynecologists. The doctor is under no moral obligation to notify her patients that she is HIV positive, but she should take all precautions to safeguard her patients against infection. In South Africa HIV-infected doctors should seek appropriate counseling with their doctors, during which time the nature of the medical practice will be discussed and resolved. Generally such doctors are advised not to engage in invasive medical procedures. Failure on the part of an HIV-infected practitioner to take such steps could result in the South African Medical and Dental Council taking severe measures to limit the practice or suspend registration of such physicians.

In America legislation has recently been evoked which makes it compulsory for HIV-infected physicians to inform their patients prior to any surgical procedure. We are morally obligated to take steps to protect immunocompromised infected physicians from being infected with various infectious agents, e.g., tuberculosis, during their work. There is a very simple and logical way of dealing with healers who are infected with transmissible agents such as those causing sexually transmitted diseases. It is said that a healer must provide health care, not only for the public, but also for himself. Failure to provide health care for himself renders him incapable of providing care to the public. A healer should be of irreproachable character. If a healer has a sexually transmitted disease it indicates he has a loose life and therefore is not entitled to treat people. AIDS has brought into the ethical arena many serious dilemmas, often with difficult solutions. If physicians cannot solve these problems among themselves, then the courts will.

Acknowledgments

I thank the following traditional healers for the information provided concerning traditional practices: Mr. Credo Mutwa, Mrs. Mercy Manci, Mr. Horatio Zungu (all from South Africa), and Mr. Tito Dladla (Moçambique). I also thank Ms. Louise Blake for proofreading and Mrs. Fatima Phaladi for typing the manuscript.

Also See the Following Articles

AIDS IN THE DEVELOPING WORLD • INDIGENOUS RIGHTS • INFORMED CONSENT • MEDICAL CODES AND OATHS • PATIENTS' RIGHTS

ALTERNATIVE MEDICINE

Margaret Whitelegg
University of Central Lancashire

GLOSSARY

acupuncture Part of traditional Chinese medicine using needles to affect energy meridians in the body.

ayurveda An ancient system of medicine practiced in India, using herbs, diet, etc.

homeopathy System of healing developed from the law of "like cures like" and which treats with minute doses of "potentized" remedies.

orthodox medicine Biomedicine; the official medical system of the Western world based on scientific principles.

osteopathy A system of healing dealing with examination, treatment, and interpretation of abnormalities of the musculoskeletal system.

ALTERNATIVE OR COMPLEMENTARY MEDICINE is difficult to define. Indeed the words "alternative" and "complementary" are a source of contention, since many people now prefer the words "complementary medicine" to signal the fact that such therapies are to be used as a complement to orthodox medicine rather than as an alternative. "Complementary" is used throughout the text since this is now the word more often in currency.

Public demand for complementary medicine has increased manifoldly in Western countries in recent years, while in the East, where the biomedical provision is still expanding, traditional methods remain a popular recourse. Researchers have suggested that the annual expenditure on complementary medicine in the United States reached $15 billion in the early nineties; for Australia estimates reached more than $1 billion (Aus) per annum. Trends throughout Europe tend to indicate a similarly large use.

An obvious feature of complementary medicine is the diverse nature of the therapies that constitute it. They vary from entire and ancient systems such as Chinese medicine and Ayurveda to more recently introduced modes such as reiki or rolfing techniques. Some therapies offer a high degree of intervention, for example, herbal medicine, acupuncture, and osteopathy, while others use approaches of a more "subtle" nature, such as homeopathy, spiritual healing, music, or drama therapy. Although the histories, philosophies, and practices within complementary medicine are so varied, common causes and shared problems arise. Some major themes in this regard are next addressed.

I. CONCEPTS DIFFERENT FROM ORTHODOXY

Despite the massive variation in history, philosophy, and practice of complementary therapies, they share a similar approach to treatment which differs fundamentally from that of orthodox medicine. The difference is between biomedicine's scientific model based on a reductionist Cartesian paradigm and the more subjective, context-based nature of the complementary perspective. Three basic areas of difference have been described: the nature of mind–body interaction, attitude to disease, and the role of the practitioner.

In terms of mind–body interaction, the biomedical perspective of practical exclusion of nonphysical factors as agents influencing either the cause or the progress of illness bases its treatment on rational and objective observation and evaluation with no interference from subjective influences. Complementary medicine, on the other hand, sees the patients and their problems as inextricably linked with their circumstances and their individual reactions to them and their lifestyles, attitudes, and environments, and will consider body, mind, and spirit in its treatment. In this context exponents speak in terms of restoring consciousness to the realm of science and suggest that it is no longer fruitful to try to reduce subjective experience to observable phenomena.

Difference in attitude to disease is characterized by the "soil–seed" debate. Disease as the cause of illness and independent of the sufferer is an approach of orthodox medicine—the "seed" thus being the causative factor. There is an assumption that all disease is generated by specific etiological agents. In contrast, in complementary medicine ill health is usually interpreted in the context of imbalance (for varying reasons) in the life force or similar holistic organizing principle to life—hence if the "soil" is healthy one will resist becoming ill. The source of the imbalance is unique to each patient. Treatment involves a supporting and rebalancing process of some sort which usually incorporates an element of encouraging the patient to find a meaningful understanding and explanation of the illness, thus perhaps allowing a redirection which will obviate the problem. The view of health is a wide one, embracing not just absence of disease, but also aspects of mental well-being. Poor vitality and low resistance are also regarded as states of ill health.

The role of the practitioner is viewed from an equally distinct perspective. While carefully and expertly treated in an orthodox medical context, the patient is nevertheless seen as a passive recipient of treatment from an expert who will make the decisions about the optimal method of care. Complementary practitioners seek a subject–subject relationship. The capacity to heal is regarded as lying in the patients themselves. Treatment is approached as a dynamic learning process where patients are encouraged to work for their own

cure, take part in their own recovery, and make their own decisions; the practitioner acts as a catalyst, providing support where necessary in the form of particular therapies.

Hence a reductionist, expert-based system, where knowledge is generated by rigorous experiment and rational analysis, is contrasted to a more relativistic approach where knowledge is seen as a social product, generated collaboratively.

II. COOPERATION OR CO-OPTION?

The relationship between orthodox and complementary medicine has changed since the beginning of the rise in popularity of the latter in the 1960s. Almost complete hostility on the part of the medical profession has given way to increasing tolerance. Change can be seen, for example, from the British Medical Association's derisive 1986 report on alternative medicine (described as an "own goal" following practically universal condemnation) to its 1993 version which talks of "therapies working alongside and in conjunction with orthodox medicine." In the USA a state-funded research institute devoted entirely to researching complementary medicine, the Office of Alternative Medicine, has been established. However, in many countries it is illegal to practice many forms of complementary medicine unless medically qualified. In others there exists some restrictive legislation, e.g., for Heilpraktiker in Germany. In the United Kingdom, practice is mainly unrestricted.

Nevertheless, relationships between orthodox and alternative medicine remain in a state of flux and debate for a number of reasons. Orthodoxy remains nervous of practitioners with no formal medical qualifications practicing treatments with little or no scientific rationale. On the complementary practitioners' part, a closer relationship with the powerful and dominant orthodoxy is not without its problems. Part of the dilemma is how to gain some form of official recognition yet remain independent of orthodox dominance. To become a "profession allied to medicine" would automatically signal subordination. The registration of osteopaths and chiropractors as recognized professions in the United Kingdom was a significant milestone on the route to autonomy, but the status of these professions when employed in a National Health Service setting remains locally negotiable. Other complementary therapies continue to work toward and/or debate the value of national professional recognition.

Some orthodox practitioners involve themselves with complementary medicine. In some cases these practitioners treat according to the alternative precepts discussed above, utilizing the wider dimensions of complementary therapy. In other cases complementary therapies are adapted to orthodox criteria and applied in a more limited and reductionist setting. Moves to incorporate alternative medicine into orthodoxy are feared by complementary practitioners as co-optive strategies, since the application of that part of complementary medicine which can be explained by present scientific knowledge within the orthodox context inevitably represents a compromised version of the original therapy. Acupuncture, for example, is limited by its principle orthodox practitioners to treatment of pain, legitimized by orthodox scientific explanation, while the practice of acupuncture as an ancient, holistic therapy which treats all ailments by application of traditional yin–yang theory is rejected and traditional practitioners using such classical methods are marginalized. Similar struggles are arising in other modalities, for example, between lay and orthodox homeopaths, or in herbal medicine where traditional herbalists use the whole plant in context, while orthodox science and the drug companies look for the active chemical for use in isolation.

The co-optive tendency is being addressed and countered somewhat by developments in education and research. Attention is increasingly focused on practitioner education, though in some cases adequate education was never lacking, and university courses are now being offered. Such efforts have obliged a new demand for a considerable and necessary scientific component to the courses, yet has encouraged simultaneously an articulation of central beliefs and thus emphasis on what is distinctly holistic and traditional about them. This new-found confidence is thus instilling a greater sense of identity which serves to resist incorporation into an orthodox mold. For orthodox practitioners wishing to practice a complementary therapy, the British Medical Association's 1993 report recommends training with a recognized complementary body. Certainly many examples of harmonious orthodox and complementary cooperative ventures do exist, but many problems remain to be solved in the area and mistrust on both sides to be overcome.

III. RESEARCH

Issues in complementary medical research parallel, to a great extent, the debates discussed above—namely how far does orthodox science set the agenda and how far can research which maintains faith with the para-

digm be successful in satisfying the demands of health authorities, practitioners, and patients.

The randomized, double-blind, placebo-controlled clinical trial has evolved as the gold standard of orthodox research. The expectations followed, then, that complementary medicine should prove itself likewise, and indeed trials have been done. As a singular method of research for complementary medicine, however, the randomized, double-blind, placebo-controlled clinical trial has been resisted. Firstly it was feared to be a tool by which orthodox medicine could expropriate suitable pieces of complementary medicine for use out of context, as evidenced by the statement of Professor Ernst, an orthodox practitioner and first professor of complementary medicine in the United Kingdom:

I think the way to go about (integrating complementary medicine into orthodox medicine) is to take one form of complementary medicine after the other and test it, and if it can be shown to work in a definite condition then it ceases to be complementary and it is orthodox medicine, and my aim would be to integrate these therapies into orthodox medicine and one day there will be only one medicine. (Medicine Now, BBC Radio Four, June 1993)

More importantly this type of clinical trial was argued to often offer an inappropriate measure of complementary therapy for it brooks no recognition of the subjectivity essential to the complementary therapeutic situation, nor, having been designed to test the effect of one drug over larger numbers of people, can it be a sensitive measure of treatments that differ from individual to individual despite a similar orthodox diagnosis. More explicitly, with the emphasis on the practitioner–patient relationship in complementary medicine, blinding in a trial would exclude essential aspects. Also placebos may compromise this close relationship when practitioners find it difficult to hand over medicines, apply an inappropriate technique, or stimulate a wrong meridian in the knowledge that their intentions toward the patients are "not the best I can do."

Criticism is also leveled at the status of scientific knowledge, which is neither timeless nor objective but is influenced by social and political context, and hence offers no superior "access to truth." The Bristol Cancer Help Centre trial is often cited in this context. A study by orthodox researchers of this popular clinic, offering complementary approaches to cancer (alongside orthodox treatment), found that its subjects, women with breast cancer, to be twice as likely to die, probably, the researchers said, on accout of some element of the alternative treatment offered there. But mistakes in the report were discovered and it was retracted, but not before a lot of damage was done to the reputation of the clinic. Lack of expertise about complementary medicine on the part of the researchers and poor scientific practice are commonly cited as reasons for the failure of this research.

Researchers in complementary medicine are increasingly aware of the need to develop a broad base of research, including that which can accommodate the context-based nature of the practices where necessary. This does not mean abandoning the clinical trial—there is no "best" method—but rather encouraging a spectrum of approaches covering a wide range of topics, using methods ranging from experimental trials to qualitative methods of the social sciences. The focus of the research must address two dimensions: firstly research with an inward focus, primarily for practitioners, to aid professional and self-development and to improve practice. In this regard the case history and case study are suggested as the gold standards of complementary medicine, since traditional knowledge on which most therapies are based rely on these as a means of accumulating expertise, as opposed to the hypothetico-deductive reasoning of modern scientific thinking. Further useful routes might be provided by, for example, audit, reflective practice, and comparative studies. Secondly an outward focus is necessary to prove the value of complementary therapies to patients, purchasers, and practitioners, and to prove efficacy in clinical conditions and safety in use. These methods may include clinical trials, pragmatic trials, outcome studies, and observational studies. Quality is a further issue in, for example, herbal medicine, and is proving sometimes difficult to control for, particularly with imported ethnic remedies. The use of remedies from endangered species, such as rhinoceros horn or tiger bones, has more recently emerged as a contentious issue.

As the ethos of research evolves, new methodologies and ideas for solutions to some problems are emerging. The development of the role of the practitioner-researcher is regarded as contributing to a research ethos in keeping with the model of society implicit in the alternative medical paradigm, allowing research in which interaction with the patient occurs. Other, quite different, directions are being considered, such as Goethean science in which the objective is approached through the subjective, but how far such ideas can be developed to offer successful research methods remains to be seen. The Office of Alternative Medicine in the USA has produced a report on research strategies for complementary medicine, suggesting some basic assumptions underpinning assessment of complementary medicine. They suggest:

- We have incomplete understanding of the world: knowledge evolves and develops
- Research methods may evolve and change as we continue to learn about the world
- Research is always feasible—and essential—regardless of the therapy under consideration
- Research rarely provides definitively unequivocal answers: there is often room for reasonable people to disagree—within limits—about the interpretation of evidence
- That said, some statements made about health are incorrect and some practices are not in the best interests of patients
- Good research aims to minimize the effects of bias, chance variation, and confounding
- Our priority is research which investigates whether treatments do more good than harm

As complementary medicine goes through the uneven process of professionalization—a necessary step to ensure protection of the public as increased numbers of people have recourse to it—a number of issues remain to be resolved. The decision has to be faced as to how far it takes the orthodox medical model as a blueprint, or whether a new model can be developed which is more appropriate for alternative philosophies. The relationship with orthodoxy has to come to an acceptable equilibrium of contact for the benefit of patients. As the academic and research ethos expands, the role of tradition versus the scientific method has to be addressed. Developments within the paradigm have to proceed, but must be rigorous enough to merit public confidence.

Also See the Following Articles

AIDS TREATMENT AND BIOETHICS IN SOUTH AFRICA • PREVENTIVE MEDICINE

Bibliography

British Medical Association (1993). "Complementary Medicine: New Approaches to Good Practice." Oxford Univ. Press, Oxford.
Eisenberg, D. M., Kessler, R. C., Foster, C., Norlock, F. E., Calkins,

D. R., and Delbanco, T. L. (1993). Prevalence, costs and patterns of use. *New England Journal of Medicine* **328**, 246–252.

Fulder, S. (1996). "The Handbook of Complementary Medicine," 3rd ed. Heineman, London.

Grossinger, R. (1995). "Planet Medicine." North Atlantic, California.

MacLennan, A. H., Wilson, D. H., and Taylor, A. W. (1996). Prevalence and cost of alternative medicine in Australia. *Lancet* **347**, 569–573.

Mills, S. (1991). "Out of the Earth: The Essential Book of Herbal Medicine." Viking, London.

Saks, M. (Ed.) (1992). "Alternative Medicine in Britain." Clarendon Press, Oxford.

ALTRUISM AND ECONOMICS

John Fender
University of Birmingham

GLOSSARY

altruism The inclination to behave in such a way as to benefit others, without the anticipation of reward from external sources; unselfishness.

asymmetric information The situation where one person knows something that other people do not (hence there is an asymmetry of information).

egoism The inclination to behave in such a way as to benefit oneself; selfishness.

externality The impinging of one agent's actions on the well-being of another, without the mediation of the price mechanism.

Nash equilibrium A situation in which each economic agent is doing as well as possible for himself, taking the behavior of other agents as given.

Pareto efficiency A state of affairs in which it is impos-

sible to make one economic agent better off without making at least one other economic agent worse off.

ECONOMICS has often been accused of assuming that economic agents are selfish and do not care for others. While there is some truth to this assertion, there is now a substantial body of work in economics which develops the idea that economic agents may display altruism in their behavior. This article reviews some of this literature, discusses what has been established, and presents some ideas for further research.

I. INTRODUCTION

Economic theory involves the construction of models which are designed to illuminate various aspects of economic behavior. Such models are characterized by assumptions; which particular set of assumptions one makes in constructing a model depends, in part, on what it is one is trying to model; assumptions relevant to one problem or set of problems may not be so relevant if one's focus of interest is somewhat different. Economic reality is, of course, extremely complex, and it is obviously impossible to model it in its full complexity; models, like maps, are inevitably selective. But we can distinguish between good and better models, just as maps can vary in quality; the important question to ask in evaluating economic models is how well they capture the crucial features of the economic problem we are interested in. Answering this question may not, of course, be easy.

Economic models typically contain various economic agents (consumers, firms, governments), whose behavior determines the collective outcome. To understand what happens in the economy it is consequentially necessary to explain the behavior of economic agents, and this is typically done by assuming that they are rational, which means that they maximize some objective function subject to appropriate constraints. (The maximization–rationality postulate has been subject to a number of criticisms, but a discussion of these is beyond the scope of this article.) In the case of consumers, the objective function is usually called a utility function, which represents an agent's preferences over a number of outcomes. An example would be where a consumer has to choose levels of consumption of a number of goods; his utility function represents his preferences over these goods (so it would attribute a higher level of utility to one bundle of goods over another if and only if he prefers the former). The consumer is invariably subject to a budget constraint, expressing the consumption possibilities that are actually available to him, which will depend on the prices of the goods, his income or wealth, etc. (He may be subject to other constraints as well, such as time and/or rationing constraints.) Carrying out the maximization, we can derive expressions giving agents' demands for the various goods as functions of a number of variables, such as prices and income.

A crucial question in the current context concerns the arguments that enter the utility function. If the variables that enter the function exclusively relate to the individual in question (his own consumption of various goods and services, for example) we say his preferences are *egoistic*. (Egoism should be distinguished from egotism. Egoism is essentially synonymous with selfishness; egotism is self-centeredness—someone who relates everything that happens to himself may be described as egotistical.) Suppose, however, that variables relating to other agents' actions or characteristics enter the function; then we might say that interdependence exists. This might arise for a number of reasons; interdependence involves what are called *externalities*, of which there are many examples: one person's playing his stereo loudly may affect others' well-being (positively or negatively), my putting my car on the road may delay other people's journeys, etc. Pollution and congestion are commonly discussed externalities. Suppose, however, that someone else's

utility enters my utility function; then, provided it enters positively, we can describe this as an example of *altruism*. If it enters negatively, we might describe this as hatred, malice, or envy; however interesting and (regretably) common negative dependence may be, though, we will not discuss it further here.

So we might be tempted to define altruism as a situation where one agent's utility depends positively on another's. However, there are further distinctions to make. There are two reasons (at least) why my utility might depend on someone else's. One is that may happiness may be genuinely affected by someone else's well-being (an example of "sympathy"). But secondly, my behavior may be as if my utility depended on someone else's not because of any direct effect of his happiness on mine, but because I believe I ought to behave in this way (a case of "commitment"). The interdependence of utility functions in this case represents ethical beliefs. Such beliefs might be susceptible to argument, debate, and persuasion, in which case the utility function would be rather different from a standard utility function, which is usually regarded as in some way "basic"—that is, dependent on tastes which are not susceptible to further analysis.

A simple formalization of the above points might proceed as follows: consider individual E, an egoist, whose utility function is given by $U_E = u_E(x_E, y_E)$, with x_E and y_E representing his consumption of goods x and y (the two goods consumed in the economy). Then we might suppose individual A, the altruist, to have a utility function of the form $U_A = u_A(x_A, y_A) + \alpha u_E(x_E, y_E)$, where x_A and y_A are his levels of consumption of x and y, respectively, and α is greater than zero. His utility function consists of two components—a self-regarding component, u_A, and an "other regarding" component, αu_E; α might be described as the "degree of altruism." The formulation can be extended to many individuals and goods in a fairly obvious way. One complication occurs when there is more than one altruist. Specifically, suppose there is another altruist who is altruistic toward altruist A; the question arises whether it is u_A or U_A which enters into the second altruist's utility function—it can plausibly be argued that if the interdependence is a case of sympathy, U_A is the relevant argument, whereas in the case of commitment, it is u_A. If we want both these examples to count as altruism, we should define altruism as the entering of at least the self-regarding component of other agents' utilities into a person's utility function.

A similar problem emerges when we consider social welfare, which we regard as the appropriate maximand for policymakers. A utilitarian social welfare function would sum individuals' utilities, but should it sum the u_A's or the U_A's? In the case of sympathy, a strong case can be made for the latter—it is surely appropriate to consider the effects on loved ones when evaluating the social costs of accidents, for example. In the case of commitment, it is less clear-cut—in fact, it can plausibly be argued that it is the u_A's which should enter into the social welfare function. (Is it right that someone should be better treated merely because some people think he should be better treated?)

In a world of more than two people, the question arises as to whose utilities should affect mine (and others). The utilities of friends, lovers, parents, relatives, and children are all plausible candidates. But what of neighbors, colleagues, fellow citizens, and members of the human race? What, indeed, about members of future generations yet unborn? Also, since we can plausibly discuss the welfare of certain nonhuman animals, should my utility depend positively on theirs? Perhaps we should expect a gradation of weights which one puts on the welfare of other beings, with one's nearest and dearest receiving the highest weights.

II. DOES ALTRUISM EXIST?

It is easy to give examples of apparent altruism. We might mention blood donation, anonymous giving to charity, voting, saving Jews from Nazis, looking after elderly relatives, martyrdom, etc. Some economists (and philosophers), who are inclined to explain all human behavior in self-interested terms, might suggest that this apparently altruistic behavior is in fact really self-interested. One possible explanation involves enlightened or long-term self-interest. Take, for example, the firm which refuses to rise prices during a shortage, or which treats its workers well. It might be argued that a firm which raised its prices during a shortage would be accused of "price gouging" and suffer a fall in demand, and profits, in the longer run. Similarly, a firm which treats its workers miserly may raise its profits in the short run, but the longer term consequences may be reduced worker morale, higher turnover, and an increased probability of unionization. However, some of the above examples of altruism may be difficult to explain in terms of enlightened self-interest. Although it is possible for a determined believer that all human behavior is self-interested to produce explanations for apparently altruistic behavior ("martyrs are maximizing their chances of salvation;" "people give to charity because it makes them feel good;" etc.), such assertions either lack empirical support or become essentially tau-

tologous. There have been a number of studies of apparently altruistic behavior which conclude that there is no plausible self-interested explanation for much of such behavior; indeed, the best explanation for such behavior is that some people do such things because they believe it to be right to do so.

But if altruism exists, the question arises how it came to exist. If evolution means the survival of the fittest then, it might be argued, we would expect to see egoism prevail; since egoists maximize their own survival probabilities, then if only the fittest survive, it would seem to follow that it will be the egoists who would tend to survive and predominate in the population. This argument is not, however, necessarily correct. The crucial point is that survival may well be enhanced by cooperation, so that if agents are predisposed toward cooperation, that may raise their survival propensities. In one researcher's models, parents have children who play prisoner's dilemma type games against each other. The prisoner's dilemma is a common problem in game theory and it is worth a brief detour in order to explain it. A typical prisoner's dilemma is shown in Table I. There are two players of the game, Row and Column. Each has to choose between two actions: "cooperate" or "defect." The table shows the outcomes or payoffs to each player given his or her choice of actions. So if Row plays "cooperate" but Column plays "defect," Row receives a payoff of 0 whereas Column receives 10. It is assumed that agents want to maximize their payoffs. What will happen? It seems that both agents' second choices dominate their first, in the sense that they thereby obtain a higher payoff, given the behavior of the other. We might therefore expect both to play their second strategies, obtaining a payoff of 1. (This outcome can be described as a "Nash equilibrium"—namely, a situation where each player is doing as well as possible for himself, given the behavior of the other. This is a natural equilibrium concept and an obvious candidate for what actually happens in the situation described. The example of the prisoner's dilemma does show, however, that a Nash equilibrium need not be Pareto effi-

TABLE I

An Example of the Prisoner's Dilemma

Row	Column	
	Cooperate	Defect
Cooperate	7, 7	0, 10
Defect	10, 0	1, 1

cient.) However, if each do this, they are both worse off than they would have been had they both played their first strategy (cooperate). A simple modification can be made to this setup. Instead of assuming that agents choose the strategy they play, it is assumed they possess characteristics which predispose them to play the game in a particular way. Altruism might hence be modeled as a propensity to "cooperate," and egoism as a propensity to "defect." A variety of assumptions can be made about how characteristics are passed from parents to children—genetic inheritance may be one mechanism, imitation another. It turns out that in many environments, altruists tend to predominate in the population. However, the issue is far from settled.

Although interesting, this work appears somewhat mechanistic, in the sense that altruistic tendencies tend to be generated in certain ways which are specified in the model, but are not derived from any underlying account of how these tendencies are produced and transmitted; producing such an account is unlikely to be easy, however.

Another, rather different, approach to the question of the circumstances in which altruism exists might develop from the argument that egoism may be "self-defeating," which would presumably imply that fully rational agents could not be egoists. If accepted, this means that the common assumption in economics that agents are both egoistic and rational would be incoherent. Unfortunately, this argument has made virtually no impact upon economics, but would seem to be a promising, but possibly tricky, avenue to explore.

III. THE IMPLICATIONS OF ALTRUISM FOR ECONOMIC BEHAVIOR

Suppose we accept the idea that some people are not entirely egoistic in all their economic behavior (an extremely cautious statement!); what, if any, implications follow? Of course, in order to answer this question, we need to know more; we need to know the extent and nature of the altruism and also something about the economic system within which it operates. It is difficult to say much at this level of generality; instead, in this section we will discuss a number of specific examples of how altruism may affect economic behavior.

Firstly, we will consider the doctrine of Ricardian equivalence; namely, that changes in the time path of taxation required to finance a given time path of government expenditures have no economic effects—in particular, no agent changes his consumption at all. An

implication is that government deficits are irrelevant to economic outcomes—only government expenditures matter. A number of stringent assumptions are required to generate this conclusion, including the following: taxes are lump-sum, there is no uncertainty, capital markets are perfect, and agents are either infinitely lived or altruistic toward their children (and the parameters of the model are such that agents actually want to transfer resources to their children). The idea is that if a tax increase is postponed, it will make no effective difference; infinitely lived agents know they will eventually have to pay a tax equal in present value to the tax postponed, and with perfect capital markets this makes no difference to their behavior. If agents are not infinitely lived, then this opens the possibility that the tax may be paid by a member of a future generation. If members of the current generation are altruistically linked to members of future generations then it can be shown that under these conditions, Ricardian equivalence still obtains; if taxes are reduced on the current generation, but raised on a future generation, then intergenerational transfers will adjust to neutralize the effect of the tax increase on economic behavior. (Suppose we start from a position where a parent, motivated by altruism, is transferring a certain amount to her child; the parent now receives a tax refund, to be financed by a tax on the child some time in the future. Under the conditions of the theorem the choice set of the parent is unchanged; she can return the child to his previous level of utility by making a transfer to him equal to the present value of the tax, and since she chose to ensure that her child attained this level of utility previously, it must still be her optimal choice after the tax change.) The theorem has been the subject of considerable controversy among economists—at issue are both the "robustness" of the theorem (how does changing the assumptions in the direction of realism affect the conclusion) and its empirical relevance. (For example, evidence exists that bequests are not made in accordance with the predictions of an altruistic model of bequest behavior.)

Another analysis of the effects of altruism on economic behavior is constituted by Becker's celebrated Rotten Kid Theorem. The idea is as follows: consider a family, only one of whose members is altruistic, but who can, and does, make lump-sum transfers between the members of the family. Then the theorem states that under certain conditions, all the members of the family will act in the collective interest of the family. Why should this be the case? Suppose one of the egoistic members of the family (the rotten kid) has an opportunity to earn an extra $100, but at a total cost to the other members of the family of $150. It might be thought that the kid, being egoistic, will seize the opportunity. However, he realizes that the altruistic member of the family will compensate those who lose, and reduce his transfer to him by more than $100. It will therefore not be in the self-interest of the kid to carry out the action—the fact of the transfer means that in effect his impact on the rest of the family is internalized. It is easy to see that the result is based on some restrictive assumptions. For example, the altruistic member of the family must be aware of what the other members of the family are doing; also, transfers must be "operative"—if the transfer is less than $100 in the first place, and negative transfers are ruled out, then again the result does not go through. A further point is that the assumption that just one member of the family is altruistic is crucial; if there are two altruists in the family, for example, then one may be tempted to "free ride" on the altruism of the other. In spite of these limitations, the theorm is relevant; it shows that for the members of a group to act cooperatively, it is not necessary for every member to be altruistic and that in some circumstances it is sufficient that just one member is altruistic. So, even if altruism is fairly rare, that does not mean its consequences for economic behavior are necessarily slight.

Further work on the implications of altruism for economic behavior considers an environment where the population consists of a mixture of altruists and egoists and analyzes the question under what conditions altruists have a disproportionately large effect on the equilibrium; takes into account moral hazard (which will be discussed further on); and considers a number of ways in which altruism may affect economic behavior, including models involving transfers and migration.

IV. THE IMPLICATIONS OF ALTRUISM FOR THE DESIGN OF INSTITUTIONS

Sometimes, perhaps less now than previously, an argument along the following lines is heard: "Capitalism is based on greed and selfishness; it is therefore an immoral system. It should be replaced by one not so based." There are a number of things that might be said about such an argument. A first point is that an economic system based on selfishness may in certain circumstances perform well. This is a common idea in economics; perhaps the most famous lines from Adam Smith are, "It is not from the benevolence of the butcher, the brewer, or the baker, that we expect our dinner,

but from their regard to their own interest. We address ourselves, not to their humanity but to their self-love, and never talk to them of our own necessities but of their advantages" (Smith, A., 1937, "An Inquiry into the Nature and Causes of the Wealth of Nations," p. 14. Modern Library, New York). The "First Theorem of Welfare Economics," which establishes that under certain admittedly highly restrictive conditions a perfectly competitive economy is Pareto efficient, has formalized this idea, which may seem surprising to many noneconomists; however, the notion that an economy of self-interested individuals may perform well is perhaps one of the central insights of economics.

Things are not that simple, though—we can all think of ways in which self-interested behavior can be harmful. Examples are crime and corruption. What is crucial is whether there is a congruence between private and social interests. This is sometimes the case in the economic system—if a firm maximizes its profits by producing high-quality goods efficiently, then there is such a congruence. On the other hand, if it maximizes its profits by producing shoddy goods and maltreating its workers, it is harder to argue that there is such a coincidence of interests. Perhaps it could be argued that the appropriate role for the government is to try to create an economic and legal framework where people can prosper by doing what is in the social interest.

However, it is never going to be the case that there will be a perfect coincidence of private and social interests. It is here that altruism may have a role. It may be difficult to police certain types of store; for example, to prevent them selling poor-quality goods. It may be that long-run self-interest improves matters. However, even this may be inadequate; so it may be helpful if shopkeepers are imbued with certain moral standards which ensure they do not cheat customers. Another example is provided by judges, who are obviously crucial for the functioning of the legal system. What is to prevent them from being corrupt—obviously if the whole legal system is corrupt, it will not be possible to punish corrupt judges! It seems, then, that it is desirable that there should be people with certain standards and principles who can be employed as judges (the argument probably applies to certain other professions, as well). It might be asked whether a judge who acts on the maxim that he will never accept a bribe is acting altruistically, in the way we have defined the term. If it is not self-interest which induces him to behave this way, he is certainly acting nonegoistically; it might be argued that such a maxim is one that tends to maximize the sum of utilities, so it is implied by a "rule-utilitarian" approach. If rule utilitarianism is an acceptable form of utilitarianism then since a utilitarian is certainly an altruist according to our definition, we can give an affirmative answer to the above question.

The first theorem of welfare economics is potentially misleading; although, given its assumptions, it may follow that self-interested behavior is all that is required to produce a socially desirable outcome, the assumptions are restrictive. The only choice variables assumed to be available to a firm are price and quantity. The possibilities of reneging on a contract or cheating customers (relying on bribing the judge, if necessary, to prevent the law being used as a remedy) are not possibilities that the analytical framework even admits.

One idea that has cropped up in the economic analysis of altruism is that altruism is a scarce resource and should therefore be allocated just as any other scarce resource, to those areas where it does most good. (The supposition here that altruism is a resource raises a number of questions. Can it be allocated like other, more conventional resources? If so, how is it produced and allocated? Perhaps altruism is better thought of as a trait, which obviously cannot be applied indiscriminately.) There are many societal tasks, perhaps, where an incentive scheme based on self-interest can perform as well as one based on altruism (provision of many private goods and services would be a relevant example, as suggested by the quotation from Adam Smith); it would seem sensible, therefore, if this is the case, for us to use the abundant resource of self-interestedness to achieve these social goals, allowing altruism to achieve goals in areas in which self-interest is less effective.

V. IS MORE ALTRUISM PREFERABLE TO LESS?

It might seem obvious that the answer to this question is affirmative—after all, how could putting more weight on others' utilities actually make things worse? However, one of the lessons of economics is that what may seem to be obvious on the basis of informal analysis may, on closer inspection, turn out to be false—this is one of the great advantages of rigorous modeling. One example from economics is that of the paradox of thrift—suppose everyone in a population raises the amount they save out of any given amount of income. But since spending in the economy falls, income may fall as well and it is possible that actual saving falls. Similarly, there may be paradoxes with altruism; we will discuss a number of ways in which more altruism can in fact reduce social welfare.

A. The Samaritan's Dilemma

Altruism may mean giving to the poor, rescuing those who have had accidents, caring for the weak and infirm, and so on. However, if it is anticipated that this will happen, people's incentives to look after themselves and provide for their retirement, for example, will be attenuated. Suppose I know that I will not be allowed to starve in my retirement—I am assured of a certain level of income, come what may. This may reduce my incentive to save; it may also increase my incentive to gamble. If I gamble and lose I may not in fact lose much. If I win, then the benefits may be considerable. But such behavior may not be socially desirable. The problem is one of moral hazard, which crops up ubiquitously in the discussion of insurance—insurance may mean that people behave in ways that are excessively risky (from society's point of view).

B. Altruism and the Enforcement of Cooperative Agreements

If the prisoner's dilemma is repeated indefinitely, agents may come to a cooperative arrangement—this is enforced by the threat of returning to the (one period) Nash equilibrium should a violation occur. Much work in game theory has involved an analysis of the circumstances in which such an agreement is sustainable. One consideration is how likely reversion to the Nash equilibrium is. The more likely this is, the more sustainable the cooperative agreement. Altruism may reduce the likelihood of reversion to the Nash equilibrium and hence make the cooperative agreement harder to sustain—altruists may appear "soft" and less threatening. This is not the only way in which altruism may affect matters; for example, if may make things better by making deviations from the cooperative agreement less desirable. But it is possible that the undesirable effect dominates.

C. The Altruist's Dilemma

It can be shown that altruism may resolve a prisoner's dilemma. But we should not conclude from this that the lesson of the prisoner's dilemma is that it shows the essential problem is selfishness, and that societal problems would disappear if people were altruistic, for it is perfectly possible to construct an "altruist's dilemma" in which altruistic behavior will make both agents worse off than they would have been had they behaved in a purely selfish manner. So altruism is not the solution to all of society's problems. The basic point is that there are coordination problems in society—alternatively, there is often a divergence between an individual's interests and society's interests, and these divergences may persist even if the individual's interests are somewhat altruistic.

D. Altruism and Imperfect Information

Imperfect (more precisely, asymmetric) information is pervasive, and of considerable relevance for ethical behavior. In the absence of asymmetric information, lying would be impossible, and it is difficult to see why honesty would be a virtue. It is easy to give examples of undesirable egoistic behavior under asymmetric information (e.g., a shopkeeper lying about product quality). Nevertheless, our aim here is to argue that altruism, or perhaps more strictly, certain types of apparently altruistic behavior, may be welfare decreasing in the presence of asymmetric information. The idea is that since a person has much more information than others about what contributes to his own utility, it may be much more efficient for society to allocate that individual a certain quantity of money and allow that individual to decide how to spend it to maximize his utility than for others to try to make his consumption choices for him. However well-meaning others may be, if they do not know his preferences, it may be harder for them to maximize his utility than for him to do so himself. This is an area where selfishness may have a comparative advantage over altruism.

VI. CONCLUSION

Although it has been argued above that there are circumstances in which altruism may make matters worse, it should not be concluded from this that it is not desirable to encourage more altruistic behavior. There are certainly many ways in which greater altruism might be desirable. But perhaps the main lesson to emphasize

from the above discussion is that the situation is complicated and it is not, in general, possible to derive simple conclusions. This is one of the reasons why further research on the topic is desirable. There are abundant areas for further research; one is the relevance of altruism in a world of asymmetric information. There is also the question of how altruism is instilled, acquired, and transferred, and the implications of answers to these questions for the design of social institutions.

Also See the Following Articles

BUSINESS ETHICS, OVERVIEW • EGOISM AND ALTRUISM • GAME THEORY

Bibliography

Bernheim, D., and Stark, O. (1988). Altruism within the family reconsidered: Do nice guys finish last? *American Economic Review,* 78, 1034–1045.

Brittan, S., and Hamlin, A. (1995). "Market Capitalism and Moral Values: Proceedings of Section F (Economics) of the British Association for the Advancement of Science, Keele, 1993." Elgar, Aldershot.

Coate, S. (1995). Altruism, the samaritan's dilemma and government transfer policy. *American Economic Review,* 85, 46–57.

Gauthier, D. (1990). "Moral Dealing: Contract, Ethics and Reason." Cornell Univ. Press, Ithaca.

Haltiwanger, J., and Waldman, M. (1993). The role of altruism in economic interaction. *Journal of Economic Behavior and Organisation,* 21, 1–15.

Monroe, K., Barton, M., and Lingemann, U. (1990). Altruism and the theory of rational action: Rescuers of Jews in Nazi Europe. *Ethics* 101, 103–122.

Parfit, D. (1984). "Reasons and Persons." Oxford Univ. Press, Oxford.

Stark, O. (1989). Altruism and the quality of life. *American Economic Review* 79, 86–90.

Stark, O. (1995). "Altruism and Beyond: An Economic Analysis of Transfers and Exchanges within Families and Groups." Cambridge Univ. Press, Cambridge.

Wilhelm, M. (1996). Bequest behavior and the effect of heirs' earnings: Testing the altruistic model of bequests. *American Economic Review,* 874–892.

Zamagni, S. (Ed.) (1995). "The Economics of Altruism." Elgar, Aldershot.

ANIMAL RESEARCH

Mark Parascandola
Cambridge University

GLOSSARY

alternatives Experimental procedures that use fewer or no animals, that replace typical animal-based procedures, or that refine existing procedures to limit pain and suffering.

animal welfare An animal's freedom from pain, and general comfort and quality of life, that welfare regulations aim to protect.

antivivisectionists Individuals and organizations that actively oppose experimentation using animals.

dissection The cutting apart and examination of the parts of an animal, usually after death.

IACUC Institutional Animal Care and Use Committee, an internal group that reviews treatment of animals and research proposals within a particular facility.

proresearch organizations Groups that actively represent the interests of medical researchers regarding the use of animals.

toxicity testing A testing process that consists of a series of experiments performed to find out if a substance or product has any harmful effects.

vivisection The cutting of, or experimentation on, a living animal.

ANIMAL RESEARCH broadly includes the use of nonhuman animals in scientific research, testing of new products, and science education. Use of animals in scientific research, particularly medical research, has a substantial history, and nonhuman animals continue to be used extensively in modern biomedical research, especially as models for human disease processes. Experimental procedures using animals are carefully regulated in most industrial nations, yet many scientists and citizens remain concerned about the well-being of these animals. Recently, there have been increasing efforts to seek out alternative research procedures that do not use animals, but it is unlikely that use of animals in research will come to an end in the foreseeable future.

The use of nonhuman animals in research raises some difficult ethical issues, and it brings out strong emotional responses. Images of animals restrained in laboratories conjure up peoples' worst fears of science gone mad, as personified by characters like Dr. Frankenstein and Dr. Moreau. But there is also the promise of new life-saving therapies and greater understanding of disease, to which past medical successes act as testimony. The challenge is not merely one of balancing moral obligations to other sentient species against the welfare of humans in need of medical care, but includes a host of difficult issues, some of which will be discussed here. In discussing relevant legislation the focus will be mainly (although not entirely) on the U.S. experience, as it provides an interesting case study of the challenges of translating ethics into policy.

I. HISTORICAL BACKGROUND

A. The Beast Machine

While experimentation with animals can be traced back to ancient times, its systematic employment as a tool for medical research did not begin until the seventeenth century. Most notable in this period was British physician William Harvey's demonstration of the circulation of the blood through experiments using various animal species. Moreover, the role of animals in the laboratory was not limited to medicine. Physicist Robert Boyle placed animals in air-tight chambers hooked up to his air pump, arguing that their subsequent suffocation demonstrated his success in creating a vacuum.

The increasing use of animals was greatly influenced by French philosopher René Descartes' concept of the "beast machine." While the Roman Catholic church spiritually divided human from nonhuman animals and had no objections to vivisection, Descartes claimed to provide a scientific rationale for making this distinction. All organisms, including humans, were held to operate mechanically like clockwork. But use of language and the possession of a rational soul separated humans from other animals, which were believed to have no awareness. The dominant view was that animal cries and vocalizations were mere creaking of machinery, and that nonhuman animals had no capacity for pain. However, the internal mechanisms were believed to be similar enough to allow experiments with animals to provide conclusions about the human body.

In the nineteenth century animals played a significant role in the development of experimental physiology, and this development in turn led to increased use of animals as sources for medical knowledge. French physiologist Claude Bernard, in his 1865 *Introduction to the Study of Experimental Medicine,* argued that experimentation with animals was a necessary part of making medicine a science comparable in status to physics and chemistry. Real sciences, Bernard observed, performed experiments, and thus nonhuman animals were to act as models for human disease in the laboratory.

For physiologists such as Bernard, the repetition and public demonstration of important physiological experiments was a necessary part of medical education. Public lectures that included live demonstrations incited significant controversy from those opposed to animal experiments. Some nations, such as the United Kingdom, have more recently outlawed public performance and advertising of experimental procedures using animals.

B. Magic Bullets

The role of animals in research was further extended later in the century with increased understanding of bacterial causes of disease. Here animals were significant not only in basic research within the new disciplines of bacteriology and immunology, but also in the development and testing of new vaccines and antitoxins, such as the diphtheria antitoxin. Animals had been used as sources for vaccine material since the introduction of Edward Jenner's smallpox vaccine in 1796, but the rapidly expanding therapeutic arsenal toward the end of the nineteenth century greatly increased the scope of medicinal use of animals.

Before the turn of the century leading pharmaceutical companies began to establish research laboratories of their own to develop new medicines. As the twentieth century progressed the number of new chemical substances introduced increased dramatically in the form of drugs, insecticides, food additives, and cosmetics. However, this rapid expansion also had some undesired consequences, including well-publicized cases of mass injury caused by tainted or poorly tested new drugs. As a result of public outcry against these dangers, regulation was enacted to require proof of safety (and later efficacy) of new products, beginning with the 1938 U.S. Food, Drug, and Cosmetic Act. Testing of new products on nonhuman animals rapidly became routine. The growth of the pharmaceutical industry and increased regulation also led to the standardization of certain procedures for testing new medicines. In particular, standardized tests for toxicity using large numbers of animals, such as the LD50 and Draize tests, significantly increased the number of animals used.

C. Animal Sentiments

Heated debate over the use of animals in research is not only a recent phenomenon. Throughout the history of medical research there have been those who voiced objections for various reasons, and with the increase in use of animals for medical experiments came increased debate. However, in the last quarter of the nineteenth century the antivivisection movement saw an unprecedented growth and influence, particularly in Britain. A number of organizations dedicated specifically to protecting laboratory animals were formed during this period, including the Victoria Street Society for the Protection of Animals Liable to Vivisection, The British Union for the Abolition of Vivisection, and the National Anti-Vivisection Society.

Antivivisectionist sentiment in the United States did not become focused until slightly later and was strongly influenced by the successes of the movement in Britain. The first U.S. society devoted to concerns about experimental animals, the American Anti-Vivisection Society, was formed in 1883 by Caroline Earle White. It was eventually followed by the formation of the New England Anti-Vivisection Society (1895), the Anti-Vivisection Society of Maryland (1898), The Vivisection Reform Society (1903), and a number of other groups. While there were attempts by these organizations to enact legislation restricting vivisection, they did not meet with the success of their British colleagues. It was not until 1966, when interest in the treatment of animals and protective legislation regained prominence, that Congress passed the Animal Welfare Act.

The publication of Peter Singer's book *Animal Liberation* in 1975 is often cited as the starting point of the contemporary animal rights movement. The book inspired many in the growing international movement for recognizing the interests of animals, and during the 1980s animal protection groups expanded their memberships at an astounding rate. The use of animals in research has been a central issue for the movement, and one that has aroused substantial public concern. In response, the research community has also formed activist organizations to represent their own concerns.

II. USE AND REGULATION

A. Categories of Use

Use of animals in experiments is typically divided into three categories: scientific research, product testing, and education. Because of their differing goals and purposes, these areas are treated differently in ethical debates over animal use and alternatives. However, the divisions between them can also be a source of controversy.

Scientific research here includes what scientists often call "basic research," experiments that are carried out to gain fundamental understanding of biological mechanisms. The investigator may simply be interested in understanding, say, how some unique species of fish digests its food. The information might be helpful for protecting a vulnerable species, but such direct applications are not necessary for the research to be funded and carried out. People commonly think of *medical* research when discussing the use of animals in research, but not all research has direct applications for human

health. However, basic understanding of biological mechanisms can sometimes lead to better understanding of disease and development of new therapies.

Product testing includes testing of drugs, cosmetics, toiletries, and pesticides for safety and efficacy. Cosmetics must be tested for any harmful effects, such as eye or skin damage. New drugs must be shown to be effective; that is, they must live up to the manufacturer's claims. Testing of a single product may require use of a large number of animals so that individual variation between the animals will not affect statistical analysis of the results. The product may also be given at various doses to establish a relationship between the size of the dose and the animal's response, because a substance that is toxic in very large quantities may be safe in smaller amounts. There is a gray area between research and testing in product development. Research leading to a new medicine may progress initially as a series of educated guesses, with the goal of understanding a particular problem. However, safety, effectiveness, and cost are also key factors at this early stage, and a pharmaceutical company may abandon a line of research because of these factors.

Two tests in particular, the Draize and LD50 tests, have generated significant controversy. The LD50 test was introduced in 1927 for the standardization of drugs such as insulin and it quickly became the leading toxicity test for all drugs. The goal of the test is to find the median lethal dose of a substance, or the dose at which half of the animals die. Hence, the nature of the test requires that animals are harmed as a result. The test also typically employed 60 to 100 animals for a single study. The Draize test, developed in the 1940s, is most famous as a test for eye toxicity using rabbits. Rabbits were used because their eyes are particulary sensitive; while this means scientists can more easily observe effects, it also means substantial suffering for the animal. Photographs of rabbits with damaged eyes and skin have been used by animal protection advocates in opposing these tests. Legislation has been introduced in a number of regions to ban these tests, and the Draize Test has been successfully banned, for example, in the Australian state of Victoria. Efforts in various countries to enact such legislation at a national level have so far been unsuccessful. However, reliance on these tests has declined significantly as a result of public pressure and the development of alternatives.

Product testing has been a leading target of criticism from animal protectionists. Some have argued that while human safety is a prime concern, many new products are of questionable value. Hence, use of animals in developing and testing such products cannot be justified. These critics ask, "does our society really need another eye shadow?" A cosmetic company might benefit from a new product line, but should one put the company's interests before those of the animals the product must be tested on? Moreover, many new products are simply "me too" items; suppose company A just put out a flavored lipstick and now companies B, C, and D want to do the same. Even new medical products that have substantial health benefits may essentially duplicate an existing product, as evidenced, for instance, by the variety of sunscreen lotions on the market. Public responses to use of animals in medical research may vary according to the perceived danger of the condition being studied. For example, a 1985 poll of 1421 adults by Medic General Research Survey showed that while 81% supported used of animals in research on cancer, heart disease, and diabetes, only 61% supported their use in studying allergies and less-threatening conditions (Orlans, 1993, p. 23). Additionally, cosmetic testing may be treated differently from testing of medicines for legislative purposes; for example, Victoria has prohibited use of animals specifically for cosmetic testing.

Animals are also used in training research scientists, physicians, nurses, and veterinarians. These various educational settings pose differing ethical and welfare concerns. Educational use is not limited to professional training, and students who have no intention of following a career in biology or medicine may be required to perform experiments on animals as part of their secondary school or college curriculum. In this case competency can be a concern, as a student who has no experience or knowledge of working with animals is more likely to unknowingly inflict pain. In the United States there is no federal law requiring a level of competency before conducting animal experiments. This is in contrast to some European countries, including Germany, England, Sweden, Denmark, the Netherlands, and Switzerland, where animal experiments by high school students are prohibited by law.

Use of animals to teach surgery is often defended by the acknowledgment that no one wants to be operated on by an inexperienced doctor. "Dog labs" have traditionally been a part of the medical school curriculum to teach physiological concepts as well as surgical skills. However, some have urged that students learn more effectively by acting as assistants to actual operations, and that they can gain basic dexterity through models and human dissections. Veterinarians, on the other hand, would seem have no choice but to practice on animals. Yet groups advocating alternatives have objected specifically to those procedures that do not benefit the animal, such as inducing a disease or performing an unnecessary surgical procedure. Hence, they have argued that procedures be performed only on animals that actually require medical attention, with students acting as apprentices to a qualified veterinarian. A number of U.S. medical and veterinary schools have adopted alternative programs, often in response to students' concerns.

B. Statistics on Animal Use

Statistics about use of animals in experiments are themselves a source of controversy, especially in the United States where the data available is particularly limited, failing to provide key information, and its reliability is questionable. In contrast, figures collected in the United Kingdom are more detailed and more likely to be verified. These numbers also have substantial political significance for groups on all sides of the ethical debate over the use of animals in research, as such statistics are relied upon to assess the current situation, suggest improvements, and gauge the progress of changes and reforms.

In Britain in 1990 3.2 million animals were used in laboratories, 79% of which were rats and mice. In the United States, however, estimates of annual animal use for research and testing have varied from 10 million to more than 100 million. The most reliable data are collected by the Animal and Plant Health Inspection Service (APHIS) of the U.S. Department of Agriculture (USDA). Research and testing facilities are required by law to report certain kinds of animal use to the USDA on an annual basis. However, they are not required to report numbers of rats, mice, and birds used, as those animals are not protected by the Animal Welfare Act. Because rats and mice make up the majority of experimental animals, this lack of data presents serious difficulties. In addition, lack of follow-up on data collection and ambiguities in the reporting forms make the available data somewhat questionable. However, it has been estimated through extrapolation that *at least* 17 to 22 million animals, 12 to 15 million of which are rats and mice, are used each year. (U.S. Congress, Office of Technology Assessment. (1986). *Alternatives to animal use in research, testing, and education.* Washington, DC: U.S. GPO). A more realistic estimate is probably upwards of 25 to 30 million (Orlans, 1993, p. 66).

There has been substantial controversy over whether these numbers are decreasing. Data from Britain, Canada, and the Netherlands suggest that numbers have been declining since 1980. In the United States, however, the picture is not so clear. Barbara Orlans (1993) has claimed that in looking at USDA data the progression is one of "halted progress." That is, while the numbers of animals used have decreased for a few years at a time, overall they appear to be either going up or remaining about the same. However, Andrew Rowan (1984) has pointed out the unreliability of that data and countered that some pharmaceutical and cosmetic companies and research institutions have reported significant reductions in animal use during the 1980s. As yet no systematic study has been undertaken.

Why are these numbers a source of controversy? Companies and research institutions, it seems, would be anxious to demonstrate their commitment to reducing animal use. The Office of Technology Assessment report has noted that demonstrating "a decreasing trend in animal use supports the position that the present system will lower animal use on its own." Yet the issue is not that simple. Animal protection groups also want to demonstrate that their efforts have made a difference in order to justify their continuing involvement, and advocates for alternatives to animal use have desired to show the success of their efforts. Moreover, it may be in the interests of those who wish to maintain their use of animals to deemphasize any further decrease to support the argument that those experiments that can be replaced with alternatives already have been.

C. Regulations and Guidelines

Most industrial countries have laws governing the use and welfare of animals in research laboratories, although standards differ significantly. Britain was the first nation to enact legal protection for animals in the laboratory with its 1876 Cruelty to Animals Act. Its current regulations, set out in the Animals (Scientific Procedures) Act of 1986, are also the most thorough. The law covers all scientific procedures that may cause pain, distress, or lasting harm to any living vertebrates (other than humans, who are protected under other laws). Strict rules are also given for licensing, care of animals, laboratory facilities, and inspection. Additional limits are placed on the number of procedures a single animal may undergo, and researchers are required to cite benefits of the research and explain why nonanimal alternatives cannot be used instead. However, some animal protectionists have criticized the law for being vague on the requirement for alternatives and for favoring "pet" animals, such as dogs, cats, and primates. Increased attention on laboratory animals in the 1980s also led to other countries enacting protective legislation; for example, West Germany and France both

strengthened earlier laws in 1986 and 1987, respectively. Australia, Canada, and most of the European community have adopted legislation of a comparable standard. Eastern European countries and the former Soviet states have not maintained effective national legislation of this standard, but that situation may be changing with greater integration into the European community.

The U.S. Laboratory Animal Welfare Act of 1966 (now simply referred to as the Animal Welfare Act) was primarily a result of public outcry over reports of theft of pets for sale to laboratories. Coverage in the popular media, including a major story in *Life* magazine, resulted in a massive response, and this issue generated more mail to Congress than either Vietnam or Civil Rights during this period. The 1966 law has been strengthened through amendments in 1970, 1976, and, most significantly, 1985.

One major element included in the 1985 amendments is the requirement that each research facility using species covered by the Act establish an Institutional Animal Care and Use Committee (IACUC). The members must include a veterinarian, a practicing scientist, and, most notably, a "community member" who is not affiliated with the research facility. Requiring a representative from outside the research field helps to ensure that the public's concerns about treatment of animals are present. The acknowledgment here is that it is not only the concerns of researchers that matter in making ethical decisions. The committee oversees inspection of facilities and reviews all research proposals that use protected species; approval is necessary for the experiment to be carried out. Policies in some countries, including Australia, Germany, Denmark, and Switzerland, specifically provide for representation on oversight committees from animal welfare groups.

One serious deficiency in the U.S. legislation is that it does not specifically protect rats and mice, which make up the majority—80 to 90%—of animals used in research and testing. The law gives the Secretary of Agriculture authority to include additional species, but so far no Secretary has done so. Because of limited federal funding and the substantial cost of enforcement it is unlikely that any Secretary will act differently in the near future. The Humane Society of the United States and the Animal Legal Defense Fund brought a lawsuit against the USDA for this "arbitrary" exclusion. A district judge ruled in favor of these organizations in 1992, but on appeal that decision was reversed on the claim that they had no legal standing as they had not been injured themselves by the policy. This ruling limits the possibility for success of other similar legal actions in the United States on behalf of nonhuman animals.

Some have argued that those species most closely related to humans require additional legislative protection; in particular, the controversial use of chimpanzees in AIDS research has focused attention on primates and the conditions in which they are kept. The nonhuman great apes—including chimpanzees, orangutans, and gorillas—have been the subject of an international movement for a more inclusive "community of equals" that would grant those species certain basic legal rights currently enjoyed only by humans. Imprisonment, torture, and killing of these animals for any purpose would be prohibited and penalized, and medical procedures and experiments would have to be carried out within limits similar to those set for human subjects. Continued pressure has encouraged more sparing use of these animals, but the proposal to grant them such fundamental legal rights remains controversial.

A significant amount of research in the United States is affected by the Public Health Service policy which applies to all facilities receiving funding from agencies of the PHS, including the National Institutes of Health, the Centers for Disease Control and Prevention, and the Food and Drug Administration. These requirements are set out in the *Guide for the Humane Care and Use of Laboratory Animals,* and they set standards for research facilities, veterinary care, and other items. First introduced as voluntary recommendations in 1963, the guidelines were made into law in 1985 as part of the Health Research Extension Act.

Regulations have been enacted not only to protect the welfare of animal research subjects, but also to protect scientists and the research enterprise. The rules governing IACUCs, for example, also impose penalties on members who violate confidentiality by passing on information about research proposals or laboratory procedures to unauthorized persons. Additionally, the Animal Enterprise Protection Act of 1992 imposes penalties specifically for activities such as breaking into a research facility or removing research animals. The original bill, stronger than what passed into law, was opposed by some groups who were concerned that it would discourage or penalize whistle-blowers who legitimately exposed welfare violations. The law is new and its effectiveness (and fairness) remains to be seen.

III. IRRECONCILABLE DIFFERENCES?

A. Pain and Distress

Pain, suffering, distress, and fear all involve subjective elements, and thus they are not easily measured. One can sometimes observe the cause of pain in someone else, such as an injury. In fact, pain is often vaguely defined as a form of discomfort resulting from injury or disease. However, one cannot directly experience another person's pain. And some feelings of pain do not directly result from physical injury, as they may be caused by emotional distress. The difficulties in measuring such phenomena do not justify denying their existence, but they have been a source of ongoing debate among scientists, animal protection advocates, and policy-makers.

Descartes' mechanistic view of animals did not attribute to them the ability to experience pain or distress of any kind, but attitudes have changed somewhat. The development of evolutionary theory in the nineteenth century helped to reduce the perceived gap between humans and other animal species. Yet scientific understanding of how animals experience pain has remained poor, and so debate over animal awareness has continued. There has also been disagreement over where the burden of proof rests. Some have argued that scientists have not successfully "proved" that nonhuman animals can feel pain, and therefore researchers should not be concerned about the cries or resistance animals may exhibit. Others have responded that in the face of uncertainty scientists ought to rely on the evidence they *do* have for animal awareness.

In particular, Rollin (1989) has argued that we already do attribute states of pain, suffering, and awareness to nonhuman animals on a regular basis. In fact, without doing so we would fail miserably in predicting and explaining their behavior. For example, we explain a dog's flight when he sees a stick that was used to beat him yesterday by saying "the dog remembers the painful experience and fears that it will occur again." Likewise, we have little understanding of how humans experience pain or fear, but we do not hesitate to attribute such states to them. Of course, other humans resemble ourselves more closely on a physical basis. But to have evidence that animals experience similar states they need not be identical to humans, only analogous in relevant ways. Hence, for animals that exhibit behavioral signs of being in pain and that have substantially developed nervous systems it is reasonable to conclude that they do share these experiences. Understanding of animal awareness has progressed substantially in recent years due to the growth of the discipline of cognitive ethology.

While some have argued that greater mental capacity makes humans more vulnerable to experiences of suffering, it also allows them to understand their predicament. One could argue that distress is often much worse for animals playing the role of experimental subjects.

Most human subjects can be informed of the experimental procedure and be assured that they will experience only a brief period of discomfort. Nonhuman animals, on the other hand, may experience substantially greater fear and distress because of their lack of understanding of the situation. Hence, even a harmless procedure may be highly stressful. For this reason special attention is required to minimize stress and ensure comfort of animal subjects.

The enactment of animal protection laws and public concern over treatment of animals shows that most people do believe that animals can experience pain and distress. And attitudes within the scientific community have changed significantly in recent years. No one *wants* to see animals suffer, and the consensus is that pain is generally something to be avoided. In this sense at least, all groups ultimately want to see an end to animal experiments that involve pain or procedures that do not contribute to the animal's health. But there are many interests involved, and animal suffering is sometimes defended on the grounds that it serves some other competing interest, such as human health. Where groups differ, as Rowan (1984) has noted, is over the time scale for eliminating use of animals in research and in how aggressively this end should be pursued.

Some nations, including Britain, Sweden, the Netherlands, and Canada, have incorporated pain scales into their legislation as a way of prioritizing welfare concerns for situations where substantial pain or suffering is involved. An experiment that required only a small blood sample would not raise the same concerns as one that involved the production of cancerous tumors. For example, the British law distinguishes between mild, moderate, severe, and prohibited procedures. Efforts to incorporate similar elements into U.S. law have failed, but the USDA census form for animal use does require that information about pain and use of anesthetics be given. According to this data in recent years more than 90% of animals used either were claimed to experience no pain or distress or were given anesthesia. Additionally, some policies, such as the 1990 Australian Code of Practice for the Care and Use of Animals for Scientific Purposes, require that researchers assume that their animal subjects experience pain in a manner similar to humans.

B. Animal Rights and Animal Welfare

Given that animals do experience pain and distress what are our obligations toward them with regard to experiments? This is where the debate and lack of consensus is strongest. It is not simply a matter of whether to use animals as experimental subjects or not, as there are a number of different views about where such use may be permitted and who should be authorized to make decisions about permissibility. Three distinct views will be presented here as an overview, but other intermediate positions have been advocated as well, and the divisions between these views are themselves a subject of debate.

Some groups have recognized that guidelines are helpful to encourage concern for the interests of experimental subjects, but maintain that formal laws are likely to be more of a hindrance to research. These advocates of self-policing support the sets of voluntary guidelines produced by government agencies and research organizations, but they are likely to oppose new legislation. They maintain that scientists who work with animals in the laboratory are best equipped to monitor the well-being of subjects. And while suffering is to be avoided, some experiments require inducing pain in animals; hence, any general regulations restricting certain procedures may prevent scientists from performing valuable experiments. For these self-policing advocates the potential benefits of medical knowledge usually outweigh the interests of nonhuman animals. This position is often defended by those known as "proresearch" groups; however, that name is misleading because most animal protection advocates support medical research that does not use animals or is carefully regulated.

Those commonly referred to as animal welfarists do support strict federal regulation of care and conditions for experimental animals. While they concede that some use of animals is acceptable in research, they maintain that all use must be carefully regulated by law. This view differs from that of the self-policing advocates who oppose such laws because the costs of compliance may place a financial burden on research centers. Animal welfarists also maintain that nonscientists can play a role in decisions about the appropriateness of a proposed experiment. For example, animal welfarists support the use of committees comprised of both scientists and laypersons to oversee all animal use. Current laws, such as the U.S. Animal Welfare Act and its amendments, do impose some such restrictions.

The primary concerns of animal welfarists are that treatment of animals meets certain basic criteria and that the experiments performed fulfill a clear and justifiable goal. Hence, researchers must both testify to the importance of their experiments and provide details of the procedures. Current laws in many countries set standards for items such as veterinary care and use of anesthetics for protected species. Animals may also suffer stress if they are prevented from exercising natural behaviors and movements; hence, laws set standards for cage sizes and surrounding environments. Some laws also prohibit unnecessary multiple surgical procedures on the same animal.

A third view, the animal rights position, opposes virtually all use of animals in research, whatever the benefits of that research may be. In this view animals have certain intrinsic rights that should be guaranteed. While rights that apply to humans are not always relevant to animals, those that are should give nonhuman animals equal standing in those respects. Hence, as we would object to performing unnecessary surgeries on humans for research purposes, we should similarly object to performing such procedures on animals. Animal rights advocates also oppose any killing of animals, however painless, unless it is done in the animals' interest (such as to quicken an unpreventable and painful death). Hence, they may accept the practice of dissection if the animals used were not killed for any human purpose. These groups are often critical of welfare laws because they feel that the regulations do not go far enough; instead, they would like to see an immediate end to animal experimentation. While they support improved care and conditions for animal subjects, they maintain that such measures are merely interim improvements that fail to relieve the true injustice. Hence, the divide between animal rights and animal welfare can seem as wide as that between animal welfare and self-policing.

As noted already, additional views exist, and what is popularly called the animal rights *movement* does not consist only of animal rights theorists. For example, utilitarianism, whose advocates include philosopher Peter Singer, does not grant animals (or humans) inviolable moral rights, but it does require that animal suffering is counted as equal to human suffering. Like the animal rights theorists, utilitarians are critical of welfare laws that allow painful procedures to be carried out on nonhuman animals that would not be permitted for human experimental subjects.

C. Justifying Animal Research

For those in the middle ground who hold that some animal experimentation is acceptable, given that it is carefully monitored, the difficulty is in deciding *which* procedures are acceptable. Even those opposed to regulations governing experimental practice may be critical of experiments that do not seem to serve any useful purpose. As a child would be discouraged from torturing a cat "to see what would happen," researchers are likewise discouraged (by their colleagues and the general public) from doing the same. In order for inflicting pain or death on animals to be justified (for those who

think it is justifiable) there must be some benefit that comes out of it. But what are these benefits and who is equipped to measure them?

One extreme position has argued that *all* past therapeutic developments were dependent upon animal research. This argument from history then concludes that animal experimentation must be a necessary component of any future medical advance as well. However, this is a difficult claim to defend, as many public health improvements, for example, resulted from observation of humans outside the laboratory. A milder version of this argument asserts that many significant advances would have occurred much later, or not at all, without experimentation on animals, concluding that many people would have missed out on valuable therapies. For so-called "basic research," which improves understanding of fundamental biological mechanisms, the benefits may seem particularly vague and distant, but some argue that it is this fundamental investigation that leads to major breakthroughs, as with the development of antibiotics. The opposing extreme makes an issue of instances where researchers have been misled into following a false hypothesis through results given by animal experiments. Yet such false trails are occupational hazards of science in general.

Particular cases, such as the discovery of insulin, have been debated back and forth, with opposing sides either extolling or downplaying the historical role of animal experiments. However, it is unrealistic to attempt to calculate how long a particular discovery might have taken if history had progressed differently, or how many humans would have suffered as a result. What one can maintain is that over the long run animal experiments have played a substantial role in the development of new therapies, and they are likely to continue to do so for some time. With increasing efforts into finding nonanimal alternatives for many procedures this role may decrease in the future.

So how are decisions to be made about which experiments justify use of animals? Should laypersons have a voice in deciding the value of answers to a particular research question? There is no reason to think that scientists are better equipped to weigh values than nonscientists are. Nonscientists may have well-developed concerns about the suffering imposed on animals, and they may decide that a lesser goal (such as development of a new cosmetic) cannot justify that suffering. However, some decisions necessarily rely upon expert knowledge. For example, poorly designed experiments can be objectionable because they do not confer the benefits of *reliable* information, and scientific expertise is required to assess quality of experimental design.

D. Risks and Reliability

Some who oppose use of animals in research, as well as some who do not, have noted that significant differences between members of different species call into question the reliability of extrapolating nonhuman animal results to humans. Animals are used in experimental science as models for human diseases; the assumption is that they are similar enough to humans that results observed in them can be assumed to hold for humans as well. The nonhuman species used need not resemble humans in every way, but only in those ways that are relevant for the experimental outcome. For example, rats differ physiologically from humans in many ways, and some of these differences affect how they react to various drugs, but the process by which cancerous tumors grow is much the same in both species. Hence, observing tumors in rats may provide useful information about cancer in humans.

However, when the claim being tested is much more human-specific, results from nonhuman animals are less reliable. Suppose a researcher wants to know what the effects are of this *particular* drug at this *particular* dose in humans. The effects of a drug in the body are dependent upon innumerable factors that interact in complex ways. In fact, that is why harmful side effects generally cannot be predicted without observing the effects of a substance on a whole animal. However, this complexity also means that small differences between members of different species can result in radically different responses to the drug. Likewise, small chemical changes in the drug given can provoke very different responses. Therefore, even if nonhuman animals have usually exhibited similar responses to humans in the past, it cannot be assumed that the same will hold for any new substance. LaFollette and Shanks (1996) discuss these concerns in detail. Sometimes, however, particular differences are desirable, as when rabbits were used for the Draize test *because of* their particularly sensitive eyes.

There are ethical issues involved here as well. First, how much risk of side effects to humans is permissible in drug testing? No method of testing (even testing on other humans) *guarantees* that the drug will be safe for *you*. But the requirements for approval of new drugs, particularly in the United States, are quite stringent, involving many tests of different kinds. The concern, though, is that these risks are not calculable, so that it is impossible to tell any individual how likely they are to be harmed by the drug. Secondly, the philosopher Peter Singer (1990) has presented an ethical dilemma for animal experiments. If one admits that the animals used really do resemble humans in fundamental ways, then it becomes difficult to justify subjecting them to treatment that we would never subject humans to without informed consent. But if one admits that humans differ in essential ways from other species, and therefore hold special rights and privileges, then the extrapolation of experimental results to humans is called into question. Proponents of animal use are likely to reply, however, that animals may be similar in physiologically relevant ways without being similar in morally relevant ways. Thus, these debates are destined to continue.

IV. THE FUTURE

Much work has been done in recent years into more humane and nonanimal alternatives to experimental procedures. While there have been numerous successes, most scientists feel that procedures using whole animals remain a necessary part of the research enterprise. However, advocates of alternatives have countered that alternatives could be developed more readily if additional incentives were provided. It is unlikely that use of animals will be replaced easily, but continued investigation into alternatives may provide the best hope for resolution for these difficult debates. Hence, it is worth saying a bit more about these efforts.

The antivivisection movement had subsided after the first decade of the twentieth century, and concerns about animal welfare were replaced by fears of unsafe products and environmental toxins by the middle of the twentieth century. In 1957 W. M. S. Russell and R. L. Burch, both British scientists concerned with reducing the suffering of animals in laboratories, co-authored *The Principles of Humane Experimental Technique*. They offered their "Three Rs" as a model: Replacement of animals by insentient material, Reduction in the number of animals used, and Refinement of procedures to reduce animal suffering, such as anesthetics. However, their call for more humane science did not lead to immediate results in the development of alternative methods. Since the 1960s animal protection advocates have pushed for increased research into alternatives, but they had little success until the 1980s.

In 1981, under the umbrella of the Cosmetic, Toiletry and Fragrance Association, a group of companies feeling pressure from animal protection advocates provided a 3-year, $1 million grant to establish the Center for Alternatives to Animal Research at the Johns Hopkins University School of Hygiene and Public Health. Two federal laws in 1985, the Health Professions Educational Assistance Act and the Health Research Extension Act, made provisions for federal funding and coordination of research into alternatives. In addition to pressures from activists, scientific developments in the 1970s strengthened the case for the replacement of certain animal tests, such as technical methods for working with tissue cultures and the Ames test for mutagens. The high cost of using animals also increased incentives for the development of alternatives, which were frequently much cheaper to carry out. Recent developments in molecular biology show promise for continuing this trend of replacing whole animals with blood and tissue samples and cell cultures. The current challenges include validating new tests, demonstrating their reliability as replacements in a variety of scenarios, and encouraging their acceptance in place of traditional animal tests for regulatory purposes.

While some old animal procedures are being replaced, new ones are being discovered, and these new avenues of experimentation will probably become the focus of future ethical and policy debates. One such avenue is the use of transgenic animals that are genetically modified to carry a gene from another species. Researchers claim that the ability to give animals traits belonging to other species, including humans, will expand the possibilities for using them as models of human disease. Additionally, some researchers hope to use organs from transgenic animals for human organ transplant operations. Developments in biotechnology may also lead to the development of insentient animals—animals not capable of feeling pain or suffer-ing—which would present additional moral and regulatory challenges. The long term success of these avenues remains unclear, and the future is complicated by the numerous ethical issues they raise. The enduring hopes and fears engendered by medical technology ensure that debate is likely to continue.

Also See the Following Articles

ANIMAL RIGHTS • HUMAN RESEARCH SUBJECTS • RESEARCH ETHICS

Bibliography

Baird, R. M., & Rosenbaum, S. E. (1991). *Animal experimentation: The moral issues.* Amherst, NY: Prometheus Books.

Blum, D. (1994). *The monkey wars.* New York: Oxford University Press.

Donnelley, S., & Nolan, K. (Eds.). (1990). Animals, science, and ethics. Special supplement to the *Hastings Center Report.* (Vol. 20, pp. 1–32).

LaFollette, H., & Shanks, N. (1996). *Brute science: Dilemmas of animal experimentation.* New York: Routledge.

Orlans, B. F. (1993). *In the name of science: Issues in responsible animal experimentation.* New York: Oxford University Press.

Rollin, B. E. (1989). *The unheeded cry: Animal consciousness, animal pain, and science.* New York: Oxford University Press.

Rowan, A. (1984). *Of mice, models, and men: A critical evaluation of animal research.* Albany: State University of New York Press.

Rupke, N. A. (Ed.). (1987). *Vivisection in historical perspective.* New York: Routledge.

Singer, P. (1990). *Animal Liberation* (2nd. ed.). New York: Avon Books.

ANIMAL RIGHTS

Evelyn Pluhar
The Pennsylvania State University

GLOSSARY

ethology The study of nonhuman animal behavior from an evolutionary and comparative perspective.

homocentrism The view that human beings are the only, or the primary, bearers of moral rights. Also known as "anthropocentrism."

moral agents Beings capable of understanding and acting upon moral principles.

morally significant beings Beings who are proper subjects of moral agents' concerns.

moral rights Justified claims against moral agents by or on behalf of morally considerable beings, e.g., noninterferene and assistance.

moral rights, basic Moral rights shared by all highly morally significant beings, e.g., the right to life, and the right not to be tortured.

moral rights, nonbasic Moral rights held by a subset of morally considerable beings, e.g., the right to freedom, and the right to equal job opportunity.

moral rights, *prima facie* Rights that may justifiably be overridden; e.g., a morally significant being's right not to be made to suffer may be overridden by moral agents if suffering is required to save the being's life.

sentient beings Beings capable of having experiences, including pleasurable and painful experiences.

speciesism The view that moral weight should be given to species membership as well as to the individual attributes of a being.

utilitarianism The view that moral agents have one fundamental obligation, viz., (roughly) to maximize nonmoral value ("utility," which has most often been identified with happiness or preference satisfaction).

ANIMAL RIGHTS would entitle certain nonhuman animals to respectful treatment by moral agents. As far as is known at present, human beings alone are capable of understanding and acting upon moral principles—i.e., of being moral agents—so it is they who would be obligated to treat, and refrain from treating, nonhumans in specifiable ways. If these nonhumans have moral rights, it follows that they are morally significant beings. It does not follow that they would have the same rights as any given human, however. Nonbasic moral rights such as the right to an education or to equal job opportunity, or the right not to be coerced into employment, are held only by those beings with the capacity to exercise those rights. Different humans may have widely different nonbasic rights; the same would hold for dogs, cows, tigers, and the like, in comparison to typical adult humans. Beings who are equally morally significant (e.g., a child and a typical human adult) need not have the same nonbasic rights. They do share certain *basic* rights, however, such as a right to life and a right not to be tortured. (Note that basic rights are *prima facie*— they are not claimed to be absolute or indefeasible. Moral agents' infliction of death or suffering upon one might be justified if it is one's own rational choice or in one's own best interests, or if moral agents cannot avoid such consequences when they act in self-defense.) The debate over animal rights is a debate about basic moral rights. Do any nonhuman animals have a *prima facie* right to life or a prima facie right not to be made to suffer at human hands?

I. THE UTILITARIAN ALTERNATIVE TO THE RIGHTS POSITION

One may hold that nonhuman animals have significant moral status without attributing rights to them, however. In fact, the contemporary philosopher who named and initiated the 20th century "animal liberation movement," Peter Singer, is himself not an advocate of nonhuman animal rights in the philosophical sense. Singer is a utilitarian. Roughly, utilitarianism is the view that moral agents have one fundamental obligation: to maximize nonmoral value ("utility," which has most often been identified with happiness or preference satisfaction). Singer traces the roots of his view to the original utilitarian, Jeremy Bentham (1748–1832), who held that society's goal ought to be the greatest happiness for the greatest number of individuals. Bentham held that any being capable of suffering (i.e., any sentient being) should have his or her experiences taken into account by utilitarian calculations. Thus, the overall utility that would be generated by a given action determines the rightness of that action. By contrast, rights theorists hold that the rightness of an act is not exhausted by the act's consequences. Individuals with basic moral rights ought to have those rights respected by moral agents, even if the sum total of happiness generated might be less than would result if those rights were violated.

Since Bentham's day, many sophisticated variations on classic hedonistic utilitarianism, which identifies utility with pleasure and disutility with pain, have been proposed. Some versions are pluralistic (identifying utility with a variety of goods, not merely with pleasure) rather than hedonistic; moreover, not every type of utilitarianism identifies rightness with the utility produced by an *act*. One might focus instead on the utility generated by following a given rule, or by following a rule that would be generally accepted by society. In his later writings, Singer himself proposes "preference utilitarianism," which stipulates that, at least for self-conscious beings, satisfied preferences, and not jut unreflective pleasures, are equivalent to utility.

It is beyond the scope of this entry to discuss the ramifications of different utilitarian theories for the moral status of nonhuman animals. This much may be said, however: According to rights theorists, any version of utilitarianism, no matter how carefully conceived it is, fails to provide sufficient protection for innocent life, human or nonhuman. Therefore, the philosophical nonhuman animal rights movement, led by Tom Regan (1983, *The Case for Animal Rights*, U. of California, Press: Berkeley), is opposed to utilitarianism.

II. CURRENT USES OF NONHUMAN ANIMALS

Let us now return to our question of whether nonhuman animals have a *prima facie* right to life or a *prima facie* right not to be tortured. Plainly, the practices of raising and killing nonhumans for food, furs, research, education, and product testing presume that nonhumans have no significant right to life. Sport hunting and trapping make the same presumption. One might hold that some animals have no serious right to life but do have a right not to be tortured. Currently, many animals used for the above purposes are subjected to conditions that would be very painful to humans. Some of the pain caused is often defended as an unavoidable consequence of procedures that are claimed to be of paramount importance to human life and health. This position is compatible with the attribution of some rights to nonhumans: one might hold that they have a *prima facie* right to humane treatment that can be overridden by the need to preserve allegedly more morally significant lives. However, no such justification is possible when the pain is avoidable or the purpose nonessential for human welfare. Those who nonetheless defend such practices as confining calves to 2-ft-wide crates or five hens to life in a cage the size of a folded newspaper, or who see nothing wrong with crushing the chest of an animal caught in a leghold trap or with beating circus animals, are assuming that these beings have no right to humane treatment at all.

Many nonhuman animals are routinely consumed for a variety of purposes. Most are killed for food. The U.S. Department of Agriculture estimates that over 7 billion animals are killed for food yearly in the United States, and this number does not include fish or seafood. Most of these animals are poultry that are raised in intensive confinement. Not all animals used for experimental and research proposes are reported, so precise figures are not available. The number is estimated at anywhere from 10 to 100 million annually in the United States. Although fewer animals are killed for their fur than used to be the case, millions continue to be trapped or farmed for that purpose. Sport hunters kill about 200 million animals yearly in the United States.

Current practices, particularly in industrialized countries, reflect longstanding assumptions about the relative moral insignificance of nonhuman animals. Although humans have always made exceptions for those animals they come to care about, for the most part homocentrism underlies our use of many nonhumans. We have taken ourselves to be the primary, perhaps the only, morally significant beings on our planet. It is instructive to examine the roots of this presumption.

III. ROOTS OF ATTITUDES CONCERNING NONHUMAN ANIMALS

A. Religious Influences

Religions traditionally reflect and reinforce a culture's deepest ideals. The place of nonhumans in various religious doctrines is therefore quite revealing. The major religious traditions of the West and the East cannot be said to have attributed rights to nonhumans. Nonetheless, some of these traditions accord a higher moral significance to nonhuman animals than others do. Indeed, some, upon first glance, appear to be the opposite of homocentric. Some 3000 years before Christ's birth, the ancient Sanskrit *Vedas* spelled out the docrine of *ahimsa*, roughly translated as, "have no ill feeling for any living being." This doctrine continues to be fundamental to many Eastern religions, including Buddhism, Hinduism, and Jainism. Whlie many followers of these religions do exhibit much more respect toward nonhuman life than others, *ahimsa* is nontheless compatible with the attribution of different degrees of moral significance to varieties of living beings. According to some transmigration doctrines, a soul that is reincarnated as a nonhuman is a former human who is thereby being punished for misdeeds. This is a homocentric doctrine, though its implications for the treatment of nonhumans

are more favorable than is the case for straightforward Western homocentrism. *Ahimsa* has been interpreted to presuppose that a soul (either one world soul or many individual souls) changes bodily identities through a succession of lives, unless and until ultimate enlightenment is obtained. The chicken you eat may be your grandmother; the fly your grandchild swats 30 years from now may be you. Compassion toward living beings thus appears to be an extension of regard for oneself and one's human loved ones. This too is a homocentic doctrine. Moreover, this compassion is compatible with some killing for human purposes: the soul cannot be killed, according to such a view, and in fact the soul may be thought to be benefited if it is released to a worthier body. Thus, even followers of *ahimsa* could consistently support some forms of animal exploitation.

The Western religious traditions of Judaism, Christianity, and Islam have been less supportive of compassion toward nonhuman animals, though not all aspects are opposed to according moral significance to nonhumans. Holy writings have been translated and interpreted in a multitude of ways, and religious leaders have held diametrically opposed views on the moral status of nonhumans. Persons who use religion to buttress their views on nonhuman animal rights typically find quotations and practices that can be interpreted as they wish. To this day, observant Jews are not supposed to hunt for sport, but the Mosaic law included provisions for animal sacrifices to honor the deity or to expiate one's sins (see, e.g., Leviticus 19:20 for an Old Testament rendering of this custom). Jewish vegetarians and nonvegetarians argue passionately for their views, based on different understandings of sacred texts. Muslims can argue similarly, pointing to different passages in the Koran, and the same holds for Christians who take different views on the moral status of nonhumans.

Perhaps the best illustration of the different positions Christians may take on this issue are the wildly opposite views of St. Francis of Assisi (1181–1226) and St. Thomas Aquinas (1225–1274). Francis was an ascetic who called all creatures his brothers or sisters, going so far as to include farm animals as participants in his worship services. To this day, many Catholics and protestants commemorate his life by bringing their companion animals to church for the "Blessing of the Animals" ritual on the anniversary of St. Francis' death. Thomas, by contrast, was devoted to the meaty pleasures of mealtime (legend has it that he was so corpulent that a semicircular hole had to be cut in his table to enable him to reach his food), and convinced that nonhumans had no moral significance in their own right (for more on St. Thomas' position, see the next section). Adherents of Western religions do not speak with one voice on moral matters, which is not surprising.

Homocentrism is the dominant theme in Western religious traditions, however. One much-discussed passage, Genesis 1:26, makes this explicit: "And God said, let us make man in Our image, according to Our likeness; and let them rule over the fish of the sea and over the birds of the sky and over the cattle and over all the earth, and over every creeping thing that creeps upon the earth" (1978. *The Ryrie Study Bible,* New American Standard Translation, translated by Charles C. Ryrie). Some argue that this implies that nonhumans exist only for human convenience and may be treated in any way whatever; others interpret it as meaning that God is giving humans "stewardship" over nonhuman animals, requiring us to use them responsibly rather than giving us carte blanche. Regardless of which way the passage is construed, it implies that the writer or writers of this verse believed humans to have a privileged moral place in creation. Those who do not regard the verse as a mere expression of human egotism debate about the special respect in which humans may resemble the deity. Do humans resemble the eternal being by having an immortal soul, albeit a finite one, as many believe? Is this the source of our alleged moral preeminence? If it is, it would be no minor matter to establish the existence of such souls, let alone their exclusive instantiation in human beings. Empirical evidence for such a claim is lacking. If holy writings make the claim, it does not follow that the claim must be true. Every holy text proclaims itself to be authoritative, not surprisingly. Whatever the truth may be, there is in fact no evidence that the author(s) of the passage believed that humans alone have immortal souls. In various passages of the Bible, souls, however "soul" may be understood, are attributed to every living being and not just to human beings, and "souls" are nowhere denied to nonhuman animals. Moreover, as Cardinal (later "Saint") Bellarmine (1542–1621) pointed out, if it were true that only humans have *immortal* souls, it would seem that the infliction of pain on nonhumans would be even *more* morally reprehensible than making human beings suffer, because they could not be compensated for their undeserved pain in an afterlife. Thus, the frequently held belief that humans alone have immortal souls is not only unsupported, it is irrelevant to the issue of nonhuman moral significance.

Other theists hold that humans resemble God by being the only rational or intelligent creatures, finite though those capacities are. Some, in fact, identify the rational capacity with the possession of an immortal soul. Could this be a major morally relevant difference

between humans and nonhuman animals? Such was St. Thomas Aquinas' contention. Since the belief that human rationality gives us a higher degree of moral significance than nonhumans is often given secular expression, let us now address Thomas' arguments in a broader context.

B. Traditional Philosophical Views on Human and Nonhuman Animal Moral Significance

St. Thomas' chief philosophical inspiration was a pagan philosopher: Aristotle (384–322 B.C.). Aquinas made it his life's work to reconcile Aristotle's writings with holy scriptures and their interpretations by church fathers. "The Philosopher," as Thomas always called him, attributed souls to all living things, but these souls were ordered from lowest to highest: the nutritive, the appetitive, the sensory, the locomotive, and the intellectual. Aristotle held that each soul a step higher on the scale retained the lower souls' capacities. Not surprisingly, the intellectual soul got the pride of place. Only humans (though not all of them!) could have such souls: "In none but him [man] is there intellect" (Aristotle, *The Parts of Animals,* Book I, Chapter I, 641b, translated by Richard McKeon in *The Basic Works of Aristotle* [1941], Random House, New York, p. 649). Beings with "irrational" souls were "inferior," he believed, and therefore properly subservient to their superiors. Hence the rational should rule the irrational, which were created by nature to serve the former. "Wild beasts," then, existed for human purposes. Half a millennium later, Immanuel Kant (1724–1804) expressed the same view:

> Now I say that man, and in general every rational being, exists as an end in himself and not merely as a means to be arbitrarily used by this or that will.... Beings whose existence depends not on our will but on nature have, nevertheless, if they are not rational beings, only a relative value as means and are therefore called things. (Kant, I., *Grounding for the Metaphysics of Morals,* pp. 35–36, translated by Ellington, J. W., 1981. Hackett Press, Indianapolis.)

Aristotle took his views to have similar implications for "irrational" humans, who ought to be slaves of their "superiors."

Aquinas added his own interpretation of the scriptures to "the Philosopher's" views, substituting "God" for "nature." "The divine likeness" between humans and God proclaimed in Genesis 1:26 is intellect, and "dominion" of humans over beasts is interpreted as the proper rule of the rational over the irrational. The latter have no values as such in God's eyes; they exist purely for the purposes of rational beings (Aquinas, *Summa Contra Gentiles*, Third Book, Part II, Chapter CXII, excerpted in Regan, Tom, and Singer, Peter [1989], *Animal Rights and Human Obligations*, Prentice-Hall, Englewood Cliffs, NJ, pp. 6–9). Although Thomas did not use the language of rights, his view entails that humans alone can be morally significant. No nonhuman animals, he explicitly tells us, can be wronged by humans, regardless of what is done to them. How does Thomas reconcile his views with the parts of the Bible that appear to enjoin kindness to beasts and birds? Ingeniously, he postulates that cruelty to nonhumans can only be wrong if it indirectly wrongs the only morally significant creatures: humans. One either damages someone's (perhaps one's own) property, or, more significantly, becomes more likely to practice cruelty against humans. Kant expressed the same view.

Many criticisms have been raised against Thomas' discussion of cruelty. Perhaps the best way to dramatize misgivings would be to imagine the following situation. Suppose that the neighbors' retarded child is playing by himself in their yard. Presumably, all agree that it would be wrong to use the child for target practice. According to Aquinas' account, however, it would be wrong because either (1) one is damaging one's neighbor's property without their consent or (2) one's action may make it more likely that you will target your rational neighbors next. Something seems seriously amiss with this account. One is instead inclined to believe that the child would be the chief victim of one's action. He is, after all, not an unattended mechanical toy, but an innocent sentient being. Why should his lack of rationality disqualify him from moral consideration? Is not the child's ability to suffer a morally relevant characteristic? If so, sentient nonhumans can also be wronged.

René Descartes (1596–1650) offered a way out of the above dilemma. He proposed that beings who are not rational are incapable of suffering. He held that nonhuman animals are merely organic machines without consciousness, unlike humans, who allegedly are amalgams of material bodies and immaterial minds (souls). Though he claims he does not deny that nonhuman animals are capable of sensation, he is denying that they can suffer. Since a nonhuman's "sensation" is supposedly not present to a mind, no experiences can result. It follows that one cannot be cruel to such a being, any more than one could be cruel to a heat-

seeking missile when one blows it out of the sky. "Thus," he reasoned, "my opinion is not so much cruel to animals as indulgent to men ... since it absolves them from the suspicion of crime when they eat or kill animals" (Descartes, R., "Letter to Henry Moore," reprinted in Regan, T., and Singer, P., 1989. *Animal Rights and Human Obligations*, p. 19 Prentice–Hall, Englewood Cliffs, NJ).

Descartes argues for his machine model of nonhuman animals by pointing out that (1) conscious beings are capable of language, whereas "beasts" are not, and (2) nonhuman animal behavior is in no way indicative of thought (Descarts, R., "Discourse on Method," Fifth Part, in *Discourse on Method and Meditations*, translation. Louis LaFleur [1960, p. 42], Bobbs-Merrill, New York. Both the premises and the inference from those premises have been roundly criticized over the years. Despite the fact that Descartes' argument has seemed implausible to many, more than a few scientists have accepted its conclusion, arguing that nonhuman animals are govered by instinct and stimuli, having no consciousness to link outside forces and mechanical responses. Some philosophers have also recently defended neo-Cartesian denials of nonhuman suffering. These new arguments have also been thoroughly criticized. Even if the Cartesian and neo-Cartesian arguments had withstood all the counterarguments mounted against them, however, an implication disturbing to many would follow: "irrational" humans, e.g., infants, would be incapable of suffering and thus have no right not to be tortured. (Until the mid-1980s, standard medical practice actually presumed this—babies were denied anesthesia even during major surgery.) Is cruelty to infants really an impossibility? How different are such humans from other animals?

IV. SIMILARITIES BETWEEN HUMANS AND OTHER ANIMALS

Humans and nonhuman animals are not very different at all, according to evolutionary theory. Unlike Aquinas and Descartes, Charles Darwin (1809–1882) saw humans as part of the animal world, with mental attributes that might be more complex but not fundamentally different from those possessed by other animals. Here we have a secular version of St. Francis' vision of the family of living beings. If all life on earth has a common origin, with differences explainable in terms of the interaction of chance events and natural selection, as evidence overwhelmingly indicates, it would be extraordinarily unlikely for humans to be the only creatures capable of consciousness. Brain activity is, of course, associated with various conscious as well as nonconscious processes. A look at the human brain itself reveals a tripartite structure: the reptilian brain, shared by all vertebrates and correlated with territoriality, homing, and mating; the paleomammalian brain or limbic system, shared by all mammals and intimately associated with emotions; and the neomammalian brain, present in more recently evolved mammals and closely connected to problem-solving and the like. Ethology, the field devoted to the study of nonhuman animal behavior from an evolutionary and comparative perspective, is rife with observations of behaviors that seem irreducible to mindless responses. Donald Griffin, the ethologist famous for discovering the principles of bat navigation, suggests that "versatile adaptability of behavior to changing circumstances and challenges" is strong evidence for consciousness (Griffin, D., "Ethology and Animal Minds," reprinted in Regan and Singer, 1989, p. 54). There is every indication that humans are not the only animals who behave as if they learn from experience. Even behaviorists assume that nonhumans can learn from experience; indeed, they take dogs, pigeons, rats, etc., to be good models for human learning. Ethologists appeal to Occam's razor: it is far more difficult to explain complex behaviors such as tool-making (a skill that must be taught to baby chimpanzees by their elders) without the assumption of consciousness than it is to hypothesize problem-solving abilities. Similarly, behavior we associate with pain in ourselves in circumstances that would indeed be quite painful to us is most economically explained as a response to pain sensations. The same applies to apparently joyful, fearful, or angry behavior.

The one capacity some humans have that might not be shared by nonhumans is the ability to make moral judgments. As far as we know, humans alone are capable of moral agency. However, here too we see evidence of continuity between our species and others. Moral agency does not spring from nowhere; it has its psychological basis in a capacity we share with a number of other animals. The ability to *empathize*, to put oneself in another's place, is necessary if one is to take moral account of the other's concerns. Humans are not the only animals apparently able to imagine the situation of another. Apart from observations by ethologists in the field and anecdotal evidence associated with companion animal behavior, apparently empathetic responses have been elicited by experiments. Philosopher James Rachels has discussed Northwestern University experiments in which a substantial majority of rhesus monkeys faced with the choice of going hungry or delivering a powerful shock to a conspecific in the next cage chose to go hungry, even for days at a time. Indeed, such behavior is sympathetic, not merely empathetic. Small human children are likewise capable of such behavior, although they are not moral agents. Once more, the dilemma for opponents of nonhuman animal rights surfaces: if moral agency is thought to be required for the possession of basic moral rights, quite a large number of humans would be morally insignificant. If we make no such requirement, the moral significance of a large number of nonhumans cannot be excluded.

In dealing with one another, moral agents take sentience, the ability to experience pleasure and pain, to be highly relevant to moral decision making. When we consider the consequences of our actions for others, we take account of their preferences, their goals, and whether they can care about what happens to them. Neurophysiological evidence indicates that all vertebrates are sentient, that all beings with limbic systems (i.e., all mammals) are capable of emotion, and that adult mammals, at least, are able to act purposefully. If the characteristics mentioned are morally relevant, what follows about the attribution of basic moral rights to nonhumans?

V. POSSIBLE POSITIONS ON MORAL RIGHTS FOR HUMANS AND CERTAIN NONHUMANS

It is plausible to hold that moral rights should be related to the capacities certain beings might have. Rocks can hardly be said to have a right to life, and plants cannot be said to have a right to humane treatment. When we look at humans and at many nonhuman animals, as we have seen, it is difficult to find a morally relevant capacity shared by all humans and only by humans. In the case of capacities directly related to rationality, we find a difference in the complexity of the capacity—a difference in degree, if you will—among species *and* among humans. We do not find a fundamental difference in kind that sets humans (some of them!) apart from all nonhumans. With regard to sentience, it is not even clear that there is a difference in degree. We have no good reason to deny that a cat—or, indeed, a human baby—subjected to a strong electrical shock experiences essentially the same pain as an adult human. Can any moral conclusions be drawn from the neurological and behavioral similarities noted above? Three moral positions are consistent with these facts.

A. Denial of Basic Rights to All

One could conclude that humans and these other animals have no moral rights at all. Philosopher Mary Midgley quotes Mortimer Adler, who sees the following implication:

> If it were to be established by some future investigations that animals differ from men only in degree and not radically in kind, we would then no longer have any moral basis for treating them differently from men, and, conversely, this knowledge would destroy our moral basis for holding that all men have basic rights and an individual dignity. (Midgley, M., 1983. *Animals and Why They Matter*, p. 139. Univ. of Georgia Press, Athens, GA)

Current evidence supports the contention that the "if" clause is fulfilled. Adler's presupposition is that nonhumans are of no moral significance; therefore, if humans are not *fundamentally* different from members of another species, they too lack such significance. Since Adler's presupposition is the very one under dispute, one need not at all draw the implication that he does.

B. Affirmation of Equal Basic Rights to Humans and Certain Other Animals

One might just as well conclude that humans and the other animals that share morally relevant properties with them are equally morally significant, possessing the same *prima facie* basic moral rights. Albert Schweitzer (1875–1965) accepted a radical version of this view, embracing the ethic of reverence for life. Attributing the will to survive to every living organism, Schweitzer took this quality to be necessary and sufficient for full moral significance: "[The ethical person] does not ask how far this or that life deserves sympathy as valuable in itself, nor how far it is capable of feeling. To him, life as such is sacred" (Schweitzer, A., "The Ethic of Reverence for Life," reprinted in Regan and Singer, 1989, p. 33). Here we see a Western version of the principle of *ahimsa*. An equal rights position is compatible with killing in self-defense, if no other option is open to us (pace pacifism). However, if I respect you right to life and you are not a threat to me, I cannot eat you or experiment upon you without your consent, even if I would otherwise die. If I do this anyway, by eating nonconsenting plants, or by testing antimalarial medicines on guinea pigs before giving them to humans, I am acting wrongly. Schweitzter, a vegetarian who fought mosquito-borne diseases in equatorial Africa by, among other measures, using test anmals, committed what he called "crimes against animals" (and plants, presumably, in the case of vegetarianism). As moral agents we can try to lessen (but never eliminate) what he calls our "guilt" by killing only when human life or health is at stake, by doing so as humanely as possible, and by succoring other life forms as best we can in all other circumstances.

Schweitzer's biocentric ethic is implausible, at least on the face of it. Does one commit a moral crime against a carrot by eating it? Or against crabgrass by plucking it out? Or against meadow plants if we let the occasional cow graze upon them? Is it truly equally criminal to cut flowers for our pleasure and to torture a puppy for amusement? After all, we, the puppy, and the cow are sentient, able to register painful experiences; plants are not. It does seem that we, who have feelings and would really mind starving, are more significant morally than poor "murdered" carrots. One can agree with Schweitzer that one should not squander life by destroying it without reason without also believing that every living thing has an equally strong claim to life. One may adopt the equal rights position without making it quite so global. One might hold that all sentient beings have basic moral rights. This position too is open to challenge. Thus, once again, we find that an equal rights position is not the only conclusion one can reach that is compatible with the similarities between humans and certain nonhumans.

C. The Unequal Rights Position

One can hold that the apparently higher degree to which humans are rational, creative, intelligent, and morally concerned entitles us to more rights than other animals. Sentient nonhumans might have the right to humane treatment, for example, but not the right to life. Another example of an unequal rights position would be the view that sentient nonhumans have some *prima facie* right to life, making it wrong for moral agents to kill them frivolously or maliciously, but a right to life which is weaker (i.e., more easily overrideable) than that which humans possess. For example, if a human needs a baboon liver transplant, the human's need overrides the life of the baboon, but a sports hunter who kills a baboon to make ash trays out of its hands would be violating the baboon's right to life. Schweitzer's suggestions that we not kill or harm animals unless human health or life is at stake, and that we carry out these actions humanely, can now be placed in a different context. These are not ways of partially mitigating crimes against beings equal in moral significance to humans—they are morally justified actions, respectful but cognizant of differences in moral significance.

An unequal rights position has been implicit in the credos of many humane organizations. The American public has become increasingly sympathetic to this position, if we are to believe an Associated Press poll released in December 1995. With a margin of error of plus or minus 3%, it showed that 66% of the 1004 American adults polled agreed that "an animal's right to live free of suffering should be just as important as a person's right to live free of suffering." This is supportive of a right to humane treatment for humans and sentient nonhumans alike. Moreover, the same percentage expressed its distaste for killing animals to test cosmetics, 59% rejected the killing of animals for their fur, and 51% opposed sport hunting. The common thread here is disapproval of killing for frivolous purposes (new cosmetic formulations, vanity, and sport). Majorities nonetheless support experimentation on nonhumans that is beneficial to humans, as well as subsistence hunting. Most also continue to eat meat, perhaps believing that it is necessary for human health, as nutritionists taught in the past. (Even the U.S. Department of Agriculture, no defender of nonhuman rights, has recognized that this is erroneous, but it is still widely believed.) The unequal rights position, if consistently acted upon, would result in better conditions for laboratory and farm animals. To some extent, this has already occurred.

If, of course, one takes the position that there is some fundamental morally relevant difference between at least most humans and all nonhuman animals, one can make a case for restricting basic moral rights to the former. Aristotle, Aquinas, and Descartes held this view. However, none of them were particularly successful in making a case for such a defining difference, and empirical evidence on humans and nonhumans suggest that we will continue to have little luck in finding one. How, then, does one choose among the rights views listed above?

VI. BASIC MORAL RIGHTS: THE DEBATE

A. How Not to Decide Who Has Basic Moral Rights

Although he is a utilitarian rather than a rights theorist, Peter Singer made the following powerful point in his early writing on animal liberation: Our decision about who is entitled to such rights should not be based on morally irrelevant characteristics. Historically, powerful humans have assigned rights on the basis of race, gender, sexual orientation, religion, ethnicity, ideology, class status, wealth, and the like. These are classic forms of bigotry. If two individuals differ primarily in terms of race, gender, etc., they should not be treated differently morally. This does not mean that they should be treated in identical ways—only women can receive pregnancy benefits. Singer puts it this way: individuals' interests, whatever they may be, should receive equal consideration (assuming, of course, that those interests do not include the violation of others' rights).

B. What Justifies the Presumption That Living Humans Have Equal Basic Moral Rights?

Let us assume for now that living humans have the same basic moral rights. What could justify the ascription of these rights to them? Several different proposals have been made.

1. The Moral Agency Argument

Philosopher and animal rights opponent Carl Cohen holds that moral rights are restricted to humans because

> [rights] are in every case claims, or potential claims, within a community of moral agents. Rights arise, and can be intelligibly defended, only among beings who actually do, or can, make moral claims against one another. Whatever else rights may be, therefore, they are necessarily human; their possessors are persons, human beings. (1986. The case of the use of animals in biomedical research. N. Engl. J. Med., Oct. 2, 865)

Philosophers of political theory are not the only proponents of this argument. An entry in The Catholic Dictionary, for example, states that humans alone can have basic moral rights because "these [rights] can belong only to persons, endowed with reason and responsibility."

What reason are we given to accept the premise that moral agents alone can be said to have rights? Philosopher H. J. McCloskey, among others, takes this to be true simply by definition, holding that only moral agents can coherently be said to possess basic moral rights. Ann S. Causey and Alan White have also claimed that it is logically impossible for nonhumans (none of them moral agents) to have rights. On the fact of it, this is a doubtful claim, implying as it does that those who do support the ascription of moral rights to nonhumans are literally contradicting themselves. Causey, however, cites philosopher Paul Taylor's classic environmental ethics book, *Respect for Nature*, in support of her contention that it is logically impossible for beings who are not moral agents to have rights. Ironically, Taylor himself points out how erroneous the definitional claim really is. He grants that there is a *traditional* concept of moral rights that does indeed apply only to moral agents, but, he stresses, this is not the only concept of rights that enjoys wide currency. According to another concept of rights, one need not be a moral agent to be a rights-bearer. Beings with a welfare, e.g., infants, have the *prima facie* right not to be harmed. Obviously, this "modified" concept is the one in use in the animal rights debate, or, indeed, in any discussion of children's rights.

It is just as well that one need not contradict oneself when one ascribes basic rights to beings who are not moral agents. Although it is highly relevant to the issue of moral *responsibility* to ask if a killer was capable of understanding the gravity of the deed, one may well wonder why moral agency should be thought to be necessary for moral *significance*. If this were the case, babies, older children, psychotics, and other mentally disadvantaged humans would possess no moral rights. The moral agency argument for rights actually contradicts the assertion that living human—not just some of them—have basic moral rights. (As we shall see, however, some opponents of nonhuman animal rights are willing to accept this implication.)

2. The Higher Intelligence Proposal

One might hold that humans are more morally significant than nonhumans because their higher intelligence makes their lives more intrinsically valuable. Intelligence is not denied to other animals, but its lesser degree (as far as is known to us) is held to warrant either the denial altogether of basic moral rights to nonhumans or the attribution of fewer basic moral rights to them than to humans. The latter position is identical to the "unequal rights" view sketched earlier.

What reason can be given in favor of such a view? It may seem self-evident that greater intelligence leads to greater moral significance. After all, it results in a more complex life and a more variegated hierarchy of preferences—an altogether richer way of experiencing and influencing the world. Such a life has more value in itself, one might hold, than the far simpler existence possible for the less aware.

On the other hand, as Paul Taylor has argued, one might be suspicious of the high value we place on a characteristic that is so closely linked to our species. Is it surprising that humans should value most what is most identified with ourselves? This can hardly be called a disinterested point of view. While this observation does not show the higher intelligence proposal to be false, it does shake one's confidence in its alleged self-evidence.

This much certainly can be said: Anyone who believes that all living humans have basic moral rights unmatched by any that nonhumans might possess must reject this account of the basis of those rights. If one's degree of intelligence largely determines one's moral significance, some nonhuman animals would be more significant morally than some members of our own species. Chimpanzees, even dogs or cats, are more intelligent than some unfortunate humans. Moreover, the view implies that more intelligent humans would possess more rights, or stronger rights, than those who are less well endowed mentally. This implication has been accepted by some, most notably Friedrich Nietzsche, but it is not a position that can consistently be held by advocates of equal (basic) human rights.

3. The Humanity Proposal

One can, finally, retreat to the position that all and only living humans have basic moral rights precisely because they are human. This is the standard homocentric view. The difficulty raised by such a view, as Singer has pointed out, is arbitrariness. Why should the characteristic of being human be any more relevant morally than being white, or male, or heterosexual?

Homocentrism is a variety of "speciesism." Speciesists think it is morally permissible to discriminate between two otherwise similar individuals who differ in terms of species membership. The term was coined by Richard Ryder and popularized by Singer himself, who characterizes it as "a prejudice or bias in favor of the interests of one's own species and against those of members of others species" (Singer, P., 1990, *Animal Liberation* 2nd ed., p. 6. Random House, New York). Speciesism, thus construed, is no more defensible than racism and sexism. James Rachels terms this position "unqualified speciesism." Can the humanity proposal be buttressed by a more defensible concept of speciesism? Rachels distinguishes "qualified speciesism" from its prejudicial cousin. A qualified speciesist holds that species membership, in itself a morally irrelevant property, is correlated with characteristics that are morally relevant. But do all humans possess morally relevant characteristics lacked by all nonhumans? The findings of ethology and moral psychology, as discussed earlier, suggest a negative answer to this question. Rachels arrives at this answer himself, concluding that human and nonhuman characteristics overlap instead of being mutually exclusive.

Other attempts have been made to show that species membership can be a morally relevant characteristic. In particular, it has been argued that any members of a species whose typical adults are moral agents should have full moral rights, even if they themselves are incapable of moral agency. Thus, a mentally handicapped human could be accorded maximum moral significance while a mentally equivalent chimpanzee would be denied it—without prejudice. Moreover, a nonhuman who is more intelligent than a human could justifiably have her organs "harvested" to save the life of that human, other things being equal, so long as her species—unlike the human species—is not characterized by moral agency.

Attributing full basic moral rights to moral agents is not controversial, given one of our standard concepts of moral rights. But how can advocates of this variety of "qualified speciesism" justify the extension of those rights to beings who are not moral agents, although they belong to moral-agency-characterized species? Various defenses of this extension have appealed to charity, potential, misfortune, kinship, and the like. Each such argument has been strongly challenged. Unless a case can be made for according moral rights on the basis of membership in a species characterized by moral agency, regardless of one's own capacities, this version of speciesism also fails to account for human rights.

4. The Sentience Proposal

The search for a lowest common denominator to justify the ascription of equal basic moral rights to living humans leads one to the sentience proposal. This was Peter Singer's original suggestion, although he is not a proponent of rights theory. Sentient beings are capable of having experiences and preferences, and they seem able to care about what happens to them, on however primitive a level. If we accord basic moral rights to them on this basis, consistency requires us to include all sentient beings within the sphere of moral consideration, regardless of their species. Moral agents should not deprive other sentient beings of life or well-being if self-defense does not demand it or if those beings' own best interests are not served by such actions (euthanasia, for example, might be in a being's best interests).

Any human who is not irreversibly insentient would have maximum moral significance in this view, so would any such nonhuman. It is unlikely in the extreme

that bacteria and sponges, for example, are sentient, and overwhelmingly probable that mammals and birds are; indeed, it is probable that all vertebrates are. Other animals are far less likely to be sentient. Empirical science is the best guide to which beings are probably capable of having experiences.

The sentience proposal forces homocentrists to examine their moral consistency. If living humans who are not irreversibly incapable of having experiences have equal basic moral rights, then so do many nonhuman animals.

C. Do All Sentient Humans Have Basic Moral Rights?

It does not follow from this that all sentient humans do in fact have basic moral rights. One may be consistent in more than one way. Bernard Rollin has argued that the current "consensus morality" accords moral significance on the basis of interests rather than rationality. Given these moral presuppositions, he holds, it could not be justified to deny significant moral status to sentient nonhumans, since they have interests too. However, some philosophers challenge that consensus morality. Rather than accept the implication that some nonhuman animals have basic moral rights *because* all sentient humans have them, they reject the premise. For example, R. G. Frey holds that only *some* humans (and *no* nonhuman animals) are entitled to basic moral rights. Frey's view has been held by many people in the past, including Aristotle, and it is increasingly popular today among philosophical opponents of nonhuman animal rights.

Frey argues that highly complex rational beings have more valuable lives than simpler beings do. He does not shy away from the implication that "infants, defective humans, and animals" may be killed in circumstances that would not justify the killing of "normal adult humans" (Frey, R. G., 1987. The significance of agency and marginal cases. *Philosophica* 39(1), 40). He expresses no enthusiasm for the consequences regarding nonrational humans; quite the contrary. Nevertheless, his consistency leads him to say,

> I remain a vivisectionist, therefore, because of the benefits medical/scientific research can bestow. Support for vivisection, however, exacts a cost: it forces us to envisage the use of defective humans in such research. (1988. Moral standing, the value of lives, and speciesism. *Between Species* 4(3), 197)

Clearly, such a view cannot be called "speciesist." Mentally disadvantaged humans as well as nonhumans are evenhandedly denied significant moral status.

Proponents of human, let alone nonhuman, rights owe philosophers like Frey an argument. A case should be made for the attribution of basic moral rights to all sentient humans. Let us now briefly look at the lines of argument that can be taken.

Tom Regan, author of the classic *The Case of Animal Rights* (1983. Univ. of California Press, Berkeley), argues that nothing less than his view, which attributes basic moral rights to "subjects-of-lives," i.e., to beings who have lives that "fare well or ill for them, logically independently of their being the object(s) of anyone else's interests" (p. 243), provides a satisfactory moral theory. Such a theory must be consistent, have an adequate scope, be precise, be simple, and conform to our reflective intuitions about rightness and wrongness. Subjects-of-lives have beliefs and preferences, even if only on a rather low level; clear cases, he holds, include normally developed mammals of at least 1 year. According to Regan, all subjects of lives, regardless of their varying mental capacities, have "equal inherent value" (i.e., equal moral significance), and that value requires moral agents to accord them maximum respect. In short, all of them, independently of their species and their value for moral agents, have equal basic moral rights. However, Regan's opponents might respond that he has biased the case against them by construing the criteria for an acceptable moral theory as he has done.

Philosopher Steve Sapontzis has made a major contribution to this debate. He argues that "three everyday moral goals," i.e., developing moral character, increasing total happiness in the world, and fairness, are advanced when nonhumans are included in the sphere of moral concern. By the same token, including sentient humans who are not moral agents would also further these goals. Sapontzis is neutral between utilitarianism and rights theory in making his case, appealing more to the advancement of virtues than to principles of obligation. He contends that, given the ubiquity of these goals, the burden of proof is on opponents of nonhuman animal rights to make their case. (The same would hold for those who, like Frey, find themselves denying rights to "defective" sentient humans).

Another way of making a case for the rights of beings with preferences, even if they are not capable of moral agency, takes its inspiration from the philosopher Alan Gewirth, although he would not endorse its extension to nonhuman animals. The argument pertains to any being capable of acting to achieve goals (i.e., to any agent).

As an agent, one has basic interests in and desires for life, health, and general well-being. Because one wants and needs these things, one also thinks that others should at the very least not interfere with one's trying to get them; i.e., one holds that others must not interfere. This is tantamount to one claiming the right to noninterference in these regards. What justifies one's insistence is the fact that, as an agent, one cannot live and thrive unless these desires can be fulfilled. But if this is what justifies one's insistence, then consistency requires one to respect others' pursuit of their goals, for they too cannot otherwise live and thrive. Thus, the argument goes, all agents should be accorded basic moral rights. Empirical psychological and ethological evidence supports the contention that numerous nonhumans and humans are agents, even though they may not be capable of the abstract conceptual thought required for *moral* agency. Now, what about humans and nonhumans who have desires and needs, as agents do, but who are unable to fulfill their desires on their own? Individuals who are too young or too physically or mentally impaired to be agents still have desires and needs that they want satisfied (e.g., food, water, warmth, shelter, and love). The fact that they cannot achieve these goals on their own does not mean that they have no rights; it means that they need more assistance than noninterference. Babies, children, many accident victims, the severely mentally retarded, the insane, and the senile are sentient nonagents. So are some very young and relatively simple nonhuman animals. If reflective agents must, to be consistent, accord rights to others with desires they want to have fulfilled, all sentient nonagents who have preferences should likewise have rights accorded to them.

As the debate about human and nonhuman animal rights continues, further responses and counterresponses to the above approaches will undoubtedly be made.

VII. IMPLICATIONS FOR THE TREATMENT OF SENTIENT NONHUMANS

If it is the case that all sentient beings have basic moral rights, many standard human practices are morally unjustifiable. Inhumane treatment of nonhumans on factory farms, in laboratories, and in the wild would not be permissible. Moreover, and far more fundamentally, we would not be entitled to treat any sentient being, no matter how humanely, as a mere commodity. If it is impermissible to confine humans for the purpose of food consumption, research, or product testing, it would be equally impermissible to do the same to sentient nonhumans. Conversely, if it is ever acceptable to kill a human being, it would be acceptable in similar circumstances to kill a sentient nonhuman (e.g., in self-defense).

Currently, animal rights activists are debating about the best strategies to pursue in order to change traditional uses of animals, from outright abolition to a more gradual approach. Opponents of nonhuman animal rights are fighting such attempts philosophically and politically. Each side needs to take the others' arguments very seriously indeed, for a great deal depends on who is right.

Also See the Following Articles

AGRICULTURAL ETHICS • ANIMAL RESEARCH • ANTHROPOCENTRISM • RESEARCH ETHICS • RIGHTS THEORY • SPECIESISM • UTILITARIANISM

Bibliography

Baird, R., and Rosenbaum, S. (1991). *Animal experimentation: The moral issues.* Buffalo: Prometheus Books.

Bekoff, M., and Jamieson, D. (1996). *Readings in animal cognition.* Cambridge, MA: MIT Press.

Carruthers, P. (1992). *The animals issue.* Cambridge: Cambridge Univ. Press.

Finsen L., and Finsen, S. (1994). *The animal rights movement in America: From compassion to respect.* New York: Twayne Publishers.

Griffin, D. (1992). *Animal minds.* Chicago: University of Chicago Press.

Hill, J. L. (1996). *The case for vegetarianism.* Lanham, MD: Rowman and Littlefield.

Mason, J., and Singer, P. (1991). *Animal Factories.* 2nd ed. New York: Crown.

Pluhar, E. B. (1995). *Beyond prejudice: The moral significance of human and nonhuman animals.* Durham, NC: Duke Univ. Press.

Rachels, J. (1990). *Created from animals.* Oxford: Oxford Univ. Press.

Rollin B. (1989). The Unheeded Cry: Animal Consciousness, Animal Pain, and Science. Oxford: Oxford Univ. Press.

Rosen, S. (1987). *Food for the spirit.* New York: Bala.

ANTHROPOCENTRISM

Tim Hayward
University of Edinburgh

GLOSSARY

anthropocentrism Concern for human interests to the exclusion of nonhumans; interpreting the world in terms of human values.

anthropomorphism Ascription of human characteristics to nonhuman beings.

human chauvinism Discrimination against nonhumans on grounds that are not rationally justified.

humanism A philosophy that asserts the intrinsic worth of humans and their capacity for fulfillment through a life governed by reason.

misanthropy Hatred or mistrust of humankind.

speciesism Discrimination on the basis of species when species is not the morally relevant criterion.

ANTHROPOCENTRISM literally means human-centeredness. In applied ethics the term describes attitudes, values, or practices which promote human interests at the expense of the interests or well-being of other species or the environment.

Traditional justifications for anthropocentrism have tended to emphasize distinctive characteristics of humans—such as having a soul, rationality, or language—that set them apart from the rest of nature and make ethics an exclusively human matter.

Criticism of the factual basis of anthropocentrism has come from natural scientific findings which undermine humans' former views of themselves as the center of the universe, the purpose of creation, or the "measure of all things," showing them instead to be a product of natural evolutionary processes, to have considerable affinities with other creatures, and to have a vulnerable dependence on ecological conditions of existence.

Ethical criticism of anthropocentrism in part draws the consequences of the scientific critique: if humans can no longer be thought to occupy a special and privileged position in the world, this calls into question their prerogative to use natural creatures and the environment however they see fit. The critique also captures increasingly widespread moral intuitions that many creatures are relevantly similar to humans and that other natural phenomena have value in themselves and not merely for us.

Thus the principled objections to anthropocentrism find increasing application in practice. Many human practices can be criticized on these grounds, including those which involve cruelty to animals, destruction of habitats, endangering species, and upsetting ecosystemic balances.

Nevertheless, there are also practical problems involved in avoiding anthropocentrism: a concern with human interests is in some ways inescapable and legitimate; applied ethics also has to deal with "hard cases" where vital human interests oppose those of nonhumans. There are also conceptual difficulties: some stem from the paradox that whereas overcoming anthropocentrism in science is achieved by increasing humans' cognitive detachment from the rest of nature, that very detachment may reinforce humans' disregard for nonhuman nature; others stem from the recognition that there are limits to how much humans can actually know about what is good for nonhumans.

Some of these difficulties can perhaps be overcome by drawing distinctions between types of anthropocentrism, for instance, between "strong" forms which are rejected because they involve unjustifiable human preferentiality and "weak" forms which are accepted because they allow only the unobjectionable features. Other difficulties might also be avoided by using a more extensive and nuanced range of terms—including such ideas as speciesism and human chauvinism—to characterize morally unacceptable ways of relating to the nonhuman world. The main purpose of the general critique of anthropocentrism is to get as clear a view as possible of what humans' obligations are in relation to nonhuman nature.

I. TRADITIONAL JUSTIFICATIONS FOR ANTHROPOCENTRISM

Anthropocentrism is the view that ethics is and must be an exclusively human affair, and that it is neither possible nore desirable to include nonhumans in the moral community. A number of considerations can be adduced to justify this position.

In the history of Western thought, the view that humans have a prerogative to use other creatures and the rest of nature as they see fit for their own benefit goes back a long way. One enduring source of support for this view has been the idea of the "great chain of being," which can be traced from Plato and Aristotle through Plotinus to Aquinas, who ordered types of being according to their degree of perfection, descending from God, through the angels, to humans, with animals and plants below them. The ethical corollary was that less perfect beings should be subordinated to more perfect ones.

Religious sources underpinned this idea; in particular, the Judaic, Christian, and Islamic doctrine of creation has fostered the belief that humans were made in the image of God and share in God's transcendence of

nature, and that the whole natural order was created for their sake. Even if in granting humans "dominion" over other creatures God did not intend them to disregard the attendant obligations of responsible stewardship, it remains the case that humans are seen as superior beings on earth.

There are also secular sources of the idea. Indeed there is a sense in which anthropocentrism can be opposed to theism: without a belief in God, humans are thrown back on their own devices, with no ultimate guarantees for knowledge or values, and can only reason as if they are the center of the world. Thus Protagoras' famous saying that "man is the measure of all things" captures the idea that people can only know that which they have the faculties and capacities to become acquainted with, and so whatever objective reality might be, reality *for us* is only such as one's mind makes it. In ethics this translates into the view expressed in Hamlet's remark that "there is nothing either good or bad but thinking makes it so." In the present context, the relativism of such sayings can be taken to refer to the idea that whatever truths—scientific or ethical— might be available to humans, they are truths valid for humans and for humans only.

Whatever their source, justifications for anthropocentrism generally appeal to characteristics of humans that mark them off from the rest of the natural world. Theists, for instance, have tended to emphasize the uniqueness of the human soul, and while they believe this is because "Man is made in the image of God," the substance of their beliefs about the human mind or spirit does not necessarily differ from that of secular thinkers. Thus the view that humans are uniquely rational beings, and that this constitutes their greatest perfection, is held not only by theologians like Aquinas, but also by more secular philosophers like Kant and atheists in the humanist tradition. Claims for human uniqueness therefore do not have to rest on appeals to divinely bestowed privilege, and philosophers have brought forward various sorts of evidence for the absence of the requisite rationality in beings other than humans.

The absence of language in other creatures indicated an absence of thought that was deemed decisive by Descartes, for instance, and Kant shared the view that language, or the manipulation of symbols more generally, was required to form the concepts which are necessary for rationality. That other creatures do not form concepts is also indicated by the fact that they do not appear to formulate intentional plans, a point illustrated by Karl Marx when he wrote that "what distinguishes the worst architect from the best of bees is that the architect raises his structure in imagination before he erects it in reality." Perhaps the most salient point about humans' unique ability to form intentions is that these can be morally good or bad.

Accordingly, the justification for anthropocentrism which is of most direct ethical significance is that it appears to be the case that only humans participate in ethical deliberations. Whether or not this is because humans, uniquely, have a capacity for moral agency, the fact seems to be that humans generally do not and cannot view other creatures as having any moral obligations, either toward one another or toward humans. It is argued, for instance, that it makes little sense to say that a cat does moral wrong in tormenting a mouse, since we do not suppose that the cat has a moral sense. Humans, then, uniquely, are the addressees of moral imperatives; only of human conduct, dispositions, or motivations is it appropriate to make moral judgments of good and bad, right and wrong. Other creatures, let alone plants or rocks, cannot do or know right and wrong. If they have no conception of right and wrong, furthermore, they are not in a position to make any moral claims against humans. This also presents an obstacle to humans unilaterally assuming unreciprocated obligations toward them: certainly, it is hard to apply the Golden Rule—"do unto others as you would have them do unto you"—if the others are so constitutionally different as to render the necessary comparison impossible.

Because of this radical asymmetry between moral agents and the rest of nature, it can be argued not only that anthropocentrism is justified, but also that to try and avoid it would be a mistake—both in practice and in principle. It would be a practical mistake since it is natural for members of one species to care about others of their own species: we do not criticize a cat for being cat-centered, so why should we criticize humans for being human-centered in this sense? Just as it would be absurd and unwarranted to think that a wild animal should care about human welfare, so is it to think that humans should direct attention from members of their own species to others. Thus if some cultures have evolved as hunters, for instance, they are not for that reason immoral. More generally, all humans consume other living entities in order to reproduce their bodily existence, and humans in all cultures must use nature in various ways in order to survive. It would also be a principled mistake to try and completely overcome anthropocentrism, for even if one is motivated to care about the fate of nonhuman entities, there are limits to how successful one might be, for there are limits to possible human knowledge of what is really good for

them, so that at best one has an unreliable, anthropomorphic, view of their good, and, at worst, such a misguided view that in trying to do good one in fact does unrecognized harm.

Rather than try to set the nonhuman world to rights, it may therefore be argued, humans would do better to concentrate on their own moral improvement, recognizing that ethics is a peculiarly human affair, concerned with right human action; if they do this, it might further be argued, they are then liable to do less harm to other beings, but for reasons connected with their own moral development. Thus an argument for anthropocentrism which many take to be decisive is that if humans become truly human-centered—in the sense of making a conscientious effort to understand themselves and their place in the world—this will yield an enlightened self-interest which provides a firmer and more reliable basis for the good treatment of nonhuman beings. Both Aquinas and Kant, for instance, believed that cruelty to nonhumans is wrong because it can foster a habit of cruelty more generally—something that is bad for humans to develop in any circumstances. Relatedly, these days it is argued humans should exercise prudence in the use of natural resources, seek to preserve species, biodiversity, and so on, for reasons that derive from their own enlightened self-interest. In short, humans have to recognize that because they live in one world with the rest of nature, if they make things go badly for its other constituents, things will ultimately go badly for them too. This view, moreover, has motivational advantages compared with attempts to appeal to an altruistic concern for nonhumans "for their own sake," regardless of their interrelation with humans.

II. CRITICISMS OF ANTHROPOCENTRISM

Despite the force and appeal of arguments justifying anthropocentrism, they are not without their problems.

To begin with, the basic presumption of human dominion on earth is the product of just one sort of cosmology; there are religions and cultures which take a quite different view: Buddhists, Hindus, and Jains, for instance, have a humbler estimate of the human place within nature and a greater solicitude for other living beings. Other cultures, including many native American ones, view the earth itself as a living conscious being to be treated with respect.

Anthropocentric assumptions are also challenged by modern science, which casts a less exalted light on the human place within nature. The idea of the great chain of being, for instance, was already revealed to be inadequate as a scientific schema in the light of the taxonomy of species put forward in the 18th century by Linnaeus—the natural historian credited by some as one of the founders, or at least founding inspiration, of the science of ecology. Further, not only is an evolutionary picture of interspecies relations more complex, it is in principle different from the teleological view usually implied by the great chain of being. Thus Charles Darwin, in *The Origin of Species,* provided evidence to refute the idea that nature exists to serve man, arguing that "natural selection cannot possibly produce any modification in a species exclusively for the good of another species."

The evolutionary view also tends somewhat to undercut claims for the uniqueness of certain human faculties and characteristics. Thus while no one would deny that humans have a particularly highly developed capacity for reason, language, and social relations, such capacities are not entirely absent in the nonhuman world. It is no longer a matter of serious scientific controversy that some animals—especially, but not only, the great apes—have social relations and are capable of thinking and even manipulating symbols. Furthermore, it is also worth recognizing that some distinctively human capacities themselves can be viewed as species-specific ways of doing things that members of other species also do in their way.

Recalling that humans are natural beings also reminds us that morality has to do with the realm of their natural being too, and that many ethical principles are intended to protect and preserve humans in their bodily existence: for utilitarians, indeed, pleasure is the highest principle; for human rights theorists, freedom from physical abuse is among the most fundamental rights. Furthermore, among humans, even those taken to lack full rational capacities—such as children and mentally disadvantaged people—are generally held to have justifiable moral claims. What this illustrates is that having the capacity of moral *agency* is not a necessary condition for being morally considerable as a moral "patient." This consideration undermines the argument that only humans can be due moral consideration. There is thus today a growing tendency to believe that moral consistency requires us to avoid harmful treatment of nonhuman beings wherever the harm is relevantly similar to a harm that would be wrong if inflicted on a human being.

Quite generally, then, just as radical differences between humans and other creatures are undermined by scientific evidence of common characteristics, so the reasons for ethically privileging humans are also undermined. There is no longer any unassailable reason to assume that only what befalls humans matters morally.

How this conclusion differs from that of an enlightened anthropocentrism is in supplying reasons for giving moral consideration to nonhumans, quite independently of whether that will also be in humans' own long-term best interest. The enlightened self-interest defense of anthropocentrism, moreover, could be criticized for an overoptimistic, and unwarranted, assumption that human and nonhuman interests ultimately coincide. In the light of this criticism, a more determined attempt to deprioritize the claims of humans may be required.

III. ALTERNATIVES TO ANTHROPOCENTRISM

Given that there are general arguments both for and against anthropocentrism in principle, it is useful to consider more specific questions about anthropocentrism in practice. For whether or not a sufficiently enlightened view of human interests may ultimately yield reasons for adequate consideration of nonhuman interests, there remain more immediate questions about what such consideration might consist of.

The reason why anthropocentrism is often criticized by environmental ethicists is that many human practices today do appear to put concern for human interests, and even for relatively trivial human preferences, above any consideration of nonhuman interests. Thus anthropocentrism appears as a problem to be solved. To understand it, therefore, means understanding what those other interests are. Certainly the idea of interests cannot be taken in too strict a sense, but it is certainly not meaningless to speak of interests of animals, or even plants, in broad terms of "unimpeded development of species capacities": since living entities are capable of flourishing, or doing badly, it is not unreasonable to impute to them "an interest" (albeit not necessarily a conscious one) in the former rather than the latter. It is more problematic to speak in equivalent terms of ecosystems, but it is perhaps not impossible, given that they too exhibit development.

Avoiding anthropocentrism in practice, therefore, means focusing on loci of value other than humans and their interests. Alternative focuses include individual creatures; living things in general, both as individuals and collectively; and ecosystems in their totality.

A. The Value of Individual Creatures

One way of overcoming anthropocentrism with respect to individual creatures is to move in the direction of sentientism. This means giving moral consideration to the interests of any sentient being—that is, any being capable of experiencing pleasure or pain, which includes all or most animals—and accepting that they have a moral claim like that of the interests of humans considered as sentient beings. What this means in practice is, first and foremost, that one is morally committed to opposing the cruel or inhumane treatment of animals. Two groups of practices which arouse particular censure are intensive stock rearing ("factory farming") and animal experimentation (vivisection), since the suffering these inflict are quite clearly not in the animals' interest. Depending on the view one takes of animal capacities, it may also be required to go beyond this and have regard for animals' social, psychological, and emotional lives. Thus many animal liberationists also argue against zoos, circuses, dolphinaria, and so on. Some animal rights campaigners go further and require an end not only to clear-cut abuses of animals, but to any *use* of them whatsoever. The grounds for this sort of prohibition goes beyond sentience to Tom Regan's "subject of a life" criterion of moral considerability. Both the sentience criterion and the "subject of a life" criterion apply to some or all animals, but not to other life forms.

B. The Value of Life

This is the focus of biocentrism, which widens the scope of concern to include not only animate creatures, but all living entities, including plants. Just as sentient creatures have certain interests which do not reduce to those of their human owners or users, so too do living entities more generally. Robin Attfield argues of trees, for instance, that they share many capacities with sentient creatures—such as respiration, ingestion, growth, self-maintenance, and reproduction. Thus if the flourishing of sentient creatures is of value, it is hard to deny that the flourishing of trees is too. However, what this means in practice may be more difficult to discern. Pursued with all consistency, one would be committed to the "reverence for life" attitude of Schweitzer who considered each organism as an individual whose suffering or death were to be avoided if at all possible. The problem is that this is not always possible. Certainly it may sometimes be—for instance, in the avoidance of the wanton destruction of an individual tree—but since we have to use trees and other plants as resources in all sorts of ways, including as food for our own survival, how do we tell when it is wanton? It may seem that our reasons are liable to be anthropocentric ones.

Nevertheless, while there may be no easy answer to such questions, there is value simply in posing them, for this means one no longer takes it for granted that human interests automatically and unproblematically can be pursued regardless of their impact on the rest of living nature. Furthermore, some of the questions can be answered. This is especially true when plants are considered not as individuals but as representatives of their species. Quite special issues arise from humans' ability to drive other species to extinction: as well as enlightened self-interest reasons for preserving biodiversity, as a genetic pool for possible future human use, there seems to many something qualitatively worse about extinguishing a species as opposed to killing an individual member of a species. There is thus a growing concern to conserve and preserve the habitats of endangered plant and animal species; even in the face of economic pressures to develop such lands, environmentalists' concerns are acknowledged to have moral weight. Indeed, as human understanding of the interrelationship between different habitats within the global environment increases, it is possible that more and more areas of relatively untouched land will be given priority over more immediate human interests.

C. The Value of Ecosystems

Ecocentrism casts the ethical net more widely still, extending moral consideration to ecosystems as a whole, including their abiotic constituents, and perhaps the cosmos more generally. Thus all natural phenomena, including rocks, mountains, and rivers, are considered deserving of moral concern. This might seem a very demanding requirement: in principle, every intervention in nature would have to be investigated for every possible ramification, which would lead to a paralysis for action. Nevertheless, ecocentric environmental philosophers, while possibly welcoming the implication that a brake should be put on human interventions in nature, have distilled certain general principles which they believe can serve as a workable guide to action.

Particularly influential is Aldo Leopold's "land ethic," whose basic principle is, "A thing is right when it tends to preserve the integrity, stability, and beauty of the biotic community. It is wrong when it tends otherwise" (1949. *A Sand County Almanac* (pp. 224–225). Oxford Univ. Press, London). Thus in considering whether to "develop" a piece of land, for instance, one must not merely consider what material or economic advantage might accrue to humans, but what the effects would be on the land itself. For Leopold, it is wrong for a farmer, in the interest of higher profits, to clear the woods off a 75% slope, turn his cows into the clearing, and dump its rainfall, rocks, and soil into the community creek. As Callicott adds, "it would also be wrong for the federal fish and wildlife agency, in the interest of animal welfare, to permit populations of deer, rabbits, feral burros, or whatever to increase unchecked and thus to threaten the integrity, stability, and beauty of the biotic communities of which they are members." (J. Baird Callicott (1993). The conceptual foundation of the land ethic. In Armstrong and Bozler (Eds.), "Environmental Ethics: Divergence and Convergence," p. 390. McGraw-Hill, New York.) In general, one should always be most cautious about interfering in the processes of ecological succession—for instance, by introducing exotic, domesticated, or genetically modified species into local ecosystems; by extracting energy from the soil and releasing it into the biota; or by damming or polluting water courses. There is also a cardinal duty to preserve what species we can, especially those predatory birds and mammals at the top of the "biotic pyramid."

The land ethic thus seems to be the most all-embracing alternative to anthropocentrism. But while it appears to encompass the concerns of biocentrism, there are respects in which it is also in tension with other nonanthropocentric value approaches, particularly those, like sentientism, which focus on the good of individual organisms. As was noted, preserving the integrity of an ecosystem can mean protecting it from certain animals, even at the cost of their welfare. In general, the holistic orientation of ecocentrism can often stand in opposition to any more individualistic concern, especially of the type characteristic of animal rights. A similar problem can arise within biocentrism, too, depending on whether it focuses on individuals, populations, or species, and, within the scope of animal concern, granting moral priority to individual animals generates no special case for the protection of members of endangered species. It thus seems that ecocentrism is in some ways opposed to concerns of other sorts of nonanthropocentrism, and that there are also tensions within and between the other alternatives themselves.

Ecocentrism may also be argued in some ways to be *consistent* with anthropocentrism. For while the land ethic officially values nature in and of itself, not for its benefits to humans or other species, its criteria of ecosystems' health nevertheless depend on human perceptions of "integrity, beauty, and stability." Other versions of ecocentrism, such as deep ecology, emphasize how humans should cultivate a relation of oneness with all that is, which in its own way also keeps humans squarely in the center of the picture. Finally, it is possible to argue that a major reason for preserving ecosystems is to preserve them as the life-support systems of humans and other species, which, as we have already noted, can be understood as a principle of enlightened human self-interest.

It therefore seems that a completely clear-cut and consistent rejection of anthropocentrism as such may be neither possible nor desirable. What also seems to be clear, though, is that a completely unbridled and unchecked anthropocentrism is unjustifiable. It may therefore be appropriate to try and draw more systematic distinctions between objectionable and unobjectionable aspects of anthropocentrism.

IV. DISTINCTIONS WITHIN ANTHROPOCENTRISM

It is helpful to distinguish between different types of anthropocentrism because while some sorts of treatment of nonhumans is morally wrong, some concern with human interests is not only unavoidable, but also unobjectionable in itself, and may even be positively beneficial for nonhumans too.

Anthropocentrism is unavoidable in the sense that anyone's view of the world is shaped and limited by their position and way of being within it: from the perspective of any particular being or species there are real respects in which they *are* at the center of it. Thus, to the extent that humans "have no choice but to think as humans," what Frederick Ferré calls "perspectival anthropocentrism" would appear to be inescapable. There is no reason, however, why this perspective should be one of hostility or even indifference toward other sorts of being. Thus it need not be objectionable in itself that we should be interested in ourselves and our own kind: humans, like members of any other species, have legitimate interests which there is no reason for them not to pursue. As Mary Midgley observes, "people do right, not wrong, to have a particular regard for their own kin and their own species." Furthermore, human centeredness may in some respects even be positively desirable: if, by analogy with "self-regarding virtues" in the individual case, being human centered means having a well-balanced conception of what it means to be a human, and of how humans take their place in the world, then it may exemplify the sorts of virtue associated with normative ideas of "humanity" and "humaneness." If, as various philosophers and psychologists have maintained, self-love, properly understood, can be considered a precondition of loving others, so, by analogy, it could be maintained that only if humans know how to treat their fellow humans decently will they begin to be able to treat other species decently. In sum, a positive concern for human well-being need not automatically preclude a concern for the well-being of nonhumans, and may in fact serve to promote it.

These considerations support the idea that human self-interest is legitimate, provided that it is sufficiently enlightened. This idea has been used by Bryan Norton to distinguish between "weak" and "strong" forms of anthropocentrism: strong anthropocentrism is objectionable because it allows the pursuit of immediate felt preferences even when this means taking an exploitative attitude toward nonhuman nature; weak anthropocentrism, however, because embodying the considered preferences of an enlightened self-interest, is capable of supporting environmental values and is thus defensible.

Nevertheless, the defense of weak anthropocentrism rests ultimately on the assumption that human interests, when adequately understood, coincide with the interests of nature more generally. This assumption may be justified in some circumstances. For instance, when an enlightened human interest in preserving a habitat, curbing pollution, or conserving resources coincides with interests of other species, anthropocentric motivations can then yield nonanthropocentric policies. It may also hold with regard to ending practices such as factory farming and the testing of cosmetics on animals if these are regarded as contrary to an enlightened human interest in a healthy and humane culture. But there are also situations where human populations need to clear other species off the land, or when a human need for basic subsistence leads to exploitation of natural resources, or when a human need for medicines can most readily be met by carrying out painful experiments on animals. In these situations the vital interests of human individuals and populations can be pitted against those of nonhumans. In these and similar "hard cases," one might expect a weak anthropocentrist's response to be indistinguishable in practice from that of a strong anthropocentrist. Certainly, only the weak anthropocentrist would perceive such cases as presenting a moral dilemma, but faced with a really hard choice, such as whether to allow an unpleasant experiment that promises to provide a cure for the cancer of a neighbor's child, even an enlightened anthropocentrist is likely to give preference to the child's interests, since doing otherwise would be misanthropic and go against the fundamental values of her position.

If weak anthropocentric principles can thus generate strong anthropocentric policies it may be helpful to introduce further criteria for identifying what is wrong with strong anthropocentrism, especially as, in practice, strong anthropocentrists could argue back from the hard cases to discredit the weak principles themselves.

One useful idea is that of "speciesism," introduced by Richard Ryder, in analogy with sexism and racism, and developed by Peter Singer. This refers to the arbitrary discrimination involved when humans are given preference merely because of their species membership, rather than for a morally relevant reason. It would be speciesist, for instance, to affirm that the suffering involved in physical torment matters morally in the human case but not in the case of nonhuman sentient beings. Unwelcome choices would still have to be made regarding the treatment of nonhumans, as they do in relation to human cases too, but the principles of the decisions could be set out in terms that are morally defensible and involve no slide into strongly anthropocentric values.

A strong anthropocentrist, however, might simply deny that any alleged similarities between humans and nonhumans are morally relevant, or argue that species membership is itself a morally relevant criterion. Someone who deploys such arguments cannot directly be accused of speciesism. The success of these arguments, though, depends on questions of fact and value that are essentially contestable. It is nevertheless possible to draw a general distinction between ways of addressing them in terms of where the burden of proof is placed. One can either assume prima facie similarities to be relevant until proven otherwise, or else one can require that relevant similarities have first to be conclusively proven—something which, given sufficiently strong assumptions about human uniqueness, is unlikely ever to happen. Adoption of this latter approach can appropriately be called "human chauvinism." Avoiding human chauvinism will always be a matter of judgment and good will, rather than the straightforward application of any unequivocal principles, but it is perhaps this, at root, which distinguishes weak from strong anthropocentrism.

V. ANTHROPOCENTRISM VERSUS MISANTHROPY

The ethical impulse to overcome anthropocentrism is sometimes portrayed by those who oppose it as a form of misanthropy. It is therefore worth pointing out that cases of environmental and interspecies harm are not always the result of anthropocentrism. It is by no means always the case that the practices or values criticized as anthropocentric actually serve humans as such: they often serve particular individuals or groups, whose interests may in fact *conflict* with the interests of humans more generally. For instance, if some humans hunt a species to extinction, this is not entirely appropriately seen as "anthropocentrism" since it typically involves one group of humans who are actually condemned by (probably a majority of) other humans who see the practice not as serving human interests in general, but the interests of one quite narrowly defined group, such as poachers or whalers. A similar point can be made regarding, say, the destruction of a rainforest, for those who derive economic benefit from the destruction oppose not only the human interests of indigenous peoples whose environment is thereby destroyed, but also the interests of all humans who depend on the oxygen such forests produce. What such considerations tend to suggest is that in some ways humans are not anthropocentric enough!

It is therefore not only conceptually mistaken, but also a practical and strategic mistake, to criticize humanity in general for practices of specific groups of humans. Misrepresenting the problem is liable to make solutions all the harder. From what has just been said about the *specificity* of environmental, ecological, or animal harms merely being disguised by putting the blame on humans in general, it should be evident that those who are concerned about such harms in fact make common cause with those concerned with issues of human social justice. The real opponents of both sorts of concern are the ideologists who, in defending harmful practices in the name of "humans in general," obscure the real causes of the harms as much as the real incidence of benefits: the harms seldom affect all and only nonhumans, and the benefits seldom accrue to all humans. Yet by appearing to accept the ideologists' own premises, anti-anthropocentric rhetoric can play right into their hands—by appearing to endorse the ideological view that "humans in general" benefit from the exploitative activities of some, the anti-anthropocentrists are left vulnerable to ideological rejoinders to the effect that challenging those activities is merely misanthropic, when in fact it is in the interests of humans more generally.

It is therefore necessary to emphasize that the critique of anthropocentrism is directed not so much against a concern of humans with the well-being of humans, but against a *lack* of concern for *non*humans.

VI. CONCLUSION

It has been shown that anthropocentrism is in some respects objectionable and in others not, and that in some respects it is avoidable and in others not. If the objectionable features were also the avoidable ones, this would be a welcome conclusion: the ethically desirable would then coincide with the practically possible. How-

ever, as the discussion of hard cases shows, it may be overoptimistic, especially in the short term, to suppose this will always be the case.

Perhaps the best way to distinguish unavoidable from avoidable aspects is to accept that humans are the *source* of ethical values but that their interests need not be the only *substance* of value. As long as the valuer is a human, the very selection of criteria of value will be limited by this fact, which precludes the possibility of a *radically* nonanthropocentric value scheme, if by that is meant the adoption of a set of values which are supposed to be completely unrelated to any existing human values. Any attempt to construct a radically nonanthropocentric value scheme is liable not only to be arbitrary, because it is founded on no certain knowledge, but also to be more insidiously anthropocentric in projecting certain values, which as a matter of fact are selected by a human, onto nonhuman beings without certain warrant for doing so. This, of course, is the error of anthropomorphism, and is likely to be attendant on any attempt to expunge anthropocentrism altogether.

To sum up, then, what is unavoidable about anthropocentrism is precisely what makes ethics possible at all. It is a basic feature of the logic of obligation: if an ethic is a guide to action, and if a particular ethic requires an agent to make others' values her values, then in an important sense they become just that, the agent's values. This is a noncontingent but substantive limitation on any attempt to construct a completely nonanthropocentric ethic. It does not follow from this that ethics should only be concerned with human interests. On the contrary, the development of environmental ethics over the past 20 years or so has provided many arguments to show how and why humans should be no less concerned about their environment and about the other living beings who share it.

Also See the Following Articles

ECOLOGICAL BALANCE • EVOLUTIONARY PERSPECTIVES ON ETHICS • SPECIESISM • WILDLIFE CONSERVATION

Bibliography

Armstrong, S., and Botzler, G. (1993). "Environmental Ethics: Divergence and Convergence," part 6. McGraw–Hill, New York.
Attfield, R. (1991). "The Ethics of Environmental Concern," 2nd ed. Univ. of Georgia Press, Athens.
Attfield, R. (1992). Development and environmentalism. In "International Justice and the Third World" (R. Attfield and B. Wilkins, Eds.). Routledge, London.

Ehrenfeld, D. (1978). "The Arrogance of Humanism." Oxford Univ. Press, London.

Ferré, F. (1994). Personalistic organicism: Paradox or paradigm? In "Philosophy and the Natural Environment" (R. Attfield and A. Belsey, Ed.). Cambridge Univ. Press, Cambridge, UK.

Hayward, T. (1997). Anthropocentrism: A misunderstood problem. *Environ. Values* 6, 49–63.

Leopold, A. (1949). "A Sand County Almanac." Oxford Univ. Press, London.

Midgley, M. (1994). The end of anthropocentrism? In "Philosophy and the Natural Environment" (R. Attfield and A. Belsey, Eds.). Cambridge Univ. Press, Cambridge, UK.

Norton, B. (1987). "Why Preserve Natural Variety?" Princeton Univ. Press, Princeton, NJ.

Routley, R. and V. (1979). Against the inevitability of human chauvinism. In "Ethics and Problems of the 21st Century" (K. Goodpaster and K. Sayre, Eds.). Notre Dame Univ. Press.

Williams, B. (1992). Must a concern for the environment be centred on human beings? In "Ethics and the Environment" (C. Taylor, Ed.). Corpus Christi College, Oxford.

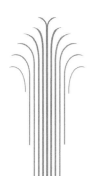

APPLIED ETHICS, CHALLENGES TO

Tim Dare
The University of Auckland

GLOSSARY

ethical expertise The idea that ethics is the sort of thing that admits of expertise and that some people have more of it than others.

monism The position that there is one and only one ultimate ethical principle.

moral deductivism The idea that uniquely correct answers to moral problems issue from deductive decision procedures.

pluralism The position that there is more than one ultimate ethical principle.

relativism The position that there are no universal ethical truths. Rather ethical truths are always true or false relative to particular cultures or situations.

subjectivism The principle that ethical statements report only the beliefs and attitudes of the person uttering the statement.

the theory/anti-theory debate The debate about the value of general ethical theories in ethical deliberation and justification.

APPLIED ETHICS is concerned with furthering our understanding, and thus the resolution, of practical issues of right and wrong.

I. INTRODUCTION

A little more than 25 years ago it was widely thought that philosophical ethics had little to contribute to such matters. This was not a matter of thinking philosophers should abandon the study of ethical theory altogether. The idea was rather that though the refinement and elaboration of general ethical theories and work on meta-ethical problems such as the meaning of moral terms might properly continue, philosophers should not suppose their efforts on these matters to have any practical value. There has been a dramatic change. Much of the most exciting ethical writing of the intervening period addresses specific moral problems such as abortion and euthanasia, many universities have applied ethics positions, and philosophers now regularly find themselves called upon to "do ethics" in the community—to serve on professional ethics committees, to produce reports for governments and institutions on ethically contentious issues, to give interviews about business ethics, and so on. Yet this dramatic change has occurred in the face of numerous and ongoing challenges. This article presents and assesses the principal challenges to applied ethics.

It is worth adding an "expansionist caveat" at the

outset. This discussion has already focused upon the role of philosophy and philosophers in applied ethics, and challenges to the legitimacy of the endeavor have tended to be similarly directed. But if correct most of those challenges will have implications not just for philosophers but for any normative theorist seeking practical consequences from their work: when engaged on certain projects, economists, social and political scientists, and lawyers may belong under the critic's spotlight as legitimately as philosophers. Hence, though I will continue to focus upon philosophy, it should be borne in mind that moral philosophers do not have a monopoly on normative theorizing nor upon the aspiration to give moral advice on the basis of such theorizing, so should not be the only targets of critics, or the only beneficiaries of a defense of applied ethics.

II. APPLIED ETHICS, ETHICAL SCEPTICISM, AND ETHICAL EXPERTISE

An influential cluster of challenges to applied ethics springs from meta-ethical views about the possibility of moral knowledge. Very crudely, the idea is that in ethics there are merely opinions, and that as a result no one can give authoritative advice as to what is right and what is wrong. This general scepticism has many forms. I am concerned here merely to give an overview and brief assessment of some of the main varieties.

A. The Challenge of Relativism

One influential variety begins from the observation that different cultures seem to have different ethical views. Some cultures think polygamy immoral, others that it is perfectly proper. Some cultures think it permissible to abandon the elderly to die, others that the elderly must be treated with particular respect and reverence. These apparent differences have led many to reject the idea of universal ethical truth. There is, the idea goes, nothing more than different cultural customs. None can be condemned as wrong or honored as right, for there is no "acultural standpoint" from which such a universal assessment could be made, or from which practical or applied ethical advice might proceed.

Cultural relativism has attracted a good deal of criticism. For now it will do to simply recite some of the more obvious difficulties. First, even granting the observations of ethical differences between cultures, it does not follow that there is no universal moral truth: it does not follow from the fact that people disagree about whether or not polygamy is wrong that there is no fact of the matter, any more than it followed from the fact that people disagreed about the shape of the earth that there was no fact of that matter. Second, even allowing, again, that there is quite dramatic ethical disagreement, it might still be the case that there is a very large area of ethical consensus. There may be some moral rules—"gratuitous killing is wrong" perhaps—held by all communities at all times. This point connects with a third: perhaps it will seem that even the rule "gratuitous killing is wrong" is not really universal. After all, certain cultures abandon their elderly to die. But the bare observation of such practices does not evidence different ethical values. Suppose attempting to keep the elderly alive in certain environments threatened the entire community. In such circumstances abandoning the elderly may not seem to be "gratuitous killing." Those who followed the practice would not show by doing so that they held radically different values to those cultures that thought the elderly should be treated with reverence and respect. Indeed, we can easily imagine circumstances in which the appropriate way to show reverence and respect was to abandon the elderly before they became a threat to the community that they themselves held important.

B. The Challenge of Subjectivism

Subjectivists claim that ethical statements report things about the utterer rather than about the world. Such statements are either merely emotional responses (so not really statements at all), or are statements only about the beliefs, desires, and attitudes of the speaker. An apparent dispute about euthanasia, according to the subjectivist, is not really about euthanasia at all, but about the feelings, attitudes, and so on of the disputants. Again, as a challenge to applied ethics, subjectivism denies the ethicist an intersubjective position from which to assess or issue advice.

This common view is both importantly right and importantly wrong. We can see how it is importantly right by contrasting ethical judgments with legal judgments. It is an integral part of our legal system that legal issues can be authoritatively settled by specified institutions. The court's role is to impose a public judgement as to what should or should not be done. There is no analogous ethical institution and to this extent the sceptical view about ethics is right. If we disagree about an ethical matter I can think you mistaken in a way that, after enough appeals, will seem merely perverse in the legal case. My moral views are arrived at by me and there is no ethical court who can overrule me. Each person's assessment of the right thing to do is *in this sense* at least as good as anyone else's. But we need to be careful about the implications of this. The idea that ethics is "personal" in the sense that I cannot be definitively overruled by others in ethical matters does not mean that ethics is personal as *taste* is personal, and the quick sketch above is importantly wrong about this. There are a number of related differences that show the cases to be importantly different. I will simply outline the central ones here.

For one thing, if my tastes change I do not suppose that I was mistaken and that I have now come to the correct view: I now like olives although I once did not, but I do not think now that I was mistaken about the taste of olives then. But this is just what I am likely to think if I change my mind over a moral matter. If I once thought abortion was always wrong and now think it at least sometimes right, then I will probably think *now* that I was mistaken *then*. The idea that ethical judgments are just matters of taste does not seem to capture this feature of moral judgments. For another, the way in which taste is personal seems to make certain kinds of disagreement over matters of taste impossible. We do not really disagree when one of us says "Olives taste good" and the other says "Olives taste bad." We can each sincerely and correctly assert our view. Expressions of ethical judgments do not seem to be like this. If they were, two people expressing what we normally take to be conflicting ethical views would not be expressing conflicting views at all. They would be like two people "disagreeing" over the taste of olives. We might think that a view of ethics that cannot explain our perception that there is a genuine disagreement between pro- and antiracists cannot be adequate. Perhaps more tellingly, if ethical judgments were just matters of taste, it would be odd and futile to try to *convince* someone that their moral views were mistaken, just as it is odd and futile to attempt to convince someone obviously enjoying their olive that they are mistaken—that they are not really enjoying it at all. But our ethical views can be changed by argument and reason. We can change our ethical views nonarbitrarily, in response to argument and discussion, in a way that seems quite mysterious in matters of taste. Ethics then is not just a matter of taste. We can make sense of the idea of genuine moral disagreement, it seems to make perfectly good sense to try to convince people they are mistaken about ethical matters, and we change our minds about such matters in response to argument and reason.

C. Ethics and the Role of Reasons

This preceding discussion seems to allow us to reject at least the simple versions of ethical scepticism and relativism, and hence to respond to the challenge those views pose to applied ethics. It does so by highlighting the role of reasons in ethics and in doing so it also tells us something about the nature of ethics and ethical expertise. As to the nature of ethics, granting a central role to reason allows us to give, at least in outline, an account of what must be true of a position if it is to count as an ethical position. If a position of mine is to count as an ethical position I must produce *reasons* for it. This is not to say that I must articulate a complex moral theory or even state a moral principle that I am following for my position to count as moral. But in practice there are certain sorts of reasons or responses which will not do: Because a mere prejudice, for instance, is precisely a belief that is not supported by reasons, I cannot offer mere prejudices in support of my position. Similarly, mere emotional reactions will not count as reasons. If all I can say in support of my claim that business is wicked is that business makes me sick or furious, I am not offering a reason that would show my position to be an ethical position. (This is not to say that ethical positions should be unemotional or dispassionate. On the contrary, we should care about our moral views. But emotional reactions should be prompted by or grounded in moral judgments and not vice versa.) And if my position is based upon propositions of fact which are not only false but so implausible that they fail even the minimal standards of evidence I impose upon others I will likely be offering not reasons but instead showing that I can think of no genuine reasons for my position at all. These will not be the only sorts of reasons that will not do in moral discourse—blind appeals to authority or precedent may well go on the list as well—but they will be enough to give a sense of the constraints posed by the requirement for reasons. The list is supposed to be illustrative rather than exhaustive.

Once we have allowed a place for reasons in moral discourse we can see that there will be other, more general, restraints as well. Perhaps most importantly, the role of reasons imposes a constraint of consistency. Consistency requires that if there are exactly the same reasons in support of one course of action as there are in support of another, then those actions will be equally right or equally wrong—they will be equally well supported or undercut by reasons. If I object to racism on the grounds that "all people are equal" then I must also object to those manifestations of other prejudice, such as sexism, that deny that principle—if I do not then it will seem that in one or other or both of the cases I am not really accepting "all people are equal" as a reason at all. My position will not in fact be based on the reason or reasons I cite.

D. The Possibility of Ethical Expertise

Recognizing the role of reasons and reasoning in ethics allows us to address another influential and related challenge to applied ethics that denies the possibility of "ethical expertise." Because there cannot be such expertise, the claim goes, nobody can purport to advise others what to do, and to the extent that that is just what applied ethicists do purport to do, their endeavor is illegitimate. But recognizing the role of reason in ethics allows us to give an account ethical expertise. Ethical expertise will consist in expertise in ethical reasoning. Just what such expertise consists in is no doubt controversial, but, again, a list of characteristics is likely to include the following:

Because ethical expertise consists of expertise at a certain form of reasoning, ethical experts will need to be proficient reasoners. They must be able to reason logically, to avoid fallacies and inconsistencies, to clarify and analyze concepts, to construct and assess arguments and positions. Of course—to hark back to the expansionist caveat offered in the opening section—philosophers do not have a monopoly on these sorts of reasoning skills, although perhaps it is fair to say that philosophy endorses them more explicitly than most disciplines. Ethical expertise will require a certain body of knowledge: knowledge of philosophical problems, questions, positions, and theories (e.g., ethical theories, theories of knowledge, views about human nature and society), knowledge of the assumptions, consequences, and criticisms of different positions or views, knowledge of types of arguments, and likely problems (e.g., fallacies like false dichotomy or ambiguity of scope). Ethical expertise will require commitment to certain values associated with good reasoning, such as commitment to understanding issues and views, commitment to reasoned support and evaluation of beliefs or claims, willingness to question key assumptions and challenge received wisdom, and interest in finding solutions to philosophical questions and problems. These values are a significant part of the ethical expert's arsenal because they amount to a commitment to *apply* the reasoning skills noted above. Being able to recognize fallacies and inconsistencies will be of no value to the ethical expert if she is not prepared to follow those skills where they lead. And applied ethicists must be well informed about the relevant facts of the cases they address. If they are to give advice on the ethics of particular fields or endeavors they must have enough knowledge of the subject area and the case at hand to appreciate the demands and problems that are either peculiar to or commonly encountered in that area.

The hope, then, is that recognizing the role of reason in ethics allows us a notion of the ethical expert. In sum, this expert will be a person who is skilled at a certain form of reasoning, who has at her finger tips a body of relevant knowledge, and who is committed to using those skills and knowledge to assess the strengths and weaknesses of moral arguments and positions. Note that there is nothing in this quick characterization to suggest that the ethical expert has some antecedent grasp on moral truth. Plato argued that philosphers should rule because they had "the capacity to grasp the eternal and immutable . . . to which they can turn, as a painter turns to his model, before laying down rules in this world about what is admirable or right or good." The expert sketched above is a more mundane character. Her skill is *procedural* rather than *substantive*. Recognizing the way in which moral positions depend upon reasoned support, she is skilled in constructing and assessing such support. Her skill and contribution does not depend upon her grasp of anything like "eternal and immutable moral truths." Rather, it is grounded in more accessible standards of reason and argumentation.

III. APPLIED ETHICS AND ETHICAL THEORY

A. The Criticism of Theory

Another cluster of challenges is more specifically directed at the role of ethical theories or principles in applied ethics, claiming, in short, that we should not turn to ethical theories for practical guidance. We need only note the fairly standard conception of applied ethics as "the application of an ethical theory to some particular moral problem or set of problems" to see the intended force of the challenge. I begin assessment of the challenge by sketching its target—the conception of moral theory and practice to which its advocates object. Providing such a sketch is a somewhat risky business, because the challengers are far from being a homogeneous group, although I shall concentrate on the core of the position upon which there is likely to be considerable consensus among "antitheorists."

First, moral theorists are said to be preoccupied with highly abstract, universal rules and principles. Annette

Baier, for example, defines a normative theory as a system of moral principles in which the less general are derived from the more general and criticises moral theorists' "prejudice in favour of formulated general rules." Second, antitheorists portray moral theory as severely reductionist; as insisting that all moral values can be gathered under some single standard. One trenchant critic of applied ethics, Cheryl Noble, maintains that this "monism" is necessary, given theorists' desire to bring the apparently endless diversity of particular judgments under a single principle or hierarchy of principles. Third, theorists are said to conceive of moral reasoning as essentially deductive: assuming that for every moral problem there is a correct decision, which will issue from a deductive procedure that rational moral agents must follow in deciding what to do. Hence Bernard Williams claims that the desire to produce "a rationalistic decision procedure" is precisely what issues in ethical theory. Antitheorists reject this deductive picture. Moral judgments are generated, they maintain, by attention not to general principles but to the paritcularities of actual cases and situations. Thus John McDowell maintains that morality is "uncodifiable" and writes that "one knows what to do (if one does) not by applying universal principles but by being a certain sort of person: one who sees situations in a certain way," and Martha Nussbaum argues for the priority of perception over rules, claiming that "to confine ourselves to the universal is a recipe for obtuseness." For the same reason antitheorists stress the importance of judgment, as opposed to deductive skill, because the competent moral reasoner will be the person who can resolve conflicts between irreducibly competing values and irresolvable claims. In sum, the clearest target of the challenge directed at the role of theory in applied ethics is one according to which applied ethics is concerned first with the elaboration of general ethical theories—egoism, utilitarianism, and Kantianism are the familiar classics—each of which purports to have discovered *the* ultimate principle of ethics, one of which selected and applied to give concrete guidance in concrete situations. Applied ethics texts that begin with a survey of the usual theoretical options no doubt contribute to the currency of the conception.

There are short and long responses to the challenge: the short one is simply to accept the critique and do applied ethics without theory. Many applied ethicists describe themselves as doing just this, embracing the antitheorist's vision more or less enthusiastically, some seeing the invitation to focus less on general principles and more upon the details of particular cases as exactly the right recipe for applied ethics, and as an opportunity

to abandon a flawed and theory-bound conception of ethics and ethical deliberation. In the remainder of this article, however, I explore a longer response to the antitheorist's challenge, outlining an approach to ethical theory and applied ethics that accepts certain aspects of the antitheorist's case but that seeks to retain some role for theory.

B. Ethical Theory for Applied Ethics

1. Why Care about Theory?

Given that many applied ethicists do at least describe themselves as doing applied ethics without theory, it may be worth beginning by saying briefly why one might hope to take the other route: why attempt to retain a role for theory and principles? There are, I think, a number of reasons.

First, antitheorists commonly claim that practices must be evaluated "from within." Eschewing recourse to theoretical criteria external to particular practices, they stress the importance of attention to loyalties, conventions, traditions, and historical and "local" explanations. But this is to severely limit the possibility of criticism of social practices. As two defenders of antitheory write "[m]oral and political norms cannot be rejected on the basis of critical standards contrary to the fundamental values and practices of the community." One reason to try to hold onto theory is that effective criticism seems at least occasionally to require us to step outside the particular practices of the communities with which we are concerned, to have recourse to general standards or principles of evaluation. This is not to say that criticism or evaluation requires "Archimedean" theoretical points. We might proceed by asking how one aspect of our practice coheres with others, but even this sort of "immanent" inquiry requires that we have some sense of which aspects of practices are more important than others and why, and these are theoretical questions.

Second, general moral principles may simply be useful to us in a variety of ways. There are obvious advantages in being able to conceive and describe "my situation" as of a kind with one already deliberated upon: Principles give me a way of accessing and considering relevant moral conflicts, of discovering and indicating how such conflicts were addressed previously, and of appreciating and advocating alternatives that might otherwise be overlooked. Subsuming my case under a general principle may save me time, effort, and anguish; I may take comfort and support from the fact that others have been down a relevantly similar path before me. Furthermore, principles may provide me with both greater grounds for confidence as to the response of others to my case, and a ready way of presenting my claims to them, because I shall at least often be less concerned that the outcome to particular cases will depend upon immediate perceptions and new deliberations.

General theories will serve similar goals, and, depending upon how one thinks moral theories function in deliberation they may do rather more beside. Suppose one thinks of moral theories not *just* as elegant and abstract sets of rules and principles, but as motivated by "actual" moral concerns and perspectives. The reason we are troubled by clashes between concerns such as those highlighted by consequentialists and deontologists, on such an account, is not because the authors or advocates of these positions have made such a fine job of constructing them *ex nihilo*. It is rather because those theories appeal to or remind us of moral concerns we have independently of the theories themselves and because they direct us to perspectives that we recognize as plausible. Here the power of the theories is to be explained by the fact that they are the careful working out of the implications and aspects of this or that plausible and antecedent concern or viewpoint. Theories would serve not as authoritative major premises in some deductive syllogism, but rather as deliberative tools, drawing attention to aspects of the case to which attention should be given and that might otherwise be ignored or overlooked. The deontological tradition draws attention to the claims of individuals to a certain sort of respect, the consequentialist to the importance of regard to the results of our actions, the communitarian to the claims of community, and so on.

2. What Must Theories Be Like?

What must be true of ethical theories and applied ethicists attitudes toward them if they are to serve the sort of role sketched here?

a. Monism and Pluralism

The approach implies acceptance of some form of "theory pluralism"—it supposes that properly conducted moral inquiry will have regard to more than one theory or principle of right action and rejects the idea that there is one uniquely correct theory or principle. Indeed, it claims that recognizing the pull or gravity of different theories or principles on moral problems is a desirable heuristic to adequate deliberation. Once we put aside the search for a single correct moral theory or principle, we are likely to find the careful and abstract statements of concern and perspectives that we find in normative

theory, useful as a reminder precisely of the complex dimensions of the cases we face.

b. Deliberative Strategies and Moral Deductivism

We must also put aside the aim of developing all-purpose, formalized moral decision procedures (although it is perhaps worth noting that it is quite hard to find theorists who have in fact pursued the aim). Moral deliberation is not the straightforward application of a favored theory or principle. Rather, theories and principles are used to clarify, to diagnose, to structure discussion. They allow us to approach moral problems from as comprehensive a position as we can manage. On this story there is no simple application of a favored theory or principle to a situation in the hope of generating "the right moral answer." Rather, theories and principles are used as one part of a process of approaching moral problems. They are tools in moral reasoning rather than self-contained machines for the generation of moral answers. Moral deliberation should be conceived of not as a matter of simply applying decision procedures consisting of lists of easy-to-follow rules, but as a matter of approaching particular cases in the light of general and perhaps competing theories and principles, of previous relevant deliberations, and of appropriate knowledge of the particularities of the case.

c. Irresolvable Problems

Applied ethicists must recognize the reality of irresolvable problems. Given competing values, it may not be possible to determine which act is morally right or which person is more admirable morally. The acceptance of the possibility of irresolvable problems does not put an end to the need for applied ethics. Irresolvable conflict, however, is likely to make the skills of applied ethicists more rather than less important. Choices must still be made in the face of such problems. Applied ethicists may help in a number of ways: They may simply alert people to moral conflict. Those caught up in difficult moral deliberations may miss points that, once alerted, they concede ought to be included in a critical assessment of the situation. Ethicists may help explain why there is a moral conflict in a particular situation, pointing to the different types of moral value that are present in the case at hand, showing why they cannot be reduced to a common denominator, and why there is no single right answer in this particular case. They may be able to point out the advantages and dangers of some responses over others, given the parties' own commitments and concerns. This may simply be a matter of telling people what happened in relevantly similar cases or may be more prescriptive. In either case those in difficult situations may be helped by consideration of how a variety of theories and values bear upon a case and how other people faced with similar dilemmas arrived at decisions, as well as by learning of the consequences of such decisions. Irresolvable problems, this is to say, may provide especially fertile ground for the skills of the ethical expert.

This may be an appropriate point to note a likely effect of theory or value pluralism. Acceptance of pluralism may be important not just because different theories at least occasionally produce different recommendations in the same case, but also because rival theories may differ about what is to count as a moral problem at the outset. Situations identified as problems by one theory may not be problems at all for the advocates of another theory: particular distributions of wealth may seem deeply problematic for (some) consequentialists but completely acceptable for rights theorists or for consequentialists of a slightly different stripe. There does not seem to be any theory-neutral way of establishing a list of moral problems let alone common resolutions. To exponents of radical versions of this latter concern, the current concerns of applied ethicists may seem to be no more than points of conflict between ethical positions that have come to dominate public ethical discourse. For the moment it will do to note that pluralism is likely to increase at least the appearance of irresolvable conflict.

d. Empirical Responsibility

A common strand in the opposition to moral theory is the complaint that it ignores the particularities of cases and practices, favoring universals while disregarding "the multiplicity and diversity of the local and historical attachments that give sense to a normal person's life." It might seem that applied ethics itself is a sufficient response to this criticism, but of course conceived of as the mere application of general principles to particular cases it fails to assuage antitheorists. Furthermore, some critics have, in effect, doubted the genuineness of philosophers' interest in applied ethics, complaining that even when philosophers do address particular moral problems, they tend to be interested in the significance of the problem for theory rather than the problem itself. At times the complaint seems well directed. It is no doubt true that some philosophical treatments of particular problems have been primarily concerned to refine and improve general theories rather than to increase understanding of the problem under consideration. Some discussions of abortion, for instance, seem concerned less with abortion per se, than with the desire

to shed further light on the intricacies of rights theories of moral obligation. When they approach particular moral problems in this fashion, philosophers are hardly involved in applied ethics at all. Suffice to say that applied ethicists must guard against a merely *instrumental* interest in the problems to which their skills are applied. Applied ethicists must approach theory with a genuine conviction that a wide variety of historical, psychological, and cultural forces are clearly relevant to any critical understanding of human morality and that such factors must be taken into account in any adequate theory. Applied ethics must take empirical matters seriously. No one who proposes to do meaningful work in applied or professional ethics can do so without first acquiring extensive empirical knowledge of the area being studied. Again, the applied ethicist requires an extensive knowledge of the values, organization, and practices of the groups or communities under consideration.

IV. CONCLUSION: THEORY AND A RETURN TO ETHICAL EXPERTISE

I have been concerned in this last section to sketch an alternative conception of moral theory with an eye to the demands of applied ethics. The conception is pluralist, rejects the hope of a universal and mechanical decision procedure, accepts the reality of irresolvable conflicts, and acknowledges the need for theory to be grounded in and responsive to sound empirical knowledge. It is intended to direct attention to an approach to ethical deliberation and applied ethics rather than to any particular normative theory or principle.

My aim has been to respond to legitimate concerns about the role of theory in applied ethics in a way suggestive for the role of applied ethicists. This last hope might be more plainly realized by linking some of the comments in these final section back to the earlier account of the ethical expertise. The conception of ethical theory and practice sketched here portrays ethical deliberation not as a matter of simply applying decision procedures consisting of lists of easy-to-follow rules, but as involving consideration of particular cases in the light of general and perhaps competing theories and principles, of previous relevant deliberations and of appropriate knowledge of the particularities of the case. I portrayed the ethical expert as a person skilled at a certain form of reasoning, who has at her fingertips a body of relevant knowledge, and who is committed to using those skills and knowledge to assess the strengths and weaknesses of moral arguments and positions. Her skill, I suggested, was procedural rather than substantive. Recognizing the way in which moral positions depend upon reasoned support, she is skilled in constructing and assessing such support. These skills are intended to allow the ethical expert to respond to the demands of applied ethics in a manner that does justice to our firmest convictions, to what we take to be our best social and moral theories, and to what we know and believe about the world.

It needs to be remembered that what we seek in the end in applied ethics are "ways of going on." But, especially given the significance of many of the issues applied ethicists face (sometimes, indeed, they will be matters of life and death) we need ways of going on that we can live with as individuals and as communities. *Pace* Plato, we do not have timeless moral truths on our shelves that can be applied mechanically to particular cases. Nor are we completely without resources to construct coherent defensible moral positions that take seriously—which is to say takes in a way that neither ignores nor accepts uncritically—the moral judgments, principles, and theories upon which our communities are founded. When we do so as applied ethicists we can give guidance as how we should go on in ways that we can live with as individuals and communities.

Also See the Following Articles

CONSEQUENTIALISM AND DEONTOLOGY • EGOISM AND ALTRUISM • KANTIANISM • THEORIES OF ETHICS, OVERVIEW • UTILITARIANISM

Bibliography

Bayles, M. (1984). Moral theory and application 10, 97–120.
Beauchamp, T. (1984). On eliminating the distinction between applied ethics and ethical theory. 67 *Monist,* 514–531.
Gert, B. (1984) Moral theory and applied ethics. 67 *Monist,* 532–548.
MacIntyre, A. (1984). Does applied ethics rest on a mistake? 67 *Monist,* 498–513.
Noble, C. (1982). Ethics and experts 12. *Hastings Centre Report,* 7–15.
Rosenthal, D., & Shehadi, F. (Eds.). (1988). *Applied Ethics and Ethical Theory.* Contains numerous relevant articles.

APPLIED ETHICS, OVERVIEW

Earl R. Winkler
University of British Columbia

GLOSSARY

contextualism A complex theory about moral reasoning and justification that deemphasizes the role of universal principles in determining right actions. In this view, moral judgments are provisionally justified by defending themselves against objections and rivals. The process of justification is essentially continuous with a case-driven, inductive process of seeking the most reasonable solution to a problem. Such justification is carried out within a framework of central cultural values and guiding norms which are seen as having presumptive validity unless they themselves are called into question by rational doubts.

conventionalism The idea that conformity with accepted or conventional moral standards and rules of a community makes actions right. This is an extremely conservative idea, as it leaves little or no room for moral progress or improvement. Hence it is usually considered a fatal weakness in a normative theory if it reduces to, or implies, conventionalism.

metaethics Contrasts with normative ethical theory.

Whereas normative ethics is concerned with deciding which actions are right and wrong, metaethics is concerned with the meanings of central moral concepts such as "good" and "right," and with an account of the logic or structure of moral reasoning and justification.

moral expertise The idea that there may be forms of moral knowledge and experience that qualify someone as a kind of expert in moral matters, if not in general then in relation to one or another area of practice, such as medicine.

normative ethical theory A systematically developed theory about the nature and the determination of moral right and wrong.

principalism A traditional view of moral justification in which a particular action is ultimately justified by showing that it conforms to a universal ethical principle which is grounded in the most abstract levels of normative theory. Most contemporary expositions of normative theory involving principalism, however, allow for the operations of reflective equilibrium theory in constructing and testing for principles.

reflective equilibrium theory A theory holding that there is a dialectical relationship between our considered moral judgments about concrete cases and our commitments to principle. Reflection on principles sometimes overrides considered judgment, and considered judgment sometimes forces revisions in our principles. What we are seeking, then, in all systematic moral reflection, is a coherent integration, or equilibrium, between our general principles and our particular judgments.

utilitarianism A form of general normative theory which holds that the rightness or wrongness of actions is wholly determined by the goodness or badness of their consequences. Classical utilitarianism defines the value of consequences in terms of their total contribution to the happiness or well-being of all those affected by an action, counting each persons' happiness as equally important with that of any other. Contemporary forms of utilitarianism may focus instead on aggregate satisfaction of individual interests or preferences.

virtue ethics A general type of normative ethical theory that displaces traditional concentration on the rightness or wrongness of action with a primary concentration on certain defined dispositions of character identified as virtues. In such a theory, virtues are seen as those dispositions that are most important in realizing some ideal, like self-realization, or that are most important to the performance of some morally justified social function, as in the practice of business or medicine.

APPLIED ETHICS is a general field of study that includes all systematic efforts to understand and to resolve moral problems that arise in some domain of practical life, as with medicine, journalism, or business, or in connection with some general issue of social concern, such as employment equity or capital punishment. There are today three major subdivisions of applied ethics: biomedical ethics, concerned with ethical issues in medicine and biomedical research; business and professional ethics, concerned with issues arising in the context of business, including that of multinational corporations; and environmental ethics, concerned with our relations and obligations to future generations, to nonhuman animals and species, and to ecosystems and the biosphere as a whole.

I. RISE OF APPLIED ETHICS

Interest in increasing our understanding of ethical issues concerning health care, business, the professions, and the environment has grown markedly over the last quarter century. When considering the main forces giving rise to this increased interest in applied ethics, one naturally thinks first of biomedical ethics, the most mature and well defined of the divisions of applied

ethics. Although abetted by the "liberation" movements of the 1960s and 1970s, biomedical ethics emerged principally in response to various issues and choices that were created by new medical technologies. The traditional values and ethical principles of the medical profession came to be regarded as inadequate in these new situations, because they often seemed to require decisions which appeared to be clearly wrong. For example, the principle of the sanctity of human life permeated the ethos and ethics of Western medicine for centuries and found formal expression in medical case law. As is now well accepted, however, a central requirement of the sanctity principle—that the physician must make every possible effort to preserve life—simply became too burdensome in the contemporary medical context to continue to support a consensus as to what is right concerning life and death decisions.

There are obvious and important differences, at a general level, between the main divisions of applied ethics. Biomedical ethics is focused within a particular institutional setting and concerns the practices of a closely associated set of professions. Business ethics is broader in scope because the field of business is so much more diverse than the medical field. Environmental ethics obviously has an even broader purview, including the attitudes and behavior of all of us, particularly our basic social patterns of resource use and consumption, and our fundamental moral attitudes toward other animals and the natural world.

In spite of these and other differences, however, business ethics and environmental ethics still have the same basic provenance as biomedical ethics. Within the context of traditional assumptions and values, modern industrial and technological processes, formerly seen as the very engines of progress, have led to global crisis. The *raison d'être* of environmental ethics is to criticize and improve the values and principles in terms of which we understand our responsibilities to future generations, our relationship to nonhuman animals and other living things, and our place in nature generally. Traditional values and principles of Western business practice have also come to seem inadequate for the complex realities of the modern world. This is particularly true regarding the social responsibilities of business, especially those concerning public health and safety and environmental risks. Scandals on Wall Street and the like may prompt endowments for ethics education in business schools, but they are not philosophically significant enough to explain the high level of interest business ethics currently attracts. A more likely explanation will concentrate on such things as the realization that the traditional corporate obligation to maximize profits for shareholders, within the limits of applicable law, can lead much too easily to exploitation, environmental degradation, and other harms.

Viewing the rise of applied ethics generally in this light, it is not surprising that as moral quandaries grew, first in bioethics and then in the other major areas, hope for progress shifted from tinkering with traditional values to moral philosophy and foundational ethical theory. At the same time, the general field of applied ethics has given rise to various subdivisions of a more concentrated kind, such as management ethics, nursing ethics, and journalistic ethics (including all news media). Likewise, the field has developed so as to incude much focused attention on ethical issues connected with a wide range of social concerns, such as discrimination and affirmative action, feminism, world hunger and poverty, war and violence, capital punishment, the rights of gays and lesbians, and so forth.

II. GENERAL ETHICAL THEORY AND PRINCIPALISM

As applied ethics has grown into an established field of study and practice, a number of important questions have arisen about the nature of the field and the problems within it. Paradoxically, perhaps, one of the most fundamental of these concerns the usefulness of ethical theory. Traditional moral philosophy has virtually identified the possibility of genuine moral knowledge with the possibility of universally valid ethical theory, and has supposed that all acceptable moral standards, of every time and place, can be rationally ordered and explained by reference to some set of fundamental principles. *Perfect* theoretical unity and systematization may be impossible to obtain, because there may be a plurality of basic principles that resist ordering. But it is generally assumed that such principles will be few in number, such that substantial and pervasive order may be discovered. A corollary to this conception of moral knowledge is the view that moral reasoning and justification are essentially a matter of deductively applying basic principles to cases.

However, contrary to the expectations created by these methodological assumptions, many philosophers who ventured into clinics and boardrooms were chagrined to discover how little usefulness this deductive approach had in the confrontation with genuine moral problems. Efforts to resolve real moral problems in medicine with some version of Kantian or utilitarian theory, for example, immediately confront the problem

of the abstractness and remoteness of general ethical principles. Of course one wants best to serve the important interests of all concerned (utilitarianism) and to respect the rights and personhood of the affected parties (Kantianism); but for real problems of practice the most important and difficult question often is how best to understand the current situation in just these terms. What, for example, does it mean to respect properly the personhood of a potential anencephalic organ donor?

In the field of bioethics, experience of this sort gave rise to a midlevel theory composed of three main principles, those of autonomy, beneficence (including nonmaleficence), and justice. This theory was systematically developed by Tom Beauchamp and James Childress in their modern classic, *Principles of Biomedical Ethics*. This theory claims that its principles are grounded in our most central traditions of normative ethical theory while also offering enough content to guide practical moral judgment in medicine. It thus purports to overcome the problem of theoretical abstractness and also to keep faith with the basic philosophical idea that applied ethics is continuous with general ethical theory. Biomedical ethics, as a primary division of applied ethics, is not a special kind of ethics; it does not include any special principles or methods that are specific to the field of medicine and not derivable from more general sources. Rather, the field of medicine is governed ultimately by the same general normative principles as hold good in all other spheres of human life. As this approach has come to dominate bioethics, it has inspired similar forms of theoretical construction in other areas of applied ethics, notably in business and professional ethics.

Gradually, however, many philosophers and others who have worked extensively in applied ethics have moved toward a rejection of the traditional idea of developing and applying general normative theory. Their experience in the field has convinced them that the appearance of universality achieved by general normative theory is necessarily purchased at the price of too rigidly separating thought about morality from the historical and sociological realities, traditions, and practices of particular cultures. A result of this separation, as already mentioned, is a level of abstraction that makes traditional ethical theory virtually useless in guiding moral decision making about real problems in specific social settings. Moreover, these critics see essentially the same problems of ahistoricism and abstraction reappearing with the standard midlevel normative theories, in bioethics and elsewhere. In addition to this, it appears to many philosophers working in applied ethics that most of the real work of resolving moral problems occurs at the level of interpretation and comparison of cases. Recourse to general normative principles, even midlevel ones, seems never to override case-driven considered judgment. On the contrary, conflict between a putative principle and the extensive consideration of cases seems always to result in refining the interpretation of whatever general principle is involved. This tendency is important in connection with contemporary efforts to refine the deductive model of moral justification by incorporation of wide reflective equilibrium theory. For it is crucial to reflective equilibrium theory and the defense of principalism that general principles override considered judgments, at least much of the time.

Concerns about ahistoricism and abstractness, and the problems of application that they create, have produced a powerful skepticism about the very possibility of constructing a perfectly general normative theory. By now this ancient philosophical quest appears to many to be inconsistent with the most immediate, natural, and defensible conception of morality. Viewed from the perspective of modern history, sociology, and anthropology, moralities are seen as social artifacts that arise as part of the basic elements of a culture—its religion, its social forms of marriage and family, its economy, and so forth. Morality is thus an evolving social instrument that serves a variety of very general ends which are associated with different domains of social life and are pursued within the context of changing historical circumstance and significant epistemic limitations. As such, a morality may be criticized in terms of how well or ill it serves identifiable and worthy social ends. But, by the same token, what is good or right in some realm of life, within a given cultural setting, must be a function of a highly complex set of conditions, including psychological factors and patterns of expectations that are themselves created by social custom and convention.

In light of the very different historical origins of diverse social forms, across so many different cultures, there seems to be no good reason to assume that all defensible moral standards will be explicable in terms of a deductive relationship to some more or less unitary set of basic principles with more or less determinate normative content. Although such a theoretical reduction or reconstruction may be possible, in spite of cultural diversity and in spite of the overwhelming failure of all previous efforts to gain general acceptance of any set of fundamental moral principles, many now regard this enterprise as exceedingly doubtful, even philosophically naive.

III. CONTEXTUALISM AND RELATED DEVELOPMENTS

Skepticism about the possibility of normative theory on a grand scale and growing doubts about the feasibility of solving moral problems by deductively applying general principles have given rise to a plurality of approaches and ways of conceptualizing problems within the field of applied ethics. One general approach to practical moral decision making that is currently gaining favor is *contextualism*. As variously developed in the current philosophical literature, contextualism has tended primarily to be critical of established beliefs about ethical theory, rather than constructive of better models of moral reasoning, but the emphasis is now shifting to include the latter. From the contextualists' point of view, it is unnecessary to strive for a universally valid ethical theory since there are more realistic ways of accounting for moral rationality and justification. In place of the traditional, essentially top-down model of moral reasoning and justification, contextualism adopts the general idea that moral problems must be resolved within the interpretive complexities of concrete circumstances, by appeal to relevant historical and cultural traditions, with reference to critical institutional and professional norms and virtues, and by relying primarily upon the method of comparative case analysis. According to this method we navigate our way to a practical resolution by discursive triangulation from clear and settled cases to problematic ones.

Moral judgments are thus provisionally justified by defending themselves against objections and rivals. So conceived, justification is essentially continuous with a case-driven, inductive process of seeking the *most reasonable* solution to a problem within a framework of shared values which are seen as having presumptive validity unless rational considerations call them into question.

Closely associated with questions concerning the usefulness of general normative theory is the question of how we should conceive of the enterprise of living and acting morally. While Kantians and utilitarians focus on following appropriate rules and principles, an increasing number of philosophers in the field of applied ethics argue that we should focus on acquiring virtues appropriate to fulfilling our roles in particular cultural and institutional settings. This conception is consistent with a general contextualist orientation in rejecting the deductive model of moral deliberation. In so far as proponents of virtue ethics are concerned with ethical theory at all, it is a much more empirically oriented theory than moral philosophers have traditionally sought. Such theory seeks to understand the instrumental effects of various ways of conceptualizing and judging action and character within the context of the social and institutional roles persons play. Unlike contextualism, however, rather than focusing directly on the structure of moral reasoning about right action, virtue ethics tends to see right action as indirectly determined by considering what actions would flow from the operation of relevant virtues.

As already emphasized, the general question which divides practitioners of applied ethics is where we should look in our quest for standards of justification for moral judgments. For some, the turn away from the deductive model of problem solving in applied ethics has spurred renewed interest in procedural aspects of group moral deliberation and decision. They have begun to consider much more seriously the question of what features a decision procedure must have if its conclusions are to be regarded as morally justified. There seems to be considerable support for the view that a justified moral judgment must represent, in some sense, a free and informed consensus of all interested parties. The central problem is to gain a fuller understanding of the nature of the biases and distortions that affect decision procedures in particular social and cultural contexts, and thus to clarify the conditions under which we can be confident that we have at least approximated such a consensus.

Clearly, rejecting the deductive model of moral problem solving does not entail rejection of all moral theory. Significant moral reform in social life depends upon securing some kind of theoretical purchase on established practice and institutional arrangements. Ethical theory in a form that is sufficient to this purpose is therefore necessary. It is necessary in many other ways as well. For example, theory of some sort is necessary even to approach the problem of moral status—what gives something moral standing such that it is an object of moral consideration in its own right? And only ethical theory can illuminate or resolve such questions as whether the distinction between killing and "letting die" is morally relevant in itself, or whether actual or hypothetical consent under certain ideal conditions is more important in justifying certain kinds of social institutions and policies. These questions, and countless others like them, simply are theoretical questions that arise naturally and unavoidably when attempting to make moral headway in a complex and changing world. Theories dealing with such questions as these, however, do not provide decision procedures for solving moral problems. Rather, they help us to extend and deepen our understanding of the complex set of moral concepts in terms of which we interpret our problems and dilemmas, and so point the way to improving our values and social practices.

The most relevant and useful theoretical constructions in applied ethics are likely to be those that are impelled by an informed understanding of the real conflicts and difficulties of practical life. The recent history of moral philosophy's contributions in the world of practice bears this out. Responses to particular theoretical issues arising in connection with problems like abortion and euthanasia, or concentrated efforts in areas like environmentalism and animal rights, have produced moral philosophy's most significant contributions to the important moral issues of the day. Moreover, the best work of this kind in applied ethics is currently exerting considerable influence on some of the most interesting work concerning ethical theory.

One of the consequences of the turn toward contextualism and virtue ethics has been a renewal of efforts to better understand the nature of practical moral reasoning and the norms governing it. This kind of exploration is presently fostering a kind of redirected metaethics. Rather than concentrating on the analysis of basic ethical concepts and the meaning of moral propositions, the focus is on the structure of actual moral reasoning, including comparisons with law and science; on the conditions for properly evaluating moral precepts and rules; and on the limits of rational decidability in morals. Metaethical theory of this kind, which might strive ultimately to systematically illuminate what abstract conditions social moralities, or their parts, must meet in order to be reasonable or defensible, may be philosophically very valuable. This kind of theory can at least serve, if not finally fulfill, a powerful intellectual desire for ordered, systematic understanding. And it could be helpful indirectly in practical terms as well.

IV. QUESTIONS OF CONVENTIONALISM, MORAL EXPERTISE, AND MORAL PSYCHOLOGY

The intensely practical and consensus-driven nature of applied ethics would alone serve to raise a question of its critical and reformative potential, but given the current trend toward metalevel contextualist accounts of moral reasoning and justification, this issue becomes acute. From such a perspective, how can applied ethics avoid being inherently conventional and conservative? How, in other words, can applied ethics secure a sufficiently critical perspective on conventional moral and evaluative practices to be capable of genuine and, if necessary, radical reform? Environmental ethics perhaps deserves special attention in this regard because so much of its thrust is directed at deep, even revolutionary, reform in moral attitudes toward other animals and the natural world.

Certain fields of applied ethics have developed to include professional consultation and the representation of so-called "ethicists" within institutional settings, on government commissions and committees, and in the media and the courts. This has resulted in much recent discussion of the whole issue of moral expertise. Can there be any such thing as a moral expert, or experts on the important ethical dimensions of certain domains of practice? Of course, if moral reasoning and decision making were primarily a matter of defending some general principle and applying it to cases in a predominantly analytical way, then, presumably, the skills associated with this process would constitute a sort of moral expertise which could be linked to certain sorts of training and preparation. In particular, training in the history of normative theory and analytic philosophy would appear especially relevant, even indispensable. On the other hand, a more contextualist approach to the process of moral reasoning will recognize a central role in moral discourse for a variety of skills and intellectual, imaginitive, and emotional resources beyond those that are typical of the moral philosopher. Psychological understanding and sensitivity will be seen as crucial, as will sociological knowledge, knowledge of religions and of legal and political realities, and so forth. This point of view, therefore, sees applied ethics as inherently multidisciplinary because it is impossible to locate all the skills and attributes necessary to progress in social morality in the training and skills that are typical of any single profession.

Interest in the issue of moral knowledge and expertise is not unrelated to a more general renewal of interest in "moral psychology," as philosophy has, in certain periods, concerned itself with this field. What, for example, are the principal sources of moral hypocrisy in our times? Or how much does the credibility of one's moral views depend on their being based on certain kinds of relevant experience? Or what general conditions support a culture in which ethics and moral values are taken seriously?

Also See the Following Article

APPLIED ETHICS, CHALLENGES TO

Acknowledgment

Much of the substance of this article is derived from the Introduction to *Applied Ethics: A Reader* (E. Winkler and G. Coombs (eds.), 1993.) Basil Blackwell, Oxford).

Bibliography

Beauchamp, T. L., and Childress, J. F. (1979) [1983]. "Principles of Biomedical Ethics." Oxford Univ. Press, New York.
Daniels, N. (1979). Wide reflective equilibrium and theory acceptance in ethics. *J. Philos.* 76, 256–82.
Jonson, A., and Toulmin, S. (1988). "The Abuse of Casuistry." Univ. of California Press, Berkeley.
Noble, C. (1982). Ethics and experts. *Hastings Centre Rep.* 12(3), 7–9.
Philips, M. (1995). "Between Universalism and Scepticism." Oxford Univ. Press, New York.
Solomon, R. (1992). "Ethics and Excellence: Cooperation and Integrity." Oxford Univ. Press, New York.
Winkler, E. (1993). From Kantianism to Contextualism: The rise and fall of the paradigm theory in bioethics. In "Applied Ethics: A Reader" (E. Winkler, and G. Coombs, Eds.). Basil Blackwell, Oxford.
Winkler, E. (1996). Moral philosophy and bioethics: Contextualism vs. the paradigm theory. In "Philosophical Perspectives on Bioethics" (W. Sumner, and I. Boyle, Eds.). Univ. of Toronto Press, Toronto.

ARCHAEOLOGICAL ETHICS

Richard R. Wilk and K. Anne Pyburn
Indiana University

GLOSSARY

applied anthropology A discipline devoted to the improvement of human life through the preservation of culture, but also through the creation of opportunities for positive cultural change.

archaeological context The association between artifacts and features that imbues them with meaning.

archaeological record The material cultural record of human life on earth.

consolidation A strategy for stopping erosion and degradation of an archaeological site or feature.

ecotourism An economic development strategy dependent on bringing in tourists to undeveloped areas. Tourist dollars help support inhabitants who gain a stake in the preservation of the wildlife that attracts visitors.

looting The intentional destruction of archaeological data for profit; usually the destruction of archaeological context.

mitigation Archaeological reconnaissance, consolidation, and data collection from endangered sites designed to allow development to proceed.

reconstruction The process of rebuilding an ancient feature or building according to its original design. In some cases this involves the restoration of paintings and furnishings.

reflexivity Self-consciousness. Social science develops theories to explain human behavior, but also analyzes the cultural origin of those same explanations. Social scientists study others, but are also conscious of studying themselves.

stewardship The protection of archaeological resources for the future, whether these are ancient buildings, sacred artifacts, or field notes and photographs.

ARCHAEOLOGY affects people in many ways, both negative and positive. The responsibilities of archaeologists to maximize the positive and anticipate and then ameliorate the negative have been the subject of heated controversy within the discipline over the last 15 years. The movement toward social responsibility has been slow and uneven, hampered to a large degree by a lack of objective information and the dominance of polemic over constructive cooperation and debate.

Some argue that archaeology has the power to deny people's access to their own past, to support oppressive ideologies, and to hasten the physical destruction of cultural heritage. It may be used to justify nationalistic aggression and ethnic or racial discrimination, to disfranchise people and damage their sense of cultural identity. Others argue that archaeology promotes environmental conservation and increases people's awareness of place, history, and continuity with their ancestors. Archaeology can warn us of the dangers of authoritarianism, support legitimate claims to land and resources, be a focus for community identity, and be a source of economic development through employment and attracting tourism.

A heightened awareness of the potential for harm has prompted efforts to write ethical guidelines for the practice of archaeology. At the same time, the public may be becoming more critical of archaeology. This should be seen as a legitimate concern given that in this country, at least, considerable public and private resources are spent on archaeological research, both for academic research (about $5 million in 1990) and through contracts from government and private companies (well over $80 million per year). Archaeology has often done a poor job communicating the results of this research to the public that pays for it, and to the people whose ancestral remains are being excavated.

Given the many recent controversies over the ethical conduct of science and a heightened public scrutiny of academics, it is not surprising that ethical issues have become more prominent in archaeology. Repressing information or avoiding scrutiny is unlikely to help in the long term; prudent discussion of ethical issues within the scientific community, and early involvement of the public in that discussion, is a better long-term solution than waiting for a crisis. The consequences of a loss of public confidence in archaeologists have already been apparent, as many countries have moved to restrict or even end the activities of foreign scholars in their territory. The controversy over the curation and reburial of American Indian skeletal remains in the United States is another cautionary example.

Research by archaeologists from the developed countries in other parts of the world is coming under particular scrutiny. North America has the largest community of archaeologists in the world, who do the most research in foreign countries. Archaeologists are the only foreign researchers in many remote places in the world; they may have an impact far beyond their numbers. At the same time their conduct and goals are subject to question by local scholars and government agencies, and by the local people who live in and around archaeological sites, often built

by their ancestors and containing remains that are key to local culture and politics.

I. LITERATURE REVIEW

There are a number of reasons, both practical and intellectual, why academic archaeologists are becoming more concerned with ethics and their relationships with the public. These include:

• Growing concern over looting and recognition that legal solutions to this problem have not been effective
• Native Americans' questioning of archaeologists' conduct in regard to native American material culture and buried ancestors
• The growing number of local archaeologists around the world who want to establish national archaeologies, often supplanting, regulating, or prohibiting the work of foreigners from richer countries
• The new linkages between archaeology and natural resource conservation, tourist development, and ecotourism promoted by both local governments and multilateral and national development programs
• The growing concern in the social sciences with the cultural and political consequences of writing history
• A reflexive and introspective trend among archaeological theorists
• The need for professional ethical standards as archaeologists have entered the world of business and government

We next summarize and discuss the different themes which have emerged within archaeology.

A. Ethics and Archaeology

Because archaeologists have considered the only objects of their study to be the dead, they have often not accepted a responsibility to the living. Types of ethical issues considered by archaeologists have revolved around investigators' responsibilities to science, to their colleagues, and toward the materials in their care. When concerned with the public, archaeologists are occupied with the formal channels of public relations, communicating their results through publication, and staying within the law. Their traditional concern with the public has been limited to discouraging looting and the traffic in antiquities.

Unlike other kinds of anthropology, archaeological work has generally been considered exempt from formal Human Subjects review.

In the late 1960s archaeologists in the United States began to see the effects of site destruction from looting and construction; their research subjects were rapidly becoming extinct. They formulated a "conservation ethic" and pushed for legislation to fund salvage and impact studies. The goal was to protect sites, and to make sure that excavation was clearly justified by scientific goals. In the long term this led to the growth of applied archaeology to undertake massive publicly funded projects, and this has posed further ethical dilemmas. Are archaeologists funded in this way loyal to the agency that pays them, to the profession and some ideal of science, or to the sites themselves? How do archaeologists publicly justify the cost of research with their academic results? But often lost in the ethical clamor of a changing profession is the voice of those who live where the resources are being excavated and "saved," and the descendants of the people whose bodies were "mitigated." To these people, often, there is not much difference between having a site destroyed by construction companies and having one "saved" by archaeologists. Local citizens might even be opposed to archaeological interference, on the grounds that it delays construction projects or land modification that promises local employment and other benefits. Archaeologists are sometimes seen as "standing in the way of progress" rather than as allies of the local community in the face of an attempt to destroy a valuable local heritage (the way they see themselves).

Perhaps archaeologists fail to effectively portray the ethical perspectives that guide their work. There have been some recent critiques of the way archaeologists write about their subject, and of the ways they may employ rhetoric for personal and political reasons. But publication of results and communicating about archaeology to the public through the media are only a small part of what archaeologists do that influences the public. Archaeology is essentially a field science that takes investigators out of their own communities and puts them, often for extended periods of time, into other communities and often different nations and cultures. The years they spend in daily interaction with local people (or avoiding interaction with them) are likely to have a larger impact on the public perception of archaeology, past cultures, and cultural patrimony than all their scholarly and popular publications. Until very recently ethical statements about conduct in the field have had little to say about anything beyond getting

permits from local governments or landowners to excavate.

B. Ethical Guidelines

The "four statements" of the Society for American Archaeology (SAA) published in the 1960s regarding ethical conduct within the discipline did not mention the public at all, and dealt only with qualifications and conduct within the profession. But the 1990s have seen a paradigm shift in the discipline as the behavior of archaeologists and the political impact of their profession have come under scrutiny (and under fire) from various public and private stakeholders and from government agencies involved in heritage management. In 1995 both the SAA and the Archaeological Institute of America (AIA) formed enlarged ethics committees to review existing statements and develop new principles. Both groups developed new statements and comparable sets of principles, but those of the SAA are more concise. They are:

1. Stewardship. The archaeological record, that is, *in situ* archaeological material and sites, archaeological collections, records, and reports, is a public trust. The use of the archaeological record should be for the benefit of all people. As part of the important record of the human cultural past, archaeological materials are not commodities to be exploited for personal enjoyment or profit. It is the responsibility of all archaeologists to work for the long-term preservation and protection of the archaeological record. Although archaeologists rarely have legal ownership of archaeological resources, they should practice and promote stewardship of the archaeological record. Stewards are both caretakers and advocates for the archaeological record. As they investigate and interpret the record, archaeologists should promote its long-term conservation. Archaeologists should use their specialized knowledge to promote public understanding and support for the archaeological record.

2. Accountability. Responsible archaeological research, including all levels of professional activities, requires an acknowledgment of public accountability and a commitment by the archaeologist to make every reasonable effort, in good faith, to consult actively with affected group(s), with the goal of establishing a working relationship that can be beneficial to the discipline and to all parties involved.

3. Commercialization. The Society for American Archaeology has recognized that the buying and selling of objects out of archaeological context is contributing

to the destruction of the archaeological record on the American continents and around the world. Commercialization of objects from the archaeological record results in these objects being unscientifically removed from sites, destroying contextual information that is essential to understanding archaeological resources. Archaeologists should abstain from any activity that enhances the commercial value of archaeological objects not curated in public institutions or readily available for scientific study, public interpretation, and display.

4. Public education and outreach. Archaeologists shall reach out to the public to: (1) enlist its support for the stewardship of the archaeological record, (2) explain and promote the use of methods and techniques of archaeology in understanding human behavior and culture, and (3) explain archaeological interpretations of the past. A variety of audiences exist for these educational and outreach efforts, including students, teachers, lawmakers, Native Americans, government officials, environmentalists, service organizations, retirees, reporters, and journalists. Archaeologists who are unable to undertake public education and outreach directly shall encourage and support the efforts of others in these activities. Archaeologists should participate in cooperative efforts with others interested in the archaeological record so that preservation, protection, and interpretation of the record may be improved.

5. Intellectual property. Intellectual property as contained in knowledge and documents created through the study of archaeological resources is part of the archaeological record and, therefore, is held in stewardship rather than as a matter of personal possession. If there is a compelling reason, and no legal restrictions, a researcher may have exclusive access to original materials and documents for a limited and reasonable time, after which these materials and documents must be made available to others. Knowledge must be made available, by publication or otherwise, within a reasonable time, and documents deposited in a suitable place for permanent safekeeping. The preservation and protection of in situ archaeological sites must be considered in the publication or distribution of information about them.

6. Records and preservation. Archaeologists shall work actively for the preservation of, and long-term access to, archaeological collections, records, and reports. Archaeologists shall also promote actions by others that lead to these ends. Archaeologists shall encourage colleagues, students, and others to make responsible use of collections, records, and reports in their research

as one means of preserving the in situ archaeological record and of providing more attention and care to the portion of the archaeological record that has been removed and incorporated into archaeological collections, records, and reports.

Publication of these principles as a special report to all members by the SAA was accompanied by a set of critical articles discussing the pitfalls of ethics in archaeological research. This document, "Ethics in American Archaeology: Challenges for the 1990s," edited by Mark Lynott and Alison Wylie, is a reasonable attempt to disseminate the wide variety of concerns voiced by the large and varied constituency of the organization. Some of these articles simply explain in greater detail the reason for the SAA's position on ethics and the phraseology of the guidelines, while others are openly critical and skeptical of the archaeological establishment. Though most contributors to the volume seem satisfied with the intent of the principles, several point out the difficult of applying ethical standards in field research.

Paul Healy gives an excellent survey of the ethical problems that arise in fieldwork, especially when conducted outside the archaeologist's own homeland, adding,

> The people of the host nation, who are perhaps the group closest to the actual archaeological remains, are the most commonly neglected in regard to archaeological research and results. For decades, professional archaeologists have made poor excuses for avoiding communication with local populations when conducting fieldwork. Thus thousands of North Americans have access to information on the prehistory of some countries, while the same information is denied the inhabitants of the archaeological sites! ... [M]any people in Third World nations find it surprising to see foreigners coming to their homeland to spend large sums of money on equipment, supplies and labor just for the sake of "research." (1984. In E. Green (Ed.), *Ethics and values in archaeology* (pp. 123–132). New York: Free Press)

These concerns are all reflected in the recent activities of the World Archaeological Congress (WAC), which has built close ties with the World Council of Indigenous Peoples and has taken as one if its missions the representation of indigenous peoples' rights to the archaeological community. This group has also published a "WAC Code of Ethics: Members Obligations to Indigenous Peoples," and has formulated and adopted the "Vermilion Accord," which establishes standards for the ethical treatment of human mortal remains (WAC, 1990. *Journal of Field Archaeology*, 17(2), 216–217). As yet, a small minority of American archaeologists belong to the WAC, and it is unknown how many actually agree with its goals and ethical codes.

Spriggs places the issue of archaeological ethics in relation to the rights of indigenous minorities in the Pacific region, but his suggestions have much broader applicability (1991. *The Contemporary Pacific* 3(2), 380–392). He says that archaeologists must engage indigenous people in a dialogue of equals on six issues: recognition of prior ownership of the land by indigenous people; consultation with and agreement of indigenous people as part of archaeological projects; presentation of results of archaeological work to local communities in a useful form; employment and training of indigenous people as part of archaeological projects; protection of sacred and traditional sites, including human burials; and differing interpretations of prehistory by indigenous people and archaeologists.

Even if archaeologists understand and consider themselves bound by ethical guidelines, the problem remains that lists of obligations are inadequate, and may do more to protect the researcher than the research subject. Nor do they tell the archaeologist what goal or group is to have priority—conservation, local people, those who pay for the research, colleagues, or objective science. And they give no advice on how to cope with conflicts between goals, beyond refusing to do the research. Ethical codes are one thing, but ethical practice is another—the codes are not a solution to the need for informed practice. The codes must be based, instead, on an understanding of practice.

In the United States, most archaeologists are trained as anthropologists and work in anthropology departments. (This is not so for classical archaeologists and those trained elsewhere in the world.) Self-critical meditations on the ethics and practice of fieldwork have become common in cultural anthropology, but they are not found in the autobiographical writings, memoirs, and fieldwork accounts of archaeologists, who rarely publish details on how they did their fieldwork. Field manuals concentrate exclusively on excavation techniques and "camp management." It is worth asking why people have so assiduously avoided writing about such an important part of archaeological practice.

II. REFLEXIVITY IN ARCHAEOLOGICAL THEORY

Some kinds of ethical issues have been raised by archaeological theorists over the last decade, as part of their dialogue with philosophers of science. As in many of the other social sciences, debate has centered on issues of relativism and objectivity, and a perceived conflict between pursuing truth and seeking relevance.

The opening to the debate can be found in John Fritz and Fred Plog's plea in 1970 to make archaeology relevant: "We suspect that unless archaeologists find ways of making their research increasingly relevant to the modern world, the modern world will find itself increasingly capable of getting along without archaeologists." (1970. *American Antiquity* 35(2), 412.) By the 1980s many archaeologists saw only the negative side of relevance; they found archaeological theory and practice to be oppressive, supporting hierarchy, authoritarianism, racism, sexism, and the continued dominance of the developed countries in the world order. They felt that archaeology had retreated into a protective shell of "scientism" and false objectivity, refusing to engage with the modern world, and therefore implicitly supporting the political and moral status quo.

The passionate debates about the scientific objectivity of archaeology that have filled tens of thousands of pages in the last 20 years have a strong ethical component. Authors disagree about whether or not archaeologists have an obligation to consider the wider social implications of their work, and whether or not the personal and political positions of researchers, or their cultural backgrounds, direct and influence their research programs and results.

Recognition of political ideology within archaeological discourse has led some archaeologists to an extreme form of relativism, where the writing of archaeology is equated with writing fiction or political polemics. A counterreaction seems to be emerging. Bruce Trigger criticizes this trend toward relativism in archaeology, finding that it denies any objective truth and sees archaeology as reification of established political interests. While not espousing a naive scientism, he argues for a "carefully nuanced commitment to empiricism" based on social responsibility (1989. *Canadian Review of Sociology & Anthropology*, 26(5), 788). Once an influential relativist, Ian Hodder now recognizes that archaeology without some notion of truth can easily become a tool of extremism and oppression, so he now favors a "guarded objectivity" (1991. *American Antiquity* 56(1), 10).

Hodder now favors an "interpretive archaeology," linked to the environmental movement, in which

> people around the world [will] use archaeology to help maintain their pasts in the face of the universalizing and dominating processes of Westernization and Western science. The physical archaeological remains help people to maintain, reform, or even form a new identity or culture, in the face of multinational encroachment, outside powers, or centralized governments. Related arguments concern the use of the past by ethnic minorities, women, and other groups to define and reform their social positions within national boundaries in relation to the dominant culture.

He then pleads for getting "the people" involved in archaeology; otherwise there will be implacable hostility as archaeologists retreat into their narrow science. But so far "the people" have had little voice in this discussion—how can we assume that they will share Hodder's goals and ambitions? And given the past record of archaeology, why should they trust professionals to look after their interests?

III. THE POLITICAL CONTEXTS OF ARCHAEOLOGY

The greater involvement of archaeologists in politics is due to more than theoretical debate. Archaeology is now deeply involved in a wide range of local, national, and international political issues, from environmental preservation, to land claims, to the world antiquities trade.

Well before the current reflexive trend, archaeology was often bent to suit political agendas in the "age of imperialism." Archaeology was implicated in a variety of racist ideologies growing out of extreme nationalist movements in the late 19th and early 20th centuries. The use of prehistory as an ideological tool of German Nazism is the best documented, although archaeology served the interests of other nationalist programs in Europe after World War I. Archaeology was also used to deny the African origins of the ruins of Great Zimbabwe, and was an instrument in the control of Australian Aborigines. In the ex-Soviet republics, archaeology is being used to justify expansionist territorial claims and ethnic oppression. Neil Silberman has discussed a number of different ways archaeology has been used by nationalist movements in the middle east, including

the marking of boundaries and the legitimization of the Israeli occupation of the West Bank. Bjornan Olsen argues that the "myth making" of present day American archaeology continues to support the interests of developed countries in the third world, an argument echoed in Matthew Spriggs' careful discussions of the political conflict over archaeology in modern Hawaii.

Contests over the meanings of history and the control of heritage have become international issues, as third world countries assert control over their own past. The efforts of the United Nations to create "World Heritage Sites" in various countries to promote conservation and to control the global trade in looted and stolen antiquities have also placed archaeology in global politics. Organizations such as ICOMOS have attempted to create guidelines for consistent government policies toward preservation.

This new political role has led some archaeologists to question whose interests are being served by their research. Michael Nassaney has described the political complexity of studying colonial period American Indians. In New England, modern Indians are seeking legitimacy and connection with the past, and they want archaeologists to support their political goals. His question is, do archaeologists have a duty to tell the "truth as they see it," or to tell stories that are politically supportive of particular people and that will ensure the financial and political support archaeologists need to continue their work? He points out ways that archaeologists have shaded their reconstructions of the past in order to emphasize continuity between modern people and ancient remains, to "toe the party line."

Much earlier, Graham Clark pleaded for archaeologists to write the history of all peoples rather than elite history or a history of only a few cultures of privilege. He hoped that as each group learned its own history, it would promote rather than inhibit the emergence of wider loyalties, a cultural "world order." His was an eloquent plea for the emancipatory power of local history, for giving people back control of their own pasts, because it "promotes human solidarity."

But in the United States, recently, the archaeological community has come into direct conflict with the interests of many Native American communities over the issue of the excavation and display of Indian skeletal remains and religious and cultural artifacts. Archaeologists now often feel caught in a dilemma, with conflicting ethical obligations to their science, to the preservation of the past, and to the sensibilities of the descendants of those whose remains they excavate.

In 1992 Trope and Echo-Hawk condemned all archaeology by whites of Indians as grossly immoral and unethical and listed the grievances of American Indians toward academic archaeology.

> ... most Indians argue that any information obtained at the expense of their burial rights and religious freedom is not worth knowing. Indians consider studies generated from archaeological curiosity as being unimportant to themselves because their tribal oral traditions adequately explain the past.... Still others detest being categorized as research subjects by non-Indians whose values, traditions, and world view are antithetical to their own. Indians point out that scholars who use Indian bodies for research gain professional prestige, promotions, and tenure without giving anything back to the tribes except disrespect, humiliation, and useless studies written in incomprehensible jargon. (1992. *Arizona State Law Journal* 24, 33–34)

They ask if scholars should stop using knowledge gained from robbing the dead, and if libraries should pull from circulation all works that contain reference to immoral archaeological research. These were some of the concerns behind the formulation and passage of the Native American Grave Protection and Repatriation Act of 1990, concerns which some archaeologists consider ridiculous or unwarranted. Similar issues and positions can be found in the controversy over the museum display of historic artifacts considered sacred or culturally important by modern Indian groups.

These issues have helped open debate about the wider ethical obligations of archaeologists and the complications that arise when one culture studies another. Andrew Gulliford argues that native peoples are only seeking a dialogue as equals in the interpretation of their heritage and the elimination of the stereotype of Indians as a "vanishing race." These are not just issues of academic freedom and the loss of "research areas," these are issues of cultural continuity and survival.

Although things seem to be changing, archaeologists have been very slow to respond to greater public awareness of the implications and impact of their work. A major impetus was the controversy over the participation of South African archaeologists in the World Archaeological Congress, beginning in 1982. For many archaeologists this was the first time modern political concerns explicitly intruded on their academic pursuits. But it certainly was not to be the last.

Since that time the World Archaeological Congress has been the major forum for discussion of the political implications of research. In 1986 they met with the explicit purpose of changing the historical relationship between archaeology and the developing world. Acknowledging that archaeology has tended to serve the purposes of elites in the developing countries, the Congress endorsed the Vermillion Accord on repatriation of burials and artifacts, and has invited the participation of large numbers of archaeologists from developing countries as well as representatives of American Indian and Australian Aboriginal organizations. They also have proposed the first WAC code of ethics, "Members Obligations to Indigenous Peoples." During the last 10 years the American Anthropological Association and the Society for American Archaeology have also sought to involve indigenous peoples in their annual conferences on panels dealing with issues of cultural property, human remains, and repatriation.

The trend is toward cooperation between foreign and local archaeologists and local and indigenous peoples in studying the past. The new "collaborative model" seeks to integrate archaeology with local history and local traditions for the pragmatic purpose of increasing public support for archaeology and site preservation, and because it will hopefully make for better and more accurate archaeology. But at present such collaboration remains undocumented and unstudied, and while its goals are laudable, we do not know if they can be achieved in practice.

IV. PUBLIC EDUCATION AND PRESERVATION

The rapid destruction of archaeological sites is a source of concern to archaeologists and governments in many parts of the world. In some regions a full 100% of the remains left by particular ancient cultures have been destroyed. But how can sites be protected? They are often large, dispersed, and in remote locations, and their sheer abundance makes policing prohibitively expensive. Many sites are destroyed for construction or agriculture, but others are despoiled in the search for antiquities to feed a voracious international market. Laws against looting are poorly enforced and the penalties are usually low compared to the possible rewards. In many areas of dire rural poverty, the temptation to dig for salable objects is strong. Beyond stricter law enforcement (which has not been very effective), the best proposed solutions involve better public relations involving public education through museum displays, television programs, and lectures; incorporating archaeology into school curricula; working with looters, amateurs, and civic groups to involve them in "legitimate" scientific research; and improving the quality of professional archaeological research and publication to better reach the public.

The public and interested amateur archaeologists are, after large-scale construction, the chief cause of site destruction. They often treat archaeologists as the enemy, as a group intent on "locking up" archaeological sites and sequestering the "relics" from public view. Archaeologists have often been guilty of poor and destructive archaeological practices and of neglecting both their legal and their professional responsibilities. At the same time, they recognize that they have to build better relationships with the public if they are to have the public support necessary for their work, and if they are to reduce destruction by amateurs.

Given all the self-reports by archaeologists of how they have improved their relationships with the public, it is surprising to find not one single objective study of the effectiveness of public education in reducing site destruction. Much of the research on natural resource conservation is relevant to this problem, for conservationists face the same problems in protecting endangered flora and fauna from local people who often want to use or sell them. The evidence shows that public education alone does not lead to preservation, at least in less affluent countries. Fencing and policing are far too expensive for most governments to maintain in the long run, especially in the face of local opposition. Many conservationists are turning to a strategy of recruiting local people in a partnership for flexible use and preservation. The major lesson is that there must be incentives for local people to participate if preservation is to work in the long run.

Development of locally controlled "ecotourism" is one option, and the sustainable harvest of wild resources for sale is another. Archaeology tourism and ecotourism can potentially be complementary, but again there has been no research on this possibility or its long-term future. Right now community control of archaeology as part of a sustainable development plan sounds like a good idea, but we have no way to judge its actual performance. Integrating archaeology with economic "development" may solve some problems, but it poses a host of new ethical dilemmas too. Similarly, an alliance between archaeologists and the emerging global network of "indigenous peoples" sounds attractive, but we do not know what problems may be emerging.

On a practical level, there is no existing research on the economic impact of archaeological work on local communities. There has been no external documentation of the involvement of local communities in excavations, and there is no publication of the experiences of archaeologists who have worked with local communities that would help those who want to plan such activities in the future. We do not have even the basis to assess the practical and ethical problems that such a program would involve.

V. ARCHAEOLOGY AND CULTURAL CONTEXT

While archaeologists have been busy reconstructing and studying the past, anthropologists and historians have made many advances in understanding the crucial role of the past in modern cultural processes. The current "process theory" places a special emphasis on the continual re-creation of social relations, but gives a prominent place to the past, as the basis of performance. Giddens' concept of "structuration" encompasses this view: "Every process of action is a production of something new, a fresh act; but at the same time all action exists in continuity with the past, which supplies the means of its initiation." (1979. *Central problems in social theory: Action, structure and contradiction in social analysis* (p. 70). London: Macmillan).

These anthropological studies of the role of the past in creating modern identity can help us anticipate many of the problems that can arise when archaeologists become involved with local and national cultures and politics. Some of the relevant cultural processes which have been identified by anthropologists and sociologists include:

- An increase in social mobility, which puts archaeology and other social sciences in the position of arbiters of authenticity. Archaeologists can challenge or support the positions of elites, because their knowledge of the past gives them the power to grant authenticity to objects, customs, and places.
- The growth of global culture—the internationalization of media and commodities—intensifies the pressure on each nation and group to find its own uniqueness. They often turn to antiquities and monuments as symbols, and scholars may come under intense pressure to help mythologize the past.
- Nationalism continues to be a strong force, particularly in the third world, where both dominant and subordinate groups seek traditions (often invented or rediscovered) that bolster their claims to legitimacy. Again, archaeology may be recruited to support these claims, or it may be attacked for failing to do so.
- The rise of ethnic movements also makes the past a

crucial symbol of identity. Group membership, political position, and claims to land and resources are often chartered by particular interpretations of past events, acts of ancestors, and migration stories. While anthropologists are beginning to study the way different peoples think about time and the past, archaeologists rarely understand how local people will interpret their findings.

The key issue for archaeologists is the struggle for control over the past. History in general has been written by intellectuals from developed countries, and most of the rest of the world's peoples have been relegated to the status of "people without history." Their past has often been depicted as static, and the remains of their ancestral civilizations have been the subject of foreign research, while the physical remains have been carried off to museums in the developed countries. Third world archaeologists have been struggling for autonomy and to recontextualize and re-present the past for local audiences, within a structure of archaeological research, methods and concepts which was built in the colonial era. Their response has often been to recast their local past according to narrow nationalist goals, and this leads to difficult relationships with foreign scholars, though they may depend on those scholars for resources for their own career development.

VI. CASE STUDIES OF ARCHAEOLOGISTS IN THE FIELD

A search for literature on how archaeologists conduct themselves in the field in relation to local people turns up very few sources. There are a few self-reported case studies by archaeologists who have successfully worked with local communities during their research, but no comprehensive studies which disclose conflicts with local people over the disposition of cultural resources, disturbance of burials, or cross-cultural misunderstandings.

The archaeology of the colonial era has acquired a deserved reputation for a patronizing attitude toward living local people and cultures. Seton Lloyd's autobiography reveals attitudes that were typical of his generation of middle-eastern research. Local people are picturesque when seen from afar, and selected members of the local aristocracy make suitable hunting partners, but most appear as troublesome workers and servants kept at a suitable distance. In one place Lloyd, responsible for the death of a driver, laments the loss of a cake as a more serious matter.

Perhaps more typical is Mallowan's recollection of digging at Ur with Woolley in 1926.

> During the excavations we employed 200–250 men.... They worked for us from sunrise to sunset with an interval of half an hour for breakfast and an hour for luncheon. It was a strenuous day's work for which they were paid at the rate of one rupee, the equivalent of about eighteen pence.... These Arab tribesmen were desperately poor and lived next door to starvation. They could hardly be expected to be possessed of any surplus energy and had to be driven along by exhortation and encouragement, and occasionally, I fear, by the sack. But the work was much coveted and was a tremendous boon. (1977. *Mallowan's memoirs* (p. 42). London: Collins)

He recounts incidents where workmen stole objects from tombs during the excavation. Later excavations in Iraq had truly adversarial relations with local people and workers, and he resorted to armed guards for safety, contending with poor excavation work and constant pilferage and theft.

Some archaeologists treated their workers well. Petrie took great pains to minimize accidents, and banned pork from his camp in accord with the Moslem sensitivities of local people. He paid his workers full market price for artifacts they found during the excavation. Such care was said to annoy other archaeologists.

The exclusion of local people from participation in the intellectual work of archaeology was justified, by this generation, by the great cultural and temporal gaps between the local people and those under study. They did not want to recognize the modern inhabitants of the region as the legitimate descendants of the ancient Sumerians, Egyptians, and Greeks, because they had already appropriated these ancients as their own ancestors. Traces of the same attitudes continue to linger in Classical and Biblical archaeology, which are supported largely by private contributions from the elites of developed countries who seek their foreign cultural roots.

Poor relationships between modern archaeologists and local people are not discussed in the literature, though they are common topics of conversation among professionals, and calls for better relations are increasingly common. In print we only see glowing accounts of close relationships and successful cooperation. Most examples come from the United States, where the cultural gulf between archaeologists and local people is relatively small. The University of South Florida's program in the Apalachicola Valley is an excellent example. The Zuni and Navajo tribes have successfully run their own archaeological programs for a number of years, and in Australia Aborigines regularly advise on archaeological projects. A more complex case comes from Truk, where a cultural anthropologist and archaeologist helped local people resist destruction of burial sites during airport construction.

Perhaps the most important recent account of community involvement in archaeology is Heffernan's 1988 book, *Wood Quay*. The community's struggle with the Irish government to preserve and excavate a central Dublin archaeological site threatened by development had profound social consequences. In fact, Wood Quay become an important political focus for Ireland, with significant impact on local and national government as a result of focusing public attention on ethnic history. In 1978, under the banner, "Save Viking Dublin," 20,000 people turned out for protest marches to stop site destruction, and a militant occupation followed. One of the important dimensions of the conflict was the ambivalence of the professional archaeological community, which initially resisted the "meddling" of the public in what they saw as their technical province. One of the causes of the political crisis was the reluctance of academics to communicate their activities and results to the public.

The particular public appeal of Wood Quay can be attributed to the startling preservation of the artifacts, the location of the site in an impoverished and disfranchised central urban neighborhood, and the way the site portrayed Viking Dublin as a cultured and cosmopolitan trading center of world importance. To a nation eager for legitimacy on the world stage, this was very powerful material. Heffernan credits the struggle to preserve the site for an emergence of popular democracy, as well as economic revitalization of the inner city. He makes an apt comparison with the excavations of the Templo Mayor of Tenochtitlan in central Mexico City. The promise of such a comparison cannot be fulfilled with the presently impoverished literature on the practice of archaeology.

VII. CONCLUSION

Archaeology is and has always been a politically charged endeavor. Research designs follow the agendas of the powerful in order to get funding and permission, and results get selectively promoted by National Geographic, Science News, and the Associated Press, depending on how they measure up to the values of the present. Most archaeologists work within the boundaries of current political requirements to get the chance to do research. Many feel that changing the world is not their responsibility, although most archaeologists harbor a belief that there are useful things to be learned from the mistakes and successes of the past. But archaeologists do have a powerful impact on the people who live in the vicinity of archaeological digs and on the people whose history connects them to research. Simply attempting to do what seems to us to be the "right thing" for local people and interested groups may work out fine sometimes, but the "right thing" will vary between cultures, and archaeologists also need to think about the "right outcome."

Sometimes this involves changing people's minds. There is a branch of anthropology specifically geared to instigating positive cultural change and preventing the deterioration of essential cultural institutions. Like the other subfields of anthropology, this one is imperfect and sometimes controversial. Nevertheless there is an accumulated body of knowledge about appropriate ways to effect change in other people's cultures that archaeologists have been extremely remiss in ignoring. These are summarized in the principles of the Society for Applied Anthropology. A complete statement of these principles can be found in *Human Organization*, the journal of the Society for Applied Anthropology, but a few points are worthy of recapitulation here. Members are enjoined to consider the impact of their research as well as the implementation of their recommendations on local people. Respect for professionals and nonprofessionals alike is inherent in every principle. Consultation with people involved and affected by research is required.

Responsible archaeology is applied anthropology. Archaeologists must research ahead of time what will be the consequences of their numbers, their money, and their interpretations, and they must shoulder the responsibilities research generates before the fact, and not try to clean up a mess with goodwill after the village factions are breaking up monuments to spite each other and the local citizenry have vowed to bulldoze anything that might bring archaeologists back to town. Research into ways to encourage site preservation is desperately needed. Sometimes this means promoting ecotourism or hiring workers through a village government. Other times archaeologists may need to distance themselves from tourist schemes and hire only from a national pool of professionally trained excavators or union laborers. Sometimes crews should include both men and women, and other times they must not; often research teams need to pay attention to dress and speech and to how behavior affects local concepts of appropriate gender roles. No one can know automatically what the correct procedures will be in any particular place; this will require specific research for each project.

Professional interest in ethics has not come a moment too soon for the discipline of archaeology. Public outreach and accountability and sensitivity to nonprofessional interest groups are the only real measures available for protecting the past. The only hope for the survival of archaeology into the new millennium lies in expanding its constituency beyond the ivory tower. Ethical considerations dictate this path, and ethical consideration will keep us on it.

Also See the Following Articles

ENVIRONMENTAL ETHICS, OVERVIEW • INDIGENOUS RIGHTS • LAND-USE ISSUES • RESEARCH ETHICS

Bibliography

Olsen, B. (1991). Metropolises and satellites in archaeology: On power and asymmetry in global archaeological discourse. In R. Preucel (Ed.), *Processual and postprocessual archaeologies: Multiple ways of knowing the past* (pp. 211–224). Carbondale, IL: Center for Archaeological Investigations at SIU.

Pyburn, K. A., & Wilk, R. R. (1995). Responsible archaeology is applied anthropology. In M. J. Lynott and A. Wylie (Eds.), *Ethics in American archeology: Challenges for the 1990s*. Washington, D.C.: Society for American Archaeology.

Vitelli, K. D. (1984). The international traffic in antiquities: Archaeological ethics and the archaeologist's responsibility. In E. Green (Ed.), *Ethics and values in archaeology* (pp. 143–155). New York: Free Press.

Vitelli, K. D. (Ed.) (1996). *Archaeological ethics*. Walnut Creek, CA: AltaMira.

Wilk, R. (1985). The ancient Maya and the political present. *Journal of Anthropological Research,* 41(3), 307–326.

World Archaeological Congress (1991). World Archaeological Congress first code of ethics. *World Archaeological Bulletin,* 5, 22–23.

Wylie, A. (1992). The interplay of evidential constraints and political interests: Recent archaeological research on gender. *American Antiquity,* 57(1), 15–35.

ARISTOTELIAN ETHICS

C. B. Megone
University of Leeds

I. Aristotle's Approach to Ethics
II. Aristotle's Method in Ethics
III. Aristotelian Ethical Theory: *Eudaimonia,* Human Nature, and Virtue
IV. *Eudaimonia,* Pleasure, and External Goods
V. Prominent Features of Aristotelian Ethical Theory
VI. Aristotelian Ethics and Applied Ethics
VII. Conclusions

GLOSSARY

acrasia Weakness of will.
eudaimonia The ultimate good, happiness.
phronesis Practical wisdom, an intellectual virtue of central importance for ethical virtue.
telos Goal or end.
theoria Contemplation or reflective understanding.
virtue (ethical) A state of character that is displayed in good actions.

ARISTOTLE certainly wrote two works on ethics, the *Nicomachean Ethics* (NE) and the *Eudemian Ethics.* He may also have written the *Magna Moralia.* Although it is a matter of dispute, the *NE* is widely believed to be the most definitive account of his views, and this entry will draw primarily on that text in developing an account of Aristotle's position. However, Aristotle was a systematic thinker. He recognized that in addressing central questions in ethics he also needed to attend to issues in the philosophy of mind and action, metaphysics (where enquiry focuses on what must, fundamentally, exist), and political philosophy. (Aristotle relies on general views most people would accept. Such reliance, though, does not preclude those views having content that is relevant to his discussions and theories in these areas.) Hence a discussion of his ethics must also draw, from time to time, on works such as *De Motu Animalium, Metaphysics* (MP), *Physics,* and *Politics.*

What follows has been divided into six main sections and a Conclusion. In the first section the broad outlines of an Aristotelian approach are presented. The second draws attention to Aristotle's views on method in philosophy, and specifically in ethics—views that obviously determine the nature of his discussion. The third section examines in more detail the answers he develops to the central questions he sets himself. In these answers Aristotle focuses on the importance of what are sometimes termed internal goods—virtues of character and of the intellect. But he is also aware of external goods such as wealth, friendship, and a good family, as well as the value of another internal good, pleasure, so in the fourth section his attitude to these goods is explained. In the fifth section some prominent features of the theory expounded are highlighted. Finally, in the sixth section, the practical implications of Aristotelian ethical theory are discussed, and specifically the influence of this kind of theory on some contemporary debates in applied ethics.

I. ARISTOTLE'S APPROACH TO ETHICS

Aristotle followed Plato and Socrates in the questions he identified as central to the study of ethics. His key question is, "What kind of life should one live?" In the *NE* he raises this question in a slightly different way in terms of the notion of an ultimate good. He observes that if there is some ultimate good at which we all aim in actions it will be of no little importance to discover it (*NE* 1094a1–26). He then notes that all in fact reach verbal agreement that the ultimate human good is a life of *eudaimonia* (*NE* 1094a14–20). Despite this verbal agreement, there is disagreement as to what *eudaimonia* consists of. So Aristotle's key question, his formulation of the Platonic question is, in effect, "What does *eudaimonia* consist of?"

Two remarks about this aspect of his approach are worth making at the outset. First, the question of what Aristotle means by *eudaimonia*, what concept he is investigating, is a matter of some dispute. What has already been said is that there is general agreement that it is the ultimate human good, but until it can be examined in more detail I shall leave the term untranslated here. Second, Aristotle raises this central issue by starting with the claim that all human action aims at some good. This, too, needs examination, but the initial point is that this starting point already shows how for him an understanding of ethics is tied to a full understanding of the nature of human action.

Aristotle also has in mind, like Socrates and Plato, a second question: "Does virtue pay?" He does not raise this question explicitly, but it is implicitly the issue in his investigation of the relation between the life of virtue and that of *eudaimonia*. The question of whether virtue pays is much like the contemporary question, "Why be moral?", save that it is expressed here in terms of the language of virtue. In adopting that language, then, Aristotle is following Socrates and Plato in developing an approach to ethics which focuses on the virtues. He is a virtue theorist. But he is not merely following authorities. Talk of virtues such as justice and courage was central to the everyday language of praise and blame in his time, with vices and other defects of character equally relevant. That language still makes sense too. In day-to-day life, cries for justice are heard worldwide, and those who are courageous, just, or wise are still commonly thought admirable. In addressing the question of whether virtue pays, the Greek thinkers recog-

nized that reflection needs to explain to us why it is justifiable to admire the virtuous. If such common attitudes are to be retained, reflection needs to show that they are not mistaken.

It is worth noting that a virtue theory such as Aristotle's has access to a rich vocabulary for ethical reflection. Aristotle's concern is not simply with right and wrong, but with courage and cowardice, wisdom and foolishness, and justice and injustice. His discussion is also one which can allow that weakness of character, or strength of character (and possibly what he terms "heroic excellence" and "brutishness" (*NE* 1145a15–20)), should be accounted for by an adequate moral theory. In these sorts of ways his approach has been held to be more sensitive than rival contemporary theories to the nuances of everyday moral debate.

Aristotle's ethics, then, has a broad framework provided by the two questions noted above. Within that framework other questions that arose for Socrates and Plato also arise for him. First, in examining what *eudaimonia* consists of he takes account of prominent existing views (see Section II for his method). In the *Republic* (540a–b), Plato had indicated that the life philosopher kings would really wish to pursue was one of intellectual inquiry or reflection (though they would be forced to engage in a more practical life for the sake of the state as a whole). Predecessors had also debated the value of pleasure in a good life, and the importance of other external goods such as wealth and friendship. Thus Aristotle is interested in the role of all these competitors in a *eudaimon* life. This arises directly from attending to his first question, but his answer to that leads him to careful discussion of the nature of both friendship and pleasure, and to focusing on the role of *theoria* (perhaps best translated as contemplation or reflective understanding) within *eudaimonia*.

Second, while Aristotle needs to spell out the nature of *eudaimonia*, clearly any account of its relation to virtue requires him also to provide a definition of virtue. Thus he faces the Socratic "What is it?" question both in relation to virtue as a whole and with regard to specific virtues. Similarly, he also needs to address the question of the relation between the virtues, whether they constitute a unity, or are in some sense identical. Then, in developing a full account, he must focus on the role of seminal virtues such as justice and courage, as well as practical wisdom (*phronesis*), an intellectual virtue particularly important for ethical virtue.

Third, the discussion of virtue leads to a discussion of motivation for action. In the early Platonic dialogues what seems to be a Socratic account of virtue is developed, one in which all desire aims at the good and virtue is thus identified with knowledge (of the good), a position leading Socrates to reject the possibility of weakness of will (as reported by Aristotle (*NE* 1145b21–35)). In the *Republic* (434e–444e) Plato develops a moral psychology that makes room for such a phenomenon, and thus will require a different account of the nature of virtue. Despite their differences, what both these predecessors make clear is that there is a tight connection between virtue and action, and in particular that an adequate account of virtue will involve a properly developed moral psychology. Aristotle follows them, too, in taking it as a constraint on the adequacy of a theory that it should give a satisfactory psychological account of defective conditions such as weakness of will (or weak character) and vice. (This is one reason for the breadth of his theory, previously noted.) Thus Aristotle's account focuses on the nature of (ethical) motivation, and in particular on the role of reason and desire in action, and so their part in a defensible definition of virtue.

Finally, Aristotle notes at the outset of *NE* that ethics is a branch of political philosophy (*NE* 1094a24–8). Thus for him the investigation of *eudaimonia* raises the question of the relation between the achievement of the ultimate good and the kind of society a citizen inhabits. This was, of course, a key theme of Plato's *Republic*. Aristotle takes the matter further through a discussion of human nature and proper human development, taken up also in the early chapters of the *Politics* (1252a1–1253a39). For Aristotle too, therefore, discussion of the virtuous individual intertwines with reflection on the just society.

If these are the issues that Aristotle's ethical theory embraces in addressing his two main questions, an outline of his approach may conclude by indicating the general nature of his response to those questions. Even a very broad indication touches on issues of contention among Aristotelian scholars, but what follows may be sufficiently general to avoid undue controversy.

Taking the two questions above in reverse order, Aristotle defends the view that virtue does indeed pay. He shows this by arguing that the active life of practical virtue, not a life of wealth or pleasure, for example, constitutes *eudaimonia*. (His response is made more complex by the fact that he also seems to view a life of *theoria*, contemplation, or active intellectual virtue, as constitutive of *eudaimonia*. The exact relation between these competitors as producers of *eudaimonia* is a matter of some dispute. For present purposes it is sufficient to say that a defensible Aristotelian theory is one that holds that an active life of practical virtue constitutes *eudaimonia*.)

Clearly this answer to his second question implies an answer to the question of what *eudaimonia* consists of. Thus Aristotle argues that virtue is worthwhile by developing his conceptions of *eudaimonia* and of virtue. His account of *eudaimonia* depends on an argument he introduces concerning human nature. This is because in his view the ultimate human good is produced when a human fulfills his nature—realizes his distinctively human potential. The distinctively human potential is the potential to live a life guided by reason, so the ultimate human good is achieved when an individual fully exhibits his potential for rationality. Thus Aristotle's answer to the first question is that *eudaimonia* consists of a maximally rational life. (The argument here is explained further in Section III.)

In order to justify his answer to the second question, Aristotle then produces and defends a conception of practical virtue such that a life of practical virtue will exhibit rationality maximally (at least in the practical sphere). Thus he argues that the virtues are states of character which enable the agent to reason (practically), and so act, fully rationally. Thus it is that the virtuous life produces *eudaimonia*. It does so because it is the fully rational life and humans are such that the ultimate human good, *eudaimonia*, is realized in a fully rational life. Thus practical virtue and *eudaimonia* are linked, in Aristotle's view, by the concept of rationality. The basis for the importance of rationality is Aristotle's teleological conception of human nature in which humans realize their *telos*, or goal, by maximally exercising reason.

As noted earlier, Aristotle is also aware of the widely held views that pleasure, wealth, friendship, and good family are valuable, and he seeks to accommodate these views within his theory. Thus he argues that the fully virtuous life is indeed pleasurable, providing an argument that depends on an analysis of the nature of pleasure. He also indicates the relevance of wealth and family for virtue. Finally he analyzes friendship, suggesting that its paradigm form is friendship of the virtuous, and indicating that its significance is related to the importance of the state in the realization of an individual virtuous life.

This rather bare sketch will be explained and perhaps made more attractive in Sections III and IV. Prior to a fuller articulation of the Aristotelian ethical position, his remarks on method in ethics need attention. These remarks help to explain how Aristotle arrives at his position, as well as revealing what he takes to be the purpose of ethical theory. Both these points are relevant to the use of Aristotelian theory in applied ethics.

II. ARISTOTLE'S METHOD IN ETHICS

In the early part of *NE* I, prior to investigating what the ultimate good might be, Aristotle makes various methodological remarks concerning the study of ethics. Later, in *NE* VII, he provides further illumination on the same topic. Some of these remarks are consistent with more general views on philosophical method expressed in other works. His views here can be divided into three categories. First he notes some constraints on the study of ethics, in particular on what sort of results can be expected in ethical inquiry. Second, there are remarks on the sort of student that can benefit from engaging in ethical inquiry. These remarks are made in the light of both where ethical discussion must begin and what its purpose is. Finally he offers a suggestion on how to assess the conclusions of a discussion. All these ideas provide insights into the nature of the philosophical study of ethics (and thus of applied ethics), as well as aiding the understanding of Aristotle's own preferred theory.

A. Precision in Ethics

Aristotle begins by remarking that different degrees of precision or clarity can be expected in different areas of study, so it will be sufficient in ethics to indicate the truth roughly and in outline. He illustrates his general idea here by noting that persuasive reasoning is evidently not adequate in mathematics, while on the other hand one should not expect demonstrative proofs of a rhetorician. Why should imprecision be expected in ethics? He appeals to the imprecision in its subject matter. First, fine and just acts exhibit much variety and fluctuation, and second, even good things fluctuate in the sense that they sometimes harm people—the courageous sometimes die as a result of their courage (*NE* 1094b10–27).

It is not clear exactly how these remarks are to be taken. There has been some discussion as to what sort of knowledge Aristotle thinks possible in ethics, and whether he thinks it comparable with scientific knowledge. Questions have also arisen as to whether these remarks support some kind of relativist interpretation of his theory. However, he does continue to talk of indicating the truth in ethics, as if there were truths here as in other areas of inquiry, mathematics, for example, but their content was less precise. Indeed perhaps the key point at this level is that Aristotle is arguing that even though results in ethics do not take the same form as those of mathematics, there is no reason to think it any less possible to discover truths and attain knowledge.

At a more practical level, the remarks do suggest that it will be hard to spell out what justice, for example, requires in terms of general rules such as "always return what you borrow" or "always keep promises." They also suggest that it might be hard to produce any systematic method, such as the classical utilitarian calculus, in the light of which to determine what act is correct on any occasion. Such a calculus does not suppose a system of rules, so is consistent with variety in that way, but it does suggest that there is a reliable universal guide to what is good, while Aristotle seems to be suggesting that even those things that are normally good are not always so. Some of these ideas are developed more explicitly in *NE* V and IX.

B. Precision and Casuistry in Ethics

In *NE*, while discussing *epieikeia* (equity) (V,10) and friendship (IX,2), Aristotle makes clear that in ethical matters (or at least problems involving justice and friendship) universal laws are not possible. Certain matters of distributive justice arise at the level of the state, and for these issues laws are needed. Even if these laws are made by just rulers Aristotle suggests they will break down: "...all law is universal but about some things it is not possible to make a universal statement which shall be correct." He indicates that in such cases the law must take the usual case, even though it is not ignorant of the possibility of error. And, as in book I, he holds that the law in such cases will be correct, "for the error is not in the law, nor in the legislator, but in the nature of the thing" (*NE* 1137b13–19). In other words, laws are needed since they will be true for the most part and thus worth having, but the ethical realm is subject to so much variation in detail that even the best generalizations will break down.

In *NE* (IX,2) Aristotle spells this out with a series of cases. For example, he asks whether one should show gratitude to a benefactor or oblige a friend, if one cannot do both, and observes that all such questions are hard. The reason is that they admit of "many variations of all sorts in respect both of the magnitude of the service and of its nobility and necessity." Nonetheless he again emphasizes the value of generalizations, noting that for the most part we should return benefits rather than oblige friends (*NE* 1164b25–33).

From a methodological point of view the main point here is to highlight the nature of the results one might expect to attain in the study of ethics. It has been emphasized that one cannot expect to discover completely reliable universal rules either about what acts are required of agents or even about the reliability of goods such as courage. The main reason for this is the enormous variation in the details of the situations agents confront. Nonetheless Aristotle also indicates that we can expect to find truths in ethics, and that the truth will be constituted in part by generalizations which are broadly reliable. These are the methodological points, but clearly these remarks have direct implications for practical decisions. If laws break down in this way, what is to be done in the unusual case? If Aristotle holds that there are truths in this area, how are they to be discerned? In other words, these remarks raise questions as to what sort of practical implications Aristotle thinks an ethical theory can have. This will be addressed in Section VI, but, broadly speaking, Aristotle's remarks in *NE* V,10 indicate that he favors a casuistical approach to those cases where the usually reliable generalization breaks down.

C. Starting Points, End Points, and Suitable Students of Ethics

Also in *NE* I,3, Aristotle argues that a young person is not a suitable student of ethics, for two reasons. First, the young do not have a certain type of knowledge that is necessary if one is to start doing ethics—they are ignorant of the actions of life. Second, they are unlikely to benefit from the study of ethics because they tend to be ruled by their passions. In the next chapter, *NE* I,4, he adds that if a student is to benefit from lectures on ethics, he must be well brought up; that is, he must have a grasp on the "that" in ethics, or at least be capable of grasping it when advised by others. The reason for this is that in ethics we must begin with those things that are evident to us (as opposed to what is evident without qualification) (*NE* 1094b27–1095b13). These remarks as to how one should begin an inquiry in ethics can be supplemented by what Aristotle says when actually investigating weakness of will in *NE* VII,1. Here he notes that we must begin by setting the apparent facts before us (*NE* 1145b2–3).

These ideas about starting points in ethics are important, and have been much discussed. The remarks in *NE* I,4 are consistent with methodological considerations put forward in the opening chapter of the *Physics,* so seem to reflect Aristotle's general dialectical method. Very roughly, the idea here is that an inquiry cannot begin in a vacuum but must take as its starting point certain widely held or prominent beliefs. The inquiry then proceeds by examining these beliefs. This certainly seems to be the procedure adopted in the investigation

of *acrasia* in *NE* VII, following the passage previously referred to, and also in the initial inquiry into the nature of *eudaimonia* in *NE* I, 4–5 (noted already), where Aristotle reviews and examines certain widely held beliefs about it.

If so, Aristotle is requiring that a student of ethics should already hold beliefs of a certain sort in advance of study. The objective will then be to examine those beliefs and, if standard dialectical method is adopted here, to seek knowledge (or understanding) by uncovering the explanations (the "whys") for those beliefs. (The position thus draws a distinction between beliefs, or opinions, and knowledge, or understanding. At the outset of an inquiry the investigator begins with widely held beliefs. If the inquiry is successful he will attain knowledge. The beliefs will be justified in the sense that he will have discovered explanations for the propositions believed.)

But what sort of beliefs must the student possess at the beginning? First, they must be beliefs acquired through experience of actions (experience of circumstances in which significant choices have to be made), and second, they must be the sort of beliefs that are acquired through a good upbringing. Some writers have supposed Aristotle to be very demanding here. They suggest that philosophical ethics is only for those who are already good. On this view a well-brought up young person's experience of actions will enable him to know already what the good person should do on any given occasion. Thus, it is said, the study of ethics will simply deepen the student's reflective appreciation of why the life he knows to be good is good.

Such a view has various repercussions, but in the present context most prominent is that it suggests that Aristotelian ethical theory will provide no practical advice at all, for the only possible students are those who need no practical advice. The "that" they must already know, prior to philosophical reflection, is what is required of them in any particular circumstance. But there are reasons to doubt this interpretation. Common sense reflection suggests that if Aristotle had held this view he would have had no students at all, for it is not clear that there is anyone who knows exactly what the right thing to do is in all possible circumstances. If such people exist there would certainly be very few of them. But in any case there are several textual reasons for supposing that this was not his view.

First, if we look at cases in the *NE* where Aristotle adopts his method, we find that he considers a range of widely held beliefs. Thus students would presumably only need to be in a position to recognize these as possible beliefs, and perhaps inclined toward one of them. It may be that in the discussion of weakness of will in *NE* VII,2 the beliefs considered are more theoretical, concerned with whether weakness of will can occur and what it consists of, not beliefs about particular practical circumstances. If so, they may all be beliefs that it is possible for an unreflective wholly good person to hold. But when it comes to the examination of *eudaimonia* in *NE* I,5, the starting points, presumably the "that," some of which a student must know in advance, include the ideas that the ultimate good is wealth or pleasure, which seem unlikely beliefs for someone who only ever makes good choices.

Also telling is the other reason given above for rejecting the young as students of ethics. Those who are young in age or young in character will be dominated by their passions, and so incapable of changing their acts in line with any knowledge their study brings. Yet, Aristotle notes, the point of ethical inquiry is action, not knowledge, a point reiterated in his discussion of virtue (*NE* 1095a4–11 and 1103b26–29). The significance of this claim can be backed up by attention to an earlier remark that knowledge of *eudaimonia* will make us more likely to hit upon what is right (*NE* 1094a22–24). Taken together, these assertions suggest that ethical inquiry (well conducted) is likely to make us change our actions (for the better) in particular circumstances. At least ethical inquiry is intended to achieve that. But if the students of ethics were all wholly virtuous already, ethical inquiry could not make them more likely to do the right actions. All their actions would already be correct.

But if the requirement here is not that students should already know what is demanded in practice, what must a young person who is well brought up believe, prior to studying ethics? One possible interpretation would take Aristotle to be setting down a minimal requirement that experience of the actions of life must have given suitable students a sense of right and wrong, or good and bad. Such a student would simply know the significance of the distinction between right and wrong. On this view, this is a prerequisite for studying ethics since any potential student unaware of the distinction would find incomprehensible the idea that some lives are worth leading, and others not. If so, the student would be unable to see the point of investigating the ultimate human good.

An alternative interpretation would be that the potential ethicist must already have some correct beliefs about which acts are right and which are wrong, and not just the simple view that there is a distinction. This may be more plausible in that, on the previous view,

all that the student has available for explanation is the existence of a bare distinction between right and wrong. By contrast, on this second view what will need explaining is why certain correct acts are right and why others are wrong, and this is the sort of thing one might expect a conception of the ultimate good to explain.

These reflections and attention to the beliefs that Aristotle in fact examines in the ethics suggest that the "that" possessed by a suitable student might include beliefs of an abstract (meta-) level, for example, concerning the link between virtue and happiness or the occurrence of weakness of will, and beliefs as to what virtue requires or what right action is in a particular case, for example, how the courageous person will act in certain circumstances. Furthermore, the student of ethics may be mistaken about at least some of these, of both types, prior to study.

Suppose then that a student must have beliefs of this sort if he is to benefit at all from studying ethics. Inquiry proceeds by examining these beliefs. How, then, does Aristotle determine when an examination of those beliefs has produced satisfactory results? What is the objective of ethical inquiry? The remarks already referred to in *NE* I,4 suggest that the objective is to arrive at a grasp of what is evident without qualification, and that this involves reaching the "whys," the explanations for the starting beliefs. But if so, how are different possible explanations to be assessed? In *NE* VII,1 he indicates that the objective is to prove (presumably by explaining) the truth of all the common opinions (all the starting beliefs), but failing this, the greater number and the most authoritative. The aim will be achieved if the process resolves the difficulties and leaves the common opinions undisturbed (*NE* 1145b3–7). In other words, the best explanation will preserve as true as many as possible of the widely held beliefs and the authoritative beliefs canvased at the outset, but will also explain the conflicts found among the starting beliefs. (Again, incidentally, this suggests that the starting beliefs in ethical inquiry need not be all true. The process of reflection can lead to their refinement or rejection.)

D. Aristotelian Method and Conservatism in Ethics

It might be suggested that this view about the objective of ethical inquiry has rather conservative tendencies. It constrains ethical theory to retain as many as possible of the widely held and authoritative beliefs existing prior to the inquiry. These beliefs determine the direction of inquiry, as well as being what the inquirer must seek to vindicate, at least so far as is possible. In this respect Aristotelian ethics might seem to differ in outlook from utilitarianism, and from any revisionist approach to ethics. The objective of the classical utilitarians was to put ethics onto a scientific base—to provide a scientifically reliable method for determining what to do. As such it was possible that the method, once discovered, might lead to large-scale revisions of practice (J. Bentham, 1789. *An Introduction to the Principles of Morals and Legislation,* chap. 1. London; H. Sidgwick, 1907. *Methods of Ethics,* 7th ed., p. 401. London).

But the degree of conservatism implied by the Aristotelian method will in fact depend on the nature of the preexisting beliefs. If there is a high degree of uniformity among these beliefs, then the method suggests that the theory should at most explain those beliefs, and thus confirm them. (Where there is unanimity, theory may be redundant altogether.) Take an example from applied ethics. Suppose that in medical practice there is widespread agreement about the importance of informed consent from patients; then the Aristotelian will simply expect ethical theory to explain that belief and will reject any theory that suggests the belief is false.

However, the method need not be particularly conservative in those areas where there is widespread disagreement among beliefs. In such cases the method will allow the theory to reject many people's beliefs, and in that respect be highly revisionary. Widespread disagreement may consist of wide variations in thought. A practical example might be the problem of abortion, where some believe it to be wrong in all circumstances, some believe it to be permissible in all circumstances, and still others hold a huge variety of beliefs between these polar positions. In such a case the Aristotelian method might expect ethical theory to vindicate only a small proportion of the beliefs held. (Some might suggest that Aristotle's defense of the importance of virtue in *eudaimonia* is another example of radicalism permitted by his method.) A different case might be where two widely held beliefs clashed, as when it is found that there is a quite general gap between the moral beliefs we assert and those we express in practice. A possible practical example might be the gap between widely expressed views about the horror of homelessness being found among people who do not take the homeless into their spare rooms. In this case an ethical theory might highlight the conflict, as well as lead to the vindication of either the asserted belief or the practice. In all these sorts of case, then, the Aristotelian method can support quite large-scale ethical change.

III. ARISTOTELIAN ETHICAL THEORY: *EUDAIMONIA,* HUMAN NATURE, AND VIRTUE

If these are the principles governing Aristotle's examination of ethical issues, how does he apply them to his two central questions? It is time to turn to a more detailed account of the Aristotelian theory that emerges from addressing these questions. What follows will explore how he develops a conception of *eudaimonia* that appeals to a conception of human nature, and how he then develops an account of virtue and the individual virtues which can show how the life of virtue is a life of *eudaimonia*. Once this has been done, some distinguishing features of Aristotelian ethical theory will be identified.

Before turning to the details, a few brief comments can be made on the general sort of ethical theory Aristotle advances. What has been said already indicates that Aristotelian ethical theory is a virtue theory, and it is there that its greatest relevance to applied ethics may be found. However, three other general features of the theory can be noted. First, it incorporates an objective conception of the ultimate good at which a human life should aim. Second, the theory is eudaemonist. Aristotle holds that the ultimate good at which a life should aim is *eudaimonia,* or happiness, though he argues for a particular conception of happiness. This does not mean that the agent should aim at *eudaimonia* in every action. Virtuous action has its own distinctive motives. But *eudaimonia* is the point of life. What this means is that a life goes better to the extent that it realizes *eudaimonia,* and less well insofar as it diverges from this ultimate good. Thus explaining the relation between virtue and *eudaimonia* provides a reflective justification of the virtuous life. The conception of the virtues is constrained by this feature of Aristotle's theory. In the end, if virtues are valuable, this can only be because they play a role in achieving this *eudaimon* life (though Aristotle also allows that "every virtue we choose indeed for themselves" (*NE* 1097b2–3)). So it must be possible to provide an account of what virtue is that reveals the way in which possession of virtue contributes to the *eudaimon* life.

Thus this second general feature also has repercussions for applied ethics, for, since the virtues may figure in applications of the theory, this eudaemonist constraint on what virtues are will have a bearing on what acts the virtuous individual performs.

Third, Aristotle puts forward a perfectionist theory.

He holds that *eudaimonia*, the ultimate good, is achieved in a life which fully realizes human nature. This aspect of the theory constrains both the account of *eudaimonia* and the account of the virtues. Thus it too has repercussions for applied ethics in the way that the second feature does.

A. *Eudaimonia*

Clarification of Aristotle's views on *eudaimonia* requires that something be said on several points. First, why did Aristotle think there was such a thing as an ultimate good, which all agree verbally to be *eudaimonia*? Second, to what English concept, if any, does this Greek concept correspond? Of what is it that Aristotle is trying to produce a correct conception? Third, the application of his favored method to the investigation of the concept needs to be outlined. A final issue arises from considering both Aristotle's initial remarks about the ultimate good and the account of it he seems to develop. This is whether he views this good as one single concrete objective or as a goal made up of, or including, several constituents.

1. The Argument for an Ultimate Good

Aristotle's argument for the existence of an ultimate good begins from the observation that every [rational] action aims at some good. If an objective is thought of as good, that will either be because it is instrumentally good, it is chosen for the sake of some further good toward which it contributes, or because it is good in itself. So, when choosing what to do, an agent's reasoning must always end at some objective thought good in itself, since instrumental goods always presuppose some further good. Aristotle's next move has been debated, but can be coherently construed as the conditional claim that if there is some ultimate good at which we aim in all actions it will be of no little importance to discover it (*NE* 1094a1–26). In other words, the fact that all our actions aim at objectives thought good in themselves leaves open the possibility that there is a single ultimate good. Thus Aristotle takes the argument to establish the point of investigating what the ultimate good is. But the argument's distinction between instrumental goods and goods in themselves also leaves open whether the concept of an ultimate good is such that its ultimacy consists in it alone, in some sense beyond all other goods, being pursued for its own sake, or whether it can be ultimate while being simply a composite of a group of noninstrumental goods (all equally noninstrumental). In addition, therefore, this initial argument leaves open whether there will turn out empiri-

cally to be just one concrete good for humans, that which is worth pursuing, ultimately in every (fully rational) action, or a range of such goods which fit together in such a way as to constitute a unity.

On this interpretation Aristotle's initial supposition that there is an ultimate good is only conditional (in various ways). He has not even tried to show that it must exist. Reflection on human (rational) action leaves open the possibility that there is such a thing and, if it exists, it would be worth knowing. This is sufficient to motivate the inquiry. Subsequent discussion may then be read as supplementary evidence that this good does indeed exist. Thus, for example, the fact that all reach at least verbal agreement as to what it is (*eudaimonia*) provides some support for its existence, and the fact that the inquiry into its existence seems to be successful constitutes further confirmation. So Aristotle does enough to show us that his first key question, the investigation of *eudaimonia*, is worth pursuing.

2. An English Translation of *Eudaimonia*

What exactly is it that Aristotle investigates once he has established that Greeks in general agree that the ultimate good is *eudaimonia*? The translation of the Greek term will both reflect and affect our understanding of Aristotle's project. One possibility is that there is no exact English translation, which might suggest that it is impossible for English speakers to conceive of the exact nature of Aristotelian ethical theory. To avoid that unsatisfactory conclusion, what is needed is a translation that accommodates the various pieces of evidence about the concept that Aristotle provides. The debate over potential candidates involves both an account of the nature of the English concepts that might serve as translations and agreement on the details of Aristotle's own conception of *eudaimonia*.

The most authoritative translations agree on the translation "happiness." This has been found problematic on the basis that some of the things Aristotle says about *eudaimonia* seem dubious if said of happiness. Thus some have questioned whether everything is pursued for the sake of happiness, and whether children or evil adults could not be happy even though lacking the virtues. It has also been suggested that happiness involves feelings in a way that *eudaimonia* does not.

Consider first the connotations of the modern term "happiness." Part of the problem with using that term here arises from the fact that happiness has become rather closely identified with some kind of fairly simple sensual feeling, as in the inquiry as to whether someone is feeling happy. Yet the contemporary concept also allows for a notion of true happiness, which picks out some stable long-term condition, as opposed to some transient condition that only mimics happiness, and this shows that happiness can be distinguished from a feeling. Once this aspect of the concept is recognized, such a translation of *eudaimonia* seems possible, at least.

Turning to the Greek concept, it is worth noting that the etymological root of *eudaimonia* lies in *eu* and *daimon,* and so relates the concept to a good demon, blessedness, or good fortune. This explains why Aristotle discusses the role of luck in *eudaimonia,* but that is compatible with the translation "happiness." We too can debate to what extent a truly happy life depends on good fortune, though ultimately we may agree with him that to think of the achievement of the truly happy life as a matter of chance is not very plausible (*NE* 1099b18–25).

What does further attention to the Aristotelian evidence on *eudaimonia* suggest? What is needed is a concept that many see as an ultimate goal, but about whose actual content there is disagreement. Turning to the first requirement, it is not implausible to suggest that what many agree on as the ultimate goal is a truly happy life. So far as the second point is concerned, the possibility of drawing a distinction between a proposed notion of happiness and true happiness shows that the concept of happiness allows just the necessary level of disagreement. Other features of the Aristotelian view, just noted, can also be accommodated. The idea that there can be mistaken conceptions of happiness makes sense of the thought that real happiness could be something unavailable to children or the evil. Finally, if happiness does involve, at least in part, some state of mind, then Aristotle, too, wants to show that pleasure, properly understood, has a part in *eudaimonia.* By the same token, once it is realized that the sort of pleasure involved in real happiness need not reduce to mere sensual pleasure, it becomes clearer how the contemplative or reflective life may be a candidate for constituting happiness. Thus all these considerations make it reasonable to suggest that the concept Aristotle is investigating is happiness (though it may help to emphasize that what is at issue is real happiness).

3. Aristotle's Method and Preliminary Inquiry into *Eudaimonia*

How, then, does Aristotle apply his method as described to the initial investigation of *eudaimonia,* or happiness? Aristotle begins his inquiry, in *NE* I,4, by considering views as to its content that have been held by the wise or the many. In other words, he canvases prominent opinions. These constitute the "that," the initial beliefs that require examination, with the objective of preserving as many of them as possible.

Of these views, several are swiftly dismissed, namely, the ideas that *eudaimonia* is a life of pleasure, one that achieves honor, or one in which the agent becomes wealthy. Wealth is a means to an end, so cannot be an ultimate good. The value of honor depends on who is bestowing it (whether they are people who honor the right sort of things), but the ultimate good must not be a secondary good in this way. The life of pleasure is not the ultimate good for humans; such a life is more suited to beasts. In this latter argument, rather briefly asserted, Aristotle foreshadows his forthcoming idea that what is good for a thing depends on the kind of thing it is. He also rules out the life of virtue, contrasting this with a life of virtuous activity. The former, he suggests, is compatible with a life asleep, for example, but what matters is not merely to possess virtue but to exercise it. Two possibilities are left: that *eudaimonia* is an active life of practical virtue, or that it is a life of contemplation or reflective understanding (*NE* 1095b14–1096a10).

These rapid dismissals may seem contrary to what the method requires. But although Aristotle rejects the idea that any of pleasure, honor, or wealth is, on its own, the ultimate good, his subsequent discussion allows that each has some relevance to *eudaimonia.* Thus he follows his method in seeking to preserve as much as possible from the initial starting points.

Of the lives that remain possibilities, the former, the active life of practical virtue, is presumably a life in which courage, justice, and so on are fully exhibited. The latter, the contemplative or reflective life, requires a little further exposition. By contemplation, Aristotle appears to have in mind not simply intellectual inquiry, but the active understanding which results from successful inquiry. To the extent that it is still possible to value such deep understanding, the idea that a life of contemplation is a life of intellectual virtue makes sense. But it may help to note that the Greek term for virtue, *arete,* can also connote excellence, so that the life of reflective understanding might be thought of as one in which (active) intellectual excellence is achieved or exhibited (which still leaves a question as to what exactly this involves).

So Aristotle is left with two prominent views not yet shown to be false. One is that a life exhibiting bravery, wisdom, justice, self-control, and other practical virtues produces or embodies *eudaimonia.* The other is that being *eudaimon* involves a life of reflection, that is, perhaps, a life in which the agent has the satisfaction of exercising his complete understanding of the world.

This would presumably be the type of life that fully satisfies man's natural desire to know (*MP* 980a21).

In the clarification of the concept of *eudaimonia* that follows in *NE* I, Aristotle is less explicit than in *NE* I,4–5 in making clear the application of his method. However, the argument for conceptual constraints on any conception, developed in I,7, relies on a shared understanding of the concept. Aristotle appeals to the fact that people will agree that the ultimate good must be complete or perfect, most choice-worthy, and self-sufficient. The brief but important argument concerning human nature, which follows in that same chapter, may be taken to rely on general views about natural kinds, themselves developed to explain facts about the natural world, understood as world of change. So the method continues to be applied, if less explicitly.

In sum Aristotle seeks an account of *eudaimonia* which explains the widely held verbal agreement that this is the ultimate good, but is also able to accommodate as much as possible in the variant beliefs as to what it substantively consists of. This is just what his method requires.

4. Inclusive and Dominant Conceptions of the Ultimate Good

The existence of the rival conceptions of *eudaimonia* (the active life of practical virtue and the contemplative life) has repercussions for an important matter in the interpretation of Aristotelian theory, for it is one reason why there has been dispute over two points already mentioned. On the one hand there is the question of whether he thinks it part of the concept of the ultimate good that it be a single good for the sake of which all else is pursued, or whether the concept allows that it could be composed of several goods, each of which is the noninstrumental goal of some subset of activities. The conceptual constraints of completeness and self-sufficiency just referred to are relevant to this question. On the other hand is the question of whether Aristotle believes there is one or many concrete goods to pursue in a human life. As already noted, these issues already arise following Aristotle's initial argument motivating inquiry into the ultimate good.

The debate is then fueled by the fact that for much of the *NE* it seems that a life of practical virtue is being advocated as *eudaimon,* but in the last book the life of *theoria,* contemplation, is once more considered, and possibly preferred. If *eudaimonia* is constituted by *theoria,* then this is compatible with (though it does not require) the view that every act in life is pursued, ultimately, for the sake of one best noninstrumental good. This good dominates all other goods. This is the heart of the dominant end view. Clearly this view of the role of *theoria* would also suggest that there was only one intrinsic good for humans. On the other hand, if Aristotle holds that *eudaimonia* is constituted by some combination of practical and intellectual virtue (and perhaps other goods too), he must hold that the ultimate good can be a composite of noninstrumental goods. This is an inclusive end view. Similarly this view of the significance of practical and intellectual virtue holds that there are a plurality of (noninstrumental) human goods.

Whatever position is taken on these issues, a similar question has to be faced by any of them. What account is to be given (within the favored view) of the relation between contemplative activity and the activity of behaving (practically) virtuously? If the latter is seen as a means to the former, how is that to be explained? And if they are both constituents of the ultimate good, how do they fit together? These questions concerning the interpretation of Aristotle's perspective are hard to resolve, and are not settled by Aristotle's appeal to human nature, which will be examined next.

In addition to the question of whether he favors a dominant or inclusive conception of the ultimate good, a more pressing issue faces Aristotle. This is whether either of the prominent beliefs above provides a correct conception of *eudaimonia.*

In what follows particular attention will be given to the active life of practical virtue, as it is more crucial to applied ethics. If that is indeed an *eudaimon* life, then Aristotle will have answered both his central questions: he will have identified *eudaimonia* and shown that the virtuous life does pay. To answer his questions in this way, he needs to explain the connection between the *eudaimon* life and the life of virtue. He achieves this by, first, producing an argument which illuminates the concept of *eudaimonia* and by, second, elaborating what practical virtue is in a way that shows how it is connected with the concept so illuminated.

B. *Eudaimonia* and Aristotle's Conception of Human Nature

The argument he produces to illuminate the concept of *eudaimonia* concerns human nature. He argues that where a kind of thing has a function, a good member of that kind is one which fully performs that function. Thus if the function of a sculptor is to sculpt statues, a good sculptor is one who sculpts statues properly. Similarly, to take an example Aristotle does not give, if the function of a knife is to cut things, a good knife is one that cuts properly. He then argues that human beings should be understood as having a function. Their function is to actively exercise reason. Hence the human good (*eudaimonia*) will be achieved by an individual that actively reasons properly (*NE* 1097b22–1098a18). Thus, to know what a good X is, it is necessary to know both what kind X belongs to and the function of things of that kind. It will be noted that this is the argument that Aristotle implicitly relied on earlier in denying that the life of pleasure is *eudaimon*, thus attacking a classical utilitarian view. (The argument can also be developed to attack preference-satisfaction utilitarianism.)

Key aspects of this argument are, first, the claim that humans have a function, and second, the claim that the human function is to exercise reason. The first claim may be denied on the basis that Aristotle's examples of a sculptor, or a carpenter, are activities which are defined by their function (as the knife is defined by its function), but humans as a natural kind do not fall into this category. Second, it may be asked on what basis the function, if there is one, is asserted to be the exercise of reason.

Both these questions require a detailed account of the argument, which is only cryptically stated in *NE*. For present purposes suffice it to say that a possible response depends on understanding humans here in the light of his general conception of a natural kind articulated in *Physics* II. Very briefly, Aristotle holds that a member of a natural kind possessses a nature, in virtue of which it belongs to that kind, and in virtue of which it is the thing that it is. (The nature constitutes the entity's essence.) This nature plays a particular role in explaining the entity's behavior. Thus, for example, an acorn has a nature which explains some of the changes the acorn can undergo, those changes which it undergoes when it develops properly. In the acorn's case, these are the changes it goes through as it develops into a fully grown oak tree, the sort of tree that best sustains the species. The nature of the acorn explains these changes teleologically. The idea is that the nature of the acorn is constituted by a particular set of potentialities. (These are a subset of all the acorn's potentialities—a subset of the ways in which an acorn can change.) When the acorn realizes these potentialities it behaves as a good member of the kind. It is in this sense that those changes are explained teleologically. It is also in this sense that an acorn can be thought of as having a function. Its function is to realize that special set of changes which are explained teleologically. And this provides the link to good acorns (as in the case of the sculptor). Good acorns are those which perform their function.

This is the sense in which Aristotle thinks of humans as having a function, such that good humans perform that function properly. A human being has a nature. This nature explains some of the changes that a human undergoes, those changes it undergoes when it develops properly, once again those that contribute to the persistence of the species. Aristotle identifies those changes as the ones that occur in a cycle of development in which the potential for reason is fully realized. How does Aristotle identify this as the key human characteristic? He relies on an analysis of empirical observation. He identifies the nature of the key developments that must take place in a human if that human is to contribute maximally to the persistence of the species. (The notion of contributing to the persistence of the species may sound Darwinian, but Aristotle's account is not arrived at by trying to explain how species came into existence through evolution. *Physics* II,8 raises doubts about such a project. The phenomenon Aristotle observes and seeks to explain is that of a stable ecosystem, and his account of natural kinds explains their behavior within that framework.) Thus his claim is that the cycle of development that a good human goes through is one in which the power of rationality is developed and exercised fully.

In *NE* only the bare bones of the argument are presented. Furthermore, the conclusion that the good human life involves the full exercise of rationality is not elaborated. In fact, unpacking what it means for a life to be fully rational is a complex matter. This is not surprising since the human case is that of the most complex natural kind, so the account of human nature needs to be correspondingly more complex. Aristotle indicates a little more about these complexities in the development of the argument in *Politics* (1252a1–1253a39). There he argues that human nature is such that the full realization of the human function can only take place in a *polis*. The basic reason for this is that humans are a gregarious species (like bees); hence their proper development involves projects shared in common. Some remarks here also gesture toward the way in which some of these shared projects involve the realization of the potential for reason.

However, the point at this stage is that a defense can be offered of the key claims in Aristotle's argument here, and thus of his conception of human nature. This in turn provides a defense of his view that the human good must be elaborated through attention to this conception of human nature, and so the view that *eudaimonia* must consist of a life which fully realizes the potential to exercise reason. *Eudaimonia* is linked to reason, so the life of practical virtue can be shown to be *eudaimon* if it can be shown that practical virtue requires the full exercise of rationality.

Before turning to the examination of practical virtue, it is worth explaining why the appeal to human nature might not be taken as settling the debate as to whether Aristotle sees the *eudaimon* life as involving some combination of the life of practical virtue and that of *theoria*, or whether he sees one of them as having a prior claim on *eudaimonia*. The argument concerning human function might be seen as supporting either view, for while human reason can be exhibited, in Aristotle's view, in practical activity, it can also be exhibited in more purely theoretical behavior. When a person exhibits fully his understanding of the world he also reasons properly. Thus Aristotle is also drawn to the second prominent view mentioned earlier, the view that the life a human should aim at is one in which he contemplates, or reflects upon, the world (*NE* 1176a30ff.). (However, more detailed examination of the function argument may suggest that it is harder to see how *theoria* can be seen as realizing the essential potential of a human being.)

As has been seen, interpreters differ in their view of Aristotle's eventual conception of the relation between these two kinds of life. His problem here is one that can still be identified with. The effort to understand the world and the life of practical virtue interact, insofar as practical virtue relies on factual knowledge and reflective understanding, so there is not a hard and fast distinction. Nonetheless these are two kinds of rational activity in which humans can engage, both as individuals and as societies. So these activities can be given distinct priority. Time can be allocated to reflection and understanding, or to more active intervention in society, and thus the question of the balance to devote to each if a life is to be *eudaimon* (adopting the Aristotelian conception of a worthwhile life) must still arise.

C. The Nature of Practical Virtue

After the initial attention to *eudaimonia* in *NE* I, the discussion of the nature of practical virtue follows at some length, with Aristotle examining both what virtue is and the nature of particular virtues. Clearly he needs to show that his account of particular virtues is consistent with his account of the generic notion.

It has been observed that Aristotle, contrary to Socrates in Plato's *Meno*, approaches the question of what virtue is by considering first how virtue is acquired. In what follows the same order will be adopted. An outline of Aristotle's views on the acquisition of virtue will be presented prior to considering the definition he offers.

The application of that definition to particular virtues will then be explored.

1. The Acquisition of Virtue

"Neither by nature, then, nor contrary to nature do the virtues arise in us; rather we are adapted by nature to receive them, and are made perfect by habit" (*NE* 1103a23–26). Thus Aristotle summarizes how the virtues are acquired. If the virtues are to constitute the realization of human nature, they must be, in a sense, in accord with human nature. But unlike most stages of the realizations of a thing's nature, human virtues require external intervention. (They will not simply occur in normal circumstances.) So Aristotle, in noting that they do not arise by nature, accepts that they are artificial, in a sense, and this is because they cannot come about unless the agent is trained by others. (This, no doubt, also reflects the fact that humans flourish in a community. The development of virtue is a shared project.) At a late stage in their development, the agent becomes capable of training himself—getting himself to do the right thing—though such training will only be necessary for those who are, at that point, less than fully virtuous.

Aristotle outlines several stages of training, or habituation, that an individual must go through if he is to acquire virtue. Reflection on *NE* I,3–4 indicates that the acquisition of virtue involves grasping first the "that" and then the "why." Thus this process appears to run in parallel with what a student must go through in preparing for and then studying ethics (see Section II). So in *NE* II,1, Aristotle emphasizes again the importance of the habits we form in youth, and thus the importance of all who affect those habits—the legislator, the teacher, and the parent.

Granted this distinction between grasp of the "that" and grasp of the "why," there are at least three stages that the young must go through in acquiring the "that." First a student must learn that a certain type of behavior is required in particular circumstances. This is learned from others, parents or teachers, for example. To know the "that" in this sense is merely to have acquired information. To know the "that" in the strong sense is to have come to enjoy it properly. There are two further stages here: first, coming to enjoy the required act, as opposed to doing it because instructed by others, and then coming to enjoy it properly, where one appreciates what it is in the action that is truly enjoyable. These latter stages involve habituation. This kind of knowledge is acquired only through trying the activity and coming to enjoy it. In this sort of process (which applies not only to the acquisition of virtue, but equally well to learning to enjoy skiing or painting), it has been said that practice has cognitive powers. The process of learning that an action is the right thing to do goes hand in hand with learning to enjoy doing it.

The last stage in which the student appreciates what it is about the action that is properly enjoyable must be closely related to a further stage in the development of virtue, namely, the point at which it is grasped why the action is virtuous. This reflective understanding must be acquired through the study of ethics, but it would seem that it might well contribute to an appreciation of exactly what it is in right action that is truly enjoyable. If so, the grasp of the "that" in this way will overlap with the grasp of the "why."

However, the main point here is that the role of habituation initially is to enable the young to grasp the "that" regarding virtue. Once that stage is attained, a second stage, just alluded to, becomes possible. This stage is the grasp of the "why" with regard to virtue, and this stage is necessary if the agent is to have a reasoned understanding of virtuous action. This may involve both a full appreciation of why a particular act is required, as virtuous, in the relevant circumstances, and an ability to grasp fully the relation between practical virtue and other key concepts, such as *eudaimonia*.

It will be possible to elaborate a little further on the nature of the acquisition process after outlining how Aristotle defines the state of virtue which results from this acquisition process.

2. Practical (or Ethical) Virtue

a. The Definition of Virtue

Aristotle offers the following definition of virtue: "Virtue, then, is a state of character concerned with choice, lying in a mean, i.e. the mean relative to us, this being determined by a rational principle, and by that principle by which the man of practical wisdom would determine it" (*NE* 1106b36–1107a2). This, then, is the condition that arises, first, from the habitual practice of right action, guided (initially) by good parents, teachers, and law, and in due course, finally, from reflection on the "that" which has been established through habit. What kind of condition is Aristotle describing?

First, virtue is a state of character (*hexis*). This is a settled disposition of the mind which disposes the agent to act in certain ways when circumstances arise to which that state of character is relevant. It is a state of character concerned with *prohairesis* (preferential) choice. (*Prohairesis* is a technical term in Aristotle's analysis of action, better translated as "preferential choice" to mark that.) Clarity thus requires the notion of preferential choice to be explained.

Children do not make preferential choices, though they act *hekousios* (intentionally). The reason is as follows. A child is capable of originating action through possessing both a desire and the relevant correct beliefs, and this is all that is necessary if the child is to act *hekousios*. But the desires of children are not preferential desires, the sort of desires that lead to preferential choices. Such desires are formed in the light of deliberation as to how to attain goals, where those goals reflect a conception of the good. Children lack such a conception of the good. They are subject only to passing desires. Thus to make a preferential choice it is necessary not only to act on a desire and a belief, but to act on a desire which derives from a conception of the good. The virtuous person has a settled disposition of the mind to make preferential choices.

But the vicious also make preferential choices, so the definition specifies more about the state of character of one who makes virtuous choices. The virtuous state of character lies in a mean relative to us. What this entails is that the agent's passions, or emotions, are appropriate, so as to give rise to actions which are appropriate in the circumstances. First of all, the doctrine of the mean does not concern moderation, but appropriateness. Second, it focuses on both the motivating condition of the agent and the actions that result. In places Aristotle seems to suggest that the emotions are primary, and thus the appropriateness of the action depends on its flowing from the appropriate emotion, because states of character (of which the virtues are one type) are "the things in virtue of which we stand well or badly with reference to the passions" (*NE* 1105b25–6; *NE* II,6). In the case of each virtue, Aristotle envisages a scale of emotional response such that there are vices corresponding to inappropriate emotions and a virtue corresponding to the appropriate emotional condition (*NE* 1105b30–1106a2, 1106b18–23). Thus, for example, there is a scale of emotional attitudes to sensual pleasure. At one extreme there is undue desire for such pleasure, and at the other there is undue indifference. These emotional conditions are associated with vices of self-indulgence and asceticism. But there is also an appropriate kind of emotional condition on this scale, and that is what is possessed by the self-controlled individual. These mean conditions involve the agent forming true beliefs about the circumstances he faces and responding with appropriate emotion, which will lead him to make appropriate choices. Thus the virtuous state of character will be a settled state of beliefs and desires, lying in a mean so as to lead to appropriate preferential choices and action.

b. Ethical Virtue, the Rational Principle, and *Phronesis*

Aristotle next suggests that this mean state of choice and character is determined by a rational principle, that by which the person of practical wisdom (*phronimos*) would determine it. This is a crucial aspect of the definition since this is the piont at which he suggests that practical virtue is a state of character involving the exercise of reason. Reason must enter into the mean state in several ways. First the agent must be disposed to form rational beliefs about the circumstances he encounters. Reason will enter into belief formation so that the agent forms those beliefs best supported by the evidence he has. But reason will also enter the emotional condition of the virtuous agent in that his motivational desires will reflect a reasoned conception of the good. To achieve this, the agent must both have arrived at a reasoned conception of the good and have desires in line with that conception (no rogue desires). As Aristotle indicates, the virtuous agent must both have true reasoning and correct desire if the *prohairesis* is to be good (*NE* 1139a22–26). Rationality governs both aspects of the virtuous state of mind. When both belief and desire are rational in this way, the agent is able to make the judgments that would be made by the practically wise person, and to act on them.

These difficult ideas can be explained a little further by considering how the acquisition of virtue leads to this state of mind. Aristotle envisages children as capable of acting on beliefs and desires, but not yet on rational beliefs and desires. Habituation will enable the child both to form more reasoned judgments as to what is worth pursuing and what is not, and to develop desires which reflect those judgments. (Presumably, the child will also need to be developing the capacity to form true beliefs of a more factual sort.) In due course the child will not pursue passing objectives simply conceived of as satisfying desires, but come to a stage where he conceives the object of pursuit as good or the object of aversion as bad. Once evaluation of that sort is possible, the next stage will be for the agent to form a reasoned conception of what is overall worth pursuing, in the light of the preliminary view of what is worthwhile. At this stage the agent will have a reasoned conception of the good. At the same time as these developments occur, motivational states will need to develop in such a way that the agent desires those objects considered good, a process in which the agent's desires come into line with his conception of the good. The result will be fully rational desires.

This account of the role of reason in virtue is further complemented by attention to the nature of *phronesis*, practical wisdom which determines the principle on which the virtuous agent acts. *Phronesis* is an intellectual virtue, defined in *NE* VI,5 as "a true and reasoned state of capacity to act with regard to the things that are good or bad for man." In *NE* VI,7 Aristotle then explains that it is the mark of the practically wise to deliberate well, "but no one deliberates about things . . . which have not an end which is a good that can be attainable by action." In other words, practical wisdom is the intellectual virtue that enables the agent to arrive at a reasoned conception of the good, a feature of moral virtue already referred to. It is also the rational faculty that enables the virtuous agent to work out correctly what to do on particular occasions in the light of that conception of the good (to calculate properly so as to reach the correct preferential choice). It thus involves reasoning about universals, reaching generalizations about what is worthwhile pursuing in life (making a conception of the good), and forming rational beliefs about particulars, all the variables of individual situations. As an intellectual virtue, it will not be acquired simply through habituation. It will require experience, particularly with regard to the ability to determine what are the pertinent particular features of each new situation. It may also be taught, perhaps through ethical study (*NE* II,1). But the previous discussion shows that it clearly depends on habituation to the extent that training provides the agent with beliefs about what is worthwhile in the light of which to form an all-things-considered conception of the good. Relatedly corrupt pleasures and pains can undermine the ability to make practically wise judgments (*NE* 1140b11–20).

c. Summary Regarding the Definition of Virtue

This discussion of the definition of virtue can now be summarized. Settled desires and beliefs, guided by *phronesis*, are what constitute the settled state of character possessed by the virtuous individual, enabling that individual to make rational preferential choices, those the practically wise would make, and to act rationally on those choices.

3. Particular Virtues

Having provided this definition of generic virtue, Aristotle now tries to show that each of the particular virtues, or each state of character widely believed to be a virtue, can be analyzed as conforming to the definition. (Given his method in ethics, his account of virtue must conform adequately to widely held beliefs as to what the virtues are.) Thus he tries to show that courage, self-control, justice, and so on are states of character constituted by relevant sets of rational beliefs and desires. Thus there is both an area of concern within an overall conception of the good (certain rational beliefs) and a scale of emotional response (relevant rational desires) that can be associated with each. The approach can be indicated by briefly outlining some of the virtues Aristotle analyzes. (It is not always easy to identify the scale of emotion Aristotle associates with a particular virtue. This problem only arises in one of these cases.)

a. Temperance or Self-Control (*NE* III,10–12)

The focus of self-control is certain physical pleasures, in particular the pleasures that involve touch—pleasures of food, drink, and sex. Thus the emotional scale in question is that of desire for these sorts of pleasures. Aristotle emphasizes that the issue here is simply physical pleasures; pains are not the object of concern of this virtue. (Naturally pleasure and pain enter into the virtue in a second way, as with all virtues.) In this area, then, virtue involves having an appropriate conception of the value of food, drink, and sex, and pursuing it accordingly. What counts as appropriate can be explained by noting that it is perfectly natural to find food, drink, and sex pleasant, but that it is possible to pursue them to excess, and this in two ways: either excessive pursuit of food, for example, quite generally, or excessive pursuit of particular tastes in food, for example, a craving for chocolate. Clearly Aristotle is appealing to widely held beliefs here, still shared, about those who overindulge. He notes that the other vice, enjoying such physical pleasures less than one should, is very rare, though the phenomena of rejecting wholesale certain types of food (e.g., vegetables), or excessive dieting, may now be more common examples. The self-indulgent are further marked by being pained when their excessive appetite is not satisfied, while the temperate agent enjoys consuming just the right amount of food or drink. What exactly this will be in particular cases will depend on a range of variables, such as the size of the agent, the type of work he does, and environmental temperature.

b. Good Temper (*NE* IV,5)

Here the scale of emotion is that of anger. Once again one of the vices is more common than the other. All would recognize the vice of irascibility, while that of undue passivity with regard to anger is unusual. However, this again provides a scale on which falls the virtue of good temper. Its nature can be made more precise by considering the excess, which can be manifested at the wrong things, with the wrong persons, more than is right, too quickly, or too long. Righteous anger will have the correct target in these various spheres. The less common vice is found in the character of the "doormat": the agent who does not even express anger in defending self or family, or in reacting to insults to self

or friends. As in many cases this vice connects with other vices, here that of undue humility (*NE* IV,3).

c. Courage

On any account it is unproblematic that courage is a virtue, but it has been debated whether Aristotle's analysis of virtue applies to it. Aristotle's analysis relates it to the emotion of fear. On this view the brave person is one who has the right amount of fear, at the right time, about the right things, for the right reason, and in the right way. The coward will be excessively fearful, where excessive fear must be analyzed in relation to the previous categories. This is complex. Some things, poverty and disease, for example, it may be cowardly to fear at all. But it is too simple to say it is cowardly to fear death; what is cowardly is to fear death in all circumstances. Thus it may be cowardly to fear death even when there is a noble goal to attain. Aristotle denies that the other vice is to be without fear, on the grounds that this is not a vice but madness. He argues that the vice is rashness, undue confidence about what really is fearful. Are both vices here associated with a single emotional scale, that of fear? Some suggest that Aristotle has now introduced two emotions, fear and confidence, and thus courage does not fit his doctrine of the mean. Perhaps this can be rebutted. Confidence about what is really fearful may amount to not fearing a thing in the right way—not fearing it in such a way as to avoid it in circumstances where it should be avoided. Courage is a difficult virtue to analyze, not least because the emotion of fear is difficult to analyze.

A further repercussion of Aristotle's overall view of virtue is that the brave person will take pleasure in brave acts, while for Aristotle one who manages to do the right thing in the face of fear, but is pained by his act, is strong-willed (*encratic*), but not courageous. For Aristotle, the pleasure taken in virtuous acts is a mark of the virtuous person's psychological unity. The pain of the encratic is a sign that part of him does not wish to perform that act, and thus an indicator that his is a character that may in due course do cowardly acts. Aristotle does not accept that the virtuous life has to be difficult for the virtuous; what is difficult, on his view, is to become virtuous.

d. Summary of Particular Virtue

What Aristotle has done here is to identify empirically a range of attitudes which can be associated with a scale of emotion, where there are widely held beliefs as to what constitute virtues and vices. He then shows that these virtues and vices can be analyzed, and defined more precisely, in terms of his general definition of virtue. This analysis also provides guidance on the nature of the reasoning that the virtuous agent engages in. Thus the self-controlled person, for example, will have to have true beliefs about the value of pursuing the sensual pleasures of food, drink, and sex; desires that correspond to those beliefs; and correct beliefs about particulars relevant to each decision. Given this, he will be able to make rational choices whenever self-control is at issue.

4. Virtue and the Exercise of Reason

The discussion above, particularly of the role of *phronesis,* has indicated that Aristotle can establish the necessary link between virtue and practical reason, and thus between virtue and *eudaimonia.* The significance of rationality for virtue has been exhibited. The virtuous agent must have rational beliefs about the facts of particular circumstances faced; a reasoned conception of the good (in the case of courage, say, this would be manifested in rational beliefs as to what is to be feared to what degree, and as to what it is worth defending or pursuing in the face of reasonably feared threats); and emotional responses that reflect the agent's reasoned conception of the good. Finally, rationality requires the absence of rogue desires (that might distract the agent from pursuit of the good). An agent whose character is rational in this way will be in a position to make rational choices, and act on those choices, thus fully realizing practical reason. Thus ethical virtue is a condition in which rationality is exhibited fully.

On this picture defective states of character, such as weakness of will or vice, involve (culpable) defects of rationality, either with regard to the agent's motivational state or with regard to the agent's conception of the good (or with regard to both).

5. Full Virtue and the Unity of the Virtues

Aristotle's definition of virtue is very demanding in the sense that it indicates that it is very hard to possess any of the virtues fully. This is because it is not possible to possess any of the virtues fully without possessing all of them fully. Aristotle makes this clear in his discussion of practical wisdom in *NE* VI, illuminating the key role of judgment in virtuous character. To possess any virtue fully the agent must be capable of exercising practically wise judgment in the area of concern relevant to that virtue. But to exercise wise judgment in any area of concern, the agent must be fully practically wise, and full practical wisdom is not itself possible without the possession of all the virtues (*NE* 1144b1–1145a11). Thus on the Aristotelian view the virtues form a unity in the sense that it is not possible to possess fully any

virtuous state of character without possessing fully all of them. To the extent that such correct judgment in all areas is an unattainable ideal, the fully virtuous life is an ideal. By the same token the life in which practical reason is fully displayed is an ideal. (The fully virtuous are like Plato's philosopher kings.) Of course that does not mean it is not worth striving to live a life as close to the ideal as possible.

6. Virtue and *Eudaimonia*

How does this discussion of virtue bear on Aristotle's main questions? He articulates and defends a definition of virtue (as a genus) such that the practical virtues are states that would be exhibited by a (practically) rational human being (*NE* 1106b36–1107a2). He argues that those conditions widely believed to be practical virtues conform to this definition. Since he has argued that the life of reason is the *eudaimon* life, this account of virtue shows that the practical virtues are indeed those characteristics that would produce *eudaimonia.*

The main features of the argument used to reach this conclusion have now been described. In the next section the role in this account for pleasure and certain external goods will be indicated. Section V will outline some key aspects of the ethical theory that results from the previous argument. Then, in the final section, the repercussions of this ethical theory for applied ethics will be discussed.

IV. *EUDAIMONIA,* PLEASURE, AND EXTERNAL GOODS

Aristotle's method requires him to preserve as much as possible in widely held beliefs, so he needs to try to incorporate within his theory the views of many that pleasure, wealth, political power, a good family, and friendship have a role in a *eudaimon* life.

A. Pleasure

Though Aristotle dismisses the life of pleasure as constitutive of *eudaimonia,* he is aware that it would be paradoxical if he were to argue that the ultimately good life need not be pleasant. He shows that it can be incorporated within his account by analyzing the nature of pleasure (*NE* VII,11–14 and X,1–5) in such a way that the life of virtue will turn out to be pleasant. For Aristotle pleasure is not a uniform category; rather, distinct pleasures are taken in distinct activities: "to each man that which he is said to be a lover of is pleasant" (*NE*

1099a7–10). On his account there is in effect a hierarchy of pleasures, their value depending on the activity they are associated with. Thus the truly virtuous take pleasure in virtuous actions (*NE* II,3). Pleasure is a mark of a person's character, rather than being a goal in itself, and the pleasures accompanying these virtuous activities are "by nature pleasant" (*NE* 1099a13), so that the life of virtue is indeed pleasant.

B. External Goods: Wealth, Power, and Good Family

Aristotle expresses the following general view about external goods: "Some must necessarily exist as conditions of happiness, and others are naturally cooperative and useful as instruments" (*NE* 1099b27–29). Thus one would expect there to be such a role for any of these goods within the life of virtue.

The importance of wealth can be explained in so far as material resources, which wealth enables the agent to attain, are necessary to satisfy the basic needs of life, food, shelter, cures for illness, education, and so on. Beyond that, leisure afforded by possession of material means may be needed to share in communal activities— discussion, drama, and so on—which contribute to the development of the powers of reason. Beyond that still, material resources may be necessary for the exercise of certain virtues. For example, in some circumstances, but not all, material goods may be necessary for generosity.

The absence of a good family can be seen as a hindrance to *eudaimonia* in two ways. Given the importance of habituation in the acquisition of virtue, it is clear that a bad family will inhibit a person's becoming self-controlled, courageous, just, and so on (*NE* 1103b23–25). More broadly speaking, a bad family may inhibit in similar ways the emotional development necessary if a young person is to share in the communal activities that contribute to the development of practical rationality.

For Aristotle the value of political power lies only in the fact that such power provides the agent with an opportunity to exercise practical reason, making laws that will help the citizens become good through habituation (*NE* 1103b3–6). Thus it is desirable, from this point of view, that all citizens have a turn in exercising power.

C. External Goods: Friendship

Aristotle's *NE* VIII–IX contains a careful and detailed discussion of friendship, distinguishing his approach from much modern ethical theory. Only a bare outline is possible here, though clearly at this point the link between ethical theory and applied ethics is very close.

For Aristotle there are three categories of friendship, and between them they cover most of the range of social interactions. Thus his discussion is much broader than might first be thought. However, his paradigm category is virtue friendshp, and his analysis of that type of friendship comes closer to an examination of what might currently be taken to be friendship. Thus he makes clear that the friendship between the virtuous is perfect friendship, and that the other two categories are only analogous to friendship, so that they are thought both to be and not to be friendship (*NE* 1156b7–8, 1157a31–2, 1158b5–6). The other categories of friendship are those formed for the sake of pleasure and those formed for the sake of utility. In the former the friends are pleasant to each other (provide pleasure to each other), and in the latter they provide each other with utility (are useful to each other).

The paradigm case, then, is that in which two people enjoy each other's company in virtue of their good character. What is enjoyed is the other's good character. As such it is more likely to be a lasting relationship since the ability of another to provide pleasure or utility may vary over time, and so is incidental to that person, but character is a more lasting feature of a person. The most perfect virtue friendship will be that of two fully virtuous people, but the category of virtue friendship will include a wide range—all those relationships where the basis is another's good character, even if the other possesses vices as well.

An example of pleasure friendship would be a relationship in which two people enjoy each other's humor, while a commercial relationship between a consumer and a market stall holder would count as a utility relationship. Aristotle observes that this category can include both legal relationships, on a contractual basis, and those which are more like mutual gift relations.

Aristotle notes various features of friendship. All are possessed by the paradigm category, but each may be found to a lesser extent, or not at all, in the other types. Thus, as noted, all friends like some good feature of the other. Friendship involves wishing the other what is good for his sake and a mutual recognition that the friends bear each other such good wishes. Friendship involves enjoyment of the other's company, spending time together, and sharing in each other's lives. Clearly a commercial relationship may involve only some of these to some degree. Nonetheless a contrast is still possible. On the one hand there is the sort of relationship in which the two parties exchange goods fairly regularly, enjoy the transactions, and wish each other well at least in the sense of wanting the other to be treated fairly in the exchange and not to be exploited. On the other there is that in which one party seeks to exploit the other—to get as much from him as possible with as little interaction as possible. Aristotle's claim that the former is a friendly contractual relationship is clearly defensible.

But if the *eudaimon* life is an active life of virtue, that does not seem, on the face of it, to require friendships. So how can Aristotle show the value of friendship within his theory? One way forward is to attend to Aristotle's remarks as to the close proximity of friendship to the virtue of justice. One might also ask why the realization of the individual's potential for reason should be found in part in a virtue such as justice which involves distributing certain goods fairly to others. The value of both friendship and justice lies, at least to a degree, in the fact that a human can only realize his nature in a polis, a community governed by justice. The exercise of rationality involves, in various ways, shared projects. This is partly because the training of the agent's desires, which leads to virtuous states of character, requires habituation both in the family and in the wider community. It is also because certain other potentials, such as the potential for language, relevant to rationality only develop in a wider community (*Politics*, 1253a7–18). Friendship is the cement that holds the requisite communities together. More directly, rationality requires friends with whom to discuss and debate—with whom, in Socratic terms, to engage in dialectic. Friendship, then, facilitates the individual's realization of this potential for rationality, and thus his achievement of *eudaimonia* (*NE* 1155a5–28).

V. PROMINENT FEATURES OF ARISTOTELIAN ETHICAL THEORY

Some general features of the Aristotelian approach to ethics can now be noted, contrasting the position with notable alternative ethical theories. First, in focusing on *eudaimonia*, Aristotle makes the whole of a life central to his ethical perspective. The key question, as noted, is what sort of life to live. Thus practical virtues are characteristics an agent needs to develop if life as a whole is to be worthwhile. This can be contrasted with an approach which makes acts directly the central focus. Thus some forms of consequentialism try to develop a method to determine what act to perform at any given time, or rules governing kinds of action to perform in relevant

circumstances. It is not that the Aristotelian perspective does not have implications for action. Virtues must be displayed in action. But acts cannot be evaluated individually, or by reference to rules; what matters is the character of the agent which leads to action, for it is the agent's character that produces *eudaimonia*.

Related to this is the fact that the Aristotelian approach is embedded in a theory of moral psychology. Aristotle's theory of virtue depends on a theory of intentional action and preferential choice within which it can be explained how virtue is a condition in which reason governs desire. This explains why the virtuous person will regularly make virtuous preferential choices leading to the acts characteristic of that virtue. This can be contrasted with some rights-based or duty-based theories of ethics which appear to pay little attention to moral psychology, and thus make it hard to see how exactly considerations of rights or duties enter into an agent's practical reasoning. The same might be said of some utilitarian theories, though it is true that Benthamite utilitarianism was based on the assumption that pleasure and pain are the basic springs of human motivation, and so was embedded in a theory of human psychology (Bentham, 1789, chap. 1). Aristotle's position differs here in offering an alternative psychological theory, in particular in developing a quite different account of the nature and role of pleasure and pain.

A third significant feature of Aristotle's approach is the emphasis on reason in ethics. Rationality enters into his scheme in two ways. At one level Aristotle seeks a rational basis which will explain and justify certain widely held ethical beliefs about the nature of *eudaimonia* and the importance of behaving virtuously. Thus he seeks an account of the key concepts, *eudaimonia*, virtue, and human nature, which will reveal their conceptual connections. But that account in turn reveals the role of reason in practical deliberation about specific acts, since the *eudaimon* life is one which exhibits reason, and in practical deliberation reason is exhibited in a virtuous state of character in which the agent's desires are rationally ordered. Such a state will lead to acts in line with rational preferential choices. This perspective can be contrasted with a Hobbesian or Humean picture in which reason is subordinate to desire: good and bad reflect the agent's desires and aversions; reason determines the means to satisfy those desires (T. Hobbes, 1651. *Leviathin*, chap. 6. London; D. Hume, 1739. *A Treatise of Human Nature* (L. A. Selby Bigge, Ed.), book II, part III, sect. III. Oxford Univ. Press, Oxford).

Finally, the Aristotelian approach is based on a distinctive conception of human nature. It is a teleological conception within which humans have a goal, and thus can flourish to the extent they achieve that goal, namely, exhibiting rationality. This implies that humans are perfectible, that they can change for the better, by realizing their potential to be rational (or for the worse, by realizing their potential to be irrational). Their nature is not, in this sense, unalterable. Again, Hobbes' view constitutes a contrast (and perhaps represents a contrasting empiricist approach). For Hobbes, humans are unalterably desire-satisfaction machines. They are driven by desires, and are better or worse only to the extent that they manage to satisfy more or fewer desires (Hobbes, 1651, chaps. 6–10). By contrast Aristotelian theory holds that humans flourish to the extent that they develop and alter their desires, at first through training by others and then through self-direction, so as to attain a condition in which their practical reasoning is rational. This is related to the way that, for Aristotle, ethical theory is related to political theory. Human nature on this view is such that its development depends on its external environment. In particular the potential to develop as a rational being can only be realized in a *polis* (a city), as just noted in discussing friendship. So Aristotelian ethics is distinguished by incorporating a particularly rich conception of human nature.

VI. ARISTOTELIAN ETHICS AND APPLIED ETHICS

What significance, then, does Aristotelian ethical theory have for applied ethics? The richness of the theory outlined means that there are various perspectives from which to discuss this question. In what follows a distinction will be made between direct and indirect implications of the theory. The direct way to consider the question is to view Aristotle's theory as a virtue theory and to ask how, if at all, that theory can be applied. A virtue theory, here, is a theory that holds that the right action in any particular case is that action which the virtuous agent would perform. Any adequate (genuinely illuminating) virtue theory will then have to give a suitably full account of the nature of virtue, as does Aristotle's theory.

An indirect perspective is provided by examining the way in which other aspects of the overall theory, such as Aristotle's theory of human nature, his account of *eudaimonia,* or his view of the relation between individual flourishing and the *polis*, might have a bearing on specific questions in applied ethics. (Of course the previous discussion has indicated that all these consid-

erations are in different ways bound up with Aristotle's view of the nature of virtue, but the line drawn here should be clear enough.)

A. Direct Implications for Applied Ethics

If Aristotelian ethical theory is considered as a virtue theory, then there have been both positive and negative interpretations of its implications for practice. In discussing these views it is necessary to bear in mind Aristotle's remarks on method in ethics, as well as the specific nature of his account of the virtues and their role in deliberation. His views on starting points, satisfactory results, and precision in ethics (see Section II) are all pertinent here.

1. Negative Views of the Practical Implications of Aristotelian Theory

As was seen earlier, one view is that Aristotle's ethical theory has no implications for applied ethics. This is because Aristotle is understood as requiring that students able to benefit from the study of ethics must already know what action is required in any particular circumstance. In other words, an appropriate student will already be disposed to make all the right choices in the humdrum decisions of daily life, as well as being clear as what to do in the more dramatic cases discussed in medical, business, media, and environmental ethics texts. This is the "that" that must be known prior to studying the "why." On this view, such knowledge is acquired through training, not through reflection. Furthermore, if a person's upbringing has led them to be disposed to make the wrong choices on occasion, no amount of reflection will change them. Such a position holds that all Aristotelian ethical theory can do is provide the already virtuous with a reflective appreciation of the worth of that life.

A rather similar view has been put forward by some writers on applied ethics, as well as interpreters of Aristotle. On this view, applied ethics courses are pointless since moral behavior depends on training, not reflection. Advocates of such a position hold that there is no difficulty telling right from wrong; the only difficulty is getting oneself to act on ones' knowledge. Such a claim is surprising given the disputes over abortion, euthanasia, and whether it is ever appropriate to cease treating, or feeding, persistent vegetative state cases, to take just some areas of dramatic applied controversy.

So far as Aristotle is concerned, it was already noted that there is reason to doubt this negative interpretation of his view, on the grounds both of common sense plausibility and of textual analysis. Similarly his texts provide no support for this attitude to applied ethics.

Clearly the earlier discussion of Aristotle has conceded the importance of habituation. But there are alternative interpretations (to that just considered) of the requirement that potential students of ethics must know the "that" prior to study. A minimal interpretation accepts that any such student must already grasp the distinction between right and wrong, and that is acquired through habituation. A second plausible view holds that habituation must have given the student some hazy conception of what is, all things considered, good or worth pursuing in life. But the question is whether ethical reflection can lead to any development in this basic conceptual grasp, and thus in turn any changes in practice. The wholly negative reply here is implausible.

Before leaving this view, it should be noted that the negative nature of this reply depends in part on a question as to the scope of applied ethics. So far in this section it has been assumed that the purpose of applied ethics is to provide guidance at least (and perhaps answers) for specific practical questions and to resolve difficult practical (ethical) problems. But it might be held that the study of applied ethics involves not merely knowing what to do, but fully appreciating why such actions are worth doing. If so, even this rather negative interpretation could allow that Aristotelian ethics can contribute something to applied ethics, for this view holds that the study of ethics will provide the "why"— the deeper reflective justification for all the particular acts performed. (This implies two levels of justification for action, the virtuous motives of the virtuous agent and the deeper reflective justification provided by the study of ethics.) To recall an example mentioned earlier, if there were general agreement about the importance of informed patient consent in medical practice, it might still be useful to understand why it is important.

a. Positive Views of the Practical Implications of Aristotelian Theory

If Aristotelian ethical theory does not merely provide a deeper understanding of the value of the good life for those who are already good, in what way can ethical reflection of the sort it involves change the student of ethics, and how can this bear on applied ethics?

As a virtue theory, Aristotelian theory suggests that the right action will be one that involves the exercise of the relevant virtue in the circumstances. Suppose a student of ethics is not yet fully virtuous; how much help with practical problems will this theory be? Some have suggested that Aristotle's particular account of the

virtues provides no help since it suggests that the act will be that which the practically wise person (*phronimos*) would perform, and this is circular. It simply advises the agent to be practically wise, rather than giving any concrete advice as to what that involves. In response to this worry, it has already been seen that Aristotle offers a much richer account of virtue than this implies, so how helpful is that account?

Begin a step earlier. Suppose that the student of ethics merely begins with the knowledge that some acts are right and others wrong; then the first effect of Aristotelian ethics will be that the student will conceive of practical problems in terms of the concepts of virtue and vice. (It is in fact quite plausible that a modern student of ethics may be in just this position.) As noted in Section I, this provides a much richer vocabulary for thinking about practical problems. The question is now not merely what action is right or wrong, but what is courageous as opposed to cowardly or rash, self-controlled as opposed to self-indulgent or ascetic. Reflecting on ethical problems using all the concepts of virtue theory will in itself have a bearing on how the agent views the problem, and thus on the factors that he takes into account in reaching a decision. Consider, for example, a patient reflecting on euthanasia. Suppose that instead of asking whether it is right or wrong he considers whether it would be brave, rash, or cowardly to seek it, in the circumstancs, and whether it would be just or unjust. Thinking in these terms forces the patient to consider what, in these circumstances, bravery and justice mean, and so what factors of the situation must be attended to in order to determine what courage and justice here require.

But it may then be queried as to how much practical help this really provides. A way of thinking about specific problems has been offered, but does this method provide any resources for determining exactly what to do? Once the agent has got as far as deciding to be brave, how does he determine what bravery concretely requires? Furthermore, how much does Aristotelian ethical theory really help here? If the suggestion is to be brave, does the patient simply rely on his pretheoretical conception of bravery, the resources he already possessed before studying ethics, or does Aristotle's theory add anything?

Clearly Aristotelian theory provides some more resources, since it provides a well-developed definition of virtue, so the question is how much practical use this definition is. The first thing to note is that this is a further place in which ethical reflection may change the agent, since it seems plausible that Aristotle provides an account of virtue which leads to revisions of the definitions of particular virtues such as courage and justice. Aristotle's account of justice (like Plato's), for example, does not simply endorse the traditional views that justice involves returning what one owes, or that it requires one to help friends and harm enemies. Justice is a matter of the proportionate allocation of honor, money, and necessities for survival (*soterian*), and the categories of friend, enemy, or creditor may not pick out the crucial criterion of desert (*NE* 1130b1–5, 1131a25–29).

So Aristotle's theory may have two related effects here. For the agent deliberating in terms of virtues it elaborates the factors he should attend to in deciding what action virtue requires. In doing this, it does not simply regurgitate the agent's pretheoretical conception of particular virtues, but may alter that conception. Of course Aristotle's methodological constraints on satisfactory conclusions require that the theory preserve as much as possible of the pretheoretical beliefs. So the theory could not completely depart from ordinary conceptions of the virtues, but revision is nonetheless possible.

This may still seem rather far removed from enabling the virtue theorist to give specific answers to applied problems. What more does Aristotelian theory suggest? To answer this question, more attention must be given to the details of Aristotle's definition of virtue. First of all, the virtues are states of characters involving true beliefs, so virtuous action requires attention to relevant facts in the circumstances. (What is meant here can include evaluative beliefs, though not directly beliefs about the human good. For example, it has been suggested that virtuous behavior toward animals requires a correct appreciation of their nature and standing.) Second, virtues are states of character which involve appropriate desires formed in the light of a conception of the good. So the virtuous agent must also have true beliefs about the good. Again, though, reference to an overall conception of the good seems a long way from what is needed to advise an agent facing a particular problem.

However, as already noted, the Aristotelian account casts further light on this overall conception of the good by incorporating within ethical virtue the intellectual virtue of practical wisdom. This, it was noted, is "a true and reasoned state of capacity to act with regard to the things that are good or bad for man" (*NE* 1140b4–6). Thus it is this virtue that enables the agent to form both the true beliefs about particulars and the overall conception of the good necessary to make fully rational preferential choices. The analysis of practical wisdom casts light on what an agent must do to form a concep-

tion of the good. It is necessary to reflect on the results of habituation. Having learned to enjoy certain quantities of food and drink, for example, or sharing goods in certain ways, or speaking the truth in certain contexts, the agent can reflect on certain general claims about what exactly is worthwhile pursuing, and how different objectives fit together into an overall conception of the good. What the agent will enjoy will be particular experiences, each involving varied circumstances. So this suggests that practical wisdom involves reaching a conception of the good through reflection on trained responses to particular circumstances. Eventually, perhaps, any conception of the good can also be refined through arriving at a deeper understanding of what makes such goals worth pursuing (this being the goal of the study of ethics).

Beyond this, Aristotle provides definitions of particular virtues, and those definitions serve to pick out more precisely what aspects of the good must be attended to in the exercise of each of the virtues. For example, the self-controlled agent is concerned with physical pleasures and pains—those associated with food, drink, and sex, particularly. So the exercise of such a virtue will have to avoid excess and deficiency in this area. Furthermore, the agent's reflections as to the requirements of self-control will need to take account of other virtues such as justice. What counts as self-control with regard to the pleasure of food may depend on the amount of food available to the community as a whole and considerations of just allocation that enter in there. Thus Aristotle's account begins to narrow what conclusions may be possible when self-control is the virtue in question.

In addition, the role of desire in the account of virtue is also important. It indicates that the agent will also have to reflect on the need to maintain a persisting virtuous character, where this means that the agent should avoid rogue desires out of line with his conception of the good. Thus the self-controlled person's current choices must be such that they do not enhance the development of undue desires for drink or sex (characteristic rogue desires).

From a practical point of view, then, the Aristotelian perspective provides a detailed account of how to reach an overall conception of the good, its relation to emotional responses and habituation, and its role in particular judgments. It indicates in some detail the considerations which, given the definitions of virtues, are pertinent to particular virtuous decisions. It points out the significance of correct empirical beliefs about particulars, if good preferential choices are to be made. Nonetheless these outlines do not indicate a precise method for reaching a judgment in each practical decision.

Thus the definition of virtue suggests some tighter constraints on the way in which a virtuous agent should reach particular practical judgments, but still the question arises as to how specific the advice is for the problems faced in applied ethics. Consider again the agent deliberating about euthanasia. Thus far the Aristotelian theory has provided a conceptual framework within which to reflect on the issue. More than that, it has provided a precise account of particular virtues, thus delineating the considerations that a just, courageous, self-controlled agent would attend to in reaching a decision. To this can be added the fact that the virtuous agent will exercise practical wisdom in making the judgment. Yet this does not seem to determine the right action in the way that certain utilitarian theories, say, might claim to do by providing a mechanism for working out exactly what to do.

b. Direct Positive Implications, Precision, and Casuistry

At this point Aristotle's remarks on method are relevant again. Aristotle held that the same degree of precision was not to be expected in ethics as in areas of inquiry such as mathematics. One interpretation of this claim has held that it supports the view that there is no simple answer to questions about the rightness and wrongness of most sorts of actions. Thus it is unrealistic to expect a virtue theory to do more than give a fairly precise account of the nature of the person who will make virtuous judgments.

As the remarks in *NE* V,10 indicated, it is a mistake to think that a rule, or set of rules, can be provided that will accommodate all the variety of considerations that practical decision making involves. However, Aristotle's remarks on casuistry there also indicated how the practically wise agent will deal with situations in which general rules break down. This supplements further his account of the practically wise's overall conception of the good. "When the law speaks universally, then, and a case arises on it which is not covered by the universal statement, then it is right ... to say what the legislator himself would have said had he been present, and would have put into his law if he had known" (*NE* 1137b19–24). This can be generalized to any case where two general claims in the practically wise person's conception of the good conflict. Suppose he holds that it is generally worthwhile speaking the truth, and generally worthwhile supporting friends, but these aims conflict in the present case. Then it seems that the agent must reflect back on past cases in which he spoke the truth, and those in which he supported friends, and consider how the generalizations relate to those cases. This will indicate the weight attaching to these principles in the past, and so inform the judgment in the present case.

On this interpretation of the Aristotelian view of applied ethics, the aim should not be to specify exactly how to reach the right decision on all occasions. No such set of guiding rules can be provided. What is needed, by contrast, is the right framework for thinking about difficult practical problems. Aristotelian virtue theory provides an adequately rich framework, fleshed out in such a way as to delimit fairly tightly the kinds of decision that might qualify as correct.

B. Indirect Implications of Aristotelian Theory for Applied Ethics

So far, Aristotelian ethical theory has been considered simply as a virtue theory. But the nature of his discussion of the virtues provides other resources that are relevant to debates in applied ethics.

Consider first Aristotle's discussion of *eudaimonia*. This is a discussion of what is the ultimate good and ultimately worth pursuing, and so must have some potential to affect practice. Aristotle's conclusion here is complex, making the relation of his discussion to practical issues more indirect, for if the life of (practical and/or theoretical) reason is what is ultimately worth pursuing, then it has to be pursued indirectly, for a rational life is itself one in which rational goals are pursued; hence the *eudaimon* life will be pursued (indirectly) by pursuing the goals of reason. Applied ethical questions will then turn on the nature of the goals of reason, and that takes us back to the decision making of the virtuous agent which has just been discussed.

Nonetheless a discussion of the ultimate good must have some bearing on the question of what all-things-considered conception of the good the virtuous agent will hold, and thus on the kind of judgments he will make in specific cases. Aristotle's discussion of *eudaimonia* is relevant here at least in a negative way, for his observations about the importance of pleasure, wealth, and honor (or public esteem) at least show that practical decisions in business or journalism, for example, which treat any of these as ultimate goods must be mistaken. His subsequent remarks about the actual place of all three in a *eudaimon* life must also help shape the virtuous conception of the all-things-considered good to be achieved by virtue.

A second aspect of Aristotle's ethical theory may also have an impact on the virtuous agent's conception of the all-things-considered good. This is the Aristotelian view that the full realization of human nature, necessary for the living of a good human life, can only take place in a polis. Thus consideration of the requirements of courage will consider the value of defending the state in the light of the fact that the state is a prerequisite for any individual to flourish, and that some states may be better constituted to promote individual flourishing than others. Similarly, action in line with the virtue of distributive justice will reflect the extent to which different distributions contribute to the flourishing of the state, and thus of each individual within it. These are still rather general constraints. However, they will affect decisions in particular practical cases. Thus ethical problems in business, for example, questions concerning the purpose of business as well as issues concerning pay and responsibility in business, will need to be considered in the light of the fact that an individual flourishes fully in a flourishing society.

This second aspect is developed in some detail by discussion of friendship. In the first place the precise analysis of virtue friendship has direct practical implications for any agent's conception of a good life. In addition the wider discussion of good social interactions again has clear implications for business ethics, and perhaps ethical issues in the media, such as the importance of privacy and honesty.

Finally, Aristotle's conception of human nature, as a set of potentialities realized fully in a life of reason, is certainly relevant to various issues in medical ethics, and may also be important in business ethics. On the medical side, attention to Aristotle's picture of human nature will be relevant to determining both the nature of human health and illness, and the quality of a life affected by ill health. (This is the quality of life measure now much discussed both in debates about resource allocation in health care and in those on the treatment of the comatose or terminally ill.)

On this Aristotelian picture, illness of any sort will consist of states which incapacitate the realization of essential human potential. Thus, first, such an account can contribute to the clarification of the concept of mental illness, and so provides a clearer view on the ethical issues that arise in psychiatric treatment. So far as quality of life is concerned, the account suggests that the current quality of a particular life will depend on the extent to which the agent is able to exercise those capacities whose exercise is involved in the living of a fully rational life. Such a perspective highlights the significance of mental health for quality of life assessments, as well as the extent to which physical incapacities prevent the agent from pursuing significant rational plans.

Furthermore, the Aristotelian picture of a human as a set of essential potentialities, whose good is found in the fully rational life that realizes those potentialities, is relevant to debates about abortion, euthanasia, and the treatment of animals, for it provides a picture within which these essential potentialities (which make a member of the species human) are fundamental in ethical reflection. This provides the resources to question the idea that personhood is what matters, not membership of the human species, a view prevalent in applied medical ethics. (Personhood is a condition characterized as a state in which capacities such as self-consciousness already exist.)

VII. CONCLUSIONS

Aristotelian ethical theory provides two kinds of resources for applied ethics. In the main it is currently deployed as a virtue theory. Such an approach seems capable of providing a framework for conceiving of specific applied problems and, within that framework, fairly tight constraints on what might count as the right judgment in each case. However, the Aristotelian approach implies that specific problems conceived in this way involve too many variables for there to be any precise mathematical calculus available in terms of which to determine what to do on each occasion. Aristotelian ethics need not hold that this undermines the view that on each occasion of judgment there is a single correct course of action.

In addition to the central notion of a virtue theory, Aristotelian ethics provides some additional considerations that can be made use of in approaching specific areas of applied ethics. Some of these feed into the deliberations about the good that will inform the judgments made by a virtuous agent. Others bear more indirectly on the reflections of such an agent. None of them determine precisely what must be done in particular circumstances where they apply, in the absence of attention to a detailed elaboration of all the particular features of those circumstances. This is consistent with the previous remarks on precision.

Also See the Following Articles

GREEK ETHICS, OVERVIEW • PLATONISM • VIRTUE ETHICS

Bibliography

Annas, J. (1995). "The Morality of Happiness." Oxford Univ. Press, Oxford.

Hursthouse, R. (1987). "Beginning Lives." Blackwell, Oxford.

Irwin, T. (1988). "Aristotle's First Principles." Oxford Univ. Press, Oxford.

Irwin, T. (1985). "Aristotle's Nicomachean Ethics." Hackett, Indianapolis.

Nussbaum, M. (1993). "Non-relative virtues: An Aristotelian approach. In "The Quality of Life" (Nussbaum M. and Sen A., Eds.). Oxford Univ. Press, Oxford.

Nussbaum, M. (1986). "The Fragility of Goodness." Cambridge Univ. Press, Cambridge.

Rorty, A. (Ed.) (1980). "Essays on Aristotle's Ethics." Univ. of California Press, Berkeley.

Ross, W. D. (1980). "The Nicomachean Ethics." Oxford Univ. Press, Oxford.

Solomons, R. (1992). "Ethics and Excellence." Oxford Univ. Press, New York.

Urmson, J. O. (1988). "Aristotle's Ethics." Oxford Univ. Press, Oxford.

ARTS, THE

David E. W. Fenner
University of North Florida

GLOSSARY

aesthetics The philosophical study of art, beauty, and the sensuous aspects of experience.

artworld The tradition, collective, or institution of all art objects, events, creators, presenters, attenders, critics, and so on.

autographic artwork A work of art that can have only one physical instantiation, such as a painting or a sculpture, and unlike a symphony, a dance, or a literary work.

censor To stop or limit the exhibition of an art object or event.

copyright The legal right not to have the copyrighted artwork manipulated (presented, published, sold, re-produced, altered, etc.) in any way without the consent of the copyright holder.

forgery The product of the act of creating an artwork in the style or manner of another artist with the purpose of presenting it as a work of that other artist.

NEA National Endowment for the Arts, a federal agency that, upon approval of an artist's application, funds the creation of art objects and events.

WE LIVE IN A CENTURY WHERE THE ARTWORLD is a world filled with tests and trials. We can, with broad strokes, treat all of these tests and trials as falling into two areas. First are the challenges that target the nature of art, whether it can be defined, whether and how art objects are different from other objects, and whether it has an essence. Second are the challenges that focus on how attenders ought to respond to this art (audience members, spectators, viewers, hearers, etc.), to its content, and sometimes to its presentational form. The first set of tests and trials may be primarily interesting to academics, critics, and contemplative artists. We can, for the sake of brevity, refer to this as the set of "academic" challenges. The second set, however, interests a much broader audience. In fact, determining how one ought to respond to the contents of some art objects interests not only all those who view the object, but even some who only hear about it second hand. In short, those art objects that demand a response demand it, potentially, from all of us. Again, for brevity, we can refer to these challenges as the "ethical" ones; ethical because they call for a value judgment and a response on the part of the attender.

I. BACKGROUND

The focus in this article will be primarily on the second set of challenges, those that have an ethical nature, no matter how narrowly or broadly made is their demand for an ethical response. However, to frame a context, we ought to begin our discussion with the first set of tests. Before the nineteenth century, definitions of art, or definitions of what made an object or an event a work of art, could focus with general acceptance on the relationship of similarity between the art object and the sensuous world. Representational theories that took this relationship as their focus, theories going back to Plato and Aristotle, could be viably considered. This changed with the advent of Impressionism. The trend was beginning then to move away from the focus on art as representing nature. The move from Impressionism, through such art movements as Pointillism, Cubism, and Abstract Expressionism to works that seem to be nothing other than formal constructs sealed the demise of representational theories of art. Art challenged such theories and, through acceptance by art audiences of more and more, it was able to push what counted as art past the point where a theory based on a similarity relationship with the world of nature was tenable.

This move away from the natural, sensuous world to greater abstraction was complemented, in the early part of this century, with a move in exactly the opposite direction. Even through the various moves of abstraction in the artworld, in defining art, one could rely on the unwavering distinction between objects of the artworld being essentially different from objects of the ordinary, functional world. Many aesthetic thinkers focused on this distinction in framing their theories. Their efforts were thwarted, however, by artists who sought to dissolve the line between the worlds of art and the everyday. Dadaists, Pop Artists, and "Ready-Made" Artists demonstrated that the line between the two worlds was not only breachable, it was illusory.

These two lines of challenge, along with the innumerable smaller and less classifiable challenges in art that the twentieth century saw set the stage in a way of great significance for the ethical challenges that the artworld faces today. Indeed, although we may separate theoretic or academic challenges from ethical ones, when viewed from inside the artworld or from an art-historical perspective, they are really on a continuum. Frequently, art objects that offered one sort of challenge also offered another.

The most controversial set of ethical tests advanced by the artworld is also the set with the widest audience. Almost everyone is concerned with decency and propriety. It used to be the case that almost everyone could tell the difference—aesthetically, artistically, and ethically—between art and, say, pornography. But today tests against the incursion of the one-time indecent or improper into the artworld are underway. Today the line between art and the obscene or prurient has been

challenged. One need only think of the uproar created by the late Robert Mapplethorpe. In general, art has become substantially less harmless. Art today not only tests and questions; in some ways, art literally threatens.

The tests in defining art are perhaps the more philosophically interesting of the lot, but the recent artworld tests of an ethical nature are much more provocative. Twentieth-century art does not merely offer tests and challenges that make connection to artists, aesthetes, or aesthetic attention. Many of these purposely go outside the boundaries of the aesthetic to make their most provocative statements. Audience members are now forced to consider works under their attention more broadly. How one ought to respond to a work of twentieth-century art is not merely an aesthetic matter. If it were simply an aesthetic matter, then many of the most provocative and engaging works of recent art would be innocuous and facile.

Simply put, it is precisely decisions that call viewers to question in themselves how they ought respond that make the arts today ethically arresting and morally exigent. Ethics is a matter of deciding what to do given a certain situation. Ethics is about action. And situations calling for audience responses of ethical sorts are in abundance.

II. CENSORSHIP

The topic of censorship has received an enormous amount of attention in America in the last three decades. It is a topic of extremes. On the one hand, there are those who wish to completely eradicate anything they (or some prescribed group) find objectionable. They wish to cut off avenues of funding; they wish to close presentation venues; they wish to vilify the creators and presenters of such objectionable art (the very labeling of these objects/events as "art" is itself convtroversial). At the other extreme are those who say that the arts ought to be entirely immune from censorship. To circumscribe a line around art over which it may not cross is to stifle the creation of art; it is to rob art of its power to challenge current views and to initiate cultural growth. At the one extreme are those who wish to reign in tightly art-funding agencies like the National Endowment for the Arts, and make museums answerable to their local communities in decisions about what may and may not be presented. At the other extreme are those who say that in art "anything goes," and "anything ought to go."

Clearly, both of these extremes are wrong and dangerous. If art is censored to an extreme, then it could degenerate into a mere reflection of the tastes and interests of the most puritanical elements of society. If, on the other hand, in art "anything goes," then real and serious harm can be done in the name of art. Physical harms (murders in "snuff films"; people screaming "fire" in a crowded theatre in the name of art), psychological harms (small children being exposed to graphic, hard-core sexual images and images of violence), and social harms (racist themes) could be committed on audiences without their consent, yet all in the name of art. The optimal position with regard to censorship lies somewhere between these two extremes. In most Western countries there is in place a tradition of liberalism with regard to self expression; this is particularly the case within the artworld. And this seems valuable. If it is, then the correct position on the censorship continuum will most probably be much closer to the extreme of the abolition of censorship rather than the extreme of total state control (supposing it is the state this is censoring). No matter where the final line is drawn, one thing is clear. Unless one asks and answers certain questions regarding censorship, one will never get close to drawing a line, no matter how initial or tentative.

What is censorship? Who censors? Why do these individuals or agencies censor? Why should one censor? Under what conditions and through what means should one censor? How deliberate or direct must an effort be to effectively constitute censorship?

A. Forms of Censorship

There are many forms of censorship. When a government dictates that a work should not exist or should never be opened to an audience, this is the most overt form of censorship. Currently, our government "censors" acts that could incite riots, the public display of overt sexual themes, yelling fire in a crowded theatre, and all acts that in their creation would seriously harm the participants. If any of these items were incorporated into bona fide artworks, then they would be candidates for direct censorship. More subtle forms of censorship exist as well. If the NEA elects never to fund a given art movement or artform, this may be viewed as a form of censorship. Others would argue, however, that for such an action to be censorship, that action on the part of the NEA would have to be deliberate and intentional with the purpose of not allowing this movement or artform a chance for exposure; just because the NEA does not fund every artist is no reason to suggest that the NEA is censoring all those who are unfunded. Nevertheless, the government does take a moral responsibility, and so is morally accountable, when it delivers to

some artists and artforms funds that others do not receive. Decisions are being made as to what is to happen with the public's money, and these decisions almost of necessity will involve more than simply what an accountant would do. These decisions will involve what the government, or agents acting on behalf of the government, decide is worthy of funding, is culturally or socially important, or is valuable as art.

Some censorship occurs on religious grounds; an object or event may be sacrilegious or sufficiently offensive to a religious body or perhaps even to common religious sentiment—perhaps even to spirituality itself—so as to be judged censorable. Serrano's *Piss Christ,* the photographic work, incidentally funded by the government, of a plastic crucifix suspended in a jar of urine, was the subject of religious and spiritual calls for censorship, or at the very least for national funding to be withdrawn (a kind of censorship in itself).

Another form of censorship is social. In direct cases, a work may threaten national security (imagine a work that incorporates state secrets that were acquired surreptitiously by the artist), or a work may threaten to incite a group of people to riot or to harm others, either manifestly or covertly. In some cases, a work may even have the effect of promoting one to harm oneself (as certain rock music has been alleged to do). In indirect cases, censorship may be deemed appropriate where the work in question attacks the moral fiber of the society or the community. If an artwork makes us less good than we would be, or were, before experiencing that work, then such a work might rightly be censored. Allegedly, pornography (which, let us stipulate here, is not art) has effects other than simply the satisfaction of prurient interests on the part of those who experience it. Could art that has themes that could be seen to appeal to sexual interests have the same ill side effects? Should such photographic works such as those of Robert Mapplethorpe be censored—or kept from children, or the public, or should they be kept from everybody at all times?

Censorship can happen in still other forms. If a gallery owner elects not to show a particular artist or artform, if a community elects not to allow such a showing, if the local school board withdraws from school library shelves certain books—books traditionally found on school library shelves—if the local television station refuses to carry certain network shows, if an exhibit is picketed.... There are many ways that censorship of artworks can occur. And in some communities, it is clear that such means of censorship are overused and are taken advantage of.

B. Who Ought to Censor?

Beyond deciding exactly what censorship is, there are other questions at the heart of the issue of censorship. The first of these is who ought to censor? This question can be answered in several different ways.

1. The Local Community

Many believe that, because different locales will sometimes differ dramatically in terms of the sensibilities of their populaces, it is the local community that is the proper group to enact censorship. What a small rural town in the Midwest holds to be appropriate may be markedly different from what is held by Manhattan's Greenwich Village to be appropriate. Censorship must, so the argument goes, reflect the local sensibilities.

2. The Religious Community

Because there is no obvious institution exclusively dedicated to caring for the ethical dimensions of people's lives and because few communities have resident ethicists, the everyday care of moral concerns frequently falls to the clergy. If they are closest to moral experts that a community will generally have, it makes sense, then, to have the clergy practice whatever censorship is necessary.

3. The Society

The state has the responsibility to protect us both domestically and from foreign invasion; does it also have the responsibility to protect us from things properly censored? On the other hand, does the state have the responsibility, given a mandate to educate its populace, to provide us with access to art? What about the possibility that some of that art may be thought properly censorable by some of that populace?

C. What Should Be Censored?

The second question can be answered more simply. *What Harms* should be censored. But, of course, the interest is in the details. The following list is made up of items that may be properly censorable. As with all such lists in this article, no final answer is offered as to which of the items listed below should appropriately be the targets of censorship.

1. What harms physically.
   a. What harms the artist's subjects, persons, property or the environment.
   b. What harms another artist's work.
2. What harms morally.
3. What harms spiritually or religiously.
4. What harms socially or divisively.
5. What harms societally or nationally.
6. What harms psychologically.
   a. Explicitness in violence.
   b. Explicitness in sexual themes.

Perhaps few, some, or all of the items in this list are appropriately censorable. This, then, would be a decision that those who are the appropriate agents of censorship might make. And given that who those agents are may differ from community to community, those items properly censorable may also differ community to community.

D. How Should Censorship Be Carried Out?

First, it is important to understand that all censorship is on a continuum with all other censorship. While authoritarian societies may censor more, and more frequently, than liberal states, each society is on the same continuum because every society, no matter how liberal, enlightened, or psychologically stable, censors something. The trick is to understand where on that continuum is the proper place to draw a line—or, more modestly, where on that continuum is the proper line drawn for *this* society at *this* time.

The old adage about obscenity—"I can't define it, but I know it when I see it"—is almost entirely useless as a means of deciding where the line is to be drawn. Clearly in many cases, perhaps all, the artist's intuitions about the propriety of a work disagree with the intuitions of those who seek to censor that artist or her/his work. It is probably the case that those who are in the most central position to enact governmental censorship, legislators and politicians, are in less of a position to act as the best judges of such things than are others. Shall the lawyers rule the artists? And yet, if the politicians are simply acting on the interests of their constituents, then we might ask why the artists ought to think themselves immune from the commonality of the views of the populace of which they are but a part.

Liberal positions—although today there exists more interest among self-described liberals for censoring items that encourage ethnic or gender disenfranchisement—have traditionally held that adults, given that they are adults, ought to serve as their own judges of what is and what is not appropriate for themselves and their families to be exposed to. Some have held that the only appropriate group to be subject to the effects of censorship is children. In the privacy of one's home, or in the privacy of a closed location, adults have the right to experience almost anything they seek to experience. So long as there exists no overt physical harm of the subjects or the audience, adults can make up their own minds.

Furthermore, some hold that censorship, in concert with the liberal position described above, ought only to be practiced on the *creation* of artworks. Only those works should be properly censored that in their creation involve harm to their subjects, as would so-called "snuff films" and child pornography. All else ought be available for the decisions to view or not to view of free and thoughtful adults.

Finally, there is the problem of the mutability of the appropriateness of censorship for a given society or community. It may well be that what is properly censorable today will not be so tomorrow. While it was right and proper for Victorians to hide the legs of tables from potentially inflamed and subsequently scandalized onlookers, we today can brave bare-legged furniture without succumbing to its temptations.

Moreover, what is properly censorable here may not be so in other societies or communities. Amsterdam's tolerances may not be the sort that could be practiced, without negative social repercussions, in cities in America or in Britain. And American tolerances may not be the sort that could be countenanced in Singapore or in Saudi Arabia. If there are such differences among place and time, then the task of censorship is an ever-present one, continually calling for attention.

III. REPRODUCTION OF ART

In this section on the reproduction of art we will discuss the problems associated with fakes, forgeries, and copies in general. While copying is obviously necessary in the creation and reproduction of many artworks and in some artforms, the former two labels are distinctly pejorative. Why? What is the moral difference between a copy and a forgery?

There are many works of art that exist, at least in a form that can be sensed, only through copies. Literature, poetry, symphonies, operas, dances, plays, lithographs, monoprints, etchings, and so forth and so on, can only be experienced by an audience through a performance, a reproduction, or a copy. These works are different in kind, then, from artworks such as paintings, sculptures, and architecture, of which there can only exist a single instantiation. There are many copies of Austen's *Pride and Prejudice,* all of them sharing in common a text, although only some sharing in common such things as print and binding. There can be many

copies of an etching, although all, given that each is signed and numbered, are different in some respect from one another. There can be a great number of performances and productions such as there are of the ballet *Swan Lake.* But unlike *Pride and Prejudice,* each may be markedly different from the others. Even within a single score, a single choreography, a single company, and a single production run, there will be differences in each and every performance.

These differences are expected and embraced by art lovers as a means of understanding and appreciating the artwork more deeply through being able to experience variations, and being in the position of comparing copies one with another. Copies are essential to the work's existing in a sensory form. And they are important enough in their differences to presenting the artwork in detail and variation to add to the experiences of audiences who see or hear more than a single copy.

Forgeries and fakes, however, do not share in the nobility of diversity that informs copies and reproductions. Forgeries and fakes, in the very naming, have an ethical dimension. These items are made with the intension that at some time they will deceive. Whether they deceive a curator, art patron, viewer, or all three, they present themselves as something they are not. For years, works of Van Meegeren were taken to be authentic works of Vermeer. Van Meegeren's works were not copies of actual Vermeer works; Van Meegeren's works were simply very closely in the Vermeer style. How such deception is accomplished, and whether fakes and forgeries suffer in respect of their aesthetic appreciation, is not at issue here. Our focus is the ethical aspect of the deception that seems a necessary part of any forgery or fake.

But what of an artist "borrowing" from another artist? "Variations on a theme," "Musical Sampling," and creating artworks "after so-and-so" or "in the style of so-and-so" are all of this kind. It has become commonplace to see the works of some artists taken over by other artists, either in collaboration of efforts, sometimes in homage to the first artist for offering inspiration or a great work, sometimes in mimicry of the former artist, and sometimes in outright misappropriation of the first artist's work in the creation of that of the second artist. As is evident, the moral implications of the use of another's work in one's own can run the gamut from being flattering to constituting stealing. Ethically speaking, how far may one go? How much of the work of another artist can one appropriate and still refer to her own work as original and separate from that of the original?

This, of course, raises the following question: What do terms like "original," "novel," and "creative" mean?

Without defining such terms at the outset, the point at which the demarcating line between flattery and stealing is to be drawn remains in question. Should a work, to be considered original, incorporate at least 50% new work? Line-drawing in percentages is problematic. Should a novel work simply include some new thought, some new expression not in the original from which it was inspired? How modest or how dramatic need be this new expression?

IV. ARTISTIC PROPERTY

This area focuses on ownership and copyrights. While this area heading may suffer from sounding too legalistic, it encompasses some of the most interesting moral dilemmas facing the artworld today.

Few of us, no doubt, have not had the opportunity to see a film that was originally produced in black and white *colorized*. While it is undeniable that film colorizers are becoming better at their craft—the first colorized films were caricatures of themselves—this does not address the point about whether they are doing a disservice to an original black-and-white film in the first place. Woody Allen, for one, has taken a strong stance against the colorizing of films. And it is easy to see from where his sentiment is borne. The nuance of shading, of the play with light and dark, that is apparent in so many films of the thirties and forties, would be severely limited in affect if colorized. Orson Welles' *Citizen Kane* is a prime example of a work that uses light and shadow in an integral way to the aesthetic nature and story of that film. Would the film be destroyed, or at least very much harmed, by colorization? What about more contemporary films such as Allen's *Manhattan* or Spielberg's *Schindler's List,* which, although color was a very clear option, were produced in black and white?

Or is it the case that artworks, like any other real properties, are possessions of their owners? If I own a table, and it is too high for my purposes, I have a right to cut the legs a bit in order to make it more functional. It is my table, and I can do with it as I like (within limits, of course; I cannot, for instance, use it to fashion stakes with which to kill the vampires I take to be sleeping in the house next to mine—actually, I suppose I can make the stakes; I simply cannot use them in the manner for which they were intended). Suppose I purchase an inexpensive copy of a painting, the sort always sold in museum bookshops and euphemistically called a print. I have the right, once I get the copy home and discover that it does not fit the frame I own, to cut

bits off of each side to make it fit. This may be aesthetically suspect, but it is still my right.

What if I own a film? What if, in the manner of Ted Turner, I purchase a film and its rights, and I wish to colorize that film? If the film is my property, why ought I not have the right to do with it as I see fit? I can, for instance, decide only to show my film ("my" film) once a decade. Few will challenge my right to do that. I can have the film formatted to fit a television screen and to fit within a 2-hour time period, and I can cut the film up with dozens of commercials. Few will challenge my right to do that. And if I want to colorize it?

The *Mona Lisa* is not for sale. It has reached that point as one of the most central members of the canon of Western art that it will most probably never again be in the position where it could be sold and owned by a single patron or a set of patrons. It, to employ the cliché, belongs to the world (or at least to France). But suppose that one could purchase it. If one did, would she be able to treat the *Mona Lisa* in any way she wished? On one side of the intuitional line about what is appropriate would be that patron's right to privately house the work; it is her right that she not allow the work to be shown. She may decide to house the work in a non-climiate-controlled room. This would be very foolish in terms of her investment, and will no doubt offend museum owners and aesthetes, but it may be her right to do so. She may wish to illuminate it brightly; she may wish to lock it in a safe. In each case, the right seems hers. Could she destroy it? That is, is it her right to dispose of it in such a way as to destroy it? Is it her right to paint on top of it, or to draw on it, or to remove the canvas from the stretchers? Can she chip away at the paint, or put pin pricks in the canvas? These latter questions test the intuition that what one possesses, what one owns, can be treated in any way that the owner believes fit. If the Louvre decided to illuminate the work too brightly, many would be up in arms over such effrontery. Artworks seem to have a protection and a right to such protection that few other possessions enjoy. One may do whatever one wishes to one's table, but one cannot torture one's livestock or pets, one presumably cannot dump down the sink the cure for cancer, and one cannot draw on the *Mona Lisa*. These are not legal encumbrances; they are moral.

Yet another topic for this area is that of how material may be published and released. This article, for instance, enjoys a certain protection, and no publisher other than Academic Press has a right to produce copies of it. This protection and others like it are in place so that the work of authors and their agents, in this case philosophers and publishing houses, are not exploited for gains that the authors, and so on, will not see. One's labor is one's own, and so benefits accruing from that labor should rightfully go to the deserving.

But what if a professor finds that there is no suitable anthology of articles available in the topic of her upcoming course? May she, for the sake of that single group of students, fashion one together for their use? May she copy just enough sets of those articles for those students and no others? What if a major in her department asks for one additional copy? Copyright law, as any teacher who uses copyrighted material can attest, is wide-ranging and not uncomplicated. The protections that we enjoy as authors are in kind the nuisances we find as teachers.

V. SPONSORSHIP AND PRESERVATION OF ART

This next area is on the sponsorship of art—where we are generally talking about social or state sponsorship—and issues of the preservation of art. Here, instead of focusing on the individual, be that the artist, patron, or viewer, we focus on the society, or, more precisely, on the state or nation. What does the state owe art, artists, and the artworld? Do the obligations that the state bears toward its citizenry compel it to diligently oversee the cultural and artistic life of that society?

Many answer yes to this question. If a society is wont to call itself civilized or advanced, then it must look after the education of its inhabitants. Part of the educational aims of such a society may be cultural in content, and so part of the state's obligation may be to provide not only for the exposure of its populace to that society's cultural and artistic history, but to provide for the continuance of the traditions and institutions that have made up the content of that history. The state must collect monies from its citizenry for education; and because artistic education is a facet of that necessary education, the state must fund art exhibitions, art institutions, artists, and art movements. In short, the state must fund art.

But how is it to accomplish this? While it is easy enough to create taxes for the benefit of art and to create agencies for the distribution of these funds, it is very difficult in the face of the number of artists working—and deserving—to decide who gets funding and who does not. Some argue that the state agencies, then, to accomplish their missions, must be in the position of being able to judge artistic and cultural value. These agencies must be able to, in a sense, look into the future to see what will be of lasting value, aesthetically as well as socially, to the society and its populace. This is a tough trick, but one that must be done *if* a society deems the funding of art to be among its responsibilities (as ours does).

The other side of the coin, of course, is that art is not properly part of the educational content of a society. Advocates of this position might say that if art is to flourish, it must be a thing embraced by the populace, and to be embraced is to be supported. If the citizens want art, let them fund it themselves, in the way perhaps that the great patrons of renaissance Florence, the Medicis and the Vatican, did. Americans pay a great deal for entertainment. If art is essentially for the purposes of pleasure, as some contend, then it is a pleasure that must rely on its own attraction for its own life. The film industry is flourishing, as is the rock music industry. If the opera or ballet is valued by the citizens, or enough of them, then the opera and ballet will flourish likewise. If they are not, then they will go the way of other artforms that are no longer practiced today. To governmentally support artforms that are not popularly supported may result in the isolation of those artforms from the very public they are intended to benefit. Such artforms may become insulated from public criticism and in doing so the governmental support may succeed in stifling and inhibiting the artistic growth of those artforms.

The key, then, is to determine, first, what role government support of the arts should take, and, secondly, exactly what value the arts, or particular artforms or movements, hold for a society. To ask the latter, one first must inquire in what context this question ought to be asked. Should the value of art be merely to strengthen the society as a political body? Should the value of art be for educational purposes only? Should art always uplift and moralize? Should art simply mirror the society, its strengths and weaknesses? Should art always challenge?

If a positive answer is offered to the question about whether the state ought support the arts, then we must ask about the nature of such an obligation. Certainly the concerns mentioned above must be addressed, but beyond these concerns lie those regarding what the state is supposed to do with the product of its investment. If the state funds art, then, one could argue, what is created is the property of the state. In the American case, the property is that of the artist, and it is hers to dispose of as she sees fit. But if the value of the funding of art is social, then there is reason for suggesting that the property, the created art, ought be looked after by the state: used in exhibitions, used for educational purposes, and stored away for continued use as the history of that society progresses.

It may be part of the mission of national museums to do just this, to house the most valuable of the works created by artists of that society (or one related in some way to that society). But what about the plethora of works that are funded and created but are not deemed valuable enough to house in national galleries? Recently, the Netherlands have experienced this difficulty. The Dutch have funded a great deal of art, with the consequence that the state is now responsible for that work. In 1992, a report came out (Marlise Simons, "Dutch State Dumping Some Non-Masters' Artwork," *The New York Times,* September 14, 1992, National Education Section) that the Dutch state was trying to "give away 215,000 works of art," which the state had funded and was currently housing. This body of work had been collected from the 1950s to the 1980s in programs where the Dutch government purchased the unsold works of Dutch artists. The government will not sell the works, for this would flood the market, ruining it for artwork currently being produced in the Netherlands. Neither will the government destroy the work, at least not until such time as all other options have been attempted, because this would suggest that the work had no value. For the same reason, then, the government will not simply give the work away. Instead, the Dutch state is trying to find homes for their vast collection in schools, hospitals, clinics, police stations, government buildings, and the like.

The Dutch are carefully attempting to assess the aesthetic and cultural merits of the works, insuring that they are not "donating the Rembrandts and Van Goghs of our time." While governments are perhaps qualified to judge the economic and social worth of objects, their's is an inescapably controversial task in the assessment of the aesthetic and cultural merits of artworks. But perhaps it is not so unique. The United States' NEA is charged with judging, at least partly on aesthetic or cultural grounds, the relative worth of projects brought to their attention for possible governmental funding. The Dutch simply have a much larger task in their hands, different in degree but perhaps not in kind from what the NEA does.

VI. ART AND ETHICS

Is there a relationship between art and ethics, between the artworld and morality? Certainly, in a trivial sense, there is a relationship: as ethical situations arise in all human activities, they certainly arise in connection with the creation of, the presentation of, and the attention to art. But perhaps this is not so trivial after all. In dealing with art, we can ask questions of an ethical nature that we may not be able to ask in other realms of human activity. For instance, is it, or can it be the case that aesthetic value in a work of art *makes up* for a lack of moral value? Is a bona fide work of art susceptible to the same moral consideration we apply to other matters? It is not, among young prepubescents, uncommon for them to question why they are forbidden to view such magazines as *Playboy* yet they are permitted—perhaps even forced—to view pictures of unclothed individuals rendered in paint on canvas or in marble? To suggest to a prepubescent or an adolescent that there are different intents on the parts of the creators of these two different items as to what they are portraying, or what reactions they mean to inspire in their audiences, is generally lost on them. They see it as they see it, and the chances that they will take a "mature" view of the art is usually a matter of unsubstantiated hope on the parts of teachers and parents. Indeed, one need only find works of art where the intent is not so modest, sexually speaking. There are works of art, some quite good, where the intent to cause sexual interest is obvious in the work. Are these objects properly shown to school children?

Take another example. With frequency, vulgarity or violence is included in a work of art to capture a greater sense of realism, or to provide a more realistic context, for the work. Shakespeare himself included vulgarity in some of his subplots to lend to the aesthetic richness or depth of those works. Most believe, at least in Shakespeare's case, that the vulgarity is not only acceptable; it is indispensable. The work would be diminished without it.

While there is clear overlap here with our earlier discussion of censorship, there is a deeper point at issue here. It may well be that in art, some events or displays that would be considered improper in nonart contexts, are accepted, even embraced.

There is, though, a second area of recent interest in the depth of the relationship between art and morality. Can it be the case, or is it the case, that art can actually make us morally better? Can art, or does some art, instruct us ethically? The answer must be yes. (I know in the case of the construction of my own early moral character, Disney films played a great role; in fact, I count on that being the case with my own son.) But art may morally instruct us in less than overt or didactic ways. Seeing the world for what it really is (at least in the experience of the artist whose work we are attending to), feeling the feelings of another in the attention to a work of art, understanding dimensions of human experience through an artwork that might have otherwise gone unnoticed—these are all ways in which art can make us morally better people.

Many believe that we grow as moral persons through exposure to art. But in the examination of such a situation, many futher questions present themselves: If this is the case, then is this instruction at the hand of the artist, or is it a function of the art object itself? Do artists have a responsibility regarding the moral enrichment of their audiences? Can a work displaying immoral themes, or incorporating immoral aspects, nonetheless be uplifting? Is all art properly criticized from a moral perspective?

For these questions, as with all the questions raised in this article, there are lots of answers. Probably there is even a plurality of good answers. The *right answers,* if there are right answers, will come only with continued attention to the questions, the nature of ethics, and the world of the arts.

Also See the Following Article

CENSORSHIP

Bibliography

Devereaux, M. (1993). Protected space: Politics, censorship, and the arts. *Journal of Aesthetics and Art Criticism* **51**, 207–215.

Eaton, M. M. (1992). Integrating the aesthetic and the moral. *Philosophical Studies* **67**, 219–240.

Eaton, M. M. (1996). Serious problems, serious values: Are there aesthetic dilemmas? In D. Fenner (Ed.), *Ethics and the Arts: An Anthology* (pp. 279–291). New York: Garland Press.

Feinberg, J. (1994). Not with my tax money. The problem of justifying government subsidies for the arts. *Public Affairs Quarterly* **8**, 101–123.

Fenner, D. E. W. (Ed.). (1996). *Ethics and the arts: An anthology.* New York: Garland Press.

Graham, G. (1991). The politics of culture: Art in a free society. *History of European Ideas* **33**, 763–774.

Sankowski, E. (1992). Ethics, art and museums. *Journal of Aesthetic Education* **26**, 1–13.

Serra, R. (1991). Art and censorship. *Critical Inquiry* **17**, 574–581.

Smith, R. A., and Berman, R. (Eds.). (1992). *Public policy and the aesthetics interest.* Chicago: University of Illinois Press.

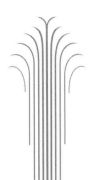

AUDITING PRACTICES

Peter Moizer
University of Leeds

GLOSSARY

altruism The theory that the right action is the one that produces the greatest benefit to others.

audit The systematic process of: (i) independently obtaining and evaluating evidence regarding assertions about economic actions and events to ascertain the degree of correspondence between those assertions and economic reality, and (ii) communicating the results to interested parties. The main example is the financial statement audit, where the auditor obtains and evaluates evidence about an organization's financial statements and then issues on opinion on whether the statements are presented fairly in conformity with established criteria, usually generally accepted accounting principles.

bias The creation of intentional errors and distortions in financial statements in order to give the impression to readers of the statements that the position is either better or worse than it really is.

consequentialism A collective term for those moral theories that state that the judgment of the rightness or wrongness, goodness or badness of an action is solely dependent on the results the action produces.

corporation An organization recognized by law that allows people to associate together so that their labor and capital are combined in a single venture. In law, a corporation is a single entity independent of its owners, which has the right to buy property, to sue or be sued without its members being held liable, and to enter into contracts.

deontology The theory that duty is the basis of morality. Some acts are therefore morally obligatory regardless of the consequences.

economic rationality The theory that individuals are motivated by their own self-interest expressed in terms of maximizing their economic wealth (as measured by the present cash equivalent of the future cash flows that will be received by the individual), while minimizing the risks attached to those future cash flows.

egoism The theory that the pursuit of one's own welfare is the highest good.

window dressing The practice of deliberately attempting to present a false picture in order to conceal an unpleasant reality.

AUDITING has a long history stretching back to the time when certain individuals had so much wealth that they required others to manage it for them. It was inevitable that a prudent, wealthy person (the *principal*), who was unable directly to supervise how his or her property was being used would arrange for some independent third party to check on how the steward (the *agent*) had employed those assets entrusted to him or her. The agent would normally be expected to give an account to the principal of how he or she had used the principal's assets in a given period. Often this would be an *oral* account of what had taken place, listened to by individuals sufficiently familiar with the agent's work to assess the accuracy of the statements made. Such a listener was called an *auditor* (from the Latin *audire*, meaning "to hear").

Early auditing also existed in formally constituted organizations. These mainly related to government activity generally, and the collection of tax revenues in particular. For example, auditors were employed in the Roman tax collection system to verify physical assets. The subject matter of auditing typically involved accounting records and systems that demanded an expertise on the part of the auditor sufficient to make a successful verification of the assets in question.

The central assumptions of auditing are that individuals are: (i) fallible human beings who are likely to make unintentional mistakes as a result of carelessness or incompetence, and (ii) *egoists* concerned principally with their own welfare who will lie to tax collectors about their wealth, and who as agents will misuse the assets of their principal for their own benefit. One of the main purposes of an audit is therefore to convince individuals that if they lie to a tax collector or, as agents, if they are lazy or steal from their principal, that such behavior will be discovered by the auditor and reported back. Some legal sanction would then follow and the individual would be punished accordingly. In medieval England, the lord of the manor was no doubt reassured by the knowledge that a *reeve* (the manorial steward who supervised the daily affairs of the manor) who had been fraudulent or who had failed to prepare an account would be tried by the manorial court and severely punished. Central to the concept of an audit is therefore the notion of deterrence. The expectation that an audit is to take place should deter a person from being either lazy or dishonest. However, within this apparently simple concept lies the conundrum that forms the basis of this article. If human beings acting as agents cannot be trusted to act in the best interest of their principals, why should auditors be trusted, given that auditors are themselves the agents of the same principals? The

problem is pithily captured in the famous quotation from the Satires of Juvenal: "quis custodiet ipsos custodes?" (who is to guard the guards, themselves?).

I. AUDITORS AND CORPORATIONS

The advent of the modern corporation has considerably altered the auditor's role. There are many types of corporations, but in this article, we will focus on the key economic institution, the joint-stock company, so called because it is jointly owned by several persons who receive shares of stock in exchange for an investment of money in the business. One of the most important attributes of a joint-stock company is the fact that the company is a person in its own right, being able to own assets and to be responsible for its own liabilities. Hence, the owners' liability to the debts of the company is limited to any unpaid share capital. The dawn of the limited liability company was in the middle of the nineteenth century, and it gave rise to the need to protect creditors from fraudulent entrepreneurs who could use the protection afforded by limited liability to avoid paying their debts. A series of court cases toward the end of the nineteenth century established that the main defense for creditors was the notion that cash could not be paid from a corporation to its stockholders (as a dividend) unless the corporation had made sufficient profits to cover the dividend. The requirement to calculate how much accounting profit had been made by a company in a year led to the need to determine how such profit should be calculated. At a simple level, accounting profit is the difference between revenues and expenses, but rules had to be invented to guide accountants about when revenues could be recognized in a particular year and how costs should be matched against those revenues (as expenses). Accounting profit was thus an artificial construct of accountants, and its meaning could be understood only by reference to the accounting conventions that had been used to generate it. The role of the auditor was therefore changed from one of listening to an agent's explanation of how assets had been used to one of commenting on the contents of the agent's financial statements. As financial statements are documents governed by convention, company auditors give their opinion using conventional, stylized language. For example, in the United States the auditor would say that the financial statements "present fairly" the financial position in conformity with generally accepted accounting principles, and in European countries the auditor would say that the financial statements show "a true and fair view" (U.K. and Ireland), "une image fidèle" ("a faithful picture," France and Belgium) and "ein den tatsächlichen Verhältnissen entsprechendes Bild" ("a picture in accordance with the facts," Germany), The indefinite article *a* is used in most European countries to denote the fact that the financial statements are giving only one view and that there are a myriad of other possible views, depending on the choice of accounting convections.

The auditor of the modern corporation has another problem not encountered by his or her medieval counterpart and this relates to the notion of corporate governance, that is, who governs the corporation. Legally, the answer is simple. The stockholders own the shares that in most cases entitle them to vote at annual general meetings on the appointment of a corporation's auditors and on the size of their audit fee. However, in practice the executive directors of a corporation prepare the resolutions to be voted upon at annual general meetings and it is relatively rare for investors to affect the passage of such resolutions. The cause of this state of affairs is the fact that the majority of shares are held by institutions run by professional fund managers who have little incentive to become involved in the running of a corporation, as their own performance is judged on how the share prices of their investments perform, not on how well they manage those investments. Given the power of directors to influence their appointment and remuneration levels, it is not surprising that when audit partners talk about their "client" they are invariably referring to the executive directors (i.e., the agent), not their real principals, the stockholders. Hence, modern auditors are effectively hired and their fees determined by the firm's executive directors, the people on whom they are reporting. There is therefore a direct economic incentive for auditors not to find or tell the truth, because to do so could jeopardize their future income in the form of audit fees and other ancillary fees derived from the corporation. In addition, there are other behavioral reasons (personal loyalties and friendships with the firm's managers) that could induce auditors not to tell the truth. In this article, we will explore the ethical motivations of auditors and the pressures on their personal integrity.

results of operations, in accordance with generally accepted accounting principles. The audited financial statements are therefore the result of a joint process using inputs supplied by both the management of the corporation and the auditor. Management produces draft financial statements and the auditor gathers evidence that either substantiates or contradicts the information contained in them.

The principal intended recipients of the auditor's opinion are the current stockholders, although it could be said that the consumers of the audit service are whoever reads the audited financial statements with a view to making some decision in relation to the corporation. As far as readers of a set of audited financial statements are concerned, the service that the auditor provides is the independent verification of the credibility of the information contained in a company's financial statements. Hence, the value of the auditor's service can be measured by the increased confidence felt by readers when using audited accounts as opposed to unaudited ones. An audit improves the quality of the information presented in the financial statements by reducing two possible distortions, noise and bias. The term *noise* refers to the unintentional errors that occur in the financial reporting process. The auditor can reduce noise in two ways: by discovering errors during the normal routine of audit testing and by increasing the standard of care adopted by employees who are conscious that their work will be subject to independent scrutiny. The second distortion, termed *bias,* refers to the creation of intentional errors by management, intent on window dressing their own performance. Bias can be introduced either by creating deliberate mistakes (such as valuing an obsolete inventory product as if it were part of the current range) or by the choice of accounting methods that do not accord with generally accepted accounting principles (e.g., defining the date on which a sale took place to be the date on which the sales order was received rather than the date on which the order was delivered to the customer). By reducing noise and bias, the auditor is helping to reduce the uncertainty faced by users when interpreting accounting information.

II. THE ROLE OF THE CORPORATE AUDITOR

The main role of the modern company auditor is to express an opinion on whether a corporation's financial statements present fairly the financial position and the

III. THE CHOICES THAT AUDITORS HAVE TO MAKE

The medieval audit included a painstaking review of every transaction. Entries were examined and traced back to underlying documents; ledger balances were checked and compared to amounts on hand and other physical evidence. It was therefore possible for the auditor to check all the transactions of the agent and to check the existence and state of all the assets of the principal. However, the modern corporation is so large that it is impossible to check all the transactions, and, hence, the auditor can examine only a small sample and verify only a small proportion of the assets, liabilities, revenues, and expenses of the corporation. In the audit of reasonably well-run corporations, the auditor can make use of the corporation's own internal systems of control that ensure that the assets of the organization are safeguarded. If the auditor is happy that the company's own control systems are working, then the auditor can rely on the outputs from the control systems. The auditor has therefore to exercise a professional judgment as to the amount of audit work that he or she considers necessary. This choice is not a simple one and involves trading off the benefits and costs of undertaking audit work. Broadly speaking, the more audit work that an auditor undertakes, the greater will be the resulting confidence that the financial statements are not misstated in a material way. However, more audit work means more time and, hence, more cost. Occasionally, more audit work means more audit fee income, because the client has been persuaded to pay a higher fee as a result of the need to perform the extra audit work, but this is unusual and it is more likely that the audit fee income is relatively fixed. Hence, the auditor has to decide how much audit work to undertake on the grounds of increased confidence and extra cost alone.

Having decided what audit work should be performed and having then undertaken the audit tests and reviews, the auditor may have to make a second choice, depending on whether the audit procedures reveal that the financial statements are misstated in some material way. If the financial statements are materially misstated, then the auditor has to decided what to do about it. There are essentially two options. The auditor can decide to do nothing, in which case the status quo is maintained. The auditor has, however, the longer-term risk that the misstatement will eventually become public knowledge (e.g., as a result of a takeover by another company) with the attendant costs (e.g., legal claims for damages, higher insurance premiums, loss of fee income as a result of the adverse publicity, loss of personal prestige and loss of self-esteem). Alternatively, the auditor can ask management to change the financial statements to correct the misstatement. This act alters the status quo and as a consequence, the management of the company could react favorably or unfavorably,

depending on how it felt that users of the financial statements would react. To a large extent, the attitude of the company management will depend on the nature of the misstatement. If the misstatement was caused by a genuine error, then the auditor is likely to receive praise for discovering it, unless the effect of the alteration is to make management's performance look significantly less favorable. However, if the misstatement was caused by some deliberate act on the part of corporate management, then the auditor would not expect a favorable reaction to his or her request to make good the misstatement. If company management refuses to change the financial statements, then the auditor has to decide whether or not to reveal the misstatement in the auditor's report. Such a course of action is bound to incur the displeasure of management and lead to an impairment in its relationship with the auditor. The effects of this are that it will be more likely that another firm of auditors will be appointed and, hence, that the audit fee revenues from this particular client will disappear.

IV. JUDGING THE QUALITY OF AN AUDIT

The value of the auditor's report ultimately depends on the quality of the work performed and the classic definition of audit quality is as follows:

> The quality of audit services is defined to be the market-assessed joint probability that a given auditor will both (a) discover a breach in the client's accounting system, and (b) report the breach.
>
> (De Angelo, L. E., 1981, "Auditor Size and Audit Quality." *Journal of Accounting and Economics,* December, p. 186.)

The value of this definition is that it stresses the twin aspects that are required of a quality audit: technical competence and independence. By *technical competence* is meant that the auditor has sufficient technical expertise to know what evidence needs to be collected and the skill to interpret it correctly, so that all the significant errors and omissions present in a set of financial statements can be identified. An *independent* auditor will ensure either that all discovered, significant errors and omissions are corrected, or that they are fully disclosed in the auditor's report. In reality, the concepts of expertise and independence can become interrelated. A dishonest auditor may choose to act in such a way that errors or omissions are not discovered that is, to behave in a technically *incompetent* fashion. An illustrious example of the practice was given in 1801 at the Battle of Copenhagen, when Admiral Nelson put his telescope to his blind eye to avoid seeing the signal commanding him to withdraw his ships from battle. He was reported as saying, "I have only one eye—I have a right to be blind sometimes: . . . I really do not see the signal!" (Southey's *Life of Nelson,* Chap. 7). Auditors can choose to act in a similar fashion by studiously avoiding those areas where errors or omissions might be found. Because the audit tests have failed to produce any embarrassing revelations, the auditor can produce an unqualified opinion without apparently compromising his or her integrity. In cases of audit failure, where subsequent events have shown that the auditor's report was incorrect, it is often difficult to decide whether the auditor made an honest mistake or whether he or she deliberately chose to act incompetently.

The practical difficulty with De Angelo's market definition is that it is not clear how the market can make its joint probabilistic assessment of technical expertise and independence. To assess the technical competence of an audit requires access to the audit working papers and requires the reviewer to assess how well the work done compares with established professional standards. However, readers of financial statements will rarely gain access to an auditor's working papers and so all the information they can obtain from the auditor is contained in the audit report attached to the financial statements. If the auditor is happy with the content of the financial statements, then an unqualified report results, but the problem for readers is that unqualified audit reports are documents noted for their consistency across different audit firms. Reading an unqualified audit report conveys the impression that the audit work carried out complies with auditing standards and guidelines, but this is only at a general level and it gives no idea of the actual level of audit quality employed. Assessing independence is even more difficult, because ultimately independence is an attitude of mind that depends on the ethical and moral beliefs of the individual audit partner. However, it is theoretically possible to discover those visible aspects of the auditor–client management relationship that might deter the auditor from disclosing a breech by management, for example, the length of time that the auditor partner has been involved with the company, the percentage of the total fees of the firm accounted for by this one audit, and any family relationships between the auditor and client management.

Apart from the formidable problems of acquiring the information necessary to make a judgment on the quality of a particular audit, there is also a more fundamental problem that relates to the nature of the auditing activity. Unlike a manufacturing process, an audit is not a well-defined activity. The auditor will have to decide which areas to investigate and in how much depth. He or she will need to decide which tests are appropriate, how they are to be conducted, and which criteria should be used to evaluate their results. However, the determination of how much audit work is appropriate is very subjective. For example,

> By far the most important consideration to the auditor in determining how much auditing depth is enough is deciding what constitutes reasonable satisfaction. To some this may seem a non-answer—too subjective, too circular to be useful. Like beauty, reasonable satisfaction lies in the eye of the beholder. But after all, this is the real world. A professional is identified by the exercise of informed, independent judgment. Were there a check-list or formula to tell us how far to go or when we have a basis for reasonable satisfaction, we would cease to be members of a profession.

(Hall, W. R., 1978, "How Much Auditing is Enough? Critique—An Auditor's Viewpoint" *Proceedings of the Arthur Young Professors Roundtable Conference,* 1978, p. 134.)

As this quotation implies, auditors have only a very approximate feel for the extent of the audit work necessary to provide a specific level of audit quality. It is very difficult to determine the probability that audited financial statements might contain a material error, even with the complete knowledge of what audit work has been done. The relationship between input (audit work) and output (audit confidence) is not sufficiently well understood to allow output audit quality to be readily linked to input quality.

V. ETHICAL INFLUENCES ON AUDITOR DECISIONS

The choices facing auditors can be simplified to two basic decisions: how much audit work should they undertake and what should they do if the financial statements are discovered to be materially misstated and the directors refuse to correct the misstatement? These choices will be made within whatever ethical framework by which the individual auditor chooses to live his or her life. In this article, two main systems of ethical thought are used to suggest how auditors might frame the choices that they have to make: *consequentialism* and *deontology*. Many other systems have been suggested (e.g., intuitionism and existentialism), but none have captured the imagination of Western thinkers to the same extent. In consequentialism, actions are judged in terms of the consequences that result, whereas in deontology the view is taken that some acts are morally obligatory. The distinction between deontology and consequentialism can be seen by asking:

> Are all the guides to conduct that we want people to follow, and all the constraints on conduct that we want them to accept, of the form—act so as to bring about X as far as is possible (consequentialism); or of the form—do (or do not do) things of kind Y (deontology)?

(Mackie, 1986, pp. 154—155.)

The debate between consequentialists and deontologists has often centered on the doctrine of "the end justifies the means" (a doctrine that teaches that evil means may be employed to produce a good result). However, such a doctrine is an extreme version of consequentialism, because it implies that the moral difference between ends and means is such that only the end is important; the means to achieve it have no moral significance at all. The more usual consequentialist view is that there is no morally relevant distinction between means and ends and, hence, that any badness in the proposed means has to be balanced fairly against the expected goodness of the end. It is therefore possible to justify the use of evil means to achieve a good end, providing that the end is sufficiently good to outweigh the bad created by the means. The deontological view differs, because it assumes that particular aspects of an action determine its moral quality absolutely. Thus, a proposed action could be analyzed in terms of its moral character and a decision could be made about whether it is morally obligatory or morally wrong on the basis of this analysis alone, without considering what else is involved. As an example, consider a conscientious objector in Britain in World War II. He could adopt the deontological principle that to kill is morally wrong, even though the consequences of all his fellow countrymen following that principle would be that Nazism would triumph.

A. Deontological Reasoning

Deontological ethical reasoning relies on the creation of certain moral injunctions by which an individual can judge whether an action is morally right. Kant used the expression "categorical imperative" to provide a test of what is an appropriate action. The best-known version of the categorical imperative is, "Act only on that maxim which you can at the same time will to become a universal law" (Flew, 1983, p. 191). This imperative does not indicate what makes an action right; it simply provides a way of seeing whether an action would be wrong—by considering what would happen if everyone acted like that. For Kant, an individual should determine whether X is one's duty by asking what if everyone were to do X, and then having decided that X is one's duty, an individual must do it, regardless of the consequences. These principles led Kant to maintain that it is never right to tell a lie: the obligation to be truthful cannot be limited by any expediency. "To tell a falsehood to a murderer who asked us whether our friend, of whom he was in pursuit, had not taken refuge in our house, would be a crime" (quoted in Flew, 1983, p 192).

B. Consequentialism and Utilitarianism

Consequentialism is an umbrella term for any of the moral theories that state that the rightness or wrongness, goodness or badness of an action is solely dependent on the results the action produces. The most famous version of consequentialism is utilitarianism. In its original formulation, utilitarianism was very simple. As J. S. Mill wrote in 1863:

> The creed which accepts as the foundation of morals, Utility or the Greatest Happiness Principle, holds that actions are right in proportion as they tend to promote happiness, wrong as they tend to produce the reverse of happiness. By happiness is intended pleasure and the absence of pain; by unhappiness, pain and the privation of pleasure. (Quoted in Flew, 1983, p. 361.)

Thus, actions are to be judged by their consequences and the amount of pleasure everyone concerned derives from those consequences; the aim is the greatest happiness of the greatest number. In recent years, the theory has been subdivided into two variants: act utilitarianism and rule utilitarianism. Act utilitarianism holds that where an agent has a choice between courses of action (or inaction), the right act is that which will produce the most happiness, not just for the agent, but for all who are in any way affected. The suggestion is that for each alternative course of action, it is possible in principle to measure all the amounts of pleasure that it produces for different persons and to add these up, similarly to measure and add up all the amounts of pain and distress it produces and subtract the sum of pain from the sum of pleasure. The right action is then the one for which there is the greatest positive or the least negative balance of pleasure over pain. Critics have pointed out that the idea of considering everyone's welfare under various alternative outcomes and compounding it involves serious technical difficulties as well as deep conceptual ones. One of them is that, except in the simplest cases, the set of people affected by the various outcomes will not be the same, and people who have to be considered under one alternative may well not exist under others.

The objections to act utilitarianism naturally lead on to the consideration of rule utilitarianism. Rule utilitarianism is not concerned to assess individual acts, but considers the utility of a rule for various types of action. The idea is to undertake the course of action that would be prescribed by the optimum set of rules, even if on a particular occasion less than total happiness would result. Thus, where the act utilitarian would ask, "What will be the outcome of my doing that?" the rule utilitarian's question would be, "What if everyone did that?" In practice, the differences between act and rule utilitarians is probably not great, because even for act utilitarians, the great majority of ordinary decisions are guided by "rules of thumb," that is, rules that sum up what it is reasonably believed will usually lead to the general happiness. It would often be either impossible or absurdly laborious to calculate in detail the likely effect on utility of each alternative in every individual case.

Although utilitarianism is the most common example of consequentialism, other forms do exist. These replace the goal of utility of happiness with some other concept of the good that is to be realized or maximized. For example, one component of the good to be realized could be the nonexistence of extreme unfairness in the distribution of advantages among persons. One effect of replacing the goal of general happiness is that the good to be realized could be specific to an individual, determined by his or her own ideals and values. Hence, the special values of particular individuals will help to determine their own mortality in the broad sense; their actions will be guided not only by what they want, but also by the need to bring about whatever they see as being good.

C. Auditor Choices from the Perspectives of Deontology and Consequentialism

In terms of auditor independence and reporting honestly, the ethical position adopted by an auditor will influence his or her decision. Thus, an auditor could follow the deontological principle that it is wrong to be dishonest. Such a person would therefore not write an audit opinion that he or she knows to be wrong, even if the consequences of issuing an honest opinion are expected to be disastrous for a large number of people. Such a person would conform to Aristotle's concept of a sincere or truthful man (*aletheutikos*):

> A man is truthful both in speech and in the way he lives because he is like that in disposition. Such a person would seem to be a good type; for a lover of the truth, who speaks it when nothing depends on it, will speak it all the more when something does depend upon it.

(Aristotle, *Ethics,* translated by Thomson, Penguin Books, 1976, p. 165.)

In contrast, a consequentialist auditor will be concerned with the consequences of issuing a truthful opinion and, hence, will have to wrestle with his or her conscience when making damaging relevations in the audit report. Perhaps one of the most damaging reports that an auditor can issue is the so-called "going concern" qualification, in which the auditor casts doubt on the organization's ability to continue as a viable entity, either because of its potential inability to meet its obligations to its creditors or because of its poor future economic prospects. One inevitable consequence of such a report is that the organization has a greater chance of going into bankruptcy. The auditor is therefore aware that his or her report can mean the breakup of an organization, which could spell considerable hardship for a large number of people. Faced with such an outcome, a consequentialist auditor may well conclude that it would be better to say nothing and produce a dishonest report, and hope that circumstances will improve sufficiently for the firm to survive. The problem of going-concern qualifications is particularly acute for a bank and auditors are particularly loathe to describe a bank as not a going concern, because to do so would cause its immediate collapse as depositors rush to get their money out.

The conclusions of the ethical analysis are therefore ambiguous. Auditors who are concerned only with performing the action that is morally obligatory (deontologists) will always report in an honest fashion, but auditors who are concerned about the consequences of their actions may on occasion report in a dishonest way. To what extent auditors do ignore the consequences of their actions is impossible to answer, because the data to answer the question is unobtainable. However, it has to be allowed that there are ethical reasons why on certain, admittedly rare, occasions an auditor may prefer to report dishonestly from entirely *altruistic* motives (i.e., taking account of the interests of others rather than the auditor's own self-interest).

However, while the preceding discussion draws attention to the fact that consequentialist auditors may act dishonestly because they think that such a course of action will bring the greatest happiness to the greatest number, the more usual threat to independence is that a consequentialist thinker will be more concerned about the consequences to him- or herself. A more plausible assumption (or at least, the assumption that the more cynical readers of audited financial statements are likely to make) is that auditors are consequential *egoists,* interested only in the effects on their own welfare. The question, therefore, that remains to be addressed is whether consequential egoists, concerned solely with their own self-interests, can be expected to behave in an independent fashion and report truthfully what they find. Surprisingly, the answer is yes in certain circumstances. These will now be discussed.

VI. THE SELF-INTERESTED AUDITOR (A RATIONAL ECONOMIC PERSON)

Perhaps the best model of a consequentialist egoist was developed by economists and termed by them "rational economic man." Rational economic individuals act in such a way as to maximize their own utility (self-interest). This goal is usually considered to have two aspects: the maximization of an individual's economic wealth, that is, the present value of the stream of future cash flows accruing to the individual; and the minimization of the risk attached to these future cash flows.

To understand the analysis, the economic basis of the auditing service needs to be understood. If a set of financial statements is produced *without* an audit, a rational economic reader will expect that the management of the organization will have biased the financial statements in some way to make the performance of the organization seem better than it actually is. There may also be errors present resulting from genuine mistakes as well as deliberate ones. However, if the same financial statements were to be produced *with* an audit, the reader would have some expectation that bias and error will have been reduced. Accordingly, the value of an audit can, in principle, be measured by how much extra confidence the reader of the audited financial statements has that they are free from the impact of

both types of error as a result of the activities of the auditor. The main form of assurance that the auditor has performed an audit of satisfactory quality is that if the auditor is subsequently found to have behaved in a negligent fashion by a court of law, then the auditor will be liable for a claim for damages. A rational economic auditor can therefore be expected to perform an audit that will reduce the chances of a successful negligence suit to a level that is acceptable to the auditor. In the language of economics, the auditor should perform audit work until the point is reached when the extra cost of undertaking more work is equal to the extra benefit that the auditor derives from that work, that is, at the point where there is only a negligible chance of being successfully sued for damages. This then represents the minimum amount of work that the reader can expect the auditor to perform.

One further point needs to be considered that relates to the reputation of the auditor or audit firm. An economic analysis of markets where reputations exist shows that those firms with a reputation for performing work of above-average quality can earn higher fees than the average. Such firms can earn a "rent" for their reputation. In the audit context, if an audit firm has a reputation for performing above-average quality work (in the sense that the financial statements of companies that it audits have a lower chance of containing significant errors), then readers will have more confidence in the financial statements. In a world of rational economic individuals who are wealth maximisers and risk minimizers, this increase in confidence means that there is less risk of error and this decrease in risk should be worth paying for (the insurance industry is built on this concept). Hence, auditors with higher reputations can be expected to earn higher fees because their reports are more highly valued. There is thus the possibility that, if an auditor performs work of an above average standard, eventually the reputation of the auditor will rise and he or she will be able to charge more for his or her services. There is, therefore, an incentive mechanism in the market for the auditor to improve audit quality, although the auditor will have to decide whether the certain costs of improving quality now are justified by the possible increase in future audit fees following the recognition of improved quality by the consumers of the audit service.

How then does this economic analysis relate to the likelihood that an auditor will report honestly? Every time that an auditor makes a statement that he or she knows to be false, that individual is risking two things: first, the costs of a successful legal action for negligence (this could be a mixture of money that has to be paid directly to the aggrieved party as a result of a legal settlement and the higher insurance premiums that will inevitably arise if part of the legal settlement is covered by insurance) and second, the costs of a loss in reputation resulting from the reduction in fee income that the auditor can command. Thus, the self-interested auditor has to balance the costs of reporting honestly (losing the audit and, hence, the future audit and other fees that would be earned from the client) against the long-term benefits of honest reporting (the avoidance of legal costs and the loss of income derived from a loss of reputation).

This analysis concentrates on the position of a single economic rationale auditor, but there is also a collective perspective, because it can be argued that auditors as a group benefit from being perceived as independent, technically competent individuals. Hence, the analysis needs to be extended to cover the audit profession and the benefits that all members could lose if one of its members were seen to be acting dishonestly.

VII. THE ECONOMIC VALUE OF A SELF-GOVERNING AUDIT PROFESSION

For a person to be recognized as an auditor, he or she has to belong to a professional body of accountants. In many countries (e.g., the U.S. and the U.K.), the professional accountancy bodies are self-governing and receive little governmental interference, which should confer substantial benefits on the audit professionals. For example, entry into the profession can be limited by examinations and practicing certificate requirements; secrecy can be encouraged; regulation of accounting and auditing practices can be carried out by the profession rather than government; and misconduct can be judged by fellow professionals. All these benefits provide a potentially higher income stream than would be possible under a government scheme and also give the profession's members more flexibility in their work. It might be expected, therefore, that there should be a strong desire on the part of the auditing profession to maintain its self-regulating monopoly and avoid governmental intervention. Government tends to respond to public anxiety, which is usually fueled by some cause célèbre, when the work of the auditing profession is deemed to be of unacceptable quality. Hence, there is the additional need to report honestly, because every occasion when dishonesty is discovered increases the possibility of government taking away the profession's self-regulatory monopoly, as well as reducing the perceived value of all audits.

One way that the profession attempts to ensure that its members behave with integrity is by promulgating and enforcing a code of ethics. Such codes lay down the minimum standards of behavior expected of members of the profession and, hence, can be said to constitute the moral rules of the profession. An egoistical explanation of the profession's morality would be that all the benefits arising from being regarded as a competent, trustworthy auditor stem from the existence of a stable, well-thought-of profession. As the observance of certain moral rules is a necessary condition of such a profession, auditors have an interest in maintaining the moral order of the profession.

However, there is also an altruistic explanation for the profession's morality that would argue that the preceding discussion based on egoism proves only that an auditor has an interest in *other* auditors abiding by the moral rules of the profession. It does not prove that it is in the interest of an individual auditor to abide by the rules, because the central argument of altruism is that the explanation of morality cannot be reduced to self-interest. The variant of the Prisoners Dilemma provided by Mackie is a good example of the point:

> Two soldiers, Tom and Dan, are manning two nearby strong-posts in an attempt to hold up an enemy advance. If both remain at their posts, they have a fairly good chance of holding off the enemy until relief arrives, and so of both surviving. If they both run away, the enemy will break through immediately, and the chance of either of them surviving is markedly less. But if one stays at his post, while the other runs away, the one who runs will have an even better chance of survival than each will have if they both remain, while the one who stays will have an even worse chance than each will have if they both run.

(Mackie, J. L., 1986, p. 115.)

In this illustration an egoistical Tom will reason that if Dan stays at his post, I will have a better chance of surviving if I run rather than if I stay, and if Dan runs then I will also have a better chance of survival if I run than if I stay. If both Tom and Dan are egoists then they will both reach the same conclusion and run, even though they have picked the inferior option. It does not matter what contracts they make with each other, because if they are both rational egoists, they will each have the same motive for breaking such agreements. The military solution to the problem is to bind the soldiers together with traditions of honor and loyalty, and the associated stigma of cowardice, as well as the penalties associated with deserting one's post. Such solutions are essentially egoistical in nature, ensuring that the individual cooperates, because of the extent of the negative consequences.

However, an altruist would argue that it is in the interest in people *for their own sake* that is a necessary condition for morality. Hence, in an altruistic analysis, both Tom and Dan would be concerned for the other's well-being and therefore remain at their post because of their regard for each other, and not because of some greater punishment that might occur. This notion of the altruistic professional is not confined to auditing, and several authors have suggested that professions may be distinguished from other occupations by their altruism, which may be expressed in the service orientation of professional men.

VIII. ANALYZING THE ETHICAL PRONOUNCEMENTS OF THE AUDITING PROFESSION

At this point, it is worth considering the ethical codes issued by the auditing profession. These tend to be framed as a set of rules of conduct that members of the profession are instructed strictly to observe. The main approach seems to be deontological, with the rules being seen as duties that are morally obligatory for members of the profession. The view that auditors should think deontologically is contained in paragraph 0.03 of Article III of *Principles of Professional Conduct* of the American Institute of Certified Public Accountants:

> Integrity is measured in terms of what is right and just. In the absence of specific rules, standards, or guidance, or in the face of conflicting opinions, a member should test decisions and deeds by asking: "Am I doing what a person of integrity would do? Have I retained my integrity?" (Quoted in Albrecht, 1992, p. 176.)

In a similar vein the first two fundamental principles in *Guide to Professional Ethics* of the Institute of Chartered Accountants in England and Wales (1996) contain the following admonitions:

1. A member should behave with integrity in all professional and business relationships. Integrity implies not merely honesty but fair dealing and truthfulness.

2. A member should strive for objectivity in all professional and business judgments. Objectivity is the state of mind which has regard to all considerations relevant to the task in hand but no other.

Occasionally, a professional body will suggest that its members should think about the consequences of their actions as in the following extract from the Institute of Chartered Accountants in Scotland (1971) *Statement of Professional Conduct No 4: Unlawful Acts or Defaults by Clients of Members,* paragraph 10:

> The council therefore recommends that members … should not disclose past or intended civil wrongs, crimes … or statutory offences *unless they feel that the damage to the public likely to arise from non-disclosure is of a very serious nature* (emphasis added).

However, such examples are rare, and the general rule for auditors is to follow the guidelines laid down by the profession. While the rules tend to be phrased in a deontological way as a series of duties that are morally obligatory for members of the profession, rule utilitarians could also be prepared to argue that it is for the best to adopt strict rules and not to deviate in particular circumstances, even when in those particular circumstances more good will result from deviance from the rules. Thus, the ethical codes and other pronouncements of the auditing profession could be seen as appealing to those members who favor either the deontological or rule utilitarianism approach to solving their ethical dilemmas, by providing those members with an agreed set of rules by which to operate. No consideration should be given to the consequences of the auditor's actions. Hence, auditors are instructed by their professional body to tell the truth at all times regardless of the consequences (*objectively* and *impartially* being synonyms for honestly). The ethical position, therefore, taken by the profession in regard to reporting any material misstatements in the financial statements is always to report them. Thus, there would appear to be an underlying tacit assumption that the ethical problem for professional auditors in a given situation is not what they ought to do, but whether to do what they know they should do. Kant seems similarly to suppose that determining what "duty" requires of an individual on a particular occasion is not a problem. The problem is resisting the temptation when duty and interest conflict.

In relation to the auditor's choice of how much audit work should be carried out, the fourth fundamental principle of the 1996 *Ethical Guide of the Institute of*

Chartered Accountants in England and Wales states the following:

> A member should carry out his professional work with due skill, care, diligence and expedition and with proper regard for the technical and professional standards expected of him as a member.

Similar statements can be found in the ethical guides of professional bodies in other countries. An auditor should, therefore, perform as much audit work as is required by the existing standards of the auditing profession. The morally obligatory act or the act that will bring about the greatest happiness from the profession's viewpoint is to do what other "competent" auditors would do.

It is perhaps worth pausing at this point to consider the basis upon which the profession formulates the technical and professional standards that it expects its members to observe. The main question to be addressed is, who should be considered when deciding what is the appropriate rule? The egoist explanation would be that the profession considers only itself. Therefore, the rule utilitarian position becomes one of formulating rules that will result in the greatest happiness for members of the profession. The consequences to others outside the profession then would not be of relevance. The deontological categorical imperative of Kant would be to act only on the maxim that you can at the same time will to become a universal law *applying to all auditors*. An altruist explanation would be that members of the auditing profession believe that the well-being of society is enhanced by a strong, well-regarded auditing profession that follows a set of rules in all circumstances. Experience might be said to show that if a profession evolves and keeps to a shared standard, society as a whole is better off.

Parker (1994) argues that both public and private interest are pursued by the profession. The public interest is readily declared, but the private interest remains submerged, yet powerful. He sees the role of ethical rules in protecting the private interests of members as a vital component of the accounting profession's continuing commitment to ensuring its own survival. This view is shared by Haskell:

> The image of the disinterested professional lingers on, but reactions to it range from mild skepticism to curt dismissal. Some modern writers regard it as a harmless myth, possessing like all myths a grain of truth and serviceable as an ideal, perhaps, but certainly not an adequate representation of

the actual motives of most professionals, most of the time. Others share Collin's hostile conviction that professionals are wolves in sheep's clothing, monopolists who live by the rule of caveat emptor, but lack the integrity to admit it.

(Haskell, T. L. (1984). Professionalism versus capitalism: R. H. Tawney, Emile Durkheim and C. S. Pierre on the disinterestedness of professional communities. In *The authority of experts: Studies in history and theory*, Indiana University Press, p. 181.)

In order to counter such cynicism, the professional bodies' response is to make their ethical "guides" into rules that, if broken, will produce sanctions against the miscreant. One example is given in the following extract from the American Institute of Certified Public Accounts' 1988 *Code of Professional Conduct* (p. 3):

> Compliance with the Code...., as with all standards in an open society, depends primarily on members' understanding and voluntary actions, secondarily on reinforcement by peers and public opinion, and ultimately on disciplinary proceedings, when necessary, against members who fail to comply with the Rules.

This quotation illustrates the central assumption of the codes of ethics of most auditing professional bodies: that they need an enforcement mechanism to make them credible. The explicit purpose is clearly to reassure a skeptical public that auditors will act with objectivity and integrity, because to do otherwise would incur the disciplinary wrath of the professional body of which they are a member. As well as imposing fines, the professional body's ultimate sanction is to expel the member and so take away his or her livelihood. Hence, while the auditing profession would like ethics to be thought of as relating to the conscience of individual auditors, it is nevertheless the case that the auditing profession retains a backstop based on the assumption that sometimes auditors will act from an *egoistical* perspective. Indeed in a study of what U.S. certified public accountants thought constituted ethics, 36% of those responding indicated that they interpreted ethics "as defined by the AICPA's Professional Code of Conduct," while 64% interpreted ethics "as a moral and philosophical framework for guiding beliefs" (Cohen, J. R., and L. W. Pant, 1991).

IX. CONCLUSIONS

Auditors' moral reasoning has been considered from two viewpoints: deontology and consequentialism, assuming that the auditor is acting in an altruistic fashion. It has been shown that deontology would imply that an auditor should always tell the truth irrespective of the consequences. However, an altruistic auditor reasoning consequentially could occasionally believe that greater good would result if he or she failed to reveal information that would have serious consequences for the client firm and its employees (e.g., by not revealing that a company is not a going concern).

The problem faced by the auditing profession is that readers of audited financial statements are skeptical about whether auditors can be trusted. Hence, the assumption that the profession and the interested government agencies have to make is that auditors are egoists interested in their own welfare. Such a view suggests that the best way to ensure honesty is either to make the costs of dishonesty so large that no one will be dishonest, or to reduce the benefits that might accrue to auditors from being dishonest. Thus, the auditing professions in advanced countries have developed codes of ethics enforced by fines and expulsion from the professional bodies, which set out to steel the auditors' resolve to avoid temptation by limiting their involvement with any one client. While they are described as codes of ethics, they are little more than instructions for behavior in particular circumstances, with penalties for failure to comply. Similarly, in order to ensure that auditors act in a technically competent and an independent fashion, legislators have allowed large legal penalties to be extracted from negligent auditors.

However, the main difficulty with this approach relates to the notion that trust can be produced by the correct use of economic incentives. The central assumption of most of the measures would appear to be that everyone's honesty has a price, and that the best way to produce honesty is to ensure that nobody is tempted to be dishonest. This notion does have the attraction of being consistent with the need for auditing

in the first place, because that is based on the assumption that company directors cannot be trusted either. Nevertheless, it does have a rather defeatist feel about it, because it implies that as a whole human beings can be trusted to tell the truth only when it suits them, but that as soon as there are incentives not to tell the truth, then dishonesty can be expected. The reality is probably that only a minority of auditors behave as complete egoists, but in order to convince a skeptical world that all auditors follow minimum standards of behavior, this minority have to be targeted by professional rules and a regime of legal penalties.

Also See the Following Articles

ACCOUNTING AND BUSINESS ETHICS • ALTRUISM AND ECONOMICS • BUSINESS ETHICS, OVERVIEW • CORPORATE RESPONSIBILITY

Bibliography

Albrecht, W. S. (1992). *Ethical issues in the practice of accounting.* Cincinnati, OH: South Western Publishing Co.

Brooks, L. J. (1995). *Professional ethics for accountants.* St. Paul, MN: West Publishing.

Cohen, J. R., and L. W. Pant (1991). Beyond bean counting: Establishing high ethical standards in the public accounting profession. *Journal of Business Ethics,* Vol. 10, pp. 45–56.

Flew, A. (1983). *A Dictionary of Philosophy,* Pan Books. London: Macmillan Press.

Mackie, J. L. (1986). *Ethics—Inventing right and wrong.* Baltimore, MD: Penguin Books.

Maurice, J. (1996). *Accounting ethics.* London: Pitman Publishing.

Moizer, P. (1995). An ethical approach to the choices faced by auditors. *Critical Perspectives on Accounting,* Vol. 6, No. 5, October, pp. 415–431.

Moizer, P. (1997). Independence. In M. Sherer & S. Turley (Eds.), *Current issues in auditing* (3rd ed.). London: Paul Chapman.

Parker, L. (1994). Professional accounting body ethics. *Accounting Organizations and Society.* **19** (August), p. 507–525.

Sen, A. (1987). *On ethics and economics.* New York: Basil Blackwell.

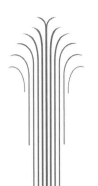

AUTHORITY IN EDUCATION

Christopher Winch
Nene College

GLOSSARY

amour propre The distinctively human love of self in which self-esteem is inextricably bound up.

argument from authority A form of inductive argument that uses the assertions of someone who is *an authority* as the major premise.

autonomy A state in which an individual is able to choose what aims in life he or she wishes to pursue.

curriculum The prescribed content of an educational process.

indoctrination A form of teaching that is thought to deprive its subjects of autonomy.

inductive logic The study of arguments that lead to conclusions that are not *certain* but only *probable* when they are sound.

instruction The giving of information by a teacher to a pupil.

normative An adjective describing phenomena that are governed by human-made rules rather than by laws of nature.

power The ability to influence others by force or various forms of persuasion.

training The inculcation of confident and settled modes of action and behaviour.

THE CONCEPT OF AUTHORITY has traditionally been discussed by philosophers in the context of political theory and of inductive logic. It is frequently argued that authority is a normative concept implying a certain entitlement to use power. Someone who is authoritative in this sense can be said to be *in authority*. For those who believe in such an entitlement, the normative connotations are positive ones; for those who do not believe in it, they are negative and the term *authoritarian* is often used adjectivally to characterize morally unacceptable exercises of authority or power, as in phrases like "an authoritarian government." Authority is also used in the sense of meaning possession of a body of knowledge, understanding, or skill. When someone possesses these attributes they are said to be *an authority*. Authority is, therefore, relevant to education in both an epistemic and a sociopolitical sense.

I. AUTHORITY AND SOCIETY

A. Social and Political Authority

Authority in the sociopolitical sense is a more general concept than political authority, where politics is conceived of as the practice of organizing and regulating human affairs through a state and legal system. There are questions as to the role of authority in human life more generally. These can be separated into two distinct and related lines of inquiry; the extent to which authority plays a role in human life and the extent to which it should. We might thus expect to see the concept of authority employed in such areas as discussions of sexual and family relationships, in questions of upbringing, training, and learning, and in questions of knowledge and belief, as well as in more overtly political debates. Authority is relevant to education not only through questions of teaching and learning (as part of a general discussion of the concept of authority), but also in politics, because the provision of education as a public or semipublic good is not just a social but a political matter, that is, it is regulated or organized by the state and set within a framework of law. Some educational philosophers, for example, J. J. Rousseau, have treated discussion of the epistemological, the domestic, and the political sphere as very closely related and largely inseparable. In Rousseau's discussion, the relationship between power and authority at all these levels is central to an understanding both of his educational and of his political theory.

Is authority necessary to any society? It is apparently a consequence of some philosophical approaches, notably those stemming from the work of the later Wittgenstein, that some form of authority is an unavoidable and essential aspect of human association. The claim is that the concept of authority is implicated in the idea of a society as such, so that any accurate description of a society would include an account of the role that authority plays in it (this does not imply that society has to be political). Some writers, R. S. Peters, for example, take the view that not every method of deciding what is wrong or right entails the exercise of authority; only those that require the participation of an authority figure or *auctor* do that. It follows from this position that social life as such does not require authority, just that, as a rule-governed system, it requires ways of deciding what are correct and what are incorrect ways of following the rules regulating that system.

In making this claim, Peters appears to be saying that authority requires an individual or *auctor*, either accredited in some way or in fact in a position to act. The presence of such an individual would constitute a necessary, but not sufficient condition for the exercise of authority for the *auctor* may fail to act in the appropriate manner by issuing information, advice, or commands. It might be denied, however that, even if there is such an individual, and even though he issues commands, counsel or information, he thereby necessarily

exercises authority, rather than power. In Peters' discussion of the role of the tutor in Rousseau's *Emile*, he writes of him as being, at least in a sense, an authority over Emile, his student. It has been argued, however, that the tutor, although in authority, through having the derivative right to teach Emile, influences him through the use of power rather than through the exercise of his authority, because he relies, for the most part, on covert manipulation or conditioning, rather than indicating overtly what is right and wrong, what is correct or incorrect, to achieve his educational aims. This suggests, in turn, that it is not merely the presence of an authoritative figure that constitutes the exercise of authority, but also the way in which the influence is exercised by the *auctor*.

However, it could be argued (and this is implicit in the work of some writers) that if this influence is exercised by showing the person being influenced what are the correct or incorrect, right or wrong, ways of going about things, then if the person or persons doing the influencing is, in some way accredited to do so (even if only in an implicit or informal sense), we can say that the influence being exercised is an authoritative one. On this view, the presence of an *auctor* is too formal a requirement; in some circumstances any individual who is not explicitly debarred from issuing information, counsel, or commands is by default an authority, provided that he is possessed of the knowledge, skill, or understanding necessary to carry out that function. Arguably, an account like that of Peters needs to be supplemented with an account of the way in which an authority exercises the power that he has, namely through the overt pointing out or right and wrong ways of going about things. If this can be done by an informal authority, then a formally constituted authoritative individual would then be neither a necessary nor a sufficient condition for the exercise of authority in general. There is, however, a further question concerning the conditions for the exercise of authority in education.

Authority can be distinguished from power through its normative connotations; the implication is that authority is a form of power that is, in some sense, legitimate. As we have seen, some have argued that this legitimated power can be distributed and informal or even implicit as, for example, in the kind of training given to a child learning his mother tongue by parents. On this view, Peter Winch's contention, disputed by Peters, that any form of society requires authority in some form or other, would appear to be correct. Authority is a necessary feature of society (which is rule governed) and of learning in a rule-governed context, where successful learning is established by correctly following the relevant rules.

Winch's account has been criticised for conflating being *an* authority with being *in* authority. From the fact that someone is an authority on their mother tongue, for example, it does not follow that they are in authority as teachers of the language. It might be replied, however, that at this basic level these two aspects of the concept of authority are not clearly distinguishable. Being an authority on one's mothertongue implies that, in a certain range of circumstances, one is entitled to pronounce on correct and incorrect usage and to give instruction. Winch's claim would then hold, as he could be interpreted as drawing attention to a basic, albeit informal, aspect of authority that resisted further differentiation. It is only when role definitions are made formal and where there is a distinct division of labor regarding the transmission of knowledge, that it becomes useful to distinguish between these two senses of authority.

According to Anscombe, there are different ways in which authority can be conferred: first, through the repeated exercise of power on a customary basis; second, through the existence of a task which needs to be carried out. Authority is exercised over young children on both these bases and parental authority arises particularly from the task vested in parents to bring up their children properly. It could be said that all that Anscombe has established is that adults in general and parents in particular are in authority in any society, but her claim would not make any sense if adults and parents were not authorities on the knowledge and skill that children need in order to become adults, for otherwise there would be no custom and parents would not be allotted such a task. In the more formal contexts of the education of older children, where a division of intellectual labor becomes necessary, the distinction is a useful one.

B. Authority, Knowledge, and Argument

The evaluation of arguments from authority is part of the subject matter of induction. Authority in argument is important because the intellectual division of labor requires it. Those who know what others need to know can transmit that knowledge. Under certain conditions, it is reasonable for others to believe what they are told by those who claim to hold such knowledge. Under certain conditions some are required to pay heed to or even to believe the pronouncements of authoritative figures. An authority deployed in an argument is a person who purportedly is entitled to transmit information, argument, or opinion. Such a person, speaking or writing either directly or through report is an authority on a subject. However, in many cases, this is not a sufficient condition for their being able to transmit information, argument, or opinion; that entitlement arises from the role (either formal or informal) occupied by such a person in their society. This situation should be distinguished from the one described above, where acquaintance with fundamental societal norms characterizes virtually all adults as authorities in both the cognitive and the social sense. In more formal cases, where, for example, there is a clearly defined intellectual division of labor and a socially defined role of teacher, the two conditions can be brought together in the requirement that for someone to be *in* authority and thus entitled to transmit information, argument, or opinion, they would first have to satisfy the requirement that they were *an* authority on particular subject matters.

C. Weber's Typology of Authority

One very influential account of sociologically different kinds of authority is that of Max Weber. Weber distinguished between three different kinds: traditional, charismatic, and legal-rational. These are ideal types of authority, rarely, if ever, to be found in their pure forms. In practice they are to be found mixed with each other in varying degrees. Traditional authority is to be found in societies that are based on large extended families headed by patriarchs or hereditary monarchs. It is wielded through familial and patronage networks and sanctioned by custom and tradition. Traditional authority, it might be maintained, is particularly dependent on clear role definitions and to a lesser degree on the expertise of the authority. Charismatic authority depends on the exceptional powers of an individual or, sometimes, of an institution. It often arises in unusual historical circumstances. Charismatic authority, because it is often dependent on the powers of an individual, may be relinquished when that individual no longer possesses such powers or when those powers are no longer seen to be important. It an also be transmuted into a form of traditional or legal-rational authority over time. Almost by definition, charismatic authority attaches particular significance to the expertise of the charismatic figure and much less to his established role in society. This suggests that charismatic leadership in its pure form is an exericse of power rather than authority. Legal-rational forms of authority depend on established frameworks of rules and procedures that, in some sense, have an objective validity such as a legal code.

The emergence of written language in the context of established procedures and a specialized bureaucracy trained to operate and interpret those procedures are preconditions for its emergence. Thus, this form of authority not only presupposes clear role definitions, but also well-delineated expertise.

In terms of our discussion so far, the authority exercised by all adult members of society in terms of their mastery of fundamental societal norms could be characterized as a form of traditional authority, although without the mystique often attached. The authority exercised by teachers in formal education systems could be described as legal-rational. It is also quite possible for a teacher in either sense to be a charismatic authority.

II. AUTHORITY AND TEACHING

The particular relevance of the concept of authority for education lies in the question of whether or not human learning is possible without authority. The issue of the importance of teaching in learning brings authority to the fore, because it is precisely the question about the entitlement or otherwise of teachers to move learning forward that becomes central. This itself breaks down into two further questions: first, of the teacher being *an* authority, namely a source of expertise; second as being a *legitimate person* entitled to teach and to promote learning. It seems that although the first might seem to be a necessary condition of the second, it is not sufficient. On this view, someone who is a teacher, then, is someone who is an authority in both senses. It needs to be added, to take account of cases such as that of Emile's tutor, that authority must be exercised in the appropriate way.

We need to turn once again to Peter's point about the accredited individual or *auctor*. It is quite possible to maintain that Peters is wrong about this necessary condition for authority in general, but right about it for education, particularly formal education. For although it can be maintained that any adult with a minimal education could suitably constitute *an authority* about the ways of the world for a young child up to the age of 4, and therefore, in normal circumstances, *in authority* to teach such matters, it is much more difficult to maintain that all minimally educated adults could fulfil this requirement beyond that point. At the next stage, it could be argued, individuals with increasingly specialized knowledge are required to fulfil the role of having sufficient expertise to be an authority capable of being a reliable source of information. If we add the requirement that an education service needs to

keep a check on who actually possesses such knowledge before employing them, then it is not difficult to see that in order to be accredited and employed as a teacher (to be in authority), one would have to have satisfied, as one condition, the requirement that one is an authority regarding a particular subject matter. Teachers, then, at least in modern societies, seem to be a form of legal-rational authority. In many cases, they are accredited both in terms of their knowledge and in terms of their expertise in getting pupils and students to learn. In order to operate (to be in authority) they both need accreditation in respect of the former attributes and a formal offer of employment.

Peters would, however, have objected to this way of characterizing the role of teacher as *auctor*. A teacher might have the role assigned to him and not be an authority on the subject matter taught. He would still, in some sense, be entitled to transmit information. Alternatively, an individual may have the necessary knowledge but lack the role legitimation; he may be an authority on the topic to be taught but lack the role that would accredit him to teach in a school, for example, but might still command enough respect to carry out the role by effectively teaching. This is why Peters is inclined to say that both being *in authority* and being *an authority* are not even necessary conditions for the ascription of authority, although apparently being an *auctor* is.

It could be said that, while Peters is right to claim that these are not necessary conditions in the strictest sense, they do, nevertheless have a strong bearing on the question as to whether we are inclined to ascribe authority to someone. Those who lack relevant knowledge or skill find their ability to perform impaired, particularly so when they are found by their pupils to lack that knowledge. In such circumstances, at the very least, their authority is impaired as their ability to get their pronouncements listened to with a degree of respect is eroded. Likewise, someone with no accredited role, but with the relevant knowledge and ability, may act in an authoritative manner and be accepted as an authoritative individual in certain circumstances. In this connection, Peters cites the butler in J. M. Barrie's play, *The Admirable Crichton*, who although formally a subordinate, is accepted as being in authority through the successful exercise of superior knowledge when the party, including his master, is shipwrecked. For someone who thinks that being in authority is a necessary condition for the exercise of authority, there are a number of possible responses to such a case. First, it could be maintained that the butler exercised power rather than authority. Second, it could be maintained that the butler assumed authority by default through his master ceding his authority in practice. There was a task to be carried out and there was tacit consent for the butler to carry out that task, which meant assuming persuasive power over the other members of the party. Third, it might be said that an unusual case such as this does not show that, in the generality of cases, being in authority is not a necessary condition of acting with authority. It might be further pointed out that although the butler initially assumed power, the customary exercise of that power eventually led to his acceptance as being in authority.

In order to be effective as teachers, people may need more than knowledge and an accepted role, they may need particular personal abilities. These would relate to being able to command attention and to gain loyalty among the class. Inevitably, charismatic powers of this kind have affective properties; pupils and students are inspired to pay attention and learn through the operation of love, devotion, awe, or fear to some extent irrespective of the truth or correctness of the subject matter taught. If teachers have, of practical necessity, to operate in this way then it ought to be asked whether or not they are entitled to do so (for their entitlement will not necessarily arise from their legal role) in view of the possible long-term effects that charismatic teaching may have on students. The problem is, perhaps, particularly acute with young children, whose acceptance of power and authority is likely to be undiscriminating. The most pressing aspect of the problem would be where a teacher is teaching something that is controversial as unquestionably true and is teaching it intentionally so as to produce unshakeable belief in his pupils through the employment of affectively loaded charismatic teaching techniques. This issue brings us to the problem of indoctrination in Section VI.

III. AUTHORITY AND THE CURRICULUM

Most would argue that there will be norms prescribing what ought to be taught that are authoritative, in the sense that they have been established by someone who is entitled to do so. These are usually called the curriculum, that is, the prescribed content of education, it is not a description of what goes on in a program of teaching, but a description of what *should* go on. Education as a social project involves someone who is in authority (a church, school board, or a government, for example) setting out the program of study. In an ideal situation, what actually takes place in schools and colleges is, then, a working through of the prescriptions in the curriculum. This need not entail that every detail of what goes on in the schoolroom is a reflection of these prescriptions but it does entail that they are duly covered.

There will be many situations where what happens in the school is only a partial or even a nonexistent working out of the curriculum. But to describe this state of affairs as the following of a curriculum is a mistake; one needs to distinguish between what is the case and what ought to be the case and the curriculum relates to the latter. However, there are situations where it is extremely difficult to physically obtain the curriculum in written or even in spoken form. This frequently occurs; where it exists only at the school or even the class level. In such a situation authority regarding what should be taught becomes informal or even implicit. The question then arises, "At what point are we still able to call this a curriculum in any meaningful normative sense?" Notice that the situation is different from that where young children pick up their mothertongue and certain basic pieces of knowledge. The school curriculum normally consists of *selected* knowledge that requires at least a degree of specialist expertise in order to be effectively taught.

If the curriculum is normative and embodies authoritative pronouncements concerning what is to be taught, then who has the authority to write it? This is a complex issue that relates to the various interests that have a stake in the control of education and the lines of accountability that they have to each other. There are four possible answers. First, parents; second, teachers and educational professionals; third, the community; fourth, the state.

Parental rights to prescribe content can be justified in a number of ways. The first is religious sanction; the second is custom, practice, and tradition; and the third is through some kind of contractual or quasi-contractual relationship between the parent and the child on the one hand and between the parent and society on the other. The first two approaches are found where religion or custom and practice sanction parental right. If they fail or fall into desuetude, however, parental rights become a problem. Locke provides an account of how parents might have such rights irrespective of religious or customary sanction. He suggests that children have rights, grounded on their interests, which they cannot fully defend or even recognize. Accordingly, those who have responsibility for them, in most cases, parents, have the *duty* to attend to those interests. Because they cannot do so except through having some ability to control the children in their care, they have derivative rights over their children that stem from the duties that they inherit in respect of their children's primary rights. It would follow from this argument that the curriculum would be one area over which the parents had rights. They would be in authority without necessarily being an authority on the curriculum.

The Lockean account is not without problems. The first of these is the limited competence of parents to write a curriculum; they may be obliged to delegate their responsibility (perhaps with the right of veto) to those who are authorities on teaching and learning and on particular subject matters. This is a particular instance of a more general issue in the Lockean account, which is that where parental incompetence or ill will can be shown, those parents forfeit their derivative rights vis-à-vis their children. Second, the interests of other members of society are implicated in the way in which any particular child is brought up. On the face of it, this gives rights to nonparents vis-à-vis the upbringing of children who are not their own. This is likely to prove to be a problem in those cases where parental interpretation of what the curriculum should consist of conflicts with the views of significant groups of other members of society who are not the parents of a particular child. In those cases where the parents concerned are in a significant minority, the majority of citizens, or the state acting on their behalf, may judge them to be incompetent or malevolent and take action accordingly. In other cases, there may be a process of negotiation whereby a consensus is reached as to the extent to which each party can implement in the public sphere the values that they espouse for their children. Whatever then emerges as the curriculum will be authoritative on this account because it will emerge as a negotiated consensus concerning the implementation of values that is then embodied in the authority of parent, state, or community; whoever, in any particular society, is charged with the provision of education.

The second answer to the question of who has authority to design the curriculum is educational professionals. Their presumed authority rests on their expertise as subject specialists and, more controversially, on their alleged expertise on how children learn. There are weak and strong versions of the case for professional control of the curriculum. The weak case asserts that they have authority through *delegation*. Because parents, communities, or the state are unwilling or unable to directly write the curriculum, teachers and educationists are entrusted to this role on their behalf. On this view, they have this authority just so long as they carry out the role with which they have been entrusted.

There are two strands to the strong argument for teacher control. The first is that teachers are the authorities (in the cognitive sense) on what should be taught and how it should be taught. The second is an argument concerning political liberty. Because, it is claimed, teachers are in fact a disinterested group, concerned only with the welfare of their pupils or students, they are best placed to write a curriculum that is both free from political interference and attends to the best interests of children. Even where the state deploys resources for education, the professionals should hold this right, it is sometimes maintained. The difficulty for holders of this position, as for very strong advocates of parental rights, is that it cannot ignore demands for accountability. If Locke is right, parents can only delegate, on a temporary basis, the right to attend to the interests of their children. Teachers remain accountable to parents. In a more general sense, if resources are provided for an educational purpose and they are accepted for that purpose by teachers, it is an elementary ethical requirement of trust and good faith that those who receive the resources from, for example, the state, use them for the purposes for which they were intended.

The third possible source of the curriculum could be the community. In those cases where a democratic state delegates curricular authority to a local body such as a school board that has been democratically constituted, the situation is much like that described for state control of education in a democratic society (see below). However, where the authority of the community is exercised (a) informally, (b) undemocratically, or (c) democratically but with a majoritarian bias, the possibility of arriving at a negotiated outcome concerning the implementation of different sets of values may be compromised. Where a community has a large majority that coalesces around a strongly held set of values that are not shared by minorities within that community, there are dangers that the dominant set of values will prevail without any form of negotiation. In this type of case, it can be maintained that the authority of the community becomes a form of *authoritarianism*, whereby authority is applied without sufficient regard to the rights of those over whom it is exercised.

The fourth possible source of authority for the curriculum is the state. It can be argued that it has such an authority if it has been delegated by, for example, the electorate, to provide education on its behalf. Once again, the authority so acquired is, on a Lockean account of representative government, a derivative one and the ultimate source of authority on curricular matters would be the electorate, which consists of parents and others. One advantage of seeing the source of authority for the curriculum in a publicly funded education system in this way is that it appears to deal with a number of the difficulties already encountered. The wishes of the electorate tend to coalesce around political programs put forward by different political parties, in which educational policy concerning the curriculum will figure. These will embody the negotiated outcomes of the combined wishes of coalitions of parents and other citizens and will constitute a proposal that can be put before the electorate as a whole, which can then choose which of these educational proposals they wish to subscribe to. In the more consensual forms of democratic polity, some of the positions in a party manifesto will at least take account of the preferences of other coalitions of interests and points of view represented by other political parties. The democratic political process, on this model, embodies the disparate interests of different sections of society and synthesizes them into policy that maximally satisfies all, given the preferences of the majority grouping. Where the representatives of the nonmajority groupings continue to have influence or have the realistic prospect of government at some point in the forseeable future, then they have a stake in the settlement of curricular matters. Where neither or these two conditions obtain, then the strict majoritarianism described above in the case of community control obtains.

Sometimes the very idea of the curriculum as prescription is attacked. The argument can be developed by questioning the right of a particular body, such as the state, to prescribe educational content. On occasions it rests on a denial that the curriculum as such should be prescriptive. The first argument can be found in John Stuart Mill's *On Liberty*, where it is argued that state prescription of content is inimical to the liberty of citizens. Mill's argument, although it does point to certain difficulties with the notion of state-controlled education, does not engage with the demand for accountability that appears to follow from the requirement that those who allocate resources for a certain purpose enjoy rights to see that those resources are used for that purpose. The second argument rests on a misunderstanding; if learning is organized into a structure that enjoys internal coherence, then someone must have the knowledge and the recognized position to be able to say what that structure is and that it is what should be taught. This person may be the individual teacher acting as an authority on his subject matter, or it may be a providing body. In either case, it is difficult to see how education could occur as a rational enterprise without some such authority. It could be argued that if one cannot distinguish between what does go on and what should go on then one has no way of evaluating the success of the enterprise or even whether it is an educational enterprise.

IV. ARGUMENTS AGAINST AUTHORITY IN EDUCATION

A. Rousseau and *Emile*

Probably the best known and most influential advocate of nonauthoritarian education is Rousseau. In *Emile* Rousseau argues that the overt imposition of one will on another is likely to be psychologically damaging, both to the one who imposes and the one imposed upon. In the overt imposition of one will upon another, the *amour propre* of both parties can suffer damage. In Rousseau's moral psychology, *amour propre* is the animal love of well-being and sense of self-preservation (*amour de soi*) with a human moral, developmental, and social dimension. An individual who is imposed upon will suffer damage to his *amour propre* through the generation of feelings of paranoid rage and resentment. The imposer, on the other hand, will suffer damage to his *amour propre* through the development of a lustful urge to dominate and to harm others for the sake of so doing. If Rousseau is right, it can be seen that the relationship between the educator and the educatee has to be handled with great care if it is not to result in harmful consequences for both. It is of no consequence for Rousseau's argument that the educator might be an authority in either or both senses. The critical point for him is that the overt imposition of will is psychologically damaging and therefore wrong. The educational project set out in *Emile* is to provide an education without the overt exercise of one will over another. In pursuing this project, Rousseau has to substitute various forms of *covert* imposition of the will of the tutor over Emile in order to enable him to learn what he wishes him to learn. In effect, the tutor has abandoned the role of teacher and has substituted for it the role of enabler, or, less flatteringly, *manipulator* of educational situations. The tutor, like any other teacher, still has an educational program and, in some sense, a curriculum (what he has prescribed that Emile shall unknowingly learn), but it is essential to the project that Emile be unaware that this program is being applied. Emile is thus put into situations that appear to rely on learning through conditioning (as when the child is taught not to break windows, through being deprived of their benefits, such as shelter from the elements) and manipulation into situations where affective considerations (such as hunger and fear) promote recollection and learning (as in the Montmorency incident). Through this program, Emile achieves what, for Rousseau, is the most prized educational goal, namely the development of a healthy *amour propre*. Rousseau, it might be maintained, evacuates authority from his educational program at the cost of introducing a total form of power that is, on many ethical criteria, unacceptable. While it is possible to see how Emile might develop a healthy *amour propre* (that is, if one is prepared to accept Rousseau's psychological assumptions and the aetiology associated with them), it can also be maintained that the program comes with considerable costs attached to it. The first is that associated with the risk of the pupil discovering that he is being conditioned or manipulated and the psychological damage that could result from such a discovery. One might well imagine that paranoid feelings of rage and resentment on the part of the pupil could be the natural response to such a discovery. The second cost is attached to the tutor. For it is impossible to conceal from him that he is imposing his will on the pupil. The exercise of guile and the resultant feeling of power that such a position could engender is likely to lead to the kind of inflamed *amour propre* animated by a lust for domination that Rousseau warns against as one of the ills besetting society.

B. Arguments against Indoctrination

It can be argued that the exercise of authority in education leads to the practice of indoctrination and ultimately to the development of individuals who are not autonomous beings. Because it is widely held that one of the main aims of education is the development of rational autonomy, *if* the exercise of authority leads to indoctrination and indoctrination is inimical to the development of autonomous beings then it follows that the exercise of authority is likely to confound the aims of education.

Indoctrination has been defined in various ways, perhaps most comprehensively by Barrow and Woods. A practice is indoctrinatory, it is held, if it embodies the following features: (a) the content of education is taught as unquestionably true; (b) it is taught in such a way as to promote unshakeable belief; (c) the way in which it is taught does not completely rely on rational persuasion; (d) the intention of the teacher is to promote unshakeable belief; (e) what is taught is, in some sense, controversial.

Criteria (a) through (d) would apply to most of the teaching that is undertaken in the elementary school,

but elementary school teaching is not, it is held, indoctrinatory because the content of the curriculum: literacy, numeracy, elementary science, history, geography, and so on is uncontroversial. The teaching of religious education in the manner described would, however, qualify as indoctrination if the subject matter were considered to be controversial. Criteria (a) through (d) rely for their effectiveness on the teacher being in authority, but even on these joint criteria, pupils would not be indoctrinated if they were taught in this way. Many would doubt that religious education is indoctrinatory even on criteria (a) through (e) because they hold that the content of religious education is uncontroversial. Let us, however, concede that criteria (a) through (d) are necessary and sufficient conditions for indoctrination to take place and that they require a teacher who is in authority for them to be fulfilled. Would it follow that an education that allowed these practices was indoctrinatory? To draw such a conclusion would be to display undue haste. The criteria may apply to particular lessons or even phases of education without their applying to the whole of the educational process. And if they apply to lessons or to phases of education, but the pupils nevertheless emerge at the end of the educational process as a whole as, in some sense, rationally autonomous beings, then it would at least be odd to say that such an education was a form of indoctrination.

In order to examine the plausibility of this suggestion we need to look more closely at the changing role of authority as education progresses and pupils become more knowledgeable, confident, and independent. In the years of elementary education it is likely that pupils will be taught in ways that suggest that the content is unquestionably true, that are designed to inculcate unshakeable belief in the truth of that content, and that are not fully describable in terms of rational persuasion. At this early stage in their education they will not think that the teacher is only an authority on a limited range of subject matter, indeed they will be quite likely to see her as an authority *tout court*.

But as children grow older they may learn, through what they observe and are told by others, that certain propositions and bodies of knowledge are, indeed, controversial, that there are propositions that although true are not unquestionably so, that beliefs can and sometimes should be subject to revision, and so on. They will also, it is to be hoped, gain some familiarity with sound and unsound versions of arguments from authority. They will come to terms with the fact that adults are not omniscient and that their role as authorities is often limited to quite restricted areas. They will learn to discriminate between situations when they should take what they are told on trust and situations when it is best that they check themselves or even question what they are told. The authority of teachers changes in secondary and tertiary education. They come to rely increasingly on rational persuasion, to admit to a limited range of competence as an authority, and to introduce topics that they acknowledge are controversial. If education is looked at as a continuous process from early childhood to late adolescence then one could view the changing character of teaching moving from one that had strong indoctrinatory features to one that contain far fewer of these features.

It is possible, however, to go farther and to maintain that this progression is a necessary one and that the indoctrinatory features of primary education are not optional extras, but central to the successful carrying out of any educational project, including one that had as its aims the development of rational autonomy. In order to be independent (minimal autonomy), to choose among various societally approved ends (weak autonomy), or ends including those that are not approved of by society (strong autonomy), a young person will need to be literate, numerate, and moderately knowledgeable about key features of the society in which he lives. He will believe that propositions relating to these are unquestionably true and, if he is to act with confidence, he must hold beliefs regarding them that are, at the very least, difficult to shake. Not all one's beliefs can be rationally justified. The conventions of literacy will be taught as norms as the way in which things are done in this particular society, they have little or no rational justification, and it is a mistake to think that they stand in need of it. In all of these areas the pupil has to accept what is said by an authority and he has to do so if he is to entertain any hope of becoming rationally autonomous.

There are, however, particular difficulties relating to the authority of the teacher in respect of moral and religious education, and these difficulties are particularly acute for those who espouse rational autonomy in the strong sense as an educational aim. The strong autonomist will maintain that an educated individual ought to be able to choose ends and values from a broader set than those that society approves of. In other words, society is not an authority (in either sense) for determining individual ends and values. It should, thus, be possible to choose moral and religious values that society does not recommend. However, if one has been brought up with unshakeable belief in moral and religious views that society approves of, one would not be strongly autonomous, because, in any meaningful sense, there would not be any possibility of choosing

any other ends than those prescribed by society. In this case, it could be argued, the authority of teachers is overextended into an illegitmate exercise of power and hence becomes a species of authoritarianism. It seems to follow then, that the deliberate inculcation of unshakeable moral or religious commitment is wrong because it conflicts with liberal educational aims. The question then arises, "Does the authority of the teacher extend to the inculcation of unshakeable moral and religious belief?"

A teacher who tells children that it is, for example, unquestionably true that it is wrong to steal is not indoctrinating, on the Barrow and Woods account, if he does not have the intention to produce unshakable belief in the child. A moral educator who thought that moral beliefs are rationally justifiable would be failing in his job if he failed to ensure that, at some stage, the children in his care did not come to realize that. For they would have failed to appreciate an essential feature of morality. But at the early stages of childhood and during the phase of elementary education it might be argued that children were only capable of moral *training* and *instruction* rather than moral *education*. Barrow and Woods say that so long as the measures are temporary, such teaching is not indoctrinatory. This would be so only when the teacher's actual intention is to produce unshakeable belief.

If the teacher of the young child is not the same as the teacher of the older child then it could be argued that a problem remains. On the one hand, if the moral trainer or instructor is sincere with the children about what he is doing he is indoctrinating because his intention is to implant unshakeable belief. On the other hand, if he does not intend to do so he might be acting in bad faith, because he is bringing the children to believe that certain propositions are unqestionably true and, in training and instructing, he is at least giving the children the impression that they should believe these propositions unquestionably when he does not think that they should ultimately do so.

This problem of indoctrination could be overcome however, if it were maintained that an indoctrinatory process can never just be a lesson or sequence of lessons but something that is a long-term project extending through the normal period of education. Then one could expect to see, as a child grew older, a decreasing reliance on the authority of the teacher and an increasing reliance on his own rationality. The educational process *as a whole* could then be seen to be nonindoctrinatory, it could be argued. So while individual teachers might sincerely try to implant unshakeable belief in the propositions that they wish the children to believe are unquestionably true, the educational process as a whole would not be indoctrinatory.

Barrow and Woods also believe that fundamental moral propositions are essentially controversial or at least not known to be true and they think that most philosophers believe this to be so. This is relevant to specialists such as philosophers and the kind of authority that it is appropriate for them to have in educational matters. Barrow and Woods' claim is ambiguous; do they mean that first-order moral principles such as that it is wrong to kill are essentially contentious or do they mean that the second-order ethical theory that allows one to derive a first-order principle is? That the second-order ethical theory is essentially contentious is hardly surprising, because it is in the nature of philosophical positions to be so. It does not follow, however, that the first-order moral principle is, or even that it is not unquestionably true even if a second-order theory chosen to underpin it were shown to be false.

If the authors mean that first-order principles are essentially contentious, then it is far from clear that most philosophers would accept this. And it is even less clear that the nonphilosophical public would. If it were generally thought that the substance of first-order moral principles was uncontentious then, even on the criteria proposed by Barrow and Woods, moral training and instruction would not be indoctrination any more than would the teaching of number facts or the rules of spelling. However, if philosophers, as a professional body, did think that first-order moral principles were essentially contentious then it would need to be asked whether or not attention should be paid to such views by the general public.

Do philosophers enjoy authority with the public regarding educational matters or are they just another group whose views may need to be taken into account when determining educational policy? One problem is that the authority of philosophers stems not so much from their ability to transmit knowledge, but in their ability to weigh up the strengths and weaknesses of arguments and to put forward persuasively their own point of view. While these attributes may give them authority qua philosopher, it could be maintained that this is the kind of authority that would be ill-suited to the making of authoritative pronouncements about matters of education. For example, if a philosopher were to say that moral principles were essentially contentious, that very statement would itself be seen as essentially contentious not only by the general public but by his philosophical peers.

One way of tackling the issue of the authority of the teacher in relation to moral education would be to adopt the position of R. S. Peters in *Authority, Responsibility and Education*, which is to say that moral beliefs must be rationally justified or at least justifiable in order to qualify as moral beliefs. It would follow that beliefs that were taught but could not be rationally justified would not be moral beliefs. But if, as Barrow and Woods maintain, moral principles are essentially contentious, it is difficult to see how they could be rationally justified. Even if they could be, it is likely that their contraries are also capable of a degree of rational justification. On the one hand, the moral educator is faced with the accusation that he exercises an *excess* of authority in relation to his charges; on the other hand, he has no special authority to transmit moral principles, but only to enable children to arrive at their own rational justification for the moral principles that they eventually choose to hold.

It is questionable, however, whether the philosophically unsophisticated public shares such a view of morality. If the authority of the public in a democratic society derives from electing representatives to carry out an educational policy and voting for the taxes necessary to provide it, then it would seem that the public has the authority to provide whatever moral education it sees fit after taking due regard for the wishes of minorities. In this situation, the authority of the philosopher qua educational policy maker will rest on his general persuasive powers with the public and with politicians.

V. EDUCATION, AUTHORITY, AND AUTONOMY

If it is the aim of a public system of education to create autonomous people, then the question arises as to what extent they should be autonomous. It is, perhaps, not difficult to see that a liberal democratic society might wish its future citizens to be autonomous in the weak sense, that is, able to make reasoned choices about ends and values from among those approved of by society. In this case, the authority of society concerning educational aims is being used to prescribe a set of aims and then to allow choice among them. Such a society might also encourage its future citizens not to regard those aims as unquestionably true but as subject to appraisal and, on occasions, revision. This could, perhaps, be particularly true of nonmoral aims and values.

The issues raised by the promotion of strong autonomy as an educational aim are more difficult. In this case, the authority of society to prescribe educational aims is to be deployed to set as an aim that the ends and values approved of by society are not a sufficient set for the future citizen to choose from. One justification for this might be that the aim of education is to produce people who are not merely autonomous, but *rationally* autonomous. It can be maintained that the ability to chose among ends and values sanctioned by society (weak autonomy) is an inadequate goal of education for the following reasons. First, the ends sanctioned by society may be morally questionable; second, they may not be fully capable of rational justification.

Someone who is rationally autonomous, it might be maintained, should be able to choose among ends according to whether or not they were morally acceptable, not just to society, but to *himself*, and to be able to do so through a process of rational justification. It could not be sufficient, it might be argued, to rely on the authoritative say-so of others for the choice of something as important as the ends of life. If a necessary condition of rational autonomy is that one can choose ends as well as means, then one must be able to make a meaningful choice from *all* the ends available, not just those sanctioned by society. To allow for anything less than an unconstrained appraisal would be to limit rational autonomy in such a way that a fundamental aim of education would be unachievable, because reason might well determine ends that were not sanctioned by society. To confine oneself to societally approved ends would be to run the risk of substituting submission to authority for rationality as an overriding educational aim.

Against this it could be argued that ther resources deployed by society would be misused if strong autonomy were adopted as an educational aim. For if a society were to use its authority concerning educational matters in order to promote aims it considered desirable, and at the same time it adopted as an aim that the desirability of such aims should be questioned and, if necessary, rejected, it could be argued that it had an inconsistent set of educational aims that could not be jointly implemented. In this case one could either jettison strong autonomy as an educational aim or jettison the other aims. The strong autonomist is not necessarily committed to this view; he does however maintain that education ought to adopt as an aim that aims should be considered that are *not* desired by society. It could be maintained that this is apparently inconsistent, committing him to the view that both socially desirable and socially undesirable aims should be pursued. However inconsistent it might be (and however paradoxical it may seem, it is difficult to show that such a view leads to a formal contradiction), it is not the same as the claim that only socially undesirable aims should be pursued, which would appear to be paradoxical, being the requirement that it would be socially desirable to pursue only what is socially undesirable; the strong autonomist is not committed to this view.

VI. CONCLUSION

The discussion of autonomy as an educational aim and the authority of society as the sovereign body to whom educators are accountable shows the tensions that exist between the liberal educator's demand that the goal of the process should be personal liberation and the view of society that education should benefit it in ways that are readily recognizable. The conflict between the desire for rational autonomy and the desire for authoritative consensus is as acute in education as it is in other areas of political theory. Authority remains a topic of central importance for ethical inquiries concerned with education.

Also See the Following Articles

AUTONOMY • CHILDRENS' RIGHTS • ETHICS EDUCATION IN SCHOOLS • RELIGION IN SCHOOLS

Bibliography

Anscombe, G. E. M. (1990). On the source of authority of the state. In J. Raz (Ed.), *Authority*. Oxford: Blackwell.
Barrow, R., & Woods, R. (1975). *An introduction to philosophy of education*. London: Methuen.
Locke, J. (1704). *Second treatise on government*.
Mill, J. S. (1910). *On liberty,* London: Dent. First published in 1859.
Peters, R. S. (1959). *Authority, responsibility and education*. London: Allen and Unwin.
Peters, R. S. (1965). *Ethics and education*. London: Allen and Unwin.
Peters, R. S. (1981). The paradoxes in Rosseau's Emile. In *Essays on educators*. London: Allen and Unwin.
Raz, J. (1990). *Authority*. Oxford: Blackwell.
Weber, M. (1978). *Economy and society*. Edited by G. Roth & C. Wittich. Berkeley and Los Angeles: University of California Press.
Winch, P. (1967). Authority. In A. Quinton (Ed.), *Political philosophy*. London: Oxford University Press.

AUTONOMY

Søren Holm
University of Copenhagen

I. The Historical Development of the Concept of Autonomy
II. Autonomy in Modern Applied Ethics
III. Critiques of the Emphasis on Autonomy
IV. Conclusion and Further Problems

GLOSSARY

autonomy From the Greek *autos* (self) and *nomos* (rule or law); self-determination, self-rule.
paternalism The act of overriding the autonomous decisions of a person with the intention of benefiting that person.
preference What a person wants to do, or wants to be the case.
respect for autonomy The moral principle that one ought to respect and not interfere with autonomous decisions.
second-order preference A preference regarding the kind of (first-order) preferences a person wants to have.

AUTONOMY is a philosophical concept of art which is playing an increasing role in various branches of applied ethics, as well as in political philosophy. Etymologically it is derived from the two Greek words *autos* (self) and *nomos* (rule or law), and therefore literally means self-

rule or self-determination. The term has been used with various technical meanings in different schools of ethics, and it is not fruitful to base a philosophical discussion of the concept on an elucidation of its meaning in common discourse, since this meaning is strongly influenced by its philosophical and political use. Almost 20 years ago Gerald Dworkin pointed out that the concept of moral autonomy is defined in at least six substantially different ways in philosophical discourse:

1. A person is morally autonomous if and only if he is the author of his moral principles, their originator.

2. A person is morally autonomous if and only if he chooses his moral principles.

3. A person is morally autonomous if and only if the ultimate authority or source of his moral principles is his will.

4. A person is morally autonomous if and only if he decides which moral principles to accept as binding upon him.

5. A person is morally autonomous if and only if he bears the responsibility for the moral theory he accepts and the principles he applies.

6. A person is morally autonomous if and only if he refuses to accept others as moral authorities, that is, he does not accept without independent consideration the judgment of others as to what is morally correct. [(1978), In *Morals, Science and Sociality* (H. T. Engelhardt and D. Callahan, Eds.). The Hastings Center, Hastings on Hudson.]

The subsequent discussions have shown that even these six definitions do not exhaust the field, and that the discussion of the exact content and limits of moral autonomy is still open. One can therefore not *a priori* assume that two philosophers writing about autonomy use the concept in the same way.

I. THE HISTORICAL DEVELOPMENT OF THE CONCEPT OF AUTONOMY

A. The Concept of Autarchy in Greek Political Philosophy

The first traces of the concept of autonomy can be found in early Greek political philosophy. An important distinction here was whether a city-state possessed autarchy (self-rule) or whether it was under the rule of some other city-state. Autarchy was seen as important because it allowed the citizens of an autarchic city-state to promulgate laws which were especially suitable to their specific situation. Autonomy was sometimes used as a synonym for autarchy, but then almost always with reference to city-states and not to individual persons.

Because most of Greek and Roman moral philosophy was not concerned with individual acts as such but more with how to build a virtuous character and how to define the virtues, autonomy never became a prominent theme in early moral philosophy.

In the medieval period discussions of autonomy were not prominent either, and the concept lay dormant until the Enlightenment period, where it was revived and connected to the growing emphasis on individualism in philosophy and in society at large.

B. Autonomy in Kant's Ethics

Autonomy is a central concept in the ethics of Immanuel Kant, but his development of the concept can best be understood if it is seen as a reaction to the development of the concept of liberty in Hume.

Hume proposed to solve the free will problem, i.e., the contradiction between the idea of human liberty and the idea of natural necessity, by dissolving it as an only apparent contradiction. If liberty is understood as freedom from external constraint, and necessity as the opposite of chance or randomness, the contradiction disappears. For Hume somebody is free if there are no external constraints on his or her actions, and this is not contradicted by the fact that his or her actions may be predictable or regular. A free will in a Humean sense

does not necessarily mean that you are the final author of your own acts, but simply that if you decide to act, you may without external constraint.

Kant reacted against this purely external conception of liberty and pointed out that freedom is more than freedom from external constraint. Kant's concept of autonomy is, like many of his other central philosophical concepts, derived through transcendental reflection. Kant observes that we believe we can judge the actions of other persons morally, and then proceeds to ask the simple question, what preconditions must be true for such a judgment to be valid?

His answer to this question is that the moral agent must have chosen his action freely and on the basis of moral principles that are also freely chosen. If these conditions are not met, then our act of judgment of the other is meaningless, because he or she is not truly responsible.

Ideal moral agency thus requires that the agent is autonomous in the sense that she has chosen her moral law for herself. Actions based on moral principles which are not self-chosen are heteronomous. Kant believes that autonomy and full rationality are coextensive, and since his criterion for ascribing rights to an individual is rationality, all autonomous beings have moral rights (as well as some partly heteronomous, but nevertheless rational, beings).

According to Kant every person has a duty to try to perfect him- or herself in order to attain moral autonomy, and a duty to respect the moral autonomy of others. This respect for the moral autonomy of others follows directly from the formulation of the categorical imperative which proscribes actions which treats others merely as means:

> Act in such a way that you always treat humanity, whether in your own person or in the person of any other, never merely as a means, but always at the same time as an end. (I. Kant, 1994. *Grundlegung zur Metaphysik der Sitten,* 7th ed. Felix Meiner Verlag, Hamburg)

It is important to note that what makes autonomy important for Kant is not primarily that it can form the basis of various rights, but that it is necessary for any claim to true moral agency.

C. Autonomy in Mill's Ethics

John Stuart Mill represents the other important strand in the historical development of the concept of autonomy, although he rarely uses the word in his writings.

In his works Mill deepens the analysis of autonomy as freedom from external constraint, but adds a line of argumentation to show why respecting the autonomy of others is valuable as seen from a consequentialist perspective. According to Mill autonomy is valuable to a person because we all prefer to be the authors of our own lives. When we are allowed to develop our own lives this in itself produces utility, and further utility is produced as a by-product when our acts are felt to be our own. It is partly on this basis that Mill can claim,

> It is better to be a human being dissatisfied than a pig satisfied; better to be Socrates dissatisfied than a fool satisfied. And if the fool, or the pig, are of a different opinion, it is because they only know their own side of the question. The other party to the comparison knows both sides. (1910, *Utilitarianism, On Liberty, and Considerations on Representative Government*. Dent, London)

For Mill autonomy is not valuable in itself, but because it directly and indirectly leads to the production of utility.

II. AUTONOMY IN MODERN APPLIED ETHICS

In modern applied ethics autonomy is a very important concept. In some theories of biomedical ethics, respect for autonomy occupies center stage as either the only or the most important moral consideration, and it also plays an important role in other branches of applied ethics.

Sociologically the growing emphasis on autonomy can be seen as a consequence of a number of social developments in the first-world countries: (a) large family structures have gradually disappeared and the "free" individual has come to occupy center stage in our thinking about society, (b) the fact of moral pluralism has been recognized on a social level and has, at least in some countries, led to a decline of state regulations specifically aimed at enforcing morality, and (c) decision making in health care has gradually been forced to conform to a more and more legalistic model where patients and caretakers are seen mainly as potential adversaries and not so much as potential co-workers.

The central role of autonomy in modern applied ethics has also intensified the debates about the two problems which Kant and Mill already grappled with: (1) What is autonomy? (2) Why should we respect autonomous choices?

A. Problems in Defining Autonomy

Modern discussions of autonomy focus on the exact definitions of an autonomous action and an autonomous agent. What are the necessary and sufficient conditions needed for autonomy?

Negative liberty (i.e., freedom from external constraint) is obviously a necessary condition for autonomous action, but is it also sufficient (i.e., are the concepts of negative liberty and autonomy coextensive)? Most moral philosophers would say no, and add that an agent also needs to choose the act in order to have performed an autonomous act. If I swat a fly in my sleep then my act is not autonomous. I am under no external constraint, but the act is pure reflex, and thereby not autonomous.

It also seems to be the case that the agent needs to be free from deception for an act to count as fully autonomous. If someone deceives me, he or she can interfere with my autonomy without interfering with my liberty.

The first of these further conditions is often expressed in terms of preferences and leads to a point of view called *preference autonomy*: An act is autonomous if and only if the agent has a preference for performing the act, and this preference is active in the requisite sense in the set of events leading to the agent's performance of the act. Many philosophers would, however, refer to the possibility of deception and claim that even preference autonomy is not sufficient for an act or an agent to be truly autonomous. Also of relevance is how the preferences of an agent have been formed. If the act is the result of a preference formed by, for instance, brainwashing, indoctrination, or deception, then it is not an autonomous act, because the preference was not really an authentic preference of the agent.

According to this view of autonomy, usually called *dispositional autonomy,* it is a necessary condition for autonomy that the agent is able to engage in second-order reflection on his or her first-order preferences and is able to change the first-order preferences as a result of that reflection (or at least able to try to change them). This view entails that there is not necessarily a direct link between each individual act of an autonomous agent and the second-order capacity of dispositional autonomy. An autonomous agent may well on occasion perform nonautonomous acts.

Dispositional autonomy is an attractive theory of autonomy and moral agency, but it is not without problems. First of all there is a problem in defining the exact content and limits of the dispositional attitude which defines autonomy. Effective brainwashing can be seen as the limiting case of inauthentic preference formation, but how much reflection is necessary before an agent can claim that her preferences are authentic and she is autonomous? Let us say that a person has been brought up in a religious family, went on to a secular university education with ample exposure to other ways of life (other sets of preferences), and has now embraced the religious views of his family. Is such a person autonomous or not?

He would probably not have chosen his present set of preferences if he had not been brought up in a certain way, but this is trivially true of most sets of preferences. If dispositional autonomy requires preferences that are fully self-chosen and authentic in the way described by Camus, Sartre, and other French existentialists, very few persons would ever be autonomous.

This example shows that it is impossible in practice to set any definite criteria for the degree of self-reflection necessary for someone to have dispositional autonomy. It may also be the case that a person is autonomous in some areas but not in others, because her reflection on her preferences has only dealt with certain areas of her preference structure.

These worries about the authentic nature of a person's current preferences and his or her ability to change them in order to become fully dispositionally autonomous could also support the conclusion that dispositional autonomy should be seen as a matter of degree and not as an all or nothing phenomenon. Such a gradualist interpretation of dispositional autonomy could be of specific interest in discussions about the moral status of children. It seems *prima facie* highly implausible to claim that children gain full autonomy, and the moral status following autonomy, at some specific point in their development. A gradualist approach seems much more sensible and can be supported by the empirical observation that children continuously develop more and more first- and then second-order preferences as they mature, and that the reasoning behind these preferences becomes gradually more sophisticated.

A final answer to the question of what preferences should count as truly authentic does, however, require a compelling theory of rational belief and preference formation, and such a theory does not seem to be forthcoming.

Accepting the dispositional account of autonomy also creates a potential problem in deciding which acts of an agent we should respect. There may be acts which are autonomous in the sense that they flow from the person's authentic preference structure, but which at the same time will impair or destroy the person's future dispositional autonomy. Entering a religious sect which uses brainwashing techniques or experimenting with addictive drugs could fit into this class of acts. Should we then respect the person's present choice, or should we respect and protect his or her dispositional autonomy? (See also Section II.D.)

B. Why Should We Value Autonomy?

Autonomy plays an important role in applied ethics because it is usually assumed that we should show special regard for the autonomous choices of persons. There is, however, at least three fundamentally different ways of arguing for this claim.

The first line of argument sees autonomy as the basis for moral standing, and thereby as the necessary and perhaps sufficient condition for the ascription of rights. This line of argument is connected to the Kantian arguments already outlined, without necessarily being strictly Kantian. Modern forms of the argument will often begin with an analysis of rights which connects rights to interests in such a way that being A can have specific right X if and only if A has an interest T which is being protected or furthered by having the right X. The next step in the argument is then to show either that autonomy is a necessary condition for having the requisite kind of interests or that being autonomous is itself an interest of this kind. A common form of this argument states that we have a basic interest in shaping our own life, and that being autonomous and having our autonomy respected are necessary conditions for our being able to fulfill this interest.

The second line of argument is basically consequentialist and connected to Millian arguments for the importance of autonomy. Autonomy is here seen as a good thing, either in and of itself (as in some forms of objective list consequentialism) or more frequently because being autonomous promotes the creation of good things in the life of the person in question. Autonomy is thus valuable primarily as a means to the creation of that which is intrinsically valuable (preference satisfaction, pleasure, etc.).

The third line of argument proceeds from the premise that we are all moral strangers. Each person has his own way of life and his own moral principles. Persons have no right to impose their way of life on others, and have no right to limit the expression of other people's way of living as long as it is not harmful to anybody. We cannot say whether autonomy in itself is valuable (because that would be to adopt the view of one specific moral community), but we have to respect the choices of others as a procedural constraint. This view has been employed in libertarian political philosophy by Richard

Nozick, is part of the foundation of mainstream liberal political philosophy, and has been employed in biomedical ethics by H. Tristram Engelhardt.

In this last line of argument, respect for autonomy will trump other moral considerations, and balancing between moral considerations will only be necessary where there is a conflict between the autonomous decisions of a number of different persons. However, the first two lines of argument do not necessarily lead to respect for autonomy as being the most important moral consideration, and there may be situations where respect for autonomy must be balanced against other considerations.

C. Autonomy in Specific Moral Frameworks

A number of moral frameworks have been developed within modern applied ethics by philosophers trying to move from grand theories to frameworks which are more directly applicable to everyday moral problems. This development has been especially prominent in biomedical ethics. Respect for autonomy is an important moral principle in a number of these frameworks. Each of the four frameworks that follow could merit a paper in themselves, but the treatment here will only briefly give an overview of the place of autonomy within each framework. They have been chosen partly because they are fairly well known by practitioners in the health care field, and partly because they have been extensively employed in the analysis of concrete problems in biomedical ethics. The first three frameworks are American, whereas the last is British.

In the four-principles approach developed by Tom Beauchamp and James Childress, and popularized in Europe by Ranaan Gillon, respect for autonomy is one of four basic moral principles together with nonmaleficence, beneficence, and justice. There is allegedly no lexical ordering of the four principles, and moral decisions about specific cases is carried out by (a) identifying the relevant principles, (b) specifying how they apply to the current situation, and (c) balancing between the considerations generated by steps (a) and (b). From the examples given by Beauchamp and Childress it is fairly clear that their principle of respect for autonomy trumps most other considerations, except perhaps where the principle of nonmaleficence is involved, or where the harm done to others is direct and immediate.

Robert Veatch argues for a system containing five nonconsequentialist principles (contract keeping, autonomy, honesty, avoiding killing, and justice) and one consequentialist principle which he calls beneficence.

He argues that the nonconsequentialist principles should be given joint lexical priority over the principle of beneficence, so that a duty of beneficence becomes operative only if the demands of all nonconsequentialist principles have been fulfilled. In this way he claims to have solved the tension between Hippocratic individualism and the utilitarian commitment to maximization. In this framework respect for autonomy can therefore only be set aside if it is in conflict with one or more of the other four nonconsequentialist principles that Veatch identifies.

The American philosopher Bernard Gert has developed a system of 10 moral rules which he argues are *prima facie* binding for every rational creature. Over the years this theoretical framework has been reworked several times. Gert's fourth rule is, "Don't deprive of freedom." According to Gert this rule is intended to prohibit interference with the exercise of a person's voluntary abilities and actions. The rule is therefore intended merely to protect the negative liberty of a person, and like Gert's other rules it can be overridden in conflict situations where other rules are involved.

The British philosopher David Seedhouse develops a theory of health care ethics based on four core values: create autonomy, respect autonomy, respect persons equally, and serve needs before wants. According to Seedhouse a conceptual analysis of health care shows that health care is centrally aimed at creating and recreating autonomy, as well as toward treating illness and disease as such. The pursuit of these goals is constrained by the need to respect the autonomy of persons and by the duty to respect them equally. According to Seedhouse it is thus equally important to promote autonomy as it is to respect autonomy, and respect for a persons autonomous choices does not necessarily trump other considerations.

D. Autonomy and Paternalism

The limits of our obligation to respect autonomous choices become important in the discussion of paternalism in medicine and social policy. When are we justified in overriding the autonomous decisions of a person in order to benefit that person? In some derivations of the value of autonomy the answer to this question is never. If either (a) we are truly moral strangers and therefore unable to speak with any justification about benefits for other persons, or (b) every person is, as a matter of empirical fact, placed in the best position to decide what is a benefit to him or her, then paternalism is never justified. If, however, we accept either (a) that persons may not know what is best for them and that others may be in a better position to judge this, or (b) that persons may not do that which is best for them even if they know what it is (e.g., they may suffer from weakness of will), then paternalistic action becomes an option. It is important to note that the central point of the paternalism discussion is the possible justification for overriding fully autonomous decisions for the benefit of the person in question. If the decision overridden is not fully autonomous, e.g., because the person is permanently or temporarily incapacitated, or the overriding act is not intended to benefit the person in question, the problem is not a problem of paternalism in the sense discussed here.

It is obvious that whether or not it is possible to justify paternalism depends on the underlying justification for the importance of respecting autonomy.

If the justification is consequentialist, and respecting autonomy thereby is a means to the creation of good consequences, there will be cases where the consequences of respecting a given autonomous choice will be so bad for the person in question that paternalism is warranted. If, however, the justification for respect for autonomy is nonconsequentialist, it will depend on the exact premises of the justification as to whether paternalism can ever be warranted.

Finally, it is important to note that paternalism is not the only potentially illicit way of influencing the autonomous acts of other persons for their own benefit. The Finnish philosopher Heta Häyry has, for instance, described the practice of maternalism in health care, where acts are illicitly influenced by making the patients aware of the great sorrow and displeasure they create among the caretakers if they perform certain acts.

III. CRITIQUES OF THE EMPHASIS ON AUTONOMY

Critiques of the emphasis on autonomy as a prerequisite for moral standing or of respect for autonomy as the basic moral value have been raised by many very different groups of moral philosophers. The three main groups of critics have been (1) communitarians, (2) feminist ethicists, and (3) European and other non-American ethicists.

The communitarian critics have claimed that the emphasis on autonomy presupposes an atomistic individualism, i.e., a view of moral agents where they are seen as totally separate, and not embedded in social relationships which precede their individuality. This "rugged individualist" is a myth, and any moral theory

building on this picture will be seriously flawed. Communitarian critics of autonomy often also point to the deleterious effects of too great an emphasis on respect for autonomy, which, in their view, will lead to a collapse of communities and eventually into a state not much different than the Hobbesian state of nature. Communities are held together by certain world views and ways of life, and they should be allowed to protect these by rules, even if these rules constrain the autonomous choices of members of the community.

The feminist critics claim that the emphasis on autonomy flows from a masculine tradition in moral philosophy, and builds on a neglect of the moral experiences of women. The feminist critique often shares part of the arguments of the communitarian critique and adds a further set of observations about the importance of caring relationships for our understanding of the moral life. The masculine emphasis on rights and duties is seen as a truncation of the moral life which must be rectified by a new care ethic which gives proper moral weight to relationships. Such an ethic will focus not on the isolated individual and his or her rights and duties, but on the individual within a set of caring relationships, and the emphasis on autonomy will be much less.

The European and other non-American critics see the emphasis on respect for autonomy as a reflection of American society and its values. This critique has mostly been directed against the four-principles approach of Beauchamp and Childress, which is very popular in biomedical ethics (see Section II.C). It is claimed that although this theory of biomedical ethics mentions four principles (respect for autonomy, nonmaleficence, beneficence, and justice), it actually emphasizes respect for autonomy to the exclusion of other values. The four principles are explicitly developed as a common-morality theory, i.e., a theory which takes its presuppositions from the common morality of a given society, and aims at a coherent formalization of this common morality. Given that the four principles are derived from American common morality, it is therefore not strange that the principles of beneficence and justice are underdeveloped. Any comparison between the American health care and social security systems and similar systems in other countries of comparable affluence shows that the American systems operate with a substantially different account of distributive justice, and that a legalistic approach to decision making is more prevalent than elsewhere. The whole derivation process of the principle of respect for autonomy therefore makes it doubtful whether the principle can be transferred to contexts outside of America if its content is not extensively redefined. It is not inconceivable that a balancing between respect for autonomy and justice would be different in societies where social solidarity and equality are more important parts of the common morality.

Critics from outside of America also point out that the doctrine of informed consent in biomedical ethics (i.e., that no intervention can be carried out without the informed consent of the patient) may owe more to American law than to an ethical analysis of the physician–patient relationship and of patient autonomy. The doctrine seems to follow immediately from the principle of respect for autonomy, but it is questionable whether most of the decisions taken by patients are really autonomous.

IV. CONCLUSION AND FURTHER PROBLEMS

Despite the critiques just outlined there is no doubt that autonomy as a necessary prerequisite for moral standing, and respect for autonomy as a core moral principle, plays a large role in modern applied ethics. There are, however, three areas in applied ethics where the emphasis on autonomy creates philosophical problems that have not yet been solved. These are: (a) autonomy and free will, (b) animal ethics, and (c) environmental ethics.

A. Autonomy and Free Will

To say that autonomy is important in the evaluation of moral acts or that autonomous choices should be respected seems to require either the existence of free will (i.e., that determinism regarding mental events is false) or the acceptance of compatibilism (i.e., the acceptance of determinism combined with the further claim that this does not preclude free will and thereby does not preclude the moral evaluation of acts). If determinism is true then all mental events and thereby all acts are caused in the same way as other natural events, and this seems initially to imply that the class of autonomous acts (i.e., acts chosen by free will) is empty. A compatibilist will usually deny this implication by trying to show that the kind of free will which is necessary for autonomy is not the same kind of free will that is precluded by determinism. It is, however, still doubtful whether a compatibilist program can succeed.

Another possible solution to the problem is to claim that moral evaluation is possible even if determinism is true and compatibilism false because our reactive moral attitudes toward others do not in any way depend on the truth or falsity of determinism. Even if all acts are determined through normal chains of physical causation we would still be justified in feeling moral resentment toward certain kinds of acts, because these moral feelings are based on the nature of human community and interpersonal relationships. This solution makes the question of moral responsibility independent of the problem of free will and turns the assessment of autonomy into a moral judgment. Such an argument could be further supported by noting that the concepts of free will and moral judgment belong to two different language games, and that the problem is caused only by mixing these two language games.

B. Autonomy and Animal Ethics

Many animals have preferences. These are expressed in various actions such as seeking out specific locations, or specific sources of food, and in avoiding noxious stimuli of various kinds. But is this sufficient for animals to be autonomous beings with a claim to moral status? The answer to this question obviously depends on whether the kind of autonomy which commands moral respect is first-order/preference or second-order/dispositional autonomy.

There is fairly widespread agreement that at least the capability for second-order reflection is a prerequisite if the autonomous choices of a person shall generate a claim to moral respect. If this is accepted only very few kinds of animals would be able to command moral respect. This does, obviously, not preclude that animals may have moral status for other reasons, or that there are things which it will be wrong to do to animals (e.g., causing them pain).

C. Autonomy and Environmental Ethics

The problems inherent in making autonomy a necessary condition for moral standing are even more acute within the field of environmental ethics than within animal ethics. Very few theories of autonomy will allow for autonomy in plants or in the nonanimate environment. The concept of autonomy is inextricably linked to the concept of action, and it seems almost senseless to attribute autonomy to entities which do not and cannot act. The environment can therefore not have moral value in itself, but only if it is valued by some autonomous agent. This is unsatisfactory for many of those interested in environmental ethics, and it is characteristic of this field that philosophers try to develop moral theories that do not rely on autonomy as a prerequisite for having intrinsic moral value. These theoretical developments are outside the scope of this paper.

Another topic in environmental ethics where autonomy becomes potentially relevant is in the treatment of the rights of future generations of autonomous beings. It has been argued that changes we now make to the environment affect the possibility for autonomous choice of future generations. This argument does, however, require the premise that we should not only respect whatever autonomous choices people make, but that we should also enable them to make autonomous choices by not restricting their opportunity range. It is doubtful whether this premise can be supported in a way which will make it useful in the argument, and it requires further argument to show that we do not only change but also diminish the opportunity range of future generations by our current actions.

Also See the Following Articles

ANIMAL RIGHTS • ENVIRONMENTAL ETHICS • KANTIANISM • PATERNALISM

Bibliography

Dworkin, G. (1993). Autonomy. In "A Companion to Contemporary Political Philosophy" (R. E. Goodin and P. Pettit, Eds.). Blackwell, Oxford.

Dworkin, G. (1988). "The Theory and Practice of Autonomy." Cambridge Univ. Press, New York.

Hill, T. E. (1991). "Autonomy and Self-Respect." Cambridge Univ. Press, New York.

Lindley, R. (1986). "Autonomy." Macmillan Education, London.

Young, R. (1986). "Personal Autonomy: Beyond Negative and Positive Liberty." St. Martin's Press, New York.

BIOCENTRISM

Kate Rawles
Lancaster University

GLOSSARY

anthropocentrism The view that we have direct moral obligations only to humans; that humans are the only beings with noninstrumental value.

biocentric egalitarianism The view that all living things have equal intrinsic value and/or inherent worth.

biocentrism The view that we have moral obligations to all living things.

ecocentrism The view that we have moral obligations to all living, and some nonliving things, including entities that are not best understood as individuals, such as ecological systems, ecological processes, and species.

inherent worth The value that an entity is held to have independently of the existence of valuers. On this usage, the claim that x has intrinsic value does not necessarily entail the claim that x has inherent worth.

instrumental value The value attributed to a being in

virtue of its usefulness to some other being, usually human.

intrinsic value The value that a being is held to have in its own right, that is, independently of its usefulness to any other being.

last man argument A thought experiment sometimes taken to offer evidence that (a) the concept of inherent worth is coherent; (b) at least some aspects of the nonsentient, living world have such worth.

sentience (Following Peter Singer), the capacity to experience pleasure and/or pain.

weak anthropocentrism The view that, while we have direct moral obligations to at least some non-humans, those we have to humans are considerably stronger.

THE CENTRAL CLAIM OF BIOCENTRISM is that moral obligations extend beyond humans to include all living things, both sentient and nonsentient. These obligations are not, or not just, indirect obligations to humans (for example, the obligation to preserve rare species because future generations of humans will have lives of diminished value if we do not); they are obligations to the living things themselves. Expressed in terms of value, the claim is that living things have *intrinsic* as well as *instrumental* value.

Biocentrism is often contrasted with *anthropocentrism*. This is the view that only humans count from a moral point of view, that we have direct moral obligations to humans alone. In the language of value, anthropocentrism is the view that humans are the only beings with intrinsic as well as instrumental value. A weaker version of anthropocentrism acknowledges some obligations to nonhumans but insists that those we have to humans are substantially stronger; that the intrinsic value of humans is much greater than that of other forms of life. Anthropocentrism of either variety is perfectly compatible with a keen concern for the environment. The ultimate justification for this concern, however, refers either exclusively or primarily to human interests and well-being. A central question in environmental ethics is whether anthropocentric accounts of our moral relationships with the nonhuman world are adequate. (A further question is whether the distinction between anthropocentric and nonanthropocentric approaches to environmental ethics is, in the end, either useful or coherent).

Nonanthropocentric views that are not biocentric include sentience-based positions, which assert that we have direct moral obligations to all and only sentient beings. Such a position is often held by advocates of animal liberation, animal rights, or animal welfare.

I. INTRODUCTION: FROM CRUSADE INTO ETHIC

An account of the history of ideas, social movements, and current conditions that has contributed to the present emergence (or reemergence) of biocentric ways of thinking is clearly beyond the scope of this article. Nevertheless, a cluster of observations can be offered that might begin to suggest some sort of trajectory toward the development of a biocentric ethic.

Moral thinking is sometimes held to progress; and this progress may be depicted in the form of an expanding circle. Moral obligation, recognized initially toward a narrowly circumscribed group, widens with the centuries to include more and more groups of beings within its reach. From a position that acknowledged such obligation only toward other male members of the same tribe, the circle has spread to take in slaves, members of other tribes, women, and children. Recent stages of development see the inclusion of sentient animals. Recognition of the moral status of nonsentient living things can thus be depicted as the next step in the history of moral development.

Such a characterization of ethical change is clearly open to diverse challenges. But that it is a characterization that biocentric writers may shape their views in

collusion with, or resistance against, is clear from the work of Callicott and Leopold, among others.

A second set of sketched observations might outline a steadily increasing interest in, and concern about, the nonhuman world. One strand of this is the romantic depiction of nature as source of wonder and spiritual replenishment. Nature as storehouse of human resources forms another. In both cases, the nonhuman world can and has come to be seen as threatened; and in ways understood as potentially damaging to human interests. Contemporary conservation organizations bear legacy to both depictions of nature and what it is that the loss of nature threatens us with—scarcity of resources, or spiritual and/or aesthetic empoverishment, or both. The crusade to save nature invites further reflection. Why, for example, should the conservation of the nonhuman be a concern of ours? Can an answer be adequately expressed in terms of human needs for material resources? Is the concern with nature as spiritually and/or aesthetically significant a comprehensive supplement to the resource view? Or does the nonhuman, natural world possess some sort of value that is independent of our various modes of valuing it?

The thought that it does is expressed by Richard Routley in what has come to be known as *the last man argument*. Various adaptions of Routley's example posit scenarios in which all conscious life forms have been destroyed, bar one human, and in which there is no possibility of conscious life evolving again. The last remaining human—a man, in Routley's example—has the option of destroying life on earth, which still supports thriving communities of trees, grasslands, and so on. The man is infected with whatever it is that has decimated his peers, and will shortly die. In the face of all this, we are to ask whether it matters if he destroys the surviving earth life. The commonly held intuition that it does is then taken as evidence that nonconscious life has some value that is not dependent on the existence of conscious valuers—and that this value is relevant to the assessment of the moral standing of these living things.

Like the Norwegian philosopher, Arne Naess, (see *Deep Ecology*) Routley is interested in resisting human chauvinism, which he understands to be the unjustifiable bias that humans manifest toward members of their own species, at the expense of others. Both Routley and Naess, who advocates *biocentric egalitarianism*, (among other things), make what might be called biocentric claims, without advancing a fully fledged biocentric theory. Such claims can also be found in the work of Albert Schweitzer (1875–1965), whose ethical position is sometimes referred to as the precursor of modern biocentric thought, and of biocentrism as an attempt to articulate a comprehensive normative position.

While Schweitzer does not offer a rigorous, philosophical defense of his claims, he articulates a particularly pure form of biocentric thinking, which the phrase, "reverence for life," is often held to summarize. Schweitzer can be described as holding the views that all living things have intrinsic value, (although he himself did not use this terminology); that the intrinsic value of nature can and should be appealed to as the basis for human ethics; and that the attitude of reverence for life would reestablish the connections between ethics and nature held to have been severed by the rise of modern industrial society. Indeed, ethics, for Schweitzer, begins when we recognize these connections, when we feel an awe and respect in the face of living things that commands our reverence and that compels us to strive to promote and preserve life in all its forms.

The attempt to work out the implications of such a position and, in particular, to offer philosophical justification for it, has been taken up by recent biocentric writers. The work of these writers will now be considered in some detail.

II. KEY EXPONENTS OF BIOCENTRISM

A. Paul Taylor

Paul Taylor's article, "The ethics of respect for nature" was published in *Environmental Ethics* in 1981. It was followed in 1986 by *Respect for Nature; A Theory of Environmental Ethics,* a book that remains one of the most comprehensive attempts to articulate and defend a biocentric position.

The core of Taylor's position is the claim that all living things have inherent value and merit moral respect, a position he contrasts explicitly with anthropocentrism. Its explanation and defense takes a number of stages, beginning with the claim that all living things have a good of their own. This Taylor explains as follows: "[t]o say that an entity has a good of its own is simply to say that, without reference to any other entity, it can be benefited or harmed." This good is objective, in the sense that it is independent of what any conscious being happens to think about it—including the being whose good is in question. For example, a certain quantity of water just is bad for a cactus plant, whether I acknowledge this or not; and one can claim that water is bad for the cactus without supposing that the cactus itself knows this to be the case.

Taylor takes the claim that all living things have a good of their own to be an empirical or descriptive one. Having such a good is a necessary but not sufficient condition for being owed moral respect. For this, an entity also has to have inherent worth: and to say that something has inherent worth is, according to Taylor, to invoke two principles: the principle of moral consideration and the principle of intrinsic value.

According to the former principle, every living being that has a good of its own merits moral consideration. The principle of intrinsic value states that the realization of the good of an individual is intrinsically valuable. "This means that its good is prima facie worthy of being preserved or promoted as an end in itself and for the sake of the entity whose good it is." To put it another way, to regard an organism as having inherent value is to believe that it must never be treated as a mere object or thing, with instrumental value alone. The combination of these two principles gives us what it means to say that a living thing possesses inherent worth. And the combination of the view that a living thing has inherent worth and a good of its own constitutes the fundamental moral attitude that Taylor calls respect for nature.

An agent who adopts the attitude of respect for nature will consider herself bound to live by a set of moral norms, governing both actions and character development, which manifest a disposition to promote and protect the good of all living things. The adoption of such life-centered ethical principles would, as Taylor points out, profoundly reorder our (human-centered) moral universe. What, then, would justify their adoption?

Taylor's view is that a set of moral norms is rationally grounded if and only if commitment to them "is a practical entailment of adopting the attitude of respect for nature as an ultimate moral attitude," and if the adopting of that attitude can itself be justified. Because respect for nature is an ultimate moral attitude, it cannot be derived from a more basic moral principle. But, just as our attitude to other humans depends on how we perceive them, so, argues Taylor, our attitude toward living things depends on what kinds of creatures we take them to be, and how we perceive our relations to them. In other words, our attitude rests on, and is supported by, a belief system that constitutes a view of nature and our place in it. So, in an attempt to justify the attitude of respect for nature, we can first articulate the worldview that supports it, and then establish whether this worldview is internally consistent; whether it is consistent with relevant scientific truths; and whether scientifically informed rational agents "can find it acceptable as a way of conceiving of the natural world and our place in it." The first step, then, is to identify the belief system that underpins the attitude of respect for nature. This Taylor calls the biocentric outlook. It has four components.

(1) Humans are members of the earth's community of life on the same terms as all the nonhuman members.
(2) The earth's natural ecosystems are seen as a complex web of interconnected and interdependent elements.
(3) Each individual organism is conceived of as a teleological center of life, pursuing its own good in its own way.
(4) Humans are not superior to any other living thing.

Taken together, these claims indicate a further crucial dimension of Taylor's position—its egalitarianism. For Taylor, all living things have an inherent worth, which is equal. The inherent worth of a human, a whale, a squirrel, a flea, and a toadstool is identical. Our tendency to construe the value of humans as greater than that of other organisms is simply "an irrational bias in our own favour .... a deep-seated prejudice." This is perhaps one of the most controversial aspects of Taylor's position.

In sum, the ethics of respect for nature has three basic elements:

(a) A belief system (the biocentric outlook);
(b) An ultimate moral outlook (respect for nature);
(c) A set of rules of duty and standards of character.

The biocentric outlook is held to support the attitude of respect for nature; from which certain nature-friendly rules and standards will follow. The biocentric outlook cannot be proved to be true, although Taylor believes it to be internally consistent and consistent also with the insights of modern science. And, while it does not prove the truth of the attitude of respect for nature, Taylor thinks that it shows that attitude to be the most fitting or appropriate one that moral agents can adopt toward the earth's wild living things.

B. Robin Attfield

Attfield, taking trees as an example of nonsentient life, seeks to establish whether and why they might be morally considerable. Like Taylor, he maintains both that trees have a good of their own, based in a more-

or-less Aristotelian notion of flourishing, and that this is necessary but not sufficient to show that trees merit moral consideration. Where Taylor appeals to the rational and scientific merits of the biocentric outlook in support of the moral status of trees, Attfield appeals to analogy with morally significant human interests—such as the interests that derive from their capacities for nutrition, growth, respiration, and self-protection—and to a version of the *last man argument*.

There are further differences between his position and that of Taylor. First, Attfield does not think that *all* living things are owed moral respect, on the grounds that not all lives are worthwhile. Second, and crucially, Attfield is not egalitarian even with regard to those lives that are owed moral respect. He maintains that diversity in capacities will lead to diversity in the amount of consideration that different beings are owed. Compared with humans and with sentient animals, there is relatively little of "positive or negative value" that "can befall" a plant. Plant interests, he therefore thinks, count for much less than those of humans and sentient animals. Attfield thus takes it that the most compelling reasons for preserving trees will refer first to the interests of humans, and then to those of other sentient animals. He concludes that while some degree of respect is due to almost all life, the interests of nonsentient life will always have a relatively low priority.

Attfield and Taylor agree that things without goods of their own cannot merit moral consideration in their own right, and that only living things have goods of their own. In addition, they share the view that the class of morally considerable beings will be restricted to individuals. Both claims are open to critical consideration.

III. ECOCENTRISM

Ecocentric approaches to environmental ethics typically "develop from the conviction that ecology must play a primary role in our understanding and valuing of nature." But, as DesJardins points out in *Environmental Ethics: An Introduction to Environmental Philosophy*, scientific ecology is a young and fast-changing discipline. Whatever implications it may have for ethics, therefore, will vary according to how ecology itself is understood. Having said that, most interpretations of ecology emphasize the importance, not of individual organisms, but of the relationships between organisms; and between organisms and their environment. The focus of ecology thus includes the abiotic as well as the biotic components of the natural world. Ecocentrists therefore tend to resist the biocentrist's exclusive emphasis on individual, living organisms, maintaining that an adequate environmental ethic must also guide us in our relations with ecological systems, processes, and non-living natural objects. Ecocentric philosophers argue that we have moral relations to these things directly; that they have inherent and not just instrumental value. An early version of this view is found in Aldo Leopold's *A Sand County Almanac*. Contemporary ecocentric theorists include Goodpaster, Johnson, Rolston, Callicott, and Rodman.

A. Kenneth Goodpaster

Goodpaster confirms the view that "being alive" is the only "plausible and nonarbitrary" criterion of moral considerability. But, in "On Being Morally Considerable," he hints that this might include entities such as the biosystem, an idea he develops in "From Egoism to Environmentalism." Here, he maintains that a genuine environmental ethic should acknowledge Aldo Leopold's concern for the integrity, stability, and beauty of the biotic community. But this, he thinks, will involve more than the extension of the class of morally considerable entities across a wider and wider range, because such extensions are always rooted in an individualistic model of ethics that is intrinsically hostile to a genuinely environmental ethics. Instead, we need to take seriously the possibility that "to be worthy of moral respect, a unified system need not be composed of cells and body tissue: it might be composed of humans and non-human animals, plants and bacteria." And this will involve exploring or developing modes of ethical thinking that are not oriented around concern for individuals.

B. Lawrence Johnson

Goodpaster refers to the respect owed to the biosystem as an integrated, self-sustaining unity. In a sense, this is to retain the individualistic flavor that he seeks to criticize. The biosystem is held worthy of moral respect in virtue of characteristics that render it similar to those individuals whose moral standing we have already recognized.

This kind of approach is developed by Johnson who, in *A Morally Deep World*, argues that "various beings other than individual organisms can meaningfully be said to have interests, and that these interests are morally significant." The beings in question include species and ecosystems.

Unlike Taylor (and others), who understand species as classes, Johnson maintains that species are better

understood as entities. He thinks, moreover, that they are the kind of entities that have morally significant interests that are not the same as the aggregated interests of their component individual organisms; and that one can assert this without introducing "metaphysical monsters." Both species and ecosystems are living processes. As such, he takes them to be characterized by a persistent state of low entropy; self-regulation and self-maintenance via homeostatic feedback processes; organic unity and self-identity. This, Johnson thinks, allows one to say that species have "well-being interests"; interests not just in surviving, but in surviving well. Ecosystems, similarly, "can suffer stress and be impaired ... can be degraded to lower levels of stability ... can have [their] self-identity ruptured. In short, an ecosystem has well-being interests—and therefore has moral significance."

This position is roundly criticized by Andrew Brennan, who claims that it rests upon a naive and scientifically outmoded view of ecosystems and species, neither of which have the characteristics that Johnson attributes to them. Brennan is particularly hostile to the claim that ecosystems have interests, because he takes this claim to presuppose a view of ecosystems as goal-directed that the scientific community has largely rejected.

A more promising approach can arguably be found in those writers who, while denying that species, ecological systems and ecological processes have self-referential interests, insist that we have obligations toward them nonetheless.

C. Holmes Rolston III

Why, Rolston asks, should we care about plants and other nonconscious living individuals, given that they cannot care about themselves? His answer is that, although plants lack a subjective life, they have an objective life of a kind that entitles them to the respect of moral agents. His account of an objective life is very similar to Taylor's. Living things, he says, have a "good-of-their-kind," as follows: "[a]n organism is a spontaneous, self-maintaining system, sustaining and reproducing itself, executing its programme, making a way through the world ... [DNA-coded information] gives the organism a *telos*, 'end', a kind of (non-felt) goal."

From here, though, the similarities with Taylor cease. Unlike Taylor, Rolston believes that species merit moral respect in addition to that owed the individual members of species. This is not because a species has interests. Rather, Rolston appeals to a form of ethical naturalism that underpins his entire position, maintaining that, as we offer appropriate biological description of species, we simultaneously uncover the correct evaluation of them. Species are dynamic life forms. The individual is a token of a type; and, from the point of view of evolutionary ecology, the species is more important. On this view, extinction is a kind of superkilling, in which not just individuals but the form of individuals is destroyed.

Rolston, while not endorsing Johnson's description of ecosystems, also maintains that ecosystems, as the generators and supporters of life, have a kind of value that he describes as systemic. Systemic value is not instrumental value. Nor is it the kind of intrinsic value, "value-for-itself," that an organism has. He describes it as "value in itself."

Rolston thus locates objective, noninstrumental value in all living organisms, species and ecosystems. He is not egalitarian, believing that humans have more value than other animals, and that, in general, value thins out as we move from conscious to nonconscious life and from animate to nonanimate nature.

D. Leopold

Aldo Leopold (1887–1948) has been described as "the single most influential figure in the development of an ecocentric environmental ethics." Leopold called for a rethinking of ethics in the light of the new science of ecology. In the course of his own life, Leopold's understanding of the nonhuman world as a world with instrumental value alone changed dramatically. *A Sand County Almanac,* published in 1949, includes spirited defense of the noninstrumental value of natural systems.

In an essay called "The Land Ethic," Leopold calls for an extension of ethics to include land, plants, and animals. The land, he argues, should be respected as a biological community to which we belong. Thus, in addition to the change in our perception of land as having only instrumental value to something with value in itself, Leopold's land ethic calls for change in our view of ourselves, from conquerors of the land community to citizens of it, as well as a shift in attention from individuals to the community as a whole. His position, which clearly involves much more than a simple extension of our ethical obligations across a broader range of entities, is often summarised in the claim that "a thing is right when it tends to preserve the integrity, stability and beauty of the biotic community. It is wrong when it tends otherwise."

Leopold tends to depict the land community as a living thing, to which qualities like health can be attrib-

uted. There is considerable debate about whether such attribution makes sense, and what concepts like health and well-being might mean, if applied to ecosystems. But here the crucial point is that Leopold does not take "living" or "having a well-being" as a criterion for moral considerability. Instead, Leopold hints that the Land Ethic will follow from an enhanced understanding of the way in which the nonhuman world is structured. These hints are interpreted and developed by J. Baird Callicott.

E. Callicott

Callicott maintains that an understanding of scientific ecology profoundly changes the way we perceive the natural world, and our relationship to it. This in turn is held to have far-reaching implications for ethics.

According to Callicott, our pre-ecological understanding of nature was of a collection of discrete individuals whose relations to one another were contingent and external. "Nature was perceived to be very much like a roomful of furniture," with humans observing it from somewhere outside. Scientific ecology, Callicott argues, has shown us that living things, including humans, are what they are because of their relations to one another. From this perspective, the natural world is not a collection of discrete individuals, but a matrix of interdependencies well described by the metaphor, "biotic community."

Drawing on arguments from Hume and Darwin, Callicott holds that ethics are rooted in natural sentiments or feelings, such as love, sympathy, empathy, benevolence and respect, that have evolved to facilitate our survival and well-being as social creatures. These sentiments have evolved in the context of the communities to which we belong, and are directed toward those we perceive as kin; toward fellow members of community; and toward communities themselves. Evolution shows us that other living things are kin, that our evolutionary history is shared with theirs. And scientific ecology, Callicott alleges, shows us that humans and all other living things are fellow members of biotic communities. Once these implications are properly absorbed, feelings of benevolence, respect, and the rest will be triggered. Thus, an extension of our ethical concerns to include the nonhuman world will follow as an extension of the love and respect we naturally feel for kin and community. This is in clear contrast to the view that extension will follow as a requirement of consistency, once we realize that nonhumans manifest the characteristic held to be a criterion of moral considerability.

F. Rodman

Rodman's article "The Liberation of Nature" was written in 1977, as an extended critical review of Peter Singer's book, *Animal Liberation* and Christopher Stone's "Should Trees Have Standing?" It remains an exciting and challenging piece of work, maintaining, among other things, that environmental ethics has been constrained by its attempts to function within traditional ethical frameworks and offering, at least in outline form, an alternative approach.

Rodman argues that Singer's extension of moral standing to sentient animals, and Stone's to living things, are both expressed in terms of the conventional ethical paradigm, which he describes as focusing on "entities, rights and obligations." Moreover, both writers, according to Rodman, transmit a double message. On the one hand, Singer and Stone argue that the moral status of certain living beings should be raised, in virtue of morally relevant characteristics that they share with human beings. On the other hand, this very argument is held to degrade the living things whose status it alleges to raise, by effectively treating them as inferior humans. "They are degraded . . . by our failure to respect them for having their own existence, their own integrity, their own grandeur—and by our tendency to relate to them either by reducing them to the status of instruments for our own ends or by 'giving' them rights by assimilating them to the status of inferior human beings." In addition, Rodman claims that the bestowal of moral status on nonhumans in this manner constitutes a subtle fulfillment of what he describes as the basic project of modernity: the conquest of nature.

A familiar but enduringly telling extract from Henry Beston suggests the beginnings of Rodman's preferred view. "For the animal shall not be measured by man. In a world older and more complete than ours they move finished and complete, gifted with extensions of the sense we have lost or never attained, living by voices we shall never hear. They are not brethren, they are not underlings; they are other nations, caught with ourselves in the net of life and time, fellow prisoners of the splendour and travail of the earth."

Rodman recognizes that "nature" is a nonteleological system in constant flux. Nevertheless, the essence of his proposal is that, instead of imposing our human-centered views upon nature, we should recognize that we and our ethical theories have a place within a larger normative order. Indeed, Rodman characterizes his ethic as the liberation of nature from the homocentric teleology imposed on it. This, he thinks, will liberate humans as well. In effect, we need a new myth about nature and our place in it, and a new attempt to recognize and resist oppression in all its forms—whether this be damning a river, repressing an animal instinct, or censoring an idea.

Rodman's article remains a challenge to much work in environmental ethics—including that written since 1977—and it raises a number of extremely pertinent questions. One question is whether attempts like those of Singer and Stone, and others reviewed here, to extend moral status to nonhumans in virtue of characteristics shared with humans, *are* inevitably and inherently degrading to nonhuman life. Others concern the extent to which an adequate environmental ethic can be articulate through the resources of conventional ethical theories, and whether and how we are to find norms in nature, while acknowledging the nature of nature as a constantly changing system.

IV. BIOCENTRIC VIEWS: CRITICAL APPRAISAL

(i) Biocentrism gives an account of the scope of ethics according to which our ethical obligations extend to all, but only, *individual* living things. It can be argued that this does not provide a framework within which the concerns of conservationists and environmentalists can be adequately expressed. Callicott and others maintain, for example, that concern for species, ecological systems, and processes does not reduce to concern for individuals, and that we have ethical responsibilities towards these entities which biocentrism fails to articulate.

(ii) A related reservation points to the biocentrists' exclusive concern with living things. Abiotic features of the nonhuman world may be valued as vital for the well-being of living things, but they are not recognized as inherently valuable, or as having moral significance in their own right. Decapitating a mountain, or changing the course of a river, may give cause for concern in so far as living things are damaged by it. But some argue that this is inadequate: that we have some sort of moral responsibilities to mountains and rivers in their own right. The force of this reservation might be felt by exploring hypothetical examples in which a mountain range is demolished without causing extensive harm to local flora and fauna.

Both objections above may be accompanied by a more metaphysical complaint. Biocentrism, it is argued, rests on a metaphysics or worldview that is held to be problematic; a common charge is that it fails to incorporate the insights of contemporary science, particularly ecology. The claim that all and only living individuals are morally significant is said to be underpinned by a view of the world as populated by diverse discrete individuals, whose relations are contingent and external. This worldview is unfavorably contrasted with one that illuminates the various relationships of interdependency that scientific ecology, arguably, reveals. Similarly, the exclusive concern with the biotic may be held to imply a worldview featuring an inert earth, on the surface of which living things run about, or out of which they grow. Scientific ecology and Gaia theory are both held to show that this separation of biotic and abiotic is a peculiar abstraction from a much more integrated reality. According to Gaia theory, for example, the biotic and abiotic have co-evolved to a degree that valuing one without valuing the other can be considered to be fundamentally mistaken.

These kinds of criticisms give rise to questions about the relationship between ethical and metaphysical commitments that are beyond the scope of this article. They also raise issues about what scientific ecology does in fact tell us about the world (some argue that it is just as reductionist and atomistic as other sciences); the extent to which science should be privileged in the formation of worldviews; and how diverse metaphysical systems are to be evaluated. It is my view that there is no simple correlation between ethics and metaphysics such that an individualistic ethics necessarily implies an individualistic metaphysics or vice versa. Nevertheless, there may be something worth extracting from the kind of criticism sketched above. An ethical position that did imply a worldview in which living things simply danced on the surface of the nonliving might be held guilty of metaphysical oversimplification. It remains to be shown, in my view, to what extent the various versions of biocentrism are in fact open to this charge.

(iii) Most biocentric positions are presented within the framework of conventional ethical theories. Attfield, for example, takes a consequentialist position; Taylor's position draws extensively on both Kant and Aristotle; Callicott develops a Humean approach. As we have seen, Rodman and other critics have suggested that it is not possible to generate an adequate environmental ethic by extending the range of contemporary theories in this way, because these theories have evolved to articulate moral claims that arise between people, and are inherently anthropocentric and individualistic. They are thus less than well suited to articulate the moral claims of nonhumans, particularly those who are extremely unlike human individuals.

V. ECOCENTRIC VIEWS: CRITICAL APPRAISAL

Ecocentric positions are not open to the criticism of individualism, or of ignoring the abiotic components of the nonhuman world. Advocates of ecocentrism claim that it does not rest on a sharp distinction between biotic and abiotic and, because such a distinction cannot be sustained, it is therefore metaphysically superior to biocentric accounts of our obligations to the nonhuman world. It may also be held to imply a less individualistic and arguably more adequate worldview. Ecocentric views are, however, subject to criticisms of their own.

(i) If ecocentrism is interpreted as recognizing moral obligations to species, ecological systems, and processes exclusively, there is a danger that the lives and well-being of individuals will be subjugated in what has been called an "ecofascist" spirit.

(ii) Most ecocentric writers suggest that our obligations to holistic entities are in addition to those that we owe to individuals. But ecocentrists then have the task of balancing competing claims and identifying the relative weight of individuals, species, and systems, when concern for each does not overlap—as it often does not. (Issues like the culling of individual animals of a common species in the interest of habitat protection bring out the problem in a particularly stark form.) The challenge of resolving conflicting interests is not one that ecocentrists are unique in facing. But including so-called holistic entities in addition to living individuals may be held to add greatly to it. Ecocentrists may respond that the issue amounts to a further reason for not attempting to generate an environmental ethic within the framework of existing moral theories—for such theories are not able to offer any means by which competing interests can be prioritized.

(iii) Ecocentrism needs to offer an account of what counts as acceptable and unacceptable treatment of the nonhuman world without postulating mythical notions of ecological integrity, balance and so on.

VI. BIOCENTRISM AND ECOCENTRISM: SHARED CHALLENGES

(i) Both types of view require a radical shift in the way we perceive ourselves, the nonhuman world and the relationships that exist between us. A major challenge facing biocentric and ecocentric theorists is to show how the demand for such a shift is to be justified.

(ii) Both views must also show that they do not issue impossibly stringent demands upon human moral agents.

(iii) Both views may be held to draw on a distinction between anthropocentric and nonanthropocentric accounts of our ethical obligations that may ultimately be unsustainable. Human well-being and that of the natural world are obviously interdependent in a number of ways. But it is also true that human and nonhuman interests often conflict. A moral theory that recognizes claims across the nonhuman world needs a sensitive and sophisticated account of how these needs are both interrelated and relatively prioritized.

VII. IMPLICATIONS FOR PRACTICE AND POLICY

In *Toward Unity Amongst Environmentalists,* Brian Norton suggests that environmentalists of most varieties can unite on a wide range of policies, (rainforest preservation would be one example), despite the philosophical differences that may persist between them. But Norton's pragmatic optimism notwithstanding, differences at the level of practice and policy will often seem to follow from the different ethical stances outlined above.

Anthropocentric approaches to environmental concerns ultimately leave the nonhuman world hostage to changing human needs and interests. Were humans to become generally disenchanted with the nonhuman world, losing interest in it as a source of wonder, beauty, information, recreation, and so on, anthropocentric environmentalists would have reason to conserve only those parts of the nonhuman world needed for human survival in a literal sense. If this is combined with the view that ecosystems are in fact less tightly woven and more adaptable to species loss than once thought, anthropocentric and nonanthropocentric environmentalists might well disagree, for example, about the relative importance of species loss compared to other things that humans value.

Policy differences may also follow from nonanthropocentric views according to where the locus of ethical concern is taken to be. For example, differences of opinion about the relative priority of individuals as against species or habitats has lead to considerable debate about the propriety or otherwise of culling. Examples include the culling of grey squirrel in Britain in an attempt to preserve the red squirrels and the culling of red deer in Scotland to preserve moorland habitat. Similarly, work of conservation bodies that focuses on the protection and preservation of species may be criticized by conservationists whose leanings are more ecocentric than biocentric. Focus on the survival of particular species of birds, for example, can lead to attempts to prevent change in certain types of habitat. A more ecocentric view might well maintain that conservationists should seek to protect the dynamism of ecological processes, rather than the outcome in terms of species that are found there at a particular slice in time.

VIII. CONCLUSION

Biocentric and ecocentric positions present the important insight that our ethical obligations are not limited to human beings alone. But expressing this insight within the framework of conventional ethical theories is extraordinarily difficult. The recognition of moral obligation toward nonhumans thus represents a major challenge to contemporary ways of thinking about ethics.

Also See the Following Articles

ANIMAL RIGHTS • ANTHROPOCENTRISM • ECOLOGICAL BALANCE • ENVIRONMENTAL JUSTICE • GAIA HYPOTHESIS • WILDLIFE CONSERVATION

Bibliography

Taylor, P. (1986). *Respect for nature.* Princeton: Princeton University Press.

Attfield, R. (1991). *The ethics of environmental concern.* (2nd ed.). Athens: University of Georgia Press.

Johnson, L. (1991). *A morally deep world.* Cambridge: Cambridge University Press.

Leopold, A. (1966). *A sand county almanac.* Oxford: Oxford University Press.

Callicott, J. B. (1989). *In defence of the land ethic.* Albany: State University of New York Press.

Rolston, H. III. (1988). *Environmental ethics.* Philadelphia: Temple University Press.

Rodman, J. (1977). The liberation of nature. *Inquiry,* **20,** 83–145.

DesJardins, J. R. (1993). *Environmental ethics; an introduction to environmental philosophy.* Belmont, CA: Wadsworth.

Norton, B. G. (1991). *Toward unity among environmentalists.* Oxford: Oxford University Press. *Environmental Values.* (1995). Vol 4, No 4, Ecosystem Health.

BIODIVERSITY

Keekok Lee
The University of Manchester

GLOSSARY

biological-species concept See *species*.

Cambrian The period of time between 550 and 500 million years ago when there was a great explosion of marine animal evolution.

diploid A cell containing two full sets of chromosomes.

eukaryotes Organisms or cells whose DNA is contained in a well-defined cell nucleus with a protein coat.

haploid A cell containing one set of chromosomes, or half the normal diploid number.

hybrid An offspring of genetically dissimilar parents.

meiosis Cell division involving the reduction of the chromosomes from two to one set, leading to the production of sex cells in the higher organisms.

Phanerozoic eon The period of time from 550 million years ago to the present, during which biodiversity has increased and existed.

polyploid A cell containing more than twice, or three or four times, the complete set of chromosomes.

prokaryotes Organisms whose genetic material is not contained within a well-defined nucleus.

speciation The process of species formation in which one population of organisms becomes two or more populations which are reproductively isolated from one another.

species A population of closely related and similar individual organisms. In the case of sexually reproducing organisms, the species refers to a population of such individuals which only interbreed among themselves but not with individuals of other species. This is the biological-species concept.

BIODIVERSITY in the widest sense is about the total variety of biota on Earth, existing at all levels of biological organization and ranging from the genetic variations between individual organisms of the same species to those between species and still higher taxonomic levels, as well as the variety of ecosystems within which individual organisms and species interact with one another and the abiotic physical conditions under which they lead their lives.

I. WHAT IS BIODIVERSITY?

In its popular sense, biodiversity is about the number and existence of different species of plant and animal life on Earth. The estimates of the size of this biota range from 3 to 10 million at the conservative end to between 10 and 100 million species at the more speculative end. Only about 1.5 million species in the plant and animal kingdoms (with animal species totalling just over 1 million and the higher plant species about a quarter of a million) have been identified by science, but even so, that knowledge is at best partial—their geographical ranges, ecological characteristics, and other properties remain unknown. Of the rest, one does not know what they are or where they are, except that on good evidence most of the terrestrial ones are to be found in the tropical forests. However, biodiversity covers five kingdoms; besides those of Plants and Animals (both being multicellular eukaryotic organisms), the three others are Monera (the prokaryotic organisms like bacteria), Protista (the unicellular eukaryotic organisms like protozoa), and Fungi (covering yeasts, molds, and fungi which are multicellular eukaryotic organisms).

Each species contains a huge amount of genetic material. Bacteria have about 1000 genes, some fungi 10,000, and many flowering plants 400,000 or more. Each species is made up of numerous individual organisms which are not identical in their genetic composition (except for the rare cases of identical twins and parthenogenesis of asexual organisms). Wide-ranging species consist of several breeding populations which possess genetic variations between as well as within the populations. It is important to stress that the extinction of any one species, the loss of a breeding population within a species, or, indeed, even the loss of an individual organism is an irreplaceable loss of genetic information. The latter two may be said to constitute loss in internal diversity; even when populations do expand again later, they will be more homogeneous in their genetic composition than their original populations.

Although genetic diversity is clearly fundamental, nevertheless, biodiversity should not be identified totally with it. Biodiversity includes but yet goes beyond genetic diversity. A species is not merely a storehouse for a set of genes. As a constituent of an ecosystem, it is more than a static collection of genetic information, but is the result of past adaptations to environmental forces and represents possibilities for future adaptations. Biodiversity is then not simply the sum of the species or subspecies that exist or the genetic variation contained therein, but also includes the web of complex relationships into which species enter both with one another and with their abiotic environment. From both the ecological and the evolutionary points of view, a species in two different ecosystems should not be con-

sidered as one unit of diversity, but two different units which stand for different genetic and evolutionary potentials. In other words, ecosystem diversity is also crucial.

A. Species Diversity: The Species Concept

As the species concept is fundamental to understanding biodiversity, a few words about it are essential and must first be given. It appears that biologists advocate different definitions of the term "species." According to Ernst Mayr, these can be grouped under four headings: the typological (or morphological), the nominalist, the biological, and the evolutionary species concepts (1988. *Toward a New Philosophy of Biology*. Harvard Univ. Press, Cambridge, MA/London). To each there appears to be objections; one concept may give a better fit in one domain of study than another. For instance, zoologists, on the whole, embrace the biological-species concept while botanists tend to remain suspicious of it. This is a reason which leads some theorists to argue that a plurality of species concepts is probably required to capture the complex patterns of variation in nature (B. D. Mishler and M. J. Donoghue, 1994. In *Conceptual Issues in Evolutionary Biology* (E. Sober, Ed.). MIT Press, Cambridge, MA/London).

B. Species Diversity: The Biological-Species Concept

However, in spite of the points just noted, the most appropriate one to use in the case of sexually reproducing organisms is the "biological-species concept," which may be defined as follows: "a species is a population whose members are able to interbreed freely under natural conditions" (E. O. Wilson, 1992. *The Diversity of Life*, p. 36. Penguin, London/New York). Two things require immediate comment:

(a) The operative phrase "under natural conditions" needs to be examined. Zoos may be and have been successful in crossing lions with tigers (a hybrid with a lion father is a liger and one with a tiger father is a tigon), but this does not mean that lions and tigers belong to one interbreeding population, no matter how genetically close they are. Under natural conditions lions and tigers have historically failed to hybridize, each preferring different habitats—lions, on the whole, favoring savannahs and grasslands, while tigers favor forests. Their respective behaviors are also different in many ways. Lions are the only social cats, living in prides and bonding with their female partners and their young. When they leave their natal prides, grown males join other groups often as a pair of brothers. The adults hunt together with the females leading. In contrast tigers are solitary. The adult males produce a scent in their urine, very different from that of lions, to mark their territories and attract female partners whom they meet only briefly for the purpose of mating.

(b) But even should adults from two species meet and breed, the hybrids they produce must not only survive to sexual maturity, but must also reproduce successfully. Sterile hybrids cannot and do not count as a species distinct from the parental ones. The biological-species definition views a species as a closed gene pool; the individuals within the population only exchange genetic information among themselves. Genetic insulation of this kind in evolutionary terms leads to hereditary traits which enable the offspring to occupy a distinctive habitat and a particular geographical range.

C. Difficulties

However, the biological-species concept is not without problems, some of which are as follows:

(a) The least serious challenge is posed by the existence of sibling species, that is, two or more populations, having split off from an ancestral species, looking and behaving so similarly that even experts may sometimes overlook certain crucial differences that render them to be reproductively isolated from one another. This is a difficulty also faced by the morphological-species concept; but while the morphological species concept cannot readily surmount this problem, the biological-species concept may be able to resolve it by more careful study.

(b) The second challenge posed by subspecies is conceptually more threatening, involving subpopulations which partially interbreed, producing fertile hybrids under natural conditions. This holds truer of plants in temperate climates which are wind-pollinated rather than of plants not thus pollinated or in the tropics, and of animals. But even with such plants, the interfertile subspecies breed more often within than between themselves.

(c) The concept has no application in the case of individual organisms which are hermaphrodites (with both ovaries and testes, capable of self-fertilization), reproduce parthenogenetically from unfertilized eggs, or are asexually reproducing plants. However, the vast majority of species belonging to the Plant and Animal

kingdoms reproduce sexually, conforming to the closed gene pool requirement.

(d) Neither is the concept meaningful in the case of chronospecies, which may be regarded as marking different stages in the evolution of the same species through time. As these were not coexisting species in time, one could not meaningfully answer the question of whether they would have bred freely under natural conditions if they had met. For instance, *Homo sapiens* is said to be descended from *Homo erectus,* taking a million years to do so. But *ex hypothesi,* they could not have met for us to ascertain if they could have bred freely.

(e) Nor does the concept apply to organisms such as bacteria belonging to the kingdom called Monera, as their genetic material is not even contained within a well-defined nucleus.

But in spite of these difficulties, any attempt to understand and explain biodiversity to a great extent has to lean on the biological-species concept, as reproductive isolation between populations is the key to the generation of biological diversity, on the whole, within the Animal and Plant kingdoms.

II. WHAT TO LOOK FOR, WHERE TO LOOK, AND HOW TO COUNT IN DETERMINING EXTANT BIOLOGICAL DIVERSITY

A. What to Look For

The number of known species of plants and animals, as we have seen, is given as 1.4 or 1.5 million, regarded readily by evolutionary biologists to be less than a tenth of living biota today. Of the known species, the ordinary layperson is usually excited only by a dozen or two of them, in particular, megafauna like the tiger, the eagle, or the panda. Ornithologists are interested in tracking down bird species, and knowledgeable gardeners are keen on rare or exotic plant species. The totality of the informed layperson's grasp probably runs only into a few hundred species. But the biosphere contains many more which only the specialists are aware of, and even more about which not even they as yet know.

As an instance in understanding the complexities underlying the observed biodiversity, take the phylum Arthropoda, embracing spiders, crustaceans, centipedes, insects, and others with jointed, chitinous exoskeletons. Arthropod species (which are far from the image of the cuddly animal) constitute more than half of the known animal species on Earth; insects, with about three-quarters of a million known species, in turn dominate the phylum, a position they have held among the small land animals for over 300 million years since the late Carboniferous period. During this period, among the plants, the angiosperms (the flowering plants), with about a quarter of a million known species, have also prospered. The insects and the flowering plants depend on one another for survival—the insects dwell in and live off every part of the plants, turning the soil, decomposing dead matter into elements which can be reused by the plants as nutrients, and pollinating them, thereby helping them to reproduce.

However, in determining biodiversity, another important dimension to bear in mind is scale. Three scales have been proposed: alpha or within habitat diversity, beta or among habitats diversity, and gamma or geographic-scale diversity. An instance of alpha diversity is the 300 or more species of cichlid fishes in Lake Victoria, one of the Great Lakes of East Africa's Rift Valley. But Lake Malawi, another of these Great Lakes, has over 500 species of such fishes—this is beta diversity. But chichlid fishes are also found elsewhere; for instance, southern India and Sri Lanka have three endemic species—this would constitute gamma diversity. Alpha diversity may be increased, but at the expense of either beta or gamma diversity. An instance of the conflict between promoting alpha diversity but at the cost of gamma diversity is Clear Lake in northern California. Twelve native species of fish used to live in this habitat, 3 of which were endemic to the lake. Fisheries managers then introduced new fish species, thereby taking the total of species to 25 and yielding a net increase in alpha diversity of 13 species. However, as a result of such introduction, only 4 of the native species have remained, and 2 native species (Clear Lake splittail and the thicktail chub) which have disappeared from the lake are also globally extinct. This shows that focusing on too narrow a scale could lead one astray.

B. How to Count

The importance of land-dwelling arthropods to other species is such that their disappearance would lead to the disappearance not only of flowering plants (and hence of forests), but also of most of the amphibians, birds, reptiles, and mammals, including the human mammal. And yet, until recently, scientists have had no way, no matter how crude and tentative, to determine the number of insect species. But since 1982 a method called the "bug bomb" has been pioneered. Assuming that the tropical rain forests harbor the great-

est abundance of insects, researchers launched an insecticide bomb in a Panamanian forest from the forest floor to the top of a tree chosen specially for the purpose in order to collect the dead and dying arthropods falling from the tree crown. They calculated that 163 species of beetles inhabited the canopy of one species of tree, *Luehea seemannii*. Estimating that there are roughly 50,000 tropical tree species, they worked out that the number of tree-dwelling beetles is 8,150,000. But as beetles are roughly 40% of all arthropods, the final number of arthropods in this kind of habitat would be about 20 million. When the arthropod species on the ground are added, the grand total came to about 30 million species of tropical arthropod. But other researchers consider this estimate to be overgenerous and have revised the figure down to anything between 5 and 10 million tropical arthropod species.

C. Where to Look

While the rain forests and especially their tree canopies are increasingly getting more attention, another space, hitherto totally unexplored, is also now attracting research interest. This is the so-called abysmal benthos, which biologists in the past, particularly in the 19th century, used to think was bereft of life. This "new" continent is the deep ocean floor, 1000 m or more below the water surface—dark, bitterly cold, and subject to the colossal pressures exerted by the water above. Yet recent exploration, aided by technological innovations, has yielded a rich harvest of macro-sized animals totally unknown to terrestrial fauna and miniscule invertebrate life forms surviving at very low metabolic rates, as well as microorganisms, like bacteria, adapted to grow and divide in very cold water under very high pressure. One informed estimate in 1991 puts the number of such species in the region of tens of millions.

But the impressive biological diversity of the plants and animals of the rain forests and the abysmal benthos could be outshone by that of the bacterial world. As earlier mentioned, given the nature of bacteria, the biological-species concept cannot be applied to their study. Microbiologists have adopted the following standard to determine what counts as a bacterial species: "a bacterial species consists of all those cells whose nucleotides are at least 70 percent identical, and hence are at least 30 percent different from the nucleotides of other species" (Wilson, 1992, 136). As late as 1989, the official list of known species was only about 4000, but research advances since then have revised it to perhaps a thousand times greater. If so, the total number of Earth's biota would certainly exceed 10 million, which is the figure often cited at the conservative end of the estimated size.

Another fruitful place to look for biological diversity among bacteria and other microorganisms is in other larger organisms, both plant and animal, dead or alive. It looks as if microbiologists have plenty of work still to do.

III. THE MECHANISMS OF SPECIATION AND FOR SUSTAINING BIODIVERSITY

A. Vertical Evolution and Speciation

To understand biological diversity, one must distinguish between two different evolutionary processes at work, namely, vertical evolution without speciation and vertical evolution with speciation. Imagine a genetic mutation in a species involving changing skin pigmentation from brown to black. If such a mutation were to bestow advantages on the individual organisms carrying it, then it could eventually mean a change from a brown-pigmented to a black-pigmented species. The species would have evolved into a new one but without a net gain in species diversity; this is vertical change without speciation. But the course of evolution could have been different. Mutations could occur which would eventually give rise to two or more species, for example, one brown, one black, and the third pink, with no genetic exchange between them. This is vertical change with speciation. In other words, vertical evolution can take place without speciation, whereas speciation cannot take place without vertical evolution itself. Another way of making the same point is to say that vertical evolution is a necessary but not a sufficient condition of speciation.

According to E. O. Wilson, Darwin's pathfinding work ultimately is concerned more with vertical change without speciation rather than with speciation, for according to Darwin's thesis of natural evolution through competition, over time and across generations, inherited characteristics which favor the survival of the individuals possessing them could transform the species so radically as to turn it into a very different one. But such a transformation involves no multiplication of species. Darwin did not have a full grasp of the processes behind the multiplication of species, although he grasped in general the distinction between vertical change on its own and the splitting of species. To start with, he was driven to rely on the notion of blending inheritance, which he then backed up with his theory of pangenesis, and not the Mendelian particulate theory which forms the basis of 20th century genetics. Therefore, he could not and did not hold the biological-species concept based on reproductive isolation as understood within the framework of Mendelian genetics, in spite of his account of the Galapagos finches. Instead, he rejected the reality of the species, regarding it merely as a convenient construct of the classifier who arbitrarily decided to include individuals which share certain similarities with, but also exhibit differences from, one another. In spite of the oft-quoted main title of his renowned book, *The Origins of Species,* full understanding of speciation eluded Darwin, according to Wilson.

B. Reproductive Isolation

Species, by and large, retain their respective identities by avoiding breeding with other species. To understand speciation, one must then understand how such reproductive isolation and genetic segregation take place in the first place. This occurs through the development of inherited mechanisms which avoid fertile hybridization between populations under natural conditions. These mechanisms include inhabiting different geographical ranges (like lions and tigers), preferring to mate in different habitats (of the flycatchers of the genus *Empidonax,* one species occupies woods and farmlands, another alder swamps and wet thickets, and yet another coniferous woods and cold bogs), breeding at different times of the 24-hr day (the females of promethea moths—*Callosamia promethea*—call from 1600 to 1800 hr, the females of polyhemus moths—*Antheraea polyhemus*—call from about 2200 to 0400 hr, and the females of cecropia moths—*Hyalophora cecropia*—call from about 0300 to 0400 hr) and at different seasons, engaging in different courtship patterns (the male jumper spiders of the Salticidae family posture and dance before the females, each species possessing a different visage and engaging in different gestures and postures to reinforce the visual signals), and emitting different mating scents (male lions give off a scent very different from that of tigers).

As we have also seen, even if the members of two species succeed in mating, their offspring might not reach sexual maturity to reproduce, or reaching such maturity, may yet turn out to be sterile. The former failure may be brought about by the fact that the hybrids are less well adapted to either of the parental habitats—open woodland or swamps—than their purebred offspring, and so may not survive to attain reproductive age. The latter may fail to form appropriate sex cells due to the incompatibility of the parental chromosomes. Following the process of cell division leading to chromosome reduction in the eventual production of sex cells, a chromosome from parental species A might find it difficult to line up with its counterpart in parental species B, as the two chromosomes differ too significantly for proper matching to take place.

The different hereditary traits—like different songs, colors, and odors—which serve as intrinsic isolating mechanisms between species start simply by being traits which adapt them to the environment rather than as mechanisms for reproductive isolation. They only eventually become so. In this sense speciation is a by-product of vertical evolution.

C. Modes of Speciation

1. Geographial Speciation

An instance of geographical speciation is the Hawaiian islands. One hundred thousand years ago, these islands were colonized by beetles, snails, birds, flowering plants, etc., arriving from the mainlands of North America and Asia. These thrived and multiplied, spreading from island to island in the archipelago, from one valley or ridge top to another. Over time, these populations, each having adapted themselves to their respective ecological niches, developed intrinsic isolating mechanisms which turned them into new and different species. A single species which was the first colonizer 100,000 years ago evolved to become hundreds of species, each one endemic only to a particular island, ridge, or valley.

Taking birds as an instance of such speciation, suppose one population built nests at certain sites in the forest which turned out to be favorable to their chances of survival and reproductive success. A very long period of geographical separation from the original bird population would lead to the evolution of a new and different species so that even if individuals from the two populations were to meet, they would not hybridize freely or with success. The new species' favored site started off by being an adaptive trait, but, when transmitted as an inherited characteristic over time, transformed itself into a mechanism to ensure genetic isolation and exclusivity.

2. Genetic Mutations and Diversity

Sometimes the genetic basis for the critical isolating difference may be traced to a very small alteration in the genes or chromosomes. For instance, some species of leafroller moths (in the family Tortricidae) are reproductively isolated by very minor differences in the chemistry of their female sex attractants, not so much even in the actual chemical substances in their composition, but only in their percentages. The males of each species only respond to a specific chemical bouquet that the females exude—even a slight deviation ensures that no mating would occur between the male and the female of two different species.

3. Polyploidy

Another genetic mode of speciation is polyploidy, that is, a two-, three-, or even fourfold increase in the number of chromosomes in each cell compared to a normal individual. Polyploidy, unlike the inheritance of adaptive traits leading to the evolution of new species, causes speciation dramatically in few generations. This is because the hybrids of polyploid and nonpolyploid individuals cannot develop normally or reproduce successfully even if they survive to sexual maturity. Polyploidy is estimated to be the cause of the origin of maybe over half of the known species of living flowering plants as well as a smaller number of animal species.

Polyploidy works as follows: prior to fertilization, the egg or sperm cell contains only one chromosome of each kind in the so-called haploid phase of the cycle in sexually reproducing species. In the next phase—the diploid phase—after fertilization, each cell contains two sets of chromosomes which form the basis for the development of the new individual. In humans, the haploid number of chromosomes is 23 and the diploid number is 46. Suppose, as in the Down's syndrome case, that instead of doubling, the chromosomes tripled in number, yielding 69, as a triploid individual organism. In the normal diploid individual, during meiosis when reduction takes place, each of the haploid 23 chromosomes in the egg or sperm can find a corresponding partner to yield 23 pairs of chromosomes. But in the triploid case, pairing is difficult, leading to the formation of large numbers of abnormal sex cells.

However, the fortune of a tetraploid individual—where the base number is quadrupled—is much more encouraging. Suppose the normal diploid number of a plant accidentally increased twice, such that each cell contains four chromosomes of each kind. In the haploid phase of the reproductive cycle, each egg or sperm will then consist of two chromosomes of each kind instead of the normal one. Suppose further that the normal individual plant has 10 chromosomes in each of its ordinary cells and 5 in each of its sex cells. The tetraploid plant will have 20 in the former and 10 in the latter. There is no difficulty for two normal diploid plants of the same ancestral species to interbreed, just as there will be no difficulty for the unusual tetraploid plants to breed among themselves. But what is not possible is for the ordinary diploid ancestor and the tetraploid derivative to interbreed—as we have seen with triploid hybrids. In other words, in species isolation by polyploidy, the triploids cannot successfully breed with the diploids or with each other, whereas tetraploids could do so with each other though not with diploids, thereby ensuring that a new species is formed which is different from the ancestral diploid species from which it is derived. In nature such doubling does occasionally take place, causing a new species to come into existence.

It is more common for polyploidy to lead to the creation of a new species when two existing species hybridize. As we have seen, hybrids are often sterile, as the chromosomes from parental species A cannot line up successfully with their counterparts from parental species B during the formation of the sex cells. But were the number of chromosomes in the hybrid to double, the problem of parental incompatibility during meiosis would be overcome as every A chromosome can now find a match with an identical A chromosome, and every B chromosome can do the same. This means that the hybrid polyploid is fertile and can successfully breed with fellow hybrids of the same type. However, it cannot breed with the original diploid ancestors from which it came.

D. Genetic Diversity

Biological diversity at one level of biological organization involves genetic diversity. Since the 1960s, a sophisticated technique called gel electrophoresis, involving the purification and identification of enzymes, has been utilized to determine the overall genetic diversity in a species. (Enzymes are protein molecules formed at the instruction of genes.) These studies reveal a very large amount of genetic diversity in the great majority of species. However, even this large estimate is an underestimation of the true amount of genetic diversity as revealed by techniques developed in the 1980s which are based on a greater understanding of the genetic code. Today nucleotide diversity based on DNA sequencing is regarded as the ultimate test of genetic diversity. A figure of 10^{17} nucleotide pairs has been speculatively put forward as the total genetic diversity among species on Earth at present. Yet even this staggering amount of biodiversity still ignores the differences between individuals of the same species. When this complexity is taken into account, the amount is increased even further.

E. Natural Selection

However, genetic mutations and diversity *per se* do not constitute the whole story of evolution and its relation to speciation. Mutations do lead to an evolutionary dead end in some cases. Natural selection will act upon the individual organisms with the new genotype, who thus display a new phenotype, exhibiting altered traits in physiology, anatomy, and behavior patterns which often affect their survival and reproductive success. If the traits caused by the mutant genes are favorable, then the new genotype will spread; if not, it will decline or disappear altogether.

F. Genetic Drift

This is a process different from that of natural selection and involves shifting the frequency of genes by pure chance, especially in a small population of individual organisms. Imagine a very small population with only five individuals containing 50% A genes and 50% B genes at a particular chromosome site. This means there will be 10 genes available to enter the makeup of the next generation. But if the inheritance of these genes is random, the following possibilities could obtain in the new population: 5 A genes and 5 B genes; 4 A genes and 6 B genes; 3 A genes and 7 B genes; and so on. In large populations, genetic drift would be weak, but in very small populations the percentages of alleles—different forms of the same gene—could change crucially even in one generation.

G. Founder Effect

One form of genetic drift leading to the formation of a new species is the founder effect. Imagine that a small group of birds fly to an island not already occupied by the species and that they come from an extant continental population where the A and B alleles exist in an equal mix of 50% each. By chance the founder birds could contain 2 A and 2 B alleles in accordance with the ratio in the ancestral population. But they could just as easily contain 3 A and 1 B; 1 A and 3 B; 4 A; or 4 B. This chance initial genetic difference conjoined with geographical isolation and the confronting of a new habitat could lead the founder population to adopt new patterns of life and adapt to a new environment, which in turn could lead quite quickly to the emergence of intrinsic isolating mechanisms, thereby ensuring its status as a new and different species.

H. Ecology and Adaptive Radiation

Science today appears to understand a good deal about the contribution of genetics, but definitely much less of ecology, to speciation.

The cichlids of Lake Victoria—earlier mentioned—are an impressive instance of adaptive radiation. Adaptive radiation involves the spread of species of common ancestry into different ecological niches. The 300 or more species in that lake have descended from a single colonizer which came from other lakes. This conclusion is based on work done in 1990 which studied the close similarity of their genetic codes. One species—*Astatotilapia elegans*—is a general feeder at the lake bottom; another—*Macropleurodus bicolor*—with a small mouth, specializes in using its pebble-shaped pharyngeal teeth to crush snails and mollusks. The Victoria cichlids could have speciated by sympatric means, that is to say, by becoming two or more species even in the absence of physical barriers between them. While these are the products of adaptive radiation in the past, the arctic char (*Salvelinus alpinus*), according to the most recent research, shows exciting signs of being on the threshold of adaptive radiation in the arctic lakes created only a few thousand years ago by the retreat of continental glaciers.

So far biological organization has been discussed at the level of the gene, the individual organism, and species. But it is important to look at others, such as the guild, community, and ecosystem levels.

A community of organisms may be defined as all the species interrelated with one another through the food chain and in other ways which could affect their respective life cycles. For instance, the goshawk (*Accipiter gentilis*) is part of a particular community of organisms living in the Black Forest; fir trees are its food web. The trees provide nourishment for moth larvae, which in turn are food for certain songbirds, like the wood warbler (*Phylloscopus sibilatrix*), which in turn are preyed upon by the goshawk. Another member of this community is the common buzzard, a European buteo hawk, whose diet includes songbirds. As a competitor, more food to the buzzard means less for the goshawk. However, the buzzard also occasionally performs, unwittingly, a service for the goshawk by abandoning its own nest, which is then taken over by the goshawk, thereby improving the latter's chances of successful reproduction. Competition and accidental symbiosis make the common buzzard and the goshawk members of the same community.

A guild is defined as all those species which inhabit the same location and which hunt or seek out the same food using similar methods. For instance, the goshawk belongs to a guild within the Black Forest community which it shares with the sparrow hawk (*Accipiter nisus*). Both are accipiters hunting small birds, flying rapidly, twisting through the forest, and sometimes soaring briefly above the trees.

An ecosystem refers to all the organisms inhabiting a particular environment, be it a lake, river, marsh, or forest, and the abiotic aspects of that environment with which the organisms interact. Ecosystemic processes include photosynthesis, nutrient cycling, and energy transfers from lower to higher trophic levels. The goshawk lives in a particular ecosystem, the Black Forest ecosystem—one dominated by fir trees as far as its biomass is concerned. That ecosystem's physical base includes granite-based soil, rocks, streams, and other small bodies of fresh water. Its biotic and abiotic elements interact, determining ultimately the flow of energy and nutrients through the system and the types and kinds of its biomass.

Within an ecosystem, the so-called keystone species plays a decisive role in determining biological diversity. Its removal or extinction would mean that other species in the community could rapidly decline or become extinct on the one hand, or dramatically increase on the other. Sometimes, species once excluded by the keystone species can establish themselves in the community, thereby changing its structure even further. The elephant (or other large herbivores like the rhinoceros) is acknowledged as such a key player in the African savannas, giving them the character they possess.

Another startling instance of the impact of a keystone species is the sea otter (*Enhydra lutris*). It was once an abundant species along the western coast of North America from Alaska to southern California until it was hunted to near extinction toward the end of the 19th century. With the disappearance of the sea otter, the abundant kelp forests also disappeared. In their place exploded the sea urchins whose main predator had been the sea otters. The sea urchins devoured most of the kelp and other seaweeds. The near-shore ocean floor was reduced to "sea-urchin barrens." Following the restoration of the sea otter, the sea urchin population declined, the kelp grew back, and other algae returned, bringing in tow squid, fishes, crustaceans, and even whales to the shores.

Studies of keystone species and their impact upon their ecosystems and communities enable ecologists to have certain insights into how faunas and floras assemble themselves. They have found that, as a rule, in the absence of a competitor, the species will expand its range—this is called ecological release, and an instance of it involves the Cocos Island finch (*Pinaroloxias inornata*). This finch shares 47 square kilometers of land (580 km northeast of the Galapagos) with only three other species of landbirds, a cuckoo, a flycatcher, and a yellow warbler. This has enabled it to spread out into multiple habitats. The obverse phenomenon is ecological displacement. In the presence of competition, closely related species yield part of their environment to others in order to survive. In the southern United States, for instance, the native fire ant—*Solenopsis geminata*—retreated to scattered woodland sites after abandoning its own prime sites to an accidentally imported fire ant—*Solenopsis invicta*—from South America. Ecological release and ecological displacement point to the conclusion that even though two species may occupy the same geographical range, they are not necessarily members of the same community or live in close proximity in the same habitat.

Ecological displacement can play a role in speciation through adaptive radiation. At first, the differences between the two closely related populations are merely phenotypic or the results of adapting to the environment, not genetic. But over generations, these traits might become part of genetic inheritance, ultimately functioning as mechanisms to ensure reproductive isolation, giving rise to two different species.

Although predation is commonly regarded as a force undermining the prey species, evidence to the contrary also exists. The starfish (*Pisaster ochraceus*) is the main predator of mollusks, including mussels, limpets, and chitons, living in rocky tidal waters, as well as of barnacles. In one case, in areas where the starfish were found, 15 species of mollusks and barnacles also existed. But when the keystone species was removed, the number of mollusk and barnacle species went down to 8. The outcome is explained as follows: in the absence of the starfish as their main predator, some of the mollusks and barnacles exploded and crowded out 7 others. In other words, these others have more to fear from their competitors than from their predator, whose presence guarantees more biological diversity than its absence.

Symbiosis is another ecological phenomenon which leads to species diversity. One form of symbiosis is parasitism. The parasite is a kind of predator which does not kill the prey outright, but ensures that its host survives, not only to support its own population, but also to support other species. The human, left to its own devices, is host to several different species of lice, (human) fleas, numerous kinds of worms, fungi, bacteria, etc. A second form is commensalism—organisms live on the body of another species or in its nest but cause neither harm nor good to the host. Lichens, mosses, and liverworts may be found on the leaves of trees in the tropical rain forests and on the plants that live on the leaves. In turn, tiny organisms like mites, barklice, and springtails may be found on them.

The third form is mutualism, where two species in close ecological relationships benefit each other, such as the protozoans and bacteria living in the hind guts of termites. The termites devour decomposing wood which, however, they cannot digest. They need the microorganisms in their hind guts to digest the wood for them. In return they provide the microorganisms not only with a home but also with a steady intake of nutrients from the wood. Mutualism is no mere curiosity as it forms the basis of the plant–fungus relationship, without which, in the history of evolution, the higher plants and animals could not possibly have emerged in the first instance or continued to persist after their initial appearance. The majority of plants have fungi in their root systems—the fungi take chemicals, such as phosphorus, from the soil which are essential nutrients for the plants. In return, the plants shelter them and give them their supply of carbohydrates. In some species, the fungi live in the outer root cells of their hosts; in others, they form dense webs around the roots. Without the mycorrhizal fungi, plants would either not flourish or die outright.

IV. THE LOSS AND GAIN OF BIODIVERSITY: NONANTHROPOGENIC CAUSES

This section looks at the loss of biodiversity when it occurs without human intervention, and then at the recovery of biodiversity after catastrophic periods of loss. But first a brief word about the history of biological diversity is in order.

A. History of Biodiversity

Three billion years ago there was no life on the land surface of Earth since the conditions were altogether unfavorable for its emergence—the ozone was missing in the stratosphere and the oxygen in the atmosphere was too thin. However, in the water things were different. Microorganisms, mainly prokaryotes whose cells do not have a clearly defined nucleus and lack other forms of cell structural complexity typical of the higher organisms, were able to survive, shielded from the lethal ultraviolet rays which descended on the land. These formed microbial mats, one of the most primitive ecosystems on Earth, made up mainly of single-celled prokaryotic organisms (which were close to modern cyanobacteria, also called blue-green algae). But from such modest beginnings, about 1.8 billion years ago, came eukaryotic organisms whose DNA was enveloped by nuclear membranes and whose cells contained mitochondria (the powerhouses of the cell, so to speak) and organelles. These soon evolved from single-celled to more complex multicelled organisms. Then in the Cambrian period, some 540 to 500 million years ago, an explosion of life-forms took place, leading to the emergence of the major adaptive types that still exist today. However, the fossil evidence, such as the Burgess Shale of British Columbia, shows that some of these forms soon died out, seemingly as nature's failed experiments.

In this critical period, animals also increased in size as atmospheric oxygen nearly reached the present-day level of 21% and a sufficiently strong ozone layer was established to shield the emerging land organisms from lethal shortwave radiation. Some 450 million years ago, during the late Ordovician period, the first vascular plants appeared, followed by invertebrate animals, with spiders, insects, mites, and centipedes forming the pioneer corp. The amphibians next emerged, followed by the land vertebrates, giving rise to the Age of Reptiles, succeeded in turn by the Age of Mammals. In short, in spite of occasional mass global extinctions, biological diversity has increased over geological time, and life-forms, on the whole, have evolved from the simple to the more complex in terms of body size, behavioral patterns, brain power, social organization, and the ability to control the environment with increasing precision.

However, it remains true that in over 550 million years of evolution, more than 99% of all species which have ever lived during each of the periods of the Phanerozoic eon have become extinct. But this near total extinction has not undermined biodiversity in the long run, as even larger numbers of species have emerged from their successful descendants. For instance, in the sequence of archaic amphibians in the Paleozoic to the dinosaurs of the Mesozoic period, the survival rate was 1 in 2000 species. Yet in spite of this low rate, the Age of Reptiles was an age of flourishing biodiversity. To take another example, when one compares the known arthropods in the Cambrian fossils with living arthropods, it is not obvious that the former exceeds the latter. And since the Cambrian explosion, there has been another great rise in biodiversity in the last 100 million years.

B. Catastrophic Loss in Biodiversity

In the last 500 million years or so, five major global extinctions have been known to exist—the Ordovician (440 million years ago), the Devonian (365 million years ago), the Permian (245 million years ago), the Triassic (210 million years ago), and the latest, the Cretaceous (65 million years ago). On top of these indisputable catastrophes, there have also been other relatively minor but still significant episodes in biodiversity loss.

With regard to the four earliest major catastrophes, dramatic global cooling is speculated to have been the cause, extinguishing many species and forcing others to retreat to less hospitable habitats, thus rendering them more susceptible to extinction from yet other causes. But as to what caused the cooling in the first place, there is as yet no consensual answer, although continental drift has been speculated.

The last of the five major catastrophes, though not the biggest, has attracted the most attention in recent years. This is the K-T extinction striding the boundary between the Cretaceous period (the youngest of the Mesozoic periods) and the Tertiary Period (the oldest of the Cenozoic periods), and which brought the Age of Reptiles to a close. One view holds that a large meteorite hit Earth, causing effects comparable to those postulated for the nuclear winter scenario. A contesting theory blames it on volcanic eruptions. Both have strengths and weaknesses given the evidence so far available. However, it is not inconceivable that both accounts may be correct. A gigantic meteorite did hit Earth, triggering volcanic eruptions, or perhaps volcanic activity happened independently but coincided with, or was followed by, a meteorite strike.

C. Regaining Biodiversity

After each of these five catastrophes, biodiversity eventually recovered to the extent which obtained before each crisis. A full recovery for the Ordovician took 25 million, the Devonian 30 million, the Permian and Triassic (taken together since they were close in time) 100 million, and the Cretaceous 20 million years. Nature did make good its loss but took 4 to 40 times longer than the average clade longevity of mammals, to which *Homo sapiens* belongs, which varies from 0.5 million to 5 million years (a clade is composed of the species and all its descendants from the time the species first fully emerged to the disappearance of the last of its descendants).

How did nature make good its loss within the last 100 million years? No complete answer exists, but part of it, at least, would include the following:

1. Species formation was optimal following the changes in the continental land masses. In the late Paleozoic era, a single supercontinent, Pangea, existed. But by the early Mesozoic, it had fragmented into two major continents, Laurasia to the north and Gondwana

to the south, with India drifting off as a separate fragment but moving steadily northward toward the Himalayan region. By the late Mesozoic, about 100 million years ago, the modern continents were formed, each isolated from the other by oceans, enhancing speciation *via* geographical isolation. As the amount of coastline increased, hospitable habitats including shallow bays for inshore bottom-dwelling organisms also increased. Both land and marine organisms flourished.

2. The emergence of tropical rain forests also was a factor. Ecologists have lighted upon what is called the latitudinal diversity gradient—species increase in number as one moves from the poles to the equator. In areas of roughly equal size, Greenland has 56 bird species, Labrador 81, Newfoundland 118, New York State 195, Guatemala 469, and Colombia 1525. Vascular plants, which include flowering plants, ferns, club mosses, horsetails, and others, and which make up 99% of land vegetation, are another example of this general principle. Of the 250,000 species known, 170,000, or 68%, are found in the tropics and subtropics. Yet another impressive statistic is that in 10 selected hectare plots in Borneo alone, 1000 species have been found, compared with 700 endemic species in the whole of the United States of America and Canada.

The same latitudinal trend obtains in shallow marine environments, with diversity increasing toward the tropics, eventually concentrating in the coral reefs, which may be regarded as the marine analogue of tropical rain forests. But rich as tropical marine life may be, it could not be said to exceed the biodiversity of the rain forests themselves—the insects alone would outdo the life-forms in coral reefs.

The latitudinal diversity gradient itself may be explained in terms of the Energy–Stability–Area Theory of Biodiverstiy which says that the more stable the climate in its seasonal fluctuations, the greater the diversity; the more solar energy available, the greater the diversity; and the larger the area, the greater the diversity. The tropics score high on each of these three biomass-enhancing scales.

Take a closer look at the first element. In temperate and especially polar regions, fauna and flora have to put up with vast seasonal fluctuations in temperature. In the winter, some of them have to hibernate, move down the mountain slope, migrate like birds to much warmer climes thousands of miles away, or shed their leaves. They have to adapt to a wide range of physical and biological constraints. Their geographial range, as a result, increases as well. This yields Rapaport's rule: the ranges of particular species contract as one travels closer to the equator or from the top of mountains down their sides. Furthermore, the more stable the climate all year long, the easier it is for more species to specialize and to exploit any niche available no matter how small. In other words, every possible niche will be occupied. In addition, a more even climate together with plenty of solar energy can support many larger life-forms than can a colder one. Smaller organisms find it possible to live on larger ones. For instance, tropical trees support lianas and epiphytes, which in turn are a source of food and shelter to many other plants and animals alike.

V. THE LOSS OF BIODIVERSITY: ANTHROPOGENIC CAUSES

The loss of biodiversity in this context may be looked at under five headings: hunting and harvesting; the pressure of population growth; habitat destruction and fragmentation; pollution and atmospheric and climatic change; and the introduction of exotics. But before doing that, two related issues need to be briefly addressed.

The first concerns the rate of species extinction through human impact. Until human appearance, it is estimated that 1 organism became extinct per 1000 years. But since 1600, roughly 400 years, over 1000 species have become extinct. And since 1960 as many as 1000 are lost per year. Some experts predict that by the end of the century 1 will be lost each hour; however, an authority like E. O. Wilson regards that to be on the low side and predicts 3 per hour, relying, in his judgment, even on cautious parameters. However, determining species extinction with any degree of accuracy is fraught with problems. Suffice it to say that given the evidence, the community of biologists agrees that the ongoing loss of biodiversity has accelerated alarmingly, particularly through habitat destruction and fragmentation brought on by pressure from human population growth.

The second issue is a methodological matter—should a species or taxon be assumed to be extant unless proved extinct, or should it be assumed to be extinct unless proved extant? While the former assumption may be appropriate for species or taxa which are well studied, understood, and regularly monitored, the latter may be said to be more suitable when these conditions do not obtain. According to the first assumption, in a recent estimate 1 bird species is said to be extinct in the Solomon Islands; yet according to the second, up to 12 species may be extinct or endangered.

A. Hunting and Harvesting

Overhunting in the past did exist—for instance, evidence in the Americas shows, in spite of the counterexplanation in terms of climatic change, that since humans arrived there during the Late Pleistocene, an estimated 45 of 120 genera (38%) of South American mammals had become extinct by about 15,000 years ago. This amounts to an extinction rate of 150 genera per million years. Of North American land mammals, 32 of 114 genera (28%) were lost. This amounts to an extinction rate of 46 genera per million years. Today overhunting and overharvesting continue, but now it is aided and abetted by more efficient technology. Animals are hunted for their bones, shells, furs, and skins, and as sources of food and drugs—some varieties of whales, rhinoceroses, and elephants, for instance, are near extinction. Plants are collected mainly for drugs; however, some are endangered as they are seen as exotic collector's items.

B. Pressure of Population Growth

Humans began their history as hunters and gatherers. As they increased in numbers, they extended their hunting grounds. When later they became sedentary cultivators, they slashed and burned vegetation for agriculture, cleared forests for houses and homesteads, and turned more and more virgin lands into permanent farmlands.

It is well to bear in mind that (human) population growth is exponential. The following figures bear out this point admirably:

Population growth	Date	Number of years
from 0.75 to 1.6 billion	1750–1900	150
1.60 to 3.3 billion	1900–1965	65
3.3 to 7± billion	1965–2000	35

To put things minimally, all these people have to be housed, fed, watered, and clothed, which can only be achieved at the cost of habitat destruction and fragmentation.

C. Habitat Destruction and Fragmentation

One need cite only two recent examples of vast habitat destruction to illustrate the point. Tropical forests in Central America have been converted into ecologically unsustainable ranches to feed the North American hamburger demand. The Amazonian forests in Brazil are primarily being opened up for mining—mines themselves, as well as the highways which provide the infrastructure for such an activity, destroy the forests.

Fragmentation renders certain sorts of species especially vulnerable, namely, large land mammals, particularly those with very low population densities and large individual ranges such as the puma and the jaguar. Such species find it difficult to survive in refuges, even relatively large ones. Species of large organisms are more susceptible to extinction than small ones because their populations are smaller and hence are less capable of rapid recovery. On the other hand, ectothermic ("cold-blooded") animals, with lower metabolic rates and long periods of inactivity, would be less susceptible to habitat fragmentation and environmental stress than endotherms ("warm-blooded" animals), whose higher metabolic rates and continuous activity render them more vulnerable to habitat adversities.

At first sight it may appear that conditions favorable to extinction, such as habitat fragmentation, may also compensate by being the stimulus for few speciation. Geographical isolation, we have seen, is one standard way of speciation. However, habitat fragmentation caused by contemporary humans are unfavorable to speciation for the following reasons: (a) the refuges may not be large enough, especially those on land; and (b) moreover, as these refuges are likely to shrink rather than expand, population expansion of the relict species is unlikely. In turn, when a population is constant or contracting rather than expanding, there is insufficient genetic variation to sustain the basis for successful selection of genetic material for species formation.

D. Pollution, Atmospheric Imbalance, and Climate Change

Again only two examples need suffice. The first concerns the destruction of the ozone layer in the stratosphere by chlorofluorocarbon (CFC) gases (a pollutant), meaning that more ultraviolet rays from the Sun enter Earth's atmosphere. An increase of such rays, among other effects, could stress species of phytoplankton and zooplankton. These microorganisms, existing in their billions spread over vast areas of the ocean, are the beginnings of the complex marine food chain. When these become scarce or extinct, so will the animals which eat them, and others higher up the chain which in turn eat these will then be endangered. Their endangerment might also upset geochemical cycles. Recent evidence in favor of this hypothesis comes from a detailed geochemical analysis of sedimentation at the time of the K-T extinction.

The second example is the so-called greenhouse effect caused by gases like carbon dioxide, CFCs, and methane which trap the heat, preventing it from escaping into space. The best estimate today is that by the year 2020, the global mean temperatures due to man-made greenhouse gas emissions will be 1.8°C above pre-industrial temperatures, with a probable range between 1.3 and 2.5°C, and by the year 2070, 3.5°C within a range between 2.4 and 5.1°C.

The threat to biodiversity posed by the predicted onset of climatic change could occur in several ways:

(1) The rise in sea level owing to the increased melting of glaciers and ice could cause the extinction of species and ecosystems in low-lying areas.

(2) The change would affect different species somewhat differently, but there would be a general displacement of species from lower altitudes and latitudes to higher ones. The displaced ones would be vulnerable to extinction as they would be faced with the difficulty of finding potential habitats at a time when predicted change is at its greatest.

(3) Changes in climate and atmospheric carbon dioxide concentrations are likely to affect rates of photosynthesis and respiration. Plants on land could in theory use up the increasing atmospheric carbon, although this response would vary with species and might decrease with time. Should the anthropogenic output of carbon and other greenhouse gases continue unhindered, then over time this could conceivably so alter the composition of Earth's atmosphere as to render it ultimately no longer supportive of life. That atmosphere preserves a constant mix of 0.03% carbon dioxide, 1.7 ppm methane, 21% oxygen, and 79% nitrogen, with a surface temperature of 13°C. By comparison, planets like Venus and Mars which have no life have no methane but atmospheres of, respectively, 96.5 and 95% carbon dioxide, 3.5 and 2.7% nitrogen, a mere trace of 0.13% oxygen, and surface temperatures of 459 and −53°C. According to the Gaia hypothesis, life itself contributes to the maintenance of Earth's atmosphere. But if human activities can have effects which might upset that homeostasis or balance, then life as we know it today could in turn be affected.

E. Introduction of Exotics

Two of the more potent exotics imported by human colonists which have wiped out endemic species have been rats and goats. Exotic animals also carry with them diseases against which native organisms have no defense. One recent spectacular extinction episode in-volves the destruction of the cichlid fishes of Lake Victoria. In 1959, the then British colonists brought in the Nile perch as a game fish. In 1985, biologists who studied the case predicted that eventually more than half of 300 odd endemic species would be eliminated by the newcomer. Furthermore, it affects the whole ecosystem—algae blooms proliferate as the algae-eating cichlids decrease, causing oxygen to deplete in the deeper waters as they decompose, thereby further accelerating the decline of not only cichlids but also crustaceans and other organisms.

F. The Sixth Ecocatastrophe?

It is commonly said that such anthropogenic changes as these could amount to the sixth ecocatastrophe in Earth's history. As we have seen, in the past, following large-scale extinctions, full recovery of biodiversity did take place, but only after a minimum interval of 20 million years; conditions encouraging recovery then obtained, thus making a significant difference to the eventual outcome. Also there were no humans then. All species are mortal; humankind could well be extinct in another 900,000 years or so. However, it is not quite like other species, as it has increasingly powerful technologies which could have the effect of making itself an exception to the rule of species mortality.

But in the foreseeable future, one very crucial condition which could affect the further loss and possible recovery of biodiversity is the unavailability of large spaces with few humans in them. Humans as a primate group are 100 times more populous than any other land mammal of similar size in the history of evolution. The human species consumes between 20 and 40% of the solar energy captured by land plants alone. Another unfavorable condition affecting biodiversity loss and possible recovery is that the tropical rain forests which abound in biological abundance are being relentlessly destroyed. In 1979, they were down to 56% of their historic cover; by 1989 that figure had dropped to slightly less than 50%, the rain forests having been reduced to about 8 million square kilometers. In 1989, the rate of destruction was about 142,000 square kilometers a year. If the same rate were to continue, they would all be destroyed roughly within 50 years. But, of course, these are only projected trends which might or might not materialize as the assumptions behind them might no longer obtain, and the future remains essentially open and uncertain.

VI. THE VALUE OF BIODIVERSITY

Philosophically speaking, two major axes need to be identified in a discussion concerning the value of biodiversity—instrumental–intrinsic value on the one hand and individualism–holism on the other. Each is an oppositional spectrum; i.e., instrumental value is defined as the antonym of intrinsic value, and individualism as that of holism.

Instrumental and intrinsic values are normally elucidated, respectively, in terms of "for the sake of" and "for its own sake." An object is instrumentally valuable to an agent if it serves as a means for achieving the agent's end; an agent is intrinsically valuable if it does not merely exist to serve the ends of other agents, but is an end in itself. A dominant tradition in Western philosophy with roots going back to ancient Greek thought holds that only humans are intrinsically valuable because they alone are beings which are rational, possess not only consciousness but self-consciousness, entertain intentions and purposes, or possess language. All other natural nonhuman beings, therefore, have only instrumental value and serve merely as means to such human projects or ends. This view is commonly referred to as anthropocentrism (that humankind is the sole locus of intrinsic value), in contrast to nonanthropocentrism, which argues that nature or at least biotic nature has intrinsic value independent of human purposes and goals.

While the previous axis raises an issue pertaining to the theory of value, the other (individualism–holism) is about an ontological matter. In this context, individualism may be understood to hold that only the individual organism which is skin-bound, easily delimitable and locatable in time and space, and monocentered is real and exists. The species which lacks these attributes is not real and cannot be said to exist, at least in the same way as individual organisms are said to be real and exist. The species is simply a convenient device for referring to a collection of individual organisms which happen to have certain features in common while also displaying differences between them—this exemplifies the nominalist species concept referred to in Section I.A. Holism denies this—the species is more than simply the aggregation of its members. Certain things which hold true of a species do not hold true of its individual members and vice versa. For instance, the average life span of a million years holds true for a mammalian species but not for any member of any one such species; similarly, a form of mental life holds true for each individual lion but not for the species of lion. Individualism seems to imply that until the demise of the last individual organism, the species itself is not extinct—in other words, the limiting case of a species of one member is not unintelligible since the species is no more than the sum of its members.

On the other hand, holism favors the view that the extinction of the species in the majority of cases may be imminent or have arrived well before the expiration of its last surviving member—the death of Martha, the last passenger pigeon, in September 1914 in the Cincinnati Zoo was neither here nor there as far as the species to which she belonged was concerned. The species can clearly survive several deaths of its individual members; however, it may be said to be endangered should its population fall below a certain critical number, the actual number varying according to the species in question and thus unable to be laid down a priori. (To further clarify, one can say that a sexually reproductive species is extinct when it can no longer continue to reproduce, and nonexistent when its last member has died. In the case of nonsexually reproductive species, extinction and nonexistence would neatly coincide.)

Another issue which has implication for environmental policy making lies in the charge of "environmental fascism" (associated with Regan) made against holism as it appears to condone sacrificing the individual (higher) mammals, as in culling some of them, in order to save the species to which they belong—to Regan, this is anathema as it violates the rights of such individual mammals to life, thereby treating them merely as means to the end of saving their species and not as ends unto themselves. It follows, then, that holism appears to sit better with a so-called conservation ethic than individualism—while the latter condemns, the former morally permits policies like culling to save either the species to which the targeted animals belong, or some other species, or the ecosystem of which their species is a part.

The two major oppositional axes together yield four different positions:

(a) *Anthropocentric individualism.* Anyone who holds that only individual humans are intrinsically valuable because they are rational, possess self-consciousness, or use language, while nonhuman individuals only have instrumental value for humans, is representative of this position. This is the position which probably underpins the so-called dominant tradition in Western philosophical thought. The remaining three challenge it to a greater or lesser extent. These have been arranged below in an ascending order of "radicalness," presupposing that a challenge to anthropocentrism is more radical than one to individualism. On the other hand, if the challenge to individualism is taken to be more fundamental, then (b) and (c) should be reversed.

(b) *Anthropocentric holism.* Bryan Norton could be said to be a candidate, although he tends to play down theoretical differences between players in the environmentalist arena.

(c) *Nonanthropocentric individualism.* Either Tom Regan, Peter Singer, or Paul Taylor could be said to be representative.

(d) *Nonanthropocentric holism.* Holmes Rolston could be representative.

On the whole, it may be fair to say that of the four positions delineated, (b) and (d) are in practice the most concerned with the value of biodiversity and the most hospitable for arguing for its protection in the long run. Consensus over holism may therefore turn out in this context to be more crucial than dissension along the intrinsic–instrumental value axis. Position (a) is the least concerned with the value of biodiversity—since nonhuman individual organisms and the species to which they belong are only of instrumental value to (individual) humans, strictly speaking (provided that technology is up to the task, and biotechnology appears to promise much on this score), it matters not whether species exist so long as whatever properties deemed to have value for human beings in nonhuman individuals and species could be retrieved before they die or go extinct. Position (c) could favor the protection and saving of species indirectly since the saving of individual organisms in certain contexts may also lead to the saving of the species themselves even if, on its understanding, species themselves are not morally considerable; neither is this position necessarily averse to the protection of habitats, as such protection may turn out to be an effective way of saving its inhabitants. For instance, Peter Singer (with Paola Cavalieri as collaborator) has come out recently in favor of putting aside some portion of the ancestral habitats of the great apes as "their homeland," so to speak, so that our most closely related cousins on the evolutionary scale can pursue their own lives, more or less, unmolested by us.

A. Anthropocentric Perspective

In general, for anthropocentrism, whether from an individualist or holist stance, biodiversity may be considered to be valuable to humankind in the following ways:

1. Strong instrumentalism. Biotic nature is a storehouse of potential raw resources such as food, fibers, and medicine—the so-called silo argument. These resources are turned into commodities whose value can be measured in monetary terms as part of the cost of production and to generate profits. In this way, the biota contributes to the advancement of human well-being.

2. Weak instrumentalism. This may be divided into two major subvarieties. (a) Biotic nature is considered as a source of amenity value as individual organisms or as parts of ecosystems, habitats, and landscapes, which in turn may be said to (i) give psychological satisfaction or religious/spiritual experience of awe to humans, whether or not these amenities are made to generate monetary value (the cathedral argument), (ii) provide recreational opportunities (the gymnasium argument), or (iii) are a source of aesthetic pleasure (the art gallery argument). (b) Biotic nature is considered to be a provider of services which constitute public/collective goods—the maintenance of biodiversity is a prerequisite for the survival and well-being of future human generations in particular (and indirectly of nonhuman species) by acting as a sink for absorbing waste, for the sustenance of the great geobiochemical and hydrological cycles (the life support system argument).

Strong instrumentalism, also referred to as resource conservation, is part and parcel of economism, including that type of environmental economics which relies solely on cost–benefit analysis, reducing all factors to monetary values. This is a controversial technique which has attracted as many detractors as admirers. To the latter it is (i) as rational a mode for the allocation of scarce resources as could conceivably be devised, and (ii) an objective yardstick, even if crudely monetary. To the former it (i) masks and distorts moral, social, and aesthetic values, turning them into what they are emphatically not, namely, economic/monetary ones (shadow pricing may be understood as a manifestation of this distortion); (ii) attaches differential weight to the preferences of present humans as opposed to those who are not yet here as the future within its theoretical framework necessarily has to be discounted; and (iii) is allied with individualism and encourages reducing biodiversity to mere genetic diversity and even nucleotide diversity—scouting the world for potentially useful plants, genes, or DNA sequences, and then storing these in a seed/gene bank or cryotorium, tends to be regarded as the most economic and, therefore, ideal solution to the perceived loss of biodiversity.

Weak instrumentalism in its first sense (a), also referred to as resource preservation, implies a far richer conception of human well-being than the crudely materialistic one underpinning strong instrumentalism. According to it, human flourishing includes what John

Stuart Mill may call the higher pleasures of the cognitive and emotive faculties. Cherishing the biota for such ends is compatible with its preservation in the form of not only individual organisms, but also as species, part of ecosystems, and landscapes. For instance, the bald eagle as a potent cultural symbol of American statehood and nationalism would demand saving not only the individual birds, but also the species itself and the habitat within which the species could thrive, rather than permitting its extinction through destruction of its habitat while simply preserving the individual birds in a zoo or its DNA sequences in some cryotorium.

Weak instrumentalism in terms of the second, life support argument (b), conjoined with holism, is most obviously implicated in the indirect saving of species and their ecosystems as part of the measures to preserve biospheric integrity ultimately for humankind. In a nutshell, it argues that while the single loss of any one species would not necessarily undermine biospheric integrity, the cumulative loss of many species within a relatively short time (when the replacement rate is far below the extinction rate) could produce an alarming downward spiral effect, as diversity begets diversity, while diminutions in diversity beget further diminutions. While it is true that the extinction by humankind of any one particular species (be it the passenger pigeon or the dodo) has not resulted in a major disaster, it does not necessarily follow that the cascading effect of biodiversity loss should be so sanguinely overlooked since its eventual outcome may be of great consequence, namely, the extinction of the human species itself. This kind of environmental risk constitutes a "zero–infinity dilemma." (Byran Norton is most closely associated with this outlook.)

B. Nonanthropocentric Perspective

Nonanthropocentrism holds that nonhumans may share the intrinsic value that humans have assigned themselves, and as such, humans may not treat nonhumans solely as means to their own ends, that is, purely instrumentally.

Nonanthropocentrists, as earlier shown, are divided into two types: (a) those who maintain that only the individual organism (such as the mammals which are subjects-of-a-life in the case of Tom Regan, those which are sentient in the case of Peter Singer, or all plants and animals which are each a teleological center of life in the case of Paul Taylor) is the locus of intrinsic value; and (b) those (such as Holmes Rolston) who hold that species and ecosystems may also be the loci of such a value.

As commented on earlier, valuing biodiversity is more intimately linked with the latter than with the former group, as the latter is concerned not simply with individual organisms as such but with the emergence and existence of species, with their ecological niches and relationships, and, therefore, with the continuance of natural evolutionary processes themselves, not merely with the extant products of such processes. But as we have also indicated, the individualist wing of nonanthropocentrism can commit itself to the indirect saving of biodiversity and even of the habitats in which the diverse species are embedded.

However, as nonanthropocentric holism poses the most radical challenge to the still presiding paradigm of anthropocentric individualism in Western thought, it is also perceived, philosophically speaking, as the most recalcitrant to defend. Reasons (some of which have been hinted at already *en passant*) include the following:

1. The appeal to particular conceptions of intrinsic value. The individualist approach singles out attributes such as sentience or mental life as being intrinsically valuable states of affairs which, obviously, only individual organisms can possess. The individual lion is sentient, a rights bearer or a teleological center of life, but the species "lion" cannot satisfy any of these criteria and hence cannot be a locus of intrinsic value. As such the individual organism may be morally considerable but not the species.

2. The appeal to empiricism. The individualist approach tacitly appeals to certain firmly held empiricist assumptions, one of which is that an entity is real if and only if it is directly observable and confrontable. As we have seen, the individual lion is monocentered and skin-bound; it is directly observable and confrontable. You can bump into it, hear it roar, or photograph it. It is, therefore, real. However, the species "lion" is neither directly confrontable nor observable. It is not monocentered and is not skin-bound. The term "species of lion" does not refer to any real entity; it is a shorthand mnemonic for referring to a mere collection of individual lions.

3. The appeal against immutable essences. It is assumed that species implies immutable essences, but this is an assumption which evolutionary biology has put to rest.

4. The appeal to authority. Darwin is cited as a biologist who upholds points (2) and (3). For him, only individual organisms exist and are real. The term "species," as already observed, is simply an arbitrary conve-

nient device to refer to individuals which closely resemble one another.

The holist rebuttal includes the following:

1. Point (3) in the previous list is an irrelevancy. Biologists who subscribe to the "reality" of species are not committed to the pre-Darwinian notion of immutable essences. The same can be said for point (4)—as earlier observed, Darwin was not primarily concerned with the phenomenon of speciation, and the biological-species concept was not available to him.

2. Direct observation and confrontability as implied in the paradigmatic meeting of an individual lion are not necessarily conditions for the status of reality—indirect, mediated observation also counts. Furthermore, other criteria of reality also obtain—as Rolston maintains, whatever produces an effect is real. A hungry lion is likely to pounce upon and devour a human; a hungry sheep is not. To understand the difference in effect, one must invoke species characteristics and differences between the lion and the sheep, not simply the individual differences between the particular individual lion and the particular individual sheep.

3. The nonanthropocentric individualist conceptions of what is intrinsically valuable and what forms the basis for moral considerability are, in turn, overrestrictive and may turn out to be just as arbitrary as the traditional anthropocentric conception. Sentientism and mental life include nonhuman mammals in their respective expanding moral circles but draw the line either at crustaceans or birds. It is true that all plants and all animals are teleological centers of life, but all three conceptions rule out species as possible loci of intrinsic value. However, if species are not understood mystically, a necessary condition for a species existing is that individual members must also exist (subject to some of the qualifications noted earlier), and if each of these members possesses intrinsic value, then it appears *prima facie* unreasonable to conclude that the species to which they belong necessarily is not also intrinsically valuable. For a start, if the species were to become extinct, there would eventually be no more intrinsically valuable members.

What naturally reproduces the valuable is itself valuable—the relationship between the reproducer of valuable entities and the entities themselves should not, however, be construed in terms of the usual means–end relationship, where the means is regarded as of mere instrumental value to the intrinsically valuable end that is pursued. The nearest helpful analogy hinting at an alternative characterization of such a relationship may be given by that between the craftsman's mold and the individual copies made from it. If each of the latter turns out to be aesthetically valuable, it is odd to perceive the former itself as of no aesthetic worth and only instrumentally valuable in the production of individually aesthetically valuable products. But the relationship between the mold and the individual copies is not that between a coffee machine and the cups of coffee it produces. The coffee machine is not meant to taste or smell like the coffee it makes, whereas the mold is meant to reproduce copies bearing the qualities it itself possesses. The relationship is more intimate than and transcends the merely technical one between a machine and its products.

The same is true of the relationship between individual organisms and the species to which they belong. One should distinguish between "producing" and "reproducing"—the former embodies instrumental rationality whereas the latter goes beyond that and is about the transmission of characteristics from one entity—a concrete material entity in the case of the mold, or an abstract entity in the case of the species—to those entities instantiating it, be these artifacts or individual organisms. However, in the case of the mold reproducing copies of the artifact, the intention is not to produce deviations from the mold among the copies, although sometimes unwitting variations could enhance the quality of the copies in question. In the case of naturally occurring reproductions, variations spontaneously occur, either through mutations which bring about a change in the genotype of the individual organism or through the random permutation of genetic material passed on by the parental organisms in the case of sexually reproducing ones.

Furthermore, while one might dispute that the relationship between the mold and its individual copies illustrates the type–token distinction, that between the species and the individual organisms unproblematically exemplifies the distinction. The individual organism as an instantiation of the species, one of its temporary loci, is a token of the type, that is, the species. As Wollheim has pointed out in the case of the type–token ontology, unlike that of universals and particulars, the properties which tokens have in virtue of being tokens of that type are transmitted to the type—for instance, the Union Jack is rectangular and colored as all individual Union Jacks which are tokens are rectangular and colored, while redness itself, the universal, cannot be colored, although all particular instances of red necessarily are colored (R. Wollheim, 1980. *Art and Its Objects*, 2nd ed. Cambridge Univ. Press, Cambridge). Individual organisms as temporary loci and tokens of the historical lineage in displaying intrinsic value are really at the same time embodiments of the intrinsic value of the historical lineage, the type, itself.

C. Humans and Biotic Kinship

Yet another view—advocated by James Baird Callicott—emphasizes the biotic kinship and continuity of humans with nonhuman organisms, though it may be held in conjunction with either the anthropocentric or the nonanthropocentric standpoint. It appeals to bioempathy on the part of humankind for the rest of the biota. This view, when understood as an empirical thesis, is particularly plausible when one bears in mind charismatic animals like the tiger, the panda, and the condor, but is presumably less plausible when one thinks of species of insects, which, after all, constitute the major components of biological diversity in the Animal kingdom. Humans might also find it difficult to empathize with plants, not to mention microorganisms. Alternatively, held as a prescriptive thesis, it begs the very question of why humankind ought to empathize with the rest of Earth's biota.

D. Transformative Values

Bryan Norton (from the standpoint of anthropocentric holism) has proposed yet another justification for the saving of biodiversity apart from merely satisfying human demands now or in the future. He distinguishes between two kinds of human demand values—mere declared preferences as opposed to "correctly identified and weighted" ones. The former may not be worthy of satisfaction for a variety of reasons, such as they are too materialistic or overly consumptive; the latter permits a criticism of such preferences, taking into account that their satisfaction has the overall impact of endangering species. These adjusted normative preferences embody what he calls transformative values. Such values, if internalized, would have the effect of changing the world from one in which human economic activities by and large imperil biodiversity to one in which humans live more in harmony with the workings of nature, so to speak. Such harmonious living is based upon realizing the following complexities: (a) humankind, in spite of its powerful technologies, is dependent on both biotic and abiotic nature; (b) the myriad relationships among the biotic as well as between the biotic and the abiotic are themselves complex and intricate, and we do not really know much about them; and (c) caution and humility in intervening and manipulat-

ing such complex systems are called for in light of inadequate knowledge and ensuing unintended consequences attendant upon such intervention and manipulation.

Transformative values are anthropocentric values. As such, in Norton's view, they are philosophically easier to defend than nonanthropocentric ones. However, a nagging doubt remains among the critics of anthropocentrism. On Norton's view, humans only cherish biodiversity because they fear for their own survival and that of their posterity. However, the biodiversity (apart from domesticated biota) that exists today, in the main, is a naturally occurring biodiversity. But a new technology has been in place for the last 20 years or so, namely, biotechnology, which can in principle produce a genetically engineered biodiversity. Suppose these substitute species could be put in place without jeopardizing the fate of humankind now or in the future. Norton, presumably, would and could have no objection to such a technological possibility. Yet to those who wish to go beyond anthropocentric values, such genetically engineered biodiversity is objectionable in principle. However, Norton would not be able to make sense of such ontological anxiety.

E. Biodiversity and Deep Ecology

The notion of biospherical or biocentric egalitarianism is part of Arne Naess's ecology program. But the prefix "bio-" does not imply biological life since deep ecology thinkers include under "life" individual organisms, species, populations, habitats, abiotic nature in the form of rivers and mountains, and all human and even nonhuman cultures. Furthermore, it is not primarily interested in advancing the notion of intrinsic value in nonhuman nature as philosophically understood. It is more concerned with transforming the biographical self into the so-called ecological self through an expansion of consciousness—such a self sees itself as the rain forest rather than the forest (whether as individual organisms, species, rocks, water, micro habitats, or the entire ecosystem) as some other entity existing outside it which it sees fit to protect or save because this entity possesses intrinsic value. The ecological self, through self-realization, identifies itself with individual lions as well as with the species lion. The implication of the deep ecology outlook for environmental policy making in the context of saving biodiversity may be spelled out as follows: Let all species (and individual organisms) flourish, subject, however, to humans being able to satisfy their basic needs. However, this invites the criticism that the qualifying clause is problematic as it begs the question of what constitutes satisfying basic human needs.

As such, deep ecology may be seen as part of the postmodernist tendency to reject human–nature dualism—humans are not apart, but part of nature. Three objections may be raised: (a) To say, "I am the rain forest," is at worst mystical. At best it is reductionist since what I and the rain forest share in common are probably atoms of carbon, nitrogen, etc. (b) It could lead to a form of egoism—in hurting or destroying the rain forest, one is hurting or destroying not the rain forest but really oneself as the ecological self. (c) Ironically, it could even amount to a form of anthropocentrism (an aspect of the thesis that human consciousness is the source of all values) since the consciousness that is being expanded to include nonhuman others is essentially human consciousness, albeit a transformed and expanded one.

F. Anthropogenic and Nonanthropogenic Views

This subsection looks at the relationship between the anthropogenic and the nonanthropogenic view of the extinction of biodiversity. We have seen earlier that there have been five major extinctions in Earth's history and before humankind evolved. The question that then arises is, if nature itself is not aversive to extinction per se, why should extinction of biodiversity by humankind be perceived to be worrying? The worry is only justified if there is a morally significant difference between anthropogenic and nonanthropogenic causes of extinction. Is it really defensible to argue that such a difference exists? The answer to this question depends on the perspective adopted—so-called postmodernism, anthropocentrism, or nonanthropocentrism.

We have already mentioned one strand of postmodern thinking which can be found in deep ecology. Another version of the rejection of human–nature dualism may be found in environmental thinkers who are not associated with deep ecology such as James Baird Callicott (1992. *Hastings Center Rep.* **22**, 16–23). On this view, everything that happens (on Earth) is natural. Therefore, any human impact on the environment is natural—the slums in Chicago are just as natural as the Great Barrier Reef, although the first is fabricated by humans and the second is not. Such a standpoint dissolves the distinction between the anthropogenic and the nonanthropogenic. Furthermore, the worry may also be said to betray a short human-related time span—nature left to its own devices would recover,

although admittedly, taking perhaps millions of years to do so. This then appears to be a quick way of dissolving the worry itself.

However, the route may be too brief. Without falling prey to any version of Cartesian anthropocentrism, a critic could correctly point out that humankind, unlike other species, is uniquely capable of grasping good and evil, as well as intentionally/knowingly destroying what is good or promoting what is evil. This means that it makes sense for humankind to pose the question of whether destruction of other species may amount to destroying something good. Posing such a question implies not so much an arrogant domination of other species as a realization that humankind may have responsibilities or duties to nonhuman others which morally act as constraints upon human activities and their impact on biodiversity.

As for anthropocentrism allied with holism, from such a perspective the extinction of species, though constituting no direct moral loss, nevertheless could have very bad consequences for us—the zero–infinity dilemma, as pointed out by Norton.

Nonanthropocentric individualism could also still regret the bad consequences of anthropogenic extinction of biodiversity, again not as a direct but an indirect moral loss, for the loss of species means ultimately the loss of individual organisms and, therefore, the loss of sentience, mental life, or teleological centers of life, which are each regarded as intrinsically valuable states. To ensure the continuing existence of golden eggs (assumed for the purpose of this argument to be intrinsically rather than merely instrumentally valuable to humankind), one must protect or save the goose that lays them even if the goose itself is not intrinsically valuable.

Nonanthropocentric holism worries because it alone bemoans directly the loss of moral worth, for the anthropogenic extinction of biodiversity amounts not merely to the loss of individual organisms, each intrinsically valuable, but their species, which are themselves also morally considerable. As each species is a unique historical lineage, a loss of a species amounts to the loss of something uniquely intrinsically valuable. From its standpoint, there is a double loss, as tokens and as type, even if in certain contexts it is prepared to condone sacrificing some tokens in order to save their type.

Also See the Following Articles

ANTHROPOCENTRISM • DEEP ECOLOGY • ECOLOGICAL BALANCE • GENETIC RESEARCH • SPECIESISM

Bibliography

Callicott, J. B. (1992). La nature est morte, vive la nature! *Hastings Center Report,* 22, 16–23.

Callicott, J. B. (1989). "In Defense of the Land Ethic: Essays in Environmental Philosophy." State Univ. of New York Press, Albany.

Ehrenfeld, D. (Ed.) (1995). "To Preserve Biodiversity—An Overview." The Society for Conservation Biology and Blackwell Science, Oxford/Cambridge, MA.

Ehrlich, P., and Ehrlich, A. (1981). "Extinction: The Causes and the Consequences of the Disappearance of Species." Random House, New York.

Fox, W. (1990). "Toward a Transpersonal Ecology: Developing New Foundations for Environmentalism." Shambhala, Boston/London.

Hunter, M. L., Jr. (1996). "Fundamentals of Conservation Biology." Blackwell Science. Oxford/Cambridge, MA.

Naess, A. (1987). Self-realization: An ecologial approach to being in the world. *Trumpeter* 4(3), 35–42.

Norton, B. G. (1987). "Why Preserve Natural Variety?" Princeton Univ. Press, Princeton, NJ.

Regan, T. (1983). "The Case for Animal Rights." Univ. of California Press, Berkeley.

Rolston, H., III (1988). "Environmental Ethics: Duties to and Values in the Natural World." Temple Univ. Press, Philadelphia.

Singer, P. (1975). "Animal Liberation: A New Ethics for Our Treatment of Animals." Avon, New York.

Taylor, P. W. (1986). "Respect for Nature: A Theory of Environmental Ethics." Princeton Univ. Press, Princeton, NJ.

Wilson, E. O., Peter, F. M. (Eds.) (1988). "Biodiversity." National Academy Press, Washington, DC.

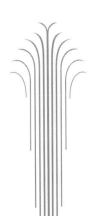

BIOETHICS, OVERVIEW

Raanan Gillon
Imperial College, London University

GLOSSARY

autonomy Literally self-rule, the ability to make decisions for oneself on the basis of deliberation. Self-determination is an alternative term. Respect for people's autonomy, to the extent that this is consistent with equal respect for the autonomy of all affected, is a component of many ethical theories in health care bioethics.

beneficence Acting so as to benefit others—a limited but universal moral obligation in many moral theories, and widely regarded as a fundamental moral obligation in health care bioethics. Acting so as to benefit oneself is also, strictly speaking, beneficence, but, given people's natural self-interested tendency to benefit themselves, self-beneficence is of less ethical interest than beneficence for others. However, in some ethical theories promoting self-beneficence/self-interest is seen as the way to maximize overall welfare.

justice The moral obligation of fairness, common to many moral theories, including much of bioethics.

Essentially justice is about treating people equally in relation to criteria ackowledged to be morally relevant. However, while that much is commonly agreed upon within most theories of ethics and bioethics, when it comes to specifying what the relevant criteria are (for example, treating people equally in relation to their needs, rights, merits and demerits, ability to benefit, or autonomous desires), there is marked disagreement in philosophy, ethics, religion, and politics.

nonmaleficence Not harming others. A moral obligation in many moral theories including much of bioethics. Needs to be taken into account together with beneficence whenever it is intended to benefit others, but is widely accepted as an independent moral obligation even when no obligation or intention to benefit is acknowledged.

person A moral category into which all readers of this encyclopedia will be agreed, by the norms of probably all moral theories, to fall. Persons, or people, owe other persons or people the highest level of moral respect. There is far less agreement about the attributes needed to be a person. Such disagreement is typified in bioethics by major disputes about whether or not human embryos, fetuses, newborn babies, patients who are permanently unconscious, and even brain dead patients on ventilators are persons. Similar disputes arise about whether any non-human animals are persons, and if so which. More theoretical philosophical debate concerns whether or not machines could be developed with the attributes of persons, and about the attributes that life-forms from other planets would need to be persons.

scope of application Even when agreement about moral obligations is achieved, there may remain radical disagreement about their scope or range of application—to whom or to what are the obligations owed? For example, while it may be agreed that there is a universal obligation that we must not unjustly kill each other, the question of what counts as "each other" may be vigorously disputed. While it may be agreed that we have an obligation to respect others' autonomy, there remains diagreement about who counts as autonomous—or sufficiently autonomous to fall within the scope of this obligation. Similarly with distributive justice, even if we accept an obligation to distribute scarce resources justly, who or even what falls within the scope of this obligation? Questions of scope are relevant to many issues in ethics generally and bioethics in particular.

―――――――――――――――――――――

BIOETHICS (as the etymology of its Greek roots implies—*bios* means life and *ethike* ethics) is the study of ethical issues arising in the practice of the biological disciplines. These include medicine; nursing; other health care professions, including veterinary medicine; and medical and other biological or life sciences. Bioethics is "applied ethics" in the sense that it is the study of ethical issues that arise or might be anticipated to arise, in the context of real activities. While medical and other health care ethics are a major component of bioethics, the latter is now widely—though not universally—acknowledged to extend well beyond health care ethics to include not only the ethics of research in the life sciences but also

- Environmental ethics, encompassing such areas as environmental pollution and consideration of the proper relationships between humans, other animals, and the rest of nature.
- Ethical issues of sexuality, reproduction, genetics, and population.
- Various sociopolitical moral issues, including the adverse effects on people's health of unemployment, poverty, unjust discrimination (including sexism and racism), crime, war, and torture.

As well as its breadth of subject matter, bioethics is characterized by the wide variety of people and disciplines actively involved. Apart from the relevant professionals such as doctors, nurses, and life scientists, and

their patients and research subjects, academic disciplines involved in bioethics include moral philosophy, moral theology, and law (perhaps the "big three" disciplines in bioethics); economics; psychology; sociology; anthropology; and history. And of course the public in general, both as individuals and in various interest groupings, and their political representatives increasingly take a direct interest in bioethical issues, as do the media.

I. HISTORICAL NOTES ON BIOETHICS

The term "bioethics" seems to have been invented—or at least first used in print—in 1970 by an American biologist and cancer researcher, Van Rensselaer Potter of the University of Wisconsin in the USA. However, the word was also used, apparently independently, shortly afterward and in a somewhat different sense, by a Dutch fetal physiologist and obstetrician working in Washington, DC, Andre Hellegers, and others who with him founded the Kennedy Institute of Human Reproduction and Bioethics at Georgetown University in 1971. Van Rensselaer used the term to refer to a "new discipline that combines biological knowledge with a knowledge of human value systems" which would build a bridge between the sciences and the humanities, help humanity to survive, and sustain and improve the civilized world. Hellegers and his group, on the other hand, used the term more narrowly to apply to the ethics of medicine and biomedical research—and indeed, in reporting these two different conceptions, Warren Reich, editor of the massive *Encyclopedia of Bioethics,* tells us that when it was first being planned in 1971 it was to have been called the *Encyclopedia of Medical Ethics.*

This division and debate are instructive in various ways about the discipline of bioethics. First, it recalls that a major component of the field of bioethics is medical and other health care ethics. Second, it shows that there is substantive disagreement about how far into what might be called general applied ethics the discipline of bioethics should extend. Third, it indicates the major developments even within the narrower subject of medical ethics that were occurring in the 1960s, in the decade prior to this debate. Before the 1960s the traditional approach to medical ethics, which was then largely limited to ethical issues arising in clinical medical practice, was for doctors in training to be told or even simply to be expected to pick up from the example of their seniors what the ethical norms of professional conduct were. Doctors were rewarded by professional acceptance if they behaved "appropriately" and punished by sanctions ranging from expressed disapproval via reprimands to, at worst, expulsion from the profession if they transgressed these norms.

In the 1960s, to this continuing norm of "professionalization" began to be added other components. The first was the involvement in the previously largely closed world of medicine of "outsiders" such as philosophers, theologians, lawyers, sociologists, and psychologists looking in on the medical profession and offering their expertise and their views. The second was the concomitant beginnings of acceptance within the medical profession that the insights offered from these varying outside perspectives could be helpful in the development of medicine. The third was an increasing realization that medical ethics needed to extend its sphere of interest beyond the clinical encounter into broader issues of social ethics in such contexts as fair and beneficial distribution of health care facilities within societies—areas of direct and necessary concern in countries such as the United Kingdom with their existing national health services—and of potential concern in countries such as the USA with their comparatively poor provision for those who could not pay for health care.

Thus by the end of the 1960s medical ethics itself was beginning to change away from being almost entirely concerned with ethical rules and codes of conduct governing clinicians to also including ethical aspects of health and illness in society. And it was also beginning to accept, however cautiously and tentatively, that people and disciplines other than doctors and medicine could have instructive and useful things to say about the broad subject area of medical ethics. In other words, traditional medical ethics was tentatively beginning to encompass both aspects of the new bioethics: the philosophically more critical, analytic, and multidisciplinary approach to ethical issues arising within the clinical practice of medicine, and the understanding that new developments within medicine and the life sciences were raising ethical issues for society as a whole. In addition, a third strand of bioethics activity was beginning to be acknowledged by some doctors and other health care professionals, notably, a sense of their obligation to become involved, as health care professionals, in trying to remedy social factors that impinged adversely on people's health—whether through lifestyle factors such as unhealthy diet, tobacco smoking, and lack of exercise; environmental pollution and other environmental hazards; overpopulation; or, even more politically contentiously, unemployment, poverty, crime, and warfare in its various forms.

Underlying all of these various strands of bioethics

from its recent origins is a further distinction, sometimes clear and sometimes fuzzy, between bioethics as previously defined as the intellectual activity of study of, reflection on, and inquiry into a range of ethical issues, and bioethics as a reforming activity intended to achieve substantive moral reforms whether at a personal or at a political level (examples might be public exposure of unacceptable health care practices, stronger entrenchment of patients rights, or abolition of nuclear weapons or land mines). While it is probably true that the large majority of people pursuing contemporary bioethics are at least in part motivated by a desire to change the world for the better, there is also a fairly clear divide between those who would do so by the pursuit and promotion of ideas, arguments, and ways of thinking and those who would add to these intellectual activities exhortation, emotional pressure, and political activity at a variety of levels. It is unclear whether the term, "the bioethics movement," which appears occasionally in the literature is intended to apply to both groups of people or more narrowly to the latter group of reformers.

The explosion of interest in medical ethics and bioethics in the 1970s was most marked in the USA where, as well as the Hastings Center (founded in 1969, originally as the Institute of Society Ethics and the Life Sciences, it started its *Hastings Center Report* in 1971) and the Kennedy Institute, founded at Georgetown University in 1971, much academic activity developed in universities and private institutes.

However, although ahead of the field, the USA was not alone in this development, and critical medical ethics activity was also beginning to be widespread if sporadic in Europe. In 1963 in the United Kingdom the multidisciplinary London Medical Group and its successors, the Society for the Study of Medical Ethics and the Institute of Medical Ethics were founded. Starting with discussion groups and study groups in UK medical schools, the Institute founded its *Journal of Medical Ethics* in 1975 and its *Bulletin of Medical Ethics* (subsequently becoming independent of the IME) in 1985. Academic courses in medical and later health care ethics first started in 1978 and began to flourish in the 1980s. Similar developments in the 1970s occurred in the Netherlands and other Benelux countries and in the Nordic countries. Development of critical medical ethics arose somewhat later in Germany, in ex-Soviet-bloc countries, and in southern Europe. In each of these three latter groups different explanations are offered for the relatively late start of modern bioethics. In Germany the experiences of the Nazi era had created a widespread reluctance to discuss critically and openly (rather than with simple and firm opposition) some of the issues being addressed in the "new" medical ethics—such as experimentation on human subjects; euthanasia; abortion, especially for genetic defects; sterilization, especially without the patient's informed consent; and the "new genetics" with all its echoes and perceived echoes of eugenics. Indeed in Germany a positive hostility was to grow toward the new "bioethics," with one leading Australian bioethicist having invitations to lecture withdrawn or withheld as a result of raucous minority protest and threats.

In the Roman Catholic countries critical medical ethics were also slow to get off the ground. One reason was that Roman Catholic medical ethics were already very well established as an important aspect of medical education in many medical schools that were within the Catholic tradition. There, the medical ethics taught was "largely a branch of traditional Catholic moral theology" (p. 982. C. Blomquist, 1978. In W. T. Reich (Ed.), *The encyclopedia of bioethics* (pp. 982–987). New York: Macmillan), and it took some time for such teaching to adapt to the new mode of philosophically critical ethics. Similar links between medical ethics and the prevailing religious culture existed where medical schools were closely integrated within other religious traditions. Thus doctors who shared the religious traditions often felt no need to accommodate the new critical approach to medical ethics teaching, which might be perceived as threatening, while doctors who did not share the religion had often turned away from medical ethics altogether, perceiving it to be a guise for the imposition of a particular religious stance which they did not share. Some such doctors went even further in their rejection of medical ethics; participating in the pervasive spirit of postwar scientific positivism, they saw medicine increasingly more as science than as art, and they perceived science to be a value-free enterprise. Ethics was thus nothing to do with science, and indeed for some of the more extreme positivists ethics was in any case strictly nonsense.

Finally, in what used to be the "Iron Curtain" countries, study of the new critical medical ethics was also slow to take off, being discouraged primarily by the prevailing state orthodoxy of Marxist–Leninism, in which medical practice was a function of the state in developing and maintaining communism. Underground opposition to Marxist ideology by the many doctors in these countries who continued to adhere to Roman Catholicism or to the Orthodox Christian faiths and their medical ethical norms was also not conducive to the new critical medical ethics.

In other parts of the world, including Africa and Asia, bioethics was also slower to develop, but by the 1990s the new multidisciplinary area of inquiry and study had become a worldwide phenomenon.

II. SUBSTANTIVE ISSUES IN BIOETHICS

As already indicated, the range of substantive issues now considered to be legitimate substrates for bioethics is vast.

A. Issues Stemming from Health Care Relationships

At one end of the scale are moral issues stemming from the relationship between patients and their doctors, nurses, or other health care workers. These include the following:

- Issues of paternalism. Is it morally acceptable for doctors to do things to patients in order to try to benefit them without obtaining the patients' informed consent? Who should decide what is in the patient's best interests if a patient and his or her doctor disagree? So far as respecting patients' decisions is concerned, is there a morally relevant difference when a patient refuses a treatment and when a patient demands a treatment?
- Issues of confidentiality. Is it morally legitimate to reveal information stemming from the consultation without the patient's consent? If so, in which circumstances and why?
- Issues of honesty and deceit. When and why, if at all, might a doctor or nurse properly lie to or otherwise deliberately deceive a patient?
- Issues stemming from patient's impaired or inadequate autonomy. When and why should children at various stages of development make their own health care decisions? When they should not, who should do so on their behalf, using what criteria, and why? How should decisions be made on behalf of adults who are substantially mentally impaired or disordered, either temporarily or permanently, and by whom? Can great distress sufficiently impair a patient's autonomy to justify overriding his or her refusal of treatment? Can the autonomy of "frail elderly" patients be legitimately overridden in their interests? If so, in which circumstances, how, and why?

B. Issues of Life and Death

Is abortion ever justified, and if so in what circumstances and why? How are moral tensions between the interests of a pregnant woman and those of her fetus—or unborn child—to be properly resolved when they arise? Why? Is the moral status of the human embryo, fetus, or newborn baby different from the moral status of more developed human beings? Why? Is it ever morally justified to kill patients? Is it ever morally justified to allow them to die? Is there ever any morally relevant distinction to be made between killing and allowing to die? Why? What is it to die? Is "brain death," with the rest of the body apparently alive as a result of being sustained by a ventilator and other interventions, morally equivalent to death in the usual sense where, as well as brain death, heart action and breathing have also ceased? What are the doctor's moral obligations to patients diagnosed as permanently unconscious but not brain dead, for example, patients in persistent or "permanent" vegetative state? How far are doctors obliged to try to keep patients alive when the probability of recovery is very low? Why? What should count as "recovery"? Why?

C. The Patient's Interests versus the Interests of Others

Should doctors always give moral priority to the best interests of the individual patient with whom they are then concerned, or may the interests of others sometimes take precedence? If so in which circumstances and why? Specific examples of such tensions include emergencies versus routine consultations or operations, and many other situations where outsiders have greater needs than the patient of the moment; medical research, where the interests of future patients may conflict with the best interests of the patient of the moment; health promotion and disease prevention where the needs of those who are not currently ill may conflict with the needs of those who are; and the requirements of medical education, both undergraduate and postgraduate (for example, the need to teach students how to examine patients and how to carry out various procedures, including operations). More obviously, tensions between the interests of the individual patient and others increasingly arise in the context of inadequate availability of resources of meet medical needs. Should doctors participate in rationing inadequate resources to their individual patients? If so why and using which criteria and processes? If not, who should carry out such rationing, why, and using which criteria and processes?

D. Issues of Distributive Justice

In asking questions like this the need to step away from the doctor–patient setting becomes particularly obvious. Distribution of scarce resources is a problem at several levels, only one of which is at the doctor–patient interaction (so-called micro allocation). At the other end of the spectrum governments must decide how much of their available national budgets to allocate to health care rather than other welfare programs, education, defense, or the arts (macro allocation). In between these two ends of the spectrum of allocation are distribution decisions at the organizational level: between different sorts of health care and other health-related activities, including teaching and research; between different hospitals or primary care organizations; and between different sectors and groups within organizations. Here bioethics becomes relevant at societal and organizational levels rather than at the level of the clinical encounter. At all these levels, however, there is a need for basic theoretical tools. In the context of fair distribution of scarce resources, for example, there is a need for an acceptable working theory—or working theories—of justice. How should the relevant agents decide that this way of deciding to distribute scarce resources is fair and that another is unfair?

E. Conceptual Analysis

In development of basic theoretical tools, conceptual analysis of the meaning—or more often meanings—of a particular concept or set of concepts is clearly a fundamental component. As obvious examples, what is meant by the terms disease, health, life, human being, person, death, brain death, and vegetative state? What is the difference, if any, between the meaning of "human being" and that of "human person"? What is meant by needs, rights, duties, and obligations? What is meant by benefit and harm in health care? What is justice in health care? What is autonomy and what conceptual distinctions are needed between it and respect for autonomy? What is meant by "care" in the context of health care? What is meant by "virtue" in the context of virtue theory, or by "nature" and "natural" when the natural is extolled and the unnatural opposed?

F. Ethical Issues in the Practice of Medical Science—The Impetus of Nuremberg

Thus even though bioethics started with critical analysis of ethical issues arising from clinical encounters, the internal intellectual momentum of that analytic endeavor has taken it far beyond its starting points. The same can be said of the critical analysis of moral issues arising from medical science. From at least the 19th century ethical issues of medicine included ethical issues of medical science, fundamentally ethical issues concerning the treatment of human (and to some extent animal) subjects of experimentation. This aspect of medical ethics was given a shocking impetus after the second world war by the revelations at Nuremberg of atrocities by Nazi doctors. This rapidly led, through the newly created World Medical Association, to an international agreement known as the Helsinki Declaration in which were enshrined the principles that informed consent had to be obtained from research subjects and that the interests of the individual patient should never be subordinated to the interests of society. Since then the ever more astounding exploits of science, and recently especially of the biological sciences in the context of organ transplantation and genetic engineering, have also pushed the concerns of bioethics well beyond their starting point within the medical sciences.

G. Bioethics, Science Technology, and Society

Quite apart from harm–benefit analyses, respect for people and their choices, and justice in the context of fair allocation of scarce resources, respect for people's rights, and respect for just laws, some strands of bioethics have become concerned with the natural and unnatural, with the effects of science and technology on the environment and on the biosphere, and with critical evaluation of that version of the scientific ethos whose self-proclaimed reductionism and purported freedom from values is perceived as more of a threat than a benefit to humanity. Such critiques in bioethics include concerns about the "new genetics," organ transplantation, especially the projected use of animal organs, and the ever increasing efforts of "high-tech" medicine and the medical equipment and pharmaceutical industries to develop methods for prolonging the "natural" life span of human beings. Sometimes such critiques are based on excessive cost, sometimes on their "unnaturalness," and sometimes as part of a broader concern about the environmental sustainability of the contemporary growth of scientific and technological interventions and their potential damage to earth's or Gaia's (Lovelock, 1979) environments and integrity.

H. Environmental Ethics

Springing from earlier roots (for example, in the transcendentalism and idealism of Thoreau, Emerson,

Aldo Leopold, and John Muir), an extensive contemporary environmental ethics movement and literature has developed (e.g. Attfield 1983, Callicott 1989, 1995, Hargrove 1989, Johnson 1991, Naess 1989, Taylor 1986). Much of this environmental ethics movement considers itself to be part of bioethics, or, as in the case of Deep Ecology (Naess 1989) and other "ecocentric" environmental ethical perspectives, considers bioethics to be part of it. Not content with the limiting of the scope of much of traditional ethical concern to the interests of moral agents, potential moral agents, or human beings (anthropocentrism), environmental ethics seeks to expand the scope of ethical concern. Disagreement arises as to what should be included as having moral status—is it all sentient animals, all living animals, or all living beings, including plants (biocentric environmental ethics), or are inanimate entities also to be included within the scope of ethical concern, for example, the biosphere as a whole, ecosystems, species, land, water, and air (ecocentric environmental ethics)?

Interleaved with varieties of environmental ethics are varieties of feminist environmental ethics, of which one group—ecofeminism—claims that adequate theories for both feminism and environmental ethics need to understand the connections between woman and nature and between the domination of women by men and that of nature by man.

Thus the range of substantive issues encompassed by bioethics is indeed vast, and some have advocated that the subject area and discipline be explicitly subdivided into relevant subdisciplines. One proposal is for the subdivision of bioethics into theoretical bioethics, concerned with the intellectual foundations of bioethics; clinical bioethics, concerned with ethical issues arising from interactions between patients and those who care for their health; regulatory and policy bioethics, concerned with rules, regulations, and laws in the context of bioethics; and cultural bioethics, which seeks "systematically to relate bioethics to the historical ideological cultural and social context in which it is expressed" (D. Callahan, 1995. In W. T. Reich (Ed.), *The encyclopedia of bioethics* (2nd ed., pp. 247–256). New York: Simon & Schuster–Macmillan).

III. DISCIPLINARY APPROACHES TO BIOETHICS

In what follows, some generalizations about various disciplinary approaches to bioethics are made without the qualifications, often extensive, that they deserve. This is an intrinsic pitfall within the "overview" enterprise, perhaps justified by the attempt to give a broad picture of the woods, even though it may fail to show the fine detail and variety of the trees and shrubs and other plants composing those woods. Overviews offer impressions and invite reflection, along with criticism and analysis, including consultation of the relevant specific entries in this encyclopedia and in the bibliography. The disciplines sketched are clinical, scientific, religious, legal, sociological, and psychological.

A. Clinical Approaches

Characterized by the immediacy of the ethical issues, a personal relationship often akin to friendship or even love (a relationship described by Campbell as, at its best, "moderated love"), clinical approaches to bioethics tend to be highly particular, situational, contextual, and partial in both senses of the term. Positive aspects of clinical approaches to bioethics at their best include the typical ethical commitment of the clinician to the individual patient, a commitment that ideally draws together all involved in the patient's health care; detailed awareness of the patient's individual problems and situation; and an ability and readiness to draw on clinical experience for predictive and management purposes. Clinical approaches to bioethics are perhaps the most ancient, and firmly established, stemming as they do from the existence and nature of clinical practice itself, and from the earliest codified deontological medico-moral obligations. Indeed aspects of the Hippocratic Oath of classical Greece remain integral parts of contemporary international and national codes of medical ethics, and also at the heart of contemporary clinical ethics.

At their worst, clinical approaches to bioethics may lack theoretical underpinnings, both scientific and ethical; they may succumb to the potential injustice inherent in excessive partiality on behalf of the individual patient; excessive paternalism is an ever present moral hazard, with patients being treated like young children and having things done to them without adequate consultation for what their clinicians regard as the patients' own good; and clinical ethics are vulnerable to inconsistency of approach, with action sometimes being too variably determined by the stance, personality, knowledge, skills, and attitudes of the individual clinician. Clinical approaches vary not only between individual clinicians and between clinicians of different cultures, but also between types of clinicians, for example, as between doctors and nurses. Such variations and their attendant conflicts can, when badly managed, cause confusion, distress, and damage to the patient, even when individual clinicians all believe themselves to be acting in the patient's best interests.

B. Scientific Approaches

Typically manifested by medical researchers, scientific approaches to bioethics aim to be as consistent as possible with scientifically established evidence and theory. At their best, when they focus on development of new treatments and diagnostic methods and on rigorous assessment of the efficacy of existing treatments and methods, they benefit patients by protecting them from unproven and potentially dangerous "remedies" and other interventions, and protect future patients by insisting on subjecting potential interventions to scientific assessment (especially, in the context of the development of new medications, by use of what medical scientists in the second half of the 20th century have regarded as the "gold standard" of such assessment, the randomized controlled clinical trial).

At their worst, scientific approaches to bioethics have a number of faults, many stemming from a reductionism whereby people and their activities, thoughts, and feelings are reduced to more or less complex combinations of scientifically analyzable components and processes. When clinicians adopt such an approach (and many contemporary doctors and increasingly nurses are also scientists, engaging in scientific research) patients may be unpleasantly confronted by what in popular parlance is termed a "clinical attitude"—cool, detached, and investigative, treating patients as biophysical problems to be solved rather than as people with problems to be solved. Such approaches have no time for unproven remedies even if the patients believe them to be helpful, and often involve hostile rejection of "alternative" health care approaches such as acupuncture and osteopathy, in the absence of scientific evidence of efficacy. In this and other contexts scientific approaches to methods of evaluation that do not involve scientific measurement—including religious, spiritual, and aesthetic evaluation—are, at their worst, highly intolerant and disrespectful. Finally, a not uncommon concomitant of a certain scientific approach to bioethics is the assimilation, and even identification, of ethics with the scientific theory of evolution. Survival of the fittest, and of the "selfish gene," becomes not only the genetic explanation for the development of ethics in humankind, but also its mistakenly reductionist substantive content.

C. Religious Approaches

Though it is even more difficult to generalize about religious approaches to bioethics, some broad positives and negatives may be discerned. At their best, religions offer a firm grounding of firmly established positive general ethical stances in which people are educated to have clear and substantive general and specific ethical obligations whose fulfillment is a religious duty. Bioethical obligations are situated within these general obligations. Moral respect for God's creation—the universe and all therein—is a common religious theme and obligation, and bioethical obligations are encompassed within such respect, sometimes under the specific obligation of stewardship for that creation. Beneficence to others is a common religious obligation, supported by the moral obligation to learn to overcome or temper self-interest by a concern to help others. Just distribution of scarce resources that aims at helping not only kith and kin and co-religionists but also all in greater need than self is another widespread religious concern of obvious relevance in the context of bioethics. Recognition of free will as a characteristic of humankind and a concern to nurture and respect it is tempered by the obligation to love God, help others in need, and treat all people as of equal moral importance—again substantive moral positions of obvious potential relevance to bioethics.

In the analysis of particular bioethical issues, religous thinkers and thinking have often been highly influential not only for their co-religionists but also for those of other religions and none. Examples include religious analyses of ordinary and extraordinary means in the context of prolongation of life; of the significance of intention in the moral analysis of action; and of the potential importance of distinguishing between acts and omissions, especially in contexts where the absence of specific prior moral obligations of beneficence does not negate general moral obligations of nonmaleficence. In addition, religious approaches tend to combine within practical morality the need for general moral principles with the need for specific applications of those general principles (casuistry); the need to combine these with obligations to educate the character to behave well (virtue ethics); and the need to make specific moral judgments only after careful attention to the stories of the people involved and to details of the specific context (narrative ethics). Indeed religious bioethicists, of different faiths, may sigh wearily, even impatiently, as they see many of the wheels of bioethics being laboriously and separately reinvented by contemporary secular thinkers.

On the other hand, at their worst, religious approaches to bioethics are intolerantly, sometimes even fanatically, rigid about received doctrines—of whichever variety they happen to be—and incapable of adjusting to new developments, or to different moral perspectives, albeit conscientiously and thoughtfully held and defended, that are opposed to their own.

D. Legal Approaches

Widely acknowledged (with the exceptions of a few legal positivists) to be based themselves on moral obligations, legal approaches to bioethics tend to reflect the moral norms of the societies concerned. At their best such legal approaches are imbued with a concern for societal benefit and harmony, along with strong commitments to the equality of all under the law. Such legal approaches enshrine the rights of the weak against being exploited and harmed by the powerful, and the rights of the individual against being victimized, whether by other individuals, by groups, or by the state. Indeed contemporary legal contributions to bioethics have been strong in developing rights-based theories of justice as underpinnings for bioethics. At their best legal approaches to bioethics argue carefully the pros and cons of contentious bioethical issues and resolve them in ways that respect to the greatest extent possible the conflicting sincerely held and carefully reasoned moral views represented in the relevant societies.

At their worst legal approaches to bioethics facilitate and enhance state oppression—for example, under German National Socialism in relation to compulsory euthanasia and to human experimentation, and under Soviet Communism in relation to misuse of psychiatry against political dissidents.

E. Sociological Approaches

Seeing themselves as scientists of societies, social scientists (sociologists) tend to try to approach bioethics in descriptive scientific mode, explaining how societal factors result in the substantive bioethical features of different societies and social groupings. At their best such approaches help to broaden the gaze of bioethics so as to look at and understand not only ethical issues arising from the personal relationships of individuals but also ethical issues stemming from societal features that cause harm and ill health. At their worst they can underestimate the moral importance of individuals as moral agents, and combine a purportedly value-free descriptive approach to social functioning, in which all perspectives on morality are alleged to be of equal value or none, with a simultaneously prescriptive political stance.

F. Psychological Approaches

Seeing themselves, for the most part, as scientists of individual psyches, at their best psychologists in their approaches to bioethics illuminate it by showing how individuals come to develop their personal stances to moral issues. At their best they facilitate self-understanding, as well as understanding of others, by all involved in bioethics, especially perhaps an understanding that much of an individual's personal stance to ethical, including bioethical, issues is a function of emotional or other nonintellectual aspects of his or her psyche stemming from personality and from environmental influences, including those of early childhood. Ethical *reasoning* is recognized to be but one component of a person's ethical stance—a component that if not necessarily the slave of the passions, as Hume put it, is at least heavily influenced by nonreasoning aspects of the mind. At their worst psychological approaches to bioethics can also manifest a relativistic, deterministic approach to morality in which the moral stance of any individual is seen entirely as a function of influences beyond his or her control, an approach that tends to negate any purpose in bioethics (or indeed in any human endeavor).

IV. FOUNDATIONAL ETHICAL ASSUMPTIONS IN BIOETHICS—PHILOSOPHICAL/ ETHICAL "SCHOOLS" OF BIOETHICS

As well as being pursued from many different disciplinary perspectives, bioethics is pursued from a variety of foundational theoretical assumptions, especially philosophical/ethical foundational assumptions. Typically articulated by philosophers independently of the various religious foundations for bioethics, such foundational ethical assumptions offer the secular "floating voter" a basis for ethical appraisal in bioethics. They also seek to offer those who are already firmly based upon a particular religious or cultural theoretical foundation a way of communicating about bioethics with those who do not share their religion, either because they have different religious beliefs or because they have none. Such foundations seek to provide a widely acceptable set of ethical theoretical assumptions, a widely acceptable approach to ethical analysis, and at least elements of a widely agreed upon ethical language suitable for the multicultural international contexts in which bioethics is pursued.

Even while reiterating earlier concerns about the dangers of generalization (and careful reading of the relevant sources will show that the generalizations that follow are no more than indications of the emphases of the relevant authors), nonetheless some groupings or "schools" of bioethics may be discerned on the basis of the importance they ascribe to different moral foundations for bioethics. Among the most important of these schools are those emphasizing the foundational importance of respect for people and their autonomy; welfare or other utility maximization; social justice; the "four principles"; and a variety of foundational approaches that either reject moral principles as foundational or find them inadequate—these include casuistry, virtue ethics, narrative ethics, various feminist ethics, and an increasing variety of "geocultural" ethics, of which only three are outlined.

A. The Foundation of Respect for Autonomy

Among early American approaches to bioethics several gave special emphasis to the foundational moral importance of respect for autonomy. Thus Veatch, within his social contract theory for medical ethics, emphasized the priority of respect for the autonomy of moral agents. Similarly (though for very different reasons) Engelhardt, developing a theory for bioethics that would enable those of different moral backgrounds to cooperate in matters of bioethics, emphasized the foundational centrality of the principle of respect for autonomy (which he later renamed the principle of permission). Important positive aspects of such emphasis are its recognition of the moral importance of respect for people, whether patients or not, as ends in themselves, not to be treated by others instrumentally, merely as means to an end. Problems with such foundational emphasis on autonomy include the tendency for this to be interpreted as encouraging atomistic, selfish, individualism, and a lack of concern and care for others.

B. The Foundation of Utilitarian Welfare Maximization

Welfare maximization—the obligation to maximize benefits and minimize harms—is a widespread foundational assumption in bioethics, and in the context of medical ethics reflects the widespread perceived obligation of doctors and other health care workers to produce as much health benefit as they can with as little harm as possible. One of the most influential (and meticulous) utilitarian philosophers in the area of bioethics is R. M. Hare, and underlying utilitarian foundational assumptions are to be found in the work of Singer and Harris. A utilitarian perspective also underlies and is challengingly argued for by Parfit. Positive aspects of utilitarianism for bioethics include its requirement of a universal duty to benefit others and to avoid harming them, and to do as much good and as little harm as possible.

Among problems with utilitarianism as a moral foundation for bioethics is that "common morality" widely perceives it to deal inadequately with several types of moral obligation. These include obligations resulting from special relationships (for example, parents' obligations to their children and doctors' and nurses' obligations to their patients), as a result of which some people should not, it is widely held, be treated merely as of equal importance with all others but should be given special priority by those who have special relationships with them and therefore special obligations to them. Similarly those in great medical need ought, it is widely thought, to be given moral priority over those in less medical need, yet welfare maximization may be ready to ignore such needs if more total benefit is achieved (for others) by doing so. And utilitarianism is widely perceived by its opponents to be too ready to subordinate respect for individuals' autonomy and other individual rights where overall maximal benefit (to others) is achieved by doing so.

C. The Foundation of Social Justice

A third moral foundation offered for bioethics is social justice. As with the other foundational principles, a wide variety of versions of social justice have been proposed, but a particularly important one in bioethics is the ideal social contract theory of J. Rawls (1971. *A theory of justice*. Oxford: Oxford Univ. Press), drawn on for his specifically health-orientated theory of justice by Daniels. For Rawls the theory of justice that rational people would arrive at behind a "veil of ignorance" (i.e., impartially because of not knowing what their own specific social roles or circumstances would be) would be based on two fundamental moral principles. The first would be an obligation to respect everyone's liberty to the maximal extent compatible with equal respect for the liberty of all. The second would be to aim at equality for all, and for deliberately created inequalities to be just only if they were both to the greatest benefit of the least advantaged and attached to offices and positions open to all under conditions of fair equality of

opportunity (Rawls, 1971, 60 and 83). Daniels emphasizes and develops the "fair equality of opportunity" component of the Rawlsian account.

Advantages of the Rawlsian approach include its combination of liberty and differential benefit to those most disadvantaged. Problems include straightforward rejection in competing theories of justice of the Rawlsian principles themselves (and their theoretical justification) and/or the "lexical ordering" ascribed to them by Rawls whereby liberty takes priority over egalitarianism. Libertarian theories of justice, for example, tend to reject any obligation to attain equality or to benefit the disadvantaged—that would be good but not obligatory. Marxist socialist theories of justice subordinate liberty to the meeting of need and the attempt to attain equality. Communitarian theories of justice may reject a Rawlsian approach on the grounds that it does not sufficiently specify a positive conception of the good linked to the needs and interests of human communities or the human community. And rights-based theories of justice may oppose a Rawlsian approach on the grounds that it is inadequately grounded in and supportive of human rights, with variations in such opposition depending on which rights are regarded as of particular importance. In brief, foundations for bioethics grounded in a moral concern for justice share a concern for treating people justly, but differ widely over the substantive theory of justice that should be applied.

D. A Quasi-foundational Approach—The "Four Principles"

An attempt to offer not a foundational approach to bioethics but an approach that tries to combine some fundamental or foundational moral principles in a way that is compatible with a variety of mutually incompatible foundational theories is the "four-principles" approach offered and developed since the 1970s by the Americans Beauchamp and Childress, and enthusiastically adopted and promoted in Europe by Gillon. Developing upon an earlier triad of three principles produced as a working framework for the ethics of medical research by a group of American bioethicists in the "Belmont Report" (A. R. Jonsen & A. Jameton, 1995. In W. T. Reich (Ed.), *The encyclopedia of bioethics*, 2nd ed., pp. 1616–1632, New York: Simon & Schuster–Macmillan), themselves drawing on a long tradition of post-Enlightenment moral theory, the four-principles approach (4PA) starts from the claim that acceptance of four *prima facie* moral principles is common to a wide range of theoretical perspectives on bioethics, and also to much of "common morality."

Thus the 4PA is offered as a common working approach to bioethics, compatible with and neutral between a wide range of competing moral theories. It is also sometimes seen as an approach that lies in between the level of relatively abstract (and usually mutually incompatible) moral theories on the one hand, and highly specific moral situations, cases, problems, and judgments on the other. The principles are respect for autonomy, beneficence, nonmaleficence, and justice. Gillon additionally emphasizes the importance of consideration of the scope of application of each (to whom or what is the *prima facie* duty owned, and why?). While there is little substantive rejection of any one of these *prima facie* principles, opposition to the approach, pejoratively dubbed "principlism" or the "Georgetown mantra," has been considerable (for example, Clouser and Gert 1994, Wulff 1994).

Criticisms of principles as foundational in bioethics emerge from a variety of alternative schools of contemporary bioethics. Some, like those already mentioned, do not reject principles but argue that these need to be grounded in a theory of ethics. Thus utilitarians ground their principles or rules within the over-arching principle of utility, or in a logical analysis of the meaning of moral terms such as "ought" (Hare); Kantians ground their principles, rules, or maxims in a Kantian moral theory; and many religions ground their own bioethical principles within their own religious ethical framework.

E. Casuistry

The newly revived school of casuistry not only points out that reliance on potentially conflicting moral principles often fails to provide a decision procedure for when those principles conflict in particular contexts, but also adds that principles emerge from consideration of cases, not the other way around. Thus it is particular cases, and decisions about particular cases, rather than principles that are foundational for bioethics. Casuistry, of which Jonsen and Toulmin are leading contemporary proponents, is the application of general moral norms to specific cases in particular contexts in the light of comparisons and contrasts with previously determined clear or "paradigm" cases.

F. Virtue Ethics

Another school of bioethics rejects moral principles as foundations for bioethics on the grounds that virtues, not principles, are the proper moral base for bioethics. Virtues, or character dispositions to act or otherwise respond well *as people*, and then as people of a certain sort (for example, doctors, parents, scientists, or accident investigators), are, according to this approach, the fundamental concerns of ethics and therefore of bioethics. This was the approach taken to ethics by Aristotle, and Aristotelian virtue ethics is enjoying a contemporary revival, with the work of MacIntyre being highly influential. One variant of virtue ethics, again importantly influenced by MacIntyre and emphasizing the necessarily socially embedded and committed nature of virtue, is communitarian ethics, a movement that at the end of the second millennium was gaining impetus in the USA, perhaps partly in reaction to that country's prevailing libertarian individualism (for example, Emmanuel 1991).

G. Narrative Ethics

Associated with virtue ethics is another school of bioethics, the school of narrative ethics, that again finds reliance on moral principles inadequate. Fundamental to bioethics in this approach is the narrative or story of particular cases, and the story is both highly specific and highly culture bound, for every culture also has its story. Everyone involved in the story has interests in its outcome and, as Brody puts it,

> The "right course of action" to resolve a problem is not necessarily the action that conforms to an abstract principle; rather, it may be the action which, without violating any moral principles, most successfully navigates all the contextual factors to move the situation in a direction that best serves the major interests of all involved parties. (p. 215. H. Brody, 1994. In R. Gillon and A. Lloyd (Eds.), *Principles of health care ethics* pp. 205–215. Chichester/New York: Wiley).

H. Feminist Ethics

Many, though not all, strands within contemporary feminist ethics also oppose reliance on moral principles, though given the wide variety of feminist approaches to bioethics, the criticisms vary. Common feminist criticisms are that moral reasoning in terms of principles is excessively abstract; fails to acknowledge the importance of the particular, of the subjective and the emotional, of the moral importance of caring and empathy, and of the responsibilities stemming from relationships; and above all fails to acknowledge and redress the oppression of women, not least in their medical care (e.g. Lebacqz 1995, Sherwin 1992).

I. Geocultural Bioethics

Just as individual religions tend to have their schools of bioethics, so too are various geocultural regions establishing their own schools of bioethics. For example, Gracia refers to a "Latin model" of bioethics appropriate to southern European nations and based more on virtues than on principles; insofar as principles are seen as relevant foundations, they may not be the quartet from Georgetown. A different quartet offered by Gracia for Latin bioethics comprises the fundamental value of life, therapeutic wholeness, liberty and responsibility, and sociality and social subsidiarity (whereby social problems are always best addressed through the smallest relevant social unit).

Further north in Europe, Wulff, while agreeing that the Georgetown principles individually "cannot be contested," claims that in practice they are used to support typically American cultural approaches to bioethics which "do not accord with the prevailing moral tradition in other parts of the western world, eg the Nordic countries" (p. 277. H. Wulff, 1994. In R. Gillon and A. Lloyd (Eds.), *Principles of health care ethics* (2nd ed., pp. 277–286). Chichester/New York: Wiley). Instead Wulff argues that the essentially Christian and Kantian Golden Rule is and should be the foundation of Nordic bioethics—and in an earlier work Wulff and his coauthors also emphasized the importance of the Danish philosopher Kierkegaard and more generally of the continental tradition of philosophy with its concerns for phenomenology, hermeneutics, and existentialism.

On a different continent, the East Asian Association for Bioethics was established in 1995 partly because bioethicists from Japan and China felt that Western approaches to bioethics were inappropriate as moral foundations for their own countries, where Buddhist and Confucian ethical norms so firmly underlie everyday morality, even in China where Maoist Marxism has had such a powerful social influence.

V. CONCLUSION

While future developments in bioethics are unpredictable, one prediction can be safely made. Whether or not we go so far as to accept Gracia's assertion to the International Association of Bioethics that "bioethics, I believe, is going to be the civil ethics of all our societies" (D. Garcia, 1993. *Bioethics* 7(2/3), 97–107), we can confidently predict that it will continue to provide a range of absorbing and important ethical concerns for

which an ever expanding audience of interest can equally confidently be anticipated.

Also See the Following Articles

ENVIRONMENTAL ETHICS, OVERVIEW • LEGAL ETHICS, OVERVIEW • SOCIAL ETHICS, OVERVIEW • THEORIES OF ETHICS, OVERVIEW

Bibliography

Attfield, R. (1983). The ethics of environmental concern. Columbia University Press, New York.
Beauchamp, T., and Childress, J. (1994). Principles of biomedical ethics 4th ed. New York Oxford: Oxford University Press.
Blomquist, C. (1978). Medical ethics history: Western Europe in the twentieth century. In *The Encyclopedia of Bioethics* (W. T. Reich, Ed.), pp. 982–987. New York: Macmillan.
Brody, H. (1994). The four principles and narrative ethics. In *Principles of Health Care Ethics*. (R. Gillon and A. Lloyd, Eds.). Chichester/New York: Wiley.
Callahan, D. (1995). Bioethics. In *The Encyclopedia of Bioethics* (W. T. Reich, Ed.), 2nd ed., pp. 247–256. New York: Simon & Schuster–Macmillan.
Callicott, J. (1989). *In Defense of the Land Ethic: Essays in Environmental Philosophy.* Albany: State Univ. of New York Press.
Callicott, J. (1995). Environmental ethics: Overview. In *The Encyclopedia of Bioethics* (W. T. Reich, Ed.), 2nd ed., pp. 676–687. Simon & Schuster–Macmillan, New York.
Campbell, A. (1984). *"Moderated Love—A Theology of Professional Care."* London: SPCK.
Clouser, K., and Gert, B. (1994). Morality vs. principlism. In *Principles of Health Care Ethics* (R. Gillon and A. Lloyd, Eds.), pp. 251–266. Chichester/New York: Wiley.
Daniels, N. (1985). *Just Health Care.* Cambridge, MA: Cambridge University Press.
Emanuel, E. (1991). *The Ends of Human Life—Medical Ethics in a Liberal Polity."* Cambridge, MA: Harvard University Press.
Engelhardt, H. T. (1986, 1996). The Foundations of bioethics, 1st and 2nd ed. New York/Oxford: Oxford University Press.
Gillon, R. (1981). The function of criticism. *British Medical Journal,* 282, 1633–1639.
Gillon, R. (1986). *Philosophical Medical Ethics.* Chichester/New York: Wiley.
Gillon, R., and Lloyd, A. (Eds.) (1994). *Principles of Health Care Ethics.* Chichester/New York: Wiley.
Gracia, D. (1993). The intellectual basis of bioethics in southern European countries. *Bioethics,* 7(2/3), 97–107.
Hare, R. M. (1981). *Moral Thinking: Its Levels, Method and Point.* Oxford: Clarendon Press.
Hargrove, E. (1989). *Foundations of Environmental Ethics.* Englewood Cliffs, NJ: Prentice Hall.
Harris, J. (1985). *The Value of Life.* London: Routledge and Kegan Paul.
Johnson, L. (1991). A Morally Deep World: An Essay on Moral Significance and Environmental Ethics. Cambridge University Press, Cambridge.
Jonsen, A. R., and Jameton, A. (1995). Medical ethics, history of; the Americans; the United States in the twentieth century. In *The

Encyclopedia of Bioethics (W. T. Reich, Ed.), 2nd ed., pp. 1616–1632. New York: Simon & Schuster–MacMillan.

Jonsen, A. R., and Toulmin, S.E. (1988). *The Abuse of Casuistry: A History of Moral Reasoning.* Berkeley: University of California Press.

Lebacqz, K. (1995). Feminism. In *The Encyclopedia of Bioethics* (W. T. Reich, Ed.), 2nd ed., pp. 808–818. New York: Simon & Schuster–MacMillan.

Lovelock, J. (1979). *Gaia: A New Look at Life on Earth.* Oxford: Oxford University Press.

MacIntyre, A. (1981). After Virtue: A Study in Moral Theory. Notre Dame, IN: University of Notre Dame Press.

MacIntyre, A. (1990) *Three Rival Versions of Moral Inquiry: Encyclopedia, Genealogy, and Tradition.* Notre Dame, IN: University of Notre Dame Press.

Naess, A. (1989). Ecology, Community and Lifestyle: Outline of an Ecosophy. (Transl. D. Rothenberg). Cambridge: Cambridge Univ. Press.

Oakley, J. (1995). Medical ethics, history of: Australia and New Zealand. In The Encyclopedia of Bioethics (W. T. Reich, Ed.), 2nd ed., pp. 1644–1646. New York: Simon & Schuster–MacMillan.

Parfit, D. (1984) *Reasons and Persons.* Oxford: Clarendon Press.

Rawls, J. (1971). "A Theory of Justice." Oxford: Oxford University Press.

Reich, W. T. (Ed.) (1978). *The Encyclopedia of Bioethics.* New York: Macmillan.

Reich. W. T. (1994). The word "bioethics": Its birth and the legacies of those who shaped it. *Kennedy Institute of Ethics Journal,* 4(4), 319–335.

Reich, W. T. (Ed.) (1995). *The Encyclopedia of Bioethics,* 2nd ed. New York: Simon & Schuster–Macmillan.

Reich, W. T. (1995). The word "Bioethics": The struggle over its earliest meanings. *Kennedy Institute of Ethics Journal,* 5(1), 19–34.

Sherwin, S. (1992). *No Longer Patient: Feminist Ethics and Health Care.* Philadelphia: Temple University Press.

Singer, P. (1979). *Practical Ethics.* Cambridge: Cambridge University Press.

Taylor, P. (1986). *Respect for Nature: A Theory of Environmental Ethics.* Princeton, NJ: Princeton University Press.

Veatch, R. (1981). *"A Theory of Medical Ethics.* New York: Basic Books.

Warren, K. (1990). The power and the promise of ecological feminism. *Environmental Ethics, 12*(2), 125–146.

Wulff, H. (1994). Against the four principles: A Nordic view. In *Principles of Health Care Ethics* (R. Gillon and A. Lloyd, Eds.), pp. 277–286. Chichester/New York: Wiley.

Wulff, H., Andur Pedersen, S., and Rosenberg, R. (1986). *Philosophy of Medicine—An Introduction.* Oxford: Blackwell.

BIOTECHNOLOGY

Michael Reiss
Homerton College, Cambridge

GLOSSARY

biotechnology The application of biology for human ends. Often divided into "traditional biotechnology"—farming and the long-established use of microorganisms in the production of foods and drinks—and "modern biotechnology"—which utilizes novel disciplines such as tissue culture, embryo transfer, and genetic engineering.

clone A collection of genetically identical cells or multicellular organisms.

DNA The chemical that carries the genetic information contained in an organism's genes.

gene therapy The intentional alteration of human genetic material for medical ends.

genetic engineering The intentional transfer of genetic material from one organism to another, usually of a different species. Synonyms include "genetic manipulation," "genetic modification," and "recombinant DNA technology."

proteins Molecules, such as the hormone insulin, that are composed of one or more chains of subunits known as amino acids; made by all organisms as a result of genes that code for these amino acids.

BIOTECHNOLOGY is the application of biology for human ends. It involves using organisms to provide humans with food, clothes, medicines, and other products. The phrase "traditional biotechnology" refers to activities like the farming of animals and plants, and the use of microorganisms in the manufacture of beer, wine, bread, yogurt, and cheese. By contrast, modern biotechnology has only become possible within the last 20 years or so through advances in novel disciplines such as tissue culture, embryo transfer, and genetic engineering.

Modern biotechnology, though it has grown out of traditional biotechnology, is distinctive in a number of regards. For one thing, its scope seems near endless. It has been claimed that it will revolutionize agriculture, medicine, the food industry, and much else besides. On the other hand, it has been argued that its potential for harm is immense. Then there is the tremendous, and seemingly ever quickening, pace of change. Finally, many aspects of modern biotechnology, such as genetic engineering, arouse deep feelings. Genetic engineering raises issues about the nature of life itself, about what it is to be human, about the future of the human race, and about our rights to knowledge and privacy.

I. THE HISTORY OF BIOTECHNOLOGY

A. Traditional Biotechnology

Traditional biotechnology has a long history. The domestication of animals and plants seems to have happened independently in the Middle East, Asia, and the Americas about 12,000 to 10,000 B.P..

Around 12,000 to 11,000 B.P., the dog was domesticated in Mesopotamia and Canaan. Within a thousand years of this time goats and sheep were domesticated in Iran and Afghanistan, and emmer wheat and barley were being cultivated in Canaan. Around 10,000 to 9000 B.P., potatoes and beans were domesticated in Peru, rice in Indochina, and pumpkins in middle America.

By 8000 B.P. the pig and water buffalo had been domesticated in eastern Asia and China, the chicken in southern Asia, and cattle in southeastern Anatolia (modern day Turkey). At the same time, einkorn wheat was being cultivated in Syria; durum (macaroni) wheat in Anatolia; sugar cane in New Guinea; yams, bananas, and coconuts in Indonesia; flax in southwestern Asia, and maize and peppers in the Tehuacan valley of Mexico. By 8000 B.P. a type of beer was being made with yeast in Egypt. Indeed, by 4000 B.P the Sumerians brewed at least 19 brands of beer—a whole book on the subject survives.

Four processes are involved in the farming of domesticated animals or plants:

• Breeding of animals or sowing of seeds
• Caring for the animals or plants
• Collecting produce (e.g., harvesting, milking, and slaughtering)
• Selecting and keeping back some of the produce for the next generation.

For more than 10,000 years, therefore, farmers have selected animals and plants. Much of this selection will have been conscious, with farmers often choosing, for example, to breed from larger and healthier individuals. Indeed, genetics is probably a much older science than is generally realized. However, much of the selection by farmers will have been unconscious, as farmers unwittingly chose, for example, animals that were tractable or tolerant of overcrowding.

B. The Relationship of Traditional to Modern Biotechnology

The fact that traditional biotechnology has such a long history might lead one to conclude that perhaps too much concern is generated about genetic engineering and other techniques of modern biotechnology. After all, traditional biotechnology often involves the transfer of genes in a way that would not happen in nature. That happens every time a farmer selects a bull to mate with cows, and every time a plant breeder dusts the pollen from one plant onto the female sex organ of another plant. Indeed, such traditional selective breeding has achieved dramatic results, as is witnessed by the many very different breeds of dogs.

Traditional biotechnology has also changed certain plants very greatly. The modern wheat used in bread making is so different from native wheats that scientists are still uncertain as to its precise ancestry. What is clear, though, is that it results from at least two interspecific crosses. In other words, on at least two separate occasions, thousands of years ago, people succeeded in breeding one species of wheat with another species. The net result is that today's bread wheat contains approximately three times the number of genes as wild wheats found in the Middle East.

However, although traditional biotechnology can result in major alterations in the genetic makeup of organisms, it differs from modern biotechnology in at least three important respects.

First, although traditional biotechnology sometimes involves crossing one species with another, these species are always closely related. To the nonexpert, the plant species crossed to make modern bread wheat all look much the same. Indeed, botanists classify them as being very closely related. This is markedly different from genetic engineering where genes can now be moved from one species to another, however unrelated, almost at will.

Secondly, the pace of change in traditional biotechnology is much slower than that in modern biotechnology. We are already at the point where a gene from one organism can permanently be inserted into the genetic material of another organism within a period of weeks. Traditional biotechnology, by comparison, works on a time scale of years.

Thirdly, genetic change as a result of traditional biotechnology happened to only a relatively small number of species, namely, those that provide us with food and drink, such as crop plants, farm animals, and yeasts. Modern biotechnology is far more ambitious. It seeks to change not only the species that provide us with food and drink, but those involved in sewage disposal, pollution control, and drug production. It also seeks to create microorganisms, plants, and animals that can make human products, such as insulin, and even possibly to change the genetic makeup of humans.

II. TECHNIQUES IN MODERN BIOTECHNOLOGY

A. Genetic Engineering

1. The Significance of Genetic Engineering

By far the most significant development in modern biotechnology, from both a scientific and an ethical perspective, is the practice of genetic engineering, which dates from the late 1970s and early 1980s.

Every organism carries inside itself what are known as genes. These genes are codes or instructions: they carry information which is used to tell the organism what chemicals it needs to make in order to survive, grow, and reproduce. Genetic engineering typically involves moving genes from one organism to another. The result of this procedure, if all goes as intended, is that the chemical normally made by the gene in the first organism is now made by the second.

2. Principles of Genetic Engineering

Suppose one wants a species to produce a protein (i.e., a biochemical consisting of a chain of subunits called amino acids) made by another species. For example, one might want a bacterium to produce human insulin so as to be able to collect and then give the insulin to people unable to make it for themselves. The basic procedure, using genetic engineering, involves the following two steps:

1. Identify the gene that makes the protein one is interested in
2. Transfer this gene from the species in which it occurs naturally to the species in which one wants the gene to be.

The first of these steps is more difficult than it may sound. Even a bacterium has hundreds of different genes, while animals and plants have tens of thousands. Nowadays, though, there are a number of ways of identifying the gene that makes the protein in which one is interested.

Two different types of approaches can be used to carry out the second step, namely, transferring this gene from the species in which it occurs naturally to the intended species recipient. One involves the use of a vector organism to carry the gene; the other, called vectorless transmission, is more direct and requires no intermediary organism.

3. Vectorless Transmission

One way of getting DNA into a new organism is simply to fire it in via a gun, i.e., biolistic (particle gun) delivery. The DNA is mixed with tiny metal particles, usually made of tungsten. These are then fired into the organism, or a tissue culture of cells of the organism. The chief advantage of this method is its simplicity, and it is widely used in the genetic engineering of plants. One problem, not surprisingly, is the damage that may be caused as a result of the firing process. A more intractable problem is that only a small proportion of the cells tend to take up the foreign DNA.

A second way of getting DNA into a new organism is by injecting it directly into the nucleus of an embryonic cell. This approach is quite widely used in the genetic engineering of animals. This method ensures that at least some of the cells of the organism take up the foreign DNA.

4. Vectors

A vector carries genetic material from one species (the donor species) to another (the genetically engineered species). Genetic engineering by means of a vector involves three steps:

1. Obtaining the desired piece of genetic material from the donor species
2. Inserting this piece of genetic material into the vector
3. Infecting the species to be genetically engineered with the vector so that the desired piece of genetic material passes from the vector to the genetically engineered species.

An example of genetic engineering by means of a vector is the infection of certain plants by genetically engineered forms of the bacterium *Agrobacterium*. *Agrobacterium* is a soil bacterium that naturally attacks certain plants, infecting wounds and causing the development of swellings known as tumors. In 1977 it was found that the tumors were due to the bacterium inserting part of its genetic material into the host DNA. This means that if foreign DNA is inserted into the DNA of *Agrobacterium*, the *Agrobacterium* can in turn insert this foreign DNA into the genetic material of any plants it subsequently attacks.

Viruses can also be used as vectors in genetic engineering. For example, retroviruses have been used in genetic engineering research on humans. Retroviruses are good candidates for this approach as they have millions of years of experience at inserting their genetic material into that of a host. A number of diseases are caused by mutations in genes expressed in bone marrow cells—the cells that give rise to our blood cells. Retroviruses have been used in attempts to insert a functional copy of the faulty gene into these bone marrow cells. The aim is to ensure that all the blood cells that descend from these bone marrow cells are healthy.

One problem with this approach, which limits the number of diseases on which it is being trialed, is that retroviruses only infect dividing cells. Many human diseases, for example, those of the nervous system, are not caused by mutations in dividing cells. A second problem is that, as so often is the case in genetic engineering, there is no control presently available as to where the gene is inserted in the human chromosomes. Instead the retrovirus inserts the desired gene more or less randomly. This has two consequences. First, the new gene may not be as effective as when it is located in its normal place. This is because genes often work best only if they are situated close to certain other genes which help turn them on and off. The second, and more dangerous, possible consequence is that the new gene may, by mistake, be inserted into an important gene, for example, tumor-suppressor genes which help prevent cancer. Disruption of the activity of a tumor-suppressor gene by the insertion of a new gene through the activity of a retrovirus has been shown in monkeys to sometimes lead to the development of cancer.

For these reasons, researchers are experimenting with other viruses. For example, adenoviruses are being used in attempts to insert functional copies of the gene which, in its faulty form, causes cystic fibrosis in humans. Adenoviruses, unlike retroviruses, do not integrate their genes into their host's DNA. This has both advantages and disadvantages. An obvious disadvantage follows from the fact that any descendants of the genetically engineered cells do not carry the functional cystic fibrosis gene. This means that once the genetically engineered cells die, the functional cystic fibrosis gene is lost with them. As a result, this approach is only likely to be effective if people with cystic fibrosis are treated with genetically engineered adenoviruses every few months. On the other hand, there is less risk of the virus inserting its genetic material into the host cells in such a way as to disrupt normal functioning or even cause cancer.

B. Tissue Culture

Tissue culture involves the growing, under sterile laboratory conditions, of cells or tissues derived from animal, plant, or other living material. It is a prerequisite for many of the techniques used in modern biotechnology.

Tissue culture based on plant material is nowadays of huge commercial importance, for example, in the horticultural trade. In particular, tissue culture can be used to produce many identical plants in a short period of time. In a standard procedure, a number of distinct small clumps of cells are taken from a plant, transferred to laboratory containers, provided with water, nutrients, and light, and allowed to grow rapidly into functioning plants. The plants so produced are genetically identical and constitute a clone. This allows features of commercial value found in only one or a small number of plants to be quickly present in larger numbers of plants. In animals, cloning can be achieved in a number of ways. The simplest procedure in farm animals is to divide an embryo, while in tissue culture, in half and then return the halves to the mother. The result is identical twins.

C. *In Vitro* Fertilization

In vitro fertilization is most commonly used as one of the treatments for human infertility, though it also sometimes used to produce large numbers of cattle embryos from desirable parents. In humans, *in vitro* fertilization leads to the production of so-called "test tube babies."

Whether in humans or other animals, *in vitro* fertilization requires the collection of suitable eggs and sperm. Egg production may be stimulated by treatment with hormone-based drugs. In mammals, eggs are collected via a surgical procedure shortly before ovulation. In the simplest form of *in vitro* fertilization sperm are added to laboratory dishes containing the eggs in a suitable medium. Fertilization occurs and after an interval of up to several days the fertilized egg(s)—which by now may have divided to form a cluster of cells—are transferred to a uterus, which may, or may not, be the uterus of the female from which the eggs were obtained.

D. Embryo Transfer

Embryo transfer entails the removal of embryos at an early stage of development from a donor female and transfer to a surrogate female. The procedure—one form of "surrogate motherhood"—is still uncommon in humans, but is quite widely used in cattle and some other farm animals.

III. ETHICAL ARGUMENTS FOR AND AGAINST BIOTECHNOLOGY

A. Consequentialist Arguments

1. What Consequences Does Biotechnology Have for Humans?

The actual (past and present) and possible (future) consequences of biotechnology are legion. Think simply of alcohol production, one of the longest established examples of biotechnology. On the one hand, consequences of alcohol consumption include much human suffering, either directly through cirrhosis of the liver, various cancers, and babies born with fetal alcohol syndrome, or indirectly through alcohol-related accidents and violence. On the other hand, alcohol is widely enjoyed by many people, provides large numbers of satisfying jobs, and is even thought now to promote physical health if taken in small quantities.

Utilitarian attempts to calculate the consequences of specific instances of biotechnology can help to clarify ethical decision making. However, such attempts will probably only rarely allow us unambiguously to decide whether or not to proceed with the technology in question. For one thing, it is difficult to accurately and quantitatively predict the consequences of new technologies.

On a broader canvas, it would be virtually impossible for humans to exist without biotechnology. This is not, of course, to imply that biotechnology should not be regulated, only to point out that even before the advent of modern biotechnology we were heavily dependent on agricultural crops, paper, and clothes made from wool and cotton, medicines derived from plants, etc.

2. Is Biotechnology Safe for Humans?

It is, of course, not possible to answer this question with either a "yes" or a "no." One can only proceed on a case-by-case basis guided by knowledge and experience. In addition, it needs to be remembered that:

- There is little, if anything, in life that is 100% safe
- "Safer" is not necessarily to be equated with "better" (it may, for example, be safer for me to read about the ethics of torture than to take practical steps to strive to reduce the extent of torture)
- By following a safer course of action in the short term (e.g., not proceeding with the genetic engineering of crop plants because of a nonzero risk that this is unsafe) one may end up with a less safe end result (e.g., more starvation or famine-induced wars).

3. Does Biotechnology Lead to Animal Suffering?

Suffering involves susceptibility to pain and an awareness of being, having been, or about to be in pain. Pain here is used in its widest sense and includes stress, discomfort, distress, anxiety, and fear. It is difficult to argue against the contention that vertebrates, and probably certain invertebrates such as octopuses, can experience pain. The extent to which animals are aware of their pain is more open to question. There is little doubt that certain of our closest evolutionary relatives, such as chimpanzees and other apes, have the requisite degree of self-consciousness. Although the extent to which other animals suffer is contentious, a growing number of biologists and philosophers accept that, at the very least, most mammals, and probably most vertebrates, can suffer. This conclusion is unlikely to surprise anyone who has ever kept a pet or has worked with animals.

Does animal biotechnology lead to animal suffering? No overall answer can be given. Take, first of all, the case of conventional farm animals such as sheep, cattle, pigs, and chickens. Under the best management regimes such animals enjoy better health than their counterparts would in the wild. It is true that some might describe their lives as being boring while their movements and certain other natural behaviors (e.g., mating) are restricted, but it is doubtful whether this constitutes suffering. However, there are countless examples of farm animals suffering as a direct result of biotechnology and poor husbandry, especially some of those kept under the most intensive regimes. For example, many chicken varieties have been subjected to such extreme artificial selection for accelerated growth that a high proportion of individuals experience bone fractures and other clinical deformities during their brief existence in battery cages.

4. What Are the Ecological Consequences of Biotechnology?

Ecological consequences of biotechnology need to be taken into account both because they often have consequences for humans and because they have consequences for other organisms too. Some countries nowadays have strict regulations about the introduction into the wild of new animal and plant varieties precisely because of the number of ecological disasters that occurred long before the advent of modern biotechnology. Indeed, literally hundreds of species are known to have gone extinct as a result of the introduction of nonindigenous species.

Fears have been expressed that modern biotechnology will contribute to further ecological damage. For example, it is possible that fish genetically engineered to be able to live in cooler waters will increase their geographic range and so displace native species. Considerable uncertainty still exists as to how significant such fears are.

B. Intrinsic Arguments

1. Is Biotechnology Unnatural?

Since at least the time of Hume it has been accepted that attempts straightforwardly to argue from what is the case in nature to what is the right course of action for humans to take are problematic. It is tempting therefore to react dismissively to objections to modern biotechnology on the grounds that it is unnatural. However, there now exist more nuanced attempts to relate to what ought to be. In addition, there is no doubt that on psychological grounds, politicians and regulators, if not moral philosophers, do well to heed such arguments. Opinion polls in a number of different countries consistently show that many people object to modern biotechnology on the grounds that it is "unnatural."

2. Is Biotechnology Blasphemous?

Some people with a religious faith either reject or are hesitant about the rightness of certain developments within modern biotechnology, maintaining that such developments are blasphemous. This is commonly summed up in the phrase, "We should not play at being God." On the other hand, it has been argued that, in some sense, we are cocreators with God. The reasoning goes as follows. Creation is an ongoing process, the universe having been in a continual state of development for some 10 to 15 thousand million years. Within just the last few thousand years, humans have begun consciously to influence the course of that continued creation in ways never before attained by any species. In any useful sense of the term, therefore, we are already cocreators with God.

3. Does Biotechnology Entail Disrespect for Organisms?

It is often argued that animals have rights and that we are not entitled to use them for our ends. A different approach is to hold that, in Kantian terms, it may be acceptable for us to use an animal's ends as our own (e.g., using a sheep to produce wool and lambs), but it is unacceptable for us entirely to ignore an animal's ends and instead use it solely as an instrument by which we attain our ends.

A number of writers have argued that it is wrong for us to violate the genetic integrity or the *telos*, in an Aristotelian sense, of organisms. Others have concentrated on the distinction between instrumental and intrinsic value. Paul Taylor has argued that all living organisms possess inherent worth, and explores the consequences of this for the resolution of conflicts between humans and other species when there is competition for limited resources.

C. Patenting

Is it right to patent genes, parts of organisms, or whole organisms? Obviously questions to do with the ethical implications of patenting are, logically, distinct from questions to do with the ethical implications of biotechnology. However, the practical reality is that the potential for money to be made from modern technology has led to a rush to patent human and other genes.

The fundamental argument in favor of patenting is that it rewards those who have put time, effort, ingenuity, or money into the invention of a new product or process. For a finite length of time (typically 20 years, though the exact length of time varies in different countries), a patent allows the inventor a monopoly right to exploit the patented invention. After this period the patent ceases.

Those opposed to the patenting of genes, parts of organisms, or whole organisms advance a number of arguments:

- It is wrong to patent life and this means that it is wrong to patent either whole organisms or their genes; the very idea is absurd, obscene, or blasphemous; living things are not "products of manufacture," but rather, the genetic resources of the planet are our common heritage
- Patenting reduces the exchange of information among researchers
- patenting encourages researchers to target their efforts where money is to be made, rather than where work is most needed.

Those in favor of the patenting of genes, parts of organisms, or whole organisms advance the following main arguments:

- Patenting is right in that it rewards the investment and ingenuity of those who develop new products
- Without such patenting there will be fewer benefits to health than would otherwise be the case

- In the absence of patenting, firms will resort to greater secrecy to protect their investment
- Patents do not interfere with pure research since experimental use of an invention does not constitute patent infringement.

Many of the ethical issues raised by the patenting of genes or even organisms are common to those already raised by the patenting of any product or process. However, it can be argued that the ability of organisms—unlike, for example, corkscrews—to reproduce and to have genes which mutate renders the notion of the patenting of organisms or their genes especially problematic from both a legal and a philosophical viewpoint.

IV. CASE STUDIES

A. Cheese Making

Cheese has been made by people for at least 5000 years. The fundamental principles have changed little over the millennia. During cheese making a number of substances are added to sour milk. One of them is rennet. Rennet is a crude extract of enzymes, of which much the most important is chymosin, also known as rennin. These enzymes act on a milk protein called casein. Their effect is to cause the milk to form a soft curd, also known as junket. Without rennet, most cheeses cannot be made.

Traditionally rennet has been obtained from the stomachs of young calves (or piglets, kids, lambs, or water buffalo calves). Rennets can be of vegetable origin, but, until recently, by far the most important source was young calves. Calves' stomachs were ground up in salt water—10 of them being required for one gallon of rennet. Calves' stomachs contain a wide range of substances in addition to rennet, so the purity was not very high. However, the gene for calf chymosin has now been inserted, by genetic engineering, into a yeast which produces a ready supply of chymosin in commercial quantities. As a result, the use of rennet obtained directly from animals has greatly decreased. In addition, genetically engineered chymosin is cheaper than traditional rennet and considerably purer.

The original gene used in the genetic engineering of the yeast came from an animal source. However, many vegetarians have endorsed genetically engineered chymosin on the grounds that its use significantly decreases the slaughtering of calves. Cheese produced through the use of genetically engineered chymosin is also approved by Muslims and Jews.

One important factor in many vegetarians' approval of genetically engineered chymosin is the fact that in practice the rennet actually used by cheese manufacturers will not contain the original calf chymosin gene, but copies of it. However, something of a diversity of views exists on this point among vegetarians. Some accept the copying stage as meaning a host containing a gene from an animal source is acceptable while others view its animal origin as meaning that the product is not acceptable.

By 1994, approximately half of the worldwide market for rennet was being supplied by genetically engineered chymosin. It is tempting to see this example of genetic engineering as a way of saving the lives of the millions of 4- to 10-day-old calves that, until recently, were killed for their rennet each year. The reality, though, is that these calves continue to be produced to keep their mothers—dairy cows—producing milk. Female calves generally themselves become dairy calves. Male calves are usually reared for meat, either as veal calves or as beef cattle.

B. Genetically Engineered Tomatoes

Tomatoes are big business, with sales exceeding those of potatoes or lettuce. However, it is generally acknowledged that today's tomatoes all too often have a poor flavor and texture. The main reason is that tomatoes are usually picked before they are ripe. The benefit of this practice is that it allows the tomatoes to be moved from where they are grown to where they are sold before they go soft. Consequently, the tomatoes are less likely to be damaged in transit. The disadvantage, though, stems from the fact that tomato flavor correlates with the amount of time the tomatoes spend on the parent plant. Picking tomatoes when they are still green leads, therefore, to relatively flavorless tomatoes.

A second problem with picking tomatoes before they go red is that they then have to be treated with ethylene before being sold. Ethylene is a natural plant growth substance and is responsible for the ripening of tomatoes *in situ*. It is supplied to tomatoes that are picked when still green as otherwise they fail to ripen. A final problem with harvesting tomatoes when they are still green is that it is all too easy to pick them when they are still very unripe. These immature green tomatoes taste even less good than the ones that result from tomatoes picked when "mature green."

For a variety of reasons, therefore, there are strong incentives for breeding tomatoes which can be picked when red. Such tomatoes should taste better and be firmer. They would not need to be treated with ethylene and might even end up costing less, as the wastage that comes from picking immature green tomatoes would probably be reduced.

From the mid-1980s a race ensued between several companies trying to manufacture and market genetically engineered tomatoes with these characteristics. In 1994 this research reached commercial fruition when Calgene's "Flavr Savr" tomato went on sale in the USA. Other companies still involved in the genetic engineering of tomatoes include Monsanto and Zeneca seeds.

The approach used relies on the fact that tomatoes take much longer to go soft if they do not produce a protein called polygalacturonase (PG). In a natural tomato, PG synthesis only takes place as the tomato ripens from green to red. Its effect is to soften the fruit by breaking down some of the compounds in cell walls between the cells of the fruit.

Preventing PG synthesis does not affect ripening, but it does mean that the fruit remains firm—just what is wanted by manufacturers and consumers. It also means that tomato sauces made from the tomatoes are more viscous and so flow less readily. This, too, is a desirable characteristic—runny tomato ketchups are not popular. Indeed, tomato paste manufacturers sometimes heat tomatoes to inactivate PG. However, this heating costs money and further reduces the flavor.

PG synthesis can now be prevented by so-called "antisense gene technology." In essence an artificial gene, made in the laboratory to be the reverse of the PG gene, is inserted into the tomato's DNA. This artificial gene effectively cancels out the effect of the PG gene and so prevents the cell from manufacturing PG. It is almost as if the PG gene had been excised from the DNA.

For those who object to such a procedure on the grounds that it is unnatural, it needs to be realized that the modern tomato, *Lycopersicum esculentum,* has already had many features bred into it by hybridizations, through traditional techniques of plant breeding, between a number of different *Lycopersicum* species. It might, therefore, be argued that the genetic integrity of the tomato has already, through conventional plant breeding, been somewhat violated.

A slight complication is that when researchers genetically engineer a species, they often add a "marker" gene which makes the organism immune to a particular antibiotic. The reason for this is that it makes it easier in the laboratory to see whether the genetic engineering has worked. In the case of tomatoes, for example, one simply has to see if the young tomato seedling is unaffected by the presence of an antibiotic such as kanamy-

cin, rather than waiting to see if the fruits the adult tomato eventually produces take longer to go rotten.

It has been pointed out, not least by the United Kingdom's Department of Health's Advisory Committee on Novel Foods and Processes, that there is a possibility, albeit a very small one, that when large amounts of foods containing these antibiotic marker genes begin to be consumed, the gene might move to disease-causing microorganisms in the gut and so make them resistant to the antibiotic too.

Most experts suspect that the chances of this happening are not great. Even if it does happen, the consequences are unlikely to be desperately serious as there are many different types of antibiotics and any one marker gene only conveys resistance to one of them. Nevertheless, the existence of a finite risk slowed the regulatory approval of genetically engineered tomatoes and other foods in the United Kingdom. In the long run, a possible solution is for companies to use other, less problematic markers. Technically this is feasible, though less easy.

C. Reproductive Techniques Applied to Farm Animals

Reproductive techniques have been applied to farm animals for over 10,000 years. Farmers have long been accustomed to breeding selectively from only certain individuals—castrating, isolating, or slaughtering the rest. Traditional biotechnology has already led to the point where turkeys are unable to mate. Instead, the males have to be "milked" by hand to obtain their semen and the females artificially inseminated.

To a considerable extent, the history of animal husbandry has been a history of the increasing physical dependence of domestic animals on humans. Modern biotechnology, which already boasts genetic engineering, *in vitro* fertilization, and embryo transfer, is likely to accelerate this trend, but it need not. It is perfectly possible that consumer pressure and/or appropriate regulations could lead to animals being given back some of their natural freedoms by the use of modern biotechnology.

D. Bovine Growth Hormone (BST)

1. Why Bother to Make Genetically Engineered BST?

Bovine growth hormone, also called bovine somatotrophin (BST for short), is a natural hormone produced by cattle. During lactation, BST causes nutrients derived from a cow's food to be diverted to her mammary glands where they are used to make milk. It is this fact that has led to an extraordinary 10-year battle over genetically engineered BST.

In the 1970s it was suggested that injecting a cow with BST might increase her milk yield. The chemical structure of BST was determined in 1973, and by 1982 genetically engineered BST had been made. A huge amount of basic and applied research has been carried out on genetically engineered BST by a number of companies, i.e., Cyanamid, Elanco, Monsanto, and Upjohn.

Injecting dairy cows with genetically engineered BST increases their milk yields by some 20%. Furthermore, it increases milk to feed ratios by some 15%—that is, the amount of milk made by the cow relative to the food she consumes goes up by around 15%. Monsanto argues that genetically engineered BST offers a number of significant advantages to dairy farmers. The main one is that by raising milk yields and increasing feed efficiency, profits are raised. Further, the technology requires no capital investment: the farmer merely injects the cows every 14 days from the 9th week after calving until the end of lactation. Finally, genetically engineered BST is virtually identical to the BST naturally produced by cows, usually differing by just one amino acid. BST is present in the resulting milk only in trace amounts and Monsanto argues that BST has no physiological effects on humans as it differs in structure from human growth hormone. In any case, the minute amounts present in milk are digested and so do not pass into the human bloodstream.

2. Arguments against Using Genetically Engineered BST

First of all, who wants or needs more milk? The number of dairy cows kept in Europe and the USA—the two regions where profitable sales of BST are most likely—fell throughout the 1980s and 1990s. This was because the demand for milk failed to keep up with the dramatic increases that took place in milk yields through selective breeding and the use of feed concentrates and other argicultural practices. It has been argued that the widespread introduction of genetically engineered BST would lead to even more farmers being put out of business.

Secondly, while it is true that genetically engineered BST itself almost certainly poses no health risks to humans, its use is linked to significantly raised levels of insulin-like growth factor-1 in the cow's milk. The consequences of this is still controversial. It has been argued that the presence of these high levels of insulin-like growth factor-1, which is chemically identical in cattle

and in humans, may trigger breast cancer in women and growth stimulation of cells in the colon. While few scientists regard this possibility as a likely one, Ben Mepham, of the Centre for Applied Bioethics at Nottingham University, has argued that legalisation of commercial use of BST in the absence of more extensive information on these questions could lead to a deterioration in public health if widespread rejection of milk were, ironically, to result.

Thirdly, does the use of BST injections harm the cow's health? Even the manufacturers of genetically engineered BST accept that its use may increase the incidence of mastitis, cystic ovaries, disorders of the uterus, retained placentas, and other health problems including indigestion, bloat, diarrhea, and lesions of the knees. In addition, its use may result in permanent swellings up to 10 cm in diameter at the injection site. Mastitis, as many women know all too well, is a painful inflammation of the mammary glands. It has the same effects in cows as in humans. Mastitis in cows is commonly treated by giving antibiotics to infected animals. Some concern has been raised at the consequences of this for human health, though these fears may be exaggerated as antibiotics have been used on farm animals for decades. A related point is that BST injections possibly put even more pressure on a cow's health in countries where farmers have little or no access to high-concentrate feeds.

Fourthly, while everybody knows that dairy farming is big business, for many people the thought that cows will be artificially stimulated by biweekly injections of genetically engineered BST for most of their lives is somehow off-putting. True, genetically engineered BST is almost identical in structure to natural BST, but to some people it seems wrong that it should be used to boost a cow's BST levels beyond what is normal. Is its use analogous to the force-feeding of geese to produce pâté de foie gras? For some people milk still retains a special aura of freshness and naturalness, perhaps because we all start our lives, once born, by living off milk. This image is tarred by the use of genetically engineered BST. It may be hard to reconcile a belief, albeit a naive one, that milk is a "natural" product with the recognition that genetic engineering is being used to direct the process.

3. The Current Legal Position

By 1996 genetically engineered BST had been licensed for use in a number of countries including South Africa, India, Mexico, Brazil, the former USSR, and the USA. Endless debates have taken place within the European Union, but in December 1994 agriculture ministers from European Union countries agreed to continue the ban on its use until the year 2000.

One of the most remarkable features of the lifting, in the USA, of the ban on the use of genetically engineered BST was that the Food and Drug Administration produced guidelines stating that any company proclaiming that its milk was produced without the use of genetically engineered BST would have to carry a long statement explaining that there is no advantage to BST-free milk. The first two American dairies that advertised their milk as "hormone-free" were promptly sued by Monsanto.

E. The Development of Animal Models for Human Diseases

Genetically engineered mice and rats are being used in increasing numbers as models for human diseases. The reason is that they are extremely useful animals on which to try experimental procedures. They have a very short generation time; large numbers can be kept easily, cheaply, and conveniently in a laboratory; and a great deal is known about their genetics. The basic procedure goes as follows. First, genetically engineer your mice (or rats) so that they mimic a human disease. Secondly, study these altered animals either to investigate the disease or to see if it can be alleviated. The hope, of course, is that what is learned about the disease from the mice or rats will be applicable to humans.

Examples of human diseases for which mouse models exist include albinism, Alzheimer's disease, atherosclerosis, β-thalassaemia, cancers, cystic fibrosis, high blood pressure, Lesch–Nyhan syndrome, muscular dystrophy, severe combined immunodeficiency, and sickle-cell anaemia. The first of these genetically engineered mice was the so-called Harvard oncomouse developed by Philip Leder and his colleagues at Harvard Medical School and patented in 1988. The Harvard oncomouse contains certain human genes which result in the majority of the individual mice in the strain developing cancers. It has to be admitted, though, that the Harvard oncomouse has not been a tremendous commercial success. Du Pont, the company which funded the research, has invested millions of dollars in the project. However, it has failed to persuade a single pharmaceutical company to sign up for deals involving the mice. Du Pont had hoped that it would be able to charge a royalty on anticancer drugs developed through studies using the mice.

However, there are instances where genetically engineered mice are proving more useful. In 1993 scientists from the Imperial Cancer Research Fund in Oxford and the Wellcome Trust at the University of Cambridge found that mice that had been genetically engineered to show symptoms of cystic fibrosis could themselves have their symptoms alleviated through genetic engineering.

Controversy exists, though, as to precisely how valuable or necessary the use of any animals, let alone genetically engineered ones, in medical research is. Some people, including the majority of medical researchers, maintain that their use is essential; others maintain that improvements in alternative approaches (including cell culture, tissue culture, and computer modeling) mean that animals are no longer needed for such work.

With regard to the effects of such procedures on the animals themselves, in the case of the oncomice, common sense, the scientific community, and the courts have all concluded that these animals suffer. Oncomice develop tumors in a variety of places including mammary tissue, blood, skeletal muscle, the lungs, the neck, and the groin. Tumors can lead to severe weight loss (40% body weight or more) while large tumors may ulcerate.

It is hardly surprising that the development and patenting of oncomice has been attacked by a large number of animal welfare and animal rights movements around the world. In addition, religious organizations are increasingly speaking out against the suffering that humans cause to animals. In some religions, such as Christianity and Islam, the animals' points of view have only really been put forth with any strength in recent decades. A number of other religions, though, have a much longer history of according priority to the nonsuffering of animals. In Jainism, the concern for *ahisma* (noninjury) goes hand-in-hand with an insistence on a vegetarian diet, while lay members are encouraged to engage only in occupations that minimize the loss of life. Within Jainism it is the monastic practice to carry a small broom with which gently to remove any living creature before one sits or lies down. In Buddhism too there has traditionally been a strong emphasis on animal well-being.

F. Human Growth Hormone

1. The Role of Human Growth Hormone

Throughout our lives our bodies produce human growth hormone. This hormone is a protein and is produced in the pituitary gland. From here it passes into the bloodstream and is carried around the body. Its main effects are on bones and muscles—growth hormone stimulates cells to increase in size or divide.

Some children produce too little growth hormone and end up much shorter than average, typically around 4 ft. in height. This condition is sometimes referred to as pituitary dwarfism, though the term is often avoided on the grounds that some people find the word "dwarfism" insulting.

In most cases, people with an abnormally low production of growth hormone end up physically quite healthy, with a body that is normally proportioned, albeit unusually small. Until the 1950s there was not anything that could be done to change their height—eating more, for example, has no effect. Then Dr. Maurice Raben at the Tufts New England Medical Center began painstakingly to extract human growth hormone from the pituitary glands of corpses. The hope was that if this was given to people with abnormally low levels of growth hormone production, they might benefit by growing more.

One of the first people treated was a Canadian called Frank Hooey. By the time he saw Maurice Raben, Frank Hooey was aged 17 and was only 4′3″ in height—the height of a typical eight and a half year old. Over the next five years he received thrice-weekly injections of human growth hormone. By the end of the treatment he stood at 5′6″, slightly below average, but well within the normal range.

Frank Hooey's treatment was a success story. However, it takes around 650 pituitary glands to produce the 2 to 3 g of human growth hormone needed for the 5-year treatment. Because of this, human growth hormone obtained from pituitaries costs far more than gold, and only a relatively small number of people benefited from the procedure.

The advent of genetic engineering has changed all this. Once the gene responsible for the production of human growth hormone was found and isolated, it was a relatively simple matter to insert it into laboratory bacteria and get them to synthesize the protein. The hormone is then collected, checked for purity, and given to people suffering from a shortage of it.

One might think that this is a perfect example of biotechnology in action. Bacteria are being used to replace a missing human protein. As being 4 ft. in height is manifestly disadvantageous, the procedure seems extremely useful and surely only someone with an extreme aversion to biotechnology could object. However, the truth is more complicated.

2. Who Uses Human Growth Hormone?

There are three main categories of people who use injected human growth hormone: children who would otherwise suffer from pituitary dwarfism and end up only about 4 ft. in height; children who would otherwise end up round about 5 ft. in height; and sportspeople.

The first of these categories, children who would otherwise suffer from pituitary dwarfism and be only about 4 ft. in height—are the ones for whom synthetic human growth hormone was originally intended. For such children there is a lot to be said for it. Growth hormone obtained by the old method of extraction from the pituitary glands of countless corpses was almost unobtainable. Further, when it was available, it was occasionally contaminated by viruses. Over a dozen cases are known where children who had received human growth hormone extracted from pituitary glands went on to develop Creutzfeldt–Jakob disease—a fatal condition caused by a virus that can infect human brain tissue.

Only about 1 in 100,000 people are pituitary dwarfs, but there are millions of children who, though taller than pituitary dwarfs, are shorter than average. What has happened since the advent of genetic engineering is that some parents have started to put their children onto programs of human growth hormone injections, hoping thereby that they will end up taller.

It might be supposed that this is not a very serious problem. After all, many parents pay for their children to receive music lessons or tennis coaching. What does it matter if some parents pay for their children to receive human growth hormone treatment?

One problem is the cost of the procedure. A full course of treatment lasts between 5 and 10 years and costs, at 1990's prices, up to $150,000. A second problem is that no one knows for certain if the treatment works. We know that pituitary dwarfs benefit, because the injected growth hormone replaces the missing growth hormone. But there are lots of reasons why children can be below average height, and some pediatricians doubt that injections of human growth hormone will help in all cases. Actual findings are unclear. There are some data which suggest that injecting short children who are not growth hormone deficient does not increase their eventual height. On the other hand, there are other data, obtained by Genentech, the leading manufacturer of human growth hormone, which suggest that growth hormone injections do increase the height of both boys and girls.

A third problem is that once you start the treatment, you have to continue. Stopping growth hormone treatment in children who are not growth hormone deficient before they have reached their adult height may cause them to grow more slowly than they did before treatment. This is because taking the extra growth hormone causes the body to temporarily stop making its own growth hormone.

A fourth problem is that even if the full treatment does cause children to grow a few inches taller, the effects on a child's self-esteem and mental health are unknown. Maybe these will be bolstered. However, it has been suggested that quite the opposite may be the case. The injections may cause children to see themselves as abnormal, with subsequent loss of self-esteem.

A final problem with injected human growth hormone is that a number of independent studies have suggested a possible causal relationship between its long-term use and leukemia. As a result, both Genentech and Eli Lilly, another company that produces human growth hormone, have changed their labeling to indicate this.

It is worth bearing in mind that half of us are shorter than the average. It is true that tall people benefit in all sorts of ways—other things being equal, tall people are more likely to be favored at job interviews, while the taller candidate has won 80% of USA Presidential election campaigns. Surely, though, society should be challenging this bias in favor of the tall rather than conniving with it by allowing parents to spend many tens of thousands of dollars in an effort to enable their children to grow a little taller. As Abby Lippman, a professor at McGill University and Chair of the Human Genetics Committee of the Council for Responsible Genetics, puts it, "Why not lower the hoops on a basketball court?"

A third category of people who are injecting human growth hormone are certain sportspeople. Some athletes have used the hormone in an attempt to increase strength, in much the same way as steroids are used illegally for the same purpose. The consequences of larger than normal doses of human growth hormone are still incompletely known, but it will not be surprising if it turns out there are harmful medical consequences. At the same time the practice, if it works, is unfair on athletes who do not inject themselves.

Recently, human growth hormone has been given to a number of people with AIDS and to large numbers of people over the age of 50. These is considerable, though as yet largely anecdotal, evidence that human growth hormone can increase muscle strength, reduce fat deposition, and reduce depression. Perhaps time will tell whether we really have found the elixir of life or whether there are significant side effects.

G. Gene Therapy

1. Somatic and Germ-Line Therapy

It is helpful to distinguish between two classes of cells found in our bodies: germ-line cells are the cells found in the ovaries of a female and the testes of a male and give rise, respectively, to eggs and to sperm; somatic cells are all the other cells in the body. The importance of this distinction is that any genetic changes to somatic cells cannot be passed onto future generations. On the other hand, changes to germ-line cells can indeed be passed onto children and to succeeding generations.

2. Somatic Gene Therapy for Human Diseases

The first successful attempts to genetically engineer humans were carried out in 1990. These attempts involved patients with a very rare disorder known as severe combined immune deficiency (SCID). In someone with SCID, the immune system does not work. As a result the person is highly susceptible to infections. Children with SCID are sometimes known as bubble babies because, until recently, almost the only way to allow them to live more than a few years was to isolate them in plastic bubbles. These bubbles protect the children from harmful germs but also, poignantly, cut them off from all social contact. In any event, at best the bubbles prolong life by only a few years.

SCID can have a number of causes. One cause is an inherited deficiency in a single protein, adenosine deaminase (ADA). The first person with SCID to be treated with gene therapy was a 4-year-old girl. She was unable to produce ADA, and in 1990 some of her white blood cells were removed and functioning versions of the ADA gene introduced into them using a virus as a vector. The improvement in her condition was remarkable. Five years later she was living a comparatively normal life, attending a normal school, and so on.

By 1995 over 200 trials for somatic gene therapy had been approved. In addition to trials on people with SCID, somatic gene therapy is being tried for β-thalassemia, cancers, cystic fibrosis, Duchenne muscular dystrophy, familial hypercholesterolemia, and hemophilia.

3. The Scope of Somatic Gene Therapy

Somatic gene therapy has been paraded as a possible cure for a great range of medical problems. It should be realized, however, that some human diseases caused by faulty genes can already be treated quite effectively by conventional means. For example, phenylketonuria is a condition which, if untreated, leads to the person being severely mentally retarded. Since 1954, though, it has been realized that the condition can be entirely prevented by giving children with the faulty gene that causes phenylketonuria a special diet. This illustrates a most important truth about human development: both genes and the environment play essential parts.

A second reason why we should not see gene therapy as the likely solution to all medical problems is that diseases such as cystic fibrosis, phenylketonuria, and sickle-cell disease are the exception, not the rule. These conditions are caused by inborn errors in single genes. However, less than 2% of our total disease load is due to errors in single genes. Most human diseases have a strong environmental component, so that genetic defects merely predispose the person to develop the condition. In addition, the genetic component is usually the result of many genes.

4. Somatic Gene Therapy for Other Human Traits

What of gene therapy to affect traits such as intelligence, beauty, criminality, and sexual preference? Will this ever be practicable? There are frequent reports in the popular press of "a gene for homosexuality" or "a gene for criminality," and it may be that much human behavior has a genetic component to it. However, attempts to find genes for homosexuality, intelligence, beauty, or criminality are, at best, the first steps to understanding the rich and complex ways in which we behave. At worst, they are misguided attempts to stigmatize certain members of society. We are more, far more, than our genes.

5. The Ethical Significance of Somatic Gene Therapy

What new ethical issues are raised by somatic gene therapy? The short answer, when we are talking about real human diseases, is "possibly none." This, for example, was the conclusion reached in the United Kingdom by the government-appointed Clothier Committee which produced its report on the ethics of gene therapy in January 1992. Because somatic gene therapy typically involves giving a person healthy DNA to override the effects of their own malfunctioning DNA, it is widely held that this is not very different from giving a person a blood transfusion or organ transplant. Of course, some individuals may choose not to have a transfusion or transplant, but very few people suggest forbidding them entirely. It is the case, though, that somatic gene therapy can be less reversible than most conventional treatments.

It is also the case that somatic gene therapy has the potential to reduce the number of ethically problematic decisions. At present the only "solution" offered to a woman who is carrying a fetus identified as having a serious genetic disorder such as muscular dystrophy is the possibility of an abortion. Somatic gene therapy may be able to offer a more positive way forward.

However, somatic gene therapy may, in time, raise new ethical issues. Suppose, despite what we have said about the complexities of human behavior, it does eventually transpire that somatic gene "therapy" could re-duce the likelihood of someone being violently aggressive or of being sexually attracted to others of the same sex. What then? One answer is to throw one's hands up in horror and agree that such "treatments" should be outlawed. However, one logical problem with this response is that most countries already spend a lot of time and effort trying to get people who have been convicted of violent crimes to be less likely to commit these again. Such people may attend education programs or receive state-funded psychotherapy, for instance, in attempts to achieve these aims. Similarly, some psychiatrists and counselors are still prepared to work with homosexuals to help them change their sexual orientation.

These two examples (violent behavior and sexual orientation) highlight two related issues. The first has to do with the social construction of disease. A disease is, in a sense, a relationship a person has with society. Is being 4 ft. tall a disease? The answer tells us more about a society than it does about an individual of this height. Some conditions are relatively unproblematic in their definition as a disease. For instance, Lesch–Nyhan disease is characterized by severe mental retardation, uncontrolled movements (spasticity), and self-mutilation. No cure is at present available and the person dies, early in life, after what most people would consider an unpleasant existence. It is the existence of conditions such as this that have even led to claims in the courts of wrongful life or wrongful birth where a sufferer, or someone acting on their behalf, sues either their parent(s) or doctor(s) on the grounds that it would have been better for them never to have been born. However, years of campaigning by activists for people with disabilities have shown us the extent to which many diseases or disabilities are as much a reflection of the society in which the person lives as they are the product of the genes and internal environment of that person.

The second issue is to do with consent. It is one thing for a person convicted of a violent crime to give their informed consent to receive psychotherapy or some other treatment aimed at changing their behavior, though even these treatments are, of course, open to abuse. It would be quite another for a parent to decide, on a fetus' or baby's behalf, to let it receive somatic gene therapy to make it less aggressive.

6. Germ-Line Therapy

At the moment it is generally acknowledged that human germ-line therapy is too risky. Researchers cannot, at present, control precisely where new genes are inserted. This raises the not insignificant danger that the inserted gene might damage an existing gene, which could lead to diseases, including cancers. We can note, in passing, that the existence, despite these problems, of germ-line manipulation in animals (i.e., non-human animals) illustrates the distinction between what is generally deemed acceptable for animals and for humans.

However, although human germ-line therapy may currently be too risky, it is difficult to imagine that this will continue to be the case indefinitely. It seems extremely likely that scientists will develop methods of targeting the insertion of new genes with sufficient precision to avoid the problems that presently attend such procedures. Nor need these new methods require much, possibly any, experimentation on human embryos. A great deal, perhaps all, of the information could be obtained through the genetic engineering of farm animals.

Further, we should realize that although germ-line therapy is sometimes referred to as "irrevocable," it is more likely, if we ever get to the point where its use is routine, that it will normally be reversible. There is no reason to suppose that if something went wrong with the results of germ-line therapy, this wrong would necessarily be visited on a person's descendants in perpetuity. The same techniques that will permit targeted germ-line therapy should permit its reversal.

One can ask whether germ-line therapy is necessary. It is no easy matter to demonstrate that something is "necessary." Value judgments are involved, so that there may be genuine controversy about whether something is needed. Is nuclear power necessary? Or the motor car? Or tigers? Or confidentiality between doctors and their patients? It is likely that most improvements that might result from germ-line therapy could also be effected by somatic gene therapy or conventional medicine. However, it may prove to be the case that germ-line therapy allows some medical conditions to be treated better.

Assuming, then, that one day germ-line therapy is both relatively safe and allows certain medical conditions to be treated better than by other approaches, would it be right or wrong?

It is sometimes argued that germ-line therapy will decrease the amount of genetic variation among people and that this is not a good thing, since evolution needs genetic variation. There are several things that are dubious about this objection. First, empirically, it is difficult to imagine in the foreseeable future that germ-line therapy is going to significantly decrease the amount of useful human variation among people. Secondly, it is possible that germ-line therapy may one day lead to even more genetic variation—as some parents opt for

certain genes in their children and other parents for other genes. Thirdly, the argument that evolution needs genetic variation is difficult to sustain faced with someone suffering as a result of a disease that is largely the result of a genetic mutation. The argument relies on possible, very distant advantages for groups of people being sufficient to override the more immediate, clear disadvantages for individuals.

Then some people have expressed the fear that germ-line therapy might be used by dictators to produce only certain types of people. The emotive term "eugenics" is often used in this context. Perhaps the major problem with this objection is that it assumes too much of genetic engineering. It is easy to overstate the extent to which humans are controlled by their genes. Dictators have had, do have, and will have far more effective ways of controlling people.

A more likely problem is that germ-line therapy will be permitted before people have grown sufficiently accustomed to the idea. The pace of technological change is so fast nowadays that some people end up feeling bewildered by new possibilities. The theologian Ian Barbour has argued that it is important that sufficient time is allowed before germ-line therapy on humans is permitted, both to ascertain, so far as is possible, that the procedure is safe and so that people may feel comfortable with the idea.

A frequently expressed worry about germ-line therapy is the extent to which future generations will be affected. Again, it is possible that this fear may be an exaggerated one. As we have said, we can overestimate the importance of our genetic makeup. Then there is the point that people already have and will continue to have a tremendous influence over future generations through everything from child-rearing patterns and family planning to books and pollution. The philosophers Robert Nozick, Jonathan Glover, and John Harris have been quite bullish about germ-line therapy, and Nozick, back in 1974, introduced the notion of a "genetic supermarket" at which parents, rather than the state, could choose the genetic makeup of their children. Harris has even argued that we may one day have a duty to carry out germ-line therapy.

There remains the worry, though, born of long experience of slippery slopes, that the road to hell is paved with good intentions. After all, suppose that germ-line therapy allowed people to choose the color of their offspring's skin. For many people, the idea is frightening and abhorrent. Indeed, it is possible that the selective use of such a practice, particularly if the procedure is expensive so that only some people can afford it, might reinforce racist attitudes in society. Despite the difficulties of distinguishing in all cases genetic engineering to correct faults (such as cystic fibrosis, hemophilia, or cancers) from genetic engineering to enhance traits (such as intelligence, creativity, athletic prowess, or musical ability), the best way forward may be to ban germ-line therapy intended only to enhance traits, at least until many years of informed debate have taken place.

Also See the Following Articles

AGRICULTURAL ETHICS • ANIMAL RESEARCH • EUGENICS • GENETIC COUNSELING • GENETIC ENGINEERING

Bibliography

Bains, W. (1993). "Biotechnology from A to Z." Oxford Univ. Press, Oxford/New York.

Cole-Turner, R. (1993). "The New Genesis: Theology and the Genetic Revolution." Westminster–Knox, Louisville, KY.

Dyson, A., and Harris, J. (Eds.) (1994). "Ethics and Biotechnology." Routledge, London/New York.

Glover, J. (1984). "What Sort of People Should There Be?" Penguin, Harmondsworth Middlesex.

Krimsky, S. (1991). "Biotechnics and Society: The Rise of Industrial Genetics." Praeger, New York.

Levidow, L. (1995). Agricultural biotechnology as clean surgical strike. *Social Text 44* **13**(3), 161–180.

Ministry of Agriculture, Fisheries and Food (1995). "Report of the Committee to Consider the Ethical Implications of Emerging Technologies in the Breeding of Farm Animals." HMSO, London.

Nelson, J. R. (1994). "On the New Frontiers of Genetics and Religion." Eerdmans, Grand Rapids, MI.

Reiss, M. J., and Straughan, R. (1996). "Improving Nature? The Science and Ethics of Genetic Engineering." Cambridge Univ. Press, Cambridge/New York.

Wheale, P., and McNally, R. (Eds.) (1990). "The Bio-revolution: Cornucopia or Pandora's Box." Pluto, London/Winchester, MA.

BIRTH-CONTROL ETHICS

Joan C. Callahan
University of Kentucky

I. Introduction and Overview
II. The Politics of Birth Control
III. The Philosophy of Woman and the Politics of Motherhood
IV. Moral Issues Associated with Contemporary Contraceptive Methods
V. Population Control
VI. Conclusion

GLOSSARY

antinatalism The fact or policy of favoring decreased childbirth.

birth control Any method used to prevent birth, including contraceptives, contragestives, and chemical or surgical abortion after implantation.

contraceptives Birth control methods that have prevention of conception (fertilization of an oocyte or egg by a spermatazoan) as their primary birth control action.

contragestives Birth control methods that intervene after conception to prevent implantation of an embryo.

pronatalism The fact or policy of favoring increased childbirth.

BIRTH-CONTROL ETHICS may be generally defined as the application of moral reasoning to issues of limiting or encouraging human reproduction.

I. INTRODUCTION AND OVERVIEW

Birth control has been and continues to be the locus of some of our most interesting and most difficult political, legal, and moral struggles. Methods for controlling fertility and controlling birth remain highly contested in society and in the courts in industrialized nations, while developing nations often seek to limit population growth as a matter deemed crucial to national survival. During the past half century, women in many societies have achieved much greater social freedom, which cannot be fully separated from the stunning advancements that have been made in birth control technology. New, increasingly reliable methods have afforded many women in the industrialized West unprecedented control over their reproduction. At the same time, poor women in these same societies are often without access to certain birth control technologies, such as abortion, because they are unable to afford them and governments will not subsidize them. This is currently the case in the United States. On the other hand, these same technologies sometimes have been imposed upon women in societies where limiting reproduction is not obviously in the best interests of individual families, for example, in societies with high infant mortality rates and where there is little or nothing available to people in the way of social security and the elderly must depend on their surviving children for support. Thus, attitudes toward and state support of individual control of reproduction vary vastly across the contemporary world. Existing social attitudes and state postures toward birth control are tied to a variety of considerations, including sexuality, politics, religion, economics, and the metaphysics (and consequent social status) of women.

Viewed historically, a similarly varied picture of birth control emerges, with the variations tied to the kinds of considerations just mentioned. For example, prostitution was often part of religion in the ancient West and Near East, where intercourse with temple prostitutes was viewed as an act of respect for a temple deity, a not atypical practice combining religion and the sexual use of women. Similarly, Greek *hetaerae* ("companions") were frequently women of relatively high social status, offering them social and economic rewards for their service to men. On the other hand, Roman *meretrices* had low social status, and were even required to dress in ways that made their occupation clear to all. Still, prostitution was accepted in Rome and it flourished in the Middle Ages, when licensed brothels served as sources of income for a number of municipalities. Indeed, it was only when venereal disease reached epidemic proportions in Western and Central Europe in the 16th century that serious efforts to control prostitution were undertaken. In contrast, the Jews rejected temple prostitution, along with the sexual practices that tended to accompany the fertility-based religions, and they developed the view that procreation is the primary purpose of sexual interaction, an attitude which carried over into Christianity. Thus, as we approached the modern world—particularly in the West, with its Judeo-Christian roots—questions regarding control of sexual interaction and birth control became deeply interlocked, and sexual interaction for purposes other than reproduction fell into disrepute. This attitude carries on today in countries such as the United States, where, for example, sexual interaction between persons of the same sex continues to be against the law in a number of jurisdictions.

Despite advances in contraceptive science made in the 19th and early 20th centuries in the West, social resistance to the development of safe, effective, and widely available contraception and nonreproductive sexual interaction has been strong. Initially dubbed "obscene," both were condemned as social evils in the Victorian Age, and contraception became associated with promiscuity and decline of family values. These attitudes reemerged in the 1990s. Many people today want not only contraceptives, but even information about reproduction, withheld from potentially sexually active teenagers. Indeed, in the United States we have seen a steady shift away from the short-lived "sexual revolution" begun in the 1960s to a renewed conservatism regarding sexual interaction and to a more and more strident opposition to sex education in U.S. public schools. And the United States is not idiosyncratic in its conservatism. As various forms of conservatism and religious fundamentalism have swept the world, contraception and other forms of birth control have fallen deeper and deeper into dispute across the globe.

II. THE POLITICS OF BIRTH CONTROL

A. Pronatalism

Religious influences on common morality and on consequent state attempts to control reproduction and sexual practices more generally can never be underestimated. In the West, religious influences underpin laws against sodomy, prostitution, fornication, and even cohabitation of unmarried heterosexual couples. In the United States, it is not surprising that two of the groups most helpful to Anthony Comstock and his Society for the Suppression of Vice were the Women's Christian Temperance Union and the New York Young Men's Christian Association. Wedded to the theological influences on state regulation of individual behaviors, including sexual behaviors, is a philosophical position which holds that one of the state's responsibilities is to protect the morals of its citizens—a view known as "legal moralism." This position, combined with the content of the Judeo-Christian tradition, continues to have a strong influence on government attempts to control sexual interaction and reproduction in the West. The current emphasis of those on the political right on so-called family values is reminiscent of the preaching of turn-of-the-century English Anglicans, who worried that contraception would "eat away the heart and drain away the life-blood" of their country and lead to "what may be called free love." The term "free love" itself reveals the traditional religious view that underpins its use, namely, the view that coitus without the "purchase price" of potential pregnancy is sinful or contrary to the will of God. Religion, then, has had and continues to have a significant influence on common morals, and when a society takes legal moralism seriously, religion has an acute influence on the content of morals that states are thought to have an obligation to enforce. Historically, the Roman Catholic church has had enormous influence in the West in this regard; contemporarily, Christian fundamentalism has overtaken this influence in the West, and other forms of religious fundamentalism have had and continue to exert pronatalist social efforts in much of the world. But religion and legal moralism are not the only considerations that influence state interest in controlling sexual interaction and individual reproduction.

Population concerns also influence law and public policy governing birth control. On the one hand, there is a tradition (with adherents as otherwise divergent as Adam Smith and Friedreich Engels) which holds that rising population is both the cause and the effect of increasing prosperity. Currently, this view is supported by theorists who argue that, in general, the standard of living worldwide has increased alongside steady increments in world population and that such population increases are accompanied by less severe shortages, lower costs for goods, and better ways of avoiding shortages. Such a position encourages governments to adopt pronatalist policies, such as disallowing contraception and elective abortion and precluding women from obtaining meaningful work outside the family.

In addition to arguments from increased prosperity, states have also adopted pronatalist policies to ensure national survival and national superiority. After the loss of French lives in World War I, for example, the French legislative assembly suppressed abortion and the diffusion of contraceptive information in order to encourage French births. In part, the concern was to ensure national survival; in part the concern was fear of Germany's population superiority.

In the first half of the 20th century, Germany was determined to increase its population from 66 to 90 million, and Italy under Mussolini was committed to entering the second half of the 20th century with a population of 60 million. The German, Italian, and French leadership well realized that depopulated or lightly populated nations are subject to control by other nations. This concern, coupled with interests in expansion and political dominance, led to strong pronatalist policies in many European nations earlier in the 20th century.

At the same time, governments sometimes adopt pronatalist policies because of their fears that birth control is otherwise harmful to the general good. Birth control (including contraception and abortion) has been held to foster decadence and selfishness, since it permits people to avoid the efforts and expenses associated with raising children, purportedly allowing them to become preoccupied with fulfilling their own self-serving interests. A society of people pursuing luxury and constant comfort is feared to be both morally and physically weak. Thus, contraception and sexual interaction become objects of state interest because of their presumed ties to the public interest. Pronatalist policies help to ensure that sexual interaction for purposes other than reproduction alone will be discouraged.

Finally, pronatalist policies are invariably associated with the control of women and the sexual access of men to women. Patriarchal concerns (i.e., concerns having to do with the dominant position of men) enter into the establishment and maintenance of gender roles, the social construction of women's (appropriate) sexuality, family structure, intolerance of homosexuality, and limits on the freedom of women to decide when they will not reproduce.

B. Antinatalism

The purported ties between sexual interaction, reproduction, and the public interest are not limited to the adoption of pronatalist policies and practices, however, and it is sometimes the case that governments adopt rigorous antinatalist policies and practices or a combination of pronatalist and antinatalist policies and practices that target different social groups. Such combinations are often linked to concerns about maintaining racial dominance within a society and the elimination of the "unfit." In the early part of the 20th century, for example, a eugenics movement grew up in the United States, and by 1932 twenty-seven states had laws allowing involuntary sterilization of the so-called feeble-minded, insane, criminal, and physically defective. Sadly, even Margaret Sanger moved away from her pioneering emphasis on reproductive choice to join the eugenicists, claiming that we needed "more children from the fit, less from the unfit." This sort of view leads to antinatalist pressures being put on the groups to be held back (or eliminated), while pronatalist pressures are put on groups to be nurtured (or expanded). Nazi Germany had such mixed policies. There, sterilization laws were adopted to preclude reproduction by "inferiors," while strong pronatalist policies and a propaganda campaign were adopted to keep women of the desired genetic heritage out of the workplace and in the home to reproduce.

China, perhaps, serves as the most striking example in the modern world of a nation with a sweeping and strong antinatalist policy. In 1979, China initiated a policy forbidding families to produce more than a single child without special permission. The policy was a result of China's concern to avoid a crushing famine in the future. But, as with strident pronatalist policies, strident antinatalist policies put individuals into conflict with their states and societies, leading to coercive and otherwise morally troubling practices. Thus, Chinese women have been pressured into abortion and sterilization, and son preference (which seems to cross virtually all societies) has led to rampant infanticide of female infants and the abandonment of older female children.

National prosperity, various concerns about national protection, and internal concerns about group primacy, then, can and do affect public attitudes and public policies relevant to encouraging or discouraging reproduction. But perhaps the most consistent influence on public attitudes and public policies regarding sexual activity and birth control is the conceptualization of woman in a given society.

III. THE PHILOSOPHY OF WOMAN AND THE POLITICS OF MOTHERHOOD

At various points in history, the medical profession has been stridently opposed to readily available contraception and elective abortion. Such opposition played an important part in the profession's gaining a licensed monopoly on providing medical care and in its rise in social authority in both the United States and Europe. But sometimes segments of the medical profession have opposed readily available contraception while supporting abortion. Margaret Sanger, for example, was surprised that the German medical establishment was not interested in helping with her goal of making safe and effective contraception widely available to women. She reported the reason, given by an unnamed German gynecologist: "We will never give control of our numbers to the women themselves. What, let them control the future of the human race? With abortion, it is in our hands; we make the decisions and they must come to us" (M. Sanger, 1938. *An Autobiography*. Norton, New York). That was 1918, but the struggle of women for authority in deciding when they will and will not reproduce continues into the present. In the United States, for example, laws continue to be passed which make elective abortion less and less accessible to women—laws requiring waiting periods, multiple visits with a physician prior to an abortion, preabortion counseling, parental notification for young women, and restrictions on late-term abortions. All of these provisions serve to restrain women's choices regarding whether they will continue their pregnancies—all serve to ensure that women will not be allowed to make these decisions without state-mandated interferences, even though the U.S. Supreme Court made it completely clear that a woman in the United States has a right to an elective abortion through the end of the second trimester of her pregnancy and a right to an abortion even later in her pregnancy if her life or health is threatened by her pregnancy (*Roe v. Wade* 1973).

The fact is that, historically and currently, women have not been afforded the reproductive authority that Sanger's sample gynecologist wanted to reserve for, in his case, male physicians. That authority has not been afforded women in no small part because of a persistent view of human nature which stretches back to Aristotle and his predecessors, according to which women, in nature and value, are very different from men. Social scientists and social theorists have argued that this traditional view is intimately linked to the intractability of the contemporary abortion debate in the West and the continuing opposition of many people to readily available, safe, and effective birth control aids. According to this Aristotelian view, the purported intrinsic differences between men and women make them naturally suited to different tasks and roles. Women are best suited to create and nourish a home and to bear and rear children. As excellent "specimens of their kind," women must foster in themselves the virtues or excellences which make them fit to do their work well. Thus, in this view, a woman's value lies in her doing well that which she is best suited by nature to do—being a wife and mother. But the ready availability of safe and effective birth control allows women to avoid their "natural" roles. When a society protects women's reproductive choice by ensuring easy access to various forms of birth control, those who subscribe to this metaphysics of woman find their world view rejected by the state. Conversely, in constructing legal restrictions on the use of and/or access to birth control technologies, the state affirms their world view. On the other hand, those who reject the Aristotelian metaphysics of woman find their world view rejected when their societies move to restrict women's birth control choices. In either case, the stakes are high. Women who believe their nature and value is tied to their roles as wives and mothers feel their very lives are devalued in a society that values and protects women's ability to avoid these roles. Women who reject the view that they have an intrinsic nature and value that is tied to these roles find their lives devalued in a society that in any way restricts women's authority and power to decide when they will not reproduce. And so it is that a conflict between these radically different world views underpins so much of the contemporary debate about birth control, and it is this conflict which explains so clearly the recalcitrance of that debate, particularly in regard to abortion.

The debate about birth control, however, also embeds other concerns, including concerns about risks to women and abuse of methods. Contemporary methods of birth control can be clustered into three kinds: (1) methods that prevent the formation or release of gametes, (2) methods that prevent fertilization, and (3) methods that prevent implantation or otherwise prevent the continued development of a conceptus. There are significant moral issues associated with methods of each of these kinds.

IV. MORAL ISSUES ASSOCIATED WITH CONTEMPORARY CONTRACEPTIVE METHODS

True contraceptive methods of birth control have as their primary action the prevention of fertilization of a female gamete (ovum) by a male gamete (sperm cell). This can be accomplished "naturally" by abstinence from heterosexual intercourse, or (less successfully) by timing intercourse, withholding ejaculation (*coitus reservatus*), or withdrawal and ejaculation outside of the vagina (*coitus interruptus*). Douches and organic pessaries (vaginal suppositories) of various sorts have been used for millennia with varying degrees of success, but none with much predictable success. Contemporary "assisted" contraception can be accomplished by the use of manufactured barrier devices (such as condoms, diaphragms, and sponges); by male or female sterilization; or by the introduction of natural or fabricated preparations, virtually invariably taken or received by women. Except for complete abstinence, the primary danger of all "natural" methods and methods deploying douches and organic pessaries is the high probability of pregnancy. Anyone for whom the avoidance of pregnancy is a high priority simply should not rely on these methods. The other kinds of methods, however, are (more or less) effective in preventing pregnancy.

A. Steroidal Ovulation Inhibitors

Exogeneous steroids that inhibit ovulation in women are among the most effective and most popular assisted birth control methods in the world. Steroidal ovulation inhibitors are currently taken by women in three ways, namely, as oral contraceptives, as subdermal implants, or as injectables.

1. Oral Contraceptives

Until quite recently, use of oral contraceptives by women was the most popular form of assisted contraception in the United States. Although far too many women do not realize it, "the pill" does not refer to a single preparation, but is a generic term that covers dozens of preparations offered under dozens of brand names. Some of these preparations include synthetic progestagens only (the "minipill") or synthetic progestagens and estrogens, which are analogous to the progesterone and estrogen a menstruating woman naturally produces and which regulate her menstrual cycle, including ovulation and menstruation itself. The primary action of all oral contraceptives is to simulate pregnancy in a women's body, thereby suppressing the ovarian changes that are necessary for ovulation.

There are at least two main moral concerns associated with oral contraceptives. First, estrogens are associated with heart disease, hypertension, and diabetes in women. This makes use of combination pills potentially dangerous for women who are predisposed to any of these maladies. However, the minipill has a higher failure rate than combination pills, and this makes pregnancy more likely for women taking progestagen-only preparations. But pregnancy is also associated with the sorts of maladies mentioned. So, women who are at risk for these diseases need to be fully informed of the dangers to them associated with both pregnancy and the use of oral contraceptives, which they often are not. Second, even though oral contraceptives have prevention of ovulation as their primary action, breakthrough ovulation and, consequently, fertilization can still occur in a woman taking an oral contraceptive. When this happens, however, pregnancies do not usually succeed because these preparations induce other changes in a woman's system which make implantation and development of a conceptus very difficult. The problem here is that when a woman's oral contraceptive is successful—she does not, as far as she knows, get pregnant despite having heterosexual intercourse—she can never know whether that success is a result of a true contraceptive action or an action that interferes with a conceptus after fertilization has occurred. In short, women who understand abortion to be the termination of a conceptus at any stage of development and who are opposed to abortion might be avoiding pregnancy through abortifacient actions of their oral contraceptives. This is a fact that is emphatically not widely known by women because it is not commonly told to them by physicians who prescribe oral contraceptives. But, of course, if women are to give adequately informed consents to taking a prescribed preparation, there is no question that they must be told that their oral contraceptive can work this way. The other dimension of this problem, of course, is that those who oppose termination of a conceptus at any point after fertilization must take as strong a stand against oral contraceptives as they take against elective surgical abortion. This, too, seems not to be very widely recognized.

2. Long-Acting Contraceptives

Like oral contraceptives, long-acting steroidal implants and injectables have suppression of ovulation as their primary birth control action. The difference is in the delivery system—the preparation is delivered to a woman's system continually over a protracted period of time, rather than arriving as a bolus, causing a sudden surge in hormone levels.

a. Implants

"Norplant" is a registered trademark of the Population Council that refers to a subdermal implant system which is manufactured and distributed by Leiras Pharmaceuticals in Finland, under license from the Population Council. It is marketed in the United States by Wyeth-Ayerst Laboratories. On December 10, 1990, the U.S. Food and Drug Administration (FDA) approved Norplant for contraceptive use in the United States nearly a decade after its approval elsewhere in the world. By the time it was approved for use in the United States, Norplant had been used by over half a million women in 17 countries, and over 55,000 women had participated in Norplant trials in over 40 countries. Planted just under the skin in six nonbiodegradable capsules. Norplant contains the progestin levonorgestrel, and is effective within 24 hr of implantation. Its main attraction is that it avoids the failures associated with so-called user error—a woman does not have to remember to take a pill. Once Norplant is in place it is effective for up to 5 years, maintenance free. Since Norplant does not contain estrogen, it avoids the risks to women associated with estrogens. And since it avoids the failures associated with "user error," it is virtually as reliable as sterilization during its 5-year period of efficacy. Unlike sterilization, however, infertility induced by Norplant is reversible, which has made it very attractive to women who want (and are medically able to) control their fertility for a prolonged period with minimal risk and minimal inconvenience but who also want to avoid permanent infertility.

Norplant's attractiveness has not been lost on family planning workers, population control workers, and U.S. legislators and judges. Within months of its approval for use in the United States, 48 states and the District of Columbia added full or partial reimbursement for Norplant to their Medicaid programs, and by the end of 1992, all 50 of the United States had made Norplant available to eligible Medicaid recipients. Within a year of its availability on the U.S. market, courts began to order the implantation of Norplant for women convicted of child abuse as a condition of their probation or parole. The moral and legal permissibility of this use of Norplant remains unsettled in the legal and ethics literatures and in the U.S. courts. Added to the debate is the recent realization that Norplant, which had originally been described as "easy in, easy out," has turned out to be extremely difficult to remove in many cases because of the formation of scar tissue around the silastic capsules. Since Norplant brings with it the negative side effects of the minipill, including weight gain, mood changes, headache, nausea, and irregular menstrual bleeding, as well as increased risks of mortality from cardiovascular maladies and some forms of cancer, many women who have it implanted seek to have it removed within a year of implantation. Much to the chagrin of physicians attempting to remove the capsules, this has proved difficult and has led to serious infections and considerable scarring for many women. Among the moral issues associated with Norplant, then, are questions of impositions upon women who might not be medically appropriate for this intervention, inclusions of risks and burdens (such as those included with removing the system) not fully realized by women who accept this technology, and risks that are not yet fully understood. One of the problems here extends back to oral contraceptives and ahead to injectables, namely, that we do not yet know what risks women are assuming when they accept exogenous steroids for virtually the whole of their lives, in the form of contraception during their reproductive years and in the form of hormone replacement therapy during their postreproductive years. Insofar as women accept these interventions, they are the only group of healthy individuals known to have pharmaceuticals prescribed for them for most of their lifetimes. That this happens to women and not to men is worth noticing, and that we do not yet know the implications of this for women is crucial to notice.

b. Injectables

In June of 1993, the U.S. FDA approved the injectable progestagen Depo-Provero for contraceptive use in the United States. Depo-Provero is quick and easy to use; one injection is 99% effective in preventing pregnancy for at least 3 months. Its annual cost is comparable to the cost of Norplant and less than oral contraceptives. These features of Depo-Provero make it highly attractive to members of some groups; for example, there seems to be a particularly strong interest in it among young women.

Unlike oral and implant systems, however, a quick return to fertility after use of Depo-Provero is often impossible, since pills cannot be stopped and capsules cannot be removed to effect a quick return to fertility. Thus, women who accept Depo-Provero have far less control over restoring their fertility than those who accept oral contraceptive or implant systems as ovulation inhibitors. What is more, timely return to fertility even after the period of known effectiveness is highly uncertain.

Depo-Provero has a troubled history, which caused its approval for contraceptive use in the United States to be held back for decades. Although studies have shown that there is some reason to believe it might be effective in preventing certain sorts of uterine cancer, studies also suggest that it is associated with elevated risks of breast cancer. This is not to be taken lightly, since breast cancer is the second leading cause of death among women (following heart disease) in the United States and much of the West.

Since contraceptive injections can be given without a women's knowledge, there are also worries about surreptitious abuses of injectables, which have been known to occur in psychiatric hospitals and refugee camps. Further, injectable systems are very attractive to those who are interested in court-ordered contraception, since they do not present the removal problems now associated with Norplant, and they do not require monitoring, as would oral contraceptives or an implant system. These features of injectable systems such as Depo-Provero make them especially attractive to courts, and this makes them particularly morally worrisome.

B. Fertilization Preventatives: Barrier and Chemical Methods

A number of birth control methods work by preventing fertilization or the union of egg and sperm by physical barrier, chemical action, or some combination of these.

It cannot be emphasized strongly enough that an often unnoticed but potentially lethal risk associated with highly effective antiovulation (and some other) systems is their inherent tendency to discourage the use of certain barrier methods, since a crucial benefit of some barrier methods is the protection they offer against the spread of sexually transmitted diseases, including HIV-AIDS. At this writing, the most useful of the barrier methods in this regard is the male condom, particularly when this is combined with a chemical spermicide.

The male condom (or sheath) is an ancient method that was used for both birth control and to prevent the spread of disease. Condoms for men are now widely available and are extremely popular among the young and the poor who are willing to use them and might

otherwise have some difficulty getting access to methods that need to be provided by health care practitioners.

Male condoms are now made with latex. An emerging problem is that cases of latex allergy are being reported in steadily increasing numbers. Negative effects on those allergic to latex are cumulative, and the allergy is often not recognized before it becomes debilitating.

Perhaps the main problem associated with condoms as a form of birth control is that they are simply not as effective as other forms, mostly because of user error. There are also the problems of aesthetics and effects on spontaneity attached to condom use. For these kinds of reasons, many men (of all ages) simply do not want to use them. This creates a special paradox for women, for if they have otherwise unprotected sex with such men, they risk pregnancy (which is never an innocuous physical condition for a woman); but if they otherwise protect themselves against pregnancy (through oral contraceptive, implants, injections, sterilization, and so on) they bear the risks associated with other birth control systems *and* they forego the significant protection from disease that can be afforded by male condom use. Given the AIDS pandemic, this protection is crucial for both men and women who are sexually active with men.

Female barrier methods have also been used since antiquity. Too often they have been both ineffective and lethal. Records of vaginal pessaries or depositories go back to the reign of Amenemhat III of Egypt's 12th Dynasty (ca. 1850 B.C.) and include such aids as crocodile dung. In Islam, elephant dung was recommended. Contemporarily vaginal pessaries include rubber diaphragms, cervical caps, female condoms, and sponges. All of these have serious problems with ease of use and effectiveness, and none of them are thought to provide significant protection from sexually transmitted diseases. Sponges that contain a spermicide appeared on the U.S. market in the late 1980s, but were withdrawn in the mid-1990s because they were relatively ineffective when used without spermicide, irritants when used with spermicides, and presented a risk of (potentially lethal) toxic shock syndrome to women using them.

In short, female barrier methods have not enjoyed much popularity since the advent of hormonal contraceptive methods for women. This is more than regrettable, however, since barrier methods remain the safest contraceptive methods for heterosexually active women who do not want to undergo surgical sterilization. They involve no introduction of exogenous hormones, and therefore they avoid the risks of these methods. Maximal protection of women's health, then, requires that nations and corporations that are developing birth control methods recognize the literally vital need for effective, easily deployable barrier contraceptives for women. The continued research emphasis on chemical contraceptives for women to the exclusion of a major research emphasis on barrier methods for women has direct and devastating effects on women's morbidity and mortality as a result of sexually transmitted diseases, including HIV-AIDS.

C. "Interceptive" or "Contragestive" Methods

1. The Debate on When Pregnancy Commences

The birth control methods we have so far considered have contraception—the avoidance of fertilization or conception—as their primary actions. Other methods have intervention after conception as their primary birth control actions. These interventions take place at different points. Some technologies intervene shortly after fertilization, preventing transport of a conceptus and/or implantation of a conceptus in a woman's uterus. Other methods intervene longer after conception and involve removing a conceptus that has implanted in a woman's uterus.

Birth control methods that act after conception but before implantation have come to be known as "interceptives" or "contragestives." In the view of those who use this language, pregnancy commences with implantation, not fertilization. The choice of these labels is quite deliberate, since they are intended to communicate that these methods intervene to prevent a pregnancy rather than intervene to terminate or abort a pregnancy. The point, of course, is to keep these methods from being understood as methods of effecting the destruction of a conceptus.

Now the problem with this sort of linguistic move is that it attempts to do away with a serious moral question by simply defining it out of existence, that is, by stipulating that pregnancy does not begin until after the time in which these methods work. But, of course, such stipulation will not satisfy those who hold that any method that intervenes after conception is, by its very nature, abortifacient. Thus, abortion (to which we shall turn shortly) remains a critical moral issue raised by these methods.

2. Intrauterine Devices and "Emergency Contraception" (or "Morning after Pills")

Intrauterine devices (IUDs) work by inducing an immune response in a woman. A device is inserted into a woman's uterus, causing her uterus and her reproductive system more generally to react to a foreign presence. This reaction impairs a number of gestational processes in a woman, including the capacitation of sperm and ovum and sperm transport (true contraceptive actions), transport of a conceptus to her uterus, and implantation within a woman's uterus.

In addition to IUDs having postconception actions, they can be particularly dangerous to women. Historically, there has been a significant association of IUDs with pelvic inflammatory disease in women and a significant association of IUDs with ectopic pregnancies (i.e., implantations of conceptuses outside the uterus), both of which are extremely dangerous to women.

At the same time, an IUD might be the best birth control methodology for a heterosexually active woman who does not want to be sterilized, who would be at exceptional risk were she to become pregnant and/or use hormonal contraceptives, and who is not willing to assume the risks of pregnancy at a given time. Some theorists object that withdrawal of IUD producers from the market after the Dalkon Shield scandal (see discussion further on) has left U.S. women with an unacceptably small list of birth control options. If it is true, as feminists tend to believe it is, that birth control is crucial to women's health, and if it is true that an IUD is the most acceptable birth control method for some women, then nations that purport to take women's health seriously need to see to it that more relatively safe and effective intrauterine devices are made available to women.

Other methods engineered to act postcoitally include the so-called morning after pill, more recently approved in the United States as "emergency contraception," which may be taken within 72 hr of unprotected intercourse and is a regimen involving four or five large doses of hormones. These interventions can act contraceptively by interfering with fertilization or "interceptively" by impairing functions necessary for the gestation of a conceptus. Again, insofar as these methods involve postconceptive actions, they raise the issue of abortion. Further, it is unclear what long-term effects these methods might have on women. Until recently one preparation which was frequently used is diethylstilbestrol, more widely known as DES. Although highly effective as a postcoital intervention, DES was problematic, not only because of its intense undesirable short-term side effects (e.g., severe nausea and vomiting), but also because it is associated with vaginal cancer in women whose mothers took it while pregnant with them. Because of this, the U.S. Food and Drug Administration suggested that female conceptuses that survive postcoital DES intervention should be aborted.

Other, newer preparations now in use combine hormones and, like DES, their primary actions induce endometrial changes that are incompatible with implantation of a conceptus. But, their long-term effects remain unknown and, like all other postcoital interventions, they lead back to the issue of abortion. This is the reason that one preparation in particular received special attention and was approved for use in the United States after roughly a decade of availability in Europe.

3. Mifepristone (Formerly RU-486)

RU-486 is the in-house name for Mifepristone, a preparation that has as its primary birth control action the binding of progesterone receptors, making maintenance of a pregnancy virtually impossible since progsterone needs to act on a woman's system in order for it to sustain her uterine lining, which is necessary to maintain pregnancy. Absent this action of progesterone, a woman's uterine lining is shed (as in ordinary menstruation), and any implanted conceptus is shed with it. Because its primary action is so clearly abortifacient, opponents of elective abortion have called Mifepristone "the abortion pill," and lobbied extensively to keep it off the market in many countries, including the United States. At the same time, a number of feminists throughout the world have lobbied equally extensively for its availability to all women for birth control purposes and to some women because of other effects it is thought to have, including positive effects of blocking the changes induced by progesterone in a woman's body, some of which are associated with increased risk of certain cancers. Indeed, some U.S. feminists have argued that the government's refusal to approve Mifepristone in the United States was actually a violation of women's reproductive liberty rights. Feminists have argued that Mifepristone ought to be available, not only because it expands birth control options for women, but also because it puts abortion in the hands of women—with Mifepristone available, it is argued, women need not submit to surgical procedures if they decide on abortion within the first 2 months of pregnancy. It has also been argued that the introduction of Mifepristone privatizes abortion in a way that is not now feasible. That is, since Mifepristone can be administered in any physician's office and the actual expulsion of a woman's uterine lining and any implanted conceptus can take place in the privacy of her home, many women will be able to avoid using abortion clinics, and thus will not be subject to the harassment and sometimes lethal risks of antichoice protestors. The massive mobilization against the ready availability of Mifepristone is largely explainable in terms of this feature of the method. Mifepristone

is, in the imagination of those who continue to subscribe to what was earlier identified as an Aristotelian metaphysics of woman, the very worst kind of birth control methodology—it is "a pill" which allows women not only to avoid motherhood, but which allows women to kill their babies in secret.

It is no small matter that Mifepristone can, in principle, be administered in virtually any physician's office. This does add substantially to the privacy of abortion and it makes it possible that early abortion will be much more readily available to women, given that there are increasingly fewer and fewer abortion clinics in industrialized nations. Further, chemical postcoital interventions such as this hold the potential for providing women with safer abortions in nations where surgical interventions are less available (i.e., where women have to travel great distances) and/or where sanitary conditions make early abortion by invasive procedure more dangerous than it is in more developed nations.

However, other feminists have argued that claims about Mifepristone's putting abortion in the hands of women are greatly exaggerated. Appropriate application of this technology, they have pointed out, involves a woman's being examined for pregnancy and her being administered the preparation in a medical facility and attended in that facility for several hours after administation of the drug. If expulsion of a woman's uterine contents is not successfully accomplished within that amount of time, she is sent home, and she must return to the medical facility for examination after the expulsion to ensure that all the products of conception have been shed successfully. If there is any residue, she will need to undergo suction abortion. Thus, even though it is true that this technology can add substantially to the privacy and availability of abortion, since it can be administered in any physician's office and can provide "cover" for physicians who would otherwise not do abortions, Mifepristone simply does not demedicalize abortion, as has been suggested by its makers and by a number of feminists who have fought for its ready availability throughout the world.

4. Menstrual Extraction

Feminists who are reserved about Mifepristone are generally among those who, historically, have been deeply concerned about the application of medical technologies to women's bodies. One suggestion these feminists offer is that women consider really (and quite literally) putting early abortion in the hands of women by developing centers where women can go for what is commonly called "menstrual extraction." Menstrual extraction is the vacuum aspiration of a woman's uterine lining. If there is a conceptus implanted, this too is extracted in the procedure. The method is relatively simple and straightforward, and can be accomplished by anyone carefully trained in the technique. Indeed, women have been helping one another "underground" with the procedure for years, using simple materials. For example, menstrual extraction has been accomplished successfully by inserting a sterile cannula about the length and diameter of a soda straw into a woman's uterus, with the cannula attached to plastic tubing. This tubing is fed through one hole in the rubber stopper of a jar, while another hole in the stopper receives tubing attached to a syringe. The syringe is pumped to create suction, and the uterine contents are thereby flushed into the jar. The procedure, which is basically a "homestyle" suction abortion, can be accomplished with relative ease during the first 8 weeks of a pregnancy. It is attractive to many feminists because it completely demedicalizes early abortion, placing it squarely in the hands of women themselves. But it is precisely this characteristic of the procedure that leads to its condemnation by groups as liberal as Planned Parenthood when is is not done by medical professionals.

D. Elective Abortion

With few exceptions, every one of the birth control methods so far discussed leads to the issue of abortion. As noted, even oral contraceptives have abortifacient actions, and all postcoital interventions potentially involve destruction of a conceptus. It is time to turn to this issue.

1. The Moral Debate in the West: The Moral Status of the Human Conceptus

In the West, the central moral position of those who have been most active in the movement against allowing elective abortion is that the human being must be recognized as a person with a full-fledged right to life from conception onward. The implication of this position for any birth control method that involves intervention after fertilization is very clear. If a public policy permitting elective abortion is not morally acceptable because conception marks the beginning of personhood (with its attendant moral and civil rights), then elective use of those methods having abortifacient actions is equally unacceptable and must be outlawed. The way the abortion debate is structured today in the West, then, makes the moral status of the human conceptus critical to the morality of abortion.

If human conceptuses are persons, this fact is not obvious since they lack the morally relevant characteristics of paradigm cases of persons, that is, characteristics that are commonly recognized to compel the recognition of strong moral rights, including the right not to be killed for reasons less than self-defense. Among these characteristics are certain mental ones, for example, a concept of a self as an ongoing being with at least some kinds of plans and stakes. Human conceptuses, embryos, and fetuses simply do not have the kinds of characterisics that compel an immediate recognition of personhood. These characteristics emerge long after birth, and this makes the matter of accepting prenatal beings that are genetically human as persons a matter of decision rather than discovery. That is, it needs to be asked whether prenatal beings that are genetically human but which do not (yet) have the characteristics of paradigmatic persons ought to be treated as persons. Since the task is one of deciding rather than discovering whether prenatal human beings should be treated as persons, the issue needs to be settled by setting a convention that establishes the point at which personhood of very young human beings is to be recognized in custom and in law.

One possible convention is to set the recognition of personhood at birth. Another is to set it at conception. Other conventions might set recognition of personhood at various prenatal stages or at various points after birth. Those who want to preclude the legality of elective abortion insist that full personhood must be recognized from fertilization onward. Setting explicitly religious arguments aside, the main secular argument given for this position is a logical wedge argument which rests on the assumption that unless beings are radically different, they may not be treated in radically different ways. It is then argued that there is just no morally relevant line that can be drawn between conception and the time a human being is unequivocally a person before which killing that human being for reasons less than self-defense would be justified and after which such killing would be be justified. The argument proceeds by starting with someone at, say, 21. It then points out that there is no radical difference between someone at 21 and at 20, no radical difference between someone at 20 and 19, and so on. The argument presses back through adolescence, childhood, infancy, through prenatality just before birth, then back through earlier prenatal stages to conception, which is the only point along the continuum of a human life where a bright line can be drawn between radically different kinds of beings, with eggs and sperm on one side of that line and new conceptuses on the other. Logic and fairness, it is argued, force us to accept that even the new human zygote is a person with the same fundamental moral rights as the mature human being.

Critics of this argument, however, point out that the foundational assumption on which it rests (that beings that are not radically different cannot be treated in radically different ways) is not acceptable. If we accept this assumption, it is argued, we will be unable to make all sorts of public policy decisions that must be made and that we believe are fair. For example, this assumption leads to the conclusion that we must give the 5-year-old the right to drink alcohol and the 7-year-old the right to drive automobiles, since bright lines cannot be found that would justify setting any drinking age or driving age. Such implications show that the wedge argument used to justify the claim that personhood must be recognized from conception onward is unsound.

2. The Infanticide Objection

However, it is often objected that this criticism of the wedge argument cannot be correct, since it opens the door to infanticide. That is, it is argued that this objection to the wedge argument not only rules out our being committed to the personhood of human conceptuses, it also implies that human infants are not persons, since infants are as undeveloped as late-term fetuses in regard to the kinds of characteristics in question.

The response, however, is that this objection is not devastating. For, again, the question is one of deciding what conventions should be adopted, and it can be allowed that even if human infants do not yet have the characteristics of paradigm persons, there are considerations that provide excellent reasons for taking birth as the best place to set the conventional recognition of personhood with its full range of fundamental moral and legal rights. Chief among these considerations is that individuals other than an infant's biological mother are able to care and are interested in caring for it. Although there are intriguing physiological changes that accompany birth, there is no change in the morally relevant characteristics of late-term fetuses and infants. All else being equal, if the life of a late-term fetus is sustained, it will develop the characteristics of paradigmatic persons. But once a human being emerges from the womb and others are willing and able to care for it, there are radical changes in what is involved in preserving its life and otherwise protecting it. And the *crucial* change is that sustaining its life or otherwise protecting it does not violate a pregnant women's rights to self-direction and physical integrity. Thus, even though birth, unlike conception, does not involve radical changes in a being itself, it is not a morally arbitrary

point for commencing recognition of personhood in custom and public policy. Taking birth as the point at which the rights of personhood should be recognized has the moral advantage of taking the actual, unequivocal personhood of pregnant women far more seriously than setting conventional recognition of personhood at any prenatal stage.

3. The Moral and Social Status of Women

Despite the obvious unsoundness of the logical wedge argument for prenatal personhood, the abortion debate in much of the world continues to be intractable. Indeed, no one actually seems to pay attention to the arguments themselves. Unhappily, the debate between those opposed to the legality of elective abortion and those who contend that abortion must be available to women if women are to be able to protect their health and are to have genuine reproductive choice too often degenerates into mere assertion and the use of loaded language that simply begs the question against the opposition. Thus, those who have appropriated the term "pro-life" for their position too often simply call human conceptuses "babies" and take the matter to be settled, while those who take what is called the "prochoice" position too often simply call human conceptuses "parasites" and take the matter to be settled. Such language on either side simply begs the question on the moral status of the human conceptus, embryo, and fetus and prevents rational discussion from proceeding.

This issue, however, is notorious for departing from rational discussion, and the very intractability of the debate has become an issue of study in recent years. More and more, feminists have suggested that no one attends to the arguments about the moral status of the fetus because this is not really what is at issue in the abortion debate. That is, feminists working on the question of reproductive rights have increasingly concluded that the *real* issue in the abortion debate is the issue of the natural, moral, and social status of women, and this is what makes the contemporary abortion debate in the West so recalcitrant. The issue of fetal personhood is a red herring that distracts focus from the real underlying issue. In much of the non-Western world, this is more obvious, where social custom and state regulation much more explicitly connect cultural views on the nature and the moral and social status of women to women's reproductive role. Conflicts between radically different views on the nature and place of women, then, get played out in social and political arenas, and it seems safe to say that there will be common agreement on the morality and legality of elective abortion only when there is prior general agreement on whether women have full value in their right, independent of any considerations of reproduction.

4. Availability: Moral Equality and the Importance of Motherhood

Government subsidized elective abortion is available to women in much of the world, particularly in nations where governments are concerned with stemming population growth. In many industrialized nations, including the United States, this is not the case. The consequence of a lack of government subsidization of safe elective abortion is that poorer women do not have ready access to it. This creates significant concerns about equality, since it is argued by many feminists and many health care providers that having elective abortion readily available is crucial to women's health. This is a sensible claim, since early abortion is safer for a woman than bringing a pregnancy to term. If only those women who have the resources to purchase an abortion are able to secure one, their health and their reproductive freedom are far better protected than the health and reproductive freedom of poor women. Thus, women's health and women's rights activists have argued and continue to argue that the moral equality of all women requires that nations make available all reasonable birth control technologies, including elective abortion, to all women who need them.

Among the objections raised against the ready availability of elective abortion, however, is the objection that women should be good mothers, and good mothers do not kill their children. Insofar as this objection assumes the personhood of human conceptuses, this position has not been justified, as already illustrated. This objection, however, can be understood less technically as an objection tied to the importance of motherhood. Women who abort, it is argued, demean motherhood.

Some feminists, however, have argued from the importance of motherhood to precisely the opposite conclusion. That is, feminists have argued that it is precisely *because* mothering is such a serious business that women must have the option of abortion. Parenting is a terrifically demanding task, even for those who are enthusiastic about taking it on. If we care about the flourishing of children, it is argued, the last thing we want to do is coerce anyone into parenting. Thus, those who support the ready availability of elective abortion also argue for this on the ground of respect for mothering and the flourishing of children.

5. New Issues in the Abortion Debate

The development of new technologies in every area has brought with it the development of new moral problems. The development of reproductive technologies is no exception, and a number of recent and emerging technologies have added new dimensions to the abortion debate.

a. Sex Selection

Attempts to ensure that a child will be of a certain sex are not new. What is new is the development of a number of "scientific" methods for selecting the sex of an offspring prior to conception. The short story is that, as of this writing, none of these methods is known to be reliable. Diagnostic procedures (such as amniocentesis and chorionic villus sampling) during pregnancy, however, are reliable in discerning sex, and termination of a pregnancy because a fetus is not of the sex desired is a reliable way of preventing the birth of a child of the "wrong" sex, which is almost invariably female. For example, even though it is illegal in India to conduct amniocentesis for abortion of a fetus of the "wrong" sex, it is well known that this is common practice in some areas of the country as a way of ensuring that girls will not be born. And China's one-child policy has led to sex-selective abortion, as well as infanticide and abandonment of many thousands of female children. This preference for sons is found throughout the world, and it raises a number of vexing questions about the morality of birth control for reasons of sex selection. For example, those who champion reproductive liberty often argue that parents should be able to choose the sex of their children if they so desire. Further, in cultures without social policies that enforce sex/gender equality, ensuring that her children are male may be the most rational decision for a woman. At the same time, however, those who focus their concerns on the position of women in societies often argue that the nearly universal preference for sons over daughters will, if it is not restrained, make the world even worse than it is now for girls and women.

Abortion for the purpose of sex selection is also importantly different from other cases of abortion in which a woman is simply unprepared to assume the role of biological or social mother of a child, since in the sex selection cases, a woman's willingness to be a parent is not in question. Thus, some supporters of the availability of elective abortion in general have also argued that abortion for sex selective reasons should not be allowed, since disallowing it does not seriously compromise a woman's reproductive liberty because it does not force her to continue a pregnancy to term when she is unwilling to assume the role of biological mother. One problem with this sort of view, however, is that disallowing elective abortion for the purpose of selecting a child of a certain sex is neither fair nor enforceable in a system where genuinely elective abortion is available, since "elective abortion" *means* that abortion can be elected for any reason whatever. Further, other analysts have argued that precluding women from seeking abortions as a way of selecting the sex of their offspring opens the door to too many other kinds of interference with women's reproductive choices—if one kind of reason can be rejected as sufficient for a woman to procure an elective abortion, what other kinds of reasons might be added to this list? Thus, even those who are morally opposed to a woman's using abortion to select the sex of her future child are often unwilling to support a policy that would disallow elective abortion for this reason.

b. Fetal Reduction

Similar issues arise with fetal reduction, which is a procedure involving reducing the number of fetuses in a multiple pregnancy. In these cases, a woman is not unwilling to become a biological (and social) parent at this time, so her basic reproductive liberty would not be sacrificed by policies that would disallow her having a fetal reduction. Thus, insofar as someone holds the position that the sole justification for elective abortion is a woman's current unwillingness to undertake the role of biological (and social) parent, they must hold that fetal reduction cannot be justified. On the other hand, fetal reduction is often defended on the ground that it is safer for fetuses and the children they will ultimately become if fetal reduction is undertaken. This is most frequently argued in cases of pregnancy involving more than two fetuses.

c. Ensuring a Stillborn

When a woman has decided she is not going to continue with a pregnancy and this decision is made relatively late in term, an abortion procedure can yield a live infant. Scientists have developed a method for ensuring a stillborn in late-term abortions. The method, known as fetal intracardiac KCl injection, involves injecting potassium chloride directly into a fetus' heart, causing instant death. Arguments supporting use of this method in later-term abortion range from ensuring the reproductive autonomy of parents and the avoidance of complex legal and psychological burdens following termination of a pregnancy to protecting the safety of women and the best interests of fetuses and the children surviving abortuses might become.

d. Coercive Abortion

A number of recent technological and legal developments set the stage for what might be understood as coercive abortion.

i. One Possible Effect of Prenatal Testing Combined with Pressure to Produce Perfect Children

Prenatal testing has become commonplace in developed nations. Indeed, in such societies woman are fully expected to accept prenatal testing and fetal monitoring as routine. In the United States, the Human Genome Project is the largest joint research project ever undertaken by the government and private enterprise. The project's goal is to map the human genome with an eye, of course, to improving the gene pool. Even though the project is far from complete, we are already beginning to see a growing number of prenatal tests for various maladies, and women are under increasing pressure to undergo these tests. However, when it is discovered that a fetus will or is likely to have a certain malady, women are then in a position where they need to decide whether or not to continue their pregnancies. In developed nations, there is already considerable pressure on women to produce "perfect" children. The now nearly daily advances in prenatal testing and fetal monitoring make this pressure all that much greater.

This is not, of course, to suggest that all women who accept prenatal testing and who abort pregnancies because of fetal anomalies are, somehow, dupes of the patriarchy or otherwise unable to make their own decisions about when to continue with a pregnancy. It merely suggests that strong cultural forces that embody deeply held biases about disability and that push in the direction of producing perfect children do exert considerable pressure on women.

ii. Insurance and So-Called Preexisting Conditions

Complicating this issue are insurance companies who threaten not to pay for costs associated with so-called preexisting conditions. Thus, for example, if it is discovered that a woman who already has a cystic fibrosis child is pregnant with another cystic fibrosis child and she is willing to birth and raise the child, it is not clear that her medical insurance company will pay for costs associated with her second child's malady. If a family will not be able to afford the medical costs associated with raising such a child, abortion might well seem like the only reasonable choice to be made.

iii. Prenatal Harm

In recent years, there have been increasing attempts to prosecute women for causing prenatal harm during their pregnancies. Many of these cases involve a woman's use of drugs during pregnancy. Laws, however, have been such as to allow prosecution only when there is a live-born child negatively affected by the behaviors of its biological mother. As states move to prosecute more and more women for causing prenatal harm, women who might be subject to such prosecution stay further and further away from the medical establishment, thereby increasing risks to their newborns, or they seek abortions rather than risk prosecution.

The bitter irony in all such cases of coerced abortion, of course, is that in any of these cases women are in a no-win situation. If they bring a pregnancy to term, they are bad mothers; if they abort, they are bad mothers.

E. Surgical Sterilization

The only forms of sterilization currently available are through surgical interventions, namely, tying, cutting, sealing, and/or removing a small portion of the fallopian tubes in a woman or the vas deferens in a man. Surgical sterilization for women is known as "tubal ligation"; surgical sterilization for men is known as "vasectomy." Such methods have become increasingly reliable. They have also become increasingly reversible, although they should still always be assumed to be irreversible.

1. Paternalism and Pronatalism, Eugenics and Antinatalism

In recent years, surgical sterilization has become the most popular method of contraception in the United States. This is an interesting shift, since until the 1970s restrictive policies and societal attitudes precluded the widespread availability of contraceptive sterilization to U.S. women. The standard rule of thumb employed by the medical profession was the so-called 120 Rule, which is a pronatalist and paternalistic rule of the first order. Unless a woman's age multiplied by the number of her children equaled at least 120 (e.g., 30 years old and four children), she generally would not be granted a request for sterilization unless it could be justified to prevent excessive pain, bleeding, high health risks associated with pregnancy, high risks of producing an anomalous child, or psychiatric illness. It has been suggested that the dramatic increase in hysterectomies in the United States during the 1960s might, at least in part, have been a result of some physicians attempt to provide contraceptive sterilization to women who would not qualify for it under the 120 Rule, much as elective abortion was provided for specious medical reasons prior to its legalization in 1973. Even today,

however, criteria for obtaining surgical sterilization in the United States vary regarding, for example, a woman's age, family status, marital status, and spousal consent. Such criteria continue to raise important questions about paternalism and pronatalism in regulation of women's access to surgical sterilization.

Surgical sterilization is highly effective; but, like other highly effective contraceptives, its very efficacy can discourage people from using condoms and spermicides, which can protect from sexually transmitted diseases, including AIDS. Also, surgical sterilization has been abused in a number of ways. The eugenic sterilizations in the United States that took place between 1927 and 1963 are notorious—nearly 63,000 people classified as insane, feeble-minded, idiots, imbeciles, and epileptics, as well as those classified as rapists, habitual criminals, persons with criminal tendencies, drunkards, drugs fiends, syphilitics, moral and sexual perverts, moral degenerates, and "other" degenerate persons, are known to have been sterilized for eugenic reasons. Surgical sterilization has also been stridently "encouraged" in China for women following delivery of a child, and population control practices in other nations have included worrisomely coercive incentives for those who accept sterilization.

2. Court-Ordered Sterilizations of Men

Just as there have been recent attempts by courts to impose birth control on women, there have been attempts and successes by courts to impose sterilization on men. Although it is not widely realized, there is an unknown number of unpublished court cases from local jurisdictions where men who have fathered a number of children but who have not contributed to their support have been given the option of sterilization or incarceration. Sterilizations have been accepted in these cases, and because none have been appealed, there has been no significant discussion of such cases in the ethics or legal literature.

3. "Fetal Protection" Policies in the Workplace

In the United States, so-called fetal protection policies have forced women to accept sterilization if they want to move into certain jobs. For example, Johnson Controls, a U.S. battery manufacturer, precluded fertile woman of child-bearing age from entering into any jobs (or entering on promotion paths to any jobs) that might expose them to toxins that could have negative prenatal or preconceptive effects on their future offspring. Not surprisingly, these jobs tended to be among the best paid in the industry. But to qualify for them, women of child-bearing age had to be able to show that they had been sterilized or were otherwise medically incapable of bearing children. In a landmark 1991 decision, the U.S. Supreme Court struck down Johnson Controls' policy and all comparable workplace policies (*Johnson Controls* 1991), contending that such policies were instances of sexual discrimination. Although this decision was in many ways an overwhelming victory for women, there is much in the case's dicta that commentators have found worrisome, including language that is likely to preclude liability of manufacturers for preconceptive or prenatal harms inflicted in their workplaces. Given current societal emphasis on fetal protection in the West and other developments in the law regarding holding women liable for prenatal harm suffered by their children, one of the worrisome consequences of the *Johnson Controls* decision is that if children are harmed prenatally by workplace toxins, their mothers will be held criminally liable for electing to work in such environments. This, of course, leads back to the problem of coerced abortion discussed earlier.

It is interesting to note that in less industrialized countries, so-called fetal protection policies, such as Johnson Controls' former policy, are virtually unheard of. One reason for this is likely to be that there is less fascination with the human fetus elsewhere than there is in the industrialized West. But another reason is that in developing nations, women are desperately needed to do various kinds of work, and industries could not function without them working in these environments. That this is a significant reason for the absence of these policies in developing nations is, ironically, suggested by the complete lack of any such policies in a number of industries in the West (e.g., cleaning industries, textiles, and agricultural products production) that consistently involve exposure to potentially hazardous substances, but where there is heavy reliance on a female labor force.

F. Male Contraception

To date, there has been little available in the way of contraceptives for men. Aside from abstinence, *coitus interruptus,* and *coitus reservatus,* the two male contraceptive options available remain condoms and surgical sterilization. Despite the fact that scientists tend to make much of how much more "rational" it is to attempt to control reproduction in women rather than men, it cannot be denied that women have borne and continue to bear far more responsibility and far more risks than do men in attempts to control birth. For example, for each new technique that is developed, thousands of women must submit to being experimental subjects. A scientific account that claims it is more rational to pursue development of methods for women serves men nicely, and this needs to be recognized. It is now widely understood that science is shot through with value assumptions, and because of this, we should not accept without question the arguments, generally put forward by male scientists, that concentration on birth control techniques for women is justified on purely objective or value-neutral grounds. The concentration on the development of birth control methods for women contributes to the restricted and burdened position of women vis-à-vis men in virtually all matters related to reproduction, and this makes that concentration morally suspect.

There is little hope for improvement in male contraception. Stronger, thinner, nonlatex condoms are on the way, and will be here shortly. Injectable preparations are in development, and there is now speculation that an injectable androgen–progestin combination, effective for 3 months, might be on the market in less than 10 years. Other vaccines are under development, with the most promising being vaccines that provide long-term interference with sperm maturation. Unhappily, these last methods still seem to be distant and are not expected to be available until after 2005. The current picture of improvement in male contraception, then, is not very bright, despite the fact that the Programme of Action of the International Conference on Population and Development, adopted in Cairo in 1994, strongly emphasizes the need for programs to encourage male responsibility for contraception (as well as for other dimensions of sexual interaction, reproduction, and child care).

V. POPULATION CONTROL

Among the most serious moral concerns arising from the risks associated with birth control technologies is with ensuring that informed consents to these risks are given. The problem cuts across all populations, insofar as the long-term risks of many methods are unknown even to those who develop, test, produce, and distribute them. But even when the risks of a technology are well known, the problem of informed consent to risks remains a serious one in developing nations where population control is a high priority.

Population control is a value that has led to selecting areas for trying out new birth control technologies when long-term risks are unknown, and it is a value that has encouraged the continued use of products known to be especially dangerous to women. In the late 1950s, for example, when G.D. Searle and Company needed to conduct trials of what became the first "pill" widely available, it turned to Puerto Rico because of the population pressures there. We now know that the hormonal doses in the earliest versons of "the pill" were much higher than needed to be effective and were quite dangerous. But the women testing them had no idea of that at the time. When there is great pressure to control population, the acceptance of previously untried birth control methods by poor, uneducated women (and more often than not, women of color) raises especially troubling questions regarding the moral equality of persons and whether genuinely informed consent to the method can be secured.

Irregularities in clinical trials and "dumping" of especially dangerous products also raise worries about birth control in nations where population control is a high priority. For example, the Brazilian Norplant trials had to be halted because of irregularities (such as using a version of the preparation not approved for the trials and failures to check for pregnancy). And A.H. Robins Company's "dumping" of the Dalkon Shield in developing nations remains an international scandal. A few months after the arrival of the Dalkon Shield (an intra-uterine device) on the market, Robins was aware of reports of adverse side effects. Hundreds of potentially incriminating documents apparently were burned, including documents related to the device's "tail"—a string that passed from the uterus into the vagina, wicking bacteria up to the uterus. Also, the Dalkon Shield was crab-shaped, with "legs" that made it difficult for the device to slip out of the uterus but which were ideal for harboring bacteria and "injecting" them into the uterine lining if the device perforated the wall of the uterus. Before being withdrawn from the market in 1975, the Dalkon Shield was implicated in 14 deaths and 223 septic abortions (spontaneous abortions accompanied by infection and high fever). Realizing that sales on the U.S. market would drop, Robins pulled it from the market and quickly sold huge quantities of the device at a large discount to the Office of Population at the United States Agency for International Development for distribution in developing nations. To this day, it is not known how many women around the world accepted this device or have died or otherwise suffered serious effects from it. In 1985, A.H. Robins declared bankruptcy as a result of the lawsuits brought against it.

It needs to be emphasized that the Dalkon Shield was an anomaly. No other intrauterine device that has gone on the open market has been nearly as dangerous. The point of the story here, however, is to emphasize the risks third-world women face when their govern-

ments are focused on population control, a focus that is often the result of governments having been led to believe that population control efforts are the price of foreign assistance.

Particularly worrisome are societies that include quotas as part of their population control policies and in which those who find "acceptors" are given attractive incentives for meeting or exceeding quotas. In some societies, too, penalties for reproducing have been replaced by incentives for accepting birth control. But where target populations are extremely poor and those "incentives" are desperately needed food and money, people have no reasonable alternative but to accept the offers extended by their governments. Where reasonable alternatives are precluded, choice is substantially diminished, and to have no reasonable choice but to acquiesce is to have no meaningful choice at all.

Although the need to limit population growth is sometimes quite real, excessive concentration on population control too often overlooks that the social conditions and economic arrangements in societies where population is taken to be the cause of poverty tend to be the kinds of conditions and arrangements which breed destitution for large segments of the citizenry. Too often, problems attributed to uncontrolled population growth are really problems stemming from the distributions of power and wealth within a society or a region. For example, the Sahelian Famine in the late 1960s and early 1970s, which led to hundreds of thousands of deaths and massive migrations southward, was not a result of inadequate resources in the region. Indeed, agricultural exports from the region actually increased during the famine years. As in this case, the problem of poverty is far too often not a problem of absolute scarcity, but a problem of the distribution of goods and services in a society or region. The focus on controlling numbers of births leads to overlooking questions about the social and economic conditions under which people tend to produce families too large for the resources to which they have access. Attempting a technological "fix" by pouring birth control technologies into so-called overpopulated nations is too simplistic a solution. As long as parents will need to rely on their children for support in their later years and as long as women are in subservient social positions (which is the case in virtually every society that is thought to be overpopulated), nations will indirectly encourage continued reproduction while directly trying to slow or halt it. The solution to "the population problem," then, lies in a holistic approach that considers a nation's major social and economic arrangements, not just its access to birth control technologies.

VI. CONCLUSION

A number of highly complex moral, legal, religious, political, cultural, class, race, regional, and gender issues continue to combine over the question of birth control. Societal attitudes toward and, consequently, access to contraception and abortion vary across nations and within nations. Governments involve themselves in regulating birth for reasons ranging from prevention of devastating famine to destruction of whole groups of people to bald imperialism. The abortion debate in much of the West continues to be cast in terms of the moral status of the human conceptus, but all indicators suggest that the real question at stake in the abortion debate is the social position and reproductive authority of women. Significant alternatives in male contraceptives continue to elude us. Throughout the world, "population control" language has shifted to "family planning" language, but too often this change is just linguistic rather than an indication of the realization that the way to preclude population problems is to create the social and economic conditions that make meaningful family planning genuinely possible for real families everywhere. In sum, the moral dimensions of birth control are, and promise to remain, very complicated and very difficult.

Also See the Following Articles

ABORTION • EUGENICS • FEMINIST ETHICS • FETUS • GENDER ROLES

Bibliography

Alexander, N. J. (1995). Future contraceptives. *Scientific American,* **273**, 136–141.

Callahan, J. C. (Ed.) (1995). "Reproduction, Ethics, and the Law: Feminist Perspectives." Indiana Univ. Press, Bloomington.

Callahan, J. C. (1996). Contraception or incarceration: What's wrong with this picture? *Stanford Law and Policy Review* 7(1), 67–82.

Correa, S., and Petchesky, R. (1994). Reproductive and sexual rights: A feminist perspective. In "Population Policies Reconsidered" (G. Sen *et al.*, Eds.). Harvard Univ. Press, London.

Correa, S., with Reichmann, R. (1994). "Population and Reproductive Rights: Feminist Perspectives from the South." Zed Books, London.

Daniels, C. R. (1993). "At Women's Expense: State Power and the Politics of Fetal Rights." Harvard Univ. Press, London.

Dixon-Mueller, R. (1993). "Population Policy and Women's Rights: Transforming Reproductive Choice." Praeger, London.

Hartmann, B. (1995). "Reproductive Rights and Wrongs: The Global Politics of Population Control and Contraceptive Choice," rev. ed. Harper and Row, New York.

Hatcher, R. A., *et al.* (1992). "Contraceptive Technology." Irvington, New York.

International Union, UAW, *et al.* v. Johnson Controls, SC 113 L Ed 2d (1991).

Knight, J. W., and Callahan, J. C. (1989). "Preventing Birth: Contemporary Methods and Related Moral Controversies." Univ. of Utah Press, Salt Lake City.

McLaren, A. (1990). "A History of Contraception: From Antiquity to the Present Day." Basil Blackwell, Cambridge, MA.

Petchesky, R. A. (1990). "Abortion and Women's Choice: The State, Sexuality, and Reproductive Freedom," rev. ed. Northwestern Univ. Press, Boston.

"Programme of Action of the United Nations International Conference on Population and Development, Cairo, 1994" (1994). United Nations Population Information Network (POPIN) Gopher of the Population Division, Department for Economic and Social Information and Policy Analysis.

Raymond, J. G., *et al.* (1991). "RU486: Misconceptions, Myths, and Morals." MIT, Institute on Women and Technology, Cambridge, MA.

Roe v. Wade, 410 U.S. 113 (1973).

Sanger, M. (1938). "An Autobiography." Norton, New York.

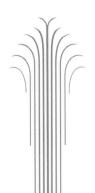

BIRTH-CONTROL TECHNOLOGY

James W. Knight
Virginia Polytechnic Institute and State University

GLOSSARY

abortifacient An agent that produces an abortion.

abortion Expulsion from the uterus of an embryo or fetus prior to the stage of viability.

birth control The act or fact of preventing birth.

conception Fertilization; the point at which the sperm cell and the ovum (egg) unite.

conceptus The products of conception; this includes embryo/fetus and placenta.

contraceptive An agent for preventing conception.

embryo The product of conception until approximately the end of the 8th week of pregnancy in humans.

fetus The product of conception from approximately the end of the 8th week (in humans) until birth.

gametes The sex cells; ovum (egg) in the female and spermatozoa (sperm) in the male.

implantation The embedding of the conceptus in the uterine lining, occurring 6 or 7 days after fertilization.

interceptive A birth control product that arrests conceptus development prior to implantation.

ovulation The release of an ovum (egg) from the ovarian follicle.

pregnancy The condition of a female during the period from conception until birth.

progestagen Any agent capable of producing physiological effects similar to those of progesterone. Progestagens generally inhibit ovulation and have other effects on the female reproductive system to prevent pregnancy.

BIRTH CONTROL TECHNOLOGY represents the endless struggle of the human species to alter the most basic design of nature—reproduction and perpetuation of the species. The constancy of our desire to control our reproductive capacities has, throughout history, also been the focal point for some of our most contentious ethical, moral, legal, and political struggles. Perhaps never in history has the need for advances in birth control technology been greater, nor the debate attendant to reproductive control harsher and more divisive, than it is currently as we approach the 21st century.

At present in the United States, over half of all pregnancies are unplanned, the teenage pregnancy rate is more than double that of European countries, the abortion rate is the highest in the developed world, and new cases of sexually transmissible diseases are increasing at the rate of over 12 million per year. These facts would seem to indicate a crying need for development of new and improved methods of birth control, greater and more widespread availability and application of existing products, and enhanced education, especially among the young, on the use of birth control products. However, numerous factors combine to thwart the ability of Americans to control their reproductive destinies. These factors, as well as a description of contemporary and potential future approaches to birth control, will be discussed in this entry.

I. INTRODUCTION AND OVERVIEW

Efforts to control human reproductive processes, from prehistory until the present day, are characterized by two constants: (1) a continuous but as yet unrealized quest for the perfect contraceptive, and (2) controversy, with reproductive control being the central focus of several contentious ethical, moral, political, and legal issues.

Dichotomies abound. For example, although reproductive capacities play such a significant role in our lives, most people know surprisingly little about the details of reproductive processes, including a lack of understanding as to how the birth control methods that they employ work to prevent pregnancy. Advances in birth control technology beginning in the early 1960s provided American women the reproductive freedom to choose societal roles other than mother and homemaker and accorded to women the freedom to engage in sexual activity without the previous fear of pregnancy. However, the promise of the birth control revolution is yet to be realized, especially in the United States where it began. Indeed, women in the United States now have fewer birth control options than women in other countries. Furthermore, the options available to American women are more expensive and more difficult to obtain. These limitations are reflected in the fact that voluntary sterilization is now the most popular form of birth control in the United States (Table I).

Limitations in contraceptive availability to the young and the economically disadvantaged, although rarely addressed in the political debate of the issues, are in large measure responsible for the facts that teenage pregnancy in the United States is more than double that in European countries, that the rate of abortion in the United States is one of the highest in developed countries, and that "welfare mothers" are available as a group that can be assailed for political advantage. Both federal and private sector funding for reproductive research has decreased almost to the point of being nonexistent. While the governments of many countries

TABLE I
Birth Control Choices in the United States

Option	%
Female sterilization	29.5
Oral contraceptives	28.5
Condoms	17.7
Male sterilization	12.6
Diaphragm	2.8
Periodic abstinence	2.7
Intrauterine devices	1.4
Other methods	4.8

Source: Contraceptive use in the United States (1989–1990). National Center for Health Statistics, *16*, 95–1250 (Released February 14, 1995)

encourage family planning and many subsidize the use of birth control, even the public discussion of birth control tends to be taboo in the United States. Although American culture exploits sex and sexual imagery in all walks of life, a prudish hesitancy to discuss the realities and consequences of sex persists and is perhaps intensifying as we approach the 21st century. In the United States, numerous factors combine to reduce the birth control options currently available, to discourage the greater application of the options that we do have, and to provide disincentives for the development of new technologies.

II. APPROACHES TO BIRTH CONTROL AND MORAL DISTINCTIONS

The world Health Organization (WHO) describes the ideal contraceptive as one that is highly effective, easy to apply, readily reversible, inexpensive, easily distributed, has no serious side effects or risks, and is acceptable in light of the religious, ethical, and cultural background of the user. To complete this utopic vision, one may wish to add that it would also prevent transmission of sexually transmissible diseases. Needless to say, there is no product that can meet those exhalted standards. The dissatisfying reality is that sexually active couples must make compromises and trade-offs among these criteria. This dissatisfaction leads to the misuse or non-use of birth control products. This, in turn, contributes to the fact that nearly one-half of the over 6 million pregnancies in the United States each year are unplanned, and that approximately 1.6 million of these pregnancies are terminated by an elective abortion.

There are three general approaches to birth control:

(1) preventing the formation or release of gametes; (2) preventing fertilization; or (3) preventing the continued development of the embryo at some point following fertilization. Although many individuals erroneously use *contraception* and *birth control* as interchangeable terms, we should not the distinction between them. While the first two approaches to birth control just described truly are contraceptive in nature, that is, the union of the ovum and the sperm cell is prevented, the third is not. Depending upon the point of embryonic development targeted, the third approach may be characterized as either *interceptive* or *abortifacient*. Although some individuals may consider the distinctions among contraceptives, interceptives, abortifacients, and induced abortion methods to be academic, to others they represent a morally and ethically crucial distinction. These distinctions largely center around the age-old question, "When does life begin?"

Although most people consider pregnancy to begin at fertilization, many medical practitioners consider pregnancy to begin at implantation (approximately 6 or 7 days after fertilization). This view is supported by the fact that prior to implantation, the tissues of the conceptus are not yet differentiated into those that will give rise to the placenta and those that will become the embryo and subsequently the fetus. Thus, according to this view, until this differentiation occurs there is not yet an embryo. It then follows from this reasoning that any birth control product that intercepts and arrests development prior to implantation is an interceptive and not an abortifacient product. This view would then imply that it is semantically impossible to consider a birth control product to be abortifacient or to induce an abortion prior to implantation. In more common usage, the term embryo is used both before and after implantation. To some, yet another distinction may be made between utilizing a potentially abortifacient product prior to having confirmation of pregnancy and the conscious termination of a known pregnancy by an induced abortion.

Two moral issues merit further elaboration. First, individuals who hold the "life begins at fertilization" view oppose destruction at any point following conception of what they understand to be a developing human being. This view generally holds as morally crucial that a unique human life begins at fertilization and hence that any intervention destructive of that life counts as aborting that life and is morally wrong. To those who hold this view, the fact that the precursor cells of an embryo do not differentiate until after implantation is irrelevant.

Second, distinguishing between true contraceptives and products that *may* employ interceptive or abortifacient modes of action is a matter of considerable importance to many women and men. While many people have no moral objection to preventing conception, they do find the termination of a potential life at any point after fertilization to be morally objectionable. For this reason, individuals need to understand not only the primary but also the *potential* secondary and tertiary modes of action of the various birth control products as they choose a product for usage. For example, oral contraceptives generally do prevent ovulation. However, so-called "breakthrough" ovulation does sometimes occur and fertilization may result. However, the pregnancy commonly will fail due to other alterations induced in the reproductive tract by the pill. Likewise, an intrauterine device (IUD) may disrupt sperm transport and survival, thereby preventing fertilization. However, fertilization does often occur but the conceptus does not survive due to the disruption within the uterus induced by the IUD. In both examples, the woman would have no way of knowing which mode of action (i.e., contraceptive or interceptive/abortifacient) was the effective one. She would only know that her menstrual cycle recurred as expected.

III. CONTEMPORARY METHODS OF BIRTH CONTROL

A. Steroidal Inhibitors of Ovulation

1. Oral Contraceptives (i.e., "The Pill")

The first oral contraceptive (Enovid, G. D. Searle Pharmaceuticals) was approved by the Food and Drug Administration (FDA) in June 1960. Shortly thereafter, several other pharmaceutical companies rushed their products onto the U.S. market. In essence, this event heralded the onset of the sexual revolution. With the advent of the pill, women at long last had a neat, simple, private, tidy, and highly effective way to avoid unwanted pregnancy. No longer did women who chose to be sexually active have to carry awkward and embarrassing (and unreliable) birth control devices, such as diaphragms and tubes of jelly, nor did they have to depend upon the conscientiousness to their male partners to provide protection. The previously unavailable freedom to enjoy a spontaneous sexual encounter without fear of unwanted pregnancy gave women an approximation of procreational sexual equality with men.

Perhaps partly because of the continued reference to oral contraceptives as *the pill,* many people tend to erroneously assume that there is only a single formulation. There are actually dozens of different formulations among the over 40 different brands on the U.S. market at present. These formulations differ in the particular type of synthetic progestagens and estrogens used, relative quantities of these steroid hormones, overall potency, potential side effects, and relative contraceptive effectiveness. Potential complications and adverse side effects of oral contraceptives can be minimized if care is taken to select the specific pill formulation that is most suitable for each particular woman based upon her age, overall medical history, menstrual history, physical condition, behavioral and health habits, and other individuating factors. This is perhaps the most practical argument against the over-the-counter availability of birth control pills, as some individuals and groups have advocated as a means to increase their availability and usage and potentially decrease their price.

There are two basic categories of oral contraceptives, the combination pill (consisting of a combination of a synthetic progestogen and a synthetic estrogen) and the minipill (progestogen only). The active components of the pill are simply synthetic steroid hormones that are similar to the endogenous hormones progesterone and estrogen produced by a woman's ovaries during her menstrual cycle and which regulate the function of her reproductive tract.

The traditional combined formulation is a constant hormonal dose taken daily for 21 days and followed by a week during which no pills are taken. Many brands include seven inert pills containing iron and vitamins that are taken during the final week of a pill cycle. The decrease in systemic hormone levels that begins after the completion of each 21-day regimen induces the changes leading to menses. These changes are analogous to the decrease in hormones that normally occur at the end of an unregulated menstrual cycle. A new cycle of pills will begin 5 days after the onset of menses.

In simple terms, the hormones in the ingested pill suppress the development of follicles on the ovaries, prevent the maturation of the ovum within the follicle, and inhibit the normal sequence of changes essential for ovulation. Because hormone levels provided by the pill are out of synchrony with normal menstrual cycle events, assorted other changes are also induced throughout the reproductive tract. For example, the characteristics of the mucus produced by the cervix is altered, making it more difficult for sperm to penetrate it. The biochemical secretions within the fallopian tube (the site of fertilization) are altered, and this alteration may result in either the failure of fertilization or the inability for proper development of the early conceptus before it moves into the uterus. Changes induced within the uterus may prevent implantation even in the (rare) instances when the other modes of action fail to be effective.

Biphasic and triphasic pills are a refinement of the combined constant formulation pills. As their names imply, rather than all 21 pills containing a constant hormone dose, biphasic pills employ two dosage levels and triphasic pills three dosage levels due the 21-day regimen. A higher dose of the hormones is contained in the pills taken during the time at which ovulation would normally occur, and a lower dose or doses at other days. One advantage of the phasic pills is the lower total amount of hormones consumed during each cycle. However, because all pills in a packet are not the same, a woman employing the phasic pills must carefully follow the prescribed sequence.

The minipill is a low-dose progestogen-only pill taken daily without a break. With the lower dosage of the minipill, ovulation is more likely to occur than in women taking the combined formulations. The minipill is especially useful for women who should not be using estrogen, such as women with a history of cardiovascular disease, hypertension, and diabetes. Since the combined pills may have an inhibitory effect on milk production, the minipill is also useful for women who are lactating.

The most significant advancement in oral contraceptives since the initial formulations of the early 1960s has been the enormous reduction in the hormone dosage. Due to the relatively short development and testing period prior to introduction of the pill, the initial pills contained extremely high levels of synthetic hormones in order to ensure their contraceptive effectiveness. Potential long-term effects of these high doses were not known. By the 1970s, evidence linking the pill with an increased statistical risk of cardiovascular disease, stroke, and assorted other health problems in women who began taking the extremely high-dose pills in the early 1960s began to accumulate. Soon after the first oral contraceptives were marketed, researchers began testing formulation with ever-decreasing levels of hormones to determine minimal effective dosages. The present-day pills contain only a small fraction of the hormone dose of those early formulations. Therefore, the health risks of the contemporary pill are far less than those from the early pill.

In addition to its 97–99% effectiveness for pregnancy prevention, the pill has many other benefits, including a more regular, less painful menses entailing a lower blood loss, a decreased likelihood of ovarian cysts and pelvic inflammatory disease, and a decreased risk for ovarian and uterine cancer. Potential negative side effects include a greater statistical risk for blood clots, heart attack, and stroke (especially among women who smoke cigarettes). Although there is not consensus among researchers, some reports indicate that taking oral contraceptives increase the risk for breast cancer, especially among women who begin to use the pill before age 18 and take it for more than 10 years. More minor side effects may include weight gain, mood changes, mild headaches, nausea, temporary irregular menstrual bleeding, and breast tenderness. Issues of potential side effects are clouded by the fact that there are so many different types of oral contraceptives and that there are complex interactions with individuating factors such as family medical history, age, smoking, and consumption of alcohol. Therefore, any generalization of what "the pill causes" must be viewed with skepticism.

Potential negative side effects of the pill are apparently exaggerated in the minds of many women. Perhaps this is attributable to the extensive media coverage given to the negative effects of the early formulations of the pill. A 1995 Gallup poll commissioned by the American College of Obstetricians and Gynecologists found that 75% of women surveyed believed that the pill caused "serious health problems." One-third of the respondents believed that the pill caused cancer and nearly as many felt that it caused heart attacks and strokes. No doubt these erroneous beliefs contribute to many women not using the pill.

2. Subdermal Implants (Norplant)

Although research on the concept of using a silastic implant to continuously deliver a progestagen began in 1967, these implants were not available in the United States until 1990. This was almost a decade after they were available in other countries. The concept of this product, marketed under the brand name of "Norplant" by Wyeth-Ayerst Laboratories, is a simple one. By placing six matchstick-sized silastic capsules filled with the progestagen levonorgestrel in a fan-shaped formation under the skin (generally between a woman's elbow and armpit), the hormone is released in a slow and constant pace, and the daily fluctuations in blood levels that occur with daily ingestion of a pill are avoided. Following placement, the implant provides highly effective birth control protection for approximately 5 years.

The Norplant system overcomes the reason for the greatest number of failures with the pill: the failure to remember to take it daily. Additionally, due to the constant rate of slow release, the total amount of progestagen released over any given time period is less than that from taking a daily pill. Hence, long-term side effects due to exposure to the synthetic hormones should be reduced.

In essence, Norplants merely represent an alternative means to oral consumption for deliverying a synthetic hormone that controls the function of the reproductive tract for the prevention of pregnancy. However, because of the lower amount of the progestagen in the woman's circulation at any given time, ovulation is not always suppressed. However, the other alterations of the reproductive system (as described earlier for the pill) prevent pregnancy in a highly efficient manner. For women to whom the distinction between true contraception and birth control *potentially* due to interceptive effects is important, it should be noted that the likelihood of fertilization (but not implantation) is greater with the Norplant system compared to combination oral contraceptives. Since potential user error does not figure into their application, the actual and theoretical effectiveness of Norplants (over 99%) are identical, a major advantage over the pill (Table II).

TABLE II

Lowest Expected (Theoretical) and Typical Failure Rates of Birth Control Options[a]

Method	Lowest expected	Typical
Total abstinence	0	?
Male sterilization	0.1	0.15
Female sterilization	0.2	0.4
Depo-Provera	0.3	0.3
Norplant	0.1	0.3
Oral contraceptives		
Combined pills	0.1	3.0
Minipills	0.5	3.0
Intrauterine device		
Progestasert	1.5	2.0
Copper T 380A	0.6	0.8
Condom (male)	2.0	12.0
Condom (female)	5.0	26.0
Diaphragm	6.0	18.0
Cervical cap	6.0	18.0
Spermicides (alone)	3.0	24.0
Periodic abstinence	1.0–9.0	20.0
Withdrawal	4.0	19.0
"Morning after" pill	—	25.0
Chance	85	85

[a] Expressed as % women experiencing an accidental pregnancy in the first year of continuous use.

The initial cheers from American women for the long-awaited arrival of a potentially revolutionary improvement in birth control that greeted Norplant in 1990 has faded to jeers from many of the more than 1 million women who have tried it, and a firestorm of controversy on several fronts now cloud its once rosy future. The first controversial issue was that of cost. Although the actual cost of the capsules containing the steroid is minimal, the company prices the Norplant kits at $345 per patient (A. G. Rosenfield, 1994. *J. Reprod. Med.* **39**, 337–342). And, although the implantation of the capsules is a simple procedure completed in 10 min or so, the average cost to the patient is $600. One reason often cited for this inflated price is the common one for all new pharmaceutical products—the necessity of recovering research and development cost. However, that claim is questionable. Trials on Norplants were conducted in the 1970s and the product was available in at least 16 other countries for up to nearly a decade and in use by over 500,000 women before it was marketed in the United States. Norplant is an excellent example of the primary financial disincentive that continues to make pharmaceutical companies hesitant to introduce new birth control products in the United States. Simply stated, if a company can sell a tested, accepted, and highly profitable product to a consumer on a monthly basis (birth control pills cost approximately 15 cents per cycle but are marketed at approximately $20 per cycle), why sell her a product that she only has to purchase once every 5 years unless it can be sold to her at a somewhat comparable profit? This is especially so when a company must be concerned with potential lawsuits from product liability claims in our highly litigious society. And this fear has been realized.

Although the potential side effects of Norplant are similar to those of the pill (e.g., weight gains, mood swings, headaches, and irregular menstrual bleeding), many women report them to be of a more severe degree. Menstrual disturbances, ranging from no menstrual period at all to continuous spotting, are common to all progestagen-only systems (including the minipill) and an unavoidable consequence of the constant delivery of progestagen without estrogen. The considerable advantage of having no estrogen in the delivery system is a reduced risk of the more serious side effects of circulatory disorders, blood clots, strokes, and perhaps breast cancer. Some Norplant users have reported infections and inflammations at the implant site. Surgical side effects unique to Norplant have caused the greatest dissatisfaction. Since the capsules are not biodegradable, they must be surgically removed. This removal has proved problematic with reports that one removal in five takes an hour or more and that one in four is painful (Nov. 27, 1995. *Newsweek*, p. 52).

Although Wyeth-Ayerst has always listed the potential negative side effects in its literature for Norplant, critics have claimed that these side effects have been downplayed in its marketing of the product. Perhaps there are many individuals who naively assume that all pharmaceutical products approved for marketing are free of any adverse side effects and who are unwilling to make the necessary trade-offs and accept the reality that no birth control product is ideal. However, the surgical complications of Norplant removal were apparently unexpected, even by doctors who implanted the devices. According to a report in *Newsweek* magazine (Nov. 27, 1995. p. 52), in the first 3 years that Norplant was on the market in the United States, there were fewer than 20 out of 800,000 users who filed legal complaints; now over 50,000 women are suing the company. This has led to a precipitous decline in Norplant sales over the past year. The FDA, the WHO, and numerous medical authorities emphatically conclude that Norplant is a safe and highly effective contraceptive and that at least 90% of the women who use it are satisfied. Certainly the fear of lawsuits has been a major reason why pharmaceutical companies have been hesitant to develop and market new birth control options in the United States. The legal assault on Norplant confirms that these fears were justified and clearly serves as a disincentive for future innovations.

The most prickly controversy associated with the Norplant system of birth control is the numerous instances of forcing or attempting to force women to use it as a means of mandating control of the procreational liberty of women as judicial punishment or as a condition to receive government benefits including welfare and public education. Since economically disadvantaged women of color have been the most frequent targets of these mandates, highly inflammatory issues of racism and discrimination are at the center of this ethical debate.

3. Injectables

In June 1993, the FDA approved the use of the injectable progestagen Depo-Provera, another "new" product to the United States market with a long history of investigation as a contraceptive dating back to 1963. Although not officially approved for contraceptive purposes until 1993, this progestagen (medroxyprogesterone acetate, MPA) had already been marketed by the Upjohn Company for 20 years as a palliative treatment for endometrial (uterine lining) cancer. Prior to U.S. approval,

Depo-Provera was already being utilized in approximately 90 countries for contraception. No doubt some physicians in the United States had unofficially utilized it for that purpose.

Depo-Provera is administered as an intramuscular injection and provides highly effective (over 99%) birth control protection for a 3-month period. Each of four annual injections costs approximately $30, making it similar in annual cost to the Norplant system and less than the pill. Like Norplant, its actual effectiveness is higher than that of the pill because the user need not do anything during the 3-month period of protection (Table II). Depo-Provera is not readily reversible. Should a woman desire to become pregnant after the injection is administered, she can only wait for it to "wear off" before fertility is restored. The 3-month period of fertility suppression is a conservative estimate, and if a woman desires to become pregnant within a year or two, Depo-Provera would not be a good contraceptive choice.

The mechanisms of action of Depo-Provera and its potential side effects (positive and negative) are similar to those of the pill and Norplant. A study by officials of the WHO suggests that users of Depo-Provera may have a higher than normal statistical risk of breast cancer. However, women who use Depo-Provera have a significantly lower risk of uterine cancer and "come out ahead" when all cancer risks are tallied.

There are other synthetic progestagens (norethisterone enanthate, NET-EN, being the most widely studied) and combined progestagen and estrogen formulations that have been studied since the early 1960s to the present day and that are utilized in other countries as injectables, providing varying durations of protection. None of these have any significant overall advantages compared with Depo-Provera.

B. Inhibitors of Fertilization

1. Physical Barriers

a. Male Condoms

Condoms are truly an ancient birth control device, having been utilized in one form or another for centuries for the dual purposes for which they remain effective—preventing the spread of sexually transmissible diseases and for pregnancy prevention. Gabriello Fallopius (1523–1562), an Italian anatomist perhaps best known for his description of the fallopian tubes (oviducts of the female) that bear his name, is credited with the first published description of the condom. Use of his "linen sheath" has been credited with helping to stem the

spread of syphilis in Europe in the 16th century. Development of the process for vulcanization of rubber in the mid-1880s that permitted mass production of condoms led to a tremendous surge in their popularity and usage.

Condoms are the third most widely used form of birth control in the United States, ranking behind only female sterilization and the pill (Table I). Because they are widely available and easy to obtain, relatively low in cost, have no side effects (other than for a very few individuals who are allergic to latex), and have no equal for preventing the spread of microbes that are responsible for sexually transmissible diseases (STDs), condoms play an especially important role as the primary birth control choice among sexually active young people. Condoms represent one of the few contraceptives readily available to minors. And condoms are the most logical birth control option for individuals who are not "pre-prepared" for sexual activity with a continuous protection method (such as taking the pill). Even if other methods of birth control are used, it is certainly advisable to also use a condom in any sexual encounter other than a monogamous relationship between two individuals known to be disease free. One criticism aimed at making hormonal methods of birth control available to young women with multiple sex partners is that they are less likely to insist that their partners use a condom, either because they feel safe in regard to their primary concern, preventing pregnancy, or because they erroneously believe that the contraceptive will also provide protection against disease transmission. Unfortunately, surveys of people with multiple sex partners—the population most susceptible for acquiring STDs—indicate that less than 10% of them use condoms during every sex act.

The chilling increase in both heterosexual and homosexual male transmission of AIDS (Acquired Immunodeficiency Disease) during the past 15 years has played a major role in spurring the increase in sales of condoms (which now totals over 450 million a year in the United States alone; May, 1995, *Consumer Rep.*) and in hastening development of more brands and options. If properly used, latex condoms reduce to near zero the risk of transmission of STDs, including the human immunodeficiency virus (HIV) that causes AIDS. One bit of good news relative to public education is a survey by the Centers for Disease Control and Prevention which found that three of every four Americans do know that latex condoms, if used consistently and correctly, will prevent the transmission of HIV and other STDs. The obvious problem, however, lies in the "if" clause.

Somewhat ironically, the oldest of our contraceptives is perhaps the one that has undergone the most dramatic improvement and received the greatest amount of research and development attention over the past two decades. Well over 100 brands of condoms are available in the United States in a dazzling array of options (nonlubricated, lubricated, spermicidal, snug, extra-large, contoured, sensitive, ribbed, studded, clear, colored, scented, etc.).

The gap between theoretical and actual effectiveness is greater for the condom than for any other birth control method (Table II). Theoretical effectiveness (effectiveness of the method itself *if* properly used and apart from user error) for the condom is quite high, 97–99%. However, actual effectiveness (effectiveness based upon subtracting from 100 the percent of women who use a given method but nonetheless become pregnant in a year's time) is only approximately 88%. Reasons for the disparity in the two figures include the facts that couples do not use condoms every time they have intercourse and that they do not follow the instructions for proper use of the condom. Breakage of the condom occurs far less frequently than does user error.

The more contentious issues associated with condoms deal with their advertising and the distribution of them, especially to minors. Although condoms are now advertised on cable television, condom ads continue to be banned on network television. This is, of course, despite the ceaseless use of blatant sexuality in advertising and the implicit and often explicit sexual encounters protrayed in television programs. While all of the potential sociological implications will not be explored here, it is certainly not surprising that condom usage is so low among at risk individuals when they are continuously exposed to the portrayal of sex on television (and in movies) as being without consequences and without ever seeing responsible sexual interaction and an intelligent discussion of protection preceding a sexual encounter modeled for them. This is compounded by the Victorian attitude toward sex education in many school systems and the reticence (or inability) of many parents to openly and honestly discuss sexual matters with their children.

b. Female Condom

The female condom is a soft, loose-fitting sheath that lines the vagina. It is made of polyurethane (not latex like the male condom) and has a semistiff plastic ring at each end. The inner ring is used to insert the device inside the vagina and serves as an internal anchor. The outer ring covers the labia area and the base of the penis during intercourse. Following a year of selected test marketing to determine acceptance, the female condom was released for widespread United States marketing by Wisconsin Pharmaceuticals in August 1994 under the brand name Reality. In Europe and Canada, the product was already available under the name Femidom.

Other than the fact that it accords women an over-the-counter product of which they have control, the female condom has few advantages and many disadvantages compared with the male condom. One advantage is that the polyurethane membrane is 40% stronger than latex; resistant to oils, allowing the use of an oil-soluble (rather than water-soluble) lubricant that may be preferred by some couples; and transfers heat and gives a more natural feel than does latex. It is also an option for those allergic to latex. However, it costs considerably more than does the male condom for a one time usage (approximately $2.50 each), requires extensive practice to properly insert, may slip around and need to be repositioned several times during intercourse, and to many is aesthetically unappealing. More importantly, although the contraceptive effectiveness under normal use was expected to be around 87% (similar to the actual effectiveness of the male condom), initial results indicate a pregnancy rate among users of 26% (74% effectiveness). This is no doubt at least partly due to the lack of familiarity with using this rather cumbersome device. Another very important point is that the female condom is not considered to provide protection to either party against STDs, including HIV transmission.

c. Diaphragm

The vaginal diaphragm, a soft, bowl-shaped rubber dome with a flexible metal rim, is an ancient female barrier contraceptive that has remained largely unchanged since the late 19th century. The diaphragm, which must be custom fitted to the particular measurements of each individual woman, is positioned in the posterior vagina, covering the opening to the cervix and serving as a physical barrier to sperm entry. Diaphragms should always be used with spermicidal gel or cream. The spermicide (generally nonoxynol-9) kills or immobilizes a substantial number of the 200 million or so sperm present in the typical ejaculate. It should be realized that regardless of the method in which spermicides are used, they only function to reduce sperm numbers and never totally eliminate all of the sperm. Actual effectiveness, even when used with spermicide, is low (80–83%). The diaphragm is, simply stated, a cumbersome, messy, inconvenient, and outdated device. Its many disadvantages are well known, especially to women who have used it.

d. Cervical Cap

The cervical cap is perhaps the perfect symbol for the state and rate of birth control progress in the United States. The cap, a small, thimble-shaped device with a small amount of spermicidal gel inside the cap, is placed directly over the cervix. It was first approved by the FDA in mid-1988. However, the cervical cap was developed in 1838, 150 years earlier, by the German gynecologist Friedrich Wilde, and has long been available throughout most of the world. It too must be custom fitted to each woman and its effectiveness (or lack thereof) is similar to the diaphragm. It does have the advantage that it can be left in place without the need for application of additional spermicide from one menstruation to just before the start of the next.

e. Contraceptive Sponge

The Today contraceptive vaginal sponge was withdrawn from the United States market by its manufacturer, Whitehall-Robins Healthcare, in early 1995. It was a polyurethane foam device saturated with spermicide and sold over-the-counter. Although it absorbed some of the ejaculate and served as a partial barrier to sperm transport, its primary mode of action was the release of spermicide (nonoxynol-9). Its reported actual effectiveness when used alone was low (75–83%), and it had numerous drawbacks, including vaginal irritation, discomfort to both partners, and causing an increased risk for toxic shock syndrome. The reason provided by the company at the time of withdrawal was that complying with more stringent FDA manufacturing and testing requirements would require modification of the manufacturing process and that these changes would take several years and result in pricing the product beyond the reach of many users.

2. Chemical Barriers: Spermicides

When used alone, the spermicidal foams, creams, gels, suppositories, and tablets currently available are only 70–76% effective at pregnancy prevention. They do add an element of effectiveness when used in combination with condoms and diaphragms. Spermicides are also useful in reducing the likelihood of transmission of agents responsible for STDs, including HIV. Agents that inhibit sperm enzymes, thereby altering sperm motility, and that interfere with other metabolic functions of sperm are under investigation but are not likely to be available in the near future.

C. Interceptive and Abortifacient Methods

1. Intrauterine Devices

The intrauterine device (IUD) has an ancient, storied, and stormy history. Although inserting some sort of object into the female reproductive tract, including the uterus, dates to antiquity, the "modern" IUD as a birth control device traces to the early 1900s. Numerous materials, designs, sizes, and shapes have been utilized over the years. The primary mode of action for all IUDs is the induction of a foreign-body reaction within the uterus that disrupts numerous reproductive events, including sperm transport, sperm capacitation, ovum transport, fertilization, conceptus movement into the uterus, and implantation. Many types also incorporate metallic ions (especially copper) that enhance their disruptive effect on sperm on progestagens that are released to elicit both localized and systemic effects. Because of the large number of events that may be disrupted, IUDs are extremely effective (98–99+% effectiveness). As described earlier, one would never know which of the potential actions of the IUD led to preventing pregnancy during any particular menstrual cycle. Research studies indicate that fertilization does occur in a significant number of cycles but that pregnancy fails prior to implantation. Women to whom that moral distinction matters should be aware of that fact before considering the use of an IUD. At present, only about 2% of women in the United States who employ birth control use the IUD. Worldwide it is one of the most commonly used options.

Despite a history of most brands of IUDs providing an effective and relatively safe birth control option, IUDs were withdrawn from the U.S. market in February 1986, and only recently have they reappeared. Their removal was largely due to the highly justified outrage and lawsuits directed against one of the many types of IUDs, the ill-designed Dalkon Shield manufactured by A. H. Robins Company. The Dalkon Shield was a crab-shaped device with sharp "legs" perfect for harboring bacteria picked up from the vagina during insertion and then injecting the bacteria into the uterin lining. This led to a painful infection that resulted in a large number of cases of pelvic inflammatory disease (PID), infertility, and at least 14 deaths. In addition, the tail of the Dalkon Shield (the string that normally trails from the IUD through the cervix and into the vagina), acted rather like a wick to continually pull bacteria from the vagina into the uterus, perpetuating the infection. The Dalkon shield was voluntarily withdrawn from the market in 1975. The predictable consequence of the lawsuits appropriately lodged against the Dalkon Shield and A. H. Robins Company (that led to their filing for Chapter 11 bankruptcy in August 1985) was a surge in lawsuits against *all* manufacturers of IUDs. Many users and potential users of IUDs failed to draw a distinction between the Dalkon shield and the many other safer varieties of IUDs. This led to a decline in sales of all IUDs and an increase in lawsuits against other manufacturers. The predictable business decision of IUD manufacturers was to remove their products from the U.S. market.

Currently there are two types of IUDs available in the United States, one that releases copper (Copper T 380A) and one that releases a progestagen (Progestasert). Intrauterine release of a progestagen has the advantage of reducing menstrual blood loss, hence overcoming one of the major negative side effects of a greater menstrual flow typical of earlier IUDs.

Certainly the IUD is not an appropriate choice for all women; however, it may be the best choice for some women. Many women experience intense cramping and spontaneously expel their IUD. It is generally most appropriate for older women who have previously had a child (the interior of their uterus is usually larger) and who are in a monogamous relationship (and hence at a greatly reduced risk for PID).

2. Postcoital Contraception (the "Morning After" Pill)

Semantical inconsistencies abound in most discussions of this method. First, as discussed previously, use of the terms "postcoital contraception" and "emergency contraceptive" are oxymoronic when discussing an interceptive method of birth control. Second, the "morning after" pill may be used up to 72 hr after unprotected intercourse (in fact, the window of effectiveness is probably even greater than 72 hr). Third, the treatment regimen typically entails four pills, not a single pill. Fourth, *all* "regular" birth control pills may be used for "emergency" purposes if administered in sufficiently high doses.

The more typical "morning after" pill is a regimen of four high-dose combined progestagen–estrogen oral contraceptives (most commonly Ovral) taken in pairs 12 hr apart beginning within 72 hr after unprotected intercourse. It is estimated to be about 75% effective in preventing pregnancy. This high dose of hormones disrupts a number of reproductive processes that are likely to interfere with either fertilization or conceptus development. Given the timing of application, the woman does not know if conception did or did not occur. This is its primary distinguishing trait from use of a product, such as RU-486, that aborts a known pregnancy.

As implied in the monikers describing this method, it is not considered a method to be used on a routine basis. In addition to being used in cases of rape, it may be appropriate as a "backup" system for cases such as condom breakage, diaphragm slippage, or simply unprotected intercourse. It should be noted that uses of high doses of the pill for this purpose have been recognized as effective for at least 25 years.

University health centers have been primary and more highly publicized dispensers of this method. Especially since student fees paid by all students support these centers and many students object to what they term a form of abortion, the availability of this service has been a recent controversial issues on many campuses.

In a somewhat unusual proactive move, an FDA advisory panel announced in June 1996 that it considered oral contraceptives to be safe and effective when used as "morning after" pills. They largely based their conclusion on the fact that for a decade women in Europe have been using the pill for that purpose. Although the FDA was clearly letting drug companies know that it would welcome an application to market birth control pills for "emergency" purposes in the United States, as of September 1996 no companies have applied to do so. Once again, fears of liability suits, negative publicity, and/or product boycotts by antiabortion groups make pharmaceutical companies reluctant to "take the bait" dangled before them by the FDA.

3. RU-486 (Mifepristone)

Not since the controversy surrounding the initial introduction of the pill has there been a birth control option that has caused the degree of excitement, optimism, outrage, condemnation, and protest as that created by RU-486. Elements of that outrage and controversy may largely be attributed to the success of those who oppose the availability of RU-486 in the United States in having it associated in the minds of many simply as "the abortion pill." Indeed, one rarely sees or hears the product discussed in the media without the moniker, *the abortion pill,* immediately written or spoken following *RU-486.* Although it can be used to induce a postimplantation abortion, RU-486 has many other potential applications that generally get ignored and obscured by the heated debate that follows the mention of this one, and no doubt which many believe to be its only, potential application.

RU-486 (the RU refers to its manufacturer, the French company Roussel-Uclaf, and the number 486 is simply an in-house designation) has the unique ability to bind to cellular receptors for the hormone progesterone at a five times greater affinity than does progesterone itself. Progesterone is essential for the maintenance of pregnancy, and, simply stated, progesterone cannot induce the changes within the uterus that are necessary for pregnancy to continue if RU-486 is occupying its receptors. Hence, the uterine lining is sloughed off, just as during a menstrual period. Since the developing conceptus requires attachment to the uterine lining for continued development, it too would be expelled. In other words, RU-486 has induced an abortion. RU-486 is generally combined with a prostaglandin, a natural product the makes the uterus contract and aids in the sloughing of the uterine contents (prostaglandins are what cause menstrual cramps). Although it can be successfully used later in pregnancy, RU-486 is generally used for induction of abortion within the first 2 months of pregnancy. RU-486 offers numerous advantages as an alternative to traditional aspiration abortions. One practical advantage is that abortion access would not be limited to the relatively few specialized abortion clinics that are currently easily targeted for protests and violence by those opposed to abortion. It is not the purpose of this chapter to address the issue of abortion, and abortion is not and should not be regarded as a method of birth control. In the best of circumstances, abortion is a physically and psychologically traumatic experience for most women. However, by all objective measures, the effectiveness (96–98%) of RU-486 as a product for elective induction of abortion and the relative absence of short-term and long-term health complications make it a highly attractive alternative to traditional methods of abortion.

However, since RU-486 binds to progesterone receptors whenever and wherever it finds them, it could also be used as an interceptive agent before pregnancy has ever progressed to the point of being established or confirmed. Its use as a "once a month" product could induce a menstrual period at its expected time—which may or may not entail an abortifacient action. Scenarios can be developed in which it could be used as a true contraceptive. Perhaps even more important are the numerous other potential and less controversial applications of RU-486 that are vitally important to women's health. For example, it may be a valuable treatment for breast cancer. As many as one-third of the cases of breast cancers contain an abundance of progesterone receptors and these tumors require progesterone to survive. Endometrial cancers and the painful excessive proliferation of endometrial cells known as endometriosis (the third leading cause of infertility in the United

States) can be successfully treated with RU-486. RU-486 can cause dilation of the cervix, allowing vaginal delivery in women who now must have a cesarean delivery. Cushing's disease, a disorder of the adrenal glands affecting both women and men that often necessitates removal of the glands, also responds to RU-486. The bottom line is that the health of American women has been imperiled because RU-486 has been banned due to *one* of its many potential applications. If it were available, RU-486 could have saved the lives of or at least benefited the health of thousands of American women. The fact that it remains unavailable is largely, if not solely, due to the hesitancy of politicians to handle the hot-potato issue of abortion.

RU-486 was first made available in France in 1988. Since that time, it has become widely available in numerous countries throughout the world. In France and the United Kingdom, over 200,000 women have had medical abortions with RU-486. Just as politicians wish to avoid the issue of abortion, so too do pharmaceutical companies. The American patent rights to RU-486 have been given to the nonprofit Population Council. No pharmaceutical company was willing to take on the controversy and liability that would greet any future attempts to market RU-486 in the United States. Clinical trials on Ru-486, renamed mifepristone, were completed in September 1995 by the Population Council. More than 2100 women who were less than 9 weeks pregnant participated in trials at 17 clinics throughout the United States. The Population Council reported "overwhelming satisfaction" among participants (Spring, 1996. *Planned Parenthood Today*).

A recommendation for approval of RU-486 for use in the United States was filed with the FDA by the Population Council in the summer of 1996. A panel of scientific advisors to the FDA voted unanimously to recommend approval (with conditions) of RU-486 on July 19, 1996. However, a final decision by the FDA on the marketing of RU-486 in the United States is pending as we go to press.

4. Methotrexate

Methotrexate is a product that is already on the market and approved by the FDA for a number of purposes, including the treatment of tumors and cancers. It was first reported in late 1993 that methotrexate could also be used to induce abortion. Since that time, numerous researchers have experimentally investigated the drug and confirmed its effectiveness as an alternative to RU-486 for induction of a nonsurgical abortion. Many scientists believe that it has outstanding potential as an abortifacient agent. Since methotrexate is already approved by the FDA for other purposes, only an application to the FDA for "supplemental indication" is necessary for consideration of its application for induction of abortion. In general, this is easier to get than is new-drug approval.

However, politics, publicity, and profit again loom as storm clouds on the horizon. To date, no pharmaceutical company has requested supplemental indication approval for methotrexate. Given the likely negative publicity potentially leading to protests and boycotts organized by antiabortion groups and the unresolved potential for future lawsuits, it is unlikely that a major company will seek such approval. In addition, because methotrexate is extremely inexpensive (approximately $4 a dose compared with about $200 for RU-486), it is unlikely to be a big profit maker.

5. Menstrual Regulation (Menstrual Induction, Menstrual Planning, Preemptive Abortion, Endometrial Aspiration, Atraumatic Termination of Pregnancy)

Without venturing too far into the semantical minefield implicit in the multitude of terms applied to this technique, in the minds of many it to some extent fills the gap between the foresight of birth control and the hindsight of abortion chosen following confirmation of pregnancy. The process is a simple, safe, highly effective outpatient procedure involving vacuum aspiration of the uterine lining within a few days to 2 weeks after the failure to commence menstruation. This procedure may or may not be an abortion since the key point that distinguishes it from a "regular" abortion is that the woman does not know for sure if she is pregnant. While pregnancy may have been the reason for her menstrual period not recurring, there are numerous other potential reasons.

Since this procedure is generally performed at a time when it is possible to discern whether or not she is pregnant, one would think that most women would want to know and avoid the procedure if they were not pregnant. However, some women choose to have the procedure performed as soon as possible and without pregnancy confirmation in order to avoid the ethical dilemma that they would see arising from aborting a known pregnancy. This approach is troubling to many, not only because it is a "head in the sand" way of dealing with an issue of considerable moral import, but also because it is important for a woman's psychological well-being that she be clear that she accepts abortion as morally permissible before employing this procedure or any of the numerous birth control methods that may have abortifacient actions.

D. Surgical Sterilization

No doubt in large measure due to the frustration arising from the deficiencies in the methods of birth control previously discussed, surgical sterilization is now the most common form of birth control in the United States (Table I). According to the National Center for Health Statistics, in 1990 (the latest comprehensive figures available) 29.5% of all American women employing birth control had tubal ligations. Add in the 12.6% of men who had vasectomies and the total percentage of women relying on some type of sterilization is over 42%. Of women in their early thirties, 47% rely on either male or female sterilization. For women in their late thirties, the figure increases to 65%. And for women over age 40, 73% rely on sterilization. Sterilization rates of women do not differ significantly by either race or level of family income. However, Caucasian men are 14 times more likely to have had a vasectomy than are African-American men. American women elect tubal ligation at a higher rate than women in any other country, with only women in China, a country that imposes a limit on the number of children that a woman may have, being a close second. The rate of tubal ligations for married women in other Westernized countries, for example, 23% in Great Britain and 15% in Holland, is far lower than that in the United States. Worldwide, 16% of all married women are protected by tubal ligation. With the repeal of state laws over the last couple of decades that previously restricted elective tubal ligation primarily to older married women who had already had children, now young unmarried women are increasingly opting for tubal ligation as a birth control method. While the exceedingly high rate of elective sterilization in the United States cannot be attributed to this fact alone, certainly the frustration of Americans over the lack of other available birth control options is a major reason for the continued and increasing trend.

There are numerous procedures and modifications for contraceptive sterilization, but all basically involve the bilateral cutting, tying, sealing, and/or removing of a small portion of the fallopian tubes (in women) or vas deferens (in men). Electro- or thermocoagulation, mechanical rings or clips, and chemical adhesives may be employed in tubal ligation. Tubal ligation prevents the ovum and sperm from reaching one another at the necessary site of fertilization in the fallopian tube. Vasectomy prevents sperm from passing from where they are stored in the epididymis into the vas deferens. Surgical sterilization approaches 100% effectiveness. Generally, there are no major long-term health risks and protection is continuous and lifelong. Although success at reversing the procedures and restoring fertility has increased over the years, both tubal ligation and vasectomy should be considered as permanent and not undertaken unless one is willing to accept termination of reproductive capacity.

IV. FUTURE METHODS OF BIRTH CONTROL

The increasing number of women and men opting for surgical sterilization, the very high rate of unwanted pregnancies (especially among the young and unmarried), the prevalence of abortions, the previously discussed issues of nonuse, underuse, misuse, and method failure, undesirable side effects of current options, and the lack of reversible options amenable to all lifestyles clearly argue that more birth control options are needed in the United States. On a global basis, United Nations' estimates predict a continued increase in worldwide population over the next 100 years, with 95% of the increase occurring in developing countries. Development of new birth control options, improvement of existing methods, and increased efforts in educating people how to properly apply current and potential future options are critical issues for the future.

A. Improvements of Current Methods of Hormone Delivery

1. Oral Contraceptives

Improvements in this now old method of revolutionary contraception has been continuous since the 1960s. In 1989, the FDA recommended removal of all references to age limits for the use of the pill by healthy, nonsmoking women. Newer formulations may now be used by women throughout their reproductive life. The pill may be available as an over-the-counter, nonprescription drug at some future date. While this would likely increase availability and usage and should decrease cost, it has the major potential disadvantage of a woman utilizing a formulation that is not appropriate for her, thereby risking contraceptive failure and adverse side effects.

Research is underway to develop a pill that could be taken orally only once a month rather than daily. This could be targeted either at the time that menses is expected (a potential interceptive action) or on the last day of a woman's period to prevent conception for the following month (a probable contraceptive action).

Such a product is probably at least 20 years away from availability.

2. Biodegradable Implants

Biodegradable systems offer many potential advantages over oral, implant, and injectable administration of hormones to control fertility. A major advantage is eliminating the need to remove the delivery system when the supply of the hormone has been exhausted. Biodegradable microspheres that deliver a measured amount of progestagen and provide protection for durations ranging from 3 to 6 months have been investigated in clinical trials and proved effective. A disadvantage of biodegradable microspheres is that they cannot be easily retrieved once administered.

Polymeric membranes allow for superior control of drug release rate compared to any nonbiodegradable system. In addition, the controlled release rate that can be achieved in these products offers the potential to minimize side effects by augmenting the amount and persistence of the drug in the vicinity of target cells, thereby reducing the exposure of nontarget cells. This makes possible the use of lower amounts of hormone and minimizes potential side effects.

One product under investigation, termed Capronor, combines the advantages of retrievable and biodegradable implants. It is a single biodegradable rod containing enough progestagen sufficient to provide contraceptive protection for a number of years, and it will eventually dissolve. However, it would be removable, and hence reversible, for a while following implantation.

3. Transdermal Delivery Systems

This approach is rather similar to the nicotine delivery skin patches now on the market to help wean smokers from cigarettes. The contraceptive hormone is delivered in a skin patch in combination with a substance that enhances skin penetration and absorption. Early trials have been associated with problems in skin irritation due primarily to the effects of the enhancers.

4. Vaginal Rings

The medicated vaginal ring is another "new" method of contraception with a history dating to the 1960s. Vaginal rings, like subdermal implants, are devices made of a biocompatible polymer, usually silastic, loaded with long-acting steroids (either a progestagen alone or a combination of a progestagen and an estrogen) that are slowly absorbed at a predetermined rate. The hormones are absorbed directly into the bloodstream through the vaginal mucus membrane. The ring is placed in the posterior portion of the vagina by the user and left in place for anywhere from 3 weeks to 3 months, or perhaps even for as long as a year. An advantage is that the user herself places and can remove the ring without the need for intervention by a physician. The ring is washable and reusable. One scheme of usage is to insert the ring and leave it in place for three weeks and then to remove it for a week to allow a normal menstrual period to occur. In essence, this is the same concept as the traditional regimen with oral contraceptives, but eliminating the need for daily intervention. The advantage of user control may also be a potential disadvantage since she must ensure its proper placement for the hormones to be appropriately released and absorbed. The position of the vaginal ring may be disrupted during intercourse, so the user needs to be rather constantly vigilant in assuring that it is properly placed.

Effectiveness and side effects of this method of contraceptive hormone delivery are similar to those of the pill. In trials to date, some women have reported localized vaginal irritation and erosion from some models. There also tends to be a disruption of vaginal microbial flora that cause a change in vaginal odor that some women (and their partners) find objectionable. N. J. Alexander predicts that a vaginal ring may be available in the United States by the year 2000 (1995, *Scientific Am.* 273, 136–141).

5. Vaginal Pills

This is in essence the same concept as the classical oral pill, but is designed to be inserted manually by a woman into her vagina rather than swallowed. It too may be a progestagen alone or a combination progestagen and estrogen. It is of a nature that would be readily absorbed into the vaginal mucosa. Reported theoretical effectiveness is over 99% and it reduces many of the undesired side effects of oral contraceptives, especially nausea. As with oral contraceptives, however, actual effectiveness is dependent upon daily administration by the user. Some women may find the method of daily delivery to be objectionable.

B. Immunocontraception for Women

The 21st century should finally see the realization of several possible options for immunocontraception in women and men. These are vaccines that would stimulate the immune system of the body to make antibodies against the functioning of selected proteins that are involved in various reproductive functions. The immune system is designed to "attack" any protein that is not native to the body. Therefore, injecting a person

with a target protein (called an antigen or immunogen) plus other substances to boost the response will result in raising antibodies that would remain in the body for variable periods of time and disrupt the normal functions of the selected antigen.

1. Vaccine against Pregnancy

Beginning around the time of implantation, the placenta of the developing embryo produces a hormone called human chorionic gonadotropin (hCG). Detection of hCG is the basis of pregnancy testing. The major role of hCG is to stimulate the continued production of the hormone progesterone that is necessary for pregnancy to continue. If the normal effects of hCG are negated, progesterone levels fall, implantation is disrupted, and pregnancy fails. Therefore, in women immunized against hCG, the antibodies would counter hCG as soon as it began to be produced and pregnancy would fail.

Several trials have been conducted examining various protocols. In one scenario, immunity against pregnancy was achieved for 1 year by two initial injections and then a booster injection yearly for continued protection. The greatest concern is reversibility. Individuating factors can affect the duration at which antibody protection declines over time. If this decline is too rapid, an unwanted pregnancy may occur due to an unknown lack of protection. If the decline is too slow, there may be a substantial period of time after the last injection before a desired pregnancy may be possible. Since this is an abortifacient approach to birth control, it should only be utilized by women who realize that and accept that mode of action.

2. Targeting the Zona Pellucida

The zona pellucida is a thick membrane that is an outer "shell" around the ovum. Penetration of the zona pellucida by the sperm is essential for fertilization. A specific protein in the zona pellucida called ZP3 has been targeted as the primary immunogenic agent. Numerous studies since the 1970s have shown that ZP3 antibodies interfere with growth of the follicle and maturation of the ovum with contraceptive results. ZP3 is responsible for binding action with the sperm at fertilization. This fact has been exploited by administering ZP3 antibodies that then bind to sperm cells, blocking subsequent fertilization by preventing them from binding to the zona pellucida.

C. Future Options for Men

While birth control options for women are limited, those for men are even more so. Other than withdrawal prior to ejaculation, the only choices available for men are condoms and vasectomy. Given the potential permanence of vasectomy, it is not a viable choice for many. Ignoring the facts that some degree of sexism may be attendant to the history of birth control research and that many men and women simply feel that birth control is primarily a woman's responsibility, there are three major physiological reasons for the inequitable emphasis on female rather than male directed approaches. First, since fertilization and conceptus development occur within women, there are a greater number of reproductive events to manipulate to prevent pregnancy. Second, since women have to centers of "brain control" of the endocrine events controlling the activities of their ovaries and men have only a single brain center of testicular control, it is easier to hormonally interrupt the events controlling female fertility without causing adverse effects on the production of the hormones needed for other body functions. Third, and perhaps most important, it is difficult to argue with the logic of attempting to prevent pregnancy by controlling the fate of a single ovum produced once a month compared with the overwhelmingly more difficult task of interrupting the continuous process of sperm production which yields 20 to 30 million spermatozoa every day of a man's reproductive life, or of trying to control their fate following ejaculation. And the fact that women generally "have more to lose" if an unwanted pregnancy should occur also argues for giving women the greater control.

1. Improved Condoms

A reduction in sexual pleasure is the major reason reported by men for not using condoms. Manufacturers have recently introduced a thin polyurethane condom and are exploring other polymers that provide less interference with sensation while continuing to provide pregnancy and disease protection. Due to the many advantages of the condom in regard to lack of side effects, reversibility, low cost, and widespread availability, improvements in this ancient method of contraception may be the ones of greatest significance for the immediate future.

2. Steroidal Inhibition of Spermatogenesis

One approach involves intramuscular injection of the hormone testosterone. Keeping testosterone at high levels leads to suppression of other so-called gonadotropin hormones necessary for sperm production. Early results are encouraging relative to suppression of sperm numbers. Disadvantages include increased irritability, acne, and the potentially more serious effect of lowering levels of high-density lipoproteins (the "good" kind of cholesterol). Adding a progestagen to the injection may reduce some of the side effects. Despite recent reports of these trials in the popular media, approval of such a regimen is 10–20 years away.

3. Inhibition of Gonadotropin-Releasing Hormone (Gn-RH)

Numerous approaches to blocking the activity of Gn-RH, which is the key controlling hormone produced by the hypothalamic portion of the brain that ultimately leads to production of testosterone by the testes, have been examined for nearly two decades. While sperm production has been decreased, the undesirable side effects of decreased testosterone leading to decreased libido, loss of muscle mass, and alterations of male sexual characteristics have been highly problematic. Replacement testosterone has been the only solution to date of overcoming these negative effects.

4. Inhibition of Sperm Maturation

Rather that directly halting sperm production, this approach would interfere with the maturation of the newly formed sperm in the epididymis where they are housed prior to ejaculation. One reason why disruption of sperm maturation may be preferable to preventing sperm synthesis is that it is easier to deliver products to the epididymis via the bloodstream. There is a natural protective barrier that prevents delivery of potentially injurious products into the testes where sperm production occurs. Also, many products directed at preventing sperm production have had toxic and irreversible effects that caused permanent rather than temporary sterility. Targeting sperm in the epididymis may avoid those problems.

V. CONCLUSIONS

J. Trussell and B. Vaughan examined factors likely to affect contraceptive use and choice to the year 2010 (1992. *Am. J. Obstet. Gynecol.* **167**, 1160–1164). They cited two predictable factors: the changing age distribution of women and the revised upper-age limit for oral contraceptive use. Less predictable factors include the number of women in each age group at risk for pregnancy, the effects of delayed childbearing, and the impact of new birth control methods. Unpredictable factors include adverse publicity about birth control methods (especially as related to health risks), concerns about STDs (especially AIDS), and changes in the availability of legal abortion. Birth control choices are also influenced by a variety of other factors, including socio-economic status, cultural background, religious beliefs, personal aspirations, health status, and individual moral and ethical values. These (and other) variables argue for a wide array of birth control options and extensive education about all possible options in order that each woman and man can make an intelligent choice as to the option that best fits their individual situation.

The demand for more effective, safer, easier to use, convenient, readily available, and affordable birth control has never been greater. Current demand will only intensify in the future years. Sadly and perhaps tragically, unless immediate steps are taken to reverse our current situation, the future of birth control in the United States is even dimmer than its present state.

What needs to be done? Government policy must be changed to one that devotes more federal agency research funding to birth control and that encourages private sector research. In our "squeaky wheel gets the grease" political system, there is no constituency pleading to congressmen to increase contraceptive research. According to a 1993 report by the Program for Appropriate Technology in Health, a nonprofit health research organization, executives of 14 major pharmaceutical companies who were surveyed reported that they believed that the market was well served by currently available contraceptives. Concerns of company executives center around the high cost and long time necessary to develop a new product, regulatory hassles, and product liability. Currently only one major U.S. pharmaceutical company has an active contraceptive research program, compared with at least 13 in the 1970s.

Politics and prudery also stand firmly in the path of progress. Political concerns pose a direct barrier to enlightenment when matters of birth control become an issue to be avoided for fear of offending the large segment of citizens (read voters) who either wish to avoid any discussion of sexual matters or believe that "just say no" is the only acceptable policy. Sexual desires, especially among the young, are not amenable to control by social agendas, political positions, or legislative action Our country's history of sexual prudery must bear a significant portion of the blame for the unprecedented high rate of teen pregnancies that politicians love to rail against for political points. Studies indicate no significant difference in sexual activity of American teens and teens in other Western countries. However, there is a dramatically higher pregnancy rate (and higher abortion rate and delivery rate) in the United States. This difference is perhaps attributable to a more open approach to sexuality, more and better preventive sex education, and an easier and freer access to contraceptive services in other countries (Rosenfield, 1994).

In this era of rapid technological progress, and in this country that spawned both the sexual and the technological revolutions, the future of birth control technology, at least for the foreseeable future, is not a bright one. The ability of biomedical science to develop options to control the reproductive process is not the impediment to progress. Dealing, as a society, with the ethical concerns associated with birth control technologies poses the greatest hindrance to future options in controlling reproduction.

Also See the Following Articles

ABORTION • BIRTH-CONTROL ETHICS

Bibliography

Knight, J. W., and Callahan, J. C. (1989). "Preventing Birth: Contemporary Methods and Related Moral Controversies." Univ. of Utah Press, Salt Lake City.

Mastroianni, L., Jr., Donaldson, P. J., and Kane, T. T. (1990). Development of contraceptives: Obstacles and opportunities. N. Engl. J. Med. 322, 482–484.

McLaren, A. (1990). "A History of Contraception: From Antiquity to the Present Day." Basil Blackwell, Cambridge, MA.

Pollard, I. (1994). "A Guide to Reproduction: Social Issues and Human Concerns." Cambridge Univ. Press, Cambridge, UK.

Service, R. F. (1994). Contraceptive methods go back to the basics. Science 266, 1480–1481.

Trussell, J., and Kost, K. (1987). Contraceptive failure in the United States: A critical review of the literature. Stud. Fam. Plan. 18, 237–283.

BRAIN DEATH

C. A. Defanti
United Hospitals of Bergamo

GLOSSARY

anencephaly A rare condition in which both hemispheres of the brain are not developed. In many cases pregnancy ends with stillbirth. The newborn babies who survive rarely last more than a few days or weeks.

brain death The clinical condition of a patient with massive damage (usually destruction) of the brain, previously defined as **irreversible coma**. This condition was chosen, by the Harvard Committee, as a new criterion of death.

brain life A concept proposed for symmetry reasons as the converse of brain death. The term indicates the beginning of conscious life during fetal development; a controversial construct.

brain stem death A concept proposed by the Royal Colleges of British Physicians and Surgeons, it means the irreversible cessation of the brain stem functions, i.e., the ability to be conscious, to breathe spontaneously, and hence to retain a spontaneous heartbeat. This definition implies that it is neither essential nor possible for the clinician to prove the permanent cessation of hemispheric functions in order to ascertain death.

neocortical (or cortical) death A term meaning the irreversible cessation of the functions of the cerebral cortex; its main clinical feature is permanent unconsciousness.

persistent vegetative state A clinical condition resulting from massive impairment of the brain hemispheres or of the cerebral cortex. The main feature of PVS is permanent unconsciousness coupled with retained functions of the brain stem (i.e., spontaneous breathing and other brain stem reflexes).

whole brain death A refinement of the previous brain death concept and endorsed by the President's Commission (1981). It means the irreversible cessation of *all* brain functions (i.e., the functions supported by the hemispheres and the brain stem).

BRAIN DEATH (BD) may be considered a paradigm of bioethics from many points of view: (a) There was a close temporal overlapping between the proposal of a new criterion of death by the Harvard Committee and the first steps of bioethics as a new, autonomous discipline. (b) The Committee itself, with its multidisciplinary composition, can be viewed, in some ways, as a prototype of the ethics committees which were started afterward. (c) An important point is that both the Harvard paper and the international debate about BD that followed typically involved many different levels of discourse—medical issues relating to the ascertainment of death, purely conceptual issues, and, above all, difficult moral problems (what is the correct approach to severely injured patients dependent on mechanical ventilation and/or permanently lacking consciousness?). This interplay among different conceptual levels, another typical aspect of bioethics, was richly expressed in the relevant literature. (d) The proposal had an enormous practical impact, having been accepted by most legislations in Western countries, and was the necessary condition of the development of modern transplantation medicine. Nevertheless, severe criticisms on the ground of empirical and philosophical reasons and frank hostility in some religious circles and among some areas of the society at large are still in place. So, even though at a first glance it may appear that the concept of BD has been a successful one, no stable consensus has been reached, and that is another typical feature of many bioethical topics. (e) Finally, the concept of BD was linked with the topic of euthanasia, at least during the first years of bioethics, and is still linked with the problem of the beginning of brain life during the development of the embryo. This in turn has important corollaries for the abortion issue. However, the question of whether the concepts of brain death and brain life are symmetrical or not has not been settled so far.

I. THE HISTORICAL FRAMEWORK OF THE HARVARD COMMITTEE PROPOSAL

The historical context in which the paper, "A Definition of Irreversible Coma," by the Harvard Ad Hoc Committee (1968. *J. Am. Med. Assoc.* 205, 85–88), was published cannot probably be better summarized than in the opening sentences of the paper itself:

Our primary purpose is to define irreversible coma as a new criterion for death. There are two reasons why there is a need for a definition: (1) Improvements in resuscitative and supportive measures have led to increased efforts to save those who are desperately injured. Sometimes these efforts have only partial success so that the result is an individual whose heart continues to beat but whose brain in irreversibly damaged. The burden is great on patients who suffer permanent loss of intellect, on their families, on the hospitals, and on those in need of hospital beds already occupied by these comatose patients. (2) Obsolete criteria for the definition of death can lead to controversy in obtaining organs for transplantation. (Harvard, 1968, 85)

In fact, this controversy was raging just then in the scientific world and among the general public after the first successful heart transplantation performed by C. Barnard in Capetown (December 1967). It is useful to remember that this historical operation was not only an extraordinary technical achievement, but equally a transgression of the usual practice and of the law: the beating heart of an (irreversibly) comatose individual was removed, so causing the death of this individual, according to the criterion then in force, in order to benefit another person. There is little doubt that this event was the *Primum movens* of the Harvard paper. One clearly recognizes two arguments in this document, the first being a mainly, but not exclusively, empirical point: resuscitation may fail not only in the obvious sense, i.e., not being able to prevent death, but also in another way, insofar as it may lead to a novel clinical state, irreversible coma, whose features are such that they raise the moral question of whether it is sensible to go on with medical treatments in order to maintain it. Secondly, there is the acknowledgment of a need, the need for organs suitable for transplantation.

An earlier draft of the Harvard paper was even more explicit about the second point and was discarded precisely because its wording exposed it to the obvious criticism that the new definition of death was merely instrumental in solving the problem of the scarcity of organs. It is useful to remember how the Harvard Committee was composed: it was a 13-member committee with a majority of doctors, but with the crucial participation of one lawyer, one historian, and one theologian. It was chaired by Henry Beecher, a well-known physician whose seminal papers on the ethical problems of human experimentation were instrumental both in establishing a new legislation for these problems and in stimulating a new sensitivity to these aspects among medical professionals. As such, the Harvard Committee was a truly multidisciplinary body and encompassed those competences (in law, humanities, and theology) deemed necessary to confer on it the authority to make a proposal with a far ranging impact on clinical practice. One does not find any philosophical discussion of the concept of death in the paper; nevertheless, there is an important quotation of a speech given by the late Pope Pius XII to a medical congress, in which two main points are made: (1) the verification of the moment of death is the task of the medical profession and is not within the competence of the Church, and (2) it is not mandatory to continue to use extraordinary means indefinitely in hopeless cases. This is an obvious political move in order to prevent possible criticisms from religious sources.

II. WHY WAS THE HARVARD PROPOSAL SO SUCCESSFUL?

Rereading the Harvard paper long after its publication, it is easy to pick out many obvious flaws. There are both problems of theoretical foundation and of internal consistency. No discussion is attempted of questions like, What is death? Is the definition of death a purely metaphysical, or also a moral, issue? Concerning internal flaws, the reason given in order to equate irreversible coma and death, i.e., permanent loss of intellect, is also valid for persistent vegetative state (PVS). Why then restrict the equation to irreversible coma and why not extend it to this no less troubling condition? Finally, even though there was a rather widespread consensus among neurologists and intensive care physicians on the clinical criteria of brain death (BD), no reliable scientific validation of these criteria (i.e., of their ability to predict true irreversibility) had been reached at that time. Why was the proposal so successful?

One can think of many reasons—the authoritativeness of the Harvard University and of the members of the Committee, its careful consideration of the interests at stake and its clever strategy aimed at preemptying juridical and religious opposition, and, above all, the need of organs and the strong support of the community for transplantation medicine. Another political reason for this success was probably the support given to BD by prolife movements in the United States, a seemingly paradoxical support if one thinks of the open opposition of prolife movements in other countries. There is obviously one sense in which a brain-dead individual, whose heart keeps beating, is still alive, and it may seem that the decision to forgo the life support treatments is an antilife move. Probably the main reason of the endorsement by U.S. movements was their hope to relieve the public pressure for euthanasia, as some of them openly acknowledged.

Alternatively, one major reason for this success may have been the far-sightedness of the Committee, i.e.,

its capacity to accept the revolutionary challenge to old ideas raised by the reversibility of the "traditional," cardiac criterion of death by modern resuscitation techniques and to work out a novel, essentially adequate conceptual response.

III. THE DEFENSE OF THE TRADITIONAL DEFINITION OF DEATH

The implementation of the BD definition in the medical practice was not without opposition. Controversies raged through more than a decade, mainly in the United States, prompting in 1981 a new official statement by another influential body, the President's Commission for the Study of Ethical Problems in Medicine. The Commission issued an important paper in which the conceptual problems of the new definition were discussed at some length (1981. *Defining Death*. Washington, DC). Its conclusion was that a practical agreement had been reached on the concept of BD and that there was a need for a common legislation. Therefore it proposed a "Uniform Declaration of Death Act" which was subsequently implemented in the legislation of many states.

Many Western countries followed this trend, but not all. In the United Kingdom, for instance, the Royal Colleges of British Physicians and Surgeons proposed the alternative concept of brain stem death (BSD), meaning the irreversible cessation of the brain stem functions, i.e., the ability to be conscious, to breathe spontaneously, and hence to retain a spontaneous heartbeat. The choice of this definition implies, among other things, that it is neither essential nor possible for the clinician to prove the permanent cessation of hemispheric functions in order to ascertain death. Moreover, no legislation was promoted in the matter and the new definition was introduced into clinical practice thanks to the authority of the Colleges.

A remarkable exception among Western countries was Denmark until the late 1980s. In fact, the Danish Council of Ethics still in 1988 had not backed the BD concept and had made instead a different proposition. It suggested considering so-called brain-dead patients not really dead, but having irreversibly entered the dying process. A parallel suggestion was to permit the procurement of organs from these patients if they had previously signed a valid donor card. In this case the removal or organs for transplantation would "become the cause of the conclusion of the dying process, but not the cause of the death of the person." (*Death Criteria*, the Danish Council of Ethics, 1989, 25) However, this interesting proposal did not prevent the Danish government from implementing a BD legislation some time after the Council's report.

Among the Eastern countries, remarkable hostility against BD still exists in the Japanese culture, where no legislation in the matter has passed so far, despite a national framework of well-developed, Western-style medicine.

On a theoretical level, it is important to note the influential attack on the BD concept made by Hans Jonas soon after its proposal. He made a case for sticking to the old concept of death. The main arguments of Jonas were the instrumental character of the Harvard proposal, aimed essentially at making easier the procurement of organs; the obscure, exoteric criteria of BD; and finally the importance of not separating the death of human beings from that of other living creatures.

BD met strong opposition from some religious sources, for instance, from Orthodox Jews, whose strenuous battle against it recently led to the implementation of a law, in the state of New Jersey, recognizing the right to conscientious objection for those not accepting the new definition.

IV. THE MEDICAL INCONSISTENCIES OF THE "WHOLE BRAIN DEATH" DEFINITION

The President's Commission, already discussed, completed in some way the work of the Harvard Committee, confirming, with a few changes, the adequacy of its clinical criteria and backing the BD proposal. However, the Commission addressed more closely the conceptual issues of the definition of death. Different options were analyzed: the "whole brain death" (WBD) formulation (death is the irreversible cessation of all functions of the hemispheres and of the brainstem), the "higher brain" version (death is the irreversible lack of consciousness, due to massive damage of the brain hemispheres), and the "nonbrain" formulations (like the "traditional" definition, based on the arrest of the circulation of body fluids). The choice of the Commission was in favor of the first one on the ground of two complementary arguments, the argument from loss of the primary organ (the brain being the critical system, viz., the integrating center of the organism, complete cessation of which means that the organism is no longer functioning as a whole, i.e., is dead) and the argument from loss of integrated bodily functioning (life is integrated functioning of the organism as a whole, and

crucial to this functioning is the interplay among brain, heart, and lungs; hence cessation of brain functions, in the peculiar condition of a ventilated patient in an intensive care unit, is a sign that death has occurred, just as cardiac arrest is a sign of death in ordinary situations). The Commission was aware that both arguments were open to several criticisms, the main ones concerning the critical role given to the brain (in fact many other organs are equally critical to the organism, e.g., the liver and skin) and the supposed irreplaceability of the brain. However, its conclusion was that, "while [it] is valuable to test public policy against basic conceptions of death, philosophical refinement beyond a certain point may not be necessary" (President's Commission, 1981, 36).

The endorsement of the WBD definition by the President's Commission does not mean that it rejected the cardiac criterion of death. In fact this criterion is still valid in most circumstances, when death occurs outside the intensive care context; simply, the validity of the cardiac criterion is dependent on the duration of the cardiac arrest, a duration that has to be such as to allow WBD to follow.

The Commission implicitly rejected the BSD definition—irreversible cessation of the brain stem functions—endorsed by the Royal Colleges of Physicians and Surgeons in the United Kingdom (1976). Moreover, it explicitly criticized the "higher brain" formulation, arguing that there are major problems in defining consciousness and personhood, whose anatomical substrate is poorly known, and that it is very difficult to diagnose irreversible lack of consciousness reliably.

However, the WBD formulation itself is open to many stringent criticisms. In fact, the demonstration of the irreversible cessation of the functions of all parts of the brain is practically impossible, as C. Pallis has shown most convincingly (1983. *The ABC of Brain Stem Death*. British Medical Journal, London). Besides, some recent empirical data, in particular the possibility of keeping biologically alive the body of brain dead people over many weeks or even months, as shown by the famous cases of two pregnant wives so assisted, the second of whom eventually gave birth to a baby, demonstrated unequivocally that modern intensive care is able to replace the integrative functions of the central nervous system, at least during some weeks or months.

Other, recently gathered empirical data show that many individuals in whom a diagnosis of BD is made following the strict criteria suggested by the Consultants to the President's Commission retain some brain activity, e.g., some autonomic reflexes and hormonal secretion. Of course this does not mean that consciousness is preserved in such individuals, much less that they are not doomed, but simply that there is a discrepancy between the clinical criteria for BD routinely used worldwide and the conceptual definition of WBD as irreversible loss of all function of the entire brain.

V. THE MOVE TOWARD A NEOCORTICAL DEFINITION AND ITS PROBLEMS

A. A Remedy for the Medical Inconsistencies of the BD Definition

If such a discrepancy exists, a possible remedy could be to revise the BD concept, equating death with permanent lack of consciousness as does the so-called cortical death theory. Note that the main argument raised by the Harvard Committee in order to back its proposal was that the individual in an irreversible coma suffers from permanent loss of intellect. In fact the present clinical criteria for BD, even though they do not prove the complete loss of all brain functions, are very strong criteria for permanent lack of consciousness.

What are the main criticisms of the cortical death theory?

A first concerns the very term of cortical death. In fact, it is simplistic to affirm that the cerebral cortex is the anatomical substrate of consciousness. Certainly many nervous centers are involved in this phenomenon, such as the thalamus and the brain stem itself; the latter is probably unrelated to the content of consciousness, but is certainly involved in maintaining wakefulness. So the term "cortical death" is an approximate one. An alternative which is less precise but more correct is "higher brain death." However, the major problem with the idea of cortical death is that, would it be accepted, not only BD but other clinical conditions would qualify as death: we are thinking particularly of PVS and anencephaly.

B. Persistent Vegetative State

Let us briefly review the clinical conditions of this state. What is PVS? Due to the development of modern intensive therapy, some patients with an overwhelming damage of the cerebral hemispheres survive, after a more or less prolonged stage of coma, in a state of absence of cortical functions, but with a relative sparing of brain stem functions. This condition is known as PVS and can be reversible, but if it lasts more than a few months, it usually can be considered irreversible. The term *permanent* vegetative state applies to such a case.

Its distinguishing feature is chronic wakefulness without awareness. Individuals in PVS seem to be awake, with open eyes, but they are unable to follow any object moving in their visual field and do not respond appropriately to any kind of stimulation. Breathing, circulation, and regulation of bodily temperature are more or less normal, without artificial support. PVS is clearly a different condition from BD. At variance with brain-dead individuals, those in PVS can survive over months and even years with only careful nursing and artificial hydration and nutrition.

Diagnosis of PVS is much more difficult than recognition of BD. No single test is available to detect PVS, and only by means of a long and skilled clinical observation is it possible to establish the typical picture of a complete dissociation between wakefulness and awareness due to a (demonstrable) massive damage of the cerebral hemispheres. The minimum length of the observation period is still controversial: 3 months are probably sufficient, if the etiology is an anoxic insult, whereas in PVS due to other etiologies 6 or even 12 months are necessary.

C. Anencephaly

What is anencephaly? It is the most severe malformation of the central nervous system, characterized by the lack of development of the cerebral hemispheres and of the cranial vault. There are different types of anencephaly. In the most common (meroanencephaly) the baby has a more or less normal face, but with the absence of a forehead. The eyes may protrude or squint, but the major defect is the lack of a cranial vault: above the eyebrows there is no skin, only a rudimentary brain covered by thin meningeal membranes. These babies have more or less functioning brain stems, and some of them are able to breathe spontaneously. If they are not given artificial ventilation, most of them do not survive longer than a few hours or days, but with mechanical assistance they can be maintained over months or years. In some respects they are similar to individuals in PVS.

A difference, of course, is the fact that an individual in PVS was previously a conscious being with a personal history; in contrast, an anencephalic baby never was nor will be. Another difference is that it is much easier to maintain a PVS individual (by artificial nutrition) than an anencephalic baby, the latter usually requiring mechanical ventilation. Finally, the diagnosis of anencephaly is an easy one and the prognosis of irreversible lack of consciousness can be made without a lengthy observation time.

Under the cortical death definition, both individuals with PVS and those with anencephaly could be considered dead. While it is now usual to pronounce a brain-dead individual as dead and to disconnect her from the respirator (and possibly to retrieve an organ from her), it appears counterintuitive to many to declare a PVS individual or an anencephalic baby as dead. In doing so it would be permissible to bury such individuals (whose bodies lack consciousness but are (usually) able to breathe spontaneously).

D. The Slippery Slope Argument

Finally, a strong criticism of the cortical theory is constructed as a "slippery slope" argument. The opponents to this theory contend that, if the concept of death was to be linked to a psychological property (consciousness) instead of biological data, it would be easy to extend the concept from PVS to other abnormal psychological states, like dementia or severe mental retardation.

Is this objection unanswerable? Certainly not. Although the concept of consciousness is intrinsically difficult to define, the diagnosis of PVS is based on the complete lack of this property, and there is no question of equating simple impairments of consciousness with PVS. In any case, there is no doubt that a change from the BD concept to the cortical one would be a momentous change, no lesser in magnitude than the previous one from "traditional" death to BD.

VI. BACK TO THE "TRADITIONAL" DEFINITION?

Recently some scholars, who formerly were in favor of the cortical definition, have argued for a return to the traditional one. For instance, P. Singer, in his last book, *Rethinking Life and Death* (1995. St. Martin's, New York), wonders if it would not be better to recognize the fact that behind the proposal of BD there was not a true problem of definition, but rather a moral problem, the problem about our duties toward the individual in irreversible coma. After a careful historical reconstruction, Singer emphasizes that the purpose of the Harvard Committee was an essentially practical one and that the Committee chose to avoid this moral problem by introducing a new definition of death.

In this sense, the strategy chosen by the Committee has some analogies with the strategy of the Warnock Committee vis-à-vis the moral status of the embryo. Their distinction between a preembryo and an embryo

stage sought to solve a substantial moral question ("What is licit to do to the embryo?") by means of a redefinition, allowing some interventions at the preembryo stage which are not permissible at the following stage.

Singer maintains that Harvard's proposal was widely accepted because of its usefulness: it did not harm brain-dead individuals, it benefited those on a waiting list for organ transplantation, and, above all, it prevented the charge of passive euthanasia being alleged against doctors who were willing to withdraw life support treatments from these patients. However, Singer argues, only a few people really believe that these individuals are truly dead, as a recent sociological inquiry has shown. Even doctors and nurses directly involved in transplantation seem not to take seriously the idea of brain death. The difficulty in understanding the concept of BD, 25 years after the Harvard paper, probably means that something is wrong with this concept. If one adds the fact that it has been proved that some (although weak and clinically not significant) nervous activities are going on in brain-dead individuals, one realizes how fragile the consensus on the BD concept is. Even though the question seems to have been settled for the moment, the need for a thorough reappraisal of the problem will appear again shortly.

In fact, Singer argues that it would have been better to face the moral substance of the question and to recognize that when life is so severely diminished as happens in so-called brain-dead and PVS patients, the respect we owe them is not incompatible with a decision to withdraw life support or possibly to retrieve organs from them for the sake of transplantation. The Harvard Committee, Singer says, was not prepared to propose such a solution, because this would have been tantamount to giving up the traditional sanctity-of-life doctrine. Other scholars partly agree with the historical reconstruction made by Singer and recognize the utilitarian motives that were behind the Harvard proposal, but refute his arguments against the BD concept and the cortical death theory. The argument concerned with misunderstanding from the general public is weak. No doubt it is difficult to comprehend the present concept of WBD, but it would be much simpler to understand the concept of irreversible lack of consciousness (many respondents to the previous inquiry clearly equated BD precisely with cortical death). The argument from repugnance ("It is repugnant to bury a breathing body"), aimed at the cortical death theory, is a typically emotivist one and rather easy to refute. Certainly it seems absurd to bury a body still breathing, but no one maintains an action such as this. Probably the most appropriate behavior, after pronouncing cortical death, would be to stop artificial hydration and nutrition; burial should be performed only after the stoppage of circulation. In any case, there is no logical relationship between ascertainment of death and burial.

VII. BRAIN DEATH AND BRAIN LIFE

A corollary of the BD issue, not thoroughly explored but logically important, is the problem of the beginning of brain life during the development of the embryo. Some scholars have tried to construct, on the ground of a supposed symmetry between the beginning and the end of life, a theory of brain life that would be the complement of the brain death theory. Their argument runs as follows: if we accept identifying human death with the cessation of the brain functions, we can hope to pick out the beginning of these functions during fetal development and so identify this moment with the beginning of the life of the human being. Obviously this beginning does not coincide with conception, but it has to be subsequent. If we manage to pinpoint this moment on purely scientific grounds, we would be able to fix a nonarbitrary boundary for the beginning of a human being. Many questions concerning abortion could be solved that way.

This idea was first suggested by Goldenring, who thought that the 8th week of pregnancy was the critical moment, because at that time brain activity begins to be integrated. Unfortunately, other scholars have proposed different chronologies, generally between the 54th day and the 70th day after conception. More recently, the stress has been laid upon the emergence of consciousness, possible to locate at about 30 to 35 weeks after conception. As one can see, disagreement is great. The reason for this is not obscure. Embryonic and fetal development is a continuous process. It is true that in this process there are some "turning points," but it is not clear at all what we are searching for: are we looking for the beginning of brain activity, whatever it may be? for the start of the integrating activity of the central nervous system? or for the emergence of consciousness? Is not our inquiry similar to the search of Aquinas for the beginning of the human form of the embryo?

Others deny the usefulness of this search, stressing the continuity of embryonal development; no "natural" boundary can be found in ontogenesis, and, in any case, no moral consequences can be directly derived from empirical data. Moreover, it is controversial that a symmetry exists between "brain life" and "brain death": embryonal development is a lengthy, complex process

under genetic control, while death (or, better said, dying), though it too is a process, has many causes and very different durations. Apart from that, BD is not a "natural" fact, but an artifact due to human intervention in the dying process.

VIII. A PARADIGM OF BIOETHICS

A. Some Characterizing Points

From what points of view can BD be considered as a paradigm of bioethics?

The first point to make is that there was a close temporal overlapping among the issue of the Harvard paper proposing the BD concept, the international debate that followed it, and the first steps of bioethics as a new, autonomous discipline (for instance, two major centers of this discipline, the Hastings Center and the Kennedy Institute at Georgetown, were founded in the years 1969–1971).

The Committee itself, with its multidisciplinary composition, can be viewed, in some ways, as a prototype of the ethics committees which have been established subsequently. No doubt multidisciplinarity, and especially the active participation of philosophers and theologians along with physicians and biologists, is a central feature of the bioethical enterprise.

Both the Harvard paper and the related literature typically involved many different levels of discourse: medical issues relating to the ascertainment of death, purely conceptual issues ("What is death?", "What does it mean to be dead?"), and, above all, difficult moral problems (what is the correct approach to severely injured patients dependent on mechanical ventilation and/or permanently lacking consciousness?). This interplay among different conceptual levels, another typical aspect of bioethics, was rather crude in the Harvard paper, but very richly expressed in many contributions to the debate. The most difficult and sensitive point seems to be whether the attempt to give a new definition of death has to be a purely ontological research or a moral inquiry, or both.

Another point to be stressed is the enormous practical impact of the new proposal, which has been accepted, during the 1970s and 1980s, by most legislations in Western countries and has been the necessary condition of the development of modern transplantation medicine. The practical success and the social and political consequences of the Harvard proposal are in many ways a model for the numerous position statements of ethical committees in other fields of medicine that followed. Nevertheless, severe criticisms on the grounds of empirical and philosophical reasons and frank hostility in some religious circles and among some areas of society are still in place. So, even though at a first glance it may appear that the concept of BD has been a successful one, no stable consensus has been reached, and that is another typical feature of many bioethical topics.

B. The Present Status of the Question of the Definition of Death

What can one say about the present status of the question of death? We presently know that no clear-cut concept of death exsisted in the past and that many doubts lingered about its ascertainment, especially during the last three centuries. At the very moment in which reliable diagnostic techniques (i.e., EKG) for documenting cardiac arrest became available, further technical advances (i.e., resuscitation) showed that cardiac arrest, once considered as the central sign of death, no longer was a valid criterion. Now we have, for the first time in history, the opportunity to stipulate a consistent definition of death, taking into account the latest development in medicine. It is not surprising that this definition (both in the WBD and in the cortical version) is in many regards difficult to comprehend and puzzling, but no less surprising and puzzling are other situations created by medical progress (suffice it to think of artificial fertilization). The novelty of situations and the inadequacy of our emotional reactions are probably not a valid argument against the new definition of death. BD (especially in the cortical death version) is a paradigm of the derangements brought about in our culture by the biological revolution.

We have been given, by technological advances, powerful means to alter the dying process, and these means have questioned one of the necessary requirements of the concept of death: irreversibility. What does irreversibility mean today? It seems to be identical to the impossibility of replacing (say, through a transplantation) the cerebral hemispheres while maintaining the memories and dispositions of that particular person.

This is not only not technically feasible today, but probably will never be so. How are we to interpret the novel situations? Why should we stick to traditional definitions? Each socially acceptable death definition has in itself a practical-evaluative component. Even the decision to identify death with the cardiocirculatory arrest was in some way an arbitrary one: it was well known that some biological activities were continuing in the corpse for some time, and only after putrefaction was the process fully completed. No present society accepts complete putrefaction as the criterion of death for exquisitely practical reasons (both moral and hygienic). Quoting J. Lachs, we can say that "death is a biologically based social status" (1988, p. 239. In *Death: Beyond Whole-Brain Criteria* (R. M. Zaner, Ed.). Kluwer, Dordrecht).

Also See the Following Articles

DEATH, MEDICAL ASPECTS OF • DO-NOT-RESUSCITATE DECISIONS • MEDICAL CODES AND OATHS • SLIPPERY SLOPE ARGUMENTS

Bibliography

Ad Hoc Committee of the Harvard Medical School (1968). A definition of irreversible coma. *J. Am. Med. Assoc.* **205**, 85–88.
Defanti, C. A. (1993). E'opportuno ridefinire la morte? *Bioetica. Rivista interdisciplinare* **1**, 211–225.
Jonas, H. (1974). Against the stream. Comments on the definition and redefinition of death. In "Philosophical Essays: From Ancient Creed to Technological Man." Prentice-Hall, Englewood Cliffs, NJ.
Lachs, J. (1988). The element of choice in criteria of death. In "Death: Beyond Whole-Brain Criteria" (R. M. Zaner, Ed.). Kluwer, Dordrecht.
Mori, M. (1992). Dalla morte cerebrale alla morte corticale: Una breve analisi degli argomenti. In "XI Corso di aggiornamento della Società Italiana di Neurologia." Monduzzi, Bologna.
Pallis, C. (1983). "The ABC of Brain Stem Death." British Medical Journal, London.
President's Commission for the Study of Ethical Problems in Medicine and Biomedical and Behavioral Research (1981). "Defining death." Washington, DC.
Singer, P. (1995). "Rethinking Life and Death." St. Martin's, New York.
Veatch, R. M. (1989). "Death, Dying and the Biological Revolution: Our Last Quest for Responsibility," rev. ed. Yale Univ. Press, New Haven, CT.

BROADCAST JOURNALISM

Margaret Coffey
Australian Broadcasting Corporation

GLOSSARY

broadcast journalism News and information gathering and dissemination on radio and television.

cable television Television programming received in the household via optic fiber cable usually on a user-pays basis.

code of ethics A statement of the values ascribed to by members of a profession.

internet A global network of computers linked through telephone lines and host computers.

organizational code of ethics A statement of values developed for and by members (employers and employees) of an organization such as a corporation or government department.

pay TV Television programming received usually by cable on a user-pays basis.

public broadcasting Radio and television broadcasting funded by subscription and/or government contribution and based on a principle of public access.

public service broadcasting Radio and television broadcasting funded by government out of taxation revenue or licence fees with a charter to provide specified broadcasting services to all citizens.

satellite transmission The sending of radio and televi-

sion signals via satellite rather than landline or electromagnetic link.

BROADCAST JOURNALISM, like any other kind of journalism, aims to disseminate information to public audiences. Technological innovation means that this information, whether in the form of news, analysis, or opinion, may reach us via radio or television, cable or satellite, or by the (pen)ultimate broadcast medium, the Internet. On the Internet, print journalism is broadcast journalism and vice versa. This fortuitous fusion brings home the fact that ethical considerations with respect to print and broadcast journalism are fundamentally the same. We ask of both that they be truthful, objective, well-informed and accurate, respectful of privacy, and uncompromised by control or influence. Outside of the technical differences and the opportunities these allow, what is distinctive about broadcast journalism is the historical context in which it has developed and out of which claims are made on its behalf.

It is widely understood that the ethical conduct of journalism is of critical importance to us. Journalism is for most people the principle source of information about the world at large. Broadcast journalism's potency is derived from its immediacy and its availability to mass audiences. In the case of television, there is the additional impact of visual images. Studies show, for example, that since 1963 Americans have quoted television rather than newspapers as their primary source of "most" of their news. Paradoxically, journalism is a source of information about our private and domestic worlds as we define these vis-a-vis the information we hear on radio or television or read in the newspaper. In democratic societies we depend upon journalism not just for information but as a point of engagement with politicians, policies, and issues. Our capacity to act decisively and effectively as citizens or as voters is influenced by how well it serves us. Indeed, nothing less than our individual self-realization as participating members of democratic societies is associated with our access to the knowledge and information journalism conveys.

Moreover, we are faced with many challenges, local and global. Whether they are to do with the survival of the environment and therefore our species, or the just distribution of economic goods (including information), the sustaining and development of democratic institutions, or the maintaining of stable, respectful relations between different peoples and cultures, our ability to face into these challenges turns upon our access to information, its quality, and our capacity to exchange it.

I. HISTORY

Broadcast journalism followed the invention of radio, its experimental popularity in the immediate aftermath of the First World War, and its established use for public broadcasting from around 1920. The earliest developments in the United States, Britain, the USSR, mainland Europe, India, and Japan sketched in an institutional organization of broadcasting which has been seriously challenged only relatively recently.

Print journalism has long enjoyed the idea of the liberty of the press insofar as it has meant freedom from licensing. However, from its early days broadcasting became subject to regulation over and above the restrictions of relevant civil laws such as those relating to defamation, contempt of court, blasphemous or obscene publications, and trespass. In the beginning, regulation was deemed necessary because of both the shortage of available spectrum and the perceived power of the radio broadcasting medium. Governments regulated to ensure a public service dimension to broadcasters' activities and varying kinds of accountability. Two major kinds of regulatory frameworks and institutional organization developed, exemplified by the broadcasting history of the United States and Britain.

A. Commercial Model

On the one hand, in the United States, commercial development went on apace when advertisers realized radio's promise as an advertising medium. Commercial radio stations burgeoned in the early 1920s. The potential for network arrangements was recognized at a very early point with the establishment in 1926 of the first (New York-based) commercial radio network. And the potential for commercial radio mayhem was countered with federal legislation. As early as 1927 the U.S. Congress passed a Radio Act which set out to inhibit monopoly—with respect to the production of radio equipment and the ownership of radio stations—and to control the allocation of radio wavelengths. The outcome of this approach was the development of four major commercial networks dependent upon advertising revenue and the securing of wavelength for educational radio broadcasting.

Television broadcasting in the United States began similarly as a commercial entertainment and information-oriented venture in 1939. War curtailed its commercial development and it was not until 1952 that the Federal Communications Commission authorized 242 channels for educational purposes. In 1962 the Education Television Facilities Act provided government funds to build new stations. By the mid-1960s a 100-station-strong noncommercial, subscriber-based, national network had taken shape under the impetus of finance from the Ford Foundation. The Public Broadcasting act of 1967 provided a mechanism for government funding of broadcasting via the establishment of a private corporation which would distribute government funds (Corporation for Public Broadcasting). Its rationale was that there were areas of broadcasting delivery which were not supported by advertising and were unlikely to be. In 1970 the already integrated network began operation as the Public Broadcasting Service and PBS now parallels National Public Radio.

Almost from the outset in the United States, the notion of noncommercially funded broadcast journalism has created controversy. (An early PBS cause celebre was the proposed Ford Foundation financed news center in 1971.) Broadcast journalism, the argument goes, requires the democratic restraints of the free market. If taxpayers' money is to be provided for public broadcasting then there must be legislative enforcement of objectivity, balance, and accountability. Strict fairness regulations must be met. The 1992 Public Telecommunications Act was an outcome of this argument: it requires the Corporation for Public Broadcasting to enforce the balance provisions of the Public Broadcasting

Act. Subsequent controversies (in 1996 over federal funding, for example) have revealed continuing suspicion of government-funded broadcasting balanced by support from those their opponents describe as leftists, liberals, or Democrats.

On the subject of regulation broadly, there is not such a neat divide between proponents and opponents. While, for example, critics of the Public Broadcasting Service demanded content regulation to counter perceived political partisanship and ambitions for PBS-led social change, some liberals support structural regulation to build rules and constraints into the structure and organization of the media taken as a whole. Their argument is that commercial media represent power and that private power may threaten liberty even as state power does. It may lead to the disproportionate representation of certain views at the expense of diversity, to inappropriate influence on public policy, or to the manipulation of the media to achieve the ends of private owners or corporations.

B. Public Service Model

In Britain, broadcast journalism has followed a different evolutionary path. While early radio initiatives were of a commercial nature, the perceived problems of "commercialization" and the need for order and control exemplified by the clamorous airwaves of the United States soon led to the view that broadcasting was best administered as a public service utility with centralized control. (Already the administration of other resources such as forestry, water, and electricity had been similarly structured.) In 1925 the British Broadcasting Corporation (BBC) was established as a monopoly, ultimately accountable to Parliament but presided over by a Board of Governors enjoined as trustees of the public interest. Broadcast journalism began on the BBC in 1926 in the print news vacuum created by the General Strike. Since broadcasting bans were applied to the leader of the opposition and representatives of organized labor, the BBC was obliged immediately to canvas issues such as its relationship to government, its notion of public service, and its means of estimating public interest. It resolved these issues by accepting the bans and reporting statements by both strikers and strike breakers. It developed a modus vivendi by which it censored itself along government suggested lines in order to forestall the imposition of government regulation. During World War II, when there was an inevitable identification of the common interest with the interests of government, there was even greater complexity in the relationship between the BBC and the British Government. Never-

theless, by the end of the war the BBC's authority as a source of news (and as a cultural institution) was firmly established. For one thing, during the war the BBC had never lied. (That does not mean it was not free of bias.) It was a public service monopoly, committed to the common interest and accountable to Parliament. As James Curran and Jean Seaton have pointed out, that meant that if government were concerned with limiting the amount and kind of information broadcast, the main pressure within the Corporation was to tell people as much as possible.

Until the 1980s broadcast journalism developed in Britain within a framework of reiterated public service notions. These included the idea that broadcasting services should be accountable and made available to everyone, and that programs should be of high quality and wide variety. Even the introduction of commercial television in 1954 occurred under the aegis of these principles, and the new Independent Television Authority was established to regulate commercial stations (ITV, independent television) virtually in the image of the BBC.

More recently there has been a reworking of the public service ideal which would detach it from the notion of a publicly funded utility. In this neoliberal view, corporate media organizations are well placed to serve the public. As Ken Cowley, Rupert Murdoch's sometime chief executive in Australia, remarked, "We take the view, as simple as it is and as corny as it sounds, that what is good for your country is good for your business and what is good for your business is good for the paper, its readers and our employers."

Another kind of reworking of the public service ideal would privatize elements of public service broadcasting organizations under some kind of regulatory oversight such as a Public Broadcasting Council. There are proposals also from the left based on a critique of existing public service broadcasting as expressive of a narrow range of perspectives. These proposals call, for example, for more representative membership of broadcasting authorities and for structures and guidelines which make broadcasters more independent of government and encourage greater ideological range and cultural diversity in program content.

Nevertheless, the paradigmatic ideas governing the broadcasting debate remain those derived from its development history. On the one hand there is the notion that broadcasting is a public good and that to be a broadcaster is to take on a public service while conscious of one's particular responsibilities toward innovation, pluralism, and quality. On the other hand, there is the idea that broadcasting belongs to the commercial arena where market forces (and minimal regulation) will ensure that the requirements of audiences, and advertisers, are met, and where it will flourish under the creative stimulus of the market. Here the broadcast journalist is understood to be a professional, with skills and marketable qualities appropriate to the profession. It is fair to say that this idea (or variations upon it) has been in the ascendant since the 1980s and has already influenced the reshaping of major broadcasting organizations (such as the BBC, the Canadian Broadcasting Corporation, the Australian Broadcasting Corporation, the New Zealand Broadcasting Corporation) and the development of communications policy in response to new technology. It has also influenced the recreation of broadcasting organizations in the former Soviet bloc.

II. RECENT TECHNOLOGICAL DEVELOPMENTS

A. Satellite Transmission

The rise of free market ideology is an important element in the rethinking of communications policy as it affects broadcasting, but the crucial factor has been the scope and speed of technological innovation. It has made redundant, for example, the pragmatic argument for regulation in the first instance, that there would be cacophony on the airwaves given the limited spectrum available. Now that satellite transmission has replaced electromagnetic signals, not only is there no comparable problem with competition, it may seem there are no boundaries either. Western-based media organizations such as Rupert Murdoch's Star TV can broadcast to Pakistan, India, or Iran. By 1994 Star TV was reaching in its target area an estimated 54 million households with receiving dishes. Such broadcasts circumvent any easily applicable state controls since they go direct to their audiences in their homes. (Either governments ban receiving dishes as in Iran or they exert political and economic pressure as with China's acceded-to demand that Star TV stop beaming BBC news bulletins into Chinese households.)

Satellite transmission has also raised questions about diversity. While it proffers a huge increase in viewer choice, its dominance by transnational corporations may be a guarantee only of (Western) cultural hegemony.

Boundaries of another sort have been abolished by the evolution of news coverage as a result of satellite transmission working in conjunction with cable net-

works in agency arrangements. Journalists with the American Cable News Network (CNN) can be anywhere, anytime, to bring to viewers anywhere in the world via local cable deliverers or major national commercial or public service networks the latest air strike, food crisis, or insurrection. Viewers everywhere hear the news stories told by Americans.

Moreover, CNN's coverage of the 1991 UN-sponsored Desert Storm war against Iraq provided instantaneous images of war which cast viewers in their homes as witnesses to missile attacks and their aftermath. In these circumstances viewers may believe there is yet another kind of boundary crossing going on: that between news and information production/consumption and journalistic /viewer complicity and voyeurism. On the other hand, viewers able to observe the death of 400 civilians in the Al-Ameriya bunker in Baghdad may have experienced the contours of citizenship expanding: it was, after all, in their names that the war was prosecuted. Why should they not see the bombing, and own to it?

B. Cable Television

The development of cable television invites comment on the hopes held for technological innovation as a means for democratizing broadcast journalism. It has been a form of television slower to develop outside the United States at least in part because of the infrastructure investment required to establish the optic fiber cables to individual households. In Australia, for example, only existing very large media companies have been able to enter the cable market, so that rather than introducing diversity the advent of cable has only confirmed Australia's existing media oligopoly. In the United States public access cable television (in a proportion of one in five cable networks) provides an enormous amount of original community programming of varying quality. Some of it may reflect less diversity than appeal to the First Amendment (which guarantees freedom of speech) as the justification for broadcasts which would elsewhere be banned (for racial vilification, for example).

Moreover the development of cable has meant that abandonment of free-to-air broadcasting as the only model. Cable television has been for the most part a commercial venture and access depends on one's capacity to pay. Hence, "pay TV."

However, there remains hopefulness about technology's democratizing potential. John Keane envisions new digital technologies as contributing to a plurality of communications media in a more democratic order where neither the state nor commercial markets exercise control, but rather publicly-funded, non-profit and legally guaranteed media institutions of civil society (1991. *The Media and Democracy*. Polity London). Certainly, one can point to the use of radio and television among people of indigenous cultures (communities of interest) to demonstrate that the new technologies may indeed offer emancipatory possibilities. Among some indigenous Australian and Canadian communities local radio and television broadcasting is a means of strengthening community cultures and of challenging the powerful incursions of satellite transmission and other Western broadcasts. Here the means of communication belong, in Keane's terms, to the indigenous public at large.

C. Narrowcasting

The next round of technological innovation is focusing on "narrowcasting" and "audience targeting" where information will be offered in response to the individual's choice. Here again the question of diversity arises. It is clear that the quantity of information available to any individual will be enormous and there will be a proliferation of access routes to information. But with existing commercial media organizations positioning themselves to take advantage of these innovations, there are questions to be asked about what diversity will mean in the age of narrowcasting and self-selected news and information.

D. The Internet

The Internet is a communications medium based on a global network of computers linked through telephone lines and host computers. It is capable of transmitting text, images, and sound. Millions of people are linked by the Internet, but unlike conventional media the Internet offers two-way communication, an absence of regulation, and freedom from commercial ownership. However, access to the Internet is dependent on the user's capacity to pay (for equipment, server provider, power, etc.).

The Internet is considered here because of its links to broadcasting: not only do forms of broadcasting—along with other activities—occur on the Net, but major broadcasting organizations have created Internet versions of themselves and make their program material available there. Broadcast journalists use the Internet as an information resource. It is possible, for example, to download texts of Australian Broadcasting

Corporation programs within hours of their broadcast, and Radio Telefís Eireann invites the downloading of voice and text news stories as a type of broadcast agency service.

In many ways the Internet is emblematic of broadcasting and the changes being induced by political and technological change. It carries a phenomenal amount of information without any organizing hierarchy of knowledge other than "user selects." It is the subject of arguments about regulation with the balance on the side of open access and freedom from censorship. (However, governments, for example, through the OECD, are investigating forms of regulation primarily to limit access.) Its utility depends on the sharpness of the user's purpose and her competence with the search engines. Its character reflects the overwhelming contribution from the United States. And it too is under pressure from large corporations attempting to take control.

III. CONVERGENCE AND CONCENTRATION

With the dominance by large corporations of the world's supply and delivery of information (and entertainment), many concerns about broadcast journalism have come to be expressed in the terms *convergence* and *concentration*.

The idea of convergence is best illustrated in the way the Internet collapses the boundaries between the distinctive identities of newspaper, radio, and television. A graphic example of convergence in the make is provided by the *Sankei* newspaper in Japan. Its new delivery system, a small box the size of an electronic organizer, may be plugged into a television at night so that each morning it downloads perhaps a thousand news articles and pictures. It is possible to scroll through these stories en route to work and have access to far more information than that provided by a newspaper. A new version will conceivably have audio and video and the user will be able to select and edit what he wishes to hear.

Convergence obviously informs the increasing concentration of media ownership and the spread of media owner activities. Media corporations are involved in telecommunications, information and entertainment (sport and film), computing, and education in addition to radio, television, and newspaper production. Needless to say, the key question here has to do with diversity: what is it and how may it be achieved?

IV. THE BROADCAST JOURNALIST

It is against this background that we must consider the professional role and obligations of the broadcast journalist.

To begin with, such persons will be most likely employed by a profit-seeking corporation and their information-gathering activities will have economic worth. They will have available impressive technological resources, thanks to which they may access information previously unavailable. He or she may be at considerable cultural and social distance from the audience: think of the CNN Gulf War reporter being heard not merely at home—in Wisconsin?—but also in Geelong, Australia, or Colombo, Sri Lanka.

A broadcast journalist will also occupy an ambivalent position in society. Public estimation of journalists is low but rhetoric from both the left and the right casts the journalist in a role central to the maintenance of democratic societies.

A. The Broadcast Journalist as Professional Employee

Journalism has come to be regarded as a profession, if different in status from professions such as law or medicine. What gives journalism its professional status, along with law, medicine, teaching, and nursing, is its relationship to a code of ethics. Its aims and its achievements are judged according to ethical ideas such as truthfulness, accuracy, and objectivity. More and more these ideas are being articulated in formal codes of ethics, the better of which address the peculiar technological context of broadcast journalism.

Implicit in the traditional idea of a professional is a notion of autonomy: this person, whose ethical commitments are held in common with the rest of the profession, nevertheless acts independently to fulfil these commitments. However, most broadcast journalists are employees whose autonomy is limited by the requirements and interests of their employer. Very often this is a large corporation whose interests will not always be best expressed in the journalist's code of ethics: corporations are explicitly about making money rather than about "telling the truth."

The fact that broadcast journalists are employees of a contracting number of employers, or alternatively that they are employees under threat when they work for "downsizing" public service broadcasting organizations, may be assumed to have some effect on journalistic culture. Lack of alternative employment opportunities and competition may foster self-censorship and a less than vigorous journalistic enterprise.

Of course the tension between a journalist's professional values and an employer's interests may be equally strained when the employer is a public service broadcasting organization. Journalists with both the BBC and the RTE are compromised by their respective institutions' adherence to government prohibition on the broadcast of interviews with members of the Irish Republication Army, a ban which is retrospective since it applies to archival material as well. Journalists with the ABC (Australian Broadcasting Corporation) found editorial decision making compromised by their employer's ratings-driven essay into "infotainment" television programming. (The issue became a public scandal in 1994–1995 and led to an inquiry and the establishment of whistle-blowing procedures within the organization.)

An increasing number of organizations are developing organizational codes of practice so that some journalists will find themselves referring to both professional and organizational codes. In Australia, for example, broadcasting organizations are required to notify the Australian Broadcasting Authority of their codes of practice as a first step in a series of measures underwriting accountability.

There is considerable discussion about the merits of professional codes of ethics versus organizational codes. As media organizations grow in size, the trend toward deregulation accelerates, and public service broadcasting is attenuated, professional journalists' organizations will be less well placed to inculcate and enforce values appropriate to broadcast journalism. It may be that, in this age of concentration of media ownership, media self-regulation through organizational codes will have a more productive impact on the quality of broadcast journalism. Such codes can at least broach at the level of the organization issues such as checkbook journalism or the improper influence of advertising or commercial consideration since they embrace those who profit from and control media activities. They may also contribute to media self-regulation across national boundaries since the nature of media organizations is increasingly global rather than local.

However, a professional code of ethics contributes toward a journalist's sense of independence no matter how comparatively weak her position. It is a reminder to all of us that there are interests and aspirations outside those of the market and corporate organizations.

B. The Broadcast Journalist and Technology

Broadcast journalists, like many other professionals, find ethical challenges in the capacities technology allows them. CNN's role in the Gulf War raised a series of such ethical questions as already mentioned. One of them had to do with what might be the proper distance from the action for a viewer.

On a more day-to-day level, broadcast journalists are able to manipulate pictures and sound for effect; they can record sound and pictures without the knowledge of their subjects, and they are able to access with technology people and areas previously inaccessible. The last two raise the issues of consent and privacy—where should the shifting boundary between what should be public and what should be private lie?

Obviously this technology may be used for good purpose, to reveal discrimination, for example. Equally obviously it is often used in breach of commonly accepted ideas about privacy and for reasons which have more to do with entertaining and stimulating audiences than with providing information. Various jurisdictions have felt the need to strengthen laws relating to consent and privacy at least partly in response to perceived problems with the media.

It is nevertheless true that television has created a culture that is less certain about the distinction between public and private and the import of what were once private differences. Alain Ehrenberg writes that tabloid television reassures as it shows that everyone is different and there are no longer any fixed norms that we are to conform to. It is a television of tolerance and what is central is that people accept the need to be true to themselves and be committed to talking about this to the television audience. Hence the kind of infotainment television where people reveal their intimate lives and the prevailing view among certain broadcast journalists that privacy is a middle-class conceit.

C. The Broadcast Journalist and Her Audience

Journalism may figure low on the scale of reputable professions but implicit in this estimation is a view of the journalist as powerful. This ambivalence is expressed in media criticism. One such critique has broadcast journalism giving us information that affects our perceptions; if it is distorted, and it often is, we will find as citizens that our capacity for choice has been corrupted. Broadcast journalism's power to corrupt the culture is a common theme in media criticism.

It is possible that media critics, audiences, and broadcast journalists themselves overestimate the latter's power. It is not clear, for example, that television pictures of the Vietnam War were responsible for opposition to the war's pursuit. Broadcast journalists are not forces in themselves. They are players in complex social and political and economic relationships. It is worth reflecting that so much of the criticism of broadcast journalism in terms of its conduct and ethics is in fact a criticism of modernity itself.

Also See the Following Articles

INTERNET PROTOCOL • MEDIA OWNERSHIP • PRIVACY VERSUS PUBLIC RIGHT TO KNOW

Bibliography

Belsey, A., and Chadwich, R. (Eds.) (1991). "Ethical Issues in Journalism and the Media." Routledge, London.

Coady, M., and Bloch, S. (Ed.) (1996). "Codes of Ethics and the Professions." Melbourne Univ. Press, Melbourne.

Curran, J., and Seaton, J. (1991). "Power Without Responsibility," 4th ed. Routledge, London.

Horowitz, D., and Jarvik, L. (1995). "Public Broadcasting and the Public Trust," Center for the Study of Popular Culture, Los Angeles.

Lichtenberg, J. (Ed.) (1990). "Democracy and the Mass Media." Cambridge Univ. Press, Cambridge.

Marshall, I., and Kingsbury, D. (1996). "Media Realities: The News Media and Power in Australian Society." Longman, Harlow/New York.

Schultz, J. (Ed.). (1994). "Not Just Another Business: Journalists, Citizens and the Media." Pluto, Sydney.

BUDDHISM

Damien Keown
University of London

GLOSSARY

ahiṃsā "Nonharming," or the principle of respect for life.

bodhisattva A saint of the Mahāyāna tradition who vows to work for the salvation of all sentient beings.

dharma Natural Law; Buddhist doctrine; Buddhist Path.

karma The principle of moral retribution.

karuṇā Compassion.

Mahāyāna The form of Buddhism prevalent in Central and East Asia. Its teachings are characterized by an emphasis on compassion, an expanded cosmology, and certain philosophical theories concerning the nature of reality.

nirvana The final state of perfection attained by the Buddha and sought by all Buddhists. A person who attains nirvana is not reborn.

paññā/prajñā Wisdom, knowledge.

Pātimokkha A code of 227 rules contained in the vinaya.

saṃsāra Cyclic rebirth.

saṅgha The Buddhist monastic order.

sīla Morality, a precept.

sutta/sūtra A discourse or sermon of the Buddha.

Theravāda The oldest surviving school of Buddhism, prevalent in south Asia.

vinaya The Monastic Rule followed by Buddhist clergy.

BUDDHISM is a major world religion whose adherents today number in the region of 500 million. It was founded in northeast India by Siddhartha Gautama (ca. 480–400 B.C.E.), who gained enlightenment at the age of 35 and was thereafter known by the honorific title of Buddha ("enlightened one"). Buddhism spread rapidly from India to parts of south Asia before the Christian era, and by the early centuries A.D. became established in China. Subsequently it spread into Tibet, Korea, Japan, and southeast Asia. As it traveled, Buddhism interacted with the indigenous beliefs it encountered and this gave rise to considerable variation in style among Buddhist schools. There may, however, be said to be a common moral core underlying the different cultural traditions.

The Buddha appointed no successor and there is no central authority on matters of doctrine and ethics, although the order of monks (*saṅgha*) instituted by the Buddha is regarded by most Buddhists as the authorized custodian and interpreter of the Buddha's teachings. The goal of all Buddhists is enlightenment (nirvana), a state of spiritual and moral perfection which can be attained by any human being who lives in accordance with Buddhist teachings. Buddhism does not believe in a supreme being or creator god, and its precepts and ethical teachings are seen not as divine commands, but as rational principles which, if followed, will promote the flourishing or welfare of oneself and others. It may therefore be regarded as a form of eudaemonism.

I. ETHICS AND MORALITY IN BUDDHISM

Although the terms "ethics" and "morality" are used interchangeably today, a distinction can be made between them which may be helpful in the context of Buddhism. In terms of this distinction (the validity of which should not be pressed too far) *morality* denotes the customs, practices, mores, and values of a society, while *ethics* is the reflection on those things from a philosophical perspective. By analogy with natural science, it might be said that morality provides the facts or data to be explained, and ethics provides the theory which tries to make sense of the facts. Its task is to ask why certain things are done, what makes some acts right and others wrong, and from where concepts like "right" and "wrong" derive their ultimate meaning and validity.

Applying this distinction to Buddhism, what is found in Buddhist sources is a great deal of morality but very little ethics. While the moral values of Buddhism are widely admired, it has invested comparatively little time in reflection on the principles which underpin its moral teachings. In the sermons of the Buddha the importance of moral behavior is spelled out clearly, as it is in the Christian Gospels. It is said (Saṃyutta-Nikāya v. 353F), for example, that you should not inflict on another what you yourself find unpleasant (the Buddhist version of the Golden Rule); that wrong actions are those motivated by greed, hatred, and delusion; that wrong actions are those which are intended to harm any being; that one should repay the kindness of beings who in the past may have been kind to one as relatives or friends (Saṃyutta-Nikāya ii. 189F); and that one should be mindful at all times of the effect one's actions might have on others. In neither the sermons of the Buddha nor the Gospels do we find extensive discussion of problematical theoretical issues, but at an early stage Christian writers took up questions of moral and political philosophy in a way that never happened in Buddhism. While the Church Fathers, notably St. Augustine, struggled to resolve the conflicts which arose between Christian, pagan, and secular values, their Buddhist counterparts such as Vasubandhu and Buddhaghosa showed comparatively little interest in exploring these themes. No doubt the influence of Greek thought and Jewish legalism provides part of the explanation as to why Christianity was receptive to these issues, and it may be that ethics, in the sense as earlier defined, is a cultural development which is unique to the West. Whatever the reason, ethics is a branch of philosophy which Buddhism simply never developed. The study of Buddhist ethics, accordingly, is a contemporary discipline born of the encounter between two ancient cultures, East and West, in the modern world.

II. CULTURAL BACKGROUND

The cultural milieu in which Buddhism evolved was itself of a unique kind. The dominant religious ideology was Brahmanism (the ancestor of Hinduism), but other important influences on Buddhism included unorthodox movements such as Jainism and the school of Sāṃkhya-Yoga. In its early formative period Buddhism defined its moral code by including and rejecting elements from both the orthodox and the unorthodox traditions of Indian thought.

A. Dharma

A concept of fundamental importance deriving from the pan-Indian heritage is Dharma. This word has many meanings and nuances, but the underlying idea is of a universal or natural law which determines both the material and the moral evolution of the universe. Every aspect of life is regulated by Dharma—the physical laws which regulate the rising of the sun, the succession of the seasons, and the movement of the constellations, and also the moral laws which regulate the operation of karma, define what is right and wrong, and determine the duties and responsibilities of every member of society. By extension Dharma also means the corpus of Buddhist teachings (since they are thought to be grounded in the nature of things), the practice of the Buddhist Path, and the spiritual realization made possible by the practice of the Path. Living in accordance with Dharma and implementing its requirements leads to happiness, fulfillment, and salvation; neglecting or transgressing against it leads to endless suffering in the cycle of rebirth (saṃsāra). Dharma is neither caused by nor under the control of a supreme being, and the gods themselves are subject to its laws. Dharma is both what is and what ought to be, and in Buddhism the term is used to denote both the natural order and the entire corpus of Buddhist ethico-religious teachings. Dharma may conveniently be translated as Natural Law, a term which captures both of the important meanings of Dharma, namely as the principle of order and regularity seen in the behavior of natural phenomena and also the idea of a universal moral law whose requirements have been discovered (not invented) by enlightened beings such as the Buddha.

B. Karma

Common to all major Indian traditions is the belief in karma, the doctrine that moral actions inevitably have repercussions on the one who performs them. Moral action is a unique class of action in that it has two distinctive effects: first, it is soteriologically transformative and modifies the spiritual status of the one who performs it, and second, it determines the good and bad fortune which a person experiences in life. Although a number of the Buddha's contemporaries denied that moral action in itself has any intrinsic significance (as many do today), the Buddha rejected this idea and emphasized that the moral life was integral to the quest for salvation. The saints of early Buddhism display the highest standards of moral conduct in their lives, as did the Buddha himself, and the goal of nirvana is inconceivable for one whose behavior is not morally perfect.

Closely associated with the doctrine of karma is belief in rebirth. In terms of this belief, which appears several centuries before the time of the Buddha, the higher forms of life (such as gods, human beings, and animals) migrate from one existence to another in accordance with their moral behavior in each existence. Good conduct is rewarded by rebirth in more auspicious circumstances, in such a way that the long course of an individual existence might be visualized as an upward or downward spiral extending over eons of time. The fact that the same living being might appear at one time as a human being and at another as an animal means that Buddhism is much more ready than Western traditions to accord moral status to nonhuman lifeforms. There is a tendency, particularly in some schools of Mahāyāna Buddhism, to see the whole of the natural order, including vegetable, plant life, and even natural phenomena, as possessing spiritual potential of some kind, however restricted.

C. Respect for Life (Ahiṃsā)

In the light of the doctrine of karma it is unsurprising to find that respect for life is a pan-Indian ideal. This ideal was promoted most vigorously by the unorthodox mendicant (samaṇa) movements such as Buddhism and Jainism, but increasingly influenced orthodox schools. Animal sacrifice, which had played an important part in religious rites from Vedic times, was rejected as cruel and barbaric, and blood sacrifices came increasingly to be replaced by symbolic offerings such as vegetables, fruit, and milk. The principle of the sanctity of life, or ahiṃsā, was sometimes taken to extremes. Jain monks, for example, took the greatest precautions against destroying tiny forms of life, such as insects, even unintentionally. Their practices had some influence on Buddhism, and Buddhist monks carried a strainer with them to make sure they did not destroy small creatures in their drinking water. In early Buddhist sources such as the Monastic Rule (vinaya), Buddhist monks are sometimes criticized by the laity for being less rigorous in the respect for life than other wandering ascetics. In general, however, although Buddhism shared the traditional Indian (and Indo-European) view of the sanctity of life, it regarded the destruction of life as morally wrong only when it was caused intentionally.

III. ETHICS IN EARLY BUDDHISM

The primary source for ethics in early Buddhism is the Pali Canon. This consists of three divisions, the most important of which contains the Discourses (sutta) of the Buddha. The second is the Monastic Rule (vinaya), which is a code of behavior for those who have taken monastic vows. The third division, the Scholastic Treatises (abhidhamma), contains material of interest for ethics, mainly from a psychological perspective, although its relevance is sometimes disguised by a terse analytical style.

In the Discourses, the Buddha's moral teachings are set out in a clear and straightforward way. The style is a cross between the Christian gospels and the Socratic dialogues, and parables and metaphors are often used to help get the point across. Ethical themes appear repeatedly throughout the Discourses, although certain Discourses are regarded as particularly significant for their moral content. The Discourse to Sigāla, for example, is of special importance for lay ethics, and is often described as "a Monastic Rule for householders." Another early Discourse, the Discourse on Brahma's Net, is a compendium of moral precepts, and may be regarded as the source of the subsequent preceptual codes. Important for its emphasis on the cultivation of a loving attitude is the Discourse on Loving-Kindness (Mettāsutta).

A. Precepts

There are five main sets of precepts in Buddhism:

1. The Five Precepts (*pañca-sīla*)
2. The Eight Precepts (*aṭṭhaṅga-sīla*)
3. The Ten Precepts (*dasa-sīla*)
4. The Ten Good Paths of Action (*dasa-kusala-kamma-patha*)
5. The Monastic Disciplinary Code (*pātimokkha*)

The most popular of these codes is the Five Precepts for laymen. The Five Precepts prohibit (1) killing, (2) stealing, (3) sexual immorality, (4) lying, and (5) taking intoxicants. The nucleus of Buddhist morality may be found in the first four, which are then supplemented by more rigorous precepts according to the status of the practitioner or to suit particular ceremonial occasions. The precept against taking intoxicants, for example, is thought to be particularly applicable to layfolk, and the Eight and Ten precepts, which supplement the basic five with additional restrictions such as on the time when meals may be taken (as well as requiring complete abstention from sexual relations), are commonly adopted as additional commitments on holy days (*uposatha*). The Monastic Disciplinary Code is a set of over 200 rules (the exact number varies slightly between schools) which set out in detail the regulations for communal monastic life. The various formulations of precepts mentioned above may therefore be regarded as a combination of moral precepts with additional practices designed to cultivate restraint and self-discipline. The large number of monastic rules requires vigilance and mindfulness at all times on the part of monks, as well as ensuring standardization and conformity within monastic communities, such that disputes and disagreements are kept to a minimum and the Order presents itself as a moral microcosm for the world at large.

B. Virtues

Although the precepts are of great importance in Buddhist morality, there is more to the Buddhist moral life than following rules. Rules must not just be followed, but followed for the right reasons and with the correct motivation. It is here that the role of the virtues becomes important, and Buddhist morality as a whole may be likened to a coin with two faces: on one side are the precepts and on the other the virtues. The precepts, in fact, may be thought of simply as a list of things which a virtuous person will never do.

Early sources emphasize the importance of cultivating correct dispositions and habits so that moral conduct is the natural and spontaneous manifestation of internalized and properly integrated beliefs and values, rather than simple conformity to external rules. Many formulations of the precepts make this perfectly clear. The precept against taking life, for example, is sometimes found in the following form: "Laying aside the club and the sword he dwells compassionate and kind to all living things." Abstention from taking life is therefore the natural result of a compassionate identification with living things, rather than a constraint which is imposed contrary to natural inclination. To arrive at such an integrated state is not easy, and involves a profound transformation of both an intellectual and a moral kind. To observe the first percept (nonkilling) perfectly requires a profound understanding of the metaphysical relationship between living things coupled with an unswerving disposition of universal benevolence and compassion. Few people are capable of either of these things, but in respecting the precept they habituate themselves to the condition of one who is, and in so doing take a step closer to enlightenment.

The virtues, as Aristotle points out, are about what it is difficult for people. The task of the virtues is to counteract negative dispositions (or vices) such as pride and selfishness. On the principle of "know thine enemy," Buddhist scholasticism constructed elaborate lists of vices (*kilesa*) and defilements (*upakilesa*), including delusion, heedlessness, torpor, lack of commitment, restlessness, anger, hypocrisy, envy, and many more. All of these things are hazards to the ethico-religious life, and lead to behavior which is contrary to the precepts, usually as a result of their egocentric bias which impairs the ability to make impartial judgments between oneself and others.

The lengthy lists of virtues and vices which appear in later literature are extrapolated from a key cluster of three virtues and their opposing vices. The three Buddhist "cardinal virtues" are unselfishness (*alobha*), benevolence (*adosa*), and understanding (*amoha*). The first two are moral virtues and the third is an intellectual virtue. Benevolence means an attitude of goodwill to all living creatures. Unselfishness means the absence of that selfish desire which taints all moral behavior by allocating a privileged status to one's own needs. Understanding means knowledge of human nature and human good as expressed in basic doctrines such as the Four Noble Truths. These teach that (1) suffering is an inherent part of life; (2) suffering is caused by craving; (3) suffering can have an end (in nirvana); and (4) the way to nirvana is by following the Eightfold Path, a way of life which emphasizes morality (*sīla*), meditation (*samādhi*), and wisdom (*Paññā*).

C. Meditation

Meditation is part of the Eightfold Path, and it plays an important role in the cultivation of the virtues. Of particular importance is a group of four meditational dispositions known as the four Sublime States. The four are love (*mettā*), compassion (*karuṇā*), gladness for others (*muditā*), and equanimity (*upekkhā*). Detailed guidance is provided in Buddhist literature as to the way in which these disposition can be cultivated and deepened. Care must be exercised in the early stages lest they be directed inappropriately and lead to selfish desire rather than being directed without impartiality. In the cultivation of love, for instance, it is recommended not to choose a person of the opposite sex as an object of affection. Surprisingly, perhaps, the first proper object of affection should be oneself. Far from being narcissistic, this involves the shrewd psychological insight that it is impossible to love others any more than one loves oneself. After developing positive feelings for oneself, the disposition is slowly extended in an everincreasing circle to friends and relations, the local community, and finally the world at large. Through this practice the mind becomes free of anger, hostility, resentment, and other negative traits which are common sources of immoral action.

The same method of practice is applied to the second and third Sublime States. Compassion is directed toward all who are experiencing misfortune with the aspiration that their suffering may soon cease, and gladness toward those in good fortune with the wish and their good fortune should remain and increase. When the first three have been developed, the practice of equanimity can begin. The importance of equanimity is that it ensures that none of the other dispositions are allowed to predominate. There is a danger for the moral life in allowing any disposition, however virtuous in itself, to become dominant. It is sometimes claimed, for example, that so long as one acts with a compassionate motive no wrong can be done. This is not the Buddhist view, and the role of equanimity is to ensure that moral judgments are not distorted by an imbalance between dispositions leading to an overemphasis on any one of them. According to the 5th century A.D. commentator Buddhaghosa, the four Sublime States should be practiced on the model of a mother with four sons: the first is a baby, the second an invalid, the third in the flush of youth, and the fourth grown up and busy with his own affairs. Her wish was that the first should grow up, that the second should get well, that the third should enjoy the benefits of youth for as long as possible, and toward the fourth—now grown up and independent—she has an attitude of even-minded observation.

D. Nirvana

The aim of all Buddhists is to attain nirvana, but there are different schools of though at to what nirvana involves. The tradition recognizes two kinds of nirvana, the kind which is attained by a person in the course of his lifetime, and the kind which is attained by an enlightened person at death. In this discussion we are concerned only with the former. The tendency has been to understand nirvana as an event in life primarily in intellectual terms as the gaining of mystical knowledge. While this is certainly part of what is involved, it leaves little scope for the important moral dimension of Buddhism. The Buddha was not just a man of great philosophical insight, but also one with a firm commitment to the well-being of others. The greater part of his life, indeed, was selflessly devoted to encouraging others to participate in the noble life envisaged in his teachings. Buddhist doctrine, for all its sophistication, is of little use unless it manifests itself in a life lived rightly. It may be more appropriate, therefore, to understand nirvana as embracing both intellectual *and* moral ideals.

It is clear that the path to nirvana, the Noble Eightfold Path, includes both these dimensions of human good under its categories of morality and wisdom. The Path also includes a third category, meditation, and we have noted the importance of meditation in the cultivation of moral virtue. It may also be noted now that meditation has the additional function of developing insight into important truths, such as the Noble Truths of suffering and its origins. What the Eightfold Path provides, then, is an inclusive program for human development which leads to the full flowering of human potential in the state known as nirvana, a state in which a person fully understands both the nature of the human condition and its potential for good, and is committed to assisting others to attain the same state of perfection.

In terms of this understanding of nirvana there is no sense in which an enlightened being "transcends" moral values or passes "beyond good and evil," as has sometimes been thought. It can be seen from the Buddha's conduct that he personally did no such thing, nor did he anywhere express the view that it would be appropriate for others to do so. The only sense in which the Buddha passed "beyond good and evil" was in not having to pause to deliberate between them: he instinctively knew the right course of action. The much misunderstood "Parable of the Raft" in no way supports the construction commonly put upon it, namely that morality is of a temporary and provisional nature, a "means to an end" and something ultimately to be discarded like a raft after one has crossed over the stream. If the Buddhist understanding of nirvana incorporates moral perfection in the way suggested above, then moral conduct is integral to the final goal. Without moral conduct, there cannot be nirvana.

E. Buddhist Values

1. Wisdom and Moral Concern

Understood in the way described above, nirvana as *summum bonum* is an inclusive final end, and the path which leads to it is nothing other than the gradual cultivation and manifestation of those virtues and qualities which compose the end. From the description of the content of nirvana just provided it is not difficult to see that two basic Buddhist values are wisdom and moral conduct. Human perfection is defined in an early text, the *Soṇadaṇḍasutta*, as the possession of these two values, which are the necessary and sufficient conditions for human fulfillment. They go hand-in-hand together; in the imagery of the text they are like two hands which wash one another. Wisdom (*paññā*) purifies moral concern (*sīla*), and moral concern purifies wisdom. Either by itself is incomplete. A person who possesses one without the other is imbalanced, and cannot be said to have attained nirvana.

2. Life

While wisdom and moral concern are explicitly recognized in all the major soteriological formulas (either as *paññā* and *sīla,* or *prajñā* and *karuṇā*), there is another basic value which is no less important in Buddhist ethics. This basic value is life itself. As already noted, Buddhist precepts forbid the destruction of life and Buddhist monks take pains to avoid accidentally destroying tiny creatures such as insects. Monks do not engage in agriculture because of the inevitable destruction of life caused by ploughing the earth. From this it can be seen that respect for life in Buddhism extends no only to human beings, as is common in other world religions, but also to animal and even insect life. The belief in karma and rebirth has had a profound influence on the Buddhist attitude to nature, and has meant that Buddhists are less ready to draw hard and fast lines between human life and other forms of life.

IV. ETHICS IN MAHĀYĀNA BUDDHISM

The rise of the Mahāyāna schools in the early centuries of the Christian era brought with it new perspectives on ethics. This involved not a rejection of the values of early Buddhism so much as a recalibration or adjustment. In particular the Mahāyāna schools felt that the scales had tipped too far in favor of wisdom and away from moral concern. Buddhism, in their view, had lost sight of the moral values exemplified by its founder, for example, in unselfishly devoting his life to the service of others. Rather than a way of life in the fullest sense, it had in their view been diverted into a quest for wisdom of a scholastic kind by an elite group leading a lifestyle divorced from humanity at large. Mahāyāna sources frequently complain about the narrowness of the "hearers" (*srāvakas*), the early followers who—in the view of the Mahāyāna—selfishly pursued a path to a private salvation, oblivious to the needs of their fellow man. Texts such as the *Lotus Sūtra* (ca. 150 C.E.) introduce new ideas about the Buddha which stressed his compassionate nature, such as in the belief that he had only feigned entry in final nirvana and had never, or would ever, abandon those still left behind. From an ethical point of view two important new teachings come to prominence at this time: the bodhisattva, and the doctrine of "skillful means."

A. The Bodhisattva

The Bodhisattva is the Mahāyāna's paradigm for human perfection. As may be expected, his qualities are modeled upon those of the Buddha, but with a special emphasis on compassion, which provides an impetus away from the life of the cloister and into the community at large.

The qualities a bodhisattva should cultivate are expressed in the form of six "perfections" (*pāramitās*), namely, generosity (*dāna*), morality (*sīla*), patience (*kṣānti*), courage (*vīrya*), meditation (*samādhi*), and wisdom (*prajñā*).

Although the sixfold formulation is original to the Mahāyāna, the virtues that compose this list are by no means new. They can quite easily be reconciled with the earlier Eightfold Path, which is itself broken down into the three categories of morality (*sīla*), meditation (*samādhi*), and wisdom (*paññā*). Thus the first three perfections can be regarded as morality in the Eightfold Path; the fifth and sixth as meditation and wisdom, respectively; and the fourth—courage or perseverance (*vīrya*)—as applying to all three categories. Instead of talking of three categories as in early Buddhism, however, Mahāyāna sources commonly speak of two, namely wisdom (*prajñā*) and compassion (*karuṇā*). The change in terminology from morality to compassion suggests that a new inflection is being introduced; whereas morality connotes self-discipline and self-control, compassion introduces an other-regarding quality. The object of compassion is always someone else. Morality is no longer essentially about observing the rules and precepts, but about setting the interests of others squarely in front of one and ensuring that attention is paid to them.

In this new formulation meditation drops out of the picture to some degree. There are two possible reasons for this. The first is that meditation may have been regarded as something practiced by an elite minority who had the leisure to devote to it. Meditation represents withdrawal and detachment, and may have been seen as a kind of aloof complacency. The second reason is that meditation is not an end in itself but a means. The goal of Buddhism is not just to be good at meditation, but to use meditation as a means to cultivate wisdom and compassion. As noted earlier, when the Buddha defined the qualities of a true Brahman (i.e., a virtuous person), he spoke only of wisdom and compassion, and did not mention meditation. The formulation of the values of Mahāyāna Buddhism as binary, therefore, makes it clear that wisdom and compassion are the essential ingredients in human perfection. One who seeks the perfection of Buddhahood, i.e., a bodhisattva, must therefore cultivate these two things evenhandedly.

The adjustment in the scale of values whereby compassion rises to be the equal of wisdom (or according to some texts, superior to it) leads to some adjustments in the understanding of Buddhist morality on the part of Mahāyāna sources. The texts begin to speak of a threefold division, such that morality consists of (i) self-control, (ii) the cultivation of virtue, and (iii) altruism. While the first two are found in the Buddhism of the "Hearers," the last is a Mahāyāna innovation. This category is evidence of the growing belief that a bodhisattva should do more than just train himself to follow the rules and do good deeds. Through altruism he must intensify his benevolence and become the servant of others, sharing in their joys and sorrows, caring for the sick, providing religious teachings, and even working miracles in order to win converts to the faith.

Serving the interests of others, however, can sometimes lead to conflict with the precepts, particularly in the case of those who are ordained. What is to be done if the needs of others require a monk to break monastic rules? For example, what if a sick parishioner needs treatment during the rainy season when monks are forbidden to travel outside the monastery? This dilemma was resolved by introducing a distinction between serious and minor offenses. While the "Hearers" were bound by all of the rules, it was felt that bodhisattvas were allowed to commit minor offenses where the circumstances required it. This was not much different than the permission granted by the Buddha himself in his last days for the Order to vary the "lesser and minor" precepts where it saw fit. According to a majority of texts, however, even bodhisattvas are not allowed to breach the major precepts such as those against killing and sexual intercourse.

B. Skillful Means

Along with the doctrine of the bodhisattva, the second important development in Mahāyāna ethics was in the doctrine of skillful means (*upāya-kauśalya*). The roots of this notion go back to the Buddha's skill in teaching the Dharma demonstrated in his ability to adapt his message to the context in which it was delivered. Thus when talking to Brahmins the Buddha would often explain his own teachings by reference to their rituals and traditions, leading his audience step by step to see the truth of a Buddhist tenet. Parables, metaphors, and similes formed an important part of his teaching repertoire, skillfully tailored to suit the level of his audience.

The Mahāyāna developed this idea in a radical way by intimating, in texts such as the *Lotus Sūtra,* that the early teachings were not just skillfully delivered, but were a device or "skillful means" (*upāya*) in their entirety. What had been taught, they suggested, was not the ultimate truth but just a preliminary to it. The preliminary phase was necessary because of the limited understanding of the "Hearers," who would have simply been unable to grasp the profundity of the true Dharma if revealed all at once. The original teachings were not false, merely incomplete. Now that the preliminary teachings had been digested, the Mahāyāna claimed, the time was ripe for the deeper meaning to be revealed.

The idea of skillful means has certain implications for ethics. If the early teachings were provisional rather than ultimate, then the precepts they contain would also be of a provisional rather than an ultimate nature. Thus the clear and strict rules encountered again and again in the early sources which prohibit certain sorts of acts could be interpreted more in the way of guidelines for those at a preliminary stage, but not as ultimately binding. In particular, bodhisattvas, the new moral heroes of the Mahāyāna, could claim increased moral latitude and flexibility based on their recognition of the importance of compassion. A bodhisattva takes a vow to save all beings, and there is evidence in many texts of impatience with rules and regulations which seem to get in the way of a bodhisattva going about his majestic mission. The pressure to bend or suspend the rules in the interests of compassion resulted in certain texts, notably the *Bodhisattvabhūmi*, establishing a new code of conduct for bodhisattvas which explicitly allowed the precepts to be broken. Even killing is said to be justified to prevent someone committing a serious crime for which they would suffer karmic retribution. Sexual intercourse is allowed for monks where rejection of a woman's advances would lead her to develop thoughts of hatred. Telling lies, and other breaches of the precept, are also permissible when the consequences would be greater spiritual development.

The principle of skillful means, then, seems to introduce consequentialist justification into Buddhist ethics for the first time. According to this principle, what is right and wrong is to be determined by reference to the consequences of what is done, and not the intrinsic nature of the act itself. Within the Mahāyāna as a whole, however, there are few, if any, sources which press this teaching to its logical conclusions with respect to normative ethics. No text explicitly states that consequences alone should guide moral deliberation, and examples which seem to embody this principle are open to interpretation at various levels. In the case of the *Bodhisattvabhūmi* (ca. 4th century C.E.), for instance, the explicit authorization to take the life of a person about to commit an offense of immediate retribution (*ānantarya*) need not necessarily be contrary to early Buddhist principles. If killing an assailant is the only way to prevent him from committing murder, then it is arguable that such an act is not against the First Precept. What is intended in such a case is to neutralize the attack, not to cause the assailant's death. That this is so can be seen from the fact that if the assailant could be restrained in some other way, the defender's purpose would be fulfilled.

Another example is found in the *Discourse of Skillful Means,* a late Mahāyāna source. At one point in this text the Buddha recounts how in a previous life he killed a man who was about to murder 500 people. This is sometimes interpreted as evidence that the doctrine of skillful means operates on the basis of consequentialist calculation. The Buddha, apparently, weighted 1 life against 500 and decided that the consequence of saving 500 lives justified the taking of 1. The Buddha's actions, however, can also be explained, as in the previous exam-

ple, as consistent with early principles without any need to introduce a consequentialist weighing of outcomes. The First Precept would remain as an absolute prohibition on the intentional destruction of life while, as recognized by the law, it would be permissible to take action (even lethal action) to safeguard one's own life or the lives of others since one's purpose in this case is to resist aggression, not to kill.

The examples mentioned above may be read in various ways but receive surprisingly little comment in Buddhist sources, demonstrating once again the presence of morality without ethics in Buddhism. It is therefore difficult to do more than speculate, as in the suggestions already offered, in an attempt to reconstruct the moral principles which underlie such cases. The moral dimension of the doctrine of skillful means, in fact, receives remarkably little attention in texts or commentaries, and examples of the use of skillful means by bodhisattvas tend to demonstrate (as with the Buddha) their skill in teaching the Dharma and the lengths they will go to save beings. The dynamic which underlies the whole notion of skillful means is compassion. Driven by compassion, bodhisattvas sometimes find themselves in conflict with the rules. But where are the rules derived from? It is important to realize that the rules are derived not simply from custom or tradition but from the other supreme value of Buddhism, namely wisdom. The rules are the product of a process of moral reasoning whose aim is to determine which are the things it is rational to do and not to do if Buddhist values are to become incarnate in oneself and the world at large. Values define success in concrete terms, and success in Buddhism is measured in terms of wisdom, moral concern, and respect for life. The precepts define the things it is irrational to do if these goals are to be attained. To act against a precept is to choose directly against these values. A person who perfects and embodies all three in the form of a being with wisdom, compassion, and eternal life (in the state of nirvana) is a Buddha. Anyone who chooses against the precepts, accordingly, alienates themselves from this ideal.

The overwhelming consensus in the Mahāyāna is that the doctrine of skillful means neither requires nor justifies the abrogation of moral norms. The doctrine crystallizes in its antinomian form under the pressure exerted by the principle of compassion. The relationship between wisdom and compassion has been explored by the Mahāyāna over the course of many centuries. This is a veritable battle for the soul of Buddhism: is it to be a religion of philosophers and mystics, or a religion of reincarnating social workers? The pendulum swings backward and forward. For much of the time compassion and the principle of "love is all you need" hold sway. At other times wisdom is in the ascendant, particularly in periods of vigorous philosophical development where schools such as the Madhyamika (2nd century C.E.) come to the fore. The conclusion must surely be, however, that both are indispensable. A human being is neither a head nor a heart, and a perfected being must be one who, like the Buddha, has perfected and *integrated* intellectual and moral potential.

V. APPLIED ETHICS

A. Monastic Ethics

The life of a Buddhist monk or nun is regulated by a code known as the Monastic Rule or *vinaya*. The Monastic Rule is a compendium of information about all aspects of the monastic Order. It describes its origins and history, the early councils, and disputes over matters of monastic conduct, and recounts how the traditions of the order arose. Embedded in the Monastic Rule is a code of over 200 articles known as the *Pātimokkha* and which provide detailed instructions as to how monks and nuns should live communally. In many respects the Monastic Rule is comparable to the Rule of St. Benedict, which was introduced in the 6th century as a model for the daily life of Christian monks. The Monastic Rule, however, is much longer than the Rule of St. Benedict. Among other things it provides an account of the circumstances as to why each rule was introduced, and of modifications which were made as new circumstances arose. The Buddha is represented as the author of the rules, although internal evidence suggests that many of them date from some time after his death. Much technical information is provided concerning the types of robes to be worn, the way dwellings should be constructed, how high beds should be off the floor, the type of mats to be used, and so on.

As well as much intricate detail on daily life, the Monastic Rule incorporates the major moral precepts such as those against taking life, stealing, and lying. The records of particular offenses under these rubrics, moreover, are a vitally important source of information from an ethical perspective. Many of the case histories reported shed much-needed light on the ethical principles which underlie the rules themselves. Whereas in the Buddha's discourses moral rules are commonly presented in summary form with little explanation, in the Monastic Rule it is possible to discern more

clearly the nature of the wrong that is done. The commentaries and discussions concerning the interpretation of the monastic rules are the closest Buddhism comes to the discipline of moral philosophy, and provide a much-needed source of clarification on many points of ethics.

It has been pointed out that the Buddhist Order is the glue which, in the absence of any overall spiritual authority, holds Buddhism together. As Buddhism spread, the Monastic Rule was copied and translated into new languages and remained the basis for monastic life, with only comparatively slight modifications. This has meant that there is a good deal of ethical unanimity across the boundaries of sect and school, and that although Buddhists may have very different understandings of the finer points of doctrine, they are often in broad agreement regarding what should and should not be done from the point of view of ethics.

B. Duties

In common with Indian moral tradition as a whole, Buddhism expresses its ethical requirements in the form of duties. The requirements of Dharma are expressed in the form of what ought and ought not to be done by individuals both in general (as human beings) and with respect to specific social roles. The most general moral duties are those found in the precepts, such as the duty to refrain from killing, stealing, and so forth. These apply to everyone without exception. Formally the precepts are undertakings, and when the precepts are "taken" in a ceremonial or ritual context, the form of words used acknowledges the free and voluntary assumption of the duty assumed. The ceremony, however, acknowledges the duty, it does not create it. The duty applies even if an individual has never heard of such a precept. It is incumbent, moreover, not only on Buddhists but on all rational beings of whatever culture race or creed. This is because Dharma is universal and timeless, and its moral authority applies whether it is recognized or not.

Examples of duties which vary with social position are the duty of those who are ordained to observe the Monastic Rule, of kings to rule justly and of subjects to obey just laws, of parents to care for their children and children to respect their parents, and of husbands to support their wives and wives to be responsible for their husbands' property. Dharma thus imposes a network of comprehensive and reciprocal duties on social relationships whereby individuals fulfill the moral obligations required of them or the commitments they have undertaken.

C. Rights

There is no word in early Buddhist sources corresponding to the notion of "rights" in the way understood in the West. The concept of a right emerged in the West as the result of a particular combination of social, political, and intellectual developments which has not been repeated elsewhere. From the Enlightenment onward it has occupied center stage in legal and political discourse, and provides a supple and flexible language in terms of which individuals may express their claims to justice. A right may be defined as an exercisable power vested in an individual. This power may be thought of as a benefit or entitlement which allows the right-holder to impose a claim upon others or to remain immune from demands which others seek to impose.

Rights are the converse of duties. If A has a duty to B, then B stands in the position of beneficiary and has a *right* to whatever benefit flows from the performance of A's duty. Although rights are not explicitly mentioned in Buddhist sources, it can be seen they are implicit in the notion of dharmic duties. If a king has a duty to rule justly, then it can be said that citizens have a "right" to fair treatment. If a husband has a duty to be faithful to his wife (Dīgha Nikāya iii. 190), then a wife has a right to fidelity from her husband. At the most general level, if everyone has a duty not take life, then all living things have a right to life; if everyone has a duty not to steal, then everyone has a right not to be unjustly deprived of their property. The logic will work in the same way for the other precepts. It might be said, then, that the concept of rights is implicit in Dharma, and that rights and duties are like separate windows onto the common good justice.

D. Human Rights

Contemporary human rights charters, such as the United Nations Universal Declaration on Human Rights of 1948, set out a list of basic rights which are held to be possessed by all human beings without distinction as to race or creed. Many contemporary Buddhists subscribe to such charters, and Buddhist leaders such as the Dalai Lama can often be heard endorsing the principles these charters embody. Certain of these rights seem to be foreshadowed in Buddhist sources: a right not to be held in slavery can be found in the canonical prohibition on trade in living beings. It is also arguable that other human rights are implicit in the Buddhist precepts. The right not to be killed or tortured, for example, may be thought of as falling under the First Precept against taking life.

On the whole, however, traditional sources have little to say about the kinds of questions which are now regarded as human rights issues. In the absence of an explicit concept of rights, of course, this is not unexpected. Nevertheless, there seems to be a curious absence of discussion about such matters, whether couched in the language of rights or otherwise. The situation has changed dramatically in modern times, and the Western language of human rights is now used regularly by Buddhists of many cultures to express their concern at outrages of various kinds. At the same time, little consideration has been given to the question of how human rights are to be grounded in Buddhist doctrine. Mimicking the West is one thing, but is there a genuine Buddhist foundation for human rights?

Human rights are closely tied to the notion of human dignity. Many human rights charters, in fact, explicitly derive the former from the latter. In many religions, human dignity is said to derive from the fact that human beings are created in the image of God, but Buddhism makes no such claim. This makes it difficult to see what the source of human dignity might be. If it is not to be sought at a theological level then presumably it must be sought at the human level. Here it would appear that for Buddhism human dignity flows from the capacity of human nature to reach perfection, as demonstrated by the historical figure of the Buddha and the saints of the Buddhist tradition. The Buddha is the living embodiment of human perfection, and it is in the profound wisdom and compassion which he exemplifies, qualities which all human beings can cultivate, that human dignity is to be found.

The Buddhist doctrine of human rights, accordingly, would seem to be grounded in respect for the human dignity epitomized by the Buddha and participated in by all to some degree. In traditional teaching this is expressed by saying that all beings have the potential to attain enlightenment (in the Mahāyāna it is often said that all beings possess the "Buddha-nature"). Since, to use the Mahāyāna formulation, all possess the Buddha-nature, it follows that all are worthy of respect, and since all are worthy of respect justice demands that the rights of each individual must be secured. Such would appear to be the foundation for a universal doctrine of human rights in Buddhism.

Also See the Following Articles

RELIGION AND ETHICS • RIGHTS THEORY • THEORIES OF ETHICS, OVERVIEW

Bibliography

Focus on Buddhist ethics (1996). *J. Religious Ethics* **24**, 2.
Keown, D. (1995). "Buddhism & Bioethics." Macmillan, London.
Keown, D. (1992). "The Nature of Buddhist Ethics." Macmillan, London.

King, W. L. (1964). "In the Hope of Nibbana: The Ethics of Theravada Buddhism." Open Court, La Salle, IL.
Misra, G. S. P. (1984). "Development of Buddhist Ethics." Munshiram Manoharlal, Delhi.
Prebish, C. (Ed.) (1992). "Buddhist Ethics: A Cross-Cultural Approach." Kendal/Hunt, Dubuque, IA.
Saddhatissa, H. (1994). "Buddhist Ethics." Wisdom Publications, Boston.
Tachibana, S. (1992). "The Ethics of Buddhism." Curzon, London.
Wei-hsun Fu, C., and Wawrytko, S. A. (Eds.) (1991). "Buddhist Ethics and Modern Society: An International Symposium." Greenwood, New York.

BUSINESS ETHICS, OVERVIEW

Jennifer Jackson
University of Leeds

GLOSSARY

contractarian theories Theories that borrow the notion of a hypothetical contract from political philosophy and seek insight into ethically problematic questions by considering how they might be answered by those making a hypothetical contract.

ethically problematic choices or issues A situation in which even people who are sensible and well-intentioned disagree or are uncertain concerning what is defensible or appropriate.

ethical relativism The view that what is ethically defensible or indefensible is relative to the beliefs or attitudes of an individual or a group—for example, a culture. The ethical relativist denies that disagreement between members of different cultures con-

cerning what is ethically defensible can be resolved by reference to independent universal moral truths.

hypothetical contract A concept used in political philosophy to clarify what a person's rights and duties are. It is supposed that insight on this may be gained by imagining what rules one would agree to live by if one were to choose these impartially, as if from behind a "veil of ignorance."

neo-Aristotelian virtues-based theory The view that certain traits of character, moral virtues, are the key to prospering in life. The virtues are said to be pervasively relevant to all roles and activities that are ethically defensible. If business is ethically defensible, these virtues should be compatible with business activity.

stakeholder theories An approach to business ethics that widens the scope of management accountability beyond the shareholders to include all who have a stake in a business. Obviously, employees, suppliers, and customers have a stake. Some would argue that there are less-obvious stakeholders, including the local community, the public at large, and, maybe, even business rivals.

utilitarianism The theory that the aim of morality is to bring about the best consequences—the greatest happiness or pleasure or satisfaction of preferences.

veil of ignorance A thought experiment for working out the rules we should live by: we are to imagine that we are choosing these rules from behind a veil that keeps us from knowing what our own position might be in this society—for example, our own age, sex, and status in society.

BUSINESS ETHICS is the study of what is ethically permissible and of what is positively virtuous, in regard to business activity. It is an attempt not only to reach conclusions but to understand what lies behind them. It is a branch of applied ethics. As such it draws on ethical theories and concepts and brings these to bear on problems and issues that arise in and for business.

I. THE INTEREST IN BUSINESS ETHICS

While some isolated examples of attention to ethical issues specifically in business can be found in the writings and reflections of philosophers from times gone by (Cicero, for example, asking whether it is unethical not to disclose to a prospective buyer of one's property that it is infested with wood worm) it is only since the early 1970s that the subject has come to be regarded as a specific field of academic study. It is now included in the curricula of most main business schools in the United States and there is increasing academic interest and activity in the field in other countries. But while the recognition of business ethics as a distinct subject area is a relatively new development, the underlying issues and problems it concerns are not all new.

Why has business ethics attracted special notice over the past quarter century? Whereas medical ethics involves issues that have always interested philosophers—for example, issues of life and death, it may not be so obvious that business practices and policies give rise to ethical problems that lend themselves to philosophical analysis. It is obvious enough that business activities impinge on our lives quite pervasively and sometimes unpleasantly. Scandals and disasters in recent years bring home to everyone how irregular or slack business practice can ruin the lives of people outside the business itself: the repercussions for Scottish highland communities of the collapse of BCCI, the widespread damage resulting from the explosion at Bhopal, and the numbers of people drowned when the *Herald of Free Enterprise* sank off Zeebruge. But the mere fact that irresponsible and mischievous business activities can cause calamities does not make the subject fit for the attention of philosophy. If the number of muggings rises sharply we do not look to the study of applied ethics for solutions. Applied ethics comes into

play where there is debate over what is ethically defensible or desirable. That muggings are indefensible is not a matter for debate. It is not philosophy that provides insight into how to get people to stop acting in ways that they already know are ethically indefensible.

Philosophy becomes relevant only where there is doubt or disagreement as to what is one's duty. Is it wrong, for example, to offer cheap travel services where the travel is cheap partly because safety precautions are relatively basic? Is it wrong to induce customers to buy items which, though noninjurious, are also frivolous? Is it wrong to fall in with customs that prevail in the country where you go to do business if those customs would be illegal and considered unethical in your own country? Is it unethical to use child labor? If so, is it also unethical to have dealings with anyone who does business with those who use child labor? Is it wrong to hire your nephew because he is your nephew and can do the job adequately even if there is another applicant who is better qualified? These are questions that actually face businesspeople. For them, they are not mere debating points.

Behind the uncertainty over what is ethically defensible in such matters and why, lie basic questions about ethics of the kind that philosophy seeks to throw light on. Are people entitled to take risks (and to invite others to take risks) provided only that they are informed? Is it ethically defensible to make money out of people's readiness to indulge themselves frivolously? Uncertainty in regard to these questions leads us to raise more fundamental questions about liberty rights and the exploitation of the vulnerable or foolish. Whether customs in other countries that offend our moral sensibilities are customs that we should respect or tolerate raises questions about the basis of moral judgments: is there a way of scrutinizing these that does not merely reflect the standards of the critic's own culture? Is it always merely arrogant to think one's own culture to be morally superior in a certain respect? Does it even make sense to say that people are mistaken in their ethical judgments? Are there certain practices that are unjust and that no one should tolerate? If so, how do we establish what practices are not merely distasteful to ourselves but downright wrong whatever anyone thinks?

Yet, if it is true that the subject has genuine academic roots in moral and political philosophy, we should expect to find throughout the history of philosophy discussion of issues that are fundamental for business ethics. And so we do: Aristotle on commutative justice (justice in exchange—in trade), Hobbes on contract, Locke on property, for example. Similarly, religions have not just *discovered* "business ethics." Misgivings about usury have a long history in Islamic, Jewish, and Christian ethics. And throughout the history of Christianity can be traced an ambivalence toward money making. Hence, it is a bit misleading to claim that business ethics is a new subject and that it is merely touched on in passing by earlier philosophers and religious thinkers.

Current interest in business ethics stems not only from the philosophically intriguing questions that underlie our puzzlement as to whether certain activities and policies in business are ethically defensible, it also stems from the changes that are occurring in business life. Over the past 20 years or so, there have been various quite substantial changes to how business is conducted and how society perceives business that themselves have fueled interest in business ethics. One might mention:

1. the changing social expectations of business—that it is expected to take over some of the social programs which hitherto have been assumed to be the responsibility of government;
2. the impact of consumer boycotts on big business and consequent efforts of businesses to justify their ethical profiles to the public at large;
3. the need for countries to agree on common standards of employment so as to be able to operate a single market;
4. the need for corporations which have cut out layers of management to spell out for their members common codes of practice;
5. the adverse impact multinationals can have on fragile economies and the extent to which they can or should become politically involved in the countries in which they operate.
6. the threat of legislation to curb what is perceived as irresponsible management and commercial practices, which is itself an incentive for firms to demonstrate their willingness and ability to self-regulate. Firms that seek to demonstrate their ability to police themselves have to address explicitly the issue of what practices or policies should be banned and why.

II. SCOPE OF THE SUBJECT

There are no sharp boundaries between what is ethical and nonethical. Codes of practice that might sound very much the concern of applied ethics, may have more to do with forms of behavior that are deemed to conform to standards of good taste and decorum than

to define what is ethically required or permitted. There may be no moral (ethical—I use the terms interchangeably) obligation to greet your customers with a smile and a "Good morning" or to keep a record of all complaints received. But these may all the same be obvious items to include in a code of good conduct.

Insofar as the law seeks to regulate our dealings with one another to actions that are not ethically indefensible, it offers a rough guide to what is accepted business practice. It is obvious, though, that we cannot settle the interesting questions about what is ethically defensible or indefensible in business by looking to the law. For one thing, the law does not tell us what is defensible, only (at best) what is thought to be. For another, the law is likely to be unclear itself just where there is ethical controversy—as over new uses of technology that make possible activities not hitherto addressed by the law. Anyway, there are many actions that are unethical, sometimes seriously so, even though the law does not forbid them. When Ford when ahead with the production of the Pinto car, knowing that its design was unsafe, it was not breaking the law as it then was. The law (for good reason) does not enforce undertakings between companies to keep prices down, yet if a pact is made and broken, the aggrieved party is likely to consider the offending party to have acted abominably. The law may forbid you to sell weapons to A, a notorious abuser of human rights, but permit you to sell to B. You may keep within the law selling to B, although you know perfectly well that B is selling to A. Negotiating your sale to A via B, may be legal but unethical. (Of course, the law serves other purposes apart from preventing unethical practices. Legal regulations may be introduced simply to maximize efficiency or for tax gathering purposes.)

Of course, we should not expect there to be sharp boundaries between different fields of applied ethics. Many of the issues that are regularly discussed under the heading of business ethics, for instance, have to do with employment ethics: fairness in hiring, firing, promotion, obligations to disabled employees or applicants, the rights and wrongs of whistle-blowing, confidentiality, health, and safety at work are issues no less for public services than for commercial businesses. Sexual harassment, or plain bullying of other kinds, can be as much a problem in a college, the marines, or the police force as in a bank or factory.

In pursuing issues in business ethics we are led into study of property rights and analysis of contract—whether, for example, a contract is ethically unsound if the parties to it are very unequal in power—is this a reason for deeming commercial surrogacy or commerce in human organs (for transplant) to be intrinsically unethical? There is also the question of how much information you are morally obliged to share when negotiating a contract. Is it, for example, unethical to buy property that you happen to know, and do not disclose, to be of much more value than the vendor realizes?

Many of the issues that are central in business ethics involve us in reflection on political theory as well as ethics: what do we mean by the phrase "equality of opportunity," and is there a basic right in this connection that any state should uphold, or is it merely a feature of a specific "Western" cultural tradition that other cultures, no less enlightened ethically, are entitled to ignore? The nature of rational choice and human motivation affects all fields of applied ethics, and leads into debate, which is familiar terrain for economists and psychologists as well as philosophers.

In deciding what the scope of our subject should be, we cannot simply analyze the relevant concepts—the meaning of ethics and the meaning of business. What we call "business" is to some extent a matter for stipulation. A case may be made for defining the concerns of business ethics much more circumspectly than has been customary. The essence of business may be deemed to be commercial enterprise that engages in the selling of goods or services simply in order to make profits. If that is basically what we take business to be about, then we can debate what activities or policies are ethically defensible in the light of its characteristic or proper aim. If you are in business you should be aiming to make a profit while conforming to the same legal and ethical constraints that everyone is bound by at work or play. In other words, you should obey the law and treat people honestly, fairly, and noncoercively.

A very interesting account of business ethics along these scope-restricting lines is to be found in Elaine Sternberg's *Just Business* (1994. London: Little, Brown and Company). She maintains that in order to understand what is ethically permissible in business one must begin with a grasp of the nature of business in the light of which one can identify what is its telos or goal. People in business are morally obliged simply to pursue that goal (which she defines as maximizing long-term value on behalf of the owner of the business) within the constraints of what she calls ordinary decency (which excludes deception, theft, coercion, violence, and illegality) and distributive justice (here thought of somewhat narrowly: that the rewards of labor should be proportional to individuals' contributions to their organization's ends). Thus, Sternberg distinguishes real businesses from other enterprises that are not single-mindedly committed to maximizing long-term owner value—for example, a family business, content to achieve a profit without being intent on maximizing it, or a charity engaging in business but alongside certain social goals that compromise its profit making (perhaps making it a policy to appoint people with a specific disability whether or not they are the candidates who are most likely to promote the wealth of the organization). In the Sternberg view, many corporations are not businesses (because they adopt other aims alongside that of increasing long-term owner value). Their having other nonbusiness aims is not unethical, she allows—as long as they are honest about their real aims.

There are some merits in settling on the narrow Sternberg definition of business. It does leave out some important questions customarily addressed within business ethics. But these can still be taken up under another heading. What is the "correct" way to define business, though, depends in part at least on what definition is useful for our purposes. Books and articles on business ethics have generally tended to adopt a broader understanding of what falls within the subject. After all, many people, who are not working for a commercial business, single-mindedly pursuing long-term owner value, are all the same *doing* business—maybe on behalf of a church, a charity, or a public service. And many of the issues that arise that are ethically intriguing crop up both in commercial and in other settings—wherever people engage in doing business. Partly, this is because much of what is discussed under the heading of business ethics is, strictly speaking, a matter of employment ethics (as we have already noted): for example, fairness in hiring, firing, and promotion; duties of loyalty between employer and employee (and ex-employees); rights of privacy—is staff surveillance or testing of staff an unethical invasion of privacy?

III. EMPLOYMENT ETHICS IN COMMERCIAL AND NONCOMMERCIAL ORGANIZATIONS

Does what is fair and reasonable treatment of employees depend significantly on whether they are working in commercial as opposed to noncommercial organizations? Consider, for example, the policy of passing over certain candidates—for a job or for promotion on account of their age—typically, because they are too old, not too young. Whether such a policy is unethical would seem to be a question for employment ethics: is this unfair treatment? And, how we answer might seem *not* to depend on whether the employee is working in a commercial or a noncommercial organization. Thus, it may be said that selecting against people on account of their age is wrong in just the same way as is selecting against them merely on account of their sex or race. All these forms of selecting may be said to offend against the moral requirement to treat each person with equal respect.

So it is often said, but should we be impressed? Is there this moral requirement? Certainly, if there is, it was overlooked by a good many philosophers (including Plato, Aristotle, Hobbes, and Hume). Even if there is this requirement, what does it imply: does it preclude selecting against those over a certain age? Of course, doing so may be foolish, may lead an organization to select against its own interests—as, for example, if the expectation that the older will be less useful is mere prejudice. But that is another matter. If the above argument is correct: it is wrong not to treat people with equal respect *and* to select against the older is to not treat *them* with equal respect, then it is indefensible for any organization commercial or otherwise to follow this policy.

On the other hand, if the above argument is not correct, then the defensibility of the policy might depend on the *nature* of the organization that adopts it. If the policy is not wrong as such, but is, all the same, a mistake—in that there is no good reason to expect the older candidates to be less useful or effective in the job, then, according to the Sternberg view, it will be wrong to follow the policy in a commercial organization, where maximizing long-term owner value is a duty for managers, but not necessarily wrong in the case of a noncommercial organization that has other aims than, or alongside, profit-making. By the same argument, in the Sternberg view, a manager in a commercial organization selecting candidates for employment or promotion not only may, but must take age into account if in fact it is relevant to the usefulness of the candidate. If, though, the organization is not commercial there need not be an obligation to choose the candidate who is most useful—in relation to profit making. Age Concern might adopt a policy of giving preference to older candidates—not because they are more "productive" but because Age Concern aims to improve the lot of older people.

IV. MISGIVINGS ABOUT BUSINESS ETHICS

Just as there are those who object to the idea that war can ever by conducted in a just, ethically defensible way, so there are those who object to the very terms "business ethics": as if, doing business is essentially unjust however it is done. Aristotle had rude things to say about business (commercial business, at any rate). As we have already remarked, Christianity has been ambivalent about money making. Usury in particular has been regarded as unethical in various religious traditions—yet so much modern business would seem to involve the lending of money at interest. In addition there are the neo-Marxian concerns about exploitation—whether property is theft, whether it is possible for the waged to earn as they deserve and to choose freely whether to work in a business and if so whether one's basic rights are compromised by one's being a waged earner.

Those who declaim business ethics as an oxymoron consider that it is not just this or that aspect of business that is inimical to the concerns of morality. They consider business life to be inherently aggressive, ruthless, and generally "not nice." Sharp practice in business is not just resignedly to be expected, it is, in this view, "good business"—hence, the comparison with warfare. It too is not nice. It is not supposed to be. It is unreasonable to rail against it, though, on this account. The usual sentiments that are supposed to govern one's dealings with others are suspended in warfare vis-à-vis the enemy. Likewise, in business, it may be thought perfectly in order to drop the usual sentiments of considerateness, fairness, and honesty—they are irrelevant.

Of course, there are those who hold that just because it is impossible to wage war without setting aside the usual (moral) sentiments, we should reject war as morally indefensible. And some may take the same line in regard to business. But at least it will be argued it is impossible and quite ridiculous to suppose war can be waged with one's moral gloves on, so to speak. Lies and coercion are the stuff of war. So either we should never wage war or, if we should, lies and deception in pursuit of victory are justified. War then will be ethically off-limits. Similarly, it may be said that business is impossible unless one is able to lie and coerce in pursuit of business advantage. So either business is unethical or ethical considerations do not apply. Compare how perfectly respectable people treat each other in the game of monopoly: they are simply out to do each other down, no mercy is shown. This is not unethical—it is after all just a game.

On the other hand it may be argued both in respect of war and of business that it is perfectly possible to engage in either without ignoring moral considerations. It is not only possible, it is morally necessary to conduct our dealings with other people justly—not only in the sense of obeying the law of the land, but in the sense of obeying "the moral law," so to speak. Even the enemy has certain moral rights and not everything that may be necessary for winning a war is justified simply on that account—not even if the cause for which one is fighting is just. Of course, we are not surprised if the moral rights of the enemy are occasionally violated—especially in the heat of battle. But even in such circumstances instances may be found of soldiers and civilians retaining their sense of justice and insisting, for example, that prisoners must not be shot however troublesome it is to respect their rights. So too in business. While it is easy and not surprising to find instances of unethical practices, it is also possible to find instances of principled regard for the moral rights of employees, suppliers, or customers even in difficult circumstances.

To be sure, instances of principled treatment of employees, suppliers, or customers may demonstrate nothing more than enlightened self-interest. The fact that some companies talk ethics, so the cynics will say, merely indicates an external interest—it is not ethics as such that concerns these companies, but the fashions, for example, for green-speak, that help to boost their profile. When ethics goes out of fashion, they will cease to talk it. While this charge no doubt applies to some firms that trumpet their moral profile, we should not simply assume that it has to be true of all.

All the same, while neither business nor warfare need be treated as moral free zones, it may still be true that certain ways of treating people are justified in the context of war or business that would not be ethically justified elsewhere. "Be nice to your enemy—or your rival, share the information with them that will be advantageous to them as well as to you" is absurd. It is not your duty to be nice to your enemy or your business rival. In either case, it may be hugely to your advantage that you have information about the weather that they do not have. You are not obliged to give them a helping hand here. Indeed, in both cases, it may be your duty not to be kind.

Cynicism about the ethical motivation of people in business may itself reflect a confusion over moral motivation. The mere fact that people in business are aiming to make money does not preclude their being genuinely committed to acting ethically, anymore than the fact that professional people make their living through their professional work precludes their being genuinely committed to the ideals of their profession. Moral motives are not automatically compromised because they are mixed. Those who are morally motivated will, though, recognize that sometimes, moral considerations constrain their money-making opportunities. Of course,

people in business as in other kinds of employment do not typically work only for the money: they expect and seek other kinds of satisfactions, pursue other aims in their work. These other aims may not be moral aims—such as to improve social welfare or reduce suffering. But nor need they be in any way hostile to such concerns. In short, cynicism about business ethics reflects either a confusion about what being ethical involves or mere prejudice towards business. Of course, insofar as "the moral law" is necessary, we need to know it and enforce it. If conforming to it can be made congenial and convenient, that is surely no bad thing.

In any case, the idea that business can operate free of *any* moral constraints is nonsense. We do business in expectation of fair dealing. Who would hire the services of a firm that boasted its amorality, that disclaimed any intention of fulfilling its undertakings? Underlying business dealings as with other dealings between people there has to be a degree of trust. Trust presupposes that people are generally disposed to be trustworthy—to honor their contracts. In the absence of trust, there is no commerce—just anarchy.

It may still be true that there are kinds of business that are inherently unjust—for example, perhaps, prostitution, drug trafficking, the fur trade, and the selling of hard pornography. It may also be true that certain types of business expose those who engage in them to particular temptations. Is it safer from an ethical standpoint to become a schoolteacher or a librarian than to become a city financier? Are some jobs more dangerous than others, more liable to corrupt those who taken them on—or is it rather that every job has its characteristic ethical pitfalls, but the pitfalls with some are more obvious than with others?

V. ETHICAL RELATIVISM AND BUSINESS ETHICS

Business ethics, according to our definition, concerns what is ethically permissible or virtuous in business—not just what is thought to be so by this party or that. Inherent in this definition is the assumption that it is possible to establish universal truths about what is permissible or virtuous. Ethical relativists reject this assumption. They note how attitudes and beliefs about what is ethically permissible or impermissible vary from person to person, from culture to culture. They claim that the idea that there is some independent universal standard or basis against which to test these different views is mistaken. Thus, they hold that it is a mistake to suppose that certain types of action are plain wrong—whoever goes in for them. Rather, one should say, that certain types of action are acceptable to some people, in some cultures, unacceptable to others, in other cultures. The differences do not mean that one culture is morally wiser than the other—just different.

Compare how in different cultures the same colors can take on different significance—white may be associated with weddings in one culture, with funerals in another. The question, "Which association is correct?" does not make sense. All that can be said is that one association is correct in one place, the other in a different place. Thus, bribery, kickbacks, child labor, and nepotism are unacceptable in some countries, acceptable in others. The ethical relativist resists the idea that either they are acceptable or they are not. The relativist holds that just where they are accepted they are acceptable.

Nonrelativists, on the other hand, insist that there are universal moral truths—about how we should live our lives. Aristotle, for example, held that there are certain traits of character, moral virtues, which we all can cultivate and need to cultivate if we are to live well. Temperance—understood as self-discipline in regard to one's physical appetites, for example, is a trait of character that every one needs, whatever culture one belongs to. Other philosophers have talked about certain obligations that have to be recognized and upheld in any society for it to provide a modicum of peace and security. The idea of human rights also appeals to a notion of obligation independent of the beliefs or attitudes of a particular society.

Insofar as the ethical relativists merely rest their case against the possibility of universal ethical truths on the observed differences of view from one culture to another, their thesis is not proven. The nonrelativist need not deny that there are such differences. It is incumbent on the nonrelativist, though, to provide an account of ethical obligations, rights, or virtues that justifies the claim that these have an authority independent of their endorsement by any particular society or culture.

Under whose ethical values, then, should a business operate? Such a question is more likely to exercise nonrelativists than relativists. But from a purely prudential standpoint, both relativists and nonrelativists can agree that insofar as success in business depends on customer satisfaction and employee morale, it pays to give heed to their ethical sensibilities—whatever you think of these. There may also be certain values that are bound to apply wherever one does business. It is difficult to imagine a business that does not need to maintain the trust and loyalty of some.

But suppose that your own views as to what is ethically permissible conflict with those of your employer's, or of your employees, or your customers, whose values should you conform to? Is it always wrong to "impose" your values? When in Rome should you do as the Romans? Relativists will merely observe here that whether you are tolerant or intolerant will depend on what your values or your culture's values happen to be. But the nonrelativist will see an important issue here: *ought* we to be tolerant? *Ought* we to agree to disagree? How are such disagreements to be rationally resolved or accommodated?

VI. CONFORMING TO, OR TOLERATING, OTHERS' STANDARDS

Does the answer to these questions depend on the nature of the disagreement? You may find yourself among people who consider an activity wrong that you regard as innocent. In such a case, if you conform, you are not acting against your own conscience. If, for example, you are working among people who consider it wrong to drink alcohol, it may be prudent for you to abjure alcohol and you can do so with a clear conscience even though you do not share their view.

But suppose that you find yourself among people who consider an activity innocent that *you* believe to be wrong. In this case, if you conform, engage in the activity, you are acting against your own conscience. Suppose, for example, you find that you cannot make any headway doing business in a certain country unless you fall in with the practice of bribery—a practice about which the people with whom you deal are unabashed but that you consider to be wrong. Is it not always wrong to do what you believe to be wrong—even if you are mistaken in your belief? In such a case you show a willingness to do evil—which is evil. You might, though, come to change your mind about the wrongness of bribery. You might decide that in *these* circumstances, bribery is not dishonest—as, for example, if it is so much the expected and tolerated way of doing business that the bribery is conducted quite openly, involves no deception. Or, you might continue to think bribery wrong even in these circumstances, but judge your conformity to be a minor not a grave wrong and one that is justified in the particular case given that it is impossible to do business unless you fall in with the practice.

There is also the possibility that although you do not yourself act in a way you believe to be wrong, you find that those with whom you are doing business do act in ways that you consider to be wrong: are you, then, morally obliged to interfere or should you simply agree to disagree? If you provide a service and some of the people to whom you provide it do wrong, you can hardly be held responsible. But suppose that you are providing people with the very means by which they are doing a wrong—*and* that this is, or should be, obvious to you. Suppose, for example, that you are selling weapons, and the buyers are notorious violators of human rights. Are you then implicated in their villainy? Or, suppose that you are selling agricultural tools but in the knowledge that these are not being put to agricultural use but being used instead to carry out massacres. Can you justify your dealings here with the claim that if you do not supply these, others will?

Is this ever a legitimate excuse? Our answer will depend on our general understanding of what morality is and of what it is that makes an action morally defensible or indefensible. From a utilitarian standpoint, morality is about producing the best consequences, maximizing happiness or the satisfaction of preferences: that is your, that is anyone's, duty. A course of action that would otherwise be wrong because of the bad consequence it would bring about, might well be defensible after all if it is evident that if you do not do it someone else will. What matters from a utilitarian standpoint is just what results, not by whose agency it results—except, of course, if it so happens that further bad consequences result if the deed is done by one person rather than another. It *may* be worse if you sell arms to these people than if I do. Perhaps, for example, you have publicly sworn that you are not doing so, as I have not. If you are found out, there will be more public indignation and undermining of trust: you gave your word. People who believed you will be angry and disillusioned.

Those who reject utilitarianism, are wont to claim that there is a morally important distinction between what we ourselves do, and what we allow others to do (here, taking the term "allow" in a broad sense to cover what we do not resist where resistance is possible). They may hold that there are some (unjust) types of actions (e.g., lying, stealing, murder, rape) that we are strictly bound not ourselves to do, even if by doing them we aim to achieve some good end, but that we are not bound in the same way to prevent others from doing. It would, of course, yield rather odd consequences, if it were held that we are *equally* bound to prevent unjust actions as we are to avoid ourselves acting unjustly. The latter duty is one we can generally comply with while pursuing our aims: it only restricts the ways in which we pursue our aims, it imposes certain constraints. The former duty, though, is very unspecific and open-ended. If we are obliged to prevent injustice wherever opportunity arises, will not this duty swallow up any freedom to pursue other aims? Will it not take over our lives? We might rather allow that we *are* under a kind of duty to prevent others from acting unjustly, but understand this duty to be of a sort that allows us discretion over how and when we act on it. Those who have the right attitude to matters of justice, then, will be unequivocally committed not themselves to engage in unjust activities, and they will mind about injustice done by others, but they will not seize every opportunity to prevent injustice. On the other hand if they pass up every opportunity to stop others from acting unjustly, we may reasonably wonder whether they really do care.

All the same there may be several pragmatic and ethically respectable reasons for not taking action against, not actively opposing, certain unjust practices in a business context. Not all unjust practices are equally grave. There can be petty theft as there cannot be a petty murder or rape. You may agree to disagree over a practice yet hope that through building trust on the basis of business dealing, you may be better able to influence those with whom you deal toward more enlightened attitudes. You may discover that what at first seemed to be an unjust practice is not so after all.

The same principles may justify different practices in different circumstances. What is a fair wage or what are reasonable safety precautions, may vary from one country to another depending, for example, on the state of its economic development. On the other hand, the mere fact that your offering of wages or of safety protection compares favorably with what employees would get elsewhere in the host country does not of itself show that your wages are fair or your safety protection is reasonable. Tom Donaldson (1989. *The ethics of international business.* New York: Oxford University Press) suggests a test to apply to check whether you could be justified in offering lower standards of pay or safety in a host country from those that apply in your home country: you should ask whether you would consider the standards you propose to apply in the host country to be reasonable, if you were in their economic position. Donaldson contrasts variations of standards that can be justified simply in terms of the relative economic development from one country to another with variations that reflect real differences of ethical view. Nepotism and bribery, for example, cannot be explained simply in terms of different priorities relating to different economic levels. Between those who consider nepotism to be wrong and those who disagree there are different views regarding what we owe our kith and kin and what we owe society at large.

Donaldson maintains that it is not wrong to fall in with different standards in a host country that are not merely based on different levels of economic development if conforming is (i) necessary if one is to do business in that country and (ii) does not involve direct violation of a basic human right. Neither nepotism nor bribery, perhaps, would involve you in a direct violation of a basic human right—although, of course, we need some way of working out what rights are basic. Suppose it is proposed, though, to discharge toxic waste into a river that flows into the terrain of a despised neighboring people who are too poor to cause trouble. If there are any basic human rights, they surely include a right against having one's water supplies deliberately contaminated.

A more problematic case would be whether you could be justified in employing children in the host country. Is there a universal human right that children should have access to education and not have to work in order to survive? Is not this a right that must be subject to economic conditions? Are some countries too poor to provide such education—what they cannot do, they cannot be morally obliged to do? Would it, then, be exploitative for you to locate your factories in these countries to take advantage of the cheap labor? Let us here understand by "exploitation," not simply taking advantage of a situation but taking *unjust* advantage of a situation. If, given the poverty of a country there is nothing unjust in their allowing children to be employed, it is not unjust for you to employ them. All the same, given that you see child labor as a regrettable necessity we might expect that you will be supportive of efforts to improve the lot of the children you employ.

Compare the situation you might face if the country in which you set up your factory discriminates against a particular ethnic group. Members of this group have access to the lowliest of jobs only and are paid a pittance compared to other workers. Here Donaldson would ask: do you *have to* conform in order to do business? If you do conform, are you directly violating a basic human right? In this case you cannot excuse the low pay on the grounds that the country is relatively poor: because it is not poverty but contempt for the particular group that accounts for the low pay they get. Is discrimination against an ethnic group a violation of a basic human right? In order to answer such a question we would need to pursue further (as Donaldson does) what we

mean by basic human rights and how these might be grounded.

VII. FRAMEWORKS FOR BUSINESS ETHICS

Applied ethics has generally been understood to involve "applying" an ethical theory to the problems, issues, or difficult choices in a particular field—for example, medical, engineering, or business, that seem ethically problematic. Of course, we should bear in mind that we know many things about what is unethical practice without recourse to any thing that one might want to call a theory. Someone in business does not have to study business ethics, does not have to know anything about theories of ethics, to know that swindling is wrong. All the same, business people may regularly come up against problems where the question, "Is this option, practice or policy unethical?" is not so easily answered. We have to start somewhere and a natural starting point for applied ethics might seem to be just those situations where people of apparent good sense and good will disagree or are uncertain. Let us call such situations "ethically problematic."

We will find a choice, problem, or issue to be ethically problematic, then, just where it seems to us that even people who are sensible and well intentioned may be genuinely uncertain as to what course is ethically defensible in the circumstances. The same theory that helps us to answers where choice seems ethically problematic, should, of course, also explain why what we consider to be ethically unproblematic *is* so (and why what sometimes seems bad when looked at in a certain light, is uncontroversially all right nevertheless).

But philosophers are bound to feel a certain unease about this recourse to theory. If this is what applied ethics is about—applying ethical "theory," are not applied ethicists trading under false pretenses? Not only are there too many theories, rival candidates, from which to start, none of these theories is the sort of thing that can be plausibly applied. "Theory" in other fields, perhaps suggests a body of systematic (largely uncontroversial) knowledge. Not so in ethics. Here, by theory, is meant an account of morality—or, perhaps, just of a part of morality, for example, of moral obligation, which seeks to explain what it is and why it matters. No doubt the understanding in question may have a bearing on controversial issues in applied ethics. But that granted, it does not provide a ready-made model that can be taken over in this or that field by practitioners as the resource they need for resolving ethically problematic decisions.

Yet practitioners in medicine, engineering, or business only turn to philosophers in the expectation of practical guidance. Will philosophers, eager to have a purchase on public policy and discussion, not be tempted to oversimplify their theories, to make out that these do "apply," lest they be excluded altogether from the ongoing debate over the controversial ethical issues?

Whereas textbooks on business ethics in the 1970s tended to begin with a survey of the main ethical theories—at least, including utilitarian and Kantian theories, more recently, there has been a turning away from these stalwarts in favor of seemingly down-to-earth less abstract accounts of ethical responsibility in business, such as stakeholder theories and contractarian theories. These might be described as "bottom-up" rather than "top-down" approaches. Utilitarian or Kantian theories start with certain very broad principles that apply to all areas of human activity—including business. Stakeholder and contractarian theories are put forward simply to clarify the ethical responsibilities of people in business starting not from broad principles but from the obligations that seem to be implicit in business transactions. Thus, the proponents of stakeholder analysis take off from their understanding of what are the fiduciary obligations of the various "players" in business. The proponents of contractarian theories in business ethics, take off from their understanding that the paradigm of obligation in business dealing is contractual.

People in business are more at home with these approaches. They can engage in debate at the level of intermediate judgments that maybe feel more solid and familiar than the foundation principles appealed to by utilitarians or Kantians. And even if these intermediate principles themselves have their foundation in this or that philosophical theory, might the tracing to foundations not be left to the philosopher theorists and be ignored by business practitioners wanting help with their problems? In debate over controversial moral issues, people do not in fact seem to make headway by appeal to very general theories of ethics any more than those who are struggling to solve a problem in mathematics go back to studying metaphysical questions about the nature of numbers. Indeed, we may feel more secure in our understanding of the intermediate principles than we are in the foundations—more inclined to trust our judgment at the intermediate level than at more abstract levels. But does either of these approaches provide a reasonably reliable and intelligible guide to ethically sound decision making in business? Let us consider each in turn.

VIII. STAKEHOLDER THEORY

One of the most favored theories in business ethics has been stakeholder theory. (Like so much of business ethics, those who proffer this theory tend to assume a management ethics standpoint. So what is put forward as a theory of business ethics, strictly speaking, is a theory of management ethics.) Ethically responsible management, it is said, involves attention to the interests of all who have a stake in the business. Thus, for example, it would not be sufficient for managers to consider only the interests of the shareholders on whose behalf they manage an enterprise.

This line of thought obviously throws up some problems. For example, just who does have a stake in a business? R. Edward Freeman (1984. *Strategic management: A stakeholder approach,* p. 46. Boston: Pitman) offers this definition of a stakeholder: "A stakeholder of an organisation is (by definition) any group or individual who can affect or is affected by the achievement of the organisation's objectives."

Now this is a very expansive definition. It embraces a firm's employees, customers and suppliers. But does it not also embrace its rivals? Indeed, by this definition as Bruce Langtry (1994. Stakeholders and the moral responsibilities of business. *Business Ethics Quarterly,* Vol. 4, p. 432) argues, just about everyone turns out to be a stakeholder in just about every business: "For, example, you do not buy your groceries at the store on the corner of Separation Street and St. George's Road in Northcote, Melbourne; your not doing so affects the achievement of the store's purpose; therefore you are a stakeholder in that corner store."

Besides the question as to who are the stakeholders, there is the question of how the various stakeholders' interests are to be taken account of. Is the idea that each stakeholder has certain rights and these must be respected? Or is the idea that the interests of all stakeholders are supposed to be aggregated so as to achieve maximum satisfaction of their preferences? If just about everyone is a stakeholder and a business has to take into account and maximize the interests of all, does the theory turn out to be a version of utilitarianism?

The stakeholder theory is put forward as a corrective to the idea that a firm only has obligations to advance the owners' interests—the interests of those who hold shares. Of course, given that other parties (suppliers, customers, employees) affect the achievement of a firm's objectives, even if it is correct to say that the primary ethical obligation of management is to advance the owners' interests, managers need to "respect" the expectations of these other parties or stakeholders. Kenneth Goodpaster (1991. Business ethics and stakeholder analysis. *Business Ethics Quarterly,* Vol. 1, p. 58) describes this interpretation of the firm's obligation to other stakeholders as a "strategic" interpretation: you respect these other interests as you "respect" the weather "as a set of forces to be reckoned with."

Now from a strategic standpoint it does make sense to extend the parties whose interests managers may need to take notice of beyond the obvious ones who have a stake in their business to everyone who affects or is affected by the business. Freeman, who offers the expansive definition of stakeholders, is clearly thinking in this strategic spirit about what managers need to do. Thus, he observes that a business might need to include as one of its "stakeholders," the local Mafia. Such a group might, after all, affect the business—sabotage its operations, threaten its employees. But stakeholders so defined are not as such *entitled* to consideration. They are not defined as those who have a *claim* on the business.

Thus, this Freeman version of stakeholder theory may be understood simply as a corrective to a myopic attitude of managers who ignore the external environment into which a business has to 'fit' in order to thrive these days. The myopic view, it will be said, is locked on to obvious stakeholders—the shareholders, the customers, the suppliers, the employees.

From this strategic standpoint, how should you weigh up the various competing interests of your stakeholders? Freeman emphasises the need for a business to define its purposes. In the light of these it is then possible to identify which stakeholders are critical to a firm's long-term success. Evidently, from this strategic perspective, some stakeholders' interests can be discounted. Suppose, for example, you are debating whether to build a filter into the chimney of your factory to minimize pollution. Suppose that on investigation, it turns out that no significant damage will be done locally. The wind will blow the pollutants over the border into a neighboring country. But perhaps the people who live there, who will be harmed, have no influence or power. They belong to a minority faction in their own country and their own government pays no attention to their problems. Likewise, suppose that no activist group is going to "make waves" in your own company in defense of the people over the border. Strategically, they may be discounted. But ethically?

Goodpaster outlines as an alternative interpretation of stakeholder theory, what he calls, a multifiduciary approach according to which the claims of all stakeholders are equally important. Those who adopt this approach will want to narrow the definition of stakeholders to those toward whom a business has some obligation. There is no fiduciary obligation to a terrorist group that poses a threat to your business. The multifiduciary view, though, may be seen as a *corrective* to a myopic view on the part of managers concerning their duties. This version of stakeholder theory basically extends the list of those to whom a business is morally accountable. Some of those who advocate this approach may talk rather vaguely about balancing the interests of the various stakeholders. Some may stipulate that all stakeholders' interests are "equally important." Goodpaster, though, insists that shareholders have a special claim, qua owners. They are not just one group of stakeholders on a level with others. It surely makes a difference that one is contractually bound to some stakeholders as one is not to others. Thus, Goodpaster argues, the multifiduciary view is untenable.

All the same, Goodpaster does maintain that a firm has moral obligations to other stakeholders that are not merely strategic, not merely derived from the obligation to shareholders. Goodpaster argues that these (nonfiduciary) obligations are just those that everyone owes in their dealings with one another—for example, the obligations not to steal, lie, cheat, or coerce. This position accords with the Sternberg view: ethically responsible management is not a question of *balancing* the interests of stakeholders. The duty of management is to advance the interests of shareholders—seeking to maximize long-term owner value. Sternberg maintains that enlightened management will be attentive to other stakeholders for what Goodpaster calls strategic reasons. She further contends that a business in pursuing the interests of shareholders is "not exempt from ordinary morality": it should always act within the side constraints of respect for distributive justice and ordinary decency. Her account of the latter seems to cover pretty much the same area as Goodpaster has in mind when he speaks of the "basic obligations" from which no agent has "moral immunity."

How then would Sternberg advise concerning the example above of a business considering whether to build a chimney to minimize pollution where those affected are over the border and have no political clout? Let us suppose that the business in question is a strictly commercial organization. In that case, applying the Sternberg understanding of what the aim of such a business is, it would seem that building a chimney might well not be defensible—it might be very costly and the business's reputation would not be endangered given the circumstances. In the Sternberg view, after all, it is the manager's duty to *maximize* the long-term owner value. Of course, the maximizing must not be at the expense of distributive justice or ordinary decency. But even taking on board these side constraints, it is not obvious that a business need always worry about the effect its operations are having on those who have no power or influence.

Sternberg observes about selling "seriously unsafe" products in the Third World that it would be "wrong, and counterproductive, to sell them in *any* market" (p. 89). But according to her theory it would only be wrong *if* counterproductive *or* a violation of distributive justice or ordinary decency—or illegal. Her examples of how wrongdoing *can* be counterproductive seem to rely on an assumption that wrongdoing is so typically counterproductive that a business is foolish, hence irresponsible, to risk it. Is that a safe assumption? Notice how the caution that acting wrongly may be counterproductive relies on public opinion. While public opinion may mobilize against a business and even a minority section of opinion may mobilize and make problems for a business, there is no ground for assuming that public opinion is always on the side of the angels. It is so easy for those who discuss business ethics to blur the distinction between acting in ways perceived to be unethical (bad for business *these* days) and acting in ways that are in fact unethical (but not seen to be so in one's society). Sternberg surmises that even if a business might get away with acting wrongly in the short term, public opinion will catch up. I think that we should not assume that public opinion is destined to become steadily more enlightened.

IX. CONTRACTARIAN THEORY

As we have seen, the stakeholder approach does not help us to resolve ethically problematic issues or choices in business management unless it is supplemented with some explanation of how managers should weigh up the competing interests of all the stakeholders. One way to gain insights on this and other questions in business ethics might be to borrow from political philosophy the notion of a hypothetical contract.

The notion of a hypothetical contract has been much used in political philosophy in an attempt to clarify the rights and duties of people in a society. Any society needs rules. Rules, to have moral force, need to be fair and reasonable. But how can we work out what rules are fair and reasonable—and whether the rules we happen to live under are so? The idea of a hypothetical contract is invoked to capture the thought that if those who made the rules were to do so from behind a "veil of ignorance," not knowing what position in society they were going to occupy, the rules they would agree to would be just. We can then imagine ourselves behind such a veil engaged in working out the rules. Having done this, we would then be in a position, it is supposed, to be able to review the rules to which we actually are expected to conform. If these do not square with those we would have chosen from behind the veil, that shows that our actual rules are not just.

But even if it is true that whatever rules would be agreed behind the veil would be compatible with justice, it does not follow that if some of our actual rules are inconsistent with those, these rules must be unjust. Behind the veil we might reasonably agree that there should be no *unnecessary* rules—no limitations of individual liberty but those required by justice. In real life, we may observe a variety of customs that inhibit our liberty. These are not merely on that account unjust. Consider, for example, a society that as a matter of custom (the reasons for which have long since been forgotten) observes a holiday on the 1st of May. This holiday will restrict your liberty in running your business. But such an arrangement is not unjust. In any society and in any long-established organization there are very many customs the point of which may be obscure but the observance of which is not necessarily unjust. The school I attended as a child had two entrances: one for boys, another for girls. We observed the rule, even though once inside the building we were not separated. The firm that you join may have a separate canteen for men and for women—both perhaps served from the same kitchen. If you ask, "Why the separation?" there may be no more to tell than that it is the tradition. The tradition might be stopped—it might fall out of favor, or prove uneconomic. But it is not necessarily unjust to maintain it.

We would be able to work out rules behind the veil because we already have some understanding of justice and of the need for rules against certain kinds of behavior. Behind the veil we would prohibit swindling. But we do not need to go behind the veil to discover that swindling is wrong. Does going behind the veil help us to resolve the ethically problematic questions in business ethics? Consider, for example, the current debate in Britain regarding the Social Chapter legislation of the European Community. On the one hand it is argued that the measures included in the Social Chapter are simply securing what are thought to be employee's rights—the right to a minimum wage, for example. On the other hand, it is argued that if such rights are established, the economy will be rendered less efficient and less competitive. Suppose we go behind the veil to try and settle the issue. Would we rule that employees have a right to a minimum wage? Would not the answer depend on whether "we" happen to be adventurous or cautious characters? It is like choosing between a safe investment with a low return and a risky investment with a high return. Being impartial (as we would be behind the veil) and understanding the alternatives does not dictate one choice rather than the other.

To be sure, much of business involves the making and keeping of contract and there are many important questions for business ethics regarding the morality of contract. For example, there are the well-known issues concerning consent—such as how informed and how free from duress contracts must be to be binding. There are the questions relating to implicit consent—such as whether acquiescence signifies consent. But this area of business ethics has to do with actual contracts, explicit or implicit, not with hypothetical contracts.

X. NEO-ARISTOTELIAN VIRTUES-BASED THEORY

There has, in the last few decades, been a revival of interest in Aristotle's writing on ethics and this has eventually had its effect on our subject.

Aristotle has little, if anything, to say about notions of consent, respect, or duty. He does not suppose we have a duty to maximize happiness or anything else. Rather, he supposes that the way to make our lives go well is to acquire certain character traits—moral virtues: these equip us for choosing well and acting well with a view to living a full human life. Courage, for example, is one such virtue. Whoever you are and whatever your circumstances, whatever society you are a member of, you need this character trait: you need to be able and ready intelligently to face dangers. The connection between having a virtue and being well positioned for living a full human life, is easier to make out in relation to some virtues than others. It sounds reasonable enough in respect of what we might call "the enabling virtues"—like courage. These traits are *strengths* of character. Whatever your aims or interests in life, you are able to act more effectively if you have control over fear. Similarly, prudence is one of these enabling virtues—enabling you to pursue your aims more effectively, whatever your aims.

But it is not quite so obvious that being honest and fair is enabling. If honesty and fairness are virtues (or aspects of a virtue—of justice) then the connection between having these traits and being well positioned for living a full human life needs some explaining—as Plato points up in the *Republic* with the story about Gyges and the ring. Assuming that it is possible to give a credible account of those traits of character that we consider to be moral virtues, justice included, might this account provide an alternative background for business ethics that could be adapted to the role of a decision-making tool?

It is, perhaps, doubtful whether this approach will prove useful to those who are grappling with ethically problematic choices in a business context. Aristotle gives an account of each virtue that describes in a general way what kind of behavior is consistent or inconsistent with exercising the virtue. But each virtue involves the use of judgment. Showing courage, for example, involves having sound judgment about what dangers one needs to face. Of course, sometimes it is obvious that a danger needs to be faced. But those choices that we find ethically problematic are just those where what is needed is not obvious to us and judgment is needed. There is in these situations no tool, no ethical grid or code, that can take the place of using judgment applied to the case in hand.

Robert C. Solomon (1992. *Ethics and excellence*. New York: Oxford University Press) approaches business ethics as a neo-Aristotelian. But he does not suggest that this approach provides a tool for decision making. He does, though, claim that understanding of virtues is helpful in other ways that bear on the issues and concerns of interest in business ethics. Thus, an understanding of the moral virtues helps us to see through the false and common assumptions that have led many theorists, especially in economics, to assume that rational choice is naturally self-interested. An understanding of the moral virtues may also be a corrective to certain misleading metaphors that circulate in business and contribute to its tainted image—business represented as a game or a war or a jungle.

On the other hand, might this approach not suggest to us that business (or a particular type of business) is inherently unethical? Suppose, for example, that honesty is a virtue. Moral virtues, on the Aristotelian account are *pervasively* relevant. Courage, for example, is not just a soldierly virtue. You need courage at school, facing up to school bullies; at work, standing up for your rights and those of your mates, in the board room, breaking bad and unwelcome news.

Likewise, if honesty is a moral virtue, it is necessary and appropriate to be honest in every role or activity that is ethically defensible. Thus, if being a policeman necessitates being dishonest, then either honesty is not after all a moral virtue or being a policeman is unethical. We might here want to refine our understanding of what having a virtue involves and what kind of activities belie having it. Is a police detective automatically dishonest because he does undercover work?

Solomon claims that honesty is not just compatible with doing well in business, it is "the first virtue of business life" (1992, p. 210). Is this a reasonable thought? Why wouldn't prudence be the master virtue? Or indeed courage? Honesty seems to take pride of place because ethics, not just business ethics, has come to seem a matter of respecting rights. But Aristotelian ethics is much broader than this. However, there is something to be said for honesty, or better, the justice of "rendering to each his due," as the central virtue. In a sense justice comes first. It is the framework in which one can be free, in business as in life—and the matter is especially important in connection with business, where one acts within a contractual network.

In any case, much needs to be done to explain what honesty involves. It is important to distinguish, for example, honesty from openness. It is surely often necessary and obligatory in business to keep secrets. The honest businessperson need not be indiscreet and may deliberately not disclose certain information that others would dearly like to know. What, then, about haggling or bluffing: are these activities that honest people will engage in? Perhaps there are at least certain situations where they will—as where such behavior is expected and accepted (consented to)—as it is in games of bluff.

But there will be other kinds of situations where it is not so easy to say what is consistent with being an honest person. Suppose that your employee comes to you for advice: he is about to take out a mortgage but seeks reassurance as he has heard a rumor that the firm is about to announce redundancies of all employees over age 55. "Is it true?" Suppose you have been told that this is to happen but you have been told in strictest confidence. If you are honest what should you say? Is it dishonest to prevaricate? Are there some situations in which other ethical requirements override the duty to be honest? Is this one?

Generosity might seem to be a virtue. But is it out of place in business? Any business? Is it ungenerous of a chief executive in a business to refuse to give money to a worthy cause? Does it not make all the difference whose money he is thinking of giving? His own money is one thing. The company money quite another. Thus, we may note that what being generous or loyal or honest requires depends in part on the context. What you owe your brother in loyalty may be quite different from what you owe a colleague or fellow member of your college.

Solomon emphasises the importance of judgment—and that this can require a sensitivity to the context, the particular circumstances. If he is right, those who handle ethical problems or dilemmas in business well will have and show judgment. But judgment is not itself a tool. Rather, if there is a tool for making decisions that are ethically sound, one needs judgment to use it well.

XI. CONCLUSION

Anyone working in the field of business ethics has to put up with continuing banter over the alleged impossibility of combining business and ethically defensible practice and policy. Contemporary discussions in business ethics, though, tend to take off from the assumption that business activity is not as such unethical. But we should not become complacent about the foundational issues raised by the radical critiques: the concerns about usury—something that disturbed Aristotle and has worried Christians, Jews, and Muslims; the concern about profiting from other people's labor; the concerns about the legitimacy of property.

Why has trade as such been thought to be unethical, or at any rate, suspect? The very essence of trade—trade for profit, it may be said, is that you buy something at a lower price than you mean to sell it. And if you are *merely* trading, what value are *you* adding to justify putting up the price? Either you are cheating the party from whom you buy who deserved more, a better price, or you are cheating the party to whom you sell, who deserved to get the goods for less. Of course, it is quite possible that you are cheating *both*. Anyway, it looks as if what you are doing is disreputable.

But, of course, it may not be true of most traders that they do nothing but buy and sell. The trader may preserve the goods bought: storage has its cost. The trader relieves one party who wants rid of a good at a certain time and keeps it in readiness for the buyer who comes to want that good at a later time. We all generally benefit from the service of traders: they facilitate the exchange of goods. There is also perhaps a false assumption behind the thought that buying at one price and selling at another is corrupt: the idea that there is the right price for each item—its real value. In fact the value of a thing may fluctuate, depending on external circumstances—fashion, for example, or the weather. Who wants ice drinks in winter (English winter, anyway)?

The radical critiques of business may be mistaken but insights may be gained through studying them— insights that may be helpful in regard to the ethically problematic questions concerning specific business practices or policies. Underlying many of these questions are conflicting views about what is fair and as to whether what is undeserved benefit or loss is unjust or simply good or bad luck. Is it unfair if Esso, Shell, and BP crowd out small independent garages by selling their gasoline below cost? Is it unfair if a firm installs covert surveillance cameras to counter petty pilfering by its staff—or is it only unfair if it does so without telling them?

There is a growing interest in this subject among people who are in business and who seek for a better understanding of the ethically problematic issues and problems that they regularly encounter in their work. Naturally, those seeking practical help look for procedures or techniques that they can apply. But if philosophy does not deliver on this front, we should not suppose that this is the only kind of help that should be looked for from it.

The fashionableness of business ethics is, of course, partly a reflection of the public interest in putting a stop to unethical business. While this interest may be good news for academics promoting the subject, it may not be altogether good news for business. The various pressures on business to be "ethical"—such as consumer boycotts, ethical shopping, and ethical investments may be largely counterproductive. Maybe, if the public always gets it right, we need not worry. If, though, public opinion is a dodgy basis for moral judgment, it is bad news for business if it comes increasingly under pressure to undergo ethical audits where the measure of what is ethical is simply whatever attitudes happen to prevail.

Also See the Following Articles

ETHICS AND SOCIAL SERVICES, OVERVIEW • SOCIAL ETHICS, OVERVIEW

Bibliography

Business Ethics Quarterly (1995). Volume 5, Issue 2 focuses on contractarian approaches in business ethics.

Coope, C. M. (1994). Justice and jobs: Three sceptical thoughts about rights in employment. *Journal of Applied Philosophy,* **11**, 71–77.

Donaldson, T. (1996). Values in tension. *Harvard Business Review,* 74(5), 48–62.

Ewin, R. E. (1995). The virtues appropriate to business. *Business Ethics Quarterly* 5, 833–842.

Jackson, J. (1996). *An introduction to business ethics.* Oxford: Blackwell.

Shaw, W. H. (1996). Business ethics today: A Survey. *Journal of Business Ethics,* **15**, 489–500.

CAPITAL PUNISHMENT

Hugo Adam Bedau
Tufts University

GLOSSARY

deterrence A punishment deters a would-be offender from committing a given offense if he or she is frightened from committing it by the thought of unpleasant consequences (being caught and punished). **Special deterrence** is the deterrent effect on a given offender created by the experience of having been punished. **General deterrence** is the deterrent effect on persons generally by the thought of their liability to punishment.

egalitarian A person who defends equality of treatment of persons as of paramount value.

equability A punishment is equable to the extent that it can be increased or decreased (as fines and imprisonment can) according to the relative gravity of the offense.

frugality A punishment is frugal to the extent that the pleasure law-abiding citizens receive from seeing it inflicted does not exceed the pain caused in the offender.

incapacitation A punishment incapacitates a would-be offender from committing a given offense if physical constraints (leg irons, imprisonment, drugs) make it physically impossible for him to commit the crime.

lex talionis The principle of making the punishment fit the crime by imitating the crime, as in "an eye for an eye, a life for a life."

marginal deterrence Of two punishments A and B, A is a marginally better deterrent than B if there are fewer criminal acts in which persons risk A than there are criminal acts in which persons risk B.

principle of utility The principle of choosing the course of action among the feasible alternatives that probably will yield the greatest net balance of good over bad consequences for the society as a whole.

profitability A punishment is profitable to the extent that as one undergoes it one also produces social benefits, e.g., by productive labor in prison.

recidivist An offender who, having already been convicted and punished for criminal acts, nonetheless commits further crimes. Thus **recidivism** is a measure of the failure of deterrence, incapacitation, and reform in a given offender's history.

remissibility A punishment is remissible to the extent that its wrongful infliction can be corrected and compensated.

retribution A punishment is imposed on retributive grounds if it is believed to be deserved (given the offender's intention and the harm caused by the offense), and its severity is proportional to the gravity of the crime.

revenge A motive out of which one acts, in retaliation for a hurt (whether deserved or not) suffered by oneself or another, without regard to limiting the quality or severity of the retaliatory act.

CAPITAL PUNISHMENT (the practice of putting offenders to death under the authority of law as punishment for their crimes) raises a wide variety of questions. Some are *empirical*; e.g., how frequently are innocent persons sentenced to death and executed? Is the death penalty a better deterrent than long-term imprisonment? Others are *legal*; e.g., what are the appropriate limits to the right of appeal by a prisoner under death sentence? What criteria should be used to assist the trial court in deciding whether to sentence a convicted offender in a capital case to death or to imprisonment? Some of the legal questions raise *constitutional* issues; e.g., does the prohibition against "cruel and unusual punishments" in the eighth amendment to the United States Constitution, if properly interpreted, forbid the death penalty? If the death penalty was acceptable to the framers and ratifiers of the Constitution, must it be constitutionally acceptable today? Still other questions are essentially *political*; e.g., should a chief executive opposed to the death penalty grant commutation of a death sentence in the face of public agitation for the prisoner's execution? Is a nominee's position on the death penalty a legitimate consideration in evaluating his or her fitness for judicial office? Some questions are *conceptual*; e.g., is there any difference between favoring the death penalty as revenge versus favoring it as retribution? Can the death penalty be said to have had a deterrent effect on those who have been executed? Lastly, there are important *normative* questions; e.g., does acknowledgment of a universal right to life invalidate the death penalty? Do the relevant moral principles in conjunction with the relevant empirical facts favor abolition or retention of the death penalty?

A fully comprehensive evaluation of the death penalty must eventually address all these kinds of questions. But philosophers may be excused if they focus their attention on the normative questions, because it is precisely these questions that lawyers, criminologists, historians, politicians, and others are most likely to ignore or dispose of superficially. Utilitarian and other consequentialist thinkers, however, must try to answer various of the empirical questions, too, because depending on what the actual facts turn out to be regarding the impact of the death penalty on the crime rate, the risk of executing the innocent, etc., their principles will require them either to favor or to oppose it. In these respects, debating the death penalty is no different from debating the merits of punishment in general or of any other particular form of punishment.

What marks the death penalty for special interest is, of course, its effect on the offender and its symbolic significance as the ultimate exercise of legitimate state power over the lives of individual citizens. Punishments of lesser severity and finality (imprisonment, fines) generally do not grip the imagination as the death penalty does. It also arouses considerable controversy despite its relative rarity. (Thus, in the United States during 1955, around a million persons were being punished in jails and prisons, of whom 3000 were under death sentence and 56 actually executed.) Historically, of course, the death penalty along with other corporal punishments (e.g., mutilation, branding) was commonly used in all nations and societies for a wide variety of crimes. Today, however, corporal punishments have generally been abolished throughout the western world, and the death penalty—repealed in all of Europe and under intense criticism in the United States despite its popularity (public opinion polls report roughly 75% or more favoring it for some cases of murder)—remains the major exception to the practice that punishments should be confined to incarceration, fines, and community service.

The principal interest among philosophers is to decide whether and under what conditions, if any, use of the death penalty is morally justified. The context for argument over its justification can take either of two forms: the appropriateness of the death penalty in a relatively ideal society (not so ideal that no felonies whatever occur, but ideal to the extent that the innocent are never punished, class and racial bias play no role in punishing the guilty, due process of law is scrupulously observed, etc.), or the appropriateness of the death penalty in some actual society, e.g., Great Britain in 1800 or the United States in 2000.

Whatever conclusion one reaches about the merits of the death penalty by focusing the discussion on an ideal society, the objection is likely to be raised that the conclusion has little relevance to the actual world in which actual people are (or might be) punished with death: Reasonable people do not try to deduce a society's decision for or against the death penalty from nothing more than such an abstract argument. Conversely, if the focus is on some actual society, warts and all, the objection will be heard that too much weight is being placed on particular details of fact, any or all of which could in principle be different, with the result that only a contingent, political (and to that extent, unprincipled) conclusion on the justification of the death penalty can be reached.

I. RELIGIOUS VS. SECULAR ARGUMENT

Popular argument over the death penalty, today as in centuries past, often relies on attempting to settle the question by reliance on Holy Writ. (The history of Christian thought on this matter is the subject of a 1997 book by James J. McGivern, *The Death Penalty Appraised: A Chronology of Christian Loss and Retrieval.* Paulist Press, Mahwah, NJ.) A cautious onlooker to the debate might wonder whether the Bible was being used only to support a moral conviction already arrived at on other (unacknowledged) grounds. Thus, Jews and Christians favoring the death penalty have often pointed to the many capital crimes endorsed in the Old Testament, and have rested much weight on the biblical passage in which God declares to Noah, "Whosoever sheddeth man's blood by man shall his blood be shed" (Genesis 9:6—the origin, incidentally, of the Mormon belief that the death penalty ought to be carried out by a firing squad, as the law in Utah required for a century). During the mid-19th century, Protestant clergy debated whether this passage was an imperative (directing civil societies to execute murderers) or a prediction (human societies are likely to punish murderers with death if they can).

However that is to be resolved (probably in favor of the imperative interpretation), opponents of the death penalty would point to other passages in the Bible, notably to the use of exile rather than death as the punishment decreed by God for Cain, the first murderer (Genesis 4:10–16). Christians particularly have often cited Jesus's defense of the woman taken in adultery, in which he invites those "without sin among you" to cast the first stone, implying that since none present is without sin, she must not be stoned, even though Mosaic law required death by stoning for adultery (John 8:3–7; what punishment, if any, she did deserve goes unmentioned).

Modern interpreters of the Bible, searching for a sound religious basis for modern-day use or repeal of the death penalty, do not rest their case on this or that biblical passage torn out of context in the manner suggested above. Rather, as is shown by the extensive and sophisticated discussion by two contemporary Christian theologians, H. Wayne House and John Howard Yoder in their 1991 book, *The Death Penalty Debate* (Word Publishing, Dallas, TX), it is necessary to take a more comprehensive view of the biblical portrait of human nature, human society, and God's will for mankind. Even then, however, reasonable interpreters attempting to take into account all the relevant evidence will have to agree—as House and Yoder do—to disagree.

Secular philosophy has little to learn from the Jewish or Christian debate over the death penalty (or from the Muslim position, which invokes Sharia law derived from the Koran to support the death penalty in Islamic societies), insofar as the debate within these religious communities rests on appeal to beliefs that only their devotees can embrace. However uncertain or controversial the moral principles are on which secular thought relies, acceptance and employment of these principles at least does not rest on an act of faith, a tradition of worship, or belief in any transcendent being(s).

These principles may be divided roughly into three groups: principles of abstract justice, such as the right to life and retributive justice; consequentialist principles, notably versions of utilitarianism; and mixed normative theories that combine features of abstract right with considerations of consequences.

II. THE RIGHT TO LIFE

For several hundred years, at least from the philosophical writings of John Locke (1690) to the Universal Declaration of Human Rights (1948) and beyond, Western thinkers have claimed that all persons have a "natural" or a "human" right to life. (Whether this is but a secular echo of or a surrogate for the biblical "sanctity of life" we need not decide here.) In recent years, especially in the context of international human rights law, statesmen and others have appealed to this right in order to invalidate laws and practices involving the death penalty, as William A. Schabas has shown in his 1993 book, *The Abolition of the Death Penalty in International Law* (Grotius, Cambridge, UK).

Philosophy, however, is bound to raise some difficulties with this approach. First, it is probably impossible to defend the right to life as an *absolute* right, in the sense that any failure to respect this right amounts to acting in a morally reprehensible manner. The right to life has never been understood to protect an unjust aggressor from being killed by his intended victim acting in self-defense and as a last resort. Most philosophers today would think the right to life does not even protect an innocent party to aggression (e.g., a baby as a hostage tied to the front of a tank about to crush a helpless and faultless victim whose only defense is to fire a tank-destroying cannon). Nor does this right imply any duty to give life-giving support to another without one's voluntary consent (as is shown in Judith Thomson's example of the dying violinist whose friends give him life support from the kidneys of a kidnapped donor).

If, as these examples show, the right to life is not absolute, then it is best understood either as a presumption, to the effect that no one may take another's life without adequate reason, or as a way of establishing the burden of persuasion on anyone who would intentionally kill another person. On either interpretation, further argument is required to decide whether there are adequate reasons for the death penalty—and so it would beg the question to appeal to the right to life to try to settle the controversy.

Second, it is quite possible to believe both that all persons have a natural or human right to life and that the death penalty is morally appropriate in certain cases. This was the position of John Locke in his *Second Treatise of Civil Government.* He insisted that although this right is natural and inalienable, it can be "forfeited"—and it is forfeited by anyone who commits a crime that "deserves" to be punished by death. However, Locke's criterion for when one forfeits one's life is quite vague, and in any case the doctrine of forfeiture is more dubious than the claim that lethal force can be justified in self-defense. Nevertheless, opponents of the death penalty cannot dismiss the idea of forfeiture for no better reason than the inconvenience it presents to them. Either the doctrine of forfeiture has to be uprooted from the theory of human rights on general grounds (unclear though it may be how that is to be done), or abolitionists must show either that (a) murderers do not forfeit their lives, because they do not deserve to die, or that (b) even though they do forfeit their lives, such forfeiture by itself does not authorize anyone to put them to death.

III. RETRIBUTIVE JUSTIFICATIONS

No doubt the strongest arguments for the death penalty rest on considerations of retribution. Retributivist thinking is more abstract and thus free from contingent facts regarding this or that society, varying crime rates, etc., all of which burden utilitarian thinking and tend to make it inconclusive.

A. Kantian Retribution

Retributive purposes and justifications of punishment take many different forms. Perhaps the best known, if not the most influential today, is Kant's in his *Metaphysical Elements of Justice* (1797). Murderers must die, he insists, because otherwise "there is no equality between the crime and the retribution." And Kant makes it clear that by "retribution" he means *lex talionis,* making the punishment fit the crime by imitating it. Although he does not say it in so many words, he holds that murderers *deserve* the death penalty; the offender deserves to suffer whatever harm he has caused the victim to suffer ("Any undeserved evil that you inflict on someone else . . . is one that you do to yourself").

Kant's retributivism, like other versions of the doctrine, places little or no emphasis on using punishments in social defense or on choosing between more and less severe punishments on grounds of their greater or lesser effectiveness in reducing crime. Nor does Kant worry about whether murderers can typically be said to have acted autonomously, so that their decisions to kill can be treated as the decisions of wholly rational agents. It is difficult to resist the conclusion that although Kant's theory tells us how to punish fairly the crime of murder in an ideal world, it tells us very little about what to do in the real world.

B. *Lex talionis*

The gravest problem for Kant's retributive theory lies in his embrace of *lex talionis.* However plausible it may be to punish murder with death, it is not plausible to punish rape with rape, torture with torture, arson with arson, etc., as Kant's contemporary, the English jurist Sir William Blackstone, pointed out in his *Commentaries on the Law of England* (1765–1770). Indeed, *lex talionis* taken strictly is extremely implausible as the principle on which to apportion punishments to crimes because it is incoherent for the vast majority of crimes.

One may reply that nonetheless it is strongly recommended for those kinds of cases where it is coherent, and death for murderers surely is the leading case. But it is not clear how one is to rebut the objection that as a principle *lex talionis* is woefully narrow in plausible application and wildly absurd or impossible in most cases, and that those who invoke it rely on it simply because it yields the result they want.

C. Proportionality

Because of the awkward consequences of relying on *lex talionis,* retributivists have preferred to rely on a principle of proportionality, according to which the relative gravity of crimes is to be matched with the relative severity of punishments. Typically, this strategy would require the crime of murder (assuming it to be the gravest crime) to be punished with the severest punishment. From this it does not follow, however, that the death penalty need be used at all. Retributive proportionality need not employ any corporal punishments; instead, the entire penalty schedule could consist of sentences to imprisonment of varying duration and deprivation.

Retributivist defenders of the death penalty object that refusing to punish murder with death fails to accord due respect and proper regard for the value of innocent life taken in murder. Without the death penalty, murder becomes just another crime only slightly worse than assault, robbery, or rape, when it is of incomparably graver nature. It is unclear how conclusive this objection is, since it seems to rest on an intuition that some will find baffling: Deliberately killing murderers is the best way to show respect for the innocent victim.

D. Other Problems

The history of the death penalty shows that it has been judged appropriate for a wide variety of crimes against the person, property, and the state. From a retributive point of view, however, it is difficult to see how the death penalty can be justified for any crime other than murder. Surely rape, robbery, arson, espionage, treason, and so on cannot be punished with death (as they have been in this century) on retributive grounds. Society has, in other words, rarely if ever contented itself with a purely retributive rationale for the death penalty; defenders of the death penalty have invoked retribution where it suits their purposes, but have not hesitated to rely on claims of superior marginal deterrence and incapacitation where they alone provide the needed result.

Even where criminal homicide itself is concerned, however, the retributivist faces unsolved difficulties. Does the retributivist propose to do away with the distinction between murder and manslaughter, i.e., between intentional and unintentional homicide? The harm done in either case is the same. Does the retributivist propose to accept or reject the legal distinction between first- and second-degree murder, i.e., between willful, deliberate, and premeditated killing and all other intentional killing? How does the retributivist propose to deal with the difference between a murderer who kills 1 victim and another murderer who kills 2

or 10? Or is the number of victims irrelevant to what the murderer deserves?

What these questions show is that a retributivist must make a variety of compromises to give practical effect to the retributivist principle. Since these compromises undermine the purity of the principle as applied, it remains obscure why one should attach preeminent status to the principle in the first place.

E. Desert

Trying to take the concept of desert seriously, as retributivism claims to do, is extremely difficult in practice, even if not also in theory. A purely *legalistic* interpretation of desert (convicted offenders deserve as their punishment whatever the law provides) poses no problems of application, but it is wholly relativistic in outcome: What prisoner X deserves today as a result of being convicted of crime C may be totally at variance with what prisoner Y deserves tomorrow (or would deserve in a contiguous jurisdiction had he been convicted there today). A *moralistic* interpretation of desert is no doubt to be preferred, but it is extremely difficult to decide in actual cases what this or that offender deserves, morally speaking. It is even unclear just what are the appropriate criteria for moral desert. No doubt guilty offenders (whether convicted or not) deserve to be punished, but what punishment they deserve—the heart of the matter where the death penalty is concerned—remains elusive.

Could a retributivist oppose the death penalty? Some have—at least they claim to be retributivist opponents of executions. They seize the issue of desert and turn it inside out, arguing that in an unjust society (all societies are relatively unjust), it is impossible to mete out punishments according to offenders' moral desert. The result (they argue) is that if you take desert seriously, you will have to oppose singling out some offenders for the irrevocable punishment of death in the spurious belief that they deserve it and that other offenders do not.

F. Conclusion

Finally, it should be noted that actual behavior shows how weak the grip of a consistent retributivism is on those who must deal with the death penalty—prosecutors, capital trial jurors, legislators, and clemency authorities especially. Persons occupying these offices show by their actual conduct that they pick and choose among murder cases, and among accused and convicted murderers, which are the ones who will get the death penalty and which will not. As there is at best little consistency from jurisdiction to jurisdiction and from case to case in the application of retributive thinking, such selectivity constantly risks being arbitrary and unprincipled. These inconsistencies may not point to any flaw in retributivism, but they do warn against overconfidence in thinking one can rely on putative retributivism in the real world of criminal justice.

IV. UTILITARIAN JUSTIFICATIONS

A. Early Utilitarians

The essence of the classic utilitarian argument over the death penalty is deciding whether the misery suffered by the condemned man (anticipating his death, followed by actually dying) and his loved ones (if any) outweighs or is outweighed by the benefits through incapacitation and deterrence the execution would provide. The classic utilitarians themselves were somewhat divided in their conclusion on the question.

1. Beccaria and Bentham

Over the past four centuries of western philosophy, few philosophers have openly opposed the death penalty; Jeremy Bentham is probably the first major thinker to have done so. Bentham's opposition to the death penalty was apparently inspired by a small but influential book published in 1764, *On Crimes and Punishments,* by the young Italian jurist Cesare Beccaria. Beccaria favored abolition, but he also favored a very severe alternative of life imprisonment without the possibility of release except by natural death. He thought the deterrent effects of dying at the hands of a public executioner were inferior to those provided by the prospect of a lifetime's loss of freedom.

Bentham agreed; first in his *Rationale of Punishment* (1775) and late in life in a short pamphlet "On Death Punishment" (1831), he argued on several grounds that the death penalty as inferior to imprisonment; it lacked "frugality," "remissibility," "profitability," and "equability," in contrast to imprisonment, and also had no indisputable advantages of deterrence or incapacitation (or so he believed, but his views on the point were unsupported by any convincing evidence). Thus, as it might be put today, Bentham believed that a cost–benefit analysis of capital punishment versus life imprisonment would lead the rational legislator to prefer the latter.

2. John Stuart Mill

A generation later, however, John Stuart Mill argued in Parliament (1868) against abolishing the death penalty entirely. Abolitionists overestimate the "humanity" of a lifetime behind bars and overestimate the inhumanity of "a short pang of a rapid death." The death penalty is to be preferred on utilitarian grounds to imprisonment for the occasional "atrocious crime." (This claim is hard to defend on utilitarian grounds; Mill had no evidence to show that only incapacitation by execution would suffice to prevent recidivism in such cases, and he is obviously flirting with retributive reasons, as he is when he attempts to tar his opponents with "effeminancy.")

B. Factors Relevant to Utilitarian Reasoning on the Death Penalty

All utilitarian reasoning about social policy, including the death penalty, is highly sensitive to the actual facts, and the facts are likely to differ over time and among societies. As a result, it is impossible to pronounce once and for all whether a utilitarian ought to favor or oppose the death penalty either in general or for some specific offense. As a case in point where utilitarian thinking on the subject can be examined, one cannot do better than consider the evidence accumulated in the United States, where the relevant facts have been studied with greater care than anywhere.

1. General Deterrence

Chief among utilitarian concerns is the deterrent effect of penalties on the general public and the evidence for or against a superior marginal deterrence for the death penalty over life imprisonment (with or without the possibility of parole release or commutation of sentence). In the United States during the 1950s and 1960s, sociologists argued that there was no evidence favoring the death penalty over imprisonment as a general deterrent: (a) abolishing the death penalty in a given jurisdiction was not usually followed by a higher capital crime rate than in neighboring jurisdictions retaining the death penalty; (b) reintroducing the death penalty in a given jurisdiction was not usually followed by a lower rate of capital crimes; (c) police and prison guards were not more frequently murdered in abolition jurisdictions than in death penalty jurisdictions.

In the early 1970s, however, new techniques of research involving multiple regression analysis borrowed from macroeconomics appeared to suggest that each actual execution in the period 1932–1970 resulted in several fewer criminal homicides. But this research—both the methods and the results—was extensively criticized, notably by the National Academy of Sciences. The authors of its report, *Deterrence and Incapacitation: Estimating the Effects of Criminal Sanctions on Crime Rates* (1978), declared, "We see too many plausible explanations for [these] findings ... other than the theory that capital punishment deters murder." Further analysis during the 1980s and 1990s has confirmed this skeptical conclusion. Few if any professional American criminologists today would endorse the proposition that the evidence shows the death penalty in the United States during the bulk of the 20th century has been a marginally better deterrent than imprisonment.

As a result, a utilitarian argument over the death penalty must conclude that, so far as the United States is concerned, there is no basis in marginal deterrence on which to prefer the death penalty to the less severe alternative of long-term imprisonment.

Some still defend the death penalty on grounds of its superior marginal general deterrence by claiming that since it is conceded on all sides that death is a more severe punishment than imprisonment, it must be a better deterrent even if only in a few undetected cases. But this a priori argument cannot be put to any empirical test, and so utilitarians and other consequentialists cannot reasonably appeal to it in an effort to offset the lack of support the death penalty as a deterrent receives from all the available empirical evidence previously discussed.

2. Incapacitation

Evidence for the incapacitative effects of the death penalty versus imprisonment is difficult to obtain. While it is reasonably clear how many capital offenses are committed by recidivist capital offenders who were not executed, it is impossible to state how many capital offenses were *not* committed because a given capital offender was executed.

By far the best empirical study of the problem involved tracing the post-resentencing conduct in prison and on parole of the hundreds of prisoners under death sentence in 1972 who were not executed because of the Supreme Court's ruling in *Furman v. Georgia* (1972). Of the 453 death row prisoners not executed whose cases were scrutinized, 7 were later convicted of a second homicide (6 while in prison, and 1 after release). On the other side of the ledger, 4 inmates on death row at the time *Furman* was decided were later shown to have been wrongly convicted.

If such statistics are generally reliable and all convicted murderers sentenced to death were actually executed, it would appear that for every innocent prisoner executed, two innocent persons would not be murdered

by recidivist murders. What a utilitarian should make of this generalization is unclear; what is clear is that inflicting the death penalty absolutely incapacitates that offender, whereas incarcerating an offender does not. This fact is bound to give a slight edge in favor of the death penalty for those who reason by appeal to consequences.

3. Risk of Wrongful Execution

For more than two centuries, the most potent argument against the death penalty has been the risk of executing the innocent. What, exactly, is that risk? In the post-*Furman* study just summarized, 4 out of 558 death row prisoners were later shown to be innocent; fortunately, none was executed. In the most extensive study undertaken to explore this problem, in which roughly 600 capital cases spanning the years 1900 through 1994 were examined, the investigators concluded that over 400 were wrongly convicted and two dozen involved the execution of an innocent person. During the same years more than 7000 persons were executed and several more thousand were convicted of capital crimes and sentenced to death.

Calculating the risk of wrongful execution from these data is all but impossible. Bentham thought this risk was the gravest objection to the death penalty; J. S. Mill agreed in theory but confidently declared that the risk of executing the innocent under British law was too remote to take seriously. More recent utilitarians (notably, H. L. A. Hart) have acknowledged the relevance of this consideration but have shown no inclination to estimate the magnitude of the problem. Nor have they suggested that only a utilitarian need worry about the risk of executing the innocent; indeed, non-consequentialists, too, must be concerned with it.

In any case, the role played in utilitarian thinking of the risk of executing the innocent must not be overstated. From the standpoint of those who oppose the death penalty and seek to vindicate their convictions by utilitarian considerations, the risk of executing the innocent can play only a small role. Any number of acceptable social practices (mining, fire fighting, space exploration) involve risk to the innocent. All parties to the death penalty controversy presumably deplore executing (or even convicting and sentencing to death) the innocent; the controversy must focus on the merits of executing the guilty. Even if there were zero risk of executing the innocent—as would be true in an ideal society (as described above)—hard-core abolitionists would presumably oppose the death penalty. Whether they could do so on purely utilitarian grounds is doubtful.

4. Racial and Class Bias

Whatever may be true in other societies or at other times, a prominent feature of the criticism of the death penalty in the United States during the past half-century has been that the death penalty as actually administered falls predictably on members of minority races (notably African Americans and Hispanics) and on those who are at the mercy of court-appointed lawyers or public defenders, overworked and underpaid officers of the court who are often inexperienced or of dubious competence. Class bias has not been much studied, but racial bias has. The most extensive empirical research on that topic has shown that in the South, the murder by a black person of a white victim is measurably more likely to be prosecuted as a death penalty case, leading to a conviction and a death sentence, than in murders where the victim and offender are of the same race or where the offender is white and the victim black.

Conceding for the sake of the argument that the facts are as described above and—more important—that they are true of the nation as a whole and are resistant to change, a purely utilitarian evaluation would attach no great weight to such bias. Evidence shows that most of those under death sentence have a prior criminal record, in many cases of grave crimes against the person. No great social loss is incurred if such persons are dealt with more rigorously by the prosecution and provided with less effective defense than other murder defendants. Utilitarians since Bentham, however, have insisted on a principle of equality ("each to count for one, none for more than one"), and if that principle is taken (as J. S. Mill took it) to be part of "the very meaning" of the principle of utility, or if it is taken as a supplementary principle, then racial and class bias inherent in a system of punishment must count heavily against it.

But in the United States, the racial and class bias of the death penalty system is part and parcel of the more inclusive racial and class bias of the entire criminal justice system. No empirical research has established that the recent or current death penalty system is *more* biased against nonwhites and the poor than is the rest of the system. All one can claim is that the *consequences* of that bias are worse in their impact on convicted offenders if the death penalty is involved than where lesser punishments are concerned. For this reason the egalitarian consequentialist is likely to prefer a system of less severe punishments.

5. Cost

Empirical studies of several different sorts during the 1980s and 1990s in the United States have tried to estimate the economic costs of a death penalty system (in which every person charged with criminal homicide is a potential death penalty defendant) versus a non-death penalty system. All these studies have concluded that a death penalty system is significantly more costly than the alternative. The most recent and perhaps the most careful such study (1993) put the additional cost per case at nearly a quarter of a million dollars ($216,000).

This additional cost has to be deeply troubling to the utilitarian, and it requires offsetting advantages lest on this ground alone the death penalty system is to be rejected. What those advantages are or might be, as judged by the utilitarian, have already been canvased: general deterrence and incapacitation. As considerations to cancel and outweigh the economic costs, they are not very promising.

Of course, it is open to the utilitarian who wants to preserve the death penalty to recommend policy changes to reduce the costs of the death penalty system. Since most of those costs occur at the trial level (not, as many think, in postconviction appeals), the imaginative utilitarian will explore ways to speed up the voir dire and jury deliberations, reduce the role of expert witnesses for the defense, and curtail funds for investigation of the crime and for bringing defense witnesses to court. But as such reforms come close to breaching the dike of due process, the utilitarian must tread carefully lest rules and practices of general application in the criminal justice system and defensible on utilitarian grounds be abandoned or severely compromised in the search for cheaper ways to conduct death penalty trials.

6. Evaluation

A utilitarian contemplating the death penalty in the United States today would be strongly inclined to conclude that it ought to be abolished for all crimes, on the ground that it violates the principle of using the least restrictive means to achieve valid state objectives. Bentham's objections to the death penalty—its lack of "frugality" and the rest—remain as true today as in his day. To these must be added the factor of outright economic cost and the evidence regarding general deterrence and incapacitation unavailable in his day. It is difficult to see how a utilitarian today could disagree with Bentham, when he wrote (1831), "The punishment of death—shall it be abolished? I answer—*Yes.* Shall there be any exception to this rule? I answer ... *No.*"

V. CONCLUSION

Over the past three centuries, philosophers have arrayed themselves across the normative spectrum in their views on the death penalty. Some believed it must be strictly inflicted on all murderers. Others wanted to confine it only to a few cases of the most atrocious crimes. Still others have conceded that although in the abstract, murderers do indeed deserve to die for their crimes, in actual practice societies are so unjust in their distribution of benefits and burdens, opportunities and responsibilities, that they are incapable of fair application of the death penalty and so must refuse to employ it. And other philosophers have favored complete abolition of capital punishment.

Philosophers do not agree over who has the burden of proof: Is it those who would change current law (whatever it is), or is it those who favor putting some criminals to death rather than confining them in prison? For the retributivist, justice in punishment comes first; for others, not taking another person's life unnecessarily comes first.

Perhaps the most important philosophical question in the death penalty debate is this: Does the theory of punishment (preferred over other theories on whatever grounds) recognize any principle that sets an upper bound to permissible severity or cruelty in punishments? Clearly, utilitarianism does not; there are no doubt good reasons for a utilitarian to oppose torture and cruel punishments, but not because any principle summarily rules them out. Retributivism, too, lacks any such principle; retributivists are willing to impose as deserved punishment whatever is appropriate given the nature of the crime—and that entails insisting on terribly inhumane and cruel punishments, given the savagery manifest in some crimes.

In this context, it is worth remembering that the United States Constitution and international human rights law do endorse such a constraining principle (prohibiting "cruel and unusual punishments," and "cruel, inhumane or degrading treatment or punishment," respectively). What kind of moral theory might best accommodate such a constraint—either as a first principle or as a special case of some more inclusive principle—remains to be seen. As things stand, we have here an interesting case where positive law breaks ground for philosophy, rather than the reverse.

Also See the Following Articles

CHRISTIAN ETHICS, PROTESTANT • CHRISTIAN ETHICS, ROMAN CATHOLIC • KANTIANISM • UTILITARIANISM

Bibliography

Baird, R. M., and Rosenbaum, S. E. (Eds.) (1995). "Punishment and the Death Penalty: The Current Debate." Prometheus, Buffalo, NY.

Bedau, H. A. (Ed.) (1996). "The Death Penalty in America: Current Controversies." Oxford Univ. Press, New York.

Bedau, H. A. (1987). "Death is Different: Studies in the Morality, Law, and Politics of Capital Punishment." Northeastern Univ. Press, Boston.

Berns, W. (1979). "For Capital Punishment: Crime and the Morality of the Death Penalty." Basic Books, New York.

Davis, M. (1996). "Justice in the Shadow of Death." Rowman & Littlefield, Lanham, MD.

Nathanson, S. (1987). "An Eye for an Eye? The Morality of Punishing by Death." Rowman & Littlefield, Totowa, NJ.

Simmons, A. J., Cohen, M., Cohen, J., and Beitz, C. R. (Eds.) (1995). "Punishment." Princeton Univ. Press, Princeton, NJ.

Sorell, T. (1987). "Moral Theory and Capital Punishment." Basil Blackwell, Oxford.

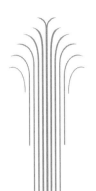

CASUISTRY

Mark Kuczewski
Medical College of Wisconsin

GLOSSARY

communitarianism A neo-Aristotelian school of thought that claims ethics is primarily a matter of a shared understanding of the good or is based upon interpersonal deliberative processes.

four-principles approach The best-known method in bioethics; also known as principlism. Principlism analyzes cases in terms of conflicts between *prima facie* duties such as respect for autonomy, beneficence, nonmaleficence, and justice.

moral taxonomy A tree-like grouping of cases arranged according to their similarity. The higher branches of the tree contain moral maxims, general concepts, and principles relevant to the cases beneath them.

morphology The general features of a case.

natural law theory A kind of philosophical position holding that God or nature inclines beings toward certain goals and ends. Happiness is thought to be action in accordance with these ends.

paradigm A clear case in which most persons would agree on the appropriate solution.

practical wisdom The virtue of the part of the intellect that deals with matters that are variable. It is often concerned with particular judgments and includes a perceptual component. Also sometimes called phronesis or prudence.

sophistry A rhetorical style of argumentation in which regard for the truth is secondary to considerations of self-interest.

teleology A system whose main feature is goal-directedness. Because human beings can make choices, teleological systems of ethics usually identify happiness with determining the highest ends of human life and making choices in accordance with them. If the belief is added that God or nature inclines human beings toward these ends, then teleological ethics becomes natural law theory.

CASUISTRY is case-based reasoning or any method of inquiry that is driven by cases rather than theory. In applied ethics, casuists argue that ethical theory is of little help in solving particular moral problems, but that with enough attention to circumstances and details, acceptable resolutions can generally be reached. Although they agree on this basic premise, casuists may differ on how to proceed in resolving particular problems.

Casuistry is a term that was discredited in philosophical circles for several hundred years but was revived by bioethicists in the 1980s, most notably in the work of Albert Jonsen. It is currently considered by many to be the quintessential method of medical ethics. The popularity of cauistry has grown and the method has become the subject of a second generation of scholarship that compares various casuistries and evaluates its relationship to other methods. Although the first generation of work in casuistry took place almost exclusively within the field of bioethics, its popularity has grown to the point that it is beginning to influence other areas such as engineering ethics.

I. THE CONTEMPORARY APPEAL OF CASUISTRY

Reasons for the widespread appeal of casuistry among bioethicists are readily apparent. Hundreds of years of debate between ethical theorists, e.g., deontologists vs. utilitarians, have produced no consensus on methodological questions. Furthermore, attempts to apply these theories directly to particular problems found that they were too general to yield useful results, or that such applications yielded rigid and blunt solutions that were insufficiently sensitive to the nuances of particular situations. This result is untenable for those who work in applied ethics. Questions must be answered, conflicts managed, and problems resolved. In bioethics, the demand was particularly acute for ethical reasoning to guide the new life and death choices that technology brought forth. The creation or revival of practical methods to deal with these matters was inevitable. Even if the word "casuistry" had not come back into vogue, this method's return seems to have been assured.

Of course, a tree is judged by its fruit in applied ethics. Bioethics, the nascent home of casuistry, has grown enormously and has produced areas of widespread agreement. Case-based reasoning has aided this progress and may provide a rational account of the development of consensus. The completeness of this account is a subject of current scholarship, and some argue that casuistry presupposes more fundamental commitments.

II. THE HISTORY OF CASUISTRY

A. Ancient and Medieval Origins

The term "casuistry" seems to have first been used in the medieval period, but this general approach to ethics has roots in the writings of Aristotle, especially his *Nicomachean Ethics* (NE). For Aristotle, ethics is a prac-tical knowledge whose characteristics differ from those of the theoretical sciences. Theoretical sciences begin with self-evident first principles and proceed through logical demonstration to deliver conclusions that obtain with necessity. In contrast, practical sciences are imprecise.

Practical investigations consider the opinions of wise persons and facts established by perception or habit as starting points and dialectically proceed to cull the first principles from such examinations. The conclusions of practical reasoning do not follow deductively from the first principles but require observation and inductive inference. Such conclusions hold only generally or "for the most part" (Aristotle, NE, I, 3, 1094b11-27). For instance, Aristotle often begins an inquiry by directing the reader to paradigmatic examples of the matter which he is exploring. Because ethics is largely about the good life, Aristotle exhorts us to look to those we credit with living well. Similarly, when describing virtues such as courage, he sets forth a paradigmatic illustration and then considers instances that bear resemblance. To recognize these paradigms, the student of ethics requires experience and a kind of developed moral judgment known as practical wisdom (phronesis). Furthermore, the exercise of practical wisdom in particular instances involves a mature perceptual capacity (aisthesis). The person of practical wisdom perceives the particular case to be of a certain type or analogous to a certain paradigm based upon its particular circumstances. These themes, i.e., paradigms, circumstances, analogy, and practical wisdom, pervade casuistry throughout the Middle Ages and in its current incarnation.

Albert Jonsen and Stephen Toulmin, in their seminal work, *The Abuse of Casuistry: A History of Moral Reasoning,* detail the rise of casuistry in the Middle Ages and its fall from grace during the Enlightenment. They argue that the practice of casuistry was mainly pursued by medieval spiritual counselors called "confessors." Catholic theologians from Augustine of Hippo to Thomas Aquinas had developed a rich tradition of natural law philosophy and theology which viewed all things as being teleologically ordered by a creator God. Each thing had its proper end in the cosmic scheme. Human beings also have their appointed place within the outline of creation provided by natural law theory. However, this kind of philosophy was too general to be very helpful to clerics who had to consider the particular acts of those in their spiritual care. They needed to fill in the outline of the natural law with paradigm cases and catalogs of variations. For this task, the moral perception and practical judgment of which Aristotle spoke would be required. According to the medieval thinkers, the faculty of conscience (conscientia) accomplished the particular judgment under the guidance provided by the virtue of prudence (prudentia).

The main tools of the casuist can be seen in the work of the medieval confessors. Prudence could identify some cases in which the goodness or evil of the action taken was clear. These paradigm cases are often helpful as the starting point of reasoning when confronted by more murky ones. Whether a problematic case is more like one paradigm than another is usually the key question in determining the moral correctness of an action. Problem cases can be grouped with one type or another based upon the characteristics of the case ("morphology"). These classificatory acts are not indubitable but are judgments about the similarity between cases and the summing of factors in a given case to determine the action most likely to be morally correct ("probabilism"). Furthermore, paradigms can be arranged according to their similarity to other paradigms, their generality or specificity, etc., culminating in a moral taxonomy of cases. Jonsen and Toulmin contend that casuistry was not derivative of natural law theology but that these classificatory schema developed largely of their own momentum. This point is crucial for casuistry's revival because few secular ethicists would be interested in a new incarnation of natural law theory.

Casuistry fell into disrepute because it became equated with sophistry. That is, certain confessors became known for cleverly using casuistic reasoning to alibi the misdeeds of their patrons. This led to a ridicule of casuistry ("abuse") as mere subjectivism and relativism. These connotations persist to the present day despite the success of the new casuistry.

B. The Contemporary Revival of Casuistry

Casuistry began its most recent incarnation when Albert Jonsen asked the modest question, can an ethicist be a consultant? He answered the question by pointing out that ethics consultants cannot bring to the bedside a theoretical system that churns out indubitable results, nor can the consultant set forth simple answers that settle cases regardless of their circumstances. Jonsen subtly pointed out that even common phrases we hear during a consultation involving duties or rights only apply in a more or less fashion and are like the common adages and maxims with which the medieval confessors worked. The consultant analyzes the case by examining all of its nuances and then sums factors that speak for one course of action or another. In the real world of moral decision making, many factors tend to work together to guide the reasoning process. Putting these

factors in perspective supports one or a few choices as likely to be morally correct. In other words, Jonsen's answer to his own question is that an ethicist can be a consultant if he is a casuist.

Jonsen and Toulmin claim that their revival of casuistry received its impetus from their work on the National Commission for the Protection of Human Subjects of Biomedical and Behavioral Research. This commission was chartered in the wake of the infamous Tuskegee syphilis experiments and was charged with creating guidelines for research involving human subjects. Jonsen and Toulmin claim that the success of the commission, which issued the landmark *Belmont Report,* was due to putting aside theoretical commitments and proceeding "taxonomically." That is, they supposedly considered one class of difficult cases at a time and compared them to simpler, paradigmatic cases. The report outlines several duties of the investigator to the subject such as respect for persons, beneficence, and justice. Similarly, Jonsen and Toulmin have remarked that cases were discussed in terms of other "mid-level principles" such as fairness and truth telling. However, these duties or principles were not used in any sort of deductive manner but were the common tongue in which cases were discussed and settled.

Before moving on to the more detailed analysis of the methods of casuistry, one point is worth noting. Casuistry depends on there being a relationship between facts and values that is intimate and viable. This presupposition is quite different from that chasm between facts and values that post-Enlightenment ethics has taken to be self-evident. Casuists assume that by analyzing the circumstances of a case closely (the facts), moral courses of action suggest themselves (values). This is a presupposition that is held dear by the Aristotelian tradition in general and thus has been the subject of analysis by other contemporary Aristotelian movements such as communitarianism and virtue theory. Because casuistry is not a theoretical account of the nature of reality, it need not offer an a priori justification of such a presupposition but is justified or condemned by the cogency of the results of the method.

III. COMMON APPROACHES TO CASUISTRY: JONSEN, STRONG, AND BRODY

A. The Casuistry of Albert Jonsen

Albert Jonsen and Stephen Toulmin revived the terminology of casuistry through their celebrated book. However, this text did not provide much instruction regarding how to use the method. Subsequently, Jonsen has provided some detailed descriptions. He has systematically outlined the working of the casuist's tools through which casuistry is supposed to provide a way to "work up" a case in a fashion analogous to the diagnostician's art in medicine.

For Jonsen, the key elements of casuistry seem to be attention to the morphology of a case, the development of a moral taxonomy, and the implicit dependence of these first two elements on a notion of practical wisdom. The morphology is the narrative or story of the case and consists of a complete description of it. The case is worked up by considering the medical indications, the patient preferences, quality of life considerations, and social and economic factors external to the patient but affected by the case.

Continuing the analogy with the diagnostician's art, the casuist classifies the case in front of him as being of a certain type, e.g., a case of euthanasia. With the identification of a type comes the recognition of relevant common moral maxims or rules of thumb that typically govern such cases. For instance, euthanasia is a type of killing and killing is governed by such moral maxims as "thou shalt not kill." Nevertheless, we also know of paradigm cases of justified killing such as those where the killing might be a kind of helping, e.g., killing a general at his request because he has been captured by the enemy and wishes to not divulge secrets. The casuist must determine whether the problematic case he is investigating is closer to those governed by the moral maxim against killing or those in which killing is justified as helping.

Classifying the case results in placing it on the tree of cases on branches that contain cases similar to this one. We noted earlier that this moral taxonomy is an idea handed down from the medieval confessors. However, the taxonomy is currently an ideal that does not exist anywhere. But, a casuist would have grounds to claim that medical ethicists have charted certain types of cases well enough that creating it is not difficult and that our reasoning in certain cases reflects such a taxonomy. It is also worth noting that in *The Abuse of Casuistry,* Jonsen and Toulmin do argue for a taxonomy that is quite general in nature at its higher levels. They argue that traditional ethical theories such as deontology and utilitarianism have failed because they did not circumscribe their proper sphere of application. These proper applications are related to the type of interpersonal relationship that is in question. At the highest levels of the taxonomy, the tree is split into an ethics of strangers governed by deontological reasoning and an ethics of intimacy in which utilitarian maxims hold sway.

Jonsen illustrates his approach using an infamous case from the medical literature known as "It's Over, Debbie." This case is one in which a resident enters a patient's room in the middle of the night to administer palliative care to a patient in great pain. The patient's chart reveals that she is terminally ill from ovarian cancer. She says "let's get this over" to the resident who administers a heavy dose of morphine. This induces respiratory depression and the patient dies within an hour.

Lining this case up under the appropriate paradigms is all important. Jonsen tells us that a paradigmatic case of euthanasia, if such exists, would involve a "competent, lucid patient with terminal illness requesting his or her personal physician to administer a lethal drug" (A. R. Jonsen, 1991. Casuistry as methodology in clinical ethics. *Theoret. Med.* **12**(4), 302). The further you wander from this paradigm, the less justified the killing is. Debbie's case seems to be far removed from this paradigm; i.e., the resident is not her personal physician and does not know if her utterance reflects a long-held wish or a momentary whim due to inadequate treatment of her pain. In this case, Jonsen does not need to tackle the harder question concerning whether there is a paradigm of acceptable active euthanasia. He simply shows that this case fails to embody the crucial circumstances of such a paradigm if there be one. This question of the existence of a paradigm is very important.

Paradigm cases, by means of analogy, can provide solutions to less clear cases. Jonsen employs the metaphor of kinetics to depict how paradigms move our thinking in problematic cases. However, this motion is not automatic. The casuist must determine if the problem case is relevantly similar to the paradigm or more similar to some other paradigm. One can claim that some sort of "principles of relevance" are needed to help with this task. However, such principles are anathema to the casuist. In place of relevance rules, Jonsen holds forth the virtue of practical wisdom or prudence.

Practical wisdom is necessary so that that casuist does not replace the principles of ethical theory with paradigms and fall back into an intellectual tyranny in their application. Instead, he must be able to recognize when the paradigm should impact the problem case and when it should not. This judgment involves weaving the circumstances of the particular case together and embedding it within the larger institutional and social context.

The circumstances of human life are, of course, mutable, but at the same time, they are embedded in important social institutions that are, if not immutable, at least relatively stable. The prudent person has the knack of recognizing that following this or that maxim, in these or those circumstances, contributes to the support of strengthening of the relevant social institutions or that, contrariwise, certain actions will undermine or modify the institution in certain ways. Similarly, actions are embedded in personal ideals, revealing or obscuring them. The prudent person also appreciates the way in which certain actions, under certain circumstances, correspond to the ideals that he or she credits. In both the social and personal realm, prudent judgment apprehends the fit of maxims and circumstances. (Jonsen, 1991. Casuistry as Methodology in Clinical Ethics. *Theoretical Medicine, 12*(4), 295–307.)

The resolution of a particular case requires experience and knowledge of many particular cases and their attendant circumstances. To determine which circumstance is the most relevant will also require an appreciation of the social and institutional context. The likely answer to the question of the existence of a paradigm is probably answerable on this basis as well.

In most instances, paradigms are uncontroversial cases in which virtually all persons can agree. However, when it comes to questions for which there is not yet a societal consensus, casuistry has two choices. (1) It may be conservative and claim that there are no paradigms where there is no general agreement. Nevertheless, as in Debbie's case, it could describe the features of a case that might be most likely to produce widespread agreement. (2) Casuistry can also take a more Aristotelian route and argue that paradigm cases are not cases on which most persons agree, but are cases on which persons of practical wisdom agree. If this is the claim, then it will sometimes be the role of the bioethicist or of an authority, e.g., the Supreme Court, to perform a prophetic role. That is, prudence will require setting forth a new paradigm and calling others to recognize it.

Although Jonsen is clearly the most renowned casuist in bioethics, his approach and terminology do not seem to have developed a large following among ethicists. His reliance on common moral adages and maxims is too open-ended for most ethicists. For instance, it is difficult to know which heading to reach for in a case such as Debbie's e.g., "killing," and Jonsen's paradigms can seem remote from the case at hand, e.g., the paradigm of the general who asked to be killed. There

is a desire for a casuistry that avoids these obscurities. The key features of casuistry are the identification of paradigm cases and the ability to draw analogies from the paradigms to relevantly similar cases. Thus, an approach to casuistry that places the emphasis on these elements is likely to be seen as maximally useful by clinical ethicists. Carson Strong has advanced such a method.

B. The Casuistry of Carson Strong: The Method of Case Comparison

Carson Strong's approach, called the case comparison method, reflects the kind of reasoning indicative of the National Commission. In an effort to make the search for maxims and paradigms less open-ended, Strong embraces general middle-level ethical concepts and principles such as truth telling and justice, etc. and role-specific duties that characterize the physician–patient relationship such as respect for patient autonomy and nonabandonment of patients. One should first identify which of these are in conflict in the case at hand. Second, identify the possible alternative courses of action. Third, compare this case with similar others to ascertain morally relevant ways in which these types of cases can differ. Finally, seek a paradigm case for each option under consideration.

Strong's method of case comparison sounds complicated but is not. Another way of stating the essential steps of this method is, ascertain which mid-level principles are in conflict, e.g., respect for patient autonomy and nonmaleficence. Then, identify paradigm cases similar to the one at hand in which each of the two principles is clearly supreme. That is, you should generate one paradigm in which it is clear that the patient's autonomy should be respected and one in which it is clear that nonmaleficence is the weightier principle. Let us take an example.

Imagine that a competent adult patient has cancer. Aggressive surgery and chemotherapy fail to stem its spread. The patient's family says that the health-care professionals should not tell this bad news to the patient since it will devastate him. The health-care professionals are not sure what to do. Strong's methodology counsels us to identify the conflicting principles in this case, i.e., respect for the patient's autonomy versus a desire to avoid harming the patient (nonmaleficence). The providers should try to arrive at a paradigm case in which it would be correct to withhold the news about the cancer and one in which they must tell him. After much hypostasizing, the providers determine that a paradigmatic case in which it is proper to withhold this news could be one in which they were completely sure the patient would not want bad news. The more sure they were about this, the more correct withholding the news would be. They determine that the only way to be completely sure would be for the patient to tell them he did not want bad news about his illness. Thus, the paradigm case would be one in which the providers go to the patient and ask if he would wish them to withhold unencouraging news about his condition so that he might be free to fight any illness or to enjoy his life without such psychological burdens. If he agreed to that plan, his case would be governed by the paradigm of nonmaleficence. Conversely, the paradigm in which patient autonomy triumphed might involve the patient asking the providers repeated and direct questions about the spread of the cancer.

It should also be noted that casuists are not committed to the concept of moral dilemmas. The solution in this problem case concerning truth telling will likely both respect the patient's autonomy and minimize the injury to him (nonmaleficence). If he tells the providers he wishes the information withheld, his autonomy is respected by honoring this wish and withholding the information will also minimize harm. If he wishes to know all the information, his autonomy is respected by giving him the informtion and it is likely that a patient who wishes to know his condition will suffer less harm by being told bad news than he would by being kept in the dark.

It is clear that Strong's method is maximally useful because it generates paradigms close to the case at hand. Practical wisdom expresses itself as creativity in generating these paradigms that can serve as the basis of agreement. The main problem that Strong's method faces also involves these local paradigms. Because the method generates paradigms very similar to the case at hand, they may be less stable and more culturally conditioned than the more general and remote paradigms and maxims that Jonsen invokes. For this reason, casuists should probably distinguish genuine higher-order paradigms from intermediate ones. Of course, when an intermediate paradigm ceases to be paradigmatic and must be replaced by another intermediate paradigm is a question for practical wisdom.

Given the austerity of Strong's approach to casuistry and the rich, elabrate machinery of Jonsen's method, one might expect that scholars would focus on the difference between these two philosophers. However, this has not been the situation in the literature on casuistry. Instead, some have mistakenly sought to draw a sharp contrast between the casuistry of Albert Jonsen and that of Baruch Brody.

C. The Casuistry of Baruch Brody: The Model of Conflicting Appeals

The contrast between the work of Albert Jonsen and that of Baruch Brody is *prima facie* inviting because Brody uses the rhetoric of ethical theory. Nevertheless, a brief exploration of the fundamental assumptions behind his terminology and method show a strong similarity to Jonsen's work. As a casuist, Brody is committed to the claim that our fundamental moral intuitions are judgments about the rightness or wrongness of particular actions, the justice or injustice of particular social arrangements, etc.

Brody points out that these basic judgments are neither evident nor indubitable for a variety of reasons, including that we may have ignored certain nonmoral properties of the situation, i.e., the circumstances of the case. These intuitions are tentative and open to revision. We proceed from a number of these intuitions to the next stage of "theory formation."

> The goal of this stage is to form a theory as to when actions are right or wrong, agents blameworthy or innocent, and institutions just or unjust. The data about which we theorize are those initial intuitions. The goal is to find a theory that systematizes these intuitions, explains them, and provides help in dealing with cases about which we have no intuitions. (B. Brody, 1988. *Life and Death Decision Making,* p. 13. Oxford Univ. Press, New York)

The good Aristotelian, i.e., the good casuist, begins with particular judgments, and proceeds to increasing levels of generality. These generalities may then aid in difficult cases when there are no clear intuitions. These generalizations make thematic what goods or principles (maxims) are at stake in related and similar cases and what features of the cases make them similar. Intuitions may also be challenged in a variety of ways such as by showing they are based upon misconceptions or misperceptions, or that they have the support of custom despite being inconsistent with our other practices. During the process of systematizing the initial, tentative judgments, one may well find that he is mistaken about some of these judgments. The systematizing process is part of the critical function of moral reflection.

For Brody, the theory of medical ethics is nothing more than a model of the physician–patient relationship. The particular model Brody develops is called the model of conflicting appeals. It takes into account that each of the traditional models of ethical theory makes an appeal to a particular good, e.g., rights, virtues, consequences, efficiency, or justice. Each traditional ethical theory appeals to one of these goods and is usually rejected because it can be counterexampled by appeals to the other goods. Thus, a model of the physician–patient relationship that can appropriately balance the claims of each provides an adequate framework for decision making in medical ethics.

The most important feature of Brody's account, the feature that makes him a casuist, is that theory does not achieve independence from the cases. Theory is confirmed by how satisfactorily it deals with cases. To the extent that it does not deal satisfactorily with cherished intuitions regarding particular cases, the theory is open to criticism and revision. Theory is created to help resolve the cases in which one has no intuitions or in which they are not clear. In these cases, theory serves a heuristic function in identifying the relevant considerations, circumstances, and maxims. However, theories cannot dictate solutions without the intuitive support that is derived from other, clearer cases.

Brody points out that there is no standard metric by which to assign objective weights to each conflicting consideration and then calculate the result. Instead, he provides several very general guidelines for the assessing of conflicting considerations but argues that that is as far as theory can go. To resolve particular cases, he advocates a "judgment approach." In this approach, he echoes Jonsen's revival of the Aristotelian notion of practical wisdom. At the core of these two casuistries is this identical concept.

One can easily see additional similarities between the casuistry of Baruch Brody and that of Albert Jonsen. In fact, it is hard to find a difference other than their respective use of the term "theory." Brody is in agreement with the taxonomic method that is so important in Jonsen's casuistry. Arranging generalizations concerning types of cases, respective goods, practices, and institutions hierarchically can be called a theory and no violence is done to casuistry in saying that it aims at theory. Brody simply uses "theory" where Jonsen would use "taxonomy."

Traditional ethical theory, the kind of theory to which casuists are averse, works in a top-down fashion from the highest level of generalization to the lowest level of particular judgments. Usually, it tries to bridge this gulf in as few steps as possible. Brody is a casuist in that he works upward from moral intuitions. The intermediate steps are important, perhaps, all-important.

Jonsen envisioned casuistry as a critique of theory. Both deontological and utilitarian considerations are relevant to moral life. The type of relationship, intimate or stranger-like, often guides which kind of consideration is more salient. Brody highlights the fact that the doctor–patient relationship embodies features of both kinds of relationship as well as a variety of other kinds of moral considerations. A "rich casuistry" will contain a variety of cases that emphasize each of the various aspects of this model of the physician–patient relationship and give guidance when appeals to the various considerations conflict.

IV. CONTEMPORARY CASUISTRY AND ETHICAL THEORY

Casuists are sometimes seen as antitheorists. If we define theory by the model of Euclidean geometry, casuists are in strict opposition to it. The geometric model views theory as a deductive enterprise beginning from first principles which are self-evident or intuitively grasped and proceeding through a chain of inferences to particular conclusions. Traditional ethical theories usually believe they are systems of values and must be worked out prior to application to the facts of particular cases. We have noted that this approach leads to ethical systems that are either too general to be of help in practical matters or too rigid to deal appropriately with particular subtleties. This casuistic critique of traditional ethical theory should not be confused with an aversion to generalization.

The moral taxonomy of the casuist is made up of generalizations covering a wide spectrum of situations. It is the belief that general statements are less reliable than the particular intuitions and practices from which they are derived that makes a casuist different from most post-Enlightenment kinds of ethical theory. All casuists argue that our moral intuitions function best at the level of the particular and it is here that most fruitful dialogue can take place. They indicate that it is the dogmatic holding of universal principles which are not based in intuition that causes irresolvable disagreements on the seemingly obvious cases. The holding of such principles preempts the inquiry into the circumstances and nonmoral properties of the case. Because casuists are not against generalizations, they are currently engaged in a number of interesting exchanges with other, practical approaches to ethics. These exchanges are among the most interesting and potentially fruitful developments in moral philosophy in recent years.

V. CASUISTRY AND OTHER PRACTICAL APPROACHES TO ETHICS

A. Casuistry and the Four-Principles Approach

Casuistry is not alone among approaches to medical ethics in being critical of traditional ethical theory. As a result, questions concerning the relationship of casuistry to these other approaches follow. The two approaches which most merit consideration are the "four-principles approach" and "communitarianism." Each bears strong similarities to casuistry and is worth being compared in some detail.

The four-principles approach, sometimes called principlism, also claims its origin in the National Commission but has become known mainly through Beauchamp and Childress' landmark text, *Principles of Biomedical Ethics*. The approach advocated in this highly regarded work can be summarized as follows. The middle-level principles of respect for autonomy, beneficence, nonmaleficence, and justice are compatible with most overarching ethical theories such as utilitarianism and deontology. Therefore, ethicists should not worry about applying theory to cases but should concern themselves with these four *prima facie* duties. The duties are said to be *prima facie* since they seem always to be in effect. However, they may conflict in specific cases. For instance, one's duty to respect a patient's autonomy may conflict with the duty to help the patient (beneficence). Medical ethics is about dealing with such dilemmas.

Advocates of the four-principles approach claim that the work of ethics is to "balance" principles in these instances. That is, ethicists must follow a procedure that determines which principle is weightier in a given instance. For this purpose, they prescribe certain prudential requirements that justify the infringement of one of the *prima facie* obligations in favor of a conflicting principle. These include being sure that there is a realistic prospect of achieving the moral objective one has chosen to honor, no alternative course of action is possible that would honor both conflicting obligations, and that we minimize the effects of infringing on the *prima facie* duty.

It is not hard to see the similarity to casuistry, although this relationship has been the subject of intense debate. The similarities were initially obscured by interpretations of the four-principles approach that saw it as a species of the top-down model of traditional ethical theory. Such interpreters then argued that the method fails to provide sufficient guidance in applying the principles to cases. If this interpretation was accurate, then principlism would be far removed from casuistry and it would simply be a failed traditional ethical theory. This is not the case.

It is clear that both casuistry and principlism agree that a top-down approach is fruitless. Moral deliberators may approach situations with general concepts such as the four principles or other mid-level moral notions but there is no algorithm for linking these notions to the particular problems at hand. The prudential maxims that Beauchamp and Childress generate are very general and require a great deal of judgment on the part of the ethicist. It is in this concept of judgment, an occasionally mentioned but underdeveloped notion of the principlists, that brings principlism into accord with casuistry and its requirement of practical wisdom. Nevertheless, it is likely this debate between casuist and principlist will continue for some time. This is largely due to the fact that the leading principlists accept the need for something like practical wisdom but continue to be uncomfortable with the notion, so they introduce new methodological machinations. It is unlikely, however, that these innovations will substantially alter the similarities between casuistry and the four-principles approach and their reliance upon a concept of practical judgment.

The four-principles approach harbors two philosophically unhealthy tendencies that casuistry avoids: (1) its language and approach are easily mistaken for traditional ethical theory, and (2) it does not develop the notion of moral judgment in the self-conscious manner that casuistry does. Furthermore, the four-principles approach is very similar to casuistry, but does not seem to add anything to the casuistic methods. Communitarian ethics, another offshoot of Aristotelian thought, holds more potential in this respect.

B. Casuistry and Communitarianism

The communitarian movement has gained widespread recognition through the work of Alasdair MacIntyre and Michael Sandel. Each of these thinkers takes contemporary social thought to task for its emphasis on the rights of the individual. They claim that the notion of the individual is too sparse a conceptual apparatus with which to resolve our current ethical quandaries. In opposition to the modern spirit, they echo Aristotelian themes including the importance of communal practices and deliberation, the role of the notion of friendship in ethics, the communal nature of the person, the existence of moral knowledge, and the need for a shared vision of the good life.

Ezekiel Emanuel has attempted to translate communitarian theory into an approach to health-care ethics. Emanuel argues that medical ethics cannot resolve questions concerning abortion, forgoing life-sustaining treatment, the allocation of health-care resources, etc., until communities arrive at agreement on shared fundamental values. Therefore, he puts forward a vision of health-care delivery that is modeled on the New England town meeting and includes the deliberation of all its participants.

When communitarians emphasize the need to arrive at a shared set of fundamental values or a shared vision of the good life prior to dealing with specific issues, their methods are anathema to the casuist. Such an approach is a form of the top-down approach of traditional ethical theory and is un-Aristotelian. For this reason, communitarians are sometimes seen to be the enemies of casuistry. However, there are also Aristotelian elements to communitarianism that make it virtually identical to casuistry.

The communitarians stress the implicit role of community in morality. Relationships and institutions have an implicit ethical dimension that forms the background of social encounters. This ethical dimension is the necessary condition of achieving the higher-order goods and purposes that make life meaningful. Philosophical ethics is the art of making this implicit ethical dimension thematic, codifying its contours, and extending its reach. Communitarians put forward a philosophical model of the person as partially constituted by and dependent upon the community. This model does not serve as a premise from which to deduce conclusions but does serve an explanatory function. That is, such a notion explains the casuist's method in exploring the process of clinical decision making and linking solutions to institutional and social goods, not simply settling all questions as questions of individual rights.

Contemporary casuistry has been accused of embracing a naive metaphysical realism. The idea that in-depth exploration of the circumstances of a case reveals the appropriate moral solutions seems to require a morally ordered universe. This universe might have been available to the medieval casuists because of their belief in natural law but is not open to the contemporary casuists. The communitarian emphasis on the implicit moral dimensions of relationships and institutions supplants the natural law. The casuist is not merely working with a given set of circumstances but works with those involved in the case to construct the case history in a certain way, to link it to the narratives of the individuals and institutions involved,

and to help all come to see how certain solutions foster the goods or end implicit within these narratives. The communitarian makes explicit the teleological dimensions of the casuist's practice. When communitarianism and casuistry are compared in this light, it is again clear that casuistry is linked to this method through the role that practical wisdom plays within each.

Communitarians such as MacIntyre often compare the person of moral knowledge to the master craftsman. Each works within a tradition that has a variety of implicit standards that are perceived and known best by those within that tradition. At the same time, these standards are not completely static but are advanced by the masters in the field. Similarly, the casuist relies on perceiving the morally relevant circumstances of the particular case and linking them to the implicit ethical dimension of the institutions within which she works. This act of classification is not static but demands interpretation and an openness to new paradigms and shifts within the social and moral milieu. Thus, the communitarian person of moral knowledge and the casuist of practical wisdom are essentially identical.

C. Casuistry and Narrative Ethics

There has also been much work in recent years on the subject of narrative ethics. This scholarship focuses on the storytelling quality of ethical methods. That is, much of what one decides about a case is determined by how we construct the story of the case, characterize the persons and issues involved, and make thematic certain circumstances. Because the "circumstances make the case" for the casuist (Jonsen, 1991, 298), and because the communitarian emphasizes the tradition or story of the community, narrative ethics may be complementary to these Aristotelian movements or may be a more fundamental art that is presupposed by them. It is clear that something similar to narrative construction substitutes for the ethical realism that the medieval natural law theorists presupposed.

Although the work within the area of narrative ethics is voluminous, comparative work on the relationship of narrative ethics to other methods in bioethics is still relatively new. However, some promising scholarship indicates that the future may be bright for further studies.

Also see the Following Articles

ARISTOTELIAN ETHICS • COMMUNITARIANISM

Bibliography

Arras, J. D. (1991). Getting down to cases: The revival of casuistry in bioethics. *Journal of Medicine and Philosphy,* **16**(1), 29–51.

Beauchamp, T. L., and Childress, J. F. (1994). "Principles of Biomedical Ethics," 4th ed. Oxford Univ. Press, New York.

Beauchamp, T. L. (1995). Principlism and its alleged competitors. *Kennedy Institute of Ethics Journal,* **5**(3), 181–198.

Brody, B. (1979). Intuitions and objective moral knowledge. *The Monist* **62**(4), 446–456.

Emanuel, E. J. (1991). "The Ends of Human Life: Medical Ethics in a Liberal Polity." Harvard Univ. Press, Cambridge, MA.

Jonsen, A. R. (1980). Can an ethicist be a consultant? In "Frontiers in Medical Ethics" (V. Abernethy, Ed.), pp. 157–171. Ballinger, Cambridge, MA.

Jonsen, A. R., and Toulmin, E. (1988). "The Abuse of Casuistry: A History of Moral Reasoning." Univ. of California Press, Berkeley.

Kuczewski, M. G. (1994). Casuistry and its communitarian critics. *Kennedy Institute of Ethics Journal,* **4**(2), 99–116.

Kuczewski, M. G. (1997) "Fragmentation and Consensus: Communitarian and Casuist Bioethics." Georgetown Univ. Press, Washington, DC.

Strong, C. (1988). Justification in ethics. In "Moral Theory and Moral Judgments in Medical Ethics" (B. Brody), pp. 193–211. Kluwer Academic, Dordrecht, The Netherlands.

Tomlinson, T. (1994). Casuistry in medical ethics: Rehabilitated or repeat offender? *Theoret. Med.* **15**(1), 5–20.

Toulmin, S. E. (1981). The tyranny of principles. *Hastings Center Report,* **11**(6), 31–39.

Toulmin, S. E. (1986). How medicine saved the life of ethics. In "New Directions in Ethics," (J. P. DeMarco and R. M. Fox, Eds.), pp. 265–281. Routledge and Kegan Paul, New York.

Wildes, K. W. (1993). The priesthood of bioethics and the return of casuistry. *J. Med. Philos.* **18**(1), 33–49.

CENSORSHIP

Bernard Williams
University of California, Berkeley

GLOSSARY

censorship Suppression or regulation of publications by a legally constituted authority on grounds of content.

first amendment Provision of the U.S. Bill of Rights governing freedom of speech.

obscenity In English law, technically "a tendency to deprave and corrupt."

pornography Publication in any form with explicit sexual content, intended to produce sexual arousal.

prior restraint A method of control that prevents material from being published.

zoning A system of controlling pornography (or another activity by permitting its sale only in certain designated areas.

CENSORSHIP includes any kind of suppression or regulation, by government or other authority, of a writing or other means of expression, based on its content. The authority need not apply to a whole judicature, and the effects of its censorship may be local. The term is sometimes used polemically by critics of a practice which would not be described as "censorship" by those who approve of it: in the USA the term has often been applied in this way to the activities of school or library boards in preventing the use or purchase of books which contain sexual scenes or teach Darwinism. It does seem that an activity has at least to be publicly recognized in order to count as censorship; interference with mail by the secret police or covert intimidation of editors would be examples of something else. Accordingly, any censorship implies a public claim of legitimacy for the type of control in question.

I. METHODS

The most drastic methods of control involve *prior restraint*: a work is inspected before it is published, and publication may be forbidden, or permitted only after changes have been made. Traditional absolutist regimes sought to control book publication by these means, and the Inquisition similarly regulated publication by Catholic writers. Legal procedures to the same effect still exist in many states for the control of material affecting national security, and in illiberal states for the control of political content and social criticism. Until 1968, theatrical performances in England were controlled in this way by a Court official, the Lord Chamberlain, whose staff monitored the script before production, demanded changes on a variety of grounds (including disrespect to the monarchy), and visited performances to see that their instructions were being carried out. In many jurisdictions, cinema films are inspected by some official agency before release, and its powers may include that of suppressing some or all of a film. However, the emphasis of these inspections has increasingly moved from suppression to labeling, the agency not so much censoring films as classifying them by their suitability for young people (in Britain the relevant body changed its name to express this).

Prior restraint is essential when censorship is motivated by official secrecy: once the information is out, the point of the censorship is lost (the British government attracted ridicule in the 1980s by trying to ban a book on security grounds which had already been published elsewhere). There are other aims of censorship, however, that do not necessarily demand prior restraint. If a work is thought objectionable on grounds of indecency, evil moral character, or its possible social effects, the suppression of it after publication may still be thought to have a point, in limiting people's exposure to it. The word "censorship" is sometimes used to apply only to methods of prior restraint, but legal provisions aimed at suppression after publication can reasonably be seen as having similar purposes and effects, and the term will be taken here to cover these procedures as well. Except in relation to media such as broadcasting, questions of principle are now normally discussed in terms of censorship after publication. It is important that censorship even in this wider sense still aims at suppression. Schemes of restriction or zoning applied to pornographic materials which require them to be sold only in certain shops and only to adults are analogous to film classification, and should be distinguished from censorship.

II. LIMITS

In 1774 Lord Mansfield said, "Whatever is *contra bonos mores et decorum* the principles of our laws prohibit, and the King's Court as the general censor and guardian of the public morals is bound to restrain and punish"[Jones v. Randall (1774)]. Although this dictum was approvingly mentioned by another English Law Lord as recently as 1962, few now would offer quite such a broad justification for censorship. In part, this is because of doubts about what "the public morals" are and by whom they are to be interpreted: pluralism, skepticism, sexual toleration, and doubts about the social and psychological insight of judges have played their part in weakening confidence in

the notion. A more basic point is that even where there is a high degree of moral consensus on a given matter, it remains a question of what that may mean for the law, and what, if anything, can count as a good reason for using the law in an attempt to suppress deviant opinions or offensive utterances.

Liberal theories claim that freedom of expression is both an individual right and a political good which can be curtailed only to prevent serious and identifiable harms. They can agree on this even though they may disagree to some extent about the main basis of these values, some emphasizing the danger of political and other power which is not transparent, some the importance of artistic and other expression, and some the ideal, influentially urged by John Stuart Mill, that it is only through an open "market place of ideas" that truth can be discovered. Liberals will agree, obviously, that the presumption against censorship is always very strong. They will differ to some extent, depending on their other views, about the kinds and the severity of harm that may in certain cases justify it. All will want to defend serious political speech; those who emphasize self-expression may be particularly concerned with protecting potentially offensive artistic activity. Those who stress the idea that free speech is a *right* (as Mill usually did not) insist that the reasons for suppression must take the particular form of a threatened violation of someone's rights.

A very strong version of such principles is embodied in U.S. law, which has interpreted the First Amendment to the Constitution ("Congress shall make no law ... abridging the freedom of speech or of the press") in such a way as to make censorship on any grounds very difficult. Mr. Justice Holmes in 1919 produced an influential formula: "The question in every case is whether the words used are used in such circumstances and are of such a nature as to create a clear and present danger that they will bring about the substantive evils that Congress has a right to prevent." Restrictions in such terms have been taken to protect even overtly racist demonstrations, let alone publications. The "clear and present danger" test is not used with regard to pornography, but the effect of Supreme Court decisions in that area has been that, at most, hard-core pornography can be suppressed. In many parts of the USA, all that the law enforces is zoning restrictions.

English law allows greater powers of suppresion than that of the USA: publications designed to arouse racial hatred, for instance, may be illegal, and the same is true in other jurisdictions. (In Germany and elsewhere, it is illegal to deny the Holocaust.)

III. PORNOGRAPHY

In the case of pornography, the main concept used in English law is *obscenity*; in a formula inherited from a judgment of Chief Justice Cockburn in 1868, the principal statute defines a publication as obscene if it has a "tendency to deprave or corrupt" those exposed to it. This professedly causal concept of obscenity implies that the rationale of the law is to be found in the harmful consequences of permitting a particular publication. However, as the House of Lords has itself observed, the courts could not apply this formula in a literal sense, and do not really try to do so. No expert evidence is allowed on the matter of causation, and in practice the question is whether a jury or a magistrate finds the material sufficiently offensive. As critics have pointed out, this not only makes the application of the law arbitrary, but reopens the question of its justification. In contrast to the principle that rights to free speech may be curtailed only by appealing to harms or the violation of rights in the particular case—the principle which Holmes' "clear and present danger" test expresses in a very strict form—only those who think that it is the business of the law to express any correct, or at least shared, moral attitude are likely to justify a work's suppression simply on the ground that it is found deeply offensive.

There has been a great deal of controversy about the effects of pornographic and violent publications, and a variety of anecdotal, statistical, and experimental evidence has been deployed in attempts to find out whether there is a causal link between such publications and some identifiable class of social harms, such as sexual crime. It is perhaps not surprising that such studies are inconclusive, and more recent advocates of censorship, such as some radical feminists, have moved away from thinking of censorship in this area on the model of a public health measure, and concentrate on the idea that certain publications unacceptably express a culture of sexual oppression. This approach tends to treat legal provisions against pornography like those against publications that encourage racial discrimination. In some systems, of course, this would still not make such censorship constitutional, even if the problem can be solved of making the provisions determinate enough for them not to be void for uncertainty.

A legal provision drafted by Catharine Mackinnon (which has not been accepted in any U.S. state, though it has influenced Canadian law) would offer a ground of civil action against publishers or manufacturers of pornography by someone who can show that she or he has been damaged by it. This procedure might be said not to be an example of censorship as it is normally understood, but it is relevant to see it in terms of censorship, to the extent that the legal action is based on the content of the material. If a woman is assaulted or raped in the course of making a pornographic film, there is already a ground of legal action; the proposals against pornography will differ from this in being essentially connected with the existence and content of the pornographic material itself.

A radical feminist outlook reinterprets the relation of pornography to other phenomena and, with that, the rationale of trying to control it. Traditional views, whether liberal or conservative, are disposed to regard pornography as a particular and restricted phenomenon, ministering to fantasy, and extreme sadistic pornography as even more so. The radical feminist thesis is that not just the fantasy but the reality of male domination is central to pornography, and that sadistic pornography involving women is only the most overt and unmediated expression of male social power. The objectifying male gaze to which pornography offers itself is thought to be implicit not only throughout the commercial media, but in much high art. It follows from this that there is a contrast of principle between pornography involving women and other pornography or sadistic material. At the same time, there is a less important contrast, not based on principle, between pornography and other material involving women. Sadistic material involving women will be seen as merely a less reticent version of what is more respectably expressed elsewhere, and if it is specially picked out for censorship, this will be for reasons of policy, somewhat as gross racial insults may attract legal attention rather than trivial ones. In practice, the claim is often made by feminists (in uneasy alliance with conservative forces) that sadistic pornography has worse social effects than other material; this returns the argument to the traditional "public health" approach and its diagnostic problems.

IV. PUBLIC GOOD DEFENSES

It is above all censorship directed against pornography that raises legal issues about artistic merit. With other kinds of censorship, in support of Church or State, it is obvious that works to be censored may have artistic merit, and even more obvious that this will be of no particular concern to the censors, who may well see a good work as more dangerous than a bad one. In the case of pornography, there has been a question, first, whether there can be a pornographic work of art at all.

It is not disputed that most pornography is of no aesthetic or artistic interest, but there is disagreement whether this is so merely because it is not worth anyone's while to make it more interesting, or because it is inherent in the content and intention of pornography. It has been argued in favor of the second view that the defining aim of pornography, to arouse its audience sexually, necessarily excludes the more complex intentions and expressive features necessary to aesthetic interest. Against this, there are in fact some visual and literary works which it is hard to deny are pornographic in terms of their content and (it is reasonable to suppose) their intention, but which have been widely thought to have merit.

There is strong pressure to use "pornographic" in an unequivocally negative way—to imply condemnation on moral, social, or aesthetic grounds. If the term is used in this way, there is a danger that different issues may be run together, and some important questions begged: it may be harder to separate, intellectually and politically, the question of whether some objectionable work has merit from the question of whether it should be censored whatever its merit.

The English law is not alone in allowing a "public good defense," which permits acquittal of a work that possesses serious aesthetic, scientific, or other such merits. It is significant that in English law a jury which acquits in a case where this defense has been made is not required to say whether it found the work not obscene or found it meritorious although obscene. The public good defense has secured the publication of serious works that were previously banned, such as *Lady Chatterley's Lover*, but there are difficulties of principle, which are clearly illustrated in the practice of allowing expert testimony on the merits of the works under prosecution. Besides the inherent obscurity of weighing artistic merit against obscenity, and the fact that evidence bearing on this has to be offered under the conditions of legal examination, the process makes the deeply scholastic assumption that the merit of a given work must be recognizable to experts at the time of its publication.

Moreover, the works that can be defended under such a provision must presumably be meritorious, which implies that they are to some considerable degree successful; but if a law is to protect creative activity from censorship, it needs to protect the right to make experiments, some of which will be unsuccessful.

The idea of making *exceptions* to a censorship law for works with artistic merit seems, in fact, essentially confused. Granted that there is a particular value attaching to significant works of art, or, again, that people have an important right to try to express themselves artistically (whether successfully or not), these concerns will not be best met by a system that provides a special exemption just for artistic merit which at a given time can be proved by experts in a court of law. If one believes that censorship on certain grounds is legitimate, then if a work of artistic merit does fall under the terms of the law, it is open to censorship: this point is acknowledged in the practice of traditional political and religious censors. If one believes in freedom for artistic merit, then one believes in freedom, and accepts censorship only on the narrowest of grounds.

Also See the Following Articles

ARTS, THE • LITERATURE AND ETHICS • PORNOGRAPHY • SEXUAL CONTENT IN FILMS AND TELEVISION

Bibliography

Coetzee, J. M. (1996). "Giving Offense: Essays on Censorship." Chicago. Univ. Press, Chicago.

Green, J. (Ed.) (1990). "The Encyclopedia of Censorship." Facts on File, New York.

"Index on Censorship" (1972–). Various issues. Writers and Scholars International, London.

Itzin, C. (Ed.) (1993). "Pornography: Women, Violence, and Civil Liberties." Oxford Univ. Press, Oxford.

Williams, B. (Ed.) (1981). "Obscenity and Film Censorship." Cambridge Univ. Press, Cambridge. [An abridgment of the report of a government committee which reported in 1979.]

CHILD ABUSE

David Archard
University of St. Andrews

Glossary

age of majority The age at which the law considers an individual to be an adult and no longer in his or her legal "minority."

battered child syndrome The title of an article by C. Henry Kempe *et al.* in *Journal of the American Medical Association*, 1962, which presented evidence of injuries and deaths due to battery by parents and guardians.

best interests of the child The principle that in all matters affecting the future well-being of the child its best interests shall be paramount.

collective abuse The abuse of children by collective agencies, such as social, political, and economic institutions or arrangements.

familial integrity The right of parents to determine, subject to certain constraints, how best to bring up their own children free from unconsented interference in the family's life.

parens patriae Literally "parent of the nation." The legitimate interest of a ruler or government in, and duty to, protect the welfare of the children within its jurisdiction.

pedophilia Literally "love of children." The desire by adults for sexual activity with young children. Stigmatized as pathological and deviant by most, it has on occasions been defended by its practitioners as an acceptable and long-practiced form of human love.

statutory rape Sexual intercourse with a legal minor who is presumed incapable of consent by reason of age.

CHILD ABUSE is a persistent and prevalent phenomenon in human history, yet only in recent times has it been identified, diagnosed, and responded to as a particular, pressing evil. There have been three key moments in the contemporary discovery of child abuse: the turn of the century, the early 1960s, and the 1970s onward (see Figure 1). Child abuse can take a variety of forms, and there are difficulties in trying to provide a single, unifying definition, especially as child abuse is presumed to be a significant wrong demanding a legal and social response. Nevertheless, single definitions are provided which range from a failure to supply a bare minimum of care to a failure to meet an optimal standard of care.

The wrong of child abuse may lie in the harm that is done to the child itself as well as to the future adult, and there may be a special wrong inasmuch as childhood must be understood in terms of vulnerability and dependence. Evaluating child sexual abuse requires an understanding of a child's innocence and its emergent sexuality.

Policy toward child abuse must respect the rights of a family to privacy, those of parents to bring up children as they think fit, and those of the child itself. The state also has a legitimate interest in the welfare of its young and future citizens. The enactment of policy must assign appropriate roles to legal, quasi-legal, and welfare agencies, take account of evidentiary problems, enforce any obligations to report suspected abuse, and consider to what extent the conditions of abuse can be identified *ex ante*.

I. THE DISCOVERY OF CHILD ABUSE

A. The Modern Discovery of Child Abuse

There can be no doubt that throughout human history children have been subjected to various forms of abuse, cruelty, and neglect. They have been sacrificed, tortured, sold into slavery, abandoned, killed at birth, mutilated, excessively disciplined, prostituted, and forced to engage in dirty, degrading, and demanding work. Nevertheless we are inclined to think of child abuse as a peculiarly modern phenomenon. Part of the reason for this is due to the way in which modernity characterizes childhood and its interests. It is principally due to the fact that child abuse has only been "discovered" in modern times. There have, in fact, been three significant stages in the contemporary discovery of child abuse.

The first occurred toward the end of the 19th century and the beginning of the 20th century. An organized movement to protect children from the "cruelty" of their parents sprang up, in both the United States of America and the United Kingdom, in the 1880s. The first systematic legislation concerning children dates from the beginning of the 20th century. Before the passing of such laws children could only be protected, as the early child protection agencies discovered, by invoking the existing animal welfare statutes. At this time child abuse was seen in terms of cruelty and neglect, the prevention of which depended upon the vigilance of the emergent voluntary child welfare organizations acting under the delegated authority of a state newly empowered to protect the interests of its youngest charges.

The second moment in the modern discovery of child abuse was in 1962 when a group of pediatricians announced their discovery of the "battered child syndrome." This followed from their suspicion that a range of injuries in children presented to doctors could not be accidental and their eventual diagnosis of a pattern of physical harms which must be attributed to parental abuse and neglect. The model of abuse emphasized the occasioning of physical wounds within a family home by abusing guardians. Its medical provenance licensed the language of pathological as opposed to normal parenting and encouraged speculation concerning both an etiological and predictive theory of abuse. Child battering was a syndrome, and the prospect of forseeing its possible occurrences lay in successfully explaining its causes.

The third moment in the modern discovery of child abuse was when the sexual abuse of children became widely discussed in the 1970s. The concern with such abuse, which many commentaries suggested might be viewed as the most serious form of abuse, continues to the present day. The widespread disclosure of child sexual abuse may be attributed in large part to the influence of the women's movement. It is natural that the attention directed to the subordination and oppression of women within the private, familial sphere by men should have been extended to include the maltreatment of dependent children. It is also inevitable that the understanding of that abuse should emphasize its sexual character and the gender of its perpetrator. The model is also constructed to privilege a feminist analysis of abusive male power, which finds its most immediate expression within the family but which also extends beyond to encompass all of society.

B. The Modernity of Child Abuse

The modern discovery of child abuse has been responsible for an increasing concern with the phenomenon, amounting almost to a "moral panic." New forms of child abuse—such as "ritual" and "organized" abuse—have been uncovered; agencies of child protection have acted zealously to disclose incidents of abuse; and the public has been ceaselessly supplied with media tales of abuse. In such an atmosphere—especially when some accusations have been retracted, others have proved groundless, and many appear implausible—there is reason to fear that a modern witch hunt is in progress. Correlatively it is reasonable to fear a period of reaction may set in with children's voices once again being silenced or their claims discounted. Such worries, on both sides, reinforce the need for a careful, judicious understanding of child abuse and the appropriate means to deal with it.

More generally, there is a tendency to believe not only that the discovery of abuse but the abuse itself is modern. Such a claim is deeply implausible. Indeed the evidence suggests that over time humanity has become less cruel and more sensitive to the needs of children.

B

Some bedtime stories are never forgotten.

Sexual abuse within the family is more common than many would like to admit. And when a child has been abused the emotional legacy is often carried into adulthood. With sensitive counselling, adults and children can often express their hidden secrets and understand the past. Such work is difficult, sometimes distressing. But we feel it's vital in giving children a fresh start.

Barnardos
Tackling today's issues

FIGURE 1 Two images of child abuse from this century and the last. The first (a) is from the 1870s. The second (b) uses a drawing by a child who has suffered abuse and was featured in a 1994 advertising campaign. Both images are reproduced with kind permission from Barnardo's Photographic and Film Archive.

There is even a story to be told of the maturation of society's adults into caring guardians after a long, dark prehistory of parental indifference, neglect, and cruelty. Lloyd De Mause offers a celebrated psychoanalytic version of this story in his *History of Childhood* (1976. Souvenir, London): "The history of childhood is a nightmare from which we have only recently begun to awaken. The further back in history one goes, the lower the level of child care, and the more likely children are to be killed, abandoned, beaten, terrorised and sexually abused" (p. 2). This kind of narrative is associated with the belief that in pre-modern times we lacked a concept of childhood, an understanding of the particular, distinctive needs and interests of human beings at this stage of their early development. Philippe Ariès's *L'Enfant et La Vie Familiale sous l'Ancient Regime* (1960) is the influential source for this widely held view.

C. The Modernity of Childhood

It is difficult to maintain that previous societies lacked a concept of childhood. Evidence for this claim is underwhelming, and many critics have offered testimony which contradicts it. What does seem plausible is that we have acquired a modern *conception* of childhood. Childhood is conceived of as radically separate from adulthood, with its own world, ways of behaving, roles, responsibilities, and characteristic features. Childhood is a time of innocence, dependence, and vulnerability, whereas adulthood is marked by knowledge, independence, and strength. The separation of the child's world from the adult's is both demanded by and serves to reinforce these contrasts.

Now, against the background of a such an understanding, it is easy to believe that children previously were cruelly treated either because they were inappropriately thought of and behaved toward as if they were adults or because adults were simply insensitive to the special needs of children as children. An important corollary of the previous claim is that parents in premodernity were cold and uncaring in their attitudes to even their own children. Historical evidence, again, can be found to discomfit this thesis: parental care for children has always been caring and affectionate; society's stigmatizing of cruelty and neglect has been a constant sign of its concern for the special needs of its young.

We have, in modern times, undoubtedly sharpened the division between children and adults. This has accentuated our concern with the maltreatment of the young. It is also true that our modern understanding of the distinctive character of childhood as a developmental stage is due to work in psychology, evolutionary theory, and anthropology. It is further true that the 20th century has seen the rise to preeminence of a universal moral and political discourse in which the special interests of children can be represented and defended. This is mostly evident in the language of human rights.

For all of these reasons it is easy to see why we should, in modern times, believe ourselves to be better guardians of our children and yet, paradoxically, think that only in moden times has the abuse of our children become systematic. There is a further point. The category of "child abuse" is a modern one, and it has been formulated within the context of modern theoretical disciplines, such as pediatrics. There are great difficulties in the retrospective employment of a recently invented concept, and there is, correspondingly, the inclination to think that a new concept brings in the wake of its application a new field of phenomena. However, to repeat, the abuse of children is not new. The systematic study of such abuse and a general, informed public concern with its occurrence are—as may be the terms through which we understand the phenomenon.

II. THE DEFINITION OF CHILD ABUSE

A. In Favor of a Narrow Definition

Agreeing on a definition of abuse is crucial for a number of reasons. First, and most obviously, how abuse is defined determines its prevalence. The wider the definition of abuse the more widespread is its incidence. In general, definitions will determine amount. No single table of figures purporting to represent the incidence of various categories of abuse could be presented which did not beg important and controversial questions about how the kinds of abuse listed were being defined.

Second, and relatedly, child abuse is a concept with clear evaluative connotations. Abuse is an evil, those determined to be responsible for it are normally condemned outright, and society is recognized to be under a clear obligation to prevent its occurrence. We have a general, though not exceptionless, understanding of greater evils as being rarer events. The more we come to think of something as common the less inclined we are to characterize it in extreme moral terms. We recognize that a wide variety of harms befall children but are disposed to represent child abuse as a special class of such harms which merit exceptional condemnation. Any moves to broaden our understanding of what child abuse is should acknowledge this disposition.

Consider an analogy with the offense of rape. The brutal, forced sexual violation of a woman is the paradigmatic instance of the crime of rape. There can be no dispute as to whether or not such an act is one of rape, and it is likely that the evidence that it has occurred will be palpable and uncontrovertible. Such an act warrants the strong, unambiguous moral condemnation of all reasonable persons. However, it is indisputable that there is a continuum of sexual behaviors which are unconsented or unwanted. There may be good reasons for extending the category of rape to include these behaviors, such as demonstrating that they display a significant commonality of undesirable male sexual attitudes to women or that the category of consent is broader than that first assumed. On the other hand, the extreme disapprobrium which attaches to the paradigmatic act of rape will most likely not extend to all the behaviors included under the extended definition. Many thus entertain the reasonable fear that the evaluative force of the category of rape is diluted by overextension of its application.

B. What Should a Definition of Child Abuse Be Like?

To the requirement that child abuse be defined in ways consistent with its present censorious import can be added at least three further important requirements. The first of these is that the avoidance or prevention of child abuse not impose unreasonable demands on those charged with responsibility for rearing children. Child abuse should not be something which occurs simply on account of the circumstances in which a child is brought up and which cannot be attributed to the actions or culpable inactions of any set of individuals. Of course it may be important for the state to assume a parental role when existing parents fail to supply an acceptable minimum of care for their children. This can be done while acknowledging that these parents may not be at fault, and that their children are the victims of circumstance rather than of abuse. That abuse has not occurred does not mean that the child does not need government protection.

The second is that what is gathered under the single category of child abuse should display a significant and substantive commonality. There is a worry that the term covers a wide variety of disparate harms to children sharing no single feature. To the extent that this worry gains ground there is reason to think that we should cease using the term and simply speak of a continuum of harms that can be occasioned to children, distinguished by their severity and causal antecedents. If there

is a point to singling out instances of child abuse it should be that they all share a special wrongness, are particularly preventable, have distinctive causes, or some combination of these features.

The third requirement of any definition of child abuse is that it should, as far as is possible, avoid the use of contested terms. The category of child abuse will not have clear evaluative implications if not everyone is clearly agreed on its evaluative content. A now familiar background principle is that law and policy, within a liberal polity, should, at least in its public explication and justification, be neutral between competing understandings of the good. An official measure should not invoke principles which are contested by those governed by the measure. Such contestation is restricted to reasonable views. No one disputes that, in this context, the pedophiliac view that adult–child sexual activity does no harm to the child should be discounted.

A definition of child abuse may run afoul of this requirement simply by its employment of terms whose application are likely to be disputed. Talk of a "normal," "adequate," or "proper" level of care is obviously contentious in this sense. It is also possible that agreement on what is meant by some central term should be combined with disagreement as to whether some practice or behavior is properly described using that term. One can agree what "harm" is but dispute whether something is indeed "harmful." Those who argue the merits of corporal punishment normally differ as to what really harms the child.

Added to this possibility is the fact that the same activity can have a different significance in contrasting social or cultural contexts. The fellating of adolescents by adult males is part of an initiation ceremony within some tribal cultures, but undoubted sexual abuse within other societies. The practice of facial and bodily scarifying by a parent is seen within one culture as an essential part of beautification, whereas in others it would simply count as gratuitous and abusive mutilation. What in both cases serves to distinguish the same practice is that in the tribal culture the adult intends, and the child understands the adult to intend, the promotion of the child's self-esteem and social status. Nevertheless, there may still be room for the claim that a practice, even though invested with the cultural meaning of enhanced status, is abusive. The example of the circumcision and infibulation of young girls within some societies is an obvious one.

The thought that our understanding of what counts as child abuse is especially subject to deep cultural and historical variation is probably unwarranted. The alleged variation is constrained by the existence of a substantial, enduring conformity of standards concerning the treatment of children. Moreover how we think we ought to treat adults is as much a matter of dispute as the question of how we should behave toward children. The formulation of *all* law and policy faces the challenge of finding agreed upon standards of behavior. Those who press the claim that child abuse is an especially disputed category run the danger either of endorsing moral relativism or counseling inaction in the face of an evident wrong.

There is a pressing reason for trying to secure agreement on what shall count as child abuse: there is now an international context within which research on child abuse is conducted and measures are pursued to eradicate it. There are also internationally agreed minimum standards of child care, such as those codified in the United Nations Convention on the Rights of the Child, which provide a benchmark for such worldwide efforts. The concern to have a single, agreed upon global category of child abuse is understandable, but the need for sensitivity to cultural difference is also crucial. The dangers of ethnocentrism in the categorization of wrongs are as evident here as they are elsewhere.

C. Approaches to the Definition of Child Abuse

In defining child abuse two approaches are discernible, though neither need exclude the other. The first is to think of abuse as a falling short of some minimally defined standard of care. The other is to think of abuse as the positive infliction of some significant harm. A single definition of abuse might combine the two. "Neglect" clearly falls under the first approach, whereas "physical cruelty" fits with the second. There may be a third approach which results from understanding abuse as misuse. There are forms of exploitative treatment of children which seem to fall short of actual injury or neglect. An example might be the use of children in public entertainment. It is of course possible to recognize that children are harmed as a consequence of such exploitation without extending the category of abuse to include misuse.

Employing then the two basic approaches, there are four broad types of child abuse recognized within contemporary legal guidelines in Western societies. These are physical abuse, neglect, sexual abuse, and emotional abuse (see Table I for some sample definitions from both the United Kingdom and the USA). For each of these subcategories it is possible to devise further constitutive subcategorizations, and it is easy to think of

some of these as the central standard instances of abuse—respectively, beating a child to the point of unconsciousness, starving a child or rearing it in filthy conditions, incestuous sexual intercourse, and severely impairing a child's psychological development. It is also easy to think of alleged instances of abuse which less clearly fall under one of these subcategories. Notoriously it is difficult to determine when the punishment of a child is no longer "justifiable" or "reasonable chastisment" and has become physical abuse. The Yanomami, who live in the forests near the upper Orinoco, kiss or suck their baby sons' penises to soothe and placate them. Within a Western context such behavior might well be classified as molestation.

The category of emotional abuse is currently the subject of the greatest disagreement, notwithstanding an acknowledgment that it should be one of the forms of serious child abuse. The dispute concerns the scope of such abuse, and this dispute in turn is fueled by the unavoidable employment of some sort of model of the normal, proper, or healthy psychological development of a child. However, it should be said that the category of physical neglect needs also to invoke some standard of a normal physical development which an abusive behavior impairs. The general issue is thus broached of how and where the benchmark of expected guardianship is set.

D. The Benchmark of Acceptable Child Care

There are three ways in which such a benchmark might be set. The first is that of a bare minimum which might be defined in terms of basic needs. Care which falls below the so defined line will result in serious damage to a child or impairment of its health or development. At the other extreme, the benchmark is defined in terms of the best possible upbringing. David Gil, for instance, states that child abuse is "inflicted gaps or deficits between circumstances of living which would facilitate the optimal development of children to which they should be entitled, and their actual circumstances, irrespective of the sources or agents of the deficit" (1975. *American Journal of Orthopsychiatry*, 45(3), 364–367). There are strong reasons for preferring the first benchmark. It conforms to the requirements that a definition of child abuse not impose unreasonable constraints on those who bring up children and that it not involve terms or claims whose meaning might be disputed by reasonable persons. Moreover, it displays a certain convergence between the two approaches to defining child abuse. Failure to meet a minimum or basic standard

TABLE I

Definitions of Abuse

Physical Abuse
- Physical abuse is defined as violence and other nonaccidental, proscribed human actions that inflict pain on a child and are capable of causing injury or permanent impairment to development or functioning. (F&K)
- Physical injury to a child, including deliberate poisoning, where there is definite knowledge or a reasonable suspicion that the injury was inflicted or knowingly not prevented. (DHSS)

Neglect
- Physical neglect is defined as the deprivation or nonprovision of necessary and societally available resources due to proximate and proscribed human actions that create the risk of permanent impairment to development or functioning. (F&K)
- The persistent or severe neglect of a child (for example, by exposure to any kinds of danger, including cold and starvation) which results in serious impairment of the child's health or development, including non-organic failure to thrive. (DHSS)

Sexual abuse
- Sexual abuse is defined as any sexual contact between an adult and a sexually immature (sexual maturity is socially as well as physiologically defined) child for purposes of the adult's sexual gratification; or any sexual contact to a child made by the use of force, threat, or deceit to secure the child's participation; or any sexual contact to which a child is incapable of consenting by virtue of age or power differentials and the nature of the relationship with the adult. (F&K)
- The sexual exploitation of children refers to the involvement of dependent, developmentally immature children and adolescents in sexual activities that they do not fully comprehend, are unable to give informed consent to, and that violate the social taboos of family roles. (S&R)

Emotional abuse
- [T]he willful destruction or significant impairment of a child's competence through such acts as the punishment of attachment behavior, punishment of self-esteem, and punishment of behaviors need for normal social interaction. (G, G&S)
- The severe adverse effect on the behavior and emotional development of a child caused by persistent or severe emotional ill-treatment or rejection. All abuse involves some emotional ill-treatment; this category should be used where it is the main or sole form of abuse. (DHSS)

Sources: DHSS: (1991) *Working Together: A Guide to Interagency Cooperation for the Protection of Children from Abuse.* HMSO, London. F&K: Finkelhor, D., and Korbin, J. (1988). Child abuse as an international issue. *Child Abuse Neglect* 12, 3–23. S&R: Schechter, M., and Roberge, L. (1976). Sexual exploitation. In *Child Abuse and Neglect: The Family and Community* (R. Helfer and C. Kempe, Eds.), p. 129. Ballinger, Cambridge, MA. G, G&S: Garbarino, J., Guttman, E., and Shelley, J. (1986). *The Psychologically Battered Child.* Jossey-Bass, San Francisco.

of child care is such as to occasion (or seriously risk occasioning) significant harm to the health and development of a child.

Between the two extreme baselines of "bare minimum" and "best possible" is a measure set by the standards of a particular community. Here the baseline is what a society deems to be good enough for its children, and care that is not good enough by this benchmark shall count as abuse. The distinction between basic needs and what is minimally acceptable within a society parallels that between absolute and relative poverty. In both cases what counts as falling below the line will vary across societies and through time. Using such a standard allows us to be sensitive to the prevailing norms within a community and to differences between communities. However, it is problematic. What one society deems good enough care for its children may be viewed as grossly unacceptable by another. Moreover it seems counterintuitive to describe as abuse behavior which more than meets the basic needs of a child but

falls just short of the high standards set in some child loving society.

This is not to say that a general concern with promoting the welfare of children is not desirable, and that it should not be served by policy initiatives. There is now a greater awareness of how children's health and development may be improved, and a greater disposition to see appropriate measures taken to this end, both nationally and internationally. The point, however, is that failure to do the best for children that we possibly can is not best described as complicity in the abuse of children. Such a description is unfair and unhelpful.

Lest it be thought that the use of "significant" to qualify the harm caused is open to some of the same sort of differing interpretations as is a benchmark of required care, we can say the following: "significant" can refer either to the degree of suffering or pain inflicted upon a child, or to the degree of impairment to the child's health and development. In the latter case the seriousness may refer to either its permanence or its departure from the expected standard, or both. Of course any such standard must be sensitive to some unavoidable differences between children, such as that between an able-bodied and disabled or permanently ill child.

E. Collective Abuse

Any definition of child abuse should not prejudge the issue of who may be held responsible for an abuse. Under the terms in which child abuse has been discovered, the greatest attention has been paid to the perpetration of abuse by individual adults, and, most centrally, by guardians. But there is no good reason to think that children cannot be abused by institutions or by society in general. Indeed it is important to recognize that this is so and that collectivities may be responsible for more extensive and more serious abuses of children than individuals. A society which conscripts its young children into active armed service or which intentionally denies them the food, shelter, education, and health care it could supply is abusing them. The "collective abuse" of children is their abuse by collective—social, economic, and political—agencies.

Two supplementary remarks are in order. First, a society cannot be termed abusive if it suffers circumstances beyond its reasonable control under which children receive less than basic care. A country which undergoes an unpreventable famine may see its children starve but is not guilty of abuse. Second, it may be the case that individual acts of abuse are more likely the poorer the economic and social circumstances in which individuals find themselves. However, that may not be sufficient to show that responsibility for the abuse shifts from the individual to his or her society.

F. Defining Childhood

In all the preceding what is to be understood as a "child" has been left unstated. This leaves open two important questions concerning the upper and lower limits of childhood. The age of majority, however and wherever that may be fixed, determines the point at which a child becomes an adult. Normally the measures which protect a child from certain kinds of abusive behavior no longer apply to someone who has come of an age. An adult may suffer physical assault or rape but not, obviously, child abuse. Although an age of majority is an all-or-nothing matter, it is fair to say that our evaluation of abuse will be proportionate to the age of its victim. The younger a child is, the more we estimate her vulnerability and dependence to be, and the more morally grave

we believe any act of abuse to be. Moreover, it may be proper to think that the earlier the abuse occurs, the more permanently damaging its effects will be. Some jurisdictions operate with a rough division between infants, children, and young persons, the ages marking the transition from the first to the second and the second to the third being set at around 7 and 12. Legal childhood nevertheless comprises all three stages with an upper limit set at 18 or 21. An understanding of child abuse as any abuse of a child of any age is acceptable so long as it remains sensitive to the distinctions, both fine- and coarse-grained, which we can make within the category of childhood.

G. Prenatal Harm

There remains the question of whether prenatal harm should be represented as child abuse. Increasingly courts are prepared to acknowledge that pregnant women may legitimately be held accountable for their actions in as much as these threaten the future health of their child. Whether such a trend bears moral scrutiny or makes for good law is one question. The separate issue, and the relevant one here, is whether the cuplable damage that may be done prenatally to a future person is properly described as child abuse. There is reason for inclining not to think that it is. The use of the term "child abuse" in this context obscures the important distinction between the postpartum child and the prenatal potential child. The latter is only a future child if it is actually born and lives. The harm that is done to a prenatal potential child is not harm done to the future child if the occasioning of the harm precedes the termination, elective or accidental, of the pregnancy. It may be insisted that harms done to a prenatal potential child are, nevertheless, harms done to a *child*. But that will be contested by others, and the ground of contestation will be the same as that which divides protagonists in the debate on the permissibility or impermissibility of abortion. Defining child abuse as including prenatal harms would thus fail to meet the requirement that any definition should, as far as is possible, avoid the use of contested terms.

III. THE WRONG OF CHILD ABUSE

No one disputes that child abuse is wrong and that it is probably a very great wrong. But what is it about child abuse that constitutes it as a serious wrong? If there is some behavior harmful to an adult then is the very same behavior done to a child morally graver? Is, for instance, the sexual abuse of a minor worse, other things being equal, than the rape of an adult? Most people would give an unambiguously positive answer, but there would seem to be two sorts of distinguishable reasons for doing so.

A. Harms to Childhood

The first reason draws attention to the distinctive and distinguishing features of childhood. These are such things as weakness, dependence, vulnerability, and innocence. The abuse of a child is a violation of what it is that makes childhood special. Moreover childhood is an unrepeatable stage in our development. Once it is over it cannot be returned to. To abuse a child is to damage the childhood of a human being, and some forms of abuse are such that a defining feature of childhood, innocence, is irretrievably lost or damaged. The entitlement of everybody to a childhood is a right to the enjoyment of one's early years in certain kinds of ways. The child is vulnerable to harms on account of its comparative weakness, immaturity, and lack of developed skills. There is a particular wrong in harming those who are more capable of suffering harm and less able to resist its infliction. Thus, some of the abhorrence felt at the abuse of a child would also be felt at the abuse of a weak and dependent adult—a sick or disabled person, for instance. Interestingly it may precisely be what is childlike about such adults that explains the similarity of our feelings. In both cases we will register our further outrage at the fact that an expectation of trust—in those who should care for others who are dependent upon them—has been so grossly violated.

However, some have criticized the modern conception of childhood for its artificially sustained representation of the child as a weak, dependent innocent. Just such a representation is what supports the continued, unwarranted separation of the worlds of adult and child. There is a danger of adults projecting onto childhood an idealized image of what they think it should be and demanding of children that their lives and behavior conform to that ideal. It may be unrealistic, and in some ways damaging, to believe that children can or should be preserved in a cocoon of innocent, ignorant dependence. Nevertheless it would be equally mistaken to think that nothing distinguishes a child from an adult, and to deny that there are respects in which a child can be damaged, as a child, by the intrusion into its life of certain kinds of behavior. It is also the case that as a matter of fact the adult enjoys greater power than a child does. To the extent that the adult exploits this power and in doing so treats the child as a means to

its own ends, it does a great wrong. It does so independently of further contentious assumptions about the nature of "adulthood" and "childhood."

B. Harms to Adulthood

The second kind of reason for thinking the abuse of a child especially wrong is that its effects endure into adulthood. The future adult is damaged by the abuse of its childhood self. Research into the precise effects of abuse continues, but no one doubts that they can be extremely serious, even debilitating, and scar the developed personality. Alcoholism, drug abuse, criminality, failed relationships, mental instability, and physical illness have all been attributed to childhood abuse. Most perniciously, adult abusers of children can often be found to have themselves suffered abuse as children. It does not of course follow that all those who have been abused as children become adult abusers. It is probably true that the character of an adult is more fixed by what is done to it as a child than by events which befall it as an adult.

C. Childhood and Self-Determination

The harm of child abuse is thus double: it is an abuse of the child and of the adult which the child becomes. However, in all of this it is important to notice an asymmetry between harm done to children and that which may be done to adults. It is standard to think of harms to adults as wrongful setbacks to their interests. At the center of the notion of what every individual has a rightful interest in is that individual's entitlement to the determination of her own actions. It is liberty and autonomy, at least for the liberal, which underpin the integrity of each self. A setback to some person's interests is wrongful if it is not consented to, and, correlatively, it is not wrongful if it is consented to. *Volenti non fit injuria* ("To one who has consented no wrong is done") is a key principle of liberal jurisprudence. However, children are not considered to be full agents capable of determining for themselves how they should live. In their case interests are defined not in terms of their own wishes and choices but at most by reference to some account of what they should or would choose if they were capable of choosing as adults. The caretakers of a child protect and promote her interests by choosing for her. This does not of course mean that the wishes of children can be entirely discounted. An emerging legal maxim is that courts should, when determining some matter touching on a child's future welfare, "have regard ... to the ascertainable wishes and feelings of the child concerned (considered in the light of his age and understanding)" (*Children Act 1989*, part I, 1, 3a). However, whereas what an adult chooses determines what is in her interests, what a child chooses is only a defeasible guide to what is in his.

There are two implications of this view which are worth emphasizing. First, it is arguable that where protecting a child's interests is not at issue then it is required that we respect a child's expressed wishes. Not to do so when the child's choices cannot be regarded as damaging her interests is an affront to her dignity. It is a form of abuse. Natalie Abrams is but one who argues for this broader understanding (1979. In *Having Children* (O. O'Neill and W. Ruddick, Eds.), pp. 156–164. Oxford Univ. Press, Oxford). Second, to treat someone as incapable of making choices is to represent her in a disrespectful way that may also be considered an abuse of her person. Paternalism—promoting the good of another in disregard of their own choices—is widely considered to be wrongful. It is the wrong of behaving toward an adult as if she were a child.

Now consider the example of statutory rape. A statutory rape law criminalizes sexual intercourse with a person below a certain age. That person may voluntarily consent to the intercourse, knowing what it is she is doing and being mature enough to understand the consequences of her action. However, her consent is discounted by the law, which presumes her incapable of consent. Feminists have expressed unease about statutory rape laws which protect young women from male sexual aggression but which also disempower those same women by ignoring their expressed sexual wishes. This raises a general worry about the protection of children. A child is sexually abused when she is subject to certain behaviors. Children do not normally voluntarily consent to their abuse. But if they do consent to sexual interactions (and even if we have good reason to think that consent is given voluntarily and knowingly) we may not acknowledge that fact. We can harm someone by overruling or ignoring their own choices. Preventing abuse means understanding what it is to be in one's minority. Continuing to treat someone as in such a state may itself be a form of abuse which disrespects what it is to be in one's majority.

IV. LAW AND POLICY REGARDING CHILD ABUSE

Given an understanding of what child abuse is and a confirmation of its wrongness, we may turn to a consideration of the morally appropriate ways of dealing with it. These must respect those general principles which determine the limits of the law and regulate the conduct of policy, such as any rights to liberty or privacy that we might determine individuals to have. But there are also more specific principles which govern the relationships between parents, children, and the state. This is not to say that children are not abused outside families and by adults other than their guardians. This is a matter which will be returned to. However, in the first instance children are normally raised by their parents, and acknowledgment of this fundamental fact must be a starting point.

A. Familial Integrity

There are at least three relevant principles: those of familial integrity, *parens patriae*, and a child's best interests. The principle of familial integrity is directed to protect the desirability of a family retaining and expressing its own particular identity against any unwarranted interference in its life. A classic legal statement of familial integrity may be found in the U.S. Supreme Court decision, *Prince v. Massachusetts* (1944): "it is cardinal with us that the custody, care and nurture of the child reside first in the parents, whose primary function and freedom include preparation for obligations the state can neither supply nor hinder" (in M. D. A. Freeman, 1983. *Journal of Social Welfare Law*, p. 71). Familial integrity comprises two principles, that of parental autonomy and that of familial privacy. Parents should be free to bring up their children as they see fit. This is subject to familiar constraints such as that they ensure that the children have their basic needs met and are not subject to significant harm. It is, for instance, thought permissible that parents should bring up their children to share their own religious beliefs, but they should not be allowed to expose their children to harms which arise from the holding of these beliefs. A Jehovah's Witness may rear his child to believe as he does but not deny his child the blood transfusion which he regards as immoral.

By familial privacy is meant the right of a family to protection against unconsented intrusion upon its activities. It is evident that the rights which the principle of family integrity grants to a family will be exercised by the parents. It is worth, therefore, remarking that the identification of a family, for the purposes of exercising such rights, with only its adult members runs the risk of discounting the interests of the children. In similar fashion the law once entertained the dangerous fiction that upon marriage a single entity, husband-and-wife, came into existence whose choices were made by only one party to that marriage, the man. Recognition that children must be protected even within the family is accorded formal status with the principle of a child's best interests.

The principle of familial integrity may be grounded in and follow from the more fundamental right of a human being to bear children. The idea is that if I bear a child (or bear a blood relation to it) I should be permitted to rear it (D. Archard, 1995. *Res Publica* 1(1), 91–106). It may rest upon broader social considerations which have to do with the proper conditions under which a society reproduces its own conditions of continued existence. A society needs future members who are capable, physically, intellectually, and morally, of assuming the burdens and duties of citizenship. The family rearing of children is the most appropriate manner of ensuring that this is guaranteed. Moreover, the alternatives to the family, which may be broadly described as "collectivist," have played no significant role in human history and are associated with unacceptably authoritarian forms of social organization.

B. *Parens Patriae*

The principle of *parens patriae* (parent of the nation) is that of the legitimate interest of the state in the welfare of its young and future citizens. It derives from the notion of the ruler as the parent, in the last instance, of his people's children. It is "in the last instance" inasmuch as the state or ruler does not aspire to usurp the parental role of the children's own guardians. Rather, the government safeguards the welfare of the children by ensuring that where a family fails in its role or a child lacks any adequate parent it will step in to assume that function. The principle of *parens patriae* is evidently founded upon the rightful interest a state has in securing the conditions of society's future existence.

C. A Child's Best Interests

The principle of a child's best interests is based on the precept that in any matter touching upon the future of a child, that child's best interests or welfare should be paramount. The principle originally arose out of custody disputes where courts were required to make a disposition of the child's future status, but it has come to be a general principle in all those legal and social policy contexts where a child's well-being is in question. It is now formally enshrined in most legislative instruments, national and international, dealing with children. It has also come to be conjoined with the princi-

ple, cited earlier, that a child's own expressed wishes should be taken account of and given a weight commensurate with the child's perceived maturity and understanding of the relevant issues.

D. How Should the State Act with Respect to Child Abuse?

Bearing in mind the existence of these three principles, each of which mutually constrains the respective operation of the others, the questions next arise of when and how a state should act in respect to of child abuse. The first of these questions concerns the conditions under which a government is warranted in acting, probably in violation of the principle of familial integrity, to promote a child's best interests and in its role as *parens patriae*. A government could seek either to prevent the abuse of a child occurring in the first place or, once it has taken place, to prevent its future occurrence.

How might the first goal be pursued? Obviously the regulations covering fostering and adoption are designed to prevent abusive guardians from acquiring parental status. A government could act to prevent the possible future abuse by parents of their own children either by complusory sterilization or by the involuntary removal of any child born to the adults into the care of another, whether by a straightforward statutory measure of compulsory adoption or from some such device as making the future payment of benefits to the adult dependent upon her agreement to have the child adopted. The second kind of action a government might take to prevent an abuse from occuring would arise from it specifying conditions under which the risk of future abuse, even where none has already taken place, is significant enough to warrant intervention. This intervention would then probably take the form of removing the child from the care of the parents. Most legislation touching on child welfare which gives a government and its agencies powers to take a child into its care does not speak simply of harm but of its risk or likelihood.

E. Predicting Abuse

The justifiability of *ex ante* action by a government with respect to child abuse is conditioned by two sets of considerations, one empirical and the other moral. The empirical considerations touch on how possible it is to predict the future occurrence of child abuse. It is plausible to think that a parent who is abusing one of his children may well, if he is not already, abuse others.

However, beyond this sort of circumstance it would be deeply contentious to believe that there is or could be a successful theory which allowed us to predict the future abusive acts of any individual. In the first place, it is always worth carefully distinguishing between a checklist of indicators that abuse is taking place from a list of supposed indicators that it will take place. Second, no universal, well-grounded, single cause, predictive theory of child abuse has been devised. The fact that some of the first attempts to understand child abuse were made by medical professionals can give rise to the misleading idea that child abuse is a pathological phenomenon with a precise identifiable etiology (see S. Montgomery, 1982. *Br. J. Social Work* **12**, 189–196). Third, any attempt to supply a psychological profile of the abusive individual must be comparatively insensitive to social and economic circumstances, which both play their part in the causation of abuse and which can change. Any plausible account of abuse must take due account of both individual and social factors.

F. Licensing Parents

The moral considerations which touch on *ex ante* regulation by government of future parenting concern the prior rights of individuals to have children. The right to form a family is an internationally recognized one which is normally accorded a considerable presumptive weight. Indeed the thought that the infertile should be assisted in their efforts to have children is driven by the belief that every human being has a powerful interest in bringing a child into existence and taking particular responsibility for bringing it up. A few have argued that parenthood should be licensed, a license being granted on the basis of an ascertainable fitness or competence to parent. However, there would be considerable practical difficulties in administering such a license, notwithstanding the impossibility of securing consensus on a standard of parental competence.

G. Dealing with the Abused Child

Children are to some extent abandoned to the care of those adults who take responsibility for bringing them up. We cannot prevent child abuse in advance of its occurring save in the most extreme of circumstances when it may be possible to identify the evident future abuser. But what of the prevention of any repetition of an abuse that has occurred? A familiar scenario would see the abused child removed from the family situation in which the abuse has occurred into some officially regulated place of safety, with

perhaps some eventual reallocation of guardianship and prosecution of the abusive parent. Or the child may be subject to some form of official supervision which broaches the family's integrity. To understand the other possible policy options it helps to draw two broad contrasts. The first is between the removal of an abused child from the "failed" family to which it cannot in consequence be returned and an acknowledgment of the familial problems the existence of abuse reveals, which may serve as an impetus to therapeutic work with that family. The second is between a legal, punitive response to abuse and a quasi-legal cooperative inquiry into its occurrence. Given these two broad contrasts it is possible to explore a number of ways in which a society can officially respond to the occurrence of abuse which take due account of the interests of all the relevant parties.

A child has an interest in no longer being abused, but it may also have an interest in remaining within its own family if that is consistent with the cessation of abuse. The removal of a child from its family may inflict harms upon that child, and this may be true independently of the abuse a child may suffer within an institutional place of safety. There is increasing evidence of such suffering to the extent that talk of "institutional abuse" is prevalent. Removing the abused rather than the abuser from the family can seem unfair to the former. Statutory removal of the child from its family may unnecessarily close off possibilities of transforming the family and rehabilitating the abuser. Society has an interest in seeing an abuser identified and punished. The child can have an interest in securing official recognition of the very fact of its abuse. But both society and child have an interest in the cessation of abuse. This may be better served by non- or quasi-legal, relatively informal proceedings in which a family can cooperate with official agencies. It may be wise to separate the bodies responsible for an establishment of issues of disputed fact and those responsible for decisions on the treatment of the child. Law courts may be better suited to the former, and nonjudicial panels for the latter.

H. The Threshold of State Intervention

The second major question broached earlier of when a state should act with respect to child abuse asks what the threshold of state intervention should be. This threshold will clearly depend upon a socially agreed definition of abuse, but most legislation in Western liberal democracies operates with some such triggering clause as "that the child concerned is suffering, or is likely to suffer, significant harm" (*Children Act 1989*, part IV, 31, 1a). Moreover, the real problem is not so much the setting of this threshold as the detection of behavior and circumstances which cross it. Respect for familial intregrity is in tension with the surveillance of intrafamilial conduct that might be abusive. A familiar complaint against social welfare agencies is that their overzealous pursuit of potential abusers, often combined with a credulous willingness to see abuse as more prevalent than it actually is, leads them to violate the legitimate rights of parents and unnecessarily to remove children from what are in fact nonabusive households. It should be added that the same agencies are publicly pilloried in the wake of any failure to have prevented some act of child abuse.

I. Detection of Abuse

It seems clear that the government cannot, alone, act to detect and thus prevent child abuse. There are a number of professionals who are in a position to monitor the welfare and healthy development of children—teachers, midwives, health visitors, doctors, hospital staff, and so on. Unfortunately many such professionals are disposed not to see abuse. Unwilling to intervene and trusting to the normal natural love of parents, they are inclined to explain away any apparent parental misconduct. There has been at least one excellent study of how child welfare agencies in the United Kingdom work with such a "rule of optimism" and succumb to the "liberal compromise" of making the best of what they do find (R. Dingwall, J. Ekelaar, and T. Murray, 1983. *The Protection of Children*. Basil Blackwell, Oxford). It is certainly arguable that all those professionally charged with the welfare of child in some regard should be under a clear obligation to report any instance of suspected abuse, failure to do so being an instance of professional misconduct.

This should not of course exempt the general public from a duty to look out for the interests of all children and not just their own. In many countries there is an unwillingness to intervene when a child is evidently being mistreated or at risk of such—on the grounds that it is a "private" matter best left to the child's own parents. Other countries, such as the Scandinavian nations, do not display such reserve, and there is much to be said for a greater assumption of collective responsibility for the welfare of children. This is equivalent to a certain "diffusion of parenting," a weakening of the prevalent assumption that whosoever a child's parents may be, they exercise exclusively all the rights that parents are assumed to have over a child. Children, it may be argued, are the proper responsibility of all of us even if, in the first instance and for the most part, it is the child's parents who exercise that responsibility.

J. Abuse Outside the Family

The preceding assumes that child abuse occurs within the family. That is not necessarily so. Children are at risk from predatory pedophiles. In an important and salutory development, the likely sexual abuser of a child was recognized not to be the caricatured stranger on the street with offers of sweets but a parent, natural or step, or a relative or a family friend. Nevertheless, that does not mean that pedophiles will not continue to operate outside the family. In a number of recent cases it has emerged that well-organized pedophiliac networks have succeeded in placing members within contexts where they can systematically abuse children. Most notably they have done so within children's homes or special schools. In some notorious instances their abuse of large numbers of institutionalized children, who are specially vulnerable and weak, has continued undetected over many years.

Calls for vigilance are insufficient. The case for evaluating all those whose job brings them into close, and perhaps unsupervised, contact with children is overwhelmingly strong. But any evaluative procedure is only as effective as the information it deploys. The case for a public register of all those known or suspected of child abuse and which may be made accessible to those agencies or employers charged with some responsibility for children is a powerful one. It does, however, raise issues of privacy, confidentiality, and a statute of limitations. Such issues are also broached if and when an official decision is made to require convicted pedophiles released from prison to register their movements, and when information about their criminal status is disclosed to a neighborhood. This is the import of the legislation, called "Megan's law" after a 7-year-old New Jersey victim of a twice-convicted sex offender living across the street, which the U.S. Congress passed and which was ratified by President Clinton in April 1996. Worries about the high rate of recidivism among child abusers and a concern that a community can only protect its children if armed with knowledge about the source of any risks are legitimate. But against these must be set the dangers of vigilantism, lost opportunities for the rehabilitation of offenders, and a progressive erosion of the rights of all publicly detested offenders.

K. Preventing Abuse

In general it is imperative that the means any society uses to effectively minimize the incidence of child abuse and punish its perpetrators should not lead to any diminution of the standards of legal protection which should be offered to all citizens, regardless of their offense. For instance, courts of law should be sensitive to the difficulties faced by children who are required to give evidence about abuse. But this should not result in someone accused of child abuse enjoying fewer legal rights than anybody else, or in a weakening of the evidentiary or probative requirements which standardly operate. The general public concern with and outrage at child abuse has developed some of the features of a moral panic. It should not further develop into a witch hunt.

Two final general comments should be made about the prevention of child abuse. The first is that concentration upon individual acts and individual offenders should not be allowed to detract from certain social preconditions of abuse. There is a significant correlation between poverty and child abuse or neglect. Sexual abuse may be classless (D. Finkelhor *et al.*, Eds., 1986. *A Sourcebook on Child Sexual Abuse*. Sage, Newbury Park, CA), but physical abuse and neglect does not appear to be (L. H. Pelton, 1978. *American Journal of Orthopsychiatry* **48**(4), 608–617). A serious commitment to the elimination of child abuse thus commits any government to a major program of social and economic reform. Similarly, recognition that children are predominantly if not exclusively sexually abused by men might help one to see such abuse as part of a more general male domination of women, and thus reinforce the case for greater sexual equality.

The second general comment is that the protection of children should not be at the expense of measures to empower them. Indeed one way to reduce the incidence of abuse is to extend the rights and powers that children have. This also requires that the "infantilizing" of children, their representation as weak, vulnerable, and dependent, which is so characteristic of the modern understanding of children, needs to be moderated. The United Nations Convention on the Rights of Children is a useful starting point, not least for that statute which accords children a voice in all matters concerning their interests.

V. CONCLUSION

Child abuse is not new, but a concern with its prevalence and multiple forms is. The desire to promote the general welfare of all the world's children should not lead to a loss of clear focus as to what child abuse is. A perspicuous, uncontroversial definition can supply the basis for a concerted global effort to reduce if not eliminate the phenomenon.

Child abuse is a terrible evil. But in understanding why it is, we need to be clear what wrongs are done to the child and what wrongs are done to the eventual adult. A grasp of the role that consent and autonomy play in this wrong is also required. Paternalism can be abusive even when it seeks to prevent abuse.

The efforts to deal with child abuse must combine law, social policy, and voluntary activity in ways that are sensitive to the needs of the child, the role of the family, and general social goals. Punitive and therapeutic ends must be reconciled. Our increasing concern with child abuse should not induce a general, moralized overreaction to the phenomenon which diminishes the defining liberal ideals of our society. It should lead to a greater assumption of collective responsibility for the welfare of children and a greater empowerment of children themselves.

Also See the Following Articles

CHILDREN'S RIGHTS • FAMILY, THE

Bibliography

Corby, B. (1993). "Child Abuse: Towards a Knowledge Base." Open Univ. Press, Buckingham/Philadelphia, 1993.
Family secrets: Child sexual abuse today. *Feminist Rev.*, Special Issue, Jan. 28, 1988.
Finkelhor, D., and Korbin, J. (1988). Child abuse as an international issue. *Child Abuse and Neglect*, **12**, 3–23
Greenland, C. (1987). "Preventing CAN Deaths: An International Study of Deaths Due to Child Abuse and Neglect." Tavistock, London.
Hacking, I. (1991). The making and molding of child abuse. *Critical Inquiry*, **17**, 253–288.
Lyon, C., and De Cruz, P. (1990). "Child Abuse." Family Law, Bristol. [for a comprehensive explanation of the British legal framework]
Parton, N. (1985). "The Politics of Child Abuse." Macmillan, London.
Stainton Rogers, W., Hevey, D., Roche, J., and Ash, E. (Eds.) (1992). "Child Abuse and Neglect: Facing the Challenge." Open Univ. Press/Batsford, London.
Stevenson, O. (Ed.) (1989). "Child Abuse: Professional Practice and Public Policy." Harvester Wheatsheaf, London.

CHILDREN'S RIGHTS

William Aiken* and Laura M. Purdy†
*Chatham College, †Wells College

GLOSSARY

instrumental reasoning Causal reasoning that judges which consequences will flow from a given act.
liberationist A proponent of the view that children should have the same rights as adults.
protectionist A proponent of the view that it is morally acceptable or morally required to recognize special protective rights for children.

THREE BASIC KINDS OF QUESTIONS occupy those who study children's rights from a philosophical perspective. First, what moral standing do children have: do they, like some animals, merely elicit duties on the part of others, or do they have interests of the sort that generate rights? Second, if they do have rights, what rights do they have? In particular, do they have a distinctive set of rights, perhaps changing over time as they develop? Or are they born with, or acquire, the same rights as adults? And third, would some entirely different model of the relationship between children

and adults make more sense than these two? For example, would it be better to think in terms of parental accountability, the cultivation of harmonious parent–child relationships, or an organic community?

I. CHILDREN'S MORAL AND LEGAL STANDING

One possible children's rights thesis is the assertion that children should be recognized as beings with independent moral worth and/or legal standing. Children seem to have an ambiguous status with regard to both moral and legal rights in contemporary Western societies: at issue is whether children's interests require independent recognition or whether their moral status is more like that of possessions or animals.

As a starting point, consider the list of rights in the United Nations' 1948 Declaration of Human Rights. Some standard security rights such as rights not to be killed or tortured or enslaved certainly seem to apply to everyone, including children. But do children enjoy other rights that are predicated of all humans, such as the right to own property alone or in association with others? Children are invisible in the discussion of most of the civil, political, economic, and social rights. Some exceptions are the rights to special care and assistance (Article 25) and the right to education; the latter, however, is qualified by the condition that parents have a prior right to choose the education that shall be given to their children (Article 26). Article 16 is still more explicit about parental authority over children; it asserts that the family is the natural and fundamental unit of society and that it is entitled to protection by society and the state. This priority of the family presents one of the major concerns in the literature of children's rights, the status of children within the family. Are children separate beings with moral worth independent of their parents or are they merely extensions or property of their parents, and thus subject entirely to parental authority? One meaning of "children's rights" invokes a denial of the second claim and a defense of the first claim such that children should be seen to have some independent moral, and perhaps legal, status within the family. Thus children's interests cannot automatically be assumed to coincide with the interests of their family, nor are their interests necessarily represented by the parent or head who speaks for the family unit. This logical and moral independence suggests that children's rights, whatever they may be, might require protection by an outside agency, such as the state.

One practical problem relevant to this issue is the question whether children have the legal standing to "divorce" their parents, as in the 1992 case of Gregory Kingsley (*The Nation*, 1993). This case centered on whether a 12-year-old could hire a lawyer to attempt to separate himself legally from his mother and attach himself to a new family. If the court recognized such standing, it would break new legal ground in the United States by supporting the position that children have substantial independent rights. Although a lower court in Florida ruled in the child's favor, that ruling was overturned on appeal. Despite this negative outcome, it is likely that children (with the help of sympathetic adults) will continue to seek the legal standing to have a say in their own upbringing.

It is difficult to say whether this innovation would be desirable. On the one hand, some children are forced to stay in abusive families, and others who seem to fall through the cracks in the child welfare system are deprived of necessary services and basic goods. Opening the door to self-help could improve their position. On the other hand, granting the possibility of such independent legal standing could prove to be highly disruptive to the cooperation, sacrifice, authority, and discipline that are needed to maintain a healthily functioning family. Furthermore, the neediest children may not be able to avail themselves of this legal opportunity because they would need the assistance of outside adults to intervene on their behalf. And this raises the possibility of inappropriate meddling by outsiders in the domestic, and so to some extent private, lives of adults; especially of those who are already disadvantaged by poverty and

who may also be members of minority cultural groups whose practices of child rearing differ from those in the dominant culture.

II. EQUAL RIGHTS

A closely related aspect of debate about children's rights concerns the nature and extent of any such independent rights for children. Do children have a unique set of rights, distinct from those of adults? Or do they have the same set of rights as adults?

Many people believe that children differ from adults in morally relevant ways. It is these differences that justify the claim that children deserve to be treated differently than are adults. So, morality would require that they be seen to have different rights and responsibilities than do adults. This position is known as "protectionism." Protectionists believe that children have a special moral status that entitles them to special moral and legal treatment. They argue that, due to lack of experience, competence and maturity, children have neither the knowledge nor self-control necessary for exercising adult rights and liberties well. Because children may not understand the likely consequences of their actions, they are more likely than adults to make decisions that lead to harm to themselves and to others. Because of their undeveloped character and lack of self-control, they may be less likely than adults to be capable of deferring gratification or resisting the harmful influence of others.

Parents are expected to take charge of their children, protecting and guiding them through their long years of development, gradually expanding both their rights and their responsibilities. Protectionists also generally support limits on children imposed by the state. Among these limits are requiring attendance in school until a certain age, prohibiting the sale of alcohol, tobacco, and other drugs or sexually explicit literature or contraceptive devices to children, imposing curfews, mandating health care such as vaccinations, and generally limiting the conditions under which children can work, engage in sexual activity, consent to abortion, refuse medical treatment, consent to be research subjects, make legal contracts, and be held legally accountable and punishable for their illegal actions. It is argued that such paternalism (or parentalism) is justified to protect and nurture children. However, protectionism need not imply the blanket acceptance of all and every possible type of restriction on children's activities. Indeed, there are good grounds for thinking that particular limits should be decided on an issue-by-issue basis so that the restriction is actually tailored to the particular child's capabilities and to the unique context of the circumstances surrounding the restriction. When restrictions are imposed parentalistically in the name of child's welfare, they should indeed primarily serve that welfare. Too frequently this type of justification can serve as a cover for the self serving interests or mere convenience of adults. In this protectionistic aspect of the debate about children's rights, the nature, extent, and moral defensibility of parentalistic limits is a central theme.

Some deny the appropriateness of any protective restrictions on children. Proponents of equal rights for children ("liberationists") may or may not deny the empirical claims about children's capacities; they deny, in any case, the moral and legal conclusions drawn from them. Liberationists emphasize the limits placed on children in contemporary Western societies, contrasting their constricted lives with their greater participation in the adult world at other times and places. It is argued that children are wronged by these limits, and that only by recognizing equal rights for children (including the right to vote) will children be able to protect themselves from such future injustice. They believe children's rights may include some protective rights, but only when these rights do not prevent children from exercising the rights open to adults. Thus, children may have special access to schooling, but compulsory schooling would violate their equal rights. Not only do liberationists maintain that the alleged negative consequences of granting equal rights to children are overblown (and so no utilitarian justification is warranted here), they also maintain that denying children adult rights is unjust. It is unjust because there are no morally relevant differences between children and adults that would justify this fundamental difference in moral standing. Because justice requires the equal treatment of relevantly similar cases, placing limits on children that are not equally placed on adults is indefensible. Of course that are many differences between children and adults, but these differences are not seen to be morally relevant. Liberationists believe that the morally relevant determining factor that is sufficient for individuals to be granted a full set of (adult) rights is whether they are capable of good instrumental reasoning, where instrumental reasoning is seen as the ability to make accurate judgments about the consequences of a given action. Protectionists deny that instrumental reasoning is sufficient and argue for more stringent standards that include the ability to make good prudential and moral judgments, attributes that children may not yet have acquired. Is the acquisition of these further capabilities morally relevant to be granted a full set of rights? Libera-

tionists can deny it either on epistemological grounds (relying on a skepticism about anyone's ability to use reason to evaluate ends) or on grounds of political philosophy (for example, liberal or libertarian theories that demand political neutrality about conceptions of the good). So they argue that the possession of instrumental reasoning alone is morally relevant in deciding moral standing. And even young children are capable of this type of reasoning.

Another reason for choosing instrumental reasoning as the criterion for equal rights is that it permits the drawing of a sharp line between the class of individuals who have equal rights and those who do not. Normal adults are capable of such reasoning and so should have adult rights. But many adults may not satisfy the protectionists' more stringent criteria of making good prudential and moral judgments. So they, like many children, would have to be excluded from those who have full rights. Otherwise it would seem that granting full rights is arbitrarily done on the basis of mere chronological age, which itself is not morally relevant. So unless those adults were, like children, deprived of adult rights, universalizability (and hence justice) would be violated. But now the line distinguishing right holders from non-right holders is very fuzzy indeed. As it turns out, the only criterion that guarantees all normal adults their rights also lets children in under the wire and so children should have a full set of rights.

Protectionists could respond to this position in a variety of ways. They might argue that there is no necessity for such a sharp dividing line between those who may enjoy adult rights and those who do not, and that there are good reasons for preferring a more stringent standard. Their argument is partly consequentialist, partly justice based. Recognizing equal rights for all those capable of any level of instrumental reasoning would be quite harmful to both children and to society at large. Raising the requirements would prevent such harm. It is true that some children, especially older children, would still be able to meet this stronger requirement, but there are alternative ways to recognize their appropriately greater liberties. Conversely, it is true that stronger requirements would exclude some adults. There are a variety of ways to deal with this fact. Extreme cases do require limits on liberty, as society already recognizes. Less extreme cases could justify the granting of full adult rights, in spite of one's failure to meet the criteria, because one has shown oneself incapable of learning about the world indirectly, and so needs the freedom to learn about it the hard way. This sad fact does not undermine the position that children (and society) generally benefit from an extended opportunity to learn to deal with the world from a relatively protected position. When children reach the age of majority (whatever that might best turn out to be) they will be granted adult rights even if they have not learned all the necessary lessons.

Liberationists could respond by underlining the similarities between arguments against children's rights and now-discredited arguments against women's rights. This analogy leads to a debate about children's basic nature. Protectionists respond that there are indeed fundamental moral differences between women and children: women are fully developed, mature humans completely capable of taking their rightful place in human society, whereas children are unfinished humans who need time and help to develop the capacity to exercise full adult rights. Liberationists may argue that if we granted children full rights we would soon see that they exercise them at least as sensibly as most adults. Or they might object that our failure to recognize equal rights for children infantilizes children; if they had equal rights, they would very soon develop the necessary capacities. Protectionists cast doubt on both theses, pointing to the questionable underlying model of human development, that is, one that sees this development as infinitely flexible and self-determining.

III. CONTROL OVER CHILDREN

What is children's role vis-à-vis the family? Liberationists argue that a child's connection with the family is voluntary. Children are to remain with their families so long as a mutually agreeable relationship can be negotiated. However, protectionists deny this contractarian approach and contend that families appropriately exercise control over children.

Many believe that family authority over children is protected by a strong right to privacy; this right undermines any interference by the state in parental treatment of children, even to protect children from what it considers abuse. However, this exceptionally strong stand for the freedom of the family from state interference assumes that the family is a single social unit with common interests rather than a collection of persons who may have conflicting interests. It also posits a "head" of the family (*paterfamilias*) who determines and represents its common interests. Both of these assumptions may be disputed. This extreme version of family rights also presupposes a libertarian political model at odds with the jurisprudence, case

law, and political reality of most modern Western states.

Weaker versions of this position hold that the state may intervene to protect children against abuse, but should leave many other decisions that may result in less than socially preferable outcomes in the hands of the family. Thus, for instance, parents can justifiably deprive their children of sex education or indoctrinate them in bizarre religious views. Frequently, the justification for noninterference with family authority is an appeal to liberalism's requirement that individuals be allowed to determine their own life plans and to pursue their own conceptions of the good without interference from the state, provided of course they do not directly harm others. But this raises problems when generalized to protect the family from interference. Although the adults' rights may be respected in this practice, it is not clear that the child's future capacity to autonomously develop a life plan and conception of the good is being respected; it could even be argued that the child is being harmed by this. By defending parental immunity from interference, respect for the rights to autonomy are being limited to the first generation. It would seem that liberal principles should justify society's intervening to guarantee children the support and education that would enable them to develop into autonomous adults (with the capacity to decide on their own conception of the good). If so, then the appeal to liberty to justify noninterference in the family seems misplaced. Nonetheless, less extreme appeals to the general principle of family privacy and noninterference are not uncommon, especially if the threat to the child is only of indirect harm. Any adequate defense of an expanded theory of children's legal rights against parental authority or actions must come to terms with this strong tradition of family sovereignty present not only in the West, but in many other societies as well.

The view that the family should have exclusive authority over children constitutes one end of a spectrum. At the other end are theories holding that the state should wield substantial direct power over children, in spite of parental wishes. Such views go back to Plato's assumption in *The Republic* that the children of the Guardians should be raised in common, without even the knowledge of their parents. More recent examples of the attempt to empower the state in this way are the Nazi position that children's primary allegiance should be to the German state, and the Soviet experiments with boarding schools for children. It is questionable whether either of these extreme views bodes well for children's welfare.

IV. SPECIAL PROTECTIONS AND ENTITLEMENTS

If liberationists are correct, few special protections for children are justifiable. Yet many contend that a crucial important function of children's rights is to provide children with protection against harm, exploitation, oppression, misuse, or neglect by others, including their parents. Children's rights could also reasonably be expected to guarantee children the prerequisites for flourishing.

One might hold that the right to protection from abuse is unnecessary because parents have natural affection for their children, and know and want what is best for them. Hence, parents can be relied on to act in ways that will prove beneficial to their children within the context of the family's values. So legal rights are not necessary to protect children from their parents.

Yet children have not always fared well at the hands of their parents. Parents have physically and sexually abused their children, exploited them for their labor, failed to provide for their physical needs (especially of female children in many cultures), put children out as sex workers, physically mutilated them, or sold them as brides. Parents have also refused children appropriate health care. Some have denied their children vaccinations against deadly diseases. Others, such as Jehovah's Witnesses or Christian Scientists, have denied their children lifesaving transfusions or therapies that would have prevented serious disability or even death. Psychological abuse and neglect of various kinds are also common.

One might therefore reasonably conclude that the state has a duty to intervene to protect children from seriously harmful treatment by parents, or by others with power over children. No special theory of inherent moral rights is required to justify this interference, because the state has an interest in insuring the well-being of its future citizens and can confer these rights of special protection from harm upon children and enforce them, when necessary, purely on the grounds of promoting the common good. Such intervention is based on a broader duty by the state to provide basic protections to relatively powerless individuals.

More controversial, but no less important, is the role of the state in guaranteeing children the goods, services, and treatment necessary for physical, social, and psychological well-being and moral agency. The issue of parental abuse, neglect, and deprivation naturally leads to controversy about the appropriate standards required, and which goods and services parents can reasonably be expected to provide.

What is necessary for physical and psychological health, as well as mental and moral development may be fundamentally disputed both within particular cultures and among different cultures. One fundamental disagreement is about proper gender roles: do young girls have a right to the same kind of education as young boys? And is female genital alteration essential, as some cultures believe, or is it, as others believe, an extreme violation of girls' rights? Other disagreements revolve around the value of severe corporeal punishment, appropriate dietary or medical practices, the type and level of education children have a right to expect, and so forth; these can often set parents at odds with the norms of a given society, and they differ radically in different societies. More generally, people disagree about appropriate levels of parental responsibility and sacrifice, as well as the extent to which other agencies such as the state should take responsibility for providing children with the necessities. Some believe families should be self-sufficient, but in many societies that is an unrealistic ideal. At the very least, public health goods like clean drinking water must be provided by the state; more expansive views posit pervasive involvement by the state in ensuring children's needs.

V. QUESTIONS ABOUT RIGHTS APPROACHES

Perhaps arguing in terms of rights is not the best means of promoting children's interests. There are, on the one hand, substantial epistemological and ontological complications involved in evoking extralegal moral rights. And, on the other, legal rights may be obscured by incoherent common law traditions and rival legislative jurisdictions. There is, in any case, a lack of clear theoretical coherence from case law and judicial review.

In addition to these problems, it has been argued that the rights approach focuses attention on the individual as an isolated and independent moral unit. Individual rights, thus construed, will often conflict with the rights of others. One problem is that there are no widely accepted ways to adjudicate between such conflicting rights. Another equally serious problem is that this approach creates an adversarial and legalistic relationship where there must be winners and losers rather than a cooperative one emphasizing compromise and the continuation of the relationship.

Thus, children and families may better be served by

different moral approaches. For example, one might instead stress parental responsibility to emphasize parental accountability and moral obligation. Or, emphasizing "caring" and the cultivation of harmonious parental–child relationships would better account for the process of helping children learn to live with and adjust to others. Yet another approach would be to envision the family as an organic community rather than a contractual association, stressing the natural process whereby children gradually emerge as individuals, maintaining their ties to the larger whole.

In response to these criticisms, advocates of rights approaches point to the history of abuse, exploitation, oppression, and neglect of children. Nor are these problems confined to the past: on the contrary, for many children, conditions are worse than ever. Advocates argue that in spite of its problems, attributing rights to children is the best way to draw attention to and begin to remedy this morally objectionable treatment. Once every child's basic needs and interests are met, there will be time to consider whether this model is optimal. Concerned for the well-being of all the earth's children, the United Nations proposed a rich set of normative guidelines for the international adoption and implementation of rights for children in its 1989 Convention on the Rights of the Child. This document is worthy of careful study.

Also See the Following Articles

AGEISM • AUTONOMY • CHILD ABUSE • FAMILY, THE • RIGHTS THEORY • WOMEN'S RIGHTS

Bibliography

Aiken, W. & LaFollette, H. (Eds.). (1980). *Whose child?* Totowa, NJ: Rowman & Littlefield.

Archard, D. (1993). *Children: Rights and childhood.* London: Routledge.

Blustein, J. (1982). *Parents and children: The ethics of the family.* Oxford: Oxford University Press.

Cohen, H. (1980). *Equal rights for children.* Baltimore: The Johns Hopkins University Press.

Ladd, R. E. (Ed.). (1996). *Children's rights re-visioned.* Belmont, CA: Wadsworth.

O'Neill, O. & Ruddick, W. (Eds.). (1979). *Having children: Philosophical and legal reflections on parenthood.* Oxford: Oxford University Press.

Purdy, L. M. (1992). *In their best interest? The case against equal rights for children.* Ithaca: Cornell University Press.

Scarre, G. (Ed.). (1989). *Children, parents, and politics.* Cambridge: Cambridge University Press.

United Nations General Assembly. (1989). *Convention on the rights of the child.*

CHRISTIAN ETHICS, PROTESTANT

John Lyden
Dana College

GLOSSARY

Anabaptism A 16th century Protestant movement that rejected infant baptism, claiming that only those old enough to express faith should be baptized, as only they could be saved by faith.

dialectical theology A movement begun by Karl Barth in the 1920s that emphasized the "infinite qualitative difference" between humans and God, as well as the depth of human sin and the need for God's grace.

evangelism A movement within Protestantism emphasizing the need for personal conversion to faith in Christ through a recognition of the "Good news" (Greek, *evangel*) of his gift of salvation.

liberation theology A contemporary theological movement proclaiming that salvation involves a total liberation involving political and economic as well as spiritual freedom.

neo-orthodoxy A movement of 20th century Protestant thinkers who rejected liberalism and sought to return to traditional Protestant views on human sin and the need for God's grace while remaining relevant to the political situation of the times.

Pietism A 17th and 18th century Protestant movement that emphasized a personal religious experience of Christ's salvation and a moral life lived in response to God's grace.

Protestantism A group of Christian churches that desired to reform Western Christianity and separated from Roman Catholicism beginning in the 16th century.

Protestant Liberalism A movement that began in the 19th century, primarily in Germany, which sought to revise Christian doctrine so that it could be brought into harmony with modern science and philosophy.

Puritanism A Calvinist movement that emphasized a personal experience of salvation by Christ; strict moral discipline and purity as the correct form of Christian life; a convenant of obedience to god, who was viewed as absolute sovereign over all; and societal reform, to convert the world to the way of Christ.

rationalism A 17th and 18th century intellectual movement that accepted reason as the chief standard for truth; it included both those who rejected traditional religion as well as those who sought to defend it as "reasonable."

Reformed A branch of Protestantism that formed in Switzerland, the Netherlands, and France, influenced most by the ideas of Ulrich Zwingli and John Calvin.

situation ethics A branch of ethics developed in the 1960s by Joseph Fletcher which claims that one cannot make ethical decisions based on rules which precede situations, but only by determining what maximizes love for all in a given situation.

Social Gospel A Protestant movement developed in early 20th century America which emphasized the social character of sin and salvation, and the need for society to be reformed along socialist lines.

PROTESTANT CHRISTIAN ETHICS refers to the systems of ethics derived from those Christian traditions which began, directly or indirectly, as a result of the Protestant Reformations of the 16th century. These movements resulted in a break from the Roman Catholic Church, which up to that time had held almost total control over the Christian churches of Western civilization. The Protestant churches had deep criticisms of both the moral practice and the doctrinal theory of the Roman Catholic church, and in order to practice Christianity in the way they believed to be correct, they felt they needed to declare their independence from the authority of Roman Catholicism. There is not, however, complete unanimity among Protestants on ethics or any other issue. The only thing that unites them unequivocally is the historic decision to break from Catholicism, and thereafter they began to disagree, at times violently, on a wide range of issues. Accordingly, to speak of Protestant ethics is to speak of a family of ethical systems which bear some common resemblances as well as many traits which distinguish them.

If there is one resemblance among them which stands out it would be the belief that humans are accepted or "justified" by God not on the basis of the good works they perform, but solely on the basis of their faith in Christ as the redeemer who brings the grace of God's salvation by his death and resurrection. Since ethics (in large part) sets forth guidelines for what works one ought to do, and Protestantism states one need do no works to be saved, Protestant ethics might seem to be an oxymoron. In fact, however, Protestants have had much to say about ethics and the works Christians ought to do—not because they need do them for salvation, but because such good works make up the way of life of those who believe themselves redeemed by Christ's promise of forgiveness and grace.

I. BEGINNINGS: THE LUTHERAN REFORMATION

A. Martin Luther

Martin Luther (1483–1546) was by most accounts the founder of Protestantism, though he did not initially intend to found a separate church or begin a religious movement. His basic belief that Christians are justified only by their faith in Christ was somewhat at odds with the dominant theology of his day, which declared that one can to a certain extent "merit" god's grace through good works. Luther's understanding of "justification by faith alone" led to his criticisms of certain Catholic practices such as the sale of "indulgences" which allegedly would aid one's salvation in exchange for the good work of a monetary contribution to the building fund for St. Peter's Cathedral in Rome. Luther wrote "Ninety-Five Theses" critiquing the use of indulgences in October 1517, and these were quickly printed in pamphlet form and disseminated to the public. Luther implied that the church was exploiting poor Germans by taking their money in exchange for vain promises of salvation, when in fact salvation comes only through faith. In time, Luther's criticisms of the Pope and the Roman Catholic Church became more serious, as he came to believe that the Church was completely corrupt and governed by Satan.

Luther's reformation, however, was far from being a simple moral reform of the church. He believed that the essential problem with the church was not its morals, but its doctrine—specifically, its failure to recognize that justification is by faith alone. For this reason, though he critiqued the ethical behavior of the Catholics, Luther's own theology may be said to have emphasized ethics less than theirs. The place of ethics and good works in Luther's theology is not always correctly understood, largely because he was so adamant that good works have no role in justification.

Luther explained his understanding of ethics, goods works, and the role of the moral law in Christian life through certain key ideas, including those of the two uses of the law, the two kingdoms, and the priesthood of all believers.

There are two uses of the law, Luther claimed, the civil and the theological. The civil use is ordained by god to keep order and to restrain evildoers in the world. This law is expressed by civil governments which develop their systems of law based on reason and conscience, not on the basis of the truth revealed in the Bible. Rulers need not be Christian to be good rulers, as they govern on the basis of principles shared by all peoples regarding the need to punish those who infringe on the public good. This use of the law then is not the sole possession of Christians, and can form a basis for ethics in all societies, whatever their religions.

The theological use of the law has relevance to Christians but only as a preparation for hearing God's forgiveness. When they consider the demands of the moral law and their inability to keep them, humans are driven to despair by their own imperfection (as Luther himself was as a young monk). Their only hope is to give up the desire to be perfect and accept their own sinfulness as well as God's love which atones for and forgives their sins.

Luther has no place for the moral law as part of Christian spiritual development per se, as there is no use of the law which pertains specifically to Christian life after the acceptance of God's forgiveness. This does not mean that the Christian will not uphold the law, in Luther's view, for the Christian will wish to follow the law to please God and serve the neighbor—but this is not done to justify oneself, nor does it mean that one is bound to the law. The Christian is free from the law, subject to none, and yet chooses to be subject to all in love. If one has experienced God's love, one will surely wish to share it with others (Luther reasoned), and this includes doing good works for the sake of others—but not for the sake of obedience to a law, or to obtain salvation.

Luther's notion of the "Two Kingdoms" further develops his ethics. There is the Kingdom of God, of which all Christians are a part, and there is the Kingdom of the world. The latter is governed by the civil law as opposed to a knowledge of Christ. The Kingdom of the world is full of sin which can be restrained only by the force of law and the threat of punishment. The Kingdom of God, on the other hand, is made up of Christians who live on the basis of love of God and neighbor. They do not require the laws of the world to be ethical, because insofar as they are redeemed they freely love others through the love of God active in their lives. This does not, however, mean that they are free to disregard the laws of the world, for they still live in the Kingdom of the world as well as in God's Kingdom. Christians obey the laws of the land because they accept the order civil laws bring to the world. For this reason, Christians can be soldiers or executioners and kill in the service of the state even though the life of the Kingdom of God rejects violence and retribution for evil. Luther justified this apparent contradiction by claiming that the Christian does not kill for himself or in sinful hatred of the other, but solely as an agent of the state which is ordained to keep order, through force if necessary.

Luther's notion of the "priesthood of all believers" also contributed to his ethics in the claim that all Christians are "priests" who serve Christ in their ordinary occupations. One does not need to be a monk or nun to serve God; one serves God best by realizing one's profession is a vocation, a calling from God to aid the neighbor by performing a useful, honest service to the community.

B. The Lutheran Tradition

Lutheran ethics since Luther has emphasized personal morals more than societal reform, not necessarily because Luther neglected the latter but because his notion of the Two Kingdoms has tended to support a separation of the Christian life from politics. Luther himself was a political conservative, as shown by his condemnation of the peasants' revolt of 1525 and his admonitions to the authorities to destroy the rebels. More importantly, however, Luther did not develop an ethical basis for criticism of the state as he tended to accept the Kingdom of the world and its use of the civil law as distinct from the ethics which govern the personal lives of Christians. It has even been argued that Nazism succeeded in Germany due to the strongly Lutheran character of the country, in that soldiers who were "only following orders" in committing atrocities without questioning their ethical basis were expressing the Lutheran idea that the laws of the world's kingdoms are distinct from the laws of God's kingdom, and as such not subject to critique by Christians. This was not the position of all Lutherans, certainly, but the lack of a Lutheran "political ethic" may have contributed to the generally passive stance the German churches took in regard to Nazism.

II. JOHN CALVIN AND THE REFORMED TRADITION

A. Calvin's Revisions to Luther

John Calvin (1509–1564) is the most significant Protestant thinker after Luther. His influence was most directly felt in Switzerland, as he controlled the Protestant community of Geneva from 1536 to 1538 and 1541 to 1564. Before this, Protestantism had already taken hold in Switzerland under the leadership of Ulrich Zwingli

(1484–1531) and others, and the Protestant churches became known as "Reformed" churches rather than "Lutheran" churches.

Calvin shared Luther's belief that all are justified before God by faith, not works, but he revised and developed Luther's theology and ethics in a number of ways. He added a third use of the law to Luther's two, this third being specifically to give structure and guidance to the Christian's life. Calvin had a more positive view of law than Luther, as he believed obedience to God and recognition of God's absolute sovereignty over all creation were crucial to Christian faith. Though Lutherans have accused Calvin of requiring good works for salvation, Calvin insisted as much as Luther had that works are not the basis but the product of faith. To follow the works of the law is required of Christians, not to be saved but to glorify God in all they do by obeying his holy will.

Calvin stressed that one can do no good work unless God's grace converts the human will from sin to obedience—thus it is truly only the "elect," those chosen or "predestined" by God for salvation, whose works are pleasing to God. Good works, while not the basis of salvation, may be signs which indicate that God's grace is at work in the one who does them.

Calvin also emphasized the concept of "stewardship," according to which we can best serve God by being good stewards and caretakers of all that God has given us. Properly speaking, everything belongs to God, but God lets us use this world and the things in it. If we use them well, for God's purposes, we are serving God and the creation in an ethical manner.

Calvin also supported the separation of church and state, as Luther had, but in practice he controlled much of the secular government as well as the church in his own Geneva. Calvin did not believe the church should meddle in state affairs, but he did suggest that a rebellion against unjust rulers might be justified on a Christian basis. This went against Luther's view that rebellion even against a tyrant is always wrong as it invites anarchy.

B. Later Calvinism

The followers of Calvin made much of his view that rebellion may sometimes by justified—most notably John Knox (1532–1572), the Scottish reformer who sought to justify rebellion against the Catholic forces of France and (during the reign of the Roman Catholic Queen Mary Tudor) England. Calvinists came to espouse a more militant political ethic than Lutherans as they sought to make the world more like God's King-

dom rather than tolerating it as separate from God's Kingdom. Calvin himself had been no more a revolutionary in politics than Luther was, but Calvinists often justified the use of force or rebellion against those who stood in the way of God's will (see below, Puritanism).

Later Calvinists also prospered economically, in part because of their clean and disciplined lifestyle which encouraged thrift and sobriety. Their ethic of stewardship led them to view their possessions as only God's possessions, held by them to show forth God's glory, and they therefore tended not to dissipate their resources but conserve and save. The sociologist Max Weber (1864–1920) claimed that Calvinism contributed to the development of capitalism through this ethic of stewardship as well as the belief that prosperity was a sign of God's favor.

III. ANABAPTISM AND RADICAL REFORMERS

The term "Anabaptism" refers to the Protestant movement which rejected infant baptism, claiming that only those old enough to express faith should be baptized, as only they could be saved by faith. Conrad Grebel (1497–1526) began the movement in Zurich, where Zwingli opposed it. Anabaptists were fiercely persecuted by the Lutherans and Reformed Protestants as well as by Roman Catholics, and this seems to have increased the Anabaptist conviction that these others were not true Christians as they did not live the Christian life. Anabaptism came to stand for a disciplined ethic, according to which those who lived immorally could be "banned" or ostracized from the community; a commitment to religious liberty and freedom of belief; and a separation of church from state. In these latter two beliefs, Anabaptists appear quite modern. In the sixteenth century, however, it was viewed as anarchy and sedition to question the state's support of the church or to allow multiple religions to exist within one state.

A. Militant Anabaptists

Some early Anabaptists reacted to the perceived impurity of Christianity with an attempt to purify it, by force if necessary. Thomas Muentzer (1489–1525) supported the peasants' revolt of 1525, an uprising which began out of their demands for fair treatment from the landowners. Muentzer claimed that because their cause was just, God would aid them in destroying the numerous opposing forces of Catholics and Lutherans. In Muentzer's view, rebellion, and force were righteous tools of God to be used against oppressors, and the state need not be obeyed by Christians when it conflicted with God's moral law. Unfortunately for the peasants, God did not rescue them and they and Muentzer were slaughtered without mercy by Lutheran and Catholic armies. In 1533 a similar incident occurred when Dutch Anabaptists declared Muenster the new Jerusalem, insisting all adults undergo a second baptism or be killed. All property was held in common, polygamy was enforced, and those who resisted were executed. Within two years the city fell to pressures within and without, and most of the survivors were killed.

This type of incident left many other Protestants with the idea that Anabaptists were violent fanatics who would enforce their rule on others as they believed they knew God's will better. Their advocacy of rebellion seemed to many a terrifying invitation to social chaos.

B. Pacifist Anabaptists

More typical of later Anabaptism were the pacifists who believed that all violence was wrong because it contradicted the ethics of Jesus. In spite of their pacifism, however, they were viewed as just as seditious as the Anabaptists who advocated violent rebellion. Their refusal to take legal oaths or serve in the military, as well as their rejection of infant baptism, were viewed as a rejection of the authority of the state—which in fact they were. The pacifist Anabaptists no less than the militants believed that the state had no authority over them regarding their views on these issues, as they were following a biblically based ethic for a separated Christian community. They insisted on a rigorous code of behavior which could not be practiced by those who were "of the world"; in this sense they rejected the world's kingdoms rather than trying to change them. Today the heritage of these Anabaptists is carried on largely by groups such as the Mennonites, founded by Menno Simons (1496–1561).

IV. PIETISM

A. Johan Arndt and Philip Jacob Spener

Pietism was a movement which developed in the 17th and 18th centuries which emphasized a personal religious experience of Christ's salvation and a moral life lived in response to God's grace. It sought to restore the role of emotion in religion which it believed had decreased since Protestantism became codified by "orthodox" Protestant theologians after the Reformation. "Orthodoxy" means "right opinion," and the orthodox Protestants tried to express exactly what one must believe in order to be saved. This led to an intellectualization of the faith and bitter fights within both Lutheranism and Calvinism over how Christian faith should be expressed. Pietism, in contrast, stressed the unity of all Protestants and deemphasized doctrinal matters to some extent. What matters is one's experience of salvation and the moral behavior which results from it.

It was in the work of Johan Arndt (1555–1621), a German Lutheran minister, that pietism first gained expression. He emphasized the need for repentance and a holy Christian life; true Christianity is expressed in love of God and neighbor more than in squabbles over doctrine. If one does not live a Christian Life, he claimed, one cannot maintain correct belief.

Philip Jacob Spener (1635–1705) supported Arndt's views and argued further that ordinary Christians should read and study the Bible in groups to develop their own personal views of the Bible. These Bible study groups, *collegia pietatis,* effectively democratized the pietist movement by allowing all to voice opinions without fear of contradiction. Pietist tolerance also insisted that Christians should show love to unbelievers rather than coercing them to faith.

After August Hermann Francke (1663–1727) founded several pietist schools, including the University of Halle, the movement grew beyond Germany to Scandinavia, Russia, England, and America.

B. Count Zinzendorf and the Moravians

One of those educated in Francke's schools was Count Nikolaus Ludwig von Zinzendorf (1700–1760). He invited a group of Moravian pietists to reside on his estate in 1722 where they founded a community and the Unity of the Moravian Brethren. Under Zinzendorf's leadership they became an influential group which emphasized an intense personal experience of being purified of sin by Christ's death on the cross. This was to be followed by internal regeneration by Christ's love which enabled believers to share this love within their communities and with the outside world

V. BRITISH PROTESTANTISM

Several important movements developed in Great Britain in the 17th and 18th centuries, all of which spread to the British colonies in America. The English (or

"Anglican") church had separated from Roman Catholicism in 1533 when the Pope refused to annul the first marriage of King Henry VIII. He responded by declaring the English Church independent of Rome and appointing his own archbishop who annulled the marriage. Henry was a staunch Catholic in doctrine, however, and it was not until his death in 1547 that real Protestant reforms were introduced. Except for a brief return to Catholicism as the state religion during the reign (1553–1558) of Henry's daughter Mary Tudor, the English church continued to be Protestant—though it remained closer to its Catholic roots than many other Protestant churches. Partly for this reason, movements arose which rejected what they perceived to be vestiges of Catholicism within the church.

A. Puritanism

Puritanism refers to a Calvinist movement which emphasized a personal experience of salvation by Christ; strict moral discipline and purity as the correct form of Christian life; a convenant of obedience to God, who was viewed as absolute sovereign over all; and societal reform, to convert the world to the way of Christ. This last came to include a commitment to education and literacy, temperance, and democracy. Puritans founded hospitals, schools, and other charity institutions for the poor.

The movement began within the Anglican church in the late 16th century when many clergy refused to accept the form of worship and church organization enforced by the state. The Anglican church was "episcopal," i.e., run by bishops (Green, *episcopoi*). Many Puritans, however, followed Calvin's view that the church should be "presbyterian," i.e., governed by councils of "elders" (Greek, *presbyteroi*) and not by a bishop—some even advocated congregationalism, the idea that individual congregations are accountable to no outside authority but God. These ideas challenged the authority of the Anglican church and worked to increase a desire for democratic reforms within the church and society. Many Puritans became separatists, advocating separation from the Anglican church, and they were persecuted for their radical social ideas.

In the 1640s, the English Parliament, supported by the army of Oliver Cromwell (1599–1658), made the state church presbyterian and tried to destroy the episcopals. The King was beheaded, the monarchy was abolished, and Cromwell was named "Lord Protector." After his death the monarchy and the Anglican (episcopal) church were reinstated, but for a time radical political and social ideas flourished under the banner of Puritanism: e.g., the "Levellers" believed that all men should have the vote, not only propertyholders (as was the case then), and the "Diggers" believed that there should be no private property, as the gifts of God's creation are to be shared equally by all. Not all Puritans were political radicals, however, and there was great variety among them in their ethical beliefs.

B. Quakers

The Society of Friends, or "Quakers," began with the idea of George Fox (1624–1691) that all have an "inner light" of truth within them. The Bible is not the final standard for revelation, as God speaks to and through each person. There was no formal authority structure among the Quakers, no ordained clergy, and no liturgy for worship services. The silent meeting form of worship allowed each individual a chance to speak if and when the spirit moved him or her, and all views were tolerated. The community reached joint decisions via a consensus process that involved each person contributing to the discussion. Quakers were and are devout pacifists, believing that one should respond to the threat of violence with love, as there is something of God in everyone which can be addressed and won over. Quakers have opposed war and slavery and worked for equal rights for women and minorities, and have come to be identified with an ethic that is politically progressive as well as nonviolent.

C. Rationalism

In the 18th century, an intellectual movement known as "Rationalism" developed which accepted reason as the main standard for truth. The development of modern science as well as biblical criticism was leading many to conclude that Christianity and the Bible were not especially reasonable, as miraculous events contradicted the laws of nature. Some rejected God altogether; others rejected traditional Christianity but held onto a belief that there is a God, one who does not want us to believe in Christ or miracles but only asks us to be moral. These "deists" emphasized the moral core of Christianity and discarded the rest of its beliefs, which they regarded as outdated superstitions.

Still other rationalists sought to reconcile traditional Christianity with a belief in reason. Among these was John Locke (1632–1704), who argued that Christianity holds truths that are above the realm of reason but none contrary to it. Human reason knows that we ought to be moral; God's revelation in the Bible does not contradict this, but supports and clarifies this basic truth. Locke accepted many traditional Christian ideas such as the miracles of Jesus, his virginal conception, and his resurrection from the dead (all taken as reasons for confessing that Jesus is the Christ)—but Locke's "reasonable" Christianity does not claim that the death of Jesus takes away human sin or that God's grace restores our freedom to do good. Rather, Locke viewed Jesus primarily as a moral teacher and example who makes the law easier to understand and to follow, allowing easy forgiveness for those who repent their sins. This law, however, can be understood without Jesus, so it is not clear that Christianity really adds anything to ethics that is not previously known by reason. Ultimately, Locke's ethics are based on reason rather than revelation, just like the deists' ethics.

Bishop Joseph Butler (1692–1752) was another Anglican who sought to show that Christianity and reason can be unified. His ethics emphasized virtues that can be known by reason, such as temperance, moderation, and most of all benevolence. The Bible adds authority to the moral law, but our own conscience and a sense of shame and duty are the basis for our obedience. Butler wanted to show that morality is reasonable and natural against the claims of Thomas Hobbes (1588–1679) that human nature is inherently selfish and unconcerned about others except insofar as necessary for personal survival. To love the neighbor, Butler argued, is not unnatural or at odds with self-love; in fact the two harmonize as one's private good (sought by self-love) increases as part of the public good (sought by benevolence, love for others). Even the commandment to "love your enemies" is rational as the desire for revenge only leads to self-destruction whereas forgiveness leads to personal as well as corporate happiness. To seek the happiness of all, the self included, is not only God's command but the commandment of reason. In Butler's view, God functions primarily as the backdrop to morality, the highest object of our love and happiness which we seek as our ground and goal.

In these efforts to show that Christianity and reason are in harmony, however, critics felt that Christianity had been reduced to reason and lost its distinctiveness. The critics of rationalism sought to restore the role of emotion and the personal experience of salvation to the Christian life.

D. Evangelicals and Methodists

1. John Wesley

John Wesley (1703–1791), the founder of Methodism, was among those who began to reemphasize the religious experience of salvation and the need for a life

transformed by Christ. As a student at Oxford, Wesley and others had founded a "Holy Club" whose members engaged in a disciplined method for spiritual life including prayer, fasting, and good works. In 1735 he traveled to the American colony of Georgia as a missionary, but was disappointed in his efforts to gain converts. On ship he had met some of the Moravian pietists, and was impressed by their confidence in God's salvation; upon his return to England, he had an experience of God's grace and mercy which gave him personal assurance of salvation and led him to begin preaching to outdoor revival meetings. The Church of England was unhappy with his independent style and theology, and Wesley's failure to accept its authority ultimately led to the separation of the Methodists from the Church of England.

Though Wesley believed like other Protestants that one is saved only by faith and not by works, he emphasized the importance of works as part of the process of sanctification by which Christians are made holy and pleasing to God. He went so far as to claim that Christians can achieve "perfection," not in the sense that they can avoid mistakes or have perfect knowledge, but in the sense that they can avoid all intentional outward sins. His moral beliefs were demanding, shaped by Puritanism, but against the Calvinists he held that we are not predestined but free to accept or reject God's grace as individuals. We choose whether we will accept salvation and live by the demands that follow from it.

Wesley campaigned against many social ills including alcohol sale and consumption, war, slavery, and poverty. Salvation was a matter of both internal experience and external behavior for Wesley, so he felt it necessary to condemn what he viewed as the sinful exploitation of the poor by the rich in English society. Methodism has continued to emphasize temperance, human rights, and the need to "feed the hungry and clothe the naked."

2. Jonathan Edwards

A revival of emotional religion also occurred in America, where it took the form of a growing "Evangelical" movement that emphasized the need to accept the "good news" (Greek, *evangel*) of Christ's gift of salvation by a personal conversion experience. The "Great Awakening" refers to a time in the 18th century when these ideas began to have significant influence. The most significant theologian of the Great Awakening was Jonathan Edwards (1703–1758).

Edwards was influenced by Puritanism as well as rationalistic philosophy in the construction of his own theology, which was an effective synthesis of numerous ideas. Edwards claimed that emotions and will (the "affections") are the root of action, but it is God who determines whether we are ruled by the true emotions of love of God and neighbor. We always choose what appears to us to be good, but a sinful person can choose only what is good for himself; with God's help, however, we can be enabled to see and choose the universal good of all. Love of God must come first, and from that comes love of the world and all that is in it. Edwards claimed (with rationalism) that it is in our nature to love God and others, but (with Calvinism) we can do this only through the power of God's grace, which turns our will to him. Edwards also emphasized the Calvinist themes of God's absolute sovereignty over our lives and the ethic of stewardship of God's creation.

VI. PROTESTANT LIBERALISM

"Protestant Liberalism" refers to a movement which began in the 19th century, primarily in Germany, which sought to revise Christian doctrine so that it could be brought into harmony with modern science and philosophy. In this aim they did not differ totally from the rationalists of a century earlier, but their revisions made a greater effort to preserve the essence of the tradition and not simply discard aspects which might seem outdated or irrelevant. Rather than abandon faith in Christ as redeemer from sin and sanctifier of Christian life, they reinterpreted these ideas to make sense in the modern world.

A. Friedrich Schleiermacher

The reputed founder of Protestant Liberalism is Friedrich Schleiermacher (1768–1834). In his view, Christian ethics (as well as doctrine) is based on Christian religious experience, specifically an experience of union with Christ as the redeemer. Christ redeems as the one who had perfect "God-consciousness," the one in whom all sin is overcome by a complete awareness of God as creator and redeemer, that upon which we ultimately depend. When we experience unity with Christ, our own sin-consciousness is overcome by God-consciousness, and it is in this that salvation consists. We are united with God through Christ, who has experienced complete unity with God.

Christian ethics, on this view, consists of describing the experience of Christians who live by the spirit of unity with Christ. Christians do not need laws to spell out what they ought to do, for they naturally do God's will insofar as they live on the basis of their conscious-ness of God. This is not solely an individual effort, however, as it is the Church which expresses the communal experience of God-consciousness in the world. In this sense, it is in the Church that Christians find the spirit of God at work.

B. Albrecht Ritschl

Albrecht Ritschl (1822–1889) developed the liberal emphasis on Christian experience by stressing its practical aspects. Christianity is not a matter of judgments of fact, as we can never know with certainty, for example, the "facts" of the nature of God. Rather, Christianity concerns judgments of value—what we value as good or bad, what we choose to do—i.e., ethics. In this sense theology is a practical matter and not a matter of philosophical speculation.

Ritschl found the practical core of Christianity in Jesus' idea of the Kingdom of God. He viewed this Kingdom as the moral ideal, a realm where God rules as Father and all human beings love one another, where every person is valued and respected. This ideal is what we should seek to actualize in the world by our own ethical efforts. Ritschl's ethics were therefore societal in scope and not merely personal. In fact, he believed that Protestantism had emphasized the personal experience of redemption to such an extent that it had neglected the ethical concept of the Kingdom of God as the ideal we should all be striving towards.

C. Adolf Harnack

Adolf Harnack (1851–1930) developed Ritschl's theology through his efforts to simplify the "essence of Christianity" to a few core ideas: the Kingdom of God, the unity of God with the human soul, and the commandment to love the neighbor. In Harnack's view, the Kingdom is not to be found in the external political realm but within each person who has experienced unity with God in love. This love is then shared with others, and so ethics is once again the core of Christian life. Harnack claimed to be basing his views on the ethics of the historical Jesus rather than later church doctrine, which he felt had needlessly complicated Christianity—but his simplifications tended to interpret the ethics of Jesus as supportive of his own middle-class German values, and ignored the rather different historical context of Jesus. Protestant Liberals like Harnack identified Christianity with the social ethics of their own culture, and so lost much of the critical challenge of Christian ethics which earlier Protestants had found in the Bible.

VII. CHRISTIAN SOCIALISM AND THE SOCIAL GOSPEL MOVEMENT

A. The Blumhardts and Swiss Socialism

The potentially radical social ethic of Christianity was not lost on Johann Christoph Blumhardt (1805–1880) or his son Christoph Friedrich Blumhardt (1842–1919), the reputed founders of Christian socialism in Switzerland. They argued that Christians are not to seek escape from the world but rather transform it, changing evil into good and conquering sin and death. This is to be accomplished in part through explicit political action (one of the Blumhardts even held political office) with the goal of achieving economic justice, understood along socialist lines. Like Ritschl, these Christian socialists emphasized the Kingdom of God as an ideal which should be brought into this world as Christians seek to improve the world and society for all.

B. Walter Rauschenbusch and the American Social Gospel

Many of the ideas of Christian socialism surfaced in the United States, taking the form of a so-called "Social Gospel" movement which emphasized societal reform as a crucial aspect of the "good news" to be brought to all people by Christians. Walter Rauschenbusch (1861–1918), the most significant thinker of this movement, claimed that both sin and salvation are to be understood in social and not just individual terms. He defined sin as the selfish neglect of others' needs, and salvation as the turn from self to God and humanity. The ideal of salvation, expressed by the Kingdom of God, embodies the hope for an end to social injustice. Rauschenbusch was a great critic of industrial capitalism, and promoted the socialist ideal that the workers should own the means of production and share in their profits. Nonetheless he held that spiritual values precede and ground material values, so he did not accept the Marxist reduction of social good to economic good. Salvation was more than just material well-being to Rauschenbusch, but he still claimed that Christians can and ought to work to "Christianize" the social order by working to end the exploitation of the poor by corporate industry. Rauschenbusch was optimistic about this possibility as he believed that social sin can be overcome by social progress, expressed in political and legislative changes.

VIII. NEO-ORTHODOXY AND MODERN PROTESTANT THEOLOGY

With the coming of the first World War, much of the optimism of Christian socialists, liberals, and Social Gospel advocates seemed discredited. The world was not getting better or closer to the Kingdom of God on earth; rather, it was getting worse, wracked by social chaos and destruction. Human sin could not be erased by social programs, for it was deep within human nature and continued to express itself in political and social evils. With the experience of the coming of Nazism and fascism and the second World War, this sense of the hopelessness of the human condition was only intensified.

A. Karl Barth

Karl Barth (1886–1965), probably the most significant Protestant theologian of the 20th century, was among the first to recognize the need for a new kind of theology. A Swiss Reformed minister, trained in liberal theology and exposed to Christian socialism, he was disgusted when his German theology professors supported the first World War. He believed that liberalism had equated the ethics of Christianity with the ethics of society, and so lacked any perspective from which to critique the society. What was needed was a theology that was biblically based which challenged society to return to Christian ethics. In the years following WWI, Barth's "dialectical theology" sought to do this by emphasizing the "infinite qualitative difference" between humans and God, the sinfulness of humans, and the human need for redemption. Humans cannot save themselves, and liberals have been foolish to believe that society can be saved by human efforts; we must rely on God entirely. This was in part a return to the ideas of Luther and Calvin, but Barth was not a political conservative; he remained a socialist, committed to economic and political reforms. He felt, however, that these could be undertaken only with the understanding that God alone will bring the Kingdom, and we cannot expect our efforts to erase sin or overcome evil.

With the coming of Nazism to Germany, Barth and other church leaders formed the "Confessing Church" which declared that Christ was its Lord and not Adolf Hitler, and so they could sign no oath of allegiance to the Fuehrer (which the state was requiring). This group protested Nazi attempts to control the church, but they did not advocate any revolutionary action against the state.

Barth revised his theology drastically in the 1930s when he came to believe that his "dialectical" theology had failed to acknowledge the human potential for good. In his emphasis on human sinfulness, he had neglected to develop the idea that God's grace can and does remake human nature so that we are free to do good and are in fact redeemed. The infinite difference between God and humans was overcome in Christ, who was both God and man and redeems our nature as such. Barth's ethics in this later period was based on the notion that God's revelation is the standard for the truth, and Christ is its norm. Christ is perfect God and perfect human, and it is from Him that we are to learn what God wants us to do. This does not mean literalistic imitation of Jesus, however, but listening for God's word to us in specific situations.

Barth influenced a range of Protestant thinkers who came to be classed under the rubric of "neo-orthodoxy." This term refers to theology which sought to return to traditional Protestant themes (such as God's sovereignty, human sin, and the need for God's grace) while at the same time remaining relevant to the situation of the 20th century. Traditional doctrines were revised, as they had been by liberals, but now the dominant tone echoed not optimistic idealism about human progress but realism about human sin.

B. Dietrich Bonhoeffer

Dietrich Bonhoeffer (1906–1945) was a German Lutheran minister who became deeply critical of German society with the coming of Nazism. Though many Lutherans accepted Hitler, Bonhoeffer protested against Nazism and even became implicated in the plot to assassinate Hitler. He was imprisoned and executed before the end of the war, and is viewed as a modern Christian martyr.

Bonhoeffer's ethics were demanding, emphasizing that faith must include obedience to God's commands which deal with life in the world. Bonhoeffer rejected the concept he called "cheap grace," the idea that salvation is only a gift with no demands attached. While some Lutherans insisted that God's grace requires nothing in response, Bonhoeffer argued that faith without obedience is not real faith. We must respond to the radical demands of the gospel with moral action, not passivity. These demands may involve self-sacrifice—in Bonhoeffer's own case, he decided to return to Germany during the war to work against Nazism even though he knew he might not survive.

Bonhoeffer's ethics were also shaped by his sense that the world has been reconciled to God through Christ, and so is already redeemed. God took form in the world in Christ, which shows that the world matters to God—and this means it should matter to Christians, as Christ now takes form in the Church which expresses the love of Christ for the world.

C. The Niebuhrs

Two brothers, Reinhold Niebuhr (1892–1971) and H. Richard Niebuhr (1894–1962), were among the most influential of American neo-orthodox theologians and ethicists. H. Richard Niebuhr's ethics stressed a responsibility before God which values all things as God does. All things in the world are valuable, but only if understood as centered in a God who transcends and grounds the world's values. Richard is also well known for his five "types" of how Christians can relate the "Christ" of their faith to the "culture" in which they live. Christians can view their faith as opposed to the culture (like Anabaptism), or as a part of the culture (like liberal Protestantism), but they may also view it as the completion of culture (as in Roman Catholic ethics), separated from culture (as in Luther's "Two Kingdoms" doctrine), or the transformer of culture (as in Puritanism). Niebuhr seems to favor the latter, part of his own Reformed church heritage.

Reinhold Niebuhr was even more influential than his brother. For him, the Christian ethic is an impossible ideal that cannot be realized in this world. The pacifist who thinks he will follow Jesus simply by always responding to violence with love has ignored the fact that one cannot always choose a course of action which avoids violent consequences. It one loves the aggressor by responding only with nonviolence, one fails to love the victims one allows the aggressor to harm. Sometimes, realism demands that force must be used to stop evil and protect the weak. This is particularly true of the political realm, which is based on power and not on love. Justice, not love, is the ideal which one should strive to achieve in the political realm—whether it is corrective justice, which protects the public by punishing criminals, or distributive justice, which apportions economic resources fairly, but not always purely equally.

The Christian ideal of love, however, remains necessary and relevant to life. One needs such an ideal to motivate political realism beyond a mere balance of competing interests to a concern for all sides. Without love as the basis for ethics, morality degenerates into a selfish concern for one's own survival or the survival of one's group. Corrective justice must still protect the rights of the criminal and treat him humanely, and distributive justice must aid those who cannot earn a living. Thus love and justice must be balanced in ethics, just as idealism and realism must be balanced.

Reinhold Niebuhr recognized, with Social Gospel advocates, that sin takes a social form in society—but he was not as optimistic as they about the possibility of eliminating social evil by policy and legislative change. Though sin is most virulent in its social forms, it is based in individuals' anxiety about their own finitude and their need to assert their power to act freely. Sin is therefore a part of human nature which can never be erased no matter how society changes. This realism about sin motivated Niebuhr's belief that the ideal of love can never be achieved, though this ideal remains crucial to constructing an ethical society.

D. Paul Tillich

Paul Tillich (1886–1965), a German theologian who moved to the United States in the 1930s, is not always classified as a neo-orthodox theologian, but he shares many of their tendencies. Tillich's theology was eclectic, borrowing from neo-orthodoxy, liberalism, and existentialism to develop his system.

Tillich believed ethics should be "theonomous," i.e., based on God's law—but this theonomy must be a synthesis of autonomy (self-legislation) and heteronomy (legislation coming from another). God's law is not simply a law imposed on us from outside by God, nor is it simply an internal ethic developed by ourselves; it combines and transcends both. Tillich also recognized that we can have no certainty regarding God's will. We trust in something as our "ultimate concern," our God, but we can never know if our faith is directed toward the infinite or only toward a finite idol. If we claim that we know God's will perfectly, we are failing to recognize the mystery and transcendence of God, making our own understanding of God into the idol we worship. True faith demands the humility which knows we are limited in our understanding and cannot claim to speak for God. Those who claim certainty in ethical matters may actually have a demonic faith, Tillich claimed, like the Nazis who regarded Hitler's will as their "ultimate concern" to which they were willing to sacrifice all other moral concerns.

Like Reinhold Neibuhr, Tillich believed that power is a reality which cannot be ignored in ethical considerations—but he understood the relationship between love and justice in a somewhat different way. Tillich believed justice and love are not in opposition but merely in "dynamic tension" with one another. Justice is the form

love takes in society, and creative justice serves the ideal of love.

E. Joseph Fletcher and Situation Ethics

In the 1960s, Joseph Fletcher promoted a view he called "situation ethics," which claimed that there are no ethical laws by which the Christian ought to make decisions, only the norm of love. One must evaluate the right thing to do in each situation as it appears by weighing various courses of action and deciding which will demonstrate the most love for all persons concerned. Fletcher distinguished his "situationism" from both "legalism" (which blindly follows traditional moral laws regardless of consequences) and "antinomianism" (which makes arbitrary decisions without reference to general principles or laws). Situation ethics allows one, for example, to justify a lie which saves a life, or even kill to save multiple lives, because such an action results in greater love.

Fletcher's view was not entirely novel, but it drew much attention and controversy. Some ethicists such as Paul Ramsey argued that though love is the primary ground of Christian morality, it is expressed in rules which precede situations. Christians are guided not merely by their own intuitions of what is loving in a given situation, but also by the rules and laws of the Christian tradition which are shaped by love. Most ethicists felt that Fletcher had oversimplified the process of moral decision making, but his views may have gained popularity precisely for that reason—as well as by the fact that they sanctioned personal judgment in an era which was questioning all authority.

IX. LIBERATION THEOLOGY

In the past few decades theology has devoted increasing concern to those who are the victims of political or economic oppression. "Liberation theology" refers to theologies which proclaim that salvation involves a total liberation involving political and economic as well as spiritual freedom. The gospel demands an end to oppression and a recognition of the exploitation of the poor, women, and minorities. Liberation theology is similar to the Social Gospel movement in these aspects, but it is more radical in its demands for societal change and in its use of Marxist and feminist social criticism. Though largely a Roman Catholic phenomenon, liberation theology has also taken Protestant forms.

A. Third World Theology

Theologians in South and Central America, Africa, and Asia have begun to recognize the heritage of colonialism in these areas and the profound influence it had on the shape of Christianity there. Imported with the oppressors, Christianity often sanctioned their actions and promoted meek passivity on the part of the oppressed. Now many Christians in these areas are rejecting this view, claiming that God actually exercises a "preferential option for the poor," those who suffer under oppressive regimes and economies. They draw on Old Testament traditions of the nation of Israel as a people of slaves freed by God, and view Jesus as one who desired to end political opporession. Liberation theology takes Protestant forms most often in countries such as South Africa which were colonized by Protestants.

B. African-American Theology

The most productive area for Protestant liberation theology has been the African-American community. Shaped by a long history of Christianity, black Americans began to question the subservience encouraged by the church in the 1950s with the dawning of the civil rights movement. The most important figure in this development was Martin Luther King, Jr. (1929–1965), a Baptist minister who organized a boycott of segregated buses in Montgomery, Alabama, and went on from there to become the national leader of the black civil rights movement. He argued that the oppressors could be overcome by nonviolent protest of the sort that Gandhi had used in India because Christian love has the power to end violence, whereas violence (in this case) will only beget more violence. King had recognized the political effectiveness of nonviolent protest methods, and so was balancing realism with idealism as Reinhold Niebuhr did in his ethics.

King was killed before the term "liberation theology" came into use, but his emphasis on the need for liberation from social oppression inspired later African-American theology. The chief difference between King and later black theologians such as James Cone is that the latter are more radical in their social analysis and more prepared to accept the possible use of violence to achieve the just end of liberation. Echoing third world theologies, Cone argues that to reject the possibility of violence on the side of the oppressed is to implicitly support the violence of the oppressor. He also focuses more on developing a theology for black people than achieving the goal of racial integration which was so crucial to King's vision. In sum, black theology after King has been more critical of white America's racism and less optimistic about achieving justice without radical methods.

C. Feminist Theology

Like third world liberation theology, feminist theology has been shaped most significantly by Roman Catholics (in particular, Rosemary Ruether), but Protestant feminist theologians exist as well. Feminist theology focuses on the exploitation of women and the need of the Church to reform itself in nonsexist ways. In the feminist view, everything from the male gender of the deity to the exclusion of women from church leadership echoes the heritage of sexism in Christianity, as women have been scapegoated as the source of evil and subordinated to males who are viewed as rightfully dominant over them. Feminists reinterpret the Bible in ways which seek to purge it of sexism, appealing to its message of liberation to all who are oppressed, including women. Some feminists have rejected Christianity altogether, turning to worship of a goddess figure, but Christian feminists try to reform the tradition in ways which preserve its essence and make it meaningful as a way of liberation for women.

X. ECUMENICAL DIALOGUE

A movement began early in the 20th century to unify Christians across denominational lines, so constructing an "ecumenical" (worldwide) Christian community. The movement was shaped most significantly by Protestants steeped in the Social Gospel movement who wanted to bring Christians together to work for peace and justice worldwide. The "Life and Work" movement, founded for this purpose, held conferences in Stockholm (1925) and Oxford (1937) which developed statements urging the unity of Christians in their ethical goals. The Oxford conference reflected the ideas of participants such as Karl Barth and Reinhold Niebuhr that both love and justice are necessary goals to work toward, and that Christians must be realistic enough to acknowledge that they cannot create God's Kingdom through their efforts on earth. The conference also criticized both communism and capitalism as inadequate ways of addressing humans needs.

The Oxford conference led to the formation of the world Council of Churches (WCC), which first met in Amsterdam in 1948. The WCC has continued to draft ethical policy statements, dealing with a range of issues including nuclear arms reduction, environmental problems, and third world rights. The goal of a "just, participatory, and sustainable society" was developed as a way of expressing the need to safeguard not only human justice and freedom but natural resources and the environmental balance as well.

XI. CONCLUSIONS

Protestant ethics contains diverse strains which cannot be easily harmonized or glossed over to present a unity. As Protestantism has evolved over the last 500 years, it has included some who wanted to abandon society, and some who wished to change it; some who focused on works as the core of Christian faith, and some who spoke little about morality. It has included liberals and moderates, conservatives and radicals. Protestants are today sharply divided on issues such as abortion and homosexual rights, even as they were once divided about slavery and women's suffrage. There will probably never be complete unity among Protestants on ethical matters, but all have claimed the bible and the Protestant tradition as their authority, and all have sought to do the will of God as they understood it.

See Also the Following Article

RELIGION AND ETHICS

Bibliography

Beach, W., and Niebuhr, H. R. (Eds.) (1955). "Christian Ethics: Sources of the Living Tradition." Ronald Press, New York.

Forell, G. W. (Ed.) (1966). "Christian Social Teachings: A Reader in Christian Social Ethics from the Bible to the Present." Doubleday, New York.

Gustafson, J. M. (1978). "Protestant and Roman Catholic Ethics: Prospects for Rapprochement." Univ. of Chicago Press, Chicago.

Keeling, M. (1990). "The Foundations of Christian Ethics." Clark, Edinburgh.

Long, E. L., Jr. (1982). "A Survey of Recent Christian Ethics." Oxford Univ. Press, New York.

Long, E. L., Jr. (1967). "A Survey of Christian Ethics." Oxford Univ. Press, New York.

McGrath, A. (1988). "Reformation Thought: An Introduction." Blackwell, New York.

Reardon, B. M. G. (1995). "Religious Thought in the Reformation," 2nd ed. Longman, New York.

Wogaman, J. P. (1993). "Christian Ethics: A Historical Introduction." Westminster/John Knox Press, Louisville, KY.

Wogaman, J. P., and Strong, D. (Eds.) (1996). "Readings in Christian Ethics: A Historical Sourcebook." Westminster/John Knox Press, Louisville, KY.

CHRISTIAN ETHICS, ROMAN CATHOLIC

Anthony Fisher
Australian Catholic University

GLOSSARY

conscience Knowledge of moral principles and their application, and the capacity to judge what to do in the here and now. Like other intellectual abilities, conscience can be mature or immature, healthy or not, integrated with passion or overwhelmed by it, well trained or distorted by upbringing; as a result it can be more or less sensitive, realistic, impartial, wise. Thus the principal goal of Catholic ethics is to form conscience according to truth.

dignity The intrinsic, equal, and inalienable worth of the human person, deserving the highest reverence and respect. Persons are created "in the image of God" as free and rational beings with a divine calling, and restored to that image by Christ's redemptive work making them children of God. Catholic ethics can thus be viewed as a response to God's call to all to live up to their dignity, to "become what you are."

freedom The capacity to deliberate and decide what to do or refrain from doing, despite internal and external pressures. The exercise of freedom shapes and expresses moral identity and destiny. Catholic ethics can be viewed as a search for those norms and virtues that enable people to exercise their freedom reasonably and responsibly.

good An object of desire and choice that fulfills the person, whether viewed as a single unitary goal (e.g., the vision of God), a multifaceted good, or multiple goods corresponding to the complexity of human nature and/or those dimensions of God in which human beings can participate. Any choice, person, relationship or situation is said to be *morally* good when it seeks or inclines to reasonable action which serves the ultimate good of persons: happiness.

grace The free gift of God of sharing his life, which sustains and fulfills people (and so is necessary even for free choice) and redeems, sanctifies, and divinizes them as adopted children of God. Grace is thus the dynamic principle of all Christian life. Theologians have commonly distinguished varieties of grace: uncreated and created, prevenient and saving, sanctifying and actual.

happiness The fulfillment of the whole person, through participation in the goods of human nature by human choice. More than just sensible pleasures or the fulfillment of private preferences even on earth, complete happiness or blessedness is only enjoyed in heaven in communion with God and the saints. Catholic ethics seeks to articulate what is involved in being rationally interested in the present and ultimate happiness of all human persons.

love A relationship in which persons make each other's good their own, sharing purposes, projects, and lives.

The call to love God, neighbor, and self is the foundation of Jewish and Christian morality. Catholic ethics can be viewed as an attempt to articulate the "logic" of love: those (respectful, nurturing, self-sacrificing, etc.) ways of acting that genuinely serve others.

Magisterium The teaching authority of the Church, restating or unfolding the implications of Christ's teaching, and exercised by the Pope, general Council, bishops, or the entire People of God. By divine assistance their authoritative distillation of Catholic faith and morals is, under certain conditions, definitive, even infallible; it therefore commands religious assent.

natural law Morality that is in principle accessible to anyone who reflects upon the structure of human choice and the nature of the human person in community. This is the basis of the common morality shared by people of good will of all religions and none, and of notions such as transcultural and transtemporal human rights.

original sin The phenomenon dramatically portrayed in The Book of Genesis as the original disobedience and consequent fall from grace of the first human beings, which explains the universal experience of alienation from or disharmony with God, others, creation, and self. The result of this sin is an internal disintegration of reason, passions, and will. This "hereditary" sin is the prototype and context of all chosen ("actual") sin.

reconciliation The restoration of right relations between persons and between the person and God following breach by sin, through the renunciation of that sin and consequent hostility, and the gifts of forgiveness and amity. Catholics celebrate this conversion sacramentally (in confession, absolution, penance, or reconciliation).

sin A freely chosen act known to be contrary to moral reason or God's law manifest to conscience. Such choices harm the sinner and others and are an affront to God. When a person deliberately and freely performs some "gravely" immoral action they sin "mortally"; when the choice is less grave, considered or free, they sin "venially."

CATHOLIC ETHICS is systematic reflection within the Catholic faith tradition upon questions of what the human person should be and do. Like all *moral philosophy* it is a search for those approaches, norms, character traits, and choices that enable people to live well individually and together; but as a species of Catholic *theol-*ogy it engages in that task by reflecting upon God's express will for humanity—found not only in the "natural law" available to all, but also in the revealed "Word of God." Catholic ethics thus offers a guide to a life that befits human nature, responds to the divine calling, and prepares people for eternal life in God's family. It seeks to educate conscience, shape virtues, and make possible wise decisions in particular cases. Catholics believe the Church has a special function in proclaiming the Gospel of Jesus Christ to every generation, interpreting it afresh and authoritatively in the light of the signs of the times, and assisting all people to understand and to live the practical implications of that "Good News." Because it preaches an eminently *practical* gospel, the Catholic tradition has long made an important contribution to applied ethics.

I. CATHOLIC ETHICS: INHERITANCE AND CALL TO RENEWAL

The Catholic tradition has long insisted that the moral law is accessible to all people of good will who follow reason's guidance, undeflected by distracting emotion, prejudice, or convention. It is thus shared by people of all religions and none, can form the basis of dialogue and common life for people of various beliefs and customs, and is properly matter for sound philosophy. But reason's full implications, and morality's practical applications, are well understood only when full account is taken of the human situation. Christians believe that our human predicament, opportunities, and calling include some realities adequately and reliably revealed only by the life and teachings of Jesus Christ, through the Church's Scriptures and tradition. All moral principles are thus matters not only for moral philosophy, but also for doctrine, faith, and theology.

A. The Scriptures

Christians believe that God is the author of Scripture insofar as he inspired its human authors; he acts in the Scriptures and by means of them; they teach without error God's saving truth. The Second Vatican Council (Vatican II) called for a Scriptural renewal of Catholic ethics: the Scriptures should be the daily food of Christian life and the subject of special study by scholars, teachers, and pastors as they seek to articulate the implications of God's word for perennial and contemporary problems.

In *The Old Testament*—those Scriptures shared by

Jews and Christians—morality is the plan of a God of love who wills the happiness of his creatures and thus reveals to them how to live well with each other and with him. The people of God are called into a special "covenant" relationship with God and moral life is at once an elaboration of the terms of that invitation and the response of the believer to it.

Thus Christians share with Jewish ethics the great commandment to love that is expanded upon in the *Decalogue* (the Ten Commandments in Exodus ch. 20 and Deuteronomy ch. 5). These norms lay the foundations for the daily life of the human person; they prescribe what is necessary and prohibit what is contrary to love of God and neighbor. This divine law (Torah) was elaborated in great detail in the Scriptures and the Jewish exegetical and teaching tradition, with specific regulations touching upon all areas of human life including worship, sex, marriage, family life, agriculture, trade, property rights, rest, social and political responsibility. Ethics are also presented through stories (the disobedience of Adam and Eve, the fidelity of Abraham, the courage of Daniel and Esther, the prudence of Solomon, the chastity of Susanna, etc.), through prophetic utterances, and in proverbial wisdom.

The prophets commonly focused their critical gaze upon idolatry of various kinds—not just of foreign gods, but of wealth, power, and privilege—and upon the quality of relationships between individuals, between communities, and with God. They preached *hesed* (love or mercy) and *sedekah* (justice or righteousness), which included harmonious community life, distributive justice, honesty, and fair dealing. The litmus test of this mercy and justice was how the *anawim* (widows, orphans, the poor, refugees, etc.) were treated, and the prophets spoke for God in condemning the predatory rich and powerful for their oppression or hard-heartedness toward the underprivileged.

In many places the ethics of the Christian *New Testament* echo those of the Old inherited from the Jews. The crucial difference, however, is that the person of Jesus Christ is presented as the paradigm and incarnation of moral truth and the imperative of discipleship. Fully God and fully man, Jesus reveals both the full extent of God's will for humanity and the full extent of human possibilities under grace. It is he who makes it possible for people to achieve their potential, to be forgiven, liberated, and transformed. His Gospel is, literally, "good news," yet it is also subversive: it turns worldly standards and expectations on their heads, calling people to repentance and self-renunciation, to take up the "cross" and follow him. His followers are to "seek first the kingdom of God," translating God's sovereignty

into attitudes and actions that transform the present human order, while recognizing that its ultimate realization is to be looked for in the future. In particular they must imitate and mediate God's inclusiveness and mercy, his loving concern for the powerless, his "preference" for the outcast. While repeating and summarizing the old law in terms of love of God and neighbor (e.g., Mark 12:28–31; cf. 1 Corinthians ch. 13), Jesus extends his disciples' understanding of all these terms, commending by word and example the kind of self-sacrificing love that he had demonstrated (e.g., John chs 13–15). He deplores hypocrisy and goes to the root of unloving behavior in the unloving heart. He liberates the believer from slavery to sin and death, and identifies those attitudes that will be the marks of his little band. In expectation of his return in judgment Christians seek to live in conformity with God's salvific plan and in hope of his promises.

Jesus presented his moral teaching in many forms: in direct teaching on life in the kingdom of God, in story form (parables), by acts of exorcism, healing, and absolution, by his own way of life and that to which he called his disciples. Perhaps his most famous ethical teaching is that collected and recorded in the Gospel of Matthew as the Sermon on the Mount. There Jesus calls his followers to lives of exemplary virtue—to be "salt of the earth," "light to the world," "bearers of good fruit," "doers of God's will," reliable teachers of others, "perfect" like God—and he elaborates on what this might mean. He begins by declaring that he has come not to overturn the old law, but to fulfill it; his "way" will require a moral depth beyond mere formal observance of precepts whether out of a minimalist legalism or a desire for the respect of others; it will be marked instead by those fundamental dispositions told in the *beatitudes* (his famous "blessed are …" sayings in Matthew 5:2–12; cf. Luke 6:20–23). Jesus then re-articulates the Decalogue in terms which at once confirm and go beyond the natural law. The precept against murder becomes a basic attitude of reverence for life and thus nonvengefulness, nonresistance, an active will for reconciliation with enemies; the precept against adultery becomes reverence for the bodies of others and for marriage, and thus opposition to sex outside of marriage, sexual impurity and exploitation, and remarriage after divorce; the precept against false oaths is unpacked as reverence for truth and thus honesty in all communications; the precept against theft becomes a reverence for created goods expressed in a boundless generosity that is never merely acquisitive, anxiously self-protective or seeking recognition; and the precepts of religion are re-presented as a call to total reliance on divine providence, and humble prayerfulness and penitence without show or pretense.

After the death, resurrection and ascension of their Lord, the apostolic generation proclaimed his Gospel in various forms and places and generated a literature, some of which was canonized as The New Testament. This included not merely restatements of Jesus' own teaching but their own understanding of its implications for their mission and for daily life. Dealing as he was with gentiles, Paul, for instance, wondered whether non-Jews and non-Christians knew the moral law; in his Letter to the Romans he concluded that by virtue of their conscience all people share in this knowledge of God's law "written on their hearts" but that without Christ's redeeming grace they are divided within themselves and inclined to sin. In his letters he responded to the needs of his particular communities by offering a great deal of moral exhortation and reproof including "household codes" of advice on diverse matters (e.g., Romans chs 12–15; 1 Corinthians; Galatians chs 5–6; Ephesians chs 4–5). Thus, already in the first century Christians demonstrated an enthusiasm not merely for moral theories and ideals but for a thoroughly "applied" or lived ethic.

B. The Tradition

Until at least the Middle Ages there existed no clear division in Christian theology between faith and practice, dogma and morals. Thus in the post-apostolic era the "Fathers" of the Church wrote very few treatises specifically on ethics; more often their moral teaching was to be found scattered among Scripture commentaries (e.g., Gregory the Great's *Moralia on the Book of Job*, ca. 580–600), homilies, spiritual conferences, letters, and polemical tracts. Such works were addressed by "shepherds of souls" to the needs of the local faithful, rather than by professional theologians to their peers. Christian ethics in this period commonly involved a creative rereading of Scriptural texts, reflection upon the practical implications of some Trinitarian or Christological dogma or of the doctrine of *oikonomia* (the consequences of divine providence and especially the Incarnation for the created order).

The Fathers brought with them the intellectual "baggage" of their surrounding world and were well positioned to challenge prevailing mores. Thus while Christians stood out against the Greco-Roman empire on many ethical matters (e.g., their hostility to apostasy, abortion, infanticide, adultery), they were in turn both influenced by and influential upon the ideas of their age. Apologists such as Justin Martyr (100–165), Clement of Alexandria (ca. 150–215), and Tertullian (ca. 160–225) were intent on showing that Christianity was no threat to society and state and that Christians lived highly moral, peaceable lives. Later writers such as John Chrysostom (ca. 349–407) and Gregory of Nyssa (ca. 335–395) emphasized the reversal of values called for by the way of the Cross. Sex, wealth, and power were to be renounced as ultimate values; Christians were called to a chaste reverence for each other's bodies and to share their material goods with those more needy than themselves; they were to be suspicious of concupiscence, lust, and avarice.

In the West, the moral theology of Augustine of Hippo (354–430) was probably the most influential postbiblical treatment for the next millennium. In his account, it is God's will that all people be fulfilled; the moral life is thus the pursuit of happiness in this life and beyond. To enable this, God shares his creativity with every human being through the gift of free will and shares his saving truth with them through the illumination of conscience. However, ever since the Fall human beings have been inclined to errors of judgment, temptations, weakness of will, and thus to sin; they would not seek their genuine good without the tutelage of God's revealed law, moderating habits and, above all, the grace granted through Christ's saving death. As a pastor Augustine addressed the moral development of his flock through pamphlets and letters on matters such as lying, marital life, and fasting.

Inheriting the ancient Greek understanding of virtue as excellence of character inclining the agent to choose well, the Fathers commonly adopted the classical "cardinal" virtues in their moral psychology and pedagogy: prudence above all, as well as justice, fortitude, and temperance. To these they added the three "theological" virtues of faith, hope, and charity described by Paul, analyzing the unity and interconnectedness of these character traits. On this account the grace of charity unifies and animates all the other virtues, and virtuous character must be cultivated if moral norms are to be readily and appropriately applied. However the Jewish-Christian notion of *metanoia* (radical conversion of heart and life) increasingly took the central place of the pagan *metrion* (a more measured, harmonious balance or "golden mean") in Christian morality. Apart from laying the foundations for Christian ethics for the succeeding millennium, the Fathers made important contributions to "applied ethics" by reflecting upon such matters as self-defense, the just war, sexual and family morality, truth-telling and promise-keeping, and the just distribution of wealth.

After the patristic era moral theology advanced more

through the work of the monastic and itinerant confessors than through academics and church leaders. Some produced influential "penitentials": books of confessional practice addressing moral psychology generally, as well as particular sins and their sacramental and penitential remedies. In the early medieval period an intellectual revival in Church and society heralded a renaissance for moral theology through the work of the "scholastics." Clerics and laity associated with the recently founded universities applied newly rediscovered classical philosophy and the tools of dialectic to the inherited "deposit" of moral teaching, seeking to articulate the first truly systematic accounts of Christian ethics.

The greatest theologian of the Middle Ages—and arguably of any age—was Thomas Aquinas (ca. 1225–1274). The Second Part of his *Summa theologiæ* was the crowning achievement of moral theology in that period. Fundamental to his approach were: a theory of practical reason by which moral principles are naturally known (natural law) and confirmed by divine revelation; an anthropology that examined the nature of human persons and thus what fulfills them; a moral psychology of virtues both natural and infused that integrate, moderate, and direct character; and a theology of grace and beatitude that empowers and motivates agents toward their final good.

Thus Aquinas inherited from classical philosophers such as Aristotle and the Stoics the idea that human beings, like all other creatures, naturally strive to fulfill their nature and that by applying reason to reality persons can discern their genuine good and appropriate norms of action; but from Christian tradition, especially Augustine, he took the insight that such reasoning is both difficult and easily distorted (by distracting passion, poor moral education, or a corrupt culture), and thus in need of being "informed" and "verified" by Christian faith. Likewise he drew from the classical tradition a picture of those good dispositions of character (virtues) that people have by temperament or education (instruction, imitation, and practice) and that incline them more willingly and ably to do the good; but from Christian tradition he added the "theological" virtues of faith, hope, and above all charity, which inform moral virtues and choices and which can be gained not only by cultivation but also by divine infusion. And whereas the classical account left to the *polis* (community) the function of educating, correcting, and otherwise enabling the person to live the good life, Aquinas attributed such healing and elevating work to divine grace mediated especially through the sacraments and teaching of the Church. The richness of Aquinas' moral

theory cannot be elaborated here. Let it suffice to note that his complex analysis of the philosophy and psychology of the human act was highly influential then as it is now, as was his teaching in particular areas of applied ethics (e.g., sexual ethics, bioethics, the just war).

Among the legacies of Aqunias taken up and further developed in the centuries that followed by other theologian-saints such as Antoninus of Florence (1389–1459) and Alphonsus Ligouri (1696–1787) were the "principle of double effect" and the distinction between "formal" and "material" cooperation. Both go to the heart of the agent's true object or intention and ultimately the permissibility of an action: in the first, as is not uncommon, a proposal has two likely effects, one desired, the other not; in the second situation, also very common, the agent's actions contribute in some way to another person's wrongdoing. The tradition has suggested that an action that has two effects is permissible if (1) it is not excluded outright because intrinsically evil (as, for example, directly killing the innocent, committing apostasy or adultery, or telling a lie would be), (2) the good effect is genuinely the one sought whereas the bad effect is at most foreseen but not intended either in itself or as a means to the good effect, and (3) the action is not excluded on some other ground (e.g., because it would be unfair to others to tolerate its bad consequences). Cooperation in the wrongdoing of others is forbidden if it involves the agent in making the wrongdoing their own goal or the intended means to their own goal (formal cooperation); but material cooperation, where the success of the wrongdoer's project is not intended but only indirectly facilitated, is sometimes, though not always, permissible.

Unfortunately such useful secondary principles and distinctions sometimes became a substitute for the richer moral theology of which they were only a part. Likewise some people took Aquinas' interest in anthropology—in particular, what the requirements of human nature might tell us about the requirements of morality—as a warrant for a morality that purported to read moral norms off nature (naturalism). Neglecting Aquinas' fuller theory of practical reason, this approach reduced natural law to norms of bodily or animal function (physicalism), to a suspicion of technological advance (as unnatural), and/or to a minimalism whereby anything not obviously inconsistent with nature is permitted.

In the centuries that followed, despite some important developments there was an increasing separation of moral from mystical, spiritual, and pastoral theology; the former unity of perspective in these areas was lost; Catholic ethics became more and more speculative, complicated, specialized, and abstract; nominalism and legalism crept into thought and practice. After the Reformation Protestant ethics developed in its own way. Dominated by the doctrines of the Fall and "justification by faith alone" (i.e., that people are saved by the gift of faith alone and not their own good works), it was pessimistic both about the possibility of natural human knowledge of the good (relying instead upon the revealed Word of God) and of any natural inclination toward it (relying upon divine grace alone and denying to human beings any merit in their actions). Catholic ethics all too often reacted by exaggerating what could be derived from reason unaided by faith, and what could be achieved by obedience to the dictates of reason and the Church, and focused increasingly upon the minutia of moral laws and their applications, and the practices of sacramental and other penances. The Council of Trent (1545–1563) restated the traditional distinction between mortal and venial sins, the former requiring full awareness, deliberate consent, and grave matter. Unrepented of, mortal sin invited damnation; repented of, it required sacramental confession and reform of life. Rival theological schools proposed various standards for resolving disputes between authorities when the moral law was doubtful (laxists, rigorists, probabilists, probabiliorists, equiprobabilists, etc.), and casuists published manuals for seminarians and confessors that proposed resolutions for very particular cases of conscience but often offered a fairly impoverished account of Catholic ethical wisdom. A legalism crept into moral theology that gave the impression that the Church's moral teaching consisted of the conventions of members of a religious organization, or the legislation of some authority supported by threats and prizes, rather than received truths about the way to human flourishing.

In modern times Catholic ethics has faced challenges from many quarters: declining religious belief and practice; the exaltation of human dignity, rights, and conscience, with a parallel diminishment of the roles of authority and tradition (the "privatization of morality"); ideologies antithetical to Christianity but each with its own valuable insights (liberalism, determinism, Marxism, Darwinism, Freudianism, existentialism, analytical philosophy); powerful alternative sources of moral instruction (media, law, public education); new technologies (transport and communications, nuclear weapons, contraception, reproductive technologies); changing socioeconomic conditions (industrialization, urbanization, unemployment, the gaps between rich and poor); cultural developments (the

"sexual revolution," individualism, hedonism, consumerism, ethical scepticism); the widely acknowledged need for a refurbishment of Catholic theology in general and moral theology in particular; and growing dissent from official Church teaching on many ethical matters, even among theologians. Catholic ethics was ripe for renewal.

C. The Call to a Renewal

From 1962 through 1965 the twentieth ecumenical council, known as Vatican II, sought both to reemphasize what was best in traditional Catholic teaching and practice and to update it in response to the needs and insights of the modern world. With respect to moral theology it prescribed "livelier contact with the mystery of Christ and the history of salvation," a firmer grounding in Scripture and tradition, and a clearer recognition that the Christian calling is heavenward in direction but earthly in its temporal enactment. It thus invited, on the one hand, a renewed Scriptural, Christocentric, and eschatological focus and, on the other, an openness to contemporary experience, the findings of scientific exegesis, the human sciences, and ecumenical dialogue. And it exhorted theologians to look for more appropriate ways of communicating moral truth to the people of their time.

In *Lumen gentium* (The Church, 1964) the Council emphasized the universal call to holiness, insisting that the pursuit of moral perfection was not the preserve of clergy and religious but the vocation of every person. It recognized that sanctity takes many forms, so that "Christians in any state or walk of life are called to the fullness of Christian life and to the perfection of love." Destined to a greater life beyond the grave, Christians are nonetheless bound to be fruitful in works of charity in this present world.

In *Gaudium et spes* (The Church in the Modern World, 1965) the Church claimed as her own "the joys and hopes, the griefs and anxieties of the people of this age, especially those who are poor or in any way afflicted" and dedicated herself to "reading the signs of the times," responding to the questions of the age, and communicating in its vernacular. Committed to the search for human happiness through respect for dignity and genuine progress, the Church expressed herself willing to work with anyone of good will toward this goal. By virtue of their natural reason (under grace) people can know moral truth; but with the special gift of revelation God's will for humanity is more clearly known and perfectly followed, because only in and through Christ can true

Box 1

Vatican II on the Moral Law—*Dignitatis Humanæ* §§2–3

The dignity of the human person is known through the revealed word of God and by reason itself ... In accordance with their dignity as persons all human beings must seek the truth and, once it is known, order their whole lives in accord with its demands ... The highest norm of human life is the divine law—eternal, objective and universal ... Human beings have been made by God to participate in this law ... They perceive and acknowledge the imperatives of the divine law through the mediation of conscience. In all their activity persons are bound to follow their conscience in order that they may come to God, the end and purpose of life. ...

human fulfillment be found. This saving truth is known infallibly by Christ's faithful in certain circumstances and they are called to make their own conscientious judgments within the community of faith. In forming their consciences they look to Church leaders who teach definitively (even when not infallibly) in morals as in faith, restating and consistently unfolding the implications of the Gospel.

The Council spoke in the midst of rapid social and cultural change, and was conscious of the growing threat of individualism and relativism. Despite its insistence on the importance of community, authority, and tradition in Christian life, many took up the Council's views on the dignity of conscience and the proper liberties of the person with greater enthusiasm than they did its teaching on moral absolutes, such as the positive norms of respect for human life, sexuality, and the poor, and negative precepts regarding abortion, euthanasia, and weapons of mass destruction.

In response to a request from the Council but in the context of "the sexual revolution" and antiauthoritarianism of "the me generation," Paul VI's encyclical on birth control, *Humanæ vitæ* (1968), met a hostile reception in many quarters, with some theologians, clergy, and laity openly dissenting. This set the stage for the polarisation of moral theology, as contending schools responded to "the crisis of '68," and for the authentic developments that have subsequently occurred.

II. RESPONSE: CONTEMPORARY APPROACHES TO CATHOLIC ETHICS

A. Christian Relativism: The Situationists and Fundamental Optionists

Many writers in the Catholic tradition have recognized the relevance of context or circumstances in assessing a moral act: if a sin at all, stealing from the rich was always regarded as less grave than stealing from a poor person; theft by a starving or drunk person as less grave than theft by a sober and comfortably off one; and so on. "Situationists" such as Protestant theologians Paul Tillich and Joseph Fletcher took up this theme from the tradition and combined it with a more contemporary exaltation of human freedom and rejection of appeals to nature, reason, authority, norms, or any other static, universalist, or objectivist standards. They denied the very possibility of norms that could spell out answers to moral dilemmas in advance: all ethical reflection is thus limited and tentative; there are always exceptions, depending upon circumstances, because truth is complex, dynamic, and perspectival; the only moral absolute is freedom or love. Thus while considering well-established norms and values when trying to discern what is the most authentic or loving thing to do in the circumstances, the agent must be willing to set aside these "rules of thumb" if authenticity, benevolence, or love is better served by doing so; external authorities such as the Church may exhort but ought not to be too "heavy-handed." What matters, in the end, is whether the person's "heart is in the right place": whether they are genuinely committed to authenticity and/or love of God and others.

In response to such theories John Paul II insisted in *Veritatis Splendor* (On Certain Fundamental Questions of the Church's Moral Teaching, 1993) that autonomy and sincerity are insufficient to establish the moral truth of a judgment of conscience. Subjectivist, individualist, and culturally relativist ethics such as situationism misunderstand the dependence of freedom upon truth and ultimately amount to a denial of the very ideas of human nature, practical reason, and revelation. Freedom of conscience is never freedom from the truth but always and only freedom in the truth; the Magisterium does not bring to the Christian conscience truths that are extraneous to it, but only highlights those truths that a well-formed conscience already possesses. Furthermore, conscience is no more exempt from confusion and error than any other intellectual faculty; evil done as the result of a nonculpable error of judgment may not be imputable to the agent, but this does not mean the act is a good one. No matter how "loving," "benevolent," or otherwise well intentioned, certain kinds of behavior are objectively wrong.

While never a mainstream approach among Catholics, situationism had its parallels in the "fundamental option" theory proposed by writers such as Karl Rahner, Bernard Häring, and Charles Curran. In this view Christians are disposed to God not simply by particular acts but by their whole orientation; this overall self-determination may be their most basic commitment(s) or even prereflective, "transcendental," and thus unchosen. Some authors propose that the realm of "good" and "evil" applies only on this level of the person's will: the less significant level of particular actions only ever constitutes "creative" attempts to express this basic orientation, or nondefinitive and relatively trivial failures to do so; the person's predominant direction will not normally be radically altered or reversed by such conduct. The "gravity" of a moral act depends, then, not on the object of the act per se but on whether it expresses or changes the agent's fundamental option; persons are to be assessed morally on the basis of this basic orientation to God and neighbor rather than their concrete behavior. Like the situationists, these writers commonly reject traditional moral absolutes, or else reject the notion that breaches of such absolutes necessarily involve grave matter.

Veritatis Splendor insists, on the contrary, that a person's most fundamental option or commitment is always freely chosen and exercised (or reshaped) by particular actions. To separate fundamental option from concrete behavior contradicts personal integrity and the revealed link between chosen acts and ultimate destiny. While certain major choices and givens commit people to core relationships and vocations, all morally significant choices actualize and limit them, orienting them (and those they influence) toward similar future choices. While prudence is certainly required in applying norms to specific situations—the applicability of positive norms will depend upon opportunity, urgency, and competing responsibilities—norms prohibiting gravely and intrinsically evil acts do not allow "creative" breaches consistent with continuing in grace and charity. Mortal sins are not limited to choices of fundamental option against God, but include any gravely disordered act that is freely and knowingly chosen. "If the object of the concrete action is not in harmony with the true good of the person, the choice of that action makes our will and ourselves morally evil, thus putting us in conflict with our ultimate end, the supreme good, God himself."

B. Christian Utilitarianism: The Proportionalists

Another 1970s attempt to "baptize" trends in contemporary secular thought was that of the "proportionalists" (teleologists or revisionists) who sought to reconcile consequentialism with traditional Christian notions such as the casuistry of "the lesser evil," the principle of double effect, and the concept of due proportion in self-defense and medical treatment. Peter Knauer, Louis Janssens, Bruno Schüller, Joseph Fuchs, Richard McCormick, and others argued that Christians, like anyone else, must reason morally by attempting an honest identification and balancing of the likely goods and evils resulting from various options. Because most acts involve both upsides and downsides, the *morally* good act is the one that seeks the greatest proportion of *premoral* (nonmoral, physical, or ontic) goods over evils; the issue is thus whether the agent has a "commensurate" or "proportionate" reason to tolerate the premoral evils. Faith adds to this intentionality (reasons and inspiration for benevolence, in particular a reference to the person's true final end), brings a certain sensitivity and clarity to assessing consequences (e.g., it places a high value on human life), and provides certain rules of thumb (e.g., the Decalogue).

What neither faith nor reason will yield, on this account, are *moral absolutes*: while some principles (such as "Do not directly kill the innocent") may be "virtually exceptionless," it is always at least theoretically possible that a situation might arise in which the greater good would be served by breaching the norm (e.g., lying to save a life; abortion in the case of rape). Sometimes a grave moral norm can properly be broken with a view to bringing about the best possible state of affairs. More often the norms in question will not be of this grave, virtually exceptionless kind but directive only, allowing various exceptions and compromises. The moral teaching of Scripture, tradition, or current church authorities plays an important role as a foil to biases, faulty reasoning and self-interest; but abstract norms from such sources should not be too easily and unqualifiedly taken as divine or objective natural law, and persons may dissent from them where they judge such norms do not apply to their situation. The limitations of human reason mean that norms are always provisional expressions that must be corrected or at least interpreted according to the totality of a concrete reality. Like the situationists, adherents to this school of proportionalism were increasingly inclined to reject traditional norms (against contraception, abortion, sex outside marriage).

Veritatis Splendor commends the efforts of these writers to articulate a morality at once rationally grounded and well suited to dialogue and cooperation with non-Catholics and nonbelievers in pluralistic societies. The Pope recognizes that the prospective consequences of an act are properly to be taken into account in choosing it, and that concern for them may diminish the evil of a particular choice. But he joins most contemporary philosophers in their scepticism regarding the very possibility of predicting in advance and balancing all the good and evil consequences of acts. More fundamentally, the encyclical reiterates the traditional position that certain kinds of behavior are absolutely prohibited by the divine and natural law; such acts are *intrinsically evil*, "irremediably" wrong, "always and per se," in every circumstance and culture, no matter how well meaning the agent or how desirable the consequences; they always represent a disordered will and cannot be ordered to God or to the person's ultimate good. As Paul wrote to the Romans, it is not licit to do evil that good may come of it. Consequentalist approaches such as proportionalism are thus logically incoherent (because of the problems of unpredictability and incommensurability), morally misleading (because they focus on motives and results rather than the specific object of the moral act), and irreconcilable with the Catholic tradition (because they allow in certain circumstances actions condemned by that tradition as intrinsically evil).

C. Christian Radicalism: The Liberationists

A third example of an attempt to "Christianize" trends in contemporary secular thought was that of the liberation theologians such as Gustavo Gutiérrez, Leonardo Boff, Juan Luís Segundo, Mary Daly, and James Cone. These writers married strands from Marxism, feminism, and/or critical social theory to elements of the prophetic and New Testament traditions and Christian social teaching. They brought this to bear upon, and were in turn informed by, the lived experience of oppressed groups such as the poor of South America and Africa, or women and Blacks in North America.

The focus of liberation theology was much more upon *orthopraxis* (doing the truth) in the struggle for liberation than upon *orthodoxy* (believing the truth). As a result, much of its energy was spent on the "conscientization" of Christians in general and the poor in particular regarding issues of justice, challenging ideologies and systems that contribute to injustice, and identifying the interrelationships between theory and practice and between context and content. Imitating God's

"option for the poor" in the Scriptures, these writers emphasize the need to look at the world and to theologize from the perspective of the marginalized, to preach good news to and for the poor, and to continue Christ's saving work by transforming society. Social change is to be achieved by various strategies such as the building of "base ecclesial communities." Liberation theologians are yet to articulate a position on most particular moral questions; insofar as they do, they commonly rely upon reasoning similar to that of the situationists or the proportionalists, asking what is the most liberating option in the circumstances or what will yield the greatest net benefit for the most oppressed.

The Congregation for the Doctrine of the Faith has issued two statements on liberation theology (*Certain Aspects of the Theology of Liberation*, 1984; *Christian Freedom and Liberation*, 1986). These documents commended the emphasis of liberation theology upon human dignity, its identification of the Church and her Lord with those who are oppressed, its insights into "social sin" and "structures of sin," and its prophetic call to action. But any tendencies to reduce faith to social action, sin to oppressive socioeconomic or political structures, salvation to liberation from these, morality to results, and heaven to a human-made utopia, were criticized.

D. Christian Psychology: Personalism and Virtue

The existentialist, phenomenological, and personalist schools that have been influential in Continental philosophy have also had their effect on Catholic ethics (e.g., W. A. Luijpen, Hans Reiner, John Paul II (Karol Wojtyla), Jean Vanier, Hans Urs von Balthasar). Reflecting upon the nature of the acting subject who personally assimilates, appropriates, and enacts moral truth, these writers have been especially attentive to anthropology (e.g., agency as "embodied self-determination," personal choice as "the synthesis of rationality and animality"), to sociology (e.g., the nature of group relationships), to mysticism (e.g., prayer, asceticism) and aesthetics, and to ordinary experiences (such as those of subjectivity, intentionality, commitment, and intersubjectivity). Resisting the tendency of such approaches to philosophical idealism, some personalists insist on a realism in line with classical (commonly Thomist) philosophy and theology. Thus, *Veritatis Splendor* talks of the natural law known to practical reason and applied by conscience in terms of "the acting subject [who] personally assimilates the truth contained in the law.

He appropriates this truth of his being and makes it his own by his acts and the corresponding virtues."

Recent years have also seen the revival of virtue ethics in secular moral philosophy. Despite its long Catholic pedigree, virtue had been neglected in modern ethical theory—with a few important exceptions (e.g., Philippa Foot, Peter Geach, Bernard Williams), some of them neo-Thomists (Jacques Maritan, Etienne Gilson, Josef Pieper). Since the 1980s writers such as Edmund Pincoffs, Alasdair MacIntyre, Charles Taylor, Martha Nussbaum, and Raimond Gaita refocused attention on questions such as the psychology of moral character, the place of moral feeling, the commitments and actions that are constitutive of the person's life-story and flourishing, and the place of communities, traditions, and practices in shaping identity and character traits. Some Catholic theologians have taken up such themes (e.g., Servais Pinckaers, Romanus Cessario). Virtues are presented as relatively stable dispositions or sensibilities that organize aspects of the human personality, integrate emotion and desires with the rational response to the good, orient agents toward reasonable conduct, and empower them to engage in such conduct easily or consistently. They are commonly residues of past acts and dispositions to engage in like future acts. The seven classical virtues (especially *phronesis* or practical wisdom) are being explored anew and in greater depth; other virtues, no longer straight-jacketed with the seven, are also being rediscovered (respectfulness, generosity, devotion, truthfulness, humility, gratitude, hospitality). The importance of virtue and vice in moral pedagogy (through imitation, habituation, role modeling, storytelling, sacramental practice, socialization), in counseling and in spiritual direction, is also increasingly recognized.

While not addressing this new direction in contemporary ethics directly, *Veritatis Splendor* noted that the "conversion of heart" necessary for a reliable conscience requires more than knowledge of moral principles. "What is essential is a sort of 'connaturality' between the person and their true good. Such a connaturality is rooted in and develops through the virtuous attitudes of the individual himself: prudence and the other cardinal virtues, and even before these the theological virtues of faith, hope and charity." Thus fidelity to the covenant and its commandments is not blind obedience but an expression of virtuous compliance and love, of human fraternity and ecclesial communion. While implicitly supportive of the revival of virtue ethics, this encyclical gives more attention to the *principles* side of the dialectic between principle and character; even if the virtuous person will know,

choose, and reveal what is morally good, true *virtues* can only be distinguished from personally or socially approved *vices* by an objective assessment of the kinds of behaviour they encourage. Thus Christian morality must be ready to criticize the model of the good person or the good life assumed or proposed at any particular time in any particular society with "the norm of truth and the splendour of goodness."

E. The Contemporary Revival of Natural Law Theory

The neo-Thomist revival promoted by Pope Leo XIII in the late nineteenth century has been carried forward in more recent years by writers such as Elizabeth Anscombe, Henry Veatch, Ralph McInerney, Benedict Ashley, Servais Pinckaers, and the English Dominicans. In this tradition but responding more directly to developments in modern philosophy, the Vatican II call to renewal, and the fallout of the crisis of 1968, writers such as Germain Grisez, John Finnis, William E. May, and Joseph Boyle have articulated a new natural law theory. Their approach is consistent with the Catholic tradition (especially Thomism), but offers some important refinements that have won the theory a place among the principal contenders not only in Catholic ethics but in secular moral and political philosophy. Many of the insights of contemporary moral philosophy, such as those of the Anglo-American analytical school, neo-Kantianism, communitarianism, personalism, and virtue ethics have been incorporated or usefully distinguished by this school.

According to the new natural law approach there are certain basic human goods that provide the real reasons for human actions: life, health, friendship, creativity, leisure, beauty, truth, religion, integrity, and so on. These goods are equally fundamental and intrinsically good; none is a mere means to any of the others; they deserve to be cherished and reverenced in every life and choice; fully realized and actualized in all human lives, they constitute happiness or flourishing (integral human fulfilment). The fundamental maxim that "the good is to be done and the evil avoided" can thus be specified as a series of underived basic principles such as preserve life, promote health, and seek and tell the truth. It requires an openness to all human goods, even those not directly pursued; it rejects any choice directly against participation by anyone in any of the goods; but it recognizes that someone's potential participation in some good will sometimes be foreseeably but unintentionally compromised by their own or another's pursuit of a good.

But an adequate ethic cannot be based solely on the basic goods because agents are often torn between competing desires for and means to these goods. The *first principle of morality* is cast by this school thus: "in pursuing the good and avoiding the evil, choose and otherwise will those and only those possibilities whose willing is compatible with integral human fulfillment." By reflecting upon what integral human fulfillment consists of, these writers have identified a series of intermediate principles (modes of responsibility) that promote such choices (e.g., the requirements of impartiality and fairness; respect for the dignity, freedom, and conscience of others; detachment, fidelity, and purity of heart). These principles exclude choices that are irrational, arbitrary, unfair, or that neglect or unfairly limit anyone's participation in these goods (e.g., the prohibitions of violent, vengeful, and prejudiced acts). The specific norms that make up the bulk of common morality can then be derived—both positive norms (e.g, treat others as your moral equals, follow the Golden Rule, help those in need, favor and foster the common good) and negative ones (e.g., do not harm the innocent, tell no lies, do not commit adultery). Such negative norms are commonly absolute or exceptionless, and this is ultimately the basis of the inviolability of basic human rights.

Ethics, in this natural law account, is no imposition of some external authority such as the Church, but a pattern of life that challenges persons to be more reasonable, more authentically themselves, and so genuinely happy. Integral human fulfillment is not merely an unattainable ideal of reason providing the basis for criticizing a will distorted (rather than supported) by feelings. Rather, it is a reality which, by virtue of God's promise and grace, can begin in this life and extend into the completed kingdom of God. There is an intrinsic relationship between every morally good act done in God's friendship and the life of heaven: even when unsuccessful, good works and dispositions are material that God has promised to raise up into a city that will last forever. Human nature's unity and dignity, and the permanence of natural law principles articulating conditions for its integral fulfillment, are guaranteed by Christ's sharing that nature with every human person, and by his having come once-for-all as teacher and savior, clarifying and supplementing morality with the revealed divine law.

In *Veritatis Splendor* John Paul II quotes with approval the teaching of Thomas Aquinas and Leo XIII that the natural law is a human participation in divine law, reason, or providence that is natural not in the sense of being a law of nature to be read merely from the behavior of animals or the teleology of organs "but because the reason which promulgates it is proper to human nature." Avoiding both the physicalism or naturalism with which some recent writers have charged classical natural law approaches, and the dualism and instrumentalism into which those very critics commonly fall, the encyclical insists upon the unity of the human person, the consequent moral significance of the body and bodily behavior, and the rational foundation of those basic goods towards which persons are naturally inclined. "The natural moral law expresses and lays down the purposes, rights and duties which are based upon the bodily and spiritual nature of the human person." Some of the precepts are universal and immutable, and "make themselves felt" to all: for example, "do good and avoid evil, be concerned for the transmission and preservation of life, refine and develop the riches of the material world, cultivate social life, seek truth, practice good and contemplate beauty." But even these norms are in constant need of better formulation and appropriate application, and our understanding of them develops organically over time. Moral acts are to be judged first and foremost by their intended object, end, or purpose, and not merely by their motivation (whether the agent is well meaning or has a good fundamental option) or their expected consequences. Christian faith illuminates the teleology of natural law—the moral life "consists in the deliberate ordering of human acts to God, the supreme good and ultimate end of the human person"—confirms its precepts, and provides a reliable source of moral wisdom where its precepts or their application are unclear.

Some neo-Thomists have complained of this new natural law theory that it lacks the elaborated metaphysics, philosophy of God, and philosophical psychology of classical natural law theory, and that it denies that there is a unitary end of human choice and a hierarchy among goods. Although clearly most sympathetic to such natural law approaches, *Veritatis Splendor* does include some comments that might be read as implicit criticisms of both the older and more recent versions. The encyclical shuns the physicalism, legalism, and minimalism sometimes found in older formulations of natural law theory; but it also challenges the new writers to be wary of any theory of intention that might seem to permit acts characterized by the tradition as intrinsically evil and to elaborate a richer anthropology, psychology, and theory of virtue. To both schools it presents a renewed challenge to be more obviously scriptural and patristic.

F. The Roman Response

Following Vatican II, Paul VI (pope 1963–1978) published some important teachings in applied ethics (e.g., on contraception, war and peace, human rights) but considered metaethical theory only en passant. John Paul II (pope 1978–) has tended to teach at both levels, elaborating some fundamental ethical principles and applying them to particular questions (human rights abuses, the arms buildup, particular wars, public executions, poverty, sexuality, bioethical controversies). The Congregation for the Doctrine of the Faith has also issued instructions on various subjects (which will be treated in Part III), while other congregations, national bishops' conferences, and Catholic bodies have issued many reflections upon the ethical issues of the day.

In response to two decades of attempted renewal of Catholic ethics, marked as much by confusion and dissent as by legitimate pluralism and genuine development, John Paul II published the letter considered above, *Veritatis Splendor*. The first papal encyclical on metaethics (fundamental moral), it is in three parts: a scriptural reflection (upon the New Testament story of the rich young man who asked Christ how to live); some controversies in metaethics; and some conclusions for personal, political, and ecclesial life. A decade before John Paul had reaffirmed the Tridentine teaching on mortal and venial sin, insisting that there are acts which repudiate God, his covenant and law, whether directly—as in idolatry, apostasy, and atheism—or indirectly—as in sins involving "grave matter" (*Reconciliatio et Pœnitentia*, 1984). In the new encyclical the same writer insisted on the intimate connection between freedom and respect for objective moral truth, on the need for a well-formed conscience, and on the existence of moral absolutes accessible to human reason and clearly elaborated in the Scriptures and tradition, some of which when broken are grave matter.

Thus while prescinding from imposing any particular theological system, recent Roman moral theology has criticized at length theories of morality that exalt human freedom and calculation beyond their proper confines, dislocating them from the norms intrinsic to human nature and reason, and/or ignoring the proper authority of revelation and community. In this view, no moral theory that would justify deliberate choices of behavior contrary to natural or revealed moral law can claim to be grounded in the Catholic moral tradition. An objectivist natural law approach with a personalist flavor is again presumed in *Evangelium vitæ* (The Gospel of Life, 1995). There John Paul II asserts that any reasonable person can come to recognize the value and inviolability of human life and argues that Catholic teaching in this area "has a profound and persuasive echo in the heart of every person—believer and nonbeliever alike—because it marvellously fulfils all the heart's expectations while infinitely surpassing them." According to this view, "even in the midst of difficulties and uncertainties, every person sincerely open to truth and goodness can, by the light of reason and the hidden action of grace, come to recognize the natural law written in the heart … [Upon such a recognition] every human community and the political community itself are founded."

The *Catechism of the Catholic Church* (1994) purports to be a "sure and authentic reference text for teaching Catholic doctrine." Divided into four parts (what Catholics believe, how they celebrate it, how they live it, and how they pray it), the third part is an exposition of Christian morality. Avoiding legalism, the metaethical section presents Catholic life as the dynamic endeavor of human persons to become fully the beings God wills and enables them to be; and Catholic ethics as the working out under grace of what persons must do in response to God's gifts and promises. It identifies in very positive terms the premises of Christian morality: creation in the image of God, with reason and will, for happiness and heaven; the cultivation of reason by knowledge of the moral law, of temperament by virtue, of the whole spirit by grace, especially in the sacraments; the possibility of sin, even grave sin, but also of conversion and forgiveness; the dignity of the conscience both individual and social; the gifts of community in general and of the Church in particular.

The Catechism then follows the tradition of subdividing ethics along the lines of the Decalogue; but the commandments are presented as the unfolding of the dual commandment of love, a positive vision and not just a series of prohibitions. The treatment of each commandment begins with a focus upon the good it seeks to reverence: God, family, authority, life, peace, sexuality, creation, truth. Against such a background defective attitudes and wrong actions emerge as vices and sins. Thus the articles on the first three commandments constitute an applied ethics of religious freedom and practice (rights and duties of faith, worship, tolerance); that on the fourth commandment, an ethic of family and civil relationships (rights and duties of parents, children, teachers, public authorities, citizens, refugees); on the fifth, a bioethic (rights and duties to reverence body and soul, to struggle for nonviolence and peace, to avoid direct killing and harming); that on the sixth commandment, an ethic of sexuality and marriage; on the seventh, a social ethic (justice, solidarity, option for the poor; prohibition of theft, abuse of animals and ecology, socioeconomic injustice); and the article on the eighth commandment, an ethics of communication (truth seeking and telling, media ethics, art ethics). Some of these precepts are presented as absolutes; all are presented as the conclusions of Catholic moral tradition and are in general most consistent with the natural law approaches. And each of the Ten Commandments is shown to have immediate relevance to controversies in contemporary applied ethics.

III. APPLIED CATHOLIC ETHICS

Space precludes treatment of all areas of traditional or recent Catholic speculation in applied ethics; what follows is merely a representative sample of the major sources, principles and conclusions.

A. Ethics of Decision-making

Christianity is an eminently practical religion: as the New Testament epistles of James and John insist, faith without works is dead and love that is not enacted is a lie. Thus the Catholic tradition provides a rich source of reflection on what is called today applied ethics—moral decision-making in the various areas of life. Unfortunately many people today, Catholics among them, see Christian morality as an unrealistic, unattainable ideal. Partly this reflects the difficulties both of knowing what is the right thing to do in some situations, and then of doing it once it is known. Both demand a determined, even lifelong effort in the face of serious obstacles (both internal and external) and, at times, personal failure. But simply because it is hard to be just, generous, honest, chaste, or courageous does *not* mean persons should settle for less. Being a good friend, spouse, parent, employer, worker, professional, or citizen is not an impossible and unrealizable ideal; even less is the effort to be these things somehow optional for the Christian. Everyone is called to holiness, and this includes the demands of practical reason to live a fully human (free, reasonable, loving) life and the demands of faith to live a fully Christian (self-sacrificing, redemptive, vocationally faithful) life.

The objective of moral reflection must always be to discover what is the right thing to do; it is irresponsible to act on the basis of a doubt if it is possible to clear up that doubt. Nor can Christians adopt a legalistic minimalism ("How far can I go without committing a mortal sin?"): like everyone else they must make a genuine effort to discern what moral truth requires in

---

Box 2

Vatican II on Moral Absolutes—*Gaudium et Spes* §27

Whatever is hostile to life itself, such as murder, genocide, abortion, euthanasia and suicide; whatever violates the integrity of the human person, such as mutilation and torture ... whatever is offensive to human dignity, such as arbitrary imprisonment or deportation, slavery, forced prostitution and trafficking in women and children, subhuman living or work conditions ... all these and the like are a disgrace, and so long as they infect human civilization they contaminate their perpetrators even more than their victims and are a negation of the honour due to the Creator.

---

the circumstances. On the other hand, God—and moral reason—never ask of anyone more than is possible for them. Christians have long recognized that there can be various impairments to moral agency (neurosis, compulsion, habit, ignorance, overwhelming passion) that limit responsibility and qualify the degree to which an objectively right or wrong act is subjectively so. Some of these obstacles can be overcome as the person matures in life and grace; others will be much more intractable. Nonetheless it is also clear that people can behave immorally by their own neglect or sinful choices.

In any moral discernment process the agent must be willing to take pertinent counsel, hearing appropriate moral authorities respectfully and praying for the guidance of the Holy Spirit, being open to challenge and conversion, and then act in accord with a well-informed and morally sensitive conscience. But how is a confused (vexed, uncertain, troubled) conscience to proceed? The Catholic tradition offers some useful pointers. Persons should look carefully and honestly at their situation in an attempt to resolve whether they have considered all the morally relevant facts and norms, whether there is an option which they have not yet adequately considered, and whether there is not in fact a clearly morally preferable option. Negative moral absolutes clarify which options are already ruled out; other options may on reflection represent the absolutizing of some inappropriate or limited promise, commitment, custom or law, or a disproportionate emotional attraction lacking rational justification and tending toward partiality or prejudice. Having ruled out such choices persons ought to consider whether the proposed action is consistent with their long-term goals and commitments, with what a virtuous person (some moral hero, a saint, above all Christ) would do in the circumstances, and with the emotional appeal each option has for them.

Of course knowing the right thing to do will not be enough to ensure that agents do it. Catholic tradition counsels persons to seek the support of others and to give themselves over to prayer and the life of the Church not only as a source of the grace of discernment, but also as a source of strength to persevere in the moral life, a source of consolation in times of trial, and a source of forgiveness and redirection in times of failure.

B. Social and Political Ethics

Catholic ethics proposes that the most basic responsibility of agents toward one another is to love them and treat them with justice and mercy. That love is to exceed the ordinary limitations of affection, the hopelessness evoked by the enormity of some social problems, and the partiality, indifference, and individualism common in the face of competing interests. It is violated by any failure of respect for the dignity and rights of others, hatred, harm or neglect of them.

The long tradition of Catholic reflection on these matters goes back to the prophetic and Dominical inheritance regarding treatment of the *anawim*, patristic reflection upon the limits to private property and duties to share and redistribute surplus wealth, and scholastic speculation on various kinds of law (divine, natural, positive) and justice (commutative, distributive, legal), and on particular questions such as usury and restitution. Beginning with Pope Leo XIII's *Rerum novarum* there has been a thoroughgoing renewal of Catholic social teaching through regular papal, curial, and episcopal publications. These documents were commonly occasioned by the concerns of their day: the condition of workers, the rise of totalitarian governments, the arms race and threats to world peace, the aspiration to a new world order marked by peace and opportunity, problems with both Marxist and capitalist worldviews. Nonetheless they established some enduring principles. Repudiating approaches that reduce justice to noninterference with others, fulfilling agreements, or treating everyone the same, Catholic social teaching has proposed a rich conception of the nature, purposes, and obligations of community life, and the need for moral rectitude, fairness, and commitment to the common good (solidarity) among the members of a community.

Among the principles that have recurred in this literature have been: the dignity of the human person; the consequent rights (reasonable expectations) of persons to those things necessary for their flourishing food, shelter, healthcare, work, a worthy standard of living, security, education, culture); the nature of persons as social and political animals who must cooperate to achieve their good; the consequent duties to respect civil rights, collaborate mutually, and act responsibly with respect to others; the intimate link between love and justice; the consequent special care (preferential love or option) for the poor and marginalized, and opposition to attitudes such as racism and sexism; the notions of community, common good, needs, rights, and duties as the context for the establishment of social, political and economic relations; and "subsidiarity" or supportive decentralization of decision-making and opportunities, so that governments complement and assist rather than hamper or replace the efforts of individuals, families, and groups to serve the common good.

In modern times individualism and collectivism, unrestrained capitalism and state socialism, have all competed for political and economic dominance and all have been rejected by the Church. Instead it has supported personal rights qualified by social obligations, a free economy together with the necessary public assistance for families and other groups, responsible and responsive government without dictatorship or rule by opinion poll, solidarity with subsidiarity, patriotism without narrow-mindedness. Having taken an active and very successful part in the critique and defeat of state socialism in many places, the Church has in recent years turned its attention toward the inadequacies of liberalism, such as its impoverished conceptions of the good (viewed as largely a matter of personal preference), of rights (limited to negative liberties), of community (an optional association, a mere means to private ends, a threat to personal liberty), and of the state (minimal in scope and "neutral" with respect to the good of its citizens). Heirs to a much richer conception of these things, Christians join all people of goodwill in seeking to promote social justice and all other aspects of the common good, and in themselves adopting a style of life consistent with social responsibility.

As citizens Christians are obliged to take an active part in public affairs, promoting social goods such as religious liberty, equal justice for all, respect for human life, protection of marriage and the family, economic justice, access to healthcare and welfare, and international justice and peace. They also have a responsibility to vote conscientiously, to obey just laws and pay just taxes, to make no unreasonable demands of government and society, and to cooperate with the criminal justice, legal, and welfare systems. Sometimes they have a duty to participate more actively in politics (e.g., to lobby

Box 3

The Social Encyclicals

Leo XIII	*Rerum novarum*	Rights and Duties of Labor and Capital	1891
Pius XI	*Quadragesimo anno*	Reconstruction of the Social Order	1931
	Divini Redemptoris	Atheistic Communism	1937
Pius XII	*Summi Pontificatus*	The State in the Modern World	1939
John XXIII	*Mater et magistra*	The Church and Social Progress	1961
	Pacem in terris	World Peace	1963
Vatican II	*Gaudium et spes*	The Church in the Modern World	1965
Paul VI	*Populorum progressio*	Development of Peoples	1967
	Octagesimo adveniens	The Church and Political Activity	1971
Latin American Bishops	*Medellin Conference Documents*	Justice and Peace	1968
Synod of Bishops	*Justice in the World*		1971
John Paul	*Laborem exercens*	Human Labor	1981
	Sollicitudo rei socialis	Social Concerns	1987
	Centesimus annus	The Centenary of "Rerum novarum"	1991
U.S. Bishops	*Economic Justice for All*	Catholic Social Teaching and U.S. Economy	1986

against the death penalty, to stand for election with a view to securing justice for some oppressed group such as the poor or refugees, to engage in legitimate protest against some wicked activity such as abortion) or to refuse to comply with manifestly unjust laws. The Gospel calls Christians to a mercy that respects the strict requirements of justice while going beyond it, overcoming injustice, and demonstrating a God-like generosity through charitable works, heroic efforts at reconciliation, and sometimes forgoing rights for the sake of others. Genuine peace and social development are fruits of this justice and mercy.

The doctrine of "the just war" that has developed since Augustine suggests that no war can be just unless several requirements are met (just cause, due authority, last resort, proportionate means, reasonable prospects of success); in modern times it has become clear that this excludes aggressive, punitive, and genocidal wars, strategies such as the nuclear deterrent, and methods of waging war such as blanket bombing and terrorism. *Gaudium et spes* declares that "any act of war aimed indiscriminately at the destruction of entire cities or extensive areas along with their population is a crime against God and humanity meriting unequivocal and unhesitating condemnation." Since the Council the popes have been outspoken critics of armed conflicts—even those authorized by "the international community"—pointing to the failures first to pursue all other sanctions and to use only proportionate force. If a war is just, citizens should participate as the law

requires but always work toward a just peace; they should almost always refuse to serve in an unjust war and may sometimes adopt a stance of conscientious objection or radical nonviolence. Governments and citizens are called to do what they can to limit the "utterly treacherous trap" of the arms race and the escalation and cruelty of wars; in particular they must work for an international order in which all war is outlawed and cooperation occurs at all levels.

C. Economic and Business Ethics

Catholic social teaching also embodies a rich tradition of reflection about rights and responsibilities regarding work, industry, property and profit. At its heart is the insistence that "the human person is the source, centre and purpose of all economic and social life" (*Gaudium et spes*). Work is seen as a basic human good through which people fulfill themselves and contribute to each other's good. Technical progress, inventiveness, entrepreneurship, productivity, and other elements of development that serve the dignity and vocation of persons are to be encouraged. Owners of enterprises, workers, suppliers, and customers have responsibilities toward each other and to their broader community. Owners, for instance, ought to ensure that their business engages in activities that genuinely contribute to the common good, by methods that are socially responsible, and with a view to a reasonable profit only, avoiding exploiting others usuriously or oppressively. Employers should treat their workers as associates in a common enterprise, recognize the priority of work over capital, provide reasonable working conditions, treat their workers fairly and mercifully, and pay a family wage (unless there are already in place social measures to meet the needs of workers with families to support). Employees properly aim to be productive, to serve the best interests of their firm, to obtain just wages and conditions, to treat management and each other fairly and mercifully, and to engage in striking and other industrial action only with just cause and as a last resort.

In *Gaudium et spes, Laborem exercens* and elsewhere the Church has insisted on the dignity of labor by which persons share in God's creative work, stamp the things of nature with their seal, realize their talents, support themselves and their families, and contribute to the wider community. From this it has argued that every person (or family breadwinner) has the right to work and to leisure, the duty to work faithfully, and the entitlement to sufficient remuneration to provide for their material, social, cultural, and spiritual life (and that of their dependents). The Church has long supported the establishment of trade unions to represent workers' interests and to contribute to the just organization of economic life.

Property ownership, wages and profits, and economic privileges and opportunities may be either publicly or privately held in particular circumstances. But ownership and entitlements always remain subordinate to "the universal destination of earthly goods": God intended the earth and all it contains for the use of everyone. This limits the rights of owners: all (and especially those with more than they need) should share their property with those who have less than they need; and all should practice careful stewardship or conservation. A number of more specific moral norms must also be observed in acquiring, saving and insuring, caring for, using, giving, lending, returning or otherwise disposing of property. Recent Catholic social teaching has been especially critical of the risks of avarice, acquisitiveness, and waste in consumerist societies, the indifference of many affluent people toward the poor, and the swing of governments away from redistributive taxation, welfare "safety nets," and foreign aid to poor nations, toward a kind of "economic rationalism" that encourages and enacts hard-heartedness and selfishness. The Church continues to call for "strenuous efforts, without disregarding the rights of persons or the natural qualities of each country, to remove as quickly as possible the immense economic inequalities which now exist and in many cases are growing" (*Gaudium et spes*) and supports the efforts of international agencies and all people of good will to support the just development of peoples.

D. Bioethics

From earliest times Christians have commonly stood out from their neighbors in their reverence for human life: they have consistently opposed practices such as abortion, suicide, and euthanasia from the scriptural, patristic, and scholastic periods through to today. In response to the new technologies and the breakdown of the Hippocratic medical ethic in many parts of the contemporary world, various authorities have issued statements in recent years: for example, Pius XII, in several addresses on end-of-life decisions; Vatican II, in *Gaudium et spes*, on several bioethical matters; the Congregation for the Doctrine of the Faith, on abortion (*Quæstio de abortu*, 1974), euthanasia (*Jura et bona*, 1980) and the new reproductive technologies (*Donum vitæ*, 1986); the Pontifical Council for the Pastoral Care of Health Care Workers (*Charter for Health Care Workers*, 1994) and the U.S. Bishops Committee on Doctrine (*Ethical and Religious Directives for Catholic Health Care Services*, 1995) both on Catholic health care; and Pope John Paul II in addresses on matters such as transplants, genetics, healthcare rights and, most recently, in the first encyclical on bioethics, *Evangelium vitæ*.

The last of these documents identifies a range of present-day threats to human life, facilitated by new technologies, ideologies, and social developments. It then draws upon natural law philosophy and Christian theology in support of the proposition that life is always a good, one of great and inestimable value: no bad condition can lessen its intrinsic goodness, dignity, or inviolability; no personal or social benefit can justify its destruction. The theological source of this dignity is shown to be in the creation, redemption, and destiny of the human being; parallel to the philosophical affirmation of the inviolability of the basic good of life is the theological affirmation that God is the Lord of life and commands reverence and love for the life of every person. After detailing the long and unbroken history of teaching on the sacredness and inviolability of innocent human life, the Pope defines as a matter of Catholic faith that the direct killing of an innocent human being whether as an end in itself or as a means to a good end is always gravely immoral. He then explores the implications of this doctrine for particular moral issues such as abortion, embryo experimentation, suicide, euthanasia, and capital punishment. The Pope is fully cognizant of the complexity of responsibility in this area: the objective evil of killing does not necessarily indicate a grave sin on the part of every perpetrator; the Church is all too aware of the pressures that draw or drive people to violent solutions to their problems and of the particular pressures suffered by pregnant women, the depressed, terminally ill, and frail elderly, and those around them. But the Church remains committed to preaching "the Gospel of Life" and to championing the cause of the victims of "the culture of death."

After rehearsing the long and unbroken Catholic tradition of opposition to abortion, John Paul II declares as a matter both of natural law and Catholic faith that "direct abortion—that is abortion willed as an end or as a means—always constitutes a grave moral disorder since it is the deliberate killing of an innocent human being." The reference to "directness" here reflects the traditional view that the death of an unborn might be tolerated where it is the unintended (indirect) side-effect of a life-saving medical treatment (such as the removal of a fallopian tube hemorrhaging from an ectopic pregnancy or the removal of a cancerous and pregnant uterus). The particular anxieties, pressures, and abandonment suffered by some pregnant women may mean that their responsibility for cooperating in this tragedy is diminished; in any case the mercy of Christ and his Church is available to all. Catholic teaching on abortion is held to apply to abortifacient drugs, destructive embryo experimentation, genetic screening with a view to aborting the handicapped, infanticide of handicapped or other unwanted babies, and disrespectful manipulations of the embryo. Despite some continu-

ing debate among theologians about the moment of "hominization" or "ensoulment," the Magisterium has adopted the prudential position that "the mere probability that a human person is involved would suffice to justify an absolutely clear prohibition of any intervention aimed at killing a human embryo" (*Evangelium vitæ*). But the Catholic tradition has increasingly assumed the stronger position that from conception the unborn child is a human person, the moral equal of all other human beings, and the Pope argues at length here and elsewhere for this.

Catholic ethics is equally opposed to suicide, assisted suicide, and euthanasia—"an action or omission which of itself and by intention causes death, with the purpose of eliminating all suffering." This is clearly distinguished from withholding or withdrawing unduly burdensome treatments and the giving of appropriate pain relief, which is not intended to hasten death—even if the shortening of life is risked or foreseen. Catholic teaching does *not* require the prolongation of life at all costs; extraordinary treatments may properly be foregone, palliative and hospice care given, and nonresuscitation ordered, especially when death is imminent and inevitable, so long as the normal care due to the sick person (foods, fluids, nursing care) is continued. It is only euthanasia, properly so-called, that is condemned as "a grave violation of the law of God, since it is the deliberate and morally unacceptable killing of a human person." Once again, the Pope is cognizant of the special factors that contribute to suicide and euthanasia: overwhelming pain, anguish or fear, the inability to find any value in suffering and desire to eliminate it at all costs, the burden upon the family, the desire to avoid impositions upon others, genuine pity. These may well lessen or remove subjective responsibility, but euthanasia remains "misplaced compassion," indeed "a disturbing perversion of mercy." No one should indulge in arbitrary quality of life judgments about their own or others' lives, on the basis of which they purport to judge that someone is "better off dead" and may be killed.

In addition to life, health—the well-integrated psychosomatic functioning of the person—is a basic human good. People should take reasonable measures to protect and promote their own and others' health. Imitating Christ "the physician of souls and bodies," the Church has become the world's oldest and largest health care provider. Catholic ethics has elaborated various norms with respect to the giving and receiving of medical treatments, opposing unwarranted attacks upon or misuses of the body (such as substance abuse, direct sterilisation whether temporary or permanent, most re-

---

Box 4

John Paul II on the Inviolability of Life—*Evangelium vitæ* §57

The direct and voluntary killing of an innocent human being is always gravely immoral. This doctrine, based upon that unwritten law which human beings, in the light of reason, find in their own hearts, is reaffirmed by Sacred Scripture, transmitted by the Tradition of the Church and taught by the ordinary and universal Magisterium. The deliberate decision to deprive an innocent human being of life is always morally evil and can never be licit either as an end in itself or as a means to a good end. It is in fact a grave act of disobedience to the moral law, and indeed to God himself, the author and guarantor of that law; it contradicts the fundamental virtues of justice and charity. . . .

productive technologies such as IVF and surrogacy, trade in organs, most research involving fetal tissue) but supporting healthy life-styles, therapeutic surgical and drug procedures, organ transplants, and gene therapy, when these comply with moral norms.

E. Sex, Marriage, and the Family

In addition to their reverence for human life, Christians have from earliest times been marked by their reverence for the human body, for marriage, and for family life. From the Scriptures, through Augustine and Aquinas, to Pius XI in *Casti Connubii* (On Christian Marriage, 1930) and Vatican II in *Gaudium et spes,* they have esteemed marriage, sexuality, procreation, and child-rearing highly, promoted chastity for people in all states of life, and celebrated the expression of marital love in sexual intercourse; they have opposed practices such as remarriage after divorce, sex outside of marriage, or unchaste or antilife sexual activity within marriage.

The "sexual revolution" since the 1960s, with its demand for readier sexual gratification, increased sexual activity outside of marriage, widespread practice of contraception, smaller family sizes, higher rates of marital and family breakdown, and openly "gay" lifestyles, presented Catholic sexual and marital ethics with new challenges. The response has been uneven. The official church has proposed traditional Christian teaching anew, drawing especially upon the Scriptures and natural law tradition, but in an increasingly personalist language, in documents such as: Paul VI, *Humanæ vitæ* (1968, noted above); Congregation for the Doctrine of the Faith, *Personæ humanæ* (On Sexual Ethics, 1975) and *Hæc sacra congregatio* (On Sterilization, 1975); John Paul II, *Familiaris consortio* (On the Christian Family, 1981); Holy See, *Charter on the Rights of the Family* (1981). Catholic proponents of "the new morality" have advocated greater freedom and some rapprochement with contemporary secular mores in this area. Writers in the natural law and personalist schools have developed a richer understanding of sexuality as a form of virtuous self-expression, of family as a basic Christian community constituting personal, social, and ecclesial identity, and of marriage and family as a basic human good and a vocation by which many lay people achieve perfection in Christ.

Contemporary Catholic sexual ethics asserts that sexuality is a bodily given, permeating and coloring personality, relationships, and activity; femaleness and maleness are complementary, grounding the reciprocity expressed in marital communion and dignifying both sexes equally. Sexual activity, properly understood, is self-expressive and self-giving, a conversation and exchange of feelings, hopes, and promises, an experience of union and transcendence, and a celebration of marital commitment. But sex can also be trivialized and abused, becoming self-indulgent, deceptive, exploitative, even abusive, thereby debasing the sexual language and becoming gravely sinful. Thus persons must cultivate *chastity,* the virtue that integrates sexuality into vocation so as to put it at the service of human happiness. Chastity enables people to put a loving and intelligent order into their passional lives and so to "say what they mean and mean what they say" with sex.

Throughout the Catholic tradition (genital) sexual activity has been reserved to marriage. It is understood to have two *intrinsic* and *inseparable* dimensions: sex is *unitive,* the "love making" of two persons, constituting and committing them as "lovers" by a mutual and complementary self-communication and self-donation by touch; and it is *procreative,* the "life giving" of two persons, constituting and committing them as a family by that same act of self-giving by which each becomes a potential parent through the other. Adultery, fornication, incest, prostitution, same-sex genital activity, contraception, masturbation, pornography—none of these activities expresses marriage and all deny one or both of the essential significances of sexual activity. Even when consensual such impoverished uses of sex involve deception and exploitation, self-deception and self-abuse, even grave sin.

From the Christian perspective, then, "sex says marriage." Marriage is the free commitment of a woman and a man to unite as wife and husband exclusively and for life; it is oriented to the mutual fulfillment of the spouses, to family life, to the building up of the community (both social and ecclesial), and to the salvation of all concerned. Following Christ's teaching on the indissolubility of marriage, Catholicism has always been very protective of the institution of marriage, whether Christian or natural. The marriage of the baptized is also held to be a sacrament, imaging Christ's relationship to his people, confirming the unity and permanence of marriage, and participating in and preparing the couple for heavenly communion. While separation or annulment (the declaration that there never was a marriage) may sometimes be in order, the Church cannot recognize the divorce of those who are sacramentally married, or their subsequent remarriage.

Within this context married couples have various responsibilities: to love, honor and serve each other, to share decision-making appropriately, to be faithful companions for the whole of life, to guard their own and each other's vocations, and to engage in chaste sexual acts, enjoying but subordinating sexual pleasure to communion, cooperating lovingly, and abstaining when there is a reason to abstain.

The vocation to marriage is also a vocation to family life. Couples should therefore procreate responsibly, using only upright methods of achieving a family (not in vitro fertilization, which disintegrates life making from love making) and of limiting family size (not contraception, which is similarly disintegrative, but natural family planning, which is not). They should raise their children lovingly and fairly, promoting their growth to physical, intellectual, social, moral, and spiritual maturity. They should bring Christian principles to bear upon every aspect of their upbringing: family prayer, home instruction, church attendance, use of media, schooling, education in sexuality, hobbies, friendships, romance, employment. Children, for their part, should love, honor, assist, and obey their parents, thereby contributing not only their self-fulfillment but to making their parents happy and holy, and so building with them "a school of deeper humanity" and "a domestic church" (*Gaudium et spes*).

F. Ethics of Communication and Education

The ethics of communication also has a robust Christian history. Christ's exhortations to truth-telling ("let your yes be yes and your no be no") were extended in patristic and scholastic teaching on the intrinsic evil of lying, and in later (but more dubious) reflection on "mental reservations" (deceiving for grave cause, by evasion but without lying). In documents since *Inter Mirifica* (Vatican II, On the Means of Social Communication, 1963) the Church has responded to the challenges of print and film, radio and television, phone and fax, computers and internet media with cautious enthusiasm.

Catholic reflection in this area begins with the premises that genuine communication is a requirement of community life, and truthfulness a requirement of such communication. People have rights to information and free speech, and authenticity requires that they seek and tell the truth. Respect for truth and for others excludes boasting and false modesty, flattery and detraction, lying and misleading (e.g., false advertising), exploitative and corrupting communications (such as pornography and propaganda), inappropriate silence about matters that should be publicized, as well as speaking when silence would be in order.

Friends have certain specific responsibilities to one another in this area: to communicate themselves honestly to each other, to respect each other's confidences and secrets, to defend one another's reputations, and so on. Parents, teachers, journalists, distributors, and other communicators also have special responsibilities by virtue of their greater access to information and their influence over vulnerable others or over public opinion and thus the political and cultural process. Civil authorities must ensure freedom of information while regulating the media as necessary for the common good. Whoever gives or receives a communication must take into account its content and circumstances, the truthfulness and completeness of what is conveyed, the manner in which the medium achieves its effect, and the potential uses of information for good or ill. All must cultivate appropriate virtues such as a passion for the truth, honesty, good judgment, modesty, taste, good humor, and piety.

Imitating "Christ the Teacher" Christians have always sought to be teachers of the truth and the Catholic Church became the world's oldest and largest provider of education. From major educational institutions to less formal kinds of instruction, the community—whether ecclesial or secular—shares with families and with students themselves the responsibility of ensuring that all have access to appropriate instruction. This includes catechesis in faith and morals, a good general education, and such specialized education as will serve well the flourishing of the student and their community. Recent documents on the ethics of education have included: Vatican II's *Gravissimum educationis* (On Christian Education, 1965), John Paul II's *Catechesi tradendæ* (On Catechesis in our Time, 1979) and *Ex corde ecclesiæ* (On Catholic Universities, 1990), and several curial documents (e.g., Congregation for Catholic Education, *The Catholic School*, 1979, and *Lay Catholics in Schools*, 1982; Pontifical Council for the Family, *The Truth and Meaning of Human Sexuality*, 1995).

In addition to the norms and virtues appropriate to the communication of any ideas, teachers have particular duties: to extend their own knowledge, research and teaching skills; to cooperate with their students and, in the case of children, their students' parents, as well as their fellow teachers; and to educate their students well. They should seek to cultivate in their students a studious and critical engagement not only with the present teaching or assessment tasks but with the whole discipline and knowledge generally; to assess and otherwise deal with their students fairly and charitably; and to participate in or at least never to undermine the broader project of the formation of the whole person, including the development of good character and right conscience.

Students, for their part, should willingly cooperate in the task of their own schooling, relating to their teachers with appropriate respect, docility, and critical-mindedness, and seeking an education both broad and deep. Norms regarding academic freedom, honesty in research and assessment tasks, collaboration between students, intellectual property, and plagiarism should be respected.

G. Environmental Ethics

From its Genesis the Judeo-Christian tradition has delighted in creation as a gift from God handed over to the stewardship and appropriate use of humanity. Despite some misreadings of this "dominion" as a license to exploit and abuse, the Scriptures and tradition have insisted on moral limits to the use of creation and the treatment of animals. Reflection upon the contemporary ecological crisis has elicited some important restatements and clarifications of the proper attitude of Christians towards their environment: there are relevant passages in John Paul II's *Christifideles laici* (On the Vocation of the Laity, 1989), his social encyclicals (listed in Box 3 above), and his 1990 message for the World Day of Peace, as well as from groups such as the U.S. Bishops (e.g., *Renewing the Earth,* 1991).

The dignity of all creation is founded upon its being created and sustained by a good God, by that God having been joined to it through the Incarnation, and by its promise of fulfillment in "the new creation" at the end of time. Thus while resisting any tendency to nature worship, Catholic tradition recognizes that respect or disrespect for creation is ultimately respect or disrespect for its Creator. In acting in and upon creation, agents experience themselves not as autonomous agents but as subcreators or cocreators with the one Creator-Provident God, not as beings that entirely transcend the created order but as creatures that share something of the nature of other living creatures and the materiality of the inorganic world. Therefore they must take into account the potential and limits of both natural resources and their own ingenuity, and the impact of their activities upon the human and subhuman environment and upon future generations.

In this account the natural environment is no mere resource with which people may do as they please: its goodness and beauty are intrinsic values that must be respected; and it is intended by God to be used not arbitrarily but for the genuine good of all. Human power, technology, and creativity ought not to be opposed to the created order as master to slave; nor should human beings be viewed as intruders or threats to their natural world. Genuine stewardship reverences, conserves, and improves upon creation, humanizing and personalizing it through human work; it does not alienate human beings from nature, pollute or destroy it unnecessarily, expropriate it selfishly and insatiably, or otherwise violate it. People should not "spoil" nature except where necessary to serve some human good in a reasonable way; they must exercise prudence with respect to agriculture, mining, polluting technologies, and so on; they must be moderate in their demands for natural resources, especially nonrenewable ones; they should prefer as far as possible renewable and recyclable resources and avoid consuming them faster than they can be replaced. The challenges of Catholic social teaching with respect to acquisitiveness, consumerism, sustainable development, and the just distribution of resources, has important implications for the natural environment.

While Catholic tradition does not support the notion of animal rights, the special characteristics of animals and the special feelings of human beings toward them occasion particular responsibilities. Animals should be appropriately protected and treated compassionately. Even where properly used for food, clothing, experimentation, games, or as pets, they should be treated kindly, not cruelly, with respect, not contempt. In addition to individual animals, attention must be paid to the protection of endangered species and the preservation of important ecosystems.

H. Ethics of Religion

Catholicism also offers a long tradition of reflection upon the ethics of religious belief and practice. Its foundations are in Scriptural injunctions (e.g., on how to relate to and worship God), the writings of the "Apologists" (who sought to show the compatibility of Christian faith and good citizenship), the teachings of the Fathers and Scholastics (e.g., on the virtues of faith and religion and the opposing vices, and on the compatibility and complementarity of faith and reason), and the doctrine and practice of the Church through to the modern era as articulated, for instance, in the several decrees of Vatican II on religious liberty, the Church, its liturgical and missionary activity, the roles and responsibilities of clergy, religious and laity, and relations with other churches and religions.

Responsibilities with respect to faith are several: to seek and receive faith with an open heart and a critical mind; to deepen it once received, assenting to the teachings of God and his Church; to guard it and respond soundly to challenges to it; to share it with others; and to live and pray that faith in all its richness. The Catholic Church relies upon a divine gift ensuring the integrity of its gospel (infallibility); but it also offers good reasons to consider faith credible. Embracing the gospel promises human beings eternal happiness; rejecting it—by wilful nonbelief, heresy, or apostasy—endangers salvation. But the responsibility to give religious assent varies and is limited in various ways (e.g., according to the authoritativeness of the teacher). Believers should seek not only to assent to authoritative teachings but also to understand their faith better through private study of Scripture and tradition and through seeking reliable catechetical formation.

The first duty of the believer is to worship God "in spirit and in truth." This requires the regular practice of private prayer and communal worship, especially the liturgy and devotions of the Church, including the sacraments. Increasingly today Catholics also engage in dialogue, prayer, and action with other Christians (ecumenism) or non-Christian believers (interfaith activity), and are mutually enriched by each other's insights, emphasizing what faith they share, without denying differences. Faith excludes acts of false worship (e.g., Satanism and cults, invoking spirits in seances, idolatry of things or of nature), superstition (e.g., reliance upon horoscopes, tarots, palms, or various "New Age" practices), and sacrilege (e.g., attacking or misusing consecrated things). Other serious sins against faith include perjury, blasphemy, vow-breaking, testing God, and similar failures of reverence for God and of fear of separation from him in hell.

Believers are also called to hope in God and his promises. Such hope is expressed in perseverance in the Christian life even in great difficulties, sharing in Christ's redeeming work, and bearing witness to him in word and deed; it is denied in grave sins such as presumption and willful despair. While hoping for the coming of Christ's kingdom at the end of time, Catholics cooperate even now with other persons of good will in building up that kingdom of love, justice, and peace; they accept responsibility for the Church's entire mission; and they seek to discern and live out their personal vocation and commitments in the face of temptation, frustration, and failure, trusting always in Christ's healing and elevating grace.

Believers must also love God and seek to deepen and express that love by acts such as: prayerful conversation and sacramental communion with God; acts of devotion, penance, and almsgiving; seeking appropriate counsel and spiritual direction; fulfilling duties of Church membership and seeking to build up the Church's vitality and peace; fostering unity among

Christians; acting charitably toward all; and preparing well for death. Opposed to love of God are: thoughtless or sacrilegious reception of the Eucharist; other inappropriate behavior at, attitudes toward, or neglect of, the sacraments; failures to pray or persevere in prayer; schism and public dissent from the Church's teachings; stubborn refusal to repent of serious sin and be reconciled with God and the Church; leading others into sin (giving scandal); and neglecting to consider and prepare for "the last things" (death, judgment, heaven and hell).

IV. CONCLUSIONS

The Catholic tradition, in reflecting upon the questions of what the human person and the Christian should be and do, has been a rich source of applied ethics. The response to contemporary challenges and the call to renewal has, however, been uneven. There remain unresolved tensions: between the goal of having a more thoroughly Scriptural, Christocentric and eschatological ethic, and the goal of articulating a common morality shared with and accessible to people of all faiths and none; between the conception of moral theology as a call to conversion to the fulness of the Christian life, and a less visionary, but some would say more practicable, conception that presents some legal minima, but that is otherwise open to contemporary life-styles and personal preferences; between the freedom of individual conscience and the demands of Church membership; between the goal of a more holistic moral, spiritual, and dogmatic theology and the academic trend to fragmentation and specialization; and between very different metaethics, with rival conceptions of freedom, conscience, the moral act, moral absolutes, and the authority of Scripture, tradition, and the Magisterium. Despite some creative developments, the Catholic ethical landscape is presently marked by radical division and dissent.

Nonetheless there are new signs of hope: a new generation of Catholic theologians and ethicists, many of them laypeople, have different concerns and are exploring new approaches. Developments in contemporary moral philosophy such as the neo-Aristotelian, neo-Kantian, and natural law revivals, communitarianism, and virtue ethics provide new opportunities for dialogue and for mining and advancing the wisdom of the Catholic tradition. The greatest challenges for Catholic applied ethics in the decades ahead will be to consolidate and integrate after a period of rapid change, to continue to listen and respond faithfully to the signs of the times, and to focus upon a new evangelization and enculturation of its ethic in a world apparently indifferent to the Gospel of Jesus Christ yet, as Catholics believe, secretly craving for it.

Also See the Following Articles

BIOETHICS, OVERVIEW • BUSINESS ETHICS, OVERVIEW • RELIGION AND ETHICS • SOCIAL ETHICS, OVERVIEW

Bibliography

Ashley, B. (1996). *Living the truth in love.* New York: Alba.
Catechism of the Catholic Church. (1994). New York: Paulist.
Curran, C., & McCormick, R. (Eds.). (1979–1996). *Readings in moral theology.* (Vols. 1–9). New York: Paulist.
Finnis, J. (1991). *Moral absolutes: Tradition, revision and truth.* Washington, DC: Catholic University of America Press.
Grisez, G. (1983–1997). *The way of the Lord Jesus.* (Vols. 1–3). Chicago: Franciscan Press.
Gula, R. (1989). *Reason informed by faith.* New York: Paulist.
John Paul II. (1993). *Veritatis splendor—The splendor of truth.* New York: Paulist.
May, W. (1994). *An introduction to moral theology.* (2nd ed.). Huntington IN: Our Sunday Visitor.
McCormick, R. (1981–1985). *Notes in moral theology.* (Vols. 1–2). Washington DC: University Press of America.
McDermott, T. (Ed.). (1989). *Aquinas' summa theologiae—A concise translation.* Dublin: Eyre & Spottiswoode.
O'Connell, T. (1990). *Principles for a Catholic morality.* (2nd ed.). San Francisco: Harper & Row.
Pinckaers, S. (1995). *The sources of Christian ethics.* Washington DC: Catholic University of America Press.
Peschke, K. H. (1993). *Christian ethics: Moral theology in the light of Vatican II.* (Rev. ed.). (Vols. 1–2). Alcester: Goodliffe Neale.

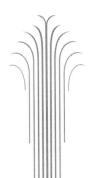

CITIZENSHIP

Daniel Warner

Graduate Institute of International Studies

GLOSSARY

citizenship The legal status confirming a person as a national of a country enjoying the rights and privileges following from that status.

cosmopolitanism The belief that an individual has duties, loyalties, and obligations beyond the particular state of which that person is a citizen.

nationalism Strong feelings of attachment to a large community usually united by history, culture, and language, most often identified with a movement toward sovereignty for that community.

nation-state A liberal ideal wherein a homogeneous community is recognized as sovereign and legally autonomous.

CITIZENSHIP is the expression of a public identity. It is at once the recognition of an official position and the ability to enjoy the rights and privileges following from that position. A citizen is one who is protected by the state and at the same time uses the state to advance claims on the basis of equality with fellow citizens.

In addition, citizenship is the subjective belonging to the public identity of a country. In a nation-state, to be a good citizen requires following the laws and participating in the life of a state as a member in good standing of the core constituency of that state.

The criteria by which citizenship is decided is one of the most important defining decisions for a state. The granting of citizenship to immigrants, for example, much like immigration or asylum policy, tells how a country views itself and the importance it gives to certain characteristics of its people. With the increasing mobility of individuals, decisions about including new citizens and excluding others who have applied for citizenship highlights country identification, especially in those countries where citizenship is considered to have a high value.

I. WHY CITIZENSHIP IS IMPORTANT TODAY

The subject of citizenship is extremely important for all states. The problem of citizenship touches on fundamental problems involving the organization of society and the place of the individual in that society. In fact, the problems of citizenship are tied to the deepest undercurrents in political and social life, and to the very basis of the structure of a state.

Historically, we can trace citizenship back to the Greeks and Aristotle, and we can see the inclusive and exclusive elements of citizenship in early times. Although not all of the population of Athens were citizens, citizenship was important for the life of the *polis*. Participation in public life was crucial for those who were deemed worthy. Indeed, citizenship was so important that much of the educational system in Athens was centered around preparing the elite to be good citizens. Public life, and hence good citizenship, had a very high priority in ancient Greece. Thus, the number of people eligible for that status was limited and the privileges accorded were rather high.

The concept of good citizenship and its privileges was extended beyond a small locality and elite during the later stages of the Roman Empire, with the exclusiveness of citizenship obviously reduced by the expansion of territorial space. While the Greeks were highly exclusive in their citizenship laws, the Romans gradually included more and more people in their citizenship laws to increase their control over their expanding Empire. For the Romans, as for later empires, the granting of citizenship was a means of separating groups from their local or tribal and ethnic affinities. The granting of citizenship to indigenous populations was a means of controlling large populations located far from the center of the Empire.

The modern concept of citizenship is intertwined with the development of the modern state in Europe and can be dated to the end of the eighteenth century. The American and French Revolutions were concerned with establishing stable political structures that included democratic practices based on notions of justice and equity. Citizenship, encompassing citizen's rights, was fundamental to the establishment of equitable and just governments based on democratic ideals. In addition, the development of welfare policies in Europe in the nineteenth century made it important for someone to "belong" to one state or city in order to profit from those benefits, just as it was necessary to distinguish those who did not belong and could not benefit.

It should be noted that at about the same time the modern concept of citizenship was developing Immanuel Kant was writing of the cosmopolitan ideal of world citizenship. Cosmopolitanism includes the recognition of the necessity for particular citizenship in a given country, but it also recognizes the duties of citizens to higher laws and eventually to a more universal form of citizenship.

The growth of the modern state and the importance of citizens' rights were related to the development of nationalism. Whereas citizenship focused on legal rights and privileges based on fundamental understandings of the individual and the individual's relation to the state, the growth of nationalism in the nineteenth century highlighted the important emotional, subjective attachment that developed in conjunction with the growth of the modern state. It was not enough to have rules of equality and privilege for citizens, it was also important for those citizens to have feelings of belonging to the bureacratic state entity. In that sense, as in ancient Greece, civic or public education became crucial as preparation for citizenship. The growth, then, of modern citizenship is closely tied to the growth of the modern liberal state and to full participation within its activities. Citizenship today, for example, is supportive of the government in mass elections in democratic countries. It is for that reason that the Greek emphasis on education as preparation for good citizenship has been extended to mass public education. Normative decisions on democratic forms of governments and the types of citizens included are crucial factors in modern political life as is the educational system that prepares students to be good citizens.

The modern liberal state does not exist in isolation. Questions of citizenship are being challenged from different sources, not only in terms of domestic pressures, but also from exogeneous sources. In the West, there are profound changes in traditional patterns of migration. The United States, for example, is receiving an influx of immigrants from Latin America and from Asia that is changing the demographic structure of the society from its original European basis. Recent discussions in France about the wearing of veils in schools also point to fundamental shifts in migration patterns away from traditional European sources, and, hence, fundamental shifts in the demographic structure of that society. The implications of these shifts are being manifested in various ways, such as the attacks on Korean-American-owned stores in Los Angeles and the rise of the National Front in France. The long-term implications of these patterns are more difficult to comprehend; it is not easy to predict to what degree and how societies integrate new members in terms of offering citizenship through naturalization. What must be noted, however, is that greater physical mobility has produced growing pressures on immigration and naturalization laws, and, hence, it has increased the importance of citizenship.

Certain countries have traditionally been immigrant friendly, especially countries like Canada and Australia, which have relatively low population densities and appear to be more open to multiculturalism and new citizens. The laws allowing new immigrants to become naturalized in these countries have been relatively flexible, inviting new migrants to enjoy the full status of citizenship. Other countries have been less friendly to new immigrants and have placed considerable barriers, including different levels of integration short of full citizenship. Recent decisions by the European Union have made it more difficult for certain groups to enter the Union, and to eventually become citizens according to the individual laws of each country.

More importantly, however, the Western integration of nontraditional members is part of a larger and more complex integration pattern. In addition to a changing migration, the West is also witnessing profound structural changes from within. In North America, we see this with the trade agreements between the United States, Canada, and Mexico. But most importantly, we are witnessing higher forms of integration within the European Union. Instead of people moving from one place to another, as in the case of migration, we are seeing European borders changing from what were once rigid brick walls to supple cell walls that will permit the free movement of people, goods, and services within a number of countries. Whereas in the case of migration people change countries, in the case of integration the borders themselves have changed in the sense of permitting freer access. Western European integration is changing the meaning of sovereignty, and, hence, of citizenship, and calls into question the very reason for migration and its significance. In the West, changing migration patterns and structural integration raise fundamental questions about traditional social attachments.

Following this pattern of integration, the differentiation of citizenship rights between different countries becomes less pronounced within economic spaces such as the European Union and the North America Free Trade Area (NAFTA). While individual citizenship rights still apply to individual countries, there are more and more commonalities involved in group citizenship within supranational organizations.

If within Western Europe and North America migration and integration have accentuated greater fluidity in social attachments toward larger units and particular citizenship laws have become less important, the situation in the East shows a marked contrast. The breakups of the Soviet Union, Yugoslavia, and Czechoslovakia have resulted in smaller social units and more localized forms of attachments wherein individual, particular citizenship rights are accentuated. The births and rebirths of various nation-states remind us that the inevitability of higher and higher forms of integration is not to be taken for granted; or, if it is, it will not be a linear progression. If one intuitively argues that societal interdependence will occur with developing technology and improved transportation—what is generally referred to as complex interdependence—the situations in the former Soviet Union, Yugoslavia, and Czechoslovakia point to another solution to the organization of social and political life. In many of the newly independent countries, normative decisions about citizenship reflect traditional animosities and exclusionary practices. In fact, the writing of new citizenship laws in the newly independent countries has accentuated the particularity of each individual country, in contrast to the commonality found in the higher integration patterns.

One could argue that state borders are being challenged throughout the world. Integration and disintegration are both dramatic transformations in the traditional spatial delimitations of the basic organization of political and social life, whether into larger or smaller units. Political theorists have debated the relationship between the individual and society within a clearly defined community, and international relations specialists and international lawyers have examined the relationship between communities defined as nation-states. Integration and disintegration call into question the society being considered by the political theorists and the nation-states being observed by the international relations specialists and international lawyers. Similar to the time of the development of the modern nation-state and cosmopolitanism, tensions between the particular and the universal can be found through the individuality of citizenship laws.

Whereas migration threatens individual identity, integration and disintegration threaten the state's identity. A citizen's identity is tied to the state that he or she is a citizen of: citizenship is the constitutive element of political identity. But, as our examples from the West and the East have suggested, states themselves are going through a form of identity crisis. In sum, then, the question of citizenship/identity in the East and the West is part of the larger crisis of identity, a crisis that is acute for both individuals and the state. While citizenship is the manifestation of a public identity, it is important to analyse how that public identity evolves, both from the structural and emotional points of view. Citizenship is membership in a state, and it is necessary to step back from a static view of a state to see how the writing and interpretation of citizenship laws are an integral and dynamic part of a state's identity.

Many of the new countries we have mentioned were not and are still not democratic. Indeed, the example of modern liberal states is far from being universal. Recognized human rights conventions and norms have fostered greater pressure on countries to assure basic fundamental rights, but these rights have not always corresponded to clear and equitable citizenship norms. Recent discussions in the Baltic States concerning citizenship for the Russian minority are an example of this problem. The High Commissioner for Minorities of the Organization for Security and Cooperation in Europe (OSCE) has dealt with several of these problems in the OSCE countries in an attempt to harmonize human rights, minority rights, and citizenship.

II. ELEMENTS OF CITIZENSHIP

But what is citizenship? What are the elements that constitute political identity? There is no general agreement on a single definition of citizenship. As the expression of public identity, citizenship encompasses two elements: it includes the existence of a public authority made up of citizens who constitute the authority, and it includes the status following from the possession of citizenship. Citizenship is at once the recognition of an official position and the ability to use the rights and privileges following from that position. A citizen is one who is protected by the state and at the same time uses the state to advance her claims on the basis of equality with fellow citizens.

As indicated in the classic description of citizenship by T. H. Marshall, this public identity can be separated into three elements: the civil, the political, and the social. The civil element of citizenship is a position from which, on the basis of equality, people can make certain claims against each other and/or against the government. The political element is that which allows an individual to participate in the decisions of the government or to be a member of that government. The social element can be summarized in terms of general welfare. In addition, Marshall saw a development in the acquisition of these elements from civil rights in the eighteenth century to political rights in the nineteenth century, and economic and social rights in the twentieth century.

What is the relationship between the civil and political elements? Can one have the civil element without the political element? To some extent, the answer is yes. African Americans in the United States did have certain civil rights before they were given the political right to vote. Foreign workers in most countries have certain civil rights even though they are not part of the political system in the sense of fully participating in elections. Moreover, one could argue that the internationalization of human rights has created a situation wherein individuals have certain rights regardless of their citizenship. Although specific citizenship is not covered by human rights conventions, all individuals have certain guarantees: human rights are citizen-specific blind; they posit a set of fundamental rights that

supersede national legislation. Human rights are carried out through the particular state mechanism, but they are universal and should not be abrogated by a specific state. Human rights may be attributed by international law, but only states may grant citizenship.

The Universal Declaration of Human Rights says: "Everyone has the right to a nationality" and "no one shall be arbitrarily deprived of his nationality nor deprived of the right to change his nationality." (Article 15. I., II.)

Article 25 of The International Covenant on Civil and Political Rights says:

> Every citizen shall have the right and the opportunity without ... unreasonable restrictions:
> (a) To take part in the conduct of public affairs, directly or through freely chosen representatives;
> (b) To vote and to be elected at genuine periodic elections which shall be held under universal and equal suffrage and shall be held by secret ballot, guaranteeing the free expression of the will of the electors;
> (c) To have access, on general terms of equality, to public service in his country.

From the human rights and natural law points of view, therefore, the civil element of citizenship can precede the political element. The political element in this sense is the forum within which the civil element is expressed. Participation in the political process of a country implies that the country has a substructure that guarantees the basic civil rights mentioned.

Both the political and civil elements are part of what could be called the "objective" element in citizenship. In terms of political theory, the objective political and civil elements are part of the vertical contract between citizens and a government. Together, these elements form the basis of the legal structure of any state and constitute the structural basis of the state. The civil and political elements are part of a common practice based on common rules; they form the structural basis of political practice. The objective, contractual structure of the civil and political elements allows the society to function insofar as the structure is actualized through practice. The civic and political elements of citizenship constitute the legal basis or skeleton of a country. They say that citizens of that country have certain duties, such as military duty or taxes, but that they also enjoy the protection of the state, public education, and so on. The objective elements describe the duties, obligations, and privileges coming from citizenship.

The third element, the social element of citizenship, is the horizontal contract in society. In other terms, we could say that the civil and political elements constitute the state, and that the social element constitutes the nation. Whereas the civil and political elements can be studied in legal documents representing the status accorded to citizens, the social element is much more difficult to discern and is tied to affective feelings of belonging that are associated with nationalism or patriotism. Although the objective element is necessary for the proper functioning of the state, the subjective element provides the sufficient affective or psychological cohesion that allows a state to function. Without the sense of belonging, the status of citizenship is insufficient to a cohesive political body and the proper functioning of a government.

The question of citizenship, therefore, cannot be studied by only looking at the legal documents and requirements for citizenship. The subjective element in citizenship leads one to examine how a society sees itself. The state, in this sense, is more than just a legal entity; it includes questions of nationality and ethnicity, and a sense of belonging through historical experience, language and religion. The subjective element is closely tied to feelings of loyalty. These feelings have often been tied to modern revolutionary movements calling for legal and political self-determination in the name of nationalism.

Today, in times of changing borders and higher forms of integration, it is this subjective element that has been the most difficult to pinpoint and capture. Given large forced migrations in the former Soviet Union, for example, questions of citizenship in the newly independent Baltic States have been most difficult. The relationship between language and citizenship, dual citizenship, residence, and loyalty have been particularly contentious in this region in the establishment of new citizenship criteria. The situation in the former Yugoslavia also shows the tense relationship between nation, nationality, and citizenship. Whereas the legal nature of citizenship can easily be amended, the subjective element is more difficult to perceive and change based on new political realities. The drawing of territorial borders is often easier than decisions concerning sentiments of populations and it is perhaps the subjective element that is the most explosive. Legal status and affective belonging are not always interchangeable.

III. CITIZENSHIP AND THE NATION-STATE

What are the possible relationships between the horizontal and vertical contracts, the subjective and objective elements of citizenship? According to traditional liberal theory, members of a given nation should be members of the same state. In other words, liberal state theory tells us that the nation and the state should be similar, hence the ideal of the nation-state. One is supposed to be a legal member and an affective member of the same country at the same time.

But, this is rarely the case and has rarely been the case in history. Although the nation-state has been hailed as the most dynamic and effective form of political identity in the modern world, we have rarely seen the legal borders of a bounded territory country coterminous with a fairly homogeneous social group. Not accepting a priori the ideal equation of the nation-state, it is important to examine three possible types of relationships between the objective and subjective elements. First, we could assert that the vertical and horizontal contracts are symmetrical, that there is a "historic fit" between the legal system of a state and the nation or community of people who reside within that state.

This ideal of the nation-state is assumed within the concept of nationalism. *Nationalism* is a political program that includes the alignment of the nation and state. It holds that groups defined as "nations" have the right to, and therefore ought to, form territorial sovereign states of the kind that have become standard since the French Revolution. Without the realization of this program of legal recognition in sovereign autonomy, "nationalism" does not attain its fulfillment. In practice the program usually means exercising sovereign control over, so far as possible, a continuous stretch of territory with clearly defined borders, inhabited by a homogeneous population that forms its essential body of citizens.

This ideal type of symmetry between the nation and the state can be placed in historical perspective. For example, Marshall maintains that the three elements, our two contracts, were united in earlier times and that each of his three elements belongs, in its formative period, to a different century. Discussions that call into question the symmetry of the nation-state and those that highlight the importance of the nation-state as an ideal lead us to question the relationship between the state and the nation.

In other words, what happens when there is no symmetry? We have referred to the nation-state as an ideal. Writers point to the fact that the ideal has been a very rare exception in history and is not relevant to our modern experience. Thus, we should recognize that, in reality, the vertical and horizontal contracts are usually separated. Whether or not the elements were united in previous times, it is the separation of the different elements—often their confrontation and/or overlapping—that confronts us today. Realistically, therefore, we must talk of the differentiation between the horizontal and vertical contracts and the subjective and objective elements. It is the separation of the two axes, the differentiation between the elements, that renders the problem of the nature of citizenship so complex. For whereas formal citizenship can be analyzed as a legal right, it cannot encompass the "imagined community" that is so crucial to statehood and belonging.

So, moving away from the initial assumed relation of symmetry, we could speculate on the separation, even accepting that at one time there was symmetry. We could say that there was initially separation, followed by a historic fit, and then a subsequent separation. One could say, for example, that an ethnic community formed a nation that became a state. In this sense, there are really two contracts. From the initial state of nature, there was the initial contract to form the community, and then there was the contract by the community to form the state. On the other hand, we could speculate that the state created the community in the sense that the governmental structure imposed a certain order that itself became constitutive of the meaning of society. The state may have been merely laws and rules, but the practice of those laws and rules created deeper attachments and involvements.

The second and third possibilities of the relationship between the different elements of citizenship assume that there has always been estrangement from the ideal. One can assume that there has always been a separation between the two contracts, and speculate about reasons for the existence of the ideal of symmetry. Whether one argues for the primacy of the horizontal or vertical axis, discussions of their primacy lead to speculation about the reasons for their continued separation, the importance or priority of the contracts, and eventually the reasons for the ideal of symmetry of the axes to form the historic fit. To see one of the elements without necessarily trying to combine the two is to deny all of the emotions of patriotism. It is to view citizenship as a commodity like any other practical association. To demythologize the ideal of symmetry and to posit estrangement as the norm is not to deny that the ideal of symmetry and the historic fit is still a powerful force. It is in this sense that one sees certain citizenships bought on the market today in terms of tax packages, or people holding different citizenships for various advantages.

The significance of citizenship, therefore, depends on a reading of the relationship between the subjective and objective elements, whether one assumes symmetry or estrangement. Whereas it is relatively simple to write laws about what is required to be a citizen, it is much more difficult to anticipate the consequences of those laws for the society at large in terms of the social element. Conversely, while it is understandable for an ethnic group to want to expand its territorial domain, the movement from ethnic group to nation to nation-state is a much larger project. Or, it may be argued, there could be the establishment of the legal state and then the creation of nationalist sentiments.

An analysis of the citizenship laws of a given country, therefore, tells us how that country conceives of the very fundamental relationship between those living within a given society and the limits of that society in terms of attachments. For example, certain states award citizenship on the basis of jus soli, birth and residence in a particular place, rather than jus sanguinis, descent no matter where the person was born or raised.

The case of Hungarians is a good example. To be a Hungarian, as far as language, history, and culture is concerned, is not the same as Hungarian citizenship, especially since the demise of the Austro-Hungarian Empire. The state of Hungary lost two-thirds of its territory and one-third of its population after World War I. In fact, the problem of the "Hungarian minority" outside Hungary points to the very difference between nation and state. In much of Eastern and Central Europe, there were nations before there were states. With the collapse of the Soviet bloc, there has been an attempt to realign the nation and state. The recent Hungarian citizenship law of 1993 recognizes the principle that all descendants of Hungarian citizens shall be Hungarian citizens if they move to Hungary, and it gives a particular status to those "Hungarians" who have lived outside the borders of the country Hungary since it lost its territories. Thus, Hungarian minorities living in neighboring countries were given preferential treatment to become naturalized "Hungarians" in an effort to realign nation and state to the liberal ideal.

IV. CITIZENSHIP AS EXCLUSION

The relationship between the objective and subjective elements within citizenship also tells us something about the limits of that society in another sense. Even if we reject the social element in citizenship, citizenship still has its limits. For, whatever we say it means to be a citizen legally, we cannot forget that citizenship is a statement of belonging that is naturally exclusive. To say that someone is a citizen of a country is to both include that person within the framework of other citizens, whether objectively or subjectively attached, or both, *and* to say that this group that person is part of is a group that excludes others. Membership in any group is a form of division between insiders and outsiders, and one cannot ignore this negative, exclusive element in a full discussion of citizenship. The granting of citizenship to some is to deny citizenship to others. As we saw in ancient Greece, the importance of privileged citizenship put a high premium on its possession with its necessary corollary of discriminating against noncitizens.

Membership as a general principle includes a decision-making process. That is, there are certain members, or the entire membership, if possible, who decide who will be new members and who will be excluded. What is important about this process is not only the form of the process itself, but the criteria on which the decision is made. The criteria are of positive and negative sorts. The positive says that a group wants a particular person to be a member either because the person is like the group or because the person is like what the group wants to be. Canada, for example, has been rather generous in granting citizenship to those who can clearly demonstrate the capacity to create employment for Canadians. The criteria established for membership also imply what people do not want; membership and nonmembership cannot be separated, just as citizens and noncitizens cannot be separated. The positive granting of citizenship to one is closely tied to the denial of citizenship for another.

The crisis of identity that we have emphasized for both the individual and the state has greatly exacerbated the importance of the negative element. Instead of talking about the constructive elements of citizenship, in terms of equality and community, in modern times we often use the notion of citizenship as a means of negative affirmation. While we see greater freedom developing in the movement of goods and services, the free movement of people (the granting of citizenship) has become more and more limited.

Myths are terribly important for nation-state building. They can be based on the heroism of past leaders or acts of group valor. Unfortunately, they can also be based on negative denial of the value of noncitizens. With greater restrictions on naturalization, we see this negative element more and more in the forefront. The exclusive element has been worsened in modern times by the current individual/state identity crisis. It is as if the pressures and uncertainties of technology and integration have caused nationalist and patriotic feelings to be based solely on the negative element.

In reaction to this negative element, one could say that all particular memberships should be abolished in order to arrive at the largest possible universal community: For certain cosmopolitans, returning to the ideals of Immanuel Kant, any form of citizenship is wrong because it inherently separates "them" from "us." ("Citizens of the World" would be an obvious exception.) What is appealing about cosmopolitanism is that it avoids the ethical dilemma of explaining why a person has greater duties and obligations to fellow citizens than to someone else. While one can easily explain closer ties to family and clan, one must also recognize that one has special duties to fellow citizens under traditional citizenship laws. Cosmopolitanism in this sense avoids the distinction between citizens and noncitizens, and the hierarchy of ethical obligations.

Separation between citizens and noncitizens in and of itself is not necessarily an ethical problem, but rather the difficulty lies in the understanding of what the separation means. One cannot argue about insiders and outsiders until one can clearly define what it means to be an insider and to be an outsider. If one is born in the United States, one is automatically a citizen of that country, not matter what one's parental status may be. This accident-by-birth citizenship begs the enormous complexity of establishing criteria for choosing new citizens, just as do lotteries and other forms of fortuitous selection. In addition, the accident-by-birth criteria highlight the problematic distinction of conventional duties toward fellow citizens and the lack of obligation toward others beyond borders.

This element of exclusion can be seen in both the objective and subjective elements of citizenship. Legally, one can be excluded from citizenship in a country but can develop profound social attachments through permanent residence. On the other hand, one can legally be a citizen of a state while remaining excluded from the dominant nation or society of that country. Indeed, one can legally be a citizen of certain countries without ever having lived in those countries.

In general, however, we focus on exclusion from citizenship in the legal sense. Each state has the right to decide on what basis citizenship in that state can be acquired. That right is an integral part of a state's self-definition. Even in ancient Greece, the cradle of democracy, out of Athens' quarter of a million population, only 40,000 people were citizens.

Nonetheless, whether it be the state's right to determine its citizenship criteria or some international authority's function to determine citizenship legally, the relationship between the subjective and objective elements cannot be decided by legislation. The relationship between the objective and subjective elements is worked out within the society and in forms of dialogue with those outside the borders. The relationship is an ongoing process that is expressed through various fora. Debates about citizenship put into focus the political identity of citizens and noncitizens in terms of the state's identity. It is in this sense that debates about citizenship are an important prism.

Also See the Following Articles

ARISTOTELIAN ETHICS • GREEK ETHICS, OVERVIEW • KANTIANISM • LIBERALISM • POLITICAL OBLIGATION

Bibliography

Hammar, T. (1990). *Democracy and the nation state: Aliens, denizens and citizens in a world of international migration.* Aldershot, U.K.: Gower Publishing Company Limited.

Heater, D. (1990). *Citizenship: The civic ideal in world history, politics and education.* London and New York: Longman.

Liebich, A., Warner, D., & Dragovic, J. (Eds.). (1995). *Citizenship east and west.* London and New York: Kegan Paul International.

Marshall, T. H. (1950). *Citizenship and social class.* Cambridge: Cambridge University Press.

Shklar, J. N. (1991). *American citizenship: The quest for inclusion.* Cambridge, MA: Harvard University Press.

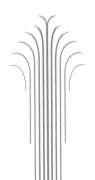

CIVIL DISOBEDIENCE

Hugo Adam Bedau
Tufts University

I. Varieties of Civil Disobedience
II. Justifying Civil Disobedience
III. The Political Effectiveness of Civil Disobedience

GLOSSARY

boycott Refusal to buy goods or services in order to protest the policies or practices of the manufacturer or seller.

civil Concerning the body politic or political aspects of a community's life; also decent, courteous conduct.

conscientious objection Refusal to obey the law or commands of higher authority because they violate one's moral convictions.

direct civil disobedience The law being violated in an act of civil disobedience (e.g., refusing to register for the draft) is the law or policy under protest (i.e., an unfair system of selective service).

indirect civil disobedience The law being violated (e.g., refusal to register for the draft) is not the law or policy under protest (i.e., the war for which the draft is instituted).

nonviolence Conduct that does not cause harm to persons or their property.

passive resistance Disobedience of the law followed by passive (unresisting) acceptance of the penalties imposed for such disobedience.

rule of law The principle that disputes are to be settled by appeal to law as determined by an independent judiciary using appropriate rules of evidence and procedure.

satyagraha Nonviolent conflict resolution involving self-purification and respect for one's opponent; originated by M. K. Gandhi. Includes passive resistance.

sit-in A tactic of nonviolent protest in which the ordinary conduct of business is disrupted (e.g., a racially mixed group occupies seats at racially segregated lunch counter in defiance of the store's policy).

tax resistance Refusal to pay one's lawfully required taxes because doing so would support government policies financed by the taxes that are deemed morally wrong by the objector.

CIVIL DISOBEDIENCE is any act in violation of the law done with the intention of frustrating or changing the law, conducted in such a manner as not to involve intentional violence against persons or property, and done in the belief that such disobedience is an appropriate tactic to achieve social justice or some other fundamental moral goal. Borderline cases arise from challenging one or more of the conditions mentioned above on the grounds that it is (or they are) not necessary.

However civil disobedience is defined, it must be done without prejudging the separate question of whether such conduct is justifiable. Not all civil disobedience is justifiable, and civil disobedience is not the only law breaking that can be justified under appro-

Encyclopedia of Applied Ethics, Volume 1

501

priate conditions. Several features of standard attempts to define civil disobedience have the effect of making such acts either harder or easier to justify. Passive resistance is defended by some as definitionally required in any act properly classified as civil disobedience. The same is true of informing the authorities prior to committing the act of civil disobedience in order to reduce the likelihood of violence and to make the purpose of the protest clear. But some would regard passive resistance or prior notice as only among the many considerations relevant to the justification of such acts.

I. VARIETIES OF CIVIL DISOBEDIENCE

The term "civil disobedience" is sufficiently broad and vague to apply to a wide variety of actual and possible cases, some of which have relatively little in common with others.

A. Individual vs. Mass Conduct

Civil disobedience may be undertaken either by an individual acting alone or by a group acting in concert. The political effectiveness of civil disobedience, however, usually depends on large numbers of participants, as in the campaigns for national self-determination in India led by Mohandas Gandhi in the 1930s and for civil rights in the South led by Martin Luther King, Jr., in the 1960s.

Persons acting alone or in small numbers are more likely to be seen as conscientious objectors, testifying by their conduct to what they believe to be an unjust law or policy but not acting with the attempt to change or invalidate the law they protest. Probably the most widely discussed case of civil disobedience in American history illustrates this problem of classification.

In 1846, Henry David Thoreau was arrested for refusing to pay the Massachusetts poll tax (he spent but one night in the local jail, his fine having been promptly paid by a neighbor). In his classic essay, "Civil Disobedience" (first given as a lecture in Concord in 1848), it is evident that Thoreau was not primarily interested in trying to change the laws and practices that he was protesting—the Mexican War, chattel slavery in the South, the Fugitive Slave Law as applied throughout the nation, and to a lesser extent mistreatment of the Indians.

Instead, he seems to have had rather different goals: to use his tax refusal as a tactic that symbolically disconnected him from the wrongs he believed the government was using the tax money to perpetrate, and to encourage others by his example to do the same, regard-

less of whether that would result in influencing the government to change its practices. In Thoreau's case and cases of conscientious objection, like refusing to report for military duty when drafted, such refusals typically lack the political purpose of changing the law, characteristic of the intention of civil disobedience.

B. Illegal vs. Legal Conduct

Whether acts, e.g., a mass rally held in a town's civic center, are classified as civil disobedience depends on whether the law forbids such acts and on what the intentions of the actors are. It is generally agreed that an act cannot be classified as civil disobedience unless some law is violated by the act: Civil disobedience is always *illegal* conduct (even if it is not properly described as *criminal*). Thus, in American society today, with "free speech" interpreted broadly by the Supreme Court and protected by the first amendment to the Constitution, much conduct that in other societies would be illegal is quite within the law here. Accordingly, nonviolent sit-down strikes and boycotts, unless they involve illegal acts, such as a violation of trespass laws, are not tactics of civil disobedience as that term is usually understood.

But whether an act is legal or illegal can itself be controversial, as is illustrated by *Walker v. Birmingham* (1967), one of the important constitutional cases arising out of the Civil Rights movement of the 1960s and decided by the Supreme Court.

Martin Luther King, Jr., and other civil rights leaders planned a mass public protest in downtown Birmingham, Alabama, scheduled for Easter weekend in 1963. But their efforts to obtain a parade permit were frustrated; the undisputed evidence shows they were denied a permit because they were planning to protest local laws and ordinances that mandated racial segregation. Birmingham officials went further and obtained an ex parte court order prohibiting the protest parade. The leaders of the demonstration decided to hold their parade without a permit and to defy the injunction; they were promptly arrested. (While in jail, King penned his famous essay, "Letter from Birmingham Jail," in defense of civil disobedience.)

In court the civil rights leaders argued that their arrest was invalid because they were unfairly denied a parade permit, the injunction was a sham intended solely to turn conduct fully within the protester's rights into illegal conduct, and in any case the segregation laws to be protested were invalid under the federal constitution. In a five to four decision, the Supreme Court ruled on technical grounds to uphold the injunction on its face and thus validate the arrests; the Court sidestepped the two fundamental issues concerning whether the denial of the parade permit was lawful and whether the segregation laws being protested were constitutional.

As seen from the standpoint of lawyers and others sympathetic to the Civil Rights movement but reluctant to endorse violation of the law (even unjust laws), the aim of the disobedience campaigns in the South (such as the one in Birmingham in 1963) was to get the local authorities to recognize the priority of federal constitutional law, especially of the "equal protection of the laws" (14th amendment). Taking that language seriously would require repeal or nullification of local Jim Crow laws, ordinances, and their selective enforcement inconsistent with such equality. On this view, there was no true "disobedience" of the law, because the "laws" being violated were themselves unlawful under the federal Constitution, the moral adequacy of which in principle was taken for granted. Local authorities, such as those in Birmingham, of course saw the matter differently; they viewed the disobedience as criminal conduct and not civil.

C. Violent vs. Nonviolent Conduct

Civil disobedience is usually thought of as nonviolent political protest; some of its most influential proponents (such as Leo Tolstoy and Mohandas Gandhi) were pacifists who preached against violence in human affairs generally and explicitly rejected it as a permissible tactic even in a good cause. But controversy surrounds the extent to which civil disobedience must be nonviolent. Some hold that an act of protest can count as civil disobedience even if it involves some violence, provided that the violence (a) was not intended by the protesters, (b) was not carried out by the protesters (rather, it was done by onlookers, opponents of the protest, or by the police), (c) was solely against property, or (d) was not very harmful.

Consider, for example, the Boston Tea Party (1773), in which local patriots disguised as Indians boarded ships in Boston harbor under cover of darkness and dumped bales of tea overboard to protest what they regarded as unfair import duties. If any intentional violence against property by definition keeps an act from being civil disobedience (because violent acts are not "civil," in the secondary sense of that term), then the Boston Tea Party is not a case of civil disobedience. However, if intentional violence is permitted so long as it is not directed against persons, then the Tea Party can be regarded as civil disobedience. (The Tea Party case raises other questions, however; if civil disobedience must be undertaken as a *public* act of political protest, then it is hard to see how those who conceal their true identity can be said to be engaged in an act of civil disobedience.)

A more troublesome case is presented by the self-immolation in the 1960s of Buddhist monks in Saigon, South Vietnam, to protest the Vietnam War (an American Quaker, Norman Morrison, died in a similar fashion outside the Pentagon in November 1965). Leaving aside whether such suicidal acts are illegal, self-immolation would not count as civil disobedience if civil disobedience must by definition be a nonviolent act.

The controversy over violence and nonviolence also shows the extent to which defining an act of civil disobedience may tacitly involve factors relevant to its justification. As a rule, violent acts are harder to justify than nonviolent acts, and so excluding violence by definition from civil disobedience tends to make it easier to justify any act of civil disobedience.

D. Direct vs. Indirect Protest

Another controversial issue is whether the law being violated in civil disobedience must itself be the law under protest. This controversy is another example of how the definition of civil disobedience relates to its justification. Some hold that only direct disobedience can be justified. On this view, the purpose of tax refusal must be to protest the principle of public taxation as such; but only a libertarian, anarchist, or nihilist could practice tax resistance in this way. In actual practice, tax resistance is typically aimed at protesting certain uses of tax revenues, e.g., to finance government weapons procurement, without any express or implied moral objections to the principle of taxation as such.

The obvious problem with most tax refusal, unless it is practiced on a wide scale and targeted at a specific public expenditure, is that its primary effect is simply to reduce overall tax revenues available to the government, thus marginally underfinancing government enterprises that most tax resisters approve of (e.g., highway construction, sewer and water supply, and police and fire protection).

Where the law broken is not the law or policy under protest, there are two dangers. First, the general public may regard such indirect disobedience as irrational, implausible, or unjustified, because the gap between the law broken and the law or policy being protested is too large. Thus, it would be virtually unintelligible to protest Congressional refusal to increase the minimum wage by refusing to file one's income tax return (contrast that with organizing a sit-in in the halls of Congress).

Second, indirect disobedience may exert little or no leverage against the laws or policies under protest. Thus, widespread burning of draft cards in the late 1960s at mass rallies to protest the war in Vietnam did not really hamper the government in carrying out the draft or the war; it was at most symbolic of disapproval and disaffiliation. It was also an ambiguous symbol: Were the cards being burnt to protest the very idea of coercive military service, or only to protest the way the draft was administered as an unfair system of selection? Or was the purpose to protest the war in which the draftees would serve? Or were there several such purposes?

On the other hand, if civil disobedience is confined to the breaking of laws that are themselves believed by the protesters to be unjust, then a vast array of law and government policies will be immune from protest by civil disobedience. For example, opponents of the death penalty can chain themselves to prison gates or trespass on prison grounds to protest an execution, but there is no law they can directly violate that will cause a halt to the execution event itself; executions are deliberately carried out within the prison in a manner that makes them inaccessible to direct protest.

E. Criminal vs. Civil Disobedience

Law breaking for selfish or purely personal reasons is criminal conduct, not civil disobedience. Disobedience of the law that is kept secret, even if done conscientiously, is not civil disobedience, because the secrecy of such acts prevents them from playing any part in the civic or public life of the community. Disobedient acts without a civic purpose, or without any principled basis, are not civil disobedience.

II. JUSTIFYING CIVIL DISOBEDIENCE

Not all acts of civil disobedience—any more than all law breaking, all lawful political protest, or all conscientious acts—are justified. As a political tactic, a given act or program of civil disobedience must satisfy several conditions before it is justified. What those conditions are, however, is controversial.

Philosophers differ over how civil disobedience is to be justified, in part because they disagree over the strength of the claim on our conduct made by the law and over the grounds of political obligation and responsibility. Traditionally and for the most part, philoso-

phers have assumed that we have an obligation or duty to obey the law, whatever it is, with the result that the burden of justification is on the law breaker. This is a burden not easily discharged. A few other philosophers, especially in recent years, have argued that there is no such obligation or duty—not even in a constitutional democracy. On their view, our only duty is to conform our conduct to correct moral principles, and any law that fails to pass the test of such principles deserves no respect or compliance (except, perhaps, on prudential grounds like avoiding arrest and other inconveniences or worse). On this view, the burden of justification falls on those who insist that there is a presumption in favor of obeying the law whatever its content may be.

As pointed out earlier, it has been argued that respect for the law (in the sense of respect for the principles defining the rule of law) is consistent with violating the law, provided one's illegal conduct is nonviolent, the authorities are fully informed in advance, and one is willing to accept whatever penalties the law imposes. Others reply that there is no good reason why breaking an unjust law, or attempting to get an unjust law repealed by breaking some other law, requires the disobedient to accept any punishment or to cooperate with the authorities at all.

In a constitutional democracy, where nonviolent political protest and participation are guaranteed by law, breaking the law is more difficult to justify than under tyrannic, despotic, or totalitarian rule. Yet nonviolent political protest is far more likely to be effective in a constitutional democracy than it is under any other form of government. It is difficult to imagine the successful efforts of the suffragettes in Great Britain and the United States in the early 1900s or of the Civil Rights movement of the 1960s except in a society that professes basic principles of political and moral equality of all persons and recognizes civil liberties and rights—precisely what nondemocratic societies reject in theory or in practice, or both.

A. The Problem of Justified Law Breaking in Ancient Athens

Civil disobedience as we know it had no place in ancient society; the idea of mass illegal protest aimed at abolishing some unjust law does not figure in classical thought. Other forms of justified law breaking, however, do. Perhaps Sophocles's *Antigone* (ca. 440 B.C.) is the earliest presentation of the problem: Ought Antigone give her dead brother Polyneices a decent burial as required by divine and customary law, despite the tyrant Creon's express prohibition of such obsequies (because Polyneices had sought to contest Creon's rulership), or ought she to comply with Creon's edict and let her brother's corpse feed the vultures? She decides to defy Creon, to her ultimate doom. (Whether Sophocles intended to side with her or with Creon or only to present a dramatic case of conflicting duties, we need not try to decide; her tragedy in any case does not constitute a philosophical argument.)

Unquestionably the first important discussion of the general problem of justified law breaking is to be found in Plato's dialogue *Crito* (ca. 380 B.C.). Socrates, imprisoned and sentenced to die as the result of conviction after trial on fraudulent charges, entertains arguments from his friend Crito, who urges him to escape from prison before his unjust death sentence is carried out. Socrates demurs; he does not dispute that his sentence is undeserved and unjust, but he argues it would still be wrong for him to try to escape. To do so, he suggests, would be to flout the authority of the laws of Athens, in conformance with which he has lived his whole life to date, and to break the implicit contract between him as a citizen and the state that requires individual obedience in exchange for social protection and nurture.

Socrates's arguments (whether or not Plato wants us to think they are conclusive) stand not only for the proposition that no selfish advantage—such as saving one's own life—is ever a good enough reason for breaking the laws of one's country, they also teach that disobeying the law even in a just cause is unjustified.

B. Christian Doctrine

1. Early Christian Thinking

In *Crito,* Socrates's argument anticipated the even stronger and much more influential doctrine in Paul's Epistle to the Romans (ca. 58 A.D.) that Christians must obey their rulers, because "the powers that be are ordained by God" (13:1). Running counter to this theme is the famous epigram of St. Augustine's, "an unjust law is no law."

As in so many other matters, the epitome of classical Christian philosophy appears in St. Thomas Aquinas. In his *Treatise on Law* (ca. 1265), Aquinas does not discuss civil disobedience as such, any more than his predecessors did, but he does examine how a Christian should react to unjust laws (the central issue of conscientious objection). His is a distinctly conservative view. He builds both on the Pauline doctrine requiring subservience of Christians to whatever rulers God has placed over them and on the Augustinian doctrine that connects law to justice. Aquinas enjoins Christians to

obey the law, however unjust it may be, unless the law requires conduct in violation of essential Christian religious tenets, e.g., worshiping false gods. And, of course, history records any number of Christians (and Jews) who went to their deaths rather than place a pinch of incense on Caesar's altar. As for lesser injustices, according to Aquinas, they are to be borne in patience, "lest a scandal [that is, disruption of social order] be caused."

The modern theory of civil disobedience has its origins in religious protests arising out of the Protestant Reformation in the 16th century. The role of conscience as the inner Word of God and thus of sincere personal convictions as the final authority over what one ought to do is a characteristically Protestant doctrine. But the attractions of Pauline doctrine remained strong, especially for Martin Luther; it was the dissenting churches—Quakers, Anabaptists, and Mennonites— rather than the main-line Protestant denominations that cultivated the doctrine of conscience and conscientious objection and passive resistance, and thus laid the basis for later secular theories of civil disobedience.

2. Martin Luther King, Jr.

In his "Letter from Birmingham Jail" (1963), Martin Luther King, Jr., offered a complex theory of justified civil disobedience. First, he defended civil disobedience as the final element in a fourfold strategy, preceded by "collection of the facts to determine whether injustices are alive," "negotiation" between the victims and the oppressors to remove the injustices, "self-purification" of the protesters to ensure that their motives were not purely self-serving, and then "direct action." (The echoes of Gandhian *satyagraha* here are no accident.) King and his associates were convinced that the fourth step (civil disobedience) was justified if the first and third had been achieved and the second had proved of no avail.

Crucial to King's argument on behalf of direct action was his belief that the laws imposing racial segregation and second-class citizenship on African Americans were unjust in several ways. First, the segregation laws did not "square with the moral law or the law of God." These laws failed that test because they "degrade human personality"; legally enforced segregation "distorts the soul and damages the personality." Second, these laws were unjust because they were "a code that a majority inflicts on a minority that is not binding on itself." Third, these laws were unjust because "the minority had no part in enacting or creating" them. King explicitly disavowed "evading or defying the law" as such (by which he meant resisting arrest or lying to the authorities about one's disobedient intentions), for that would lead to "anarchy." He concluded by saying, "I submit that an individual who breaks a law that conscience tells him is unjust, and willingly accepts the penalty by staying in jail to arouse the conscience of the community over its injustice, is in reality expressing the very highest respect for law."

Whether or not one agrees with King's four-step procedure to justify civil disobedience, or with his criteria of unjust laws, it is plain that his theory brings to the surface considerations relevant to justifying civil disobedience superior to those that can be teased out of such earlier writers as Aquinas or Thoreau. And while it is evident that King formulates his theory of justification within the framework of Christian thinking, no great difficulty attends revising and restating his theory in purely secular terms (Bedau, 1969, pp. 78–79).

C. Secular Theories of Justification

Several different kinds of moral theories and moral principles can be invoked to justify acts of civil disobedience. Three at least deserve brief mention.

1. Utility, Natural Law, and Conscience

It is always open in theory for a utilitarian to argue in a given case (whatever may be true in general) that more good than bad would accrue (or more harm would be avoided) by disobeying this or that law as a tactic for getting it repealed in favor of a new law or policy that better serves the general welfare. For anti- or non-utilitarians, of course, such an argument is unpersuasive, since it suffers (in their view) all the familiar difficulties of utilitarianism generally, chief among which is making in advance reliable calculations of future consequences. And it is worth noting that the classic utilitarians, notably Jeremy Bentham and J. S. Mill, never used their utilitarianism to justify breaking unjust laws.

Other theorists, working in effect in the Aristotelian tradition, would appeal to natural law—cross-cultural, universal moral principles—and argue the justifiability of breaking the law nonviolently when a society's positive law is inconsistent with the natural law. Since the advent of utilitarianism two centuries ago, natural law theories have waxed and waned in popularity among legal theorists; in recent years Ronald Dworkin's views beginning with his 1977 book, *Taking Rights Seriously* (Harvard Univ. Press, Cambridge, MA) perhaps best represent this tradition.

Finally, some thinkers would accord to individual conscience a final authority, though the incipient anarchic consequences of such a view will make more cautious thinkers look elsewhere. If each person's conscience is the final authority on right and wrong conduct, then it appears we may have to embrace the paradoxical consequence that certain acts of law breaking are both right and wrong, because the dictates of personal conscience vary radically in many cases.

2. John Rawls

Many writers since the Civil Rights movement and the Vietnam War have offered versions of a purely secular theory of justified civil disobedience. Unquestionably the most influential of these is to be found in the writings of John Rawls, especially his 1971 book, *A Theory of Justice* (Harvard Univ. Press, Cambridge, MA). On Rawls's theory, an act of civil disobedience in a constitutional democracy is "a last resort," and if such acts are to be justified, four conditions must be met: (1) the aim must be to secure society's compliance with a fundamental principle of social justice; (2) the protesters must have tried lawful methods of reform (assembly, petition, election) to no avail; (3) the protesters do not make claims for their tactics and goals inconsistent with allowing others with similar grievances to use similar tactics to secure their goals; and (4) there is some reasonable prospect that the protest will be successful.

Condition (1) rules out using illegal tactics in pursuit of relatively unimportant goals, or goals that cannot be defended on grounds of their justice. Condition (2) rules out impulsive or premature use of illegal tactics to secure a just goal that reasonable patience using lawful means could have obtained. Condition (3) rules out any presumption of special privilege to break the law in a just cause. And condition (4) rules out causing social turmoil when there is no prospect of accomplishing the goals being sought. As Rawls observes, "we may be acting within our rights [in breaking the law to protest injustice in society] but nevertheless unwisely if our conduct only serves to provoke the harsh retaliation of the majority" (1971, pp. 376). In other words, here as elsewhere, what we have a *right* to do may not be what we *ought* to do.

Of course, there is room for disagreement over the interpretation of these conditions, their scope, and their meaning. (In particular, much turns on how Rawls defines and justifies the principles of social justice that are built into his first condition, a topic to which he devotes the bulk of his book.) And it is possible for reasonable people to disagree over the facts relevant to one or more of Rawls's four principles, though it is easy to see that each of these conditions (or something very like them) is necessary to justify law breaking in a constitutional democracy. Dropping any of these conditions immediately raises questions about how the civil disobedience could possibly be justified given the social costs it usually involves. It is equally difficult to see what further conditions might be needed in the belief they are necessary to make the set of conditions sufficient for justification. What changes would be required to adapt Rawls's criteria to justify civil disobedience undertaken in something less than a nearly just society or in a society not governed by a democratic constitution is another matter. When the whole society is governed unjustly, some form of revolution may be called for in which individual or mass illegal protest would play a very different role (if any) from the one it can play in a constitutional democracy.

III. THE POLITICAL EFFECTIVENESS OF CIVIL DISOBEDIENCE

Has civil disobedience played a constructive role in any nation's political affairs? There is little doubt that using Rawlsian criteria and facts generally available, various tactics of civil disobedience were amply justified as part of the long campaign to invalidate locally enforced racial segregation and in trying to get the national government to withdraw its armed forces from Southeast Asia.

The question of the political effectiveness of civil disobedience is more complex. When it merges into conscientious objection, it will not often have much political effect. To take a hypothetical case, a warden who refuses to administer a lawful execution in his prison, because he believes the death penalty is a violation of human rights, will be relieved of his duties and replaced by an official with no such qualms. While one can imagine all prison wardens and staff refusing to participate in lawful executions, there is no record of any such conduct and little likelihood of such concerted action in the near future in any American death penalty jurisdiction. Without widespread organized refusal, individual acts of protest and disobedience of this sort are unlikely to have political effect—which is not to deny their significance for the dissenters or their influence on sympathetic bystanders.

Civil disobedience can be a powerful tool of public education in a constitutional democracy; this fact tempts activists into taking extreme measures even when they anticipate that their efforts may ultimately be ineffective. The more extreme the act of disobedience, the greater likelihood of publicity in the media; the greater the publicity, the greater the likelihood of public reflection and debate on the rationale of the disobedience—or so the argument goes in theory. Under a Nazi or Stalinist tyranny, however, civil disobedience is likely to be of no avail. The authorities will have no respect for the protesters just because their conduct is public, remains nonviolent, and appeals to principles of justice; the protest will go unnoticed by the government-controlled media and the protesters will be summarily arrested and given harsh punishment. In 1989, the Chinese government literally crushed nonviolent illegal student protest in Beijing. Even in South Africa, India, and the United States earlier in this century, civil disobedience produced reforms only in conjunction with a larger strategy of education and pressure carried out within the law. Civil disobedience by itself in Great Britain and the United States during the Cold War, however, had some effect in curbing atmospheric nuclear bomb tests, but it had little effect on nuclear disarmament. On a wide range of lesser issues, many of them local and not widely publicized, selective, nonviolent law breaking has achieved some notable successes— but, again, usually only in conjunction with lawful efforts publicizing the goals and the strategies of protest.

Perhaps the two most recent efforts at fairly large-scale civil disobedience in the United States have been organized by Operation Rescue, the militant antiabortion group, and by ACT-UP, the AIDS action group known for its disruptive tactics. They are instructive examples when political effectiveness of civil disobedience is under scrutiny.

Beginning in 1987 in Binghamton, New York, Operation Rescue has organized blockades of several hundred abortion clinics around the nation under the banner of "rescuing" the unborn from an undeserved death. Between 1988 and 1990 more than 25,000 protesters were arrested in actions claimed to be "nonviolent in word and deed." Operation Rescue does not, however, describe its blockades as "civil disobedience," arguing that civil disobedience is always "political," whereas rescuing fetal life is not. Be that as it may, there is no evidence that Operation Rescue has so far managed to reach the conscience of the majority and reduce popular support for the availability of abortion services over and above what lawful antiabortion protest has achieved. To be sure, abortion clinics and their staffs have been much threatened and inconvenienced by rescue blockades, but it is quite unclear how many abortions Operation Rescue has actually prevented, as distinct from diverting them to unblockaded clinics.

ACT-UP, also organized in 1987, focused its agenda on forcing pharmaceutical companies to scale down the price of its expensive medications so that more HIV-positive and AIDS-infected patients could purchase them, and on forcing the government to test and approve such drugs more rapidly. Its tactics (including breaking up news conferences and board meetings) have apparently worked. They certainly helped publicize the plight of those with AIDS and helped make progress toward its two main goals. Whether ACT-UP's tactics also won the hearts and minds of the government and industry officials who attempted to carry on business as usual, or only frightened them into partial compliance with ACT-UP's goals, is less clear.

As these two cases suggest, judging the political effectiveness of acts or campaigns of civil disobedience in a constitutional democracy is not easy. Such disobedience is usually carried out in conjunction with other activity wholly within the law (news conferences, demonstrations, or leafleting), so isolating the effects arising solely or mainly from civil disobedience is well nigh impossible. In the Civil Rights and anti-Vietnam War movements, individual and mass disobedience were essential aspects of citizen protest; in the former case, the movement could not have succeeded without direct illegal action. Much the same must be said about the impact of Gandhian *satyagraha* in obtaining self-rule for the Indian subcontinent earlier in this century. Historians and social scientists need to look at other cases where the evidence is less clear, in the hope that such scrutiny will teach us more about the circumstances in which civil disobedience can be politically effective.

Also See the Following Articles

ABORTION • CAPITAL PUNISHMENT • PACIFISM • THEORIES OF JUSTICE: RAWLS

Bibliography

Bedau, H. A. (Ed.) (1991). "Civil Disobedience in Focus." Routledge, London.
Bedau, H. A. (Ed.) (1969). "Civil Disobedience: Theory and Practice." Pegasus, New York.
Carter, G. M. (1992). "ACT UP: The AIDS War and Activism." Open Magazine, Westford, NJ.
Greenawalt, K. (1987). "Conflicts of Law and Morality." Oxford Univ. Press, New York.
Haksar, V. (1986). "Civil Disobedience, Threats and Offers: Gandhi and Rawls." Oxford Univ. Press, Delhi.
Harris, P. (Ed.) (1989). "Civil Disobedience." Univ. Press of America, Lanham, MD.
Kraut, R. (1984). "Socrates and the State." Princeton Univ. Press, Princeton, NJ.
Rawls, J. (1971). "A Theory of Justice." Harvard Univ. Press, Cambridge, MA.
Yoder, J. H., *et al.* (1991). Symposium on civil disobedience. Notre Dame J. Law Ethics Public Policy 5, 889–1119.
Van den Haag, E. (1972). "Political Violence and Civil Disobedience." Harper and Row, New York.
Zinn, H. (1972). "Disobedience and Democracy: Nine Fallacies on Law and Order." Vintage Books, New York.

CIVILIAN POPULATIONS IN WAR, TARGETING OF

Gabriel Palmer-Fernández
Youngstown State University

I. The Practice of Targeting Civilian Populations in War
II. The Protection of Civilian Populations in War

GLOSSARY

absolutism To determine the moral value of an act, absolutist moral theories consider whether that act is commanded by God, required by a promise made, is in accordance with widely accepted rules or the rights of persons, or can be consistently willed as a universal law. Absolutist moral theories typically deny what consequentialism asserts—that an action is right as a function of what it will produce.

combatant A legal and moral category requiring that a person, to be considered a combatant, be commanded by another responsible for subordinates, have a fixed distinctive insignia recognizable at a distance, carry arms openly, and conduct operations in accordance with the laws and customs of war.

consequentialism Consequentialist moral theories hold that the ultimate criterion of what is morally right is the value of what is brought into being. An act is right if it happens to bring about a better state of affairs than acting otherwise—if it will produce, or is intended to produce, at least a greater balance of good over evil as any alternative action. Such moral theories depend on a comparative evaluation of alternative courses of action.

just-war tradition The dominant moral tradition in the

West that governs the rights of states to go to war and the conduct of soldiers in war. It is divided into two parts, the *jus ad bellum,* which considers the conditions under which war is compatible with morality, and the *jus in bello,* which regulates the actual waging of hostilities.

noncombatant immunity A *jus in bello* principle that distinguishes between combatants and civilians with the consequence that the latter, also called noncombatants or innocents, are immune from deliberate military attack. It is sometimes also called principle of discrimination and is generally regarded as an absolutist principle.

obliteration bombing Air-bombing raids, strategies, or policies that fail to distinguish between combatants and noncombatants. It is sometimes also called area, carpet, terror, or mass bombing. Many jurists and moralists consider this kind of attack a prohibited form of warfare.

principle of double effect A principle that distinguishes between the direct and the indirect effects of an action. It asserts (i) that a person is morally responsible only for the direct (or intended) effects and (ii) that indirect (or unintended) evil effects (e.g., the death of civilians), when they are neither the means to or themselves the end, are allowable.

principle of proportionality A principle of the just-war tradition that appears in two forms. First, as a norm of the *jus ad bellum* the principle of proportionality states that the harms which accompany the use of force must not be so great as to outweigh the

Encyclopedia of Applied Ethics, Volume 1

values defended by force. As a *jus in bello* norm this principle requires that one weigh the harms caused by a particular tactic or strategy against whatever advantage is gained by such means. It is generally regarded as a consequentialist principle.

CIVILIAN POPULATIONS have undergone misery and death in the millions due to 20th century wars of extraordinary scope. Blitzkriegs, obliteration bombing, the threat of nuclear annihilation, guerrilla wars, terrorism, and the recent rise of ethnopolitical conflicts can easily create the impression that the immunity of civilian populations from deliberate military attack belongs to some distant past. That would be a mistaken impression, however. Despite the truth of the assertion that a distinguishing feature of modern war is the slaughter of the unprotected, the principle of noncombatant immunity originated in the 16th and 17th centuries, particularly in the writings of Francisco Victoria and Hugo Grotius, and gradually developed in the body of international law, the tradition of the just war, and in the Hague and Geneva Conventions. But the future relevance of this principle is far from clear. If it is the case that future wars will take the form of widespread indiscriminate destruction by the use of nuclear weapons, terrorist attacks, or ethnic warfare, then the important distinction between combatants and civilians is bound to break down, and the principle of noncombatant immunity may indeed belong to the past.

Thus the clear definition and justification of the principle of noncombatant immunity are major concerns of legal and moral theorists. However, those theorists face a significant problem. The principle is useful only if we can establish a distinction between combatants and civilians, that is, between who may and may not be deliberately killed in war. Civilians, this principle asserts, may not be deliberately killed in war because they are innocent. But the meaning of innocence in war is controversial. Absent a clear definition of who is innocent and why, it will be very difficult to say who may and may not be deliberately killed in war.

I. THE PRACTICE OF TARGETING CIVILIAN POPULATIONS IN WAR

The manner and method of waging war are partly a function of the technology available to a nation. In the days of dynastic wars a battlefield was often safely removed from civilian populations, and the number of deaths was greater among soldiers than civilians. Civilized war, legal and moral texts tell us, is confined to hostilities between armed forces.

> It is with good reason that this practice has grown into a custom with the nations of Europe, at least with those that keep up regular standing armies or bodies of militia. The troops alone carry on war, while the rest of the nation remain at peace. (E. de Vattel, 1740. *The Law of Nations; or Principles of the Law of Nature (in French), iii, p. 226. J. Newbery, London)*

But today death in war has a far wider range. The emergence of modern means of waging war—the airplane, the missile, and chemical, biological, and nuclear weapons—have not only increased the lethality of war, but also expanded combat over large areas and gradually included greater sectors of the civilian population.

It must be recognized, however, that civilians have always faced some risk in war, even when their material contribution to war has been slight.[1] In ancient as well as in modern times, civilians have been attacked along with soldiers. Sometimes they come under direct attack in order to kill soldiers taking refuge among them; at other times, they are directly attacked because of a critical importance identified with them–namely, the morale of a nation, the collapse of which, it is said, leads to surrender. Such is plainly the case in sieges, where war extends beyond the combatant population and the death of civilians, usually by starvation and dehydration, is a means to hasten the enemy's surrender. The long history of siege warfare suggests that attacking civilian populations is a time-honored method of war, for example, the siege of Jerusalem in 72 C.E. or Leningrad by German forces between 1941 and 1943, where more than 1 million civilians died of starvation or disease.

One distinguishing and very troubling feature of 20th century warfare is the extent to which civilians are deliberately put in harm's way. The cities of Hiroshima and Nagasaki were destroyed by a single atomic bomb. This weapon was new and revolutionary. But the havoc, misery, and death that that single weapon caused was only a more effective means of implement-

---

[1] The risk is only getting larger. Civilian deaths in war have increased dramatically in this century. In World War I, 5% of deaths were civilians; in World War II, 48%; in Korea, 84%; and in Vietnam, 90%.

ing a strategy that had vigorously been pursued against Germany in World War II (WWII) by more conventional weapons, and perhaps had its origins when the Austrians, in the mid-19th century, launched unmanned bomb-carrying air ballons at the city of Venice. The air balloon was a poor weapon—it drifted with the wind. But it had the potential to cause significant panic in civilian populations—as it did, for example, in May 1915, when Germany bombed London by using a propeller-driven dirigible. Guilio Douhet, an Italian officer, predicted some years later in his 1921 book, *The Command of the Air,* that "now it is actually populations and nations," and not their armies, "which come to blows and seize each other's throats (1942. Translated by D. Ferrari, p. 195. New York). For Douhet and his disciples, which included Hugh Trenchard and Charles de Gaulle in Europe and Billy Mitchell in the United States, the first and most vital target in an air war naturally was the enemy's own strategic bombers. But they were quick to point out the bomber's potential for defeating an enemy with a decisive "knockout blow" and for creating havoc, misery, and terror in the civilian population. The capacity to strike from the air—either with airplanes or with missiles—is the single most important element in 20th century warfare. It delivers the war directly to the enemy's civilian population.

A. Strategic Air War and Civilian Populations in Europe

The experience of strategic bombing during WWII shows clearly how the horror of war moved from soldiers to civilians. When the war broke out, the major belligerents restrained themselves from air bombing of the enemy's heartland. The restraint was reflected in an August 1939 communiqué of British and French officers expressing their lack of intent to bomb civilian population as such. But the restraint was short-lived. Precision bombing required daylight low-level attacks, where flak proved deadly. British Bomber Command soon learned that to be effective it had no option but to fight in the dark. By the fall of 1940, British bombing of German territory was an indiscriminate and nocturnal event. For similar reasons, after September of 1940, Germany was also using its Luftwaffe's bombers only at night. But nighttime bombing was extremely inaccurate. When conducted over a city these raids were more likely to miss than to hit any military or industrial site. Indeed British assessment of bombing campaigns over Germany estimated that only one-fifth of its bombers placed their payloads within 5 miles of the specified target. Deficiencies of bomb-aiming technology coupled

with the circumstances in which missions were conducted brought a dramatic change in the nature of modern war: *targeting cities themselves.*

By early 1941, the British Air Ministry issued new orders to Bomber Command. Indiscriminate bombing which had been condemned at the beginning of the war became operational policy. Primary targets would no longer be conventional military objectives, but the morale of the civilian population and especially the residential areas of the industrial workers. Bomber Command was instructed to employ its power on those targets without restrictions: lay down a carpet of bombs over urban and industrial areas in which conventional military targets would be hit, but only incidentally and as a bonus to the mass, indiscriminate killing of civilians. As a matter of policy, death and destruction were brought to civilians in order to destroy their morale. That was certainly the case, for example, in the second bombing of Hamburg where incendiaries started thousands of fires throughout the city, creating terrific winds as the fires sucked for more oxygen and sending charred bodies and debris flying through an atmosphere of nearly 800° centigrade.

As the British had before them, Americans also discovered that daylight precision bombing was a misnomer. Even when the target was discrete—for example, railroad yards and industrial plants—heavy damage to the surrounding residential areas was unavoidable. American commanders at first resisted British policy of bombing civilian populations. Yet the results of American raids were hardly distinguishable from British nighttime indiscriminate bombing. The U.S. Strategic Bombing Survey estimated that 80% of U.S. daylight bombing missions missed by a fifth of a mile or more. As the war progressed, U.S. targeting policy took the form of British obliteration bombing in an attempt to destroy German civilian morale. The climax of targeting civilians in Europe came at Dresden, near war's end. On February 13 and 14, 1945, British and then American forces bombed this German city teeming with homeless refuges from devastated rural towns and advancing Soviet armies. Some 50,000 civilians were killed in those raids.

War in the 20th century became indiscriminate war when the British Bomber Command and then the U.S. Army Air Force adopted the policy of deliberately targeting civilian populations, i.e., the urban and industrial base of a society. As *Target Germany,* a 1943 U.S. Air Force book, put it,

> The physical attrition of warfare is no longer limited to the fighting forces. Heretofore the home

front has remained relatively secure; armies fought, civil populations worked and waited.... [But now] we have terror and devastation carried to the core of a warring nation. (p. 19. Simon and Schuster, New York).

Germans, too, tested the morale of British civilians through shock and terror, first by the use of bombers and then by the V-1 and V-2 flying bombs. Though totally ineffective for attacking military targets, these precursors to the intercontinental ballistic missile were, as Goebbels said, awe-inspiring weapons of murder.

B. Strategic Air War and Civilian Populations in Japan

American targeting of civilian populations culminated in a campaign of terror and fire-bombing of Japanese cities. As in Europe, American air strategy at first gave priority to the Japanese air industry and advocated precision bombing of conventional military targets. But attempts to strike these targets from high altitudes proved to be no more successful than in Europe. When Curtis LeMay assumed command of the 20th Air Force in Japan, he was instructed to give targeting priority to cities rather than industrial targets. Bomb loads would consist of incendiaries—i.e., fire bombs—rather than high explosives, with the purpose of striking at the will of the Japanese people to continue the war. With the success of limited fire-bombing raids in January and February of 1945, the American Air Force undertook a campaign of fire-bombing the city of Tokyo in early March 1945 that destroyed nearly two-thirds of the city's commercial district and killed an estimated 100,000 civilians. This and other nighttime incendiary raids on Japanese cities killed more civilians than the atomic bombings of Hiroshima and Nagasaki, both of which were a late emphasis upon the supposed effect of targeting civilian populations by indiscriminate attack.

The post-World War II debate on the effects of strategic bombing gives a mixed assessment to the assertion that air power will deliver victory in modern war. Britain's own bombing survey after the war suggests that targeting civilian populations was successful only in disrupting German transport and communications systems. It did not induce the effect on civilian morale that it hoped for. American's own postwar bombing survey expressed similar doubts about the effectiveness of obliteration bombing in Europe. Matters are somewhat different with the atomic bombing of Hiroshima and Nagasaki. The same American postwar survey

claims that the Japanese would have surrendered even if the atomic bomb had not been used. The air war against Japan had already been won, and its defenses were fragile. Yet others maintain that the speed with which surrender followed the bombings of Hiroshima and Nagasaki supports Douhet's thesis that air power would prove decisive in modern war.

C. The Threat of Nuclear Annihilation

Notwithstanding the partially negative assessment by postwar bombing surveys, targeting civilian populations with weapons of massive and indiscriminate destruction was enshrined in American nuclear strategy. As it emerged in the postwar years, American policy of nuclear deterrence aimed at enemy cities. At first, during the Eisenhower years, this policy called for the immediate launch of the entire U.S. nuclear arsenal in response to enemy aggression. The single target list included cities in the former Soviet Union, China, and satellite states, and made no distinction among military, industrial, and civilian targets. As President Eisenhower himself put it, we "cannot afford to preclude [ourselves] from using nuclear weapons even in a local situation, if such use will best advance [our] security interests" (J. L. Gaddis, 1982. *Strategies of Containment*, p. 190, Oxford Univ. Press, Oxford). Expected fatalities of a massive nuclear retaliatory strike were estimated between 360 and 425 million civilians.

Other nations, of course, pursued their own nuclear programs—Great Britain, France, and the former Soviet Union, for example. But it became increasingly clear that targeting civilian populations, i.e., massive nuclear retaliation against cities themselves, would result in mutual suicide, absent adequate defenses against enemy missiles. Exploration of a flexible nuclear response and advocacy of a "no-cities" strategy were therefore sought in the late 1950s and early 1960s. Robert McNamara, Kennedy's Secretary of Defense, announced in February 1961 that basic military strategy in general nuclear war would target conventional military objectives and seek the destruction of the enemy's military and nuclear forces, and not the civilian population. Targeting only the enemy's forces rather than the enemy's cities (sometimes referred to as counterforce/no-cities) was short-lived, however. By the fall of 1962, McNamara began to favor an entirely different strategic posture, and by the end of his tenure as Secretary of Defense, had come about-face, advocating the very ideas which, upon coming into office, he had criticized and dismissing the counterforce/no-cities doctrine as having only a very limited role in deterring a nuclear-armed adversary.

Subsequent development of U.S. nuclear weapons policy has emphasized either a selective and flexible response to enemy aggression or some form of massive retaliation in which cities themselves are targeted. Whichever of these strategies one adopts, its activation will surely lead to the indiscriminate killing of civilians. Withholding direct nuclear attack from civilian populations has played an important role in the development of nuclear strategy. Yet doctrines of selective and flexible response are fraught with dangerous destabilizing first-strike possibilities and retain the threat of widespread civilian slaughter by the possession of a large nuclear reserve force. McNamara may well have been correct when he said that nuclear forces are totally useless, except to deter one's enemy from using them by the threat of massive retaliation. If ever deterrence fails and nuclear war breaks out, then nuclear weapons will have failed in their purpose and at least one nation will be in ruin.

D. Ethnopolitical Conflict and Civilian Populations

To appreciate fully the extent and manner in which civilian populations are targeted in modern war, it is necessary to consider, finally, the recent rise of ethnopolitical conflicts. Since the end of WWII, such conflicts have become increasingly prominent in various parts of the world—in Bosnia, Liberia, Sierra Leone, the Caucasus, and Sri Lanka, for example. Armed hostilities between ethnic groups, some observers contend, indicate that the kinds of war we will see in the future will not be wars between nation-states with armed forces as their agents fighting along geopolitical lines. Instead, armed conflicts in the early 21st century will likely occur between groups that define themselves along ethnic (sometimes also religious) lines and make claims on behalf of collective interests against nation-states and other political actors.

The facts seem to support those contentions. First, the number of groups involved in serious ethnopolitical conflicts has increased dramatically in the post-World War II period: from 26 groups between 1945 and 1949 to 70 in the 1990s, with the greatest increase in the 1960s and 1970s (36 and 55 groups, respectively). The main issue in most of these conflicts is the contention of power among ethnic groups in Third World nations. Second, the 50 ethnopolitical conflicts in the 1993–1994 period alone caused some 4 million deaths, the vast majority of which were civilian, and displaced nearly 27 million people. And third, this type of conflict is very likely to increase in the near future as there is greater communal contention for power among ethnic groups in several of the world's regions, particularly in poor and weak states like those of Africa, most notably, Burundi, Rwanda, Zaire, Angola, and Sudan. One can anticipate that forced resettlement of groups, mass repression, genocidal massacres, guerilla warfare, and other forms of political violence will directly effect large numbers of civilian populations.

II. THE PROTECTION OF CIVILIAN POPULATIONS IN WAR

Recent developments in military technology and strategy make possible destruction of a kind and magnitude previously unimaginable. Incendiaries; gas, chemical, and nuclear weapons; and the capacity to strike from the air, coupled with a strategy to destroy industrial centers and weaken the enemy's resolve to fight, create a mode of warfare that brings certain death to combatant and civilian alike. These facts have led contemporary jurists and moralists to stress a principle that stretches back to the early modern period. It appears first among a group of Spanish theologians of the 16th century, was developed by several Dutch jurists of the 17th century, and was then incorporated into the body of international law. Since the 1970s, as moralists, both secular and religious, have reflected on the massive and indiscriminate power of modern means of warfare, the principle of noncombatant immunity has taken special importance. It is this moral principle which determines that civilian populations are not legitimate targets of war.

A. The Just-War Tradition, International Law, and the Principle of Noncombatant Immunity

The dominant intellectual tradition concerning the morality of war consists of a set of principles that together are referred to as the just-war tradition. The origins of this tradition may be traced to ancient philosophers and jurists, for example, Plato and Cicero. But it was the 5th century Christian theologian St. Augustine who gave us the first systematic formulation of the conditions under which war is compatible with morality. Augustine's formulation of the just war was refined over the centuries, and by the high middle ages had become official teaching of the Roman Catholic church. Today that tradition is embodied in secular international law and informs much of the public debate on the morality of war.

The just-war tradition distinguishes between questions concerning when a state has a right to wage war (referred to usually in the Latin as the *jus ad bellum*) and those on how war is to be waged (the *jus in bello*). For a war to count as just, the following conditions must be satisfied: (i) there must be a just cause; (ii) the war must be waged with the right intention; (iii) the decision must be made by a legitimate authority; (iv) there must be a formal declaration of war; (v) there must be reasonable hope for success; (vi) war should be the last resort; and (vii) it must satisfy the requirement of proportionality. Even when the *jus ad bellum* conditions are met, there remains the further question of how war is to be waged, that is, the *jus in bello*. The just-war tradition requires that the manner of waging hostilities satisfies the principles of noncombatant immunity—civilians must not be deliberately attacked or killed, and fighting is to be directed solely against the armed forces of the enemy—and of proportionality—the means employed in fighting must not be so destructive as to outweigh the good to be achieved.

In its modern secular version, just-war thinking has increasingly stressed one justification for going to war. The injustice which war should seek to correct is the crime of aggression of one state against another; hence the only justification for war is self-defense. This view is found also in modern international law and in Article 51 of the United Nations Charter, which permits the use of force for individual or collective self-defense. Early formulations of the just war, however, allowed the use of force for reasons other than self-defense, for example, to protect the innocent from attack, to restore rights unjustly denied, to reestablish an order necessary for peaceful and decent human existence, and to punish an evildoer.

Since the 16th century, the principle of noncombatant immunity has defined the most important limit on the manner of waging armed hostilities. This principle depends on the distinction between combatants and civilians, and is interpreted as a prohibition against the deliberate killing of civilians, who are usually referred to as innocent, in contrast to combatants, who are referred to as guilty or culpable and are therefore legitimate targets of deliberate attack. But the earlier formulation of the just war had nothing resembling this prohibition. Indeed, some argue that Augustine thought there was little, if anything, wrong in the deliberate killing of civilians, if the necessities of a just war demand it. For Augustine, so it is argued, the requirement to vindicate justice obviates all other considerations, even when the innocent may suffer. Just as Lot's family in the Book of Genesis is an exceptional innocent mi-

nority in the wicked city of Sodom, Augustine believed that in an injust state there will be only a minority of truly innocent people. Furthermore, because innocence is an interior disposition that cannot necessarily be ascribed to any individual with certainty, one cannot know who are the truly innocent. So, Augustine counsels the soldier and public functionary to do what is required for justice, and to let God on the last days separate the wicked and the guiltless. Some improvement on the protection of civilian populations in war is found in the work of the 13th century theologian Thomas Aquinas. Though he relied heavily and explicitly on Augustine, Aquinas unequivocally states that it is unlawful deliberately to kill the innocent. But Aquinas' clear condemnation of killing civilians must be weighed against his doctrine of double effect, which allows for the incidental or unintended deaths of civilians in war—what is usually referred to as collateral damage.

It was the Spanish theologian Francisco Victoria who presented to date the most powerful prohibition against the deliberate killing of the innocent and, at the same time, a justification for overriding that prohibition:

> The basis of war is a wrong done. But a wrong is not done by an innocent person. Therefore war may not be employed against him.... [Furthermore] it is not lawful within a State to punish the innocent for the wrongdoing of the guilty. Therefore this is not lawful among enemies. (1917. De indis et de iure belli reflectiones. In *The Classics of International Law* (J. B. Scott, Ed.), p. 178. Carnegie Institute of Washington, Washington, DC)

Victoria defined the class of innocents as all persons who do not directly take part in the waging of hostilities and included in it all children, women, farmers, foreign travelers, clerics, and "the rest of the peaceable population." He understood, however, that this prohibition is hardly attainable in all circumstance and that in war sometimes innocents are killed. To determine whether the killing of innocents is ever permissible, Victoria relies on Aquinas' principle of double effect, but with greater restriction that Aquinas himself employed. Victoria says,

> Sometimes it is right, in virtue of collateral circumstances, to slay the innocent, even knowingly, as when a fortress of a city is stormed in a just war, although it is known that there are a number of innocent people in it and although cannons and other engines of war cannot be dis-

charged ... without destroying innocent together with the guilty. The proof is that war could not otherwise be waged against even the guilty and the justice of belligerents would be balked.... In sum, it is never right to slay the guiltless, even as an indirect and unintended result, *except when there is no other means of carrying on the operations of a just war.* (Italics added. Victoria, 1917, p. 179)

Victoria's restriction on killing civilians is stricter than Aquinas' in at least two ways. First, he requires that there be no other way of "carrying on the operations" of a war, and second, the killing of civilians is to be limited to the prosecution of a war known to be "just." When there is doubt regarding the justice of a war, then war is to be fought with greater retraint and the immunity of civilians should not yield to the necessities of war. The principle of noncombatant immunity might then function as a moral absolute.

While Augustine, Aquinas, and Victoria were the formative figures in the medieval and early modern formulation of the just-war tradition, it is the work of the Dutch jurist and theologian Hugo Grotius, often referred to as the founder of international law, that exercised the most profound influence on the modern secular development of that tradition. Much like Victoria, he lays great emphasis on the immunity of civilians from direct attack: "One must take care, so far as possible, to prevent the death of innocent persons, even by accident (H. Grotius, 1962. *The Law of War and Peace,* translated by F. W. Kelsey, bk. III, chap. 11, XVI, 2, p. 741. Bobbs-Merrill, New York). In this class of innocents, Grotius includes children, women, the aged, farmers, clerics, and prisoners of war. We have here a clear rule prohibiting direct attack on civilians. But this rule is not absolute. Grotius says, "We may bombard a ship full of pirates, or a house full of brigands, even if there are within the same ship or house a few infants, women, or other innocent persons who are thereby endangered." He cautions, however, that one

must also be aware of what happens, and what we foresee may happen, beyond our purpose, unless the good which our action has in view is much greater than the evil which is feared, unless the good and the evil balance, the hope of the good is much greater than the fear of the evil. (Grotius, 1962, bk. III, chap. 1, IV, p. 601)

In all this, Grotius depends on the principles developed by his medieval predecessors, namely, noncombatant immunity, the *jus in bello* requirement of proportionality, and double effect.

Grotius, however, departs from the medieval tradition in two ways that are of great importance for the modern understanding of the just war. First, for him, the *jus ad bellum* is met by a formal declaration of war by the sovereign of a nation-state that includes the reasons or causes leading to war without reference to any substantive understanding of justice, thereby making, far more possible than Victoria had, the possibility that both sides to an armed conflict can be just. In the absence of a shared understanding of justice, as the Roman Catholic church had provided for the middle ages, the modern world of separate and sovereign nation-states has no criterion for appeal to determine the justice of a war other than a system of laws that prescribe proper conduct in international relations. The other departure is this. Augustine and Aquinas had given primary attention to the *jus ad bellum.* But Grotius seems far more interested in restricting the methods and conduct permissible in the prosecution of war—that is, the *jus in bello.* This emphasis on the means permissible in war is particularly well suited to the modern secular world of nation-states and their competing political interests, a world profoundly different from the societal conditions of religious strifes that led to the Thirty Years' War and dominated the period of Grotius' own life. Force is justified, as Grotius put it, "to protect rights and maintain order (1962, bk. I, chap. 2, I, p. 73). He thus limits the legitimate causes for war. But far more important has been the prohibition against deliberately killing civilians and the stringent conditions under which that prohibition may be overridden. These contributions still apply to recent discussions of the *jus in bello* and are embodied in existing international law.

A topic of contemporary debate is whether a clear and morally relevant distinction can be made between combatants and civilians, that is, between who may and who may not be deliberately killed in war. Plainly there will be persons who fall into grey areas such that their immunity from deliberate attack might not be clearly established, for example, musicians in an army band, cooks, electricians, and others whose roles may not have a distinctively military character, or civilians working in munitions or airplane factories, as well as research engineers and physicists improving weapons delivery systems whose labors contribute much to the war effort. It is difficult to determine, moreover, whether the political leadership of a nation that commands the armed forces to war should be considered combatants or civilians. In spite of these areas of indeterminacy, it is assumed that this distinction can and ought to be made, and therefore may be regarded as a morally relevant distinction.

This important distinction between combatants and civilians is recognized by modern international law, the Hague Conventions of 1907, and is quite explicitly incorporated into the 1977 provision attached to Article 51 of the Geneva Convention of 1949. That provision states:

> The civilian population as such, as well as individual citizens, shall not be the object of attack. Attacks or threats of violence the primary purpose of which is to spread terror among the civilian population are prohibited. Indiscriminate attacks are prohibited. Indiscriminate attacks are (a) those which are not directed at a specific military objective; (b) those which employ a method or means of combat which cannot be directed at a specific military objective; or (c) those which employ means or methods of combat the effects of which cannot be limited as required by this Protocol: and consequently, in each such case, are of a nature to strike military objectives and civilians or civilian objects without discrimination. Among others, the following type of attack [is] to be considered as indiscriminate: an attack which may be expected to cause incidental loss of civilian life, injury to civilians, damage to civilian objects, or a combination thereof, which would be excessive in relation to the concrete and direct military advantage anticipated.[2]

Obviously the bombings of Hamburg, Dresden, Tokyo, London, Coventry, and other instances of obliteration (carpet, terror, or area) bombing, including the atomic bombing of Hiroshima and Nagasaki, are prohibited by the above. International law, as articulated by Hague and Geneva Conventions, embodies very strong humanitarian principles, and the protection of civilians is one of its most important tasks. But from the moral point of view, simply drawing a distinction between combatants and civilians is not sufficient to establish that crucial moral difference wherein the former may and the latter may not be deliberately killed. What needs to be determined is why it is morally wrong to

deliberately kill civilians, and why it is permissible—indeed, some will say a positive duty—to kill combatants. The standard answer is that civilians may not be deliberately killed because they are innocent. Now, what does innocence in war mean?

B. Who Is Innocent in War?

The international law and the just-war tradition consider civilians to be innocent and therefore illegitimate targets of deliberate attack. What does it mean to say that civilians are innocent? What is the sense of the word "innocence" when applied to civilian populations in war? When one says that civilians are innocent, does one imply that combatants, i.e., noninnocents, fighting in a just war are guilty of a wrongdoing and for that reason may deliberately be killed? Clearly innocence does not have the same sense as when used to describe, say, children or those we might consider exemplars of the moral life. If it were the former, then we know innocence is short-lived, for children soon become adults; if the latter, then it is applicable only to extraordinary individuals. Either way, innocence would describe only a small segment of a civilian population. When applied to civilians in war, innocence must have a meaning different from its ordinary one and refer to some distinguishing fact about civilians in respect to war. What might that fact be and how is it related to some morally relevant sense of the word "innocence"?

Two approaches to the problem of innocence in war are evident among contemporary moral theorists. I refer to them as the *moral* and the *role-functional* views. The one determines innocence and guilt by reference to the justice or injustice of a war, while the other looks to a person's participation in war. Most theorists assume that the distinction between permissible and impermissible targets of deliberate attack coincides with the distinction between the guilty and the innocent. But if the moral and role-functional views define these terms in different ways, then we have less than a clear distinction between those that may and those that may not be deliberately killed in war.

1. The Moral View

The moral view determines innocence and guilt on the basis of the justice or injustice of a war. The important question of who is and who is not a legitimate target of deliberate attack is therefore a function of the (in)justice of a war. Elizabeth Anscombe says,

> What is required for the people attacked to be non-innocent in the relevant sense, is that they should themselves be engaged in an *objectively*

---

[2] 1993. Protocol additional to the Geneva Convention of 12 August 1949 and relating to the protection of victims of international armed conflicts. Protocol I, part IV, chap. II, Article 51, in *International Conventions on Protection of Humanity and Environment* (G. Hoog and A. Steinmetz, Eds.) p. 289. Walter de Gruyteer, New York.

unjust proceeding which the attacker has the right to make his concern; or—the commonest sense—should be *unjustly attacking* him. (Italics added. 1981. In *Ethics, Religion, and Politics,* p. 53. Univ. of Minnesota Press, Minneapolis)

A plausible interpretation of this view maintains that in a conflict one side is necessarily engaged in an "objectively unjust" procedure. Hence, soldiers on that (unjust) side lack the necessary condition of a just cause and are guilty of fighting an unjust war, even when they fight in accordance with the rules of war. It seems, moreover, that combatants fighting on the unjust side—call these "unjust combatants"—act just as badly in killing enemy soldiers—call these "innocent combatants"—as if they were killing children, the aged, and the infirm. Whatever they do in such a war, they do it inescapably without justice. Those who fight for a just cause, on the other hand, are morally innocent, and when they fight in accordance with the rules of war they fight with—or, better yet, on behalf of—justice.

This view is subject to at least two objections. First, it is far from clear how we are to attribute justice to one side in an armed conflict. There will certainly be cases where the injustice of a belligerent is clear and we can, with medieval and some modern writers, for example, Aquinas and Vanderpol, maintain the criterion of fault as the essence of the just-war tradition. The *jus ad bellum* concern with a just cause for war should then be easily and clearly established. Yet the criterion of fault might not be discernable in every war, and we might have to entertain the possibility of doubt and ignorance regarding a just cause. Victoria, for example, long ago stressed the difficulties in establishing objectively the antecedent causes to a war and, moreover, allowed soldiers who in "good faith follow their prince" to fight in an unjust war when the injustice is known only to the ruler. In this way, he says, soldiers "on both sides may be doing what is lawful when they fight (Victoria, 1917, 177). But in Anscombe's view, it appears that when the criterion of fault or justice in a war cannot be clearly established, then it would be impossible to determine who the innocent and the guilty are and, by extension, who may and may not be deliberately killed. Such a war, then, could not morally be fought.

The second objection is this. There is the assumption, at least in modern democracies, that citizens have a positive duty in justice toward the state—for example, to obey its laws. If citizens fight in a war in accordance with this duty, then they cannot be acting against justice, and all soldiers who fight from duty are innocent and thereby immune from deliberate attack. We may suppose, however, that there is a duty prior to obedience to the state to discern the justice of a war. Citizens, before becoming soldiers, must to the best of their ability determine this important matter. Those who do not and simply obey the state might be guilty of an injustice, whether or not their cause is just, and are thereby legitimate targets of deliberate attack. On the other hand, those who do come to the conclusion that their cause is just, whether or not it is objectively so, are innocent soldiers and may not be deliberately killed. And of these there may be very many in any war. As Jenny Teichman observes, in this account of innocence and guilt

> there will always be in any war quite a large number of innocent soldiers.... The only way of avoiding the conclusion that killing the soldiers who are on the right side is the same sort of thing as killing unarmed civilians is either to redefine innocence and non-innocence more radically than Anscombe has done, or drop the notions and construct a distinction in some other way. (1986. *Pacifism and the Just War,* p. 66. Basil Blackwell, Oxford)

It is further supposed by proponents of the moral view that killing in war is justified on the model of punishment. That is the model given us first by Augustine and then by other Christian writers, and it is frequently appealed to by politicians and citizens. The contrast between *moral* innocence and guilt also suggests it. Those who have no legitimate cause in fighting are unjust combatants and may not morally kill opposing (innocent) soldiers. When these unjust combatants kill innocent soldiers they commit an act on par with murder. Just as some people say society has a right to punish those guilty of murder by killing them, so too soldiers fighting for a just cause may similarly punish unjust combatants for their crime. But this model of killing in war seems far from adequate. Because most soldiers fight from duty to the state, they do not seem to be the proper objects of punishment. Rather the political leadership that orders, and the citizens who encourage, the troops to fight are likely to have a greater share of responsibility for the war, and hence to be guilty of initiating and supporting injustice. If this is even remotely correct, then many legitimate targets of deliberate attack in war will lie in the civilian and not the combatant population. Waging such a war would then be very practically impossible.

2. The Role-Functional View

An alternative view determines innocence on the basis of a person's engagement in the business of war. To say that some persons are innocent is just another way of saying that they are harmless and not involved in violent action. The root of the word "innocence" has this sense to it: *nocentes,* a Latin word that means harmful, coupled with the prefix *in,* yields the meaning "harmless" or "one who does not injure." So, while it is always wrong to deliberately kill the innocent, some people, because of what they do, are guilty and lost their immunity from deliberate attack. Some moral theorists have therefore assumed that the terms "innocent" and "guilty" are equivalent to a person's role as civilian or combatant, respectively. That assumption is evident, for example, in the work of Paul Ramsey, who says,

> The distinction between the "guilty" who are legitimate targets of violent repression and the "innocent" who are not ... is reducible to degrees of actual participation in hostile force.... [The principle of noncombatant immunity] takes into account a person's specific function, or lack of function, in the war itself in order to save as many as possible from being absorbed into the thrust of war. (1968. *The Just War,* pp. 153, 164. Scribner, New York)

Thomas Nagel, too, has argued that in discussions of war innocence "does not mean morally innocent but currently harmless.... So we must distinguish combatants from noncombatants on the basis of their immediate threat or harmfulness (1974. In *War and Moral Responsibility* (M. Cohen, T. Nagel, and T. Scanlon, Eds., pp. 19–20. Princeton Univ. Press, Princeton, NJ).

According to the role-functional view, innocent persons are not engaged in an activity that is immediately violent or threatening, and do not contribute directly to, nor are they within a chain of command that may engage them in, war-related violence. The guilty, on the other hand, are those who put in mortal jeopardy others' lives or contribute in a relevant way to those who do. There are then two major categories of people in wartime: combatants who are guilty of posing an immediate mortal threat, and civilians who are innocent of posing any such threat. In the former category we might include certain types of civilians who are not combatants strictly speaking—for example, munition workers, engineers and physicists who work in the war industry, and perhaps political leaders who initiate wars and order soldiers to fight in them. In the latter category we might include military chaplains, cooks, and medical personnel who do not contribute directly to the war effort but assist the soldier as a person.

The international law of war as specified in Geneva Conventions and Hague Regulations is roughly compatible with the role-functional view. A combatant is any person satisfying four requirements: is commanded by a person responsible for subordinates, has fixed insignia, carries arms openly, and conducts operations according to the laws and customs of war. Such persons have the right to kill other combatants and are themselves legitimate targets of attack. Note the lack of reference to the justice or injustice of a war in this definition of combatant status. Unlike the moral view, the role-functional view and the law of war hold *jus ad bellum* and *jus in bello* judgments to be, as Michael Walzer puts it, "logically independent," allowing "for a just war to be fought unjustly and for an unjust war to be fought in strict accordance with the rules (1977. *Just and Unjust Wars,* p. 21. Basic Books, New York). But the international law of war, unlike the role-functional view, makes a modest though important appeal to the *jus ad bellum* when it requires for combatant status that war be formally declared. Without this appeal to a formal declaration of war, we could not draw a further and important distinction between a soldier and a combatant, and absent that distinction it would be hard to say why the killing of soldiers who are not in war (call these "noncombatant soldiers")—for example, the killing of U.S. soldiers in Lebanon and, more recently, in Saudi Arabia—is wrong.

Even when the distinction between soldiers and combatants is established, one must explain why a combatant fighting in a just war is guilty of some injustice such that she may be killed by soldiers of the opposing side. How does it come to be that all combatants are guilty and may be killed while all civilians are innocent and may not? How can we establish a morally relevant distinction between the innocent and the guilty? In its ordinary sense innocence is said to be a condition of moral purity, of being uncorrupted by evil, or of not being culpable for some injustice. But obviously this is not the sense Ramsey and Nagel have in mind. Theirs is an innocence emptied of moral content. For them, what is crucial in determining innocence and guilt is a person's *role* regarding the waging of hostilities. Therefore innocence and guilt coincide with the role of civilian and combatant, i.e., with being illegitimate or legitimate targets of deliberate attack.

Proponents of the role-functional view will admit that the terms "innocent" and "guilty" are, as Ramsey says, "misleading," and then they might go on to make a further and finer distinction: while a soldier fighting in a just war might be *formally* innocent (i.e., morally innocent of injustice), he is nonetheless *materially* or causally culpable of a direct and immediate mortal threat. This distinction allows the use of the terms "innocent" and "guilty" without the usual connotations of moral innocence and guilt, and should be understood, as Michael Walzer says, as "term[s] of art" ascribing moral innocence and guilt to no one. Yet if one cannot ascribe moral innocence or guilt, how can killing be justified?

Merely occupying a role is not sufficient to justify killing. Killing, after all, is a most serious act and it should have a very clear justification. Unlike the moral view, the role-functional view justifies killing in war not on the model of punishment, but on that of self-defense against a mortal threat. Nagel says, "The attack is aimed specifically against the threat presented by a dangerous adversary.... The prosecution of conflict must be directed to the cause of danger" (Nagel, 1974, 18, 20). The implication here is that killing is justified only to repel an immediate mortal threat to one's life and that it is otherwise unjustified. But if self-defense provides the model on which killing in war is justified, we should have to admit that soldiers seldom, if ever, go to war to defend themselves and that therefore there are relatively very few cases when killing in war is justified—the threat justifying self-defensive action must be immediate and lethal. Should one try to extend the cases in which killing is justified, one is likely to raise the question of who is responsible for a war. Perhaps then the political leadership, that seems more morally responsible than most combatants, would become legitimate targets of deliberate attack. At any rate, to kill deliberately a person who is not an agent of danger—i.e., a civilian—is beyond the scope of justifiable killing, while to kill an agent of danger—i.e., a combatant—is justified as self-defnese. It is important to note that self-defense justifies only the killing of "the cause of danger." But it does not justify the killing of combatants as such.[3]

This account of innocence and guilt does not draw upon ordinary meanings of those terms, nor does it appeal to the *jus ad bellum* concern with the justice of a war. Any ordinary meaning of the word "innocence" applied to war will likely include so many combatants and exclude so many civilians that it would make the just prosecution of a war impossible. Moreover, any definition of guilt drawn from the *jus ad bellum* concern with the justice of a war will, like the moral view, allow innocent soldiers on the right side to kill guilty soldiers on the wrong side, but will render the killing of the former by the latter as morally equivalent to the killing of children, the aged, and the infirm. Unless this view draws the line between innocence and guilt on the distinction between civilian and combatant—i.e., refers to one's role as agent of a mortal threat—it could not distinguish between who may and may not be deliberately killed in war.

One wonders at this point whether the concept of innocence is at all useful and whether a suitable moral concept is available. Barrie Paskins' and Michael Dockrill's modified Kantian concept of respect for persons is suggestive of a solution. Might it do the important work the language of innocence and guilt wants to do? For them, treating people as ends rather than as objects, as mere means to an end, leads to a "very important distinction between two kinds of death in war":

> Some people, in virtue of what they are doing, can regard death in battle as, however terrible, neither more nor less than suffering the consequences of their own actions. Some other people who might be killed in war do not have this thought open to them. The distinction coincides pretty closely with that between combatant and noncombatant. For the combatant must recognize that death in war would be a fate internally connected with the activity in virtue of which he is a combatant. But, except in very special circumstances, this does not apply to the noncombatant.... Because of the internal connection between combatancy and being killed, a combatant has the option and opportunity to regard the prospect of death in war as meaningful: written into what he is doing is a connection with being killed that gives his own death a meaning.... But the death in war of a noncombatant does not have any such guaranteed meaning. (B. Paskins and M. Dockrill, 1979. *The Ethics of War,* pp. 224–225. Univ. of Minnesota Press, Minneapolis)

To assume that death can have any "guaranteed meaning" is highly problematical. That aside, Paskins and Dockrill make an important point: soldiers in war

---

[3] Ramsey, unlike Nagel, holds not only a self-defense justification of war, but also a second and much broader justification that allows the use of force to "maintain a just endurable order in which [women and men] may live" and to protect the victims of injustice—or as he puts it, "to deliver as many of God's children from tyranny.... [L]ove for neighbors threatened by violence, by aggression, or tyranny, provided the grounds for admitting the legitimacy of the use of military force." It is doubtful that this second justification for the use of force challenges my classification of Ramsey within the role-functional view. Even when force is used to defend others, or a political system, the justification for killing another extends only to, as Ramsey says, "the bearer of hostile force"; that is, the agent of danger. (Ramsey, 1968, 143–144)

know they take on a high risk of, and might even expect, death. It is in the nature of their activity. Killing them does not fail to respect them as persons engaged in purposeful activities. As Nagel puts it, "A coherent view of this type will hold that extremely hostile behavior towards another is compatible with treating him as a person—even perhaps as an end in himself (Nagel, 1974, 14). But civilians do not take a similar risk nor have the same expectation. So for them, death in war is not related to any activity or goal they might pursue, and deliberately killing them fails to respect this fact about their lives. A view of this type, however, seems hardly distinguishable from the role-functional view—note the emphasis on the role of combatants in the above quotation—and may face similar difficulties.

C. May Innocents Ever Be Directly Killed?

No explicitly moral justification for the British policy of strategic bombardment of cities was given during World War II.[4] Yet there are now some people who think that it was justified. What moral justification might that policy have? If the killing of innocent people is morally wrong—is murder—how can a policy that aims deliberately to kill innocent civilians be justified? It is a simple matter of logical consistency, one might object, that because murder is by definition the unjustified killing of innocent people, the bombing of German civilians is incapable of justification. Yet perhaps, others say, there are rare moments of grave crisis when the innocence of persons does not render them immune from deliberate attack.

The deliberate killing of innocent civilians, unlike the destruction of the enemy's combatants, is not a legitimate goal in war. But large-scale killing of civilian populations is in some circumstances justifiable, according to some interpreters of the just-war tradition. In those circumstances the principle of proportionality,

rather than noncombatant immunity (or discrimination), is usually appealed to. That principle is said to require that the harm done by military force be proportionate to some military goal. It prohibits gratuitous harm—i.e., harm that does not serve a military aim—but allows a great deal of harm so long as a legitimate war aim is served. So stated, proportionality is a consequentialist principle that weighs, say, the loss of civilian lives against victory. In Germany, the bombing of cities killed over 300,000 civilians. From the point of view of the *jus in bello* absolutist principle of discrimination, British bombing of German cities was nothing short of murder. Whatever end or goal is supposed to have been achieved by that policy does not justify the deliberate killing of civilians. But the just-war tradition as well as the international law of war contains this second and more permissive *jus in bello* principle that looks not at the distinction between precision and obliteration strategic policy. When applied to the bombing of German cities during WWII, this principle asks whether the military goal sought by strategic bombing justifies the civilian casualties it produced.

1. Supreme Emergency

In *Just and Unjust Wars* Michael Walzer offers the most respectable defense available for the deliberate killing of innocents in war. In several sections of that book and elsewhere, Walzer examines Britain's predicament shortly after the outbreak of WWII. He contends that unless Bomber Command was used systematically against German cities, Britain would very likely suffer defeat and an immense evil power would be let loose on the world. The bombers coupled with a policy of terror bombing against German civilians offered the only hope to avoid defeat by an enemy who posed, as Walzer says, "an ultimate threat to everything decent in our lives (1977, 253). What should one do? Kill tens of thousands of innocent civilians—children, the aged, and infirm—in order to stop a Nazi triumph, or respect the lives of innocent persons knowing that an age of barbaric violence will come to every nation in Europe?

Walzer gives a controversial response to this dilemma. In the life of nations there are rare moments of supreme emergency when the rights of innocent persons must be violated if a nation is to avoid defeat. In those rare moments military success might be so critically important that justice is more properly measured by the evil one prevents than by evil done. Walzer's proposed solution to such desperate times is that political leaders may take whatever measures are necessary to meet the task. He says,

---

[4] An exception is William Temple, Archbishop of Canterbury from 1942 to 1944, who defended the bombing of German and Italian cities on the simple thesis that, as Stephen L. Lammers puts it, "citizens of all modern states are implicated with the actions of their state" (S. L. Lammers, 1991. William Temple and the bombing of Germany: An exploration in the just war tradition. *J. Religious Ethics* **19**(1), 71–92). We should note also that very few criticisms of city bombing were advanced in the moral literature of the day. Public opinion in England strongly supported city bombing: 76% of those polled in areas that had not suffered city bombing—e.g., Cumberland, Westmoreland, and North Riding—approved of the RAF adopting a policy of bombing the civilian population of Germany, while only 45% of Londoners approved and 47% disapproved. The remaining 8% were undecided.

[C]ommunities in emergencies seem to have different and larger prerogatives [from individuals]. I am not sure that I can account for the difference, without ascribing to communal life a kind of transcendence which I do not believe it to have. Perhaps it is only a kind of arithmetic: individuals cannot kill one another to save themselves, but to save a nation we can violate the rights of a determinant but smaller number of people. (1977, 254)

Before one can justify the deliberate killing of innocent civilians, however, a nation has to face an evil of an ultimate nature. Simple military necessity will not do. The threat has to be such that defeat of the defending nation will result not merely in the establishment of a new balance of power, but in the triumph of evil, of a power so terribly awful that everything decent is radically jeopardized. Nothing less than an evil of this kind can justify the claim of emergency and the deliberate killing of innocent civilians. Accordingly, the threat must be, first, imminent, and second, not simply the loss of honor, but of a most serious nature.

With the criteria of imminence and seriousness of danger, Walzer distinguishes between the legitimacy of British bombing of German cities between 1940 and 1942, and the continuation of this practice during 1944–1945, when Britain was no longer in a condition of emergency, making the attacks on the cities at the end of the war immoral. It is important to note that Walzer's defense of British bombing does not diminish the injustice done to innocent German civilians. The decision to bomb the cities was made at a time when Germany posed a rare danger to the survival of Britain and defeat was ever present. It was a response to a condition of supreme emergency. But while a condition of supreme emergency justifies extreme action, an important wrong was nonetheless committed against German civilians. He says,

> Supreme emergency describes those rare moments when the negative value that we assign— that we can't help assigning—to the disaster that looms before us devalues morality itself and leaves us free to do whatever is militarily necessary to avoid disaster.... [Its essential feature is this:] that we recognize the evil we oppose and the evil we do and set ourselves, so far as possible against both. (Walzer, M., n.d. Emergency ethics)

Walzer's doctrine of supreme emergency and his defense of British bombing policy are subject to various lines of criticism. Here are two in outline form. First, in *Just and Unjust Wars* Walzer asserts that the rules of war are derived from individual rights. These rights, he argues, are more basic than considerations of utility. Yet when the stakes are high, utility has a certain priority over individual rights. Here, if anywhere, the ends to be achieved justify the means. But if utility overrides individual rights when a nation faces great disaster, why not follow utilitarian calculation all the way and consider the interest not only of one but of all communities, or, as Grotius says, "of the whole human race"?[5] It seems that if Walzer considers only the interests of one nation, say, Britain, he has to show why it is morally preferable that innocent civilians in this, rather than in another nation, say, Germany, survive. Second, whether absolutists and consequentialists moral principles, e.g., discrimination and proportionality, can be reconciled is a matter of great theoretical importance. Each contains quite different ideas about the content of morality. The first clearly is concerned with what we do to others, while the other attends to what happens to certain values and interests when we adopt one course of action over its alternative. When and on what grounds do we choose one understanding of morality over another?

Walzer describes supreme emergency as a very rare moment. It was the unique circumstance facing Britain that justified the deliberate killing of innocent civilians. Given the great evil Britain had set to defeat one could only choose the more permissive morality, knowing all the while the evil one does: become "murderers," he says, "for a good cause" (Walzer, 1977, 323). But the fact is that Walzer thinks supreme emergency is not that rare at all. Supreme emergency has become in the nuclear age, Walzer says, "a permanent condition" (1977, 274). One might then assume that a nation may do, or threaten to do, in this permanent condition of emergency just what Britain was justified in doing in the period 1940–1942. If this assumption is correct, then Walzer's argument is self-defeating, justifying on a permanent basis what initially was justified only for a rare and unique event—namely, the killing of civilians.

---

[5] The entire sentence reads, "Kings who measure up to the rule of wisdom take account not only of the nation that has been committed to them, but of the whole human race." The implication here seems to be that the political leadership of a nation must consider war's consequences not only for its own citizens, but also for the entire international community. (Grotius, 1962, Prolegomena, 24, p. 18)

2. The Principle of Discrimination, Terrorism, and Ethnopolitical Violence

As noted in the first section of this article, there are forms of political violence other than war between states that aim deliberately to kill civilians. Terrorism is usually understood to be one of those forms. Although there are some vexing questions regarding the definition of terrorism (e.g., is it different from freedom fighting, guerilla warfare, and other forms of political violence carried out by nonstate agents?), the application of just-war principles to acts of terrorism yields an unequivocal condemnation. To the extent that terrorism is designed to create fear and despair among civilians by sabotage, assassination, subversion, and other violent acts with indifferences to the legal and moral rules governing the use of force, terrorism is condemned on *jus ad bellum* and *jus in bello* grounds, for example, formal declaration of war and discrimination. The international law of war concurs with this judgment, and Protocol I of 1977 to the Geneva Conventions extends no legal protection to terrorists. Violence is sanctioned when carried out between groups of combatants who wage hostilities in accordance with the rules of war and distinguish themselves from civilian populations. Terrorists, however, do not fight in accordance with those rules, nor do they distinguish themselves. But, as some commentators contend, there may be a bias in the just-war tradition and the law of war in favor of the system of states such that violence by nonstate groups is immediately rendered an impermissible use of violence. Such bias, some say, is fairly obvious in standard definitions of war that allow only states to engage in armed hostilities by armies of combatants as their agents recognized as such by international conventions.

From the point of view of the just-war tradition what distinguishes terrorism from acceptable forms of violence is that its victims are persons who in no way, either morally or causally, are responsible for the harm inflicted on them. Rather the targets are often innocent members of the civilian population, as in the bomb attack at Harrods in London in 1984 and the Achilles Lauro incident in 1985. Terrorism is a form of political violence, so it is different from other uses of violence, say, for private gain. But terrorism is an objectionable use of violence because it is by its nature indiscriminate. For the sake of some political objective it aims deliberately to maim and kill civilians and other persons by virtue of their religion, ethnic heritage, or nationality. Even when the distinction between the innocent and the guilty cannot be clearly drawn, the killing of civilians by terrorist attacks treats them as mere things, as instruments in a political struggle, and fails to respect them as agents and persons.

The same conclusion can be shown to follow from the principle of discrimination applied to ethnopolitical violence. As noted in the first part of this article, since the end of WWII violence between ethnic groups has been steadily increasing, and total civilian casualties number in the millions. Gradually we are moving from nation-state conflicts fought along national borders to conflicts where the borders are determined by linguistic, religious, and ethnic differences, for example, between Hindus and Muslims in India, Turkic Muslims and Slavic Orthodox Russians in Central Asia, and Orthodox Christians and Muslims in the former Yugoslavia. Indeed we face a new and very troubling type of armed conflict without governments and armies as their agents fighting among themselves according to established rules of war. In this new type of conflict we encounter a breakdown of the traditional division of government, armies, and civilians. To the extent that such conflicts do not adhere to this important division and deliberately kill civilians because of their ethnic or religious identity, they are not a form of war. The law of war and the just-war tradition concur that these conflicts are nothing short of murder on a grand scale.

D. May Innocents Be Indirectly Killed?

The word "killing" describes an action the result of which is someone's death. It is not a moral term as such. From the moral point of view, what we wish to know is whether an act of killing is justified or not. An act of killing that is not justified we call murder. So murder is, by definition, the unjustified killing of a human being. As a general rule, deliberately killing innocent persons is unjustified—is, in other words, murder. Yet it is said that sometimes not all killing of innocent persons is murder. In some circumstances the killing of an innocent person, though reasonably foreseen as a result of the course of action one undertakes, is not murder because death was neither the means to some end, nor itself the end, one intended to bring about. There are a number of controversial issues regarding life and death that are frequently discussed in just this way, including therapeutic abortions, e.g., the removal of an ectopic pregnancy or cancerous uterus that results in the death of the fetus, and palliation of a dying patient by use of morphine hastening the patient's death. In cases such as these, the death of those who have done no harm—who are innocent—although tragic, is said to be permissible.

Consequentialist moral theories typically define a right action by reference to the state of affairs that action brings about. Roughly, an action is right if it happens to bring about a better state of affairs than acting otherwise. It does appear that when deliberating on what one ought to do, a person needs to consider (and is likely responsible for) all reasonably foreseen direct and indirect effects of a given action. The former usually refers to what a person intends to bring about, and the latter to what is foreseen but unintended—often referred to as a secondary or side effect to the action. For the consequentialist, the direct–indirect effects distinction is relatively unimportant. Both effects are the result of one's action and are to be assessed in terms of the state of affairs they produce. For the absolutist, however, the distinction is of great significance. A person, the absolutist will say, is responsible for the direct, but not for the indirect (or unintended) though foreseen, effects of her action. If an action, say, obliteration bombing, aims directly to bring about the death of innocent civilians, then that action is wrong—is, in other words, murder. But when the intention is, say, to destroy an enemy shipyard, a munitions factory, or a communications center (all legitimate targets of deliberate attack) and innocent civilians are killed, their death is a secondary or indirect effect of legitimate military conduct. Their death is, so the view goes, coincidental and collateral.

It is the principle of double effect that makes the just-stated distinction between intended (or direct) and unintended (or indirect) consequences. For example, I perform an act A that intends good G and foresees some evil effects E. Assume that I want to bring G about and have no wish for E, nor is E part of my intentions. E just happens. The principle of double effect is ready to say that I am not morally responsible for E, which is merely a side effect even if foreseen. But matters are different when E is my intention or a means for G, or when E is disproportionate to G. When E is my intended end or a means to some end, or when it is needless, this principle condemns my action. So, intending or using evil, or inflicting needless harm even for a good end, makes the act morally wicked. According to Anscombe, this principle is

> absolutely essential to Christian ethics. For Christianity forbids a number of things as being bad in themselves. But if I am unanswerable for the foreseen consequences of an action or refusal, as much as for the action itself, then these prohibitions will break down. If someone innocent will die unless I do a wicked thing, then on this view I am his murderer in refusing: so all that is left to me is to weigh up evils. Here the theologian steps in with the principle of double effect and says: "No, you are no murderer, if the man's death was neither your aim nor your chosen means, and

if you had to act in the way that led to it or else do something absolutely forbidden." Without ... this principle ... the Christian teaching that in no circumstances may one commit murder, adultery, apostasy (to give a few examples) goes by the board. These absolute prohibitions of Christianity by no means exhaust its ethic; there is a large area where what is just is determined partly by prudent weighing up of consequences. But the prohibitions are bedrock, and without them the Christian ethic goes to pieces. (Anscombe, 1981, 58)

One does not, however, have to be a Christian or theist of any kind to adopt this principle. Any absolutist system of morality is likely to have some dependence on it: some things are absolutely wrong and may never be done even if the heavens are about to fall. So, one may not perform an act that is absolutely prohibited (say, torture) to save someone else's (an innocent's) life. But the principle of double effect does allow the indirect and proportionate killing of innocent persons. How does a principle which belongs to an absolutist system permit the killing of innocent persons in war?

Consider one application of this principle. Suppose orders are issued to bomb certain important enemy military targets, say, a command, control, and communications center, a munitions depots, and several highways and bridges used for military transport. Bombing these targets will kill combatants, an action permissible in war. But suppose that a number of civilians are also likely to be killed. They either live or work nearby the munitions depots and bridges. It is, of course, wrong to deliberately kill these civilians. But the principle of double effect says that absent the intention to kill them, their death, though an evil, is not a moral evil but a side effect of a legitimate act of war. Acts that produce such evils are said to be justifiable when (i) the action is either morally good or indifferent, (ii) the intention of the agent performing the action is upright, (iii) the evil is causally related to the intended good, and (iv) there is proportionately grave reason for allowing the evil to occur. Supposing that all four conditions are satisfied in the above example, then the death of civilians is incidental to the act and considered collateral damage.

Indeed that was the reasoning evident in official statements by the U.S. chain of command in the 1991 war against Iraq. We were told repeatedly during that war that the U.S. choice of targets was designed not to hit civilians directly. So, the principle of discrimination was adhered to. Moreover, many of the weapons used in that war—so-called "smart weapons"—gave the assurance that hitting targets within cities would not be hitting the cities (i.e., civilians) themselves. There was no intention, nor need, to rely on WWII strategies of obliteration bombing against civilians. Yet reports attested that due to continual strikes, oftentimes of the same target, particularly in Baghdad near civilian areas, a significant number of civilian casualties were produced. Is there a threshold at which indirect and foreseen effects gain at least the appearance if not the reality of intended aims, when it no longer makes sense to say that civilian casualities are collateral or incidental to permissible conduct in war? At which point do collateral civilian deaths become disproportionate to legitimate military conduct?

Combatant casualties in this war were rather high. Intelligence sources estimated that some 150,000 Iraqi soldiers were killed. The vast majority of them were conscripts who cannot be held responsible for the war. The same sources estimated that civilian casualties may have been equal to combatant deaths. Is this number of civilian deaths acceptable on proportionality grounds? Suppose that American bombing did not intend to kill civilians, only to destroy various aspects of Iraqi infrastructure having some military value. How shall we think of a highway or bridge, an electric power plant, or sources of communication that have some military value but are used regularly by civilians? What if the destruction of those targets has a greater impact on a society than on its armed forces? Are these civilian or military targets? Destruction of infrastructure targets in Baghdad has to date affected the health and living standards of civilians more than the military. To say that these are strictly military targets and so the misery their destruction causes is collateral seems, on consequentialists grounds, to be an evasion of responsibility.

These remarks suggest the following criticism of the principle of double effects. It is extremely difficult to determine what are the intended and unintended effects of a course of action. The fact that our actions often have more than their intended effect does not necessarily mean that we have no responsibility for their unintended effects. When we know our actions bring about the death of innocent persons, even when they are indirect, it seems too narrow a sense of responsibility to say that those deaths, though tragic, are permissible. Is it really possible to engage in a course of action knowing that civilians will be killed and say that their death is only incidental and that one therefore is not responsible for them? To be sure, responsibility may admit of degrees. In some circumstances a person may be less responsible for what is allowed to happen than for what she does. That is an important distinction. But when what is allowed to happen is some 150,000

innocent deaths, as was the case in the war against Iraq, the magnitude seems disproportional to any legitimate military goal, and those deaths begin to take the form of a deliberate action.

This line of criticism is particularly well suited to debates on nuclear deterrence. Some argue that a policy of nuclear deterrence is an effective way to prevent nuclear war. By threatening unacceptable loss to a potential adversary, whatever gains might obtain from aggression are offset and a sort of peace is retained. It has been the readiness to use nuclear weapons that has produced peace in Europe since the end of WWII. But this claim is highly controversial. That to date there has not been a nuclear war is no real evidence that deterrence has this preventive function. Europe has enjoyed other periods of peace without nuclear weapons, even when European governments were more militaristic than now—for example, the 40 years of peace after the Franco-Prussian War of 1871. It is a common and simple fallacy to mistake what is not the cause (deterrence) of a given effect (absence of nuclear war and peace) for the real cause. From the moral point of view what is important to determine is the morality of nuclear deterrence. If nuclear weapons are immoral means of warfare because they cannot satisfy the principle of discrimination and will produce effects disproportionate to any goal, and if it is immoral to intend what one may not do, it seems then that nuclear deterrence is itself immoral. Nations ought, therefore, to disarm themselves immediately and unilaterally of these weapons of mass destruction. Proponents of deterrence argue, however, that so long as a nation does not deliberately aim nuclear weapons at civilian populations but rather at military targets—so-called "counterforce deterrence"—however many civilians deaths result from the use of these weapons are only collateral and incidental to legitimate military conduct. It is the principle of double effect that, for the absolutist, opens this line of reasoning. For the consequentialist, however, even when deterrence aims only at strictly military targets, the side (i.e., unintended) effects of a nuclear attack are hardly different from the intended end. Indeed, if an adversary's fear of collateral damage is one of the things that deters, it is then one of the means by which deterrence is achieved. And means to an end are always intended actions. So, the killing of civilians is intended even in counterforce deterrence.

Acknowledgments

I am grateful to my colleagues Drs. Cynthia Brincat and Thomas Shipka, and to two anonymous reviewers, for their detailed and helpful comments on an earlier draft of this paper.

Also See the Following Articles

MILITARY CODES OF BEHAVIOR • NUCLEAR DETERRENCE •
NUCLEAR WARFARE • TERRORISM • WARFARE, CODES OF

Bibliography

Clark. I. (1990). "Waging War: A Philosophical Introduction." Clarendon, Oxford.

Cohen, S. (1989). "Arms and Judgment: Law, Morality, and the Conduct of War in the Twentieth Century." Westview, Boulder, CO.

Detter De Lupis, I. (1987). "The Law of War." Cambridge Univ. Press, Cambridge.

Holmes, R. L. (1989). "On War and Morality." Princeton Univ. Press, Princeton, NJ.

Johnson, J. T. (1981). "Just War Tradition and the Restraint of War." Princeton Univ. Press, Princeton, NJ.

Lackey, D. P. (1984). "Moral Principles and Nuclear Weapons." Rowman & Allanheld, Totowa, NJ.

Miller, R. B. (1991). "Interpretations of Conflict: Ethics, Pacifism, and Just-War Tradition." Univ. of Chicago Press, Chicago.

Palmer-Fernández, G. (1996). "Deterrence and the Crisis in Moral Theory." Peter Lang, Berlin/New York.

Van Creveld, M. (1991). "The Transformation of War." The Free Press, New York.

CODES OF ETHICS

Jane Pritchard
University of Central Lancashire

GLOSSARY

client A person for whose benefit work is carried out by a professional. For medical practitioners, a client may also be called a patient. The term "client" can be compared and contrasted with a customer or consumer, who is the object of business and/or commerce as opposed to a profession.

code A collection of aspirations, regulations, and/or guidelines that represent the values of the group or profession to which it applies.

ethics Moral philosophy generally or a particular philosophy; the term can be used interchangeably with the word "morals."

Kantian An adjective deriving from Immanuel Kant; used to describe Kant's own work and to describe the work of other philosophers and theories which share Kant's priorities and approaches, notwithstanding that they may differ quite significantly from Kant's work itself.

nontraditional professions A large group of professions generally including accountancy, banking, engineering, management, social work, and almost all varieties of "white collar" work. All forms of artists and sports people may be called professionals, but it is suggested that in such case the word is used in a different way to mean either not-amateur or expert.

practice The work or business of a professional. Interestingly, while many nontraditional groups have claimed professional status, few have adopted the word "practice" to describe their work. A professional who is in practice may be called a practitioner.

profession A group of workers having common values and aims. Philosophically the word may be used to indicate a common moral purpose, for example, doctors may have a duty to promote health which is understood as a moral good. Professions may be self-governing, that is, without interference or supervision from people or bodies who are not members of that profession. The word is used popularly to describe any group of workers having specialized knowledge and training, for example, computer scientists or broadcasters.

professional Like "profession," this word can be used to indicate a moral dimension to work carried out or the individual doing that work, or it can be used similarly as words such as "expert" and "conscientious." In the moral use a professional will have a duty to try to do beneficial work for a client. In the wider sense it may be used to describe any member of a service rather than a manufacturing industry. That said, many professionals are employed in every aspect of industry and commerce.

traditional professions A group of professions generally including, but not be limited to, medicine, law, the church, and the armed forces. Education may be included although this can also be classified as vocational along with nursing.

CODES OF ETHICS are those bundles of intentional or behavioral requirements that members of a profession or other group must comply with in order to remain part of the group. A code can be formal, that is, written, or informal, not presented in written form but nevertheless identifiable as prescribing certain agreed upon standards of practice and values usually through common training and peer pressure. Whether or not a written code exists, the expression "code of ethics" can extend beyond the document itself and include disciplinary functions and variations in practice, either written or informal. In the same way the code can draw on the underlying but shared morality of the group members. This might be of great importance in the interpretation of what a general principle means in terms of a particular profession.

Codes will vary from one group to another. Where a code contains details of disciplinary procedures for breach of its provisions, this may be an indication that the code belongs to a self-governing, structured profession, for example, law or medicine. Where codes are short and contain a list of very general moral aims it may be an indication that the code is aspirational or that the particular profession is little more than a loose association of members with common interests. Codes can be written for the benefit of members, clients, and/or the public at large. They may be used for various purposes from licensing, to compliance, to marketing. It may be helpful to see these different uses as ranged on a continuum from quasi-legal requirements through moral prescriptions to mere advertising puffery. Very often a particular code will comprise a combination of these features and serve a number of different purposes.

I. INCREASED USE OF CODES

Interest in codes of ethics has increased tremendously in the decades since the second World War. One reason for this in relation to research and medical practice is that they were seen as a way of protecting patients and participants against a repeat of the kind of inhumane experimentation carried out by Nazi doctors during the war. Once the spotlight fell on research practice it became clear that unacceptable procedures were very widespread. There were experiments being carried out in many other countries as well which failed to look after the participants. The ethical issues of research and scientific practice are now firmly on the agenda. Generally, there is much greater awareness throughout the developed world that respect for human rights must be considered at every stage of research. The adoption of a code of ethics can play an important part in putting that awareness into practice.

Public interest in ethical conduct has widened from medicine to almost every sector of modern life, including the work of other professions, the business and service industries, and public service. While most of the traditional professions have had codes for a long time, many codes have been revised and extended. Professional groups can no longer assume that clients will accept as good practice what they say is good. Clients are much more aware of their own rights. Better communications and wider media coverage of legal cases of professional negligence and malpractice have combined with this to level out the balance of power between professionals and clients. A code of ethics can be an important vehicle to help maintain this delicate balance.

The use of codes of ethics extends far beyond professional barriers. It is common for trade associations to adopt them, sometimes in a bid to acquire professional status. Corporations and institutions may have codes of ethics which warrant to their customers and to the public what practices and priorities compose the corporate image.

Increased use of codes is the result of a variety of reasons. Codes themselves come in a variety of forms and serve several different functions.

II. THE FORM OF CODES

Codes come in many different forms and may be formal (written) or informal (oral). They bear a variety of names: codes of ethics, codes of professional conduct, and codes of practice are the most common forms. A code of ethics may also appear in the form of a charter or mission statement. While the names are used interchangeably, three broad categories are usually identified which give insight into the purpose of the code.

N. G. Harris and M. S. Frankel both identify three groups, but their divisions are slightly different. Harris's code of ethics corresponds exactly to Frankel's aspirational group. They differ in their classification of the other two. Frankel distinguishes between educational and regulatory codes, whereas Harris includes both aspects in his code of conduct, though they serve different purposes. The main difference in classification is not in the content but in who the reader of the code is. Harris combines educational and regulatory clauses in a code of conduct which he classifies as a document prepared for the benefit and regulation of the members of the group. Harris's third group, codes of practice, is distinguished by being written for nonmembers. These might be members of the general public, customers, students, or clientele of the group and may include the members too. By acknowledging this, Harris identifies a category which is halfway, as it were, between a code and a charter or mission statement. Charters and the such are generally imposed on or designed for the public at large rather than any special group. The different classification is unimportant in practice, as both writers correctly point out that most codes are a mixture of all categories and can appear in almost any form. The following paragraphs follow Harris's classification.

Codes of ethics usually consist of a short set of principles, for example, "every member shall conduct themselves with the utmost honesty and integrity." They are very general in nature. This group can be classified as aspirational. The provisions of this type of code are so broad that it is likely that all such codes will be similar although the groups adopting them may be very different, from doctor to engineer, and school teacher to licensed victualler. How a code of ethics acquires meaning in terms of the practice of a particular group will vary from one group to another. Understanding what constitutes the "utmost integrity" for dentistry, for example, may be learned through professional education, apprenticeship, or discussion with other dentists, and most likely through all of these things. Development of such understanding may happen gradually over a whole career. Generally a code of ethics will be prepared for members of a group as an internal document. It will be addressed to professionals or employees rather than clients or customers. See Section V for an interpretation.

Codes of conduct are also prepared for use within the group membership. They are more detailed than codes of ethics and give details of how a general duty will be manifested in practice. They may include detailed regulations for special procedures, for example, what to do in an emergency or in what circumstances a general duty may be breached by the requirements of stronger specific duties. An example of a special circumstance may be that the public interest may sometimes justify breach of a general duty of confidentiality to a company or client. Disciplinary provisions may be included in this sort of code. The detail of codes will be referred to again in Section III. In reality codes vary so much that it is helpful to look at actual examples. Codes of conduct can be extremely lengthy and sometimes contain extensive commentary on how the group interprets certain stipulations in practice. They can be both educational and regulatory.

Codes of practice are documents which, like codes of conduct, are more detailed and specific than codes of ethics. They are distinguished from these other two kinds of code by being written for a wider readership than members alone. This can include clients, customers, and members of the general public. They warrant to the readership the standards of practice that can be expected. It will be a matter of degree whether this warranty amounts to a promise or an aspiration. In the former case a complaints procedure may be in place whereby customers can complain of failures to realize standards specified. In some cases there may be included provisions for compensation to be payable. The inclusion of complaints procedures may be an indication of the degree of commitment on the part of the group or organization to adhere to the provisions of the code. There will be tremendous variations in the content of codes of practice as well as in the commitment with which they are embraced. Inevitably there will be some codes of practice which are little more than advertising puffery.

III. THE CONTENT OF CODES

While individual codes can be very different from one another, a large number of codes contain a basic corps of very similar aspirations. Common clauses relate to the need for honesty, fairness, and confidentiality in relation to a client's affairs. Many codes, particularly those which apply to health care or social welfare, often contain references to the principles of beneficence, nonmaleficence, respect for autonomy, and justice. Professional codes typically contain a provision whereby a member should not do anything which brings the profession itself into disrepute. This is interesting because it is not for the benefit of a particular client but for the benefit of other professionals and their clients and for the image of the profession in the eyes of the public at large. There could be instances where this kind of clause causes conflict between the interests of an individual client and the member's duty to the profession as a whole.

It is clear from Section II that the different forms of codes will vary greatly in length and detail. Most codes, though, share the feature that they begin with general principles and then move to an expansion of how such principles translate into the work of the particular group. Thus it can be argued that codes are used in a way that is top down, moving from principle to practice. As such it could be argued that codes do not adapt very easily to a bottom up or case study approach to work, moving from particular circumstances toward deciding which principles to apply.

IV. THE FUNCTIONS OF CODES

A code of ethics can have a variety of functions. The different types of code and their contents discussed in Sections II and III in part make the main function of a particular code explicit. In a similar way some of the functions of codes are implicit from the theoretical framework, discussed in Section V, in which they operate. Codes are not absolute documents and many comprise a variety of features and have several functions. When discussing the functions of codes inevitably one is talking about what codes could do and sometimes do rather than describing how any particular code operates.

Codes of ethics can be seen as a mark of a profession. Harris ascribes the increase of the use of codes in part to this function alone. Codes can also be used as a warranty to customers and clients of how a business will conduct itself in regard to certain basic moral principles like honesty and fairness. In the context of a particular group, a code of ethics can provide an important focus for group loyalty and shared values.

It should not be assumed that all the functions are positive. One negative function of codes is that, rather than improving standards of practice, they may actually serve to reduce them. This could happen in at least two ways. Firstly, if a code is adopted in a superficial way, for example, as a marketing tool in order to give the impression that a business intends to behave morally, it may be treated with contempt. Alternatively the same code may be put in place to avoid statutory regulations being imposed on a business or industry. Thus by pretending to have moral standards, legal constraints are sought to be avoided. In these circumstances employees or customers seeking to implement the provisions of the code are likely to find their actions out of step with what management requires. The code, by misleading people about managers' intentions, makes the situation worse than had it never been adopted at all.

A second situation where a code could have a negative effect takes place with complete sincerity. Where codes contain so much detailed information about what standards are required and what conduct will constitute those standards, there is a danger that the people who apply such a code will conform so thoroughly and precisely that the effect is that they, in fact, suspend the moral dimension of their work. They apply the provisions of the code in exactly the same way as detailed legal regulations are applied. As such the provisions of the code are not treated as guidelines which ought to be followed but as laws which must be followed, allowing no room for the exercise of professional discretion.

There is a delicate and fine balance to be maintained between what ought to be done by a professional who has the expertise and experience to make independent decisions about what is required in particular circumstances and what the law or, arguably, an overprotective, governing body prescribes must be done in all circumstances all of the time. The ability to maintain this balance without overbearing regulation can be seen as a central feature of a professional as opposed to some other kind of worker. What a professional is or could be will be discussed more fully in Section V. The difficulty in practice, and why this possible feature of codes, and indeed too-rigid law, is regarded as a negative function, is that it inhibits the worker from being free to respond to unforeseen circumstances. The human beings who make up a clientele, while they may be similar, do not operate in standard or predictable ways. What is good for one cannot be assumed to be good for another. This is a danger of any standardization involving people, and care should be taken that codes of ethics do not make the position worse rather than better.

V. THEORETICAL FRAMEWORK OF CODES

Interpretation of how the broad principles set out in codes of ethics translate into conduct will be different from one group to another. In Section II it was suggested that a code acquires meaning for members through discussion, education, and training. While this may be true, it is not true to say that all readers of codes have an adequate opportunity of understanding how a code ought or is intended to be interpreted. Edgar says in relation to a social work code that interpretation necessarily operates outside the scope of the code itself. This is a general feature of codes and is acknowledged to be problematic. In the context of traditional and more structured nontraditional professions there is an opportunity to discuss interpretation of the code because qualification for membership in the group requires long training at the outset and, in many cases, continuing education as a condition of the renewal of a certificate of registration or practice. That is not to say that the opportunity is necessarily taken. Section VI will look at some individual examples by way of illustration. Some corporations hold training sessions on interpretation when a code of ethics is introduced. A significant number of codes are adopted without any guidelines on interpretation at all. The code of ethics may be the main vehicle for the expression of the group's values and norms, but what these mean in practice may not be clear and/or may only be understood through practice over a period of years. As such, codes must be seen as signposts and partial tools in the ethics of an organization or group and by no means as ends in themselves.

Interpretation may take place on an ad hoc basis, each case being dealt with in accordance with the decisions and moral opinions of the individual in charge, or through the application of a consistent and coherent ethical theory. Probably every possible variation between these two extremes will apply in practice.

How a code is interpreted will depend on the moral beliefs of the group. These may be implied or explicit. They may also emerge from the moral beliefs of individuals in the group. The predictability of beliefs held by members of a group may in part depend on how well the culture of the organization is articulated. There is a certain circularity between group culture and codes whereby in some cases the culture will come before the code is adopted and sometimes afterward. This will impact how the code is or can be interpreted in practice. If the code is written out of and reflects the moral values of a culture then a correct interpretation can be obtained by looking at that culture. In this situation the code is a codification of values already held by an organization. The culture has made the code. If, however, the code has been formulated with the intention of trying to change the culture of an organization, then interpretation must not come from going back to the existing culture but must come from outside the organization or be imposed by new management policies. In this sense the code makes the culture. In the latter situation training in how to translate the provisions of the code into practice will be essential if the code is to succeed. In the former case training will not be so important, as interpretation draws on the existing values of those to whom the code applies.

Historically membership of the traditional professions was drawn from the same cultural and social background. It was almost always the case therefore that members of a group shared values and had a common understanding of what was moral. That is not to say that members all behaved morally or did not have differences of opinion, but the expectancy of cultural understanding was very high. As such, professions were most likely to come under the first category previously referred to. Thus any code reflected existing and shared values of a group. A code of ethics was perhaps helpful but was not an essential source of information on their values.

The position today is very different. There are both more associations with codes and their membership is much more varied. Society itself is much more diverse and communities are made up of people from different religious and cultural backgrounds. Members of a group may hold a great variety of different views. As such, groups are more likely to fall into the second category and to adopt a code which sets out values to which they as a group aspire. In these circumstances training is likely to assist members to understand and identify with the values of the group.

What kind of training is appropriate will vary from group to group and will also be subject to external constraints like time and resources. The subject matter of the training may be techniques in problem solving, group dynamics, and case work, and may include varying degrees of moral philosophy.

There is a lot of room for discussion about how moral philosophy relates to codes of ethics. Harris argues that professional codes are underpinned by Kantian moral theory, although Chadwick disagrees that this view is based on a correct interpretation of Kant's work. Other codes may be deliberately written in adherence with the principles of a particular theory. Yet others may reflect a variety of different moral positions and lack any coherent or consistent analysis, having emerged out of practice and the need to respond to different situations. Many codes are written in a composite way, which may include adherence to general principles but may be revised to accommodate changes in law, practice, or current thinking. The more specific the provisions of a code, the more likely it is that a code will need to be revised in response to external changes. The making of codes can be both proactive, in that they prescribe change that is desired, and reactive, in that they respond to changes which are mandatory.

One aspect of the debate about codes, how they are or should be formed, involves a discussion about what constitutes a profession. The theoretical framework, uses, and functions of codes will vary in accordance with how "profession" is defined. If a narrow view of profession is adopted which allows only those groups which have an intrinsic good intention to be classed as a profession, then a code must necessarily reflect that central moral function to be of any value at all. This view might not be limited to the work carried out, but may extend to the person doing the work. Thus a professional is a good person by definition. Medicine has the central value of promoting health. Some could argue that this is the only value appropriate to medicine, and thus a code of ethics is not required because that is all it would say. Codes of conduct may still be appropriate for giving practical advice on standards of behavior. Others could take a much wider view and include in the term profession any group that has a common expertise or access to a particular body of knowledge. In such a classification there is no essential moral position applicable to the members or the work carried out by those members. A code of ethics may thus be an important vehicle whereby moral values and required standards of practice are communicated both by and to the members. It may be the only source of moral limitation placed on members. In this kind of classification an individual professional has no essential moral nature.

VI. THE EXPERIENCE OF CODES BY DIFFERENT GROUPS AND CONCLUSIONS

The variations in the use made by different groups of codes of ethics can be illustrated by a brief look at two groups of workers, namely, doctors and nurses. Inevitably there are differences in the experience of these groups in different countries, but even so it seems likely that the overriding implications of the experience of those groups in the United Kingdom and the United States can give insight into codes and professionalism generally. There are quite significant differences between the groups in these two countries anyway.

All nurses in the United Kingdom must be registered with the UKCC, which is itself constituted by statute. The UKCC has wide powers relating to the training, guidance, and discipline of its members. As such, all nurses must adopt the various codes of ethics and conduct specified by that body. There is no equivalent body in the United States, and membership in the American Nurses Association (ANA) is voluntary. Generally there is very little training or discussion of ethics in a formal way. Members of the ANA adopt its code as a condition of membership. While the ANA has some powers in relation to guidance and representation of nurses, many

aspects of nurses' education, registration, and discipline are dealt with by different state boards. Partly as a result of this position there is scope for much greater variation in the standards of practice and moral points of view of nurses in the United States than those in the United Kingdom.

At the same time it could be argued that there is more scope in the United States for nurses to exercise professional discretion, and thus it is easier for them to argue that nursing is a separate and independent profession. On the other hand it is now compulsory that trainee nurses in the United Kingdom all have some training and discussion of ethics both generally and in relation to the interpretation of their code. As such nurses in the United Kingdom are increasingly aware of the significance of ethics to their work and the impact of their code. They also have a strong group identity. Both groups of nurses have scope for the exercise of some professional discretion, but in a wide variety of circumstances must subject their professionalism to the discretion exercised by doctors.

Doctors in the United Kingdom, while subject to various advisory and disciplinary bodies and even some specific ethical guidelines, do not subscribe formally or uniformly to any code of ethics. The public perception of doctors both historically and currently is that they are professionals. Doctors in the United States do have a code, but there is scope for diversity as practice registration is dealt with by individual states. They are publicly perceived as professionals and would seem to have a high degree of scope for the exercise of professional discretion. Doctors in the United Kingdom receive very little formal training in ethics before qualification. That received afterward will be extremely variable and largely voluntary. While there is more opportunity for U.S. doctors to receive training in ethics or to discuss the issues in a formal way, it cannot be said that it is necessarily part of the experience of all doctors.

The experience of codes of ethics and professionalism of these two groups is diverse both in relation to that of the same professionals in different countries and in relation to the other group. This difference exemplifies the great variety found in codes of ethics in terms of use, form, content, and theory. Nevertheless, even though there are great differences, it is possible to gain an impression at least of how codes of ethics operate across the board. That an example has been used from health care should in no way be taken as excluding non-health care workers from the typicality of the experience. That typicality is diversity.

Also See the Following Articles

MEDICAL CODES AND OATHS • THEORIES OF ETHICS, OVERVIEW

Bibliography

Chadwick, R. (Ed.) (1994). "Ethics and the Professions." Avebury, Aldershot.

Edgar, A. (1994). Narrating social work. In "Ethics and the Professions" (R. Chadwick, Ed.). Avebury, Aldershot.
Frankel, M. S. (1989). Professional codes: Why, how and with what impact? *J. Bus. Ethics* **8**, 109–115.
Gorlin, R. A. (Ed.) (1994). "Codes of Professional Responsibility," 3rd ed. The Bureau of National Affairs, Washington, DC.
Harris, N. G. E. (1994). Professional codes and Kantian duties. In "Ethics and the Professions" (R. Chadwick, Ed.). Avebury, Aldershot.
Harris, N. G. E. (1989). "Professional Codes of Conduct in the United Kingdom: A Directory." Mansell, London.
Koehn, D. (1994). "The Ground of Professional Ethics." Routledge, London.

COERCIVE TREATMENT IN PSYCHIATRY

Ron L. P. Berghmans
Institute for Bioethics

GLOSSARY

coercive treatment The application of treatment
against the will of the patient.
paternalism Actions in the interest, but against the
wishes of a person.
psychiatric advance directive A document stating the
wishes of a person with regard to future psychiatric
treatment in case of incompetence.

COERCIVE TREATMENT IN PSYCHIATRIC CARE is
an issue of ongoing legal, ethical, and societal debate
in many countries. Although historically speaking psychiatry and coercion have always been connected to
each other, this connection has existed along with
movements criticizing the use of coercion in psychiatric care.

Illustrative examples are of Philippe Pinel in France,
Samuel Tuke in England, and Vincenzo Chiarugi in
Italy around the turn of the 18th and 19th centuries.
In 1793, so the story is told, Pinel liberated the lunatics
in the Bicetre from their chains. The British Quaker
Tuke introduced the concept of moral treatment in the
Retreat in York. And in Florence in 1788 Chiarugi
asserted boldly that it is a supreme moral duty and
medical obligation to respect the insane individual as
a person.

Although the use of coercion in psychiatric treatment
is generally inspired by benevolent motives, the misuse
of psychiatric hospitals, techniques, and medications
with the aim of repressing political dissidents was
widely practiced in the former USSR and illustrates
the potentiality of abuse of psychiatry for political or
other reasons.

The application of coercive interventions, as a mode
of external causation with therapeutic intent, was regarded by Aristotle as a proper means of treating the
insane. Speaking of children and the insane, in *Eudemian Ethics* he states, "They are in need not of arguments, but, in the former case, of time to grow up,
and, in the latter case, of either political or medical
chastisements—for the administering of drugs is a form
of chastisement no less than beating is" (M. Nussbaum,
1994. *The Therapy of Desire. Theory and Practice in
Hellenistic Ethics*, p. 6g. Princeton Univ. Press, Princeton, NJ).

Rational deliberation and practical reasoning, in the
view of Aristotle, are not within the reach of lunatics

who are guided by their emotions. These emotions lead to beliefs which cannot be corrected by rational argument or persuasion.

In contemporary society, it is predominantly by way of legal regulation that the reasons for and limits of psychiatric coercion are described and enforced. In a number of jurisdictions legal reform in mental health care has led to the recognition of the right of the mentally ill to refuse treatment.

Although these legal regulations themselves are based on moral values, such as the principle of respect for individual autonomy, they also raise a number of ethical questions. An important question concerns the limits of the autonomy of the mentally ill and the moral justification of coercive interventions, i.e., involuntary commitment and coercive treatment.

In mental health care the ethical debate with regard to coercive psychiatric treatment is concerned with conceptual issues as well as care issues. One of the major conceptual issues is the issue of competence or decision-making capacity in the mentally ill. Practical care issues are centered around the ethical acceptability of coercive psychiatric treatment in the community (outpatient coercive treatment) and the use of psychiatric advance directives as instruments guiding the provision of psychiatric care.

Before addressing these issues, attention will be paid to the concept of coercion and to the moral values involved in coercive psychiatric treatment. Then the moral justification of coercive psychiatric treatment will be addressed. Central to the moral evaluation of psychiatric coercion is the issue of competence or decision-making capacity. This will be analyzed in the next section. Then some morally relevant considerations regarding the form, content, and limits of coercive treatment in psychiatry will be outlined. Lastly, the moral issues involved in psychiatric advance directives are discussed.

I. THE CONCEPT OF COERCION

Feinberg makes some helpful conceptual distinctions with regard to the concept of coercion (J. Feinberg, 1986. *The Moral Limits of the Criminal Law,* Vol. III, *Harm to Self.* Oxford Univ. Press, New York/Oxford). On the scale of different ways of getting a person to act as you want him to act, the following strategies can be distinguished: compulsion proper, compulsive pressure, coercion proper, coercive pressure, manipulation, persuasion, enticement, and request. Somewhere on this scale there is a cut-off point where simply "get-ting" a person to act in certain ways becomes "forcing" him.

In order to simplify matters, different types of behavior control can be reduced to one of the three following paradigmatic cases: (1) rational persuasion, (2) manipulation, or (3) coercion.

Rational persuasion is being employed if a person tries to influence the behavior of another by causing him to openly consider and reevaluate his intentions toward a certain act without bringing to bear any pressures of incentives extraneous to the rational evaluation of the likely consequences of that act from the point of view of the self-interest of the person being asked to act.

The attempt of a person to influence a subject's behavior takes on a manipulative character if the communicative approach taken loses a straightforward and open quality. The primary intent of the manipulator is to produce or engineer the needed assent by bringing pressure to bear, in a deliberate and calculated way, on what he presumes to be the manipulable features of the subject's motivational system.

In coercion, sufficiently strong incentives to act are provided that it would be unreasonable to expect any person not to so act. Coercion may take the form of an offer or of a threat. A coercive offer may be an irresistible incentive because of the extreme attractiveness of the offer to the subject. A coercive threat generally involves the promise of some extremely unattractive result (some significant evil) if the coercee does not act in the way the coercer wants him to act.

In the most extreme sense, coercion may not even involve an act of the coercee, but may simply imply a total separation between the act and the will of the coercee: this is typically the case if physical power is used, as in the case of compulsory psychiatric treatment.

In both persuasion and manipulation, the subject of the attempted behavior control is left a volitional element of discretion with regard to his actions; there is some amount of freedom to refuse or assent. In coercion, this volitional, discretionary element is absent; the coercee is simply forced to act, and is in no way responsible or liable to moral censure for so acting.

What is morally problematic or offensive about the use of coercion? In the case of coercion the subject is distracted from pursuing his own goals and purposes by effectively limiting his range of opportunities for action. Coercion thus reduces freedom of choice and voluntariness with regard to the goals and purposes a person values in his life. Coercion is a threat to the moral view of persons as autonomous and responsible agents who are entitled to act upon their own conception of the good and the good life and can be considered accountable for these actions. In societies stressing the value of respecting the autonomy of persons, from a moral point of view coercion is *prima facie* wrong.

Given these morally relevant features of coercion, it follows that coercion in general, and psychiatric coercion in particular, is in need of justification.

II. THE JUSTIFICATION OF COERCIVE PSYCHIATRIC TREATMENT

With regard to the justification of coercive psychiatric interventions, it is possible to distinguish broadly between two moral principles: the *harm principle* and the *principle of paternalism*. In the United States a parallel distinction is made between the state's *police power* to protect others from a person's actions and its *parens patriae power* to protect people from their own actions.

The harm principle, which goes back to the work of John Stuart Mill, implies that coercive interventions are morally justified if a person poses harm to others. In the famous words of Mill, "That the only purpose for which power can be rightfully exercised over any member of a civilized community, against his will, is to prevent harm to others" (1859. *On Liberty*). Obviously, Mill's principle does not focus on psychiatric coercion and the mentally ill, but on the use of power in general toward all citizens of society. [In fact, by implication Mill excluded the mentally ill from his libertarian guiding principle.] Mill's principle applies solely to the use of power in order to prevent a person from harming others.

From the harm principle a limited justification of psychiatric coercion can be inferred: it is morally justified to prevent a person from harming others, even if in order to succeed it is necessary to apply force. The harm principle justifies the use of liberty-limiting interventions such as involuntary commitment or seclusion in emergency situations. Coercive treatment (i.e., forced medication) with the therapeutic intent to treat the disorder underlying the behavior which created the emergency in general cannot be justified by reference to the harm principle, because it involves an infringement of the physical and mental integrity of the person.

To justify coercive treatment the principle of paternalism needs to be applicable. The principle of paternalism refers to the use of coercion toward a person in order to prevent him from harming himself. The justification of paternalistic coercion in general, and particularly paternalistic psychiatric coercion, is a complex question for which different kinds of moral reasoning have been proposed.

A number of these lines of justification are consent-based strategies. They are attractive because they try to provide a justification for the use of coercion by eliminating the central morally troublesome feature of coercion, which is the absence of the free consent of the coerced person. The following consent-based justification strategies can be distinguished: (1) the appeal to past consent, (2) the appeal to future consent, (3) the appeal to "real will," (4) the appeal to presumed will, (5) the appeal to rational consent or will, and (6) the appeal to self-binding.

Without discussing these strategies in detail it can be stated that all have more or less serious shortcomings. Past consent in general is considered to be revocable by the consenting person because of a change of mind. The appeal to future consent (sometimes coined the "thank you" theory) suffers from conceptual and empirical defects. Conceptually, consent-after-the-fact (i.e., the paternalistic intervention) cannot be separated from the effects of the intervention as such. Thus, an appeal to future consent might lead to the justification of morally offensive practices such as brainwashing. Above that, empirical research shows that a significant number of subjects of coercive paternalistic psychiatric interventions do not express feelings of gratitude or consent-after-the-fact. Appeals to "real will" or "presumed will" suffer from inescapable subjective and speculative aspects, and the reference to "rational will" ultimately leads to circular reasoning. Finally, the appeal to self-binding is too restricted in order to succeed as a general moral justification of paternalism. It presupposes the expression of future-oriented consent of the subject to specific paternalistic actions. This issue will be addressed separately in a later paragraph.

Another type of moral justification of paternalistic (coercive) psychiatric treatment is not consent-based, but also refers to the moral principle of autonomy or self-determination. It is the argument which appeals to the preservation or enhancement of autonomy in order to justify paternalism. Although this line of moral reasoning certainly has force in case of children who have (still) partially developed capacities for autonomy (and paternalistic parental duties, in fact, are based on this consideration) there are several objections to this argument if it is applied to adult cases. There are two major objections. The first concerns the implication that in case there is no reason to believe that autonomy will be preserved or enhanced, the paternalistic intervention would be unjustified. This would mean that coercive actions toward incompetent persons that aim at preventing them from harming themselves, but do not preserve or enhance their autonomy, are unacceptable. Secondly, the argument opens the door to paternalistic actions toward competent persons if it is reasonable to believe that their already existing capacities for autonomy could be enhanced. Given that many people are not fully autonomous in an ideal sense, but nevertheless sufficiently autonomous to have a justified claim toward others that their self-regarding choices and actions are respected, this would imply a significant widening of the range of paternalistic interventions. In conclusion, preservation or enhancement of autonomy is neither a necessary nor a sufficient condition for the justification of paternalistic intervention.

A more promising line of moral argument for the justification of paternalistic psychiatric interventions is what can be coined the *balancing strategy*. Within this strategy a balance is sought between primary ethical values of respect for individual autonomy and self-determination and concern for the individual's well-being. Of central importance for this line of moral reasoning is the distinction between strong and weak paternalism. In cases of weak paternalism, the paternalist discharges the wishes, choices, or actions of the paternalized because the latter suffers (or is presumed to suffer) a defect, disturbance, or limitation of his decision-making capacity. Strong paternalism, on the other hand, involves interventions for the good of a person whose decision-making capacity is not disturbed or restricted. Strong paternalistic actions generally are not considered to be morally justified, because they involve an infringement of the freedom and autonomy of the person involved. Weak paternalistic actions may be morally justified if capacities for autonomous choice and action are restricted or disturbed and the subject risks harm to self. In these cases concerns for individual well-being gain greater weight.

It is now possible to briefly sketch the necessary elements for the justification of paternalistic psychiatric treatment. These are the following:

1. Risk of harm to self
2. Defect of decision-making capacity
3. Reasonable prospect of benefit for the person involved
4. Failure of alternative, morally less troublesome ways to benefit the person involved
5. Application of the least restrictive intervention(s) which may lead to the intended good for the person involved
6. Application of measures and goals which are most in line with (or least in conflict with) the known

values, attitudes, desires, and life plan of the person involved.

III. AUTONOMY, CAPACITY, AND COMPETENCE

Central in the moral justification of coercive treatment in psychiatry are the concepts of competence and decision-making capacity. How should these concepts be understood in the context of psychiatric care? Before addressing the issue of the assessment of decision making in practice, some preliminary points need to be mentioned.

Firstly, the fact that a person suffers from mental illness does not necessarily imply that he or she lacks decision-making capacity. Secondly, decision-making capacity as a moral concept cannot and should not be considered as a trait or characteristic of an individual person, but as an attribute which is attached to an individual with regard to a specific choice or action. It is contextual and relative to choices and actions.

A. Standards for Decision-Making Capacity

Regarding the standards for the assessment of decision-making capacity, different proposals have been made. Three broad standards or tests can be distinguished:

1. The simple ability to express a preference
2. Abilities to understand information, to appreciate one's situation, and to act on (rational) reasons
3. The ability to reach a reasonable decision or a reasonable outcome.

Implicit in all three standards are different conceptions of freedom and rationality. The first standard broadly distinguishes between people that totally lack the ability to express themselves (i.e., the unconscious, the permanently comatose, and severely mentally handicapped or demented patients) and others. In view of this standard we ought to respect choices and actions that are dangerous to persons and are based on false beliefs, a lack of relevant information, or imperative hallucinations, simply because of the fact that the person's choice or action is considered his or hers. On the other hand, the third standard places a heavy burden on the decisions and actions of persons. It rests on the fiction of some sort of ideal, hypothetical and disinterested, highly rational observer being able to make an objective and morally neutral calculus of the balance between goods and harms that are at stake in a particular decision or action. By focusing on the outcome of the decision-making process in terms of reasonableness or welfare maximation, this standard disregards the fact that decision-making capacity at least refers to a process of reasoning (the second standard). Given these considerations, from an ethical point of view some version of the second standard (or process standard) seems best fitted to serve as an adequate standard in the context of a balancing view.

This, however, does not imply that there is one single test to assess decision-making capacity in individual cases. The choice for a variable standard for the assessment of decision-making capacity—taking into account the relativity of capacity to the decision at hand—morally seems the best way to balance the interests of the patient (expressed in the moral principle of beneficence) and the rights of the patient (expressed in the moral principle of respect for autonomy). The application of a variable standard implies that in different situations and contexts different criteria for the assessment of decision making may be in place, taking into account differences with regard to the decisional capacities of the patient as well as regarding the interests that are at stake and morally relevant characteristics of the intervention which is considered.

B. Psychiatric Conditions Affecting Decision-Making Capacity

As already mentioned, it is important to recognize that suffering from mental illness does not automatically imply incompetence or lack of decision-making capacity. The relationship between mental illness and decision-making capacity is more complex. Assessing decision-making capacity is specific to the particular circumstances and individual characteristics of the mentally ill person. With regard to the latter, the type of mental illness may play a significant role. In order to illustrate this, the ways in which different psychiatric conditions may affect autonomy and decision-making capacity will be briefly discussed.

One example is paranoia. Although the practical reasoning of the paranoid person may be perfectly intact, the premises or presumptions on which his reasoning is based are deeply false. Although ultimately counterproductive, a paranoid delusion involves the withdrawal into a private world and the commitment to a private ideology in which it is impossible for the person to test her perceptions and inferences against anyone else's. In a comparable fashion a depressed person's reasoning and choice (i.e., a refusal of treatment) may

be based on a severely negative image of the self and the surrounding world. These negative thoughts may refer to the present, the future, or the past. Other examples of autonomy-subverting psychiatric conditions are compulsive hand washing and pathological gambling. Although the choices and actions resulting from such conditions cannot be considered unintentional, they are generally not what the person wants or prefers.

Particular psychiatric conditions thus may exert a controlling influence on the actions and choices of a person, making a person do or choose a course of action she does not want or prefer. They not only reduce autonomy, but leave a person no other choice than the one he or she makes, as is the case in a person who acts on the delusion of being a very bad person who needs eternal condemnation and punishment.

IV. SOME MORALLY RELEVANT CONSIDERATIONS REGARDING THE USE OF COERCION IN PSYCHIATRY

In this section, some further moral issues regarding coercive treatment in psychiatry are briefly discussed. First the issue of neurosurgical interventions for the treatment of mental illness is addressed. A second issue concerns coercive treatment in the community, and the third deals with the segregation between involuntary commitment and coercive treatment.

A. Neurosurgical Interventions

An issue which still attracts much attention is the use of organic therapies, particularly psychosurgery, or in contemporary language, neurosurgery for mental disorder. Introduced in 1935 by the Portuguese neurologist Egaz Moniz, "prefrontal leucotomy" (or lobotomy) became very popular in the 1940s and 1950s as a result of the work of the North American surgeons Walter Freeman and James Watts. The operation, involving the piercing of a hole in the skull in each temporal brain region through which a leucotomy knife was inserted and swept up and down in arc, was used mainly for institutionalized patients with a diagnosis of schizophrenia. It is estimated that by the mid 1950s some 50,000 operations had been carried out in the USA and some 10,500 in England and Wales. After growing evidence of adverse effects, including intellectual impairment, disinhibition, apathy, incontinence, obesity and epilepsy, and with the introduction of specific and effective psychopharmacological agents in the 1950s, there was a marked decline in the use of psychosurgery.

At present, as a result of the fact that not all mental disorders respond to psychopharmacological agents, there exist stereotactic neurosurgical procedures, combined with neuroimaging techniques, that produce a more limited lesion in the brain and avoid the disabling effects of the earlier procedures. Also, the indications for neurosurgery for mental disorders are limited, e.g., intractable obsessive compulsive disorder and major depressive illness, although there are relatively recent examples of the use of neurosurgery for the treatment of humans with deviant sexual behavior in the former Federal Republic of Germany, which is considered dubious on scientific, clinical, and ethical grounds (G. Schmidt and E. Schorsch, 1981. *Arch. Sexual Behav.* **10**(3), 301–323).

Is it ever justified to apply such an irreversible and invasive organic therapy against the will of the patient, i.e., as coercive psychiatric treatment? In order to answer this question it is necessary to take a closer look at this type of intervention. What are the morally relevant characteristics? Firstly, it is an irreversible intervention. Although small brain areas generally are involved and destroyed, it is necessary to consider that there is no way back from the surgery. The coagulated brain cells cannot be restored to function. Secondly, neurosurgery may involve an irreversible change of the personality of the patient. Opponents of the application of neurosurgery for mental disorder have argued that it is questionable whether patients considered for this form of treatment ever are able to give their free and informed consent. They argue that because of the severity of their mental disorder the consent is illusory—which raises doubts about their decision-making capacity—and, apart from that, that it is questionable whether any person can give morally valid consent to an intervention which may lead to irreversible personality changes.

Counter to the first claim, it can be argued that decision-making capacity does not depend on the severity of the disturbance or psychopathology of the patient, although it is known that professionals in mental health care generally tend to assume such a direct and reverse relationship between capacity and severity of mental illness. Contrary to the second argument, it can be argued that there are other situations in which society does not object to the choice of a person to become "different" or "someone else." In the context of severe and debilitating suffering which may have persisted for many years in the absence of effective treatment, it can be reasonable that a person consents to neurosurgery in the face of possible personality changes because this is weighed against the possible benefits of treatment.

Nevertheless, the issue of coercive neurosurgical treatment remains. In the light of the earlier mentioned morally relevant features of neurosurgery, it is doubtful whether it is ethically justifiable to operate against the wishes of the patient. In case the patient is considered competent to refuse treatment (based on the application of the aforementioned variable standard), this refusal ought to be respected. In case of a refusing patient who lacks decision-making capacity, coercive neurosurgical treatment could possibly be justified in cases of last resort, if this is the only means to lessen severe and enduring suffering of the patient.

B. Coercive Treatment in the Community

An important topic of debate with regard to the limits of coercive treatment in psychiatry concerns the acceptability of coercive treatment of mentally ill patients staying in the community. Traditionally coercive treatment has been limited to the confines of psychiatric clinics and mental hospitals.

With the growing availability of effective treatment for chronic mental illnesses such as schizophrenia and affective disorders, in industrialized countries a move toward deinstitutionalization and community mental health treatment developed. Since the 1960s this has led in the United States to significantly shorter lengths of stay in mental hospitals resulting in a 75% reduction in inpatient censuses in public mental hospitals. Because of the fact that a large part of the proposed community facilities were never created, and because a significant number of the discharged chronically ill patients continued to be unwilling to accept treatment voluntarily, the so-called revolving door patient became visible as a by-product of mental health reform. This was reinforced—not only in the United States, but also in other western countries—by the reform of commitment laws designed to limit the use of involuntary hospitalization and to protect the mentally ill against psychiatric power.

These developments have led to debates concerning the introduction of coercive treatment of mentally ill people staying in the community. The morally troubling issue is that some mentally ill persons who could, with supervision and treatment, cope in the community in a number of jurisdictions may be left to deteriorate until they—if ever—become a serious danger to themselves and/or others. Some commentators take the view that this has resulted in great harm and avoidable deterioration in patients who lack insight into their condition. Another consequence is that clinically committed civil or criminally insane patients stay longer than medically necessary in the mental hospital.

In the debate regarding coercive treatment of mentally ill people in the community, three types of such treatment can be distinguished:

1. Conditional release from clinical commitment
2. Substitute for clinical commitment
3. Prevention of involuntary commitment to a hospital (preventive outpatient commitment)

The third type of coercive community treatment, preventive outpatient commitment, is the most controversial. The goal of preventive outpatient commitment is to intervene at an early stage in order to prevent further deterioration of a mentally ill person's condition. It is a form of psychiatric coercion in which the state intervenes by requiring a mentally ill person to receive psychiatric treatment before the person's mental illness deteriorates to the point that inpatient hospitalization is required and the usual commitment criteria are met. Thus, a logical implication of preventive outpatient commitment is the lowering of commitment criteria (Miller, 1991). There is not a strict dangerousness criterion, but broader "need for treatment" criteria, as, for instance, in the state of North Carolina, where the outpatient commitment statute requires that mental illness must be present, that the person is in need of psychiatric treatment, that deterioration of that mental illness will inevitably occur (ultimately leading to inpatient civil commitment), and that the mental illness is preventing the person from voluntarily seeking psychiatric care.

Critics oppose this broadening of commitment criteria, and also criticize the assessment of inevitable deterioration. From a moral point of view, however, some broadening of commitment criteria is not necessarily unjustified in the light of the possible benefits involved for the patient. If a patient has insufficient capacity to refuse beneficial treatment, it can be defensible to use coercion if there is risk of harm, even if this harm does not involve the person's life being at stake.

The problems regarding the assessment of "inevitable deterioration" are comparable to the issue of the dangerousness prediction by psychiatrists. The capacity of psychiatrists to reliably predict dangerousness has been challenged for many years. Many reviews have emphasized both the poor success rate of predictions and the false-positive problem in predicting any phenomenon with a low base rate. Nevertheless, in practice psychiatrists are asked to make such predictions which may result in the compulsory commitment of citizens. If prediction of inevitable deterioration is difficult, what type of evidence might be used? One, and possibly the best, type of evidence seems to be past history and experience. If predictions of deterioration are operationalized by requiring evidence of prior deterioration which required rehospitalization, criticism based on the alleged inability of clinicians to predict anything and fears that outpatient commitment will be used (and even abused) indiscriminately can be minimized.

C. Segregation of Involuntary Commitment and Coercive Treatment

As already discussed, the harm principle justifies liberty-limiting interventions which aim at the prevention of harm to others. A refusal of treatment cannot be overruled unless the principle of paternalism also can be invoked.

In some jurisdictions this has led to the segregation of involuntary commitment on the one hand and coercive treatment on the other. This segregation may involve that a person is compulsorily admitted to a mental institution and deprived of his liberty because of the danger he poses to himself or others, but he cannot be coercively treated because in the institution he is not dangerous and/or he competently refuses treatment. This can lead to a moral dilemma: a person who is treatable and committed cannot receive proper treatment which may be of benefit to the mental disturbance that caused the danger which initially led to the commitment.

In order to provide a way out of this possible dilemma it has been proposed to link decisions to commit and to coercively treat a mentally ill patient. In this proposal, treatability—and not danger to self or others—would become a central justification for involuntary commitment, and the underlying rationale for committing people should be to treat them to avert their suffering serious deterioration.

Although this proposal has appealing features, it also raises a number of questions, not the least of which is the issue of how to conceptualize and operationalize the criterion of treatability. It certainly deserves further debate.

V. PRIOR CONSENT TO COERCION: THE PSYCHIATRIC ADVANCE DIRECTIVE

Advance treatment planning for mental illness is one of the issues of debate in contemporary psychiatry. As is well known, there is a number of mental illnesses that have certain periodic features. The most prominent are the manic-depressive psychoses, but we can also think of young chronic schizophrenics.

People who suffer from manic depression often can benefit from treatment and live a life that can be in many respects satisfying. However, even if the patient complies with the necessary lithium medication, a breakthrough of a manic condition cannot always be prevented. It is also a well-known fact that sometimes these patients stop their medication, and that by doing so a manic condition can be triggered.

In such cases, some of these patients refuse treatment or supervision because they lack insight into their actual condition. They think there is nothing wrong with them and have the opinion that not they, but the people around them are acting crazy. They undertake actions that are harmful to themselves or to people in their environment. For instance, they may be extremely insultive to their neighbors, act sexually disinhibited, or embark on unresponsible financial transactions. If not in the short run then in the long run this behavior may be extremely destructive for individual self-esteem, private and social relations, employment, etc. However, in a number of cases the patient does not meet the legal criteria for involuntary commitment or coercive treatment. His or her actions may be harmful, but not (extremely) dangerous to himself or others.

Through the use of psychiatric advance directives, it would be possible for mentally ill persons who are competent and with their disease in remission to give prior consent to treatment at a later time when they are incompetent, have become noncompliant, and are refusing treatment. This prior consent justifies the paternalistic overruling of current wishes of the patient. Obviously, in order to guarantee patient rights it is necessary to apply certain procedural safeguards against misuse and abuse of psychiatric advance directives. But ultimately respecting prior competent wishes, even if this goes against the current wishes of the patient, may be a just way of balancing the moral principles of respect for autonomy and beneficence.

VI. IN CONCLUSION

Coercive treatment in psychiatry is a complex issue raising a number of medical, legal, ethical, and policy questions. Societal developments have led to a strong emphasis on the moral principle of respect for the au-

tonomy of persons. The mentally ill have been given liberty rights which have traditionally failed them under the guise of paternalistic psychiatric beneficence. In a number of jurisdictions this has led to a right of mentally ill people to refuse treatment. Recognizing a "right to be left alone" may be devaluated to a "right to rot" if communities and mental health professionals use this liberal principle to legitimate indifference and lack of compassion. On the other hand, psychiatric coercion, although generally motivated by good intentions, involves *prima facie* a morally offensive action. In particular in mental health care, interventions may deeply intrude into the physical and mental integrity of the subject. In these cases moral reasons reaching beyond the presumed best interest or benefit of the patient are needed to provide an ethical justification of coercive treatment.

Also See the Following Articles

ADVANCE DIRECTIVES • AUTONOMY • PSYCHIATRIC ETHICS

Bibliography

Adler, N., and Gluzman, S. (1993). Soviet special psychiatric hospitals. Where the system was criminal and the inmates were sane. *British Journal of Psychiatry,* 163, 713–720.

Brock, D. (1993). A proposal for the use of advance directives in the treatment of incompetent mentally ill persons. *Bioethics,* 7, 247–256.

Buchanan, A. E., and Brock, D. (1989). "Deciding for Others. The Ethics of Surrogate Decision Making." Cambridge Univ. Press, Cambridge, UK.

DeGrazia, D. (1994). Autonomous action and autonomy-subverting psychiatric conditions. *The Journal of Medicine and Philosophy,* 19, 279–297.

Foucault, M. (1961). "Folie et deraison. Histoire de la folie a l'age classique." Plon, Paris; (1973). Madness and Civilization: A History of Insanity in the Age of Reason." Random House, New York.

Fulford, K. W. M. (1989). "Moral Theory and Medical Practice." Cambridge Univ. Press, Cambridge, UK.

Haworth, L. (1986). "Autonomy. An Essay in Philosophical Psychology and Ethics." Yale Univ. Press, New Haven/London.

Kleinig, J. (1984). "Paternalism." Rowman and Allanheld, Totowa, NJ.

Kligman, M., and Culver, C. (1992). An analysis of interpersonal manipulation. *The Journal of Medicine and Philosophy,* 17, 173–197.

Lavin, M. (1995). Who should be committable? *Philosophy, Psychiatry & Psychology,* 2(1), 35–47.

Miller, R. (1991). The ethics of involuntary commitment to mental health treatment. In "Psychiatric Ethics" (S. Bloch and P. Chodoff, Eds.), 2nd ed., pp. 265–289. Oxford Univ. Press, Oxford.

VanDeVeer, D. (1986). "Paternalistic Intervention. The Moral Bounds on Benevolence." Princeton Univ. Press, Princeton, NJ.

COLLECTIVE GUILT

Gregory Mellema
Calvin College

I. Collective Guilt and Moral Responsibility
II. Collective Guilt and Moral Taint
III. Collective Guilt in Existentialist Thought
IV. Collective Guilt and Contemporary Society

GLOSSARY

collective guilt The guilt attaching to a collective group for a harm for which the collective is either responsible or for which the collective is tainted due to the wrongdoing of a moral agent or agents outside the collective.

collective responsibility Responsibility for a state of affairs borne by a collective consisting of two or more moral agents.

metaphysical guilt A term coined by Karl Jaspers to describe a collective guilt based upon the idea that a person's identity is shaped by the group, that choices of people affect others in the group, and that guilt is produced as a result of this process.

moral taint That which results from the transferring of the contagion of an agent's moral wrongdoing to others who are connected to this agent.

original sin The sin committed by Adam, the first man, for which the entire human race is allegedly held accountable.

shared responsibility Responsibility for the same state of affairs borne by two or more moral agents.

stain A term employed by Paul Ricoeur for moral taint.

COLLECTIVE GUILT attaches to a group consisting of moral agents as the result of the group bearing moral responsibility for a harm which has occurred. Collective guilt can also attach to a group of those who are tainted by others bearing moral responsibility for a harm. Typically, the collective to which the guilt attaches will subsequently experience guilt for this harm. Suppose several students from the same high school bear collective responsibility for murdering a victim, and they subsequently feel guilt for this state of affairs. Their guilt may be described as a collective guilt. However, those who are tainted by these actions, such as other students from the same high school, may also experience feelings of guilt for this harm. If so, they likewise experience collective guilt.

Two features of this account are noteworthy. First, although guilt is typically experienced when collective guilt attaches to a group, one need not have the experience of guilt in order to be a member of such a collective. And even if the members of such a collective experience guilt, this is not to say that they must be aware of experiencing guilt. The possibility is left open that they experience guilt in a less than fully conscious manner. Furthermore, the guilt experienced by those to whom collective guilt attaches is typically not a sense of personal guilt for a harm. Second, collective guilt is always relative to a harm which has in fact occurred. Those who attempt to bring about a harm and fail do not bear collective guilt for this harm, for it does not occur, though they can bear collective guilt for attempting to produce the harm, for this state of affairs does occur.

In addition, at any given time a person might belong to various collectives which are collectively guilty for various states of affairs.

Collective guilt cannot attach to those who neither belong to a collective responsible for a harm nor are tainted by the actions of those who do belong to such a collective. Such people are sufficiently remote from the harm that guilt fails to attach to the collective to which they belong. Accordingly, feelings of guilt are not reasonable or appropriate in this type of context. Of course, people can have feelings of guilt which are unreasonable. But some connection must exist between these people and those responsible for the harm for them to share in the collective guilt and for their feelings of guilt to have a legitimate basis.

There is a great deal of controversy over what this connection consists in. Some have maintained that collective guilt for the sin of Adam, the first man, extends to the entire human race. The Doctrine of Original Sin, as it is sometimes called, teaches that all human beings have in some manner sinned through Adam and have come to bear guilt for the sin which caused evil to enter the world. The collective which is guilty for the fall from Paradise, then, is judged to be all human persons, past, present, and future. All of humanity is said to bear collective guilt for what Adam did in the Garden of Eden.

Two questions are raised by the assertion that all of us bear collective guilt for Adam's sin. First, to what degree do people experience guilt for this sin? Although the experience of guilt is not a necessary condition for membership in a collective which bears guilt, it is plausible to suppose that at least some people will experience guilt for Adam's sin if the doctrine of Original Sin is a true doctrine. No doubt some people will attest that the guilt they experience for this sin is real, but there will certainly be others who deny the experience of guilt for this sin. Regarding this latter group, one who supports the notion of collective guilt for Adam's sins may wish to argue that the experience of guilt in certain people is less than fully conscious.

A second question is this: What connection exists between the sin of Adam and others of the human race? For collective guilt to occur, members of the human race must at least be tainted by the sin of Adam. How, then, does this take place? Theologians who have attempted to answer this question have produced accounts of this connection which are not always easy to comprehend, and it is safe to say that the Doctrine of Original Sin is a notion which remains controversial.

Other Biblical accounts also seem to embody cases of collective guilt which rely on the tainting of many people as the result of one person's sin. In the book of Joshua a man named Achan returns from a battle with possessions of those who have been conquered, in spite of having been forbidden to take them. Achan returns to his tent and buries these possessions in a hole. When he is discovered to have done this, Achan is put to death. But members of his extended family are likewise put to death. Here many will be inclined to raise questions about the severity of the punishment. But for present purposes, the point of this account is that it is an example of being tainted by the wrongdoing of those to whom we are related by birth.

I. COLLECTIVE GUILT AND MORAL RESPONSIBILITY

One of the ways guilt attaches to a collective is when a collective bears responsibility for a harm which has occurred. In the literature there are two primary ways in which collective responsibility is characterized. First, collective responsibility is sometimes characterized as the sharing of responsibility for the same state of affairs by two or more individuals. Second, collective responsibility is sometimes characterized as the view that a nonhuman entity, a collective which is composed of human beings, bears responsibility for a state of affairs. The primary difference between these two notions is that an individual who does not bear responsibility for a state of affairs cannot be a member of a collective bearing responsibility for this state of affairs in the first sense, but it is possible for this individual to be a member of a collective bearing responsibility for it in the second sense.

The first conception of collective responsibility can be illustrated by a case in which several people deface a public building by spraying graffiti on it. Each person bears moral responsibility for a common state of affairs, the defacing of the building, and hence they share responsibility for this state of affairs. Individuals who share responsibility for a harm do not always bear the same degree of responsibility for the harm. But when this type of collective responsibility occurs, each member of the collective bears at least some degree of responsibility. Consequently, the members of the collective bear collective guilt as the result of their participation.

The second conception of collective responsibility can be illustrated by a variation of the same example. Here the members of an established gang deface a public building by spraying graffiti on it. But in this example not all of the members participate in the activity. Some members spray the building, others offer words of encouragement to those spraying the building, and others simply stand and watch. Of those who stand and watch, some secretly wish that the others would stop spraying graffiti and find something else to do of a less destructive nature. However, they do not express this wish, for they do not want to risk being expelled from the gang.

In this example it is plausible to judge that the members of the gang form a collective which bears moral responsibility for the defacing of the building. But the responsibility of the collective does not automatically distribute to all of its members, as in the case of shared responsibility. Here those members of the gang who wish that the others would stop defacing the building arguably do not bear responsibility as individuals for the defacing, for they wish that the building not be defaced. If so, then the gang could be divided into those who bear individual responsibility for the defacing of the building and those who do not. But all the members of the gang still belong to a collective which bears moral responsibility for the defacing of the building (since those who wish that the others not deface the building are members of this collective as long as they do not in any manner express dissent to the actions of fellow gang members).

The collective which bears moral responsibility is not itself a human being, but it is composed of human beings. Of the human beings who compose it, some bear responsibility for the defacing of the building and some do not. Unlike shared responsibility, the responsibility of a collective does not invariably distribute to all of its component members. But the members can nevertheless constitute a group which bears collective guilt.

Some philosophers have held that a collective can bear moral responsibility for a state of affairs even if no member of the collective bears responsibility for the same state of affairs. D. E. Cooper proposes the example of a club which closes due to lack of *esprit de corps* among its members. He argues that the members are collectively responsible for the closing, but no individual member need bear responsibility for the closing. If cases such as this are possible, and there is considerable dispute as to whether or not they are, then collective guilt is likewise possible in situations where no member of the collective is responsible for the harm producing the guilt. Then several people could bear collective guilt for a harm for which none of them bears individual moral responsibility.

Those who support the notion of collective responsibility are far more inclined to countenance cases in which at least one member of the collective bears responsibility for the outcome for which the collective itself bears responsibility. Consider the collective of German citizens during the second world war. It has often been claimed that the German people were collectively responsible for the occurrence of the Holocaust. The vase majority of German citizens played no role in the events which led to the deaths of countless Jews, and hence they do not bear responsibility as individuals for the Holocaust. But various Nazi officials bear responsibility as individuals for the Holocaust as the result of their individual contributions to the events of the Holocaust. Accordingly, the collective of German citizens consists of some who bear responsibility and others who do not. The same is presumably true of those German citizens who experience collective guilt for the Holocaust: some but not all bear individual responsibility for it.

II. COLLECTIVE GUILT AND MORAL TAINT

The other way that a collective comes to experience collective guilt is through being morally tainted by those who bear moral responsibility for a harm. Moral taint results when harm is produced by a certain person or group of persons, and the contagion of their wrongdoing is transferred to others who have had no involvement in bringing about the harm. Those German citizens who played no role in the events of the Holocaust were tainted by the wrongful actions of the Nazi officials who were involved in these events. These German citizens bear no moral responsibility for the events of the Holocaust, but, because they are tainted by the actions of the Nazi officers, they are in a position to experience and bear collective guilt.

Anthony Appiah has led the way in philosophical circles in explicating this concept (his account is similar to an account of moral stain offered by Paul Ricoeur, but it is considerably clearer). According to his account, a person who is tainted by the wrongdoing of another moral agent experiences a loss of moral integrity. When a person who happens to have some connection to us produces harm, then our own moral integrity can be affected. Appiah applies moral taint to an understanding of the issue of divesting shares of stock in companies doing business in South Africa in the 1980s. A shareholder in such companies was not in any manner responsible for the harmful effects of apartheid, but he or she was nevertheless tainted by those practicing apartheid. Consequently, shareholders in these companies experienced a loss of moral integrity.

Appiah believes that a feeling of shame is appropriate when one is tainted by the wrongful acts of others. Feeling a personal sense of guilt is not appropriate to the situation, for one has no personal involvement. But the appropriateness of a feeling of shame makes possible collective guilt. Because I and several others feel shame over the wrongful actions of one to whom we are connected, the possibility exists that collective guilt attaches to us. Of course, it is not a foregone conclusion that collective guilt attaches to people whenever they are tainted by the wrongful actions of another. Frequently people feel neither shame when they are tainted nor a sense of collective guilt. But the presence of taint is a condition which makes collective guilt possible.

From this it follows that experiencing a sense of collective guilt is not the same as experiencing a personal sense of guilt. Those holding shares of stock in firms doing business in South Africa need not feel a personal sense of guilt for the harmful effects of apartheid, but they can experience collective guilt. If they experience guilt at all with respect to apartheid, the guilt appropriate for them to experience is collective in nature. And the type of guilt appropriate for those German citizens who experience guilt as the result of being tainted by the harmful actions of Nazi officials is collective guilt.

III. COLLECTIVE GUILT IN EXISTENTIALIST THOUGHT

In his book, *Sharing Responsibility*, Larry May argues that 20th century existentialist thought can shed much light on questions connected with moral responsibility and moral taint. The understanding of the concept of responsibility in 20th century existentialist thought is shaped largely by the writings of philosophers such as Jean-Paul Sartre, Karl Jaspers, and Hannah Arendt. Writing in the years immediately following the second world war, they tried to come to terms with the widespread failure of their fellow citizens to prevent the horrible actions of the Nazis. May notes that they turned to existentialist thought in an effort to explain this profound failure, and they likewise appealed to the resources of existentialist thought to design an adequate theory of responsibility. To their way of thinking, an adequate theory of responsibility is marked by its ability to take seriously society and the problems which afflict it.

Inspired by this tradition, May develops an existentialist approach to questions of group or collective responsibility. His approach is built upon the notion that groups have a very powerful influence over their members, and specifically over their attitudes and behavior. As the result of belonging to the group, one's personal values undergo a transformation; people belonging to groups discover that the members influence and transform the values of one another. And along with this sharing of attitudes and values comes a sharing of responsibility for group actions. May argues that belonging to groups also tends to make people insensitive to certain harms in such a way that they come to share responsibility for these harms.

Sometimes groups are responsible for inaction. May refers to situations in which the members make a decision not to act as a collective omission. There are also cases in which people with the ability to form a group to prevent a harm from occurring fail to act, and he refers to this phenomenon as collective inaction. These putative groups can frequently be judged collectively responsible for their inaction, or even for the harms they fail to prevent. The members of these putative groups are not necessarily guilty for their inaction or for these harms; it is more appropriate for them to feel shame for their inaction or collective guilt for these harms. May emphasizes that there is the potential for great social good when people seek solutions of a collective nature, since groups are far more likely than individuals to be able to prevent significant harms from occurring.

May's discussion is intended to push to the limit how we ought to think of agency and responsibility. People who are the products of Western culture tend to think of agency in individualist terms and to think of responsibility as set at a very modest level, and May is attempting to challenge these ways of thinking. He quotes Hannah Arendt as stating, "This taking upon ourselves the consequences for things we are entirely innocent of, is the price we pay for the fact that we live our lives not by ourselves but ... [within] a human community." This statement provides a basis for understanding why the German people feel shame and a sense of collective guilt for the actions of Nazi officials. Because we live in a human community, Arendt believes that there is a sense in which we take upon ourselves the consequences of the harmful acts of others. Although the German people were entirely innocent of the actions of the Nazi officials, existentialists such as Arendt can help us to understand why they experience collective guilt.

Another existentialist writer who has much to say about guilt in the context of groups or collectives is Karl Jaspers. Jaspers's discussion is framed in terms of a particular type of guilt known as metaphysical guilt, and, although he does not offer a precise definition of this notion, it is quite evident on the basis of what he says that this notion is related to the notion of taint.

Consider these words from his book, *The Question of German Guilt:*

> There exists a solidarity among men as human beings that makes each co-responsible for every wrong and every injustice in the world, especially for crimes committed in his presence or with his knowledge. If I fail to do whatever I can to prevent them, I too am guilty.... That I live after such a thing has happened weighs upon me as an indelible guilt. (1961. Translated by A. B. Ashton. p. 36. Capricorn Books, New York)

Jaspers speaks here about a type of guilt which is neither legal, political, nor moral. He describes it as a guilt which attaches to people for failing to prevent wrongs and injustices in the world. And the expectations for them to prevent these wrongs and injustices is high. Even if they must risk their lives to prevent injustices, the failure to do so weighs upon them in the form of guilt which is indelible.

In this passage Jaspers also makes a startling statement that human beings are "co-responsible" for every wrong and injustice in the world. People are first and foremost coresponsible for wrongs and injustices that are known to them. However, to a certain extent they are coresponsible for *all* wrongs and injustices in the world. Commenting upon this passage, May states that Jaspers comes dangerously close to stating that each member of the human race shares responsibility for all of the world's harms.

Two important ideas underlie the notion of metaphysical guilt in Jaspers. The first is that a person bears metaphysical guilt only through being a member of a group or groups. An important element of Jaspers's thought is that people's identities are shaped partly through their group memberships. Who they are is shaped in part through the various groups to which they belong. For this reason it makes sense from an existentialist point of view to judge that some people in a group are implicated by the actions of others in the group.

But there is more to metaphysical guilt than membership in groups. The second important element of metaphysical guilt is that individuals make choices regarding the behavior of others in their groups. If others in one's group are causing harms, then one must make a choice whether to act to prevent the harms, at least to indicate disapproval of the harmful behavior, or to do nothing. If one does nothing, then one has failed to distance onself from these harms, and metaphysical guilt will attach to one who fails to distance oneself from these harms.

Choosing whether or not to distance oneself from the harms which others in one's group are causing is also closely connected to one's identity as a person. In a real sense one is choosing who to be when one makes this choice. Metaphysical guilt in this manner is not only based upon one's actions, but it is based upon the concept of choosing to be a person of a certain type. If a person chooses silence when others are perpetuating harms, then the person's choice of silence is the choice to be a certain kind of person. This type of choice is a crucial part of what enters into how Jaspers conceives of metaphysical guilt.

It is different with moral guilt. There are situations in which one incurs both moral and metaphysical guilt by choosing silence when others are perpetuating harms. But it is possible for one to incur metaphysical guilt without incurring moral guilt. Sometimes the only way to prevent or speak out against certain harms is to risk one's life; these cases are of special interest to Jaspers. One who chooses silence in these cases incurs metaphysical guilt, as has already been seen. But Jaspers seems to believe that it would be a mistake to judge that one incurs moral guilt as well in situations of this type. Although metaphysical guilt and moral guilt are frequently incurred jointly, they are not always.

It is a consequence of these ideas that Jaspers views moral guilt quite differently from moral responsibility. Moral guilt is not necessarily borne by people who choose silence in the face of harms, but responsibility (or, more precisely, coresponsibility) for every wrong or injustice in the world is shared by everyone who fails to speak out against them. Thus, there are presumably many instances in which one's silence renders one responsible for harms brought about by others, even though one does not bear moral guilt for these harms. In the end, it is not clear to what extent responsibility is comparable to metaphysical guilt in Jaspers's thought, but responsibility is definitely broader than moral guilt.

In May's opinion, shame or taint are the moral concepts which come closest to metaphysical guilt. When someone bears metaphysical guilt because of wrongs committed by others, it seems that one can likewise describe the situation as one in which the moral agent is tainted by this wrongdoing. Of course, Appiah denies that taint involves guilt, but it is moral guilt that Appiah has in mind in making this denial. Metaphysical guilt, by contrast, seems to attach to people in the scheme of Jaspers in the very sorts of cases where Appiah would postulate the appearance of taint.

Jaspers's notion of metaphysical guilt is not, however, exactly the same as what Appiah describes as taint. As pointed out already, metaphysical guilt is also bound up with the matter of choosing one's identity. One's choice of whether to distance oneself from the harmful acts of others is partly a choice of who one is. Whether one comes to bear metaphysical guilt in Jaspers's scheme is partly a matter of one's relationship with other moral agents and partly a matter of what one has done in terms of choosing an identity. Taint is characterized by Appiah in terms of one's relationship with other moral agents, and, regarding the choosing of one's identity, his account has nothing to say. This is not to say that the choice of one's identity is completely irrelevant on Appiah's account; by choosing to be a certain kind of person one will take actions which may preclude one's being tainted. But whatever relevance we can find here is only incidental; by contrast, it appears to be essential to Jaspers's understanding of metaphysical guilt.

May's preference is to think of taint along the lines of what Jaspers suggests. He agrees that Appiah is correct to think that taint is the right concept to employ in cases where people react with silence to the harmful acts of others with whom they are associated. But it is preferable to take into account the question of who one is. The optimal way of understanding taint is that it is determined not only by what one does but also by who one chooses to be.

Appiah describes a case in which one of the co-owners of a store is carrying a box of knives up the stairs from the storeroom while the other co-owner is about to sell a knife to a youth who, they both know, plans to use the newly purchased knife for murder. The co-owner coming up the stairs knows that if he hurries, his partner will sell the youth a knife from the new box; otherwise, his partner will select one from the top shelf. Appiah believes that the partner is tainted by the stabbing if and only if the knife used in the stabbing comes from this box. Hence, on Appiah's view, if he delays in coming up the stairs he escapes taint.

But there is more to the story from the perspective of Jaspers. Suppose the partner decides to bring the box up at once, but he does not do so because the telephone begins to ring. Although the partner's choice to bring the box up at once does not result in his actually doing so, he does make a choice. This may appear to be a trivial choice, but those in the existentialist tradition have repeatedly urged that choices such as this are choices of who one is. The partner is choosing to be a certain kind of person, the kind of person willing to be connected with a stabbing. For this reason a follower of Jaspers will argue that the choice itself is enough to taint the partner. Regardless of whether he follows through on his choice, he is nevertheless tainted.

The view one takes about examples of this type has large implications for collective guilt. For, once again, collective guilt presupposes collective responsibility or moral taint. If one neither belongs to a collective responsible for a harm nor is tainted by the harmful acts of another, then no reason exists for ascribing collective guilt. If the youth murders a person with his newly purchased knife, then if the knife was not from the new box, the co-owner is not tainted by the murder (in Appiah's view), and there is no reason for the co-owner to experience collective guilt.

IV. COLLECTIVE GUILT AND CONTEMPORARY SOCIETY

People frequently express the judgment that groups or collectives are guilty for what has taken place or for what has failed to take place. In debates on abortion, for example, those holding a prolife position sometimes judge that society bears collective guilt for the occurrence of legal abortions. It is sometimes maintained that all human beings bear collective guilt for the atrocities of war which occurred in places such as Bosnia. And the dramatic rise in violent crimes committed by teenagers and preteenagers is another area in which society might be said to bear collective guilt.

On the basis of the foregoing discussion, it is dubious that society as a whole bears collective guilt for abortion, civil warfare in other nations, or a rise in crime, for it is unlikely that all members of society are connected to these states of affairs either by taint or by collective responsibility. Moreover, it is sometimes a matter of controversy whether the alleged harms (such as legal abortions) are in fact harms.

Nevertheless, ascriptions of collective guilt for problems in contemporary society are important to take seriously. For although they are sometime exaggerated, they frequently contain a core element of truth. Many people in our society are closely enough connected to the problem of teenage violent crime to warrant membership in the collective which experiences guilt. Thus, although society as a whole does not warrant membership in this collective, a sizable segment of society arguably does. And an additional segment of society no doubt is connected to the crimes committed by teenagers through taint.

As May indicates, many of society's problems can be adequately addressed only when the collective nature of responsibility for these problems is acknowledged. Accordingly, the collective guilt experienced by those collectively responsible for or tainted by these harms serves as a motivator to undertake solutions for these problems.

This line of thinking suggests that collective guilt has the potential for playing a very positive role in contemporary society. While the term "collective guilt" often suggests something negative or even sinister in human life, there is clearly a positive dimension to the role it plays in the life of a community. As a community we can band together to find solutions to the problems that we and others experience. On an individual level, the experience of guilt can motivate a person to actions of a positive nature. But the effectiveness of an individual's solutions to the problems of society is limited. Collective guilt, by contrast, has the potential for motivating an entire group to undertake the solutions of societal problems on a large scale.

There are problems of a practical nature which arise when a group undertakes to solve the problems of society. Perhaps the greatest challenge lies in the initial organization of a group of individuals into a unit which can undertake to solve these problems. But the presence of collective guilt is a factor which makes this organization more manageable than otherwise, for it motivates individuals to desire to participate in groups which can find solutions to these problems.

Collective guilt also has the potential for leading a group of individuals to a greater self-understanding. The experience of guilt can function to shake a group out of its complacency, force it to concentrate upon a harm which has occurred, and take a new look at itself and its relationship with the harm. The collective guilt experienced by the German citizens for the events of the Holocaust led these citizens to ask questions about themselves and their relationship with these events

which they would not have been motivated to ask in the absence of collective guilt. In the end they achieved a greater understanding about themselves and about human nature in general.

In some cases collective guilt has the potential for playing a type of purifying role in the consciousness of a group. When the group confronts the feelings of collective guilt and examines its relationship to the harm which has given rise to the experience of collective guilt, there is an opportunity to give expression to feelings of regret or remorse for the events associated with the harm. Depending upon the precise circumstances, this process could reasonably be regarded as a type of purifying process. Collective guilt resulting from the phenomenon of moral taint is perhaps not the type of collective guilt for which this designation would be appropriate. But when collective guilt results from a situation in which a group bears collective moral responsibility for harm, there is reason for the members of the group to express feelings of regret or remorse, and this can result in the consciousness of the group undergoing a process of purification.

Bibliography

Appiah, A. (1987). Racism and moral pollution. *The Philosophical Forum* 18, pp. 185–202.

Arendt, H. (1987). Collective responsibility. In "Amor Mundi (J. W. Bernauer, Ed.), p. 50. Martinus Nijhoff, Dordrecht.

Cooper, D. E. (1968). Collective responsibility. *Philosophy* 43, pp. 258–268.

French, P. (1992). "Responsiblity Matters." Univ. Press of Kansas, Lawrence, KS.

Jaspers, K. (1961). "The Question of German Guilt, translated by A. B. Ashton. Capricorn Books, New York.

May, L. (1992). "Sharing Responsibility." Univ. of Chicago Press, Chicago.

May, L. (1987). "The Morality of Groups." Univ. of Notre Dame Press, Notre Dame, IN.

Morris, H. (1976). "On Guilt and Innocence." Univ. of California Press, Berkeley.

Ricoeur, P. (1967). "The Symbolism of Evil," pp. 8–9, 35–37. Harper & Row, New York.

COMMUNITARIANISM

J. Donald Moon
Wesleyan University

GLOSSARY

civic republicanism A tradition of political theory opposed to monarchical rule, advocating a form of rule in which citizens participate in deliberation regarding the common good. In much of the republican tradition, the stability of the polity depends upon the virtue of the citizens, particularly their willingness to put the common good over their private ends, their courage in defending the state, and their capacity for wisdom and good judgment. Because not everyone had or could have such virtues, classical republicans tended to restrict citizenship to those who had (or were presumed to have) those virtues, notably propertied males.

common good A value or end shared by members of a collectivity. For some, the common good is merely aggregative, the sum of the goods of individuals. For others, the common good is the good of a group considered as a collectivity.

conception of the good A general term denoting one's understanding of the standards and values that make a life worthy and fulfilling. Related terms include the human good, conditions of human flourishing, and ideals of excellence.

liberalism A tradition of political theory including Locke, Kant, Bentham, Constant, Mill, Dewey, and Rawls. Although internally diverse, the core commitments of liberalism include the moral equality of all people, constitutional and limited government, a secular basis for political authority, and the primacy of values such as freedom, justice, and representative democracy. While acknowledging that the state must play crucial roles, liberals are committed to a social order in which important activities (such as religious worship, family life, cultural affairs, economic production and consumption, and education) are organized through the voluntary association of individuals and groups, rather than being authoritatively controlled or coordinated through the state. "Liberalism" in this sense should not be identified with "liberalism" as used in American politics today.

COMMUNITARIANISM as a self-consciously formulated political doctrine has emerged only in the past 20 years, while "community" has been a core value for virtually all political theorists since systematic reflection on political life began. In the past theorists took the importance of community for granted, focusing on the kind of community that would promote human flourishing. But with the decline of face to face communities and the rise of individualism in modern, complex societies, the very existence of community has come to be a major concern. Communitarians hold that many of the basic institutions of our society must be strengthened, that the emphasis on individual rights in our culture must be supplemented and corrected by a focus on responsibilities, and that the good of the community and the integrity of its traditions should be promoted by a variety of means, including the deliberate use of public policy. Communitarians are particularly critical of liberalism, especially "political" or "minimal" liberalism. In their view, it has become the "public philosophy" of modern, democratic societies, particularly the United States, and so has contributed to these trends. What is required is a new public philosophy incorporating what is best in the liberal tradition, but correcting its excesses. Communitarianism is now a public and political movement, with its own organization (The Communitarian Network), its own journal (*The Responsive Community*), and (as of the summer of 1996) over 250 web sites on the Internet which include "communitarian" in their titles or descriptions.

I. THE CRITIQUE OF LIBERAL INDIVIDUALISM

Communitarianism first emerged within academic political theory as a critique of liberalism. Oddly, the first theorists who were commonly identified as "communitarian" (typically include MacIntyre, Sandel, Taylor, and Walzer) do not describe themselves as communitarians; Sandel, for example, prefers the term "civic republican." To a large extent communitarianism has been defined by interpreters and/or critics, so any account of the movement is apt to be controversial, as different observers focus on different aspects of the movement.

Most communitarians find much to admire in the liberal project, but they argue that liberalism rests upon an impoverished view of human nature and freedom, and that the primacy it accords to rights and justice, particularly in Rawls's influential account, cannot provide a sufficient grounding for social life. In his *Theory of Justice,* Rawls had argued that the basic principles of justice which should be used to govern the major institutions of a society (particularly the state and the economy) are the principles that individuals would agree to in what he called the "original position."

This is a setting in which free and equal people come together to decide upon the principles of justice to govern their ongoing social life. Because people disagree among themselves on many important matters, including especially the values which constitute a good life, a life of human flourishing, and because they have

somewhat conflicting interests about how the fruits of social cooperation should be distributed among different people, Rawls argues that we need to find a "fair" procedure through which people could discover or construct mutually acceptable principles to govern their common affairs. In the original position, Rawls imagines that participants are ignorant of their own particular identities: they do not know what their talents and interests are; they do not know their race, sex, gender, or social class; and they do not know what their ultimate ends in life are. Because they know nothing about themselves, whatever decisions they reach would necessarily have to be impartial, unbiased by particular interests. Because the original position is constructed in accordance with the requirements of fairness, not advantaging any particular type of person, interest, or disputed view of the human good, it expresses the liberal commitment to a society based upon the ideal of mutual respect.

Rawls argues that participants in the original position will agree on two principles of justice: the first establishes a scheme of "equal basic liberties," and the second regulates the extent of social and economic inequalities. People will accept these principles because they presuppose only those capacities and aims that everyone shares, notably the desire to live in a society under rules that all can regard as just, while being able to form and to pursue the different aims and ideals that different individuals believe to be necessary for a good life. Thus, people will recognize that the basic institutions of society must make room for different individuals to pursue different ideals, and so they would agree to place restrictions on the state and would call for an extensive arena of social life in which individuals will be free to pursue their own, separate ideals and values. This sphere of "civil society" will be protected by a system of rights, creating a space in which people may pursue their distinctive individual (and group) ends. For the same reason, the basic norms of the society must be "neutral" among these different ends in the sense that they are not adopted in order to promote any particular conception of the good, which would unfairly burden those who do not share that conception.

Because Rawls's fundamental principles are not justified by reference to some ideal of human excellence or conception of human flourishing, and because his theory leads to a conception of society in which individuals enjoy a basic system of rights which provides them extensive areas of negative liberty, areas in which each is free to choose important aspects of his or her way of life, he characterizes his theory as one based on the "priority of the right." In contrast to most other forms of political theorizing, this version of liberalism does not seek to arrange social and political institutions in such a way as to enable people to achieve the good life, or at least as good a life as possible, in part because people do not agree about what a good life requires.

Communitarians fear that unless people are united by deeper and richer ties than those of mutual respect, they will not be able to reach agreement on principles of justice, and even if they did, they would not be moved to observe them. Social order, they argue, requires more than justice. Because of the primacy it accords to individual rights and the limits it imposes on the polity, the liberal project is self-defeating.

Much of the communitarian critique focuses on two supposed shortcomings of liberalism: the first concerns what is taken to be the ontology of liberalism, specifically its reliance on an atomistic concept of the self, "unencumbered" by essential attachments to others; the second is the liberal commitment to universality. Unfortunately, much of the debate has centered on these two issues, which occlude the genuine and important questions that communitarians have raised about modern forms of social and political life, and the political commitments that liberals endorse. I will briefly review the first two sets of issues, and in the next section turn to the third.

A. The Unencumbered Self

Liberalism in all its variety valorizes the "individual" in one way or another. In *On Liberty*, John Stuart Mill argued not only that "the free development of individuality is one of the leading elements of well-being" (1989, p. 57. Cambridge University Press, Cambridge), but that it is only through the cultivation of one's individuality and autonomy that one develops "the qualities which are the distinctive endowment of a human being" (p. 59). Similarly, Kant held that the mark of a mature person was having the courage to make one's own decisions, based upon one's own reasoning, without relying upon the authority of others. Both utilitarians, for whom individual well-being is fundamental, and social contract theorists, who invoke the image (or fantasy) of society as resulting from the free agreement of presocial individuals pursuing their own ends, view society in instrumental terms. And so, in a way, does Rawls's conception of the original position. In these images, society is seen as "external" to the individuals composing it, a set of means they employ to achieve their goals and, at the same time, a set of limits or constraints on what each can do because of the potential resistance of others. The ideal arrangement of society, then, enables individuals to achieve their private ends as effectively as possible.

Communitarians charge that these pictures ignore the fact that we are and can only be social and historical creatures, whose capacities, values, aspirations, and identities result from our being born and raised in particular communities. Society is not external to the self; rather, we are constituted by our membership in particular social groupings. Liberals are simply wrong in thinking that individuals are capable of "choosing" their "conceptions of the good." The self, communitarians insist, is not "prior" to its ends, for one's fundamental aims and purposes are part of one's identity, rooted in one's life history, most of which is given and in no sense chosen. Even when we take the time to reflect on the course and meaning of our lives, we do not so much "choose" our ends as "discover" what they are. When we make particular decisions, when we choose a course of education, decide to accept a job or start a business, have children, or whatever, we make these choices by reference to our goals and other aspects of our identities, which we must take as given if we are to reach any decision at all. And it could hardly be otherwise, for one's life is so complex, rich, and nuanced that one can never know oneself fully. No matter how much one might engage in a process of self-examination, one can only illuminate certain aspects of oneself, and—so long as one is not spiritually dead—it is always possible that one will surprise oneself, coming to see something that had been hidden. If we cannot fully know ourselves, the idea that we could "choose" who we are, that we could be fully "self-determining," is absurd.

Needless to say, the valorization of such mythical choice is even more wrongheaded; not only is the ideal of radical self-determination unachievable, but it takes our attention away from the conditions that are necessary for a meaningful life. If we could abstract ourselves from all social contexts and experience the "absolute freedom" to choose our own identities and way of life, what we would actually experience would be pure "terror," a void in which we would have no basis for making any choices at all, as Hegel observed long ago. As one communitarian, Daniel Bell, puts it in *Communitarianism and Its Critics,* "if you ask yourself what matters most in your life, . . . the answer will involve a commitment to the good of the communities out of which your identity has been constituted" (1993. P. 94. Oxford Univ. Press, Oxford).

This line of criticism is not unique to contemporary communitarians; variants of it have been put forward since Rousseau first presented an utterly compelling critique of the "atomistic" understanding of society in his *Second Discourse* in 1755. That we are social and historical creatures, whose identities are in essential ways "constituted" by our membership in different social groups, can hardly be doubted. If liberalism rested on an understanding of the "self" as radically unsituated, capable of freely choosing its own ends, it would hardly merit attention. But liberalism does not presuppose this ontology.

There are many varieties of liberalism. Some, such as John Stuart Mill's, is based upon a particular view of human flourishing, one in which autonomy and choice are central, and liberal practices, particularly negative liberty, are defended on the grounds that they are necessary to exercise and develop "the distinctive endowment of a human being." In Mill's view, it is precisely because we are powerfully shaped by social forces that (in a mature society) social and political institutions should provide as much negative liberty as possible.

Similarly, Rawlsian liberalism does not rest upon an atomistic conception of the self. As previously explained, it seeks to provide principles of justice to regulate a morally pluralist society. It holds that the only principles that can do so are those which are not predicated upon a particular "conception of the good," but which accord equal standing to all citizens, regardless of the particular values and identities they embrace. Thus, if an individual were to change her identity, converting from one religion to another, or altering her sexual orientation, her standing as a citizen would not change. For political purposes, the individual (or the self) is conceived of as "prior" to her ends, but this is perfectly compatible with the recognition that any particular individual has a certain character that is, in many fundamental ways, unchosen and unchangeable. The "priority" that Rawlsian—or what he now calls "political"—liberalism insists upon is not rooted in a particular ontology (a particular conception of human nature); rather, it is political. Our rights (and duties) should not depend on our constitutive attachments, but merely upon our capacity for moral agency.

To this response, communitarians counter that if we are not "unencumbered selves," if one's own good is deeply tied to the good of the communities of which one is a member, why should we base the political order on such a narrow view of the self, and why should we confine it to securing the rights and promoting the interests of selves so narrowly conceived? Bell, for example, argues that we should dismiss "liberalism's absurd and counter-intuitive restrictions on the legitimate functions of government" (1993, 13), and use our political institutions to promote the flourishing of the communities which constitute us and through which we realize ourselves, even if these measures would limit the rights that liberals seek to protect.

This brings us to the heart of the opposition between political liberals and communitarians. For liberals, the critical issue is the fact of value pluralism. If we were all members of a single community (or set of related communities), sharing a view of the conditions of human flourishing, then there would be no obstacle, at least in Rawls's theory, to using the state to promote those conditions. His very conception of justice as fairness presupposes that people have conflicting interests rooted in different views of the human good. It is not that we are "unencumbered selves," but that we are encumbered in many different ways.

It is crucial to Rawls's view that these differences reflect reasonable disagreement; he insists that people share the ability to reason—to reach conclusions based on a rational assessment of the evidence—but he argues that the grounds on which judgments of the human good are made (both theoretical and practical) are seldom so compelling as to preclude reasonable disagreement. The evidence may be conflicting and so hard to assess, people may disagree about the weight to be assigned to different factors, or different normative considerations may be found on both sides of an issue. Although the public use of reason may be adequate to resolve many issues, there will be others that cannot be settled in this way. Rawls's position, then, does not rest upon skepticism (as the term is commonly used) or value noncognitivism, but on the recognition that our deepest convictions about the nature and meaning of human life involve questions of such scope and complexity that we cannot claim that our own particular answers are rationally demonstrable, so that those who disagree with us can be dismissed as irrational or irresponsible.

It is also crucial to note that political liberalism rests upon a particular understanding of morality and moral motivation. It presupposes that we want to act only in ways that we could justify to others, particularly those who are affected by our actions. Thus, if the norms governing our relationships are ones that no one subject to them could "reasonably reject," then we can regard ourselves as justified when we follow those norms. Only someone who accepts something like this view of morality is likely to find the Rawlsian effort to discover mutually acceptable principles of justice to be at all plausible.

This account of moral motivation is closely related to Rawls's understanding of political legitimacy. In

Rawls's words,

> Since political power is the coercive power of free and equal citizens [acting] as a corporate body, this power should be exercised, when constitutional essentials and basic questions of justice are at stake, only in ways that all citizens can reasonably be expected to endorse in the light of their common human reason. (1993. *Political Liberalism, pp.* 140–141. Columbia Univ. Press, New York)

When I cannot endorse the grounds on which power is exercised, then I am a victim of superior force, and a sociopolitical order resting on force in this way cannot be a legitimate one.

If through discussion and argument the views of citizens came to converge on a unified understanding of the good, using the state to advance it would not violate Rawls's principle of political legitimacy. But liberals insist that there can be no appeal to a single conception of the good without an account of how these disagreements can be resolved, which in turn requires an account of moral or evaluative knowledge which explains how an adequate level of public justification and agreement on values can be achieved. Absent a method to overcome such disagreements, political theories premised on a unitary view of value are implicitly recipes for tyranny.

The key issue, then, is whether the extent of reasonable pluralism in modern societies is so great as to make a democratic politics premised on a unified conception of the good impossible. This is a matter on which both communitarians and liberals are divided. Some communitarians, such as Bell, seem to hold open that possibility, while others, such as MacIntyre, are skeptical. In *After Virtue* (1984. 2nd ed. Univ. of Notre Dame Press, Notre Dame), MacIntyre rejects the liberal solution to pluralism, insisting that a just and stable society can only be based on a shared moral framework including an account of the human good, which leads to the conclusion that modern politics can only be, as MacIntyre puts it, "civil war carried on by other means" (253). We will return to this issue in Section II.

B. Universality

Communitarians also fault liberalism for claiming to offer a set of universally valid political principles, principles that are normatively binding at all times and places. Liberals, communitarians charge, seek to ground political principles in universal features of human nature and rationality, and so neglect what is really crucial in our moral experience. Just as we are social and historical creatures, so our moral lives are constituted by the system of beliefs, concepts, and values which make up a "community's shared understandings." Rather than seeking an "Archimedean point" from which we can judge the structure of society as a whole, social criticism should be (and can only be) directed at interpreting our "shared understandings." By enabling us to see how some of our practices conflict with our "deepest" understandings of ourselves, such grounded criticism can be instrumental in reforming those practices. The success of the American Civil Rights Movement, for example, was rooted in part in the ability of its participants to appeal to the deepest elements in the "American Creed," which conflicted with the racist practices embodied in Jim Crow laws.

Obviously this is an enormously complex issue, but like the ontological argument it does not really divide liberals and communitarians. In his most recent work, Rawls has cast his arguments as interpretations of the self-understandings of contemporary western democracies, and eschews universalist pretensions. Other liberals, such as Brian Barry, have argued that the interpretivist position rests on a mistake, and that we cannot reject universalism without falling into incoherence. At the same time, to the extent that communitarians advance a substantive account of the human good which can be realized only in certain forms of society, they at least implicitly adopt a universalist perspective. Nonetheless, the view that political argument is and can only be interpretative raises serious questions, particularly in the context of societies marked by significant value pluralism, whose "traditions" incorporate conflicting moral values. How, we might ask, can such conflicts be adjudicated if we can only appeal to the authority of the conflicting traditions themselves?

It would be question-begging to require a general answer, and different "interpretativists" (who may or may not describe themselves as communitarians) offer different accounts. The intuitive idea, as Bell explains it, is that such conflicts can be resolved by appealing to the "deepest" self-understandings of a community by offering "an interpretation of shared meanings" that the community will eventually come to accept (1993, 65). There are, however, many different ways in which the notion of "deepest" may be understood. In one sense, our "deepest" self-understandings are those to which we cling most tenaciously—those we most resist changing. But the self-understandings that are deepest in that sense may not be ones we care to affirm. As an individual, for example, one might find certain judgments or views to be so deeply embedded in one's character and experience that they are virtually impossible to shake off, such as attitudes about sexuality or one's body. Yet one might come to the conclusion that these attitudes are irrational and even destructive, and undertake a systematic program—such as entering psychotherapy or a religious order—to rid oneself of them.

In response, it might be argued that one's deepest self-understandings are those that, after serious reflection, one is prepared to affirm, regardless of the psychic power of other beliefs and attitudes. In this view, our deepest self-understandings are those for which we can give fully reasoned justifications. If we offer that answer, however, we open up a great deal of space for the kinds of criticisms of received traditions and authority that liberals have always demanded, and which (at least some) communitarians have found wanting. But if we do not make that move, then we appear to leave the notion of "deepest self-understandings" obscure.

The problem with both the argument about ontology and the argument about universality is that they fail to grasp the real issues that divide liberals and their communitarian critics. Liberals and communitarians do not necessarily take opposed positions on these philosophical questions, nor do these philosophical positions directly lead to substantive political judgments. To a great extent, the attention paid to these issues has been a diversion from the real disagreements between liberals and communitarians, to which we now turn.

II. COMMUNITARIANISM AS A PUBLIC PHILOSOPHY

The animating spirit of communitarianism, it might be argued, is a concern with the health of the group, which dictates the approach it takes to substantive issues of public policy. It is not that communitarians reject freedom and individuality; on the contrary, they believe that these characteristically liberal values cannot be realized unless a society is united by traditions and institutions embodying a rich array of substantive ends. Looking at contemporary western, particularly American, society, communitarians criticize the emphasis placed on individual rights and insist that rights must be balanced by a concern with responsibilities. In the absence of a coherent, functioning social order, individuals cannot even enjoy their rights, and social order is not possible unless its members acknowledge and discharge the claims it makes upon them. Communitarians believe

that social order requires a stronger form of unity than is possible in a framework that gives pride of place to justice, seeking to accommodate moral pluralism by ensuring that the basic structure of society is "neutral" among the different systems of value encompassed by the society. In short, a viable society must partake of the qualities of a community. But what is a community? And what is required to sustain one?

A. The Concept of Community

Ironically, there has been little discussion of the nature or forms of "community" by communitarians. Some, such as Michael Walzer, view the nation-state as an overarching form of community, holding that one of the principal goods a community distributes is "membership" in the community itself. Others, such as Alasdair MacIntyre, deny that the state, or at least the modern state, can be a community in any real sense, precisely because of the triumph of modernist, particularly liberal, political and moral theory, a triumph that has caused the moral disorder or our time. For MacIntyre, the only genuine communities today are nonpolitical, such as religious or ethnocultural groups which sustain traditions and practices that embody and promote a common good for their members.

1. Constitutive Communities

Responding to this criticism of communitarianism, Daniel Bell has delineated three types of community— what he calls communities of "place," "memory," and "face-to-face personal interaction governed by sentiments of trust, co-operation, and altruism" (1993, 14). Each of these is (partially) "constitutive" of the individual, in the sense that they define one's identity. Because humans have a "need to experience [their lives] as bound up with that of 'constitutive communities'," and because "what matters most in [anyone's] life" involves "a commitment to the good of the communities out of which [one's] identity has been constituted" (1993, 94), sustaining such communities is morally essential. To this point in the argument, few liberals would seriously demur. The key issue is how the coercive power of the state may be used to achieve this worthy objective.

Granted that our lives are meaningful only when we live within rich networks of human relationships, it does not follow that the proper role of the government is, for example, to enforce the norms that establish these networks. Indeed, liberals would point to the variety of the communities that Bell names, and to the fact that different individuals participate in different communities, to argue that the role of the *political* community must be limited, lest it undermine the goods that can only be secured in other forms of community. To restrict the role of the state does not necessarily damage constitutive communities, but may even be a condition of their flourishing. As Marx pointed out in his essay, "On the Jewish Question," religious belief and commitment are very strong in the United States, even though the state plays a smaller role in supporting religion than in most other countries.

2. Sustaining Communities

Of course, communitarians would not endorse any and all use of state power designed to promote particular communities. Indeed, the list of policies that Bell offers appears to be well within the bounds of liberal discourse. Among other things, he proposes that the right to veto building projects which clash with the architectural styles of an area be given to communities of place, that mandatory civilian national service for young adults (to enhance the nation-state) be instituted, and that "political support" for threatened linguistic communities be provided to communities of memory, and that stricter divorce laws be passed to enhance communities of face-to-face interaction, specifically families. But just as communitarianism is not a species of totalitarianism, so liberalism is not radical libertarianism. Liberals do not oppose *any* use of political power to advance communal goals, but, in Rawls's words, only those uses of power, "when constitutional essentials and basic principles of justice are at stake," that could not be endorsed by all citizens (1993, 139–140). This restriction does limit the ways in which communal goals may be pursued, but the kinds of policies Bell proposes do not in any obvious way raise issues of constitutional essentials or basic principles of justice.

Consider, for example, the case of divorce law reform. Bell does not explain what he has in mind by "stricter" divorce laws, but it is hard to see how making divorce more "time-consuming," thereby "allowing for a certain period of reflection before the knot is permanently untied," would by itself violate liberal principles. Indeed, this proposal is similar to a number of policies that mandate a waiting period before a major decision is taken, such as entering a marriage or borrowing a substantial sum of money—policies designed to ensure that the decision reflects a genuine choice, and is not the result of impulse or unreasonable pressure. Moreover, since dissolving a marriage affects others, notably the couple's children, there may well be a strong case on a liberal conception of justice to reform many aspects of contemporary American practice, particularly those involving child support and the division of marital property.

This does not mean that liberals could countenance any "reform" of family law designed to strengthen families. Liberals would oppose policies that would make divorce impossible or prohibitively costly, or that would deny women equal rights to own property, receive an education, or pursue a career. These proposals would threaten basic principles of justice, but they do not appear to be on the agenda of most communitarians.

B. Communitarian Reasoning

If liberals and communitarians are not necessarily divided by the importance they attach to community, and if they sometimes reach the same conclusions, they often do so for different reasons. I would suggest that the real differences between them concern the modes of political reasoning they employ. Communitarians, not surprisingly, tend to begin with the needs of the group, and analyze issues from that perspective. For example, when communitarians support individual rights—rights that can be invoked against the group itself—they often do so by arguing that such rights are necessary to realize social values that are embodied in central institutions and governing traditions of the society. The differences between liberal and communitarian forms of political reasoning can be seen by considering two examples, the issue of freedom for consensual sexual relationships and freedom of speech and expression.

1. Sexuality

Because sexuality is so important to one's identity and fulfillment, liberals are deeply suspicious of any abridgment of one's freedom to engage in consensual sexual relationships, including policies that restrict same-sex relationships. By contract, communitarians can come down on either side of this issue. As Philip Selznick argues in his book, *The Moral Commonwealth* (1992. Univ. of California Press, Berkeley), "the individual's interest in freedom of choice [does not] overcome the community's interest in vindicating its beliefs," so long as "there is a genuine consensus on ... the wrongfulness" of the conduct (408). The American Supreme Court (in *Bowers v. Hardwick,* 1986) allowed a Georgia law prohibiting sodomy to stand, invoking two strands of communitarian reasoning. First, it held that homosexual conduct was not connected to valued social practices or institutions such as "childrearing and education, family relationship, procreation, [or] marriage," and second, that the moral traditions of our society have long condemned homosexuality. From a communitarian perspective, the "expression of cultural identity" can justify significant restrictions on individual liberty.

But the communitarian perspective does not require such restrictions. Michael Sandel, in *Democracy's Discontent* (1996. Harvard Univ. Press, Cambridge, MA), suggests that "homosexual intimacy" may share some of the virtues of "heterosexual intimacy." "[L]ike marriage, homosexual union may also be 'intimate to the degree of being sacred ... a harmony in living ... a bilateral loyalty,' an association for a 'noble purpose'" (104). This line of argument has been used, for example, to justify the extension of civil marriage to gay couples. By showing that homosexual relationships can realize goods similar to those achieved through conventional marriage, the majority may come to "some appreciation of the lives homosexuals live," while the liberal argument can at best "win for homosexuals ... a thin and fragile toleration" (107).

While communitarianism does not necesssarily commit one to the exclusion of those who do not fit "mainstream" categories, it should be noted that the form of argument it employs does lead to real limits on the extent to which different ways of life can be accommodated. In this case, an argument can be constructed to include homosexuals within the community, but only to the extent that their practices can be assimilated to mainstream practices. Within the gay community there are a number of different voices, including those who reject the "marriage" model, celebrating instead a way of life in which one has multiple sexual partners, or one in which the boundaries and nature of sexuality are systematically transgressed, for example, through flamboyantly violating sexual roles by actions such as cross-dressing and assuming both male and female modes of speech and behavior. It is hard to see how a communitarian argument could be extended to include people within these subcultures. While the communitarian form of argument can embrace a certain degree of pluralism, it is less inclusive than liberalism.

2. Speech

The question of free speech represents another area where liberal and communitarian forms of reasoning can lead to different results. Liberalism has historically been associated with a very strong commitment to free speech, rejecting any content-based regulation of speech (except in cases of obscenity or defamation), and insisting that permissible regulation of speech (regarding time, place, and manner) be neutral among different points of view. As Charles Fried puts it, "State regulation of unwelcome expression is the punishment of pure ideas or beliefs—the outlawing of having ideas or beliefs, or of letting people know that you have them" (1992. In *The Bill of Rights in the Modern State* (G. Stone, R. Epstein, and C. Sunstein, Eds.), pp. 236–237. Univ. of Chicago Press, Chicago). He goes on to argue that "in a free, just society (a liberal society) no one may be compelled to adopt or to deny any particular theory of the good" (236–237). For that reason, the state may not "forbid communications that may convince an audience to modify its conception of the good" (236–237).

Communitarians also endorse freedom of speech, but they tend to arrive at this position from quite different premises. In *The Partial Constitution* (1993. Harvard Univ. Press, Cambridge, MA), Cass Sunstein argues that "the free speech principles should be viewed through the lens of democracy" (12). The key idea is that of "popular sovereignty"—the ideal of a citizenry collectively shaping its fate through deliberative processes leading to informed and rational judgments. In this view, special protection must be accorded to political speech, since restrictions on political speech would undermine the deliberative character of democratic politics. But other forms of speech would receive less protection, and could be restricted if a legislative majority viewed them as harmful. Such harms could include the effect of speech in shaping people's values and beliefs in undesirable ways. For example, if pornography is viewed as reflecting and promoting hostile attitudes toward women, it could properly be regulated or banned. Similarly, communitarians can argue for content-based restrictions on speech which would limit the right of people to express doctrines of racial or religious superiority. In cases such as these, liberals and communitarians may and often do hold different positions. But even where they reach the same conclusions, they employ different modes of reasoning. This can be seen in the approach they take to democracy, a form of government both strongly endorse.

C. Democracy and Self-Government

Because authoritarian regimes institutionalize inequality between rulers and ordinary citizens, only a democratic form of government is compatible with the liberal commitment to equal rights. Moreover, because democracy is possible only if citizens have the capacity and the willingness to participate in political affairs on equal terms with others, liberals recognize that the cultivation of the virtues of citizenship is a legitimate objective of the state. In this area, the state should not be "neutral" among competing conceptions of the good, for the good of democratic self-governance is a necessary condition for a liberal polity. The liberal commitment to democracy, it must be stressed, is based upon—and limited by—certain basic principles. In particular, liberals insist that democratic government must be limited government; political power must be exercised in accordance with certain procedures, and it must not be used to violate basic rights. There must be an extensive sphere of "private" life within which individuals are free, in association with others, to pursue their own, often conflicting, conceptions of the good. Liberals often worry about the rights of minorities, and are ambivalent about theories of popular sovereignty, which can be used to justify a majority's imposing its views on a minority, when the minority has reasonable grounds for rejecting those views.

In contrast to liberals, many communitarians draw their inspiration from the tradition of civic republicanism, which celebrates the participation of citizens in collective processes of deliberation about the common good as essential to human flourishing and freedom. For example, in *Democracy's Discontent* Sandel draws on the republican tradition to argue "that liberty depends on self-government" (1996, 5), making democratic self-governance the primary value, in contrast to the liberal approach. But Sandel does not break entirely with liberalism, as he acknowledges that republican politics have historically been repressive and exclusive, denying full citizenship to large categories of people such as women, racial and religious minorities, and workers on the grounds that these groups do not have the capacities or the virtues necessary to full citizenship. Like liberals, he affirms equality and value pluralism. Thus, he would limit the role of the state only to the promotion of those virtues necessary for democratic citizenship.

Where he differs from liberals is in his account of what these virtues and capacities are. For most communitarians, self-government is a demanding condition, possible only when citizens are united by a strong sense of the common good based upon a common identity, and so it requires some degree of cultural and moral homogeneity. As Sandel puts it,

> To deliberate well about the common good requires more than the capacity to choose one's ends and to respect others' rights to do the same. It requires a knowledge of public affairs and also a sense of belonging, a concern for the whole, a moral bond with the community whose fate is at stake. To share in self-rule therefore requires that citizens possess, or come to acquire, certain qualities of character, or civic virtues. (1996, 5–6)

Liberals believe—or hope?—that the limited aims of politics can be realized by a citizenry united by little more than mutual respect. Because communitarians view the requirements of democratic self-governance to be so demanding, the role of the state in cultivating the virtues of citizenship will be much more extensive than liberals would allow.

These differences are in part normative and conceptual, rooted in communitarian commitments to the idea of a common good, the importance of "constitutive communities" in human well-being, and in a view of freedom as participating in public life. In large measure, however, they are broadly empirical, resting on different readings of the democratic experience. Communitarians tend to see modern democracies as threatened by a growing sense of alienation, cynicism, and powerlessness on the part of citizens. This condition cannot be overcome unless citizens place greater priority on their public and civic identities and activities, working with others to solve their common problems. And they can do that only if they see themselves as members of communities, sharing a cultural identity and a common fate with others. Where liberals view the political "expression of cultural identity" with suspicion, seeing it as a form of illegitimate exclusion of those who are "different," communitarians fear that liberal minimalism will lead to the erosion of the cultural traditions that make a liberal-democratic society possible in the first place.

III. PLURALITY AND COMMUNITY

The forerunners of modern communitarianism include the traditions of civic republicanism and conservative criticisms of modern and industrial society. The former celebrated the self-governing city-states of ancient Rome and Greece, and envisioned a society of virtuous citizens united in their absorption in public life. The latter deplored the destruction of organic, face-to-face groups united by ties of kinship, religion, tradition, and mutual obligations between the sexes and among those of different social statuses. Common to both is the assumption that community requires likeness; it is rooted in what is common. In adapting these traditions to contemporary experience, communitarians must find ways to reaffirm community in the face of high and growing levels of diversity in modern society. And they must do so in a world that is increasingly interdependent, a world in which effective responses to common problems can often be found only at national or even international levels, where there is not even the semblance of community in any traditional sense. It is a world that liberal theory was designed to address, and that communitarian thinkers have in the past rejected.

Communitarian thinkers are beginning to grapple with these issues, moving from the critique of liberalism to offering an alternative account of how plurality may be accommodated. Ironically, the communitarians' focus on the health of the group is both an impediment and a resource. It is an impediment in a multicultural setting, where the valorization of any particular identity excludes those who do not share it. But it is also a resource for communitarian theory, since the problem of accommodation often involves managing the relationships among groups taken as distinct entities, rather than their individual members.

The "liberal strategy" for accommodating ethnocultural and religious diversity is largely one of separation and neutrality. The role of the state is limited to providing for a system of justice and the provision of certain public goods, and the promotion of specific religious and cultural values becomes the task of various religious and cultural communities, among whom the state is to be neutral. Thus, in *What It Means to Be an American* (1992. Marsilio, New York), Michael Walzer describes American politics as "separated not only from religion but from culture itself or, better, from all the particular forms in which religious and national culture was, and is, expressed," a "freedom that makes it possible for America's oneness to encompass and protect its many-ness" (30–31). The rights and responsibilities of individuals are the same for all, and no public or political recognition is given to the religious or cultural differences among them.

In some circumstances this strategy does not seem to address the problem of accommodating diversity. In *Multicultural Citizenship*, Kymlicka argues that language differences resist solution through a strategy of separation and neutrality. The state must conduct its dealings in some particular language(s), and therefore speakers of minority languages will inevitably face burdens that are not borne by others. Notoriously, systems of equal rights can lead to very unequal results when applied to people in different situations. As Anatole France noted, in what has become a cliche, "the law, in its majestic equality, forbids the rich as well as the poor to sleep under bridges, to beg in the streets, and to steal bread." In these circumstances, calls are often heard for "group rights" to supplement or even displace the system of individual rights.

The term "group rights" is somewhat ambiguous. Sometimes it refers to rights that can only be exercised by a group, which requires that there be a structure of authority through which the group can decide how the rights in question are to be exercised. The rights of a nation-state in the international system, for example, are "group rights" in that sense, such as the right to go to war in self-defense. Many native American peoples in the United States and Canada enjoy group rights within territories reserved to them, such as the right to hold property, manage business enterprises, and enforce certain norms. Group rights of this sort confer powers to the group (or its leaders) vis-a-vis its own members and others groups.

In other cases the phrase "groups rights" refers to norms permitting or requiring differential treatment of individuals based on ascribed membership in particular groups. In Quebec, children of non-Anglophone parents must be educated in Francophone schools, while English-speaking parents are free to send their children to either English or French language schools. In systems of group preference, spaces may be reserved in government, in schools, or in places of employment for members of particular groups, who may be selected on different criteria or may be required to meet different standards than members of other groups.

Although it is not impossible for liberals to accept group rights, either in the form of empowering the group as an entity or in the form of permitting differential treatment of members of different groups, they can do so only with difficulty, for group rights undermine the condition of common citizenship and, on the face of it, violate the basic commitment to equality. From a communitarian perspective, however, it is much easier to find a justification for group rights. In particular, group rights can be used to strengthen the group in order to sustain it as a "constitutive community." Group rights related to language, for example, may be used to reduce the pressures the speakers of minority languages face to assimilate the majority language, or even to penalize them if they try to adopt the majority language, thereby preserving the cultural integrity of the group and its role in the lives of its members.

Liberals tend to worry that defining one's rights and so one's life prospects by reference to one's ascribed membership in a particular group can actually lead one to adopt an identity as a member of that group. Contrary to widespread belief, group identities are not "primordial," and one of the most powerful factors contributing to the formation of such identities is a sense of common fate that can result from differential treatment based on some ethnic or other ascribed characteristic. As one's fate comes to be determined by the fact that one "is" an "X"—a Jew or black or a resident of a particular region—that fact becomes salient in a way that it might not have been before, and can even become a basis for political mobilization. Thus, far from merely reflecting given identities, political structures which involve differential treatment based on group membership can actually give rise to such identities. The obvious danger, then, is that group rights can cause differences to become ossified, exacerbating the conflicts between groups and inhibiting the formation of new forms of community.

Contemporary communitarians, confronting an increasingly diverse and interdependent world, tend to reject the idea that the value of community can be realized only through some specific type of community, such as locality, religious group, ethnicity, or national state. Rather, they seek to invigorate communities of different types and at different levels, including families, religious and cultural groups, associations of civil society, political parties, localities, nation-states, and even transnational groups. Thus, responding to liberal concerns, they would endorse a system of group rights to promote community, so long as it is not so rigid that it prevents adaptation to changing circumstances.

IV. CONCLUSION

Although often taken to be sharply opposed positions, liberalism and communitarianism are distinguished more by their central concerns or worries, and by their styles of political reasoning, than by contrasting ontologies of the self or views about moral universalism. Communitarians worry that the emphasis on individual rights and self-realization in modern societies has led to a neglect of the social and cultural conditions necessary for the emergence of strong individuals, individuals capable of exercising the rights which liberals prize. They worry that liberalism offers a one-sided view of the values that can and must be realized through political action, and that a society that really implemented a liberal public philosophy would be incapable of reproducing itself over time. Communitarianism has reinvigorated earlier forms of criticism of modern society, and has contributed to the emergence of more nuanced, less doctrinaire forms of liberalism. Although communitarianism has not (or not yet) taken the form of a systematic, integrated account of modern political life, it has enriched our understanding of modern society and extended the terms of discourse in important ways.

Also See the Following Articles

FREEDOM OF SPEECH • KANTIANISM • LIBERALISM • THEORIES OF JUSTICE: RAWLS

Bibliography

Avineri, S., and De-Shalit, A. (Eds.) (1992). "Communitarianism and Individualism." Oxford Univ. Press, Oxford.
Daly, M. (Ed.) (1994). "Communitarianism: A New Public Ethics." Wadsworth, Belmont, CA.
Etzioni, A. (1993). "The Spirit of Community." Simon & Schuster, New York.
Kymlicka, W. (1990). "Contemporary Political Philosophy." Oxford Univ. Press, Oxford.
Mulhall, S., and Swift, A. (1992). "Liberals and Communitarians." Blackwell, Oxford.
Sandel, M. (Ed.) (1984). "Liberalism and Its Critics." New York Univ. Press, New York.

COMPUTER AND INFORMATION ETHICS

Simon Rogerson
De Montfort University

GLOSSARY

information systems A multidisciplinary subject that addresses the range of strategic, managerial, and operational activities involved in the gathering, processing, storing, distributing, and use of information, and its associated technologies, in society and organizations.

intellectual property rights Rights that encompass confidential information, patents, trademarks, and copyright.

software A general term encompassing all programs that are used on computers; it can be divided into **systems software**, which controls the performance of the computer, and **application software**, which provides the means for computer users to produce information.

teleworking Working in flexible locations and at flexible times using computers while ensuring that the needs of the organization and of the individual are catered for.

COMPUTER AND INFORMATION ETHICS came into being as computer technology advanced and people started to become aware of the associated pitfalls that threatened to undermine the potential benefits of this powerful resource. Computer fraud and computer-generated human disasters were indicative of a new set of problems arising from this advancing technology. Perhaps the earliest recognition of this new set of problems was Donn Parker's "Rules of Ethics for Information Processing" (1968. *Communications of the ACM,* **11,** 198–201). By the mid-1970s such issues had been grouped together under the term "computer ethics" (coined by Walter Maner) that represented a new field of applied professional ethics dealing with problems aggravated, transformed, or created by computer technology. Deborah Johnson (D. G. Johnson, 1985. *Computer Ethics.* (1st. ed.). Englewood Cliffs, NJ: Prentice-Hall) defined computer ethics as being the study of the way in which computers present new versions of standard moral problems and dilemmas, causing existing standard moral norms to be used in new and novel ways in attempt to resolve these issues.

This is a narrow scope of computer ethics that focuses on the application of ethical theories and decision procedures used by philosophers in the field of applied ethics. Gradually this scope has been extended, as illustrated by James Moor's definition of computer ethics as the analysis of the nature and social impact of computer technology and the corresponding formulation and justification of policies for the ethical use of such technology (1985. In T. W. Bynum (Ed.), *Computers and Ethics.* Oxford: Blackwell).

Encyclopedia of Applied Ethics, Volume 1

The current broad perspective of computer ethics embraces concepts, theories, and procedures from philosophy, sociology, law, psychology, computer science and information systems. The overall goal is to integrate computing technology and human values in such a way that the technology advances and protects human values, rather than doing damage to them (T. W. Bynum, 1997. *Information ethics: An introduction*. Oxford, Blackwell). The term "information ethics" is becoming widely accepted as a better term for this area of applied ethics. This is because, firstly, the computer has evolved into a range of forms including the stand-alone machine, embedded computer chips in appliances, and networked components of a larger, more powerful macro-machine, and so the word "computer" is now misleading. Secondly, there has been an increasing convergence of once-separate industries to form an information industry that includes computers, telecommunications, cable and satellite television, recorded video and music, and so on.

I. THE UNIQUENESS OF COMPUTERS

The case of a company operating a nationwide network of service engineers illustrates what can go wrong if the implications of using computer systems are not carefully and fully investigated. The company had been suffering from several thefts of its service vehicles when parked at night. The attraction was not the expensive, though specialized, service equipment in the vehicles, but the engines of the vehicles themselves, which apparently had a high resale value. The company decided to attach electronic tags to the vehicles, enabling vehicle movement to be monitored from a central office. At night it was possible to place an electronic fence around the vehicles, and should an attempt to move the vehicle beyond the fence occur an alarm was triggered at the central office and the police alerted. The system proved highly successful and thefts were reduced dramatically. The management of the company then realized that this system could be used to monitor indirectly the movements of the sales engineers throughout the working day, providing information about abnormal activity instantaneously and without the knowledge of the engineers. The computer manager was briefed to develop this spin-off system, and therein lies the problem—the legitimate use of technology giving rise to the opportunity of questionable unethical action by the company which would affect every service engineer and ultimately anyone who used a company vehicle. The computer manager was placed in a very difficult position because of the conflict in professional responsiblity to the company on one hand and to the employees as members of society on the other.

This situation arose because of the uniqueness of computers. While spying on employees can be done without the use of computers, it is the power of computers that makes such activities viable in this situation. According to Walter Maner (1996. *Science and Engineering Ethics*, **2**(2), 137–154), the characteristics of the computer's uniqueness include storage, complexity, adaptability and versatility, processing speed, relative cheapness, limitless exact reproduction capability, and dependence on multiple layers of codes. This uniqueness has resulted in a failure to find satisfactory non-computer analogies that might help in addressing computer-related ethical dilemmas. Indeed this is an area that raises distinct and special ethical considerations that are characterized by the primary and essential involvement of computers, exploit some unique property of computers, and would not have arisen without the essential involvement of computers.

There is a need to discover new moral values, formulate new moral principles, develop new policies, and find new ways to think about these distinct and special ethical considerations, particularly in the organizational context (Maner). The sections that follow consider the major issues within information ethics with the exception of issues specifically related to the Internet.

II. PRIVACY AND MONITORING

Privacy is a fundamental right because it is an essential condition for the exercise of self-determination. Balancing the rights and interests of different parties in a free society is difficult. Problems of protecting individual privacy while satisfying government and business needs are indicative of a society that is becoming increasingly technologically dependent. Sometimes individuals have to give up some of their personal privacy in order to achieve some overall societal benefit.

Organizations are increasingly computerizing the processing of personal information. This may be without the consent or knowledge of the individuals affected. Advances in computer technology have led to the growth of databases holding personal and other sensitive information in multiple formats, including text, pictures, and sound. The scale and type of data collected and the scale and speed of data exchange have changed with the advent of computers. The potential to breach people's privacy at less cost and to greater advantage continues to increase.

There are two important types of privacy: consumer privacy and employee privacy (R. A. Spinello, 1995. *Ethical aspects of information technology*. New York:

Prentice Hall). Consumer privacy covers the information complied by data collectors such as marketing firms, insurance companies, and retailers; the use of credit information collected by credit agencies; and the rights of the consumers to control information about themselves and their commercial transactions. Indeed the extensive sharing of personal data is an erosion of privacy that reduces the capacity of individuals to control their destiny in both small and large matters. Organizations involved in such activities have a responsibility to ensure privacy rights are upheld. Consumer privacy focuses on the commercial relationship. Expanding this concept to client privacy includes consideration of non-commercial relationships where privacy is equally important. For example, medical, penal, and welfare relationships have, without doubt, serious privacy relationships. According to Spinello the issues that need to be addressed regarding movement of consumer data (and client data) can be summarized as:

- Potential for data to be sold to unscrupulous vendors
- Problems with ensuring the trustworthiness and care of data collectors
- Potential for combining data in new and novel ways to create detailed, composite profiles of individuals
- The difficulty of correcting inaccurate information once it has been propagated in many different files

Employee privacy deals primarily with the growing reliance on electronic monitoring and other mechanisms to analyze work habits and measure employee productivity. Spinello explains that employees have privacy rights which include the rights to control or limit access to personal information that he or she provides to an employer; to choose what he or she does outside the workplace; to privacy of thought; and to autonomy and freedom of expression.

In the modern workplace there are increasing opportunities to monitor activity. It is important to ensure that the use of monitoring facilities does not violate employee privacy rights. Some of the potential problem areas are:

- Personal computer network management programs that allow user files and directories to be monitored and to track what is being typed on individual computer screens
- Network management systems that enable interception and scrutiny of communications among different offices and between remote locations
- E-mail systems that generate archives of messages that can be inspected by anyone with authority or the technical ability to do so
- Electronic monitoring programs that track an employee's productivity and work habits

- Close circuit television surveillance systems that are computer controlled and have extensive archiving facilities and digital matching facilities

A modification of the data protection principles within the United Kingdom's Data Protection Act (1984) provides a framework that can be used to address the issue of privacy, develop a reasonable privacy policy, and ensure that the development and operation of information systems (IS) are sensitive to privacy concerns. The modified principles are as follows (E. France, 1996. *Our answers: Data protection and the EU Directive 95/ 96 EC.* Wilmslow: The Office of the Data Protection Registrar): (i) Personal data shall be processed fairly and lawfully. (ii) Personal data shall be collected for specified, explicit, and legitimate purposes. (iii) Personal data shall not be further processed in a way incompatible with the purposes for which they are collected.

(iv) Personal data shall be adequate, relevant, and not excessive in relation to the purposes for which they are collected or further processed. (v) Personal data shall be accurate and, where necessary, kept up to date. (vi) Personal data shall not be kept longer than is necessary for the purposes for which they are collected and further processed.

(vii) An individual shall be entitled, at reasonable intervals, without excessive delay or expense and under no duress, to be informed by any controller when he or she processes personal data of which that individual is subject and to certain information relating to that processing; to access the personal data of which the individual is subject and to any available information as to their source; and to knowlege of the logic involved in any automatic processing of data concerning him or her involving certain automated decisions; and, where appropriate, to have such personal data rectified, erased, or blocked, and to have details of such rectification, erasure, or blocking available to third parties to whom personal data have been disclosed.

(viii) Appropriate security measures shall be taken against unauthorized access to, or alteration, disclosure, or destruction of, personal data and against accidental or unlawful loss or destruction of personal data.

III. INFORMATION PROVISION

Information has become one of the most valuable assets, for it is through information that people gain knowledge that can then be used in both current and future decision-making activities. Information is concerned with communicating a valuable message to a recipient. Thus information must be clear, concise, timely, relevant, accurate, and complete. A message which has no value to its recipient is simply termed data. The majority of information provision is likely to use computer-based IS. The integrity of information is reliant upon the development and operation of these systems. The responsibility for these activities is a complex issue. For example, it is not clear whether IS provision is a service or the supplying of a product, nor is it possible in the case of a large IS for a single individual to fully understand it, and therefore no single individual can be held responsible for the whole system. It often turns out that an organization together with several individuals within that organization have a shared responsibility.

It is important to understand the nature of responsibility, which, according to D. G. Johnson, comprises four concepts (1994. *Computer ethics* (2nd. ed.). Englewood Cliffs, NJ: Prentice-Hall):

1. Duty—a person has a duty or responsibility by virtue of the role held within the organization
2. Cause—a person might be responsible because of undertaking or failing to undertake something which caused something else to happen.
3. Blame—a person did something wrong which led to an event or circumstance
4. Liability—a person is liable if that person must compensate those who are harmed by an event or action

Specific responsibility issues often include several of these concepts. For example, a computer programmer knowingly reduced the testing procedure for a program in order to meet a deadline by not using the supplied test data that were for very infrequent cases. This resulted in a major operation failure several months after implementation. In this situation the programmer was to blame because failure to complete the specified testing had caused the program malfunction, and it was the programmer's duty and responsibility to ensure adequate testing. In this circumstance the programmer may be found legally liable.

One practical way of dealing with responsibility is to assign it to individuals involved in information provision within an organization. Individuals can be grouped into three broad categories: development, implementation, and maintenance of IS; collection and input of data; and output and dissemination of information. Responsibility clauses should be included in each job specification within these three areas of organizational work. Each clause should explain the extent of responsibility. Both management and nonmanagement jobs should be covered. Individuals should be adequately briefed on their responsibilities regarding the authenticity, fidelity, and accuracy of data and information. They should be encouraged to accept such responsibilities as part of their societal responsibilities. Should an undesirable

event occur it should be considered on its own merits, and responsibilities can be identified using the responsibility framework already in place.

IV. SOFTWARE AS INTELLECTUAL PROPERTY

Intellectual property rights (IPRs) raise complex issues which organizations have to address. IPRs related to software and data are particularly difficult to assign and protect, and require careful deliberation before executive action occurs. Society has long recognized that taking or using property without permission is wrong. This extends not only to physical property but also to ideas. It is generally accepted that software is a kind of intellectual property and that to copy it or use it without the owner's permission is unethical and often illegal.

Ownership might not be clear. Johnson (1994) argues that a consequentialist framework is best for analyzing software IPRs because it puts the focus on deciding ownership in terms of affecting continued creativity and development of software. Software may be developed by a number of people, each making a contribution. Individuals might have difficulty determining which elements belong to them and to what degree they can claim ownership. Individuals may be employees or contractors. The development of software on behalf of a client raises fundamental IPR issues. It is important that agreement concerning the ownership of IPRs is reached at the onset before any development commences.

If an organization or group of individuals invests time, money, and effort in creating a piece of software they should be entitled to own the result by virtue of this effort and be given the opportunity to reap an economic reward. For the sake of fairness and equity, and to reward initiative and application, one should have the right to retain control over intellectual property and to sell or licence the product. However, the extent of these rights is debatable. Parker, Swope, and Baker explain that there is a responsibility to distribute software that is fit for the purpose for which it was developed, so the owner does not have the right to distribute software that is known to be defective and that has not been thoroughly tested (D. B. Parker, S. Swope, & B. N. Baker, Eds., 1990. *Ethical conflicts in information and computer science*. Wellesley: QED Information Sciences). Software embodies ideas and knowledge that can often benefit society as a whole. To have unrestricted rights may curtail technological evolution and diffusion, which will disadvantage the consumer and society. For example, there may be a piece of software that is deemed to be societally beneficial but which is withheld on commercial grounds. It is questionable whether the owner has the right, simply on grounds of optimizing economic gain, to withhold distribution. Some reasonable limit must be placed on the IPR so an equitable balance is struck. For example, currently copyright legislation in the USA protects the expression of an idea and not the idea itself. This constraint appears to achieve a balance between the right to private property and the furthering of common good.

There is reasonable agreement in countries of the West that individuals or groups of individuals have intellectual property rights regarding software. The law in many countries recognizes that computer software is worthy of protection because it is a result of a creative process involving substantial effort. The principal instrument of protection is copyright. However, the interpretations in other countries and situations are sometimes different. For example, IPR safeguards in countries of the Far East are minimal mainly due to a different philosophy that tends to treat intellectual property as communal or social property. In economically poor developing countries the view often taken is that the right to livelihood takes precedence over other claims on which IPRs are based. It is only when prosperity increases that there is a shift from a social wellbeing interpretation of IPRs to one with more emphasis on the individual. Such differences will have an impact on organizations involved in international trade and must be considered carefully.

V. ORGANIZATION STRUCTURE AND THE LOCATION OF WORK

With the advent of computers there has been a shift from traditionally stable organizational structures toward more flexible working arrangements. New computer-enabled working practices are creating more dynamic structures that are highly flexible and capable of responding to environmental uncertainty. For example, with the advances in telecommunications and IS, many jobs can be redefined as telework, which involves working remotely via a computer link. Many organizations are now using teleworking, communal office desks and computers, and geographically dispersed virtual teams to reduce organizational operating costs, but there may be serious disadvantages in this. For example, teleworking might result in the breakup of social groups in the workplace and the disenfranchising of those without the resources to participate. This may detrimentally affect organizations and society in the long term.

The impact of computer-enabled work will continue to grow. Work that is capable of being transformed into computer-enabled work must have a low manual labor content, be undertaken by individuals rather than teams, require minimal supervision, be easily measurable, and not depend upon expensive or bulky equipment. This means that there are many activities that might be organized as flexible computer-enabled work, including:

- Professional and management specialists such as accountants, design engineers, graphic designers, general managers, and translators
- Professional support workers such as bookkeepers, proofreaders, and researchers
- Field workers such as auditors, sales representatives, insurance brokers, and service engineers
- Information technology specialists such as software programmers and systems engineers
- Clerical support workers such as data entry staff, telesales staff, and word processor operators

Without doubt there are opportunities for benefit gains through the use of computer-enabled work for both organizations and individuals. However, this change in work practice raises many ethical dilemmas, and as computers evolve the dilemmas will continue to change. The following list illustrates some of the dilemmas and questions that may arise:

- The ability to employ people and sell goods and services globally through technological support may result in localized ghettos comprising people who have redundant or overpriced work skills and people who cannot afford the goods and services produced. Does an employer have a responsibility to the local community to ensure such ghettos do not exist or are minimized?
- Is it right to exploit low labor costs in the economically poor areas of the world, ignoring the injustice of wage differentials and an employer's responsibility to the community in which its employees live?
- Given the access to a global workforce and an increased need for flexibility to respond to the dynamic needs of the marketplace, the permanency of jobs and job content are likely to change. Is this acceptable to individuals, and how might organizations support individuals in coping with this often stressful situation?
- Computer-enabled communication only supports some of the elements of human communication. The loss of non-verbal communication or body language and the creation of electronic personalities could have an impact on the way people interact. Will this have a detrimental effect on individuals and the way they work?
- The workplace provides a place for social interaction at many levels. Individuals cherish this interaction. Commuting provides psychological space that separates work from home, which is important to some people. The move to teleworking radically changes this situation, potentially causing social isolation and disruption

in home life. How can organizations safeguard individuals when adopting teleworking?

VI. COMPUTER MISUSE

As computers become more widely used, the risk of misuse and abuse increases, and the impacts of such acts are likely to be greater. For example, in the United Kingdom there was a threefold increase in the number of computer abuse incidents reported in 1993 compared with 1990, with virus infection, fraud, and illicit software accounting for 40% of the total incidents. Computer abuse covers a wide spectrum of activity, as summarized as follows (Audit Commission, 1994. *Opportunity makes a thief.* London: HMSO):

- Fraud through unauthorized data input or alteration of data input; destruction, suppression, or misappropriation of output from a computer process; alteration of computerized data; and alteration or misuse of programs, but excluding virus infections
- Theft of data and software
- Use of illicit software by using unlicensed software and pirated software
- Using computer facilities for unauthorized private personal work
- Invasion of privacy through unauthorized disclosure of personal data and breaches of associated legislation, and disclosure of proprietary information
- "Hacking" through deliberately gaining unauthorized access to a computer systems, usually through the use of telecommunication facilities
- Sabotage or interfering with the computer process by causing deliberate damage to the processing cycle or to the equipment
- Computer virus infections by distributing a program with the intention of corrupting a computer process

Spinello (1995) argues that organizations and individuals are ethically obliged to protect the systems and information entrusted to their care and must strive to prevent or minimize the impact of computer abuse incidents. He suggests that those stakeholders at greatest risk from a computer abuse incident might be party to decisions made concerning security arrangements. He argues that computer abuse offenses should not be treated lightly, even if the detrimental outcome is negligible, because, at the very least, valuable resources will have been squandered and property rights violated. Spinello also points out that a balance has to be struck regarding stringent security measures and respect for civil liberties. There is a dual responsibility regarding computer abuse. Organizations have a duty to minimize the temptation of perpetrating computer abuse, while individuals have a responsibility to resist such temptations.

VII. DEVELOPING INFORMATION SYSTEMS

Developing a computer-based IS is frequently a complicated process requiring many decisions to be made. As well as economic and technological considerations, there are ethical and social issues that need to be taken into account, but these are sometimes overlooked. It is generally accepted that IS development is best undertaken using a project team approach. How the project is conducted will depend heavily upon the perceived goal. The visualization of this goal should address many questions, including:

- What will the goal of the project mean to all the people involved in the project when the project is completed?
- What will the project actually produce? Where will these products go? What will happen to them? Who will use them? Who will be affected by them and how?

These types of questions are important because through answering them an acceptable project ethos should be established and the project's scope of consideration defined, so that consideration of ethical and societal issues is included, as well as that of technological, economic, and legal issues. The problem is that in practice these fundamental questions are often overlooked. It is more likely that a narrower perspective is adopted, with only the obvious issues in close proximity to the project being considered. The holistic view promoted by such questioning requires greater vision, analysis, and reflection. However, the project manager is usually under pressure to deliver on time and within budget, and so the tendency is to reduce the scope and establish a close artificial boundary around the project.

Within computing there are numerous activities and decisions to be made, and most of these will have an ethical dimension. It is impractical to consider each minute issue in great detail and still hope to achieve the overall goal. The focus must be on the ethical hotspots where activities and decision making include a relatively high ethical dimension because they are likely to influence the success of the particular information systems activity and promote ethical sensitivity in a broader context. The scope of consideration is an ethical hotspot and is influenced by the identification and involvement of all stakeholders both within and outside the organization.

The widespread use of and dependence upon IS within organizations and society as a whole means that the well-being of individuals may be at risk. It is therefore important that in establishing the scope of consideration of an IS project the principles of due care, fairness, and social cost are prevalent. In this way the project management process will embrace, at the onset, the views and concerns of all parties affected by the project. Concerns over, for example, deskilling of jobs, redundancy, and the breakup of social groupings can be aired at the earliest opportunity. Fears can be allayed and project goals adjusted if necessary.

An IS project is dynamic and exists in a dynamic environment. Appropriate information dissemination is essential so that the interested parties are aware of occurring change and assignments can be adjusted accordingly. Being over-optimistic, ultra-pessimistic, or simply untruthful about progress can be damaging not only to the project but also to both the client and the supplier. This is true whether the supplier and client are in the same or different organizations. Typically, those involved in this communication would be the project team, the computer department line management, and the client. An honest, objective account of progress which takes into account the requirements and feelings of all concerned is the best way to operate. Thus the second project management ethical hotspot has to do with informing the client. No one likes to get shocking news, so early warning of a problem and an indication of the scale of the problem are important. The key is to provide factual information in non-emotive words so the client and project manager can discuss any necessary changes in a calm and professional manner. Confrontational progress meetings achieve nothing. The adoption of the principles of honesty, non-bias, due care, and fairness help to ensure a good working relationship.

Turning to the overall development process, there are numerous methodological approaches to information systems development. Few deal adequately with the ethical and societal dimensions of the development process, instead tending to stress the formal and technical aspects. Consideration of the human, social, and organizational consequences of system implementation must not be overlooked during the development process. Management should encourage systems developers to adopt the principles of non-bias, due care, fairness, and consideration of social cost and benefit. In particular they should include the social design of computerized systems and work settings in the overall systems development project; build systems that are attractive to those whose work is most affected by them; and undertake information systems development in parallel with any necessary reorganization of work, taking into account changed responsibilities, relationships, and rewards.

VIII. COMPUTER PROFESSIONALISM

In discharging their professional duties, computer professionals are likely to enter into relationships with employers, clients, the profession, and society. There may be one or several of these relationships for a given activity. Quite often there will be tensions existing between all of these relationships, and particularly between the employer and societal relationships. There are three skills that a computer professional should possess so that professional duties might be undertaken in an ethically sensitive manner: (1) the ability to identify correctly the likelihood of ethical dilemmas in given situations; (2) the ability to identify the causes of these dilemmas and to suggest appropriate, sensitive actions for resolving them, together with an indication of the probable outcomes of each alternative action; and (3) the ability to select a feasible action plan from these alternatives.

Codes of conduct can be useful in helping computer professionals discharge their duties ethically, because the code provides a framework within which to work, and indicates to the new professional what are acceptable work practices. An excellent example of a code of conduct is that adopted by the Association for Computer Machinery (ACM) in 1992. The extract in Box 1 shows one of the 24 imperatives and its associated guideline that sets the overall tenor of the code and relates to many issues of computer and information ethics, for example, those raised in this article about the location of work and privacy.

Focusing on obligations makes it possible to consider carefully the implications of advancing computing technologies. There are four types of obligations for computer professionals: those as a supplier, those as a client, those as an end user, and those as a member of the community (W. R. Collins, K. W. Miller, B. J. Spielman, & P. Wherry, 1994. *Communications of the ACM*, 37, 81–91). These obligations can be summarized as follows:

Obligations as a supplier to the client are to provide a reasonable warranty and be open about testing processes and shortcomings. Those to the end user are to provide clear operating instructions, give reasonable protection from, and informative responses to, use and abuse, and offer reasonable technical support. Obligations to the community are to ensure reasonable protection against physical, emotional, and economic harm from applications, and to be open about development processes and limits of correctness.

Obligations as a client to the supplier are to negotiate in good faith, facilitate adequate communication of requirements, and learn enough about the product to make an informed decision. Those to the end user are to provide quality solutions appropriate to the end user's needs within reasonable budgetary constraints, be pru-

Box 1

Extract from the ACM Code of Ethics and Professional Conduct

Imperative: 1.2 Avoid harm to others.

Guideline: "Harm" means injury or negative consequences, such as undesirable loss of information, loss of property, property damage, or unwanted environmental impacts. This principle prohibits use of computing technology in ways that result in harm to any of the following: users, the general public, employees, employers. Harmful actions include intentional destruction or modification of files and programs leading to serious loss of resources or unnecessary expenditure of human resources such as the time and effort required to purge systems of "computer viruses."

Well-intended actions, including those that accomplish assigned duties, may lead to harm unexpectedly. In such an event the responsible person or persons are obligated to undo or mitigate the negative consequences as much as possible. One way to avoid unintentional harm is to carefully consider potential impacts on all those affected by decisions made during design and implementation.

To minimize the possibility of indirectly harming others, computing professionals must minimize malfunctions by following generally accepted standards for system design and testing. Furthermore, it is often necessary to assess the social consequences of systems to project the likelihood of any serious harm to others. If system features are misrepresented to users, co-workers, or supervisors, the individual computing professional is responsible for any resulting injury.

In the work environment the computing professional has the additional obligation to report any signs of system dangers that might result in serious personal or social damage. If one's superiors do not act to curtail or mitigate such dangers, it may be necessary to "blow the whistle" to help correct the problem or reduce the risk. However, capricious or misguided reporting of violations can, itself, be harmful. Before reporting violations, all relevant aspects of the incident must be thoroughly assessed. In particular, the assessment of risk and responsibility must be credible. It is suggested that advice be sought from other computing professionals.

Reprinted with permission of the ACM, 1515 Broadway, New York, NY 10036-570
Email: acmhelp@acm.org

dent in the introduction of computing technology, and represent the end user's interest with suppliers. Obligations to the community are to acquire only products having reasonable public safeguard assurances and be open about product capabilities and limitations.

An obligation as an end user to the supplier is to respect ownership of rights. Those to the client are to make reasonable requests for computing power, communicate needs to the client effectively, and undertake to learn and use the products responsibly. Obligations to the community are to make a conscientious effort to reduce any risk to the public and encourage reasonable expectations about computing technology capabilities and limitations.

Obligations as a community member are to become aware of the limitation of computing technology, encourage effective economic and regulatory frameworks, support societally beneficial applications, and oppose societally harmful applications.

Organizations are an essential part of society. Those in charge of organizations have a responsibility to ensure that when computers are applied in pursuit of business objectives it is done so in a balanced manner that accounts for the needs of both individuals and society, as well as those of the organization. Senior executives must strategically manage computer usage to ensure that issues such as privacy, ownership, information integrity, human interaction, and community are properly considered. Computer professionals and their managers must be trained so that they are sensitive to the power of the technology and act in a responsible and accountable manner. The adoption of a broader approach that addresses economic, technological, legal, societal, and ethical concerns will help to realize a democratic and empowering technology rather than an enslaving or debilitating one, both now and in the future.

Also See the Following Articles

COMPUTER SECURITY • CONFIDENTIALITY, GENERAL ISSUES OF • INFORMATION MANAGEMENT • INTERNET PROTOCOL • PROFESSIONAL ETHICS

Bibliography

Berleur, J., & Brunnstein, K. (Eds.) (1996). *Ethics of computing: Codes, spaces for discussion and law. A handbook prepared by the IFIP Ethics Task Group.* London: Chapman & Hall.

Bynum, T. W., & Rogerson, S. (Eds.) (1996). Global information ethics, special edition. *Science and Engineering Ethics,* 2(2).

Huff, C., & Finholt, T. (Eds.) (1994). *Social issues in computing: Putting computing in its place.* New York: McGraw–Hill.

Johnson, D. G., & Nissenbaum, H. (Eds.) (1995). *Computer Ethics and Social Values.* Englewood Cliffs, NJ: Prentice-Hall.

Langford, D. (1995). *Practical computer ethics.* London: McGraw–Hill.

Rogerson, S., & Bynum, T. W. (Eds.) (1997). *A reader in information ethics.* Oxford: Blackwell.

COMPUTER SECURITY

Eugene H. Spafford
Purdue University

GLOSSARY

Big Brother A personification of the government of a nation, with the sense that this government intrudes on the privacy of individual citizens and observes or records their activities. (From the character of Big Brother, an omnipresent, Stalin-like dictator in the George Orwell novel 1984.)

break-in In the context of computer use, the act of illegally or improperly gaining access to confidential information or to restricted computer sites; also known as *computer burglary*.

hacker Originally, a person highly skilled in computer use, especially an amateur or hobbyist who carries on computer activities as an amusement or challenge, as opposed to a person who is employed to work with computers; currently, in popular use, a person who uses computer expertise in a frivolous or harmful manner, as by intentionally spreading computer viruses or improperly gaining access to confidential information.

vandalware A noncommercial software program that is intended to allow the user to damage or interfere with the operation of other computers.

virus A noncommercial software program that is intended to replicate itself on a host computer, without the knowledge of the user of that computer, so as to damage or interfere with the computer's operation.

RECENT INCIDENTS OF UNAUTHORIZED COMPUTER INTRUSION have brought about discussion of the ethics of breaking into computers. Some individuals have argued that as long as no significant damage results, break-ins may serve a useful purpose. Others counter with the expression that the break-ins are almost always harmful and wrong.

I. INTRODUCTION

On November 2, 1988, a program was run on the Internet that replicated itself on thousands of machines, often loading them to the point where they were unable to process normal requests. This *Internet Worm* program was stopped in a matter of hours, but the controversy engendered by its release raged for years. Other recent incidents, such as the "wily hackers" tracked by Cliff Stoll, the "Legion of Doom" members who are alleged to have stolen telephone company 911 software, and the growth of the computer virus problem have added to the discussion. What constitutes improper access to computers? Are some break-ins ethical? Is there such a thing as a "moral hacker"?

It is important that we discuss these issues. The continuing evolution of our technological base and our increasing reliance on computers for critical tasks suggests that future incidents may well have more serious consequences than those we have seen to date. With human nature as varied and extreme as it is, and with the technology as available as it is, we must expect to experience more of these incidents.

In this article, I will introduce a few of the major issues that these incidents have raised, and present some arguments related to them. For clarification, I have separated a few issues that often have been combined when debated; it is possible that most people are in agreement on some of these points once they are viewed as individual issues.

II. WHAT IS ETHICAL?

Webster's *Collegiate Dictionary* defines ethics as: "The discipline dealing with what is good and bad and with moral duty and obligation." More simply, it is the study of what is *right* to do in a given situation—what we *ought* to do. Alternatively, it is sometimes described as the study of what is *good* and how to achieve that good. To suggest whether an act is right or wrong, we need to agree on an ethical system that is easy to understand and apply as we consider the ethics of computer break-ins.

Philosophers have been trying for thousands of years to define right and wrong, and I will not make yet another attempt at such a definition. Instead, I will suggest that we make the simplifying assumption that we can judge the ethical nature of an act by applying a deontological assessment: regardless of the effect, is the act itself ethical? Would we view that act as sensible and proper if **everyone** were to engage in it? Although this may be too simplistic a model (and it can certainly be argued that other ethical philosophies may also be applied), it is a good first approximation for purposes of discussion. If you are unfamiliar with any other formal ethical evaluation method, try applying this assessment to the points I raise later in this article. If the results are obviously unpleasant or dangerous in the large, then they should be considered unethical as individual acts.

Note that this philosophy assumes that *right* is determined by actions and not by results. Some ethical philosophies assume that the ends justify the means; our current society does not operate by such a philosophy,

although many individuals do. As a society, we profess to believe that "it isn't whether you win or lose, it's how you play the game." This is why we are concerned with issues of due process and civil rights, even for those espousing repugnant views and committing heinous acts. The process is important no matter the outcome, although the outcome may help to resolve a choice between two almost equal courses of action.

Philosophies that consider the results of an act as the ultimate measure of good are often impossible to apply because of the difficulty in understanding exactly what results from any arbitrary activity. Consider an extreme example: the government orders 100 cigarette smokers, chosen at random, to be beheaded on live nationwide television. The result might well be that many hundreds of thousands of other smokers would quite "cold turkey," thus prolonging their lives. It might also prevent hundreds of thousands of people from ever starting to smoke, thus improving the health and longevity of the general populace. The health of millions of other people would improve as they would no longer be subjected to secondary smoke, and the overall impact on the environment would be very favorable as tons of air and ground pollutants would no longer be released by smokers or tobacco companies.

Yet, despite the great good this might hold for society, everyone, except for a few extremists, would condemn such an *act* as immoral. We would likely object even if only one person was executed. It would not matter what the law might be on such a matter; we would not feel that the act was morally correct, nor would we view the ends as justifying the means.

Note that we would be unable to judge the morality of such an action by evaluating the results, because we would not know the full scope of those results. Such an act might have effects favorable or otherwise, on issues of law, public health, tobacco use, and daytime TV shows for decades or centuries to follow. A system of ethics that considered primarily only the results of our actions would not allow us to evaluate our current activities at the time when we would need such guidance; if we are unable to discern the appropriate course of action prior to its commission, then our system of ethics is of little or no value to us. To obtain ethical guidance, we must base our actions primarily on evaluations of the actions and not on the possible results.

More to the point of this article, if we attempt to judge the morality of a computer break-in based on the sum total of all future effect, we would be unable to make such a judgment, either for a specific incident or for the general class of acts. In part, this is because it is so difficult to determine the long-term effects of various actions, and to discern their causes. We cannot know, for instance, if increased security awareness and restrictions are better for society in the long term, or whether these additional restrictions will result in greater costs and annoyance when using computer systems. We also do not know how many of these changes are directly traceable to incidents of computer break-ins.

One other point should be made here: it is undoubtedly possible to imagine scenarios where a computer break-in would be considered to be the preferable course of action. For instance, if vital medical data were on a computer and were necessary to save someone's life in an emergency, but the authorized users of the system could not be located, breaking into the system might well be considered the right thing to do. However, that action does not make the break-in ethical. Rather, such situations occur when a greater wrong would undoubtedly occur if the unethical act were not committed. Similar reasoning applies to situations such as killing in self-defense. In the following discussion, I will assume that such conflicts are not the root cause of the break-ins; such situations should very rarely present themselves.

III. MOTIVATIONS

Individuals who break into computer systems or who write *vandalware* usually use one of a few rationalizations for their actions. Most of these individuals would never think to walk down a street, trying every door to find one unlocked, then search through the drawers of the furniture inside. Yet, these same people seem to give no second thought to making repeated attempts at guessing passwords to accounts they do not own, and once onto a system, browsing through the files on disk.

These computer burglars often present the same reasons for their actions in an attempt to rationalize their activities as morally justified. I present and refute some of the most commonly used ones in what follows; motives involving theft and revenge are not uncommon, and their moral nature is simple to discern, so I shall not include them here.

A. The Hacker Ethic

Many hackers argue that they follow an ethic that both guides their behavior and justifies their break-ins. This hacker ethic states, in part, that all information should be free. This view holds that information belongs to everyone, and there should be no boundaries or re-straints to prevent anyone from examining information. Richard Stallman states much the same thing in his GNU Manifesto. He and others have further stated in various forums that if information is free, it logically follows that there should be no such thing as intellectual property, and no need for security.

What are the implications and consequences of such a philosophy? First and foremost, it raises some disturbing questions of privacy. If all information is (or should be) free, then privacy is no longer a possibility. For information to be free to everyone, and for individuals to no longer be able to claim it as property, means that anyone may access the information if they please. Furthermore, as it is no longer property of any individual, that means that anyone can alter the information. Items such as bank balances, medical records, credit histories, employment records, and defense information all cease to be controlled. If someone controls information and controls who may access it, the information is obviously not free. But without that control, we would no longer be able to trust the accuracy of the information.

In a perfect world, this lack of privacy and control might not be a cause for concern. However, if all information were to be freely available and modifiable, imagine how much damage and chaos would be caused in our real world by such a philosophy! Our whole society is based on information whose accuracy must be assured. This includes information held by banks and other financial institutions, credit bureaus, medical agencies and professionals, government agencies such as the IRS, law enforcement agencies, and educational institutions. Clearly, treating all their information as "free" would be unethical in any world where there might be careless and unethical individuals.

Economic arguments can be made against this philosophy, too, in addition to the overwhelming need for privacy and control of information accuracy. Information is not universally free. It is held as property because of privacy concerns, and because it is often collected and developed at great expense. Development of a new algorithm or program, or collection of a specialized database, may involve the expenditure of vast sums of time and effort. To claim that it is free or should be free is to express a naive and unrealistic view of the world. To use this as a justification for computer break-ins is clearly unethical. Although not all information currently treated as private or controlled as proprietary needs such protection, that does not justify unauthorized access to it or to any other data.

B. The Security Arguments

These arguments are the most common ones within the computer community. One common argument was the same one used most often by people attempting to defend the author of the Internet Worm program in 1988: break-ins illustrate security problems to a community that will otherwise not note the problems.

In the Worm case, one of the first issues to be discussed widely in Internet mailing lists dealt with the intent of the perpetrator—exactly why the Worm program had been written and released. Explanations put forth by members of the community ranged from simple accident to the actions of a sociopath. A common explanation was that the Worm was designed to illustrate security defects to a community that would not otherwise pay attention. This was not supported by the testimony during the author's trial, nor is it supported by past experience of system administrators.

The Worm author, Robert T. Morris, appears to have been well-known at some universities and major companies, and his talents were generally respected. Had he merely explained the problems or offered a demonstration to these people, he would have been listened to with considerable attention. The month before he released the Worm program on the Internet, he discovered and disclosed a bug in the file transfer program *ftp*; news of the flaw spread rapidly, and an official fix was announced and available within a matter of weeks. The argument that no one would listen to his report of security weaknesses is clearly fallacious.

In the more general case, this security argument is also without merit. Although some system administrators might have been complacent about the security of their systems before the Worm incident, most computer vendors, managers of government computer installations, and system administrators at major colleges and universities have been attentive to reports of security problems. People wishing to report a problem with the security of a system need not exploit it to report it. By way of analogy, one does not set fire to the neighborhood shopping center to bring attention to a fire hazard in one of the stores, and then try to justify the act by claiming that firemen would otherwise never listen to reports of hazards.

The most general argument that some people make is that the individuals who break into systems are performing a service by exposing security flaws, and thus should be encouraged or even rewarded. This argument is severely flawed in several ways. First, it assumes that there is some compelling need to force users to install security fixes on their systems, and thus *computer burglars* are justified in "breaking and entering" activities. Taken to extremes, it suggests that it would be perfectly acceptable to engage in such activities on a continuing basis, so long as they might expose security flaws. This completely loses sight of the purpose of the computers in the first place—to serve as tools and resources, not as exercises in security. The same reasoning would imply that vigilantes have the right to attempt to break into the homes in my neighborhood on a continuing basis to demonstrate that they are susceptible to burglars.

Another flaw with this argument is that it completely ignores the technical and economic factors that prevent many sites from upgrading or correcting their software. Not every site has the resources to install new system software or to correct existing software. At many sites, the systems are run as turnkey systems—employed as tools and maintained by the vendor. The owners and users of these machines simply do not have the ability to correct or maintain their systems independently, and they are unable to afford custom software support from their vendors. To break into such systems, with or without damage, is effectively to trespass into places of business; to do so in a vigilante effort to force the owners to upgrade their security structure is presumptuous and reprehensible. A burglary is not justified, morally or legally, by an argument that the victim has poor locks and was therefore "asking for it."

A related argument has been made that vendors are responsible for the maintenance of their software, and that such security breaches should immediately require vendors to issue corrections to their customers, past and present. The claim is made that without highly visible break-ins, vendors will not produce or distribute necessary fixes to software. This attitude is naive, and is neither economically feasible nor technically workable. Certainly, vendors should bear some responsibility for the adequacy of their software, but they should not be responsible for fixing every possible flaw in every possible configuration.

Many sites customize their software or otherwise run systems incompatible with the latest vendor releases. For a vendor to be able to provide quick response to security problems, it would be necessary for each customer to run completely standardized software and hardware mixes to ensure the correctness of vendor-supplied updates. Not only would this be considerably less attractive for many customers and contrary to their usual practice, but the increased cost of such "instant" fix distribution would add to the price of such a system—greatly increasing the cost borne by the customer. It is unreasonable to expect the user community to sacrifice flexibility **and** pay a much higher cost per unit simply for faster corrections to the occasional security breach. That assumes it was even possible for the manufacturer to find those customers and supply them with fixes in a timely manner, something unlikely in a market where machines and software are often repackaged, traded, and resold.

The case of the Internet Worm is a good example of the security argument and its flaws. It further stands as a good example of the conflict between ends and means valuation of ethics. Various people have argued that the Worm's author did us a favor by exposing security flaws. At Mr. Morris's trial on federal charges stemming from the incident, the defense attorneys also argued that their client should not be punished because of the good the Worm did in exposing those flaws. Others, including the prosecuting attorneys for the government, argued that the act itself was wrong no matter what the outcome. Their contention has been that the result does not justify the act itself, nor does the defense's argument encompass all the consequences of the incident.

This is certainly true; the complete results of the incident are still not known. There have been many other break-ins and network worms since November 1988, perhaps inspired by the media coverage of that incident. More attempts will possibly be made, in part inspired by Mr. Morris's act. Some sites on the Internet have restricted access to their machines, and others were removed from the network; I have heard of sites where a decision has been made not to pursue a connection, even though this will hinder research and operations. Combined with the many decades of person-hours devoted to cleaning up afterwards, this seems to be a high price to pay for a claimed "favor."

The legal consequences of this act are also not yet known. For instance, many bills were introduced into Congress and state legislatures in subsequent years as a (partial) result of these incidents. One piece of legislation introduced into the House of Representatives, HR-5061, entitled The Computer Virus Eradication Act of 1988, was the first in a series of legislative actions that had the potential to affect significantly the computer profession. In particular, HR-5061 was notable because its wording would have prevented it from being applied to true computer viruses. The passage of similar well-intentioned but poorly defined legislation could have a major negative effect on the computing profession as a whole.

C. The Idle System Argument

Another argument put forth by system hackers is that they are simply making use of idle machines. They argue that because some systems are not used at any level near their capacity, the hacker is somehow entitled to use them.

This argument is also flawed. First of all, these systems are usually not in service to provide a general-purpose user environment. Instead, they are in use in commerce, medicine, public safety, research, and government functions. Unused capacity is present for future needs and sudden surges of activity, not for the support of outside individuals. Imagine if large numbers of people without a computer were to take advantage of a system with idle processor capacity: the system would quickly be overloaded and severely degraded or unavailable for the rightful owners. Once on the system, it would be difficult (or impossible) to oust these individuals if sudden extra capacity was needed by the rightful owners. Even the largest machines available today would not provide sufficient capacity to accommodate such activity on any large scale.

I am unable to think of any other item that someone may buy and maintain, only to have others claim a right to use it when it is idle. For instance, the thought of someone walking up to my expensive car and driving off in it simply because it is not currently being used is ludicrous. Likewise, because I am away at work, it is not proper to hold a party at my house because it is otherwise not being used. The related positions that unused computing capacity is a shared resource, and that my privately developed software belongs to everyone, are equally silly (and unethical) positions.

D. The Student Hacker Argument

Some trespassers claim that they are doing no harm and changing nothing—they are simply learning about how computer systems operate. They argue that computers are expensive, and that they are merely furthering their education in a cost-effective manner. Some authors of computer viruses claim that their creations are intended to be harmless, and that they are simply learning how to write complex programs.

There are many problems with these arguments. First, as an educator, I claim that writing vandalware or breaking into a computer and looking at the files has almost nothing to do with computer education. Proper education in computer science and engineering involves intensive exposure to fundamental aspects of theory, abstraction, and design techniques. Browsing through a system does not expose someone to the broad scope of theory and practice in computing, nor does it provide the critical feedback so important to a good education. Neither does writing a virus or worm program and releasing it into an unsupervised environment provide any proper educational experience. By analogy, stealing cars and joyriding does not provide one with an education in mechanical engineering, nor does pouring sugar in the gas tank.

Furthermore, individuals "learning" about a system cannot know how everything operates and what results from their activities. Many systems have been damaged accidentally by ignorant (or careless) intruders; most of the damage from computer viruses (and the Internet Worm) appear to be caused by unexpected interactions and program faults. Damage to medical systems, factory control, financial information, and other computer systems could have drastic and far-ranging effects that have nothing to do with education, and could certainly not be considered harmless.

A related refutation of the claim has to do with knowledge of the extent of the intrusion. If I am the person responsible for the security of a critical computer system, I cannot assume that *any* intrusion is motivated solely by curiosity and that nothing has been harmed. If I know that the system has been compromised, I must fear the worst and perform a complete system check for damages and changes. I cannot take the word of the intruder, for any intruder who actually caused damage would seek to hide it by claiming that he or she was "just looking." In order to regain confidence in the correct behavior of my system, I must expend considerable energy to examine and verify every aspect of it.

Apply our universal approach to this situation and imagine if this "educational" behavior was widespread and commonplace. The result would be that we would spend all our time verifying our systems and never be able to trust the results fully. Clearly, this is not good, and thus we must conclude that these "educational" motivations are also unethical.

E. The Social Protector Argument

One last argument, more often heard in Europe than the United States is that hackers break into systems to watch for instances of data abuse and to help keep "Big Brother" at bay. In this sense, the hackers are protectors rather than criminals. Again, this assumes that the ends justify the means. It also assumes that the hackers are actually able to achieve some good end.

Undeniably, there is some misuse of personal data by corporations and by the government. The increasing use of computer-based record systems and networks may lead to further abuses. However, it is not clear that breaking into these systems will aid in righting the wrongs. If anything, it will cause those agencies to become even more secretive and use the break-ins as an excuse for more restricted access. Break-ins and vandalism have not resulted in new open-records laws, but they have resulted in the introduction and passage of new criminal statutes. Not only has such activity failed to deter "Big Brother," but it has also resulted in significant segments of the public urging more laws and more aggressive law enforcement—the direct opposite of the supposed goal.

It is also not clear that these are the individuals we want "protecting" us. We need to have the designers and users of the systems—trained computer professionals—concerned about our rights and aware of the dangers involved with the inappropriate use of computer monitoring and recordkeeping. The threat is a relatively new one, as computers and networks have become widely used only in the last few decades. It will take some time for awareness of the dangers to spread throughout the profession. Clandestine efforts to breach the security of computer systems do nothing to raise the consciousness of the appropriate individuals. Worse, they associate that commendable goal (heightened concern) with criminal activity (computer break-ins), discouraging proactive behavior by the individuals in the best positions to act in our favor. Perhaps it is in this sense that computer break-ins and vandalism are most unethical and damaging.

IV. CONCLUDING REMARKS

I have argued here that computer break-ins, even when no obvious damage results, are unethical. This must be the considered conclusion even if the result is an improvement in security, because the activity itself is disruptive and immoral. The results of the act should be considered separately from the act itself, especially when we consider how difficult it is to understand all the effects resulting from such an act.

Of course, I have not discussed every possible reason for a break-in. There might well be an instance where a break-in might be necessary to save a life or to preserve national security. In such cases, to perform one wrong act to prevent a greater wrong may be the right thing to do. It is beyond the scope or intent of this article to discuss such cases, especially as no known hacker break-ins have been motivated by such instances.

Historically, computer professionals as a group have not been overly conconcerned with questions of ethics and propriety as they relate to computers. Individuals and some organizations have tried to address these issues, but the whole computing community needs to be involved to address the problems in any comprehensive manner. Too often, we view computers simply as machines and algorithms, and we do not perceive the serious ethical questions inherent in their use.

When we consider, however, that these machines influence the quality of life of millions of individuals, both directly and indirectly, we understand that there are broader issues. Computers are used to design, analyze, support, and control applications that protect and guide the lives and finances of people. Our use (and misuse) of computing systems may have effects beyond our wildest imagining. Thus, we must reconsider our attitudes about acts demonstrating a lack of respect for the rights and privacy of other people's computers and data.

We must also consider what our attitudes will be towards future security problems. In particular, we should consider the effect of **widely** publishing the source code for worms, viruses, and other threats to security. Although we need a process for rapidly disseminating corrections and security information as they become known, we should realize that widespread publication of details will imperil sites where users are unwilling or unable to install undates and fixes. Publication should serve a useful purpose; endangering the security of other people's machines or attempting to force them into making changes they are unable to make or afford is not ethical.

Finally, we must decide these issues of ethics as a community of professionals and then present them to society as a whole. No matter what laws are passed, and no matter how good security measures might become, they will not be enough for us to have completely secure systems. We also need to develop and act according to some shared ethical values. The members of society need to be educated so that they understand the importance of respecting the privacy and ownership of data. If locks and laws were all that kept people from robbing houses, there would be many more burglars than there are now; the shared mores about the sanctity of personal property are an important influence in the prevention of burglary. It is our duty as informed professionals to help extend those mores into the realm of computing.

Also See the Following Articles

CONFIDENTIALITY, GENERAL ISSUES OF • ELECTRONIC SURVEILLANCE • INFORMATION MANAGEMENT • INTERNET PROTOCOL • PRIVACY VERSUS PUBLIC RIGHT TO KNOW

Bibliography

Adelaide, J. P. B. et al. (1990, March). Is computer hacking a crime? *Harper's Magazine,* 280(1678):45–57.

Baird, B. J., Baird, L. L., Jr., & Ranauro, R. P. (1987, December). The moral cracker? *Computers and Security,* 6(6):471–478.

Denning, P. J., et al. (1989, January). Computing as a discipline. *Communications of the ACM,* 32(1):9–23.

Denning, P. J. (Ed.). (1991). *Computers under attack: Intruders, worms, and viruses.* Reading, MA: ACM Books/Addison-Wesley.

Hoffman, L. (Ed.) (1990). *Rogue programs: Viruses, worms, and Trojan horses.* New York: Van Nostrand Reinhold.

Landreth, B. (1984). *Out of the inner circle: A hacker's guide to computer security.* New York: Microsoft Press.

McIlroy, M. D. (1990). Unsafe at any price. *Information Technology Quarterly,* IX(2):21–23.

Schwartz, J. (1990, April). The hacker dragnet. *Newsweek,* 65(18).

Seeley, D. (1989, January). A tour of the worm. In *Proceedings of the Winter 1989 Usenix Conference.* The Usenix Association.

Spafford, E. H. (1989, June). The Internet Worm: Crisis and aftermath. *Communications of the ACM,* 32(6): 678–698.

Spafford, E. H. (1989, September). An analysis of the Internet Worm. In C. Ghezzi and J. A. McDermid (Eds.). *Proceedings of the 2nd European Software Engineering Conference,* pp. 446–468. Berlin/New York: Springer-Verlag.

Spafford, E. H., Heaphy, K. A., & Ferbrache, D. J. (1989). *Computer viruses: Dealing with electronic vandalism and programmed threats.* Arlington, VA: ADAPSO.

Stallman, R. (1986). *GNU EMacs Manual,* pp. 239–248. Cambridge, MA: Free Software Foundation.

Stang, D. J. (1990, March). *Computer viruses.* (2nd ed.). Washington, DC: National Computer Security Association.

Stoll, C. (1989). *Cuckoo's egg.* New York: Doubleday.

Tucker, A. B., et al. (1991). Computing curricula 1991. Piscataway, NJ: Published by the IEEE Society Press.

CONFIDENTIALITY, GENERAL ISSUES OF

Mary Beth Armstrong
California Polytechnic State University

I. Nature of Professions and Role of Confidentiality
II. Deontological Arguments for Confidentiality
III. Special Case—Whistleblowing
IV. Summary

GLOSSARY

confidentiality A rule or duty requiring one entrusted with private or secret matters to refrain from divulging them.
deontological Of or pertaining to the theory of duty or moral obligation.
negative duty Duty to refrain from certain actions.
positive duty Duty to perform certain actions.
prima facie At first sight, before further examination.
profession A vocation or occupation requiring advanced training in some liberal art or science, and usually involving mental as opposed to physical work.
utilitarianism The doctrine that the worth or value of anything is determined solely by its utility.
whistleblowing To reveal secret and detrimental information, usually outside of one's normal channels of communication or outside of one's organization.

THE ESSENCE OF CONFIDENTIALITY is the keeping of secrets. When one person confides secret information

to another, the recipient of the secret may or may not have a duty to keep the secret confidential. Such a duty might be created by a promise to the first party by the recipient of the secret. Thus, the duty to keep information confidential might arise under the more general duty of promise keeping, which will not be discussed herein because it is a topic unto itself. Role relationships may also create a duty to keep secret information confidential. Clients, patients, penitents, employers, etc., reveal secret information to professionals, for example, with the expectation that the role professionals play will create for them a duty to keep the secret information confidential. This article will concentrate on the role-related duty of confidentiality by professionals.

I. NATURE OF PROFESSIONS AND ROLE OF CONFIDENTIALITY

Sociologists differ among themselves concerning the nature of professions and the attributes shared by professionals. Usually, however, agreement can be found on four fundamental attributes of a profession: expertise, monopoly status, public interest ideal, and self-regulation.

Professionals have special knowledge, usually of a theoretical nature. This expertise is manifested when they offer advice to their clients/patients. Society acknowledges the need for the expertise and limits practice of the profession to those who can demonstrate their expertise and obtain a license to practice. But

Encyclopedia of Applied Ethics, Volume 1

knowledge is power, and power in the hands of a few can cause harm to the many. So, in exchange for the license, professionals must promise to use their expertise to benefit, not harm, society. Thus, the public interest ideal, which is often expressed in a code of ethics, is the profession's promise to act in the public interest. Self-regulation is a privilege granted to professions in exchange for the fulfilment of their duty to regulate their own members.

Of particular interest to this discussion is the third attribute discussed above, the public interest ideal. Keeping professional secrets or confidences has long been considered to be in the public interest. Arguments defending professional confidentiality are based both on deontological reasoning and on utilitarianism. Deontological justifications are based on notions such as privacy, autonomy, promise keeping, loyalty, and role-related duties. Utilitarian arguments stress the positive benefits to society when professionals can be trusted to keep confidences. One court summed up some of those benefits as follows (*Hammonds v. Aetna*, 1965):

> Since the layman is unfamiliar with the road to recovery, he cannot sift through the circumstances of his life and habits to determine what is information pertinent to his health. As a consequence, he must disclose all information in his consultations with his doctor—even that which is embarrassing, disgraceful, or incriminating. To promote full disclosure, the medical profession extends the promise of secrecy.

II. DEONTOLOGICAL ARGUMENTS FOR CONFIDENTIALITY

A. *Prima Facie* Duties

Professional confidentiality is recognized as a *prima facie* duty, and is therefore morally binding on professionals unless it is in conflict with equal or stronger duties. Justification for the claim rests on the premises of promise keeping (i.e., the implicit promise of all professions to act in the public interest), individual autonomy over personal information, and respect for relationships among human beings and for intimacy. Sissela Bok (1982. *Secrets: On the Ethics of Concealment and Revelation*. Pantheon Books, New York), points out that even though the premises supporting confidentiality are strong, they cannot support practices of secrecy that undermine and contradict the very respect for persons, human bonds, and the public interest that confidentiality was meant to protect.

Beauchamp and Childress, in their text on biomedical ethics, assert four requirements for justified infringements of a *prima facie* duty:

1. The moral objective justifying the infringement must have a realistic prospect of achievement
2. Infringement of a *prima facie* principle must be necessary in the circumstances, in the sense that there are no morally preferable alternative actions that could be substituted
3. The form of infringement selected must constitute the least infringement possible commensurate with achieving the primary goal of the action
4. The agent must seek to minimize the effects of the infringement

The most common objective justifying infringement of confidentiality is that of preventing harm or not causing harm. Thus, the interests of clients/patients/penitents to whom the professional owes the *prima facie* duty of confidentiality are pitted against the interests of others in society (or society itself) who may be harmed if the professional secret is kept.

B. Positive and Negative Duties

Another way to analyze duties is to distinguish between positive and negative duties. Although there is some controversy in the literature regarding the appropriateness of this distinction, nevertheless it is included here in an attempt to help order the duties related to confidentiality issues. In general, positive duties are obligations to bring about good or be meritorious, and they generally require some action on the part of the professional. Negative duties, however, are duties to not harm or not do bad, and most often require inaction or compliance with rules defining one's role. Negative duties are seen as more obligatory than positive duties. Thus, keeping professional secrets, a negative duty, would be a stronger duty than the positive duty to take action to prevent harm, assuming that the magnitude of the potential harm to society is equal to the magnitude of the potential harm done to the client/patient/penitent by revealing the confidence.

Negative duties do not always trump positive duties, however. Ruland and Lindblom argue that the positive–negative duty distinction serves as the basis for a strict ordering of duties. They describe four criteria for policy makers who might determine when professionals should be bound by the negative duty to maintain confidentiality and when they should reveal the secrets to prevent an impending harm. The criteria are relentlessness, nature of responsibilities, uncertainty of outcomes, and magnitude of consequences.

1. Relentlessness

Relentlessness refers to the dischargeability of a duty. Since one cannot perform all positive acts of beneficence, some would argue that positive duties are relentless and thus never obligatory. Ruland and Lindblom, however, argue that positive duties are obligatory in circumstances that are less than relentless. For example, even though accountants cannot be held to a duty to disclose all information of benefit to the public, they may have a duty to disclose certain limited sets of information.

2. Nature of Responsibilities

As circumstances change, so might the nature of the responsibilities faced by certain individuals. For example, if one were to witness a person crying for help while apparently attempting to keep from drowning, one might have a positive duty to attempt to save the individual. This duty to help would be particularly strong for a lifeguard on duty. If one were not a lifeguard, but were a champion swimmer, the positive duty might still be strong. For a nonswimmer there would probably be no duty to help, nor might there be for a mother with small children playing by the water's edge, especially if others are present who could help the victim. Thus, the strength of a positive duty is affected by who else might share the responsibility and by the nature of the shared duty.

3. Uncertainty of Outcomes

The strickness of a positive duty is related to the probability that something bad will occur or that something good will not occur if the duty is not fulfilled. Usually if one violates a negative duty the result will almost always be harmful, whereas if one does not perform a positive duty, a bad result can be avoided by other means. However, there are circumstances in which failure to act on a positive duty will have an almost certain outcome. When these circumstances occur, they could change the relative strictness of a positive duty to act.

4. Magnitude of Consequences

As the magnitude of the harm increases for a positive duty, and the magnitude of harm is decreased for a negative duty, the positive duty can be seen to outweigh the negative duty.

Beauchamp and Childress essentially combine the last two criteria above when they state that it is necessary to consider both the probability and the magnitude of harm and to balance both against the rule of confidentiality, as follows:

Probability of harm	Magnitude of harm	
	Major	Minor
High	1	2
Low	3	4

Beauchamp and Childress state that as the assessment of the situation approaches 1, the weight of the obligation to breach confidentiality increases. As the situation approaches 4, the weight decreases. Cases 2 and 3 are more troublesome. However, they see no moral obligation to breach confidentiality in case 2 (high probability of a minor harm) and conclude that, in case 3, some form of risk–benefit analysis is called for. They also imply that reasonable doubts ought to be settled in favor of preserving confidentiality.

Unfortunately, this discussion does not give guidance to help assess the probability of harm or its magnitude. Nor are types of harm distinguished (e.g., bodily harm, loss of wealth, or damage to reputation). Presumably such guidance and distinctions are to be made by individual professional practitioners in concrete situations, based upon guidelines by their professional organizations. Hopefully, such guidance would include rules governing commonly encountered situations within a particular profession, and ideally such rules would be well conceived and based upon the same concepts described herein.

III. SPECIAL CASE—WHISTLEBLOWING

A. Description

One special form of confidence breaking, termed "whistleblowing," requires additional analysis because it is most often associated with professionals (such as engineers or accountants) working as employees inside an organization, as opposed to professionals working outside of an organization as consultants or contractors. Whistleblowing can be internal, as, for example, when a professional takes his/her concerns to someone "over the head" of the professional's supervisor, perhaps even to a board of directors. External whistleblowing, however, is the more commonly understood form of whistleblowing, and in these cases individuals take their secret information outside of the organization to authorities (such as law enforcement or regulators) or to the media. According to Peter Drucker (1981. *Public Interest* **63**, 18–36), whistleblowing is just another name for informing, and the only societies in western history that encouraged informers were bloody and infamous tyrannies. In Drucker's view, under whistleblowing, under the regime of the informer, no mutual trust, no interdependencies, and no ethics are possible. Ralph Nader, on the other hand, views whistleblowers as heroes and whistleblowing as a necessary component of corporate accountability.

B. Characteristics

Sissela Bok also paints a negative picture of whistleblowing. She states that three elements, each jarring, and triply jarring when conjoined, lend acts of whistleblowing special urgency and bitterness: dissent, breach of loyalty, and accusation.

Dissent is the act of alerting the public to a risk perceived by the whistleblower but denied by those in authority. *Breach of loyalty* is perceived because the whistleblower comes from within, which is quite different than exposure from without. *Accusation* points the finger of responsibility to certain persons within the organization because of their negligence, greed, or incompetence.

C. Appropriate Circumstances

All three elements just discussed impose requirements on the whistleblower: of judgment and accuracy in dissent, of exploring alternative ways to cope with improprieties that minimize the breach of loyalty, and of fairness in accusation.

Thus, Bok sees whistleblowing as a valid means of last resort to discharge a duty to protect the public interest if (1) the threat of harm is imminent and serious, (2) existing avenues for change within the organization have been exhausted, and (3) the whistleblower makes his/her accusation openly, so those criticized have the opportunity to defend themselves. The third requirement may be particularly burdensome, since fairness to the accused may result in unfairness to the whistleblower. Some states and organizations, as well as the federal government, recognize this imbalance of power and have enacted whistleblowers' protection acts to safeguard the rights of whistleblowers.

Richard DeGeorge (1981. *Busi. Professional Ethics J.* 1(1), 1–14) lists similar criteria to consider before blowing the whistle. For him, engineers in large corporations are *permitted* to go public with information regarding public safety if:

1. The harm that will be done to the public is serious and considerable

2. They make their concerns known to their superiors

3. If, getting no satisfaction from their immediate superiors, they exhaust the channels available within the organization

For an engineer to have a moral *obligation* to alert the public, additional requirement are:

4. She or he must have documented evidence that would convince a reasonable, impartial observer that the engineer's view of the situation is correct and the company policy is wrong

5. There must be strong evidence that making the information public will in fact prevent the threatened serious harm.

IV. SUMMARY

In summary, confidentiality is a *prima facie* obligation, but not an absolute obligation. Some may argue about when and in what circumstances confidentiality should yield to other duties, especially duties to protect the public from harm, but few would see professional confidentiality as an absolute duty. Whistleblowing, a special form of confidence breaking, is especially troublesome for professionals in a corporate–employee relationship because of the additional loyalty duties required by that employment relationship. Individual practitioners in any profession need policy and rule makers who will help them apply some of the theory mentioned herein to particular sets of circumstances. This implies, of course, that policy and rule makers themselves are well grounded in the philosophical underpinnings of confidentiality.

Also See the Following Articles

CONFIDENTIALITY OF SOURCES • PRIVACY • WHISTLEBLOWING

Bibliography

Armstrong, M. B. (1994). Confidentiality: A comparison across the professions of medicine, engineering and accounting. *Professional Ethics* 3(1), 71–88.

Beauchamp, T. and Childress, J. (1989). *Principles of Biomedical Ethics*. 3rd Edition. Oxford: Oxford University Press.

Pearce, R. (1996). To save a life: Why a rabbi and a Jewish lawyer must disclose a client confidence. *Loyola L. A. Law Rev.* 29(4), 1771.

Ruland, R., and Lindblom, C. (1992). Ethics and disclosure: An analysis of conflicting duties. *Crit. Perspec. Accounting* 3, 259–272.

Stewart, T. (1994). AIDS and murder: Decisions regarding the maintenance of confidentiality versus the duty to protect. *Law Human Behav.* 18(2), 107.

CONFIDENTIALITY OF SOURCES

Michel Petheram
Open University

GLOSSARY

consequentialism The view that the value of an action derives entirely from the value of its consequences. The best-known form of consequentialism is utilitarianism.
House of Lords The final court of appeal in the United Kingdom for both civil and criminal cases.
promise A declaration that one will or will not do something.

WE ARE entrusted with other people's secrets; we entrust others with our own. This entrusting requires that we or they do not pass on the secret information contained in these avowals, and this keeping of confidences is something we all value. Professional people, including journalists, often receive such confidential information. But in the case of journalists the information is to be made public; it is the source of the information that is required to be kept confidential. Much valuable information comes to journalists from individuals who wish to keep their identity secret.

A civil servant passes to a newspaper a document that reveals that the government has lied on a particular issue. If her request for anonymity is not observed, she will lose her job. A journalist investigating drug dealing in a town obtains an interview with one of the drug dealers; the police then demand that he give them the name of the dealer, so that they can prosecute him.

Because, for journalists, obtaining information is their raison d'etre, this practice of confidentiality has long been recognized. Journalists further believe that if they were not able to offer confidentiality, then many of these sources of information would not make themselves available. Some journalists have been prepared to go to prison to defend a promise of confidentiality.

I. THE VALUE OF CONFIDENTIALITY

Journalists themselves often express a strong belief in the need for confidentiality of sources. A recent account of journalism in the United Kingdom by noted journalist Raymond Snoddy remarks: "It is impossible to exaggerate the importance for a journalist of being able to obtain information in confidence from a private source and then being allowed to protect the confidentiality of the source" (Snoddy (1992). *The good, the bad and the unacceptable*. London: Faber). The author also refers to the still secret identity of "Deep Throat" who helped Woodward and Bernstein in the Watergate investigation. Conrad Fink in *Media ethics* describes confidentiality as "an essential tool of the trade" (p. 47) (Fink

Encyclopedia of Applied Ethics, Volume 1

(1988). *Media ethics.* New York: Mc-Graw-Hill). To turn to more official views, the Society of Professional Journalists, Sigma Delta Chi, from the United States, says in its code of ethics, dating from 1973: "Journalists acknowledge the newsman's ethic of protecting confidential sources of information." Less platitudinous was the 1934 code of ethics of the American Newspaper Guild, which says: "Newspapermen shall refuse to reveal confidences or disclose sources of confidential information in court or before judicial or investigating bodies." In Great Britain the National Union of Journalists, in its code of conduct, says that "a journalist shall protect confidential sources of information."

Surveys of the press in the 1970s indicated that a substantial number of newspaper stories are based on information that could only be obtained through confidential reporter–source relationships (Van Gerpen (1979). *Privileged communications and the press.* Westport, CT Greenwood Press). The *Wall Street Journal* reckoned that 15% of its articles are based on confidential information. Memoirs of journalists and journalistic textbooks all refer to the necessity of preserving the confidential relationship between reporters and their sources.

It should be noted that the issue of confidentiality arises for other professions. Doctors, lawyers, and priests are traditionally recipients of information that the donor, so to speak, does not wish to have passed on. It is hard to see how the relationship between lawyer and client can work at all, without such an understanding. As modern society becomes more complex, with more information being recorded, other professions come to hold confidential information, such as bank managers, accountants, social workers. But, as mentioned above, the relationship between reporters and sources is rather different, in that it is a means to making information available to the public, whereas the other relationships are to keep the information itself confidential.

II. THE PHILOSOPHICAL ARGUMENTS

A. Sissela Bok

The most substantial discussion of confidentiality is to be found in the book *Secrets* by Sissela Bok in the chapter "The Limits of Confidentiality" (Bok, S. (1986)). In this she argues that the justification for confidentiality rests on four premises, of which three support the general practice of confidentiality, and the fourth supports professional secrecy in particular. The first premise is that of individual autonomy over personal information; people can have secrets. The second holds that it is not only natural but often also right to respect the secrets of intimates and associates, secrets that might have been shared with one, and that human relationships could not survive without such respect. The third premise asserts that a pledge of silence, should one be made, creates an obligation beyond the respect already provided for by the two previous premises, for persons and for existing relationships. Such a promise raises the stakes. But then, as Bok points out, there may be times when these premises have to be overriden, for example, if maintaining confidentiality would lead to violence being done to innocent persons, or to someone becoming an unwitting accomplice in crime. In such circumstances, she says, a promise of silence can be breached. But her fourth premise "enters in to add strength to the particular pledges of silence given by professionals. This premise assigns weight beyond ordinary loyalty to professional confidentiality, because of its utility to persons and to society."

This point about the social utility of the silence of the professional is important, because it is easy for professionals in any field to advance confidentiality as a shield (the medical profession is particularly prone to do this). An absolute insistence on confidentiality can be unreasonable. It can be used as a means for deflecting legitimate public attention. (And indeed it is often this kind of confidentiality that journalists frequently need to breach to discover something of public concern.) Bok concludes her chapter: "The premises supporting confidentiality are strong, but they cannot support practices of secrecy—whether by individual clients, institutions, or professionals themselves—that undermine and contradict the very respect for persons and for human bonds that confidentiality was meant to protect." A system of ethics cannot excuse any group from the rules of moral reasoning predicated simply on the role of that group within society.

So Bok believes that confidentiality is not an absolute value; it is something that can be overridden by other, weightier considerations.

B. Other Arguments

Another way of setting up the argument is in a two step argument as follows. The first step is to say that confidentiality is justified in journalism because it is necessary to do the job, it is a tool of the profession. The second step is the claim that journalism itself is important, that is, to give the justification for the profession.

The first step is a consequentialist one; but does the second step have to be consequentialist? For example, a doctor may argue for the practice of medicine as a whole, not simply that it is concerned with the reduction of pain (consequentialist) but that it shows respect for the individual's physical integrity (nonconsequentialist). When the argument takes a consequentialist turn, we will have to compare the benefits of revealing confidences in problem situations with the benefits of keeping them, and then it is clear how well the two-step argument succeeds.

But if a plausible nonconsequentialist defense of professional activity can be put forward, it may be possible to argue that the two-step argument introduces values that are more important than social utility and therefore should not be weighed crudely against the benefits of disclosure. (Bok's discussion was couched in terms of social utility.) Whether it is possible to put forward a nonconsequentialist justification of journalism is doubtful.

The argument most frequently proposed by journalists to defend their activity is in terms of aiding the functioning of democracy by creating or ensuring well-informed citizens. This is clearly a consequentialist approach. A second line of argument often invoked is that freedom of speech and thereby journalism aid the pursuit of truth. This again is a consequentialist argument, but also rather more double-edged, in that if one is pursuing truth, one is appealing to the virtue of making things known, whereas in this instance the journalist wishes to conceal information.

The harsh truth seems to be that as journalists themselves invoke social utility (usually by appeal to the "public interest"), they have no moral high ground of values that override this utility to fall back on.

Finally, it may be said that what is at stake here is the keeping of a promise, and this can be considered an obligation or a duty, irrespective of the consequences. And it is a duty that is widely acknowledged. So, because breaking promises is wrong, it is wrong to break a promise of confidentiality. But does the keeping of a promise have an absolute force? Although a perhaps simplistic evaluation of the consequence of an action is avoided when we refer to duty, this does not of itself avoid moral conflict. Here, as happens in many other areas of life, the duty of promise-keeping can be in conflict with other duties, or with other's rights, such as the right to a fair trial.

III. THE LEGAL ARGUMENTS

Some of the confidential professional relationships mentioned earlier are considered important enough to receive recognition by the law, for example, those be-

tween lawyers and clients, priests and penitents, bank managers and clients. Journalists have this legal protection in Sweden, but not in the United Kingdom or the United States.

Journalists feel that they are often summoned to court without serious alternative attempts by the police or the courts to obtain for themselves the information they want. In these circumstances, the press claims that it is being used as an investigative arm of government.

A watershed decision was made in the United States in 1972 in what is known as the *Branzburg* case, which resulted from the refusal of a journalist to give the names of his sources for an article on drug use. A majority in the Supreme Court ruled to deny constitutional protection for the reporter–source relationship. According to this judgment, reporters had no privilege under the First Amendment to refuse to testify before grand juries.

"The great weight of authority is that newsmen are not exempt from the normal duty of appearing before a grand jury and answering questions relevant to a criminal investigation …. These courts have … concluded that the First Amendment interest asserted by the newsman was outweighed by a general obligation of a citizen to appear before a grand jury or a trial pursuant to a subpoena, and give what information he possesses …. We are asked … to grant a testimonial privilege that other citizens do not enjoy. This we decline to do." (Quoted from Hulteng (1985). *The messenger's motives* (2nd Ed.). Englewood Cliffs, NJ: Prentice-Hall). One of the judges, however, dissented from this judgement: "A reporter is no better than his source of information. Unless he has a privilege to withhold the identity of his source, he will be victim of governmental intrigue or aggression. If he can be summoned to testify in secret before a grand jury, his sources will dry up and the attempted exposure, the attempt to enlighten the public, will be ended." (Ibid.)

Following this dissenting opinion, many lower federal courts and state courts in the United States have protected journalists. This judge had proposed a three-part test, which should be met before government could compel grand jury testimony from a journalist. First, there should be probable cause to believe that the journalist has information "clearly relevant to a specific probable violation of the law." Second, that the information sought could not be obtained by alternative means less destructive of First Amendment values. Third, there should be a "compelling and over-riding need" for the information.

However, according to Van Gerpen (1979), p. 177, there is a substantial record of case evidence that a so-called "chilling effect" set in after the 1972 case. There were concrete illustrations of stories that were not published because assurance of confidentiality could not be extended to sources.

In the United Kingdom the issue is covered by the Contempt of Court Act 1981, section 10. This lays down that a court may not require journalists to reveal their sources "unless it is established to the satisfaction of the court that it is necessary in the interests of justice or national security or for the prevention of disorder and crime." Some have argued that this requirement is too wide, especially the phrase "in the interests of justice" (Robertson and Nicol (1992)). There have been few cases in the courts: one occured in 1990 when a journalist was fined £5000 for refusing to disclose a source. The case went all the way to the House of Lords, where one of the judges argued: "no one has a right of conscientious objection which entitles him to set himself above the law if he does not agree with a court's decision. That would undermine the rule of law and is wholly unacceptable in a democratic society. Freedom of speech is itself a right which is dependent on the rule of law for its protection and it is paradoxical that a serious challenge to the rule of law should be mounted by responsible journalists."

In reply, journalists might say that this is to beg the question about where their responsibility lies and that their dispute is not with the system of justice itself, but with the interests (for example, governments or large corporations) that are using the system to protect themselves.

Overall, it is not that journalists wish to put themselves above the law, but a question of where the burden of proof should lie, and what conditions need to be fulfilled to require a journalist to reveal his source. If they are too easy to meet, then it becomes likewise easier to intimidate the press, so that they are less able to carry out their socially useful tasks. Part of the problem in the United Kingdom is that there is no written agreement, comparable to the First Amendment in the United States and Freedom of Information Acts elsewhere, on the role of the press.

IV. PROBLEMS WITH SOURCES

So far, we have been assuming, with journalists, that the reporter's privilege of keeping confidences is a good thing. It may sometimes, perhaps often, be necessary. However, in principle, sources should be made known. For one thing, the reader is often only able to judge the value of the information provided, if he or she is able to evaluate the source from which it comes. Confidentiality can act as a smokescreen. As an editorial

from the *Washington Post* put it (1969, December 2. Quoted in Hulteng, 1985. *The messenger's motives* (2nd Ed.). Englewood Cliffs, NJ: Prentice-Hall):

"Walter and Ann source (née Rumor) had four daughters (Highly Placed, Authoritative, Unimpeachable, and Well-Informed). The first married a diplomat named Reliable Informant. (The Informant brothers are widely known and quoted here; among the best known are White House, State Department, and Congressional.) Walter Speculation's brother-in-law, Ian Rumor, married Alexandre Conjecture, from which there were two sons, It Was Understood and It Was Learned."

Thus, confidentiality deprives the audience of the opportunity to decide for itself how much faith to put in the information. In other words, the names of the sources are an important part of the story.

In addition, news sources act from a variety of motives, not all of which are praiseworthy. They may be providing information out of self-interest or for revenge. How is the journalist to know whether this information has been altered, edited, or selected out of context? What interest is he serving? There is a very real danger that journalists and through them the public can be deceived by this use of confidentiality. In the United Kingdom, the government uses a system of informal unattributed briefings to the press, known as the "lobby system." This has allowed governments and individual politicians to manipulate the news to the point of "disinformation" (Cockerell, M., et al., 1984. *Sources close to the Prime Minister: the hidden world of the news manipulators*. London: Macmillan). "When journalists are presented with secret information about issues of great import, they become, in a very real sense, agents for the surreptitious source." (Epstein (1974, April 20). The American press: some truths about truths. *The National Observer*).

It may not be in journalists' long-term interests to connive in such practices. The extensive use of unattributed sources promotes distrust and even cynicism toward reported stories. Journalists should not let their desire to obtain information undermine the long-term credibility of the information they present to their readers. More generally, journalists stand for openness in public discourse; they challenge secrecy. They should, therefore, avoid it in their own practices; reliance on reporter's privilege can lead to accusations of hypocrisy.

V. CONCLUSION

The main consequence of all this is that because a journalist may be in the position of being taken to court to divulge a source, he or she should be very careful about promising to protect a source's anonymity. One textbook of media ethics has put it quite strongly: "Never promise to protect a source's anonymity unless you are prepared to go all the way—to jail, even—to keep your promise. Whatever the source's motives, you must be known far and wide as a completely reliable, ethical reporter who stands by a promise .... No reporter can work effectively without complete trust from sources" (Fink, 1988, *Media ethics,* Mc-Graw-Hill, New York).

The practical consequence of this ethical burden is that in many newsrooms, editors have taken it upon themselves to make the decision as to whether a news source should be granted anonymity, and so reporters must ask permission of their editors. One of the main considerations in making such a decision will be, how important or valuable is the information being offered?

It may be useful to note what journalists think of confidentiality. In a survey carried out in the United States in the mid-1980s, publishers, editors, and journalists were asked about their view of the issue. Twenty-five percent of the total said that a pledge of confidentiality to a source should always be kept no matter what the circumstances, even if it means a long jail term for the reporter and heavy financial cost to the newspaper (although, interestingly, this broke down into 40% of the journalists, 18% and 20%, respectively, for publishers and editors, who worry more about financial consequences). A further 62% thought as a whole that a pledge of confidentiality should always be taken seriously, but it can be violated in unusual circumstances (Meyer, P. (1987). *Ethical journalism.* New York: Longman). Unfortunately, a survey of this kind does not give the answer to the question that immediately arises, in what circumstances? For if a journalist is not going to follow the rigorous course of action suggested above, then this is just what a source seeking a pledge of confidentiality needs to know.

Here it may be useful to return to the three part test suggested after the *Branzburg* case (see Section III). Two of the conditions are relevant. First, the information should be relevant to a specific violation of the law. When a case like this arises, one would expect a newspaper to have worked out a policy as to whether it would resist or comply with a demand to reveal confidentiality, and if to comply, whether it would argue its case up to the highest appeal court. The second condition was a "compelling and over-riding need." These are difficult to specify. Obviously, if the promise of confidentiality concerned a life or death situation, then life should be preserved. Another consideration follows from the fact that a promise of confidentiality requires trust on both sides. If it should turn out that the information provided under the promise of confidentiality should be false, then the journalist or newspaper may reasonably no longer feel bound to his or to its side of the bargain.

In view of these considerations, and taking into account the fact that individuals can vary considerably in how seriously they take their promises and the weight that they then give to reasons for overriding their promises, the source who seeks confidentiality would be advised to act on the principle of "caveat emptor" and inquire as fully as possible into the journalist's or newspaper's attitude to their promises of confidentiality.

Nevertheless, it is clear that, whether the ethical argument is in terms of consequences or of duty, promises of confidentiality should be kept. The doubts raised in Section IV suggest, not that such promises may be broken more easily, but that they should be given more carefully and less frequently.

Also See the Following Articles

CONFIDENTIALITY, GENERAL ISSUES OF • PRIVACY • PRIVACY VERSUS PUBLIC RIGHT TO KNOW

Bibliography

Bok, S. (1986). *Secrets.* Oxford: Oxford University Press.

Day, L. (1991). *Essays in media communications: Cases and controversies* (chap. 6). Belmont, CA: Wadsworth Publishing.

Robertson, G., & Nicol, A. (1992). *Media law* (3rd ed.). London: Penguin.

Van Gerpen, M. (1979). *Privileged communication and the press.* Westport, CT: Greenwood Press.

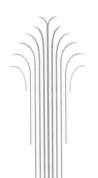

CONFLICT OF INTEREST

Michael Davis
Illinois Institute of Technology

I. What Is Conflict of Interest?
II. What Is Wrong with Conflict of Interest?
III. Strategies for Dealing with Conflict of Interest
IV. Appearances, Loyalties, Gifts, and Bribes
V. History of Conflict of Interest

GLOSSARY

adverse interest A private interest giving one a reason to act contrary to one's duty as agent or trustee; not necessary for a conflict of interest.

agent A person authorized by another person, the principal, to act in the principal's behalf and continuously subject to the principal's control.

apparent conflict of interest A situation in which a person does not have the conflict of interest in question but someone else would be justified in concluding that the person does.

bias A deflection of judgment in a determinate direction.

conflicting interests Same as conflict of interests; not necessarily a conflict of interest.

conflict of commitments A situation in which a person has at least two commitments and fulfilling one will make fulfilling the rest impractical; not necessarily a conflict of interest.

conflict of interests A situation in which two or more interests conflict, whether within one person or between persons; not necessarily a conflict of interest.

conflict of roles A situation in which satisfying the demands of one role precludes satisfying the demands of another role that one also occupies; not necessarily a conflict of interest.

disloyalty The fact of acting contrary to one's duty as agent or trustee.

fiduciary A person having a duty to act in another's behalf. Both agents and trustees are fiduciaries.

trustee A person having a duty to act in another's behalf, especially with respect to property, but not subject to that other's control. Trustees are fiduciaries but not agents.

CONFLICT OF INTEREST is a situation in which some interest of a person has a tendency to interfere with the proper exercise of his judgment in another's behalf. Although often financial or familial, the interest creating a conflict of interest can be friendship, enmity, or anything else having a tendency to bias judgment (without rendering it incompetent). However, mere bias or prejudice does not entail a conflict of interest. Conflict of interest is also distinguishable from conflict of commitments, conflict of roles, partiality, loss of independence or objectivity, and disloyalty. What is wrong with a conflict of interest is that it renders one's judgment less reliable than normal. Conflict of interest creates an usual risk of error. Depending on how it is handled, the conflict may also constitute negligence or betrayal of trust. Some conflicts of interest should be avoided; some, escaped; some, disclosed and managed. The term

Encyclopedia of Applied Ethics, Volume 1
Copyright © 1998 by Academic Press. All rights of reproduction in any form reserved.

589

"conflict of interest" (as used here) seems to be a recent coinage.

I. WHAT IS CONFLICT OF INTEREST?

A conflict of interest is a situation in which some person *P* (whether an individual or corporate body) has a conflict of interest. *P* has a conflict of interest if and only if (1) *P* is in a relationship with another requiring *P* to exercise judgment in the other's behalf and (2) *P* has a (special) interest tending to interfere with the proper exercise of judgment in that relationship. The crucial terms in this definition are "relationship," "judgment," "interest," and "proper exercise."

A. Relationship

Relationship (as used here) is quite general, including any connection between *P* and another person (or persons) justifying that other's reliance on *P* for a certain purpose. A relationship may be quite formal (as is that between a United States Senator and her constituency) or quite informal (as is that between friends). A relationship can last a long time (as familial relationships generally do) or only a minute (as when one directs a stranger to a distant address). The relationship required must, however, be fiduciary, that is, involve one person trusting (or, at least, being entitled to trust) another to do something for her—exercise judgment in her service.

B. Judgment

Judgment (as used here) is the ability to make certain kinds of decision correctly more often than would a simple clerk with a book of rules and all, and only, the same information. Insofar as decisions do not require judgment, they are "routine," "mechanical," or "ministerial"; they have (something like) an algorithm. The decision-maker contributes nothing special. Any difference between her decision and that of someone equally well trained would mean that (at least) one of them had erred (something easily shown by examining what they did). Ordinary math problems are routine in this way.

Where judgment is required, the decision is no longer routine. Judgment brings knowledge, skill, and insight to bear in unpredictable ways. Where judgment is necessary, different decision-makers, however skilled, may disagree without either being clearly wrong. Over time, we should be able to tell that some decision-makers are better than others (indeed, that some are imcompetent), but we will not, decision by decision, be able to explain differences in outcome merely by error—or even be able

to establish decisively that one decision-maker's judgment is better than another's.

Anyone sufficiently adept in the exercise of judgment of a certain kind is competent in the corresponding field. Each profession is defined in part by a distinct kind of judgment. Accountants are especially adept at evaluating procedures for reporting finances; civil engineers, especially adept at predicting the likely serviceability of physical structures; teachers, especially adept at judging academic progress; and so on.

Judgment is not only an attribute of professions. Any agent, trustee, or other fiduciary may exercise judgment. One may even exercise judgment in a relationship as mundane as watching a neighbor's children while he answers the phone. But not every relationship, not even every relationship of trust or responsibility, requires judgment. I may, for example, be asked to hold a great sum of money in my safe until the owner returns. I have a great trust. I am a fiduciary upon whom the owner may be relying for her future happiness. But I need not exercise judgment to do what I should. My duties are entirely routine (however much the money tempts me). I need only put the money in the safe and leave it there until the owner returns and asks for it.

C. Interest

An interest is any influence, loyalty, concern, emotion, or other feature of a situation tending to make *P*'s judgment (in that situation) less reliable than it would normally be (without rendering *P* incompetent). Financial interests and family connections are the most common interests discussed in this context, but love, prior statements, gratitude, and other "subjective" tugs on judgment can also be interests (in this sense). So, for example, a judge has an interest in a case if one of the parties is a friend or an enemy, just as he would if the party were his spouse or a company in which he owned a large share. Friendship or enmity can threaten judgment as easily as can financial or family entanglements.

D. Proper Exercise

What constitutes proper exercise of judgment is generally a question of social fact including what people ordinarily expect, what *P* or the group *P* belongs to invites others to expect, and what various laws, professional codes, or other regulations require. Because what constitutes proper exercise of judgment is a social fact, it may change over time and, at any time, may have a disputed boundary. For example, physicians in the United States today (probably) are expected to give substantial weight to considerations of cost when deciding what to prescribe, something not within the proper exercise of their judgment in 1960.

What is proper exercise of judgment also varies from one profession to another. For example, a lawyer who resolves every reasonable doubt in favor of an employer when presenting the employer's case in court exercises her professional judgment properly; an industrial chemist who does the same when presenting research at a conference does not. Chemists are supposed to serve their employer by serving the truth (not, like lawyers, to serve the truth by serving their employer).

What is proper exercise of judgment may also vary from one employer to another. For example, one company may leave its employees free to choose their flight even though the company is paying for it; another may require employees to choose the least expensive flight consistent with arriving on time. Because employees are agents having a general duty not to waste their employer's resources, and because choosing among flights generally involves judgment, the employees of the second company will have less room for conflict of interest than employees of the first. They will have less room for conflict of interest because their employer has restricted the domain of proper judgment more than the first did.

II. WHAT IS WRONG WITH CONFLICT OF INTEREST?

A conflict of interest is like dirt in a sensitive gauge. All gauges contain some dirt, the omnipresent particles that float in the air. Such dirt, being omnipresent, will be taken into account in the gauge's design. Such dirt does not affect the gauge's reliability. But dirt that is not omnipresent, the unusual bit of grease or sand, can affect reliability, the ability of this gauge to do what gauges of its kind should (and generally do) do. Such "special" dirt might, for example, cause the gauge to stick unpredictably. Insofar as dirt affects a gauge's reliability, it corresponds to the interests that create conflicts of interest. So, a conflict of interest can be objectionable for at least one of three reasons:

First, P may be negligent in not responding to the conflict of interest. We expect those who undertake to act in another's behalf to know the limits of their judgment when the limits are obvious. Conflicts of interest *are* obvious; one cannot have an interest without knowing it, although one can easily misjudge how much it might affect one's judgment. Indeed, people with a conflict of interest often esteem too highly their own reliability (much as might a dirty gauge used to check

itself). Insofar as P is unaware of her conflict of interest, she has failed to exercise reasonable care in acting in another's behalf. Insofar as she has failed to exercise reasonable care, she is negligent. Insofar as she is negligent, her conduct is morally objectionable.

Second, if those justifiably relying on P for a certain judgment do not know of P's conflict of interest but P knows (or should know) that they do not, P is allowing them to believe that she is more reliable than she is. She is, in effect, deceiving them. Insofar as she is deceiving them, she is betraying their (properly placed) trust. Insofar as she betrays their trust, her conduct is morally objectionable.

Third, even if P informs those justifiably relying on her that she has a conflict of interest, her judgment will be less reliable than it ordinarily is. She will still be less competent than usual—and perhaps appear less competent than members of her profession, occupation, or avocation should be. Conflict of interest can remain a technical problem even after it has ceased to be a moral problem. Even as a technical problem, conflict of interest can harm the reputation of the profession, occupation, avocation, or individual in question.

A. Not Bias

Conflict of interest is not mere bias. *Bias* (in a person) is a deflection of judgment in a certain direction. Bias, whether conscious or unconscious, is relatively easy to correct for. For example: If a gauge has a bias, we need only add or subtract a set amount to compensate. The gauge is otherwise still reliable. If a person is biased, we can simply discount for the bias ("take it with a grain of salt," as we say).

Conflict of interest is not bias but a *tendency* toward bias. Correcting for a tendency is much harder than correcting for a bias. Consider our gauge again: Because of the special dirt in it, it has a tendency to stick. How do we correct for that tendency? Do we accept the first reading, strike the gauge once and then accept the new reading, strike it several times before accepting a reading, average all the readings, or what? How are we to know when we have what we would have had were the gauge as reliable as it should be?

B. Not Conflict of Commitments or Conflict of Roles

A conflict of interest is not a conflict within one's commitments or between one's roles but between some (special) interest and the proper exercise of competent judgment in accordance with some commitment or role.

So, for example, I do not have a conflict of interest just because (in a fit of absentmindedness) I promised to give a talk today after promising to attend my son's soccer game scheduled for the same time. That conflict of commitments or roles does not threaten my judgment (although I must decide between them).

I would, however, have a conflict of interest if I had to referee at my son's soccer game. I would find it harder than a stranger to judge accurately when my son had committed a foul. (After all, part of being a good father is having a *tendency* to favor one's own child.) I honestly do not know whether I would be harder on him than an impartial referee would be, easier, or just the same. What I do know is that, like the dirty gauge, I could not be as reliable as a "clean gauge" would be.

The same would be true even if I refereed for a game in which my son did not play but I had a strong dislike for several players on one team. Would I call more fouls against that team, fewer (because I was "bending over backward to be fair"), or the same as a similarly qualified referee who did not share my dislike? Again, I do not know. What I do know is that an interest, my dislike of those players, is sufficient to make me less reliable in the role of referee than I would otherwise be. Conflict of interest does not require a clash of roles; one role (referee) and one interest (a dislike of some players) is enough for a conflict of interest.

C. Impartiality, Independence, and Objectivity

We often describe an inability to judge as someone less involved would as a loss of "impartiality," "independence," or "objectivity." Such descriptions often pick out a conflict of interest, but just as often they do not. One can, for example, fail to be impartial, independent, or objective because one is biased or under another's control.

III. STRATEGIES FOR DEALING WITH CONFLICT OF INTEREST

Virtually all professional codes, and many corporate codes of ethics as well, provide some guidance on how to deal with conflicts of interest. Unfortunately, many say no more than "avoid all conflicts of interest." Such a flat prohibition probably rests on at least one of two mistakes.

One mistake is assuming that conflicts of interest can always be avoided. Some certainly can. For example,

a public prosecutor might, upon taking office, put his assets in a blind trust. He would then not know what special effect his official decisions would have on his finances. His "objective interest" could not affect his judgment. He would have avoided all conflicts of interest arising from his investments. He cannot, however, avoid all conflicts of interest in that way. He cannot put all his interests, including his family and friendships, into a blind trust. The prosecutor may not, for example, be able to avoid having a case in which a member of his family is the defendant's attorney, a witness, or even the defendant.

The other mistake upon which a flat prohibition of conflicts of interest may rest is the assumption that having a conflict of interest is always wrong. *Having* a conflict of interest is not like stealing money or taking a bribe. One can have a conflict of interest without doing anything wrong. To have a conflict of interest is to have a moral problem. What will be morally right or wrong, or at least morally good or bad, is how one resolves that problem. There are two approaches to the problem (apart from trying to avoid those conflicts that should be avoided).

A. Escape

One approach to the problem posed by a conflict of interest is *escape*. One way to escape a conflict of interest is to redefine the underlying relationship. So, for example, a prosecutor foreseeing certain conflicts of interest might "recuse" himself, that is, establish procedures so that all litigation involving his assets, family, and the like that pass through his office bypass him. Another way to escape a conflict of interest is to divest oneself of the interest creating the conflict. If, for example, the conflict is created by ownership of stock in a certain corporation, one can sell the stock before making any official decision affecting it (and have nothing to do with the stock for a decent interval thereafter).

Escape can be costly. So—to continue our example—recusing gives up the public advantage of having the prosecutor contribute to certain official decisions. The prosecutor will not even hear of matters he would ordinarily decide. Divesting avoids that cost, but perhaps only by imposing a substantial personal loss (because, say, the prosecutor would have to sell a stock when its price was depressed). If the prosecutor cannot afford divestment, and recusal is impractical, he may have to choose a third way of escape, withdrawal from the underlying relationship: he may have to resign his office.

B. Disclosure

The other approach to resolving the moral problem posed by a conflict of interest is to *disclose* the conflict to those relying on one's judgment. Disclosure, if sufficiently complete (and understood), prevents deception. Often disclosure also allows those relying on one to adjust their reliance accordingly (for example, by seeking a "second opinion") or by redefining the relationship (for example, by requiring recusal for a certain range of decisions). But, unlike escape, disclosure as such does not end the conflict of interest; it merely avoids negligence and betrayal of trust.

Procedures for disclosure can be quite elaborate. For example, the city of Chicago now requires every employee of the executive branch with significant responsibilities to fill out annually a two-page form disclosing close relatives, business partners, and sources of outside income. The forms are open to public inspection.

Disclosure may itself generate problems of privacy and confidentiality. For example, if a condition of holding a certain public office is that the official list everyone with whom she has a business relation, she may have to provide significant information about people who, having nothing to do with government, thought they could avoid having their business relations put into a public record.

C. The Best Approach

What should be done about a conflict of interest depends on all the circumstances, including the relative importance of the decision in question, the alternatives available, the wishes of the principal, client, employer, or the like, the law, and any relevant code of ethics, professional or institutional. Some conflicts should be avoided; others escaped; and others disclosed.

Generally, conflicts of interest are easier to tolerate when they are "potential" rather than "actual." A conflict of interest is *potential* if and only if *P* has a conflict of interest with respect to a certain judgment but is not yet in a situation where he must make that judgment. Potential conflicts of interest, like time bombs, may or may not go off. A conflict of interest is *actual* if and only if *P* has a conflict of interest with respect to a certain judgment and is in a situation where he must make that judgment.

In a friendly divorce, for example, the parties may prefer a less-expensive proceeding in which they share a lawyer to a more-expensive one in which each party has its own. The lawyer who undertakes to represent both parties in such a divorce can, of course, foresee that a dispute about the house, car, savings account, or dog may turn ugly. From the beginning, the lawyer would be risking a moment when trying to put her professional judgment at the disposal of one party while trying to do the same for the other would affect the judgment in ways hard to predict. She would, that is, have a potential conflict of interest as soon as she agreed to represent both parties. But, while the divorce remained friendly, she would have no actual conflict of interest.

The lawyer should, of course, be sure that the parties understand the risks, as well as the benefits, of sharing a lawyer before she agrees to such an arrangement. Among the risks is her precipitous withdrawal from the proceeding should the divorce turn ugly. She would have to withdraw if the divorce turned ugly because an actual conflict of interest would make it impossible for her to serve her clients as her profession wants lawyers to serve clients. The profession's code takes precedence over the clients' wishes.

IV. APPEARANCES, LOYALTIES, GIFTS, AND BRIBES

A. The Appearance of Conflict of Interest

Many potential or actual conflicts of interests are, out of politeness or timidity, misdescribed as "apparent conflicts of interest" or "merely apparent conflicts of interest." The term "apparent conflict of interest" should not be wasted in this way. A conflict of interest is (merely) *apparent* if and only if *P* does not have the conflict of interest (actual or potential), but someone other than *P* would be justified in concluding (however tentatively) that *P* does. Apparent conflicts of interest (strictly so called) are no more conflicts of interest than counterfeit money is money.

An apparent conflict of interest is nonetheless objectionable—for the same reason that any merely apparent wrongdoing is objectionable. It misleads people about their security, inviting unnecessary anxiety and precaution. Apparent conflicts should be resolved as soon as possible. An apparent conflict of interest is resolved by making available enough information to show that there is no actual or potential conflict. One might, for example, answer a charge of financial interest by showing that one does not own the property in question. Where one cannot make such a showing, the conflict of interest is actual or potential, *not* (merely) apparent.

B. Disloyalty

Disloyalty is neither necessary nor sufficient for conflict of interest. Disloyalty and conflict of interest are only loosely connected.

You can, of course, be loyal and have a conflict of interest. A loyal agent who cannot reasonably avoid or escape a conflict of interest respecting some affair on which her judgment is to be deployed would disclose the conflict to her principal. Having fully disclosed it and received the principal's informed consent to continue as before, she may continue, even though her judgment remains less reliable than it would otherwise be. There is no disloyalty in that; yet, the conflict of interest remains.

One can also be disloyal without having a conflict of interest. For example: If, being too greedy, you embezzle money from your employer, you are disloyal. You consciously fail to act as a faithful agent of your employer. Although your greed is certainly an interest conflicting with your employer's interests, conflict of interest does not explain why you took the money or what was wrong with taking it. You did not need to exercise judgment on your employer's behalf to know that you should not embezzle your employer's money. There is a conflict of interests here, that is, a conflict between one of your interests and one of your employer's, but no conflict of interest.

C. Gifts and Bribes

Gifts are an important subject in any discussion of conflict of interest. Gifts are a way of recognizing and reinforcing friendship. Because gifts have this function, they can also establish bonds of interest where none should exist, for example, between a judge and a litigant or between a company's head of purchasing and the company's most ambitious supplier. For that reason, many governments, businesses, and other institutions have policies limiting business gifts to mere tokens. Some forbid such gifts altogether.

A "gift" *demanded* is a bribe (or "grease payment"), not a gift (strictly speaking). Bribes as such do not create a conflict of interest. A *bribe* is a payment (or promise of payment) in return for doing (or promising to do) something one should not do (or, at least, should not do for that reason). Where bribes affect judgment (as they often do), they affect it in a definite way, that is, in the direction promised. Affecting judgment in a definite direction creates a bias, not a conflict of interest.

Bribe *offers*, however, often do create a conflict of interest. I may, for example, be so enraged by your offering me a bribe that I can no longer reliably judge your skill.

V. HISTORY OF CONFLICT OF INTEREST

Too frequently, discussions of conflict of interest begin with the biblical quotation, "Can a man have two masters? Can a man serve both God and Mammon?" This is the wrong way to begin. The reason one cannot have two masters is that a master is someone to whom one owes complete loyalty, and complete loyalty to one excludes any loyalty to another. Having only one master *is* a strategy for avoiding all conflict of interest, but a strategy making the concept of conflict of interest uninteresting. We must worry about conflict of interest only when having two or more masters—or, to say it without paradox, having none—is normal. Conflict of interest is an interesting concept only where loyalties are regularly and legitimately divided.

Beginning a discussion of conflict of interest with that biblical quotation makes conflict of interest seem an idea as old as the bible. In fact, the term—and, apparently, the idea—are barely half a century old. The first court case to use the term in something like our sense was decided in 1949 (*In re Equitable Office Bldg. Corp.*, D.C.N.Y., 83 F. Supp. 531). The *Index of Legal Periodicals* had no heading for "conflict of interest" until 1967; *Black's Law Dictionary* had none until 1979. No ordinary dictionary of English seems to have had an entry for "conflict of interest" before 1971. The first philosophical discussions of the term also date from about that time.

"Conflict of interest" seems to have begun as a mere synonym for "conflicting interests." This older term designated a clash between a *public* interest (say, impartiality in a receiver or trustee) and some *private* "beneficial" or "pecuniary" interest (say, a receiver's hope of buying property at a bankruptcy sale he administers). The private interest was often said to be "adverse" (that is, opposed) to the public interest. Only in the late 1960s did lawyers begin explicitly to connect the term "conflict of interest" with judgment.

The term "conflict of interest" began to appear in codes of ethics in the 1970s. Today the term is so common that we would find it hard to do without it. Yet, if "conflict of interest," both the term and the concept, are as new as they seem to be, we are bound to ask, "Why now?" So far, we have no authoritative answer. The history of "conflict of interest" has yet to be written.

Also See the Following Articles

BUSINESS ETHICS, OVERVIEW • CORPORATIONS, ETHICS IN • LEGAL ETHICS, OVERVIEW

Bibliography

Carson, T. L. (1994). Conflict of interest. *Journal of Business Ethics* **13**, 387–404.

Davis, M. (1993). Conflict of interest revisited. *Business and Professional Ethics Journal* **12** (Winter), 21–41.

Donaldson, M. S., & Capron, A. M. (Eds.). (1991). *Patient outcomes research teams: Managing conflicts of interest.* Washington, DC: National Academy Press.

Luebke, N. R. (1987). Conflict of interest as a moral category. *Business and Professional Ethics Journal* **6** (Spring), 66–81.

McMunigal, K. (1992). Rethinking attorney conflict of interest doctrine. *Georgetown Journal of Legal Ethics* **5** (Spring), 823–877.

Parley, L. (1995). *The ethical family lawyer: A practical guide to avoiding professional dilemmas.* Chicago: Family Law Section, American Bar Association.

Porter, R. J., & Malone, T. E. (Eds.). (1992). *Biomedical research: Collaboration and conflict of interest.* Baltimore: Johns Hopkins University Press.

Pritchard, Michael S. (1996). Conflicts of interest: Conceptual and normative issues. *Academic Medicine* **71** (December), 1305–1313.

Rodwin, M. A. (1993). *Medicine, money, and morals: Physicians' conflicts of interest.* New York: Oxford University Press.

Spece, R. G., Shimm, D. S., & Buchanan A. E. (Eds.). (1996). *Conflicts of interest in clinical practice and research.* New York: Oxford University Press.

Stark, A. (1995). The appearance of official impropriety and the concept of political crime. *Ethics* **105** (January), 326–351.

Wells, P., Jones, H., & Davis M. (1986). *Conflicts of interest in engineering.* Dubuque, IA: Kendall/Hunt Publishing.

CONFUCIANISM

Julia Po-Wah Lai Tao
City University of Hong Kong

GLOSSARY

dao The way.
hsiao Filial piety.
li Conventional principles.
ren Humaneness.
shu Fairness, empathy, to extend oneself.
te Ethical virtue.
yi Rightness.
zhong Benevolence, being true, to exhaust oneself.

CONFUCIANISM is one of the most influential philosophical schools in China. It is, however, not a unitary discourse. Scholars have identified four major discourses of Confucianism : Classical Confucianism (the early Confucians), Medieval Confucianism (the Han-Tang Confucians), Neo-Confucianism (the Song-Ming Confucians), and New Confucianism (the contemporary Confucians).

Classical Confucianism developed during the Zhou epoch in Chinese history. It is represented by the thinking and teaching of Confucius and his followers who lived during the Zhou epoch (1111–249 B.C.). The background was the decay of the central power of the Zhou king, the dissolution of the patriarchal feudal system, and the crisis of conventional morality. Faced with such a crisis, Confucius tried to find a new moral basis for rescuing ethical life. This entry will focus on the discourse of Classical Confucianism to provide a discussion of the conceptual explication and basic structure of the Confucian system of ethical thought.

I. BACKGROUND

Confucianism is not a unitary discourse. Scholars have identified four major discourses of Confucianism: Classical Confucianism (from the early Confucians, 551–479 B.C., to Hsun Tzu, 298–238 B.C.); the Medieval Period (from the Han Dynasty, 206–220 A.D., to the Tang Dynasty, 618–907 A.D.); Neo-Confucianism (from the Sung Dynasty, 960–1279 A.D., to the Ming Dynasty, 1368–1644 A.D.); and New Confucianism (the contemporary Confucians in the 20th century). Classical Confucianism is represented by the thinking and teaching of Confucius and his followers who lived during the Zhou epoch in Chinese history (1111–249 B.C.). It was a time of decay of the central power of the Zhou king, the dissolution of the patriarchal feudal system, and the crisis of the inherited tradition in the middle of the first millennium B.C. in China.

The decline of the Western Zhou kingdom brought with it serious threats to its firmly established hierarchies and the conventional ritual rules of propriety (*li*). The rules of proper behavior according to social position had turned out to be fragile and had lost their binding force. War was the most evident expression of the crisis and tore the world asunder as traditional certainties disintegrated. The challenge faced by the Zhou philosophers was the crisis of the established conventional rules of propriety. It is also the period known as the "hundred schools" in Chinese philosophy, distinguished by the many controversies of the age, made possible by the breakdown of traditions and received opinions. It is therefore no accident that the peak of Chinese philosophy fell into this period, which is also known as the "warring states period" (481–221 B.C.).

Confucianism is the most influential of the many schools which emerged during the Zhou epoch in trying to provide an answer to the challenge of its age, precipitated by the decline of conventional morality. The task of Confucius (551–479 B.C.) and his followers was to find a new moral basis for rescuing ethical life. The theoretical foundation of the Confucian position is found in a representative text, the *Lunyu* (the *Analects*), or the "collected sayings" of Confucius. The *Lunyu* is the founding document of the school which prefigures all the different directions into which it developed. Commonly considered the main and reliable source of Confucius's teaching, it bequeaths to Classical Confucianism a large and complex ethical vocabulary which constitutes by far the most comprehensive and the most influential ethical program in China. This article will focus on the discourse of Classical Confucianism to provide a discussion of the conceptual explication and basic structure of Confucianism as a system of ethics.

The ethical vocabulary which the *Lunyu* bequeathed to the Chinese contains both basic and dependent concepts. The basic concepts are the most important, comprehensive, guiding ones. They are not amenable to the simple expedience of translation and require careful conceptual analysis and interpretation. Dependent concepts derive their ethical import by reference to the basic concepts. Their complex interrelationships constitute the core structure of the Confucian ethical system. Confucius's concern is not only to develop a vocabulary of ethical categories; he also searches for a unifying, pervading ethical perspective to ground morality.

One major obstacle to the explication of the conceptual framework of Confucian ethical thought is the absence of definitions of important terms and basic categories in classical Confucian discourse. As a general rule, the Confucian explanation of the use of ethical terms is context dependent, addressed to a particular rather than a universal audience. There is a lack of interest in context-independent explanation of the use of technical terms. As Theodore de Barry observes, "for the Chinese the idea is not so much to analyze and define concepts precisely as to expand them, to make them suggestive to the widest possible range of meaning" (W. T. de Bary, Ed., 1970. *Self & society in Ming thought*. New York: Columbia Univ. Press, P.V.). Confucian reasoning and argumentation are also highly inexplicit. These special features of the Confucian ethical scheme render the explication of the conceptual framework a task of philosophical reconstruction of the meaning, status, and relationship of the basic notions and dependent concepts, including their presumed interconnection or interdependence in Confucian ethical thinking.

II. BASIC CONCEPTS AND STRUCTURE

A. *Dao*—The Way

The Confucian ethical framework comprises five basic concepts: *dao* (the way), *te* (ethical virtue), *li* (conventional propriety), *yi* (rightness), and *ren* (humaneness). They are formulated as abstract principles which are amenable to specification in particular contexts. *Dao* is the center of Confucian ethics—it is the one unifying and pervading principle and ideal of Confucianism. Confucius says, "My way [*dao*] is pervaded [*guan*] by one" (*Lunyu* 4:15) (1972. *A concordance to the analects of Confucius*. Reprint. Harvard–Yenching Institute Sinological Index Series. Taipei). Unlike other basic terms, *dao* is most distinctive in the Confucian system as an abstract, formal term in the highest generic sense. It is subject to specification by way of other value principles such as *ren, li,* and *yi* in the Confucian system.

In the *Lunyu*, *dao* is sometimes used as a verb, meaning "to guide," and sometimes it is used as a concrete noun, meaning literally "road." In the latter sense, it can be rendered as "way." But in distinct Confucian ethical usage, it is *dao* as an abstract noun that is meant, and more especially, in an evaluative rather than a descriptive sense. It refers to the ethical ideal of a good human life as a whole, or the ideal of human excellence. In this understanding *dao* is functionally equivalent to the ideal "way of life."

B. *Te*—Ethical Virtue

The ideal Confucian way of life is a well-ordered society based on good government responsive to the basic needs of the people. Special emphasis is placed on harmonious human relationships (*lun*) in accord with *te*, virtues or standards of excellence. To realize this ideal, Confucianism stresses character formation or personal cultivation of virtues (*te*). The ultimate goal is to bring human action into harmony with *te*. In Confucian ethical thinking, the notion of *te* is a conception of ethical virtues that can contribute to an achieved condition of an ethically well-cultivated person, a *zungzi*, with commendable character traits in accord with the ideal of *dao*. It can also call into existence a condition that is deemed to have peculiar potency or power of efficacy in influencing the course of human life. Confucius once remarks that "the virtue of the *junzi* [ethically superior or paradigmatic individual, gentleman] is like the wind; the virtue of the small man is like grass. Let the wind blow over the grass and it is sure to bend" (*Lunyu* 12:19).

The specification of *te* in the Confucian system can take the forms of *ren*, *li*, and *yi*. In this sense, *te* is an abstract noun like *dao*, but it also depends on *dao* for its distinctive character. *Ren*, *li* and *yi* are generic focal terms. They convey distinct, though not unrelated, centers of ethical concern. Other categories, such as filiality, respectfulness, and fraternity are dependent terms. Their ethical import depends on direct or indirect reference to one or more of the generic terms. *Dao* as an ideal provides the unifying perspective.

C. *Li*—Conventional Propriety

The notion of *li*, or rites, focuses on the ritual code. The ritual code is essentially a set of rules of proper conduct pertaining to the manner or style of performance. They are originally the unwritten rites and customs of the prestate communities and tribes.

In Confucian ethics, the *li* set forth the rules of ethical responsibility. As a set of formal prescriptions for proper behavior, they have a threefold function: delimiting, supportive, and ennobling (A. S. Cua, 1966. "The Conceptual Framework of Confucian Ethical Thinking," *Journal of Chinese Philosophy*, 23, 165). The delimiting function is primary in that the *li* set constraints and define what is permissible and impermissible behavior. They serve to prevent human conflict. It is recorded in the *Lunyu* that "of the things brought about by *li*, harmony is the most valuable"(*Lunyu* 1:12). *Li* delineate the boundaries of pursuit of individual needs, desires, and interests and set forth rules of pro-

ceeding in an orderly fashion to promote unity and harmony. This orderliness consists of social distinctions or divisions in various kinds of human relationships (*lun*), namely, the distinction between ruler and minister, father and son, the elder and younger, husband and wife, and among friends. Thus, *li* function as negative moral rules which stipulate the conditions of the eligibility or permissibility of actions.

The *li* also have a supportive function which is to provide guidance on conditions or opportunities for satisfaction of desires or interests within the prescribed limits of action. They provide socially acceptable channels or outlets for the fulfillment of desires and needs. They contain rules that enable us to implement our desires by redirecting the course of individual self-seeking activities, without suppressing the motivating desires.

The ennobling function of *li* is "cultural refinement." They are oriented to the education and nurturance of emotions or their transformation in accord with the spirit of *ren* and *yi*. This explains the Confucian emphasis on music and the arts. Confucius says, "Be stimulated by the odes, take your stand on *li*, and be perfected by music" (*Lunyu* 8:8). In the ideal case, they give expression to the ethical character and enrich a *li* performance by according it an aesthetic dimension. The *junzi* lives by rites: "Courtesy not in keeping with what is *li* becomes laborious bustle; caution not in keeping with what is *li* becomes timidity; courage not in keeping with what is *li* becomes brashness; and forthrightness becomes rudeness" (*Lunyu* 8:2).

But the fact that people need transmitted conventions for finding their orientation does not mean, however, that they could exclusively rely on them. From a Confucian viewpoint, conventional propriety is indispensable, for without it people would be "without any standing," as the *Lunyu* states. Yet the rules of proper behavior had lost their binding force since the decline of Western Zhou society in Confucius's time. He thus advocated a "return to propriety" (*fu li*) which is only possible if a man "overcomes himself." In the all important matter of where a gentleman takes his stand, Confucius says, "Take your stand in the *li*" (*Lunyu* 8:8), and "unless you study the *li* you will not be able to take your stand" (*Lunyu* 6:13)

But there is no simple, precise formula for the process of self-definition. On the one hand, it is important that there should be an objective norm to which to refer. On the other hand, Confucius shows a clear distrust of mere instinct or impulse; some recourse must be had to an external norm or measure. Confucius once said of himself, "I have no preconception about the permissible and the impermissible" (*Lunyu* 18:8). Quite naturally, one may raise the question of justification for such judgments in exigent circumstances.

D. *Yi*—Rightness

The ethical significance of *yi*, in part, is an attempt to provide a rationale for the acceptance of *li*. *Yi* focuses principally on what is right or fitting. The equation of *yi* with its homophone *yí* meaning "appropriateness" is explicit in *Zhong Yong* (1980. Liji zhengyi. In Ruan Yuan, shisanjing zhushu. Reprint Peking: Zhonghua), Section 20, and generally accepted by Confucians: "*Yi* means *yí* [appropriate]. To honor the wise is the greatest exercise of it. *Yi* is that everybody does his due [*yí*]" (*Guanzi*, 1978. Dai Wang. Guanzi jiaozeng. In zhuzi jicheng. Vol. 5. Hong Kong. Zhonghua 36, p.221).

As a central concept of classical Confucian ethics, *yi* is frequently translated as "justice." "The absence of distinctions and justice is the way of beasts," says the *Liji* (11, 1456c). *Yi* has also been rendered as "rightness," "sense of duty," "oughtness," and "integrity." The variety of proposals coincides with actual variations in the meaning of *yi*, which can be aptly explained by the difficulty of determining what is "just" in the first place.

The coincidence of the term with that which is due or appropriate (*yí*) is a very common connotation of *yi*, the just, and it is quite characteristic of the classical Chinese understanding of justice. The identification of *yi* and *yí* corresponds to Plato's and Aristotle's notion of *dikaiosyne* (justice). (H. Roetz, 1993, *Confucian ethics of the axial age: A reconstruction under the aspect of the breakthrough toward postconventional thinking.* State University of New York Press, p. 127) For Plato, justice is "having and doing what is a man's own and belongs to him," and "doing one's business and not being a busibody" (*Republic* IV, 433) For Aristotle, justice is "the virtue through which everybody has his due, in accordance with the laws" (*Rhetorica,* 1366b). The meaning of this understanding of justice becomes plain in Aristotle's *Politics:* "It is clear, then that some men are by nature free, and others slaves, and that for the latter slavery is both expedient and just (*dikaion*)" (1255a1). For Aristotle, the just can go together with equality and inequality alike. This is very different from Rawls' contemporary notion of "justice as fairness," which defines justice as comprising the idea of general *equality.* As for the Confucians, they are committed to an egalitarian anthropology which upholds the conviction that all people are equal by birth. Nevertheless, despite their egalitarian anthropology, the social bonds and separations predetermined by given inequalities of their society do play a role in their idea of justice.

> What is the just for man? That the father is kind and the son is filial, that the elder brother is good to the younger brother and the younger brother respects the elder brother, that the husband is just [*yi*] and the wife is obedient, that the elder are gracious and the young are docile, that the ruler is humane and the subject is loyal—these ten things are called the just for man. (*Liji* 9, 1422c)

The notion of justice in these quotations is oriented to a particular social station. *Yi* in this sense is close to *li.* The meaning of justice is the maintenance of a hierarchical order representing the *general* structures of hierarchical social relations. *Li* describes the detailed code of the corresponding appropriate forms of conduct.

But *yi* is not just a conventional rule in the sense of "everybody pays his due." In the Confucian literature, *yi* is not always relative to social position. What is right or fitting depends on reasoned judgment. As Xunzi puts it, "the person concerned with *yi* follows reason" (*Xunzi,* W. Xianqian, 1978. In *Zhuzi jiaheng* (Vol. 2, p. 15). Hong Kong: Zhongua). Thus, *yi* may be construed as reasoned judgment concerning the right thing to do in particular exigencies. Hard cases for deliberation are those that can be resolved by an appeal, not to an established rule of *li,* but to one's reasoned judgment of what is the right or fitting thing to do. When queried as to what a person ought to do when his sister-in-law is drowning, given the *li* requirement of his age that male and female are not to touch one another in giving or receiving anything, Mencius, one of Confucius's most influential followers, emphasizes weighing the circumstances rather than endorsing compliance. This appeal has nothing to do with building an exception to a rule of proper conduct but has to do instead with appealing to one's sense of rightness in exigent situations. Courage to uphold the interest of the underprivileged is emphasized in Confucius's teaching to his disciples, who are told that it would be "cowardice not to interfere when justice is at stake." (*Lunyu* 2:24, 4:16) The Confucian ideal *junzi,* is an independent intellectual who cannot be bent by authority and power. In the name of justice, Confucian philosophers constantly polemize against the search for private profit. In the *Lunyu,* the terms *yi* and *li* (profit) contrast with each other: "A gentleman listens to the argument of justice, a mean man listens to the argument of profit" (4.16). "He who seeing a profit yet thinks of justice ... can be regarded as a complete person" (14.14).

This double character of justice helps to explain why there are many divergences in the use of *yi*. An emphasis can be laid on its conventional, restrictive aspect as well as on the interest of the greater whole. Both sides can conflict with one another if the general interest necessitates suspending what would be appropriate according to one's social station. However, a basic idea remains: justice brings into effect the interest of all against the egoism of individuals. Confucius says, "In dealing with the world, the gentleman is not invariably for or against anything. He is on the side of what is *yi*" (*Lunyu* 4:10).

E. *Ren*—Humaneness

Ren or humaneness is the nonegoistic fundamental ethical norm in Confucianism. "Confucius regards humaneness the highest," testifies the *Lushi chunqiu* (1978. In *Zhuzi jicheng* (Vol. 6, 17.7, p. 213). Hong Kong: Zhonghua). Confucius says, "There are only two ways: humaneness and inhumanity" (*Mengzi. 1972*. In *A concordance to Meng Tzu* (2A7, 4A2). Reprint. Harvard–Yenching Institute Sinological Index Series. Taipei). What humaneness has to add to a life embedded in the transmitted rules of propriety and good manners is love, active sympathy, and respect for the other as a being like oneself.

1. Humaneness as Love and Compassion

The central account of humaneness in Confucianism is love. The first direct identification of both is found in *Lunyu* 12:22. Fan Chi asks what humaneness is. Confucius says, "To love men [*ai rén*]."

Ren means to embody love. (*Mozi* 40, p.191) (S. Yirang, 1978. In *Zhuzi jicheng* (Vol. 4). Hong Kong: Zhonghua)
A person of *ren* loves others. (*Mengzi* 4B28, p.165)
To love men and to be advantageous to this, this is called *ren*.
(*Zhuangzi* 12, p.183) (G. Qingfan, 1978. In *Zhuzi jicheng* (Vol. 3). Hong Kong: Zhongua)
Ren means love. (*Xunzi* 27, p.324)
To love all people together in one's heart, this is called *ren*.
(*Xinshu, Daoshu*, p.928) Q. Yuzhang, 1974. *Jiazi xinshu jiaoshi*. Taipí: Zhongguo wenhua zazhi she)

The Confucian concept of love is distinguished by its insistence on an element of justice within humaneness.

To someone who asks, "What do you think of repaying injury with virtue?" (*Lunyu* 14:34), Confucius says, "With what, then, shall virtue be repaid: Repay injury with straightness [*zhi*], repay virtue with virtue." *Zhi*, by itself is a virtue, which can also be rendered as "justice." The Christian ideal of loving one's enemy is absent in Confucianism. To repay injury with straightness, then, and not with injury, is to uphold an element of justice within humaneness. It incorporates the righteous anger at inhumanity into humanity itself. This insistence on justice is necessary in Confucian ethics, because of the absence of the notion of a trancendent God to preside over an otherworldly last judgment (Roetz, 1993, p. 129). Justice and humaneness are the two sides of a coin. The humane person in Confucianism is characterized by impartiality and a sense of justice.

The Confucian concept of love is also distinguished by the importance of the family. *Hsiao*, filial piety, is considered to be the root of humaneness. According to Mengzi, "The reality of humaneness is service to the parents. To love parents [*qin qin*] is humaneness (*Mengzi* 4A27, 6B3, 7A15).

Family love holds a special status here, and it even seems to be the very essence of humaneness. In Confucian ethics, the family is of special importance as the place of the first exercise of virtue, but it is not ruled out to gradually expand the range of the ethical commitment. The family remains a place of primary responsibility, but it is not the only one. On the contrary, the affection which is assumed to grow naturally in it shall become the model for treating others in general, though never at the price of abandoning one's parents. Family morality is no end in itself. If love is not to prove blind to the problem of justice, the unequal primary distribution of love must not entail a restriction of morals to the family; there needs to be an ethical commitment also to strangers. Mengzi therefore advocates the transition from the family to the well-being of all, which he conceives as the "extension" of affection or of feelings of care. He writes about how family love is open to enlargement to include "love of the other" in this way:

> Treat the aged of your own family as is due to the aged, and then include [*yi*] the aged of others in this treatment. Treat the young of your own family as is due to the young, and then include [*yi*] the young of the others in this treatment. Then you can make the world go round in your palm.... Therefore, if one extends [*tui*] one's kindness, it will suffice for the protection of the whole world. If one does not extend one's kindness, it will not even suffice to protect wife and

children. It is just one thing in which the ancients greatly surpassed others: they knew how to extend what they did, and this is all. (Mengzi 1A7. The quotation is from Shijing 240:2)

The emphasis on family love within a general "love for people," which is especially found with Mengzi, aims at a foundation of morality for the ethical life, rather than a limitation on the ethical life. Confucianism does not advocate ethical particularism. Confucian humaneness in no way encourages a particularistic attitude, setting limits and excluding strangers. In another reading of humaneness in Mengzi, humaneness is an extension of the natural compassion which everyone feels in view of the hardship and misfortune of others. Not to be able to bear the suffering of others and to feel fundamentally alarmed when witnessing it—the most poignant picture is that of the child about to fall into a well (Mengzi 2A6, p.200)—becomes a starting point of ethics just as fundamental as the natural affection for kin. Mengzi writes:

All men have a heart which cannot bear the suffering of others ... My reason for saying that every man has a heart that cannot bear the suffering of others is this. Suppose a man suddenly sees a child about to fall into a well. In such a situation, everybody will have the feeling (xin) of alarm and compassion. This is not because he wants to enter into good relations with the parents of the child, or because he wants to gain praise in his neighborhood and among his fellow students and friends, or because he dislikes the cry of the child.

Compassion is one of the central expressions of humaneness. To share the suffering of others, to be overwhelmed by their pain, and to feel alarm and compassion in view of the fundamental vulnerability of human beings are the spontaneous emotions of a humane heart which Mengzi and the ancient literature have ascribed to a person of ren.

2. Humaneness as Respect for the Other

Humaneness also entails an attitude of equal respect which does not distinguish between individuals, but precedes any status- and role-specific treatment of others. On a question regarding humaneness, Confucius answers, "Outside your door [in public], behave as if you were receiving a high guest. Employ the people as if you were performing a great sacrifice" (Lunyu 12:2). Humaneness is also independent of the sentiment one may feel for the concrete person (Roetz, p. 132):

A humane person will by all means respect [jing] others. For respecting others there is a way. If one deals with a capable person, one will esteem and respect him. If one deals with an incapable person, one will fear and respect him. One will respect a capable person with intimate affection, but will respect an incapable person from a distance. *Respect is the same in both cases, but the feelings are different.* If one is loyal, trustworthy, upright, and guileless, and does not injure the other, then one will behave right with whomever one comes into contact. This is the disposition of a person who has humaneness. (emphasis added. Xunzi 13, pp.169–170)

Respect (jing) is an attitude of seriousness, honesty, and attentiveness when dealing with the other. It expresses an attitude of respect that every human being, regardless of his or her capabilities and ethical qualities, is of the same value. It is this abstraction of "human" which makes up the moral substance of the concept of humaneness in Confucian ethics. Humaneness therefore stands above particularism and social hierarchies. Humaneness further provides a formal basic pattern of horizontal respect in its specification as the "Golden Rule" (Roetz, p. 132).

3. Humaneness as the Golden Rule

If we seek for a center of the Lunyu, this center will be humaneness in its reading as the Golden Rule. It incorporates a formal, abstract procedure into Confucian ethical reasoning. As a concise, intuitively plausible and generalizable formula for moral conduct, it also plays an important role in philosophical ethics up to the present:

Zigong asked, "Is there something which consists of a single word and which can, because of its nature be practiced for all one's life?" The Master said, "I should say this shu: What you do not want for yourself, do not do unto others." (Lunyu 15:24)

Here Zigong is asking for a general maxim, to serve as a general guide to conduct for a whole lifetime. For such a maxim, Confucius recommends shu. In everyday language, shu means "forgiveness." In the Hanfeizi (Wangxian shen. 1978. Hanfeiji jijie. In zhuzi jicheng, Vol. 5. Hong Kong: Zhonghua), shu is the cardinal virtue of the pacifist Song Xing and synonymous with kuan, "tolerance," or "leniency" (Hanfezi 50, p.352). Shu has also been translated as "sympathy," "altruism," and "mutualness." But shu has mostly been rendered as "reciprocity" or "fairness" in sinological literature. The maxim is repeated in *Lunyu* 5:12 and 12:2. Zigong says, "What I do not wish others to do unto me, I also wish not to do unto them." Confucius answers, "What you do not wish to be done to yourself do not do to others."

The negative, "Do not do unto others what you would not have them do unto you," has been called the "Silver Rule," because it offers a negative version of the Golden Rule, "Do unto others what you would have them do unto you," as found in the New Testament. But it is important to note that the negative version does not necessarily represent the "lower" form of ethical behavior. There is in fact less danger in the negative version of projecting into the other person wants which he or she does not have. What is essential is that the establishment of a reciprocal relation between the self and the other is also accomplished by the negative version. Moreover, in *Lunyu* 6:30 we do find the idea of treating others like ourselves not only in the sense of refraining from action, but also in our active doing:

> A humane person, wishing to establish himself, will also establish others. And wishing to achieve perfection, he also perfects others. To be able to take the near as analogy, this can be called the method of humaneness.

Active sympathy stands at the heart of the Golden Rule. The Golden Rule is the method of humaneness. It is a measure for moral conduct. It represents a formal procedure rather than a virtue. The formal element of the Golden Rule recognizes that the moral nature of an action relates to its generalizability. This is achieved by the fictitious changing of positions of the self with the other on the simple basis of the self's generalized wishes (Roetz, p. 135). This procedure does not depend on any conventional values. It assumes a symmetry in relations, while there can be a great asymmetry in love and particularly in compassion. For Mengzi, the archetype of humaneness is not the consideration of granting the other the same which I claim for myself, but the unconscious, spontaneous reaction to save a child about to fall into a well from imminent death. Mengzi's assumption of an innate moral capacity in *zi* has a strong egalitarian trait: by the very possession of one and the same good nature capable of active sympathy, every man is a moral being deserving *direct* respect.

F. *Dao*—The Unifying and Pervading Ideal

Humaneness is the core of the ethical teaching of Confucius. It stands above propriety. It roots morality in the formal procedure of role taking, not in traditional virtue, transcending the horizon of one's own cultural heritage. It recognizes the other as a human being like oneself and thus comprises an element of *equality*. Confucianism is more than mere conventional norms. As Confucius once said, "if a man has no *ren*, what has he to do with *li*?" (*Lunyu* 3:3). But *li* allows the development of *ren* in a social context. Given that *dao* is the ideal of the good human life as a whole, *ren*, *li*, and *yi*, the basic Confucian ethical principles comprising the notion of *te*, are constitutive rather than merely instrumental means to its actualization. In other words, the actualization of *dao* requires a coordination of three equally important centers of ethical interest and endeavor. The connection between these foci is one of complimentarity rather than subordination. Thus *ren*, *li*, and *yi* are mutually supportive and adherent to the same ideal of *dao*.

As discussed earlier, during the crisis of the mid-Zhou era, *li* was increasingly seen as superficial and forced. But for the Confucians, the rules of propriety are indispensable. The fact that people need transmitted conventions for finding their orientation does not mean, however, that they could exclusively rely on them. For this reason, *li* is thus supplemented by *ren*. *Ren* and *li* stand in a complimentary relation. *Lunyu* 12:1 identifies *ren* with conduct in accordance with *li*, while *Lunyu* 3:3 declares *li* meaningless without *ren*. For Confucius this vacillation shows that humaneness is not to be played off against the conventional ethos. Both are indispensable. Individual rules of propriety may be suspended according to circumstances, but *li* or the ethical life as such is not replaceable. It is the ethical etiquette which constitutes human culture as distinct from mere nature. There would be no human society without *li*. *Ren*, however, provides the necessary corrective which is to protect the conventional ethos against degenerating into a superficial and exploitable formalism once again. While it does not make sense to ask which is the more important concept, humaneness can be regarded as the higher norm, inasmuch as it helps to keep propriety uncorrupted, and it is in this sense that it is also the center of *Lunyu* and Confucian ethics. Confucius proclaims, "A decided scholar and a humane person will never try to save their lives at the expense of humaneness It may happen that they give their lives in order to accomplish humaneness" (*Lunyu* 15:9). Confucius does not see any fundamental contrast between *ren* and *li*:

> Yan Yuan asked about humaneness. The Master said, "To overcome one's self [*ke ji*] and to

return to propriety [*fu li*] is humaneness. If one day one will overcome the self and return to propriety, then the whole world will turn towards humaneness. Humaneness can only come from the self—how could it come form others?"

Yan Yuan said, "I beg to ask for the concrete steps." The Master said, "Do not look at what is contrary to propriety! Do not listen to what is contrary to propriety! Do not speak what is contrary to propriety! Do not put into action what is contrary to propriety!" (12:1)

If, as a man, one does not possess humaneness, what is propriety good for, then? (3:3)

Since humaneness can only come from the self, moral cultivation of the inner "self" is emphasized in Confucian ethics. The formation of the self and its conscience is based on the very mutuality which is expressed in the Golden Rule:

> The Master said, "Shen! My way [*dao*] is pervaded [*guan*] by one." "Yes!" said Zengzi. When the Master has gone, the disciple asked, "What does he mean?" Zengzi said, "The way of our teacher is *Zhong* and *Shu* [benevolence and fairness], and that is all." (*Lunyu* 15:24)

Zhong also has the meaning of "doing one's best," "exhausting oneself," "being true," and "sincerity" and *shu* has also been rendered as "consideration of other people's feelings and interests," "extending oneself," and "empathy." In this light, Confucian ethics displays a concern for both self-regarding and other-regarding virtues. It also expresses the interdependence of the Confucian "self." One cannot learn humaneness except by loving others (*Lunyu* 6:22, 12:12, 12:22, 19:3). An integral part of the moral life is the interrelatedness of human beings. In living the Confucian life, one has to respond appropriately to those with whom one has a relationship; one is responsive to other people and mutually responsible for one's relationships according to the role(s) one might fill in that relationship. It is the principle of humaneness which provides the procedure for making reasoned judgment according to the requirement of *yi* in exigent circumstances.

III. CONFUCIANISM— ABSTRACT MORALITY AND CONVENTIONAL MORALITY

With the principle of humaneness, the Confucian ethic makes a great demand on moral conduct. To put the Con-

fucian program into practice constantly requires decisions and choices. Decision and choice are topics in Confucianism and Chinese philosophy in general. The fact that decisions have to be, and can be, taken is related to one's freedom to shape one's surroundings, choose alternatives, and escape from established ways. This kind of choice presupposes an autonomous basis of judgment in people. Yet, that decision and choice are important at all for Confucianism has often been denied, the denial being linked to the assumption that the notion of an individual capable of free decision is lacking. True, the Confucian self is not an atomic isolated entity, but stands in interdependence with its social environment. But this does not rule out that the self can be detached from the society to which it owes its existence, and is capable of conceiving still other and better forms of living. In *Lunyu* 9:26, Confucius says, "It is possible to deprive a whole army of its generals. But it is not possible to deprive even a common man of his will."

The protagonist of the Confucian ethics is positively a "person" in the sense of a self-responsible autonomous being with his or her own dignity. The autonomous being will do his or her best to fulfill his or her social role, but he or she is more than that. The subject of Confucian ethics is not essentially or even exclusively defined by the social role. A very frequent motif in ancient Chinese literature is independent action, the practical counterpart of self-reflection. In Mengzi 3B2 we read,

> ... he who dwells in the wide house of the world [in humaneness], has his stand at the correct position of the world, and walks the great path of the world [justice], who if he reaches his ambitions, strides his way alone, who cannot be led to dissipation by wealth and high position, led astray by poverty and mean conditions, and bent by authority and power—such a man is called a great fellow.

Here we find one of the most noble and emphatic of classic proclamations of uncompromising dedication to abstract moral norms. A classic grounding of the freedom of judgment and decision is later found in Xunzi in the following description of the "heart" (*xin*), the organ of thinking:

> The heart is the ruler of the body and the master of the wondrous intelligence. It gives commands, but it does not receive any from anywhere. It prohibits and permits by itself, it decides and chooses by itself, it comes active and stops by itself. Thus the mouth can be forced to be silent or speak, and

the body can be forced to bend or stretch itself, but the heart cannot be forced to alter its opinion.... Therefore I say: The heart is free and unrestricted in its choices. (*Xunzi* 21, p.265)

The human mind's autonomy to choose and reject according to its own discretion can hardly be expressed more clearly. In Confucian thinking, *xin* refers to the inclination to behavior (heart-mind). One does not find in Confucianism an inherited Greek psychology which divides the ego into the rational and the emotional. Neither is there a dichotomy between the mind and the heart. Confucian anthropology, correspondingly, also denies any relevant natural distinction between people. "People by nature are close to one another, and by daily practice [or by custom] diverge from one another" (*Lunyu* 17:2). "A sage and I are of the same kind," and "anybody can become a Yao or a Shun [Sage kings of the past]" (*Mengzi* 6A7, 6B2).

Confucius does not promise any reward to the moral actor except for safeguarding his self-respect, staying free from shame, and inner happiness. The *Lunyu* refrains from a religious and a cosmological grounding of morality. In the *Lunyu* it is stated, "Man can make the *Dao* great. It is not the *Dao* can make man great" (*Lunyu* 15.29).

Human endeavor for the "great" decides what the *dao* will be. Human beings are what they make themselves; hence the emphasis on self-cultivation. Confucianism gains its critical attitude and its distance from the given world without any appeal to a transcendent God.

Confucianism embodies a principle of autonomy which is equal to that in the liberal moral tradition in the West. The *Lunyu* knows the concept of a "self" that stands its ground against the misunderstandings and the hostility of others. It can be self-critical and sit in judgment on itself. For Mengzi, critical self-reflection which leads to the realization that one has been upright will enable one to "withstand thousands or tens of thousands." A Confucian *junzi*, says Mengzi, "strides his way alone," if necessary, and cannot be "led astray by poverty and mean conditions and bent by authority and power." In *Lunyu* (13:23) we read, "a *junzi* harmonizes but does not conform. A mean man conforms, but does not harmonize." The Confucian ideal is that both moral mental attitude and ethical responsibility can be made compatible with each other—an ideal which culminates in the utopia of the "Great Community" (*da tong*) where the specific care for the individual contest of life no longer competes with the interest of the greater whole.

Confucianism certainly is not a clan or a morality role with no universal principles. Because family love

holds a special status in Confucianism, scholars such as Bertrand Russell are of the view that "Confucian emphasis on filial piety prevented the growth of public spirit" (1922, *The Problem of China*. London: Allen & Unwin, p.40). In fact, Confucianism ethics do not subscribe to particularistic assumptions, but rather to universalistic ones. In Confucianism, family and state stand in close relationship. But they also conflict with each other. It is recorded in Mengzi 7A35,

> Tao Ying asked, "When Shun was Emperor and Gaoyao judge, what would they have done if Gusou [Shun's father] murdered a man?" Mengzi answered, "Gaoyao would simply have arrested him." Tao Ying: "Then Shun wouldn't have prevented that?" Mengzi: "How could he? Gaoyao had received the mandate for that." Tao Ying: "What would Shun have done, then?" Mengzi: "For Shun, to abandon the empire would have been the same as to throw away worn-out sandals. He would have stolen away with his father on the back, settled somewhere at the cost, lived there happily to the end of his days, and would have forgotten the empire.

Forced to make a decision, Shun takes the side of his father. But he did not bend the law in favor of the father. He gives up the position in which his solidarity with the father would incur a violation of law. The *Lunyu* recorded the reverse case of a crime of the son. We are told that Shi Que from the nobility of Wei ordered the death of his son for having made common cause with an assassin. The decision meets the approval of the *Zuozhuan*, which comments that "great justice [*yi*] exterminates kinship" (*Zuo zhuan*. Yin 4-6, p. 11. In *Chunqiu*. 1966. Harvard-Yenching Institute Sinological Index Series. Reprint Taipei: Chinese Research Aids Centre). "Great justice" can overrule kin relations in favor of public interest, with the exception of the commitment to the parents. In Western law, too, one finds the privilege of declining to give evidence against one's closest kins.

Being a relationship-based philosophy, what is important for Confucius is that one acts responsibly within one's social and cultural environment and according to the roles one occupies in the variety of relationships one engages in. This does not mean that each person is completely constituted by the roles he or she plays. Rather the quality and the meaning of a satisfactory Confucian life are based on how one fulfills the responsibilities within each relationship.

IV. CONFUCIANISM— VIRTUE-BASED MORALITY AND RIGHTS-BASED MORALITY

Confucianism from the beginning has been a critical philosophy. Confucius, Mencius, and Hsun-tzu complained that the ancient practices that constituted harmonious civilization had been corrupted so that people no longer were filial, capable of true friendship, or socially responsible. They searched for a higher standard to ground the social, conventional *dao*. They argued for a moral anthropology, *xin*, described as moral sentiment:

> The feeling of compassion is the beginning of humaneness. The feeling of shame and disgust is the beginning of justice. The feeling of courtesy and modesty is the beginning of propriety. The feeling of right and wrong is the beginning of knowledge. Man has these four beginnings, just as he has his four limbs. He who has these four beginnings and declares himself incapable [of virtue] has done violence to himself.... If one knows how to bring them to completion, it will suffice to protect all within the four seas. If one does not bring them to completion, it will not even suffice to serve one's parents. (Mengzi 2A6)

Inherent in human nature is the potential for excellence, the source of our human worth and dignity. Human beings have intrinsic value. Confucius says, "Heaven is the author of the virtue that is in me" (*Lunyu* 7:23). On this view, man's nature is a "given" that exists from birth. For Confucians, human beings are worthy because they can become morally perfect through self-cultivation. There is no interpretation that human behaviors are completely determined. Confucianism attaches great autonomy to the individual self because of its belief that the individual is an active self capable of reaching a state of moral autonomy and achieving "*ren*."

Confucianism is a moral theory of human dignity without a notion of abstract universal human rights. In contrast to a liberal rights-based morality, Confucianism provides a radically different picture of morality. Being a morality based on virtue, what Confucianism takes seriously is not rightful claims of self-assertions, but the virtues of caring and benevolence. It is in essence an ethics of care. In contemporary Western social ethics, moral problems are posed, debated, and solved largely within a discourse of rights. There is even the claim that we cannot do moral philosophy without rights—"there

cannot be an acceptable moral theory that is not rights-based" (J. L. Mackie, 1984. "Can There Be a Right–Based Moral Theory?" in *Theories of Rights*, Jeremy Waldron (Ed.), Oxford: Oxford University Press, p. 176). In the West this is due to the dominance of liberalism as a moral and political thesis which takes liberty as the fundamental source of other values. Liberals contend that all moral and political values and principles are to be derived from the ultimate source of liberty. They therefore endorse the principle of noninterference and regard all rival visions of life as equally good.

There is no concept of abstract universal rights in Confucianism. In modern Western liberal thought, individual rights or human rights are role-detached rights which are held equally by every human regardless of social role and position. Confucian understanding of rights is role attached and relationship based. The notion of the human subject being prior to, and independent of, experience is a necessary requirement of moral agency in Western liberalism. It holds that a human being is fully autonomous only if one is free to discover what is distinctive about oneself as an individual. To liberals, the central goal of morality is finding terms of peaceful coexistence among persons with different conceptions of the good. The underlying belief is that people are capable of self-direction because of the faculty of reason. Individual persons have worth and dignity because of their capacity for "purposive agency" and "moral autonomy." In Western liberalism, moral agency and individual selfhood are closely associated with the claiming of rights.

In contrast, moral agency and the self of the individual in the Confucian tradition are constituted by the web of unique role relations which one possesses and by the way concrete responsibilities are performed by the self in each particular set of role relationships. It is in one's role relationships and role performance that the self finds the source of one's sanctity as a human being and the basis of one's self-esteem, worth, and fulfillment. Personhood is an achievement, rather than a given, or a right of birth. The life to which a person is given is not given ready made. Confucian ethics therefore emphasizes self-cultivation, self-development, and self-transformation.

Liberals conceive human worth in terms of moral autonomy. Confucians conceive human worth in terms of moral perfectibility. The model liberal society is composed of distinct individuals who are morally autonomous, rational, and sovereign in their choice, and protected from interference and constraints in the pursuit of their way of life and personal projects. The Confucian model society is a community of virtuous characters dedicated to the pursuit of the virtues of good faith, friendly relations, and caring for others, and the fulfillment of reciprocal obligations. Confucianism is a universal morality of autonomy and harmony—not an abstract individualism but an organic holism as envisioned in the *da tong* (Great Community):

> When the great *Dao* prevailed, the world belonged to the general public. They chose the worthy and capable, were trustworthy in what they said, and cultivated harmony. Therefore, people did not love only their own parents and did not treat only their own children as children. Thus the aged could live out their lives, the grown-ups all had their function, the young could be reared, and the widowed, the lonely, the orphans, the crippled, and the sick all found their care. Men had their roles, and women their homes. They hated casting away goods, but not necessarily to keep them for themselves. They hated leaving their strength unemployed, but not necessarily to employ it for themselves. Therefore, scheming had no outlet, and theft, rebellion, and robbery did not arise, so that the outer doors were left unlocked. This is called the Great community [*da tong*]. (*Liji* 9, *Liyun*, p.1414b)

V. CONCLUDING REMARKS

Confucian ethics poses a distinction between *individualism* and autonomy. As a moral thesis, it is unique in its claim of an autonomous capability of moral judgment and action without relying on external authority. At the same time, it emphasizes human connectedness rather than separateness of persons. The Confucian moral theory is a theory of human dignity without a notion of universal human rights. *Ren* or humaneness is regarded as the defining characteristic of human beings, not some kind of abstract right. Justice is not the search for just relations between contingently related individuals. Justice is the search for response to express our caring, our connectedness, and our interdependence to maintain the web of relationships which stand at the heart of being human. On the Confucian view, individual rights have to be interpreted within a broader framework of reciprocal obligations. Personal autonomy has to be underpinned by a shared conception of the good society. Liberal justice has to be founded upon a foundation of mutual care and concern. The relevant ethical question is not, "What is just?", but "How should one respond?"

To the Confucian, it is our sympathy, our other-regarding sentiments, and our moral capacity to feel for others which define our humanity. Confucianism supports the contemporary feminist view that compassion is a moral virtue, not a mere instinct or an intuitive feeling. It involves a sense of shared humanity, of regarding the other as a fellow human being. Because compassion involves a sense of shared humanity, it promotes the awareness of equality. The other-regarding ethic of Confucianism is distinguished by its lack of commitment to a notion of transcendence. There is lack of a notion of *creatio ex nihilo* which one finds in alternative other-regarding moral systems such as Judeo-Christianity. It emphasizes that the moral and spiritual achievement of human beings do not depend on tricks, luck, some esoteric spells, or external agencies. Instead, the emphasis is on continuous self-development and acting responsibly within one's ethical and cultural environment according to the role one occupies in the variety of relationships one engages in.

As human beings, we are not only deeply affected by our caring obligations and relations with others, we are also partly or largely constituted by these relations and obligations. In the Confucian vision, "the self develops its contours, unfolds its characteristics, takes shape, becomes actual and individuated through engaging and interacting in a network of role relations with others" (Tu Weiming, 1985. "Selfhood and Otherness in Confucian Thoughts" in A. J. Marsella, G. DeVos & F. L. K. Hsu (Eds.) *Culture and Self: Asia and Western Perspectives.* New York: Tavistock, p. 230).

As a living ethical tradition, Confucianism grounds morality neither in religion nor in reason, but in humaneness and humanity. Its ethical universalism is firmly embedded in the Golden Rule of humaneness, the assumption of equal human worth, and the emphasis on reasoned judgment according to the principle of *yi*. They provide the moral resources for Confucianism to further continue its universalist legacy of tradition to evolve into a universal morality.

Also See the Following Articles

RELIGION AND ETHICS • TAOISM

Bibliography

Chi-chao, Liang (1930). *History of Chinese political thought during the early Tsin period.* Trans. L. T. Chen. London: Kegan Paul.
Dawson, R. (1981). *Confucius.* Oxford: Oxford Univ. Press.
Dawson, R. (1993). *The analects.* Oxford: Oxford Univ. Press.
de Bary, W. T. (1991). *The trouble with Confucianism.* Cambridge, MA: Harvard Univ. Press.

Fingarette, H. (1972). *Confucius—The secular as sacred*. New York: Harper & Row.

Hall, D. L., & Roger, T. A. (1987). *Thinking through Confucius*. New York: State Univ. of New York Press.

Kung-Chuan, Hsiao (1979). *A history of Chinese political thought*. Trans. F. W. Mote. Princeton, NJ: Princeton Univ. Press.

Lau, D. C. (trans.) (1979). *The analects*. Harmondsworth: Penguin.

Munro, D. J. (1969). *The concept of man in early China*. Stanford: Stanford Univ. Press.

Schwartz, B. I. (1985). *The world of thought in ancient China*. Cambridge, MA.: Harvard Univ. Press.

Waley, A. (trans.) (1938). *The analects of Confucius*. New York: Vintage Books.

Wing-tsit, Chan (1963). *A source book in Chinese philosophy*. Princeton, NJ: Princeton Univ. Press.

Yu-Lan, Fung (1948). *A short history of Chinese philosophy*. New York: Macmillian.

Yu-Lan, Fung (1953). *A history of Chinese philosophy*. Trans. D. Bodde. Princeton, NJ: Princeton Univ. Press.

CONSEQUENTIALISM AND DEONTOLOGY

Matthew W. Hallgarth
United States Air Force Academy

GLOSSARY

altruism The view that egoism is not enough for morality, and that taking into account other persons' interests, for their own sake, is a necessary condition for morality.

a priori Means "before." In philosophy, the fact of knowing a proposition prior to experience, that is, without referring to experience to verify its truth. It has been hotly debated over the centuries whether *a priori* knowledge is even possible.

categorical imperative Kant's phrase for an absolute moral obligation, of the unequivocal form, "Do X," always. He proposes three tests to ascertain what these are.

consequentialism Any ethical theory that argues fundamentally that right action is an action that produces good results or avoids bad results.

deontology Literally means the "science of duty." It refers to any moral theory that emphasizes that some actions are obligatory irrespective of the pleasurable or painful consequences produced.

egoism The view that actions are right that satisfy self-interest.

foundational A fundamental assumption or axiom of a particular theory. A foundational assumption of Kant's ethics is that humans are autonomous.

libery (harm) principle Mill's principle that utility is maximized in societies where the guiding hand of the state is restricted to intervening in one's personal life only to prevent harm, one to another, but not to prevent you from harming yourself. It prescribes minimum limits to human and government sovereignty consistent with his principle of utility.

maxims What Kant calls a "subjective principle of action." These are the rules people operate by when they perform actions. Maxims that are indeed moral ones have to meet certain criteria.

prima facie On the face of it, at first glance, out of context. For example, killing human beings intentionally is *prima facie* wrong, although it is actually permitted in a just war.

summum bonum Latin for "highest good." A good that is an end in itself, and not a means to a higher order good. In Artistotle's theory, health is not the *summum bonum* because it is a means to the *summum bonum,* which is *eudaimonia* (happiness).

teleological Emphasizing design, goals, ends, that is, purposiveness in nature. Teleological ethical theory grounds moral obligation in observations about the design, goals, ends, and purposes of human beings. All consequential moral theories are teleological.

utilitarianism An altruistic variety of consequentialism that holds that good results are results that maximize benefits and minimize harms, even if this entails self-sacrifice. Usually, benefits is translated "pleasure," and harm is translated "pain."

utility principle Foundational moral principle espoused by Mill and Bentham. Acts are right if they maximize happiness for the greatest number of people. By happiness is meant maximizing pleasure and minimizing pain, unhappiness is vice versa.

CONSEQUENTIALISM refers to any of a class of normative theories that will argue that morally right action is action that produces good results. Theories of this type are teleological, in that they assume first an empirically grounded, natural theory of human good as a prelude to deriving moral obligations. Consequential theories in various ways always subsume moral obligations under the higher umbrella of a question best answered through observation, "What, given our environment and what is obvious about human nature, is good?" By understanding what our design suggests constitutes the ultimate goal of human action, our moral obligations logically follow as the "right" way to achieve that goal.

The word *deontology* originates from the Greek words *deon* (duty), and *logos* (science). Hence, it means the science of duty. In everyday reasoning the notion of duty is not a particularly divisive concept. When a person makes a decision, he normally chooses based on a common-sense assessment of his interests and the interests of others in light of his other long- and short-term commitments, a job, the offices he holds, previous promises, and various other obligations. However, a theoretical approach to the concept of duty is often very technical and the subject of much debate.

Deontology refers to any of a class of moral theories, the most noteworthy of which comes from the influential philosopher Immanuel Kant, which argue that there are some moral obligations which obtain absolutely, irrespective of the consequences produced. Whereas the teleological moral theories of the ancient Greeks and the modern utilitarians emphasized the instrumentality of moral obligation as conducive to individual and corporate happiness, or the good life, answering the question "What is good?" deontological moral theories ground moral prescriptions in terms of the question, "What is right?" For deontological theories, the moral law is absolute and supreme. If considerations for one's well-being or the well-being of others contradicts a rationally acceptable moral law, obedience to the law is obligatory and must prevail. This is doing your duty for the sake of the duty alone. Kant even went so far as to say that lying to save the life of a friend is wrong. Unlike the observationally grounded consequential theories, Kant's position is that moral laws are understood *a priori* and then implemented by the practical reason

humans use to regulate action. Although we can go back as far as the Stoics to see a budding concept of deontology mentioned as fundamental to the moral life (e.g., their avowed duty to live according to nature), we find our fullest, most influencial spokesperson for deontological morality in the person of the eighteenth-century philosopher Immanuel Kant.

I. CONSEQUENTIALISM

Variations among consequential theorists are nearly always rooted in different assessments of human nature. If, generally speaking, consequential theories argue that right action produces good results, consequentialists remain a good deal removed from consensus. Just what *is* the good? What is the good result we are obligated to seek? How a consequentialist answers this question depends on the different answers given to foundational teleological questions such as these: Are humans necessarily selfish? Is it in their capacity to act autonomously? and, Are they able to put reason above inclination? Consequential theorists posit a variety of answers to these questions, and their answers imply vastly different normative obligations, both individually and collectively. Each, however, is consequentialist in consistently grounding obligations in the view that right action is that which produces good results. If there is any consensus among consequential theorists, it is a very general sort of agreement, based on observation, that humans are naturally driven to live a full life, to, in some sense, flourish as a human being in a community. This flourishing is what Plato calls justice, Aristotle calls *eudaimonia,* Hobbes calls peace or security, and the utilitarians call happiness.

Aristotle skillfully captures what each of these theorists generally mean by the natural human drive to live a full life, to flourish. He observed that there are many human goods that people strive for, such as health, money, friendship, power, and fame. A middle-aged man cuts down on his fat intake for health reasons, a young man saves to buy a motorcycle, a rich person creates a foundation to support philanthropic causes, and a young music student diligently practices the guitar. However, Aristotle was astute enough to ask if, among all good things, there is a highest human good, or *summum bonum.* It would be something all people want, not as a means to other goods, but as an end in itself. This ultimate goal would be the final desire of all human striving, that is, justice, security, *eudaimonia,* or happiness. Each of these posited "ends in themselves" serve as proposed theoretical definitions of what it means to flourish as a human being.

Consequential theorists will universally agree that the *summum bonum,* this ultimate end of human striving, is not amenable to *a priori* logical proof. Nevertheless, a close observation of human behavior shows that all human pursuits are a means to, or constitutive of, living a full, flourishing life. This inability to logically prove an ultimate end of human striving, is, Mill argues, the case with all questions of ultimate foundations. Foundational principles are, at their best, generalizations inferred from empirical observation. At their worst, they are ad hoc assumptions used to derive pet obligations a particular theorist feels strongly about.

So, consequential theorists generally agree that right action is that which produces good results, but disagree on the details of what the nature of this *good* is because they disagree on fundamental questions about human nature. Additionally, consequential theorists disagree on a deeper practical issue concerning the good. Who's good gets precedence when a moral agent makes decisions about alternatives that each produces good results, contributing to this variously defined idea of what constitutes human flourishing? Should the good of the self come first? Are we obligated to sacrifice for the sake of a greater good of the community? Are the criteria for human flourishing objective (e.g., good job, talents, utilized, healthy family) or subjective (maximize pleasure/minimize pain)? What is the state's proper role in creating conditions where activity that produces good results are maximized? What is the proper integration between concerns for the common good and my private good? Practical considerations like these are the source of much of the debate in consequentialist circles. Now it is time to survey the chief varieties of consequential theory. For the sake of brevity, the quintessentially famous consequential theory called "utilitarianism," championed by Jeremy Bentham and John Stuart Mill, will be most substantively addressed.

A. Egoistic Consequentalism

Egoistic versions of consequentialism argue that when moral agents consider courses of action, they will be or should be motivated by self-interest, irrespective of aggregate consequences produced for the community, that is, unless those community consequences best satisfy self-interest. Self-interest is the egoist consequentialist's answer to the scope question, Who's good counts when I have to decide between competing actions that produce good results. Notice the operative words "will be" or "should be."

The egoistic consequentialist who holds that agents "will be" motivated by selfish considerations must defend the view that persons are motivated by self-interest, necessarily. This is a descriptive theory, and normative talk about "should and ought" loses most of its moral force. On this account, it makes no sense to call for sacrifice when sacrifice, unless it produces something the self wants (like honor), is impossible. In this view, the only two normative issues at stake are those of method and the level of community intervention. The first suggests that agents ought to be taught to think clearly and critically so as to best calculate what the self wants and the most effective method to achieve it. This might, as Hobbes argues, entail cooperation given some assurance to personal security enforced by the state. The second issue concerns the community's need to structure an adequate system of rewards and punishments in order to steer its citizens' necessarily hedonistic drives in directions that effectively balance self-interest with the larger community's interest.

An egoistic consequentialist who argues that humans "should" pursue personal interest admits that humans are not determined by self-interest considerations in moral decision-making, but they should be. This variety of egocentric consequentialism is prescriptive about its hedonism, arguing that beneficial consequences are maximized for society and the individual when persons pursue their own ends, that is, mind their own business. Ann Rand would fit in here. This view defends a belief in human autonomy but criticizes personal and social altruism as more harmful than good, and hence wrong by consequential standards. The prohibition (twentieth) amendment to the U.S. Constitution serves as a good example of an idealistic and socially atruistic law that was morally wrong in contradicting the individual and hence the common good. Illegalizing liquor made more people feel oppressed on a personal level and eroded respect for law on the public level. It produced bad results. Prescriptive egoistic consequentialists have the same concerns over method and community intervention as the descriptive egoistic consequentialist, although the prescriptive variety has, in accepting a notion of human autonomy, a broader range of alternatives than personal and social conditioning.

It should be noted that egoism as a set of consequentialist theories vaguely defines a range of views that might, depending on interpretation, include a large host of positions. The character-centered theories of the Greeks, most notably Plato and Aristotle, are often referred to as enlightened egoist positions, because they argue, I think quite well, that the path of virtue and excellence is, given human nature, *the* way human beings are fulfilled in this life. In Plato's case, this virtue produces the good result of harmony of soul and harmony in the community, which Plato essentially defines as personal and corporate justice. The social contract positions of the ancient Hebrews (via Abraham), Thomas Hobbes, and lately John Rawls serve as popular religious and rational models for how the human person can achieve the good results of right relationship with God, security from the brutality of anarchy, and distributive justice. These can also be interpreted as egoistic positions, although based on diverse metaphysical assumptions about the origin of the universe and what motivates human nature and why. With each of these theories, note the agreement on the premise that right action is action that produces good results. What this good is and who's good is most important generates the disparity in these positions.

B. Altruistic Consequentialism

Altruistic consequentialism is really a euphemism for utilitarianism. These theories argue that in situations where self-interest and the interests of the community clash, the self is obligated to sacrifice its interests for the good of the community, assuming of course that the benefits obtained by the larger community exceed those to be gained by the self. Utilitarianism typically answers the question, "What is the good?" as actions that promote happiness, with happiness defined as acts that maximize pleasure or minimize pain. This is a prescriptive formulation with greater normative force, because it defends the human capacity to freely choose the greater good even to the detriment of self-interest. Both Bentham and Mill fall into this camp. Mill even goes so far as to say that personal sacrifice for the greater good of the community is the highest virtue that can be found in human beings. "Though it is only in a very imperfect state of the world's arrangements that anyone can best serve the happiness of others by the absolute sacrifice of his own, yet so long as the world is in that imperfect state, I fully acknowledge that the readiness to make such a sacrifice is the highest virtue which can be found in man." However, Mill argues, unless the good results are produced, the sacrifice is intrinsically worthless. "The utilitarian morality does recognize in human beings the power of sacrificing their own greatest good for the good of others. It only refuses to admit that the sacrifice is itself a good. A sacrifice which does not increase, or tend to increase, the sum total of happiness, is considered wasted." Mill insists that the

need for these sacrifices is symptomatic of an imperfect world, although in the best social conditions this dilemma infrequently presents itself. A society properly educated and ordered according to consequentialism (his principle of utility) is to Mill the best framework for harmonizing the interests of the individual with those of society. More on how Bentham's and Mill's positions cash out in a moment.

C. Idealistic Consequentialism

This version of consequentialism is the brainchild of G. E. Moore. Also called ideal utilitarianism, it likewise makes good results the criteria for rightness and wrongness in moral decision-making, but argues that the attempt to define what the good is is futile, because good itself is indefinable. Hence, it makes sense that he refuses the strivings of humanity to a specific good such as, for example, gaining pleasure and avoiding pain. Moore espoused instead a richer view of human consciousness in his *Ethics*. By Moore's account, goodness is an intrinsically indefinable quality or property that may issue from many experiences such as contemplation, gaining new knowledge, or aesthetic enjoyment. The real debate here is whether these human experiences are actually reducible to gradations of something like pleasure and pain. For it seems Mill's emphasis on quality in his consequential scheme can and does absorb the intellectual and the aesthetic into a higher order of pleasure. One's view on this issue depends on the efficacy of Moore's argument for good as an indefinable quality. It has exerted considerable influence on the philsophical community. A detailed account of Moore's position would require another essay.

D. Consequential Decision-Making

Let us assume for a minute that some variety of consequentialism in its descriptive or prescriptive forms is true. Each theory makes some good arguments. How are moral agents to calculate the possible good results of their moral decisions so as to determine what course of action is morally right in a situation? And what is the larger community's role in facilitating the best possible accomodation between competing claims of maximizing self-interest and maximizing the common good? To restate an earlier formulation, "If good results indeed determine what action is right, what makes those results good, and who's good counts?" Jeremy Bentham and John Stuart Mill, the quintessentially famous consequential thinkers, serve as good examples to illustrate how moral obligation using a results model can be worked out. For a full view of different ways consequential morality is cashed out, familiarize yourself with the ancient Greeks, the social contract theorists, in addition to the following utilitarians.

1. Bentham

As an example of disputes over consequential moral decision methodology, consider the altruistic consequentialists, that is, utilitarians, Jeremy Bentham and John Stuart Mill. Bentham was a philosopher and legal reformer interested in changing the British legal system into what he argued was a fairer model that meted out rewards and punishments according to the beneficial or deleterious consequences produced by the questionable act. Bentham was frustrated by the fact that a hungry peasant in Britain would get 20 years in prison for stealing an apple from a street vendor, while a more affluent white-collar criminal (e.g., Michael Milken), who caused much greater harm to society, would get a relatively mild sentence.

Bentham, like many other minds in the nineteeth century, was enamored with the accomplishes of science and held out high hopes for the scientific method's ability to also solve moral and social problems, in addition to practical problems of health, food, and industrial production. To support his self-avowed legal consequentialism, Bentham wrote *Introduction on the Principles of Morals and Legislation,* a carefully written guide on his method for correct consequential moral decision-making. In this book, Bentham developed what he called a "hedonic calculus," a quantifiable scheme whereby levels of pleasure and pain could be rigorously and accurately assessed to determine the consequential effects for the various alternatives in a moral decision. The choice that produced the most pleasure or the least pain, as evaluated using various criteria like intensity, duration, and propinquity, identified the correct moral course of action. Fairer laws would be established, and social rewards and punishments would be meted in proportion to quantifiable results verified by this calculus.

Now this might seem, *prima facie,* how we do in fact make many of our moral judgments. It seems to work in simple cases, like what game to play with friends. And yet, Bentham's method is vulnerable to criticism using some simple case situations. For example, suppose a person is a compulsive peeping tom because that person enjoys voyeurism. In Bentham's calculus, if the victims are ignorant, the agent does not get caught, and his actions generate intense pleasure, it seems the act is not only acceptable, but a moral obligation according to the calculus. Examples like these defy common-sense perceptions about justice and rights. The same difficulty would emerge in other cases as well, for example, the justifiability of carefully framing an innocent person for a crime to satisfy a community's desire for justice, and hence, to maximize corporate pleasure.

2. Mill

Mill's famous brand of consequentialism owes much of its substance to Bentham's ideas, for Bentham knew Mill as a child and was a friend and colleague of Mill's father. Mill figured out Bentham's vulnerability to the aforementioned criticism and thus offered some cogent amendments to Bentham's views, while at the same time retaining the position that consequences, in terms of levels of pleasure and pain, is nonetheless the foundational principle of moral action.

Mill argued that restricting pleasure to quantifiable pleasures ignored quality as a vital consideration in the moral situation. This concern for quality in the agent's attempt to maximize personal happiness is not a novel idea in Mill. Epicurus supported a similar position in suggesting that pleasures of the mind are superior (purer) than bodily ones. They are not, as Epicurus says, "mixed." Epicurus argues that bodily pleasures are usually accompanied by associated evils as well, for example, hangovers for alcohol and jealousy for physical love.

Regarding this quality/quantity issue, Mill asks a now-famous question, "Is it better to be a pig satisfied than Socrates dissatisfied?" According to Bentham, it seems one ought or will (Bentham seems at times to equivocate between descriptive and prescriptive statements) choose the quantifiably pleasurable life of the pig, while, as Mill asserts, no one who has experienced both sides of this dilemma would choose the more vulgar existence. Figuratively speaking, only the pig would. This qualitative factor has plenty of mundane practical applications too. For example, should I read pulp fiction or a classic? Listen to Mozart or to pop music? Watch *Citizen Kane* or championship wrestling? If you ask people who have experienced each, who know and understand each, the higher quality pleasure is preferred. Mill puts it plainly, "Of two pleasures, if there be one to which all or almost all who have experience of both give a decided preference, irrespective of any feeling of moral obligation to prefer it, that is the more desirable pleasure."

Another way the quantity/quality issue is broached in contemporary discourse is in the distinction between act utilitarianism (consequentialism), and rule utilitarianism. Bentham's emphasis on the quantifiable assessment of acts placed him in a position to have to accept problematic examples to remain consistent. Mill tried to overcome this by arguing that a holistic determination of beneficial consequences required asking this general question, "What general types of acts, as a rule, tend to maximize beneficial consequences over time?" When you take counterintuitive cases like the peeping tom example and generalize them into a social norm of behavior, what, *prima facie,* seems at first to support the consequentialism, it turns out, thwarts it when viewed as an acceptable pattern of behavior over time. The common good is dimished. Hence, peeping tom behavior is wrong, in spite of exceptional cases.

What Mill has done through his emphasis on consequence maximizing rules of behavior is to salvage the possibility of making respect for human rights consistent with consequentialism. Let us suppose that researchers are very close to discovering a cure for sudden infant death syndrome, or SIDS, and the discovery of this cure will save 10,000 infant lives per year. Also suppose that the only way this cure can finally be discovered is through painful and fatal experimentation on 10 healthy newborn infants. Although Bentham, as an act consequentialist, would have to justify this experimentation, Mill as a rule consequentialist would not. For what would a society be like if acts of this type, as a rule, were generally accepted? This rule, by ignoring a right to life, would make people insecure and afraid, perhaps rebellious, and thus, would significantly diminish the collective happiness of that society.

Therefore, according to Mill's richer, rule-oriented, quality-emphasizing consequentialism, persons should take the responsibility for developing an enlightened notion of self-interest that emphasizes seeking pleasures of quality. Likewise, the state should structure educational policy and the broader system of social rewards and benefits according to higher concerns for quality in maximizing the common good. This includes respecting rules that honor human rights in ways that cultivate the tenuous balance between personal and community happiness.

Mill also amends Bentham's consequentialism by more cogently broaching the difficult task of harmonizing personal autonomy in pursuing one's own ends (pleasures) with the state's mandate to maintain a civil community life (corporate pleasure). He does this through his proposed "liberity principle," or "harm principle," as it is also called. Based on astute observations about what makes human beings happiest as members of a community, the "harm principle" places a (happiness maximizing) limit on the autonomy that adults may exercise in pursuing their ends in a community, while at the same

time limiting the state's prerogative to intervene in the personal lives of its citizens. Persons may do anything free of government intervention to the extent that their behavior does not harm someone else. The government may not intervene in someone's life to protect that person from himself. Mill argued that the happiness of individuals and society is maximized when persons are at liberty to partake of even potentially self-destructive behaviors. Thus, on Mill's account, smoking should remain legal, but may be banned in restaurants. Mill articulated it this way, "Mankind are greater gainers by suffering each other to live as seems good to themselves, than by compelling each to live as seems good to the rest." By Mills account, this "harm principle" is therefore a necessary condition for harmonizing beneficial consquences for person and society.

E. General Criticisms

Following are several general criticisms of consequential moral theory. Many more specific criticisms that apply to specific consequential theorists, that is, the Greeks, Hobbes, Rawls, Moore, and so on, deserve further study but are beyond the scope of this essay.

1. A common criticism of all versions of consequentialism concerns measuring levels of pleasure and pain produced in a moral decision. Exactly how do we measure it? Whether you focus on quantity or integrate quality considerations, it is still nearly impossible to accurately predict which act over time will maximize good consequences. And in Mill's argument that we should concern ourself with act types as a rule, we at best can only claim to have a general idea as to which act types tend to produce the best results. But specifically in practice, how can I possibly determine accurately what impact by moral decision might have on, say, my yet unborn grandchildren? To calculate, it seems I am forced to construct arbitrary boundaries on the range of calculation. At worst I am pressured by time considerations to make a decision without adequate time to make a thorough assessment. These considerations can and often do countermand the purpose of consequentialism. Mill answers this criticism merely by appealing to man's expanding wisdom over time, arguing that we have had thousands of years of collective human experience to inform us as to which decisions to make. In a limited sense, this is true.

2. Another criticism of consequential morality concerns the fact that, to be consistent, it is forced to be exclusively forward looking. This is problematic. For example, suppose a criminal violates Mill's harm princi-

ple and murders an innocent civilian in cold blood. The culprit is convicted of the crime beyond a reasonable doubt. If only consequences matter, the sole, justifiable concern of the judge sentencing the convict must be future concerns, for example, satisfying the public's need for security from this person's maladjustment, quenching their justifiable desire for justice, or the need to make the punishment harsh enough to deter other potential felons. But what about backward-looking reasons? What about the appropriateness of punishing the culprit for some asocial behavior done in the past, such as murder? We naturally think of the past as critically relevant to the moral domain, especially situations of this type. This problem of needing to be forward looking also works with less heinous moral issues like promise keeping. A promise made in the past is morally important despite the fact that breaking it for some future enjoyment might increase the total of pleasure. These issues demonstrate some problems consequentialists have with (intrinsically valuable?) concerns for justice.

3. In still another criticism of consequentialism, R. M. Hare in his book, *Freedom and Reason,* argues that the supposed distinction between act and rule consequentialism collapses into the act variety. In the aforementioned peeping tom example, Hare would argue that if act consequentialism justifies peeping tom behavior, it follows that rule consequentialism will justify it too. For in all situations with the same conditions, one can easily say that, as a rule, one ought to act this way. Hare argues that when rule consequentialists reject these types of exceptional cases, they do so by altering the parameters of the situation. In the peeping tom example, the rule consequentialist would have to assume the behavior will become public knowledge with the instigation of the rule, and this redefines the situation being analyzed. If Hare is right, consequentialism's tenuous connection to human rights remains.

4. A final criticism of consequentialism concerns the common-sense notion that motives have intrinsic moral value, something the consequentialist denies. A rule consequentialist will instead extol the virtues of good motivation as an instrumentally valuable state of mind that tends, more often, to produce good results. Suppose someone is drowning in a lake at a public park. One person knows the victim to be rich and famous, and hopes for both publicity and wealth from rescuing the individual. He is a good swimmer and he successfully rescues the struggling swimmer. In a similar case suppose the victim is neither rich nor famous. In this case a different person comes along who recognizes a duty to protect life regardless of personal gain and risk. But this person is a weak swimmer. He attempts the rescue and they both drown. In these cases, the consequentalist will ascribe greater moral value to the first scenario. To Mill, the latter rescuer's good intentions are "wasted." There is an inherent virtue and a nobility about the latter situation that most recognize, but that consequentialists must dismiss to remain consistent. A later contemporary of Bentham and Mill, Henry Sigwick, cogently addresses this last criticism by drawing an important distinction between notions of right and wrong and praise and blame. In the drowning example, Sidwick would argue that this agent's action was morally right in that it produced good results. However, the agent still merits blame for acting from a blameworthy motive. Likewise, the latter agent did something wrong in not producing beneficial results, though he nevertheless is of praiseworthy character for owning pure motives in the situation. The consequentialists' reluctance to ascribe intrinsic value to motives and difficulty in accounting for criticisms based on justice and rights introduces the discussion of deontological ethical theories, a wholly different class of moral theories. They argue that obedience to moral principles is an absolute obligation, and not instrumentally contingent on the production of beneficial results.

II. DEONTOLOGY

A. Kant

We will confine the lion's share of the discussion of deontology to the well-articulated, rigorously defended duty ethics of Immanuel Kant, with some time later devoted to the deontology of W. D. Ross. It was Kant's contention that if moral obligation was going to be universally binding on humanity in the truest sence, it had to be grounded in bedrock, logically, consistent, *a priori* rational principles. To pull this project off, Kant works out a deontic scheme not dependent on empirical observations about human behavior or the world humans inhabit. In this way, Kant salvages, he thinks, the right to assume the truth of human autonomy.

1. Moral Law versus the Law of Nature

Why does Kant insist that genuine moral living consists of a rational dedication to do one's duty for duty's sake alone, independent of the consequences produced? One way to look at Kant's thinking on this position is to elucidate his emphasis on the importance of making moral obligation something that is ontologically above the system of nature.

Kant lived in the optimistic excitement following Newton's scientific discoveries. During this period, many eminent philosophers genuinely thought it was a matter of time before science would discover the causal relationships that explain every phenomenon that occurred in the universe. To Kant, this was a troubling hypothesis for moral responsibility. Consequential morality, Kant argues, grounds moral obligation in observations about the desires, strivings, and ends of human action. If this were true, Kant showed, then moral obligation was confined to the natural order, and being confined thus, would inevitably be predictable in terms of cause and effect. If this were true, the deliberations and strivings of humanity would ultimately reduce to a descriptive behaviorism, and hence destroy the deeper meaning of words like "ought" and "should," "praise" and "blame." Genuine human morality, Kant argues, must be grounded in rational principles beyond the predictable causality of laws of nature, in an authentic, autonomous human will dedicated to duty for duty's sake, in spite of the predictable vicissitudes of natural inclination.

An example will help. Envision three persons watching the Jerry Lewis Telethon. The first person watching gives money because he needs a tax deduction for that fiscal year. The second individual sees a crippled little child on the television, is moved with pity, and, in tears, sends in a donation. The last person has indifferent emotions about the need but recognizes a rational obligation to help if she can. Most people, consequentialists included, would say that the second person's decision to give has moral value. Kant disagrees. In his deontological view, only the third person's motives have moral worth, because they are rationally dedicated to dutiful obedience to moral principle. The second person's motives lack moral worth because they are grounded in a contingent, behavioral law of nature, not in an autonomously chosen will. It just so happens that this second person's particular physical constitution is susceptible to pity, which is ultimately no different than the way a lion's particular constitution makes it inclined to ruthlessly kill and eat zebras for food. In the case of the pitiful giver and the lion, praise, and blame are irrelevant, even though the constitution of the second person is, no doubt, socially useful. The second person, moved by the same predictable class of forces that motivate a serial killer or a compulsive gambler, does not give a genuine moral response.

2. Intentions

Kant's contrast between the moral law and the law of nature explains why deontological morality is grounded in human motivation and not in consequences. Ascription of moral worth rests totally with the agent's intentional state. Kant says, "There is only one thing that is good without qualification, and that thing is the good will." There are many things, Kant states, that are viewed as good, for example, intelligence, good fortune, character traits, and so on. But these things can be used for evil ends unless they are under the control of a person with the "good will." Only this is intrinsically valuable. "Considered in itself, [the good will] it is to be esteemed beyond comparison as far higher than anything that it could ever bring about merely in order to favour some inclination or, if you like, the sum total of inclinations." Kant takes this still further. "Suppose the good will is "impotent" and wholly incapable of bringing about whatever it tries to accomplish. He says that "even then it would still shine like a jewel for its own sake as something which has its full value in itself." To transcend the predictable system of nature, the "good will" must be autonomous and thus rationally generated, because it is reason alone that enables the human person to overcome myriad variations of inclination and desire.

3. Good Will and Maxims

Kant sets humans apart as unique beings endowed with a special capacity to make genuine moral decisions grounded in a rationally governed, autonomous will obedient to moral laws, irrespective of natural desires or inclinations to the contrary. But what are the true moral laws? And how does the error-prone person assess the true ones? In Kant's terminology, reason communicates to the mind things it should do according to rules he calls maxims. How does this process work? To illustrate, suppose I am leaving the grocery store and I notice that an elderly lady is encumbered with a load of groceries by the store exit. I decide it is my duty to open the door for her. In this case, Kant argues, my mind is operating according to a subjective principle of action, a maxim, of the following form, "When I infer that a person needs help and I have the capacity to help, I have a duty to help." Acting according to maxims is not necessarily a conscious mental activity, although the mind is continually making such judgments about alternatives of action according to these principles for action. Naturally, not all maxims necessarily cash out absolute moral laws. The aforementioned person moved by pity to give to the Jerry Lewis Telethon is acting according to a maxim of action, but the maxim is not a moral law and the intentions have no moral worth; it does not express a "good will." In this case, the person acts according to a contingent maxim grounded in a predictable and natural cognitive dissonance, "When something moves me with pity or sympathy, take action to assuage guilt or restore homeostasis." This is not an autonomous, rational response.

4. Categorical Imperatives

Kant's deontological morality, as you might suspect, offers a rational test the agent can use to determine if the maxims the mind and will deliberate on are in fact maxims of genuine moral worth. Maxims of supreme moral worth take the form of what Kant calls "categorical imperatives," that is, they are necessary, and of the unconditional form, "Do X!" not of the contingent form, "If you want Y, do X."

Human lives encounter scores of conditional maxims too, and by not being categorical, are not necessarily wrong. These are the prudential judgments that make up most of life. For example, we know that physical fitness is desirable as conductive to a long, vigorous life. Hence, an exerciser might operate according to the hypothetical maxim, "If you want to be healthy, get some regular exercise." Kant calls these types of maxims hypothetical imperatives. Thus, although we can argue with some success that people have a duty to exercise, we cannot argue that they have an absolute moral duty to do so. Categorical imperatives as a different species, are optionless.

Kant's criteria for determining whether a maxim for action is a genuine universal moral principle, remember, must be grounded in *a priori* principles to avoid begging a key question of objective rational foundations. His three criteria rely on the principle of contradiction, and each is a necessary condition to ascribing categorical moral value of the maxim at stake.

1. Universalizability: Act only on that maxim through which you can at the same time will that it should become a universal law.
2. Means/ends: Act in such a way that you always treat humanity, whether in your own person or in the person of any other, never simply as a means, but always at the same time and end.
3. Autonomy: Act so that you treat the will of every rational being as a will which makes universal law.

To briefly illustrate how these criteria (tests) work, let us look at Kant's example of promise keeping. A person in desperate need is driven to borrow money to get by. He reasons that he will promise to pay back the money without ever really intending to do so. Could breaking a promise ever be a universal moral law? It

would contradict itself. For if every promise were broken, the purpose of the principle would become meaningless and inert, for no one would promise anything, knowing beforehand that each promise would be meaningless. Truth is, the capacity to break promises is paristic on the moral law of promise keeping, and requires the assumption of the morality of promise keeping to sustain itself. Because breaking promises cannot be universalized without contradiction, the issue is settled. The promise must be kept because keeping one's word is an absolute moral law.

And yet when a maxim cannot be universalized without contradiction, it will also fail the other criteria as well. In the breaking of a promise, the person also violates Kant's second criteria for categorical assessment, for in the breaking of the promise, one is treating someone as a means only, and not at the same time an end. The word "only" is of practical importance here, because in our many personal interactions we usually rely on other persons and groups as a means without violating a moral rule. If the destitute person were to pay back the money as promised, he nevertheless would still use the giver as a means to get out of a tough situation, but he would not be using that person as a means "only." As Kant states, "For then it is manifest, that a violator of the rights of man intends to use the person of others *merely* as a means without taking into account considerations that, as rational beings, they ought always at the same time to be rated as ends, that is, only as beings who must themselves be able to share in the end of the very same action." Finally, if a maxim for action fails to meet the first two criteria for categorical imperatives, it will fail the third one also, to "treat the will of every rational being as a will which makes universal law." In short, because each rational agent is an autonomous will given the capacity to know and obey moral laws, they are entitled to the respect and dignity due to a being of that type. Hence, in the case of promise breaking, the maxim contradicts itself, treats humanity as a means only, and fails to accord the dignity and respect due to the lender as a rational, autonomous agent.

5. Human Nature

The concept of duty as primary in deontological moral systems entails a unique view of morality in light of true facts about human nature. Kant offers a rational methodology to determine whether the maxims a moral agent acts upon are in fact absolute moral rules. And yet, the notion of duty is important in that human beings are a species that often chooses to follow other inclinations in spite of its knowledge of moral obligations. This is an important difference between the teleo-gical position of the consequentialists and the deonto-logical thinkers. The Greeks and the utilitarians were concerned to understand what, for human beings, is moral given reliable observations about their specific nature as creatures. Deontological morality, as evidenced in Kant, is concerned with what is moral *in spite* of the nature of human beings. Genuine morality applies to all rational beings, of which humans are an imperfect and easily distractable example. The concept of duty would be unnecessary, in Kant's view, for perfectly rational beings, for those beings would always understand the purely reasonable moral law and act on it. Humans though, as imperfectly rational beings, require the concept of duty as a practical motive for action that is necessary to subordinate conflicting human desires to the rational, autonomous, law-abiding will.

This analysis again suggests why intentions (good will) are morally valuable while consequences are not. Right and wrong motivations can obtain in situations where the correct action is executed by both parties. A shopkeeper can be honest in his business practices because he wants his business to be successful, or he can be honest because he recognizes a rational obligation to dutifully obey the moral law. The first motive merely coincides with what duty requires and lacks genuine moral value, while the latter motive expresses obedience to an absolute moral maxim that expresses a good will, and hence, has genuine moral worth. Such examples are not meant to be complicated and Kant himself argued that this perspective on duty was neither original nor esoteric. Everyone, he argues, knows that doing something you are morally obligated to do and doing something you want to do are two different things. And we all know that the former is meritorious in a unique way; the latter is not.

6. Perfect and Imperfect Duties

Thus far in the discussion of deonology, particularly Kant, one might think that duties are duties, period, and hence must be obeyed. This is true of categorical imperatives. But if you reflect a minute, you can no doubt think of situations where different duties seem to conflict and a decision must be made as to which one to fulfill. In these cases, Kant recognizes an important distinction between what he calls perfect and imperfect duties. This distinctive allows us to resolve many of our moral dilemmas.

In short, perfect duties are defined as negative duties, that is, associated with the moral requirement not to cause harm. In many, if not most cases, this implies a

right to redress, including many times, state interven-tion, if the violation of a perfect duty harms you. Perfect duties are phrased as maxims that lend themselves easily to verification as categorical imperatives by Kant's three tests for moral maxims. If someone punches you in the nose for no apparent reason, they have violated a perfect, categorical duty. The rule, "Everyone ought to punch anyone in the nose whenever they are so inclined," cannot be universalized without contradiction, treats humanity as a means only, and violates the dignity and respect due to rational, autonomous moral agents. The same analysis holds for most other negative duties, such as the duty not to steal, to lie, to murder, to molest, and so on.

Imperfect duties refer to positive duties, that is, prudentially bringing a positive consequence to a situation. When these duties are phrased in the form of maxims, they most often do not cash out as categorical moral obligations. They are hypothetical, and hence are of the form, "If you want X, do Y." With imperfect duties, we can only say with assurance something like the following: "It is praiseworthy to do acts of this *type*." However, in specific situations, the failure to fulfill the imperfect duty does not entail a right to compliance or enforcement by the receiver. If you are driving down the highway and you notice a motorist stranded with a flat tire, do you have a categorical duty to stop and help? No, and yet it would be nice to help, and further-more, we praise people who do acts of this type when they can. Likewise, you would laugh if the stranded motorist claimed a right to your help in fixing the flat, and expected the state to fine you if you did not stop to assist. The duty to give to charity would also classify as an imperfect duty. You can argue generally that per-sons should give to charity, but as a member of the Boy Scouts of America you cannot expect that any individual is categorically obligated to give to your organization, nor could you expect the police to arrest those who did not give to your cause. And yet, persons who have a "good will" will help in similar ways.

7. The Virtues of Kant's Deontology

This has been a rough-and-ready recount of Kant's complicated rational scheme for the real possibility of a genuine human morality grounded in an autonomous will that is above the predicatable system of nature. His views derive from an exhaustive metaphysical and epistemological philosophy that attempted to overcome David Hume's incisive arguments against all attempts to demonstrate the possibility of certain knowledge. Kant's deontology does have practical virtues that deserve mention.

1. Kant was wise to emphasize the valuable role that intention plays in the ascription of praise and blame to moral agents.

2. His desire to ground morality in an autonomous will that somehow can "rise above" the predictable system of nature is foundationally crucial to our belief in moral responsibility. This is just as important today as it was in Kant's time. For a universe in which human behavior is reducible to merely a higher order of animal behavior, minimizes morality to a need for conditioned social control and abdicates a rich view of personal accountability.

3. His view respects contemporary notions of human rights. The tests for assertaining categorical moral rules omit any opportunity for violating the dignity and respect due all rational agents, regardless of perceived social benefit. Rational, autonomous persons who "can do otherwise" deserve respect due free agents who possess genuine moral responsibility.

4. His deontology correctly requires that persons never treat themselves as unique or special, deserving consideration as exceptional cases. Such a consistency requirement entails that if I have reasons for doing something categorically moral, those reasons must be adequate for anyone reasoning in that or similar cases.

5. Finally, Kant's deontology, in defending a rich view of human freedom, lends itself to support for the classic notion of justice, that is, to get what you deserve. Moral agents who, through decisions subject to possible discipline by a rational, autonomous will, forsake performing their perfect duties, forfeit their rights to be treated with the dignity the categorical imperative mandates. Hence, a thief, in violating an absolute moral law, loses his right the similar treatment under that law, and may be incarcerated. This perspective supports the common-sense notion that we punish people precisely for injustices they committed in the past, and not just to deter the behavior in the future. There is genuine accountability here.

8. Criticisms of Kant

Kant's deontology is not without its opponents. Here are some of the criticisms commonly raised.

1. One criticism of Kant's ethics is that he ultimately assumed the freedom of the will without proof. Given our observations about the human condition, it is viewed by many as more tenable to postulate determinism over freedom, regardless of what that does to human morality. In Kant's case, he seems to make a pragmatic decision that moral responsibility is so important that this justifies the assumption of human freedom.

2. Many reject Kant's contention that genuine moral worth is grounded in a purely rational activity of the will married to an impersonally calculable logical consistency. Kant does not try to hide this. And yet, his view of intentionality, though rigorous, fails to capture much of what we admire as moral motivation, such as the admiration of maternal instinct judiciously applied.

3. Another criticism of Kant concerns the issue of maxims. When humans act, Kant says that we act according to subjective principles of action called maxims. What he never does is argue for a consistent way to form these maxims prior to assessment via the three tests for categorical imperatives. Once again honesty serves as a good case in point. Suppose I am unemployed and tempted to steal to feed my family. If I phrase the maxim generally, "It is OK to steal," I am breaking a categorical moral law by the three tests. But Kant does not really specify that I cannot phrase the maxim anyway I wish, such as "I may steal to feed my starving family when I know I will not get caught, and when I can reasonably assume that others in the same position are not doing the same." Universalize this maxim, and there is no apparent practical contradiction. Here we seem to have a case where a maxim fails the first test but passes the second and third ones.

4. Kant insists that moral situations never, if thought out carefully, cash out as genuine dilemmas over conflicting categorical imperatives. Otherwise, the status of absolute moral rules as a class would be in jeopardy. During the Second World War, Dutch fishermen hid Jewish fugitives in their boats and ferried them to safety over in England. Often, SS patrol boats and submarines would stop these fishing boats. When Nazi captains asked the fishermen if there were Jews on board, what were the fishermen to do? If the maxims, "It is wrong to lie," and "Permitting the murder of innocent people is wrong," are both viewed as categorical imperatives, as I think they must be, then we have a genuine categorical dilemma. In these cases, most Dutch captains viewed it as permissible to sacrifice absolute honesty to save innocent life. Kant has trouble with these types of scenarios.

B. W. D. Ross's Twentieth-Century Deontology

The persistence of problematic dilemmas for Kantian deontological thinkers is, in many respects, accounted for by the amendments made to deontological thought in the twentieth century by W. D. Ross. Consequentialist thought dominated ethical debate in the nineteenth and early twentieth centuries until Ross rearoused philosophical interest in the notion of duty.

An influential gadfly that prompted Ross in this area was an article by H. A. Prichard entitled, "Does Moral Philosophy Rest on a Mistake?"

1. "Plain Man" Intuition

Prichard argues that this "mistake" of moral thought is to base our ethical obligations on the good to be achieved as compared to alternative courses of action. As a matter of fact, Prichard argues, we do not appreciate an obligation because of arguments that support it, but merely by a sense of direct awareness of the importance of the obligation. This analysis, directed at the consequentialists, also criticizes the rational, calculative methodology of Kant. Prichard grounds obligation in human intuition, and this intuition often contradicts reasoning about results, and also rejects dry recourse to rational speculation based on the principle of contradiction.

Ross accepts Prichard's argument for intuition and uses it to ground his deontological morality in the principle of *prima facie* duty. According to Ross, the terms "right" and "good" are distinct, irreducible, indefinable objective qualities, consistent with G. E. Moore's position. An act is either right or wrong, but it is motives that are good or bad. On this account, there are four possible conclusions in assessing the moral quality of an agent's response in a situation. Ultimately, and this is where Ross is most easily subject to criticism, a person by intuition "knows" which course of action is right and which motive connotes a "good" one. But because right and good are indefinable, there is no need to analyze further, as the consequentialists do in making good an instrumental quality.

How does Ross's view work in practice? Well, he argues that the "Plain Man" understands his duty in a situation according to Prichard's notion of immediate awareness. So, if a murderer stops at my front door and asks, "Is your child here, I'm going to kill him?" the "Plain Man" knows intuitively that this situation justifies a lie to save life. This is how Ross tries to overcome exceptional cases that plague the Kantian scheme. The aforementioned Dutch fishermen example is another case in point. The "Plain Man" or average Joe will just "know" that his duty to be truthful may be suspended for a more stringent duty, in this case to save Jews from concentration camps.

Ross addresses an obvious concern closet critics should have about the nature of intuition. Obviously, many people intuit very badly, and they often rationalize things they want into morally acceptable decisions. Ross's answer to this is to point out that the intuition he has in mind is developmental. Hence, education

and practical training are vital to molding the intuitive faculty into one that makes good moral decisions. Is this still what we would call intuition? Well, in a way, yes. Here is an example that illustrates how it should work. As a adolescent, many children go through a period where they do not respect their parents, (although they are good parents by all normal standards), they think their parents owe them more than they receive, or they surmise that their parents are overly conservative and have habits that are distinctly passé. But if the parents are patient, they remain hopeful that the children will "grow up" and eventually "understand" why they are like they are. In the mind of the maturing adolescent, and this comes at different times for different children, it will just "dawn" on the child that his parents are not as unfair, dumb, or passé as he thought. He will just "see" it, usually as a response to understanding the good reasons behind the parent's actions through encountering adult situations himself, such as having children of his own, or working out a personal budget. In this case, Ross would say the intuition of the maturing person has positively developed. Upon "understanding" the reasons behind the parents' actions, the adolescent might recognize a *prima facie* duty of gratitude to his parents, perhaps even a duty of reparation for past injuries inflicted out of ignorance. Although it is true that as humans, we use reason to make moral deliberations, the point of understanding is intuitive in Ross's sense. Remember how you have worked and worked to figure out a difficult math problem, only to have the whole solution just "dawn" on you. This is what Ross means by intuition.

2. *Prima Facie* Duty

Prima facie duty (duty on the face of it) refers to a duty one must perform, unless it conflicts with a more important duty intuitively recognized. In a situation where two or more *prima facie* duties conflict, the one my "Plain Man" intuition tells me I must perform is what Ross calls the "actual duty". In the absence of a conflict of duties in a moral situation, any *prima facie* duty is the agent's actual duty. Thus, in the case of the Dutch fishermen, the duty to be truthful is the actual duty in cases where no other exceptional circumstance warrants overriding it for a more important obligation, such as saving innocent life.

Ross argues that there are seven *prima facie* duty types, and each is an obligatory actual duty unless there is a conflict with a greater *prima facie* duty. This list is the duty types Ross observes, though he is humble enough to say that this list could be incomplete. The seven *prima facie* duties are as follows:

1. Fidelity: Keep promises and commitments.
2. Reparation: Correct past wrongs.
3. Nonmaleficence: Duty to prevent harm.
4. Beneficence: Duty to increase general pleasure.
5. Justice: Duty to prevent unfair distribution of benefits.
6. Gratitude: Duty to repay kindness, and
7. Self-improvement: Duty to better oneself.

In this list, Ross admitted the complexity of the moral domain in human affairs. Another example will help demonstrate how he cashes these duties out in practice. Suppose a nurse makes an appointment to give a lecture on Friday at 6 p.m. at a gathering of oncology nurses for the Nurses' Association. En route to the engagement, she witnesses an automobile collision with life-threatening injuries. If she stops and renders assistance, she will miss her engagement, but if she makes her appointment, someone will likely die. Ross would say this nurse has a conflict between the duties of fidelity and nonmaleficence. Irrespective of consequences, (making the engagement might create more general utility), the nurse will know intuitively that in this case the duty of nonmaleficence overrides the duty of fidelity. She has an actual duty to stop and render assistance. However, after the assistance is complete, her failure to fulfill her *prima facie* duty of fidelity obligates her to a duty of reparation, that is, to call and explain the situation to the Nurse's Association and probably offer to speak again at a later date. Likewise, the Nurse's Association should recognize a *prima facie* duty of gratitude for the call and demonstrate an understanding of her predicament as a duty of beneficence. This intuitive weighing of our various duties, Ross, argues, is in fact how we work out our morality in practice. Though it has its weaknesses, it does offer a practical explanation for the moral complexity humans encounter day to day.

3. Criticisms of Ross

The main criticisms of Ross are as follows:

1. An intuitive method for moral decision-making is unreliable and often inconsistent
2. Much of his notion of *prima facie* duty is left undefined, that is, the "Plain Man" must figure out on his own which of the seven duties apply and which one overrides which.

Regarding the first criticism, Ross argues that by intuition, he means self-evident in the sense in which mathematical axions are self-evident to those familiar with them. Also, if the system of *prima facie* duties seems unsystematic, that is because that is how we, in fact, reason about moral issues. In this sense it is descriptive. Ross argues that though his deontology is apparently less systematized than consequentialist positions, they are in reality no less precise in practice. In practice, the principle of utility is at least if not more difficult to cash out in actual decision situations, and is based on a principle that is not how humans really think about moral issues. Besides, Ross does have a governing principle of action implicit in his deontology. An act is morally right (i.e., an actual duty), if and only if it is a *prima facie* duty, and no other conflicting act represents a more stringent duty.

Also See the Following Articles

ACTS AND OMISSIONS • EGOISM AND ALTRUISM • KANTIANISM • UTILITARIANISM

Bibliography

Aristotle. (1925). *Nicomachean ethics.* (W. D. Ross, Trans.). London: Oxford University Press.

Abraham E., Flower, E., & O'Connor, F. (Eds.). (1989). *Morality, philosophy, and practice: Historical and contemporary studies:* New York: Random House.

Bentham, J. (1948). *Introduction on the principles of morals and legislation.* W. Harrison (Ed.). London: Oxford University Press.

Brennan, J. G. (1973). *Ethics and morals* New York: Harper and Row.

Hudlin, C. W. (Ed). (1949). *Moral traditions in moral philosophy.* Dubuque, IA: Kendall/Hunt.

Kant, I. (1948). *Groundwork of the metaphysics of morals.* (H. J. Paton, Ed. and Trans.). London: Hutcheson & Co, Ltd.

Mill, J. S. (1979). *Utilitarianism.* G. Sher (Ed.). Hacket Publishing.

Mill, J. S., (1947). *On liberty.* A. Castell, (Ed.) Arlington Heights, IL: AHM Publishing Co.

Rachels, J. (1993). *The elements of moral philosophy.* (2nd ed.). New York: McGraw-Hill Inc.

Ross, W. D. (1930). *The right and the good.* Oxford: Oxford University Press.

Solomon, R. C. (1984). *Ethics: A Brief introduction.* New York: McGraw-Hill.

CONSUMER RIGHTS

Jan Narveson
University of Waterloo

GLOSSARY

consumer The ultimate user of a product or service.

criteria The set of standards by which a product is to be evaluated.

descriptions The information presented by the seller to characterize his product to the consumer.

market view The view that rights are based on consumers and producers both acting to make exchanges on mutually agreed terms.

normal performance Performance within a known and accepted range for the type of good in question.

risk Probabilities of adverse effects stemming from use of a consumer product.

socialist view The view that producers may be com-pelled by society to supply the needs of consumers; rights are politically derived.

standards Established categories of degrees of performance: "fair," "good," "superb," etc.

transaction An exchange, mediated by communication, between seller and buyer; in a free market, this exchange is voluntary.

CONSUMER RIGHTS are a function of business, which is a set of transactions between buyers and sellers. At the end of the line in the "buyer" direction is the consumer, the one who uses the item or the service purchased for his own purposes, such as to satisfy his own hunger. The ultimate *buyer* may not be the ultimate *consumer,* as when a mother buys food for her children, but we will assume for simplicity that they are the same person. Of course, much buying of things to be used is done by producers as well, yet the function that grounds the whole thing is that of the "ultimate" consumer. We produce, generally speaking, in order that we may "consume"—though much "consumption" does not use up what is used, but merely uses it. It is the rights of the consumer *as* consumer that we are interested in here: what do producers owe to these people who seek, pay for, and use their products?

What is a "right" in these contexts? The general answer is that if the seller fails to fulfill the requirements in question, that is grounds for complaint and possible remedial action. To say that one person, A, has a right against another, B, is to say that some aspect of A and A's relation to B is such as to create a requirement—a duty or liability—on B's part. If B fails to live up to that requirement, then he owes it to A to make good on the deficiency, or possibly some kind of penalty or punishment is in order. Just how those should be effected will not be discussed in this article, but it is obviously an important subject for research and action, legal or otherwise.

I. TWO VIEWS ABOUT THE BASIS OF CONSUMER RIGHTS

We can depict two broadly differing general outlooks on consumer rights. On one type of view, it is the social purpose of an economic system to satisfy consumers. They are what it is "for"; the consumer has priority over the producer, and the buyer over the seller. On this view, there is no particular necessity that producers should produce for their own benefit; all are to produce, insofar as they can, in order that all may consume, simply insofar as they need or want the items produced.

An important variant view is that we are to bring about the "best" for the consumer—but not necessarily in the consumer's own judgment of what is best for him. On this view, the notion that what the consumer has are "rights" is marginalized, and would be replaced by a theory about what is good for people, whatever they may think about it. Such views make customers into children and will not be considered further here. We will assume the liberal view, on which the consumer is "sovereign" so far as his own interests, needs, and values are concerned.

On the other view of consumer rights, the socioeconomic system should not attempt to favor consumers at the expense of producers: it treats all people alike, with their many distinctive interests. Some are interested in producing for its own sake, others produce for profit, and still others may play a money-making "game," as if for its own sake. The rights of consumers, this view holds, must be designed with a view to the whole community; thus, neither consumers nor producers have authority or social preference, as such, over the other. Producers produce for whomever or whatever they want to produce for. Thus, unless they happen to be specially motivated to produce for certain particular others, inducing them to produce for particular people will require an inducement by those people, in the form of an offer of something sufficiently desired by the potential producer that a prospect of receiving it will

motivate him to produce the desired goods. Usually this inducement is money; again, for simplicity, we will assume that for present purposes.

This second view is the free-market view of production and consumption; the former view is approximately that of Marxists and other socialists. Familiar outlooks also hold that some production is to be "socialized" while other production is to be handled by the free-market system. Large issues are involved in resolving the dispute between socialists and free-market defenders, and of course there would be many shades of opinion from out-and-out socialism to the out-and-out free market. However, the second, or free market, view portrays consumers as we normally understand them. What is special about the consumer is that he is "on his own": it is the consumer who decides what and whether he will buy, and what and whether he will consume, within the limits of his budget. Meanwhile the producer is not obliged, but only induced, to satisfy the consumer's interests. This general outlook is really what frames the whole idea of *consumer* rights, so far as most of us are concerned.

With this background, what is the consumer to expect from those who supply the things he wants? There are two quite different viewpoints that follow from the distinction drawn in the preceding discussion. On the first view, the consumer is entitled, as it were, to everything, for example, excellent performance with ironclad guarantees and total safety ("zero risk"). He can expect them because producers have no individual freedom; they are simply required to produce. On the free-market view, on the other hand, the consumer's entitlements are determined by the *agreements* he makes with the producers or sellers of the goods he buys. The producer owes the consumer what he has agreed to give him—no less, but no more. On this view, the consumer must determine what he wants and whether the package offered by the seller is going to give it to him. It is up to the producer to judge whether what the consumer offers as an inducement for him to supply the desired thing is enough of an inducement to do so. In short, both parties must decide what the price shall be.

Might the consumer do better with a package of rights that impose much heavier duties on producers? To think so is to ignore the fact that rights are expensive. Making an item "perfectly" safe typically costs several times as much as making it merely very safe; many consumers would prefer less safety at a lower price. The same goes for other things we might hope to secure for the consumer. Thus the second view, paradoxically, enables producers to supply the consumer with more of what he or she actually wants.

If we think that morals are reasonable arrangements among human beings, rather than some sort of transcendental dictates from on high, we will see that the second viewpoint is preferable to the first. Socialized control over producers—as if each of them had a moral duty to satisfy consumers as much as possible, regardless of its effects on the producer's interests—is counterproductive to consumers as well as producers.

II. TRANSACTIONS

What is a fair treatment of consumer rights, then? The beginnings of the right answer are achieved when we recognize that the buyer–seller relation is a *transaction* in which one party offers goods or services and the other money (or, as in barter, some other goods or service, but here we assume for convenience that all purchases are made with money). Each person in the transaction is trying to better his situation to the maximum extent possible; each makes whatever deal he can on the basis of his own interests. This gives us our fundamental requirements. First, each must observe the rule that the offer, in whatever specific way it is made, is such that the other party can expect to come away better off, in terms of his own preferences, than when he entered. If the customer is not satisfied, he has no reason to buy; if the merchant is not happy, he has no reason to sell. The meeting point—a kind of Aristotelian mean—is achieved when both are sufficiently pleased that the deal does indeed go through. The other fundamental duty is that each person carry through on his commitment: the seller to deliver the goods as agreed, and the buyer to pay the price agreed.

III. DESCRIBING THE GOODS

The key to understanding consumer rights on this general conception lies in the fact, easily overlooked, that transactions depend crucially on *communication* between the parties concerned. Since neither is forced or duty bound to participate, and each is out to make the best bargain he can, transactions of this kind require communication. The seller *offers* his wares or services, possibly by displaying them, but more likely by describing them, in such a way as to convey to the consumer that his goods are of the kind wanted by the potential purchaser: a car, a mixing bowl, a lecture on quantum mechanics, etc. Because the purchaser must respond in light of the information he can gather, including whatever he is supplied by the seller, this basic supply-

ing of a general description under which the good is offered by the one, and acquired or rejected by the other, is the first place at which mischief could be done. The seller could describe his good as "F" when it is not in fact an F, but something else.

IV. "LET THE BUYER BEWARE"?

Is there any basic rule about this? One suggestion is that none is really needed, since the consumer, after all, is a free agent who need not make the purchase at all. Or to put it another way, the "rule" is the famous *caveat emptor* ("Let the buyer beware!"). This rule would throw *all* the responsibility on the consumer—it is "his lookout," as they say. But there is a problem in this: it would make the acquisition of goods a much more expensive process than it need be—not in terms of higher purchase prices in money, but in terms of the customer's time and effort devoted to making his purchase. Moreover, if we knew that in general we could expect nothing in the way of responsibility for his product from the seller, that would be a very effective incentive not to buy at all—hardly what the seller wants!

Caveat emptor is a "bottom-line" right, and as such is indeed basic: it is the right to say "no"—to "vote with one's feet." Certainly it affords the basic protection of the consumer. But attention to the basic terms of free exchange enables us to do better. There is every reason to assign some basic responsibility to those who make claims about their products. Instead of "caveat emptor," we can hold that the seller has the responsibility to see to it that his product is to be *as claimed*. Even tagging the good by a general name—"tire," say, or "ladder"—supplies a general description, and therefore one that could be misapplied. This misapplication could be morally objectionable. Let us see just how.

V. MISDESCRIPTION

When is duplicity or bad faith involved? The basic answer to this is that the word—"car," "lecture," or whatever—will designate the goods or services in virtue of what is supposed to be good *about* them. Let the letter "F" stand for this basic label or tag. It designates the "function," as the ancients called it, of the offered goods or services. Virtually all goods have names of that type—names indicating the function they are ostensibly to perform. In some cases, the item actually offered is, for example, fake: it simply does not perform that function *at all*. What was claimed to be money is actually counterfeit; the supposed computer is merely a cleverly painted box. Obviously that is wrong. The consumer is entitled to the truth in this regard: those who supply something wholly different from what is claimed misuse language, and thereby misuse *people*.

However, there are subtler ways in which we can violate reasonable requirements on these matters. When you say that the item is "an F," you are conveying that it has a certain purpose or function: "this is an iron" implies that "this item is for flattening clothes"; calling it a "car" implies that it is for transportation; and so on. Descriptions of the "functional" type are ubiquitous in the business world, for the obvious reason that we go to the market in order to satisfy various fairly definite desires, and sellers seek to make their livings by giving us what we want—which they can only do by designing and marketing things that will meet those particular desires.

What, then, is involved in saying, "This is an F"? When "F" is a *functional* term, the answer is fairly easy, for to apply a functional term is to supply the essentials of the answer: if this thing is *for* accomplishing F, and if it will not do that, then the purchaser has a complaint. He has "been had." Anyone knowing the meaning of the term will know what a vacuum cleaner is for; to be sold something so described is to be licensed to expect that it will in fact suck up loose dirt. And so on.

VI. CRITERIA AND STANDARDS: "NORMAL PERFORMANCE"

We may distinguish two dimensions along which the implications of F-ness may be concretely spelled out. First, the description of x as having function F implies certain *criteria* of evaluation. If it is a car, certain questions, how comfortable?, how fast?, how economical?, and several others, come quickly to mind as relevant. Which criteria are more *important* than others is another matter; buses, trucks, off-road vehicles, racing cars, and so on each have more specialized transportational purposes. A functional description carries with it the relevance of certain general criteria, and also opens up questions about which more specific criteria are applicable. The customer must query and negotiate about the latter, but the former are simply given—no one needs to raise any such questions. If what was alleged to be a tennis racket breaks in half upon even mild contact with the ball, it is a poor racket, or even, at the limit,

"not a racket at all." It is the functionality of the descriptive terms that makes the latter something close to a synonym for the former.

In order to do that, however, we now need to introduce another dimension. Once we have criteria of performance, the next question is, how well does the item perform by those criteria? Fuel economy is a criterion of merit in an automobile, but how much is how good? There is a narrower question of special importance: how much is "*good enough*"? Here we will need empirical facts. Given an array of these, we can sort cars into "average," "miserly," "gas guzzler," and so on. Performance will range all the way from hopeless to superb. Considering this, can we say any more, just on the basis of the functional language in which consumer goods are described, about what the consumer is *entitled* to?

Indeed we can. Consider that the seller has it within his power to augment, specify, or amend the description of his goods to any degree he likes. Suppose, though, that he does not take advantage of this liberty: the consumer asks for an F, and the seller hands him item x, without further comment (or just, "OK, here's one!"). It is reasonable to suggest that what the consumer has a right to assume he is getting is an F that is, broadly speaking, "normal." Were it no so, e.g., definitely substandard, say, or on the other hand the best F ever made, clearly it is in the seller's and consumer's mutual interest that the seller should *say* so—at least if the price asked is also in the "normal" range. The question, "Well, you didn't ask for one that *worked*, now, did you?" is ruled out. To ask for an F *is* to ask for an F that "works"; that is, one that does to at least a modest degree what Fs are supposed to do. If it does not even manage that, the consumer has a legitimate complaint.

If F is, for instance, a mountain, then the idea that it is "supposed to do" anything in particular has no basis in the sheer semantics of the term. In such cases, discussion of what it is wanted for would have to be carried on. (It might be theological, say, in which case if the consumer were of a different religion from the seller, the discussion may be quite protracted!) But in "consumerland," what we normally buy are things made by people and made under quite definite auspices. To do that is to hook into fairly specific commitments about what the things are "supposed to do" and, very roughly, how well they are supposed to do it. The point, then, is that the consumer's minimal right is to get what was asked for, as described by the language then current and known to be current, or by whatever other beliefs are known to be shared between them. Anything else, if intentional, convicts the seller of mendacity, duplicity, insincerity, or even fraud.

VII. SETTING VS. IMPOSING STANDARDS

The question of normal standards of performance suggests the idea of setting up commissions, regulatory agencies, and so on with the power to specify standards. Such activities can make it easy to infer the relevant criteria and standards by which to appraise the goods in question. A four-star restaurant can be expected to have *very* good food of the kind it offers; Joe's No-Star Hamburger Stand cannot.

A danger about agencies that are actually given regulatory powers, as distinct from the power simply to specify normal standards, is that they will impose requirements so stiff that meeting them will materially raise the price of the item, or eliminate it from the market altogether, when some consumers would prefer not to pay that price. They might prefer to do without the item altogether rather than pay for the one with all the required "bells and whistles," or to have one meeting less rigorous standards at a considerably lower price. This raises another major issue: do consumers have the right to whatever services would-be suppliers are willing to supply, at least so long as they do not harm others? An affirmative answer offers a challenge to many current beliefs about these matters.

VIII. OTHER VIEWS

This last point brings up such things as seat-belt legislation, the prohibition of many drugs or of asbestos, and a host of other cases in which current laws either prohibit something the consumer would like to have and would be willing to pay for or give him his choice between an item he does not want or is not willing to buy at the postregulatory price and no item of that kind at all. In all these cases, we have *imposed* standards set by people who claim to know better than the consumer what is good for him. Such standards must be based on views of what is good for people that depart from market freedom and treat people not as sovereigns but as "subjects," the regulatory agency or government taking the role of nanny or priest. They are, in short, antiliberal. As previously remarked, it is quite unclear that the notion of "rights" is properly applicable to theories of that kind, and therefore that notions of "consumer rights" would properly describe them.

IX. LIMITATIONS FROM THIRD-PARTY RIGHTS

On the other hand, it is clear that protection of persons outside a particular transaction is a proper source of rights in this area. The free-market view holds that so long as the agreement between buyer and seller is fully voluntary, no objection can be made to its provision. However, advocates of such a view also agree that if party A wishes to sell party B an atomic bomb, the rest of us should have something to say about it.

Here two useful comparisons are of interest. First, consider the plumbing standard that, in many localities, requires that if you want twin basins in your bathroom, each must have a separate drain line to the basement instead of the much less expensive method of draining both into the same line. Second, there is the law in Minnesota requiring that anything claimed to be "ice cream" must conform to the original specifications of what was so called before commercial manufacture of ice cream became common, with the result that anything sold as ice cream in Minnesota will be equal or superior to the most expensive, exotic ice cream available in, say, New York City.

The Minnesota law attests to the role of descriptions, but also raises a question of semantics. By 1990, the term "ice cream" had come to be applied to any number of imitations, most sold at much lower prices than real ice cream would require. Nevertheless, the legislators in that state could point to a "literal" meaning in which x is not really "ice cream" unless it is made with cream. The legislators did not forbid the sale of alternative substances which in other states would be designated "ice cream"—the manufacturers merely have to call it something else.

We may consider the Minnesota law as high-handed but not out of bounds: consumers expecting iced *cream* when they ask for ice cream are protected effectively by this law, but those whose expectations are governed by familiar looser uses will find higher prices for possibly unwanted higher quality. A modest linguistic adjustment puts buyer and seller on mutually agreeable terms. The twin-line plumbing regulation, on the other hand, genuinely makes it impossible for people to have twin sinks in their bathrooms without great extra expense. No legitimate purpose is served by the requirement—it is just a boondoggle for the plumbing union. It does not protect people outside the transaction between the householder and his plumber, nor does it serve the interests of the purchaser, as those are seen by the purchaser. Such a regulation, then, seems to violate consumer rights, whereas forbidding the sale of atomic bombs on the open market to all comers is justified on a principle that even the most radical "libertarians" accept.

That principle is that voluntary activities are permissible so long as they do not endanger the rights of others outside the transaction: forbidden are what are called "third party" harms, or "negative externalities." Such parties were not consulted, and did not contribute to the production of the good transferred in the exchange, yet they experience the ill effects it generates as a by-product, or are forced to go to extra expense to protect themselves from those effects. That is unfair. If one is going to produce a good, then, one must take responsibility for whatever evil is generated as well. Voluntary activities are permissible so long as they do not endanger others outside the transaction: unwanted effects on third parties must be avoided. While the consumer is a party to the transactions being considered here, and therefore not "external" to them, it is a concern of everyone that we not be damaged by the transactions of others. Both consumer and producer rights are limited by whatever general duties toward all people there may be. And while people differ to some extent on what those duties are, there is one such general duty that no one will deny: the duty not to inflict involuntary harm on others. We may not kill or damage others or their property, and contracts between others do not modify that duty. On the contrary, the rights of contractors themselves, including consumers, may be seen to stem from that very same principle. Market transactions are protected by norms against violence and fraud.

X. RISK TO HEALTH

We need to distinguish at this point between the consumer or purchaser in his role, strictly, *as* consumer and purchaser, and that same person in his role as a person. In this way we may invoke a right of consumers that limits transactions independently of the points about descriptions of goods already discussed. This right is the very general right *not to be harmed,* as in the "Law of Nature" of John Locke, which "forbids us to harm another in his life, health, liberty, or property." Some possible harms would be a function of deficiencies in the transaction of the kinds discussed before: the product may not be as described. Others, however, have little direct relation to those. Among these, the most obvious concerns health. Products might, unbeknown to the consumer, be likely to damage his health in some way. If it is known that they might do so, the producer must warn the consumer of such risks, and is deficient if he does not.

How does this relate to the consumer as consumer? The answer is that everyone is reasonably presumed to be concerned about his own health, since health plays such a significant role in almost everything we do. And there are myriad ways in which a product could be damaging to health, most of which the consumer cannot be expected to know about in detail. Yet he enters into transactions in hopes of emerging better off, not worse off. If his health is put at serious risk by his purchase, unbeknown to him, then this basic purpose of his consumer activities is to that extent defeated.

Risk to health, however, is an extremely variable effect. In general, risks are probabilities of damage—not certainties. *How* probable must it be that the consumer's health will be damaged, and how serious must that damage be, before his purchase becomes contrary to his interest in making it? This is a relevant question because, on reflection, it is reasonable to suppose that virtually every voluntary exchange between people could conceivably damage one party's health in some way. Yet many of these risks are trivial. And others, while decidedly not trivial, are nevertheless accepted by parties to bargains as unfortunate but unavoidable further costs to be taken into account. The smoker, for example, may well know that his consumption of cigarettes could damage his health, and seriously; yet for all that he may think that the benefits of smoking to him outweigh those risks. In the liberal view that underlies market transactions, it is his right as a consumer to bear such risks, so long as they are not seriously misrepresented to him by the seller.

This gives us the key to our understanding of the consumer's rights in this respect. We must say that the product must be such as not to "significantly" damage his health. That is to say, any risks entailed must be low enough so that it is reasonable to assume that its presence would make no difference to the consumer's voluntary behavior. Risks to health that are extremely low may be ignored. For example, if our product is no riskier than just about anything else that we know the consumer does anyway, then it is not a risk that we need bother to mention, even if we are aware of it—and a law, say, that prohibited imposition of such levels of "risk" would be unreasonable. Further, if it is a "standard risk" that this product has, one that any user of it is likely to be aware of, then there is again no liability on the part of the producer stemming from the specific right of the consumer he deals with for failing to mention it in the transactional process.

XI. SELLER VIGILANCE: HOW MUCH?

How much effort must producers make to become aware of possible risks and to inform consumers about them? It is very difficult to answer such questions in a precise way. However, it is plausible to say that the broad answer is, "not very much." Producers are not medical researchers, and cannot reasonably be expected to be. We all act against a background of normal knowledge, and producers operate, in addition, against a background of knowledge of what they produce that is well above normal for people in general. Efforts to increase that knowledge are expensive, and when the history of the product is well known and no significant risks have as yet emerged, are surely not worth doing. The costs of such research, after all, must be borne by the consumer, who may quite reasonably not be willing to pay them. Normal liability for products, then, is a function of prevailing knowledge of the relevant kinds. That knowledge tends to increase in the contemporary world, and a producer could be deficient in keeping up with its progress; at some point, then, he could be failing in a responsibility. But this responsibility cannot be very great. Beyond some point, the consumer will prefer to pay a lower price and take more risk than to purchase from suppliers who devote so much attention to risk reductions that their products become unacceptably expensive.

XII. CONCLUSION: THE CONSUMER'S RIGHTS AS CONSUMER

Our general conclusion is that the consumer is entitled to the goods he has bargained for, in a condition that he can reasonably expect on the basis of normal practice or from what was specifically agreed to with the seller or producer. Other accounts of consumer rights, which may accord rights greatly in excess of what has been sketched here, have the shortcoming that meeting the demands they impose is likely to be so expensive as to motivate consumers to cease purchases, and thus for producers to refuse to engage in production of what consumers want. If people are forced to produce nevertheless, they become to that extent slaves; if they are allowed to cease producing the things in question, the consumer suffers. In a free society, either is unacceptable. Any basis for such further rights would have to take us beyond the area of *consumer* rights as such. Thus, the previous account presents the basics of consumer rights insofar as the righholders are consumers.

Also See the Following Articles

BUSINESS ETHICS, OVERVIEW • CORPORATE RESPONSIBILITY

Bibliography

Boylan, M. (Ed.) (1995). "Ethical Issues in Business." Harcourt Brace, Forth Worth, TX.
Dejardins, J., and McCall, J. J. (1996). "Contemporary Issues in Business Ethics," 3rd ed. Wadsworth, Belmont, CA.
Shaw, W. H. (1996). "Business Ethics," 2nd ed. Wadsworth, Belmont, CA.

CONTRACTARIAN ETHICS

Paul Kelly
London School of Economics

I. Ancient and Medieval Origins
   of Contractarianism
II. The Social Contract and Political Legitimacy
III. Hypothetical Contractarianism: Kant and the
   Contractarian Derivation of Morality
IV. The Contemporary Reemergence of
   Contractarianism: Three Approaches
V. Conclusion

GLOSSARY

agreement motive The basic motive presupposed by contractualist justifications of moral obligation or distributive justice; namely, the desire to justify one's actions in terms that others could not reasonably reject.

consent A form of agreement whereby the members of a political community or the moral subject agree to a set of norms or rules governing their activities. The authority of these rules is derived from the agreement or consent of those to which they apply. Consent can take two forms. **Express consent** is the intentional agreement of a person through a contract, a promise, or an oath. **Tacit consent** is agreement to a norm or practice inferred from the acceptance of the benefits of that norm or practice.

contractualism A term used to distinguish hypothetical contractarian defenses of moral obligation and justice from contractarian defenses of political obligation.

hypothetical contract A way of justifying moral and political norms by considering what might be agreed to if certain artificial or ideal conditions apply. This way of thinking about moral and political obligations does not justify by showing how they *are* derived from a real agreement; instead, it attempts to reveal the character of such practices by treating them *as if* they were the result of an agreement.

impartiality The ideal underlying one strand of hypothetical contractarianism. Impartiality theories treat each member of a hypothetical agreement as having an equal standing or veto on the terms of the agreement by detaching the grounds of the agreement from self-interest, the passions, inequalities of power and advantage, or special attachments to others.

mutual advantage This form of hypothetical contract assumes the parties as self-interested agents, each attempting to maximize his own advantage through a common agreement. The terms of such an agreement must therefore be to the advantage of all the participants, although not necessarily equally beneficial.

original position The characterization of the circumstances of a hypothetical agreement. The concept was given currency by John Rawls.

state of nature The circumstances prior to an agreement in classical social contract theory. It usually refers to a situation prior to any moral or political authority to enforce obligations. It is sometimes used to refer to circumstances prior to any moral norms or conventions.

veil of ignorance The device used by Rawls in his account of the original position to guarantee an impartial agreement. The veil deprives the participants of any particular knowledge about themselves and all but general knowledge about their circumstances.

CONTRACTARIAN ETHICS uses the idea of an agreement, contract, or bargain either to show us where moral and political norms come from, or why such norms are obligatory and binding, irrespective of their historical origins. As a way of both explaining and justifying moral obligation, the contract tradition is one of the oldest as well as most versatile traditions of ethical theorizing. Today, as the most common form of moral and political theorizing adopted by antiutilitarians and antirealists, the contract tradition is used to do three things: to explain the origin and content of moral obligation; to serve as a philosophical explanation of the nature of moral obligation; and to address the political problem of distributive justice. In each case these different modern uses of the idea of a contract all develop and expand insights derived from the history of this complex and evolving ethical tradition.

I. ANCIENT AND MEDIEVAL ORIGINS OF CONTRACTARIANISM

Although ethical and political contractarianism as a clear, recognizable tradition is a modern phenomenon going back no earlier than the sixteenth century, most historians of the contract tradition find antecedents much earlier in ancient Greek and Medieval thought. Among the Greeks the idea of morality being based on an agreement is connected with the distinction drawn between "nature" and "convention" by the Sophists. An emphasis on the conventional or artificial origins of morality naturally leads to an explanation of the point of the convention or the reasons individuals have for respecting moral norms when they are recognized to be merely conventional. Thus, we find in the reported arguments of Antiphon, Hippias, Glaucon, or Thrasymachus intimations of the claim that the political community, or the norms of morality serve the interests of the members of such communities. The examples of Glaucon and Thrasymachus as reported in Plato's *Republic* are certainly not endorsements of the contractual justification of political and moral norms, but by criticizing the justification of conventional norms as serving the interests of all, such thinkers raise, albeit only to criticize, what seems clearly an emergent contractualist argument. The cases of Glaucon and Thrasymachus are particularly interesting as sources of what appear to be Greek antecedents of the contract tradition because Plato introduces their ideas in the early part of the *Republic,* which is devoted to the nature of justice. Justice is, of course, the issue that lies at the heart of the post-Rawlsian resurgence of contract theory in our own time. However, where modern thinkers have used the idea of a contract or agreement to provide a defense of reasonable norms of social cooperation, and thus show that some version of justice is rational (Gauthier) or reasonable (Rawls and Barry), Glaucon and Thrasymachus try to deny such an agreement is rational because it subordinates the strong to the interests of the weak. In Plato's dialogue, Glaucon introduces the story of the Ring of Gyges—a magical ring that makes the wearer invisible, and therefore able to do whatever he wishes—to show that it is only the force of law and the fear of conventional sanctions that grounds obedience, not any recognition of interest or advantage, nor the claims of reason. Glaucon and Thrasymachus are introduced by Plato as foils for Socrates' own account of justice in the soul and the state, so not too much weight can be attached to the report of these Sophistic arguments. What is clear is that both thinkers respond to what appears to be a widely shared account of the conventional defense of morality as being justified in terms of the mutual advantage of all members of the political community. This does not take the form of appealing to an explicit foundational contract, but to modern minds that are more prepared to see a hypothetical contractarian format implicit in an argument from mutual advantage it does suggest intimations of arguments that were to gain currency much later on.

Although the Sophists such as Glaucon and Thrasymachus give us at best intimations of contract arguments through their critiques of justice, a more unambiguous ancient Greek use of the contract device can be found in Plato's *Crito*. The *Crito* relates the tale of Socrates following his death sentence for impiety and corrupting the youth of Athens with his philosophical inquiries. One of Socrates' friends and benefactors, Crito, comes to see him to persuade him to flee Athens before his death sentence must be carried out. The dialogue turns into a discourse on political obligation. Socrates rejects Crito's appeals to flee the unjust sentence, and one of the arguments he uses raises the idea of a contract between him and the "laws." To flee his sentence, even though it is not in his interest to accept it (and it is clearly presented in the dialogue as an unjust and politically motivated decision) would be to break an agreement with the "laws" who gave him life, just because it no longer served his immediate purposes. An agreement with the "laws" (who are personified and can speak for themselves in the dialogue) is like a genuine contract or promise in that it cannot be revoked merely because of the inconvenience—even an extreme inconvenience—of keeping one's obligations. The argument is certainly one of the clearest invocations of the idea of a contract between citizen and political community. This all falls short of modern consent-based theories of political obligation of the sort we find in John Locke in the seventeenth century, because Socrates does not suggest that the agreement or promise is the source of the "laws." The "laws," and, therefore, the political community, have some sort of independent moral existence that Socrates is also recognizing, whereas Locke uses the contract to explain the origin of political authority and municipal law. This point has led many recent commentators to argue that the *Crito* has more affinities with an alternative communitarian tradition that subordinates the individual to the political community, an argument that is most closely associated with G. W. F. Hegel (1770–1831) in the early nineteenth century and that has been taken up recently by critics of contemporary contractarian theories of justice, such as Michael Sandel, Charles Taylor, and Alasdair MacIntyre. Nevertheless, the idea of a binding agreement between citizen or subject and political authority that transcends the claims of self-interest is one that was to have continuing relevance in the development of the tradition.

There are many other ancient sources of contractarian thinking, which while not directly contributing to the emergence of a recognizable modern tradition nevertheless continued the appeal of the device of the contract, covenant, or agreement to explain the origins of political society, or the bindingness of morality. The Old Testament deploys the image of a contract or agreement to describe God's relationship with his chosen people; to take only one example, there is the covenant between God and Noah not to destroy the world as long as certain conditions are fulfilled. Much of the narrative of the Old Testament can be read as a tale of fidelity and infidelity to this agreement on the part of the children of Israel. Alongside Biblical contractarian metaphors, a nonreligious source is Roman Law. Both the Bible and Roman Law, along with the recovery of Classical Greek ideas explain in part the deployment of contractarian language in the medieval period. However, where the Greek sources suggest the use of the device to explain and legitimize conventional moral norms, the most common use of the device in the medieval period is much more narrowly political, explaining the relationship between rulers and ruled. This form of contractarianism is best described as *constitutional* contractarianism, as it is not used to explain the nature of political society as resting on consent, but rather it is used to argue that the ruler has an obligation to rule in the interests of his subjects and that this places limits on the extent of his authority. The agreement here is only metaphorical, for few medieval thinkers go as far as to suggest that legitimate authority is a genuine grant from the people in the way modern doctrines of popular sovereignty do. That said, the idea of a contract or agreement is used to show that the ruler should rule as if he has been granted authority by a contract with his subjects. Again, the contractarian device is implicit in the account of the relationship rather than as with Hobbes, Locke, and Kant, in the language and concepts deployed; nevertheless, given the prevalence of idea it is unsurprising that it should shape the ways in which thinkers conceptualize political relationships. That said, we can find clear evidence of contractarian language in writers such as Manegold of Lautenbach in the eleventh century, who claims that the tyrannical ruler breaks the contract by virtue of which he has appointed; this is reminiscent of Locke's later theory of consent.

The ancient Greeks and writers of the medieval period provide interesting intimations of a tradition, and it is unsurprising that we should find such echoes of modern ideas in premodern settings given that no idea or concept springs fully formed into philosophical discourse without a long and complex gestation. Nevertheless, these intimations suggest disparate uses of the device. It is not until the early seventeenth century that contractarianism as a recognizable tradition emerges onto the scene as a philosophical response to very peculiar political circumstances.

II. THE SOCIAL CONTRACT AND POLITICAL LEGITIMACY

Why contractarianism should have achieved such a dominant position in the early seventeenth century is open to considerable scholarly debate, depending largely on how significant one wishes to see the rupture between the medieval and the modern world. However, two broad reasons for the emergence of the modern contractarian tradition can be found in the upheavals wrought by the Protestant Reformation and by the discovery of the new world. The former reinforced the significance of individual choice and responsibility in morality that had always been implicit in Christianity. With the Reformation came a challenge to the primacy of external moral authority located in the institution of the Church; individuals had sole sovereign responsibility for their own salvation. An institution such as a church could, therefore, only have the status of a voluntary association freely entered into by men in order to pursue the goal of salvation and the good life for which they alone were responsible. But what happens when these individuals run up against an authority that demands actions and beliefs that individuals might judge an obstacle to that goal? By liberating individual judgment and responsibility for salvation the Reformation created profound political problems by pitching Catholics against Protestants, or Protestants of different sects against each other in fundamental controversies over the good life, moral obligation, and political order. If individual conscience is sovereign, then no political sovereign can impose as obligations those things that any individual might recognize as obstacles to salvation. But if the individual is the sole authority of what constitutes an obstacle, this undermines the possibility of political order and it gave rise to anarchy and the religious wars that raged throughout the sixteenth century.

What was needed was a recognition of a law of nature written in all men's hearts or reason, which would allow for moral obligation and political order independently of individual judgment. But it was precisely this that the discovery of the New World seemed to threaten. For rather than supporting a common natural moral order, acquaintance with new civilizations appeared to show that there was almost nothing that one society might find obligatory that another found repugnant and wrong. These discoveries appeared to many to support a scepticism about the possibility of any kind of moral norms.

Although this can only be a crude sketch of a very complex story, it is fair to see the twin problems of political disorder and moral scepticism as underlying the rise to prominence of the contract tradition. This can be most clearly seen in the work of Thomas Hobbes.

A. Thomas Hobbes (1588–1679)

Hobbes's greatest work, *Leviathan* (1651), is a response to the twin challenges of political disorder and moral scepticism. Hobbes is not a moral sceptic, although he is sometimes presented as one. He is clear that the content of moral norms is discoverable by reason; thus, he rejects the view that the content of morality is always local and relative to a particular community. But aware of the challenge posed by knowledge of other cultures and beliefs, he cannot claim that reason alone can discover a complex system of moral laws such as we find in medieval Thomism, for these have clearly not been discovered by a good portion of the world that in other ways does not seem to be without the common faculty of reason. Whatever reason delivers must be available to all; thus, Hobbes claims the fundamental right of nature is to self-preservation; man is forbidden by reason to do that which is destructive of his life, or that which takes away his means of self-preservation. This right of self-preservation gives rise to the law of nature that he describes as a "theorem" to indicate that it is not a moral law but a prudential maxim concerning the best way to secure self-preservation and freedom from fear of a violent death. While he uses the term law of nature, to describe this theorem he admits that as a deliverance of reason it is not a law at all. Thus, while moral laws have reason as the source of their content, they require something more to transform them into obligations.

Hobbes's account of obligation is voluntarist, in that he claims the lawlike quality of moral obligations that makes them action-guiding is not to be found in their content but in their source. The normativity or action-guidingness of morality depends upon a supreme legislative will that requires obedience by imposing sanctions on noncompliance. Moral obligations are like laws, they are binding because of their source and not because of their content, although as we have seen Hobbes did not think the content of morality was merely arbitrary as some commentators suggest. What then is the source of moral obligation's lawlike character? For medieval voluntarists, God is the legislator, and it is because he imposes sanctions on disobedience that morality acquires its lawlike character. Hobbes clearly cannot make this move, because it would appear to open the way for the liberation of individual judgment discussed earlier, with each individual judging him- or herself under threat of sanctions for not acting in accordance with conscience; however, he does not unequivocally deny that God is the ultimate source of morality. Instead, Hobbes locates the source of moral obligation in the will of the sovereign legislator or *Leviathan,* a "mortal" God, who can impose his will on his subjects. It is to account for the origin of the sovereign that Hobbes appeals to the idea of a social contract. Thus, he does not use the idea to explain the content of morality, but rather how moral obligation can be normative or action-guiding.

The contract argument works in the following way.

Hobbes posits the law of self-preservation as a dictate of reason; he then constructs a famous account of a presocial state of nature as a state of war. In the absence of a political sovereign to impose order each person will act to secure his (seventeenth-century moral theory is not gender neutral) own preservation. This results in conflict as each person is partial to his own advantage and will prefer himself over others. Similarly, he will come into conflict over the resources he needs in order to secure his own preservation, and as there is no moral or political authority, there can be no legitimate claims to ownership or possession that are exclusive. Whatever you hold in your hand, I may take if I need it to preserve myself. Hobbes also posits natural equality that complicates the natural condition. For although men are not all of equal physical power, there is no person so strong that he is not vulnerable to the stealth of the weak when he sleeps. Differences of skill, wit, and circumstance all contribute to make men equal in the state of nature: equally vulnerable, that is. This natural equality leads to diffidence, or fear and suspicion of one's neighbor. Diffidence, in turn, encourages men to attack first when they have the advantage, rather than waiting until they are vulnerable or in need, and this inevitably leads to a state of constant war between every man. For Hobbes, the prepolitical state is not a state of society but one of constant war and struggle ending only in death.

This characterization of the state-of-nature as a state of war, coupled with the rational desire for self-preservation leads to a modification of the law of self-preservation into two further laws of nature. These claim that men should seek peace and that they should be willing to give up as much of their liberty right to all things when others do likewise, and accept in return as much liberty against others as one is willing to allow against oneself. Thus, reason and the warlike state of nature provide men with a prudential reason to enter an agreement with one another to create the sovereign power who will secure peace and order by imposing his will on all men alike. In making this agreement to institute the sovereign whose will makes moral and political norms possible, individuals move from a presocial state of chaos to one of society.

It is important to stress two aspects of this agreement: first, it is an agreement among individuals to set up the sovereign, and not an agreement between subjects and their sovereign. The contract is to create civil or political society by authorizing a sovereign. Second, because the agreement is not between subjects and ruler Hobbes's contract theory does not provide a consent-based theory of political obligation. Moral and political laws are obligatory because they are imposed upon us;

their obligation is not conditional upon our consent, whether express or tacit. The sovereign's authority is absolute—that is what it is to be sovereign; consequently, Hobbes's response to the problem of the diversity of religious beliefs is to subordinate religion to the political sovereign and allow him to determine what is and is not required. The sovereign's authority is absolute because although men retain their residual right to self-preservation that can be exercised against a sovereign when he requires that they submit to a violent death, this cannot be seen as a limitation on sovereignty, which must entail the right to impose sanctions including death to enforce the law. If the right of nature was a constraint on sovereign power, then the sovereign could not impose the death penalty or require military service in wartime and thus function as a sovereign.

Hobbes uses the contract device to explain the source of obligation and not the content of morality; however, his positing of an absolute sovereign authority as the answer to the problem of the action-guiding character of morality creates a genuine problem. If sovereignty in the moral and political sphere is absolute and unconditional, then there can be no principled limit upon its exercise; potentially, the sovereign can make up any "moral" obligations he pleases. Hobbes's voluntarism that distinguishes between the source of moral obligation and its content creates a problem of political legitimacy that is the characteristic concern of subsequent contractarian theorists, most notably John Locke.

B. John Locke (1632–1704)

Locke's argument in the second of his *Two Treatises of Government* (1689) is not explicitly directed at Hobbes, but rather at a different defense of absolutism advanced by Sir Robert Filmer. Nevertheless, one can see the problem of legitimacy that exercises Locke as one bequeathed by Hobbes to subsequent contract thinkers. For Locke, like Hobbes, the contract is not the source of morality; unlike Hobbes, he does not even use the contract device to account for the normativity of the law of nature. Natural laws for Locke are genuinely lawlike and therefore action-guiding, as they have their origin in the will of God. This divine will is discoverable by ordinary human reason and, once recognized, is binding upon the will. That said, Locke spent much of his philosophic career agonizing over a philosophic account of the content of natural law and the epistemology necessary for its discovery.

Locke's concern is not with the foundation or obligatoriness of moral norms; his concern is more narrowly political. He is more interested in what form of political rule is compatible with our preexisting moral rights and obligations. That is, he is concerned with setting the boundaries to political rule and challenging defenses of political absolutism. Locke's argument also begins in the state of nature, but his account of it differs from Hobbes's. The Lockean state of nature is prepolitical but not presocial. In it men have genuine obligations, rights, and duties, institutions such as private property exist, and with it industry and trade. Why then do we need a political society? The answer is that it is a response to the inconveniences of the state of nature. In the state of nature each individual has the executive power of natural law, which means that each individual is entitled to interpret breaches of natural rights and duties and to impose sanctions, not only as a means of self-defense but also against third parties who violate natural rights to life, liberty, and property. The inconvenience of the state of nature arises because in imposing punishment individuals have to rely on their own judgment of proportion and justice. This gives rise to charges of partiality and disproportion, inciting redress and revenge, as individuals value their property above the life or liberty of others. Consequently, the legitimate exercise of the executive power of the law of nature creates the potential for a state of war. If each person acts as judge and jury in his or her own case, there is a tendency to disorder and instability. It is for this reason that individuals contract to leave the state of nature and to establish civil society. In doing this individuals agree to pool their natural executive power to collectively secure their individual rights. This is only the first stage of his contract argument. Once civil society is created the members agree by majority vote to establish a constitution; a further agreement between the property holders is then required to determine the appropriate level of taxation.

The first and second stages are the most important in Locke's theory, for these show that, contrary to Hobbes, not only is the establishment of civil or political society the result of an agreement, but more importantly the constitution of government is itself the consequence of a separate agreement. In agreeing or consenting to a constitution, individuals do not alienate their natural rights to an arbitrary sovereign power like Hobbes's sovereign; they cannot do that because their right to life, liberty, and, by implication, property are enjoyed as a trust from God. Instead, government's role is to protect such rights impartially and to give precision to their interpretation. However, while the protection of such rights explains the utility of government, it does not fully explain its legitimacy; this must have its root in an act of will or of consent. The legitimacy of govern-

ment is contractual. Obligation to government depends upon consent, because all are born free as bearers of natural rights, no one is born subject to government. But not everybody can have expressly consented to the establishment of government: what about subsequent generations? Does Locke expect the foundation of government to be ratified formally by each succeeding generation? If so, what are the boundaries of a generation? To overcome such difficulties Locke introduces an infamous distinction between *express* and *tacit* consent. *Express* consent is a clear expression of will in a promise or an oath of allegiance. This form of consent is preferred by Locke. But *tacit* consent, which is all that most will ever be able to give, is to be inferred from the acceptance of certain benefits of government. By appealing to the idea of *tacit* consent as a form of agreement he potentially broadens the concept to the point where it becomes indistinguishable from rival accounts of political obligation. Despite its problems, consent theory remains one of the standard arguments for political obligation and legitimacy, both philosophically and in the public domain.

In Locke's theory, the social contract is used as a metaphor for a complex historical account of the emergence of the institutions of civil society, money, and private property. His second level theory of the origin of government has a stronger air of historical reality about it. There must have been an original contract if government is to be legitimate. Whether Locke really believed this is a matter of scholarly controversy, but many minor contractarians of the same period certainly did believe in social contract theory as a historical account of the origin of legitimate government. Challenges to social contract theories as historical explanations of morality or political obligation, such as David Hume's (1711–1776) in *Of the Original Contract* (*Essays Moral and Political,* 1742), did not, however, lead to the abandonment of the theory; instead, we find that two of the most profound contractarian theorists, Jean-Jacques Rousseau and Immanuel Kant, salvage the tradition by freeing it from the blind alley of speculative history.

C. Jean-Jacques Rousseau (1712–1778)

Unlike Hobbes and Locke, Rousseau has two distinct contract theories: the first is to be found in a *Discourse on the Origins of Inequality* (1755), in which he mounts a sustained critique of the tradition. Whereas his predecessors offer the state of nature as a philosophical construct Rousseau offers an evolutionary anthropology that presents the state of nature, not as a situation of anarchy and inconvenience, but rather as a situation of primeval innocence that is corrupted by property, politics, and civil society. His point is that appealing to state-of-nature arguments does not work, because either they incorporate passions and motives that can only have a social basis into the presocial state, thus making the appeal redundant, or else what we can know about our natures independently of social influence is such that it can play no part in explaining the origin or legitimacy of political and moral institutions. Alongside this indictment of appeals to "nature" to ground political society or a basic moral law, Rousseau also depicts the idea of a contract—an "evil contract"—to explain how it is that the rich acquire the consent of the poor in the creation and unequal distribution of private property. The evil contract turns the idea of the social contract into an account of the emergence of the very vices and antisocial passions that in its classical form it is supposed to overcome. Thus, in turning social contract theory on its head Rousseau at the same time as being one of its greatest theorists, is also one of its most profound critics.

Alongside this critique Rousseau develops an alternative account of the social contract to explain the possible reconciliation of freedom as self-rule, or not being subject to the will of another, and popular sovereignty, which would seem to entail precisely such subordination. This reconciliation is achieved by means of a "conversion" contract developed in *The Social Contract* (1762). This contract employs the notion of the "General Will." Rousseau's argument is called a "conversion" contract because it assumes that in the process of constituting itself as a political association, individuals undergo a conversion—or transformation of character and motives—that enables them to distance themselves from their particular self-interested wills and through the concept of the General Will they identify themselves with the community and will only follow those rules that apply generally to all members of the community. This involves conceiving oneself as primarily a citizen rather than as a presocial individual. Insofar as willing, the General Will merely involves willing that which one truly desires as a citizen and member of the community; one is not subordinating oneself to the will of others but merely recognizing one's true interests. In this way Rousseau thinks he can reconcile freedom and popular sovereignty. Rousseau's concept of the General Will was intended to create a system of continual rather than one-off consent. It does, however, have a paradoxical character in that genuine freedom is acting in accordance with impartial rules even when these seem to conflict with one's perceived private interests. One's

freedom is, therefore, an objective matter rather than a subjective judgment, and this grounds Rousseau's claim that individuals can be "forced to be free," thus leading to allegations of totalitarian tendencies in his thought.

Although Rousseau's contractarianism has an ambiguous character—according to some commentators betraying the insights of Lockean consent theory—the real significance of his conception of the General Will can only be seen in the transformation it receives at the hands of Immanuel Kant. Whereas Rousseau transforms the social contract as a political device, with Kant the tradition becomes the recognizably modern ethical tradition familiar from the work of contemporaries such as John Rawls and T. M. Scanlon.

III. HYPOTHETICAL CONTRACTARIANISM: KANT AND THE CONTRACTARIAN DERIVATION OF MORALITY

Although the "classical" social contract tradition of the seventeenth and eighteenth centuries began with Hobbes as an attempt to explain the authority of moral norms it quickly became a *political* tradition concerned with the legitimacy of sovereign authority and the grounds of political obligation. As such it would seem far removed from the concerns of modern ethical theory. However, the contractarian tradition enjoys a central place in contemporary ethics; that it does so is largely the responsibility of the German philosopher Immanuel Kant (1724–1804). As with almost every other field of philosophy in which he wrote, Kant transformed the terms of modern moral philosophy. Consequently, though he contributed to the "classical" tradition of seventeenth and eighteenth century contract theory his contribution goes way beyond the *political* concerns of Hobbes, Locke or Rousseau.

Kant's contribution to the development of contractarian thinking is to be found most clearly in *The Metaphysical Elements of Justice* (1797) and in *The Groundwork of the Metaphysic of Morals* (1785). The former work develops the idea of the contractarian device as a hypothetical thought experiment. In the writings of Hobbes there is a certain ambiguity over the reality of the original agreement, although given that he tries to present the acquisition of sovereign power through conquest as a form of binding agreement on the part of the conquered, it does appear that Hobbes took the reality of the contract seriously. Similarly, for Locke and Rousseau, although in different forms, the legitimacy of political rule could only be derived from actual consent. The problem with such theories is that they either broaden the idea to such an extent that anything, even agreement at the point of a sword (in Hobbes), could count as a promise or contract, or else they make the theory depend upon a spurious historical narrative that once disproved seems to undermine the possibility of either political obligation or legitimacy. Kant brilliantly avoids these problems by denying that a contract has to take place, or that political and moral obligation is derived from some kind of real contract. Political authority and moral practices have complex and diverse historical origins, often in force or in fraud. What matters is not how they came about but what could give them authority. Here, Kant departs from the voluntarism of Hobbes and Locke. The authority of moral and political norms is not derived from an external lawgiver such as the Leviathan or God (in Locke's case); rather, the authority and legitimacy of moral norms is derived from their being recognized as the dictates of pure practical reason, and it is this process of recognition that Kant argues has the same form as recognizing the deliverances of a hypothetical contractual agreement. Kant's argument is indebted to Rousseau in that he claims the authority of laws and moral norms is derived from their contractual form, but unlike Rousseau he does not require that this contractual form emerges from a self-legislating political community governed by the "General Will." Instead, for Kant the legitimacy of laws and moral norms is guaranteed so long as those norms are such that rational men *could* have consented to them as the outcome of a hypothetical agreement. And this process of consent is simply the recognition of the reasonableness of the moral law. In making this argument Kant frees the contract tradition from its origins in voluntarism. Now the contract is not an example of a choice, even a hypothetical one; rather, it becomes a device for describing how we recognize authoritative reasons. It does not matter whether these reasons originate in the will of a monarch whose authority is derived from conquest or birth, or from a republican constitution. What matters is that the laws could be the subject of the consent of reasonable men. Thus, the contract device becomes for Kant a purely hypothetical test for determining the legitimacy or genuineness of putative moral and political norms, dispensing with the need for accounts of the state of nature. As such the contract device is able to serve as a thought experiment, free from the challenges of historical sceptics such as David Hume. It is in this hypothetical guise that the contractarian device has been used in subsequent moral theory.

The second significant development of the tradition that has its roots in Kant's theory is found in his moral philosophy, in particular in *The Groundwork of the Metaphysic of Morals*. In this short work Kant sets out to defend the autonomy of moral obligation. Kant does not ask the traditional question, do we have any moral obligations, and if so, how? Instead, he takes the practice of morality for granted. We do have moral obligations, the task is to show what they are and where their necessary authority resides. Unlike Hobbes and the voluntarist tradition he does not explain moral authority in terms of externally imposed sanctions, but neither does he locate the source of obligation in the internal sanction of interest or desire, for these are merely contingent and transitory and cannot ground the lawlike quality of moral obligation. Morality cannot be based on prudence or mutual advantage, because this would always allow us the possibility of a reason to defect from moral norms when they significantly disadvantage us. Such a justification would undermine the possibility of the moral law. Instead Kant provides an account of the authority of the moral law in terms of the categorical imperative: "Act only according to that maxim through which you can at the same time will that it should become a universal law." Thus, the action-guiding character of morality does not depend upon self-interest or mutual advantage, but on the rational will, the will always to act on norms that can be willed as a universal law. The categorical imperative echoes Rousseau's "General Will," which distinguishes between the subjective will and the impartial willing of the "General Will." However, again Kant does not suggest the categorical imperative is embodied in a particular form of political community; rather, it is a hypothetical test of the "moral obligatoriness" of norms, not an account of where they came from. It may well be the case that norms concerning promise keeping and truth-telling have the source in conventional practices based on a convergence of interest, but what transforms these conventional norms into moral norms is that they can be willed as universal laws. Where this connects with the hypothetical contractarianism of *The Metaphysical Elements of Justice* is that the universalizability test of the categorical imperative, with its commitment to the idea of impartiality, provides a content for the idea of reasonableness that he appeals to there. Legitimate laws are those that could be characterized as resulting from a hypothetical agreement between reasonable men. But what does Kant mean by reasonable in this context? He certainly does not mean men who wish to maximize their individual or collective advantage. Instead, the idea of reasonableness is closely connected to the ideal of impartiality, so that a reasonable agreement would be one that did not depend on advantage, inequality, or self-preference, but could be justified to anyone, whatever their position. Moral justification for Kant takes the form of requiring reasonable consent, but where reasonableness is defined not in terms of advantage but rather as impartiality based on the rational will.

Kant's use of the contract as a purely hypothetical device and his appeal to universalizability as a form of impartial consent transformed the contract tradition. However, immediately following Kant the contractarian methodology fell into abeyance as a result of challenges from utilitarianism, Hegelian communitarianism, and Marxism. That Kant's theory did not have a more immediate impact is largely due to his difficulties in showing that men could actually be moved to act in accordance with the categorical imperative. How was it that men could have an overriding reason to act that was not reducible to some internal motive such as interest or desire? Kant had attempted to show how morality could be distinguished from prudence, but some argued only at the cost of making the action-guiding character of moral norms wholly mysterious. The elaborate metaphysics of Kant's theory of moral psychology, which became the target of Hegel and his Idealist successors, need not detain us here, but its perceived weakness does at least go some way to explain why Kant is often presented as the end of the "classical" tradition of contract theory.

IV. THE CONTEMPORARY REEMERGENCE OF CONTRACTARIANISM: THREE APPROACHES

Although the contractarian method did not disappear completely, the dominant methods of moral theorizing post-Kant were utilitarian, and idealist. The social contract as a political device continued to have some significance among political theorists, but even here the onslaught it received from the combined forces of utilitarians, Marxists, and Hegelian-inspired idealists left it as little more than an historical curiosity, the prerogative of historians of ideas, but not a dynamic tradition of argument in its own right. Throughout the first part of this century as ethical theory became increasingly concerned with the analysis of moral language and less with substantive moral issues such as what rights, duties, and obligations we have, the contractarian method seemed increasingly an irrelevance rather than a discredited theory. All this was to change with the work

of the American philosopher John Rawls. In a series of important articles published from the 1950s onward and then later with the publication of his highly influential *A Theory of Justice* in 1971, Rawls succeeded in reinstituting normative political philosophy as a central component of ethical theorizing. Unlike so many of his contemporaries, Rawls was not simply concerned with providing an analysis of concepts such as justice; he was concerned with what justice requires. That is, what principles should distribute the benefits of social cooperation. The transformation that Rawls brought about in moral and political theory is considerable. But what is also especially significant about his work is that he consciously located his own theory of justice in the tradition of social contract theory going back through Kant, Rousseau, and Locke. Rawls's theory not only made the social contract device respectable, but also made it a dynamic contemporary tradition of ethical theory to rival the hegemony of utilitarianism and intuitionism.

Since the publication of Rawls's *A Theory of Justice* other contemporary moral philosophers have gone back to the "classical" social contract tradition of the seventeenth and eighteenth centuries for inspiration. David Gauthier, in his 1986 book *Morals by Agreement,* draws heavily on a rival version of the contract tradition to Rawls. Whereas Rawls is more influenced by Kant and Rousseau, Gauthier draws on Hobbes. More recently, T. M. Scanlon has developed a Kantian contract theory of moral obligation; however, although he like Rawls is inspired by Kant, his interest is different and he uses the device in a significantly different way. A critical analysis of the contractarian method in ethical theory over the last 25 years would produce a tale as complex and as varied as that of the "classical" tradition in the seventeenth and eighteenth centuries.

Most standard surveys of contemporary contractarianism tend to divide the rival theories into two camps: the broadly Hobbesian "mutual advantage" theories, and the broadly Kantian "impartiality" theories. There is much to be said for this classification, not least the fact that it neatly connects the contemporary versions with the two main strands of the "classical" tradition. However, in order to convey the full variety of contemporary contractarian ethics, it is also useful to offer a tripartite classification based upon the goal or motive of each theory and theorist. This classification distinguishes between "moral foundationalist" theories such as that of Gauthier; "philosophical" theories such as that of T. M. Scanlon and B. J. Diggs; and "political" theories such as that of John Rawls or Brian Barry. Each will be considered in turn.

A. Moral Foundationalist Theories: Gauthier and Buchanan

The contractarian arguments of both David Gauthier (*Morals by Agreement,* 1986) and James Buchanan (*The Limits of Liberty,* 1975) offer a response to the challenge of moral scepticism; both see moral rules as derived from rational constraints on self-interest. It is this derivation of morality from prudence that connects their theories with a Hobbesian version of the contract tradition. Although strictly speaking Gauthier and Buchanan depart from Hobbes's argument in that they make the content as well as the authority of moral rules the subject of an agreement, whereas Hobbes used the agreement only to explain the authority of moral norms. For both Gauthier and Buchanan values are all reducible to preferences and desires, and individual actions can be most economically explained in terms of desire satisfaction. Individual agents may claim to be motivated by altruism and regard for others, but the model of man as a egoistic utility maximizer remains the least metaphysically demanding account of human motivation. If all that has value is individual utility maximization, then no one individual has a reason to regard an action that harms another person as a consequence of pursuing his interest as inherently wrong. Similarly, taken as an individual no one person has a reason to respect private property or the distribution of resources if it does not advantage him. Why then do we need morality? The reason is the simple Hobbesian one that if each person attempts to maximize his own advantage without regard for others the result will be chaos and each person will be the worse off. Even the strong and the wealthy will have to spend a disproportionate amount of their resources on security rather than on consumption and enjoyment. Self-interested individuals, therefore, have a reason to accept conventions concerning respect for property, promise-keeping, and the rule of law as a condition of maximizing their own advantage. Thus, for Hobbesians such as Gauthier and Buchanan, insofar as there can be moral rules this must be because these rules are to the mutual advantage of those to whom they apply. (Whether such a situation can be characterized as a society is a matter of controversy.) Gauthier claims such conventions can be "generated as a rational constraint from the nonmoral premises of rational choice." The content of the conventions will also reflect the relative differences in bargaining power of the participants. As there are no moral norms prior to this rational derivation of morality, there cannot be any moral constraints on the contract as a mutual advantage bargain. Instead, the bargain/contract applies to the distribution of the "economic surplus" in society that is the difference in the economic product of a society that results from social cooperation, and could not, therefore, be the result of uncoordinated individual actions. As such the bargainers bring with them their individual property holdings, and, therefore, at least potentially considerable inequalities of power and influence. This may seem to make any such bargain "unfair," but as Buchanan points out the moral value of "fairness" is something that cannot be appealed to, given the sceptical premises from which the Hobbesian starts.

The subtlety and originality of Gauthier and Buchanan's resurrection of a Hobbesian contract has generated an enormous secondary literature. Gauthier's argument in particular has been responsible for encouraging, along with Rawls, a greater dialogue between ethics as a branch of philosophy, and the related disciplines of economics and political science. However, his argument has also generated considerable criticism. Gauthier claims to be able to derive moral norms from a minimal common rationality, the desire of individuals to maximize their own advantage. If his argument is successful it would have considerable significance for the future of moral philosophy. But quite naturally many have contested this, by either showing that the argument does not work or that what it yields is not morality. Many have pointed out that if individuals are strongly motivated to maximize their own advantage they will retain a strong incentive to "defect" from morality when they can get away with it. Hobbes certainly recognized this problem, which is why he relied ultimately on the sovereign to guarantee morality. Gauthier does not follow Hobbes that far. Furthermore, Gauthier and Buchanan's bargaining model of an agreement severely disadvantages children, the weak, and the handicapped; in fact, it disadvantages all those who are the beneficiaries of mutual cooperation but who cannot be contributors to it, and this is precisely the class of person that morality is supposed to protect. As they have little bargaining power and often little physical power their consent can be bought extremely cheaply in ways that do not maximize or even secure their advantage. Such problems do not necessarily prove fatal, given the sceptical position that Gauthier and Buchanan commence with. Reason may well deliver little but a pale imitation of morality, but unless alternative theories prove more successful in explaining the origin and obligation of moral norms, it may well be the case that Gauthier's "Morals by Agreement" is the only morality we can have.

B. Philosophical Contractarianism: T. M. Scanlon and B. J. Diggs

Whereas Hobbesians such as Gauthier and Buchanan use the contract device to show how we can ground some moral norms on the basis of prudence, an alternative and less sceptical approach is adopted by writers such as T. M. Scanlon and B. J. Diggs. Both writers adopt a more Kantian perspective in that neither starts from a position of scepticism; furthermore, unlike the Hobbesian bargaining situation, they also replace the use of natural physical equality with a conception of substantive moral equality as the ground of the agreement. The contractarian device is used to a very different effect by both Scanlon and Diggs. Their concern is not to ground morality as such, but as with Kant to provide a philosophical account of the nature of moral obligation (Scanlon) or of respect for persons (Diggs).

In his 1982 article "Contractualism and Utilitarianism" T. M. Scanlon offers the contract device of a hypothetical, reasonable agreement as an account of moral wrongness. This account is, he argues, better able to make sense of what we mean when we judge something morally wrong. He does not offer the contract device as an account of the meaning of moral terms, but rather as a metaethical theory about what wrongness consists of. His contractualism is offered as a rival to utilitarianism as a metaethical principle, although he concedes that the content of moral norms justified by both theories may well converge. This has the effect of making his argument more abstract and philosophical than either the "foundationalist" argument of Gauthier or the more politically urgent argument of Rawls. Scanlon's argument has implications for the questions that concern both Gauthier and Rawls, but his primary concern is different; as such it can best be distinguished as he describes it as a "philosophical" or metaethical rather than a substantive theory designed to tell us the content of our moral norms and obligations.

Scanlon's contractualist account of the nature of moral wrongness can best be summed up in his own brief formulation: "An act is wrong if its performance under the circumstances would be disallowed by any system of rules for the general regulation of behaviour which no-one could reasonably reject as a basis for informed, unforced general agreement." This idea of reasonable rejection gives everyone a potential veto and thus a ground of consent to moral norms. But like Kant, this rejection must be reasonable. One cannot "reasonably" reject a rule or system of rules because it

conflicts with some self-interested objective. A Nazi cannot "reasonably" reject a system of equal rights because it conflicts with his desire to persecute Jews. Reasonableness for Scanlon, and also for Diggs, involves the recognition of equal moral status by treating each person impartially, rather than as an instrument to one's own ends. Diggs, too, uses the idea of reasonable agreement as an account of how we can make sense of our moral intuitions to accord a certain moral priority to the person.

Why should we adopt this impartialist perspective? For Scanlon and Diggs, the issue can be sidestepped, as both assume a moral motivation underlies the practice of morality. For Scanlon, this motivation is simply the "agreement motive" that is the desire to justify one's actions in terms that others cannot reasonably reject. This is, crudely put, a conception of Kant's categorical imperative purged of the precarious metaphysics of the self on which he built it. It is a purely empirical question of how widespread this motive is; therefore, it is something that philosophers can put to one side.

There remains one major ambiguity in the account I have given. Scanlon's account of moral wrongness appeals to the idea of impartial agreement, and therefore appeals to a Kantian form of the contract tradition. However, what does reasonable rejection consist of? Some critics insist that one cannot make sense of the idea independently of morality; thus, for someone who regards a certain form of behavior, for example, homosexual acts, as morally repugnant, it might well seem that the criminalization of such acts is not something that could be "reasonably" rejected, although many may wish to reject it. Scanlon attempts to get around this appeal by "informed" general agreement, where informed agreement would be epistemologically rigorous disallowing arguments based on faith or authority or factual error. The problem with such a response is that it makes it difficult to show just when any conventional rule or system of rules might actually satisfy the philosophical test of moral wrongness. An unduly rigorous metaethical principle will always be subject to challenge from a simpler procedure such as that offered by utilitarianism. That said, the influence of Scanlon's argument, and to a lesser extent that of Diggs, is that they have placed contractarianism and not merely substantive moral argument at the heart of metaethics.

C. Political Contractarianism: Rawls and Barry

John Rawls's *A Theory of Justice* is often credited with the resurrection of the contract tradition in contemporary philosophy, and it is still regarded by many as definitive of modern contractarianism despite the work of Gauthier, Scanlon, and others. Rawls's argument differs from these others in that he is not concerned with metaethical issues or with grounding the whole of morality on prudential rationality. Instead, his is a political concern: the problem of justice. The problem of justice as he presents it is one of justifying fair terms of social cooperation between men and women who differ about fundamental ends or the good life. In other words, Rawls is concerned with the problem of reasonable disagreement about ultimate ends and values; he does not assume that such disagreement is a sign of there being no objective values at all. Consequently, a theory of distributive justice is an important component, but only one component, of a complete and adequate moral theory. The goal of fair terms of social cooperation is important, because if people cannot agree on ultimate ends, they can at least consent to the political institutions and rules that govern them as long as those rules are seen to be fair. The governing idea is similar to that of a game, where one of the participants may not like the outcome (if they lose) but where they can at least agree that the outcome is a fair one as it is the result of rules that all parties can accept.

Rawls uses the idea of a social contract in its Kantian form as a reasonable agreement, as his metaphor for a just society; thus, his theory is contractarian at its deepest level. He quite explicitly places his theory and his understanding of the problem of justice in the tradition of "classical" contract theory, by which he means Kant, Rousseau, and Locke (he deliberately excludes Hobbes from this tradition as he rightly sees Hobbes as not having a theory of consent). As well as using the contract as a metaphor for a just or fair society, Rawls also uses the contract as a device to legitimize the two principles of justice that he thinks will guarantee that the basic structure of a society (its basic rights and institutions) will be fair and thus a legitimate basis for consent. His defense of the content of the two principles of justice is independent of the contract argument, but he is left with the problem of what special authority his two principles have, rather than, say distributive principles derived from the principle of utility. The problem of the legitimacy of the two principles of justice—that each person is to have an equal right to the most extensive basic liberty compatible with an equal liberty for others, and that social and economic inequalities be arranged so that they are both to everyone's advantage and attached to positions open to all—is solved, he claims, by showing that they are principles that would be chosen in an initial fair-choice situation.

To demonstrate this part of his argument he constructs a hypothetical contract in which the participants are to choose in an original position those principles that should govern the basic structure of their society. However, this choice cannot simply be an unrestricted bargain, or else the principles chosen would merely reflect the unequal power and bargaining position of existing societies and could not therefore be the basis of free, uncoerced consent. To rectify this problem Rawls introduces the "veil of ignorance." This is a constraint that denies the participants in the original position specific knowledge about their goals and life plans, knowledge about their social position, and all but general information about their society. The "veil of ignorance" has the effect of turning a rational calculation of advantage into a situation of impartial and, thus, fair choice, as no one will be able to seek his advantage at the expense of others. Inequalities may well be justifiable in such an agreement, but only insofar as they are to the benefit of the worst off in that society.

Rawls's argument has been the subject of extensive criticism and comment, so much so that it would hardly be an understatement to claim that the subsequent development of normative political theory in the English-speaking world has been as a commentary on aspects of Rawls's argument. Two issues in particular are relevant here: first, whether choice behind the veil of ignorance would result in Rawls's two principles and not some utilitarian principle; and second, whether the contract device does any real work. The first issue has been taken up, because Rawls appeals to considerations external to the original position, namely, the strains of commitment argument to preclude the choice of utilitarian distributive principles. This argument allows one to exclude principles that one would find overburdensome when one returns from the hypothetical choice situation to the real world. It is suggested that because utilitarian principles might require accepting burdens for no other reason than aggregate utility, they could not be the grounds of reasonable consent over time. The second issue is related and it questions what work is being done by the contract in the original position. It is claimed that the whole contract argument can only provide a motivation to accept the principles of justice as fair if we already have that motive, because all it does is model a fair decision procedure; it does not provide us with a reason for adopting an impartial perspective when determining what rules should govern social interaction. As the original political problem of justice is reasonable disagreement over ultimate ends, then surely must this not also extend to the commitment to impartiality?

An alternative theory that has attempted to respond to and carry further Rawls's original political project of grounding fair terms of social cooperation, but without appeal to the original position, is to be found in Brian Barry's recent work, *Justice as Impartiality* (1995). Like Rawls, Barry is concerned with the problem of justice as arising from reasonable disagreement over fundamental ends and purposes. However, unlike Rawls and following Scanlon, Barry argues that the impartialist contractual solution to the problem of justice depends upon the prevalence of the "agreement motive" as the solution to the problem of why one should adopt the perspective of impartiality. This is precisely the issue that, it is argued, Rawls's original position contract does not answer. Barry makes the further claim against Rawls, that if the Scanlonian "agreement motive" does obtain (and this is an empirical matter), then there is no need for the elaborate device of the original position contract, as a Scanlonian reasonable agreement will actually do all the work that Rawls wants. Barry's argument retains the deep contractarianism of Rawls by seeing the idea of a society as a fair or reasonable agreement, as the only principled response to the political problem of how people who disagree about fundamental ends can live together on acceptable terms. He merely replaces the elaborate device of the original position contract with a Scanlonian contractualist agreement in which individuals are asked to choose only those principles to govern their affairs that no one can reasonably reject.

Barry's argument is a complex mix of both Rawlsian insights into the task of justice with Scanlonian insights into the contractual nature of reasonable agreement. Nevertheless, in its political emphasis on the problem of pluralism about ultimate ends, Barry's argument is much closer to that of Rawls and it demonstrates how significant the contractarian method remains to one of the fundamental problems of moral and political philosophy.

V. CONCLUSION

The work of Rawls, Gauthier, Scanlon, and many others amply demonstrates the continued vitality and diversity of the contractarian tradition in modern ethics. That tradition in its Hobbesian and Kantian strands demonstrates the vitality of insights derived from some of the greatest philosophers of the modern period. That said, despite the centrality of the contract device to both the moral and political strands of contemporary ethical

theory, there have been signs that its significance is once again on the wane. The main challenge has been directed towards the Scanlonian-type "reasonable agreement" versions of contractualism. It is argued that the concept of "reasonableness" cannot provide a purely impartialist ground for moral or political principles because "reasonableness" itself has to have a moral content, or it presupposes precisely the values it aims to justify. This is the argument of communitarian critics of contractarianism, such as Michael Sandel, Alasdair MacIntyre, and Charles Taylor, as well as cognitivist antirealists such as Ronald Dworkin and Perfectionists such as Joseph Raz. Many, although not all on this list, are in sympathy with some of the substantive conclusions of Rawls-type contractarianism, but they reject the contractarian method he adopts to ground his principles. Although Rawls in his later works has conceded much to such critics, others such as Barry have been rather more robust in defending a contractualist position. If it is the case that contractarianism may be falling out of fashion among moral and political philosophers, it remains an enormously versatile and important tradition with many able defenders. And as its history shows, it is a theory that has never been off the center stage for very long. To write its obituary would be both premature and extremely unwise.

Also See the Following Articles

GREEK ETHICS, OVERVIEW • RIGHTS THEORY • THEORIES OF JUSTICE: RAWLS

Bibliography

Boucher, D., & Kelly, P. (Ed.). (1994). *The social contract from Hobbes to Rawls*. London: Routledge.
Hampton, J. (1986). *Hobbes and the social contract tradition*. Cambridge: Cambridge University Press.
Kavka, G. (1986). *Hobbesian moral and political theory*. Princeton: Princeton University Press.
Kelly, P. (Ed.). (1996). *Utilitas* (Vol. 8, No. 3). *Special Issue on Justice as Impartiality*.
Korsgaard, C. (1996). *The sources of normativity*. Cambridge: Cambridge University Press.
Kukathas, C., and Pettit, P. (1990). *A theory of justice and its critics*. Cambridge: Polity Press.
Kymlicka, W. (1990). *Contemporary political philosophy*. Oxford: Clarendon Press.
Lessnoff, M. (1986). *Social contract*. London: Macmillan.
Medina, V. (1990). *Social contract theories: Political obligation or anarchy*. Savage, MD: Rowman and Littlefield.
Vallentyne, P. (Ed.). (1991). *Contractarianism and rational choice*. Cambridge: Cambridge University Press.

CORPORAL PUNISHMENT

Burton M. Leiser
Pace University

GLOSSARY

deterrence The theory that the punishment of one person will serve as an example to others, and deter, or discourage them from committing similar offenses.

flogging Inflicting pain by whipping or by using a cane.

insubordination A refusal to comply with the rules or laws set down by some authority.

lex talionis The law of retaliation, an ancient Babylonian law, adopted by other civilizations as well, that prescribes punishments for wrongdoers exactly like the offenses they committed; popularly known as "an eye for an eye."

maiming Cutting off or mutilating part of a person's body.

perjury Testifying falsely under oath.

retribution The theory that punishment is "payment" to the offender for the offense he has committed; that an offender *deserves* to be "paid back" for what he has done.

CORPORAL PUNISHMENT is an expression derived from the Latin *corpus*, body, and *punire* to punish. *Pun-*
ire is closely related to another Latin word, *poena*, from which we get the English word *penalty* and also the word *pain*.

Corporal punishment is thus the infliction of pain upon a person through something that is done upon his or her body. The notion of *punishment* qualifies this, however, in a rather significant way. Punishment is generally considered to be a harm or deprivation that is imposed upon someone by a person who possesses authority, and is justified by the victim's having violated some rule or law that the authority has a right to enforce. Therefore, a person who leans too far out a window and falls out, breaking a leg in the process, has certainly suffered bodily harm, but has not suffered corporal punishment. Similarly, one who contracts lung cancer after a lifetime of smoking suffers grave bodily harm and terrible pain, but these are not thought to be punishments. They are merely the results of his or her habit. In general, the natural consequences of an individual's behavior are not thought to be penalties, although they may be very painful indeed.

Corporal punishment is thus distinguished from capital punishment (the death penalty), fines (deprivation of property), and imprisonment (deprivation of liberty).

I. KINDS OF CORPORAL PUNISHMENT

A. Flogging

In recent years, "corporal punishment" has generally been used almost exclusively to refer to spanking or flogging, particularly of children by their parents, of students by their teachers, or of prisoners by penal authorities. In the broadest sense, the term can refer to any bodily harm that is inflicted upon a person as a kind of penalty. Apprentices—young workers who were learning their trade—were often flogged by their masters when they did not perform up to the master's expectations. Naval personnel were subject to flogging, often with a cat-o'-nine tails (a whip made of nine knotted cords attached to a handle) when they were disobedient, drunk, or rowdy. Slaves were beaten cruelly and mercilessly by their masters. In some countries, such as Singapore, corporal punishment by caning (forcibly applying a rattan cane to the bare back of the prisoner, often resulting in severe welts and the flaying of the victim's flesh) or flogging is still employed regularly as the penalty for certain offenses.

In its broadest sense, "corporal punishment" may also refer to *torture* or *maiming*.

B. Torture

Torture is the infliction of particularly painful and ultimately deadly forms of treatment. Extremely horrifying treatments and devices have been employed in order to cause gradual escalation of the pain and suffering and to break the will of even the strongest victims. A few examples:

- The Chinese water torture: Placing the prisoner in an immobile position and causing water to drop incessantly on his face and forehead.
- Repeatedly forcing the prisoner's head under water and holding him there until he is on the verge of drowning.
- Depriving the prisoner of sleep for prolonged periods of time.
- The rack: A device upon which the prisoner was stretched, by all four limbs. As a wheel was slowly turned, the prisoner's arms and legs would gradually be stretched further and further, until eventually, they would be pulled out of their sockets.
- The iron maiden: A metal casket into which the prisoner would be placed. As screws on the outside were gradually tightened, spikes on the inside of the device would slowly press upon the prisoner's flesh, and eventually pierce his body, causing excruciating pain and ultimately causing him to bleed to death or die because his internal organs were crushed or pierced. A smaller version of this device was a spiked band that would be placed around his head.

- Electric shock treatment, particularly applied to the breasts of women and to the genitals of men and women.
- Various drugs designed to cause the prisoner to suffer delusions, dizziness, nausea, diarrhea, and terror.

Torture is most often used, not as a form of punishment, but as a means of extracting confessions or information from the victim. However, it may be used as a way of inflicting great pain upon a prisoner in retaliation for what is deemed to be a particularly grievous offense. Prisoners of war have often been tortured by their captors long after it must have become obvious that they had no useful information to divulge.

C. Maiming

Maiming is the amputation or mutilation of a part of a person's body. Many kinds of maiming have been practiced over the centuries as forms of punishment, and some are still in use in certain parts of the world.

In some parts of the Islamic world, for example, including Saudi Arabia, Kuwait, and Afghanistan, theft is punished by amputation of the thief's hand, usually by an ax or a sword.

Rapists and fornicators (men who have had sexual intercourse with unmarried girls) may be punished by being castrated (having their genitals cut off). Slanderers (those who spread vicious lies about others) have been punished by having their tongues cut out or being fastened to their cheeks. In some societies, certain crimes have been punished by cutting off the offender's ear or his nose, by blinding him, or by branding him with some distinctive mark on his face or forehead.

II. JUSTIFICATIONS FOR CORPORAL PUNISHMENT

Whipping and other forms of corporal punishment have been practiced since ancient times as a means of disciplining wayward children, slaves, women, convicts, workers, and others who were too weak to defend themselves. Many attempts have been made to justify the use of the lash or other means of disciplining people who were deemed to be disobedient or insubordinate. The following are among the justifications that have been used.

A. Corporal Punishment Has Respectable Ancient Roots

One of the most common justifications has been the claim that corporal punishment has been practiced from time immemorial.

Ancient codes of law, such as the Code of Hammurabi (a Babylonian lawgiver who lived about 3800 years ago), prescribed the *lex talionis*, the law of retaliation, which called for "an eye for an eye, a tooth for a tooth, a wound for a wound," and so on. That is, if a person caused another to lose the vision of an eye, his own eye would be blinded.

The same formulation is found in the law codes of the Biblical books of Exodus and Deuteronomy, but the context (especially in chapter 21 of Exodus) suggests that the ancient Hebrews were not applying the rule literally. Instead, it seems that they were thinking in terms of money damages, as we do in our civil law courts, rather than maiming or corporal punishment. Thus, if one person caused another to lose his vision, he would not be blinded in return. Instead, the court would assess what he should have to pay his neighbor to compensate him for his loss. The same would apply to a person who knocked out another's tooth, caused him to lose the use of an arm or a leg, or even caused him (accidentally) to lose his life. In our own law, such monetary compensation falls under the law of torts, or civil damages, and is quite distinct from criminal penalties. Although one might think that it is impossible to calculate the financial equivalent of a person's eye, his arm, or—most especially—his life, the fact is that in our civil courts, juries try to make such calculations every day, particularly in accident cases and in medical malpractice cases. We have replaced maiming or other forms of corporal punishment with what our society deems to be a more civilized approach to doing justice to people who have suffered physical harm through the negligence—and in some cases even the intentional acts of others. The first evidence we have of such an approach appears in the Biblical book of Exodus.

The Bible is not entirely free of references to corporal punishment, however. In the Book of Proverbs, the inspiration for generations of parents and schoolmasters was articulated quite simply: "He who spares the rod hates his son, but he who loves him disciplines him early" (Prov. 13:24). If that was not emphatic enough, the author of Proverbs added, "If folly settles in the heart of a lad, the rod of discipline will remove it" (Ibid., 22:15.). These ancient proverbs have often been paraphrased, "Spare the rod and spoil the child." Such authority has been cited for generations by those who seek justification for using corporal punishment on their children, their students, or others who are in their charge.

B. Corporal Punishment Builds Character

Beyond the mere authority of the Book of Proverbs is the rationale it offers for inflicting corporal punishment upon children in particular, but also, perhaps, on others who are in need of strict discipline. The implication of those proverbs is that suitable early application of the rod is an effective and useful corrective to bad behavior. Young children who are inclined to misbehave are particularly in need of discipline, it is argued, and when all else fails, a swift blow to the child's posterior is certain to get a child's attention. Every child, it is assumed, will soon realize that similar behavior in defiance of the rules will lead to similar, or even more severe punishment, and will therefore avoid the undesirable behavior.

Christians, Jews, and other students of the Bible are not alone in using such a rationale. Menander, a student of the great philosopher, Aristotle, and a distinguished Greek dramatist who lived in the fourth century B.C., wrote, "The man who has never been flogged has never been taught." Thus, he suggests that flogging is not only useful for correcting wicked behavior. It is absolutely essential for inculcating an inclination to behave properly. One may infer, therefore, that every parent, teacher, or other person who has the moral training of others in his hands has a positive obligation to use corporal punishment on his charges in order to improve their character and make them more amenable to obedience and conformity to the rules and laws of their society.

Going beyond the general usefulness that corporal punishment is supposed to have in building good character, some authorities have claimed that it is essential for religious salvation. Cotton Mather, the great Puritan leader in colonial America, claimed that one is "better whipped than damned." It was believed that children were naturally inclined to sin. Early Puritanical and Calvinist religious thinkers believed that as God was a stern disciplinarian who used his enormous power and wrath to extract obedience to his commandments. In the same way, they believed, human authorities must use stern discipline upon children and others who are prone to habitual misbehavior. It was the only way to instill in them a proper fear of the awful, dreadful consequences of sin.

Noah Webster, the eighteenth-century American educator, journalist, and publisher who compiled and published the first Webster's dictionaries, wrote:

> The rod is often necessary in school; especially after the children have been accustomed to disobedience and a licentious behavior at home. All government originates in families, and if neglected there, it will hardly exist in society; but the want of it must be applied by the rod in school, the penal laws of the state, and the terrors of divine wrath from the pulpit. The government of both families and schools should be absolute.

In the 1840s, the American poet Walt Whitman wrote that flogging was so frequent and so severe that in one Brooklyn school, 40 boys were thrashed in one morning, and a little girl was "so cut and marked with the rattan over back, neck, and shoulders, for some trifling offence [sic], that the livid marks remained there for several days."

It was believed that children from some homes (most likely those from impoverished or immigrant families) were so "primitive" that they were insensitive to any kind of punishment other than "the stimulus of bodily pain, or the humiliation that attends its infliction."

C. Corporal Punishment Sets a Good Example for Others

A further justification for corporal punishment is its alleged usefulness as a deterrent. That is, it is not only useful in reforming the disobedient child or adult and persuading him or her to behave properly. It also sets a powerful example for others who may be inclined to violate the rules. Those who see the pain and humiliation that was suffered by the person who has been subjected to flogging or other forms of corporal punishment will be less inclined to risk facing such a punishment themselves. The father who spanks his oldest son may well warn his younger children at the same time, "This is what will happen to you if you misbehave as Johnny has done." In a community that tolerates wife-beating as a form of discipline by their husbands, reports of beatings inflicted by some husbands might, at least theoretically, incline other women to greater obedience to their husbands. Similarly, it is assumed that prisoners who have watched guards whipping or punching other inmates for their infractions of the rules will be more inclined to refrain from similar violations themselves.

D. Corporal Punishment Is a Form of Retribution

In addition to reform and deterrence, retribution is believed to be one of the principal purposes of punishment. While reform and deterrence look toward the future, holding that punishment is intended to persuade the offender (in the case of reform) or others (in the case of deterrence) to obey the rules in the future, retribution looks to the past. The theory is that a person who has violated the law or some official rule *deserves* to suffer some loss for having done so. The penalty that is to be applied to him or her is supposed to be "fitting" to the offense committed. It is not always very easy to design a "fitting" or "suitable" penalty for each offense, but in general, an effort is made to find a penalty that is deemed to be "proportionate" to the offense.

This concept of proportionality is easy to grasp, but more difficult to apply in practice. It can be summarized fairly easily by observing that we try to fashion penalties in such a way that they are neither so severe as to be perceived as brutal or grossly excessive for the crimes committed, nor so light and trivial as to be meaningless. Thus, for example, 10 years behind bars for parking overtime is grossly excessive. A $5 dollar fine for robbing a bank or committing murder would be ridiculously inadequate. It is usually much easier to identify penalties that are disproportionate than it is to specify those that would be deemed to be most appropriate.

In the criminal law, some offenses do not easily lend themselves to equivalences. A thief may be required to restore the goods he has stolen plus some further value (perhaps three or four times the value of those goods) by way of punishment. (*Lex talionis* may prescribe that a murderer may be executed in retaliation for the life he took. In Hammurabi's code, one who murdered a neighbor's daughter was punished by having his own daughter slain. In the Hebrew Bible, a perjurer (one who had testified falsely against his neighbor) would be sentenced to suffer the penalty that would have been inflicted upon the person against whom he testified if he had not been found out. So if his testimony would have resulted in the execution of the original defendant, he would be executed. And if it would have resulted in the original defendant's having to pay a heavy fine, the same fine would be levied against the perjurer. But what if the penalty could not possibly be imposed upon the perjurer?

Suppose, for example, that the perjurer had testified that a priest was an illegitimate child—that he had been born to an adulteress. The priest would have been disqualified for the priesthood and all of the privileges that went with it. A similar penalty could have been imposed upon the perjurer if he had been a priest: He could have been deprived of his priestly privileges. But if he were an ordinary layman, obviously it would have been impossible to impose such a penalty upon him. What, then, could one do? The answer was: Flog him.

People seem to like to affix numerical equivalents to penalties as well as to most other things. Numerical measurements confer a kind of precision, subjectively at least, to human endeavors. Just as legislators and judges can set numbers to the length of prison time to be served for various offenses (30 days, 6 months, 25 years), those who have been able to impose corporal punishment on people who were under their control and authority have been able to set a number that they no doubt believed to be somehow appropriate to the offense: 30 lashes, or 40, or whatever seemed suitable.

E. Corporal Punishment Is More Humane than Imprisonment

In our society, imprisonment has become the standard form of punishment for most major crimes against individuals or the state. Minor offenses may be punished by the imposition of fines, and occasionally some creative judges experiment with other kinds of penalty. But for the most part, prison is the "solution" we have found to the crime problem. The modern prison system arose out of the religious theory of penitence. It was believed that if a wicked person were subjected to harsh conditions and deprived of many of the good things of life, he would repent of his sinful behavior and become a better person. For this reason, our prisons were originally called "penitentiaries."

The prison system has obviously not been a very happy solution, for although it keeps the convicted criminal off the streets for a period of time, many experts have concluded that it is rather unsuccessful in rehabilitating most prisoners, and that it has not significantly deterred others from following in their footsteps. Indeed, it has been suggested that in some communities, young people regard having "served time" as a badge of honor. Far from being penitent and learning to live honorably while serving time, many convicts emerge with enhanced knowledge of the criminal life and its techniques, and new contacts in the underworld who can help them to become reestablished and to become more proficient than they were when they were caught. Thus, prisons have come to be known as schools of crime.

This leaves completely aside the question of the cost of incarceration. Hundreds of millions of dollars are currently being spent on the construction of new jails and prisons. The cost of keeping a single prisoner locked up for one year is estimated to run between $20,000 and $35,000 per year—as much as tuition and other expenses at the finest Ivy League colleges.

In light of these considerations, some experts have suggested that for some crimes, at least, flogging or some other form of corporal punishment might be more rational than imprisonment. It would be much less costly. The criminal who is flogged would be free to resume his normal activities immediately, and would thus not lose his job or have his family life disrupted. It would make an immediate, unforgettable impression on the criminal himself. And it would serve as an example to others who might contemplate similar crimes in the future.

III. ARGUMENTS AGAINST CORPORAL PUNISHMENT

A. The United States Constitution and Other Laws

Some people have argued that the Eighth Amendment to the United States Constitution, which prohibits "cruel and unusual punishment," applies to corporal punishment, which they regard as cruel and unusual.

The United States Supreme Court, however, has held otherwise. Insofar as school children and convicted criminals serving prison terms are concerned, the Court has held that the Eighth Amendment simply does not apply to them. The Court has declared that school children are adequately protected by the oversight provided by school boards and school administrators, and by the opportunity they have to sue individuals who overstep the bounds of decency and reasonableness or who are abusive in their use of corporal punishment. Furthermore, the Court has ruled that there is reasonable ground for believing that corporal punishment may have the effect for which it is intended.

Another concept that has affected legal thinking about this subject is the doctrine according to which the school stands *in loco parentis*, in the place of the parent. This doctrine can be traced back to the English common law, which was in effect long before the American War of Independence, and is the basis of much American law to this day. The doctrine means that a child's parents convey to his or her tutor or school the same authority as they have over the child, including their own right to discipline the child. Of course, they cannot convey greater authority than they have themselves, which means that they cannot convey authority to be cruel or abusive toward the child.

Some courts have held, however, that the teacher stood *in loco parentis* when parents hired their own tutors or sent children to school voluntarily. Now, however, when parents have no choice but to send their children to school and most children go to public schools whether they want to or not, the school does not stand *in loco parentis* because the parent has been compelled by the state to send the child to school. Courts taking such an approach have held that if a parent specifically states that she does not want her child subjected to paddling or spanking, the school has no right to permit teachers or others to discipline the child in that way. Others, however, have held that parents cannot interfere with a school's inherent right to maintain order in its classrooms and on its premises, and that where state law permits paddling, schools may do so, with or without the parent's consent.

It is reasonable to conclude that the law is in a confused state on the issue of corporal punishment in the schools. There appears to be nothing in the Constitution to prevent school authorities from employing corporal punishment, so long as state law permits them to do so. The states are not uniform in their statutes dealing with this issue. Some states have outlawed corporal punishment completely. Others permit it, but with provisions against cruel or abusive behavior by teachers and other persons who are in positions of authority.

In other areas, such as corporal punishment of prisoners as a disciplinary measure, there is general agreement in the courts that so long as the punishment is not clearly abusive and is measured and suitable to the prisoner's offense, it is permissible.

B. Corporal Punishment Does Not Reform

Some psychologists and other opponents of corporal punishment have argued that corporal punishment is ineffective as an instrument of reform. Those who use it expecting the culprit to mend his ways are simply misguided, they say. On the contrary, a person who is paddled or whipped or caned is likely to be made even more angry and defiant and less likely to repent or atone than if he had been reasoned with or treated more humanely.

C. Corporal Punishment Does Not Deter and Is Counterproductive

Opponents of corporal punishment claim that corporal punishment does not deter others. For major offenses, it is simply not enough. For minor offenses, it strikes them as being too little to have any significant deterrent effect. Moreover, the person who administers the punishment (in schools, most often the child's teacher) is thereafter perceived to be cruel and heartless, and loses the respect of those whose respect is vital if a good and constructive relationship is to exist.

In schools, it has been suggested, the fear and humiliation brought about by corporal punishment leads students to drop out, to vandalize school property, and to vote against education funding when they become eligible to vote. During the nineteenth century, reformers contended that the whipping of sailors was responsible for rebellion and bloody mutinies. The same was said about major rebellions in prisons.

From an educational standpoint, it has been argued, corporal punishment teaches precisely the wrong lessons. Whether it is administered by parents, teachers, or other persons in positions of authority, the lesson derived from it is that it is right to beat people and to cause them great pain. The lesson that people in authority should be trying to impart is that such behavior is wrong, that acts of aggression are to be avoided, and that the way to solve problems is through open discussion and the use of reason rather than a resort to brute force. And finally, according to some experts, it may induce post traumatic stress disorder, a disability that people sometimes suffer after war, rape, or major natural disasters. This disorder leaves them unable to function normally, and often leads to very serious aftereffects, including total withdrawal, inability to communicate effectively, and other grave symptoms that can interfere with future development and make a normal life impossible for them.

D. Corporal Punishment Is Unjust

Contrary to those who claim that corporal punishment is suitable from a retributive point of view, it is argued that corporal punishment is unjust, that it offends contemporary concepts of decency and human dignity, and that it is incompatible with civilized conduct.

Long before the Civil War, a judge in Indiana, dealing with a case involving a schoolboy who had been whipped by his teacher, predicted that one day, the use of the rod would be prohibited by public policy because it is inherently evil. Instead, he said, the teacher will be compelled to resort to "the resources of his intellect and heart." He believed that the particular evil of corporal punishment lay in the natural tendency of those who used it to become so overwhelmed by passion that they became brutal and excessive.

> The husband can no longer moderately chastise his wife; nor ... the master his servant or apprentice. Even the degrading cruelties of the naval service have been arrested. Why the person of the school-boy, "with his shining morning face," should be less sacred in the eyes of the law than that of the apprentice or the sailor, is not easily explained.

In his book, *The Pilgrim's Progress*, Richard Henry Dana offered a particularly sadistic portrait of a ship's captain's use of the lash. As he was flogging one of the men on board his ship, the captain danced around the deck screaming, "If you want to know what I flog you for, I'll tell you. It's because I like to do it!—because I like to do it." Similarly, in *Uncle Tom's Cabin*, Harriet Beecher Stowe described the sadism of the slave owner and how he communicated it to the slaves he appointed as overseers, who became as savage and brutal as his bulldogs.

Such sadism was often shared by the spectators, and aroused concern about the effects on them. It was believed that schoolboys who flocked around whipping posts and seemed to enjoy the floggings they witnessed were learning precisely the wrong lessons.

IV. THEORIES OF HUMAN NATURE AND CORPORAL PUNISHMENT

If man is seen as innately inclined to evil, then it may make some sense to think that his evil impulses can be driven out of him by harsh punishment. On the other hand, if people are believed to be essentially rational creatures who sometimes go wrong because of environmental factors over which they have no control, then it may be more sensible, if our purpose is to improve them, to appeal to their rational faculties than to subject them to cruel and painful whippings.

Reformers have always singled out and emphasized those cases in which persons who have violated the law and been treated humanely have reformed, while those who were treated harshly became ever more rebellious and insubordinate. They like to compare the classroom of the harsh teacher whose students are restless and always waiting for an opportunity to do mischief with that of the kind and gentle teacher, whose students continue working and maintain perfect order even when she is out of the room. Convicts are, in their opinion, basically decent people who can be reached by gentle persuasion, while they will only grow more incorrigible if they are treated cruelly and will look for opportunities to do even greater damage whenever they have the chance.

Such philosophical theories as determinism and free will may have a major impact on public policy, on the development of the law, and on the disposition of individual cases, although occasionally astute or skeptical judges, legislators, and citizens may turn the intended impact of such a theory on its head, as the following story indicates:

Clarence Darrow, a renowned Chicago attorney, used to argue that criminals should not be punished because the world is completely deterministic. That is, everything that occurs is brought about by preexisting conditions, and no person possesses free will, or the ability to make choices that are independent of conditions and events that had come before. Because every act we perform is predetermined and beyond our control, he said, it makes no sense to blame any of us for what we do, or to punish us. Criminals are not at all responsible for what they do, and therefore, the law ought to provide for rehabilitative treatment for them rather than cruel and harsh penalties. If they were at all moved by morality, he insisted, judges would see the soundness of this argument and be lenient toward the defendants who are brought before them. To this, legend has it, one judge responded, "Mr. Darrow, assuming that your theory of determinism is correct, it must apply to judges as well as to criminals. On your theory, judges cannot help but do what they do and are no more morally responsible for their verdicts than criminals are for the crimes they commit. I presume, therefore, that you will not blame me or think that I am being unduly vengeful when I sentence your client to be hanged."

Despite the changes that have taken place over the past two centuries, corporal punishment continues to play a large role in the lives of millions of people throughout the world. Parents continue to believe that it is an effective means of disciplining their children, that it will "teach them a lesson they'll never forget." Even when it does not improve a child's behavior, some parents get a kind of malicious pleasure from beating a willful child and "giving him what he deserves." Children who experience such forms of punishment are often inclined to follow the same practices with their own children, and so the system is perpetuated. Our experiences as children carry over into other realms of activity as we grow older. What works with children ought to work with adults, we think. So when adults violate the rules of our society, we conclude that they ought to respond to physical punishment. Because adults can usually tolerate more physical pain than children of tender years, and because they are more likely to be fixed in their ways, the punishment must be escalated if it is to have any effect at all. When crime and violence run riot and no other measures seem to work, it is quite natural that people will turn to methods they know from their own experience tend to work at least some of the time. Everyone has felt pain, and everyone knows how prone we are to give up some things we might want in order to avoid painful consequences.

But others, believing in the ultimate perfectibility of human beings, are prepared to take their chances with the ultimate instruments of civilization: reason, rational discourse, and human kindness. They are convinced that if children are brought up in loving homes, and if their school environments are permeated by an atmosphere of caring, they will grow to be responsible citizens without ever experiencing harsh discipline.

Despite vast amounts of research into the efficacy of corporal punishment, there is no consensus as to whether it works over the long run. But even if it does, a strong argument can be made that the various forms of corporal punishment are ultimately unethical, despite its ability to instill fear and terror in the hearts of those who are subjected to it.

Thus, corporal punishment continues to be practiced, except where it has been outlawed—and sometimes even there.

Also See the Following Articles

CAPITAL PUNISHMENT • CHILD ABUSE • CHILDREN'S RIGHTS • FAMILY, THE • JUVENILE CRIME

Bibliography

Bolmeier, E. C. (1976). *Legality of student disciplinary practices.* Charlottesville, VA: The Michie Company.

Glenn, M. C. (1984). *Campaigns against corporal punishment: Prisoners, sailors, women, and children in antebellum america.* Albany: State University of New York Press.

Greven, P. (1991). *Spare the child: The religious roots of punishment and the psychological impact of physical abuse.* New York: Alfred A. Knopf.

Hyman, I. A., & Wise, J. H. (Eds.). (1979). *Corporal punishment in American education: Readings in history, practice, and alternatives.* Philadephia: Temple University Press.

Hyman, R. T., & Rathbone, C. H. (1993). *Corporal punishment in schools: Reading the law.* Topeka, KS: National Organization on Legal Problems of Education.

Newman, G. (1983). *Just and painful: A case for the corporal punishment of criminals.* New York: Macmillan.

Paquet, R. A. (1982). *Judicial rulings, state statutes and state administrative regulations dealing with the use of corporal punishment in public schools.* Palo Alto, CA: R & E Research Associates.

Valle, J. E. (1980). *Rocks & shoals: Order and discipline in the old navy 1800–1861.* Annapolis: Naval Institute Press.

CORPORATE RESPONSIBILITY

Celia Wells
University of Wales, Cardiff

GLOSSARY

aggregation A situation in which the conduct or knowledge of a number of individuals is combined to establish corporate fault.

alter ego A senior corporate officer whose actions and mental state are regarded as those of the corporation itself.

legal personality The fact of endowing a corporation with separate legal status.

nominalist theory The theory that a corporation has no separate legal status of its own but is an aggregation of legally responsible individuals.

reactive fault Assessing fault from a corporation's remedial action following harm-causing activity.

realist theory The theory that legal personality is a valid concept reflecting a corporation's existence separate from its members.

respondeat superior The fact of attributing the wrongdoing of all corporate employees to the corporation.

tort A civil wrong for which remedy may be sought.

vicarious liability The fact of attributing the wrongdoing of an employee to the employer.

CORPORATIONS are legally deemed to be single entities, distinct and separate from all the individuals who compose them. Legal personality means that corporations can sue and be sued, hold property and transact, and incur criminal liability in their own name and on their own account. Not all business enterprises are incorporated (partnerships, for example, are unincorporated groups, as are most clubs). Similarly, not all corporations are business enterprises (universities and local government bodies may be incorporated but are not necessarily engaged in business). However, because debate about corporate responsibility tends to concentrate on business corporations, and in particular on their responsibility under criminal laws, this will be the primary focus of this article.

I. INTRODUCTION

A. Corporations

Corporations play a central role in developed economies and there is wide agreement that they have responsibilities, including social responsibilities. Three general positions on the responsibility of corporations in this sense can be identified, each importing different notions about the scope and character of any obligation to act responsibly. The first view is that businesses should perform acts that promote society's good; the second that they should act such as to prevent social harms from occurring; and the third that they should maximize company profits within the limits set by the law.

This general concept of social responsibility is concerned with the purposes for which corporations should act, and therefore with the limits of their freedom to act. Corporate responsibility as understood in this article, however, is of a rather different kind. Here the term is used to connote the means by which liability is attributed to a corporation for conduct done in its name.

Consideration of the concept "corporate responsibility" clearly raises questions as to the meaning of the two words, "corporate" and "responsibility." It may help to rephrase the expression as "the responsibility of corporations," in order to emphasize that it is the corporation that is the more challenging concept. The idea that a nonhuman entity might have responsibilities and incur legal liabilities or penalties requires explanation. The scheme adopted here is to discuss the theory of legal personality in the second section, and then to use the third section to consider some of the issues raised by the concept of responsibility and the appropriateness of applying it to corporations. Using those discussions as a background, the next area to explore is the legal attribution of fault to corporations. This is approached from both descriptive and evaluative standpoints. The issue of corporate punishment is addressed in the final section.

To begin with, a brief typology of legal regulation is necessary.

B. Legal Regulation

The range of solutions, both actual and potential, to the problem of attributing responsibility to a corporation varies according to the area of law concerned. To begin with there is an area of law that is itself known as "corporate law." This covers such matters as the formalities required in order to establish a company recognized by law, the procedures for their functioning, the duties of directors, and the role of shareholders. Questions in relation to the proper governance of companies have come to the fore in the last decade, a development connected with, and running parallel to, the concerns about corporate responsibility that are central here. In other words, corporate law regulates the corporation's relationship with its own "members," in contrast to those legal duties and responsibilities that regulate its relationship with outsiders. Many of those external duties and responsibilities apply equally to individuals and to incorporated bodies. The civil law of obligations—contract and tort—applies to corporations as it does to individuals. There is nonetheless a question as to how responsibility is to be attributed to the corporation in these areas. That, however, has been regarded

as relatively unproblematic, largely because those areas of law do not rely on a notion of fault, or where they do (as in the tort of negligence, for example), it is an objectively assessed fault liability (see Section III below).

Criminal law in some of its guises applies to corporations as it does to individuals. However, it is here that many of the difficult questions arise as to how a legal entity such as a corporation can be responsible. Criminal law is preeminently concerned with standards of behavior enforced, not through compensation, but through a system of state punishment negotiated via standards of fault such as intention, knowledge, and subjective recklessness. Whether and how that system should be applied to corporations thus attracts more controversy than does the ascription of civil liabilities (see Section IV below). There is a further type of criminal law, however. Unlike laws against murder, assault, and theft, for example, which apply universally to all persons of sound mind, there are schemes created specifically to regulate areas of business activity. Trading standards laws, health and safety laws, and environmental protection laws all fit this category. These regulatory schemes share some characteristics of the criminal law—such as utilizing the criminal procedural and penalty structure—yet in other ways are quite different, and are certainly perceived as distinct, from mainstream criminal law. Those differences are often reflected in the rules relating to corporate responsibility. It can be noted that jurisdictions that do not recognize corporate criminal liability (or have not until very recently), such as many in continental Europe, avoided the difficulties that might otherwise have arisen in regulating business enterprise by establishing a stream of administrative regulation. These regulatory schemes, despite their different classification, actually share many of the characteristics of regulatory criminal law.

II. THEORIES OF LEGAL PERSONALITY

Whether a corporation is to be endowed with legal personality is one of three interrelated questions that need to be addressed if a corporation is to be found responsible for criminal offences. Can a corporation be a person in a descriptive sense, in a moral sense, and in a legal sense? In many ways the first two are the most challenging and they are considered in Section III below. The latter question gives rise to a ready answer—law can and, as we shall now see, does accord to corporations a separate status.

All human beings have legal personality although

their responsibilities and rights may vary according to their age and status. A group of people—for example, a club, association or partnership—does not generally have a legal existence separate from its individual members. Blackstone explains, in this passage, why this may cause problems and how they may be overcome:

> As all personal rights die with the person; and, as the necessary forms of investing a series of individuals, one after another, with the same identical rights, would be very inconvenient, if not impracticable; it has been found necessary, when it is for the advantage of the public to have any particular rights kept on foot and continued, to constitute artificial persons, who may maintain a perpetual succession, and enjoy a kind of legal immortality. These artificial persons are called bodies politic, bodies corporate (*corpora corporata*), or corporations: of which there is a great variety subsisting, for the advancement of religion, of learning, and of commerce; in order to preserve entire and for ever those rights and immunities, which, if they were granted only to those individuals of which the body corporate is composed, would upon their death be utterly lost and extinct (Blackstone. (1765). *Commentary on the Laws of England,* 1, 455).

The origins of both separate personality, and the connected development of limited liability, can be found in Roman law. However, it is ironic that limited liability emerged at that stage in order to protect the public property of municipalities, whereas its clear function now is to protect private investors from the claims of third parties.

Despite this long history of endowing certain organizations with separate legal personality, there has been an increasingly lively debate as to its theoretical basis. Are corporations merely, and nothing more than, collections of individuals, as the "nominalist" view would hold, or does the corporation have an existence and meaning as well as a legal personality of its own, as the "realist" view contends? The early corporations had little in common with business organizations and were more like guilds functioning as a mechanism to control the right to engage in specific business activities. The transition to the modern business corporation with its division between capital and management dates from the resolution of the East India Company in 1612 that trading was to be carried out by the corporation rather than by individuals acting under its umbrella. By the nineteenth century, investors were protected through

limited liability, and corporations began to be sued in tort for some of the injuries they caused. Yet, beyond accepting that the corporation was legally distinct, there was remarkably little agreement, or in some cases concern, as to the theoretical base. Holdsworth, the renowned legal historian, found the whole business a bore and thought English law had escaped "very lightly touched" by speculations as to whether the company was nominally or fictionally separate, or in reality so (Holdsworth, W. (1944). *A History of English Law* (3rd Ed.), ix, 70. London: Sweet and Maxwell). The common law, for Holdsworth, had only ever possessed one theory of corporate personality, that it was to be treated as far as possible like a natural man. Certainly, in the early days, an anthropomorphic conception of the corporation informed legal determinations. Later, this taken-for-granted approach began to cause real difficulties. Establishing who or what comprises the "corporation" proved to be a far from simple matter.

Particularly in relation to criminal law, with its reliance on moral fault, there is still a struggle between the nominalists and the realists, a struggle that affects the rules by which responsibility is attributed. Because, in the nominalist view, the corporation does not exist apart from its members, any blameworthiness or responsibility can only derive from the culpability of an individual servant or employee. That still leaves to be decided whether the corporation will be responsible for all of its employees or for some of them (see Section IV, below). For the realist, on the other hand, the corporation does represent something beyond the individuals comprising it and this opens up completely different avenues for attribution.

One of the paradoxes of corporate personality is that, while it addresses the temporality of human lives, by allowing the corporation to continue as property holder after the death or disappearance of any particular group of original members, the very nature of the company is that it can be dissolved. Legal personality may bring freedoms as well as responsibilities but they are alienable. And in general the protections imported by legal personality outweigh any corresponding responsibilities or obligations. This can be usefully borne in mind in considering the corporation as a moral person.

III. CORPORATIONS AS MORAL PERSONS

It is one thing to say that a corporation has the legal status to own property, make contracts in its own name, even be sued in negligence in its own name, and another to say that it can be morally responsible. Deeming the corporation a legal person may facilitate the attribution of responsibility, but by itself that mechanism does not answer core questions about the nature of blame and its applicability to a nonhuman person. These are vital matters to resolve if corporations are to be held liable for breaches of law that require proof of fault, as do the majority of criminal laws. It is those questions with which this section is concerned.

A. Metaphysics

Is it important whether a corporation is described as a person in any other (nonjuristic) sense? Some argue that a metaphysical theory is unavoidable despite its evasion by lawyers who concentrate on the consequences rather than the appropriateness of using the term. Modern philosophical thinking associates personhood with human beings. That does not necessarily preclude an organization from being regarded as a person, especially if the organization is regarded as nothing more than a group of human beings. The real question is whether that group can be regarded as an individual in the sense of an indivisible whole.

B. Moral Personhood

Even if we accept that (some) organizations have a separate existence, and are not merely aggregations of human beings, does that mean they are moral persons as well? Certainly, one step in the argument that organizations may be regarded as capable of moral decision-making and therefore susceptible to moral blame (and thus to criminal accountability), is acceptance of the proposition that they are not just collections of people. The next step involves consideration of ideas central to moral accountability, such as agency, rationality, and autonomy. Can they apply to an organization?

One of the main proponents of corporate moral personality, Peter French, seeks to compare organizational decision-making structures with the human mind, so that corporate intentionality is regraded as comparable with human intentionality. For others, this is seen as too restrictive and fails to exploit the potential of developing different criteria for ascribing organizational responsibility (see below). These proponents of organizational accountability distinguish between different types of groups, between conglomerates that do attract such accountability and aggregates (mere collections of people) that do not. Corporations qualify as conglomerates because, among other things, they have internal decision procedures. For others, moral personhood is so closely dependent on human capacities for emotion and evil that it cannot, by definition, apply to an organization.

An alternative approach is to start from the opposite end altogether. Instead of asking whether the corporation is like a human being, we could question how far human beings fit into the assumed picture of isolated actors, divorced from their social context. This reflects a theory most closely associated with Hegel who "tried in many different ways to show that the formation of what might appear to an individual to be his or her own particular intention or desire or belief already reflected a complex social inheritance that could itself be said to be evolving, even evolving progressively, with a 'logic' of its own" (Audi R. (Ed.). (1995). *Cambridge Dictionary of Philosophy*, p. 314. Cambridge: Cambridge University Press).

C. Concepts of Blame

It will be helpful at this point, therefore, to subject to closer scrutiny some of the key ideas underlying concepts of blameworthiness. Because a major area of controversy is whether an organization, or corporation, can per se be held responsible in criminal law, it is important to clarify the core concepts of blame.

Accountability is a fundamental principle here. Corporations traditionally fell with animals, children, and the insane as nonaccountable. Fault ascription presupposes rationality and autonomy. Rationality implies that an agent acts for reasons and that those reasons both rationalize the action and causally explain it. Autonomy suggests an agent with causal power over her body and an inextricable link is thought to exist between fault ascription, autonomy and human bodies.

It is clear that an account in this form will exclude corporations. Could a different form of argument rule them in? Three possible lines suggest themselves. One explanation is that the exclusion of corporations results from the vagaries and accidents of history, culture, and language. We should perhaps not be surprised that the language of attribution or fault ascription reflects the fact that the main subjects of law have been human persons. (In recent history, that is; animals have not always been regarded as inappropriate subjects for punishment.) Deploying the descriptive language of an individualist rationality and autonomy will inevitably limit the debate about corporate responsibility, a debate that should be conducted at a different level. A more useful notion than autonomy might be that of a unified actor or decision-maker.

Second, the individualistic account of rational behavior makes a number of challengeable assumptions about human behavior. As suggested here, ideas of responsibility cannot readily be separated from the social contexts in which they develop. People do not necessarily think *as* individuals but as products of particular cultures and social institutions. A closely related argument casts doubt too on the aptness of the underlying assumptions of mentalism and autonomy in the conventional account of individual responsibility.

Here we need to spell out in more detail the particular form of accountability adopted in systems of criminal law to reflect the concern already noted with rationality and autonomy. Criminal laws tend to be eclectic in their use of fault terms. Key features in criminal culpability are the subjective mental states of intention, knowledge, and recklessness. Here the prosecution will be expected to prove that the defendant herself realized that her actions would inevitably lead to a particular result, (intention); that she herself was aware of particular circumstances, (knowlege); or that she herself was aware that her actions might have that result or that a circumstance might exist (recklessness). Although many systems also utilize objective fault terms such as negligence (that the defendant's behavior fell short of that expected of a reasonable person even though she had not adverted to the relevant risk), and even discard the need for a mental state altogether in some cases (usually dubbed strict liability), the underlying basis for distributing different fault elements is not always explicit. The objective is to ensure that people are not punished for causing results for which they should not be blamed. The means of achieving that objective is more problematic than sometimes admitted. While we might agree that the actions for which a person might be held responsible consist of more than their bodily movements (and therefore more than in the unforeseen or unforeseeable results of these movements), attempting to divine the additional factor in hidden mental states may be a misconceived task.

IV. RESPONSIBILITY ATTRIBUTION

In general, three different theories for attributing blame to corporations compete for attention. The first is based on the agency principle whereby the company is liable for the wrongful acts of all its employees. United States federal law employs a principle of this type, *respondeat superior,* while English law limits the application of vicarious liability to certain regulatory offenses. The second theory of blame attribution, which English law utilizes for all other offenses, identifies a limited layer of senior officers within the company as its "brains" and

renders the company liable only for their transgressions, not for those of other workers. The third locates corporate blame in the procedures, operating systems, or culture of a company. Company culture theory is beginning to achieve judicial recognition in Australia and in England.

The first two theories have in common that they seek in different ways to equate corporate culpability with that of an individual and both are therefore derivative forms of liability. Further, the second version adopts an anthropomorphic vision of company decision-making. The third theory, on the other hand, exploits the dissimilarities between individual human beings and group entities.

A. Vicarious Liability

In the civil (as opposed to criminal) law, an employer or principal is liable for the acts of any employee or agent. Criminal law has generally accepted this avenue of blame attribution in a limited range of strict liability offences. A full-scale vicarious liability principle is endorsed in South Africa as well as in the federal law of the United States, thus confirming that there is no difficulty in applying the vicarious principle to offenses both of strict liability and of subjective knowledge. However, in the United States, it has to be remembered that jurisdiction over many criminal law matters lies at the state level. Some states follow the federal rules, while others (mostly those that have adopted the Model Penal Code) adopt more closely the English common law binary scheme. Under this, vicarious principles apply to certain regulatory offenses only.

To render a corporation vicariously liable, the employee's conduct must be within the scope of the individual's employment or authority. Vicarious liability is regarded as too rough and ready for the delicate task of attributing blame for serious harms. It has been criticized for including too little in demanding that liability flow through an individual, however great the fault of the corporation, and for including too much in blaming the corporation whenever the individual employee is at fault, even in the absence of corporate fault. This summary of the drawbacks of vicarious liability neatly encapsulates one of the major problems in any discussion of corporate responsibility—how to conceptualize "corporate" fault. Vicarious liability attracts criticism as a mechanism for attributing fault because it is felt that there is some other way of measuring "corporate culpability." The key question is to identify that way.

B. Alter Ego (Identification) Theory

It was not until the middle of this century that English law contemplated a form of corporate liability that could apply to serious offenses such as fraud, theft and manslaughter. Vicarious liability was a judicial development, and the courts had rejected the idea that a corporation could commit a serious offense such as a felony. One of the objections to finding corporations liable for such offenses was that they required proof of a mental element of intention, recklessness, or negligence. For the purposes of corporate liability for this type of offense, English courts changed direction half a century ago and developed the *alter ego,* or identification theory, under which certain key personnel are said to act as the company (rather than on behalf of it, as is the case with vicarious liability). The underlying theory is that company employees can be divided into those who act as the "hands" and those who represent the "brains" of the company. The anthropomorphic approach has its origins in the following observation by Viscount Haldane in an earlier civil case:

[A] corporation is an abstraction. It has no mind of its own any more than it has a body of its own; its active and directing will must consequently be sought in the person of somebody who for some purposes may be called an agent, but who is really the directing mind and will of the corporation, the very ego and centre of the personality of the corporation. That person may be under the direction of the shareholders in general meeting; that person may be the board of directors itself, or it may be, and in some companies it is so, that that person has an authority co-ordinate with the board of directors given to him under the articles of association, and is appointed by the general meeting of the company, and can only be removed by the general meeting of the company ((1915) *Lennard's Carrying Co Ltd v Asiatic Petroleum Co*).

Translated into the criminal sphere, this became the basis for the identification principle, which essentially meant that a company would be liable for a serious criminal offense where one of its most senior officers had acted with the requisite fault. Expounded in the leading case of *Tesco v Nattrass* (1972), this limited the relevant personnel to those at the center of corporate power.

The recent emergence of corporate responsibility as a topic of debate reflects concerns about the safety of workers and of members of the public. Disasters such as rail crashes, ferry capsizes, and chemical plant explosions that can be attributed to corporate enterprise operations have led to calls for those enterprises to be prosecuted for manslaughter. It is the cultural origins in changing perceptions of risk and hazard from various sources as well as the legal acceptance of these demands that are of interest. They have also led to doubts about the appropriateness of the two theories of corporate responsibility hitherto recognized by legal systems. One of the more egregious examples of poor safety attitudes was seen when in 1986 a car ferry left the Belgian port of Zeebrugge with its door open and capsized with the loss of nearly 200 lives. The subsequent inquiry in England, where P&O Ferries was based, found a history of open-door sailings and management disregard of obvious safety measures such as a system of indicator lights informing the bridge whether the door was closed. Although P&O was prosecuted for manslaughter, itself an historic event, it proved impossible to convict the company because of the restricting identification theory. It was the very fact that safety was not taken seriously within the company, that no director had responsibility for safety, that made the identification theory a clumsy tool of attribution.

Vicarious liability, as we have seen, is indeterminate in its sweep. It has rarely been applied to serious offenses such as manslaughter. Identification liability regards the transgressions of only a limited number of people within the company as relevant to the attribution of culpability to the company itself. The rhetoric of identification liability asserts not merely a difference of degree between the two principles. It is said that under identification theory, the errant company officer acts as (rather than on behalf of) the company. However, on closer scrutiny, the distinction is of less substance than at first appears. In both vicarious and identification liability, the individual company employee can be prosecuted in her own right, and in each case, the company can only be liable if fault is found in one individual.

As Fisse and Braithwaite cogently conclude:

[The Tesco] principle is highly unsatisfactory, mainly because it fails to reflect corporate blameworthiness. To prove fault on the part of one managerial representative of a company is not to show that the company was at fault as a company but merely that one representative was at fault .... This compromised form of vicarious liability is doubly unsatisfactory because ... it is difficult to establish corporate criminal liability against large companies. Offenses committed on behalf of large concerns are often visible only at the level of middle management whereas the Tesco principle requires proof of fault on the part of a top-level manager. By contrast, fault on the part of a top-level manager is much easier to prove in the context of small companies. Yet that is the context where there is usually little need to impose corporate criminal liability in addition to or in lieu of individual criminal liability (1993, p. 47).

The limitations of these theories have led to a debate about more appropriate mechanisms for establishing corporate culpability, especially with regard to attempts to bring manslaughter prosecutions.

C. Holistic Theories

Variations in size, structure, and decision-making policies and practices among corporations does not prevent the possibility of isolating two broad models of corporate process. Both make it difficult to trace corporate behavior to any one individual. Under the organizational process model, specialization of tasks within an organization leads to a diffusion of responsibilities. The second model, that of bureaucratic politics, is where decision-making is a bargaining process among individuals. Both models should alert legal systems to the need to seek additional forms of culpability attribution. The ideas considered in this section all have in common an attempt to escape from company liability derivative on the wrongdoing of one individual. In other words, they aim to capture the "corporateness" of corporate conduct.

1. Aggregation

In many large organizations, task specialization means that, even among officers senior enough to count for *alter ego* purposes, one individual director will not have access to all the information on which to base a finding of knowledge or negligence. This was the case with P&O Ferries following the Zeebrugge disaster. Aggregation of pockets of knowledge from a number of individual employees has been accepted in U.S. federal courts. However, it has not been adopted in jurisdictions reliant on the more restrictive identification theory for knowledge-based offenses. While aggregation might appear attractive, it presents two difficulties. Reliance on individual, albeit disaggregated, knowledge suggests an incomplete shift to "corporateness"; and it relies on a fiction (that, if A knows that p while B knows that q, this allows knowledge of "p and q" to be ascribed to the corporate person). Aggregation of knowledge is an incomplete solution. The two organizational models referred to earlier suggest that a scheme of corporate liability has to look further than individuals (atomized or aggregated) to the corporation's structure itself.

2. Systems Theory

A developing theory for attributing fault to a corporation is based on internal decision-making structures. This owes its philosophical debt to Peter French who identified three elements in such structures: a responsibility flow-chart, procedural rules, and policies. Later theorists have been less concerned with matching corporate systems with human intentionality.

A legislative example can be found in the Australian Criminal Code Act of 1995, which seeks to establish standard principles for federal offenses, eventually extending to similar situations under state law. Under the code, intention, knowledge or recklessness will be attributed to a body corporate whenever it expressly, tacitly, or impliedly authorized or permitted the commission of the offense. Such authorization or permission may be established, inter alia, where its culture encourages situations leading to an offense. "Corporate culture" is defined as an attitude, policy, rule, course of conduct, or practice existing within the body corporate generally or in the part of the body corporate where the offense occurred. Thus evidence of tacit authorization or toleration of noncompliance or failure to create a culture of compliance will be admissible.

3. Reactive Fault

In this third nonderivative theory, corporate culpability is not sought in antecedent fault. Instead, fault is inferred when a corporation fails to take reasonable remedial measures in response to a harm-causing act or omission by any of its employees. This brings three particular advantages. It avoids the problem of proving antecedent fault; it gives the corporation an opportunity to show remorse and rehabilitative measures; and it introduces a forward-looking dynamic to the problem of corporate harm.

V. PUNISHING CORPORATIONS

Even if the conceptual problems can be overcome awkward questions will be asked about the efficacy of corporate punishment. Fines are ineffective, it is said; corporate prosecutions allow guilty individuals to escape penalty and the target is misdirected because "innocent" shareholders, employees, and consumers bear the real costs. One simple answer to the suggestion that corporate liability is ineffective is to point to the extraordinary efforts corporations frequently employ to avoid conviction.

To the objection that corporate liability can shield individual miscreants, the answer is that this not inevitable and that the structure of liability and its practical execution should ensure that individuals and corporations are appropriately dealt with. A distinction has to be drawn between intended and unintended fallout. Shareholders are often introduced into the discussion as "innocent" but this emotive terminology obscures the very role that brings them into the net in the first place; their financial involvement and thus their intimate "interest" in the company cannot be written out of the account. When it comes to unintended effects, then the argument against corporate sanctions gains strength. It is again important to remember that the rhetoric of individual responsibility is not borne out in reality; the families of offenders (often women and children in particular) are the hidden victims of individual punishment. In each case the question that is raised is whether those indirect, secondary costs are outweighed by the benefits (however they are calibrated) of the primary criminal sanction.

An important question is whether the activities of corporations concern us sufficiently to impose upon them criminal penalties. The real problem is that, if a deterrent effect is sought through financial penalties, rather than through adverse publicity or other remedial measures, the size of the penalty might have to be so great that the unintended side effects would indeed be intolerable. The almost exclusive reliance on fines in some jurisdictions has contributed to this sense of powerlessness. However, within some systems there is evidence of more imagination and commitment to overcome the limitations of financial penalties. It is trite to note that a company cannot be imprisoned. A combination of a fine and the incarceration of directors may be the most effective punishment. Fines are not the only option for the company itself. Equity fines (which effectively dilute the value of the company's shares), corporate probation, adverse publicity, and community service are all options.

Corporate probation is used in the United States in addition to or as an alternative to fines. Sanctions are aggravated by factors such as the aggregate harm or gain from the illegal activity and the involvement or condemnation by "high level personnel." Against "criminal purpose organizations" a power to execute (corporate capital punishment) is available. Sentences are fine-tuned to reflect culpability. Corporations that have effective programs to detect violations, that report them when they occur, and that accept responsibility are rewarded with a lower fine. Guidelines thus seek to ensure that criminal penalties act as more than externally imposed costs.

A further dimension to corporate sanctions is the recognition that their effectiveness is increased if they are combined with prosecution and punishment of senior managers within the company. And paradoxically, despite a resistance to the notion of corporate liability, the civil law jurisdictions of Europe sometimes show more willingness to prosecute company directors following corporate negligence. The common law recognizes corporate liability but is reluctant to employ it. What is evident is a tendency to harmonize. France and the Netherlands both now allow for corporate prosecutions and in the common law states, the issue of corporate responsibility is much more than a theoretical possibility and companies are alert to the threat of a manslaughter prosecution.

To conclude, corporate responsibility presents a conundrum. However hard one looks for the essence of the corporation, the role of individual employees, managers, and directors cannot be above scrutiny. Because most economic activity is carried out by corporations, their potential for causing injury, both physical and financial, to their employees, their customers, the general public, and the national economy cannot be overstated. Corporate defendants are highly motivated and well placed to exploit the metaphysical gap between "the company" and its members.

Also See the Following Articles

CORPORATIONS, ETHICS IN • LEGAL ETHICS, OVERVIEW

Bibliography

de Doelder, H., & Tiedemann, K. (Eds.). (1995) *Criminal liability of corporations.* Dordrecht: Kluwer Law International.
Fisse, B. & Braithwaite, J. (1993). *Corporations, crime and accountability.* Cambridge: Cambridge University Press.
French, P. (1984). *Collective and corporate responsbility.* New York: Columbia University Press.
Stone, C. (1975). *Where the law ends: The social control of corporate behavior.* New York: Harper.
Wells, C. (1993). *Corporations and criminal responsibility.* Oxford: Clarendon Press.

CORPORATIONS, ETHICS IN

Harvard University

 II. Traits of High-Performing Firms
 III. Promoting Corporate Innovation and
   Risk Taking
 IV. Promoting Corporate Responsiveness
 V. Creating Conditions that Foster
   Organizational Trust
 VI. Creating an Ethical Corporate Culture
 VII. A Realistic View of Business Ethics
 VIII. Public Policy

GLOSSARY

corporate culture The shared attitudes, values, and philosophy that influence how the managers and employees in a given organization think and act.

ethical business firm A company that has earned the respect and trust of its employees, customers, suppliers, investors, and others for striking an acceptable balance between its economic interests and the interests of all parties affected by its actions.

organizational trust Members' confidence in a firm's integrity and commitment to ethical behavior, including people's genuine concern and respect for each other.

ETHICS IN CORPORATIONS holds a curious place in the minds and hearts of many managers. On the one hand, it stands on a pedestal, something to admire and to exhort. On the other hand, it has a negative aura, something associated with contentious problems, another brickbat for business practitioners to dodge. After all, the pursuit of corporate ethics can cost money, lose sales to less scrupulous competitors, drain management time and energy, cause discontent where none existed, and give rise to unrealistic expectations as to how a corporation should or should not function. The problem with this thinking is that it ignores the risks and opportunity costs of not acting to ensure ethical behavior. Companies have been fined and their operations restricted by court orders; executives have been jailed. Loss of good will in the trade, personal embarrassment, and other negative consequences can result from misconduct. The benefits are also readily apparent. They include: the sense of personal pride and satisfaction that people can derive from being part of a fair-minded organization; the avoidance of costly litigation and crippling scandals; improved corporate relationships with customers, suppliers, investors, and the community at large; and, most important, the generation of conditions that favor individual and organizational creativity and initiative. The experiences of some of the world's most successful companies reveal ethical behavior to be a critical factor contributing to long-term superior performance. A growing realization of this causal relationship

Encyclopedia of Applied Ethics, Volume 1
Copyright © 1998 by Academic Press. All rights of reproduction in any form reserved.
661

among business leaders is likely to do more for moving ethics from window-dressing status to core concern than preaching and punishments could ever accomplish.

I. CORPORATE EXCELLENCE

Our analysis starts with the questions: "What is it that sets corporations who compete successfully over the long-term apart from the pack?" "Why are so many of the world's large corporations like fancy cars with powerful V-8 engines running on only three or four cylinders?"

To answer these questions, we need to consider how firms gain and sustain competitive advantage. As the world's highest market-value corporation ($137 billion as of May 1996) and one of its most successful enterprises over the past 15 years, General Electric (GE) can shed some light on achieving corporate excellence. CEO and chairman of the board Jack Welch begins his letter in the 1993 annual report by telling shareholders that despite economic weakness in several of the company's global markets, GE posted its best results in a history stretching back more than a century. After citing a list of impressive accomplishments with respect to revenues, earnings, cash flow, productivity, and the like, he goes on to explain the reason for this level of performance:

> We run this Company on a simple premise: the only way to win, in the brutally competitive global environment in which we operate, is to get more output from less input in all 12 of our businesses and, by doing so, become the lowest-cost producer of high-quality goods and services in the world.

> We believe the only way to gain more output from less input—to grow and win—is to engage every mind within our businesses—exciting, energizing, involving and rewarding everyone.

This important theme is restated in the chairman's letters in the 1994 and 1995 annual reports:

> Using 100% of the minds and passion of 100% of our people in implementing the best ideas from everywhere in the world is a formula, we believe, for endless excitement, endless growth and endless renewal.

Our dream, and our plan, well over a decade ago, was simple. We set out to shape a global enterprise that preserved the classic big-company advantages—while eliminating the classic big-company drawbacks. What we wanted to build was a hybrid, an enterprise with the reach and resources of a big company—the body of a big company—but the thirst to learn, the compulsion to share and the bias for action—the soul—of a small company.

With reference to the tendency for people in large corporations to build layers and walls between themselves and others that "inhibit creativity, waste time, restrict vision, smother dreams and, above all, slow things down," Welch points to the need for leaders at every level who can energize, excite and coach rather than enervate, depress and control. He explains:

> To be blunt, the two quickest ways to part company with GE are, one, to commit an integrity violation, or, two, to be a controlling, turf-defending, oppressive manager who can't change and who saps and squeezes people rather than excites and draws out their energy and creativity. We can't force creativity and energy from our teams—they have to give it—but we have to have it to win.

> We delayered. We removed ... much of the extensive command structure and staff apparatus we used to run the Company.... We cleared out stifling bureaucracy, along with the strategic planning apparatus, corporate staff empires, rituals, endless studies and briefings, and all the classic machinery that makes big-company operations smooth and predictable—but often glacially slow. As the underbrush of bureaucracy was cleared away, we began to see and talk to each other more clearly and more directly.

II. TRAITS OF HIGH-PERFORMING FIRMS

A. Ambitious Goals

Welch's comments reveal several traits that high-performing firms share. One is a highly spirited organization with aggressive goals. Welch describes the excitement that high hurdles can generate in an organization:

Across this Company, stretch targets are making seemingly impossible goals exciting, bringing out the best from our teams.

Stretch *does not* mean "commitments are out." Stretch can only occur in an environment where everyone is totally committed to a rigid set of core values—integrity, trust, quality, boundaryless behavior—and to outperforming everyone of our global competitors in every market environment.

Stretch *does* mean we are not fixated on a meaningless, internally derived, annual budget number that does nothing but make bureaucrats comfortable.

A stretch atmosphere replaces a grim, headsdown determination to be as good as you *have* to be, and asks, instead, how good *can* you be?

This same explicit attention to aggressive goals can be found in every highly-successful company. One example is the Johnson & Johnson (J&J) statement of strategic direction that then-chairman James Burke had issued in 1980:

We are dedicated to exceptionally high growth. To achieve this we must be well-positioned in growth markets, and each management must be aggressively innovative and strive to grow faster than the markets in which it competes.

Important as it is, getting an organization excited and stretched is only part of the challenge, and possibly not the most difficult. Once the firm is a leader in its field, with high returns, management then has to guard against organizational complacency and arrogance. Left unattended, these attitudes can spread like cancer, crippling corporate effectiveness and leading to performance setbacks. Many formerly leading companies, notably General Motors and IBM in recent years, fell victim to these organizational nemesies.

B. Ample Business Opportunities

A second trait of outstanding firms is the continuing ability to generate an adequate supply of attractive business opportunities to satisfy the organization's performance expectations.

The GE annual reports give some idea of the attractive business prospects that the company is looking to develop:

GE revenues from outside the United States continued to outpace our domestic growth. In Europe, they totaled more than $9 billion in 1994. More importantly, our businesses are well positioned for another year of significant net income growth as the European economy continues to recover ... Globalization continued with double-digit top-line growth in the key emerging markets of Mexico, India, China and Southeast Asia.

This is a Company focusing on huge growth opportunities as we look to the millennium—a GE that renews itself constantly, exhilarates itself with speed and freshens itself by constant learning.

GE is well known for investing heavily in markets with high growth potential (e.g., medical electronics, financial) and abandoning less promising businesses, despite its leadership position and long association (e.g., small appliances, TV). Less well known is Welch's near-obsession with improving operations as a way of enhancing competitive advantage. He describes GE's principal approach to achieving operating excellence as follows: "No matter how good we are in any particular operation—and we generally are pretty good—we always find someone else who does it better. We now search out the leaders in each case—whether inventory control or new product introduction techniques— and try to learn from them. This effort has released a flood of ideas that is improving every operation in our company and, more importantly, is creating great excitement. I see each of these improved abilities as an operating tool and am doing everything possible to ensure that GE continues adding more and more to its tool kit."

In effect, the ability to position the organization so that it can achieve exciting goals calls for effective business strategies, adequate resources, superior operations, and management leadership open to risk-taking and prepared to move fast. It also calls for management's readiness to entertain and even promote radical solutions, as Welch notes in discussing the nature of the challenge associated with stretch goals:

The CEO of Yokogawa, our Japanese partner in the Medical Systems business, calls this concept "bullet-train thinking," i.e., if you want to double its speed, you have to break out of both conventional thinking and conventional performance expectations.

C. Clear Standards of Behavior

A third important trait in this kind of highly charged corporate environment, as implied in Welch's brief reference (cited earlier) to the consequences of an integrity violation in GE, is the presence of clear limits and prohibitions to help focus energies in productive paths and to safeguard against improper actions. Welch's admonition regarding integrity violations was also forcefully stated in his letter to shareholders in GE's 1992 annual report:

> ... there is one boundary that we continue to maintain, strengthen and make clear to everyone—the boundary that says that no matter how hard we compete—here and around the world— not one foot must ever step outside the line of absolute integrity.

Most firms spell out unacceptable behavior—such as giving or receiving valuable gifts in the normal course of business, improper charging of time on project work, sexual harassment, and so on—in corporate codes of conduct and other company directives. Normal management supervision, management and financial control systems, and internal auditing all serve to ensure compliance. Companies can also employ organizational safeguards to deal with specific temptations, such as the practice of having more than one signature for large checks.

Such activities treat integrity in a narrow sense. They emphasize compliance with laws and regulations. Welch, however, defines integrity in much different terms, as having to do with basic human behavior characterized by openness and trust. Indeed, an examination of outstanding corporations reveals their ability to discourage improper behavior by inspiring concern and respect for others. For example, Johnson & Johnson's success in animating its credo—with its emphasis on serving customers, employees, the communities in which it operates, and the share owners—helps the organization to have a positive mindset about what one should and should not do to conduct business in a proper way.

The emphasis on trying to do what is right rather than not doing what is wrong might seem a quibble. The distinction, however, has important practical implications. The problem with proscriptions, as so evident in the tax courts, is that no set of complex rules and regulations can prevent some smart, determined person from finding a loop hole or some way around. The more complex the situation and the more at stake, the less likely are prohibitions to work. In contrast, while also vulnerable to pressures and uncertainty, people inspired to do things right are more likely to find courses of action involving acceptable behavior, if only because they struggle to this end.

It is important to understand how these three elements—ambitious goals, ample opportunities, clear standards of behavior—interrelate with each other. The stronger the pressures for performance, the greater must be the availability of valid business opportunities so as not to frustrate the organization. The less able the firm is to provide enough business opportunities to satisfy organizational ambitions, the greater the need for limits and controls to prevent people in the organization from taking improper actions to meet their goals. In effect, the combination of business opportunities and organizational safeguards must be adequate to channel the pressures for performance in constructive directions. When they fall short, companies risk involvement in questionable actions. Just consider the experiences of companies like Prudential Securities, charged with defrauding 400,000 investors, C.R. Bard, charged with illegal alteration and marketing of catheters, and National Medical Enterprises, charged with filing $522 million in fraudulent psychiatric claims. Bad companies? Amoral managers? The answer is generally no. These companies, along with most of the other firms that have committed legal and ethical improprieties, pride themselves as sound and upright organizations. Their fault probably lay in not accommodating their pressures for financial performance with adequate legitimate business opportunities and sufficiently strong safeguards.

Some people point to less ambitious corporate goals as one possible way to avoid these kinds of problems. But corporate excellence implies superior performance and, in turn, demanding goals. Because safeguards rarely add directly to financial and operational performance, the means for achieving such goals, then, has to be in generating attractive business opportunities.

Along with hustle, adequate resources, and their fair share of good luck, the way leading firms generate a continuing supply of attractive business opportunities is by means of *innovation and responsiveness*. Such firms are innovative with respect to their products and services, their business strategies, and their operations. And the results of this innovation are responsive to the needs and interests of their customers, suppliers, and other significant parties, and to the opportunities and threats relevant to their businesses.

III. PROMOTING CORPORATE INNOVATION AND RISK TAKING

Consider what it takes for a company to be innovative and self-renewing over time. Clearly, it must have smart people who understand the business and are capable of foreseeing potential opportunities and threats. This condition applies both to the people who are in a position to initiate new business undertakings and those who can commit the necessary corporate resources. Having able people, however, is in itself not enough.

People in an organization, able as they might be, also have to be *willing* to create and advocate innovative ideas. And senior-level managers have to be willing to ferment fresh thinking and commit resources to attractive but unproven, and usually unprovable, initiatives. But as any experienced manager knows, major innovations in business normally involve considerable uncertainty and risk. They require making decisions with incomplete information, challenging established views, and facing an uncertain chain of events and outcomes. They can also mean upsetting established relationships with suppliers and customers, unsettling entrenched approaches to manufacturing and marketing products, and realigning the power and influence of individual managers.

Because intended benefits of major organizational changes are generally far more uncertain than the associated costs, a case can always be made for maintaining the status quo or for making marginal or tentative adjustments. Advocating bold strategic moves and highly innovative proposals typically carries personal risks, because the creative analysis can rarely be proven— depending as it does on conjectural insights and difficult judgments—and because radical changes are likely to meet with opposition. Consequently, many good ideas never see the light of day because of the originator's fears of being discredited as naive, confused, foolhardy, or worse. And even where bold initiatives are approved and put into play, the champion still runs the risk that the effort might fail because of inadequate organizational support, radical competitive reactions, or some other unpredictable development. It is little wonder that people's reluctance to run such a gauntlet of career risks is possibly one of the most underrated obstacles to innovation in medium and large business firms.

While certain organizational processes—such as the use of teams, appropriate measures of performance, and rewards for success—can encourage innovation, people's willingness to stick out their necks is strongly influenced by their downside risks ... how they expect to be treated should difficulties arise or their proposed course of action fail to meet expectations. They must believe that their superiors respect them and will treat them in a positive and constructive manner.

They must also be able to trust others in the organization to act responsibly and in good faith in dealing with innovation and change. For new business ideas to succeed in practice, what is of vital importance in all but the smallest firms is an organization disposed to cooperation and support rather than to internal suspicion and petty bickering. The successful outcome of major business initiatives by one unit in an organization often depends on the willingness of other operating and functional departments to give constructive advice and encouragement during the early stages, while new ideas are still imperfect and vulnerable, and needed support when problems arise during implementation.

Feeling valued and secure, people are more willing to put forward unconventional ideas and to engage in constructive give and take. But gaining this kind of trust depends on well-established organizational values by which people act with integrity and treat others with consideration and dignity when things go wrong as well as when they go right.

Senior management's willingness to back new ideas and its attitude toward failure go a long way in explaining J&J's impressive record of success. The Medipren story characterizes the manner in which initiative and failure are handled. When a group of managers in 1986 proposed launching a nonprescription pain reliever containing Ibuprofen, then-Chairman James Burke opposed the idea, arguing that the competition had too great a head start. But when his subordinates continued to advocate the move, he gave permission to proceed. In July 1992, Johnson & Johnson stopped selling Medipren. According to the executive who had overseen the launch, no one was penalized for the failure. This outcome was in keeping with senior management's view that corporate growth necessarily involves the legitimate risk of backing some losers in the search for winners. This same attention to encouraging risk-takers and treating them with respect is also evident in the following comments by David Aycock, former president of the highly successful Nucor Corporation:

> The most destructive force with respect to innovation is to make scapegoats of the people involved in a failed initiative. When management approves a project, it assumes a co-responsibility. It should share in the blame—if there is to be blame—as well as in the glory.

In effect, to unleash the creative energies of an organization, its people must trust that they are treated with respect under any circumstance, so long as they act sensibly and responsibly.

IV. PROMOTING CORPORATE RESPONSIVENESS

Promoting corporate responsiveness is not unlike promoting innovation, only different people are also involved. Corporate responsiveness depends in part on gaining critical insights about relevant future developments from customers, suppliers, and other outsiders who are in a position to provide good information on a timely basis. This kind of information is more likely to be given when these parties hold the company in esteem and expect a fair exchange of value. Customers might hope for improved products or services or simply to ensure the health of a good supplier. Suppliers might hope for an improved relationship that could lead to larger or more secure purchases. All outsiders are likely to expect a *quid pro quo* in exchanging valuable information and a reassurance that the receiver would never willingly use the information in a way that might hurt them.

Once again, we are dealing with trust. Senior management's reputation for fair-mindedness as well as for business savvy can help to inspire such cooperative relationships.

V. CREATING CONDITIONS THAT FOSTER ORGANIZATIONAL TRUST

The logic is compelling. For people to expose themselves in promoting new business opportunities and new ways of doing things, they have to believe that the potential personal rewards outweigh the personal costs and that they are not risking their careers. This means that they have to trust their bosses, peers, and others in the organization to be supportive.

For long-term, sustained corporate excellence, this trust must be based on ethical and moral principles. It is true that unscrupulous firms can reap financial success by being innovative and taking bold risks. But one need only read Michael M. Lewis's account of Salomon Brothers in the 1980s to appreciate that "honor among thieves" can be fickle. Based on fear or greed, this honor can unravel when individuals find it to their advantage to act in their own self-interest. And the very possibility

of this unraveling diminishes the level of trust that people engaged in unethical activities can have in each other. In contrast, the really great corporations are those where senior managers succeed in motivating their people to behave ethically in all their business dealings.

Consistency and comprehensiveness are important dimensions of ethical behavior. Trust cannot be built on isolated or selective acts of good will. I cannot fully trust people who treat me well on some occasions and shabbily on others, depending on what is in their best interest. Nor can I fully trust people who might treat me well but treat others uncaringly, because such behavior invites questions as to why one is receiving special treatment and when might it be my turn to be used or abused. A cartoon depicting a car repair shop with a sign stating, "We overcharge the other customers and pass on the savings to you!" reveals the folly of regarding moral integrity and sincerity as anything but all-inclusive and seamless.

VI. CREATING AN ETHICAL CORPORATE CULTURE

Creating an ethical corporate culture turns out to be far more difficult than many business practitioners realize. For one thing, management has to set out with the right reasons. Too many U.S. corporations initiate ethics programs primarily to stay out of trouble. Rather than energizing, this negative perspective—characterized by a legalistic approach involving detailed formal codes of conduct, training sessions focusing almost exclusively on employee proscriptions, and threats of termination, fines, and jail—tends to stifle an organization. A typical reaction is the cynicism expressed by a dedicated and accomplished middle-senior level line manager of a leading U.S. chemical manufacturing company to the requirement that he attest in writing once a year to having read and agreed to the company's code of conduct, "I don't even read all that garbage anymore. All the Mickey Mouse is just so that top management can cover its collective rear-end."

This heavy-handed approach is not at all what goes on in companies that really motivate their people to conduct business in an ethical manner. In these companies, senior management lays out the firm's obligations to employees as well as the employees' obligations to the firm. For these managements, encouraging good behavior is as important as discouraging bad behavior, and business ethics is seen to pertain to any decision or action that has an impact on someone or other, and not to be limited to those actions that might lead to costly legal or public consequences for the company.

A. Informed Leadership

Creating and maintaining a corporate culture where trust can thrive is the job of senior line management. This means that these managers have to be informed, committed, and involved. The task cannot be delegated to some staff person or department. The companies most successful in achieving organizational pride and commitment to mutual respect are those where senior managers have consciously developed sensitivity to and understanding of the ethical dimensions of their decisions by encouraging open discussions of these matters. Business leaders who succeed in promoting high standards of behavior keep informed about ethical issues relevant to their companies by exchanging views with many different people and addressing specific situations rather than moral abstractions. As a result, their values and ethical concerns are perceived throughout their organizations as meaningful and sincere. While management's concerns alone will not ensure a company's ethical performance, they represent the critical starting point in giving direction and setting the right tone for the entire process of managing corporate ethics.

B. Successful Management

Senior management must also ensure that the business is well managed in all other respects. Poor operating performance invites attempts to overstep the line of acceptable behavior in order to avoid the consequences of failure. As one senior manager perceptively noted: "The most unethical behavior in business is poor management."

C. Promoting Ethical Behavior

With a foundation of ethical sensitivity and a well-directed business in place, top management is then in a position to promote organizational concern for the interests of all parties affected by the firm's operations. As would be true in introducing or upgrading most organizational processes, senior managers would give inspirational talks, provide training, and assign staff responsibilities to gain organizational commitment. However, in attempting to shape basic organizational values, they should never limit themselves to such special efforts, as happens in many companies boasting ethics programs. Instead, they must be prepared to involve the powerful, core organizing and motivating mechanisms already in use in directing and operating the firm, such as reporting relationships, planning and control systems, and performance evaluation. Human nature being what it is, if ethical behavior is not explicitly measured, and rewarded, it is not likely to receive the serious attention that it requires.

D. Ethical People

Creating the organizational trust that can enable the creativity and risk taking essential to corporate excellence is every bit as demanding of senior management as would be to redirect corporate strategy or to restructure the organization. No ethics program, however good, can succeed if the people involved do not value the basic ethical precepts that the company is espousing. Business ethics ultimately depends on the moral inclinations of the people doing the work of the corporation. For this reason, the great firms staff and surround themselves with outstanding people who are honest and fair-minded. Proper staffing calls for recruiting people with strong moral values as well as strong business skills. It also calls for helping them to connect their personal values to their work activities. And, finally, proper staffing requires senior managers to place operationally qualified people who are also skillful in providing moral leadership in positions where they can have the greatest effect on others in the organization. Former U.S. Treasury Secretary and Unisys CEO W. Michael Blumenthal had this point in mind when he noted that he was most likely to run into difficulty in hiring and promoting senior level managers when he put "intelligence and energy ahead of morality."

The idea of staffing an organization with outstanding people who are honest and fair-minded can sensibly be extended to include the selection of influential third parties—legal and financial advisors, management consultants, advertising agents, suppliers, strategic alliance partners, and even major customers—who are likely to uphold and support rather than subvert the company's ethical climate. In avoiding dependencies on unscrupulous outsiders, senior management eliminates potential sources of unhealthy temptations and pressures.

Figure 1 provides an overview of the basic argument in this paper. In practice, business leaders must start with the four prerequisite actions for a corporate culture of respect and fairness.

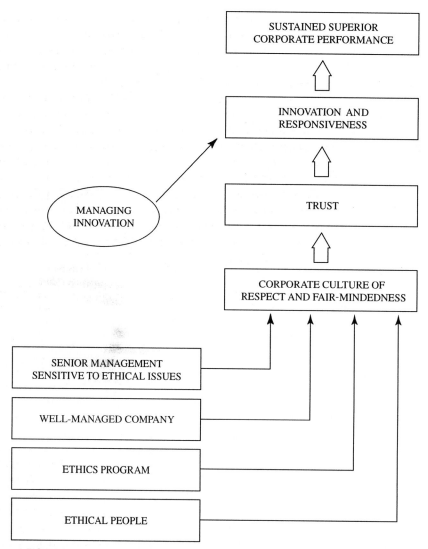

FIGURE 1   Overview of the Relationship between Ethics and Corporate Performance.

VII. A REALISTIC VIEW OF BUSINESS ETHICS

Business ethics poses somewhat of a dilemma for many business practitioners. On the one hand, it is something wholesome and uplifting and is quite often placed on a pedestal by its advocates and devotees. On the other hand, it is usually connected with troubles and can invite unfair criticisms about the way the company is run. For a realistic view of business ethics it is necessary to recognize its practical limits and the full burden that its diligent application requires as well as the potential benefits.

To behave ethically does not require a person or an organization to become a bleeding heart, engaging in every good cause that one encounters. Just where the dividing line between business ethics and philanthropy or social awareness lies can be difficult to define. For example, in a cover story on managing by values at Levi Strauss, *Business Week* asked if the company's emphasis on "values" distracted it from the nuts and bolts of running its business. It quoted a Levi's director as expressing concern with the risks of management getting carried away with its lofty vision of how to run a modern corporation: "There's a danger that this will degrade into a touchy-feely, I-don't-want-to-offend-you, creativity-stifling style of management. . . . the challenge for Levi's is to be sure that decisions are not just 'nice' decisions, but decisions that are meant to enhance shareholder value." This comment calls attention to the importance of selecting suitable and discarding inappropriate issues when acting in the name of business ethics. For a CEO arbitrarily to include marginal or controversial causes without troubling to gain broader support runs a risk of discrediting the whole process.

Relatedly, it is also important not to create false expectations regarding the benefits that business ethics provides. Having an ethical firm in which trust abounds does not ensure innovation and risk-taking. These desired outcomes also depend on organizational processes that encourage, select, strengthen, and carry out the breakthrough innovative ideas that excellent corporations seek. IBM is a good example of a highly ethical company that lost its way by becoming stodgy and myopic in its technological responsiveness.

As noted earlier, it is also possible for firms to be innovative—at least in the short run—without being ethical or having the kind of organizational trust discussed above. In this regard, some people have questioned the appropriateness of GE as a reference company in arguing the critical importance of trust and ethics to corporate excellence. They ask, "How can GE be considered an ethical company with a track record that includes a recent indictment for anticompetitive actions in the industrial diamond business, a \$350 million scandal in its Kidder, Peabody unit, and several alleged violations over the years in the aerospace business?"

This history is instructive in several regards. First, allegations are no proof of wrongdoing. Corporations are open to attacks that are malicious, mistaken, or simply the outcome of conflicting interpretations of law or evidence as well as to those that are justified. In the industrial diamond litigation, for example, a federal judge took the almost unprecedented step of throwing out the government's case against GE for lack of evidence. Attacks that are unwarranted can nonetheless severely undermine the credibility of senior management's ethical leadership unless firmly countered in word and deed.

Second, in any large, dynamic company, no matter how well managed and how firmly committed to the ethical conduct of business, ethics violations are bound to occur as the result of ignorance, error, or self-serving on the part of individual employees. When a firm is guilty of wrongdoing, management needs to own up and take corrective actions quickly. In this connection, according to a GE spokesperson, when a GE employee schemed with an Israeli general to divert government money for their own use, GE promptly informed the government, cooperated fully in the government's in-

vestigation, took decisive actions against those who had allowed the scheme to continue, and promptly settled with the government rather than enter lengthy litigation. In the Kidder, Peabody fraud, GE considered itself to be the victim when a single employee allegedly inflated his profits in order to improve the appearance of his performance.

How quickly and competently senior management deals with ethical violations determines the impact that they are likely to have on the organization's commitment to high standards of behavior. In this connection, the Israeli and industrial diamond cases were used throughout GE for instructional purposes to indicate that employees who commit wrongdoings will be punished and those who are innocent have nothing to fear. According to sources in the company, this message has been communicated with passion and repetition. To reinforce the message, the annual human resources review takes into account each manager's commitment to integrity.

Perhaps most important to this discussion of GE's ethical character is the recognition that managers engaged in elevating ethical standards of organizational behavior face many added difficulties when compared to those in companies with well-established ground rules. Welch is clearly out to change the GE culture by attempting to replace a century-old tradition of managers measuring their self-worth by the number of their subordinates and by being "on top of things" with a new spirit of delegation and empowerment. In calling for integrity, he is also setting limits to the macho, hard-driving, got-to-win values that have long dominated managers' behavior. To his credit, Welch recognizes the challenge he faces in gaining organizational adherence to a new culture: "The top group of 36 or so people are living the new values. We behave like a group of friends who are ready to help each other whenever needed. Getting this spirit deep in the GE organization is still a problem. Flattening the company's organization helps some to penetrate the lower levels with this message."

In any organizational transition of this magnitude, it is easy for people to be torn between new edicts and old norms and to be unsure about how to reconcile stricter standards of behavior with unrelenting goals for performance. Mistakes are bound to happen. What is critical is how Welch and other senior managers go about changing these organizational values.

Continually emphasizing integrity—both in talk and in print—is one way Welch seeks to strengthen this underpinning to the GE culture. He highlights its importance in every appearance at the GE Management

Development Institute and made it the centerpiece of his closing remarks at the annual operating managers meeting on January 5, 1995. On compliance and integrity, he said:

> We want you to use the diamond case as a positive, uplifting experience. For those who follow the policies, who live by the law, we will stand behind them and support them to the hilt. We'll put our reputations on the line, our Company and our personal reputations to battle for them. For those who don't, there is no support.... Be sure your employees know exactly where you stand on compliance. You must walk the talk with no chance of a misunderstanding of just exactly where you stand. There is no shortcut to being the best in business and at the same time being the most ethical in the business community.

Welch concluded his talk to the operating managers with an uplifting rationale as to why integrity can and will dominate the GE culture:

> You and I all have a myriad of options. We could be doing anything we want. We are here because we choose to be here.... Why would you be in a culture that wasn't the absolute best? You'd never participate in a place that didn't have the highest integrity in the world.... You're here because you like stretch, you like high performance, you like to be the best, you like to win—and you hate to lose. You are the very best, and you wouldn't be in a place that had any ethics that were wrong for anything in the world.

Welch clearly recognizes that the quest for integrity at GE calls for his direct leadership and deep personal involvement. Progress can be slow, setbacks can happen, and the effort is unending. But the payoff is well worth the effort. Business experience clearly shows business ethics to be a necessary condition for sustained, long-term organizational innovation and responsiveness. As Jack Welch concluded his letter to shareholders, "... people, excited ... and inspired ..., have an absolutely infinite capacity to improve everything." The great challenge for business leaders is to tap this capacity, and trust is critical to this end.

VIII. PUBLIC POLICY

Experience shows that high-minded appeals for virtuous business dealings, however much good they do,

fall far short of promoting universal concern for the common good. Recourse to laws and regulations also fail to curb many legal and ethical transgressions and abuses. What is also needed is to have business leaders understand the critical role that ethical behavior plays in generating long-term corporate success and consequently to favor responsible business practice as a matter of self interest.

To develop such understanding, public and private institutions and individuals engaged in protecting and promoting the common good must launch major efforts to educate business practitioners—managers and employees—the world over about the basic connections between business ethics, organizational trust, and sustained corporate success. Explaining how to foster ethical business behavior in large corporations is a crucial part of the message in light of the subtle and unforgiving managerial challenges associated with this process. Indeed, many business leaders who acknowledge business ethics as relevant to their firms' operations fall prey to underestimating the difficulties associated with developing true organizational commitment to this cause. This error perhaps has done more to undermine progress in motivating responsible business behavior than anything else.

Publicizing and celebrating highly successful business leaders and companies that have reputations for conducting business with high ethical standards is an effective means for calling attention to the potential benefits of responsible business practice. One way to start is by featuring articles and stories in business and general news media that describe their accomplishments and the reasons for their successes. Prominent and highly regarded local executives and firms along with exemplary global corporate heads and organizations can serve as powerful inducements and attractive models for other firms. In time, such parties can be showcased through awards at local, regional, national, and global levels, much as the Deming Awards recognize companies for achieving superior quality standards or Nobel and Oscar awards celebrate individual achievements.

To further inculcate the concepts in common thinking, teaching materials and curricula that examine the role of ethical business behavior in supporting innovation and responsiveness—key ingredients for long-term corporate success—need to be developed for executive education and degree programs. In parallel with management education, individual business firms need to be encouraged to develop and offer in-house development programs that inform employees as to why and how they should behave so as to contribute to a trusting corporate culture.

Peer pressure within the business community is likely to be one of the most powerful means for encouraging higher business standards. In medieval times, the guilds performed this function to a degree. No successor institution has ever filled the subsequent void. Along these lines, then, a longer term policy objective might be to form a business elite that would provide leadership in merging self-interest and the common good. The following explanation of General Mills' heavy involvement in community services illustrates this point:

The maintenance of the Company headquarters in the Minneapolis-St. Paul business community has kept General Mills in an environment that has consistently encouraged responsibility to society, support of the arts, education, and social services, and enlightened attitudes toward competitive practices and employee relations. Aggressive activities by executives heading the area's leading companies have resulted in companies competing with each other in support of community activities. The senior officers of many of the area's leading companies work together on the boards of non-profit organizations and encourage, if not cajole, each other to high levels of community involvement.

Bridging the apparent gulf separating self-interest and common good is not a matter of force fitting but rather one of inspired business practice. Developing socially responsible solutions to difficult business challenges is far more difficult than adopting conventional, self-serving, *caveat emptor* responses. But the extra effort can lead to long-term corporate success, as Welch argues, by "tapping an ocean of creativity, passion and energy that, as far as we can see, has no bottom and no shores."

Also See the Following Articles

CONSUMER RIGHTS • CORPORATE RESPONSIBILITY • EXECUTIVE COMPENSATION • IMPROPER PAYMENTS AND GIFTS • MERGERS AND ACQUISITIONS

Bibliography

Aguilar, F. (1994) *Managing corporate ethics*. New York: Oxford University Press.

Aguilar, F. (1992). *General managers in action* (2nd ed.). New York: Oxford University Press.

Andrews, K. (1988) "Ethics in policy and practice at general mills," In *Corporate ethics: A prime business asset*. New York: Business Roundtable.

Lewis, M. (1989). *Liar's Poker*. New York: Norton.

Waters, J. and Bird, F. The moral dimensions of organizational culture. *Journal of Business Ethics*. **6**, 1, 15–22.

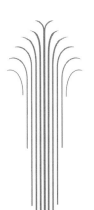

COURTROOM PROCEEDINGS, REPORTING OF

Rupert Read,* Max Travers†
*University of Manchester, †Buckinghamshire College

GLOSSARY

defendant The accused person in a court case.

freedom of speech The right to speak or write whatever one wishes, so long as the speech itself does not constitute a harmful *action*.

journalistic practice What journalists—reporters—actually do.

party In a legal case, the person(s) on one side or another of it.

plaintiff The accusing person in a court case, "the complainant," "the wronged party."

rape-shield laws These are laws designed to protect—"shield"—an alleged rape victim from having to reveal her *prior sexual history* to the court (thereby also restricting the availability of that information to the press). The term is also sometimes used to refer to laws shielding her from having to have her *identity* revealed to the public.

COURTROOM PROCEEDINGS, that is, what happens in courts of whatever type, are generally highly routin-ized and routine affairs (although of course not without consequence to the parties to them). The reporting of such proceedings is normally a similarly routine matter—if it occurs at all, it will generally be very brief and entirely uncontroversial. It will be a public record of certain ordinary matters of public record.

In major trials, court cases of distinctive public interest, the (more detailed) reporting of the proceedings will take on additional importance. In particular, concerns may arise about the prejudicing (in one direction or another) of the trial by widespread or biased reporting. It is then that the mode of (and any limits imposed upon) the reporting of courtroom proceedings is most likely to become a matter of distinctive ethical interest.

I. INTRODUCTION

The extent to which the press should be allowed to report courtroom proceedings has been an issue for public debate and discussion in America for many years and is increasingly becoming an issue in Britain. This review will examine some possible applications of ethics, as a branch of applied philosophy, in this area of human conduct. It will begin by providing a historical account of the relationship between courts and the press in America and Britain, providing illustrations of how both reporting, and restrictions on reporting, have been viewed as a problem. It will then consider the ways in which different philosophical perspectives can perhaps assist in clarifying the issues raised in these debates. Finally, it will consider the prospects for incorporating ethical standards into this area of journalistic practice, and it will make a critical point about the purpose of ethical codes in the professions.

II. THE RELATIONSHIP BETWEEN COURTS AND PRESS IN AMERICA AND BRITAIN

American courts have only recently taken measures to prevent journalists gaining access to the courtroom, as a result of growing public concern about the prejudice suffered by defendants in a number of trials during the 1960s. Restrictions on the freedom of the British press to report court proceedings date back to the eighteenth century, and give judges wide powers to hold journalists in contempt of court for publishing material that prejudices the outcome of trials. The objective of courts, and legal authorities, in each country has been to preserve the principle of "the open court" (i.e., public access to whatever is going on in the courtroom—which is regarded as a fundamental safeguard of justice), while at the same time preserving the right of the defendant to a fair trial. It is recognized by all commentators that it will not always be possible to reconcile these two principles, and that there will always be some potential for conflict between the press and the courts.

A. Restrictions on the Press in America

In America, the two opposing principles relating to reporting courtrooms are enshrined in the U.S. Constitution. The First Amendment states that "Congress shall make no law ... abridging the freedom of speech, or of the press." The U.S. Supreme Court has stated that "with respect to judicial proceedings in particular, the function of the press serves to guarantee the fairness of trials and to bring to bear the beneficial effects of public scrutiny on the administration of justice" (*Cox Broadcasting Co. vs. Cohn,* 420 US 469 (1975)), and journalists continue to rely on this Amendment to oppose reporting restrictions imposed by particular courts (see, for example, *Nebraska Press Association vs. Stuart,* 427 US 539 (1976)).

The Sixth Amendment, on the other hand, provides that "in all criminal prosecutions, the accused shall enjoy the right to a speedy and public trial, by impartial jury of the State and district wherein the crime shall be committed." The extent to which freedom to report under the First Amendment prejudices this right has always been a matter for concern and debate in American public life, especially since the infamous Lindbergh baby kidnapping trial in the 1930s, in which some accused parties were given a severe "trial by the press" before and alongside their actual trial in court.

In its investigation into the 1963 Kennedy assassination, the Warren Comission roundly criticized journalists for their irresponsible reporting of police leaks in the course of the investigation, complaining that—as a result—"it would have been a most difficult task to select an unprejudiced jury, either in Dallas or elsewhere." The case that produced most public discussion of the issue, and resulted in legal change, was that of Dr. Sam Sheppard, an osteopath who was convicted of murdering his wife in 1954. The Supreme Court ordered a retrial 12 years later on the grounds that the media had prejudiced his right to a fair trial. The court noted that:

> Much of the material printed or broadcast during the trial was never heard from the witness stand, such as the charges that Sheppard had purposely impeded the murder investigation [through refusing to take a lie detector test] and must be guilty since he had hired a prominent criminal lawyer; that Sheppard was a perjurer; that he had sexual relations with numerous women; and finally, that a woman convict claimed Sheppard to be the father of her illegitimate child. As the trial progressed, the newspapers summarized and interpreted the evidence, devoting particular attention to the material that incriminated Sheppard, and often drew unwarranted inference from his testimony (Kane, P. (1992). *Murder, Courts, and the Press: Issues in Free Press/Fair Trial,* p. 18. Carbondale: Southern Illinois University Press).

According to another account:

> At one point, a front-page picture of Mrs. Sheppard's blood-stained pillow was published after being re-touched to show the alleged imprint of a surgical instrument—inferentially, her husband's (Gerald, E. (1983). *News of crime: Courts and press in conflict.* Westview, CT: Greenwood Press).

The Supreme Court in the Sheppard case* urged that judges should make more use of their existing powers

---

* New DNA evidence, available only in 1997, suggests more strongly than ever that Sheppard was in fact innocent.

to protect defendants by measures such as changing the venue of trials, sequestering juries, or enabling the defense to make greater use of voir dire (a procedure designed to select jury members uncontaminated by the influence of the media). They were also asked to be more proactive in controlling the release of information by the district attorney's office and the police, and in using court orders to prevent the press publishing prejudicial stories. This was also the central recommendation of the American Bar Association's Reardon Committee in 1966, which drew up professional standards for lawyers and judges in their dealings with the press. These included placing an obligation on the media not to report a defendant's previous convictions before or during a trial.

Since 1966, there have been a whole raft of Supreme Court appeals relating to this issue. Some have been brought by *defendants,* complaining that they have been denied their constitutional right to a fair trial (O. J. Simpson, for example, could and very probably would have tried to appeal on these grounds, if he had been convicted of murdering his wife and her companion in his infamous 1995 criminal trial). Others have been brought by the press, seeking to protect their first amendment rights against "gagging orders" (e.g., *Nebraska Press Association vs. Stuart,* 427 US 539 (1976)). Finally, there have been a few suggestions recently that the increasingly fine-grained nature of the spotlight that the media is able to apply to the evidence and so on in high-profile cases may—if the defense uses the opportunity effectively—work against *plaintiffs,* through making it more difficult to successfully prosecute high-profile defendants (here again, the O. J. Simpson case has been said by some to be a case in point).

In general terms, it would seem that the Supreme Court sees its role as preserving the freedom of the press wherever possible, so that the onus lies on judges to find ways of protecting the rights of defendants without placing blanket restrictions on reporting. However, journalists have tended to argue that the press has the more difficult task of defending freedom of speech against the institutional power of the courts.

B. Restrictions on the Press in Britain

The desirability of open justice is an important principle of long standing in British law. Eighteenth-century jurist Jeremy Bentham argued that it was important for the courts to be open in order to ensure that judges behaved properly and fairly in their public duties:

Publicity is the very soul of justice. It is the keenest spur to exertion and the surest of all guards against improbity. It keeps the judge himself, while trying, under trial.

According to Robertson and Nicol, society derives a number of other important benefits from having an open system of justice:

The prospect of publicity deters perjury: witnesses are more likely to tell the truth if they know that any lie they tell might be reported, and provoke others to come forward to discredit them. Press reporting of court cases enhances public knowledge and appreciation of the working of the law, and it assists the deterrent effect of heavy sentences in criminal cases. Above all, fidelity to the open-justice principle keeps Britain free from the reproach that it permits 'secret courts' of the kind that have been instruments of repression in so many other countries (Robertson, G., & Nicol, A. (1992) *Media Law* (3rd ed.), p. 15. Hammondsworth: Penguin.).

This common-law principle is the British equivalent of America's First Amendment, although freedom of the press to report courtroom proceedings is significantly curtailed by a number of statutory and common law exceptions. To give some examples: *in America,* it is left to the discretion of the court whether to make orders preventing the press disclosing information about the identity of the alleged victims in rape trials, or of juvenile defendants, and the court has discretion to allow the media to televise courtroom hearings. *In Britain,* the Criminal Justice Acts of 1987 and 1991 govern the position on reporting juveniles (although one aim of the 1996 Criminal Justice Act, which is gradually coming into force, is to remove this protection from convicted 16- to 18-year-olds, with the aim of adding "public shaming" to the punishment they receive from the courts). The Sexual Offences (Amendment) Act 1976 responded to a decade of campaigning for a change in the law, by making it an offense to identify the complainant in rape cases. Section 41 of the Criminal Justice Act 1925, which makes it an offense to photograph or make sketches in court, effectively prevents televising court proceedings.

However, the most far-reaching restriction operating on journalists in Britain, at least in principle, is the law of contempt, which is now governed by the 1981 Contempt Act. This gives judges or the attorney general the power to impose an unlimited fine or to imprison journalists for up to 2 years for influencing the result of a court or tribunal.

It is worth noting though that when British courts have had to decide whether actions by the media amount to contempt, they have tried, wherever possible, to maintain the open-court principle, by finding that, although stories in the press may be prejudicial, they still need not affect the outcome of trials. The judge in the Jeremy Thorpe murder case dealt with the problem of two prejudicial books by asking prospective jurors to stand down if they had read either of the books.

But perhaps the best example of the reluctance of British appeal court judges to support the widespread use of contempt orders can be found in their views about the susceptibility of jurors to media influence. In the trial of two well-known London gangsters, the Krays, the judge observed that "I have enough confidence in my fellow countrymen to think that they have got the newspapers sized up and they are capable of looking at the matter fairly and without prejudice even though they may have to disregard what they read in a newspaper" (see p. 342 of Robertson and Nicol, 1992). In another case, the Court of Appeal noted that juries tend to forget reporting that took place a long time before the trial. This was because "an inward-looking atmosphere built up during the trial and the jury and judge tended less and less as the trial proceeded to look outwards and more and more to look inwards at the evidence and arguments being addressed to them" (*Gee vs. BBC* (1986), 136 NLJ515, CA).

Robertson and Nicol argue that, notwithstanding this judicial reluctance to restrict the press, journalists and editors in Britain take the threat of being held in contempt seriously, to the extent of being unduly cautious in reporting news relating to the courts, in a way that would astonish journalists in America. There has, however, been a flurry of recent cases that have considerably raised the temperature of debate in Britain.

Perhaps the most-influential of these cases was that of the Taylor sisters in 1994, in which their conviction for murdering Alison Shaughnessy, the wife of Michelle Taylor's former lover, was quashed by the Court of Appeal on the grounds that the outcome of the trial had been affected by reporting in a number of tabloid newspapers. One front-page article in *The Sun* showed a still photograph taken from a video of Alison Shaughnessy's wedding that appeared to show Michelle Taylor kissing the groom full on the mouth (whereas the video viewed as a whole shows that it was an innocent "peck on the cheek"). This was published under the title "Cheats' Kiss." The Taylors spent 11 months in prison, and in 1995 made an (ultimately unsuccessful) attempt

in the High Court to force the attorney general to make a contempt order against the offending newspapers.

Since then judges have become more outspoken in criticizing the press. When there was extensive newspaper coverage of the previous convictions of Geoff Knight (the boyfriend of the soap opera actress Gillian Taylforth), the judge abandoned the trial, complaining that "I have absolutely no doubt that the mass of media publicity in the case was unfair, outrageous and oppressive." In a very recent case, the trial of six prisoners charged with breaking out of Whitemoor prison was abandoned in January 1997 as a result of the press publishing details of the involvement of five defendants in the IRA and the previous convictions of the sixth. The judge ordered the newspaper editor concerned to report in person to the court, along with the prison officials who provided the story, in order to explain why they should not be held in contempt. (Ironically, the barrister representing these defendants has suggested that the collapse of the case may represent a cover-up that prevents the public from hearing about an allegation that prison officers colluded in the escape.)

III. REPORTING COURTROOM PROCEEDINGS: AN ETHICAL PERSPECTIVE

As should be evident from the case studies considered above, it is extremely difficult to envisage the creation and enforcement of a general purpose ethical perspective on issues around the reporting of courtroom proceedings, a perspective that would be genuinely *cross-cultural* (for even between Britain and America there are deep differences as to what counts as a matter for ethical concern in this regard), and that would be able to cope with the different and specific issues raised by the *variety* of cases that any such perspective would have to handle.

Any attempt to apply, say, Utilitarian—or even Kantian—considerations to a case in which an issue has arisen as to whether reporting of a trial should be restricted by either self- or other-imposed censorship must take fully into account how the *weighting* is to be undertaken of the public right to know, the check on dishonesty in the court, the rights of the defendant and of the plaintiff to privacy, and to a fair trial, and so on. Such weighting will need to be undertaken in the light of the concrete sociopolitical context of the court and of the question that is being tried in it. It may well be, then, that the complex perspectives of the various institutional forces involved (i.e., the judge, the journalists, the parties to the case, etc.) are more evidently well-founded and grounded in reasonable precedent, than are any theoretical ethical perspectives that can be brought to bear on the issues from outside of them.

However, there may be ethical issues relating to the reporting of courtroom proceedings that are not *recognized* as significant or important by the courts or media in America or Britain, and it is possibly in *this* regard that an applied ethics perspective can be most useful, in at least helping getting these recognized *as* issues, *if* politicians or movements are not already effectively doing so. Two potential examples are:

A. Reporting Rape Trials

There is a law protecting the identity of complainants in Britain, although this is still largely a matter for the discretion of judges and the press in America. However, some—for example feminist critics of the legal system—might want to argue there are wider ethical issues, which are not recognised in debates about courtroom reporting. Soothill and Soothill (1983, Prosecuting the victim: A study of the reporting of barristers' comments in rape cases. *The Howard Journal,* 32, pp. 12–24) suggest that the media tend to portray rapists as "deviants," whereas in fact rape is a "far-reaching social problem" that affects women much more ubiquitously than the special circumstances of a rape trial might suggest. This is a much broader political critique of the role of the media, which is neglected by writers on the fair trial/free press debate. Thus, a group who might have a reasonable complaint about the media in relation to rape trials (and arguably more generally: see Lorraine Dusky (1997), *Still Unequal: The shameful truth about women and justice in America.* New York: Crown Press), are women plaintiffs. They are often exposed in the courtroom to allegations of sexual impropriety, and so on; and the harm this may cause is argued by feminist legal theorists to be massively magnified by currently operative reporting methods and newspapers' assumptions about women.

However, another group who might have just cause to feel aggrieved are the defendants. Someone accused of a crime may suffer all kinds of damage to livelihood and reputation, even if the trial ends in an acquittal and there is no bias or prejudice in the reporting. It might also be argued that the anonymity given complainants to varying degrees in rape trials, which is intended to make it easier for victims to come forward, may also make it easier to make ill-founded allegations.

B. The Myra Hindley Case

Hindley, one of "the Moors Murderers," was convicted of enticing and murdering young children in Northern England in the 1960s, and was sentenced to life imprisonment. Despite strong evidence of her having undergone a personal transformation, of having been successfully "reformed," successive British Home Secretaries have turned down her appeal for parole, partly on the grounds of public opinion. It could be argued that the media have been partially responsible by reprinting extracts from the trial, including photographs of her and her accomplice Brady taken at the time of the murders. This is perfectly legal, but supporters of Hindley and critics of the judicial system might argue that nevertheless the press are acting unethically.

IV. ETHICAL ARGUMENT AND JOURNALISTIC PRACTICE

Academics in the field of applied ethics tend to present philosophy as a means of attaining a clearer—or more rational—understanding of difficult moral dilemmas than is available to the ordinary citizen, without a philosophical training. Here are two typical statements, from a textbook on philosophy of law, and an introduction to media ethics respectively:

Legal philosophy provides clarity, intellectual order and structure and standards of rational (often moral) criticism and evaluation. It thus gives insight into the relevant questions to ask when laws are being discussed, or legal reforms are proposed, and it can help to introduce reason into areas where passion often dominates (Murphy, J., & Coleman, J. (1990) *Philosophy of Law: An Introduction to Jurisprudence.* Boulder, CO: Westview Press).

Too often … students and practitioners argue about individual sensational incidents, make case-by-case decisions, and do not stop to examine their method of moral reasoning. Instead, a pattern of ethical deliberation should be explicitly outlined in which the relevant considerations are isolated and given appropriate weight. Those who care about ethics in the media can learn to analyze the stages of decision making, focus on the real levels of conflict, and make defensible ethical decisions (Christian, C., Rotzoll, K., & Fackler, M. (1991). *Media Ethics: Cases and Moral Reasoning* (3rd ed.). New York: Longman).

In media ethics textbooks, students are usually asked to consider real or invented case studies in which there is no clear answer on dilemmas which arise in the course of day-to-day practice, and are not governed by a professional code of conduct or by law. Christian *et al.*, for example, use the example of a fire in a gay cinema, in which two local newspapers took a different view on whether they should print the names of people killed in the fire. Other examples might include the question of when it is ethical for a journalist to lie in order to obtain information that might benefit the public.

The study and discussion of ethics has only recently been taken up by bodies responsible for training journalists, and one can view this sociologically as part of a wider trend toward professionalisation in America and Britain. As Max Weber and others have noted, codes of ethics function as "gatekeepers," and are one means by which occupational groups seek to enhance their status and economic position in society; while, as many studies have shown, practitioners on the ground frequently fail to live up to the ideals envisaged by their professional associations.

In the case of the legal profession, Carlin showed that firms at the bottom end of the profession could not afford to be ethical (and indeed regarded "ethics" as a means used by firms at the top to prevent competition, by enforcing impossibly high standards). Ethical breaches which formed a routine part of practicing law in these firms for business and doing disreputable things for clients. Travers in his study of a firm of criminal lawyers representing legal aid clients, found that rules such as avoiding conflicts of interest were simply not feasible for this type of practice, in which prosecution witnesses were regularly ex-clients, and that breaches were ignored by the local courts.

The gap between professional ideals and actual practice is arguably similar in journalism; the British quality press often criticizes the tabloids for damaging the reputation of journalism as a profession. It seems unlikely that ethical reasoning (in the sense of weighing up the moral pros and cons of alternative actions) plays much part in journalistic practice when the latter is dictated by the need to "scoop" rivals in a vicious circulation war; although the necessary empirical studies of news gathering, and editorial decision-making have not yet been undertaken by British or American sociologists.

What one might predict such studies might well find, if they focused on the way in which the media report courtroom proceedings, is that editors and journalists routinely do not view this as an ethical issue, and certainly rarely if ever as one requiring the services of a philosopher, in that they see no ethical or moral problem in their task of reporting news, and in so doing making money for their proprietor. One would also imagine that they regard the law not as the embodiment of ethics, but as an obstacle they have to work with, in order to avoid being held in contempt by the courts. On this view, which is admittedly cynical about the role of ethics in the professions, teaching journalists skills of moral reasoning, while it might be worthwhile educationally, should not be expected to produce any great transformation in journalistic practice. And it may require sustained political will, including a wide-ranging critique of the organization of the media in contemporary "open" Western cultures—rather than (or—at least—as well as) intelligent applied ethics discourse—to successfully alter or "ethicalize" any aspects of legal journalism that are considered to be problematic or, more plainly put, wrong.

Also See the Following Articles

CONFIDENTIALITY, GENERAL ISSUES OF • FREEDOM OF THE PRESS IN THE USA • PRIVACY VERSUS PUBLIC RIGHT TO KNOW • RAPE • TABLOID JOURNALISM

Bibliography

Bunker, M. (1997). *Justice and the media: reconciling fair trials with a free press*. Mahwah, NJ: Lawrence Erlbaum Associates.

Carlin, J. (1976). *Lawyer's ethics: A survey of the New York bar*. New York: Russell Sage Foundation.

Fish, S. (1994). *There's no such thing as free speech ... and it's a good thing too*. New York: Oxford University Press.

Mill, J. S. (1869/1991). *On Liberty and Other Essays*. Oxford: Oxford University Press.

The Guardian (1997, January 24, p. 7). Editor faces judge as IRA jail break trial collapses.

The Guardian (1995, July 31, p. 6). Judgement day: Unprecedented high court action after two year's imprisonment.

Travers, M. (1991). *The reality of law: An ethnographic study of an inner-city law firm*. Doctoral dissertation, University of Manchester.

CRIME AND SOCIETY

Susan Dimock
York University

GLOSSARY

crime An offense against law.

deterrence A theory of punishment which claims that legal punishment is justified insofar as it facilitates future compliance with the law by deterring potential offenders.

excuses Excuses recognized in law exclude a person who has acted contrary to the law from liability to punishment, typically because the act was done unintentionally or nonvoluntarily; crimes committed under the influence of insanity, by accident, or because of coercion are typically excused, for example.

law A purposeful code of rules enacted and enforced by a governmental authority.

legal positivism The theory that positive law has the status of law just in virtue of having been enacted by the proper political authorities in a society according to some conventionally recognized procedure.

legal punishment The intentional imposition of an avoidable loss imposed by legal authorities upon an offender for an offense.

liberalism The theory that insists that political institutions be arranged so as to allow each individual the liberty and opportunities needed to realize as fully as possible his or her conception of the good life.

mitigation A reduction of the sentence a criminal is liable to after the determination of legal guilt has been established, due to the special difficulties which the particular criminal may have faced in conforming to the law; great temptation, provocation, and seriously deprived childhood circumstances may be taken to mitigate the sentence which ought to be imposed upon a particular offender.

natural law The theory that there is an eternal and self-justifying moral code binding upon all peoples, to which positive (humanly enacted) law must conform.

retributivism A theory of punishment which claims that legal offenders deserve punishment just in virtue of having committed a past offense, and that such punishment may be imposed even if doing so is not justified on utilitarian grounds.

teleological retributivism Theories that apply teleological considerations to the law, thus arguing that law serves some function, and then arguing that criminals must be punished to enable the law to perform its function.

teleology The belief that all things have an end or function, and that they cannot be fully understood without reference to that end or function.

therapeutic models of crime and punishment Models that treat crime as illness and seek to prevent crime by rehabilitating or treating those who suffer from the illnesses which result in criminal tendencies.

utilitarianism The moral theory that enjoins individuals to choose that action, rule, or law which will maximize the happiness or welfare of those affected by it.

CRIME is something which people care passionately about. Crime generates significant costs, both for the victims of crimes and for others, and significantly reduces the quality of life for members of a society. It is not surprising, therefore, that both philosophers and social scientists have devoted sustained attention to the subject of crime. But while social scientists have principally been interested in discovering what causes crime, as well as what its effects are on people variously affected by it, philosophers have been more interested in the question of how we ought to understand crime and our typical response to it, which is legal punishment. I shall be more concerned in this article with the philosophical than with the sociological and psychological questions which crime raises.

Although this entry title is "Crime and Society," I believe it will be most perspicuous to begin this paper with a discussion of society before moving on to discuss crime and our responses to it. This is because one cannot adequately understand crime without some conception of society and the role of law within it. Only once we have examined the proper place of law in society can we evaluate various approaches to crime, which we will do by examining various theories of punishment. The purpose of the discussion is to examine how liberal societies ought to understand crime law and punishment.

I. LIBERALISM

The conception of society with which we shall work is a broadly liberal one. I shall briefly describe a liberal conception of society (not the unflattering caricature that some communitarian, feminist, and Marxist critics have presented) which captures the most salient features of classical and contemporary explications of liberalism—from John Locke, John Stuart Mill, Ronald Dworkin, John Rawls, Joseph Raz, Will Kymlicka, and others of their ilk.

A. Equal Respect for Persons

Liberals begin with a conception of human individuals as the locus of value. What ultimately matters, from the moral point of view, is the happiness or well-being of people. And, moreover, the happiness or well-being of each person matters equally. The paramount principle of the resulting political morality is that the equal value of human well-being must be respected.

What exactly the entitlement to equal respect comes to is understood differently by diverse liberal theorists, of course. Those who believe that respecting the equal value of individuals requires treating the happiness or welfare of each as equally important may be drawn to utilitarian or welfarist theories. Others, who believe that respecting individuals equally requires ensuring that they enjoy equal opportunity to pursue their own happiness, will be more concerned with the distribution of opportunities and resources in society than in the final distribution of satisfactions. Still others hold that showing equal respect for individuals requires respecting their natural rights which prevent the sacrificing of the interests of some for the betterment of others. Finally, some liberals insist that respecting the value of each individual requires imposing only those restrictions on their freedom that each could rationally agree to be constrained by as a means to their own good.

B. Impartiality between Competing Conceptions of the Good

Central to the liberal insistence upon the equal value of human beings is their belief that showing equal respect for individuals entails a duty of impartiality for competing conceptions of the good. Liberalism is thus the doctrine most suited to the social reality of moral pluralism. Pluralism involves the existence of irreconcilable moral disagreement about the good, and particularly irreconcilable conceptions of what constitutes a good life. Pluralism is a fact in virtually all modern countries, and liberalism was an historical reaction to this social fact. Liberals insist that showing equal respect for individuals requires adopting a stance of impartiality between competing conceptions of the good life, or at least between reasonable conceptions of the good life. Those conceptions of the good which justify the oppression or subordination of some groups in society for the good of others cannot be tolerated in any peaceful society which is founded on the recognition of the equal worth of all people, and so such conceptions of the good as are represented in Nazism or the Klu Klux Klan, for example, must be denied. But there can be many others which represent reasonable comprehensive moral doctrines which must be tolerated even by those who think that they are fundamentally misguided. It is important to note that this insistence upon impartiality between competing conceptions of the good is not based on moral skepticism, or on the belief that we cannot adequately judge the truth or reasonableness of competing conceptions of the good; rather, it is based upon the liberal belief that human welfare is the central moral value and that a necessary component of human welfare is to be found in having the freedom to define for oneself what constitutes a good life.

C. Liberty

This concern for ensuring impartiality between competing conceptions of the good leads liberals to place paramount importance upon individual liberty. Ensuring the maximum liberty for each compatible with a like liberty for all follows from the commitment to impartiality. This is so not only because individuals must be free to pursue their own conception of the good without interference from others, but because they must be free to examine, challenge, and criticize both their own conception and those of others. Thus the state especially must guarantee the maximum equal liberty to each individual if it is to maintain impartiality. This underwrites the liberal commitment to such basic freedoms as freedom of religion, association, speech, and conscience.

D. Limited Government

Finally, from liberalism we also get a picture of the proper relation between the people and their government. Government must be for the people (and this has typically been taken to be best served by insisting further that government be by the people as well). That is, governments are charged with impartially serving the interests of their citizens, rather than the interests of the governors or those of particular groups. Furthermore, government must be limited in power, for it must exercise only so much power as is needed for it to fulfil its task of serving the interests of the people.

These themes have come together in the liberal insistence that society be governed by the rule of law. A society governed by the rule of law is one governed by settled standing laws, promulgated to and binding on all. It is also characterized by the insistence that all people are equal before and under the law. To ensure this the administration of legal justice is to be constrained by considerations of due process, which ensure that anyone accused of an offense has a fair opoportunity to defend herself, that people will only be held legally liable for those offenses for which they are responsible, and the like.

II. LIBERALISM AND THE LAW

These central liberal tenets give rise to a conception of individuals as having a natural entitlement to equal concern and respect from their governments, and to a conception of justice which requires that the basic institutions in society be arranged so as to allow all persons an opportunity for full and equal participation in the political, economic, and cultural life of their country, and the maximum freedom to pursue their individual conceptions of the good life consistent with the rights of others.

This conception of society, and particularly the liberal insistence upon governmental impartiality between competing conceptions of the good life, might at first blush be thought to raise questions about the moral legitimacy of using law to regulate the behavior of members of society: in prohibiting various actions through law and making their performance the subject of coercive sanctions, is the government (or the majority it represents) not imposing its conception of the good on citizens who may hold dissenting opinions? In prohibiting racial discrimination, for example, is the state not thwarting the ability of racists to pursue their conception of the good?

The short liberal answer to this question is that only those conceptions of the good which are reasonable need be respected. While there has been considerable disagreement concerning how to understand the requirement of reasonableness, at least one element of it seems uncontentious on liberal principles: the liberty claimed by any individual or group must be compatible with a like liberty for all. Those whose conception of the good supports the subordination or oppression of others in society cannot claim that their conception must be respected, for they fail to respect the value of others and their freedoms; they claim a greater degree of freedom than they would be willing to allow to others.

A. Why We Need Law

This is, as I said, the short answer. In order to understand the fuller liberal response to concerns over the legitimacy and proper role of law, we must briefly examine why we need law at all.

Many things might be thought to define our nature as human beings, at least in part. One is that we are social creatures, whether by nature or by nurture. Another is that we are vulnerable to violence at the hands of our fellows. Furthermore, we are avaricious, desiring a great many things which are insufficiently supplied by the hand of nature to satisfy our individual desires.

This last is tied to two other very important facts about us: we compete for scarce goods, both material and nonmaterial, and it is often the case that together we can cooperate in such ways to increase the overall stock of goods which are desired so as to better serve our individual wants than we can by engaging in noncooperative competition.

Our vulnerability to violence, as well as our need for mutually beneficial cooperation, has ensured that to live well together we must institute social rules which provide a general prohibition on force and fraud and define the terms of social cooperation. Such rules also need to be enforced. This is so, not merely because it is taken as conceptually true that rules must include provisions for some sanction against those who break the rule, but also because we recognize that each of us may be subject to temptation to break the rules by which we maintain social peace and cooperation. If there were not temptations to cheat, the rules would be superfluous. Moreover, it must be recognized that society cannot tolerate widespread disobedience to the rules which limit violence and protect cooperative arrangements, for violence and breaking of agreements tend to be self-perpetuating acts in some important sense. Violence breeds violence for a number of reasons: to be the victim of violence leads individuals to take a peculiarly self-interested perspective; it leads to anticipation and fear of more violence, both for the victim and for the perpetrator who fears retaliation; it makes defensive violence more likely; it weakens the ties of mutual concern and respect which must bind together the members of a peaceable society; and it breeds retributive emotions such as resentment and even hatred. Similarly, having faith in the commitments of one's fellows is absolutely vital to a functioning community. General veracity is needed for any meaningful sense of community, and a general commitment to promise, contract, or agreement keeping is needed for the stability of mutually beneficial cooperation. Without trust that our fellows will generally do as they have agreed to do, we should be incapable of sustaining many of the good things in life. And, again, breaches of agreements take on a certain momentum of their own, once this practice becomes at all widespread: breach of promises leads to distrust and suspicion, which thereby makes the victim of the breach less willing to enter into other cooperative schemes without adequate assurance of performance from his partners, which in turn breeds suspicion and lack of goodwill, which reinforces the original distrust, etc., and the perpetrator of such breaches must also find it more difficult to trust his fellows for similar reasons.

In choosing to regulate behavior through the use of a system of law and punishment, we have chosen to leave individuals with the ultimate freedom to choose how they shall act. By imposing penalties on some behaviors, the law provides an additional reason (distinct from any other moral, prudential, or political reasons they may already have) to do as the law requires. Yet ultimately it is up to individuals to decide whether they will obey the law or break it and thereby accept the risk of being punished. Contrast this method of behavior control with early childhood conditioning, imposed drug therapy, or constant surveillance, and it becomes apparent that the rule of law comports well with basic liberal principles.

Such a policy is attended with serious risks, however, for people will break the law, at least so long as we are characterized by our limited goodwill toward others and our situation is one of competition with others for scarce goods. Insofar as our societies continue to fall short of the ideals of liberal theory, as they currently do, and so are characterized by gross inequalities of wealth and political power, extreme poverty, and restricted opportunities for many, racial and gender inequalities and other forms of social injustice, the risk that some will choose to engage in criminal activities will be even higher. Yet liberal societies do not typically view the "causes" of crime in a strictly deterministic way; they typically reject the idea that there are criminogenic social conditions which inevitably drive people to crime. Rather, the presumption is that crime is voluntarily undertaken by those who could have kept to the law. The onus of proof is on those who would argue that a specific criminal is not responsible for her crime to show that it was done in one or another of the excusing or mitigating circumstances recognized in the legal code in her society, such as insanity, nonvoluntary compulsions, intoxication, provocation, accident, mistake, duress, and coercion. In the absence of one of these conditions being relevantly operative, the presumption is that individuals both can obey the law and are responsible for failing to do so.

None of this is to deny that there are a great many factors which contribute to crime: from poverty to systematic exclusion from a range of benefits in society on arbitrary grounds, from peer pressure to thrill seeking, and from hatred to greed. Within liberal societies such factors are taken only to contribute to crime, not to cause it. Because people can be inclined to crime by these and a myriad of other reasons, the coercive enforcement of law is needed.

Law, we might say then, is a purposeful code of rules designed to regulate the behavior of those subject to it so as to make possible peaceful and mutually beneficial social interaction. By making certain acts illegal, and attaching penalties to their performance, the law attempts to reduce if not eliminate the incidents of those acts being performed.

B. The Creation of Crime

This way of organizing our affairs and regulating our interactions with others makes possible a unique problem, however; unique, that is, only to those capable of engaging in rule-governed practices: what to do with those who break the rules. This is a problem generated by all rule-governed activities. It is only against the background rules that many offenses or breaches can be defined. For example, the breach of moving a pawn four spaces in a single move can only be understood as a violation against the rules of chess. What response is appropriate to such offenses must be determined from within the activity of chess, moreover. The law likewise gives rise to a particular range of offenses, which we call crimes. Crimes are breaches of the law (usually only that branch of law known as the criminal law, as distinct especially from tort law but also from property law and contract law); without the institution of law we would lack the notion of crime. This is not to say that we would not have other categories of wrong and harm, but just that the notion of crime is inseparably linked to the concept of law. Moreover, the conception of law with which one operates will itself provide a particular conception of crime and the wrongfulness which crime involves. Breaches of the law are not viewed in the same light as breaches of the rules of etiquette, for example, nor like breaches of the rules of hockey. Gentle correction may in order for the first breach, and a five minute penalty for the second. Punishment, by contrast, is what is imposed for violations of the criminal law.

Legal punishment is an avoidable loss intentionally imposed by legal authorities upon an offender for an offense. The offense, upon which such a loss (the penalty) is conditioned, is a violation of a legal rule or principle. The determination that such an offense has occurred must, furthermore, be established by some public process of inquiry. It is important that the state (legal authorities), rather than the victims of crime, say, impose punishment for the violation of the laws which prohibit violence and make cooperation possible. For crime is an offense, not just against the victim of the crime (if there is one), but also against society as a whole. Victims may rightfully seek restitution for the harm they suffer through the actions of criminals

through civil law, or they may waive this right, but it falls to society to punish offenses against it. To understand the idea that crime harms society in general, we need only note that the conditions of peaceful society with our fellows are in the interests of each person in society, and insofar as crime threatens that good, everyone is harmed.

The primary harms created by crime fall on the victims of crime and those who care about them or depend on them; victims bear the primary costs of crime, which may include loss of life or physical maiming, impairment or pain, loss of time, loss of future income or wealth, loss of future enjoyments, loss of property, and the psychological costs of being victimized. For reasons that we shall consider under Section III.E, it is important for one's society not to acquiesce in anyone's being treated in this way, and so it is proper that the state punish criminals for the harms they do to their victims.

It is even more obvious that the state should assume the role of punishing when one takes into account the secondary harms which crime inflicts upon everyone in society. These include many of the same psychological harms suffered by victims of crime: fear, impotence, anger, mistrust, etc. The members of society must also bear the costs of maintaining the enforcement apparatus of law; taking into account just the central institutions of the police, the courts, prisons, and noncustodial forms of confinement, this is a substantial price. And criminals show that it is not enough by engaging in crime in spite of that apparatus being in place. So citizens purchase locks and alarm systems, buy extra insurance, and stop going out at night. The criminal acts wrongly in forcing others to bear these costs, and society rightly punishes this injustice.

C. The Limits of Law

The question to which we will turn next is, What is the proper limit of law? Should the law be used to regulate sexually "deviant" behavior, abortion, minority religions, euthanasia, etc.? These are controversial questions. In this debate concerning the proper limits on the use of law, four broad positions can be discerned.

1. The Harm Principle

Those who accept the harm principle accept that it is legitimate to use the law to limit the liberty of individuals in order to prevent them from harming others. Acceptance of this principle, thus understood, is very widespread. In arguing that the purpose of law is to secure nonviolence and make possible voluntary cooperative relations between people, we have been accepting this principle. The harm principle has often been taken to mean more than this, however, for its most famous formulation by John Stuart Mill stated that the prevention of harm to others was the *only* legitimate use of the law. Most liberals recognize that this may be unduly restrictive. When understood this latter way, the harm principle stands opposed to three other principles concerning the proper limits of the law.

2. Paternalism

Those who accept this principle accept that the law may be used to limit people's freedom to harm themselves. Laws requiring the use of seat belts, prohibiting the use of life-destroying substances (such as heroine or crack cocaine), or prohibiting suicide are typically justified on paternalistic grounds: we prohibit these behaviors to protect people from themselves, for their own good, just as we impose restrictive rules on children to prevent them from harming themselves. Mill and many other liberals have argued that paternalism is not permissible when dealing with competent adults—that it denies them the respect they are due as individuals. While most societies have allowed some restrictions on individual freedom for paternalistic reasons, it remains true that such restrictions require special justification within a liberal framework, where the onus of proof is on those who would treat others paternalistically to show that the danger to be prevented is serious, that some individuals are vulnerable to that harm if left free, and that the freedom to be restricted cannot figure centrally in any reasonable conception of the good.

3. Legal Moralism

Those who defend legal moralism, such as Lord Patrick Devlin, hold that the liberty of individuals may also be restricted to prevent them from engaging in immoral behavior. Now most serious crimes are both immoral and harmful to others (the victims of the crimes). For legal moralism to be distinct from the harm principle, then, it must require that some actions be prohibited on the grounds of their immorality, despite the fact that they are victimless, that is, though they harm no identifiable person(s). Sexual morality provides useful examples. Homosexual behavior between consenting adults, heterosexual relations between unmarried persons, voluntary prostitution, sadomasochistic acts, and the like have all been thought by a sizable majority of people in western societies at one time or another to be immoral behaviors, yet there may be no victim of such activities. Legal moralists insist that it is enough to justify limiting the freedom of people to engage in such activities that the majority of people in their society find them morally intolerable. Such a view typically rests upon the claim that society has a right to defend its shared morality against activities which might undermine its authority. Such a position seems to deeply conflict with the basic tenets of liberalism, and legal moralism has slowly been rejected as a legitimate use of the law.

4. The Offense Principle

The final defense for the use of law to restrict the liberty of individuals which we will consider concerns the use of law to prevent offense to others. It is not clear, however, that offense actually functions as an independent ground for restricting the liberty of individuals, rather than reducing to either the harm principle or legal moralism. Many people have sought to restrict access to pornography and other obscene material on the grounds that it is offensive to some members of society. But surely for the offensiveness of some material to be serious enough to justify restricting it, it ought to count as harmful to the group offended by it. I may offend my fellows with either my breath or my fashion sense, but neither offense is likely to count as sufficiently serious to allow others to determine how I will conduct my oral hygiene or whether I shall wear white after labor day. Only those offenses which diminish the welfare of others in some significant way, i.e., which harm them, can justify restricting the liberty of individuals to do as they will. If some are not being directly or indirectly harmed (by being made an unwilling audience to such things as they find offensive, say, or through the indirect effects which the viewing of pornographic materials may have on rates of violence against women), but rather are offended by the mere idea that others are viewing such material, then this seems to reduce to legal moralism. Some people find the behavior of others to be so seriously immoral that the mere knowledge of their behavior is offensive and so they claim that the law must restrict their liberty.

These are the disputed grounds on which we may limit the liberty of some through the use of law. Where should the liberal come down on these questions? Which principles should she accept? They ought to, and for the most part do, favor the harm principle as basic, and a restricted version of paternalism so as to ensure that the law maintains its impartiality to competing conceptions of the good life.

III. THEORIES OF LAW, CRIME, AND PUNISHMENT

Different conceptions of law have been offered in the western tradition, and each theory of law offers not only an understanding of the nature of law, but also an account of what makes criminal behavior wrong and what the correct response to such wrongdoing is. While we cannot here canvas all the possible theories of law, or even all of those which have received sustained attention in western history, a brief excursion into the philosophy of law will shed light upon which conception of law and corresponding theory of punishment is most consistent with the liberal principles we have identified as the hallmarks of western society.

A. Natural Law

Historically natural law was the dominant conception of law in the western world. According to this way of understanding law, it is an ordinance of reason directed to the common good. Furthermore, law is a system of rules the purpose of which is to reinforce through public rules and sanctions a transcultural and eternal moral law which is binding upon all peoples. The purpose of law is to regulate human behavior so as to prevent moral wrongdoing. Natural law theorists held, then, that there is a necessary connection between the content of the law and the content of the correct moral code, such that every law serves a moral end (to prevent morally wrong acts from being done or to ensure that morally required acts are done). The very idea of an "immoral law" is considered a conceptual confusion for such thinkers; there could be no such thing. Law is just a human enactment of the requirements of morality, and so the two (morality and law) could never diverge so as to allow for immoral laws.

The natural law conception of law entails a particular conception of legal wrongdoing (crime) as necessarily also being a moral wrongdoing (sin or vice); in the language of law, it conceives crimes as *mala in se,* that is, as acts which would be wrong independently of and prior to their being made illegal. And it usually recommends a particular response to such wrongdoing, which has come to be known as retributive punishment. Punishment is a response to the moral wrongdoing of legal offenders, and on the retributive conception of punishment, those who commit such wrongs must be punished because they deserve it. It is morally fitting or just that those who do wrong suffer harm (that good

be returned for good, evil for evil). Punishment ensures that those who violate the law and thereby commit a culpable moral wrong suffer the harm they deserve.

This conception of crime, as well as the retributive response to crime for which it calls, has been rejected by most theorists over the past couple of hundred years. While historically natural law theorists were content to justify punishment as the "fitting" response to actions which offend against a self-evident, or at least self-validating, moral law, we cannot be so complacent. We can no longer be sure of the existence of such a law, let alone its precise content. Nor can we be sure that the positive legal code of any particular society coincides with such a law, even if it were to exist. And, finally, even if there were such a moral code, knowable by the likes of us, and our legal system did not deviate from it in any substantial way, we cannot be sure what the fitting response is to the various offenses it makes possible.

Besides the general problem of providing a convincing theory of the moral code to which all positive legal codes must conform, there are other serious problems with the natural law position. In the first place, such theories have difficulty accommodating offenses which are merely *mala prohibita*, though these may serve legitimate legislative purposes; these offenses are wrong only because they are illegal. Furthermore, not all moral wrongs should be prohibited in law and made punishable by the state (for example, lying to a friend without a valid excuse is surely immoral, but ought not to be made illegal as well). If natural law theorists are committed to saying that all and only those actions which are *mala in se* ought to be legally prohibited, then they will have difficulty justifying both *mala prohibita* offenses and explaining why some moral wrongs are treated differentially (not punishable within the positive law) from others.

There are more important objections to the natural law position as well. First, we seem to be faced with countless examples of legal systems which contain morally repugnant laws, yet in spite of this they seem to be genuine laws. The claim, made by St Augustine among others, that "unjust laws are no laws at all" seems to answer questions of the substantive morality of particular laws with an illegitimate stipulative definition.

Furthermore natural law theories seem incapable of providing a convincing justification of punishment, resting as they do simply on the intuition that moral wrongdoing deserves a punitive response. Desert and cognate concepts, while clearly relevant to discussions of punishment, are not sufficient to justify such a practice. Yet desert is the tie which has most closely connected retributive theories of punishment to the natural law conception of law.

The notion of desert which is central to this version of retributivism within a natural law framework has been terrifically difficult to defend, and all desert-based retributivists face the problem of attempting to move from the claim that, because offenders deserve punishment, it is somehow permissible or obligatory that the state ensure that they get what they deserve. Since the state is not typically charged with the task of ensuring that individuals get what they deserve, we would require an account which provides a differential justification of punishment—which explains why the state ought to ensure that those who behave culpably by committing moral wrongs get their just deserts while those who commit no such wrongs may have to wait for their just rewards. Thus the natural law theorist would have to provide a substantive theory of justice which explains not only why criminals deserve punishment, but also why the state must ensure that they receive their just deserts. In doing so, however, the natural law theorist would have to admit teleological considerations into her theory, for now punishment would be justified insofar as it achieved some good—the attainment of justice—and not merely because it is the self-evidently fitting response to wrongdoing. This should not be overly surprising, however, because natural law theories have an important teleological component built into their very notion of law as an ordinance made for the common good, but it does create a tension between their theory of law and their theory of punishment. It is clear, whatever the problems internal to natural law theories, that this conception of law is incompatible with a liberal political morality. It cannot accommodate the fact of moral pluralism, nor can it make room for the injunction of impartiality. If there is one moral code to which law directs us to conform, liberal freedom is misguided as an ideal.

B. Legal Positivism

Legal positivists insist that whether something counts as a law is not determined by its moral quality, but by its pedigree, as well perhaps as its having certain other formal features. Thus laws are laws in virtue of being directives of a law-making authority; they may also have to be of some specified generality, promulgated, etc. What is of most importance, though, is that legal positivists deny that there is any necessary connection between law and morality. Laws may promote morally reprehensible ends. Thus we can no longer infer that those who commit legal offenses are thereby guilty of moral wrongdoing or that it is fitting that they be punished under some grand theory of justice. Indeed, under positivism, there is no guarantee that punishment, any more than law, secures any good at all.

Positivists have typically tried to defend punishment by developing a functionalist theory of punishment. There are serious problems with such an approach, however. Consider, for example, a function commonly attributed to punishment by positivists such as H. L. A. Hart: the function of punishment is to maintain conformity with the law, or to deter violations of the law. The crucial problem with such a view is that without the assumption that the law itself is morally justified, the fact (if it is a fact) that punishing increases conformity with the law does not provide a moral justification for punishing. And such an assumption of the moral validity of the law is precisely what positivists cannot avail themselves of due to their insistence on the separation of law and morality.

The problem alluded to here will cripple any attempt to develop a specifically functionalist justification of punishment within a positivist conception of law. For at most such attempts can provide a functional, but not a moral, justification of punishing; functionalist justifications can work as moral justifications only if the purpose attributed to punishment can be shown to be justified as a moral good. By contrast, within a natural law framework, if one could demonstrate that punishment increases obedience to the law, then one would thereby have also shown that punishment contributes to a moral good, namely conformity with the moral law. For a positivist, there is no similarly straightforward way to move from a functionalist to a moral justification of punishing. On the contrary, the recognition that a legal code may be immoral seems to doom all such attempts. Whether the function of punishment is deterrence, rehabilitation, repentance, education, or what have you, unless we have reason to believe that the actions being deterred are morally bad, or that the lessons being learned are morally good, then the fact that punishment performs such functions cannot provide a moral justification for punishing.

C. Utilitarian Theories of Law and Punishment

The rise of legal positivism has made room for alternative theories of law and punishment, however. Many have been offered within the framework of utilitarian moral theory. Utilitarianism has had a venerable history within western philosophy, at least since its formulation by Jeremy Bentham, and many of its proponents offer it as the moral theory most compatible with liberalism. Utilitarians hold that the action, rule, or law which is morally best is that which maximizes the happiness, pleasure, welfare, or preference satisfaction of those affected by it; hereafter, for the sake of brevity, I shall speak of the interests of individuals as the value which utilitarianism enjoins us to maximize. Because utilitarianism evaluates the morality of actions, rules, or laws on the basis of their consequences—how they impact the interests of those affected—it is a species of conseqeuntialist moral theory. Many important theorists have argued that the question, Should we have a legal system at all?, and if so, What laws should we have?, are best answered by utilitarian reasoning. It is clear that human interests are better served if we live under the rule of law than if we live in a state of unrestricted freedom, and so the existence of a legal system is justified on utilitarian grounds. What laws should we adopt? Only those which maximize the happiness or welfare of those who are bound by them. In this way utilitarians attempt to accommodate the central tenets of liberalism: they insist that everyone's interests who will be affected by law must be equally considered, and only those laws which best serve the aggregated interests of all are to be permitted. They assume a presumption in favor of liberty, recognizing any restriction on freedom as bad, and insist that only those restrictions which promote the interests of all to the highest degree possible are to be enacted. Insofar as the resulting legal system serves the interests of all, it satisfies the demand for impartiality and provides a moral justification for the resulting laws. Utilitarianism also provides a plausible justification for respecting the central aspects of the rule of law, limited government, and the insistence on responsibility as a necessary condition of justifiable punishment in most cases.

There is one overwhelming criticism that can be launched against utilitarian theory in general, and as applied to law in particular: it stems from the fact that utilitarianism is an aggregative theory which seeks to maximize human interests understood in terms of net utility. Net utility is calculated by summing all of the benefits accruing to each person who will be affected by a law, and subtracting all of the aggregated harms done to each by that law; the result is the net utility of the law. Now utilitarianism tells us to maximize net utility. But net utility concerns only the overall consequences of a law, while it is indifferent to the distribution of utility to different people. This means that certain individuals, who have unusual interests or needs, may find that their interests are repeatedly subordinated to the interests of larger minorities or the majority; even

more worrisome, but stemming from the same source, the interests of some may be sacrificed for the good of others, in such a way that some are made significantly worse off in order to make others, perhaps already quite well-off, even happier.

Utilitarians claim that their theory can offer a justification of punishment, insofar as punishment has good consequences, but this too is problematic. The effect of punishment which is most often offered by the utilitarian by way of justification is deterrence. By punishing those who break the law we deter those individuals from committing future crimes; known as specific deterrence, this benefit may be achieved both by incapacitating the criminal and by inspiring sufficient fear in him who is punished that he will not risk being punished again by breaking the law in the future. More importantly, by punishing criminals we also achieve general deterrence; that is, we deter others who might be tempted to break the law by holding out the threat of punishment if they follow their inclinations. As well as achieving the good of deterring potential violations of the law, punishment may also have other beneficial consequences which the utilitarian could point to: it may appease the desire for revenge felt by the victims of crime and others, it may serve to educate members of society in the norms which govern their society, etc.

There are many problems with the deterrence theory of punishment. In the first place, it is possible to deter others from crime even by punishing the legally innocent. Conversely, general deterrence can be achieved so long as it appears that we punish criminals; we need not actually do so. Furthermore, there are some cases in which it will clearly do no good to punish a particular offender, perhaps because he is clearly and sincerely repentant and because no one else knows of his crime (so he cannot serve as a bad example to others); in such cases, utilitarian considerations seem to suggest that we ought not to punish. These conclusions—that we may punish the innocent or refrain from punishing the guilty—seem to conflict with our basic notions of justice.

Defenders of deterrence theory have tried to answer these concerns by distinguishing between the justification of the practice or institution of punishment (which is utilitarian because having a system of punishment results in good consequences of reducing criminal activity) and the justification of a particular action falling under that practice (which involves the punishment of particular offenders, and ought to be guided by retributive considerations as required by the practice). Whether such hybrid theories rescue deterrence theory from the charge of injustice is a matter of dispute.

Deterrence theory faces other problems as well. It depends upon a particular conception of the potential offender as a rational calculator who weighs the expected benefits of the crime against the probability of being caught and punished at some specified level of severity. This is an unrealistic picture of many criminals: many criminals are poorly educated or even illiterate; many suffer from mental disorders of varying severity or from substance abuse/addiction; many others overestimate their chances of escaping detection or punishment, or underestimate the severity of their punishment if it will be inflicted; and many of the most violent crimes are committed in the heat of passion, under provocation, duress, or severe economic or peer pressure. Such offenders seem unlikely to be capable of the rational calculation that deterrence theory presupposes. Those who would defend deterrence theory typically respond to such criticisms by arguing that these cases show only that, for these individuals, specific deterrence may fail. Indeed, we know for all those who have rightly been punished that specific deterrence did fail. Nonetheless, they say, others will have been deterred by the punishment of those who were not. Belief in general deterrence is not undermined by the kinds of facts I have been citing.

Though we cannot know what the general deterrent value of punishment is, let us assume for the sake of argument that punishing some offenders does deter a significant number of others from committing crime. This is clearly a benefit, both to those who were deterred and to society more generally. But there is a serious worry here. Are we not using those who are punished for the betterment of others? Are we not sacrificing the interests of some for the well-being of others? (This is the same worry that we identified in discussing utilitarian theories of law, of course.) It would seem so. And this is difficult to reconcile with our commitment to liberal values, especially with our demand that every person is entitled to equal concern and respect from their government.

Deterrence theory raises a different problem as well, which arises at the level of deciding what penalties are appropriate for which crimes. Western societies have long been committed to what is called the principle of proportionality in setting penalties: it states that the gravity of a crime ought to be proportionate to the severity of the sentence to which one is liable for committing that crime. Deterrence theory, if consistently followed, would run afoul of this principle. For what penalty ought to be set for a particular crime on this view is determined by what is needed to deter people from doing it. Generally, the deterrent value of any

threat depends upon two factors: the likelihood that it will be imposed and the negative utility of it, that is, how unpleasant the punishment will be. If we hold the likelihood of being apprehended and punished constant, then the only way to increase the deterrent value of punishing some crime is to increase the severity of the penalty. Now surely the crimes we most need to deter are those to which a great many people are tempted, as well as those which are particularly harmful in each instance. It would seem, then, that theft or tax evasion ought to be treated on a par with murder or rape. Furthermore, given how low our detection and conviction rates for most crimes actually are, we ought to impose much more severe penalties on those offenders who are caught (assuming that we are unwilling to devote the resources necessary to significantly raise the level of conviction). Such thinking may indeed be behind the trend in sentencing evident in western countries in this century, which is characterized by an increasing use of penal incarceration as punishment, longer prison terms, and a recent increase in the use of the death penalty in jurisdictions which still allow capital punishment.

D. Teleological Retributivism

There has been a noticeable return to retributive thinking in the philosophy of law of late. While retributivism has probably never fully lost its sway on the minds of ordinary citizens when reacting to crime, it did suffer decades of abuse at the hands of theorists. Those who advocated retributive principles were accused of everything from hate mongering to inhumanity to naivety. At best retributivism was based on a theological foundation and so was best left to God; at worst it was an ill-masked attempt to justify simple revenge.

What is this doctrine, the proponents of which were deemed worthy of such scorn? At its core it is the view that offenders deserve punishment just in virtue of their past offense, regardless of any good consequences (deterrence, education, rehabilitation, etc.) which their punishment might contingently bring about. Modern retributivists do not claim, however, that the offender's desert stems from violating an eternal moral code (as did the natural law theorists), nor do they claim that punishing offenders does no good. Rather, they claim that punishment does serve some important good, though to understand what that is requires that we look to their conception of law itself, for only against this can we see what makes criminal wrongdoing wrong and how punishment rights that wrong.

Though many versions of what I have called teleological retributivism are currently being proffered and debated, I will concentrate on just two which seem representative of the type and particularly well-suited to liberal society. First, contemporary retributivists begin by constructing a functionalist theory of law. Though functionalism was originally associated with natural law theory, it is consistent with legal positivism as well, and the theories I discuss are compatible with a positivist understanding of law. On such views, one attempts, through conceptual analysis and an examination of the actual workings of a particular legal system, to identify the function which the law serves. That the law serves any particular function is, of course, a contingent matter under positivism, yet we may nonetheless identify such a function. The goal, then, becomes to identify the function of legal systems within liberal societies. Once we have identified it, furthermore, we must then assess its moral acceptability as well as determine whether punishment is necessary for it to serve that function.

One such attempt is to be found in the work of Jeffrie Murphy, Herbert Morris, and Michael Davis, which I call the "unfair advantage theory." They argue that law is a system of restrictions, compliance with which benefits everyone, for the kinds of reasons we considered under the heading Why We Need Law (II.A). The cost of those benefits is individual restraint. Law abidingness ensures that everyone bears a proportionate share of the burden; but those who violate the law take an unfair advantage over the law abiding, for they enjoy the benefits of law without bearing the costs in individual restraint. The criminal, on this view, commits the injustice of being a free-rider; crime, whatever else it involves, necessarily involves upsetting the balance of burdens and benefits which the law provides. Punishment, insofar as it imposes a loss upon the criminal, a burden with the law abiding do not have to bear, reestablishes a fair distribution of burdens and benefits in society. Thus punishment is both required and justified.

An alternate contemporary theory of this type is that which I call the "trust-based theory." On this account, law functions in liberal societies to maintain basic trust in society. Such trust makes possible peaceful, mutually beneficial cooperation, even among strangers. Crimes are those actions which undermine societal trust. The criminal, on this view, harms not only his victim (if there is one) but society more generally by undermining the conditions of trust in society. Punishment is needed to correct this wrong, insofar as it functions to reaffirm for the members of the society the commitment to trust within it and an unwillingness to allow its members to be victimized without protest.

Both of these views, it seems, are compatible with liberal political values. They recognize society as a cooperative venture for mutual advantage, which requires that each individual conform to a set of basic rules. The justification for such rules, though, is that they benefit each person individually. The price of such benefits is compliance, and those who fail to comply must be punished.

E. The Therapeutic Model of Crime and Punishment

All of the theories we have examined thus far have agreed that punishment is a justified response to criminal wrongdoing. We come now to examine two approaches to crime which hold that punishment as such is not justified. The first, which will be our focus in this section, concentrates on reforming the criminal, while the second concentrates on compensating the victim.

One nonpunitive forward-looking approach to punishment, concerned with affecting crime prevention through the treatment and rehabilitation of offenders and those at high risk of being offenders, often goes under the name of the therapeutic model of punishment. Hailed at first as a humane alternative to punitive punishment, those who advocate a therapeutic approach to crime control offer a very different response to crime than do either retributivists or deterrentists.

The therapeutic model is most often associated with Lady Barbara Wootton and Dr. Karl Menninger. On this approach, considerations of responsibility and *mens rea* are treated as irrelevant in determining our response to criminal behavior. That response is to be purely forward-looking, oriented to the goal of rehabilitation. The sole goal of such theories is to prevent crime and serve public safety; this is to be achieved by the reform of criminals and others with criminal tendencies. The central problem of crime control, these theorists argue, is how to identify, detain, and treat potentially dangerous citizens.

This emphasis on crime prevention has obvious appeal. Surely it would be better to ensure that our fellow citizens live within the law in the first place than to wait until they have engaged in harmful behavior and then visit them with punitive hardship for doing so. Despite its initial attractiveness, the approach is so fraught with problems that it has largely been abandoned.

The first set of problems encountered by rehabilitation or therapeutic models, like their forward-looking utilitarian cousins, stem from their inability to meet important demands of justice. If the goal is crime prevention, it would seem that preventive detention even of those who have not yet committed any crime must be allowed, and indeed it has been by many defenders of this view. This is to empower psychiatrists and other health practitioners, who are to be in control of the diagnosis and sentencing of offenders and potential offenders for the most part, to detain individuals even if they have committed no crime; such a view offends against considerations of justice, as well as our commitment to visit people with ill only for their overt acts. Such an approach would certainly completely undermine the constraints of procedural due process which characterize a society under the rule of law.

Preventive detention on the basis of criminal tendencies is also a very dangerous practice for any society to allow. It depends upon being able to identify some people as potentially dangerous independently of their overt acts. This is usually done by group membership, where simply being a member of the class of vagrants, blacks, homosexuals, Catholics, or what have you is sufficient for a person to be labeled dangerous; any policy which allows group membership itself to be grounds for detention can only reinforce the prejudice and injustice which makes the members of some groups more likely to commit crimes in the first place, or to be seen to be more prone to crime. Likewise, diverging moral values may be taken as a sign of probable criminal tendencies and so dangerousness. Allowing preventive detention of some on the basis of moral disagreement is clearly incompatible with liberal political values.

It is important to note that a therapeutic approach to crime prevention involves other problems as well. Even if it is confined to those who have committed crimes, the goal of rehabilitation is problematic, for it leads to a policy of indeterminate sentencing: one must detain criminals for as long as they pose a danger to society, that is, until they have been rehabilitated. Indeterminate sentences are the only way to affect this goal. This violates procedural due process, as well as offending the principle of proportionality. It further undermines another principle of justice which has been a hallmark of liberal political systems and is the concomitant of equality under the law, namely, that like cases be treated alike.

Finally, we must wonder about the motivation behind the therapeutic response to crime. The view of criminals that underlies the theory seems to be that of individuals who are ill or otherwise ill-equipped to restrain themselves as required by the law—the victims of mental disease, unconscious compulsions, or nonvoluntary responses to challenging social circumstances. The view seems to be that criminals cannot help committing crimes. But this seems unlikely in vastly many cases, unless we assume that criminal behavior itself demonstrates the operation of illness or compulsion. Such an assumption would simply beg the question of whether criminals are responsible for their crimes, however. Furthermore, such an assumption is contrary to human dignity. This is true not only theoretically, but practically as well. For the therapeutic model of detention allows not only for the involuntary deprivation of liberty characteristic of punishment, but also involuntary treatment, that is, enforced therapy for rehabilitative purposes. Procedures of enforced therapy include the administration of electric shocks, aversion therapy, a myriad of drug treatments, and psychosurgery. Such invasive, personality-altering treatments, when imposed against a person's will, not only fail to respect the inherent dignity of persons, but may themselves constitute "cruel and unusual" punishments, something liberal societies have long rejected; to impose such treatments on those who have committed no wrong is an abomination.

F. Restitution

The restitution approach to crime denies that criminals deserve punishment. Rather, they insist, the victims of crime deserve compensation. The correct response to crime, therefore, is to ensure that criminals compensate their victims for the loss which the criminal has imposed upon them. Randy Barnett has been a principal spokesperson for this view.

On the restitution model the distinction between criminal law and tort law largely collapses: on both, those who cause damage to another are required to compensate those to whom the damage has been done. No further punitive response is justified. This is a radical suggestion, and it is not without difficulties.

First, of course, there is the serious question of how damages are to be assessed and the level of compensation set. What is the proper compensation for rape or battery? How can one provide restitution to a murder victim? These are difficult, but perhaps not unanswerable, questions. They do, however, raise a second concern, which is that this view seems to reinforce a certain commodification of values which many find an objectionable feature of western democracies, for it requires that we be able to identify the monetary value of such goods as physical security, freedom from pain, and life and limb.

More worrying still, to institute a system of compensation in place of punishment raises serious questions of justice. Suppose that it is decided that the appropriate compensation for rape is $200,000.00. If one is wealthy, one may must just pay this cost (as well, perhaps, as one's share of the cost of maintaining the courts, police, etc.) and one would have discharged one's liability. But many crimes are committed by those who are poor. They are to be forced to make compensation over time. If they cannot find sufficient employment in the community, they may be forced to work within labor projects established for this purpose, either in closed or open custody. It would seem, then, that very different losses may be imposed upon individual criminals depending upon their financial resources. This offends the liberal commitment to equality before and under the law, the requirement that like cases be treated alike, and the principle of proportionality. While the restitution model is meant to provide justice to victims, who are admittedly lost sight of on the other models of punishment we have examined, it seems to do so at the cost of injustice to criminals.

Finally, ensuring restitution for victims of crime does nothing to protect the members of society from dangerous criminals. The wealthy rapist may simply go on his way. If the purpose of punishment is to protect individuals from force and fraud, exacting compensation from those who engage in such behavior is an inadequate response to crime. This is not to deny, however, that victims ought to be compensated for their losses by those who have imposed them; we need to retain our tort law and make it more assessable to victims of crime. It is to deny that we can safely abolish the use of criminal law and legal punishments.

Also See the Following Articles

LIBERALISM • PATERNALISM • UTILITARIANISM

Bibliography

Cragg, W. (Ed.) (1992). "Retributivism and Its Critics." Franz Steiner Verlag, Stuttgart.
Cragg, W. (1992). "The Practice of Punishment." Routledge, London.
Dagger, R. (1993). Playing fair with punishment. *Ethics* 103(3), 473–488.
Davis, M. (1992). "To Make Punishment Fit the Crime." Westview.
Dimock, S. (1997). Retributivism and trust. *Law Philos.,* 16(1), 37–61.
Duff, A., and Garland D. (Eds.) (1994). "A Reader on Punishment." Oxford Univ. Press, Oxford.
Ellis, A. (1995). Recent work on punishment. *Philos. Quart.* 45(179), 225–233.
Feinberg, J., and Gross, H. (Eds.) (1995). "Philosophy of Law." Wadsworth, Belmont, CA.
Frey, R. G., and Morris, C. W. (Eds.) (1991). "Liability and Responsibility: Essays in Law and Morals." Cambridge Univ. Press, Cambridge.
Gorr, M., and Harwood, S. (Eds.) (1995). "Crime and Punishment: Philosophical Explorations." Jones & Bartlett, Boston.
Tunick, M. (1992). "Punishment: Theory and Practice." Univ. of California Press, Berkeley.
Walker, N. (1991). "Why Punish?" Oxford Univ. Press, Oxford.

CUSTODY OF CHILDREN

Carol Levine
The Orphan Project

GLOSSARY

"best interests of a child" The standard by which a judge, after considering all relevant factors relating to a child's custody, determines what placement, on balance, is most likely to support a child's need for continuity, stability, and nurturing.

custody planning The process of determining placement of a child when a parent is unable to provide care.

gestational motherhood The process by which an egg from one woman is fertilized and implanted in another woman's uterus and carried to term.

guardian A person legally charged with taking care of a minor.

guardian ad litem A person appointed by the court to represent a minor's best interests in a specific litigation or decision-making process.

in vitro fertilization A procedure in which a woman's egg is fertilized by a man's sperm in a laboratory and then implanted for gestation.

joint or shared custody A legal arrangement in which both parents share the legal or decision-making power over their children.

kinship foster care A formal arrangement similar to nonrelative foster care, in which a child's kin is certified to act as the foster parent and receive the regular foster care rate. This is permitted only in some states.

mediation An informal process, conducted by a trained individual (not usually a lawyer), that helps family members agree on an acceptable custody arrangement for their child. In a nonconfrontational way, it focuses on problem solving within a family system.

permanency The goal of child custody arrangements, i.e., a home where a child can receive love and support represents a permanent and stable custody situation.

standby guardian laws State statutes that permit a parent with a chronic, life-threatening or terminal illness to name a guardian to take over the care of her children in case of death, incapacity, or another such event.

surrogate or contract motherhood An agreement between a woman and (usually) an infertile couple in which the woman agrees to become pregnant by being artificially inseminated with the husband's sperm, to give birth to the child, and to give it to the couple to adopt.

CUSTODY is the arrangement by which adults, usually parents, exercise control over the person and property

Encyclopedia of Applied Ethics, Volume 1

of a minor. An adult may have physical and legal custody of a child, which means that the child lives with that adult, who makes decisions about the child's education, health care, religious training, travel, and so on. In some cases one person has physical custody, while another has legal custody. If a parent has sole custody, he or she is completely in charge; the other parent may have visitation rights. Joint custody usually means that both parents have to consult about major decisions, even though one may be the residential custodian.

Most custody decisions arise from divorce proceedings. More than 20% of all American children under the age of 18—13 million—live with a divorced single parent or with a remarried parent. Modern reproductive technology and the practice of contract or "surrogate" motherhood have created new and perplexing dilemmas. With an estimated 2.5 million infertile couples in the United States, adoption is one route out of childlessness. An estimated 2 to 4% of American families include an adopted child. Custody disputes may arise in adoption proceedings. Finally, parental death or incapacity due to AIDS or other causes has led to new problems in placing children. All these situations pose ethical as well as legal and social challenges. The ethical issues include questions such as the relative value to be placed on biological, rather than relational, continuity as the basis of a custody decision; the extent of the child's involvement in and consent to the decision; how to assess competing interests in determining a child's "best interests," and the role of expert witnesses in child custody proceedings.

I. CHANGING STANDARDS FOR CUSTODY DECISIONS

A. Historical Background

Conflicts over the custody of children have an ancient history. In the Bible (1 Kings 3:12–28) King Solomon made one of the best-known judicial decisions. Two women came before him, both claiming to be the mother of a 3-day-old boy. Both had given birth at the same time in the same house but one baby died. Both women claimed to be the mother of the living child. King Solomon called for a sword to divide the infant in two. One woman agreed, saying the child should be neither hers nor the other woman's. The other woman begged the king to give the baby to her rival rather than kill him. This woman, the King announced, was the true mother and she was awarded the child. This case, the text asserts, proved that King Solomon's prayers to judge his people with an "understanding heart" had been answered.

Except for the dramatic threat of the sword, the situation has contemporary overtones. Grief at the death of an infant, appropriation of another baby, a custody proceeding to determine the child's placement, a judgment about the child's best interests—these are the stuff of real life, as well as of modern fiction.

Although custody practices varied somewhat in the ancient world, the most powerful tradition in terms of modern practice has been Roman law. The Roman doctrine of *patria potestas* gave unlimited power to the *paterfamilias*—the father, or oldest male in the family. Originally, fathers even had the right to sell their children (except into slavery) or kill them if they were unwanted or a burden. Even without this ultimate weapon, fathers had total legal control over their children, and mothers had none. Children were considered property; because women had no property rights, they also had no rights over their children.

This absolutist view of paternal authority began to weaken in the mid-nineteenth century, as advocates for women's rights championed reforms. As childhood began to be defined in a modern conception as a distinct life stage with psychological as well as physical needs, women's roles as nurturers assumed new, albeit still unequal, importance. In addition to new emphasis on the mother–child bond, social changes such as industrialization and urbanization separated home from workplace. In these new economic arrangements women were often deemed the more appropriate custodians.

By the end of the nineteenth century the doctrine of paternal power had been replaced by "maternal preference" or the "tender years" doctrine. That is, young children were perceived to be better off with their mothers than with their fathers if the parents did not stay together. States defined "a child of tender years" in many different ways, some limiting the definition to infants and young children under the age of 7, others including any dependent minor.

Preference for the mother was not unlimited. If, in divorce proceedings, a woman was shown to have engaged in adultery or other misconduct, her children, no matter how "tender" in years, were likely to be taken away from her. In general, children were awarded to the parent who had the strongest case for divorce, with no regard to the particular relationship between parent and children.

B. The "Best Interests" Standard

By the 1960s the standards began to change again. Fathers' groups complained that they were unfairly excluded as potential custodians. Women's groups complained that a sex-based standard violated the equal protection guarantee of the Constitution. In the 1970s there was a new emphasis on psychological factors affecting child development. In their enormously influential "best interests" trilogy, published in 1973, 1979, and 1986 Goldstein, Freud, and Solnit stressed the importance of continuity, a child's sense of time, and the limits of law and prediction. They advocated placing a child with the "psychological parent." They later argued that state intervention should be kept to a minimum, as the "least detrimental alternative." The final book focused on the roles of professionals in the child placement process. Other writers have criticized their views as overly focused on a nuclear family model, which fails to recognize culturally diverse structures, and on a single psychological parent, when children may have several significant adult figures in their lives.

While the "best-interests" standard has clear advantages over those used in earlier eras, it is so broad and so vague that it is difficult to implement in practice. Many custody decisions are made amicably by parents. If, however, parents cannot agree, and a case comes to court, a judge will make the final determination. But on what evidence? And, when evidence conflicts as it often does, what values come first? There may be lawyers for both parents, with a parade of expert witnesses testifying that the child's best interest is to be placed with the "good" parent rather than the one who has proven his or her "unworthiness" by bad deeds, bad moods, or bad checks. Determining who has been the child's primary caretaker—a common test in many states—can become just another version of the "maternal preference" standard, because in most cases the primary caretaker is the mother. Real or purported sexual abuse is often used as a trump card. Attorneys appointed to represent the child's best interests (guardians *ad litem*) or the child's preferences may have great legal skills but no experience or training in evaluating a child's developmental and emotional needs. Judges may be swayed by their own experiences, stereotypes, and prejudices in making decisions. The subject of the hearings—the children themselves—may or may not even be questioned about their preferences. In fact, their preferences may be transitory, manipulated, or inconsistent with adults' views. In sum, the historical progression from paternal to maternal preference to "best interests" has eliminated some inequities, but has made custody cases more complex and subjective.

The adversarial nature of child custody cases that come to court has disturbed many child advocates. It is all too easy for children to become pawns in divorce disputes; and the process that appears to decide their best interests is fraught with potential for manipulation or power differentials. In any adversarial relationship, there are winners and losers. No matter who is awarded custody, the children lose some relationship with the other parent. Moreover, it is difficult to maintain a loving relationship with both parents when the child's loyalty to one has been undermined.

Mediation is one option that tries to avoid the excesses of the adversarial system. This process, conducted by a trained mediator, tries to achieve a consensus in a nonconfrontational way by focusing on problem solving within a family system. Sometimes a decision may be that joint custody, or shared custody, is the best solution. Mediation does not always work, however. Critics say, for example, that it perpetuates the power imbalance that characterized the marriage.

II. NEW REPRODUCTIVE TECHNOLOGIES AND CONTRACT MOTHERHOOD

As contentious as divorce proceedings can be, at least the basic facts of parenthood are not usually at issue. The dispute is most often between the biological mother and father. New reproductive technologies and the practice of contract or surrogate motherhood have added a new layer of complexity. The "mother" may be the woman who provides the ovum, or genetic material; the one who gestates the embryo and gives birth to the child; or the one who nurtures and cares for the child after birth. While paternity is not so often at issue, the "father" may be a sperm donor or the husband who provides sperm for artificial insemination in a woman who has agreed to bear his child and give it to him and his wife to adopt and raise.

The most famous case involving surrogacy was the 1987–1988 "Baby M" case in New Jersey. Mary Beth Whitehead was hired by William and Elizabeth Stern, an infertile couple, to conceive a child with Mr. Stern's artificially inseminated sperm. When the baby was born, Mrs. Whitehead refused to give her up as agreed. Ultimately the New Jersey court ruled that although the contract was invalid, the adoptive parents should have custody; the surrogate mother retained visiting rights.

In 1988 the New Jersey Supreme Court ruled that surrogacy contracts are invalid, comparing them to "baby selling." Legislatures in other states have also barred or restricted surrogacy contracts, although the laws often are murky.

In 1993 the California Supreme Court in the case of *Johnson v. Calvert* became the first court to consider the custody of a baby with two potential mothers—the woman whose egg had been fertilized by her husband's sperm in vitro and the woman who had carried the implanted embryo to term. The court upheld the contract but did not rule on whether the genetic or gestational mother was the "natural" mother. It declared that whichever woman was the "intended" mother should have custody of the child.

When embryos are created in vitro, that is, fertilization takes place in a laboratory and the embryos are frozen for future use, there may be disputes about their fate if the parents divorce, or disagree about their disposition. These cases clearly raise the question of whether the embryos are "future children," whose custody should be determined by a best-interests standard, or property, whose disposition should be determined by contract law. The Tennessee case of *Davis v. Davis* in 1992 illustrates this struggle. Initially a divorce court viewed the dispute about the frozen embryos of Junior and Mary Sue Davis as a child custody case and awarded the embryos to Mrs. Davis, because the best interests of the embryos involved being born and she intended to have them implanted with the hope of bringing a pregnancy to term. She later decided against implantation and wanted to donate the embryos to a fertility clinic. An appellate court did not accept this view and treated the embryos as property, in which each party had an equal right. The embryos could not be implanted or donated without the father's consent. The Tennessee Supreme Court rejected both views, declaring that the embryos were neither children nor property but had an intermediate status based on their potential for development. The characteristics and limitations of this status were left largely undefined by the court.

Although there have been many attempts to regulate the increasingly complex reproductive technologies, most controversies are decided on a case-by-case basis, with few principles to guide the decisions or to shape future policies.

III. ADOPTION

If King Solomon's decision is the prototype of custody decisions, then the story of Moses is the prototypical adoption story. The Bible (Exodus 2:2–10) tells how baby Moses' mother placed him in a basket at river's edge to avoid the Egyptian Pharaoh's intent to kill all Hebrew baby boys. He was found and adopted by Pharaoh's daughter. Moses later returned to his people and led them out of bondage. This story too has contemporary resonance: an interreligious adoption, and a reunion with a birth family, in this case, a birth people.

In Roman times, unwanted babies were frequently left in places where strangers might find them and adopt them. Such children were often treated as equals to natural children; they were granted a special, privileged status of *alumnus*, a dependent whose relationship with parents did not arise from blood, law, or property. Birth parents were permitted to reclaim children if they paid adoptive parents for the care they had delivered, but the bonds of affection that developed between adoptive parents and children were also recognized. In modern times, a distinction developed between "code law" and "case law" countries. In countries dominated by the 1804 Napoleonic Code, such as France and Latin American nations, adopted children were given information about birth parents and permitted to keep their original name. Countries such as the United States that followed the example of English common law emphasized blood ties and did not permit strangers to adopt. Only in the 1920s did American states begin to legalize adoption, and then only with closed records.

About half of all adoptions take place within family units: stepparents adopting the children of their new spouse, grandparents adopting grandchildren, other relatives making legal their informal caregiving and custodial arrangements. Another 20% are adoptions of foster children. Adoptions involving nonrelatives raise questions about the relative weight to be given to genetic linkages, the tension between confidentiality and need for health and other information, and the rights of children to know the circumstances of their birth, and if they choose, to find their birth parents.

Adoption practice has changed dramatically in the United States in the past few decades. Most stranger adoptions until the 1960s and 1970s involved newborns who were as much like the adoptive parents in appearance, religion, and background as possible, were placed in a new family with the aim of severing all ties to their past, and were surrounded by secrecy. As infertility became more common as a medical and social problem, adoption became a solution for childless couples, rather than as a placement for poor or orphaned children as it had been in the past. Adoption laws were passed to protect the confidentiality of the adoptive parents, and to remove the stigma of illegitimacy from the children.

Birth parents had few or no avenues to reclaim their children, or even to find out what happened to them.

With the development of contraception, the legalization of abortion, and decreasing stigma surrounding unwed motherhood, the supply of newborns, especially healthy White infants, decreased. As a result, adoptions involving children who are different from their parents in religion, race, ethnicity, and country of birth have become more common. Furthermore, standards about who can adopt have loosened considerably. Older couples, single men and women, gay and lesbian couples, couples of modest means—all can under some circumstances become adoptive parents. Given the differences between parents and children, the fiction that the adoptive parents are the birth parents is much less frequent. Moreover, children are now told much more directly and at an early age that they are adopted.

Nevertheless, controversies remain. The rights of fathers, particularly fathers who were not notified of the adoption or even told that they were fathers, have featured prominently in some cases. The U.S. Supreme Court in 1976 gave birth fathers equal rights to consent to adoption. The case of Baby Jessica is a celebrated example of the power of this decision. Born in February 1991 to Cara Clausen, an unwed mother in Iowa, Jessica was adopted at the age of 6 days by Roberta and Jan DeBoer, a Michigan couple. They believed that both the birth mother and father had given up their rights. In fact, Ms. Clausen had lied about paternity and the baby's father, Dan Schmidt, learned about the baby only several weeks later. Then began a long and bitter court battle to determine custody. By 1992 the birth parents had reunited and married. The final decision, made by the U.S. Supreme Court in 1993, returned Jessica to them. She was renamed Anna Schmidt. In this case, the courts saw a father's rights to his child as paramount.

While so-called "open" adoptions, in which birth parents remain in contact with their children, have been seen as an alternative to traditional patterns of secrecy, state laws so far have failed to give birth parents any legal rights in these arrangements. Some advocacy organizations, such as Concerned United Birth Parents, promote the primacy of biological ties and the right of children to know and to be reunited with their birth parents. Other advocacy organizations, such as the National Council for Adoption, support adoptive parents' rights to confidentiality and to the protection of laws that make adoptions final after a specified time.

Among the most controversial practices are interracial and international adoptions. Most childless couples seeking children are White; most children available for adoption are African American, biracial, or from other ethnic minorities. Opponents to this type of adoption argue that Black children raised in White families lose their Black identity and have difficulty growing up in a world that does not accept them either as Black or White. Supporters claim that children need love, nurturing, and protection, all of which can be provided equally well by White as well as Black parents. Furthermore, White families can give Black children opportunities to develop cultural identity. Children mired in foster care, with multiple placements and no continuity of care, are denied the benefits of family life. The most recent attempt to address this controversy is the 1996 federal welfare reform bill, which gave a boost to interracial adoptions by providing that states receiving federal funds may not discriminate on the basis of race in adoption. A special law, the 1978 Indian Child Welfare Act, gives Indian tribes the exclusive authority to consent to adoptions of Indian, or part-Indian children.

International adoptions, while becoming more common, are also controversial. In these cases children are removed from their native lands and birth families, and grow up in a totally different culture. Opponents claim that these children will suffer the loss of their language, cultural background, and family identity as a result of this dislocation. Proponents claim that these children have often been abandoned, do not receive good medical care, and might die or otherwise suffer lifelong consequences if they are not removed. For example, there has been considerable publicity about the plight of girl babies abandoned in Chinese orphanages because their parents, limited to one child, want a boy. With the breakup of the Soviet Union, children from Eastern Europe are being adopted by American families. Korea and Latin American countries are other sources. The circumstances under which some birth parents give up their children in these countries may involve less than voluntary, informed consent. At the same time, unscrupulous entrepreneurs may misrepresent the status or health of babies to potential adoptive parents.

Before a child can be placed with adoptive parents, the rights of the birth parents must be terminated legally. If the parents are dead or have been adjudged unfit because of child abuse or mental illness or other reasons, this may be just a formality. But in many cases a parent may be ambivalent, contest the termination, and delay closure. This again pits the interests of birth parents against potential adoptive parents, leaving the child without permanency and stability. In some cases arrangements can be made for the birth parent to visit the child, but these are not legally enforceable once the adoption is final. Termination of parental rights may be the best option, but legal papers do not erase a child's past attachment to a birth parent, even if it was filled with psychic and physical pain.

In 1994 the National Conference of Commissioners on Uniform State Laws proposed a Uniform Adoption Act, a model state statute. The Act has been adopted in one state and is under serious consideration in some others. It generally favors the interests of adoptive parents in being assured that an adoption is final; to the degree that this coincides with the child's interests, it can also be seen as sensitive to children's interests. It attempts to specify the rights and obligations of biological fathers and sets a 6-month limit for fathers who were not informed to contest the adoption. The model statute also urges courts to deal with adoption cases speedily and it emphasizes the importance of established parent–child relationships in determining preferences for custody.

Child welfare agencies have become much more flexible and responsive to the varying needs of children and parents as a result of societal changes, public pressure, and advocacy from all perspectives. Nevertheless, old practices and beliefs die hard. Regulation by government agencies should be concerned with ensuring that private adoptions (without agency intervention) meet acceptable standards and that nonprofit agencies work toward sensitive and speedy assessments.

IV. CUSTODY PLANNING FOR TERMINALLY ILL PARENTS

The death of a parent is a traumatic event in any child's life. When the other parent survives, and has enough resources to support the children emotionally and financially, custody does not usually become an issue. The surviving parent retains legal custody. In single-parent families, or cases in which the surviving parent lacks resources to care for the children, other relatives may step in. Foster care, either with kin (as is permitted in several states) or with nonrelatives is a last resort.

In recent years the increased mortality due to AIDS among women, especially African Americans and Latinas, has created a new set of custody issues in a population already struggling to deal with the impact on families of drug use, violence, and poverty. An estimated 100,000 or more children and youth under the age of 18 will lose their mothers to AIDS by the year 2000. Traditionally in the communities hardest hit by AIDS and drugs, as in ethnic, racial, and religious minorities, informal placements with relatives are preferred to any involvement with lawyers and courts. As long as no

medical, educational, or serious behavioral problems arise, these arrangements work well enough. When there is a crisis, or even under ordinary conditions such as entering school, the informal placement may be jeopardized and the child may be removed by child welfare authorities. Informal arrangements can also be legally challenged by another relative—for example, a long-absent father who now wants custody.

To try to ensure greater stability and permanence in placement after a parental death, and to keep children from entering the costly foster care system, several states have passed "standby guardian" laws. Although they vary in detail, these laws provide that a parent with a chronic, life-threatening, or terminal illness may name a guardian to take over the care of her children in case of death, incapacity, or another triggering event. Unlike a regular guardianship proceeding, the parent does not have to give up custody at the time. And unlike a will, in which judges have great discretion in accepting or rejecting the deceased parent's choice of guardian, the future guardian is approved by a judge while the parent is alive and can give her reasons for choosing this person.

Standby guardianships, however, have some limitations. There may not be a suitable person to name, or the named person's ability or willingness to be a guardian may change in the months or even years from the initial discussion. In states such as New York, where a parent may choose simply to designate a standby guardian on paper without going to court, the designation is viewed as evidence but does not guarantee the judge's decision. Finally, court approval of a standby guardian generally makes that person ineligible for any financial benefits, such as kinship foster care, that might be essential to support the child. This provision in itself poses an ethical dilemma for society: a custody plan that offers greater likelihood of continuity and permanence for an orphaned child than an informal arrangement also deprives the guardian and the child of potential financial support.

Although it is in the child's best interests for a parent to plan for future custody, insofar as it is possible, sometimes parents' wishes may conflict with what others believe is best for the child. A mother's dying wish may be for her eldest daughter who is only 17 to take responsibility for the younger children and to keep them together. The mother's wish may be understandable but unachievable. Adolescents are seldom equipped, financially or emotionally, to take on long-term caregiving responsibilities. Or a father may choose as guardian someone whose past history indicates a poor chance of fulfilling the role because of mental or physical illness, or someone he has just met. In these cases, the situation is often complicated because there is no one else more obviously suited to the role. The alternatives then become a risky choice as guardian or the risks of foster care placement. Many foster parents do an excellent job; however, foster care typically involves multiple placements, where the quality of caregiving varies considerably.

V. CONCLUSIONS

Although genetic relationships have long been the basis of social organization, family structures have changed throughout history. The nuclear family, considered in the United States for many decades to be the norm, is no longer the typical family structure. Many children live in families with one genetic parent, that parent's married or unmarried partner, or with their grandparents, other relatives, foster parents, adoptive parents, and other combinations of adults and children. The child custody system is slowly catching up to social changes by recognizing that for some children it is not possible or desirable to live with their biologic parents and that alternative relationships can be mutually supportive. At the same time the power of blood ties remains. This basic identification is now supported by rapidly developing genetic research that provides important health and perhaps even behavioral information. It is likely that this tension between genetic links and psychological bonds will remain in the child custody arena. Neither exists without the other; both should be considered in making custody decisions.

Mental health professionals who become expert witnesses in child custody cases have a special responsibility to weigh the impact of their testimony not only on their adult clients but also on the children who are the subjects of the proceeding. Because the "best interests" standard is so broad, the professional may influence the decision by selecting certain factors to present and by not discussing others. Judges may be convinced by the professional's authoritative manner rather than by the substantive information.

The expectation of confidentiality that prevails in the therapeutic setting does not fit well with the adversarial nature of a legal case. If the client waives the confidentiality privilege in order to bring his or her own therapist to the courtroom, information may be revealed that may be damaging to the client's case. Yet, if the therapist is not called, it may seem as though the client has

something serious to hide. To advance the client's case in court, the therapist may be forced to jeopardize the therapeutic relationship. In situations in which there is no prior therapeutic relationship, the professional may not have the time or the access to sensitive information on which to make a reasoned recommendation.

Children are not property, although they are sometimes treated as if they are; neither should they be pawns in parental disputes, although they almost always are. Murray (1996. *The Worth of a Child.* Berkeley: University of California Press) presents three models of parenthood: children as property, the parent as steward, and mutualism in the parent–child relationship. Stewardship, he says, is preferable to property ownership because a good steward acts to manage the resource—the child—to further its interests. But even this concept fails. Mutualism emphasizes the "central importance of the *relationship,* without losing sight of the individuality of the parties" [emphasis in original]. This sense of mutual commitment—the very essence of family—should be the basis of a new ethic of parenthood that values children for their inherent worth and for an ethic of custody decision making that places this value above all others.

Also See the Following Articles

ADOPTION • CHILDREN'S RIGHTS • CONFIDENTIALITY, GENERAL ISSUES OF • FAMILY, THE • REPRODUCTIVE TECHNOLOGIES • STEWARDSHIP

Bibliography

Archard, D. (1993). *Children: Rights and childhood.* London and New York: Routledge.

Bartholet, E. (1993). *Family bonds: Adoption and the politics of parenting.* New York: Houghton Mifflin.

Blustein, J. (1982). *Parents and children: The ethics of the family.* New York: Oxford.

Boswell, J. (1988). *The kindness of strangers: The abandonment of children in Western Europe from late antiquity to the Renaissance.* New York: Random House, Inc.

Goldstein, J., Freud, A., Solnit, A. J., & Goldstein, S. (1986). *In the best interests of the child.* New York: The Free Press.

Guggenheim, M., Lowe, A. D., & Curtis, D. (1996). *The rights of families.* Carbondale, IL: Southern Illinois University Press.

Peters, J. K. (1996). The roles and content of best interests in client-directed lawyering for children in child protective proceedings. *Fordham Law Review* 64(4), 1505–1570.

Shiono, P. H., & Quinn, L. S. (1994). Epidemiology of divorce. In *The Future of Children: Children and Divorce* 4(1), 15–28.

Stolley, K. S. (1993). Statistics on adoption in the United States. In *The Future of Children: Adoption* 3(1), 26–42.

DARWINISM

Peter Munz
Victoria University of Wellington

GLOSSARY

adaptation The suitability of an organism for its environment.

altruism Unselfish, cooperative behavior, initially believed to be inexplicable in terms of the theory of evolution by competitive natural selection, but in recent years seen to be, like everything else, the result of evolution by natural selection.

culture The habits and beliefs that are present in a society without explicit plan or agreement.

eugenics The science of the production of good or improved offspring.

evolution The general view, directly opposed to creationism, that all forms of life have developed or emerged gradually or saltationally over a long period of time.

innate knowledge Knowledge and cognitive dispositions for the acquisition of knowledge present at an organism's birth before its exposure to the world.

mutation A change in the phenotype brought about by a change in the germ cells. Such changes are heritable. More broadly, the concept can be used to refer to the invention of new theories.

natural selection The nonrandom survival and reproductive success of a small portion of those members of a population that possess characteristics adapted to their environment.

neo-Darwinism Originally August Weismann's version of Darwinism without the inheritance of acquired characteristics. Later used as a general description of all other amendments made after the New Synthesis.

New Synthesis The title of a book by Julian Huxley summing up the body of Darwinian theorizing as it stood in the mid-20th century.

ontogeny The development of an organism from the fertilized egg to the adult stage.

paradigm An overarching perspective that gives rise to, guides, or inspires "normal science," which can be tested, while the paradigm itself is believed to be immune and, strictly speaking, neither false nor true.

received view of science The body of canons of research methods believed to be capable of delivering true theories by proceeding from simple observations to general theories which can be verified. These canons are also referred to as Baconian Principles.

social Darwinism The body of social, political, and economic theories which seized on Darwin's notion of competition for limited resources. It developed in the wake of Darwinism and led to emphasis on individual achievement and quality, and considered displays of altruism an impediment to cultural and economic progress.

sociobiology Originally the title of a 1976 book by E. O. Wilson but now generally used to refer to the study of cultures and societies as biological phenomena.

species A reproductively isolated group of organisms that are capable of interbreeding with each other.

uniformitarianism The view that all changes in biological, geological, and societal conditions proceed at a gradual, uniform pace according to general laws of biology, physics, chemistry, and sociology.

DARWINISM is the entire body of theories that developed in the wake of Darwin's theory of evolution by natural selection, which went a long way toward explaining that in evolution there is natural or automatic design without a Designer. It not only revolutionized biology but acted as a powerful solvent of traditional religious belief. Its long-term impact on the shape of modern culture and that culture's ability to yield economic rationalization cannot be exaggerated. It embraces not only Darwin's original theory, many single parts of which have turned out to have been false, but also a large number of subsequent theories, some of which have, in turn, also been abandoned; some of which are giving rise to major controversies about the motor of evolution, its pace, and the respective degrees of accident and necessity in evolutionary change; and some of which keep on inspiring research and discoveries in the life sciences as well as in the social sciences. All in all, Darwinism has proved an enormously fertile research program, yielding ever and ever more positive results in all conceivable directions. Last but not least, it has made a profound impact on our understanding of the nature of scientific discovery and the status of science as well as on our understanding of old philosophical problems of knowledge and perception and the crucial role of innate ideas and of cognitive dispositions.

I. INTRODUCTION

Darwinism is neither a doctrine nor an ideology. It is best described as a paradigm in Kuhn's sense—as a framework inside which one can do a lot of normal science. The most pointed and concise formulation of the paradigm, in the words of the American psychologist Donald Campbell, is that all life has evolved from a common ancestor by "chance mutation and selective retention." As Ernst Mayr has observed, the powerful significance of the new paradigm lay in the way in which it shifted attention from typology to population thinking. Darwin started to think of species not as fixed morphological types, but as populations of diverse individuals, the mean characteristics of which keep changing by selection. In this way his paradigm centers on the mutability of species—a mutability which explains how all diversity is a development away from an original cell and how every species is the descendant of another species. Such a paradigm is an overarching theory, capable of accommodating and of inspiring many other theories and able to tolerate the refutation and modification of many of its subtheories. As Kuhn indicated in his *Structure of Scientific Revolutions* in 1962, new paradigms arise when old ones are being overtaken by new discoveries which cannot be accommodated by the old paradigms.

The major pre-Darwinian reigning paradigms about the history of the earth and the presence of organic life were the Paradigm of Linnaeus, in which all species were listed as permanent, stable presences, and the Paradigm of Catastrophism, in which the past changes of both species and the earth were explained as the results of sudden, unpredictable, and irregular catastrophes such as earthquakes, floods, or meteorites.

The Linnaean paradigm explained nothing at all and was compatible with the traditional Biblical story, which was becoming doubted by more and more people during the 18th century. The catastrophic paradigm came to be questioned by the newly developed geology of Hutton (1726–1797) and Lyell (1797–1875), according to which the history of the earth was better explained as the result of the uniform operations of the laws of physics on rocks and water.

At the same time, the idea that at least living organisms had evolved over a long period rather than been created by God at the beginning of time was being considered more and more seriously, not least by Erasmus Darwin (1731–1802), Charles Darwin's grandfather, and by the Frenchman Lamarck (1744–1829), who was, however, more concerned with one special mechanism of adaptation than with the course of evolution itself from unicellular beginnings to the complexities of primates and *Homo sapiens sapiens*.

During the 18th century there also had been thoughts of evolution as a gradual unfolding of a predetermined blueprint, as in Goethe's *Urpflanze* or in Diderot's vision of seminal fluid as the microcosm which contained all future development *in nuce,* so to speak. In these paradigms, phylogeny was modeled on or thought of as an analogy of ontogeny. It was against this background that Charles Darwin (1809–1882) developed his revolutionary paradigm of evolution, which explained everything that was explained in the Linnaean and the catastrophist paradigms and a great many phenomena that were not.

The body of ideas contained in Darwin's new paradigms have changed over the years. The original Darwinian theory of the instability of species held that all species had descended from a common ancestor; there then came the revival inspired by the discoveries of Weismann and de Vries at the beginning of our century; then there was the so-called New Synthesis formulated by Julian Huxley in the middle of the 20th century; and during the second half of the 20th century, there is Neo-Darwinism and the so-called "Darwin industry," an ever-increasing production of books on Darwin and the implications of his paradigm for molecular biology, genetics, social culture, morphogenesis, and ethics, and both statistics and games theory are fruitfully applied to bring out further implications.

II. DARWINISM IN BIOLOGY

During his voyage around the world as the official naturalist and the gentleman companion of Captain Fitzroy, R.N., Darwin collected an enormous amount of information about species, both living and fossil. He gradually noticed that their distribution both in space and in time was not random, but that every fossil and every living organism he had come across was somehow fitted to the special environment in which it had been found. It was not only that fish were in water and birds in the air, but that, for example, the many finches on the Galapagos Islands were really different species which had developed special characteristics in response to the islands on which their ancestors had landed.

It is a telling comment on Darwin's courageous method that when he collected information about those finches on the Galapagos Islands which were to play such a large part in his arguments about the specific adaptation of organisms to a specific environment, his own collection was too inexact to allow an important classification of those finches according to their spatial distribution. Darwin had to wait for the more precise classification of the Galapagos birds by John Gould to see the point that each of the islands had its own special kind of finch.

And finally, it turned out much later and long after Darwin, when more accurate measurements were taken, that one could tell from the shapes of the finches' beaks the shapes the berries had on each island on which those finches were living. So the conclusion that the finches were fitted in minute detail to the special environment in which they were thriving is inescapable. But there was nothing in Darwin's own observations to make that conclusion inescapable.

After his return to England, Darwin kept mulling over his observations, and, in the back of his mind, he was wondering how the observation that species were not randomly distributed could be linked to the idea that evolution had taken place. He certainly knew that the possibility of evolution had been mooted. What was lacking was a knowledge of the mechanism by which it could have taken place.

Another thought that Darwin kept turning over was that if evolution had taken place and that if all of today's organisms had descended from earlier ancestors, then the received opinion that species were stable and permanent groups of organisms must be wrong. Darwin worked forward to the idea that species are mutable and transient, that earlier species had become extinct and new ones had developed from the older ones, and that today's species might eventually give way to descendants which were different species. In order to confirm his idea that species are mutable he started to collect a vast amount of information from farmers who, he knew, had been breeding both animal and plant organisms for centuries in order to generate offspring which had specially suitable qualities—such as hens that laid more eggs and sheep that grew a specially suitable kind of wool. He used this information to confirm in his own mind the idea that species are mutable and that Linnaean taxonomy, though not mistaken, could not be explanatory and ought to be replaced by one that was.

It was well known how farmers were achieving the selection of suitable characteristics by artificial breeding. But in nature, who had been the farmer? How could species change by natural means? What was the mechanism and what was the natural, as opposed to the articifial, incentive? In October 1839, he came across the famous treatise by Malthus (1760–1834) about population growth and pressure. Malthus explained that the supply of food was insufficient to nourish an ever-increasing population and that from time to time human beings had to be wiped out in great numbers by pestilence and war or other calamities. In short, Darwin got the idea from Malthus that resources are always limited and that the survival of individuals, be they animal or plant, depended on competition for those limited resources. If there is competition, obviously, some organisms manage more successfully than others, and those that manage more successfully are more likely to have more offspring than the others.

But there was still one element missing from the

puzzle. If there is competition, there have to be differences even between the organisms of the same species. Competition between species requires no special explanation. If one species has got suitable beaks and another does not, and if they are living in the same environment, then the species with the suitable beaks for the berries that are available in that environment will thrive more than the ones without such a suitable beak. But if species are mutable and new species develop from old species, then there must be variety among the members of each and every single species. And then the penny dropped.

In his *Autobiography,* written toward the end of his life, Darwin reported that he remembered "the very spot in the road, whilst in my carriage" where the thought occurred to him. If the single organisms of every species are slightly different from one another, then those that are better fitted to the environment than others must eventually breed better and faster and leave more offspring so that, over a long period of time, the species changes its characteristics and turns into a species in which the single members are better and better adapted to the environment. Thus he arrived at the conclusion that the competition between individual members of a species is a process of natural selection of those that are the best fit to the particular environment in which the species is living.

In this way he was able to explain how it happens that species are mutable and that all the species we know today are descended from other species which had been their ancestors. To put it bluntly, he explained how modern man was the direct descendant of a species of primates and how these primates had had ancestors that did not even look like bipedal primates, let alone mere vertebrates. What is more, he was able to explain how such natural selection, by bringing about the survival of the fittest, was the direct cause of the fact that every single species is adapted to the environment in which it is living.

In this way the new paradigm was put together. The salient features were (1) species are mutable and are descended from earlier ancestors, (2) the mechanism of mutability and descent consists of natural selection, and (3) the result of natural selection is adaptation of every species to the environment. These are the basic rudiments of the new paradigm which afforded for the first time an opportunity for an explanation of a wide variety of different geological and biological phenomena, and for this reason displaced all older paradigms, even though this did not happen at once. But it is telling that the very first edition of 2500 copies of Darwin's *Origin of Species by Means of Natural Selection* in 1859 sold out in a matter of weeks. This paradigm, with a large number of refinements and modifications over the past century, has proved unexpectedly fruitful beyond Darwin's own wildest expectations. But it would be wrong to think of this increasing fruitfulness as a straight line of increasing success and acceptance. Far from it.

Bishop Wilberforce's campaign against Darwinism is too well known to deserve further treatment. The bishop simply objected because Darwin's theory of evolution contradicted the Bible. It was a storm in a teacup, even though in parts of the USA Wilberforce's campaign was taken up again 100 years later and led to the famous Tennessee court case. But there lurked an element in this campaign which was not known to either Darwin or Wilberforce which went far beyond conflict with the Bible, for it was chastening even to people who were willing to doubt the Bible. When knowledge of the human brain increased, it followed from Darwin's theory of evolution that there is one part of the human triune brain which is common to humans and reptiles, ancestors which had evolved long before the earliest primates.

More important than Wilberforce's protests was the fact that both Darwin and his closest friends and collaborators also had their doubts. As to Darwin himself, he kept wondering how an organ such as the eye could have evolved, for the adaptiveness of the eye depended on a combination of several features—the lens, parts of the brain, the hollows in the skull—none of which were adaptive by themselves and, according to literal Darwinism, ought never have been selected for survival. To Darwin such complex organs were a mystery. But there was more. Darwin was completely ignorant of the mechanics of heredity and therefore kept wondering how a characteristic which was proving adaptive in one generation could ever be passed on to the offspring of that generation. As a result he had to fall back on the theory of Lamarck which had postulated that acquired characteristics are hereditary and are acquired because the organism *strives* to acquire them. Darwin had discounted Lamarck's theory of the acquisition of useful characteristics but kept harking back to the heredity of acquired characteristics.

Today we know that Lamarck was wrong because acquired characteristic cannot be passed on to the next generation. But Darwin did not know that and had to make do with that part of Lamarckism. Even more disturbing was the fact that Darwin did not know how old the earth was and kept wondering if there had been enough time for evolution to have taken place according to his principles and to have led far enough to produce humans. And finally, many of Darwin's closest friends, living as they were in pre-Kuhnian days, realized that there was no observational basis for what they took to be a theory rather than a paradigm, and that the absence of such a basis made the theory highly speculative.

As a result of such doubts and of the lack of further evidence, Darwinism went into a sort of decline until the beginning of the 20th century. It was only then that corroborating theories and corroborating evidence came to the fore. The first serious revival came when it was found that Darwin had been wrong to wonder about the available time, for it turned out that the earth was indeed old enough to allow for Darwinian evolution to have occurred. There was also the discovery by Mendel (1822–1884) of the Laws of Heredity and the checkered history of their reception. The Mendelian discovery that hybridization produces new characteristics is considered one of the pieces that had been missing in Darwin's own original theory. These laws did not prove Darwinism to be right, but they showed much better than Darwin had been able to show new characteristics can emerge.

Then there came the Dutch botanist Hugo de Vries, who in 1889 provided a much better explanation of the emergence of new species than had been availabe to Darwin. De Vries suggested that selection does not work so much on individual differences within a species, but that from time to time a real mutation occurs which produces new characteristics. His theory stated that these new characteristics emerge by genuine saltation and that it was these mutated forms which, if adaptive, could become the origin of a new species. Before de Vries, Darwinism had simply relied on the fact that all single individuals of a species are slightly different. But such individual differences are usually minute as far as evolution is concerned. What was needed to make Darwinism plausible was an understanding of the real nature of the occurrence of individual differences. And soon on the heels of Mendel and de Vries there came Weismann's theory in 1896 that cells contain a "germ plasm" which is transmitted intact in reproduction and which determines how the body will grow. This plasm could not be affected by the body and therefore Weismann put paid to the prominent place Lamarckism had occupied in early Darwinism.

Last but not least, there was A. R. Fisher's amendment of original Darwinism in his 1930 book, *The Genetic Theory of Natural Selection,* in which he consolidated the theory of evolution by explaining that natural selection acts primarily within species and not exclusively by competition among species. With that book he provided a genetic basis for the all-important idea that species are mutable—something which Darwin

himself had not been able to do. All these discoveries, far from falsifying all or any part of Darwinism, gave it new life and showed how fruitful Darwin's original paradigm was. The more biologists discovered about the nature of life, the easier it became to fit these discoveries into Darwinism's overarching paradigm of evolution by random mutation and selective retention.

As if this was not enough there came in the middle of the 20th century the growth of molecular biology and, eventually, the discovery of the double helix of DNA. This gigantic discovery of the molecular structure of genes not only fitted the Darwinian paradigm, but provided enormously strong evidence for its truth. With the discovery of that molecular structure there came the so-called Central Dogma, which stated that DNA can pass instructions to the organism's proteins, but that the organism's proteins cannot influence the composition of the genes. This Central Dogma not only refuted the Lamarckian elements in Darwin's own thought but also provided a perfectly viable explanation of why random mutations occurred and why they were being offered to the environment for selection: every time a portion of DNA changes hands (or ought we say, more correctly, changes bodies?) there is a likelihood of errors occurring during the copying process. This explains why species change in a way in which original Darwinism could never have explained. And what is more, our knowledge of DNA also explains why there was an advantage in sexual reproduction and why sexual reproduction was more likely to generate mutations than simple cell division. All in all, as the century went by, discovery after discovery made the Darwinian paradigm more and more credible, even though many facets of the original subsidiary theories, due to what Kuhn calls "normal science," kept being changed.

Apart from the scientific changes that keep being made, there are also more purely philosophical controversies surrounding the interpretation of Darwinism. The English biologist Richard Dawkins, in his *Blind Watchmaker* of 1986, has set himself the task of providing minute evidence and hundreds of examples as to how the Darwinian paradigm of evolution by chance mutation and selective retention can indeed explain the seemingly improbable fact that, starting with unicellular organisms, evolution has led to such complex organisms as human beings.

In contrast, the American paleontologist Stephen Jay Gould has forcefully argued in a series of books and articles that Darwinian evolution is a nonlinear process and that it is so improbable to have led to human beings that, far from being probable, it was pure chance that it did. Gould insists on the pure contingency of evolution.

Darwin himself had been in at least two minds about this. In some places he considered that the continuing process of evolution never led to progress, and in many other places he thought that it did and that not only were human beings progress over primates, but that among human beings, the British "race," as he called it, was progress over other forms of human life.

As to Gould's forceful insistence on contingency, there may be a genuine misunderstanding here. Th. Dobzhansky explained long ago that in Darwinism there are two elements, contingency and necessity. Mutations are contingents, but once emerged, the selection by the environment of the mutation is not all that contingent. If a fish, to make up a crude example, were born by some chance mutation with lungs, it would not be selected to live long enough to breed. The lack of selection follows by necessity from the properties of water. Gould's pan-contingency, according to which selection as well as mutation is purely contingent, is untenable, or at least incompatible with Darwinism.

Darwin himself was aware that his paradigm implied design, for this is what adaptation amounted to. His paradigm merely differed from the creationist paradigm in that, e.g., the fit of gills to water and lungs to air was not the result of a divine Designer, but the necessary outcome of natural selection. Darwin himself relied on the notion of natural selection to bring about design and fit, although he did supplement natural selection with the idea of sexual selection. In very recent times the idea that natural selection is supplemented by sexual selection has been given a wide berth.

But there have been endless debates and disagreements about the randomness of natural selection. On one side there are the theories which stress the accidental and unplanned nature of evolution, and on the other, theories which stress the noncontingent elements. The accidental nature of design is at the heart of R. A. Fisher's statistical genetics in which gene frequencies are modified by natural selection. On this side there is also M. Kimura's notion of genetic drift, which makes evolution "neutral" because many amino acids and nucleotide substitutions are random fixations or nearly neutral mutations. S. J. Gould has suggested that the process of evolution is not the slow continuous process envisaged by Darwin, but the result of punctuated equilibrium. That is, evolution comes in leaps and starts, and then stays stable for long stretches of time, only to speed up again after long intervals.

On the other side we have Brian Goodman who argues that organisms are not mere survival machines or carriers of genes, selfish or unselfish as the case may be, but that their evolution is, on the contrary, in part controlled, as D'Arcy Thompson proposed as early as 1917, by the geometry of biological form. In a similar vein it has also been proposed by Stuart Kauffman that we are actually "at home in the universe" because not even mutations are random occurrences, but result from the innate tendencies of complex systems to exhibit order spontaneously. Kauffman shows with lots of examples that such autocatalytic processes are at work in the very nature of matter. Not only do they produce living organisms, they also make them evolve along the lines in which they have evolved, so that the entire process is more or less predictable. A similar noncontingent view of Darwinian evolution is contained in the so-called "Anthropic Principle," which states that evolution as such and the course it has taken are a necessary consequence of the way the universe first came into being. If it had come into being in a different way, that Principle states, the evolution of life would not have been possible. Further, once life had emerged, it was only a matter of time for beings with large brains like humans to evolve.

We must conclude with the observation that the Darwinian paradigm has proved immensely fruitful; that it is strengthened, not weakened, by new discoveries; and that the broad debates about contingency and necessity, accident and design, and punctuated equilibrium and autocatalytic processes are all conducted in the shadow of the paradigm because they are what Kuhn calls "normal science," pursued on the assumption that the original Darwinian paradigm is tenable. No observations have been made which cause disquiet about the Paradigm itself—disquiet which could eventually lead to the substitution of a new paradigm.

III. DARWINISM IN THE HISTORY OF SCIENCE

According to the canons of scientific knowledge as they have been developed in the modern era since Francis Bacon (1561–1626) and formulated as "The Received View" as recently as 1977 by Frederick Suppe, Darwin ought never to have arrived at his theory. These canons demand that scientists do not make hypotheses, let alone guesses. Scientists ought to collect observations and, when they have collected enough observations which display recognizably similar features, they ought to proceed by induction to formulate a general theory. If this path is followed, the results are certain, and only those results that are thus certain are entitled to be called "science." If it turns out that the results are false, then there must have been a failure in the method by which they have been arrived at.

Scientists themselves, until quite recent times, have paid lip service to these canons, and any departure from the canons, even though this occurred very frequently, was considered "politically incorrect." However, historians of science have shown that no scientist worth his mettle has ever observed these canons. On the contrary, knowledge is arrived at by courageous guesses about almost random observations. These guesses are then subjected to rigorous and untiring efforts to falsify them. And even if they fail to be falsified, they are still not certain to be true, but are considered to be working hypotheses and taken to be provisionally true. This is a more realistic account than the "politically correct" orthodoxy that there is a "right" method which yields certain truth.

To mention just one example, I. B. Cohen has shown in his magisterial *The Newtonian Revolution* of 1980 that Newton's actual practice differed very widely from the politically correct scenario ("hypothesis *non fingo*") to which he pretended to have adhered. In any case, Karl Popper, in his *Logic of Scientific Discovery* of 1934 (English translation in 1959), had shown that the Baconian canon could not possibly have been observed and that there is not and need not be a "correct method." In 1962 Thomas Kuhn, in his *Structure of Scientific Revolutions,* enlarged on Popper by making a very convincing case that the pursuit of "normal science" was completely dependent on and relative to an initial paradigm which owed its presence to anything but the observance of the Baconian principles and "The Received View."

The rise and history of Darwinism is especially instructive for the philosophy of science. Darwin admitted in his *Autobiography,* which he wrote late in life, that he had not abided by the politically correct Baconian canon. In this self-portrait he explained that he had made a very large number of observations about the spatial and temporal distribution of species and paid brief lip service to the established view of scientific method by stating that he had made these observations according to "Baconian principles." But then he immediately proceeded to tell the truth and let the cat out of the bag. He said that these observations had demanded an explanation and that it came to him in two separate flashes.

The first flash which led him to the hypothesis, unsupported as it was by the observations themselves, that there was competition for survival and the selection of the fittest (meaning "most adapted to a specific environment") occurred when he happened to read Malthus' text for his "amusement." It was, so he implied, an accident that he came across Malthus and that Malthus led him to formulate the main part of his paradigm. But he was still left with the problem as to what was the criterion of selection. The solution to this problem came in another flash, suddenly and out of the blue, and was not supported by observations at all—though, he added, this was not strictly true, for he did make a large number of observations by gathering information from farmers all over England as to how they bred certain characteristics by *artificial* selection. He used these systematically gathered observations in order to support his final theory, but only after the hypothesis about descent by modification had flashed through his mind.

However, there is a snag of which Darwin was not aware. Artificial breeding as practiced by farmers does produce new characteristics. For example, one can artificially change cabbages to yield, e.g., cauliflowers and brussels sprouts. But, and this is the all-important point, sprouts and cauliflowers can again be crossed and are fertile to produce offspring; that is, they are not really new species at all. Artificial breeding, in short, does not support the theory that species are mutable. Nevertheless Darwin used these observations of artificial breeding as evidence that one can change species, that species are unstable, and that one species can change into another species. He believed artificial breeding to be genuine evidence for the mutability of species. But in this he was wrong, or at least his notion of what constitutes a species was wrong.

A species is a group of organisms which can produce offspring. They are fertile. We define a species in this way. Artificial breeding can change characteristics inside a species, but it cannot transcend a species and produce a new species. For this to happen one needs a mutation in the DNA of at least some members of a species. This was unknown to Darwin, though it is well known to us and has led to the science of genetic engineering. We thus arrive at the astonishing conclusion that the most important piece of evidence he used to support his theory that species are mutable was wrong. The hypothesis that species are mutable, as we have seen, is absolutely crucial to the very notion of Darwinian evolution, but the evidence which Darwin collected and on which he based his conclusion proves nothing of the sort.

It was only long after Darwin that the real reason why species are unstable was discovered. Thus Darwin did not follow the correct method, which stated that one has to arrive at a theory by using induction from a large number of correct observations. The very history of Darwin's discovery of his paradigm, that is, of Darwinism, is therefore living proof that the Baconian principles were wrong and that Popper and Kuhn were right. The hypothesis precedes the guess, and the truth of the guess does not depend on the observation of the canon, but on the courage to make a guess—the guess can turn out to be correct even though the observations which have inspired it are false. The initial observations by themselves are neither here nor there. Darwin's observations of the spatial and temporal distribution of organisms would have allowed for different explanations and certainly did not compel, as Bacon's principles would have demanded, the conclusion which Darwin proposed. Moreover, Darwin showed considerable courage, for as he himself admitted, there was ample room for doubt. He was very conscious of the fact that he was guessing and that none of his many observations added cogently up to his hypothesis.

When he was deeply immersed in his great work on barnacles he wrote to his friend Hooker on June 15, 1850, that "systematic work would be easy were it not for this confounded variation [in individual barnacles] which, however, is pleasant to me as a speculist, though odious to me as a systematist." And Hooker himself had written to him in April of that year, "I remember once dreaming that you were too prone to theoretical considerations about species and unaware of certain difficulties in your way, which I thought a more intimate acquaintance with species *practically* might clear up."

His friend Hooker was not a "speculist" and so it was Darwin, not Hooker, who created the paradigm. Darwin, the "speculist," had the courage to proceed to guess and speculate even though the evidence was far from conclusive. As far as he knew, the earth was not old enough to allow for the evolution of primates, let alone of hominids, to have taken place. And his ignorance of the mechanics of heredity made it extremely unlikely that characteristics which proved adaptive in some organisms in one generation could be passed on to the next generation so that a new "species" could emerge. By the received Baconian standards of what counts as science, Darwin failed. But since he did not fail, and since his proposal that evolution proceeds by competition and selective retention has proved a most fruitful paradigm into which a vast number of subsequent discoveries could be fitted, Darwin, among other things, provided a living example of how science really progresses and how knowledge grows. The explanatory power of Darwinism has increased and is increasing in spite of his failure to follow the received canon. Darwin demonstrated that the philosophy of science propounded by Karl Popper in the 1930s is a valid philosophy of science.

The case of Darwin's paradigm forces us to make an important amendment to Kuhn's theory of the nature of paradigms. According to Kuhn, all theories are relative to a paradigm, and a paradigm itself cannot be compared to reality. This means that a paradigm is an assumption or model which stands entirely on the fact that it allows a lot of normal science. It is abandoned when the normal science it generates ceases to yield satisfactory explanations and when the dissatisfaction tends to outweigh the satisfying theories it leads to. The example of Darwin's paradigm contradicts this part of the Kuhnian philosophy of science, for the Darwinian paradigm, pace Kuhn, is falsifiable. It depends, of course, on how the paradigm is formulated. If it is taken to mean the survival of the fittest, it may be little more than a tautology, though a very fruitful one. As a tautology it is obviously not falsifiable. If it is formulated as the view that species are mutable, it could, in principle, be falsifiable, but as Wittgenstein once remarked, nobody has ever watched the transmutation of a species. In this formulation it is at best a metaphysical theory because one cannot really describe the kind of observation that might falsify it.

But consider a different formulation. If the paradigm is taken to be the view that all species are descended by modification from an initial cell, the paradigm becomes very falsifiable. In this formulation, the paradigm implies the proposition that there could not have been *homo sapiens* 300 million years ago. Now, if one were to find a human fossil in a rock sediment of 300 million years ago, the paradigm would be falsified. We must therefore conclude, against Kuhn, that there are at least some paradigms which are falsifiable.

But there is more to come. It has turned out that the Darwinian paradigm can be applied not only to the evolution of organisms, but also to our *knowledge* of the evolution of organisms, as well as to our knowledge of the evolution of knowledge in general, that is, physics, geology, psychology, sociology, and so forth. In Darwin's paradigm every organism that survives to breed and leave offspring is more or less adapted to its environment. In other words, it embodies knowledge about its environment. An organism must therefore be seen as an embodied theory about its environment. If an organism emerges which is badly adapted or not adapted at all, it cannot surive and so it becomes—to use Popper's terminology—falsified.

This scheme can be extended to knowledge itself. Knowledge consists of theories about the environment, and one can see that theories which are formulated by human minds are disembodied organisms. If they are not true, they will eventually be falsified and will not survive, just as embodied theories, that is, biological organisms, that do not adapt do not survive. Popper has thus added a new dimension to the original paradigm. The emergence of organisms is random, but their survival depends on the degree of their adaptation. An adapted organism is therefore a correct solution of the problem of survival.

In the same way, a theory is a hypothetical solution of a problem. As long as it fails to be falsified, the problem of survival in a given environment is solved. In Popper's version, the quintessence of Darwinism is problem solving. Every organism, in becoming adapted to an environment, changes that environment in so far as it itself becomes part of that environment, thus creating new problems for other organisms as well as for itself. Each solution makes new problems and each new problem calls for another solution.

IV. DARWINISM AND PHILOSOPHY

Darwin was not a philosopher and did not pretend to be one. Nevertheless he was incisive enough to understand that if his theory of evolution was true, then there would be important and crucial implications for philosophy. In his *Notebooks* he made two crucial entries. He stated that if one understands the baboon (i.e., at least one of our ancestors), one would realize that Locke was completely wrong. Locke had taught that our minds are, at birth, a *tabula rasa*, and that whatever we know gets poured into it by sense experience after birth. Darwin realized that if we are descended from primates, some of their mental equipment or their cognitive apparatus must have come down to us just as their eyes and parts of their nervous system have. It follows from Darwinism that much knowledge, or at least the equipment to acquire knowledge, is indeed innate and not the result of exposure to the world. The mind is, at birth, not an empty bucket.

Darwin's second entry concerned Plato. He said that Plato had taught that man's soul had preexisted before it entered the body at birth. He suggested that we substitute "monkeys" for "preexistence"—meaning Plato was not entirely wrong, and not nearly as wrong as Locke. Souls and their imaginary ideas had not just "preexisted" as Plato had thought, but some of these imaginary ideas we call our mind are derived from our ancestors and have been passed on to us because they are adaptive. Darwin was discriminating and not evenhanded. He rejected Locke out of hand but suggested that we merely have to amend Plato.

With these succinct remarks Darwin expressed the idea that every sound theory of knowledge would have to take into account the facts which follow from evolution by natural selection. That is, all organisms come into the world with faculties and senses adapted to their environment and that these adaptations are not acquired during their lifetime, but are the result of millions of years of natural selection, so that all organisms are born with them. All that can take place after birth and exposure to the environment is a bit of fine tuning. These philosophical implications were taken up and explicitly propounded, and their consequences systematically explored, by the Nobel prize-winning ethologist Konrad Lorenz in his *Behind the Mirror* of 1973 (English translation, 1977).

There are, in addition to the general philosophical orientation of Darwinism, a number of further and quite specific implications which I will list, though not necessarily in their order of importance.

Darwinism, by its insistence on selection, made an enormously important contribution to our understanding of the method of information transfer. The common sense view which had been widely broadcast and almost universally accepted was that information is transferred by copying, and that we learn by following instruction. In Darwinism it is the other way round. Information is transferred by a selection from an abundance of random and maverick proposals, and those that contain the correct information are selected.

This selectionism has proved enormously fruitful. It has completely changed our understanding of the mechanics of immunity responses, and Gerald M. Edelman has used the idea to explain the growth of the nervous system. We are born, he argues, with a rich abundance of neurons. After exposure to the world, a vast number of these neurons atrophy because only some connections between neurons are selected by the environment. This theory is a direct application of Darwinism to our understanding of the operations of the brain and the rest of the nervous system.

In the philosophy of Karl Popper (1902–1994), selectionism plays a similar role. Popper argues that knowledge grows by the almost wild-cat emergence of proposals, some of which are selected for retention because they fail to be falsified by the environment. We do not learn about the world by taking instruction and by waiting around patiently, but proceed by making guesses and then allow the world to select those that best correspond to it.

The Darwinian conception of adaptation contains the germ for a sound and viable theory of truth. It is widely believed that one can call a proposition "true" if it corresponds to the facts it describes. But this is easier said than established. If one starts instead with the notion of adaptation one can form a better understanding of the relationship between a proposition and the facts it purports to correspond to. In an important sense an adapted organism is a "true" theory about the part of the environment it is adapted to. But no adaptation, as S. J. Gould never tires of informing us, is perfect. It depends, to start with, on the relative presence or absence of competitors. If, for example, there are no competitors, an organism does not have to be minutely adapted in order to survive. The same goes for the notion of truth. There can never be perfect correspondence between a verbal proposition and the "facts" it is supposed to be about, because words simply do not and cannot "correspond" to anything other than further words. But if we think of truth in the way Darwinism thinks of adaptation, we will be able to reach a better understanding of what is meant when one claims that a proposition is true.

Darwinism has also made a major contribution to the old and perennial problem of whether there is a "real" world, that is, a world other than the world we perceive. In a sense, the belief that there is, is a contradiction in terms, and idealists of all shades have never lost time to insist on the contradictoriness of realism. But with Darwinism there is now very good ground for being a genuine realist. The presence of the living organisms from the earliest single cell to modern humans is a mirror image of the real world. The real world, over millions and millions of years, has, by natural selection, allowed certain organisms to survive and breed. Every organism is a sort of mirror of that world. Crudely speaking, fish mirror water, and birds mirror air. If there were no photons, we would have no eyes, and if there were no sound waves, there would be no ears. One can learn a lot about the shape of the steppe by studying the hoof of a horse. In short, the presence of life is proof that there is a real world over and above what we can perceive, and what is more, we can learn a lot about its properties by looking at the living organisms that are adapted to it. If this is so, our knowledge of those properties does not have to rely entirely on our ability to look at the world.

Darwinism also throws a new light on a very old puzzle. Philosophers ever since Plato have wondered about the relation between particular objects or events and the universal concepts, words, or general theories under which we subsume them in order to describe and refer to them. This is a no-win situation. If we start from universals, we can never get more than many identical particular events or objects. If we start from *genuinely* individual particulars, we can never reach a

universal summary. Since there are genuinely individual particulars, and since no two objects or events are so alike that they could be taken to be the clones we get when we start with universals, the influential philosopher Richard Rorty maintains that universal concepts or theories are figments of the human imagination which serve no purpose other than to make life difficult or create jobs for philosophers. But this view cannot be correct for the simple reason that Rorty himself could not express it in so many words unless there were legitimate universals or words with universal meanings and universal reference. In Darwinism there is a much better, if not exhaustive, understanding of this relationship.

In Darwinism genuinely individual particulars play a crucial role. If there were no absolutely individual particular organisms, evolution could not have taken place, for evolution depends on the natural selection from a vast array of individual differences. But the mechanics of selection and the survival of those organisms that are selected obey universal laws. In Darwinism, in short, it is not a question of either particulars or universals. The presence and interaction of both genuinely individual particulars (that is, particular organisms which are not clones, i.e., not so many instances of a universal) and universals are the essential feature of evolution. And if evolution had not taken place, we would not be here today to wonder about the relationship between particulars and universals.

Philosophers, especially those interested in history and the development of cultures and societies, have often wondered whether such development is determined or whether, at any one moment, people are free to alter the institutions and beliefs they have been born into. The great debate has always been whether there are laws of development or whether development follows unpredictable paths.

It was tempting right from the inauguration of the new paradigm to talk, as Herbert Spencer did, of a "Law of Evolution," the irresistible operation of which had caused life to develop from simple cells to ever-increasingly complex organisms which, when the human stage was arrived at, were being forced by that law to develop toward ever greater perfection. One could think of the operation of such a law of evolution as a gradual unfolding of a cellular germ which contained, right from the beginning, all the potential that was to evolve. Alternately, one could think of such a law as the expression of a universal, cosmological force which, though incomprehensible, was irresistible. Darwinism sheds a very special light on that problem.

In the Darwinian paradigm, there is no law of evolution—neither in the sense of an unfolding nor in the sense of an irresistible cosmic force. On the contrary, in the Darwinian paradigm all changes are the result of the routine operations of general natural laws, and none of these changes are necessary or predictable. For this reason Karl Popper was quite wrong when in his *Poverty of Historicisim* (1957) he included Darwinism among the "historicist" pseudo-sciences in which it was held that there is such a developmental law which forces changes in a certain and predictable direction. Popper eventually retracted this charge, and indeed Darwin's conception of evolution and history conforms to the strictest scientific standards according to which changes are the result of the operation of ordinary natural laws and not the result of a single developmental law.

Nevertheless, even by these strict scientific standards, changes are not totally random, and at any one moment the future is not entirely unpredictable, for the prevailing conditions at any one moment allow only for a limited number of changes to take place. This applies to the history of thought and science as much as to organic evolution. If we think of inventions of new beliefs and new institutions as an analogue to mutations, we can soon see that while there is a lot of freedom for new mutations and inventions to take place, there are also very severe limitations on such freedom.

At any one moment, the opportunities for mutations that stand a chance of being selected are limited. To make another crude example, while an elephant could be born with a mutation that yielded a longer trunk or harder tusks, the chances of an elephant being born with a mutation that made its baby into a bird is negligible. In other words, mutations, though random and unpredictable, can only make use of the opportunities that are already present.

One is tempted to conclude that the same applies to human institutions and beliefs. A feudal society with its *curia regis* could change into a parliamentary democracy, and a parliamentary democracy could easily change into a totalitarian dictatorship. But a society organized along clan structure is not likely to "mutate" into a society which consists of an assembly of individual persons with equal rights which could be joined freely by other individuals from different societies.

It follows from these considerations that the more specific and complex adaptations become, the fewer the opportunities for further mutations. This shows that while there are no laws of development (i.e., there is no "historicism," to use Popper's term for laws of development), the future is never wholly undetermined and certainly not as undetermined as Popper maintained,

because the opportunities for changes are circumscribed by present conditions. Admittedly, this is a somewhat speculative thought, but one should not underrate the Darwinian elements which support it.

V. SOCIAL DARWINISM

It is no surprise to find that as soon as Darwin's thoughts about competition for the struggle for survival became known, they were seized by enthusiasts and distorted. Herbert Spencer (1820–1908), a contemporary of Darwin, immediately seized the opportunity of using Darwinism to make a social philosophy. Already in his *Social Statics* of 1851, Spencer had jumped the gun eight years before Darwin's own *Origin of Species* and had proclaimed that "evolution" (The term was coined and popularized by Spencer earlier and more than by Darwin!) was a law of necessary progress which underlay the whole of organic creation. Civilization was part of nature and of a piece with the development of the embryo and the unfolding of a flower. It guaranteed that evil would ultimately disappear and man would "become perfect."

In order to promote this idea and make it plausible, Spencer started to propagate the slogan, "the survival of the fittest." In suggesting that the most fit is not only likely to have more offspring, as Darwin had done, but is more entitled to survive as an individual than his or her competitors, Spencer injected a solidly unethical, not to say immoral, element into Darwinism. Where Darwin had suggested that there is competition inside every species and that competition would eventually produce a different species, Spencer thought up a whole array of catch phrases about nature and society and formulated a general theory about the development of the universe from an initial state of homogeneity toward a higher state of greatly diverse complexity.

In his posthumous autobiography Spencer eventually declared that people who multiply beyond their means take the road to extinction and will die off in droves as (referring to the great Irish Famine) "we have recently seen exemplified in Ireland." Those who remain are the "select of their generation." Spencer was, if there ever was one, a real enthusiast whose idea of tragedy was, as he himself confessed in his autobiography, a theory contradicted by a fact, for he ought to have known that the Irish Famine was to a large extent not only a natural disaster but that its "selective effects" were brought about by the policies of the British government. One way or another, all this was not incompatible with what Darwin had suggested, but changed its emphasis and led to Tennyson's further poetic slogan that "nature [is] red in tooth and claw."

With such a slogan and the Spencerian thought about survival of the fittest, the ground was laid for a social philosophy which insisted that societies should not be controlled and marshalled by governments, but rather that individual members should be allowed to compete by all means available to them to down other individuals, prey on them, and take advantage of their weaknesses, and that by that mechanism, societies in which only really worthwhile individuals survive would emerge.

It is a moot point whether this translation of Darwinism to social thought was an adaptation, a mere translation, or a downright travesty of Darwinism. Darwin himself was tolerantly bemused by Spencer and sympathized with the broad idea that there was evolution from simple beginnings to great diversity. But he also knew that while he saw this progress and the changes it necessitated as the result of the uniform operation of ordinary natural laws, Spencer thought of it as the result of an irresistible law of development—precisely a form of what Popper was later to call and reject as "historicism." Whichever way, it became readily popular and generated two powerful movements.

The first movement was what we commonly now call "right-wing" politics. Such politics, in which individual effort is encouraged and in which governmental and traditional restraints on such efforts are removed, is not the direct or sole result of Darwinism. There was a solid pre-Darwinian basis which goes back, for want of a better single source, to Adam Smith's teaching in Britain and to the 18th century "laissez-faire" school of thought in France. But the advent of Spencer's version of Darwinism cannot be underestimated. At the very least it provided a pseudo-scientific underpinning, and with that underpinning it has reached new heights in our own day with the attack on the welfare state and the New Deal in the USA. These attacks are often supported by an appeal to the Darwinian principle that one ought to allow natural selection free play and not support the poor by handing out benefits or other forms of social security. The New Deal and the welfare state, it is argued by social Darwinists, are a useless and ultimately self-defeating interference with the process of natural selection through which the poor, the sick, and the unintelligent would die out. Spencerian Darwinism is a major factor in the influential political and economic thought of Karl August von Hayek.

In contrast to the advocacy of total freedom for natural selection, another movement inspired by social

Darwinism advocates new and unprecedented heights of active interference. This second movement, which, like the first, is also promoted by Spencer's underpinning of Darwinism, is the eugenics movement. In eugenics the thought that there is a possible biological basis to disease and to mental and psychological attitudes and propensities is taken very literally. As a result it came to be proposed that Darwinism taught that one should breed human beings artificially and subject their sexual activities to scientific control in order to avoid or, at least reduce, the incidence of disease, poor intelligence, psychological deviance, and criminality.

The trouble with that application of Darwinism to social policy is not that it is pseudo-scientific. In so far as there are hereditary factors in these social maladaptations, it is a perfectly reasonable thought that controlled breeding, even though it interferes with individual freedom, might produce more stable, more peaceful, and more prosperous societies. The trouble with eugenics lies in its practicability. It is one thing to assert, probably correctly, that there are hereditary factors which could be eliminated by artificially controlled breeding, but quite another to believe that we know enough of the precise genetic factors that make for lack of intelligence and other forms of asocial behavior. It is true that in many simple cases such as sickle-cell anemia a lot of progress has been made and that controlled breeding might one day eliminate this dreadful disease. But when we come to complex phenomena like "intelligence," we are completely in the dark. There is no telling what unintelligent behavior really consists of and which genes ought to be eliminated in order to avoid it. What is more, the many facets of "intelligence" are almost certainly not all genetic. There are cultural and psychological dispositions which make for intelligence, and cultural and psychological factors which prevent intelligence. It is an unfounded assumption that we know that such phenomena as intelligence, creativity, altruism, and egotism are purely genetic and that we have enough detailed knowledge of genes to use artificial breeding to promote or eliminate them. In spite of these considerations, the movement keeps coming up time and again to produce a large literature.

The link between authentic Darwinism and Spencer's version should not be dismissed lightly. Darwin showed friendly tolerance of Spencer. One must not think that Darwin was duped. In his *Descent of Man* of 1871 he himself used eugenic arguments. He argued that parents who are wealthy and in poor health, and therefore short-lived, are likely to produce children who are not healthy. But these children will inherit their wealth early in life and therefore breed more children than they might have otherwise. Hence, they will pass on their own poor health to an even larger number of children.

It does not matter that Darwin applied the theory of the inheritance of acquired characteristics in this argument. What matters is that he was not wholly innocent of the social implications of Darwinism and that Spencer's flamboyant literary activity was not a total travesty of Darwinism. But there is more. Darwin himself lived in the midst of the industrial and commercial revolution of Victorian Britain, and the great Exhibition of 1850 was appreciated by him and his whole family as a symbol of the progress of wealth and well-being. It is very likely that his ready appreciation of Malthus had something to do with the fact that he belonged to a wealthy family which was the immediate beneficiary of that industrial and commercial progress, and there is certain evidence that he was appreciative of the way the growing British Empire was spreading that kind of progress around the world.

Some historians have made the most of these connections, and there is an entire school of thought which believes that Darwinism was in reality the ideology of the Victorian middle class, engaged in ever more and freer enterprise to enrich themselves and to prosper. But it is one thing to detect, as many biographers of Darwin have done, the inspirational power of that kind of socioeconomic progress and quite another to use it to judge the value and truth of Darwinism. Newton, it has been alleged, was inspired to think of the force of gravity, which acts at a distance, by the fact that he longed for his mother from whom he was separated when he was a toddler. But this theory about the inspiration of his theory of gravitation, if correct, does not function as proof of its truth or as proof that it was nothing but an ideology for deprived children.

Similarly it has been suggested that the indeterminacy principle of quantum mechanics owed its inspiration as well as its power to carry conviction to the indeterminate, fluid, and uncertain sociopolitical environment of the German Weimar Republic in which it was conceived by Heisenberg. But again, it should not be argued that this climate added to or detracted from its validity. For the same reasons we must disentangle the optimistic climate of mid-Victorian Britain in which Darwinism was born from the philosophical and scientific reasons for its validity and continuing fruitfulness.

VI. DARWINISM AND THE HISTORY OF CULTURES

Darwinism played a crucial role in the development of modern industrial and postindustrial cultures and social orders by cutting away the religious foundations on which the ancient regimes had rested. Just as Copernicus had shown that we are not in the center of the universe, Darwin taught us that we had not been specially created by God in the Garden of Eden, but that we are not all that different from apes, who in turn were second cousins to reptiles and cabbages. His theory of evolution helped to disenchant and thus clear the way for economic rationality by destroying not only religious belief, but the institutions which had supported such belief and which were still standing in the way of economic rationality and profit maximization. At the same time he also provided a new and different kind of enchantment and enthusiasm for science, for it has to be admitted that in many important ways the thought that primates have evolved from unicellular organisms and that we humans have evolved from primates is a great deal more awe inspiring than the idea that God manufactured us from a lump of clay. But if he helped to destroy the old order and make room for the technologies and industries which are supporting an ever-growing human population, he also laid the foundations for an entirely new view of the development and evolution of cultures.

Ever since Greek and Biblical times, it has been recognized that cultures change and that these changes come in a certain order so that the relationship between the passage of time, the earlier and the later, is not random. For the most part it was thought that the cultures of the past were better or happier than the cultures of the day, although in some cases it was believed that the good old days might become restored in the future through some miracle, as in the case of Christians, or in the case of Karl Marx, through the advent of the great proletarian revolution.

During the 18th century these largely metaphysical versions of the successions of the qualities of cultures came to be replaced by more sober and realistic accounts in which there was a gradual change and a gradual progress from early primitive conditions of hunter–gatherer cultures to pastoral cultures, and from pastoral cultures to industrial and commercial, capitalist cultures. These changes, it was believed, had nothing to do with biology or with the fact that humans are special kinds of animals. They were controlled, on the contrary, by institutional factors and by the modes of making a living.

Eventually during the 19th century these versions were elaborated into genuine stories of progress toward intellectual and spiritual enlightenment. The main motor of these changes in the appreciation of these sequences is to be found in the writings of the French philosopher Auguste Comte, and, largely through his influence, there came a veritable avalanche of histories of cultural change and even of cultural evolution (see Box 1).

Box 1

As the titles of the following texts indicate, the accent was on civilization and on societies, so that human beings as biological organisms were completely neglected: Henry Maine's *Ancient Law* (1861); E. B. Tylor's *Researches into the Early History of Mankind* (1865); John Lubbock's *Origin of Civilisation* (1870); Lewis H. Morgan's *Ancient Society* (1877); H. T. Buckle's *History of Civilization in England* (1857–1861); and, in the middle of the 20th century, Arnold Toynbee's massive 13-volume *A Study of History*.

With Darwinism, the center of interest focused not just on the changes in cultures, but on the origins of culture (see Box 2). Why, we were now asking, is there any culture at all? The change of orientation is the direct result of the realization that human beings are, at least to start with, animals, and that culture must therefore be a biological phenomenon. If one wants to understand it and the changes it has undergone since its inception, one has to start with its origins. These origins must be linked to the period in which primates

---

Box 2

With the burgeoning of Darwinism we find that the titles of such books as listed in Box 1 started to change. They were now called *Shadows of Forgotten Ancestors* (Sagan); *Man, the Promising Primate* (Peter Wilson); *Man, the Ethical Animal* (Mary Midgley); *Man, the Moral Animal* (Robert Wright); *The Chosen Primate* (Adam Kuper); *The Lopsided Ape: Evolution of the Generative Mind* (M. C. Corballis); *The Origin of Humankind* (Richard Leakey); *Sociobiology* (E. O. Wilson); *The Rise and Fall of the Third Chimpanzee* (Jared Diamond); and *The Adapted Mind* (J. H. Barkow, Leda Cosmides, and J. Tooby).

---

started to become hominoid, eventually hominid, and, finally, human.

It is part of the story of Darwinism and the growing employment of the Darwinian paradigm that before we reached the books in Box 2, there was a very powerful reaction against the eugenic, social Darwinian, and racist elements in social Darwinism. This reaction took the world of anthropology by storm, and whatever its failings, it must be realized that it was motivated initially by the very ethical consideration that eugenics and other racist and unethically competitive features of social Darwinism were unacceptable. It was no accident that the first and chief promoter of this anti-Darwinian reaction was Franz Boas, a Prussian Jew who had emigrated to the USA toward the end of the 19th century.

The Boasian school insisted that culture was a unique phenomenon which had nothing to do with biology. Each culture was the sole and complete determinant of human behavior and mentality. Each culture was different from all other cultures, and the rules and norms prevailing inside every culture were relative to that culture and could not be judged from the outside, least of all in terms of their adaptation to an environment, and most certainly not in terms of whether they dealt successfully with our animal nature.

In the wake of Boas, even though not directly influenced by him, there developed the antievolutionary and nonhistorical anthropology of both Bronislaw Malinowski (1884–1942) and A. R. Radcliffe-Brown (1881–1955) in Britain, and the structural anthropology of culture of Claude Lévi-Strauss (1908–) in France. The most widely read, nonevolutionary, nonbiological works in this category are Margaret Mead's *Coming of Age in Samoa* (1928), Ruth Benedict's *Patterns of Culture* (1934), and Bronislaw Malinowski's *Argonauts of the Western Pacific* (1922).

If one is working inside the Darwinian paradigm, none of these works can tell us much about human cultures, for they do not take into account that culture, like everything else in this world and like the universe itself, has evolved from simple configurations into vastly complex constellations. In Darwinism the process of evolution, whether neutral or for the good or bad, is continuous. If one wants to understand culture, one has to first consider the primates who preceded humans and seek to understand why they managed without cultures where humans cannot. As a result, the biology-oriented anthropologists all start with a consideration of those characteristics of primates which were integrated into culture, though in a modified way. But after this initial start, which is common to them all, the paths have diverged.

On one side there are those who have remained, strictly speaking, zoologists. In their view all elements to be found in human cultures are extensions and adaptations of the characteristics of primates. The first to explore this idea was E. O. Wilson, who endeavored to find the roots of cooperation and altruism, without which human societies cannot function any more than animal societies, in the prehuman world—hence his derivation of the social instincts from biology. Darwin himself had thought that human ethical standards might be derived from the herd instincts of animals, but Thomas Huxley, one of his closest collaborators, had argued in 1894 that "ethical progress ... depends on combating nature."

But since then biologists have changed their minds and prefer to think that ethical human dispositions, though seemingly altruistic and often unselfish, are really derived by natural selection from the struggle for survival, because in many circumstances it pays an individual to be unselfish rather than selfish. In this development of Darwinism, a paper by R. L. Trivers, "The Evolution of Reciprocal Altruism" (1971. *Quart. Rev. Biol.* **46**, 35–57), has become a classic, and Trivers' argument has been explored in many directions and details, not least by the sociobiological work of E. O. Wilson.

The tendency to see all characteristics of human culture as special adaptations of primate behavior is most keenly expressed in the recent writings of the Californian zoologists Leda Cosmides and John Tooby. In their work, humans are presented as well-developed primates, and in this view there does not appear to be a need for what we have come to call the social or cultural sciences. It is enough to know biology in order to understand how it is that humans have developed logical reasoning, calculus, and quantum mechanics. Tooby and Cosmides do not think of themselves as "zoologists," but as psychologists, and are doing, if one takes them at their own valuation, social science.

On the other side are those anthropologists who recognize that with bipedalism and the development of the brain's frontal lobes an entirely new element has come into being. It is this new element which is responsible for the fact that humans in their cultures have become, as Peter Wilson argues (1980. *Man, The Promising Primate,* New Haven, Yale Univ. Press, New Haven, CT), paranoid, can wage wars, can make peace, can think up religion and science, can prohibit incest, and can invent political institutions which control decision-making processes. All these abilities are absent in primate societies, and their presence and role in human cultures are due to the mutations which have brought about the emergence of hominids and eventually *homo sapiens sapiens.* In the works of this school of thought, culture is different from primate organization, but is clearly based on, and necessitated and facilitated by biological mutation.

None of these schools of thought are likely to be the last word in the fruitful extension of Darwinism to the emergence and development of cultures, for in both schools it is taken for granted that human culture is an improvement on, and an extension of, primate life. But there is one important biological facet which neither of these two schools of thought has taken into account. Not every biological mutation which is eventually selected for survival—as culture definitely has been—is necessarily by itself an adaptive advantage. One might, on the contrary, think that culture is a secondary phenomenon, a form of damage control. Without it, maybe the mutations which have led to bipedalism and the larger frontal lobes of the brain would have been an unmitigated disaster and their bearers—or perhaps victims would be a more fitting term—would have died out soon after the mutations had taken place. From the point of view of social science, it may well be that the most fruitful contribution of Darwinism is the realization that for purposes of orientation and cooperation, humans are not to be seen as a single species—as a purely biological point of view suggests—but should be seen as both Richard Sennett and Erik H. Erikson have suggested independently: divided into societies which are quasi-species.

If one sees human societies as artificial species, social science becomes placed very firmly into a biological, Darwinian framework. We are accustomed to thinking of humans as one species. Strictly speaking, and using the definition of species as a group whose members are sexually compatible, all human beings are such a group. But in another sense we would gain a lot by looking upon every human culture or society as a special species, or, more accurately, as a quasi-species which replicates artificially the characteristics of natural species.

To start with, societies/cultures, like species, are not types but populations, and are, in the sense of Darwinism, as mutable as species. Inside the society/culture, sexual congress breeds true offspring—"true" in the sense that the young are nurtured into the habits of their parents, just as mice breed other mice. Further, sexual congress with members of other societies/cultures is prohibited by law or custom, so that we get the same effect as we get in different species where mice cannot breed with elephants. And, finally, the members of other societies are, like the members of other purely biological species, considered and treated as potential food, or at least as prey, ready to be exploited. While altruism is a biologically programmed essential ingredient in social cooperation, there also have to be boundaries where cooperation and altruism stop and preying begins. If we look upon the initial mutations which brought about the changes from primates to hominids in this way, we remain firmly within the Darwinian paradigm. We can thus avoid the pitfall of the anthropologists of the first group who considered culture as a nonbiological phenomenon, and can also improve on the second school of thought in which culture is nothing more than an extension of animal characteristics.

Also See the Following Article

EVOLUTIONARY PERSPECTIVES ON ETHICS

Bibliography

Dawkins, R. (1986). "The Blind Watchmaker." Longman, London.

Desmond, A., and Moore, J. (1991). "Darwin." Michael Joseph, London.

Ghiselin, M. T. (1969). "The Triumph of the Darwinian Method." The Univ. of Chicago Press, Chicago.

Gould, J. S. (1989). "Wonderful Life." Penguin, Harmondsworth.

Hull, D. L. (1973). "Darwin and His Critics. The Reception of Darwin's Theory of Evolution by the Scientific Community." Harvard Univ. Press, Cambridge, MA.

Maynard-Smith, J. (1958). "The Theory of Evolution." Penguin, Harmondsworth (rev. ed. available as "CANTO," Cambridge Univ. Press, Cambridge, UK).

Mayr, E. (1991). "One Long Argument. Charles Darwin and the Genesis of Modern Evolutionary Thought." Harvard Univ. Press, Cambridge, MA.

Munz, P. (1989). Taking Darwin even more seriously. In "Issues in Evolutionary Epistemology" (Hahlweg K. and Hooker C. A., eds.). SUNY Press, Albany.

Munz, P. (1993). "Philosophical Darwinism." Routledge, London.

Plotkin, H. (1994). "Darwin Machines." Harvard Univ. Press, Cambridge, MA.

Popper, K. R. (1972). "Objective Knowledge." Clarendon Press, Oxford.

Ruse, M. (1986). "Taking Darwin Seriously." Blackwell, Oxford.

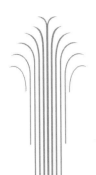

DEATH, DEFINITION OF

Alexander Morgan Capron
University of Southern California

I. The Origins and Content of the Modern
   Standards
II. Challenges to the Prevailing Standards

GLOSSARY

anoxia The absence of oxygen supply to the tissues.

apnea The absence of the impulse to breathe, which leads to an inability to breathe spontaneously.

brain death An imprecise though commonly used term that connotes either (a) the cessation of all brain functions, (b) the cessation of higher brain functions, or (c) the determination that a person has died, based on (a) or (b).

brain stem Also known as the "lower brain," the portion of the brain (made up of the midbrain, the pons, and the medulla oblongata) that links the brain and the spinal cord, and that controls spontaneous, vegetative functions (such as breathing, swallowing, and the sleep–wake cycle) and also plays a role in mediating "higher brain" functions such as consciousness.

common law The law generated by judges in deciding cases.

EEG An electroencephalogram measures electrical activity in the higher centers of the brain; a "flat EEG" means that no electrical activity is detected.

higher brain The portions of the brain (principally, the cerebrum and its outer shell, the cortex) responsible for cognition, feeling, memory, and consciousness.

PVS Persistent vegetative state, a noncognitive condition, caused by injuries to the cerebrum or brain stem, in which patients go through a sleep–wake cycle but are unaware, and can breathe, chew, swallow, and even groan but show no signs of consciousness, perception, or other higher functions.

spinal reflexes Those reflexes that originate in the spinal cord, such as knee and ankle jerks, and that may persist even after cessation of functions in the brain, including the brain stem.

UDDA A model statute, the Uniform Determination of Death Act, proposed in 1981 for adoption by the states by the American Bar Association, American Medical Association, President's Commission for the Study of Ethical Problems in Medicine and Biomedical and Behavioral Research, and the National Conference of Commissioners on Uniform State Laws.

vital signs The traditional signs of life, particularly breathing and heartbeat, which are used in diagnosing death.

whole-brain death The death of a human being determined by the irreversible loss of functions in the entire brain, including the brain stem, in contrast to death declared based on only the loss of functions in the higher brain but not the brain stem.

WHEN DOES DEATH OCCUR? This age-old question has become a modern one thanks to recent medical advances. In the 19th century, improvements in physicians' diagnostic methods, particularly after the development of the stethoscope, gave determinations of death greater certainty, quieting ancient fears of premature burial. Medical developments since the 1960s have had the opposite effect, though the questions now do not concern the accuracy of clinical measurements but their interpretation. Techniques used to support vital functions in critically ill and injured patients until they can function on their own again produce the traditional "vital signs" of heartbeat and respiration in some patients whose brains have been irreversibly damaged. The task of "defining death" does not involve exploring the meaning of death (and life), but the narrower and more practical task of setting standards to determine when death has occurred in patients whose circulatory and respiratory functions are artificially sustained—in other words, patients who in the absence of such support would be recognized as dead by the traditional cardiopulmonary measures. Both the heart–lung and the brain standards have been established by clinicians and recognized by the law. Though widely accepted, the standards—and the situations in which they apply—are not always well understood by the public. They also face philosophical and practical objections in academic circles.

I. THE ORIGINS AND CONTENT OF THE MODERN STANDARDS

A. Artificial Support and Organ Transplantation

1. A New Category of Patients

The need for a new basis for determining death arose in the 1960s along with the development of techniques to support breathing and heartbeat in very sick, hospitalized patients, particularly those who had suffered trauma to the head as well as those who had experienced a stroke or cardiac arrest. Such events can cause cerebral edema (an accumulation of fluid and swelling in the brain tissue), which in turn generates pressure that prevents blood from circulating to the brain. Brain cells can be damaged if deprived of oxygenated blood for even brief periods. Thus, edema and other pathophysiologic mechanisms can cause the brain to cease functioning even when the damage to other organs is less severe.

As it became apparent that artificial support, such as mechanical ventilation, could restore and then indefinitely maintain breathing and heartbeat in some patients, physicians began to wonder when they could

cease treatment, a question to which the answers were far less clear at that time than they are today. One answer to the dilemma of when to cease treatment was clear: when a patient has died, further treatment is neither required nor, indeed, appropriate.

Many techniques to prolong life—including drugs to maintain blood pressure and body temperature as well as devices to support breathing, blood flow, nutrition, and hydration artificially—have been developed as means for preserving functioning in very ill or badly injured patients until they recover. But this objective often cannot be achieved, as the famous Harvard Medical School Ad Hoc Committee on Brain Death noted in 1968: "Sometimes these efforts [to save the desperately injured] have only partial success so that the result is an individual whose heart continues to beat but whose brain is irreversibly damaged" (1968. *Journal of the American Medical Association,* **205,** 337–340). Some of these patients have only suffered harm to their higher brains; they will remain persistently unconscious but can eventually breathe without mechanical support. Others, however, have suffered more extensive damage involving the centers in the brain, particularly the brain stem, that are responsible for breathing and bodily regulation. These patients do not respond to their environment and are profoundly unconscious. Indeed, an early study by French physicians Mollaret and Goulon described this phenomenon as *le coma dépassé* (beyond coma). Without artificial support, these persons would be regarded as dead, yet with that support they continue to manifest the traditional vital signs of heartbeat and respiration.

2. Public Attention Catalyzed by Heart Transplantation

Had the problem of artificial "vital signs" in bodies that had lost all brain functions remained of concern largely to physicians when they assess artificially supported patients, a new diagnosis of death based on lack of brain functions might have slowly been incorporated into the general understanding of death. But the first human-to-human heart transplant in South Africa in December 1967, followed by dozens of cases around the world in the ensuing months, catapulted the "definition of death" into the public arena and linked the two topics in the public mind, even though the new "definition" is used more frequently in ordinary cases of life support than in cases in which organs are removed to be transplanted.

It is easy to see why the public was astonished when a beating human heart was plucked from a body that had been declared dead so that Dr. Christiann Barnard could transplant it into another patient. How could the donor, whose heart was beating, be dead, while the recipient, whose own heart had been removed, was considered alive?

While Dr. Barnard and other heart transplant teams pushed boldly ahead, physicians generally were concerned that the brain-based criteria for diagnosing death did not follow the accepted legal standard, which at the time was the complete cessation of all vital functions, including breathing and heartbeat, without reference to whether such functions arose naturally or as the result of medical intervention. Two issues were thus presented. First, by what techniques could the absence of brain functioning be determined, and were they as reliable a method of determining death as the older techniques? Second, was it appropriate for physicians to proceed on the basis of a medical consensus about these techniques or did more formal steps need to be taken to bridge the gap between the medical and the general view of death, as embodied in the law and in popular understanding?

B. Establishing Diagnostic Criteria for Death

1. Varied Criteria to Measure a Single Phenomenon

The methods used to establish loss of brain function differ somewhat from country to country. In the United States physicians utilize clinical signs and confirmatory laboratory tests such as the electroencephalogram (EEG) to measure the absence of any activity in the entire brain, while British neurologists measure the loss of functioning in the brain stem in patients with coma of known origin, and experts in other European countries focus on preconditions for brain function, such as intracranial blood circulation. All of these methods, however, aim to establish the same condition, namely that the functioning of the brain (including the brain stem) has so fully and irreversibly ceased that in the absence of artificial support the patient's heart and lungs would not function. In effect, by measuring whether a person's brain has ceased functioning, physicians create a new window through which to view the phenomenon of death when their own interventions obscure what could otherwise be seen through the window of cardiopulmonary function.

The reliability of observations made through the new window was carefully established through studies of comatose patients in whom cerebral unresponsivity and unreceptivity and the absence of brain stem reflexes were measured clinically, apnea occurred when the res-

pirator was withdrawn, and tests established the absence of blood flow to the brain or a "flat" EEG. Because the concern is with brain functions, the observation of spinal reflexes is not inconsistent with a diagnosis of death.

The criteria developed to diagnose death stress the importance of knowing the origin of the coma (whether through injury, anoxia, or otherwise) both to rule out reversible causes of responsivity (such a sedation, hypothermia, and neuromuscular blockade) and to determine how long the patient must be observed and subjected to which clinical or confirmatory tests. The standards promulgated by the Harvard committee in 1968 required repeat testing after 24 hr, but as the diagnostic procedures were further refined, different standards were established for different categories of patients, for some of whom 6 hr of observation suffices.

2. The Implications of the Standards

While attention in discussions of determining death is usually focused on brain-based criteria, most determinations of death continue to be based upon the traditional heart–lung criteria. Like the brain-based criteria, the latter have two components, the full cessation of relevant functions and the irreversibility of the cessation.

Both brain and respiratory–circulatory criteria are framed in terms of functions, not the organs that usually perform the functions; for example, a conscious person who requires mechanical assistance to breathe would not be regarded as dead even if his lungs were unable to operate, so long as his respiratory function could be sustained artificially. Certain forms of intensive medical care in effect substitute for brain functions as well, though no full replacement has been created for all functions of the entire brain. Moreover, since brain cells do not regenerate, once cellular activity has been lost it will not be regained, and damage to the normothermic adult brain is usually irreversible after even a relatively brief (e.g., 10 min) period of anoxia. Nonetheless, care must be taken in the use of terms such as "brain death" which suggest that the death occurs in a single organ, when what is really at issue is the determination of death for an organism based upon the irreversible cessation of functioning in a particular organ, such as the brain.

Another implication is that what is important in all cases is the loss of the particular function, not the destruction of cells, much less the total absence of activity in some cells in the relevant organ. Indeed, were the standard for death set at destruction of the brain rather than loss of functions, no clinical tests now exist that could establish such destruction before cardiac arrest.

Individual cells or groups of cells—even in neurologic tissue—may continue to function after death of the organism as a whole. A familiar example is that fingernails and hair continue to grow briefly after death. Some challenges to the brain-based "definitions" of death are based on findings that certain biologic processes (such as the secretion of hormones) persist for a period in the brains of persons determined to be dead by currently accepted standards. The existence of cellular activity is not inconsistent with a diagnosis of death, however, provided that the vital function in question has ceased and cannot be replaced, and that the cellular activity itself is not a central function of an integrated organism.

3. The Bifurcated Standard

The UDDA and comparable statutes elsewhere, including Australia, recognize two standards for the occurrence of death, one based on cessation of brain functions and the other on cessation of blood flow and breathing. This "bifurcated" standard is based on the notion that either means of determining death can be used in appropriate circumstances to measure the same phenomenon, namely, death of the organism as an integrated whole. The duality of the standard sows the potential for confusion because it can be misunderstood to establish two kinds of death, "heart–lung death" and "brain death." Yet this problem is probably inevitable because only a small percentage of patients are diagnosed as dead based on direct assessments of brain functions, so the two methods of determining death will continue to exist. Any confusion resulting therefrom would not be eliminated simply by rewording the statute, but needs to be specifically addressed.

The Law Reform Commission in Canada proposed a different approach, under which the irreversible cessation of brain functions would be the sole "definition" of death, but this standard could be met not only by showing directly that brain functions are absent, but also "by the prolonged absence of spontaneous cardiac and respiratory functions." This approach has also been endorsed by a number of commentators, who see it as conceptually superior. Some, such as James Bernat, propose that the "definition" actually be "the permanent cessation of the functioning of the organism as a whole," while cessation of brain functions play the role of the "criterion for death," intermediate between the definition and the two distinct sets of tests ("cardiorespiratory" and "neurological") by which death would actually be diagnosed (J. Bernat, 1992. *Journal of Clinical Ethics,* 3, 21–26).

While these approaches are attractive in underlining that human death is a single phenomenon, their concep-

tual clarity is dependent on general understanding of the brain's particularly important role in integrating functioning of the whole organism and of its great vulnerability to injury, particularly through loss of blood flow, so that uncorrected loss of breathing and heartbeat either shows loss of brain functions or foretells such loss. Yet, as a President's Commission concluded in rejecting the Canadian approach, "most of the time people do not, and need not, go through this two-step process. Irreversible loss of circulation is recognized as death because—setting aside any mythical connotations of the heart—a person without blood flow simply cannot live" (1981. *Defining death.* Washington, DC: U.S. Government Printing Office).

C. Translating Medical Criteria into Legal Standards

Although the establishment of criteria and tests to diagnose death is a matter of technical complexity best left to physicians and other scientists, the underlying objective is not to determine the biological status of cells or organ systems, but rather the social status of a human being as a living being or a dead body. Thus, by the 1970s, even as studies proved that the clinical measurement of absence of brain functions was as reliable as the traditional measures for cessation of heart–lung functions, a consensus emerged that it would not be appropriate to leave the matter of "redefining" death to the medical community alone. Instead, society needed to respond formally by setting the framework within which physicians would apply any particular criteria and tests.

1. Judicial Revision of the Standards

Just as countries differ in the methodology employed by physicians in diagnosing death, they have also followed different paths in establishing legal standards. In some jurisdictions, the process was left to the courts. The existing common law standard of "absence of all vital functions, including breathing and heartbeat" had been articulated by earlier judges in deciding cases in which the moment of death was important, such as in disputes over estates and the like. Beginning in the 1960s, courts were called upon to update that standard to reflect more accurately new scientific findings and medical procedures.

The process by which this updating occurred was not always smooth, however. One impediment to action is the courts' lack of scientific understanding, but equally important is the judicial attachment to existing, well-settled rules. Deference to precedent is usually desirable, both to simplify litigation and to provide predictable legal standards, but the result was that as late as 1968, an appellate court in California decided to adhere solely to the heartbeat-and-breathing standard even though these functions were being artificially maintained in the person in question.

Several cases in the United States in the early 1970s illustrate how problematic it was to rely on the judiciary as the primary means to make law on this topic. For example, in *Tucker v. Lower,* a case that came to trial in Virginia in 1972, the brother of the donor in an early heart transplant sued the physicians, alleging that the operation was begun before the donor had died. The physicians had declared the donor dead when his brain functions ceased, even though medical interventions maintained normal pulse, blood pressure, respiration, and other vital signs in the donor. While the trial judge initially planned to follow the traditional common law standard (absence of all functions, including breathing and heartbeat), the jurors returned a verdict for the defendants after the judge—without explanation—changed his mind and allowed them to find that death had occurred when the brain ceased functioning irreversibly.

Two other examples arose from heart transplants in 1974 in California. The persons charged with homicide for causing the donor's death in each case attempted to claim the surgeons' removal of the still-beating hearts rather than their own acts was the cause of death. One trial judge accepted this argument as being compelled by the existing definition of death, but his ruling was reversed on appeal, and both defendants were eventually convicted.

2. Statutory Standards

While law revision was left to the courts in some places, such as Great Britain and several states in the United States, most jurisdictions in the United States, Canada, and Australia turned to the legislature to establish the legal standards for determining death. The legislative process has several advantages: it allows a wider range of information to enter into the framing of standards for determining death; it offers an avenue for participation of the public; and it provides prospective guidance and dispels public and professional uncertainties about the law, thereby reducing the likelihood of cases against physicians for malpractice or homicide. In the United States, the best known statute, the Uniform Determination of Death Act (UDDA), was proposed in 1981 by leading medical and legal groups and the Presidential Bioethics Commission. It is now law in more than half

of U.S. jurisdictions, while virtually all the rest have some other, essentially similar statute. The UDDA provides that an individual who has sustained either (1) irreversible cessation of circulatory and respiratory functions, or (2) irreversible cessation of all functions of the entire brain, including the brain stem, is dead. A determination of death must be made in accordance with accepted medical standards.

The UDDA represents an incremental rather than a radical restatement of the traditional understanding of death that ties together the accepted cardiopulmonary standard with a new brain-based standard that measures the same phenomenon. From the outset, some commentators suggested that the need to develop a statute presented an opportunity truly to "redefine" death; as will be discussed, further on that view was usually associated with the suggestion that patients who had lost function of their higher brain centers should be regarded as dead. None of the adopted statutes has accepted this argument.

Another feature of the statute is that it operates at the level of standards rather than that of medical criteria or clinical tests. The result is a law that is sufficiently precise to set forth the public understanding of what constitutes death but not so specific that it is tied to the details of contemporary technology. It sets forth the general standards by which death is to be determined but leaves the medical community to establish and apply appropriate criteria and specific tests for determining that the standards have been met, recognizing that techniques may change in light of experience and further study.

The standards set by the UDDA are unvarying in two senses: they apply to all situations in which human death needs to be determined, and they are the same for all persons. An accepted standard for determining death is needed to resolve a number of issues: appropriate medical care, the timing of organ removal, homicide, life insurance benefits, probating a will and transferring property, taxes, and marital status, to name a few. In theory, varying policy objectives might dictate different standards in particular context, but just as the traditional heart–lung standard was employed across all situations, so too does the UDDA rather than attempting to "define" death separately (and perhaps inconsistently) in a myriad of statutes.

Using a single definition for all purposes does not preclude relying on other events besides death as a trigger for some decisions, it simply means that "death" means the same thing in all contexts, so that the same person is not "alive" for life insurance purposes but "dead" according to the criminal law. Most jurisdictions make provision, for example, for the distribution of property and the termination of marriage after a person has been absent without explanation for a period of years, even though a person "presumed dead" under such a law would not be treated as a corpse were he or she to turn up alive. Likewise, in order to increase the number of transplants, some people have argued that in certain circumstances surgeons should be able to remove organs before the donor has died; such a statute would authorize acting before death rather than creating a separate meaning of death.

The second aspect of uniformity is that the standards for determining death apply equally to all people, without reference to their social status or wealth, the circumstances in which they are hospitalized, or their potential social utility as an organ donor. Only one jurisdiction, New Jersey, has departed from this objective; under a statute adopted in 1991, people whose religious beliefs would be violated by the use of brain-based criteria are allowed to have their deaths declared solely on the traditional circulatory–respiratory basis.

II. CHALLENGES TO THE PREVAILING STANDARDS

By the middle of the 1980s, nearly all jurisdictions (the major exception being Japan) had legally recognized the medical consensus that death can be determined in most people by the traditional measures of heartbeat and breathing and in artificially supported patients by measures of total brain function. Still, challenges to the prevailing standards continue to be raised by some philosophers and physicians, and some developments in organ harvesting seem to contradict the premises of the UDDA and similar statutes.

A. Whole-Brain versus Higher Brain Functions

1. The Difficulties in Implementing a Higher Brain Standard

The UDDA specifies that death occurs when "the entire brain, including the brain stem," ceases functioning. Some patients, such as those in a persistent vegetative state (PVS), who usually never regain consciousness even when vigorously supported, do not meet this whole-brain standard even though they have lost all higher brain functions associated with consciousness and interaction. Many people would agree that certain features of consciousness (or at least the potential for

consciousness) are essential to being a person as distinct from merely a human being. Should the law equate a loss of personhood with death? A related question rests on the ontological proposition that to be a particular individual means to have a personal identity, which depends on continuity of personal history as well as on self-awareness. If the loss of consciousness destroys such identity, does that mean the person has died, even if the body continues to live?

Society has thus far answered both versions of the question—which is essentially whether the loss of higher brain functions should allow death to be declared—in the negative. Some of the reasons for doing so are clinical, since it is more difficult (some would say impossible) to diagnose the permanent loss of higher brain functions with the same degree of certainty as the loss of whole-brain or circulatory–respiratory functions, though advances in diagnostic methods may eventually overcome this problem. More basically, the very concept of what functions pertain to the higher brain is highly contested. For example, the specific characteristics deemed by philosophers to be essential for personhood have varied widely from John Locke's focus on self-awareness to Immanuel Kant's requirement of a capacity for rational moral agency. Thus, one higher brain standard might encompass only those such as PVS patients who lack any capacity for self-knowledge, while another would include senile or severely retarded patients who cannot synthesize experience or act on moral principles.

Furthermore, the difficulties in making accurate predictions that neocortical functions will not return following certain injuries pale in comparison to diagnosing that an irreversible "loss of personhood" or "loss of personal identity" has occurred. Simply put, neurologists have no way of directly correlating concepts such as "loss of personhood" with particular neurological structures whose condition could be measured.

If Culver and Gert are correct that "death can be applied directly only to biological organisms and not to persons" (C. Culver & B. Gert, 1982. *Philosophy in Medicine*. New York: Oxford Univ. Press), absence of consciousness and cognition could still be relevant in deciding, for example, whether—and if so, for how long—patients who lose (or never achieve) personhood or who have lost their personal identity should continue to receive life-prolonging treatment. Unlike the situation in 1968, when medicine first began formally to address the question of terminating treatment for artificially supported patients, most people would not now regard changes in the "definition" of death as a principal or particularly useful way to address the issue. Additional guidance has been developed by courts and legislatures as well as by professional bodies concerning the cessation of treatment in patients who are alive by brain or heart–lung criteria, but for whom further treatment is considered (by the patients or by others) to be pointless or degrading. In a word, "when to allow to die?" is a very distinct question, from an ethical as well as a policy viewpoint, from "when to declare dead?"

Furthermore, any move to treat some or all persons who lack consciousness and other higher brain functions as dead because they lack "personhood" or "personal identity" would lead either to burying spontaneously respiring bodies or to having first to take affirmative steps, such as those used in active euthanasia, to end their breathing, circulation, and the like. The statute proposed in 1976 by philosopher Robert Veatch, which equates death with cessation of cerebral function, recognized that this would be unacceptable to most persons. Therefore, he included a "conscience clause" that allowed people, while still competent, or their next of kin to decline to have death determined on the higher brain standard. No jurisdiction has adopted a higher brain standard, nor does the "conscience clause" in the New Jersey statute encompass that standard.

2. Attempts to Classify Anencephalic Infants as Dead

The closest policy makers have come to allowing death to be determined on higher brain grounds arose in the context of several highly publicized attempts to transplant organs from anencephalic infants. These babies are born without a neocortex and with the tops of their skulls open, exposing the underlying tissue. When, as is often the case, their brain stems function, they can breathe on their own and may even show basic reflexes, such as sucking. While they can survive for long periods with vigorous support, in most cases they are provided only comfort care and expire within 2 weeks.

In 1987–1988, Loma Linda Medical Center in California tried to obtain more organs, particularly hearts, from this source. The physicians placed anencephalic infants on respirators and waited until death could be diagnosed neurologically (a procedure that was controversial in itself because the reliability of such determines in very young infants is questioned). In the end, no organs were transplanted because the infants either did not expire within the 2-week period specified in the protocol or, if the respirator were delayed, the intermittent episodes of anoxia that damaged their brain stems (and permitted death to occur) also caused deteriora-

tion in other organs that rendered them useless for transplantation.

In several other instances, women who expected to give birth to a baby with anencephaly publicly sought authorization to allow harvesting of organs immediately after birth, so that their child's death could at least give another sick child the chance to live with a transplanted organ. But in the only case to produce an appellate decision, the Florida Supreme Court in 1992 declined to create a special standard of death for anencephalic infants.

In deciding not to expand the standards for death to include anencephalic infants, nor to amend the organ transplant acts to allow premortem harvesting from these infants, judges and legislators were clearly aware of two slippery slopes. First, as the pediatricians caring for the potential Loma Linda donors found, parents and physicians of other infants with severe anomalies and limited life expectancy would regard these children as comparable on relevant grounds to the anencephalic infants as organ donors. Second, the change in the standard for determining death could not be limited to infants, since the salient criteria—absence of higher brain function and limited life expectancy—apply to many other persons (such as patients with severe brain injuries or advanced Alzheimer's disease) as well. The decision to accept anencephaly as a basis for declaring death would thus imply acceptance of a higher brain standard for diagnosing any and all patients, with the attendant problems of regarding a spontaneously functioning body as "dead."

B. Changing Clinical Criteria

Some commentators have suggested that society should rethink brain death because some bodies determined to be dead on neurological grounds exhibit functions—such as hypothalamic–endocrine function and cerebral electrical activity—that indicate that not all functions of the entire brain are absent. Some of these findings may suggest that the tests for brain death need to be expanded to encompass additional factors if the presence of these factors indicate that the orgaism has not lost its integrative functioning. But since some organic activities persist in dead bodies, the real question is whether any particular finding—such as the secretion of a hormone—demonstrates the persistence of a function that is as physiologically integrative as the others whose absence is part of accepted brain-based diagnostic criteria. Certainly, if these functions continue in persons who are declared dead under cardiopulmonary standards, then their presence does not show that the clinical criteria for the brain-based standards are inaccurate or incomplete, and neither a "redefinition" of the standards nor a change in criteria would be needed.

C. The Importance of Irreversible Cessation

The UDDA and comparable rules set forth diagnostic rather than prognostic standards: that death has occurred, not that it is likely to occur. Thus the requirement of irreversibility is an essential component of both standards for determining death. In the case of circulation and respiration, artificial support can sometimes stimulate a resumption of functioning that seemed to have ceased, so a judgment of irreversibility depends upon an effort at reversal having been made or clearly having been judged futile.

Yet a protocol developed at the University of Pittsburgh in 1992 and similar efforts at other medical centers to increase the number of donor organs seriously compromise the irreversibility criterion. Under the protocol, patients dependent on life support who desire to be organ donors are disconnected in the operating room, which leads to cardiac arrest. After 2 min of asystole (lack of heartbeat), death is declared based upon the "irreversible cessation of circulatory and respiratory functions," at which point blood flow is artificially restored to the organs which are to be removed, to keep them viable for transplantation. Yet the failure to attempt to restore spontaneous respiration (and circulation) functions in non-heart-beating "cadavers" shows that death has not occurred according to the existing criteria. The requirement of "irreversible cessation" must mean more than simply the physician chose not to reverse. If no attempt at restoration is made, a declaration of death is not appropriate, though a prognosis can be made that death will occur if available means of resuscitation continue to be withheld. Thus, rather than contradict the existing "definition of death," the Pittsburgh protocol departs from it. As Truog argues, "the reluctance of the Pittsburgh team to extend their protocol in ways that would be acceptable for dead patients could be an indication that the patients may not really be dead after all" (R. Truog, 1997. *Hastings Center Report*, **27**(1), 29–37). (Truog himself favors abandoning "brain death" and allowing organs to be transplanted from anesthetized patients who had consented to being organ donors.)

D. Public Concern and Confusion

Even after 30 years of public awareness that the irreversible cessation of brain functions is one means of determining death, substantial confusion persists on the whole subject. Some of the confusion probably has its origins in the linkage of the definition of death to organ (particularly heart) transplantation, especially when it appears—as in the protocols described previously—that physicians may be altering the standards in order to increase the number of eligible donors. While such efforts may have laudable goals, they also undermine confidence in both the certainty and the uniformity of the standards for determining death. Ironically, as Sanner has reported, uncertainty about death determination decreases the number of people willing to consent to organ donation.

Although virtually all reported cases of misdiagnoses of death involve determinations based on misreading circulatory and respiratory signs in patients who were not on ventilators, public anxiety focuses on brain death. Part of the confusion can be traced to the very terminology, which wrongly suggests the existence of a special, separate category of death—or worse, that brain death is almost but not quite death. It is not unusual for newspaper accounts to describe a "brain-dead" patient being disconnected from "life support," after which she expired.

Unfortunately, the difficulty of speaking of "death diagnosed on neurological grounds" or of "a brain-based determination of death" probably means that the term "brain death" will not disappear. Also unfortunately, this term is sometimes used even more loosely to describe a patient who has been unconscious for a long time, though breathing spontaneously; thinking only of the loss of the ability to communicate and to perceive the world, family members and others may understandably feel that their comatose relative is "brain dead." Indeed, this has even lead to the popular use of the term to describe people (particularly celebrities) as "brain dead" when they commit some particularly dimwitted act.

But the problems with the present definition of death go beyond its colloquial misuse. It has been shown that even medical and nursing personnel have difficulty in applying the concept of death to artificially maintained bodies that manifest many of the traditional—and readily perceived—signs of life: a moving chest, pulsing blood vessels, and warm, moist skin. Closer examination by the trained eye reveals the difference between such bodies and living beings (closed eyes or a fixed gaze, the lack of cortical reflexes when the eye or ear is stimulated, and so forth), but that may not always, or not immediately, overcome the sense that death has not occurred.

Clearly, continuing efforts are needed to educate people (including health care workers) that death is a single phenomenon which can be measured at least as accurately by determining that brain functions have permanently ceased in patients who are artificially maintained as by examining for absence of heartbeat and respiration in other persons. Meanwhile, no jurisdiction that has accepted brain-based determinations of death (as virtually all Western countries have done, either through law or through accepted medical practice) has seen fit to abandon this standard either to return to the older, circulatory–respiratory standard alone or to incorporate a standard based solely on higher brain functions.

Also See the Following Articles

ADVANCE DIRECTIVES • DEATH, SOCIETAL ATTITUDES TOWARD • DO-NOT-RESUSCITATE DECISIONS • EUTHANASIA • ORGAN TRANSPLANTS AND DONORS • PATIENTS' RIGHTS

Bibliography

Capron, A., & Cate, F. (1997). Death and organ transplantation. In M. Macdonald, R. Kaufman, A. Capron, and I. Birnbaum (Eds.), *Treatise on health care law* (pp. 45–60). New York: Bender.

Sanner, M. (1994). A comparison of public attitudes toward autopsy, organ donation, and anatomic dissection: A Swedish survey. *Journal of the American Medical Association, 271,* 284–288.

Veatch, R. (1976). *Death, dying and the biological revolution: Our last quest for responsibility.* New Haven, CT: Yale Univ. Press.

Youngner, S., & Arnold, R. (1993). Ethical, psychological, and public policy implications of procuring organs from non-heart-beating cadaver donors. *Journal of the American Medical Association, 269,* 2769–2774.

Youngner, S., Landefeld, C., Coulton, C., Juknialis, B., & Leary, M. (1989). "Brain death" and organ retrieval: A cross-sectional survey of knowledge and concepts among health professionals. *Journal of the American Medical Association, 261,* 2205–2210.

Zaner, R. (Ed.) (1988). *Death: beyond whole-brain criteria.* Dordrecht, Netherlands: Kluwer Academic.

DEATH, MEDICAL ASPECTS OF

David Lamb
University of Birmingham

GLOSSARY

anencephaly A condition affecting neonates where there is a spinal chord and a brain stem, but no cerebral hemispheres.

anoxia The absence of oxygen in arterial blood or tissues.

brain stem The part of the brain that connects the cerebral hemispheres to the spinal cord.

death The irreversible cessation of integrated life; the end of life.

electroencephalograph (EEG) A technique for measuring electrical activity in the brain.

life Definitions of life are problematic, insofar as there is no universally accepted meaning of "life." But from a medical standpoint life depends on integration of the following physiological functions: ingestion, digestion, absorption, respiration, distribution, metabolism, excretion, and egestion.

persistent vegetative state (PVS) A chronic condition resulting from either cerebral anoxia or impact injury to the head. Patients in a PVS may have intact brain stems, and if adequately nursed may survive for years. Lacking function in the cerebral hemispheres, they show no behavioral evidence of awareness; they are said to be "awake but unaware."

THE MEDICAL ASPECTS OF DEATH are inescapably bound up with philosophical, metaphysical, and ethical issues. Unless these issues are addressed, then attempts to empirically verify death or provide guidelines for the diagnosis of death will be meaningless. Technical data alone cannot provide answers to what are essentially metaphysical and moral questions. Criteria for death and arguments about more reliable tests for death must be related to some overall concept of what death means, for at stake are our notions of "personhood," "humanity," "life," and the boundary between duties appropriate toward a living being and duties appropriate to a corpse. Clearly these questions raise issues which are frequently determined by clinical facts, but they nevertheless transcend them, for they involve a whole background of moral, political, and legal considerations which ultimately relate to what is *meant* by "death." This article will focus on the interplay between the moral and the philosophical issues relating to death and its medical aspects. The first section will consist of a brief historical review of modern medicine's role in our understanding of death. The second section will address the conceptual issues which underpin medical approaches to death. Different concepts and their respective criteria and tests will be evaluated in the third section, and some of the moral problems generated by recent formulations of the concept of death will be reviewed in the final section.

I. DEATH AND MEDICINE: AN HISTORICAL REVIEW

A. Death and Medical Science

From the earliest of records, the traditional view, enshrined in common sense beliefs, was that death occurred with the last breath of life. This view is expressed in the Hellenic Judeo-Christian and Islamic religions, and it predates modern scientific medicine. The notion of death is, of course, central to the major religions, but while they express concern over the integrity of the body and its postmortem disposal, they have not addressed the practical medical aspects associated with the diganosis of death (see Table I). As a general rule people have entrusted their physicians with the task of determining the boundaries of physical life.

Nevertheless, the determination of death has been, and continues to be, a problematic issue, and doctors have frequently been accused of being out of step with public perceptions of death. Doubts concerning the medical profession's competency to diagnose death have been expressed throughout the history of modern medicine. But as a general rule doubts concerning the reliability of medical criteria and tests for death have

emerged with the introduction of new medical techniques. Moral problems have also tended to be more acute during periods when neither the medical profession nor the public have fully understood the implications of certain developments in medical science.

The modern scientific era in medicine has its intellectual roots in the 17th century when pioneers such as Harvey, Gassendi, and Descartes advanced mechanistic theories of life. Living beings were depicted as complicated mechanisms, and analogies were drawn between physical systems of the day and living organisms. Thus bodily functions would be depicted in terms of mechanical devices, the most successful model being Harvey's mechanistic account of heartbeat and circulation of blood. The Cartesian account of the living organism is, perhaps, the most familiar one. According to the Cartesians the living being was a machine which was powered in certain respects by a mind or soul.

From the 17th century onward the mechanistic view of life has dominated scientific medicine, and concepts of death have rested upon mechanistic analogies. Thus the patient is dead when the machine packs up, when the cardiac pump no longer functions, or when the central computer is irreversibly dysfunctional. As a rule mechanistic ideas about life and death have not affected religious notions of death as the separation of the immortal soul from the perishable body; death can be presented as the boundary between the extinction of physical life and the beginning of spiritual life. The

TABLE I
Definition, Criteria, and Tests for Death

Definition	Criteria	Tests
Nonmedical concepts		
Exogamy	Marriage outside the clan or caste	Production of a marriage certificate
Missing, presumed dead	Missing in wartime	No evidence of existence over a specified period of time
Separation of soul from body	No criteria	No tests
Medical concepts		
Irreversible loss of the capacity to maintain circulation	Irreversible cardiac standstill	No recordable pulse or blood pressure, asystole on ECG
Irreversible loss of personhood	Loss of higher brain function, and mental function	No evidence of awareness, isoelectric EEG, PET scan abnormalities
Irreversible loss of the function of the whole organism	Irreversible metabolic arrest of every cell in the body	Microscopic evidence of destruction of every cell in the body
Irreversible loss of integrated functioning of the organism as a whole	Irreversible loss of brain function (irreversible apnoea with loss of the capacity for consciousness)	Clinical signs of a nonfunctioning brain in the context of specified preconditions and exclusions

TABLE II

Physiological Components of Death

1. *Systemic death.* Entails criteria and tests indicating total and irreversible cessation of heart beat and respiration. Traditionally accepted as a yardstick of human death, it is currently regarded as a prognostic indicator that total stoppage of the brain is imminent.

2. *Whole brain death.* Entails criteria and tests indicating total and irreversible stoppage of integrated brain function. This includes cessation of all neuronal components in the intracranial cavity, both cerebral hemispheres, the brain stem, and the cerebellum.

3. *Brain stem death.* Entails criteria and tests indicating total and irreversible death of all structures above the foramen magnum. This involves irreversible loss of consciousness and capacity for spontaneous respiration.

physician is concerned with the former, the priest is concerned with the latter. Despite cultural and religious diversity throughout the world, people have placed tremendous moral importance on the boundary between life and death. Medical concepts of death, so it is generally agreed, are primarily concerned with the physical and observable manifestations of an organism (see Table II).

B. Uncertainties Concerning the Diagnosis of Death

Doubts concerning the reliability of medical criteria and tests for death have accompanied developments in scientific medicine. These doubts have been strongly expressed in controversies over the transplantation of vital organs, such as the heart and lungs. Developments in resuscitative technology led to a spate of claims throughout the 1960s concerning patients who had been "brought back to life" and to consequent discussions concerning the uncertainty of medical criteria for death. There are parallels between the uncertainty created by techniques of cardiac resuscitation in the 20th century and the uncertainty which accompanied the development of artificial resuscitation in the 18th century.

Around 1767 enlightened doctors and reformers began to organize "humane societies" to teach the newly discovered technique of "artificial respiration" for the purpose of resuscitating victims of drowning or suffocation. Artificial respiration had a dramatic effect on popular perceptions of death and the dying process. By 1796 the London Humane Society alone had claimed to have resuscitated over 2000 people. The fact that so

many apparent "deaths" could be reversed prompted suspicions regarding the possible numbers who had been diagnosed as dead and were consequently buried but nevertheless might have been resuscitated by the miraculous new technique. Misunderstandings over the nature of resuscitation generated confusion and disenchantment with the medical approach to death.

Of course today we understand a great deal more about resuscitation and can measure, with some reliability, the extent of damage which will occur if a brain is starved of oxygen for a given period. During the 18th century medical science was ignorant about anoxic insults to the brain and doctors knew very little about oxygen and its properties. Today we are aware that artificial respiration has limits and that it will not restore life to a person whose brain has been destroyed. In the 18th century many of those who marveled at the miracle of artificial respiration were unable to consider this fact. Thus artificial respiration was appealed to by skeptics who maintained that medical criteria and tests for death were unreliable. Some critics went so far as to say that putrefaction was the only sure sign of death.

As resuscitative techniques developed throughout the 18th century other interventions in the dying process were employed. According to one concept of death—the irreversible loss of the capacity to maintain circulation (see Table I)—resuscitation would include measures to restore motion to the blood, such as violent shaking of the patient and thumping victims of drowning accidents. The introduction of smelling salts in 1721 was seen as an aid to resuscitative techniques, and later electric shocks were administered to restore heart, nerve, and muscle functions. In 1755 Giovanni Bianchi used electricity to resuscitate a dog. The first human to be electrically "resuscitated" was in 1774. By 1800 electrical resuscitation had joined artificial respiration as a means of convincing many doctors, as well as the lay public, that existing criteria for death were unreliable.

Although little was understood about electricity at the time, exponents of electrical resuscitation convinced many people that traditional medical methods of diagnosing death were inadequate. Giovanni Aldini, Professor of Physics at Bolognia, gave public demonstrations of electroresuscitation, and in 1803 Londoners were thrilled by the twitching and wheezing Aldini evoked from the electrified corpse of an executed convict. With the mysterious force of electricity available, who could trust the doctor when he diagnosed death? Aldini had a tremendous impact. Mary Shelley mentions him in the beginning of her book, *Frankenstein.* Her work vividly portrays the ethical and emotional terrors posed by the new resuscitative technology—not to mention organ transplantation a century later—and the uncertainty medical science had created regarding the public's understanding of death.

Problems with the medical diagnosis of death were to persist throughout the 19th century. Efforts were directed to solve problems with patients in coma, suspended animation, and related conditions such as catalepsy, asphyxia, ecstasy, and trance—the latter of which was examined by the notorious Franz Mesmer, who argued that in trances the soul was free to leave the body. Hence Mesmerism cast further doubts on the certainty of a medical diagnosis of death. Mesmerism not only brought about a state of apparent death, its practitioners also claimed the ability to restore the dead back to life.

With further technical innovation came further concerns regarding death. The introduction of inhalation anesthesia in 1846 generated concern over the boundary between life and death. There were also reports of "fasting girls" who allegedly spent long periods in death-like states without ingesting or excreting. By the late 19th century there was widespread panic across Europe and the USA concerning the indeterminacy of medical diagnosis in the face of possible reversals of death. The author Edgar Allan Poe gave expression to widespread public fears in stories such as the *Tell Tale Heart*. In response to the panic, governments passed laws to extend the interval between death and burial. Open caskets with around-the-clock guards were often featured in 19th century European burials. Stories of "revived" corpses being rescued by grave robbers whet the Victorian appetite for sensationalism and horror. This was the context in which laws requiring death certificates emerged.

During the first half of the 20th century public confidence in the medical profession's ability to diagnose death returned. This period also revealed a more optimistic attitude toward science, and scientifically trained doctors were trusted by their patients. However, the latter half of this century has seen a return to a more questioning attitude toward scientific medicine. Fears are once again expressed that medical science has blurred the distinction between life and death. Phillipe Aries expresses this as follows:

> Death has been dissected, cut to little bits by a series of little steps, which make it impossible to know which step was the real death, the one in which consciousness was lost, or the one in which breathing stopped. All of these little silent deaths have replaced or erased the great dramatic act, and no one has the strength or patience to

wait over a period of weeks for a moment which has lost part of its meaning. (1976. *Western Thoughts Towards Death from the Middle Ages to the Present,* pp. 88–89. Marion Boyors, London)

Since the late 1960s the era of heart transplantation has focused the minds of the medical profession and the public on the criteria for death. In most countries neurological criteria have replaced traditional cardiorespiratory criteria for death (see Table II). But while the medical profession has generally accepted brain-related criteria for determining death, this move has encountered a degree of public anxiety. Nevertheless, one fundamental point has emerged from the history of confusion and uncertainty regarding the diagnosis of death: until the development of neurological criteria for death, no one had seriously examined the concept of death in its medical context. Doctors had sought to diagnose death without explicity addressing the philosophical problem of relating their (usually implicit) concept of death to the criteria and tests they employed when diagnosing the deaths of their patients. The idea of a defintion of death, in medical guidelines and legal statutes, appears to have emerged simultaneously with brain-related definitions of death.

II. CONCEPTUAL ASPECTS OF MEDICAL DEFINITIONS OF DEATH

A. Philosophical Requirements for a Definition of Death

Unlike the concept of disease, the concept of death cannot be exclusively determined by medical criteria. This is because it is related to more general philosophical beliefs concerning the *meaning* of life and death. While there is a consensus that the determination of death is a matter for medical science, the decision that doctors should have this responsibility nevertheless reflects a philosophical position regarding death, namely, that it is empirically decidable. Moreover, an acceptable medical definition should be compatible with well-established cultural and religious beliefs about life and death. The following suggestions specify the requirements for a medically based definition of death:

1. *Death must involve a recognizable and irreversible physical transformation.* Any well-grounded medical concept of death must be linked to an irreversible physical change in the status of an individual which can be

clearly and unambiguously determined by empirical means. It follows that if a patient, declared dead according to a particular concept of death, were to recover, then either the concept would be medically unsatisfactory or the criteria meeting it had been inadequately applied (see Table I). From the medical standpoint it is not possible to say that the patient was dead but is now alive; what has to be said in such cases is that the patient was alive all the time but was mistakenly diagnosed as being dead. Science excludes miracles, and scientific medicine can only operate with concepts of death which specify an irreversible physical dysfunction (see Table II).

2. *A definition of death must be selective.* Philosophers and physicians have often debated whether death is an event or a process. But strictly speaking, from a biological point of view, death involves a process which begins when one or more vital organs cease functioning and ends when the whole organism has decayed, when every single cell in the body is undergoing putrefaction. No society or cultural tradition has ever seriously endorsed a situation where death could be determined at either extreme of this continuum, and the medical profession is consequently empowered to employ selective criteria. Thus doctors have sought to identify a stage in the ongoing course of events when the individual organism no longer functions as an integrated whole. It has long been recognized that residual functions may persist after death, that muscles will respond to percussion for several hours postmortem, and that skin, bone, or arterial walls may remain viable for transplantation purposes for a day or more. Spinal reflexes may persist beyond the death of the brain, and do so when no cardiac activity can be demonstrated.

It is therefore essential, when considering medical criteria for death, that a sharp distinction is maintained between death of the organism as a whole (irreversible loss of integrated function) and death of the whole organism (total destruction of every cell). The latter has never operated in practice, and most of the confusion regarding apparent reversals of death, which was considered in Section I, stemmed from a failure to appreciate that criteria for death are selective and based on a definition which requires criteria for irreversible loss of function of the organism as a whole.

3. *A definition of death must be universal and holistic.* The requirement for universality implies that the criteria must be unambiguous and the results of tests repeatable. It also implies that the mechanism of death be the same for all people whether in the backwoods or in a well-equipped intensive care unit. Taking into consideration cultural beliefs and values, a medically grounded definition of death will attach significance to both mental and physical attributes of a dying person, recognizing that among the important features of life are integration and organization. Thus death is not strictly equated with the loss of the vital functions of any one or more organs, but with the loss of the capacity to *organize* and *integrate* vital functions. The claim that the elimination of certain functions—for example, those of the skin, heart, or kidneys—may lead to death is not the same as saying that the loss of those functions *is* death. A patient undergoing dialysis is not dead, although she may die if she forgoes dialysis. But she will then die—directly or indirectly—of the cerebral consequences of renal failure. The functioning of the organism as a whole will have been severely compromised.

B. Medical Criteria for Death

Medical criteria for death should refer to basic biological functions. This is so because medical criteria are meant to be universal. Thus the poetic expression, "cowards die a thousand deaths," while making a point about the psychology of fear, would be meaningless in an intensive care unit where there is only one notion of death which applies to all humankind. The relationship between different definitions of death—some of which are nonmedical—and their criteria and tests is shown in Table I.

Medical criteria for death refer to specific functions which must be totally and irreversibly lost. The tests for death involve examination procedures used to ascertain whether the criteria have been met. Both criteria and tests must be unambiguous, depending upon accepted medical and biological facts. They should be reliable and repeatable and provide a clear yes/no answer. Criteria and tests for death are meaningless unless related to some overall definition of death (see Table I).

III. CARDIOCENTRIC AND BRAIN-RELATED DEFINITIONS

A. Problems with Cardiorespiratory Concepts of Death

A medically grounded definition of death, it has been argued, must specify an irremediable and irreversible physical state. It must be selective, such that death can be recognized before total destruction of all cellular components. It must reflect a holistic view of life, recognizing that life is bound up with the capacity to organize and integrate essential functions.

Traditionally doctors have operated with cardiorespiratory conceptions of death, and criteria and tests have involved evidence of irreversible cardiac arrest and absence of pulse and respiration. However, during the 1950s and 1960s, successes in cardiorespiratory reversal generated a major scientific and ethical problem: the problem of the "beating-heart cadaver," where ventilation to asystole was becoming distressing to doctors and relatives, as a clear boundary between life and death was no longer apparent. The need for clarity in the definition of death and states approaching death was given urgency by improvements in the management of patients in coma. Before the introduction of techniques such as intravenous hydration, nasogastric feeding, and artificial ventilation, few survived long in a state of deep coma. Such patients either rapidly recovered or died. But improved techniques of life support meant that severely brain damaged patients could be kept alive for longer. These improvements occurred at the same time as developments in organ transplantation, which had led to a demand for cadaver donors. Moreover, it was becoming increasingly obvious that artificial continuation of cardiac and respiratory activity, under certain conditions where brain function had irreversibly ceased, was not equated with the maintenance of life, and was of no benefit to the patient. In cases of this kind, conventional cardiorespiratory criteria had proven incapable of giving a clear unambiguous answer to the question of the borderline between life and death. The way forward lay in considering the importance of the brain. Although the terminology was in a state of flux during the late 1960s and 1970s—doctors spoke of *coma depassé,* irreversible coma, cerebral death, and neocortical death—the construct "brain death" did achieve a degree of precision that allowed a pragmatic use of the term.

B. What Is Brain Death?

Brain death has been recognized by the medical profession in most countries where sophisticated facilities for intensive care have evolved. Nevertheless, the issues bound up with brain death, its meaning and diagnosis, continue to generate controversy both within and outside of the medical profession. Many of those who oppose brain-related criteria for death do so because of a perceived linkage with organ transplants, as it is sometimes argued that brain death is an artificial construct to facilitate easier access to transplantable organs. This issue will be addressed in Section IV. There is also both medical and philosophical controversy with regard to the appropriate definition of brain death. In the literature on this subject, three distinct formulations of brain death have been promoted: "higher brain," "whole brain," and "lower brain" or brain stem formulations.

1. Higher Brain Formulations

The higher brain, or cerebrum (See Fig. 1), is generally associated with consciousness (thought, memory, and feeling), movement, and speech. Irreversible loss of higher brain function is a feature of the persistent vegetative state, a condition in which patients are unaware of their environment, but may have the capacity to breathe spontaneously. Those who argue that death should be equated with the loss of higher brain functions base their case on the fact that such a loss strips a patient of his or her psychological capacities and attributes. It follows that arguments supporting higher

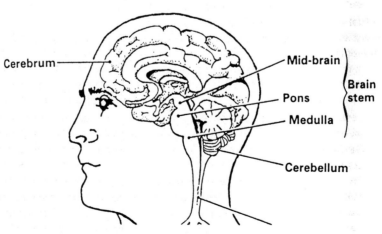

FIGURE 1   Diagram of the brain stem.

brain formulations will be connected with criteria seeking to describe the minimum necessary qualities for personhood (see Table I). However, such a concept of death would not relate in any way to the fact of continuous spontaneous respiration. The case for personal identity criteria for death has been advanced as a modern version of Cartesian dualism, with consciousness, and its connection with the "higher brain structures," assumed to be (morally speaking) distinct from the other bodily mechanisms. Priority is therefore given to the loss of consciousness, a view which in its extreme form attributes no significance to continuous bodily functions. Hence R. Puccetti suggests that corpses are really of two kinds, "the vast majory that cannot breathe unaided and a small minority that can nevertheless do this" (1988. In *Beyond Whole Brain Death* (R. M. Zaner, Ed.), p. 85. Kluwer, Dordrecht).

Opponents maintain that it is immoral to regard a being that is capable of unassisted breathing as dead and ready for burial or cremation. In practice medical authorities tend to regard patients in long-term persistent vegetative states as candidates for the selective withdrawal of life-prolonging therapy.

2. The Whole Brain Formulation

The whole brain formulation is expressed in the USA's Uniform Declaration of Death Act, which was adopted by Congress following a recommendation from The President's Commission for the Study of Ethical Problems in Medicine and Biomedical and Behavioral Research. It requires the existence of a state characterized by the "irreversible cessation of *all* functions of the entire brain, including the brainstem" (1981. *Defining Death*. Washington, DC). Having met criteria for whole brain death, the expatient has no capacity for consciousness, spontaneous respiration, heartbeat, or temperature control. Insofar as these functions persist, they are performed by the technical apparatus, not by the patient. Once it has been shown that the loss of these functions is irreversible, there should be no problem in recognizing death.

3. The Brain Stem Formulation

The whole brain formulation has been challenged, at the conceptual level, by the brain stem formulation implicit in the United Kingdom's guidelines for the determination of death which were issued by the Medical Royal Colleges and their Faculties in 1976 and 1979. It is claimed that irreversible loss of brain stem function is equivalent to the state required by the whole brain formulation, since survival of the brain stem is needed to generate the capacity for consciousness and the ca-

pacity to breathe. Despite the most vigorous form of therapy, an individual cannot survive with a dead brain stem. With irreversible cessation of brain stem function there can be no integrated functioning of the brain, and consequently brain stem death is perceived as the "physiological kernel" of whole brain death. Properly diagnosed, in the context of the recommended preconditions (the patient must be in a comatose state of known origin, require a ventilator, and suffer from irremediable structural brain damage) and exclusions (reversible causes of a nonfunctioning brain stem, among which are hypothermia and drug intoxication), the diagnosis of brain stem death yields unambiguous clinical criteria which can be objectively tested.

IV. MORAL PROBLEMS ATTENDING THE DIAGNOSIS OF DEATH

In the interests of scientific accuracy and ethical propriety it is essential to separate questions related to the conceptual and factual aspects of determining death from questions regarding the value of the patient's residual life and further questions concerning the need for transplantable organs. The following questions highlight the moral debate on medical aspects of death.

1. *Is the patient dead?* Once the definition, criteria, and tests for death have been clearly established, this question becomes one of medical diagnosis. However, medical diagnosis is not indifferent to public opinion, reflected through its laws and guidelines which provide an ethically acceptable framework within which doctors can work.

2. *Should the patient be allowed to die?* Whereas the scope of the first question is limited to objective clinical evidence, and draws upon established medical facts, this second question may involve ethical, religious, and economic considerations, and may involve answers which reflect different moral attitudes to the quality of residual life. Questions concerning whether the patient is alive or dead, like questions concerning pregnancy or meningitis, demand a yes/no answer. But answers to the question, "Should the patient be allowed to die?" are not immediately clear-cut. They entail a wide range of possibilities, ranging from the withdrawal of some, but not all, forms of therapy, to the controversies surrounding proposals for physician-assisted suicide and ethical debates regarding the withholding of futile therapy. (cross reference, euthanasia) When deciding if the patient is dead, deference to the authority of the physician is required. When deciding whether the patient

should be allowed to die, one may have to refer to legal, ethical, economic, and political matters, as well as to the known wishes of the patient, relatives, and others.

3. *Should the need for transplantable organs influence decisions about the determination of death?* Tremendous pressure exists for more transplant donors, and this pressure is likely to increase. A physician treating a terminally ill patient can be subjected to conflicting moral obligations when it is known that the organs of that particular patient can be used to save the life of another. To avoid potential conflicts between the attending physician and the requirements of the transplant team, practices have evolved which ensure that the donor's physician should have no role in the transplantation procedure itself. This has become known as the "dead donor rule," or separation principle of organ transplantation. According to this principle, neither costs of therapy nor the potential benefits to organ recipients should influence the implementation of criteria for death—the objective of which is to enable a physician to terminate treatment when there is no longer a patient to treat. In this view stories about "human vegetables" lingering on for months (while their organs could be used to save other lives) must never be allowed to influence criteria for determining death. The fact that others might benefit from the organs of dying patients (or patients in persistent vegetative states and anencephalic neonates), so the argument goes, is no reason for the assimilation of these states with death.

To avoid the need for transplant organs interfering with decisions concerning the diagnosis of death, some countries have proposed tougher guidelines for a determination of death when transplantation is under consideration. Thus the 1984 Report of the Swedish Committee on Defining Death recommends angiographic tests whenever transplantation is envisaged. Other countries have insisted that a whole team of doctors must agree over the diagnosis of death in the case of a potential donor (see the discussion on public fears of premature diagnosis in Section I).

The reason for these extra provisions was no doubt to allay public fears of a premature diagnosis of death and hasty removal of organs. But critics have pointed out that these very requirements may create public anxieties rather than avoid them, as they introduce the notion that there is a special kind of death awaiting potential organ donors.

While some philosophers and physicians have maintained that criteria for death should be linked to organ retrieval, and that the donor should be given an opportunity to opt for criteria for death in circumstances which facilitate an autonomous desire to donate organs, prevailing opinion supports the "dead donor rule." In medicine, the requirement for objective criteria for death, and hence cessation of therapy, must be shown to be independent of any extraneous considerations. If organ transplantation had never developed, or if there were sufficient funds to ventilate every dying patient indefinitely, it would still be seen as a scientific and ethical objective to seek reliable criteria for death. As the Report of the Conference of European Health Ministers (Strasbourg, 1987) noted, "it would be preferable by far for man's future survival to have to abandon transplantation than to agree to remove organs from individuals who are not really dead."

Also See the Following Articles

BRAIN DEATH • DO-NOT-RESUSCITATE DECISIONS • EUTHANASIA • LIFE, CONCEPT OF • ORGAN TRANSPLANTS AND DONORS

Bibliography

Arnold, R. M., and Youngner, S. J. (1995). The dead donor rule: Should we stretch it, bend it, or abandon it? In "Procuring Organs for Transplant" (R. M. Arnold, S. J. Youngner, R. Schapiro, and C. M. Spicer, Eds.), pp. 218–234. Johns Hopkins Press, Baltimore.

Lamb, D. (1996). "Death, Brain Death and Ethics," 2nd ed. Avebury, Aldershot.

Lamb, D. (1996). "Organ Transplants and Ethics," 2nd ed. Avebury, Aldershot.

McCullagh, P. (1994). "Brain Dead, Brain Absent, Brain Donors." Wiley, Chichester.

Pallis, C., and Harley, D. (1996). "ABC of Brainstem Death," 2nd ed. BMJ Publishing, London.

DEATH, SOCIETAL ATTITUDES TOWARD

David Wendell Moller
Indiana University

GLOSSARY

modern death A term for ways of dying that are shaped by medical and technological intervention and that are filled with images of loneliness, unrelieved suffering, meaninglessness, and confusion.

negotiated death A term reflecting the fact that a mosaic of competing interests often juxtapose patients, physicians, loved ones, and outside parties against each other, and the way the person dies will depend on how the conflicts are resolved.

physician-assisted suicide The act or fact of physicians helping dying persons to kill themselves with the merciful intention of relieving intolerable suffering.

sting of death A term for the icy horror that humans feel when facing the inevitability of death that is either exacerbated or relieved by prevailing folkways of dying.

thanatology revolution A cultural movement that stems from a recognition and rejection of the human indignities of modern technological dying.

traditional patterns of death Ways of dying that are sustained and defined by ceremony, spiritual and cultural meaning, and broad presence of communal support.

DEATH is inevitable, and it is the nature of being human, especially the "mixed blessing" of human consciousness, that gives rise to awareness of the self and to the inescapable knowledge that one day the self will be extinguished. From the very beginning, human beings have had to live with the imperatives of being human, a salient part of which includes knowing that life is fleeting and that every individual's life is temporary and perishable. From this inevitable face-to-face encounter with mortality, humanity has created a wide array of cultural and social patterns of dying, death, and mourning. In Western society, which is the focus of this essay, death traditionally held a central and deeply meaningful place in relation to the folkways of everyday living. In ways that were encompassing and powerful, despite vicissitudes of form and style, traditional patterns of death provided moral certainty and guidance for individuals in their encounters with mortality. In fact, the rituals and folkways of traditional patterns established death as a public and meaningful part of community life. In this framework, dying persons were deeply anchored by traditional cultural expectations and ceremonies that escorted them and their loved ones through the dying process. In this way, the regular inclusion of death, sorrow, and suffering in day-to-day

Encyclopedia of Applied Ethics, Volume 1

life provided for a collective defense against mortality that enabled humanity to tame the sting of death in a communal and, for the most part, comforting way.

However, during the 20th century, especially its second half, sweeping changes occurred not only in the styles and ways of death, but also in the relationship between human beings and mortality. In dramatic ways, dying, death, suffering, and mourning have lost their cultural significance and have become increasingly invisible and privatized in the modern social context. As will be explored in greater depth, a new attitude has emerged that promotes new ways of envisioning and talking about death and includes such terms as "denial," "avoidance," "fear," and "isolation." In addition, new images and themes have also emerged, reflecting the redefined relationship between the styles of living and the styles of dying. This contemporary imagery includes themes of bureaucratization, medicalized dying, death as an enemy, cultural repression of grief, unrelieved pain, violations of human dignity, and patients entangled and languishing in a technological web of tubes, wires, and imposing machines. Additionally, the moral certainty which was a cornerstone in the traditional patterns of death has given way to ambivalence, dissensus, and enormous complexity. Indeed, the simplicity and assurance that traditionally accompanied individuals through their journey of dying and death have become relics of the past and supplanted by recurring normlessness, turmoil, and confusion. Ironically, however, from this context of denial and dehumanization, a counteremphasis on openness and "death with dignity" has emerged. In this regard, the field of thanatology has been established as a subspecialty in medicine, the death-with-dignity movement has received popular cultural attention, and the hospice movement has been successful in establishing a widely available alternative to institutionalized, high-tech death.

I. TRADITIONAL PATTERNS OF DEATH AND DYING

The most brilliant chronicler of the history of Western patterns of death is Philippe Ariès. In his classic works, *The Hour of Our Death* and *Western Attitudes Toward Death,* he traces the evolution of humanity's relation to mortality, identifying five evolving, yet distinct historical stages: the Tame Death, the Death of the Self, Remote and Imminent Death, the Death of the Other, and the Invisible Death.

In the era of the Tame Death, which spanned the 5th to the 11th centuries, death was governed by familiarity, acceptance, and ritual. In this framework of familiarity, it was believed that individuals could sense when death was near, thereby enabling them to prepare for life's ending. One of the central characteristics of the Tame Death was that death provided warning of its arrival; in this regard, appropriate death could never be sudden and unanticipated. Suddenness of death was an indisputable source of shame. If, for example, a woman was struck down and killed by lightning or drowned unexpectedly, the very suddenness of her death cursed her with an irreversible stigma, resulting in the systematic erasure of her existence from the collective memory of the community forever.

It may seem strange that in an era where death was so pervasive and familiar that quick and unanticipated death would be feared so deeply that no one dared to talk about it. However, it needs to be remembered that the ability to anticipate death provided a forewarning—a shielding social armor—that enabled the community to gather and protect itself, whereas sudden death shattered the sense of communal order that helped individuals and their loved ones to confront mortality. In this world, death was not only anticipatable and familiar, it was also a public occurrence. The dying person was the center of a group of people. It was in this context of community that rituals and ceremonies were extensively used to comfort the dying person and to enable the community to say farewell. In this way, the icy horror of death was tamed by the rituals and familiarity that established an aura of serenity at the deathbed, and humanity was able to collectively face and bear the burden of mortality.

The image of peace and serenity in death also extended into the grave. Although, in the early part of the Tame Death, the dead body was a source of superstitious fear, that dread of dead bodies quickly gave way to a comfortable acceptance. Mass graves which were often partially or fully open to public view, along with charnels where the regularly exhumed bones of the dead were stored, were prominent features that defined the medieval cemetary. Of special significance is the fact that a great amount of social and commercial activity took place in the cemetery, in direct proximity to the open graves. This remarkable relationship between the living and the dead bespeaks an intimacy with death that would most certainly horrify modern people, who are accustomed to the dead body being sterilized and rendered mostly invisible to everyday life. It is also important to note that it was generally believed that although the dead body was decaying in an open, mass grave, the "deceased person" peacefully slept in a garden of flowers awaiting the resurrection when all would be saved and gain entrance into heaven. It is similarly interesting that remnants of this image persist today, as it is common practice to surround the casketed dead body with flowers in contemporary viewings and funerals, and to envision the deceased as being in a state of restful and peaceful slumber.

Around the beginning of the 11th century a twinkle of the cultural values of self and individualism appeared. In the broader cultural and social context, themes of personal responsibility and moral and legal wrongdoing, as well as the corollary sanctioning of individual behavior, were developing. For the first time in the history of society notions of the self begin to take on cultural meaning. Associated with this cultural revolution was the idea that not all lives and deaths were the same. The fate of the individual dying person, therefore, was no longer lost in and bound to the collective destiny of humanity. In this framework, in this era of the Death of the Self, the notion of biography emerged. Biography as a cultural and social notion was rooted in the belief that one's life was the product of personal choices, and that one could be held accountable for the choices one made. During this period, the idea of biography became a defining component of the deathbed. It was believed that, at the time of the resurrection of the body, the life choices of a person would be tabulated and summarized as either good or bad. If, in the overall calculation of a person's life, good outweighed evil, all evil would be erased and the person's life would be judged as wholly virtuous and deserving of salvation. The same was true of a person whose life was judged to be sinful. He would be remanded to hell where he would be gleefully greeted by the devil who presented him with a biographical sketch of his life in which all his good deeds had been expunged and only the evil ones remained.

During the 15th century, as part of an evolution within the Death of the Self and development of the cultural idea of individualism, new concepts of judgment, reward, and punishment emerged. Judgment would no longer occur at the time of ressurection, in the unknowable vastness of the cosmos, but rather at the confines of the earthly deathbed. The rich and beautiful image that surfaced was of a dramatic spiritual contest between good and evil. This battle was waged in the bedroom of the dying person where it was believed that the temptations of evil actually clashed with the forces of goodness and purity. The dying person was both participant in and witness to this struggle. In this scenario, the hour and manner of death became

the key to salvation. If one died a virtuous death, salvation was secured. If, on the other hand, during the relentless struggle for the soul of the dying person evil triumphs, he would be quickly cast into hell facing an eternity of damnation and suffering.

As Ariès correctly points out, the moment of death became the crucial juncture where one irretrievably either won or lost all. In this mysterious and explosive spiritual contest, a sense of drama and urgency became part of the dying process that redefined the assurance and quiet that characterized the Tame Death. For the very first time a terrifying risk to death was experienced. And, although Ariès argues that this terror was limited to fears of the afterlife and did not extend to a fear of death itself, it is safe to argue that we were witnessing anxiety and disquiet becoming associated with death in an unprecedented fashion. It is not, therefore, inconceivable to believe that some very unexpressed and primitive fear of death itself was aroused by the terrifying consequences of the spiritual struggle at the deathbed. In this regard, it may very well be that our modern full blown fear of death has its embryonic origins in the Death of the Self.

Another important manifestation of the Death of the Self grew out of the fact that humans took great pains to remind themselves of the frailty of life. Themes of the macabre became widespread, and cultural icons of the time were filled with deathbeds, decomposition, and gruesome skeletons. Literally, images of death, in its most naked forms, dominated the European landscape from the 14th to the 16th centuries. As I observe in *Confronting Death: Values, Institutions, and Human Mortality* (D. W. Moller, 1996. New York: Oxford Univ. Press), the poetry, paintings, woodcut art, drama, and stories of the time were dominated by images of disfigured corpses, rotting skin, and dead bodies covered with shreds of worm-eaten flesh. Additionally, in what amounts to a departure from the earlier era of the Tame Death, sudden death became culturally acceptable and visible. This growing appeal of unexpected death was reflected in the popularity of the "Danse Macabre"—the "death play" of the times—wherein ghastly looking skeletons would frightfully appear, survey the living, and without warning, select certain individuals to be their partner in the eternal dance of death.

Upon first reading, the images of the Death of the Self may appear bizarre and revolting. Yet, there are some interesting parodies and parallels that can be found in the modern ways of death. The deathbed in modern context is a place of enormous alarm and inquietude. Unlike the traditional patterns of the Death of the Self, where fear and dread of the deathbed were related to forebodings about the afterlife, the modern deathbed is typically distinguished by a sense of loss, agitation, confusion, and nervousness about the facts of death itself. The images of spiritual struggle have been replaced by images of physical catastrophe and personal suffering. One only need consider the immense technological battle against death that is waged daily in the intensive care units of America's hospitals to understand that the modern deathbed is filled with intense drama and struggle of a physical, not spiritual, nature.

It is also fascinating that while most images of death in the modern context are mechanized and antiseptic, a fascination with the macabre persists. Sherwin Nuland in his book, *How We Die,* effectively explains this irony when he observes that despite our anxiety and fear we are irresistibly attracted to death and its terror. Despite the fact that we are inclined to cover our eyes in the face of death, we just cannot help but sneak a peak! And, when we do seek a glimpse, we often do so by journeying with delight to death's macabre side. Grotesque and frightening physical images are a staple in horror films, Hollywood thillers, and novels. In a certain yet mysterious way, the horrifying deaths of Ron Goldman and Nicole Simpson in the 1990s, along with the images of the celebrity defendant charged in their brutal murders, captivated the cultural consciousness of America for an astonishing period of time, becoming a regular entrée in the menu of tabloid and mainstream news media. To be sure, our popular obsession with Jeffrey Dahmer, Charles Manson, David Berkowitz, Ted Bundy, and other serial killers reveals an ironic fascination with unimaginable horror and tragedy in the face of death—in the face of furious and sudden death. Thus, while the forms of the macabre have changed in graphic ways, images of sudden death and of the grotesque physical facts of death continue to attract and titillate the cultural interest of contemporary individuals.

As the 16th century began, many attitudes and practices remained the same. Open graves and charnels were present everywhere, images of the macabre remained, and the *artes moriendi* were prominent at the deathbed—but the deathbed itself lost its miraculous and awe-inspiring ambience. In fact, the new attitude which emerged drew and expanded upon the idea of biography and personal accountability that originated in the previous era. In this new framework, however, the triumph of sacredness and virtue at the moment of death was replaced by an emphasis upon virtuous daily living as the means to salvation. And, as the moment of death lost its theodic urgency, the deathbed experience be-

came less traumatic and assumed a greater quality of calmness and tranquility. Corresponding to the decline in the drama and importance of the deathbed was the rising significance of living life in constant preparation for death. In an era where sudden death was still widely emphasized, one needed to vigilantly ready oneself for death. In this regard, death was perceived as being imminent. However, although individuals lived in a close and intimate relationship to their own death and its spiritual consequences, the reality of death was seen to be a proximate but future occurrence. Simply, the prevailing idea seemed to be that while one constantly must prepare for death through righteous daily living, and one also recognized that while death was inevitable and could happen at anytime, one tended to believe that it would not happen "just now." In this matter, although death was clearly perceived as an immediate call to live well, it was cast as a somewhat vague and future happening. Death thereby became both pressingly imminent yet safely remote, and Western society moved into the era of Remote and Imminent Death.

One especially remarkable development during the era of Remote and Imminent Death was the growing interest in physical death and the dead body. Two salient themes in this regard emerged: (1) the dead body as a means of furthering scientific knowledge, and (2) the dead body as a source of macabre eroticism. In the shadow of the Industrial Revolution, in a world where the currents of science strengthened daily, the dead body was increasingly perceived as a vital source of knowledge about life and its mysteries. Issues of physical anatomy were discussed everywhere and dissections and lessons in anatomy occurred so frequently that they became a fashionable art form. In fact, they were so central to the cultural life of the community that the affluent built private dissecting rooms in their homes, and the anatomy lessons themselves became popular social events to attend. This in turn created a demand for dead bodies which led to blackmarketing enterprises and thievery from the graveyards. In regard to the second point of emphasis, it is important to remember that it was the qualities of serenity and peacefulness of the deathbed that endowed death itself with an irrefutable beauty. It is also crucial to note that physical images of the macabre continued to be widespread, and, with the rapidly growing emphasis on the scientific, physical facts of death, the dead body itself was becoming a source of cultural preoccupation. It is in this context which highlighted the physicality of death, conjoined with the fact that death itself was perceived to be pastoral and beautiful, that the corpse began to elicit erotic regard and attention. In this cultural milieu, the passions of eros merged with the cultural predilection for thanatos. In this world where the stirrings of imagination prevailed, and where instances of actual sexual encounters with the dead are part of the historic record, nercophilia emerged as a significant theme but was mostly contained within the boundaries of imaginative faculty and fancy.

In the 20th century, where death is virtually invisible to the texture of everyday cultural life, the images of the era of the Remote and Imminent Death seem odd and perverse. However, these shocking images which appear so contradictory to prevailing canons of aesthetic taste have been and continue to be a part of the cultural mix of contemporary life. Anatomy continues to be important to modern society, but its place and context have been redefined. The widespread cultural passion for anatomy that established dissection as a fashionable social activity for many has been transformed into a matter of specialized, professional importance. Anatomy labs filled with cadavers continue to exist and play an important role in our contemporary scientific development, but they are reserved for students and professionals in the health care and mortuary field. Thus, what is at play here is not an elimination of the images of the traditional era, but a natural social evolution, consistent with the modernizing of Western society, that has made anatomy all the more societally and scientifically important while intensely specializing and restricting its role.

The idea that the corpse could rouse and stir erotic desire is most alien to modern persons who with caution and trepidation push the very image of the dead body to the margins of personal and social consciousness. But once again, despite our own fear of the sight of death and disgust at the idea that the dead body can elicit erotic desire, we still cannot resist sneaking a peak. For example, as I note in *Confronting Death,* themes of loving the dead continue to have an enticing and captivating role in American popular culture. Dracula and his sexual harem of the undead continue to delight modern readers and theater and moviegoers with their sensual seductions of the living. Many of the aforementioned Hollywood-produced thrillers, that entertain tens of millions every year, also have strong and vivid erotic impulses intimately blended with the terror of murder, blood, and dismemberment. Popular works of fiction, from celebrated authors such as Anne Rice, Stephen King, Sidney Sheldon, and Caleb Carr, adroitly blend images of the macabre and the sensual in ways that are beguiling to the modern reading public. These examples are just a few, but illuminate the fact that on a fantasy and surrealistic level the forbidden territory of necrophilia continues to arouse and attract the cultural interest of modern individuals.

The beginning of the 19th century is associated with a dramatic decline in the images of the macabre that persisted for so many years. During this period of time, the fourth and final phase of the traditional patterns of Western death came into existence. In this age, which Ariès terms the Death of the Other, images of the physical facts of death were replaced by more ethereal images of romanticized and sentimentalized death. In this framework, the beauty of death resided not in its physical nature, but in its spiritual and interpersonal significance.

The landscape of the broader society was changing vividly and in direct correlation with pandemic growth in industrialization and urbanization. One of the direct by-products of the social metamorphosis was the contraction of broad ties of social community into smaller intimacy attachments, thereby limiting the "public character" of the deathbed. Interestingly, as the size of community diminished at the deathbed, the impact of death became more profound for the survivors. In this age, where the anguish of loss was quietly intensified and personalized, dying became a spectacle infused with great pain and suffering. Almost bewildering and certainly paradoxical is the fact that the beauty of death was contained in the urgency and torment of the process itself. Consistent with broader folkways in the Victorian way of life, sorrow was embraced as an opportunity for personal and spiritual elevation, as well as a testing ground for one's ability to meet the requirements of personal, cultural, and social responsibility. Animated and theatrical expressions of grief were not only expected, they were a cultural imperative for appropriate death. For this reason, material and emotional extravagance in dying, grieving, and mourning became representative of the age.

The concentration and intensification of grief marked a truly notable departure from previous eras and established a direct segue to contemporary styles of dying. Although fellowship, religion, and ritual remained strong sources of support, the careful observer can readily perceive the emergent howling of death and the scurrying of Victorians as they struggled to quiet its enormously emotional and disturbing presence. One can also sense the growing detachment and insularity of the deathbed from the broad connections of social community as a prelude to the social exile, loneliness, and solitude of the contemporary dying experience. Although harnessed by grandiose and melodramatic ritual, one can intuit a nascent transfiguration of the face of death itself. No longer tranquilly accepted, death was becoming unbridled—that is to say "untamed." Thus, although dramatically dissimilar to patterns of death that prevail in the 20th century, Victorian death served as a preface to the emergence of modern death and its corollary growth of patterns of denial.

II. MODERN DEATH: ICONS OF DENIAL AND INDIGNITY

During the 20th century dramatic and sweeping changes took place that not only redefined the ways of death but also the overall relationship between humanity and mortality. In great part, dying, suffering, and mourning have lost their significance in cultural life and increasingly have become invisible and privatized. Consider, for example, the modern inability to speak directly about matters of death and dying. Euphemisms such as "passed away," "kicked the bucket," "bought the farm," and "is with God now" are regularly used in order to avoid directly speaking about death. Medically based euphemisms are also widespread and are equally duplicitous: "the patient has expired," "respirations have ceased," "the patient is no longer with us," and "the patient has gone sour" are typical phrases used by physicians and nurses that circumvent direct use of the words "dying," "death," and "dead." Additional evidence of the fact that dying, suffering, and death have become invisible processes in American cultural life is found in the very vernacular that scholars use to describe the place of death in society. This intellectual language includes terms like "denial," "fear," "avoidance," "closed awareness," and "isolation." In this regard, the collective American tendency is to isolate and depersonalize the realities of death from the everyday flow of cultural life, which represents a clear and significant departure from traditional patterns which embraced death openly, emphatically, and directly.

In the modern organization of death, new issues and themes now surround the deathbed and establish its present definition and shape. Prevailing issues at hand include bureaucratic organization of dying, medicalization of dying, death as an adversary, patients lingering, emotional neutrality of professional caretakers, and technologically rooted dehumanization of dying persons. In this contemporary context, the process of high-tech, medicalized death has become both standard and dominant in the management of dying individuals. It also coincides with the growing unease with death and dying in the broader society. In this framework, a conspiracy of silence has emerged, and in a striking way,

dying, suffering, and death have become largely disguised and concealed from everyday patterns of living. Coinciding with this trend toward invisibility and privatization is the vanishing of norms and rituals that once helped to sustain and guide individuals and loved ones through the dying process. It is precisely this cultural devaluation of the meaningfulness of death that underlies the broad social trend that has relegated the management and control of death to a technological and medical model. The burden of care, once reserved for loved ones in a communal setting, has now been transferred to the technocratic arena of the hospital, and is assumed by paid professionals.

In this milieu of high-tech, bureaucratized death, the deathbed itself has become a place of enormous expense, confusion, and unrelieved suffering. Studies have shown that physicians, who are the dominant actors in shaping the course of modern death, are themselves uncomfortable with the human and emotional side of dying. Trained in the heroics of technological intervention, physicians are often the last to accept the proposition that good patient care often means the decision not to begin or extend treatment in order to prolong life. The result is that one-half of all Americans presently die in a tangle of anxiety-provoking tubes and machines. In addition, physicians commonly do not listen and respond to what patients want, communicate inadequately and with half-truths about bad news, and are insufficiently attentive to the matters of pain control and relief of suffering. The conclusion of certain studies is that the prevailing emphasis on never ending procedures and remorseless technological attacks upon disease leave families emotionally and financially drained, and patients filled with anxiety while longing for equanimity in dignity.

In this framework, the organization and the culture of the modern hospital are frequently at war with patients' wishes. Physicians, who spend an enormous amount of time and energy learning the technocratic skills that are the hallmark of their profession, are ill-prepared and generally disinclined to communicate openly, directly, and supportively with dying persons and their families. It should also be recognized that in the technocratic culture and bureaucratic climate of the modern hospital physicans who are interested in caring for the psychosocial needs of dying persons all too often find themselves unsupported and disregarded in their caring activities. Student physicians who are under phenomenal and highly competitive pressure to learn the science and technology of medicine, and interns and residents who are struggling through the demands of 90-hr work weeks, often find that the burden of psychosocial care obtrudes upon the time and energy that must be expended to master the knowledge and skill required of a modern physician. As a consequence, a patient's personal account of illness and the related private issues of coming to the end of life are dismissed as irrelevant by physicians who translate the human meanings of dying into a series of technologically based treatment regimens. The patient as a person, and the human sufferings that are associated with dying and death, is normally disregarded in this organization of care. In the rush to provide the very best technical care possible, physicians have become deficient in their ability to actively listen and respond to the concerns of dying patients.

Some scholars have suggested that personal and professional arrogance lies at the heart of this insufficiency of caretaking. While there may be some element of truth to this view, the matter is much more complicated. The source of the problem goes far beyond the personal and professional character of physicians, and resides in the structure of modern medicine and its dependency on science and technology. In the process of technological brinksmanship, which defines much of modern medicine, the identification and treatment of disease is systematically isolated from the person who is sick. Clearly, in this scenario, the contemporary, medical management of death is far removed from the web of ritual, fellowship, and meaning that supported the dying person and the surrounding community during the eras of the tamed and traditional ways of death.

However, it is important to note that reinterpreting the human dimensions of dying as medical and technical matters is functional within the modern, bureaucratized system of care, and is emblematic of the general cultural tendency toward death avoidance. More specifically, the more medical activity is restricted to a biomedical focus, the more attention is diverted away from the sweeping and emotionally charged personal issues of dying and death. Thus, the confrontation with mortality that profoundly challenges the psychosocial and emotional lives of dying persons and their loved ones becomes a largely unspoken, constrained, and evaded part of the physician–patient and physician–family relationships. It should also be recognized that patterns of avoidance also tend to characterize dying persons' relationships to loved ones and the ties among loved ones themselves. The result of these patterns of evasive interaction is to deprive all of the participants of ongoing systems of support and to isolate and privatize much of the sufferings of dying and loss in the personal and private worlds of individuals. What is at stake is

the management of the potentially volatile psychosocial and emotional dynamics of dying in a way that enables unimpeded flow of professional and bureaucratic activity. The internal dynamics of patients and their families become largely inconsequential to the central focus of the medical activity, which is not the dying person, but rather the disease and symptoms in the body in the bed. Thus, it is a consequence of the restrictive technological focus of their training and the organization of medical work that physicians tend to become dismissive of and hardened to the personal, psychological, and social facts of dying.

The crucial point to recognize is twofold: (1) the technological and medical management of death is closely linked with the broader cultural environment of uneasiness with dying, suffering, and loss, and (2) the failings of the psychosocial abilities of physicians are far more related to structural issues rather than personal inclinations. It should also be pointed out that in today's cultural climate and medical world, where there is so much angst in openly confronting the human dynamics of dying, and where there are so many conflicting tensions about competing treatment options, the relationships between dying patients and physicians have become complex and confusing. For example, while physicians have been increasingly criticized for impersonal, impolite, and uncivil regard for dying patients, dispassion and detachment are essential to good patient care and sound professional judgment. The problem which arises is when the culture of medical education and work fails to adequately address the bridging of technological focus with recognizing patients as persons with legitimate and compelling human needs. It is out of the systematic unwillingness to address seriously the bridgeability of the dual professional responsibilities of detachment and active respect for personhood that the gross indignities of modern dying surface. In this regard, skillful and successful care of dying persons must successfully negotiate between the competing demands of objectivity and empathy, between professional expertise and compassion, between detachment and intimate involvement, and between care of the body and care for the person.

In the absence of an institutionalized basis for acquiring systematic knowledge and skill on how to balance the employment of technology against consideration of the patient as a human being, the ability to provide consoling and beneficent care for the dying is a highly individualized phenomenon. Those physicians who excel in their care of dying patients as persons do so because of their extraordinary resources as a person, or because they have been personally and deeply touched by an exemplary teacher.

Our modern cultural context of denial and technologization is replete with cases where the modern, technocratic ways of death have exacted a huge human toll on dying persons and their loved ones. Confronted by a world that is unfamiliar and complex, patients live in an isolated state of pain, dysfunction, and helplessness. They regularly worry about what they are not telling me, feel ugly, worthless, and depressed, feel physically and emotionally scarred by their illness and the relentless technological invasion of their bodies, worry about being a burden to loved ones, and desperately try to make some sense out of all the suffering. Even those patients whose lives are successfully prolonged by technological intervention are generally embittered by the price they have to pay to gain some extra years or months of life.

Those who actually survive severe, life-threatening illnesses of long duration seldom have good memories of their experience with the system of medical care. Loved ones who witness the emotional and physical roller coaster of long-term illnesses are overwhelmed by their own personal sense of helplessness and of not knowing what to do or say. They navigate with frustration and sometimes anger: the impersonalism of the bureaucracy, the evasiveness and elusiveness of physicians, the parade of strangers who wander in and out of their loved ones' room, the confusing array of specialists, and the ever changing coterie of interns and residents. They resent being pushed to the corner of a room or out into the hallway as their role as decision makers and caring persons is replaced by the expertise and ministrations of the professionals. Paradoxically, however, despite their need to be actively involved in the caretaking of their dying loved one, they are often overpowered by a sense of inadequacy, confusion, and inexperience. They commonly find the physical and emotional pain of dying unbearable to witness, and they retreat from the deathbed into an isolated world of anguish and loss. This withdrawal not only intensifies their feelings of alienation and suffering, but their loved ones as well.

In short, the overall picture of the modern dying experience is dramatically different from traditional patterns of death. It not only lacks the serenity and support of the earlier patterns but is infused with graphic images of harshness, ugliness, and savagery. In this regard, the overarching point to be made is that the natural sorrow and pain of dying, once ameliorated by traditional folkways, is intensified by contemporary cultural forces of isolation, denial, and meaninglessness; they are also are worsened by the neglect, inattention, and indifference of technology focused physicians to the humanity and personhood of dying patients.

III. MODERN DEATH: REVOLT, CHANGE, AND COMPLEXITY

The modern model of death, rooted in a culture of denial and dominated by technological procedures, has been subject to increasing social and ethical criticism. Not only has the current age of technological death given rise to enormous suffering and indignity, but it has also spawned a confusing array of conflicts, choices, and uncertainties. In this context, ironically and paradoxically, as physicians have been dulled by the bureaucratic routine and technological focus of patient care and correspondingly have become dispassioned and hardened to suffering, the broader culture is increasingly filled with individuals that are intensely anxious and worried about the indignities and suffering that characterize modern dying. It is precisely the prevalence of this anxiety and growing discontent that became the prelude to a cultural movement of criticism, rejection, and reform.

The pioneering and perhaps best-known critic of medicalized death is Elisabeth Kübler-Ross. Her book, *On Death and Dying* (1969. New York: Macmillan), received widespread attention when it was first published. In a tone of lament that runs throughout her work, she questions the lack of sensitivity and compassion in the contemporary medical treatment of dying persons, and rejects the dominant heretofore uncontested pattern of technological death. In fairly straightforward style she presents an image of the gruesomeness of modern death, namely, its loneliness, mechanization, dehumanization, and impersonalization. This portrait struck a chord in the quietly worried American public. Her contrast of how dying persons may cry out for peace, rest, recognition of their sufferings, and for dignity, but instead receive infusions, transfusions, invasive and exhausting procedures, and technologically driven plans of action, was recognized by many as having relevance to their own personal experiences. Of perhaps even greater importance is her continual allusion to the idea of "death with dignity," an idea that is quite matter of factly presented and seems readily achievable in her analysis. Her rather uncomplicated view of serenity, acceptance, and personal courage, so often absent from the modern death experience, were of great and understandable appeal in a society terrified of the indignities of technological dying.

In this way, Kübler-Ross was a catalyst for the opening of the societal floodgates of anxiety and denial. It is also important to note that the general cultural atmosphere at this time was convulsed with criticism of the ability of the materialistic and technological foundation of American life to satisfy the human spirit. Thus, in relation to the great turbulence and revolt of the sixties, a cultural movement that challenged the humanity of medicalized dying began to emerge. Seemingly overnight, thanatology courses on campuses were designed and taught, textbooks began to proliferate, movies and theaters began to probe the previously taboo topics of suffering and death, self-help and support groups burgeoned, and a body of popular and scholarly literature on dying emerged—some of which, ironically in this age of denial, would become best-sellers. It was these happenings that were part of and gave birth to the thanatology revolution and the death-with-dignity movement. And, as we shall see, while this movement was able to create some opportunities for greater peace and ease in dying, it also brought to life a whole new set of dilemmas and complexities that themselves are filled with new forms of anguish and suffering.

A main component of the cultural rejection of technological death is the hospice movement which began in earnest during the 1970s. Contrary to the life-prolonging focus of medicalized dying, the hospice movement seeks a palliative, spiritual, and humanistic alternative. In this way, the hospice as a philosophy and system of care seeks to reclaim the solace and support that were provided by the rituals and patterns of traditional death. Although the concept of hospices has grown enormously during the past decade and specialized programs have emerged to serve select populations such as children and persons with AIDS, only about 10% of patients currently die in a hospice. Thus, while the growth of the hospice clearly reflects a renunciation of the prevailing ways of medicalized death and a desire to humanize the care of dying persons, problems of access, availability, and acceptability seem to be limiting its effectiveness. Since most hospice care is home care and requires the presence and commitment of the primary caretaker, many families are not equipped or willing to assume the responsibility of caring for a dying loved one. Additionally, there is a clear underrepresentation of select populations, most notably minorities and persons with AIDS.

While the hospice movement has gained many vociferous advocates over the past 20 years, there is a lack of convincing and reliable studies on the effectiveness of the hospice as a universally viable system of care. Several questions are relevant here. For example, are the claims of dignity achieved by hospice advocates influenced by the type of persons and families that select hospice care in the first place? That is to say, do special kinds of individuals tend to choose hospice care, and if so, are their distinctive personal qualities mainly responsible for dignity achieved? Do hospices socialize patients and families into behaving in accord with the ideals of the hospice? In this regard, do dismay, anger, and fear become submerged in a "feigned" but expected display of courage and dignity? On a broader level, the future of hospices will be significantly modified by the turmoil and changes presently occurring in the broader system of health care. Increasing bureaucratic regulation, financial cutbacks imposed by managed care, and the growing likelihood that in time to come hospices will evolve into for-profit, commercial enterprises are destined to have a transforming impact on both the philosophy and the reality of care. One final issue needs to be mentioned. In our age of death, denial, and secularized patterns of daily life, it is unlikely that a system designed to achieve death, even a peaceful one, will ever receive widespread support. In this way, the hospice is likely to remain a useful, yet highly individualized option in the modern organization of dying.

Another consequence of the cultural repudiation of technological dying, and in some ways an inherent part of technological development and application, is pluralistic-negotiated death. Pluralistic-negotiated death is an outgrowth of the convergence between the moral complexities that emerge from the development and success of technological systems of care, and the recent development of the death-awareness, death-with-dignity movement. As sociomedical change makes it more possible for patients and families to negotiate to obtain information, they become more empowered to make choices about how pain will be managed, about the use or nonuse of technology, and where death itself will take place. More patients and families are negotiating directly with physicians and other involved professionals regarding the patterns and course of treatment. Clearly, while the emergence of negotiated death offers possibilities of empowerment which did not even exist a scant decade ago, it, too, brings a new anxiety and confusion to the dying process. In contemporary society, where there is a movement toward the individualizing of death (which, of course, is reflective of the great cultural drift toward individualism), it is increasingly difficult to identify the best choice of action, and often the interests of patients, families, and professionals are in conflict. This moral and cultural anguish is clearly evidenced by the number of recent decisions that have been made at the state, federal, and Supreme Court level that were necessary to resolve, legally at least, profound conflict about the ways of death.

While these public and controversial cases reflect and contribute to the anxiety of dying in our modern era, on a less dramatic plane negotiations and conflict over how people should and will die are being waged in private, isolated circles all over the country. These negotiations typically can involve physicians, family members, hospital administrators, and even lawyers. They may concern discussions about halting therapies, choices about alternative and competing options, how aggressive to be in terms of technological levels of commitment, and may involve decisions about disconnecting life-sustaining equipment for comatose patients, who may or may not have left directives for their own care. These sometimes informal and ad hoc, and at other times more formal, negotiations may take several forms: families against physicians, family members against patients, patients against physicians, family members against family members with patients and physicians as anxious onlookers, physicians against other physicians, etc. Much less obvious than these patterns of interpersonal, interrole conflict is the enormous internal dissonance and confusion that all of the preceding parties experience in their uncertain, modern confrontation with death. In addition, the possible presence of attorneys and other outside interest groups may worsen an already confused and messy scenario.

One dramatic outgrowth of the jumbled and bewildering world of negotiated-pluralistic death is the recent movement toward the right to die and physician-assisted suicide. In the past decade there has been a visible movement to enable dying persons to determine the manner of their death, allowing them to choose to die free from "life-sustaining" heroics. Even more dramatically, efforts designed to instruct the terminally ill on how to commit suicide have made their way into mainstream cultural life, and a movement is currently underway that would legitimize a role for physicians in helping incurably sick persons to die. In an age of pluralism and individualism, and in response to the indignities of high-tech death, many have been seeking more flexibility and greater options in the modern styles of dying. It is important to interject that this movement is supported by patterns in the broader culture which encompasses themes of self-determination, personal empowerment, and secularized systems of meaning. In this milieu, especially in the face of the insufficiency and inadequacy of present patterns of care and the prevalence of unrelieved suffering, increasing arguments are advocating reform both in the law and in the practice of medicine. In fact, concern about the savageness of modern dying has grown to such a degree that some patients and physicians are decrying current prohibitions against assisted suicide as being cruel and inhumane.

I do not mean to imply that the movement toward establishing a right to die and a right to assisted suicide has evolved unchallenged. To the contrary, the issue is enormously contentious on many fronts, and there are strong and equally vociferous arguments against legitimizing and legalizing assisted suicide. The most straightforward of these is that killing, in any form, is inconsistent with the role of healer that defines the professional character of physicians, nurses, and other health care providers. The advocates of assisted suicide respond that physicians are purveyors of comfort as much as they are healers, and that active euthanasia is an option to be considered in the struggle to relieve suffering.

Opponents have then taken the argument to a deeper level and suggest that even if individualized, particular acts of assisted suicide may be moral and merciful, the precedent that is established by the legalization of assisted death is dangerous and destructive. They point to possibilities of abuse, neglect, misuse, and overuse. In this regard, it is argued that informal practices and pressures would overshadow the formal protections and safeguards built into the system of free and informed request and consent. For example, families exhausted by the responsibilities of caring for a loved one may unconsciously or consciously advocate the path of euthanasia. Dying patients may themselves feel a burden to others and decide to kill themselves because they feel unwanted and useless. In the current environment of desperately trying to control the costs of health care, the option of enduring life rather than having to continue to pay to care for it may become an attractive societal goal. Also, if expectations develop that pressure dying persons to elect assisted suicide, it is also likely that these expectations may extend to persons other than the terminally ill. Timothy Quill, one of the most reasonable and persuasive advocates for assisted suicide, is on record stating that the system of physician-assisted suicide should be expanded to include the chronically sick and people with disabilities.

Thus, while the image of Dr. Kevorkian and his suicide machine has been in media headlines for the past few years, a much more serious and litigious debate over the mortality and "side effects" of legalizing assisted suicide is being waged in legal, medical, and ethical circles. This debate, however, seems to be taking place in an already evolving pattern toward the acceptance of assisted suicide. Studies have shown that a majority of the American public supports the right to assisted suicide for dying persons. Some studies are beginning to suggest that physicians are becoming increasingly open to and supportive of the merits of assisted suicide, and some are already engaging in the practice, albeit illegally so. In this regard, although opposition from the political and religious sectors will remain strong, it is likely that the courts will gradually begin to legalize the right to assisted suicide. This, in turn, with the battle over safeguards and informed consent that will inevitably ensue, will make the personal experience of dying all the more fraught with staggering and worrisome choices for everyone.

IV. EASING DEATH'S STING: A CONCLUSION

The human confrontation with death is universal and inescapable. In earlier times in Western society, dying and death were more benign and meaningful experiences than they currently are. Indeed, despite variation in style and form, the rituals and practices of death were deeply connected to folkways, mores, and traditions that established dying as a meaningful part of the cultural life of the community. These patterns were directly shaped by the role that religion and community played in defining the everyday cultural climate. In direct contrast, the modern model of death is derived from two great social transformations: (1) the abdication of community to cultural values of individualism and privacy, and (2) the triumph of a secular, scientific world view over religious and spiritual explanations for life and death. As a consequence of these permutations in social life, dying has increasingly become taboo and ugly—an ironic form of modern pornography. Thus, in the contemporary social environment, where death is no longer tamed by community, spirituality, and cultural systems of meaning, technologically based efforts to defeat death and extend life have become pervasive. This cultural embrace of technological intervention as a prophylactic of death has given rise to prolonged and intensified suffering, and previously unknown indignity in the dying process. Thus, not only has death and dying become culturally intolerable in the modern setting, the actual human experience has become increasingly intolerable for dying persons and their loved ones.

In recent decades, a thanatology revolution has begun and is seeking to reverse the horror and indignities of modern dying. The death-with-dignity movement, with its specific components of hospice care, pluralistic

dying, and right-to-die advocacy, seeks to reign in and control the prevailing harshness and savagery of modern death. Paradoxically, the motivations of this movement seem strikingly similar to those of past eras, namely, to transmute the terror of death into a palliative and endurable experience. In this framework, of what some have called the "happy death movement" it is not just dying without fear that is the ultimate prize, but rather the ability to transform the dying process into a final opportunity for growth and happiness. Yet, despite even the most dedicated and honorable attempts to ease the turbulence that surrounds modern death, the contemporary human experience with dying remains full of suffering, fear, and indignity, and is replete with anxiety, confusion, and normlessness.

Thus, while the traditional patterns of death were able to successfully ease the sting of death, through elaborate use of rituals, constraints, and meaning sets, death's sting seems especially piercing, on both the individual and a social level, in this age of denial, technological sophistication, and ethical dissensus. In the words of Goëthe, "Death is, to a certain extent, an impossibility that becomes a reality." Historically, as we have seen, Western society went to great lengths to confront death as a reality in order to make it possible. In our contemporary world, however, patterns of cultural life so tenaciously avoid and complicate the realities of death, that dying in the modern context has become seemingly impossible to bear.

Also See the Following Articles

DEATH, DEFINITION OF • DEATH, MEDICAL ASPECTS OF • DO-NOT-RESUSCITATE DECISIONS • EUTHANASIA

Bibliography

Ariès, P. (1991). *The hour of our death.* New York: Oxford Univ. Press.
Beauchamp, T. (1996). *Intending death: The ethics of assisted suicide and euthanasia.* Englewood Cliff, NJ: Prentice Hall.
Becker, E. (1973). *The denial of death.* New York: The Free Press.
Callahan, D. (1993). *The troubled dream of life: Living with mortality.* New York: Simon & Schuster.
Cassell, E. (1991). *The nature of suffering and the goals of medicine.* New York: Oxford Univ. Press.
Gorer, G. (1965). *Death, grief, and mourning.* New York: Doubleday.
Kübler-Ross, E. (1969). *On death and dying.* New York: Macmillan.
Moller, D. W. (1996). *Confronting death: Values, institutions and human mortality.* New York: Oxford Univ. Press.
Moller, D. W. (1990). *On death without dignity: The human impact of technological dying.* New York: Baywood.
Quill, T. (1993). *Death and dignity: Making choices and taking charge.* New York: Norton.
Tolstoy, L. (1960). *The death of Ivan Ilych.* New York: Signet.

DEEP ECOLOGY

Carl Talbot
University of Wales, Cardiff

GLOSSARY

anthropocentrism The normative ethical claim that the nonhuman world only has value insofar as it is instrumental in satisfying human desires.

biospherical egalitarianism The proposition that all organisms (and even all things) in nature are deserving of equal consideration.

ecocentrism The view, commonly opposed to anthropocentrism, that the acceptability of environmental practices should not be established solely in reference to human welfare, but should consider the effects of such activities on life as a whole.

ecosophy A philosophy of ecological harmony that guides everyday life.

holism The theory that all the various parts of a system are internally related in such a way that the whole, of which they are a part, is more than the sum of these parts, in the sense that the whole has characteristics that are not explainable by reference to the properties and relations of its parts.

identification The process by which the individual self becomes aware that it is part of a single, unified nature.

intrinsic value Nonderivative value which resides in a thing as a result of the nature of the thing itself.

self-realization As employed by deep ecologists, this term denotes the process whereby the individual self becomes ever more aware that its interests are identifiable with those of nature as a whole. As a norm it prescribes this process. It also denotes an ultimate goal, or aimed for perfection.

vitalism The doctrine that there is an essential, creative principle within the process of nature.

DEEP ECOLOGY, as a concept, emerged as one half of a typology formulated by the Norwegian philosopher Arne Naess in 1973. Since that time many environmentalists have advanced deep ecology as the philosophical foundation of authentic environmental policies. The typology seeks to distinguish environmental approaches according to whether or not they address environmental concerns from an anthropocentric standpoint, that is, one which is concerned only with the environmental impact of practices on the well-being of human beings. Shallow ecology, the other half of this typology, even in its most enlightened form, is concerned only with human-centered considerations; for example, conservation strategies are promoted with a view to securing the maintenance of natural resources for continued human consumption.

Deep ecology, by contrast, identifies anthropocentrism as the fundamental cause of environmental destruction, arguing that human are not different and apart from nature, but that all nature, including humans, is a unified whole. When evaluating the environmental acceptability of human practices, deep ecology does not restrict itself to asking what the effects on human interests are, but asks what are the consequences for all of nature. For guidance in these matters deep ecology upholds the belief, summed up in Barry Commoner's "third law of ecology" (B, Commoner, 1972. *The Closing Circle*. Bantam, New York), that "nature knows best," and that any change to a natural system caused by human activity is likely to be harmful to that system. Deep ecology therefore promotes a lifestyle which seeks to harmonize with nature.

I. THE BASIC TENETS OF DEEP ECOLOGY

A. The Critique of Anthropocentrism

Arne Naess has claimed that what is distinctive about deep ecology is its policy of asking ever deeper, more fundamental questions about matters of environmental concern, in order to arrive at the presuppositions underlying environmentally destructive activities. We take the issue of pollution to illustrate this insistence. Deep ecologists argue that shallow approaches to this problem are limited to evaluating and alleviating the effects of pollution on human health, accompanied by technological endeavors to dissipate, or reduce, the harmful consequences of pollution. In contrast, deep ecologists contend that their approach requires them to assess pollution from a point of view that considers its effects on the whole of nature. What is more, deep ecology goes further by questioning the value assumptions of modern society which drive a progressive expansion of the production and consumption of material goods, and whose technologies and industries are identified as the causes of pollution.

Deep ecologists believe that their more penetrating analysis is further exemplified when one considers the use of natural resources. The shallow approach is characterized as emphasizing the security of resources for humans (for the most part, those belonging to the present generation of affluent societies). The conservation of resources is entrusted to market forces which will supposedly place high premiums on scarce natural resources, thereby retarding their overexploitation. Deep ecology, in rejecting this analysis, questions the very notion of a "resource", arguing that no natural object should be viewed only as a resource for human aspirations. Concerned with the well-being and flourishing of all of nature, deep ecology argues that human use of the environment ought to be governed by an understanding of the consequences of such use on the long-term maintenance of ecosystem integrity, with a view to encouraging the future health of all life.

Whereas the shallow approach to such environmental problems as pollution and resource depletion is only occupied with human-centered concerns about its effects on human health and future opportunities, deep ecology rejects what it sees as this superficial, short-sighted perspective in favor of an "ecocentric" approach which questions the effects of such destructive activities on life as a whole.

B. The Unity of Nature

Unlike shallow ecologists who stress the essential difference between humans and nature, deep ecologists argue that this dualism is misconceived. Often citing conceptual resources from Eastern mysticism, the spiritual practices of "primal" peoples, the philosophies of Spinoza and Heidegger, the late 19th and early 20th century organicism of theorists such as J. S. Haldane (J. S. Haldane, 1884. *Mind* IX, 27–47), the vitalism of Henri Bergson (H. Bergson, 1935. *The Two Sources of Morality and Religion*. Macmillan and Co., London), and the discoveries of modern quantum physics, deep ecology claims that there is no world of discrete things, only a single unity. Organismic analogy is employed by deep ecologists to convey their holistic understanding of nature where all life, and the various habitats it occupies, are considered part of the "superorganism" Gaia, or the "expansive self." A number of basic assumptions make up this holistic account: the whole is more than the sum of its parts; the whole determines the nature of its parts; no understanding of the parts can be achieved in isolation from the whole; and the parts are dynamically interrelated and interdependent. In this way the nature of any one thing in the world is determined by its relations with every other thing and its relation to the whole. Naess calls his particular brand of holism "relationism", as he believes that an organism is defined (i.e., is what it is) by its relations with all the other parts of its environment and nature as a whole; thus he argues that "an *organism is interaction*."

In line with its holistic loyalties, deep ecology rejects as inadequate and unsuitable the analytical method of modern science insofar as it assumes that discoveries about the nature of a thing can be made by isolating it and exposing it to experimental scrutiny. Deep ecologists are quick to stress the "nonanalytical" nature of deep ecology's understanding, and wish to replace the scientific ontology (that is, its account of the nature of being) of modern society with an account of the world as a "relational field". In this model there are no discrete objects, only the flux of a world of relations and interactions.

All too often this understanding of deep ecology has encouraged rather obscure accounts of how we are able to gain knowledge about nature. Naess, in rejecting the methods of scientific inquiry, asserts that our knowledge of the world is not analytical but "experiential"; that is, it takes the form of impressions of the unity of nature. This experiential knowledge is the product of a specific esoteric epistemological faculty, the idea of which, for Naess, has its theoretical roots in the writings of Spinoza, and which provides us with a spontaneous intuition of natural unity. It is this intuited experience of the oneness of nature that forms the fundamental premise of deep ecology. This would seem to make the attainment of knowledge as it is generally understood impossible, for to know something about any part of nature we must first have knowledge of nature as a whole.

C. Biospherical Egalitarianism

Deep ecology argues that if we recognize the essential unity of nature, such that the character of all forms of life is determined by their relations with all other life, and that any one organism is merely a particular instance of the total field of relations, then certain ethical conclusions naturally emerge. If all organisms are part of the same unified nature then they all deserve equal consideration. This ethical proposition of the equal validity of every organism to realize its own good is termed *biospherical egalitarianism*.

Deep ecologists have attempted to extend the remit of this ethical principle by stretching the term "life" beyond its biological usage; so, for example, Naess has argued, "The intuitive concepts of life sometimes cover a stream, a landscape, a wilderness, a mountain, an arctic [sic] waste" (A. Naess, 1984. *The Ecologist* 14, 202–203). This claim is possible, deep ecologists believe, because value is not assigned by humans, nor is it dependent on biological assertions about, for example, the relative complexity of an organism's structure (as the arguments of many who wish to extend moral consideration or rights to some, or all, nonhuman animals propose), but is posited by the intuition that all of nature is fundamentally one and the same. So, for example, according to deep ecology the intrinsic value of a whale does not arise from the perceived comparable

complexity of its nervous system to that of humans, but is a consequence of the intuited unity of nature.

If biospheric egalitarianism is taken at face value its prescriptions seem wholly impracticable, as the well-being of one form of life necessitates the killing of other forms of life for its sustenance. Therefore, deep ecologists attach a qualification: biospherical egalitarianism, *in principle*. Deep ecology is not claiming that the interests of, for example, humans may never override the interests of nonhuman nature. Rather deep ecology is rejecting what it sees as the anthropocentric assumption that human interests always win out. Naess suggests a possible formulation for decision making when interests conflict: "A vital need of the non-human living being A overrides a peripheral interest of the human being B" (1984. *Environ. Ethics* 6, 267).

II. A "PLATFORM" FOR DEEP ECOLOGY

Deep ecologists are keen to assert that the deep ecology movement is not founded on a single "dogma"; rather they prefer to view it as a common ground, or "platform," that is shared by a diverse array of supporters. In an effort to characterize this platform Naess and G. Sessions have proposed a set of principles which they consider basic to deep ecology, and which are given in Table I.

While heralding their theory as radically new, deep ecologists share the urge to paint an authentic patina of age. Usually ignoring the historical specificity of the favored sources, deep ecology seeks confirmation of its account in an eclectic collection of philosophies, religions, and belief systems, old and new, in an effort to build a broad base of support, and in some respects, present itself as the culmination of, and, perhaps, even successor to, an aged and universalistic lineage. The platform of deep ecology is supposed to represent the derived views which adherents of the many religions and philosophies, who make up the supporters of the deep ecology movement, have in common.

III. THE PHILOSOPHY OF DEEP ECOLOGY

A. The Distinctiveness of Deep Ecology

It is possible to discern three uses of the term "deep ecology." There is a methodological sense where deep ecology represents the policy of asking ever deeper questions about ecological relationships so as to arrive at the fundamental assumptions that inform them. It is

TABLE I

The Basic Principles of Deep Ecology

1. The well-being and flourishing of human and nonhuman life on Earth have value in themselves (synonyms: intrinsic value, inherent value). These values are independent of the usefulness of the nonhuman world for human purposes.

2. Richness and diversity of life forms contribute to the realization of these values and are values in themselves.

3. Humans have no right to reduce this richness and diversity except to satisfy vital needs.

4. The flourishing of human life and cultures is compatible with a substantial decrease of the human population. The flourishing of nonhuman life requires such a decrease.

5. Present human interference with the nonhuman world is excessive, and the situation is rapidly worsening.

6. Policies must therefore be changed. These policies affect basic economic, technological, and ideological structures. The resulting state of affairs will be deeply different from those of the present.

7. The ideological change is mainly that of appreciating life quality (dwelling in situations of inherent value) rather than adhering to an increasingly higher standard of living. There will be a profound awareness of the difference between big and great.

8. Those who subscribe to the foregoing points have an obligation directly and indirectly to try to implement the necessary changes.

Source: Devall, W., and Sessions. G. (1985). *Deep Ecology: Living as if Nature Mattered.* Gibbs M. Smith, Salt Lake City, UT.

not clear, however, that this practice is distinctive of deep ecology and that ecocentric policies will necessarily result. There is also a popular sense of deep ecology which expresses a general ecocentric orientation toward environmental matters giving rise to the platform of deep ecology. While this sense of deep ecology is characteristically opposed to anthropocentrism, there is nothing that differentiates it from other positions which, though opposing anthropocentrism, do not share deep ecology's philosophical assumptions.

Responding to this, the deep ecologist Warwick Fox has argued that what makes deep ecology a truly distinctive approach to environmentalism are these philosophical assumptions that guide it, formulated in a large part by Naess in what he terms his "Ecosophy T." While deep ecology often cites the findings of ecological science in support of its position, its premises are metaphysical, not scientific.

B. Self-Realization: The Fundamental Norm of Deep Ecology

As has been seen, deep ecology's starting point is an intuition—the immediate, spontaneous experience of the unity of nature. It follows from this intuition that "all entities are constituted by their relationships"—that there will come an increased "identification" with the world of which we are a part. Enlightened by the intuition of nature's oneness, deep ecologists suggest that the individual self "matures" as its interests become ever more identified with the interests of nature as a whole. In this way, realization of the potential of the individual self becomes inextricably bound up with the realization of the interests of the whole of nature, or what deep ecologists call the "expansive self."

Thus we arrive at the "fundamental norm" of deep ecology—self-realization. This enterprise consists of the process of formulating an identification of the personal self which goes beyond an identification of self-interest with the individual, or with the interests of other humans, to an identification of one's interests with those of nature as a whole. In this way deep ecology seeks to harness self-interest by claiming that our interests are synonymous with those of the expansive self that is nature. In terms of our environmental obligations, the defense of nature becomes equivalent to the defense of ourselves, when our self is identified with the expansive self.

Other ecological norms such as "diversity of life," "complexity," and "symbiosis" are, so deep ecologists contend, derived from this fundamental norm of self-realization to the extent that they contribute to the realization of this expansive self. It is this philosophical account which, it is claimed, makes deep ecology a distinctive approach to matters of the environment.

C. Superseding Ethics?

More recently Fox has attempted to refine Naess's philosophical sense of deep ecology by emphasizing what he considers to be its distinctive psychological theory. Fox maintains that the conclusions of deep ecology emerge from its theory of human psychology. Eager to dissociate deep ecology from environmental ethics, as it denotes approaches concerned with the discussion of values in nature, Fox contends that the moral prescriptions which arise from ethical theories of intrinsic value in nature are necessarily directed at a "narrow, atomistic, particle-like conception of self," whereas deep ecology relates its metaphysical vision to a "wide, expansive, field-like conception of self." Consequently, according to this account of deep ecology, moral obligations founded on the recognition of intrinsic value will be superseded by what Fox calls "natural inclination":

[Deep ecology is] not concerned with the question of the logical connection between the fact that we are intimately bound up with the world and the question of how we should behave, but rather with the psychological connection between this fact and our behavior. [Deep ecologists'] analysis of the self is such that they consider that if one has a deep enough understanding of the way things are (that is, if one empathically incorporates the fact that we and all other entities are aspects of a single unfolding reality) then one will (as opposed to should) naturally be inclined to care for the unfolding of the world in all its aspects ... given a deep enough understanding of this fact, we can scarcely refrain from responding in this way. (W. Fox, 1990. *Toward a Transpersonal Ecology*, p. 247)

This philosophical sense of deep ecology (which Fox has called his own version of transpersonal ecology) avoids moral prescription and instead seeks to invite us to share its adherent's ontological vision; having moved beyond our narrow, selfish interests by the acceptance of nature's unity, acts of environmental concern will not be the result of moral obligation, but rather care for nature will "flow naturally" with the realization that one's self is but "an aspect of a single unfolding reality," thereby rendering ethics "superfluous."

There does, nevertheless, appear to be some confusion in the literature of deep ecology as to whether questions of value and moral prescription have a place in the theory and practice of deep ecology. Clearly the platform of deep ecology is pregnant with the language of value and obligation, and Naess describes "self-realization" as the "fundamental norm" of deep ecology. Deep ecology seems quite inconsistent on this matter, though for the most part Naess, at least, seems to accept complementary roles for ontology and ethics. And as Richard Sylvan has suggested, attempts, such as Fox's, to shift the emphasis of environmental philosophy from ethical to ontological concerns might be seen as "a regressive attempt to move environmental philosophy to anthropic experiential concerns" (R. Sylvan, 1990. *Discuss. Papers Environ. Philos.* **18**, 54), insofar as our care for the environment, in such an account, is founded on the *human* experience of its oneness.

IV. DEEP ECOLOGY AND SOCIAL CHANGE

A. The Call for a New "Religion"

Deep ecologists claim the destruction of the natural world results from a modern anthropocentric con-

sciousness which mistakenly leads humanity to believe that nature is a resource for human ambition. Consequently, this degradation of nature will cease when we embrace a new consciousness which recognizes our spiritual oneness with all of nature. Thus the target of deep ecology's social critique is the idea of anthropocentrism: "The target of the deep ecologists' critique is not humans *per se* (i.e. a general class of social actors) but rather human-centredness (i.e. a legitimating ideology)" (W. Fox, 1989. *Environ. Ethics* **11**, 24).

Deep ecologists seek to change humanity's anthropocentric consciousness, which, they argue, drives our ambition to dominate and exploit nature, by inviting people to change their idea of nature by an experiential encounter with the fundamental oneness of reality. The idealism that informs this analysis leads deep ecologists to call for a new "religion" or "spirituality" which teaches a holistic, harmonious account of the human–nature relationship. Social change, it seems, is to be achieved by the missionary work of deep ecologists with their invitation to spiritual enlightenment. Unlike, for example, a Marxian account which would identify the project of the domination and exploitation of nature with the economic goals of a capitalist class, deep ecology claims that environmental destruction results from a wayward psychological impulse of humanity as a whole. Subsequently the project is not primarily one of political and economic change, but one of psychological or spiritual reorientation; deep ecology seeks to exorcise the ideas of anthropocentrism, production, consumption, etc., from the collective human consciousness.

B. Nature's Prescriptive Force

According to deep ecologists the appropriate social behavior is prescribed by an understanding of nature's own values. They espouse and promote a new paradigm summed up in such slogans and principles as "nature knows best," and "change to a natural system brought about by human activity is likely to be detrimental to such a system". This normative code asserts nature as the ethical authority, with the study of nature's interactions providing the source of values and prescriptions. These prescriptions fall into three general classes whereby the appropriate attitude toward nature which humanity ought to adopt is one of awe, reverence, and humility; the appropriate goal of humanity is to realize a harmonious relationship with nature which will result in the least impact on ecological systems; and the appropriate goal for human inquiry is to discover the values of nature so that humanity may learn how best to pursue an existence which involves the minimum intervention in ecological systems.

Despite the assurances of many deep ecologists, one only needs to be acquainted with a few examples of their literature to see that much of their theory leans heavily on the narratives of ecological science such as "natural stability" and "carrying capacities." Deep ecologists frequently recruit the vocabulary of ecological science; their models of nature often reflect those used by ecology, and in defense of their conclusions deep ecologists regularly cite the findings of this science. The problem with this practice is that deep ecology does not make clear how norms such as "live in harmony with nature" are to be interpreted, nor does it seem to take account of the often transitory and contingent nature of scientific principles and models.

C. Misanthropy

Deep ecology's account of nature's normative force is also utilized as a political program. Natural values are to be applied to human culture such that thinking about social organization is to be conducted, as Kirkpatrick Sale advises, in "biotic" rather than "social" terms. This has led deep ecologists to claim a "neutral, privileged" ground outside of human concerns. Where in early history human conduct was ruled by nature through nonhuman beings such as elementals, spirits, and demons and natural locations such as oracles, in deep ecology nature's prescriptive force is transmitted by the pseudo-scientific vocabulary of "natural harmony," "stability," "diversity," etc. While modern religion and emergent capitalism secularized and "despiritualized" nature, allowing for its wholesale exploitation, deep ecology aims to resuscitate the veneration of a spiritualized nature. By importing nature's normative force into human society, deep ecology seeks to submerge the human world into the natural world.

The understanding of the essentially destructive character of human activity and the belief that "nature knows best" have lead some deep ecologists to make explicitly misanthropic remarks. For example, in his theory of Gaia, J. E. Lovelock argues that

> our humanist concerns about the poor of the inner cities or the third world, and our near-obscene obsessions with death, suffering and pain as if these were evil in themselves—these thoughts divert the mind from our gross and excessive domination of the natural world. (1989. *The Ages of Gaia*, p. 211)

Other campaigning groups have offered an account of famine as "nature seeking its own balance." Understood as a natural phenomenon, in this account, famine is not only inevitable but also good, insofar as society's continued well-being depends on our nonderivation from established natural conditions.

Publicly the theorists of deep ecology have distanced themselves from these direct declarations of some members of its campaigning factions, but nevertheless they do seem to find support in the theory of deep ecology. Deep ecology's psychological or spiritual solution to the problem of environmental degradation requires a "psychological maturity" of the self, that is, "a deep understanding of the way things are". This deep understanding will prescribe (though deep ecologists prefer the nonforceful, "incline") our behavior as that of acceptance and accommodation to the "will of Nature". Just such an exorcism of social activity from history, leading to its subsequent naturalization, is a stated aim of deep ecology. For as Fox informs us, "deep ecologists have been attempting to get people to see that historical and evolutionary outcomes represent 'the way things happen to have turned out'—nothing more" (1989, 24).

It is deep ecology's contention that there is a pervasive basic striving implicit in nature: the urge toward self-realization. It is nature's creative purpose to travel toward the aimed-for perfection of self-realization; thus purpose, creativity, and historical momentum are naturalized, becoming the possession of nature as the Absolute Subject. In this way deep ecology's conception of nature underwrites a moral economy which cites the appropriate social behavior as consisting of a retreat of human activity from the realm of "wild" nature (this is often summed up by those deep ecologists influenced by the philosophy of Heidegger in the slogan, "let it be"; see, for example, B. Zimmerman, 1983. *Environ. Ethics* 5, 99–131). This normative vision has led deep ecologists to support demands for the international designation of wilderness preserves, though these moves have been met with hostility by many indigenous peoples whose homelands have been subject to the attention of these projects and who have been displaced and dispossessed as a result (R. Guha, 1989. *Environ. Ethics* 11, 71–83). The application of natural values to human society has led deep ecologists to claim a "neutral, privileged" ground outside of human concerns, but its critics have argued that this depoliticization of the environmental crisis, and the move toward psychological analysis rather than class analysis of its causes, results in deep ecology being blind to matters of social and environmental justice. Romanticized as a common ideal for all, deep ecology's project of spiritual rehabilitation may obscure the social relations, founded on economic class, gender, and race, which, it can be argued, play a considerable part in determining the real character of environmental despoilation and the distribution of the detrimental impacts of this process, such as pollution, which studies by environmental justice groups have shown to be distributed disproportionately in society.

Also See the Following Articles

ANTHROPOCENTRISM • ANIMAL RIGHTS • BIOCENTRISM • BIODIVERSITY • DEVELOPMENT ISSUES • ENVIRONMENTAL JUSTICE

Bibliography

Bradford, G. (1989). "How Deep is Deep Ecology?" Times Change Press, Ojai, CA.

Devall, B., and Sessions, G. (1985). "Deep Ecology: Living as if Nature Mattered." Peregrine Smith Books, Salt Lake City.

Fox, W. (1989). "Transpersonal Ecology: Developing New Foundations for Environmentalism." Shambala, Boston/London.

Giha, R. (1989). Radical American environmentalism and wilderness preservation: A third world critique. *Environ. Ethics* **11**, 71–83.

List, P. C. (Ed.) (1993). "Radical Environmentalism: Philosophy and Tactics." Wadsworth, Belmont, CA.

Luke, T. (1988). The dreams of deep ecology. *Telos* **76**, 65–92.

Naess, A. (1973). The shallow and deep, long-range ecology movement: A summary. *Inquiry* **16**, 95–100.

Naess, A. (1989). "Ecology, Community and Lifestyle." Cambridge Univ. Press, Cambridge.

Pepper, D. (1996). "Modern Environmentalism: An Introduction." Routledge, London.

Sylvan, R. (1985). A critique of deep ecology. *Rad. Philos.* **40/41**, 2–22.

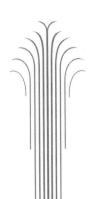

DEVELOPMENT ETHICS

Nigel Dower
University of Aberdeen

GLOSSARY

aid Transfer of resources on noncommercial terms (as grants or concessionary loans), either by governments (official aid), international financial institutions, or by individuals' donations through aid agencies to promote development in poorer countries (the South) or more particularly to alleviate absolute poverty. Various ethical theories require such aid.

development (a) A process of socioeconomic change, primarily and centrally a process of economic growth, which, to some significant degree, is the object of public policy and planning. This, it will be argued, is broadly the dominant conception of development. But behind it lies a less specific, but explicitly normative definition of development as: (b) A process of change in a society that, in the eyes of thinker, is a change that ought to happen (e.g., from a worse state to a better state)—in certain respects parallel to the earlier idea of "progress." As will be noted, it is possible to offer rival conceptions of development dependent on the normative criteria adopted.

distributive justice A principle of social justice that requires that resources and wealth should be so distributed as to meet the needs of all people in a society. Applied to the world as a whole, distributive justice requires aid and economic relationships generally to be such as to meet the basic needs of all people.

economic growth Growth in the economy of a country enabling its inhabitants to have access to a materially higher standard of living. Economic growth is the central feature of the dominant paradigm of development, but is rejected as the most important feature by many thinkers in development ethics.

global society A social order on a global level in which effective cooperation to facilitate development, particularly development directed toward the alleviation of extreme poverty, can take place. The ethical arguments of many forms of development ethics stem from a global ethic, which assumes both some universal values (often including some diversity of expression) and cosmopolitan obligations, and argues for the effective establishment of an appropriate global society.

North–South relations The relations between richer countries in the industrialized "developed" countries of the world ("the North") and poorer "developing" countries ("the South"). Ethical issues are raised both about aid programs and about the general trading and investment policies of the North in the South.

well-being The condition in a human being of flourishing. This is a central normative idea in terms of which development should be defined, about which rival ethical theories provide different accounts.

DEVELOPMENT ETHICS is systematic, disciplined reflection on the ethical basis of authentic development. Development ethicists generally agree on the centrality of the alleviation of extreme poverty, but also question the adequacy of the conventional "economic growth" model of development, both in what are called "developing" countries and "developed" countries. Economic growth needs supplementing with a principle of distribution and is only a means to human well-being defined in other more complex ways. Different philosophical theories are offered to provide the basis for these values (such as Kantianism, neo-Aristotelianism, and rights theories). All accounts of development, conventional or otherwise, presuppose some set of values. The issue of relativism needs to be considered, although most development ethicists would prefer to defend a form of universal values that incorporates some degree of pluralism and cultural diversity. At the global level development ethics raises issues about global society and the existence of global obligations, and thus considers the justification for aid, at the governmental and personal level, and the appropriate forms that international trade and investment should take.

I. INTRODUCTION

As a self-conscious area of academic enquiry, development ethics is of very recent origin (some 15 years standing), and its emergence more or less parallels the establishment of the International Development Ethics Association (1984), which has helped give some public identity to it. This is not to say that individual thinkers such as Lebret and Goulet were not talking about ethical or value issues in development, formulating ethical strategies for development, or even using the phrase "development ethics" for some while before that. Indeed, the central questions with which development ethics deals—having to do with the nature of the good life, the principles underlying an appropriate social order, and the ethical demand for change—have been around ever since inquiry into the human condition began.

Although, as we shall note later, the range and complexity of the issues covered by development ethics has enlarged, it essentially emerged from critical ethical reflection on the process of socioeconomic development in poorer countries (variously called "underdeveloped," "developing," "the South"), which since the Second World War were seen as the object of international aid programs. As Denis Goulet, a pioneer in the field of development ethics, put it, development ethics is concerned with "the ethical and value questions posed by development theory, planning and practice" (Goulet, D., (1977). *The uncertain promise*, The Apex Press). It includes both a consideration of the *what* of development (kinds of goods/benefits) and the *how* of development (kinds of processes of acceptable social change).

As the later discussion will illustrate, from the point of view of those who see themselves engaged in development ethics, nearly all discourse about development, including that of the dominant paradigms that stress economic growth at the core of development, is implicitly normative or evaluative in character. But it is characteristically those thinkers who for one reason or another have become dissatisfied with what is done and pursued in the name of conventional development, who actually see themselves engaged in development ethics.

II. AREAS OF AGREEMENT IN DEVELOPMENT ETHICS

Almost all those thinkers, whether academics, agency workers, planners, or the poor themselves, who see themselves engaged in development ethics will agree on a number of shared presuppositions. I shall first point these out briefly before turning to areas where there are disputed issues and dilemmas fraught with uncertainty (see Box 1).

Box 1

Areas of Agreement in Development Ethics

A. Development is *ethical* in character

B. Development Ethics is *multi*disciplinary

C. Reduction of *poverty* is central to authentic development

D. Development is ultimately *human* development

E. What is appropriate is *context*-sensitive

F. Conventional Development qua *economic growth part of the problem*

A. Ethical Component

Development theory and practice contain an ethical component, and it is important to make this explicit. Many disagreements about development are about different value premises, rather than disagreement about the "facts," for example, about what means will really achieve agreed-upon ends.

B. Multidisciplinary

Development ethics is a multidisciplinary field, involving inputs drawn from many different disciplines, such as economics, sociology, law, politics, and philosophy. It is also a field that deals with issues that arise at many different levels, from what happens at the local community level to issues in international relations.

C. Reduction of Poverty Central

The reduction of extreme poverty lies at the heart of what development ought to be about, both in the sense of being a primary goal and in the sense that the reduction of poverty provides the key reason ethically for development. Whatever else justifies international aid and more generally cooperation, the commitment to reducing world poverty—which affects 1 billion, or approximately one-fifth, of the world's population—should be seen as central.

D. Humanistic Account

A humanistic account of development in terms of the "flourishing" or "good life" of individual human beings and of a societal common good should be given, which is significantly richer than any account of development as overall economic growth, and is inconsistent with authoritarian solutions to development that deny liberation and undermine the human spirit.

E. Contextual Sensitivity

Development strategies need to be contextually sensitive. That is, what patterns of development are appropriate for any given community or country may vary from place to place, depending on circumstances, culture, stages of development, and so on.

F. Conventional "Development" Part of the Problem

In one sense "development" itself is part of the problem. That is, what is done in the name of development, conventionally understood, may actually be an impediment to proper, authentic, or integral human development.

Let us now look at the "conventional" approach to development that arose after the Second World War, and see how dissatisfaction with it led to the emergence of critical ethical reflection on it and eventually to what is called development ethics.

III. WHAT IS DEVELOPMENT? THE DOMINANT PARADIGM

In the dominant view of the last 50 years the key question has been primarily about the processes of socioeconomic change within economically poorer countries (developing countries/the South). There have in fact been two concerns of the international community since World War II. First, enabling the poorer countries to catch up with industrialized countries and thus to reduce the gap between the industrialized world and the nonindustrialized world; and second, tackling absolute poverty—that is, not just relative poverty but a condition of malnutrition, disease, short life expectancy, and generally harsh living conditions below any reasonable level of decency, a condition that many hundreds of millions were suffering. The two goals of reducing the gap between rich and poor countries and tackling conditions of absolute poverty are not of course the same, because aiming at or achieving one could occur without aiming at or achieving the other, and vice versa. But it was generally assumed that the two went together and mutually supported each other (at least in the long run). Because both goals were clearly desirable and matters of general consensus in the international community, the ethical basis of it all was, if reflected on at all, seen as self-evident.

What then dominated thinking and planning were economic growth models. General improvements in the economy of poor countries will lead to the reduction of inequalities between countries and to the reduction of extreme poverty. This is not to deny that there were various rival theories about how best to achieve this, and as the development decades progressed, different theories took precedence. An early approach (still favored by some) was one according to which general economic growth will benefit everyone, including the very poor, by a process in which wealth, largely stimulated in the richer sectors, "spreads" or "trickles down" to all in society (a modern variant of Adam Smith's "hidden hand" mechanism).

However, others felt that this needed to be modified because it was evident that poverty reduction did not automatically follow from economic growth without some kind of intervention or direction from central institutions such as governments. Modifications (within mainstream development economics/studies) of this economic growth model included "growth with equity" (i.e., growth with mechanisms, generally state-directed ones, to redistribute wealth in favor of the poor), and "basic needs" theories, again targeting the poor with programs designed to meet basic needs.

Because the goals (overall growth and poverty alleviation) were seen as self-evidently good and mutually supportive, the mainstream debates about models of development were not usually seen as ethical debates or as involving "development ethics." Rather, the various debates about rival models were seen primarily as debates about appropriate *means* to the same goals, that is, debates about what policies, institutions, and so on did *as a matter of fact* pursue the twin goals most effectively. As such much debate in development thinking is about *empirical* issues (and this remains true to this day). But the positions adopted were in fact also informed by ethical assumptions, and these were made more explicit as challenges to them emerged.

IV. QUESTIONING THE DOMINANT PARADIGM

By the beginning of the eighties, both philosophers outside development studies and some within the field (such as, notably, Amartya Sen) were self-consciously questioning the ethical foundations of development, both the appropriate means of pursuing it and the ends. There were in fact various aspects or phases to this.

A. Normative Accounts of Development

Various writers began to stress the humanistic assumptions underlying development discourse—in this respect Denis Goulet, writing books long before the 1980s, was a pioneer. There are two features to what I am calling the humanistic emphasis: first, that in the last analysis it is individual human beings whose lives go well or badly; and second, that an account of human well-being is needed that is considerably richer than accounts of increases in economic well-

---

Box 2

Development

Development is a comprehensive economic, social, cultural, and political process that aims at the constant improvement of the well-being of the entire population and of all individuals on the basis of their active, free, and meaningful participation in development, and in the fair distribution of benefits resulting therefrom.

Source: United Nations. (1986). *Declaration on the right to development*, 41/128, from Preamble, paragraph 2.

---

being. In the 1990s, the *Human Development Reports* of United Nations Development Program have quite explicitly in both title and content stressed the range of criteria for assessing and measuring progress in the good life (see Box 2).

Development is concerned with progress in human well-being/flourishing. Economic growth and industrialization are only means to certain ends, and they are only justified if they achieve those ends; if they do not, as the critics would claim they sometimes do not, then they are not justified, and may even be inappropriate if they frustrate the attempts of poor people to achieve well-being. It should be noted that even improvements in indicators such as higher calorie intake, easier access to water, or better housing are also *means to ends*, not ends in themselves. Generally, of course, such things do lead to better lives, but it is not self-evident that they do. Easier access to water may indeed have advantages, but if the presence of the well or pump upsets traditional patterns of life in the village, there may be costs as well that need to be taken into account.

It is not clear then that development understood in conventional terms does always advance human well-being. Once this has been accepted, various other things held to be self-evident also become questionable. Does the South necessarily have to imitate or catch up with the North? If it is not clear that the image of the good life offered by the model of development in the North—materialism, consumerism, liberal choice, and so on—is satisfactory, why should countries with other kinds of values, often religious, seek to imitate the North? Perhaps there are other ways of tackling extreme poverty (bad in almost any value scheme) that do not depend on wholesale commitment to economic growth or liberal markets.

All sorts of "alternative" models of development, based on value and factual premises rather different from those of the economic growth paradigm are offered (many linked to ecological visions, feminist perspectives, as for example, in the writings of Vandana Shiva). Some theories of development will seek primarily to enlarge the criteria for evaluating development: economic growth (or growth with equitable distribution) will still be seen as necessary, but its adequacy or sufficiency in giving an account of the key values or goals to be sought will be questioned. Other theories will be more radical, questioning the centrality or necessity of economic growth (at least for sectors other than the very poor), but present alternative models of change (which may involve growth in other things). All these theories will make much more of other criteria such as freedom, equality, rights, community, political participation, a healthy relationship with the environment, and so on. At the extreme there is the rejection of "development" altogether as an appropriate object of pursuit. Thus, for instance Wolfgang Sachs and others in *The Development Dictionary* (1992. London: Zed Books) see development discourse as ineradicably linked to the global economy that "homogenizes" cultures, and therefore they reject it as an important organizing concept for identifying desirable social change (see Box 3).

As I note in the next section, these critical responses to the dominant paradigm of development are all based on alternative value systems that have in more recent years led to more sustained philosophical reflection on what the bases of these are. But what also emerged from these alternative approaches is an important feature: the criticisms of the economic paradigm are not merely criticisms of it as applied to poorer countries in the South. They are in effect (if not in primary focus) criticisms of that paradigm *as applied to rich countries as well*. In other words development ethics is not really about ethical issues to do with the South, it is about development anywhere.

B. Grassroots/Planning Issues

The increasingly sophisticated exploration of the ethical foundations of development is not confined to abstract or general issues of overall policy, but informs much discussion of more specific situations, planning decisions, and grassroots development projects. Again, the dilemmas involved in these can be seen as dilemmas about moral values and priorities, not merely about the most effective means of achieving agreed ends. Often projects in which modern techniques are introduced come into conflict with traditional communal values. Policies that meet the immediate needs of poor people may be seen as problematic when issues of sustainability are considered. The promotion of the status of women comes up against various forms of cultural resistance. The policy of giving aid in conflict situations may be questioned if that is likely to fuel the conflict. (Des Gasper is one writer who focuses of identifying the details of such dilemmas. See, e.g., Gasper, D. (1994). Development ethics: An emergent field? In Prendergast, R., & Stewart, F. (Eds.). (1994). *Market forces and world development*. Macmillan).

What focus on such dilemmas brings out are two important features of development ethics. Because development is by definition a process of change, for which there would be no justification if it were not from a worse state to a better state, development decisions are being made in situations of *transition in an imperfect world*. Even if thinking about development often has a reference to an idea of full or perfect development and the values that would be fully realized in it (a modern way of thinking about "utopia"), the hard ethical issues in development have to do with the real world of change in conditions that are not merely marked by extreme suffering but also by human imperfections—prejudice, ignorance, fear, greed, power, and the social, political, and economic structures that reflect them. These form the backcloth to many of the real dilemmas in decision-making.

Box 3

Approaches to Development

A. Economic growth as central:
   Free market with trickle-down effect
   With mechanisms for equitable distribution
   Focus on poverty reduction/basis needs.

B. Economic growth as necessary but not sufficient:
   Importance of other criteria as well as economic growth: e.g., liberty, rights, participation, equality, community, respect for the environment.

C. Radical alternatives:
   Economic growth in general neither necessary nor sufficient: redefinitions of authentic development or rejection of development altogether.

V. PHILOSOPHICAL EXPLORATION

A. Normative Positions in Philosophical Ethics

During the last 10 years, mainstream moral philosophy has entered the development stage to a significant degree. Three kinds of questions can be identified. First, if development is about change from a worse state to a better state and this involves centrally the improvement of the lives of human beings, by what criteria do we measure that improvement: what is the good life, human well-being, or flourishing? This has been the primary focus of discussion. But two further kinds of question arise. Part of what makes a society move from a worse state to a better state is the general nature and quality of its social structure and relations, how human well-being is distributed in the society, what kinds of liberties and rights are in place, what kind of moral culture exists, what values of democratic participation established, and so on. Third, ethical questions can be raised about the pursuit of development by a country in terms of its *external* relations to at least three things: the environment, future generations, and other countries in the world. (See Dower, N., in R. Attfield, and B. Wilkins (Eds.), 1993, *International justice and the third world.* London: Routledge).

The book *Ethical Principles for Development: Needs, Capacities and Rights* (ed., Aman (1992), Montclair), based on a conference on the same theme a year before, reflects accurately the kind of involvement of moral philosophers in development thinking. Three of the main philosophical approaches are indeed those of needs (represented there, for example, by Peter Penz), rights (represented, for example, by Jim Nickel), and capacities (represented by David Crocker). The needs approach, picking up on an earlier "basic needs" strategy (associated with Paul Streeten) stresses the importance of an account of needs, sharply to be distinguished from wants and luxuries, in which to ground the priority of action to address extreme poverty. Interest in rights theories also has a dual purpose of providing an account of the essential elements of human well-being, but also providing the basis for, in the words of Henry Shue, "everyone's minimum reasonable demand upon the rest of humanity" (Shue, H., 1996. *Basic rights: Subsistence, affluence and US foreign policy.* Princeton: Princeton UP).

The "capacity" or "capabilities" approach has gained prominence in recent years as providing a neo-Aristotelian account of human flourishing. The approach found in the writings of the Indian development economist-cum-philosopher Amartya Sen has been given philosophical development in the writing of thinkers such as Martha Nussbaum and David Crocker. The central concern is to map out the central capacities that are exercised in "functionings" and so to provide an account of human well-being that, while placing sufficient emphasis upon physical well-being, also brings in properly psychological and social capacities and functionings.

Another approach of importance in this debate is what can be called the Kantian approach, which stresses the fact that human being are rational agents whose well-being is exhibited in the properly developed exercise of rational choice and autonomy. As a prominent exponent Onora O'Neill ((1989) *The faces of hunger.* Allen & Unwin) argues that extreme poverty undermines the properly developed exercise of rational agency. Thus this approach gives a good theoretical basis for the thesis that helping the poor is essentially a matter of *empowering* them.

These are only a few of the approaches that can be taken. For instance, utilitarianism can also provide a basis for identifying what the essential elements of well-being are (happiness, preference, satisfaction, etc.) and a rationale for the distribution of well-being in society (i.e., that which maximizes well-being). Similarly, a liberal theory like that of John Rawls in *A Theory of Justice* (1971, Oxford UP) provides a relatively "thin" account of what human good consists of (the exercise of choice to achieve each person's conception of the good), an account of the primary goods (wealth and liberty) needed for this, along with principles for the distribution of these primary goods in society. What is perhaps striking about utilitarian and liberal theories (including those that stress the importance of free markets) is the fact that relatively uninformative accounts of what the good consists of are provided ("preference satisfaction," "doing what you want/choose"), as compared with the earlier-mentioned accounts (Aristotelian, Kantian). The latter, like many other even more substantive or specific accounts of the good found, for instance, in certain religiously based ethics or various kinds of ecological ethic, press for a richer account of what (real) human well-being consists of, and hence of what constitutes real development. Indeed, although this is an oversimplification, it can be said that the value theories lying behind the dominant "economic growth paradigm" tend to be utilitarian or liberal, and part of the increase in the active philosophical engagement with the bases of development partly arises precisely from a dissatisfaction with the adequacy of the relatively thin account of human good presupposed in the dominant accounts. After all, if one thinks it is adequate to say that human well-being consists of getting what you want or exercising choice, then it seems self-evident that more wealth enables you to get more of what you want or to exercise more choice, so it is obvious that economic growth is desirable. It is this inference that much of the recent philosophical discussion precisely questions.

It will be apparent that once the level of discussion engaged in is that of basic moral theories about the good and the principles of social order, the implications are not merely about appropriate criteria for change in developing countries, but apply equally to richer countries. Indeed, much of what motivates philosophical inquiry into the appropriate basis of social change stems from an unease about the priorities and commitments of rich countries themselves.

Of course, one source of that unease stems precisely from the relationship that rich countries have with poorer countries, both in terms of their aid programs but also much more significantly in terms of their wider economic relationships. For instance, if more aid is to be given or economic relations should be such as to benefit poorer countries more, this it may be argued requires a willingness to reduce economic growth in the North, or even to question its dynamic altogether. Another source of unease though about the economic growth policies of the North stems from a concern about the way of life in the North considered in its own right being too affluent, too materialistic, or too consumerist, and so there is a desire to consider more explicitly the essential values that, the thinker claims, should underlie policy in the North. A third area of concern that invites a reexamination of the basic values underlying development in the North stems of course from concern for the environment—protecting Nature now and the well-being of future generations—hence the immense interest in *sustainable* development.

B. Metaethical Considerations about the Nature of Development Discourse

In the previous section we looked at several ways in which philosophers bring moral philosophy into the discussion of values underlying development. These have been primarily *normative*—that is, rival theories are presented about the content of the values and their justification. But there is also a range of ethical and more generally philosophical issues that can arise in connection with thinking about development, which are not so much to do with defending a particular value approach as examining some of the more theo-

retical assumptions and issues lying behind the discourse.

Consider for instance conceptual issues about the meaning of "development": what are its links with the idea of "teleology" (as shown in the development of an acorn into an oak, to use Aristotle's example), with the idea of evolution (in biology) or progress (as in Victorian thinking about progress)? What is the significance of the fact that development refers both to the current process of change and also to a future state of having achieved development, and what is the relationship between the two?

It is apparent from much of the discussion above that many thinkers are keen to stress that their account of development presupposes values of various kinds—hence the interest in development ethics. But perhaps the ethical dimension is not, as it were, an optional extra that some thinkers are keen to bring in, but can be, and is, excluded in much other thinking, such as in that of many who accept the dominant growth paradigm. Perhaps it is significant that all attempts to *define* development, at least where development is being regarded as an object of policy or planning, that is, as something to be chosen and intentionally pursued, are implicitly if not explicitly ethical or evaluative. Dower, for instance, has argued that we should define development as "a process of socio-economic change which *ought* to happen." This is the "thin" account (or "concept") that underlies any thinker's attempt, conventional or otherwise, to give a thick account (or "conception") that is justified as being what the thinker thinks ought to happen (Dower, N. (1989). *What is development? A philosopher's answer.* Glasgow: Centre For Development Studies).

C. Universalism, Particularism, and Relativism

A third kind of consideration (crossing the metaethical/normative division) is of immense importance, and this concerns what may be called the issue of relativism, particularism, and universalism. Much of the ethical concern about development has come from an unease that the patterns of development that are dominant in the North are not appropriate to social change in the South, and that in many ways what is happening with the strengthening of the global economy is the destruction of traditional cultures, worldview and value systems, even though such local or traditional value systems are in fact right for those cultures and the appropriate bases for whatever change needs to take place. In other words, the values that should underlie social change vary from society to society. What is happening in the global economy is but the latest manifestation of European cultural imperialism, or "Eurocentrism." Most but not all writers in development ethics share this unease, but in varying degrees and with different views of its theoretical significance.

One response, noted earlier (by Sachs), is to see the idea of "development" closely tied to the European value system, itself born of the Enlightenment and the idea of "universal reason," and thus, in the name of celebrating diversity and the need to defend traditional value systems against the encroachment of global capitalism, to reject the idea of development altogether as an appropriate vehicle for articulating desirable social change. (Much of the language of Latin American liberation theology reflects this, rejecting development in favor of "liberation.") But those within development ethics, who retain a commitment to the central concept but recognize that rival values can be built into it, can also make the point that diversity of cultures and norm within them are to be defended in the name of development (as Goulet and Verhelst do). This is because it can be claimed that the kinds of social change that ought to happen or it would be good to happen, will be different in different places, and will, for instance, depend upon the values already accepted by the people in question.

But the recognition that much diversity needs to be accepted and defended (in the face of the "homogenizing" tendency of international economics) can stem from two very different theoretical positions, relativism and universalism incorporating diversity. The relativist position, in modern times often identified with postmodernism, essentially rejects the idea of a universal value system of any kind (because there is no vantage point from which to achieve it), and claims that values are relative to different countries or culture (or in the extreme, different individuals), so it is impossible to provide any general ethical theory (such as the ones indicated above) that could apply to all societies, and hence to all processes of change called development. The values underlying each society's appropriate social change are internal to that society and its traditions, history, and current situation. It is possible of course for a development ethicist to adopt this position. There is nothing in the general position of being interested in the ethical issues in development that precludes such a position. On the whole, however, those interested in development ethics do not adopt this position, but rather the universalist position that incorporates diversity,

pluralism, and particularism. This stems from both a belief in a universal value core itself and also from a belief in the validity of universal norms of global responsibility, for example, of the rich to support authentic development in the South, norms that are problematic on a purely relativist position.

Most thinkers interested in development ethics prefer to identify some kind of universal value framework and then accommodate various kinds of diversity within it. Thus, those who advocate a neo-Aristotelian or Kantian or "rights" approach are generally keen to show that their theories are at a sufficiently high level of generality as to allow significant variations in different societies' development: these variations are expressions of or interpretations of the underlying value in different social contexts. It would not be their intention to see their theory as projecting an essentially Western value theory onto other parts of the world, although their critics might argue that, despite their intentions, they are doing just that.

Indeed, this might be a criticism made by many development ethicists of the dominant economic paradigm insofar as it is premised on a liberal or utilitarian value framework. That is, the advocate of the free market and the Northern model of economic transactions might *claim* that this is premised on the *universal* value of the freedom of the individual to pursue his own conception of the good or seek his own preferences (which might be culturally influenced in different ways). But from the point of view of the critic, this very model of the individual rational chooser is not neutral as between different forms of cultural life, but advocates a very distinctive and particular form of cultural life in contrast with more communalist conceptions or ones in which certain religious value are central. (Consider the clash between Western materialism and Islamic theocratic ideals.)

Although most thinkers in development ethics do set out to develop some kind of nondogmatic universal value theory, it should be noted that, just as nothing in the idea of development ethics precludes relativism, so nothing in the idea precludes an attachment to a dogmatic idealism of some kind or other that the thinker knows full well is not actually accepted in many of the societies for which it is recommended. Thus, a highly specific religious model of appropriate change, or a model dominated by an ecological vision, or a model advocated by an avid secular liberal defender of free choice, might be advocated for all societies, with the quite specific and intended implication that what is dominant and accepted in most countries at present is simply misguided (see Box 4).

Box 4

Ethical Theories and Development

A. Normative positions concerning the good life/
   social order
       e.g., Kantianism; Aristotelianism; basic
       rights needs theories, utilitarianism, Rawl-
       sian liberalism.

B. Meta-ethical issues
       Links with teleology, evolution, progress
       Evaluative nature of definitions of devel-
       opment.

C. Relativism vs. universalism concerning the
   values inherent in development.

VI. INTERNATIONAL DEVELOPMENT ISSUES

I now turn to various issues that arise at the international or global level. These are the issues that arise if
one considers international ethics insofar as it has a
bearing on development issues. I shall define international ethics as the ethics of the relationships between
states and between individuals living in different parts
of the world. Ethical issues germane to our enquiry
have been identified and discussed by a number of
writers, both within the disciplines of philosophy and
international relations and outside them, and although
these issues would now be seen as clearly belonging to
the remit of development ethics, they have been to
some extent discussed without being seen as part of
development ethics—partly because these issues arose
before development ethics had emerged as an identified
subdiscipline. The two main issues to be focused on
are the ethics of aid and the ethics of international
economic relations.

These both have a direct bearing on development
in the following ways. Aid clearly is directed (whatever
the motive) to the development of the recipient country, whether to the overall development of the country
as a whole or to the specific development projects
of the very poor in those countries. Either way, clarity
about what development is and what values underlie
it is rather important, because aid is only a means
to some good that it promotes, and it takes its value
from the value of the "end." Similarly, the kinds and
levels of economic relations that rich countries or its
actors such as transnational companies exercise have

a distinct bearing on the kinds and levels of development that takes place in a poorer country. If, therefore,
we have a view as to what is an appropriate kind
of development for such a country, we may come to
recognize that international trade and investment is
not, either in its intentions or in its consequences,
adequately achieving this development (or is actually
impeding or undermining it). Then we will have
reason ethically to criticize it and seek ways of modifying or controlling it.

A. The Ethical Basis of Aid

Most writers concentrate on the ethical basis for an
individual's giving aid to help alleviate distant poverty.
The assumption is generally that this provides the basis
for a parallel argument that rich countries should give
official aid to poorer countries. While this assumption
requires defense (because on the face of it the duties
of government are shaped by more complex considerations, such as the preference of their electorates on the
one hand, and on the other the existing international
code of practice and existing agreements), it is assumed
in what follows. (It should also be noted that there is
often a further difference between private giving and
government aid. Most private giving is directed to projects for the poor and is justified on the grounds that
the very poor are helped; whereas much if not most
government aid is directed to the overall economic improvement for the poor country and may be justified
on those grounds, without specific reference to poverty
alleviation as its justification.)

Various ethical bases for aid have been given, many
of them not surprisingly the same as the ones given
above for the internal ethical basis of development.
Thus, Beitz extends Rawls's theory of social justice for
a domestic society to a global society, and he argues
that the condition of mutual economic interdependence
is such that it requires the principles, most notably
the "difference principle," to be applied globally. Thus,
ideally the world ought to be so organized that the least
well-off (the poor in the South) are better off than
they would be under any other global arrangement. He
recognizes that we are far off that point, but should
move gradually towards it. Henry Shue's theory of socially basic rights to subsistence, security, and liberty,
which imply the correlative duties on the part of others
generally not to deprive people of their rights, to protect
them from standard threats of deprivation, and to come
to the aid of those deprived of their rights, provides
the basis for global action to alleviate global poverty.
Onora O'Neill in *The Faces of Hunger* uses a Kantian

argument to support the claim that the rich should take action, including political action against existing power structures, to empower the poor (see above).

But perhaps the most famous single example of an ethical argument used to get the rich to give their money (and, no doubt, their time, effort, and resources generally) is Peter Singer's famous article entitled "Famine, Affluence and Morality" ((1971) *Philosophy and Public Affairs*), reprinted many times because it sets out a clear argument and replies to objections with a clarity that has hardly been matched since, although many papers have been written. The central argument in this depends upon a simple premise: "if it is our power to prevent something bad from happening, without thereby sacrificing anything of comparable moral importance, we ought, morally, to do it." Although Singer himself is a utilitarian, he fashions this principle, which is the major premise of the argument, in such a way as to include, as he sees it, both consequentialists and nonconsequentialists.

All the above arguments are essentially forward-looking arguments, in the sense that they do not depend on looking back on the situation and asking "how did the current level of extreme poverty come to exist?" They are dependent on acknowledging (a) that it exists, whatever its causes, (b) we in the North (those of us reasonably well-off) have the capacity to give or support (effective) aid, (c) so we ought to do so. (How much and in what ways is a matter for further debate. Certainly not all take the extreme "as much as you can" line of Singer's argument.) But it should be noted that some arguments for giving aid are backward-looking (to recall W. D. Ross's well-known conception) in the sense that they depend on the recognition (which is somewhat controversial) that countries in the North engaged in and continue to be engaged in exploitation of the South (colonialism and neocolonialism) and therefore ought to make amends/restitution/recompense for the injustice done. If individuals give aid on this basis, they do so as beneficiaries of or as part of larger causal chains of such exploitation, not because they themselves are the active perpetrators of it.

There are, however, various arguments lined up against all these arguments (quite apart from rejection of the assessment of exploitation in the last-mentioned argument). They fall broadly into three kinds of arguments: those that do not accept a general duty of generosity (anywhere), those that do but restrict it to the domestic domain and so deny a global responsibility, and those that claim that aid generally does not work.

First, it is not self-evident that our basic moral code has to include a general duty to help others. The main function of morality is to refrain from harming others in various ways or to refrain from interfering with their rights, and although we can have particular duties of positive care, for example, as parents to children or when we are under a contract to care for someone, there is no general duty to help others; so *a fortiori* there is no duty to help others in other parts of the world.

Second, although most development ethicists themselves, as noted above, would see it as a corollary of their commitment to universal values to argue that we have duties of care the *scope* of which is world-wide, it is by no means self-evident that this is so. Arguments from relativists, and those conventionalists and communitarians who take the strong line that moral duties arise out of social convention or the traditions of a particular community, will lead to conclusions of different kinds, that our duties to peoples in other parts of the world are either nonexistent or marginal compared with those to members of one's own society. Parallel to these arguments, there is the quite specific argument belonging to international relations theory called "international scepticism," according to which, because of the nature of the international system of independent states, for example, the fact that there is no "common power" to enforce rules, there is no morality between them, only an arena of contending powers, so *a fortiori* there is no duty to give aid or further the development of other countries.

Third, there is a cluster of arguments to the general effect that aid either does not generally, or cannot, work and so there is no duty to do what is impossible. Such arguments have either to do with the general nature of aid, with the argument that it necessarily creates dependency, or they have to do with the long-run ecological consequences of aid, particularly emergency food aid. (Garrett Hardin is particularly well-known in this regard.) (See Box 5.)

B. Trade/Economic Relations

Aid programs are of course only a very small part of the total impact of rich countries on the economies of poor countries; most of the impact is the result of trading relationships, investment policies in the Third World, including the making of loans and then requiring debt repayment. These impacts may be direct through the policies of governments and their agents or through the activities of transnational companies and banks that are based in a rich country but operate in other countries.

Many writers have examined these relationships and have noted the inequality of wealth and power

Box 5

The Arguments for Aid

1. Forward-looking arguments: if we have the capacity to help, we ought to help: e.g.,
   Extended benevolence (Singer)
   Kantinaism
   Basic rights
   Global social contract.

2. Backward-looking argument:
   Restitution for past (and present) Exploitation.

The Arguments against Aid

1. No general duty to help others anywhere

2. Obligations to help are exclusively/primarily to members of one's own society; therefore global obligations nonexistent/marginal

3. Aid does not work.

involved, and the creation of dependency and periphery status (especially those of Marxist orientation, such as Frank). Some writers have criticized this inequality with great moral passion such as Hayter (Hayter, T. (1983). *The creation of world poverty.* Pluto Press), while others have, in a more theoretical mode, attempted to construct ethical theories with which to criticize the patterns of power in the name of global distributive justice. (See, e.g., Beitz, C. E. (1979). *Political Theory and International Relations.* Princeton: Princeton UP). In the 1970s the so called group of 77, the block of developing countries at the United Nations, promoted the idea of a "New International Economic Order" (which was adopted by the UN), which in many ways reflected the interest in the ideas of global distributive justice and a new distribution of power in the world. Although the intellectual foundations of the idea of the NIEO may still be valid, it did not survive as an active vehicle of change. In fact, the 1980s were a period in which the inequalities of power in the world got greater. The harsh consequences of the "recycling" of oil-surplus money through loans to the South began to be felt, with the pressures of debt repayments becoming and continuing to be a major burden on countries in the South. These debt repayments were one factor in the continuing of and growth in levels of extreme poverty.

C. World Development and Globalization

The phenomenon of globalization has an important bearing on how we think about development issues. The processes associated with globalization—increasing world markets, global communication through the media and through the Internet, the development of international institutions and regulations, the increasing impact of international NGOs (nongovernmental organizations)—all contribute to the emergence as a social reality of something that may be called "world society." Thinkers over the ages have often postulated the idea of a "civitas maxima" ("the greatest society"), and indeed many moral theories, like the ones discussed above, at the heart of development ethics, precisely suppose that we all, in ethical terms, belong to one moral order or one moral community, whether or not the reality of a world society exists, and that if it does not, then one's moral theory supports movement in the direction of achieving it.

What is happening in the world, despite many other factors such as ethnic struggles, can be seen as a gradual but marked move in the direction of the emergence of a world society. This is not to say that what is emerging is what cosmopolitan idealists would like, because the strengthening of the world economy is, as noted earlier, producing homogenization of cultures (and therefore the undermining of traditional cultures), it is reenforcing global inequalities, and it is also putting pressure on the global environment.

However, the bearing of this on development is important. The phrases "world development," "international development," and "global development" have certainly been in use for some time, but the exact meaning of these phrases has remained ambiguous. On the one hand these phrases can refer to the overall process in the world as a whole in which *separately* the various processes of development in different countries occur. It is a byproduct and has a *summative* function. On the other hand, they can refer to the framework within which international cooperation occurs in order to promote development in particular countries, especially in the South. (Thus, aid programs can be seen as international development). But with the process of globalization a third sense can be identified as emerging, although it is often implicit.

If the world as a whole is to be thought of as one (emerging) society, then the development of that society is an object of prescriptive interest. "What kind of world do we want?" is really a question about development, albeit about the development of the largest unit—the whole world. The issues are not, of course, merely about economic growth in the world as a whole or with the priority of poverty alleviation, but about the values to be sustained and promoted in the world as whole, the kinds of diversity to be accepted or celebrated, the kinds of global institutions (not merely international ones) that need to be fostered to give expression to global governance. Global governance is not, after all, the same as world government, because there may be many different ways of ordering our common affairs at a global level. (See, e.g., the Commission on Global Governance, (1995), *Our Global Neighbourhood*. Oxford: Oxford UP.)

An important dimension of this, of course, is concern for the environment and the need for sustainable development. Environmental issues in the modern world are, of course, crucially global in reach, and effective measures often require actions by all countries. So any effective way of fostering sustainable development needs to be global in scope and conception. Such measures are, therefore, in logic and ethical requirement, about global development, even if this language has not been taken up very much as yet. That is, environmental protection requires global development, not merely the development of this or that country, considered in isolation.

This level of enquiry belongs to the emerging agenda of development discourse and development ethics. But it also illustrates another more general point. Most thinking hitherto about development has assumed that the *primary unit* of development is the nation-state (and other units have been defined intranationally or internationally in terms of it). This is because development as an object of prescriptive interest is something subject to human control, at least to some degree. Nation-states have had that kind of control. But development can be about any size or shape of human association that can, by its corporate or collective decision-making, affect the way its own future goes. So if we are now seeing a changing world order in which the nation-state has a less central place, there will not only be greater interest at the global level but also greater interest in what

happens at more local levels. It is not merely that these trends are happening, whether we like it or not. There are moral arguments for moving toward a greater sense and reality of global society as well as a returning to a greater sense and reality of local community. But these arguments are really about development because they are about desirable social change in the world as a whole.

Also See the Following Articles

DEEP ECOLOGY • DEVELOPMENT ISSUES, ENVIRONMENTAL • DISTRIBUTIVE JUSTICE, THEORIES OF • ENVIRONMENTAL ETHICS, OVERVIEW • WORLD ETHICS

Bibliography

Aiken, W., & LaFollette, H. (Eds.). (1995). *World hunger and moral obligation* (2nd ed.) Engelwood Hills: Prentice-Hall.

Aman, K. (Ed.). (1991). *Ethical principles for development: Needs, capacities and rights*. Montclair: Institute for Critical Thinking.

Attfield, R., & Wilkins, B. (Eds.). (1993). *International justice and the third world*. London: Routledge.

Crocker, D. A. (1991). Towards development ethics. In *World development* (Vol. 19, No. 5, pp. 457–483).

Daly, H., & Cobb, J. B. (1989). *For the common good: Redirecting the economy toward community, the environment, and a sustainable future*. Boston: Beacon.

Goulet, D. (1995). *Development ethics—A guide to theory and practice*. New York: Apex Press.

Hausman, D. M., & McPherson, M. S. (1993). Taking ethics seriously: Economics and contemporary moral philosophy. *Journal of Economic Literature*, **XXXI**, 671–731.

Riddell, R. (1987). *Foreign aid reconsidered*. London: James Currey.

Sachs, W., et al. (Eds.). (1992); *The Development Dictionary*, London: Zed Books.

Sen, A. (1992). *Inequality re-examined*. Cambridge: Harvard University Press.

Sen, A., & Nussbaum, M. (1993). *The quality of life*. Oxford: Clarendon Press.

Shiva, V. (1989). *Staying alive: Women, ecology and development*. London: Zed Books.

Verhlest, T. (1990). *No life without roots: Culture and development*. London and New Jersey: Zed Books.

UNDP (1991–1995). *Human Development Reports*. New York.

DEVELOPMENT ISSUES, ENVIRONMENTAL

Nigel Dower
University of Aberdeen

GLOSSARY

development (a) A process of socioeconomic change, primarily and centrally a process of economic growth, which, to some significant degree, is the object of public policy and planning. This, it will be argued, is broadly the dominant conception of development. But behind it lies a less specific, but explicitly normative definition of development as: (b) A process of change in a society, which, in the eyes of thinker, is a change that ought to happen (e.g., from a worse state to a better state). As we shall see, it is possible to offer rival conceptions of development dependent on the normative criteria adopted, and environmental considerations play an important part in those alternative conceptions.

environment The physical world that "surrounds" a person or group of people and on which human beings depend for life as physical beings. This may be called "nature" or the natural world, so long as it is understood that this includes matter and indeed living things modified by human skills and technology. (Note the contrast with a broader sense: "that which surrounds someone or a group of people in terms not just of the physical environment but in terms of social reality—laws, moral codes, institutions, systems of knowledge, art, etc." In this sense an environment is essentially a "field of significance," mediated by culture and knowledge.)

global ethics An ethical approach according to which the whole world is regarded as one moral domain or community: the scope of our moral obligations extends in principle across this one community.

quality of life The overall character of a person's life assessed in term of how well (or badly) that person achieves well-being. The criteria by which this is assessed are complex and a matter of disagreement; some, for instance, stress economic or material standing, others stress factors such as relationships, community, and liberty.

resources Types of things that have a significant use value. Natural resources refer to those substances in nature that have a significant use value, but resources can also refer to things like finance, knowledge, skills, and so on.

sustainability The capacity that something has to be sustained into the future (either indefinitely or for a timespan indicated by the context). The term is applied to development, society, industry, agriculture, cities, and so on.

DEVELOPMENT has been conventionally seen as economic growth and the increase in the material standard of living of human beings. Environmental ethics has focused upon the natural world as a source of value and upon our responsibilities to future generations. The pursuit of development and the protection of the environment are often seen to come into conflict with each other. Various attempts, including different accounts of *sustainable development,* are made to integrate the two set of concerns. An overall ethical theory, characteristically global in scope, is usually presupposed, and many thinkers, except for the very optimistic, see the need for more explicitly normative accounts of development in terms of quality of life understood in ways that go well beyond the economic paradigm.

I. CONVENTIONAL APPROACHES TO DEVELOPMENT

The strategy of the article will be first to consider the standard ethical presuppositions lying behind development (in sense (a)) and behind concern for the environment, and then to identify areas of conflict and possible areas of reconciliation. This will lead to a consideration of some global issues and a reevaluation of development.

A. Development as Economic Growth (with Equity)

In this century, and in particular since the end of the Second World War when the language of "developed" and "underdeveloped" became well established, it has generally been understood that among the publicly agreed goals of any society has been the pursuit of economic growth, and hence that this determines one of the key roles of government. Economic growth enables people to have access to more wealth and hence to achieve a better quality of life—longer, healthier, more enjoyable, and so on. It has generally been assumed that countries in the industrialized parts of the world (the "developed" world, often referred to, with little attention to geographical accuracy, as "the North") have achieved a satisfactory level of development (although still continuing to grow), and that countries in other parts of the world ("underdeveloped," "less developed," "developing," "the South") need to catch up, both because of the gap between countries as such and also because of the existence of extreme poverty (currently affecting about 1 billion people or a fifth of the world's

population). The presumption has been that the North provides the model for the South to follow or emulate.

However, issues have arisen (a) over the adequacy of thinking of development as economic growth, for example, whether "growth with equity" would be better or whether "basic needs strategies" need to be built into it, (b) over whether free markets adequately distribute wealth to all (by "trickle down" or "hidden-hand" mechanisms) or should be complemented by more active interventionist policies (progressive taxation and welfare provision), and (c) at least before 1989, whether capitalism or state-controlled economies delivered the goals of development better. With the emergence of what is now called "the global economy," there is in many ways even more general agreement, at least among governments, businesses, and international agencies such as the World Bank, not only about the idea of development as sustained economic growth but also about the appropriate means of pursuing it—namely, the free market.

B. Ethical Basis for Pursuing Development

There are two kind of ethical basis for this commitment to development as economic growth. The first one is based on the function of government. It is perhaps worth noting that in earlier eras this would not have been seen as a function of government. For example, in early contract theories such as Locke's, the function of government was the protection of life, liberty, and property, through the provision of security from external attack and of internal order. The origins of the transformations are complex but two things are worth noting: first, the rise of modern science with its power over nature through technology to improve the material conditions of human beings; second, the Enlightenment belief that it was good and possible to use reason to improve the human condition. The nineteenth century conception of the "idea of progress" is an outcome of this and leads to our ideas of development (which may be seen as another term for progress). If governments are there to promote the interests of their nationals and these interests include economic growth, and this is even more clear for any government with a democratic mandate from their citizens who *want* increasing economic prosperity, then there is a general ethical rationale for a commitment to development so understood.

The second ethical basis for development comes from the fact that development is either directly about the reduction of extreme poverty or is largely justified as a general process in terms of such reduction. There is a large literature concerning the ethical basis for poverty reduction, both within countries (e.g., John Rawls's idea of "social justice" (Rawls, J., (1971) *A theory of justice*. London: OUP.) and through international cooperation. (For a survey, see, e.g., Riddell, R. (1987). *Foreign aid reconsidered*. London: James Currey.)

II. ENVIRONMENTAL ETHICS

A. Environmental Problems

Environmental ethics as an active field of inquiry has arisen in the last 20 years as a response to the recognition that human practices are affecting the physical environment in a number of disturbing ways, and that therefore we need collectively to change our practices. The facts to which environmental ethics is a response are briefly:

a. The destruction or damaging of the natural world—harming of nonhuman life, reduction of wilderness areas, destruction of species—and, increasingly, technological manipulation of life-forms, and

b. The *finiteness* of ecosystems and the planet as a whole in respect of: the depletion of non-renewable natural resources, the limited capacity of the biosphere to absorb the effects of human activity (pollution, too much carbon dioxide emission, overuse of lands and waters) without deleterious change; and the areas in which renewable resources are produced, so that an upper limit of sustainable yield of food, timber etc. has to be accepted and hence ultimately an upper limit to *population* levels (see Box 1).

B. Ethical Bases: Nonhuman/Future Generations/Global Dimensions

The ethical responses have for the most part centered on *why* we should care about how we treat or relate to

---

Box 1

The Finiteness of the Biosphere

Three Dimensions:

(a) Finite nonrenewable resources
(b) Finite capacity to absorb effects of human activity without deleterious change
(c) Finite areas for sustainable production of renewable resources.

Box 2

Environmental Ethics

Three issues concerning the scope of moral responsibility:

(a) Humans only or nonhuman life?
(b) Present generations only or future generations?
(c) Local interests (in our society) only or global interests?

---

the physical environment. The main issues (discussed elsewhere) touch on (a) whether we should care for the environment because other life-forms in nature, and maybe nature itself, have a value, worth, and moral status *independent of our interests* (biocentrism), or should care for it because it is in our collective interests as humans to protect it (anthropocentrism); (b) whether the basis of concern for human well-being is properly grounded in the interests of current generations, that is, those human beings currently existing, or rather in the interests of (distant) future generations as well. (c) The third issue is whether moral concern is for the well-being of those in one's own society or is in the interests of humankind as a whole. Thus, many environmentalists would assert three dimensions:interspecies, intergenerational, and international, to the scope of moral responsibility (see Box 2).

The third "local/global" issue is much less attended to, partly because it is easy to assume that because environmental problems are often global in scope and require internationally agreed responses (as in the Montreal Protocol (1988) on ozone-layer depletion), our duties are also *to* all humanity, not to members of our society (who might be affected by changes globally), and partly because there is such general consensus that environmental ethics is global in scope. ("We" need to cut back on fossil fuel emissions is taken to mean "we in the world" generally rather than "we in the U.K.," etc.). This actually makes it easy to fail to notice how this assumption actually comes into conflict with what is also commonly assumed about development and international relations, which we will note later on.

C. Second Type of Ethical Issue: Challenge to the Economic Growth Paradigm

There is however another important type of ethical debate within environmental ethics that cuts across the three types of issues identified above. Irrespective of the reasons why one advocates measures to protect or care for the environment, there is the question: does protecting the environment, adequately or properly caring for it, require *radical or substantial change* in the ways we act, for example, in patterns of consumption and ways of using the natural world, and in the ways we depend on others to act to sustain our way of life, for example, patterns of industrialization, or can it be done without such radical changes? That is, does a commitment to the environment involve a radical departure from the ways we behave, at least in the industrialized North, and about the ways we think about values and our way of life, about ideas of the good life, about social institutions, about the role and interpretation of economics in public life, in short *about our commitment to development as growth?* Or can we, through other kinds of measures, important as they may be but still not really disturbing the modern economic paradigm, such as the "greening" of industry, remain committed to "continuing more or less as before"?

Consider the IPAT formula ($I = P \times A \times T$) suggested by Paul and Anne Ehrlich as a way of understanding the Impact (I) of human beings on their environment as a function (roughly) of the number of people (*Population* $= P$), their general level of material *Affluence* (A) and the kind of *Technology* (T) used to sustain the well-being of the population. If we want to reduce the negative impact, which variable do we change? So far as the industrialized North is concerned, the general response is to change the T variable by suitable "greening of industry" measures. But the radical approach will say that challenges in A are equally important (see Box 3).

These issues cut across the more central issues in environmental ethics in the following way. Someone who adopted a biocentric, global approach and cared about future generations could still advocate economic growth, if he or she though that such growth could be environmentally nondamaging and that our "consumer" paradigm of the good life was consistent with proper *respect for nature.* But for a variety of reasons most do

not. Conversely, someone who adopted an anthropocentric approach and even had little interest in future generations might advocate serious questioning of economic growth and of consumer paradigms simply because of the effect on currently existing generations of humans of our cumulative impacts on the environment. Many so-called "optimists" do not.

III. AREAS OF CONFLICT

There are several ways of showing conflict between those committed to development and those committed to environment care.

A. Limits to Growth

The idea of growth and the idea of conserving or preserving may be seen as in conflict with each other. The very title of the famous Club of Rome report (Meadows, D. (1972) *Limits to Growth.* London: Earth Island), which sparked much of the debate in the 1970s, suggested a conflict at root between the dynamics of development, which is growth, including the growth in the use of nonrenewable natural resources, and the constraints that an essentially finite world imposes on that. Other thinkers, such as Herman Daly, have pressed the case for the "impossibility theory," that it is impossible for the world to continue indefinitely using up resources, putting more pressures on the environment through pollution, and so on (*see*, e.g., Daly, H., (1991), *Steady-state economics: The economics of biophysical equilibrium and moral growth,* pp. 149–51, San Francisco: Freeman). This entails the politically controversial view that it may be impossible for countries in the South to attain the standard of living of countries in the North. It should be noted here that unless one supposes, for Hobbesian reasons, that it is all right for countries to retain their wealth in an international competitive environment in which not all countries can achieve this, the implication of this view is that morally the North needs to cut back, not grow, *for reasons of social justice,* even if it did not need to do this anyway because its practices are unsustainable (even without the South catching up). In the 1970s the main focus of conflict was over the possibility of running out of nonrenewable resources, but in more recent years the issue has had more to do with levels of pollution and land degradation.

The conflict noted above is not strictly a conceptual one but an empirical one, because, of course, what is meant to grow is an economy, and what is to be conserved or sustained is a healthy resource-full environment. Strictly speaking these two are perfectly compati-

---

Box 3

The IPAT Formula

I (Impact) $= P$ (Population) $\times A$ (Affluence) $\times T$ (Technology)

Source: Ehrlich, P., & Ehrlich, A. (1991), *Population explosion.* London: Hutcheson.

ble, if economic growth can be pursued in ways that conserve the base—which is precisely what the "optimists" will argue. Indeed, there are several strands to this approach. Writers like J. L. Simon argue as follows: first, it is important to stress that humans themselves are the "ultimate resource"; that is, as resourceful, clever creatures, capable of creating new technologies, adapting our desires and preferences, we will find solutions to environmental problems as we continue to pursue human progress. To talk of "limits" to natural resources is misleading, because a natural substance is only a resource or an important resource relative to human interests—not all that long ago oil was not a resource—so that as some types of thing we call resources run out, we will find other things to take their place as "resources". Linked to this point is an issue raised by Pearce (Pearce, D., et al., (1989) *Blueprint for a green economy,* London: Earthscan) concerning sustainable development: for development to continue, what do we need to sustain—a natural resource base (i.e., a total stock of natural capital) or rather, as the optimist will claim, a sufficient capital base combining natural capital and human capital, the latter being made up of skills, knowledge, institutions, industrial infrastructure, and so on? From a radical perspective, the claim that humans are resourceful and adaptable is seen as naively optimistic (as a reason for discounting other concerns) and a variant on the "technological fix" or an undue reliance on technology to find the solutions to the problems it has helped to create. The above remarks have a bearing on another area of conflict, *population* policy—do we or do we not need to curb population growth? If it is to be checked, is this done appropriately by birth control programs or proper socioeconomic development for the poor?

Clearly there is a whole range of positions on a continuum between the out-and-out optimist who does not think we need to make any real adjustment to the pursuit of development for all countries—that is, to global growth (because the environment *as a whole* will continue to serve human needs adequately, even though parts of it are clearly damaged, etc.) and the position of those who think that the pursuit of universal growth is quite impossible and therefore a radical reevaluation of human priorities is called for. Many will see the need in varying degrees for serious changes, certainly in industrial and technological practices, if not in Northern life-styles more generally. Part of the difficulty in interpreting the much-used phrase "sustainable development" is that the phrase covers a whole range of positions (see below).

Strictly speaking, there are several responses one could make to the recognition that universal growth is impossible:

a. One could accept that in a "win-lose" world it is necessary to defend one's corner: if much of the world cannot (realistically) catch up, then that is tough luck. (There was a suspicion of this approach perceived by delegates from the South at the Stockholm Conference on the environment in 1972, who thought that the North was more interested in conserving its future than helping the South catch up.) This in effect involves denying a "global ethic" or an ethic of global responsibility.

b. One could accept that all countries continue to pursue economic growth now, well aware that in the not-too-distant future tensions over diminishing resources, such as water supplies, will multiply. It is reckoned in any case that more military conflicts in the future will be fought over environmental issues. (Many would read the Gulf War as at least in part about the control of oil supplies.) This involves denying that we have responsibilities to future generations.

c. In rejecting that it is ethically acceptable to pursue one's own country's development in disregard for other countries and/or the future (i.e., in rejecting (a) and (b)), others will attempt seriously to modify the pursuit of growth (as a part of the overall goal of global growth) so as to accommodate both the goals of other countries and also the constraints and values derived from our environmental understanding.

B. Rival Worldviews

The conflict identified above between development goals and environmental constraints is just that: a matter of limits imposed by the environment on the pursuit of development. But there are other conflicts that do not depend on this fact but upon other considerations that have to do with broader worldviews. Even if what counts as a natural resource depends upon its usefulness to us at a particular time, it remains a deep part of our Western tradition to which development discourse gives expression, to think of nature as a bundle of resources or as a provider of resources or as a waste sink; its value is essentially instrumental, and it is there for us to master and exploit. Much of the recent environmentalist thinking, whether inspired by a nature-centered approach, or a more enlightened human-centered approach (one, for instance, that sees spiritual and aesthetic appreciation of nature as vital human interests) rejects that whole way of thinking about nature, and indeed questions the tendency to assimilate "environment" with "nature." Rather, nature is to be seen as an object of appreciation, reverence, or respect, and our relationship to the rest of nature should be more as plain citizens of the *biotic community* (the graphic and influential image in Aldo Leopold, (1949), *A Sand County Almanac,* London: Oxford UP) than as masters of it. On these views part of the problem with development is that it is the product of the Western enlightenment tradition in which man, as the only truly rational being (as suggested by Kant and Aristotle earlier, among many others) or being possessed of a soul (Descartes' dualistic metaphysics) is set apart from the rest of nature in a kind of dualistic antithesis.

C. Implications of Accepting Limits to Growth and/or Rival Worldviews for Development

If the pursuit of economic growth is seen as needing to be checked, severely reduced, or generally questioned, what implications does that have for our understanding of development? There are here two strategies possible. One is to give up the whole idea of development as essentially flawed or necessarily imbued with the values of the global economy. This is for instance the approach of writers like Wolfgang Sachs. The challenge is then to provide some alternative concept or conceptual package through which to articulate acceptable change. On the other hand, there is an alternative strategy, adopted for instance by many members of the International Development Ethics Association (IDEA), of taking up the challenge of redefining development in ways that make economic growth less central for all and making environmental constaints and values more integral to the conception of development itself. (It should be noted that these approaches do not deny the importance of such economic growth as is needed to enable the very poor to escape their poverty. Indeed, if anything, special emphasis may be put on precisely this, in contrast to the more general goals of growth as a global goal, especially for rich countries.)

D. Development as Setting Limits on Environmental Protection

Conversely, of course, commitments to development, insofar as they are seen as ethically defensible or necessary, will set limits to the degrees and kinds of environmental protection that are seen as ethically required or politically realistic. If development as economic growth is seen as a commitment of public policy, how can, for instance, measures to protect the environment justifiably go beyond the public expectations behind that policy? Even if development is not seen simply as economic growth, development is firmly rooted in the idea of "human" development, of progress in human well-being. Thus, any environmental perspective that does not take this into account has to be questioned from the point of view of a development thinker.

E. Strategies for Responding to the Conflict

There is little doubt that there are many intellectual conflicts like the above between those who pursue development and see environmental protection as essentially pragmatic ("exploit it well now so that we can go on exploiting it later") and those for whom environmentalism is about a new approach to nature (and ourselves). Whether or not these conflicts are resolvable depends upon how far each party is willing to acknowledge that there are important values on the other side to be given some weight.

Clearly a defender of orthodox development must: (a) first, in relation to resource/pollution constraints, *either* deny there is conflict, *or* if there is, argue for disregard of the future or of other countries on the grounds of a right to collective self-defense (or of a denial of a *global ethic* altogether); *or* be prepared to modify his position on growth; and (b) second, in relation to rival worldviews, *either* defend his view as correct (and dismiss the others as unimportant, etc.) *or* be willing to incorporate these views into a revised conception of the "goods" that development pursues.

Conversely, a defender of a radical environmentalism must: (a) first, in relation to resource/pollution constraints, *either* deny the propriety of development as growth *or* be willing to reach a compromise strategy that combines to some extent the goals of development with the goals of environmental protection (*sustainable development* being, of course, one such attempt to combine the two); and (b) second, in relation to rival world views, *either* reject the development package and much of the value system in our Western tradition *or* be willing to acknowledge that the social and economic concerns of human beings, which development serves but which do not have direct reference to the environment, are important and legitimate and need incorporating into an agreed package. We need now to look more closely at some of the theoretical issues involved in attempting to integrate them into one package. In what follows I shall consider various attempts to combine the two sets of values, first looking at the more

Box 4

Summary of the Range of Views

A. Robust defense of development as sustained economic growth, based on:

Either (i) rejection of value of one or more of the following: nonhuman life/future generations/global responsibility;

or (ii) very optimistic reading of environmental prospects;

or (iii) both.

B. Integration of "human" values in development with "environmental" values into an overall ethical approach requiring significant changes. What is called "sustainable development" (and other accounts) covers a range of positions:

either (i) greening of industry, and so on, but no real change to the goals of development;

or (ii) substantial changes to northern way of life;

or (iii) rejection of economic growth and acceptance of other criteria for quality of life, leading to redefinitions of development.

C. Robust affirmation of ecological values and rejection of "development values," based on:

Either (i) an affirmation of real human values as drawn on or consistent with ecological values;

or (ii) a misanthropic rejection of human concerns.

practical positions, and then at more theoretical issues underlying them (see Box 4).

IV. ATTEMPTS TO INTEGRATE THE TWO

A. Sustainability

Many thinkers in the last 20 years or so have tried to integrate the two sets of concerns into a coherent policy and rationale. The World Council of Churches popularized the idea of a "just and sustainable society," combining sustaining the environment with economic justice. "Sustainability" became a key concept, being applied to many things such as sustainable agriculture and sustainable cities. Its application directly to development was

given a large impetus by the Report of the World Commission on Environment and Development (WCED (1987), *Our Common Future*. Oxford University Press, commonly referred to as the *Brundtland Report*), and continues to be the focal point for international agreements, such as *Agenda 21* of the World Summit on Environment and Development in Rio de Janiero in 1992 (the "Earth Summit"), and Charters such as the *Business Charter for Sustainable Development* (1991) of the International Chamber of Commerce (ICC).

B. Other Approaches: Small Is Beautiful

Before saying more about sustainable development as an organizing concept for coordinating the two sets of concerns, I should add that other attempts are made too. The philosophy behind Schumacher's influential approach (Schumacher, E. F. (1973). *Small is beautiful*. London: Blond and Briggs.) was very much that of integrating environmental concerns with the kind of development projects that helped to alleviate world poverty. An organizing concept for this and many other concerns was that of *intermediate/appropriate technology*; because what was advocated was a kind of technology that met both genuine human needs and was environmentally beneficial. Ideas of ecodevelopment, feminist critiques of economic development partly in the name of more caring or nurturing relationships with nature, and proposals for a "new economics" by, for example, the New Economics Foundation (in the U.K.) are among a large array of "alternative" visions of how to order our economic affairs in such a way as to be really in harmony with nature.

C. Sustainable Development

The idea of sustainable development stands out as prominent, both because of its popularity and because it represents a wide range of perspectives, from the radical to the conventional. It started off as being an idea from the alternative culture, but has since the *Brundtland Report* essentially been adopted, some would say coopted, by governments and businesses, in whose intellectual hands the continued commitment to economic growth is unshaken and for whom precisely what is to be sustained or is capable of being sustained is *development as growth itself*.

The phrase is one those that immediately triggers one set of responses (because of the history and circumstances of its becoming accepted) but, in terms of what it explicitly says, is somewhat different. Almost anyone when presented with the phrase will think, "That's about the protection of the environment into the future." But what it actually says is "*development* that is capable of being sustained." Even the most well-known and popular definition of sustainable development in the *Brundtland Report* avoids any explicit reference to the environment: "Sustainable development is meeting the needs of the present generation without compromising the ability of future generations to meet their needs." (WCED, 1987, p. 8.) Clearly here, as in most discussions of sustainable development, the assumption is that what is critical for later generations to be able to meet their needs is a healthy environment with sufficient natural resources. We must ensure that what we do to or with it does not undermine the environment for its part in providing them with this. But even here, for this to be achieved, it hardly follows that the environment *as it is* has to be sustained. Much invasive action on the environment, such as large-scale mining or forest clearing, which might be anathema to many environmentalists, might be seen by developers to be consistent with ensuring that there will be adequate resources to meet the needs of future generations. In any case, as I remarked earlier, one of the key issues is what is being passed on to later generations—a stock of natural capital or a combination of natural and human capital (see Box 5).

D. Ecological Inputs into the Goals of Development

One way of seeking to integrate the two sets of concerns is to make environmental values part of the goals of development. That is, environmental values do not merely set external limits to development; they can, for many, inform the very character of development. If one thinks, for instance, as many environmentalists do, that nature is valuable or that living things in nature are valuable, then public policy ought to supplement or extend the goal of development with the goal of promoting or respecting natural value (not just human interests). Second, if many citizens actually *want* an environment to which they can relate, aesthetically, spiritually, or recreationally, or want to get back to a general sense of relatedness to *nature,* which modern technological attitudes in particular and worldviews of man as separate from nature in general impede, then the whole paradigm of development as economic growth is severely questioned. Third, if there comes to be an ethical recognition that future generations matter and that the impacts of one's own country's economic policies may cause problems in other parts of the world that are unacceptable, then these values will affect the very rationale of development.

Finally, ecology also provides us with a model of diversity, because flourishing ecosystems contain much diversity in some kind of equilibrium. Its diversity is crucial; it is not a problem. Perhaps in thinking about development, both in respect of different development paths of different countries and in respect of the acceptance of diversity within "multicultural" societies, the ecological model has an important place. Certainly, given that the global economy is currently causing what has been called the "homogenization of cultures" in the name of a single, liberal, free-market model of development, respect for diversity of cultures and of "collective experiments in living" would be indispensable. An Indian activist, Coreen Kumar de Sousa, once remarked (at a conference) about the *Brundtland Report,* "I do not accept that we have our common future. Rather we have our futures in common." Here as in other respects, those led by firm and explicit ethical reflection are led to complementary positions over development and the environment. The key debates should be, and increasingly are, not between advocates of human development and advocates of ecological care, but between these groups adopting common cause and those who advocate growth in the global economy.

Whether, however, the attempt to integrate the goals of development with the goals of environmental protection into an integrated policy results in a thinker's adopting a radical critique of current growth policies or in endorsing "green" growth policies, there are normally two kinds of reason for adopting the strategy of integration, one theoretical and one pragmatic.

Box 5

Sustainable Development

Sustainable development involves meeting the needs of the present without compromising the ability of future generations to meet their own needs.

Economic growth provides the conditions in which protection of the environment can best be achieved, and environmental protection, in balance with other human goals, is necessary to achieve growth that is sustainable.

Source: International Chamber of Commerce. (1991). *Business charter for sustainable development,* Introduction.

V. REASONS FOR INTEGRATION

A. Theoretical Considerations Leading to Integration into an Overall Ethical Theory: Both Commitments Valid

Most thinkers caring for the environment will acknowledge that the interest that humans have in maintaining and where possible (particularly in the case of the poor) improving their material lot is not unreasonable. Thus, they will recognize that the duties we have toward the environment and the duties we have to fellow human beings now are both *valid* (or "true," if a traditional view that moral statements state moral truths is accepted). Intellectual integrity requires an overall account, and thus requires an attempt to pursue both goals in such a way that they can be made to coincide, where possible, and to provide some guidance on how to resolve conflicts where they cannot be made to coincide. Likewise, with those coming from the direction of an interest in development, most development thinkers will also see the need to combine concerns for the environment with development goals simply because their moral theories recognize that both sets of duties are valid, and intellectual honesty requires some kind of integration.

At any rate it seems clear that whereas some time ago development theorists were not really required to have worked-out views about environmental value and conversely environmentalists could content themselves with saying why we ought to protect the environment, it behooves all theorists now to answer the following questions:

—"Does the policy you propose meet the ethical requirements for environmental care?"
—"Does your policy meet the ethical requirements for the reasonable realization of human needs and aspirations, especially those of the poor?"
—"How does your ethical theory guide you in dealing with difficult cases of conflict?"

Any thinker interested in both the environmental perspective and the development perspective will, *if he is to be a consistent moral thinker,* need to work out or accept an *overall ethical theory* within which the various concerns can be justified and integrated. Many thinkers nowadays, especially philosophers interested in the application of ethical theory to these issues, see themselves as providing a properly worked out normative theory that gives expression to the range of concerns we have identified.

It is also possible, of course, for a theorist to see him- or herself as starting from neither initial position (or from both, as in the case of the author), and thus seeking to develop an adequate overall ethical theory in which the humanistic concerns of development and the wider concerns that have to do with future people and the nonhuman world are properly articulated.

It is not necessary, of course, to accept the need to do this, and for two rather different reasons. Someone in one camp can simply reject the ethical claims in the other as invalid. Environmentalists may reject the normative framework of development discourse altogether, and they might even adopt a thoroughly misanthropic approach toward human well-being (e.g., the claim that humans are a cancer; views dubbed by critics as "environmental fascism," etc.). Developmentalists may reject any normative theory concerning the moral standing of nonhumans and future generations, and only allow ethical concerns about the environment to enter the picture in terms of standard economic consequences for those in society now (the group whose development is in question), and, if a robustly realist view of international relations is assumed (discussed below), regard the effects on distant people now as morally irrelevant or unimportant too (except insofar as it affects their own development).

It is also worth noting that, even if a theorist himself attempts to construct or find an overall ethical theory in which these concerns are integrated, it remains the case that many people do not do so and either reject other perspectives or fail to acknowledge them. What then? Part of the challenge of modern complex pluralistic societies is to find a way of accommodating different normative perspectives and worldviews. For instance Rawls's later theory of *overlapping consensus* (in *Political Liberalism* (1993), OUP) can cover not only the acceptance of *diversity* in a multicultural society (e.g., diversity of religious and ethnic kinds), but also diversity of ethical perspective such as between those who advocate growth and those who reject it (and a range of positions between). But this is still an overall ethical theory, one that deals with conflicts of values between people, rather than within any individual thinker.

B. Pragmatic Considerations: The Issue of Motivation

Quite apart from the requirements of intellectual integrity, there is a further important consideration that has gained prominence in recent years under the rubric of "environmental politics," "the new economics," and so on. Basically the question here has to do with *motivation:*

how to persuade people to act so as adequately to protect the environment? People may be persuaded by the moral arguments that they ought to do many things to help protect the environment, but they may find it difficult actually to do much about it, for instance, because it is not generally done (so there is no feeling of reciprocation or solidarity), or because action may be at what they see as a significant cost to themselves. It is therefore, speaking pragmatically, quite hopeless to present arguments for changing life-styles as austere demands, because if we are realistic about the structure and patterns of human motivation, we must accept that, while a few may do so, most will not.

It is therefore vital that concern for the environment is seen as consistent with the continuing *quality of life*. Thus, it is important both that, as far as is possible, the goals of development (as the maintenance and improvement of well-being) are seen as closely linked to care for the environment, and also that alternative conceptions of quality of life, less linked to material affluence, are seen as more acceptable. Much recent writing on development ethics, for example, by Denis Goulet is concerned to advocate, often in the form of reminders of past wisdom, a nonmaterialistic conception of well-being, stressing community, relationships, and so on, as the core of development. (Eric Fromm's (1979) *To have or to be?* London: Sphere Books, is a seminal work in this vein, although not explicitly about development.) Part of the point here is that even if there were not environmental reasons, conceptions of well-being less tied to material wealth are seen as inherently preferable anyway.

Green politics is likewise faced with the challenges and complexities of turning what often appears to be very idealistic into hard and realizable policies. (*See*, e.g., S. C. Young, (1993), *The politics of the environment*, Chorleton: Baseline Books.) Much effective environmental protection really requires legislation to ensure compliance and thus reciprocity of effort, but legislation requires democratic processes that in turn depend on sufficient voters supporting relevant party-political programs.

It might be thought that the challenge of persuading people to see environmental protection as consistent with their quality of life was only really a problem for those advocating radical changes. For someone who thinks that all we need do is to change some of the background practices (e.g., in industry) but not to change affluent life-styles to any significant degree, there is no problem. To some extent this is true, but an analogous problem does exist for all those committed

to the greening of industry: how to get businesses to comply with new tougher environmental standards. Although some advocates of business ethics press for the "stakeholder" analysis, according to which a business has responsibilities to all types of stakeholders, such as those who are affected by the activities in question, the more traditional theory (which represents in the real world what usually happens anyway) that businesses are legitimately guided by the profit motive alone is still widely accepted. If that is, as a matter of fact, what largely determines the policies of businesses, then there are two key factors that shape the way businesses operate: enforceable environmental law and consumer demand. For either of these factors to bring about effective change, changes in public values are needed. New laws require democratic consensus. New business policies based on changes in consumer preference require informed and motivated consumers. The challenge of combining the moral arguments with enlightened self-interest remains.

VI. GLOBAL ISSUES

Even if we accept that the central concern of a society's development is with the well-being of human beings living in that society, it can also be argued that among the goals of that society (including its government) should be precisely the goals that recommend themselves to environmentalists—namely, respecting nonhuman life, care for future generations, and concern for fairness in dealings with other countries. Not all environmentalists would necessarily accept all three, although there is most general agreement about the *global* scope of our obligations. Indeed, this aspect is least attended to, perhaps because it seems self-evident that from an environmentally holistic perspective national borders are irrelevant and global effects require global solutions.

A. Cosmopolitan Theories of Global Ethics

But when applied to development, the implications are far-reaching. An environmental ethic is essentially a global or world ethic. Like many of the traditional ethical theories, such as natural law theory, Kantianism, or utilitarianism, it assumes that morally speaking we belong to one world community. We are *cosmopolitans* ("citizens of the world") even if we do not properly recognize this. But the implications of this for our understanding of international relations are considerable, and question the assumptions of the dominant "internationalist paradigm," which assumes the legitimacy of each state pursuing its own national interests, *including its commitment to development,* within a fairly limited framework of international norms. This takes us into the field of "international ethics," which of course I am only touching on here, but which, together with development ethics and environmental ethics, is one of the large growth areas in applied ethics in the late twentieth century.

B. Environmental Sovereignty or Common Heritage of Mankind

A cornerstone of the dominant paradigm of international relations is sovereignty. One aspect of sovereignty often claimed is something called environmental sovereignty—the right of a nation or jurisdiction to control the use of the natural resources within its territorial borders. The *UN Declaration on the Right to Development (1986)* asserts that peoples have a right to exercise "full and complete sovereignty over all their natural wealth and resources." Because much of the natural wealth of the world is in the South, this may be a useful check on attempts by those operating from the North to control it. But from a theoretical point of view, particularly one informed by ecological values, it is troubling. It is not at all clear morally that if we adopt a global ethic, whatever its standing in international law, a country has a right to do just what it wants with its resources, if, for instance, its misuse of them has bad consequences for others outside that country. Take, for instance, a tropical rain forest. Does a country like Brazil morally have a right to do what it will with it, given the potential loss of genetic information or the disturbance to the global weather system that destruction of much of it would cause? By the same token, of course, resources that a country like the United States comes to possess because they were bought on the international market, like oil, would also be subject to the same proviso.

What these two cases illustrate is that, apart from the propriety of a global ethical standpoint from which to make judgments of appropriate or inappropriate use, ownership, whether by a person, an organization, a people or a state, does not confer *absolute rights* of use and disposal. In what ways and how far environmental factors should restrict rights to property is an issue that needs and receives attention. Linked to this is another issue: was Locke right to suppose that in "mixing our labour" with natural materials we added 99% of their value? From an ecological perspective this is highly questionable for a variety of reasons. But if Locke is wrong, then the "right to property" theory partly founded on it is also partly questioned.

C. Is Nature to Be Seen as a Pool of Resources Anyway?

Should then the Brazilian rainforest be seen, ethically, as on all fours with the resources of the deep-sea bed, the "common heritage of mankind," to use the language of the *UN Convention on the Law of the Sea* (UNCLOS (1982), New York)? But this too has its problems, because it suggests that *the natural world as whole is there for the use of humankind as a whole.* It repeats in different language the assumption that nature is a bundle of resources for human use. Of course we cannot avoid altogether thinking of the natural world as the supplier of the resources we all need, but the idea of a common heritage or common resources is for many environmentalists questionable, unless there is a proper corrective to the one-sidedness of it in terms of the importance of other kinds of relationships that we have toward the natural world.

VII. THE EVALUATIVE NATURE OF DEVELOPMENT

A. Development Ethics: Philosophical Approaches

Implicit in much of what has been said above is a certain understanding of "development discourse," which now needs to be stated explicitly. Philosophers have become very interested in recent years in the ethical foundations of development. There are three issues in particular: the general normative basis of development as a process of socioeconomic change, the issue of why the reduction of extreme poverty should have moral priority, and the ethical basis of international aid and trade. Rival accounts based on central philosophical theories are argued for. Thus, for instance, Aristotelian, Kantian, Rawlsian, utilitarian, natural law or human rights accounts are given and compared. Although none of these theories is explicitly concerned with the environment, most writers are sensitive to the need to take environmental concern into account. Some who are explicitly concerned with the latter develop theories of ecophilosophy to transform or extend these main-line Western theoretical approaches so as to be sensitive to biocentric considerations.

B. The Liberal and Statist Value Assumptions Underlying the Dominant Development Model

One of the important things that the upturn of interest in normative theories in development has done has been to put the defenders of the conventional model of development as growth on their metal, thus forcing them to defend the model in terms of its basic ethical presuppositions. Several characteristic defenses of this model are worth identifying: first, what makes the process of socioeconomic change *good* is that more people have access to more wealth, which leads to the greater exercise of choice and thus happiness/well-being, defined in terms of preference satisfaction. Second, as noted in Section I, governments have a duty to enable this to happen, because that is what electorates want them to do. Third, the duty of governments has implications for foreign policy, because its primary and usually overriding allegiance is to the economic well-being of its citizens. Similarly, multinational companies have duties vis-à-vis their shareholders to maximize profits in foreign operations, within the frameworks of international law or domestic law, such as they are.

What essentially emerges from the dominant development paradigm is its essentially *liberal* and *statist* assumptions—liberal because of a minimal conception of the good and because of the central value of economic liberty, statist in that it is assumed that the primary unit of development is the state, and that each state has a right to pursue its own development. (Consider the 1986 *UN Declaration on the Right to Development*.) It is these assumptions that are both highlighted and generally opposed in the philosophical engagement with development. Many examples of alternative value assumptions about development have been indicated earlier in the article.

C. Concept and Conceptions of Development

What emerges is that *there is no ethically neutral account of development;* insofar as development is a process of change subject to human control (e.g., by governments with a mandate to act on behalf of their people), what we call "genuine" or "real" development presupposes our value system. The initial definition of development as economic growth is not the neutral definition of development, but a particular if dominant conception of development, combining a set of values with a set of factual assumptions about what is possible and what works in the world. It might after all be right, but it is not right by definitional fiat. It may be helpful to say that whereas there are numerous rival *conceptions* or

"thick" definitions of development, there is a "thin" definition or *concept* of development, which might run as follows: development is a process of change in a society that ought to occur. What ought to be made to occur? That is what one's ethical theory will determine. This allows for the possibility of diverse models of development for different countries. It also significantly shows that development in the South need not be thought of as "catching up with" or "imitating" the North.

Nor are these wider reflections restricted to academic speculation. Many international documents put emphasis now on the diversity of criteria relevant to judging appropriate development. The influential *Human Development Reports* of the UNDP (United Nations Development Program) bear witness to this, as does the 1986 *UN Declaration on the Right to Development* (see Box 6). The very title "human development" does, however, show a Janus-faced character. "Human" signals the recognition that the human person is the central subject of development, and this involves many dimensions of value in addition to economic or material standing. On the other hand, in stressing "human," such accounts still bear witness to the humanistic origins of even the more enlightened kind of development thinking. This is not to say that such accounts and reports are not sensitive in all sorts of ways to environmental considerations, but they do not go as far as many thinkers would wish to go in including ecological values in the dynamics of social change.

The fact that accounts of development are open to rival evaluative inputs has important consequences for the environmentalist. So long as development is seen essentially in economic growth terms, with all the assumptions that go along with that, and the environmentalist is putting forward a rival perspective (and is not someone merely adapting the growth mechanism from

---

Box 6	

Development

Development is a comprehensive economic, social, cultural, and political process, which aims at the constant improvement of the well-being of the entire population and of all individuals on the basis of their active, free, and meaningful participation in development and in the fair distribution of benefits resulting therefrom.

Source: United Nations. (1986). *Declaration on the right to development,* 41/128. From the Preamble, paragraph 2.

within that paradigm), there seems to be little meeting of minds and a kind of impasse of incommensurate worldviews. But if it is recognized that what we call development or justified social change incorporates our values, whatever they are, then the way is open to incorporate environmental values into one's conception of development itself.

What thinking about the environment does is to contribute to the opening up of the discussion on the ethical foundations of development. But at the same time it has to take seriously that discourse of development, if it is to be effective and open to the truths about human well-being that that discourse contains.

Also See the Following Articles

DEVELOPMENT ETHICS • ENVIRONMENTAL ETHICS, OVERVIEW • LAND USE ISSUES

Bibliography

Aiken, W., & LaFollette, H. (Eds.). (1995). *World hunger and moral obligation* (2nd ed.) Englewood Cliffs, NJ: Prentice-Hall.

Aman, K. (Ed.). (1991). *Ethical principles for development: Needs, capacities and rights.* Montclair: Institute for Critical Thinking.

Attfiield, R., & Wilkins, B. (Eds.). (1993). *International justice and the Third World.* London: Routledge.

Brown, C. R. (1992). *International relations theory—New normative approaches.* London: Harvester.

Daly, H., et al. (1989). *For the common good: Redirecting the economy toward community, the environment, and a sustainable future.* Boston: Beacon.

Ekins, P. (Ed.). (1986). *The living economy.* London: Routledge.

Engel, R., & Engel, J. (Eds.). (1991). *Ethics of development and environment.* Boulder, CO: Westview Press.

Goodin, R. E. (Ed.). (1994). *The politics of the environment.* Aldershot: Edward Elgar.

Goulet, D. (1995). *Development ethics—A guide to theory and practice.* New York: Apex Press.

O'Neill, J. (1993). *Ecology, policy and politics.* London: Routledge.

Pearce, D. W., et al. (1990). *Sustainable development: economics and environment in the Third World.* Aldershot: Edward Elgar.

Redclift, M. R. (1989). *Sustainable development: exploring the contradictions.* London: Routledge.

Robinson, N. A., et al. (Eds.). (1992). *Agenda 21 & the UNCED proceedings—International protection of the environment,* Proceedings of United Nations Conference on Environment and Development, IUCN.

Sachs, W., et al. (Eds.). (1992). *The development dictionary.* London: Zed Books.

Simon, J. L., et al. (Eds.). (1995). *The state of humanity.* London: Oxford UP.

UNDP. (1991–1995). *Human development reports,* New York.

DISABILITY RIGHTS

Anita Silvers
San Francisco State University

GLOSSARY

Americans with Disabilities Act (ADA) 1990 U.S. civil rights legislation that protects against disability discrimination.

compensatory rights of the disabled Entitlements or exemptions assigned as benefits to compensate for impaired individuals' disadvantages.

disability Originally, the condition of having fewer rights or more limited or truncated rights than other classes of people. In current usage, the condition of having functional limitations occasioned by physical, sensory, or cognitive impairments.

Disability Discrimination Act (DDA) 1995 U.K. disability rights legislation.

equal rights of the disabled Protection of equal physical and social access but, also, distribution of resources that can overcome functional limitations so as to equalize capabilities.

group-differentiated rights Rights that pertain only in virtue of membership in a subset of the population.

handicap A prevention or impediment of fair access to social participation and equal opportunities.

medical model of disability The concept that disablement is a disadvantageous state of individuals resulting from their physical or mental defects.

minority model of disability The concept that disablement is a disadvantageous social environment responsive to the normal majority rather than the impaired minority.

moral model of disability The concept that disablement is a disadvantageous state, usually a visible impairment, visited upon individuals as retribution for their progenitors' or their own erroneous conduct or flawed character.

social model of disability The concept that disablement is a state of society that disadvantages impaired individuals, not a state of impaired individuals that disadvantages them in society. Thus, the dysfunction attendant on (certain kinds of) impairment is artificial and remediable, not natural and immutable.

PEOPLE WITH PHYSICAL, SENSORY, OR COGNITIVE IMPAIRMENTS are said to be disabled. To describe someone as disabled means the individual has functional limitations, but sometimes also imputes incompetence, dependence, and the inability to exercise rights in virtue of the individual's limitations. People with disabilities often are assigned group-differentiated entitlements or exemptions—special rights that are supposed to compensate for their disadvantageous impairments. But people with disabilities now also claim an equal right to full social participation. Their social equality is furthered by group-differentiated protective rights prohibiting the obstruction of their physical and social access. Their equality also is furthered by a general distributive right to resource allocation that can normalize their primary functionings.

I. WHY DISABILITY RIGHTS?

Originally, having a disability meant having fewer, more limited, or more truncated rights than other classes of people. In today's vernacular, however, disability is identified exclusively with being physically, sensorily, or cognitively impaired. This is because such individuals customarily are regarded as being so naturally inferior that they are ineligible to be equally protected by the law. Their impairments defeat their appeals to rights, so to speak. Either they are denied rights others possess because law or tradition deems them incompetent, or else their impairments bar them from meaningful exercise of those rights. So to be disabled has come to be identified with having a physical, sensory, or cognitive impairment, even though the original meaning of the term gave it a much wider application.

To compensate for the impairments that disadvantage them in society, individuals with disabilities may claim entitlement to group-differentiated protections or benefits, or to exemptions from normal standards. These are rights that arise from and pertain to their deficits and are seen as responsive to their special needs. However, contemporary social construction theory reconceives disability as emanating not from individuals' defects but rather from social policy so flawed that it disadvantages the minority of individuals who are impaired.

Under this latter conception, persons with disabilities, whether they can be assimilated to other people or whether they remain intractably different from others in the way they live their lives, have the same need for and equal right to full social participation, including the enjoyment of self-determination and equal respect. They may assert their right to the reform of social practices that debar them from equal opportunity for education, employment, recreation, and family life. This right affords them a strong claim to structures and infrastructures that facilitate their civic, commercial, and personal flourishing, such as wheelchair-accessible built environments, communications systems that one does not have to hear to use, and the transmission of information in alternative modes accessible to touch and hearing as well as sight.

If disability is an artifact of unfavorable social arrangement, the disabled should need fewer special benefits and exemptions as they are offered greater access to the usual social goods. This is because social arrangements will be altered so their natural differences will no longer translate into social disadvantages. However, commentators concerned that no amount of environmental alteration can make some disabled people sufficiently competitive caution against eliminating provisions for their sheltered maintenance.

II. DISABILITY, DIFFERENCE, AND MORAL IMAGINATION

"Dilemmas of difference appear irresolvable," warns Martha Minow, writing about inclusion and exclusion in American law. "The right to be treated as an individual ignores the burdens of group membership; the right to object to.... group membership reinvokes the trait that carries the negative meanings" How do we "redress the negative consequences of difference without reenacting it?" Minow asks (Minow, 1990).

Given that their difference from other people is inescapable and can be concealed—if at all—only at formidable cost to energy and self-esteem, the existence of people with physical, sensory, or cognitive impairments tests certain philosophical positions. For example, that equality may bestow group-differentiated rights on the disabled challenges philosophical positions that privilege normal functioning by magnifying it into a standard against which the disabled shrink into invisibility.

Many kinds of philosophical considerations, both ethical and epistemological, are invoked with the assumption that those whose condition or state is being analyzed fall within the parameters of normal functioning. This is the standard of the common speaker or so-called normal rational agent. Accounts of impartial, objective, and just judgment usually require that one balance one's own standpoint, with its special interests and needs, by affording equal weight to what others want to see or want to do from the viewpoint of their special interests and needs.

Of course, you can't really know what it is like to be me, so the exercise here is to abstract by imagining what other persons' ambitions in view of their interests and needs *normally* would be were they in my place or I in theirs. But performing major life functions such as moving one's body is so intimate an element of the fabric of our experience that one cannot accurately imagine how to live otherwise. Nor is the inability to envision what one's ambitions or desires would be in such an event merely a matter of the degree to which one's own experience of impairment fails to approximate that of a defective agent.

For sometimes vast differences in functioning are occasioned by relatively small differences in impairment, while at other times relatively severe impairments are only minimally dysfunctional. There is no fixed proportional relation between the two, nor can one insightfully project from one's own normal experience to a much more restricted version of one's life.

Now, what we view as within our reach in the world around us—and thereby what we take as the objects of our ambition—is directly a product of the scope of our functioning. This explains why disability, understood as functional limitation, is thought to alter people so profoundly that their abnormality or singularity marginalizes them and renders them of little account from a philosophical point of view. For the prospect of being so limited paralyzes the normalizing imagination required to operationalize impartial judgment to such a degree that one cannot effectively reproduce how such a person experiences the phenomenal world. One can empathize with someone so much more seriously limited than one's self, yet not be able accurately to put one's self in his place.

Individuals perceived as irreparably impaired thus come to be seen as being beyond the scope of philosophical investigation because they cannot be presumed to engage in normal functioning. This being so, it becomes apparent why modern moral, social, and legal thought does not dismiss disability, as it does some other contingent differences, as being accidental to a person's moral being and negligible to the moral status of the individual. Disability emerges as a crucial attribute just because having a (severe) impairment defeats a condition assumed to be necessary to rational systems of judgment, namely, that reasons for action must not be opaque to normal adults. In a philosophical framework that operationalizes universalizability by normalizing, impairment cannot help but matter.

So to be disabled is to be seen as so substantially different from other persons as to disrupt the deployment of universalized judgment. It is this dislocation that challenges philosophy in its treatment of disability and in its consideration of the moral and social status

the disabled deserve. For it is one thing to account for group-differentiated entitlements and exemptions bestowed to compensate for insurmountable inferiority, but another, in view of the opacity of the disability experience, to comprehend how people with disabilities can command and exercise rights securing equality, whether these are global or group-differentiated.

III. WHAT IS A DISABILITY?

In Western society, to be disabled is to be disadvantaged regardless of how much success one achieves individually. Costs always are extracted if one is seen as a member of a poorly regarded group. This is the generic implication of "disability."

To illustrate this general point about the perils of being identified with a devalued group, during the nineteenth century and earlier, the law specified that being a woman be accounted a disability. That is, regardless of their personal competence, all women were disabled from owning property, retaining custody of their children, and voting. These limitations were justified by characterizing women as belonging to a group of persons whom nature made too weak and silly to execute such transactions and responsibilities successfully. Even if some women are demonstrably stronger or more competent than some men, the state was supposed to have an overriding interest both in protecting society from the typical woman's hapless attempts at independence and in shielding the characteristically helpless members of this class from demands that would overwhelm them.

In its original usage, then, saying that someone has a disability entails that the individual is not owed normal opportunity, autonomy and respect. During this period, progressive U.S. legislation and judicial decisions challenged racial segregation by affirming that race is no disability, that is, that differences in race do not justify differences in social participation, in opportunity, or in protection under the law. But there has been little opposition in this same period to considering physical, sensory or cognitive impairment to be a disability that permits diminished legal safeguards and justifies reduced opportunity. Only very recently have public beliefs regarding both the causes and the results of impairment shifted sufficiently to facilitate reparative legislative action. The 1990 Americans With Disabilities Act and the 1995 (U.K.) Disability Discrimination Act strive to sever the entailment between disability and disadvantage.

IV. WHO IS DISABLED?

To arrive at what considerations support the rights of those disadvantaged because they are disabled, it is crucial to understand who constitutes this group. But defining who is disabled is a matter of remarkable contentiousness. This is because being designated as disabled is never neutral.

Depending on the social environment, it can mean being stigmatized and barred without question or recourse from opportunities that other citizens take for granted as their right, whether these be employment, education, recreation, or family life. But it also can mean acquiring entitlements that strike other citizens as privileging, whether these be protective care, or financial assistance, or exemptions from fees or performance standards. In the former situation, people struggle against being thought to be disabled; in the latter, they struggle to be verified as disabled.

Whether a person desires to be identified as disabled probably varies with whether she thinks other people will apply this characterization as an incentive for helping her or instead as an excuse to deny her opportunity. Some people with significant impairment—for example, many people who are Deaf (that is, members of Deaf culture as well as hearing impaired)—insist that they are not disabled but simply differ from other groups in respect to the language they use to communicate.

In contrast, other groups of people—for instance, those with such conditions as dyslexia or attention deficit disorder—struggle to be viewed as disabled in order to be cared for consonant with their deficit. There are organizations of visually impaired people that describe blindness as just an inconvenience, while there are organizations of people with myalgic encephalomyelitis (chronic fatigue syndrome) that describe ME as profoundly debilitating. In general, people seem more comfortable characterizing their impairments as disabilities when they can invoke group-differentiated disability rights to mitigate the social disadvantage disability invokes.

A. The World Health Organization Definitions

During the 1970s public policy considerations generated strong concern about the propriety of the terminology designating persons with physical, sensory, and cognitive impairments. The terms "disability" and "handicap" were often confused. As a concession to the discomfort the very thought of impairment visits on most nondisabled people, the use of euphemisms such as "differently abled" or "challenged" or "having special needs" was promoted.

In 1980, the World Health Organization adopted a trilogy of concepts meant to increase precision in the discussion of disablement. The International Classification clearly distinguishes among "impairment," "disability," and "handicap": "impairment—any loss or abnormality of psychological, physiological, or anatomical structure or function; disability—any restriction or lack (resulting from an impairment) of ability to perform an activity in the manner or within the range considered normal for a human being; and handicap—a disadvantage for a given individual, resulting from an impairment or disability, that limits or prevents the fulfillment of a role that is normal, depending on age, sex, social and cultural factors, for that individual."

This conceptual scheme has been used extensively in rehabilitation, education, statistics, policy, legislation, demography, sociology, economics, and anthropology. It provides that someone may be impaired without being disabled, and disabled without being disadvantaged, but whosoever is disadvantaged through disability suffers this state in virtue of being abnormal or functioning below the normal range.

These definitions are fashioned primarily to guide how rehabilitative health care and other social services should be allocated. But they have been subject to vehement objections from segments of the disability community. Most generally, the definitions are thought to blame the victim by locating disability in the deficits of impaired individuals rather than in the failure of society to treat such individuals equitably. The WHO definitions are believed to characterize impaired people as a problem to which the first response should be to seek a cure, if this cannot be achieved then to pursue restoration of the maximum function possible, and, finally, if these preferable options fail, to consign the still-impaired individuals to a facility for long-term care.

Equally problematic is the way this conceptual trilogy reifies a relative benchmark into an absolute standard. How people normally carry out an activity or fulfill a function is a matter of custom, not of nature, and is much dependent on which people are dominant and which subordinate in the group. In today's world, for instance, no single way of traveling five miles prevails. Where autos are abundant, the blind are dysfunctional travelers while the one-legged function nearly normally; where the prevailing mode of travel is to walk, the reverse is the case.

To respond to these complaints, changes in the latter

two elements of the WHO conceptual trilogy are offered in the Standard Rules on the Equalization of Opportunities for Persons with Disabilities, adopted by the UN General Assembly in 1993:

> The term "disability" summarizes a great number of different functional limitations occurring in any population in any country of the world. People may be disabled by physical, intellectual or sensory impairment, medical conditions or mental illness. Such impairments, conditions or illnesses may be permanent or transitory in nature.
>
> The term "handicap" means the loss or limitation of opportunities to take part in the life of the community on an equal level with others. It describes the encounter between the person with a disability and the environment. The purpose of this term is to emphasize the focus on the shortcomings in the environment and in many organized activities in society, for example, information, communication and education, which prevent persons with disabilities from participating on equal terms.

These emendations are meant to acknowledge both individual's needs (such as rehabilitation and technical aids) and the shortcomings of society (various artificial obstacles to social participation). But some disability activists still are concerned that these definitions are too centered on the individual's deficits and that they construe disability as a medical rather than a social problem. For the definitions may not yet adequately clarify the interaction between societal conditions or expectations and how successfully individuals function.

B. The Moral Model of Disability

Although who is a minority and how minorities are treated differs significantly from nation to nation, almost invariably the group most marginalized in respect to both social and personal areas of achievement consists of those with serious physical, sensory, or cognitive limitations. In respect to other differences among people—whether these derive from sex, race, or cultural heritage, each kind of difference is thought in some locales to justify social inequities between groups, but for other places and peoples the same difference is dismissed as contingent, external, and of no consequence in excusing injustice.

In contrast, in almost all places and among most people, individuals who are impaired are assumed to be, by the very nature of their condition, inferior. From antiquity, the traditional explanation for their disadvantage supposes that there is some moral flaw, not necessarily theirs but perhaps that of their progenitors, for which failing they must suffer.

C. The Medical Model of Disability

In the modern era, the progressive approach to justifying the disadvantage visited on such impaired individuals substitutes a physiological or mental deficit for the moral flaw blamed by antiquity. This medical model fixes on reducing the numbers of people with disabilities by preventative or curative medical technology. Despite its scientific associations, the medical model resembles its predecessor in its assignment of responsibility, for impaired individuals' deficits are attributed to their inadequate health precautions or their bad genes, that is, once more to their own or their ancestors' failings.

Although beneficial for those who otherwise would be bereft of treatment, this medical model of disability obstructs those whose impairments defy medical restoration by restricting them to roles of dependence as the recipients of failed care. But currently, their status is being reconceptualized so as to shift the locus of their handicap from personal shortcoming to public failure. This alteration is fueled by recognition that impairment is no sufficient condition of social failure.

D. The Social Model of Disability

That is, individuals with precisely the same kind and degree of impairment attain vastly differing levels of social performance. To illustrate, the success of persons with these impairments shows that deafness bars neither the composing nor professional performing of music; visual impairments do not prohibit scientific careers; and although some individuals with mobility impairments are thought to be unfit for employment, others with identical impairments have thrived in most sorts of work including the presidency of the United States.

The theoretical impact of these accomplishments has been to transform the notion of "handicapping condition" from a state of a minority of people that disadvantages them in society to a state of society that disadvantages a minority of people. This social model of disability transfigures individuals with disabilities from patients into persons with rights that, when acknowledged, are expected to (a) compensate for or (b) eliminate the social disadvantages that are attendant upon their being a minority. The social model of disability thus traces the source of this minority's disadvantage to a hostile environment and treats the dysfunction attendant on (certain kinds of) impairment as artificial and remediable, not natural and immutable. Their environment is inimical to them because in respect to almost all social venues and institutions, people with disabilities are neither numerous nor noticeable.

E. The Minority Model of Disability

During the past half century, both national and international movements to secure greater social participation for people with disabilities have grown in vigor and in success. These activities are not novel. For from antiquity and in quite diverse cultural settings, from the medieval guilds of the blind to the organizations formed by injured veterans following dozens of wars to San Francisco State University's International Whirlwind Network of village wheelchair makers in developing nations, where impaired individuals have fashioned a positive group identity, creating and promoting a distinctive and comprehensive way of life, they have improved their socioeconomic condition.

The minority model extends and politicizes the theory promoted by the social model of disability by arguing that the functional limitation associated with impairment varies with the degree to which the social environment respects the differences of the minority of individuals who are impaired. To improve their functionality, this model recommends, people with disabilities should employ the same organizational strategies other minorities have used to adjust the social environment to accommodate their differences.

Speaking very generally and glossing over national differences, the last 50 years have advanced the class of persons with serious physical, sensory, or cognitive limitations so they enjoy an unprecedented (for this class) degree of opportunity to participate in society—in work, in education, in public and family life. The success of their movements is manifested variously: for instance, in the increasing availability of curb ramps and wheelchair taxis, the appearance of televised subtitle captions to translate aural into visual communication, or the tightening of Internet standards to ensure that graphical user interfaces do not keep digitized information from the voice-output computers used by visually impaired individuals.

These are among the displays of their presence that now combat the historical invisibility of persons with disabilities. They emerge in a climate suited to dislodge the traditional practices that subordinate individuals with disabilities to hostile social and built environ-ments. For the adaptive devices listed above reverse the expectation that impaired individuals should conform to the environment by accepting the limitations their disabilities impose if they cannot overcome them. Mandating accessibility—requiring that cities ramp curbs, that television sets contain caption decoders, that software manufacturers attach alt-tags to graphics—furthers the idea that where exclusionary circumstance bars the disabled, their isolation must be remedied by making the environment more accommodating to them.

V. TWO KINDS OF DISABILITY RIGHTS

Claims made by and for persons with disabilities as to their rights arrange themselves in two broad categories, each with its own history and each reflecting a different model of disability. Into the first category fall rights assigned to compensate impaired individuals for their natural disadvantages. In contrast, rights encompassed by the second category protect against artificial disadvantages, those society imposes on disabled people because of their impairments. Which of these holds more promise for ameliorating the historic isolation of people with disabilities will depend on whether their marginalization is the inescapable result of their own unalterable deficits or, instead, grows out of hostile social arrangements that can be rectified.

To analyze claims for disability rights (or for that matter any group-differentiated rights that pertain to being in a minority), it is useful to bring together the perspectives of those who would claim such rights with those who would be constrained by the selfsame claims. Assessing assertions about disability rights then will turn on seeing what claims both are useful in advancing the disabled minority and also exert a compelling call on the nondisabled majority.

So, first, the comparative plausibility of the two broad approaches to disability rights will be influenced by what the majority of individuals, those with no serious physical, sensory, or cognitive deficit, consider they could owe to the minority, that is, to people who are in physical, sensory, or cognitive deficit. And, second, the relative importance of these kinds of rights will depend on what the minority, that is, those who are impaired, imagines the majority to owe them. Third, the coherence of these perspectives will emerge from how well each group's members understand how the members of the other group are situated.

Combining these criteria suggests that strong disability rights are those advanced by the disabled, appreciated by the nondisabled, and framed by a realistic and respectful mutual understanding. To the extent claims of rights pertaining to being disabled meet these conditions, they will be both important and plausible.

While not inconsistent, the two broad approaches to disability rights are unlikely to prove equally important and plausible in application. For the view of impairment embedded in the first category of disability rights implies that sheltering the disabled from social responsibility is protective of them, while for the second category it is prejudicial to isolate the disabled from the usual social demands. As well, whether the preferable program is to level the social playing field in ways that afford fair access to social participation by people with disabilities, or whether it is unrealistic to expect these individuals to take the field at all, let alone triumph on it, turns on whether the disadvantages consequent upon their limitations are contingent or necessary, artificial or natural.

And responses to these questions raise further issues. If it is the constructed physical and social environment that converts their limitations into defects, what claim does the disabled minority have on the nondisabled majority for shelter from such socially imposed disadvantage? On the other hand, if being physically, sensorily, or cognitively impaired makes individuals naturally inferior, does any ground other than compassion incline the nondisabled majority to offer compensatory benefits to the disabled minority?

A. Entitlements and Exemptions

Of the two broad groupings of disability rights, the more familiar is organized by the idea that the disabled are owed benefits correlative to their natural disadvantages. Claims of this sort often are institutionalized as entitlements or exemptions. To illustrate, in Canada discrimination based on disability is globally prohibited under broad national and provincial constitutional and human rights law, whereas special specific entitlements and exemptions to compensate for disability include medical and disability tax credits, disability benefits for those eligible under the Canada Pension Plan, extended social assistance for those whom disability places in long-term need or renders unemployable, and services and care under various provincial social service and private insurance plans.

"From the thirteenth century," writes Deborah Stone in *The Disabled State,* "it has been widely held that indulging, exempting or shielding (people with disabilities), or placing them in specially protective care, is more realistically to their benefit than giving them access to merely equal treatment" (Stone, 1984). However,

it is an error to imagine that pure beneficence prompts the assignment of this category of rights. For it is as a convenience for the able bodied that the earliest instances of protective or compensatory disability rights appear. With the breakdown of feudalism in Europe in the thirteenth and fourteenth centuries, laboring people gained geographical mobility, yet the need for place-bound laborers remained pressing. Consequently, laws were enacted which forbade able-bodied working persons from traveling from town to town without special authorizing documents.

But disabled individuals were exempted and encouraged to depart in order to afford able-bodied persons relief from their protracted presence. From the able-bodied's point of view, this provision could be viewed as a dispensation to a privileged class, while for the disabled it was a mechanism for expelling them from the ranks of workers. Thus, the exception granted individuals in virtue of a disability operated not so much to liberate this minority as to free others from having to interact with persons regarded as nonproductive. (Het Dorp, the Dutch village for disabled people, is a contemporary manifestation of the propensity for isolating these individuals from other people. Originated in the 1960s as a self-contained community that would allow disabled people to manage their own affairs, it became widely viewed as a "disabled ghetto" because it could not escape imposing an "institutional" life-style on its inhabitants. Like other institutions intended to shelter the disabled, Het Dorp could not escape being a totalizing environment.) Observing that sheltering the disabled frees the nondisabled from having to interact with them introduces a more generalized thought about compensatory rights, namely, that the nondisabled confer entitlements on the disabled for their own advantage, not to advance those less fortunate.

In the West, modernizing laws reconceived persons with quite different disabilities by grouping them into a single inferior class, one that the dominant class found it to its own advantage to treat exceptionally, and one that consequently excited the envy of other subordinated groups. From this institutionalizing process emerged the concept of "the disabled." Simultaneously, groups like the guilds of the blind who joined together to hire guides, work at certain crafts, and visit the sick disappeared in Western Europe. (But guilds of blind musicians and fortune-tellers survived for many further centuries in China; and in Japan guilds of blind acupuncturists, and of masseurs who often doubled as money-lenders, flourished from the seventeenth century onward. Members of these organizations were offered special opportunity to practice their professions, much as in the United States today food concessions in state buildings often are reserved for lease by blind vendors.)

In Western countries, then, protection for the disabled shifted (to some degree) from a private and family-centered responsibility to a public duty of charity. How generously this obligation is satisfied has become a sign of the community's affluence as well as its compassion. (In other places in the world, however, the locus of care for people with disabilities remains family and kin, whose reputations depend on how well they bear their burden.)

By the seventeenth century, the virtue of according charitable benevolence to those in need clashed outright with the fear of creating a class of drones. Consequently, there emerged the idea that individuals with physical, sensory, or cognitive impairments were "deserving" poor, those who would have worked but for their unfortunate impairments. These were people whose families should have cared for them, but who were forced to turn for care to the state, thereby displacing their expectation of support from an affectional to an institutional object. (This idea is widely preserved today, for instance, in contemporary Swedish law, which counts the disabled, along with children, the elderly and immigrants, as a "weak" group with whose special protection local governments are charged.) To be a member of this class was to be preferred to the undeserving, willfully malfunctioning poor, although careful attention to character was mandated to keep a disabled person from slipping over the line.

Although thought to be owed care, the disabled had to be treated so as to make their condition seem unattractive to those capable of work. So any claim they had for obtaining subsistence or care came to depend on their abandoning claims to self-determination. That is, to be considered as deserving of support they did not earn, the disabled had to be thought of as incompetent and to accept the restrictions this designation entails. For instance, in view of their definitively deficient state, the disabled could not be envisioned as sufficiently responsible to use whatever means charity bestowed on them effectively. So another social group emerged: care-givers, persons whose profession it became to channel charity by administering it properly to damaged individuals.

1. The Right to Be Sheltered

Thus, as a social class, the disabled have been defined not only as nonproductive but they are the means of production for members of another group, professional care-givers. To demonstrate their commitment to contain the costs of benevolent practices, to discourage drones, and to prove their competent professionalism, care-takers need to alter some of their charges so that they no longer claim to need care. To mitigate the risk of rehabilitation's depleting the supply of those to be cared for, institutionalized care-taking also tends to see more and more types of persons as inadvertently rather than intentionally unproductive and to contend that they have a right to continued support befitting their disadvantage.

But to exercise this right may be to retreat from claiming other rights, namely, one's prerogative to be a self-esteeming, self-respecting, self-determining agent. This is the cost of making claims to be entitled to care plausible to one's prospective care takers. In Sweden, for example, the *boendeservice* system provides centralized attendant service in semi-institutional settings for seriously disabled people. To try to gain a competitive edge over other residents so as to obtain a higher priority for their personal care, residents vie with each other to develop personalities that are nonoffensive and appealing to the staff. Proposals to adopt the independent living model disseminated by the World Institute of Disability (housed in Oakland, California) have met with skepticism about whether disabled people can manage their attendant care by themselves.

More than a quarter-century ago, Robert Scott studied the behavior of visually impaired people who were dependent on social agencies and reported his findings in *The making of blind men: A study of adult socialization.* Scott observed that in a system in which being cared for is the primary way the disabled relate to the able-bodied, it becomes socially incumbent upon the former to profess incompetence even where they are more competent than the former. Ron Amundson expands on this point:

> the "sick role" ... relieves a person of normal responsibilities, but carries other obligations with it. The sick person is expected to ... Regard his or her condition as undesirable. These requirements resonate with the attitudes of society towards disabled people.... One interesting correlation is that able bodied people are often offended by disabled people who appear satisfied or happy with their condition. A mood of regret and sadness is socially expected (Amundson, 1982).

In a social environment arranged to defy their very survival, individuals with disabilities may place a premium on cultivating their entitlement to protection and support from the nondisabled. But confining themselves to a subservience that prevents their fully flourishing may be the price the disabled have to pay for the nondisabled to acknowledge these claims for care. Consequently, once their survival is guaranteed, as is more securely the case in the most highly economically developed nations, self-determination and independent living become increasingly attractive as the primary goals. (While some argue that the eugenics-driven Nazi eradication of people with disabilities shows how survival is the single important issue for people with disabilities regardless of the economic context, others point to the post-World War I economic stresses in Germany as at least partially responsible for this atrocity, which, of course, expanded to engulf other minority groups.)

B. Equality

In contrast, the second broad grouping of disability rights presumes that people with disabilities are equal to the nondisabled in their capacity to flourish in competitive environments. The historian Joan Scott remarks: "Equality, in the political theory of rights that lies behind the claims of excluded groups for justice, means the ignoring of differences between individuals ... This presumes a social agreement to consider obviously different people as equivalent ..." (1990. Deconstructing equality-versus-difference. In M. Hirsch & E. F. Keller, *Conflicts in feminism*. New York and London: Routledge).

But the differences attendant upon serious impairment so resist being thus dismissed through social agreement that it is hard, and perhaps even inappropriate, to conceptualize individuals with disabilities as identical to others. Even the most powerful democratic theory may offer people who are impaired no more than a pretense of equality. In this regard, the philosopher Charles Taylor comments:

The basis for our intuitions of equal dignity (is) a universal human potential, a capacity that all humans share.... our sense of the importance of potentiality reaches so far that we extend this protection even to people who through some circumstance that has befallen them are incapable of realizing their potential in the normal way—handicapped people ... for instance (Taylor, C. 1992. *Multiculturalism and the politics of recognition*. Princeton: Princeton University Press).

From this perspective equality seems to be no more than a fiction for whoever cannot or will not be homogenized or function in the normal way. But whether giving differences their due means we must retreat from the goal of inclusiveness is equally a troubling question. In respect to physical, sensory and cognitive impairment, how do we satisfy a principle of neutrality (understood as the requirement to be indifferent to difference) toward disability without victimizing the disabled person by inappropriately disregarding how her needs, expectations, and outcomes differ on account of her limitations?

1. Equal Protection and Civil Rights

The 1990 Americans With Disabilities Act constitutes an attempt to resolve this dilemma of difference by making the equal protection guaranteed to citizens by the U.S. Constitution's Fourteenth Amendment meaningful to individuals whose physical or mental impairments substantially limit one or more major life activities. The ADA offers legal recourse against the prevalent propensity to view such impairments as excusing the inferior treatment of those who endure them. The ADA establishes both a ground and a process that liberates the disabled minority from social arrangements that artificially disadvantage the members of this class.

The ADA takes a minimalist approach to achieving social equality for the disabled: it constrains the nondisabled majority from actions that deny the disabled access to opportunity for social participation. In enacting the ADA, the United States Congress determined that:

historically, society has tended to isolate and segregate individuals with disabilities, and despite some improvements, such forms of discrimination against individuals with disabilities continue to be a serious and pervasive social problem ... individuals with disabilities ... have been faced with restrictions and limitations, subjected to a history of purposeful unequal treatment, and relegated to a position of political powerlessness in our society based on characteristics that are beyond the control of such individuals and resulting from stereotypic assumptions not truly indicative of the individual ability of such individuals to participate in, and contribute to society.

The American Congress diagnosed that "the continuing existence of unfair and unnecessary discrimination and prejudice denies people with disabilities the opportunity to compete on an equal basis and to pursue those opportunities for which our free society is justly famous." The Congress declared that "the Nation's proper goals regarding individuals with disabilities are to assure equality of opportunity, full participation, independent living, and economic self-sufficiency." The ADA gives all those who have or are regarded as having a physical or mental impairment that substantially limits major life activities the right to invoke legal protection against being denied participation in employment, public services, and public accommodations.

Although the right to be protected against discrimination based on one's perceived or actual disability may not seem to be an aggressively affirmative approach to equalizing, it actually is quite a "thick" right. For the ADA famously designates as discriminatory failures to adjust environments that otherwise exclude the participation of qualified individuals with disabilities. So equal protection here gives people with physical, sensory, and cognitive limitations claim under American law to extensive modifications of existing practices and sites that currently debar them. Thus, the ADA levels without homogenizing, for leveling the entrance to a building so as to make it accessible does not erase the differences in how guide-dog owners, wheelchair users, and Olympic sprinters travel through it.

In the everyday life of persons mobilizing in wheelchairs, their inequality, both as experienced by them and in the eyes of others, manifests itself not in the inability to walk but in exclusion from bathrooms, from theaters, from transportation, from places of work, and from life-saving medical treatment. Suppose that most persons used wheelchairs? Would we not have built ramps rather than staircases? Suppose most were deaf? Closed-captioning would be open and would have been the standard for television manufacture in the United States long before July 1, 1993.

The ADA sets neutralizing the historical inequality of people with disabilities as the benchmark against which to assess whether current practice is just. By hypothesizing what social arrangements would be in place were persons with disabilities dominant rather than suppressed, so that the arranged environment (both physical and social) welcomes rather than ignores them, it becomes evident that systematic social exclusion of the disabled is a consequence not of their natural inferiority but of their minority status.

Failure to provide accommodation illegitimately impinges on the negative freedom of disabled users. That is, the absence of access to transportation limits impaired people's ability to compete for employment and other social goods. The limitation is arbitrary: access to this social necessity is absent only because impaired people happen to be a disregarded minority rather than an influential majority. Were a majority rather than a minority of users disabled, the initial

designs of public transportation would have had to accommodate them or there would have been too few riders. As an expression of the right to equal protection, the ADA requires that the disabled be given at least whatever access is readily achievable, for it is even more egregiously arbitrary to deny easily realized access. (On a case-by-case basis, access more difficult to achieve may also be required.)

Related legislation adopted by the U.S. Congress offers added insight into the discrimination against disability that must be arrested if the disabled are to increase their social participation. For instance, the 1988 Air Carriers Act intervenes to relieve travelers with physical or sensory impairments from being ill treated on the basis of their disability. This legislation, fleshed out by Department of Transportation regulations, gives passengers a claim to have certain kinds of adaptive equipment, such as wheelchairs and guide dogs, treated as extensions of their bodies rather than as luggage. The Act also constrains airlines from imposing special restraints on the travel of passengers with disabilities in the absence of demonstration that the particular passenger poses a specific hazard. This provision protects people with disabilities from the injurious consequences of being stigmatized as burdensomely or dangerously incompetent travelers just because they are disabled.

From a public policy point of view, the ADA, the Air Carriers Act, and similar legislation (such as the United Kingdom's 1995 Disability Discrimination Act) focus on acting affirmatively to maintain a replete array of alternative or adaptive modes of accessing the usual social options. This strategy protects individuals from being denied, for no other reason than that they are or are thought to be disabled, access to opportunities provided for everyone else. But the mandate is to respond only in order to repair the social arrangements that marginalize people with disabilities. To satisfy their other needs, they must pursue opportunity just as other people do.

Consequently, although they respond to the historical exclusion that makes employment available to only a small percentage of individuals with disabilities, neither the ADA nor the DDA mandate the provision of compensatory income for people with disabilities. For there is no reason to think that such an arrangement would obtain were the disabled the majority instead of the minority. Were most people disabled, it would surely be very difficult for the able-bodied minority to care for and sustain so many of them. Were the nondisabled in the minority, it is less rather than more likely that they could guarantee to provide subsistence for the disabled. Nor is there anything arbitrary or inequitable in their supplying no such care.

2. Equal Capability and Distributive Rights

To model disability rights on civil rights presumes that the disabled are capable of flourishing without special care just as long as they have meaningful access to social opportunity. That is, if freed from arbitrary barriers, they will fare as well as the nondisabled in a competitive environment. But is this realistic? To some it seems a dangerous delusion.

Equality of opportunity, it is argued, can do no more than level a field on which only the highest-functioning impaired people can thrive. If left to compete with the nondisabled on a level playing field, they suppose, most impaired people, and particularly those with the most limited physical and/or cognitive capacity, are incapable of advancing even if barriers vanish. The civil rights model thus seems to favor those who are capable of functioning competitively as long as the environment supports their alternative or adaptive modes of functioning. (The DDA excludes from protection those who, however impaired, nevertheless function sufficiently competitively to avoid unfavorable treatment. It focuses on those whose impairments elicit unfavorable treatment from employers and thus do less well than they would if their environment did not resist the participation of people with disabilities.) But it ignores those whose impairments make them incapable of competitive functioning. If this is so, appealing to equality seems not to go very far in increasing the social participation of people with disabilities.

However, freedom to function unimpeded by practice or rule does not exhaust the approaches to equalizing functioning. For it is not just by eliminating barriers to alternative or adaptive modes of functioning that transforming social arrangement can transfigure functioning. While it is true that leveling the playing field of opportunity does not automatically level the capabilities that people must possess to profit from opportunity, such mitigating measures as rehabilitative treatment, medication, and orthotic, prosthetic, and other personal assistive devices can improve an impaired person's capabilities so as to raise her level of functioning. But what considerations should decide if such measures are taken?

Supporters of the view that equality must offer more than unrealizable opportunity sometimes suggest that an additional dimension to leveling the playing field exists—namely, that, in a competitive society, equitable social arrangement levels the capability of individuals

to leave the starting gate, even if doing so involves an initial unevenness in how goods and services are allocated. Seeking a principle of equitable distribution of resources, the economist Amartya Sen argues that unequal allocations are intuitively correct if they equalize individuals' capabilities for primary functionings. To illustrate, he finds nothing objectionable in allocating more resources to a needy cripple to buy a wheelchair to raise the level of her mobilizing up to that normal for the society in which she wheels than are given to needy able-bodied individuals who can attain that same degree of mobility with no extraordinary allocation of resources.

This is so even if the impaired individual believes herself as well off as others—that is, as equal to them—regardless of her deficits and will not be gratified to receive a wheelchair. For the point is to empower individuals' capability equitably, not to equalize their outcomes. In this case, providing the wheelchair mitigates the degree to which paralysis impairs the individual's capability to function, that is, to engage in all the activities calling for mobility. In sum, the argument is that democratic values impose a social obligation to equalize people's capability to function well, although whether or not they actually do so falls to them individually.

In this view, then, the appeal to equality gives people with disabilities a distributive claim to whatever mitigating measures will help to normalize their functioning. This claim takes precedence over other people's desires for goods that merely gratify or enhance them. Although some of the remedies such a distributive right secures may be identical to those which otherwise are described as benefits, satisfying a right directed at securing equitable capability to function should not be confused with tendering care. For it is through the lens of paternalism, which presumes the perpetual dependence of people with disabilities, that care is seen as an entitlement, while it is to promote their ultimate independence that the equalization of their capabilities for functioning is proposed.

Normalizing capabilities enhances positive freedom by increasing the scope of a person's functionings. Persons with physical, sensory or cognitive impairments may suffer more than others from defective capabilities (although a wealthy but impaired person conceivably may be more capable than a poor but able-bodied one). If this is so, people with disabilities may have greater occasion than others to seek to be restored or rehabilitated through mitigating measures. Nevertheless, a right is not group-differentiated just because members of a particular group are more likely than others to exercise it. A right pertains not to some persons but to everyone alike if all equally can exercise it should the occasion arise to do so.

In 1993, the United Nations endorsed a set of principles about the human rights of people with disabilities. This resolution, called the "Standard Rules on the Equalization of Opportunities for Persons with Disabilities" is not binding on member countries but is considered an expression of enlightened policy. Focused on securing full social participation for people with disabilities, with meaningful exercise of the rights enjoyed by others, this document somewhat indiscriminately recommends all of the approaches to rights we have discussed here. But it cautions that compensatory support systems can have a chilling effect on whether people with disabilities are offered and seek opportunity for employment.

3. The Right to Health Care

If persons with disabilities have a right to rehabilitation because their impairments reduce their capability to function sufficiently well to compete, then whosoever is equivalently reduced in capability should equally enjoy a claim to restoration. This makes health care that restores functioning a social good because it is an important instrument for furthering democratic ends. On this idea is based the view that restorative health care is a right secured by considerations of distributive justice. Preventative health care, understood to be an effective means to containing the costs of restorative health care, becomes in this view a derivative but similarly important right.

But for individuals with disabilities something troubling attaches to assigning an egalitarian purpose to the provision of health care. It appears to be the desire to be freed from the company of the disabled that informs claims on the just distribution of means for achieving normal capabilities. That is, if impairment causes inequality by reducing personal capabilities, but public policy drives toward securing equality through restoring personal capability, then to achieve equality is, ultimately, to eliminate or circumvent impairment. For people with disabilities, justice demands a cure. For people without disabilities, the existence of incurables is perceived as a failure of justice.

But many persons with disabilities cannot be fully or even significantly restored. So unlike the right to equal access to the social and built environment, the right to equal capability to function whatever the environment fails to address individuals who cannot achieve normal capability through restorative treatment or mitigating means. This is because the latter approach levels by erasing rather than by embracing difference.

The civil rights approach advances those who despite their impairments can function competitively, albeit not normally, but fails those whose impairments prevent their functioning competitively. In contrast, the distributive rights approach advances those who can be restored to normal function but fails those who cannot be. Moreover, by equating being equal with being normal, and thereby elevating normal functioning over alternative or adaptive functioning, the latter approach undercuts the former one.

Additionally, there is an unsettling similarity between the distributive rights approach's emphasis on approximating normal functioning and the importance that quality of life metrics likewise attach to being normal. Treatment allocation procedures that rely on so-called quality of life measures notoriously deny health care and other goods to the disabled on the ground that impaired individuals' compromised capabilities help but reduce their overall well-being below that of "normal" people, making them less attractive candidates for the allocation of any benefit that must be rationed. In health care allocation systems that rely on these quality of life metrics, being impaired in some ways that defy medical restoration automatically threatens one's eligibility for various kinds of care because the system's conceptual framework assumes that to be impaired is without question to have an inferior life.

For the irreparably impaired, it is difficult to see why the distributive right to be returned to normal is a more effective route to equality than is the civil right to command respect despite abnormality. How can laying claim to the right to be altered so as not to be an individual with a disability be central to any person's self-respecting self-identity as an individual with a disability? Thus, promoting the equitable distribution of capabilities does not also argue for recognizing a group-differentiated right pertaining to the disabled minority.

Rather, the distributive rights model invites homogenizing. For both those who are impaired and those not yet so, this approach to equality promotes the right to be free of the disabled minority. This is not to deny that the disabled and the nondisabled equally may have a claim on rehabilitative health care. It is only to say that if access to health care is considered a right for anybody, it must be presumed to be a right of able-bodied and disabled equally, albeit one that individuals with disabilities may exercise more frequently.

VI. EQUALITY OR ENTITLEMENT?

Contemporary approaches to disability rights are centered by the notion that people with disabilities are owed social inclusion through full recognition of, rather than despite, their impairments. From this perspective, nothing could be further from a compliment than telling an impaired person "I never think of you as disabled because you have overcome your limitations." The imagery of overcoming is much associated with disabled people who, through courage and good character, transcend their seeming limits.

But for those who cannot undertake or do not aspire to such a strenuous style of life, rights that can be exercised only in virtue of heroic striving appear at best vacuous. Appealing to equality to guide public policy regarding people with disabilities is feared to be a retreat from policies that shelter them back to policies that are indifferent toward them. There is all the difference in the world between conceiving of people with disabilities as equal and thereby as deserving only such special treatment as is needed to reform social practice that excludes them, and thinking of them as deficient and thereby as deserving of special benefits, entitlements and exemptions to sustain them in their exclusion. Policies informed by the former view controvert the beliefs about people with disabilities that motivate the latter view; policies that promote the latter view enfeeble the attitudes needed to implement the former view.

These conflicts surface clearly in worries about the effectiveness of the U.K.'s Disability Discrimination Act. In spirit, the DDA resembles the ADA. The DDA is animated by the conviction that systematically less favorable treatment is the cause of the inferior social participation of people with disabilities. Deleterious differential treatment of people because of their disabilities is discriminatory under this law if it can be removed or made insubstantial by a reasonable adjustment, or if it cannot be justified. (Some feel that the DDA is weaker and vaguer than the ADA. Its national enforcement mechanisms differ markedly, but to a great extent this arises because employee complaints are handled differently in the U.K. than in U.S. employment law. The DDA relies much more heavily on the well-developed U.K. mechanisms for employment grievance resolution and adjudication, while the ADA invokes antidiscrimination regulatory action fashioned to enforce earlier civil rights legislation.)

A. Individual and Collective Rights

In the United States, people with disabilities struggled for equality in exercising the individual rights assured by the U.S. Constitution, while in the United Kingdom people with disabilities struggled for the collective right to control the services provided by the social service system. Vic Finkelstein, organizer of the U.K.'s Open University's course, "The Disabling Society," remarks that the emphasis on individual rights issued in fewer services but strengthened disabled individuals' power to control them (including the appointment of people with disabilities to positions of power within the social service system) while the emphasis on collective rights resulted in a much more comprehensive service system but with no ground for individual control.

In the United Kingdom, enhanced attention to individual disability rights has been cotemporaneous with the curtailment of the welfare system. For instance, with the coming of the DDA the British Government repealed several key elements of the 1944 Disabled Persons (Employment) Act, including the employment quota system that required employers to reserve 3% of their labor force for workers with disabilities. In theory, the DDA should eliminate those discriminatory practices that bar people with disabilities from social participation so as to reduce the need for such entitlements.

But critics point with despair to the DDA's lack of independent enforcement mechanisms. They believe the British public long has recognized discrimination against people with disabilities but has no desire to stop it. Therefore, to rely on the normal protection afforded by, for instance, the Industrial Tribunal, while abandoning the special protection of sheltered work situations is unrealistic, the critics insist.

B. Disability, Competence, Compensation

This debate illustrates that the difficult choice facing people with disabilities is not just how to seek their rights but, even more fundamentally, which kind of rights to seek. The conflict within U.S. law between the ADA and worker compensation provisions portrays the problem plainly. Although the regulations are consistent in language, the conceptions of disability that underlie them prove incompatible in application. The benefits obtainable under worker's compensation accrue in virtue of impaired individuals being conceived of as unable to work, while the protections afforded under the ADA depend on impaired individuals being conceived of as fully qualified to work.

Physicians diagnosing disability for the purpose of obtaining work injury compensation are trained to emphasize how great a loss of competence the worker has suffered. But in so doing, they document that the worker cannot perform tasks essential to the job, thereby establishing that it is far from discriminatory to deny employment to this person whom disability disqualifies from work. U.S. courts also have been loathe to prohibit an employer who is compensating a worker for being too impaired to do a job from considering the impairment in relation to other job assignments the worker may seek. At root, conflicts between worker's compensation rights and ADA rights are propelled by antithetical beliefs as to the competence of the disabled.

C. The Right to Education

In general, claims of people with disabilities to special benefits and to equal opportunities clash because the public is conflicted as to whether to interact with impaired individuals as equals or instead as dependents with special needs. In the United States, this debate is played out in the educational development of youngsters with disabilities. The Individuals With Disabilities Education Act (covering grades K through 12) provides that the learning needs of students with disabilities be met, where "needs" are understood to include separate settings if required and skills (such as toileting) usually acquired prior to entry into formal schooling. On the other hand, the Americans With Disabilities Act (covering all public and private providers of educational programs) makes no provision for special needs of students with disabilities but requires that reasonable accommodation be made to give them access to whatever programs benefit nondisabled students.

Under the IDEA, sign language interpreters are considered a support for those deaf youngsters who cannot otherwise perform adequately in school but not necessarily a right of those whose performance is at least average despite having only the partial access to information to be obtained through lip reading. But under the ADA, sign language interpreters are considered a necessity for all deaf youngsters regardless of how well they perform in the absence of signers; the assumption is that those who perform well without signers nevertheless deserve the opportunity to excell by having the same full access to information their hearing peers enjoy.

However, under the IDEA, learning disabled students receive academic coaching if they claim this as a special need. Under the ADA, regardless of learning disabled students' needs, tutoring is required for them only if there are tutoring programs for all students, in which case learning disabled students conceivably could prevail in claiming that tutoring must be available in a form equitably accessible to them. Because the IDEA does not extend through university level, whereas the ADA covers all educational programs regardless of level, disabled students who have been accustomed to having their needs met in special programs offered by their schools sometimes lack the skills of self-reliance needed to pursue equal access to regular programs.

Their difficulty manifests another aspect of the dilemma faced by activists who desire to extend and expand the scope of group-differentiated rights pertaining to the disabled. The choice lies between competing as a group for benefits that minimally support all but fail to cultivate the development of the most talented, and competing individually for opportunities that have been opened to all but fail to support the well-being of the least talented. This division is another example of the gap between group-specific rights to outcomes and group-specific rights to opportunities.

D. The Right to Life and the Right to Die

Access to life and control over life are the most fundamental opportunities in the human experience. Whether people have a right to live and to die regardless of disability is a matter of much controversy that divides disabled people from each other and from the general public as well. In the United States, some disabled individuals with nonterminal conditions have sought court approval of their right to have assistance in dying.

They argue that their suffering is unbearable, either in virtue of their medical condition, or else because society forces them into a useless and isolated dependence. They deny that anyone is obligated to continue suffering to satisfy other people's aversions and fears regarding death. They urge that if their lives are not their own, they should at least enjoy autonomy in deciding whether to live or to die and that their bodies should be at their own disposal in, at least, this ultimate case. In making this argument, they express a distaste for feeling and being felt to be burdensome, an attitude that a 1996 Gallup poll identified as the prevalent reason half of the American public favors assisted suicide.

In the past, U.S. courts have been disposed to agree with such arguments. Some decisions hold to be assisted to die is an equitable application of the acknowledged right to refuse life-saving treatment. Other courts see individuals as entitled to dispose of their lives because there is no state interest sufficiently strong to deprive them of this right. Against this it now is argued on appeal that the state has an interest in protecting those most vulnerable from being killed.

In this regard, some prominent disability activists

deplore the ease with which both the courts and the public assume that suffering certain kinds of impairments certifies the rationality of killing one's self. These activists see the legalization of assisted dying in nonterminal cases as telling disabled people they are obligated to die in order to relieve others from the burdens of caring for them. Because they are subject to so much repression and contempt in their daily lives, they feel these attitudes must also be embedded in the desire of nondisabled people to facilitate death for persons regarded as incurable. They rightly recollect that the Nazi extermination of unwanted kinds of people was initiated by a program of mercy killing which targeted people with disabilities. And they regard the traditional social practices of sterilizing people with disabilities (regardless of whether their conditions were inheritable) or denying them the right to marry as equally revealing of how the lives of people with disabilities have been devalued.

Disability rights activists are more divided in rejecting the practice of abortion. For the public at large is more convinced of the rationality of terminating a fetus because it might be impaired than about the rationality of terminating a person who actually is impaired. So it would seem that abortion, not assisted death, is the more frequent locus of rejection of life with disability and consequently that its unopposed practice is more critical in sanctioning the social disregard of people with disabilities. But disability activists tend to focus their fears more narrowly on the technology for identifying individuals as potentially disabled, for instance, the mechanisms for genetic testing and counseling.

And they are not alone in their uneasiness about the social consequences of the current genemapping effort (the Human Genome Project). The social consequences of being divulged to be potentially impaired while one is yet healthy and functioning appear so threatening as to recommend to many that this research be curtailed. For it is widely acknowledged that to be labeled potentially disabled, even if one is not yet nor certainly so, is so devaluing in other people's eyes as to diminish one's self-esteem and reduce the quality of one's life.

The extent to which individuals whose disability has yet to actualize are protected by current law from discrimination responsive to their prospective conditions is still obscure. (Amendments to provide protection through the DDA against discrimination based on future disability were consistently defeated. Current case law is insufficient to determine whether the ADA offers protection against discrimination provoked by the results of genetic testing.)

VII. REFORMING PHILOSOPHICAL DISCOURSE TO SPEAK CLEARLY OF DISABILITY

Legislation like the DDA and the ADA precedes philosophy by outlawing the inferior or less favorable treatment of individuals in virtue of their impairments. But if legislative action is to transform both personal expectation and social practice, philosophy must uncover a powerful and persuasive theoretical commonality of experience that bridges impairment without invoking the normalizing imagination. This will be an experiential core expressed through a discourse freed from the tyranny of the normalizing standard.

A discourse purged of disability discrimination will recoil from conflating impairment with having fewer rights or less competence to exercise one's rights. A discourse liberated from disability discrimination will not compel or facilitate inferences to the inferiority or the exclusion of people with disabilities, nor presume them to be incompetent. A discourse revised to combat disability discrimination will frame policy language that promotes, rather than precludes, equitable levels of social participation by people with disabilities.

This program challenges the discourse developed to convey modern philosphy's obsession with normalizing. But having engineered a rationalist discourse that disregards difference so as to diminish whoever is irritatingly so, one from which people with disabilities disappear whenever talk turns to justice, happiness, or self-realization, philosophy now owes the disabled a language in which to speak of them does not predispose that we must speak ill. In such a reformed way of speaking, we will be much clearer about how to assign disability rights, and how to assume disability responsibilities as well.

Also See the Following Articles

DEATH, MEDICAL ASPECTS OF • DISCRIMINATION, CONCEPT OF • DISTRIBUTIVE JUSTICE, THEORIES OF • RIGHTS THEORY

Bibliography

Amundson, R. (1992). Disability, handicap, and the environment. *Journal of Social Philosophy* **23** (1).

Bickenbach, J. (1993). *Physical disability and social policy.* Toronto and London: University of Toronto Press.

Colker, R. (in press). *Hypercapitalism.* New York: New York University Press.

DeJong, G. (1984). *Independent living & disability policy in the Netherlands: Three models of residential care & independent living.* New York: World Rehabilitation Fund.

Doyle, B. (1996). *Disability discrimination: The new law*. Bristol: Jordans Publishing Ltd.

Hahn, H. (1987). Civil rights for disabled Americans: The foundation of a political agenda. In A. Gartner and T. Joe (Eds.), *Images of the disabled, disabling images*. New York: Praeger.

Jones, M. & Marks, L. E. (Eds.). (in press). *Disability divers(ability) and legal change*. Dordrecht and Norwell, MA: Kluwer.

Kavka, G. (1992). Disability and the right to work. *Social Philosophy and Policy 9* (1).

Miles, M. (1996). Community, individual or information development? Dilemmas of concept and culture in South Asian disability planning. *Disability & Society, 11* (4), pp. 485–500.

Minow, M. (1990). *Making all the difference: Inclusion, exclusion and American law*. Ithaca and London: Cornell University Press.

Morris, J. (1991). *Pride against prejudice*. Philadelphia: New Society Publishers.

Oliver, M. (1990). *The politics of disablement: A sociological approach*. New York: St. Martin's Press.

Rioux, M. (1991). Exchanging charity for rights. *Entourage, 6* (2).

Rioux, M. (1994). Towards a concept of equality of well-being: Overcoming the social and legal construction of inequality In M. Rioux and M. Bach (Eds.), *Disability is not measles: New research paradigms in disability*. Ontario: L'Institut Roeher Institute.

Silvers, A. (1994, June). Defective agents: equality, difference and the tyranny of the normal. *The Journal of Social Philosophy*. Twenty-fifth anniversary issue.

Silvers, A. (1995). Reconciling equality to difference: caring (f)or justice for people with disabilities. *Hypatia*. Special Issue on Feminist Ethics and Social Policy. P. DiQuinzo and I. Marion Young (Eds.).

Silvers, A. (in press). Women and disability. In A. Jaggar & I. M. Young (Eds.), *The Blackwell's companion to feminist philosophy*. Oxford: Blackwell's.

Stone, D. (1984). *The disabled state*. Philadelphia: Temple University Press.

United Nations, (1993). *Standard rules on the equalization of opportunities for persons with disabilities*, G.A. res. 48/96, 48 U.N. GAOR Supp. (No. 49) at 202, U.N. Doc. A/48/49 (1993).

Wendell, S. (1996). *The rejected body: Feminist philosophical reflections on disability*. New York and London: Routledge.

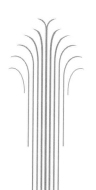

DISCOURSE ETHICS

William Outhwaite
University of Sussex

I. Justification of Norms
II. Applications

GLOSSARY

action, communicative vs. strategic Communicative action is defined by Habermas as action oriented by and/or in pursuit of mutual understanding; strategic action is concerned with manipulating others so as to produce effects, by speech or other means.

communication community A group of scientists or, more broadly, other language users in communication about some subject.

discourse Used by Habermas in a semitechnical sense to refer to the systematic examination of problematized validity claims; also more generally as in "discourse ethics."

ideal speech situation A hypothetical state of optimal communication that would make possible a fully justified consensus; in Habermas's model, an implicit aim of all sincere communication.

performative contradiction A self-refuting utterance such as "I don't exist"; more broadly, a practice such as presenting arguments for the impossibility of rational argumentation.

universalization The principle that moral principles and maxims for action should be applicable to all relevantly similar cases.

universal pragmatics An approach to discourse distinguished by the fact that the utterances (rather than sentences, as in most linguistics) it studies are not tied to specific and variable contexts.

validity claims In addition to specific claims about matters of fact or morality, Habermas claims that all assertoric utterances presuppose the intelligibility, truth, legitimacy, and sincerity of their assertion.

DISCOURSE ETHICS or communicative ethics is an ethical theory, or more precisely a theory of the justification or grounding of moral norms. It was developed from the mid-1970s by the German social philosophers Karl-Otto Apel, Jürgen Habermas, Albrecht Wellmer, and others, and it was taken up in the 1980s by a number of American theorists, notably Seyla Benhabib, Kenneth Baynes, Thomas McCarthy, and William Rehg.

I. JUSTIFICATION OF NORMS

Both Apel and Habermas were concerned with the developing of contemporary philosophy of language, in particular John Austin's speech act theory, as extended by John Searle and others, into a basis for a critical social theory opposed both to empiricist social science (and technocratic social planning) and to its counterpart, as they saw it, in emotivist theories of moral discourse. One of Apel's first contributions to discourse ethics, "The *a priori* of the communication community and the foundations of ethics," forms a metaethical complement to an earlier article on "The communication community as the transcendental presupposition for the social sciences." Apel's strategy has been to derive a "transcendental-pragmatic" foundation for ethical principles from an analysis of the preconditions of argumentation: "The logical validity of arguments cannot be tested without, in principle, positing a community of scholars who are capable of both intersubjective communication and reaching a consensus." The communication community is a precondition of scientific inquiry, dependent as this is on public communication. It also implies a minimal ethics of mutual recognition and the pursuit of agreement on ethical as well as on factual matters: "... the *rational argumentation* that is presupposed not only in every science but also in every discussion of a problem, in itself presupposes the validity of universal, ethical norms."

Apel's argument draws heavily on the American pragmatist philosopher C. S. Peirce. Peirce's "community of scholars," Apel stresses, is necessarily open-ended, because it must include anyone who might make a relevant contribution. An argument such as Apel's relies upon reflection on the pragmatic, as opposed to merely formal, preconditions of human communicative activity. Whereas analytic philosophy focuses on the "*logical (syntactic-semantic) presuppositions for statements or propositions*" a transcendental-pragmatic analysis focuses in a more naturalistic way on the *activities* of communication and argumentation. The "fact of argumentation" provides "an irreducible, quasi-Cartesian starting-point."

This approach can be illustrated by Apel's conception of what he came to call performative contradiction, later taken up and extensively used by Habermas. The sentence "I do not exist" is grammatically correct, but its utterance is paradoxical, as is the utterance of the English sentence "I can't speak English." Similarly, there is a performative contradiction implied in, for example, engaging in argumentation while claiming apodictic certainty for one's own assertions and refusing to countenance opposing views. (We see this, in negative form, when someone refuses to enter into argumentation with a supporter of, say, genocide, on the grounds that to begin discussion would suggest an openness to debate, and a willingness in principle to be convinced, which could not be reasonably expected in such a case.) Argumentation, in other words, simply *means* the problematization of claims in the course of discussion. It is thus a starting point in the sense of an irreducible (*unhintergehbar*) fact that provides the basis for an ultimate justification or grounding (*Letztbegründung*) of certain norms of reciprocity—a minimal ethics.

The communication community is not merely a precondition for a minimal ethics. Apel makes the further claim that communication is also "the indispensable *medium* for the grounding of norms which can achieve consensus." In the modern world, at least, no individual, nor for that matter a ruling party or bureaucracy, can usurp the role and responsibility of the individual moral subject in forming his or her moral judgments "in solidaristic cooperation with others." The notion of individual responsibility is not of course new; it is central to Kant's conception of practical reason. What *is* new, however, is the emphasis on dialogue and cooperation that Apel sees as being no less necessary in moral reflection than in the practice of science. (A Robinson Crusoe's moral reflection on whether he could justifiably kill animals for food would be no less dependent on his earlier socialization in his moral communities of origin than would his linguistic capacity on the language communities in which he had previously lived.)

This second aspect of Apel's arguments has been developed more fully by Jürgen Habermas. Habermas had argued as early as 1973, in *Legitimation Crisis,* that "the validity of all norms is tied to discursive will-formation." As he put it more recently, it is a feature of the modern world that "in place of exemplary instructions in the virtuous life and recommended models of the good life, one finds an increasingly pronounced, abstract demand for a conscious, self-critical appropriation, the demand that one responsibly take possession of one's own individual, irreplaceable, and contingent life history." Habermas is less concerned with, indeed fundamentally skeptical of, Apel's attempt to furnish an ultimate foundation for moral norms. He characterizes his starting point as "universal pragmatics," as distinct from Apel's more directly Kantian expression "transcendental pragmatics." Every use of language in a genuinely communicative context (as opposed to the issuing of orders or the mere production of effects by linguistic means) involves certain presuppositions: that what we say is intelligible, that what we assert or presume to be the case is in fact the case, that we are sincere in what we say and morally entitled to say it. As Habermas shows with the homely example of a professor asking a seminar participant to fetch a glass of water, even a simple request, understood not as a mere demand but "as a speech act carried out in an attitude oriented to understanding," raises claims to normative rightness, subjective sincerity, and factual practicability that may be questioned. The addressee of the request may reject it as illegitimate ("I'm not your servant"), insincere ("You don't really want one"), or mistaken as to its existential preconditions (availability of a source of water). Speech acts can be classified according to the illocutionary effect that is primarily intended by the speaker: Habermas distinguishes between constative (assertoric), expressive (experiential), and regulative (imperatives, intentional sentences, e.g., promises) speech acts and sentence forms. Corresponding to these are what Habermas calls world attitudes: an objectivating, neutral attitude to facts in the world, an expressive attitude to the speaker's own subjective world, and a norm-conformative attitude to legitimate expectations.

At the back of every act of communication is the implication that we can reach a consensus on the validity of these claims. Ultimately, Habermas claims that we can only distinguish, as a matter of principle, between a genuine and a false consensus if we presuppose the possibility of an unconstrained dialogue to which all speakers have equal access and in which only the "force of the better argument prevails." This is what he called for some time the "ideal speech situation." Of course, Habermas admits that actual contexts of argumentation do not often, if ever, correspond to the ideal speech situation. Yet it is more than just a fiction, or a regulative idea in Kant's sense of the term, because we do in fact have to assume its possibility. "So far as we accomplish speech acts at all, we stand under the curious imperatives of that power which, with the honourable title of 'reason' I aim to ground in the structure of possible speech. In this sense I think it is meaningful to speak of an immanent reference to truth in the life-process of society."

Habermas's concept of validity claims covers both the domain of factual truth and that of moral or expressive statements. It is here that Habermas's consensus theory of truth becomes particularly important. Like Apel, Habermas is strongly influenced by Peirce's conception of an ideal community of investigators as the ultimate and counterfactually presupposed reference point for both factual and moral claims. What is true or right is what such a community would assent to after full exposure to all the relevant evidence and an unlimited opportunity to discuss it. Truth, as we have seen, Habermas analyzes as a "validity claim"—indeed the paradigmatic one. The discursive redemption or cashing (Einlösung) of truth claims cannot, Habermas argues, be carried out by a direct comparison of utterances with reality, as postulated by correspondence theories of truth. Propositions are not like pictures, which can be more or less like what they represent; "truth is not a comparative relation." The alleged correspondence between true statements and reality can only be expressed in state-

ments. Truth must therefore be defined in terms of a projected consensus:

> I am entitled to ascribe a predicate to an object if and only if any other person who could enter a discussion with me would ascribe the same predicate to the same object. . . . The condition for the truth of statements is the potential agreement of everyone else. . . .

This may seem a roundabout account of truth compared to one that makes "Habermas is in Frankfurt" true because Habermas is, in fact, in Frankfurt rather than New York. But whatever the problems of this theory, it is easy to see why it appeals to Habermas: first, it embodies a forward reference to an intersubjective consensus, and perhaps to a rational form of life. Second, whereas correspondence theories of truth cannot easily be extended to cover the domains of ethical and aesthetic judgments, such as "murder is wrong" or "château-bottled wine usually tastes nicer than vin ordinaire," it is not impossible to imagine a rationally founded consensus on such judgments. Although, Habermas insists, the validity of norms or the sincerity (Wahrhaftigkeit) of expressions of subjective feelings must not be confused with propositional truth, we do not do justice to the meaning of normative validity if we simply say that truth and falsity are not relevant to ethical statements.

> When I state that one norm should be preferred to another, I aim precisely to exclude the aspect of arbitrariness: rightness and truth come together in that both claims can only be vindicated discursively, by way of argumentation and a rational consensus.

Habermas' model thus contrasts with the ethical subjectivist position according to which moral prescriptions are constrained only by requirements of consistency and practicability. Habermas notes that a discourse ethic is based on the claim "that (a) normative validity claims have a cognitive meaning and can be treated like truth claims, and that (b) the grounding of norms and prescriptions demands the carrying through of an actual dialogue and in the last instance is not possible monologically, in the form of an argumentation process hypothetically run through in the mind." Habermas thus makes two related claims for his discourse ethic. First, that it expresses our moral intuitions, at least as these bear on the process of discursive justification of norms. Second, this focus on normative consensus, as opposed to abstract universalizability means that a discourse ethic, unlike Kant's, can go beyond a pure concept of justice to include the more universal structural aspects of ways of life that relate to communicative action itself. Thus, even a moral philosophy that confines itself to justifying and elucidating the "moral point of view" and avoids preempting the concrete moral decisions of social actors, includes a kind of vision of the good life—at least as a form of life that embodies these modes and norms of moral-political reasoning.

Habermas argues that his model of discursive validation does not apply to all the validity claims raised by speech acts. Understandability, in particular, is not simply raised as a claim that could be satisfied; it has to be satisfied if in fact the communication is to count as successful. Second, the consensus theory of truth, based on the pursuit of consensus, applies only to claims to truth and rightness.

> Claims to sincerity (*Wahrhaftigkeit*) can only be validated in actions. Neither interrogations nor analytic dialogues between doctor and patient can count as discourses in the sense of a cooperative search for truth.

Discourses are themselves of various types: hermeneutic discourses concern questions of interpretation; theoretical-empirical discourses concern "the validity of empirical claims and explanations," and practical discourses concern the application of methodological or other standards.

These forms of discourse are distinguished from those of "aesthetic" or "therapeutic" critique. In therapy, sincerity or insincerity are not *grounded* but *revealed* by consistency or inconsistency with action. And aesthetic judgments do not so much imply the direct grounding of standards of value as the bringing of objects into relation with those standards.

> Above all, however, the type of validity claim attached to cultural values does not transcend local boundaries in the same way as truth and rightness claims. Cultural values do not count as universal; they are, as the name indicates, located within the horizon or lifeworld of a specific group or culture. And values can be made plausible only in the context of a particular form of life.

Habermas's line of argument can thus be seen to run between formal theories of the universalizability of moral judgments and substantively loaded ethical theories (Aristotelian or Hegelian) of the "good life."

Few people would question Habermas's analysis of aesthetic judgments, but that of moral–practical ones is more contentious. In the positivist tradition, or more broadly for any ethical subjectivist position, practical discourse is constrained only at best by requirements of consistency and practicability. Habermas' position here is somewhat equivocal. He is "inclined ... to a cognitivist position," but because he also upholds a consensus theory of truth it is not quite clear what he means here by "cognitivist." He often relies on a reference to the everyday participant's position. "No one would enter into moral argumentation if he did not start from the strong presumption that a grounded consensus could in principle be achieved among those involved." According to the alternative conception, judgments about justice and morality cannot be disentangled from broader ethical conceptions. In other words, Habermas's and Apel's position falls squarely on the battlelines between those who uphold an essentially Kantian notion of universalizability, such as R. M. Hare and, in a related application to social justice, John Rawls, and the "contextualists" or "communitarians" who stress the embeddedness of moral principles in cultures and ways of life, where these are themselves seen as objects as well as sources of moral value. This ongoing controversy is in many ways a replay of the opposition between Hegel and Kant. Habermas's strategy is essentially to socialize Kant's individualistic moral theory in such a way as to meet Hegelian objections, or at least to point in the direction of their resolution, while Apel's position is closer to traditional transcendental philosophy.

Running through his essays of the 1970s is a line of development in Habermas's thought from communicative competence to a broader concept of interactional competence, which in turn develops into a theory of communicative action. One of the central elements of Habermas' theory is the distinction between the genuinely communicative use of language to attain common goals, which Habermas takes to be the primary case of language use and "the inherent telos of human speech," and strategic or success-oriented speech, parasitic on the former, which simulates a communicative orientation in order to achieve an ulterior purpose. Although communicative action is not identical with moral action, it is consistent in some sense with taking the moral point of view and shares some of its basic pragmatic features. Communicative action is oriented both by and toward mutual agreement, including often a consensus on what is to be done.

For Habermas, then, as for Apel, it is precisely the diversity of world views and value systems in the modern world that requires us not to give up on the idea of a universalistic justification of moral norms. Such a justification is provided, Habermas argues, by what he calls the "discourse principle" (D), that norms are valid if "all those affected could agree to them as participants in a rational discourse." This discourse principle can be applied both to morality, the concern of much of Habermas's work in the late 1970s and early 1980s, and to law, to which he has also devoted his attention in his most recent work. As we have seen, he differentiates between moral and more broadly ethical issues on the basis that the former must be assessed in radically universalistic terms, while the latter admit of cultural variation. Ethical issues are concerned, he argues, with the identity and the favored ways of life of specific collectivities. It follows, therefore, that what has come to be called discourse ethics should more properly be called a discourse theory of *morality*. (Habermas has however continued to use the term discourse ethics, as I have done in this article.)

A discourse ethics framed in this way is claimed by its supporters to retain the basic sense of Kantian universalizability, while transferring the locus of universalization from the individual moral subject to the concrete collectivity of those concerned. As Thomas McCarthy put it, "The emphasis shifts from what each can will without contradiction to be a universal law to what all can will in agreement to be a universal norm." Habermas restates the Kantian universalizability criterion in the form of a principle that he calls U, according to which a norm is morally right if "*All* affected can accept the consequences and the side effects its *general* observance can be anticipated to have for the satisfaction of *everyone's* interests (and these consequences are preferred to those of known alternatives." This does justice both to our post-Wittgensteinian sense that the use of language, including moral language, is an intrinsically public activity, and also to the practical point that the best way of ensuring that we take other people's interests and concerns into account is to ask them, rather than second-guess what we take to be their likely response. (Anyone who has missed a meeting and found himself "put down" for some disagreeable task will feel the force of this point.)

Discourse ethics also enables us to meet certain of Hegel's objections to Kant to the effect that moral views are grounded in the discourse and practice of concrete human communities and cannot be addressed in abstaction from them. Discourse ethics thus enables communities to, as it were, draw the practical consequences from this fact by reflecting, in a postconventional way, on their needs and aspirations. What in Hegel is underwritten by the evolutionary advance of the human spirit

becomes a fallible and open-ended, but still hopefully progressive, process of refinement of intuitions and customs. Discourse ethics therefore also reflects the ethical value widely attached to open discussion in modern societies. As Habermas explained in an interview,

> I am not saying that people ought to act communicatively, but that they *must*. When parents educate their children, when living generations appropriate the knowledge handed down by their predecessors, when individuals cooperate, i.e., get on with one another without a costly use of force, they must act communicatively. There are elementary social functions which can only be satisfied by means of communicative action.

Communicative action, he insists, is not the same as argumentation; the latter term denotes specific forms of communication: "islands in the sea of praxis," but the expansion of communicative action at the expense of more authoritarian traditions forms a necessary basis for argumentative discourse to become more widespread. As he put it in another recent work, "What seems to me essential to the degree of liberality of a society is the extent to which its patterns of socialization and its institutions, its political culture, and in general its identity-guaranteeing traditions and everyday practices express a noncoercive form of ethical life in which autonomous morality can be embodied and can take on concrete shape.

At the same time, however, it is not clear how *much* discusssion a discourse ethics commits us to, nor how this might best be institutionalized. Habermas's characteristic response is to point to the variety of fora in modern societies, ranging from academic symposia to television debates and parliamentary assemblies, in which specific moral and ethical issues are argued out. Democratic law-making provides the means to back up and implement certain moral and ethical decisions, as well as those on more technical issues. Democratic legislation operates according to agreed-upon rules, such as majority voting, which in turn may be problematized or modified in certain contexts. (Many constitutions, for example, require more than a simple majority on matters considered particularly important, and the Council of Ministers of the European Community for a long time required unanimity on certain questions.)

As we have seen, Habermas claims that a principle such as (U) 'acts like a knife that makes cuts between "the good" and "the just." This, however, is hardly convincing: it seems clear that a quintessentially "moral" issue such as abortion is also embedded in "ethical" issues to do with the position of women, as was starkly revealed at the time of German reunification by the clash between East and West German abortion law. The practical difficulties of differentiating between moral and ethical issues raises in a sharper form the "Hegelian" or communitarian question of whether discourse ethics, at least in the form represented by Apel and Habermas, has been too "Kantian" in its emphasis on justice rather than on issues of the good or the good life. Albrecht Wellmer and Seyla Benhabib have tended in different ways to stress these dimensions of community and mutual recognition, at the expense of what they see as a spurious rigorism in Apel's and, to a lesser extent, Habermas's formulations. Paradoxically, such critiques tend to redirect attention to the communication community that was central to Apel's model, though this is now conceived in sociologically fuller and more adequate terms.

II. APPLICATIONS

There is a sense in which discourse ethics makes *all* ethics into applied ethics: as Wellmer put it, 'what is "applied" is the moral principle itself.' The important issues will tend in practice to be concerned not with the fundamental grounding of basic norms but with discourses of application concerned with the overlapping scope of conflicting norms. Both Apel and Habermas have recently paid particular attention to such issues. Apel has developed what he calls "part B" of his discourse ethics: whereas part A is concerned with the formal justification of moral norms, part B is an "ethic of responsibility tied to history" (*geschichtsbezogene Verantwortungsethik*). This begins with the recognition that the communicative *a priori* which makes possible both (moral) philosophy and (empirical) science is at the same time a historical feature of our modern culture. This implies further that we have to consider how far modern societies do in fact provide the conditions for moral judgement and action of the kind discussed here. And this raises both specific paradoxes to do with the appropriateness of moral action in immoral contexts and broader questions as to how far even the most attractive modern societies approximate the conditions set out in the discourse ethic model for the exercise of moral reflection. (In looking at modern societies, it is hard not to be struck by the ways in which the very substantial democratization of everyday social interaction coexists with new divisions, separations, and antagonisms between the haves and the have-nots, locally and globally, that breed increasingly cynical attitudes on both sides.)

Habermas too has pursued issues of application in both ethical and legal contexts, relying heavily in the latter on the work of Robert Alexy. He remains however extremely cautious about any attempt to blur the distinction between his explication of the "moral point of view" and concrete practical issues. Wellmer, by contrast, has plausibly shown how difficult it is to distinguish in any case between justification (*Begründung*) and application.

Discourse ethics does not offer, then, a practical solution to concrete moral or ethical issues, so much as a set of recommended practices within which such solutions may be pursued. In this of course it resembles democratic theory, which it has also complemented and enriched—notably in its contribution to the conception of deliberative democracy. This to some extent resolves the issue raised both in Germany by Wellmer and in the United States by a number of critics as to whether discourse ethics should be understood more in relation to politics and the public sphere than in relation to morality in a strict sense. His discourse ethic is, Habermas concedes, necessarily somewhat formal. It is based on a procedure, that of practical discourse, rather than specific ethical prescriptions. It draws a sharp distinction between questions of justice and questions of the "good life"; the latter can only be addressed in the context of diverse cultures or forms of life or of individual life projects. On the other hand, a universalistic morality can bridge the division between morality and law, in that both are based, in varying ways, on a relation to discourse. In Habermas's most recent major book, *Between Facts and Norms* (*Faktizität und Geltung*), he develops the implications of this model for a theory of law and the democratic state. A variant of the same discourse principle on which he had based his ethical theory also forms a foundation for a legitimate political order, and it can thus be shown, he suggests, that democracy is a condition for genuine legality.

Discourse ethics might also be said to generate certain constraints on the professionalization of applied ethics. Whereas a more traditional deductive (e.g., deontological) or consequentialist (e.g., utilitarian) ethics might give priority to the contribution of experts, the implication of discourse ethics is that experts will tend to be confined to a maieutic role of facilitating and clarifying discussion, as well as making their own contributions *as participants*. Here again, discourse ethics meshes in with what is arguably a greater sophistication of modern societies in relation to professional expertise. We are now perhaps less likely to take an expert opinion on trust, and more likely to expect to be confronted with the need to evaluate opposing expert opinions—including those of expert evaluators of first-order expertise. In the discourse ethics model, the everyday practice of moral reasoning is shown to be continuous with professional meta-ethical disputes, and this is perhaps one of the strengths of the model for a world such as ours. Discourse ethics may not be the successor to Kant's theory of practical reason that many theorists have wanted, but it may still be, as Habermas once said of philosophy, the best available "stand-in and interpreter."

Bibliography

Apel, K.-O. (1980). *Towards a transformation of philosophy* (G. Adey & D. Frisby, Trans.) London: Routledge and Kegan Paul.

Apel, K.-O. (1993). L'éthique du discours comme éthique de la responsabilité. *Revue de Métaphysique et de Morale* **98**, 4, 505–537.

Baynes, K. (1992). *The normative grounds of social criticism: Kant, Rawls, and Habermas.* Albany: State University of New York.

Benhabib, S., & Dallmayr, F. (Eds.) (1990). *The communicative ethics controversy,* Cambridge, MA: MIT Press.

Habermas, J. (1984/1987). *The theory of communicative action* (Vols. 1–2). London: Heinemann, and Cambridge: Polity.

Habermas, J. (1984). *Vorstudien and Ergänzungen zur Theorie des kommunikativen Handelns,* Frankfurt: Suhrkamp.

Habermas, J. (1989). *Moral consciousness and communicative action.* Cambridge, MA: MIT Press.

Habermas, J. (1986). Law and morality. *The Tanner Lectures on Human values,* VIII, pp. 217–279.

Habermas, J. (1993). *Justification and application.* Cambridge, MA: MIT Press.

Habermas, J. (1994). *The past as future.* Lincoln: University of Nebraska Press, and Cambridge: Polity.

Habermas, J. (1996). *Between facts and norms.* Cambridge: Polity.

Habermas, J. (1996). On the cognitive content of morality. *Proceedings of the Aristotelian Society* XLVI **3**, 335–358.

Passerin d'Entrèves, M., & Benhabib, S. (Eds.) (1996). *The philosophical discourse of modernity; Critical essays.* Cambridge: Polity.

Rehg, W. (1994). *Insight and solidarity. The discourse ethics of Jürgen Habermas.* Berkeley, Los Angeles, and London: University of California Press.

Wellmer, A. (1986). *Ethik und Dialog. Elemente des moralischen Urteils bei Kant und in der Diskursethik.* Frankfurt: Suhrkamp.

White, S. (1988). *The recent work of Jürgen Habermas: Reason, justice & modernity.* Cambridge: Cambridge University Press.

DISCRIMINATION, CONCEPT OF

David Wasserman
University of Maryland

GLOSSARY

affirmative action The general name for a variety of policies that target people of a particular race, ethnicity, or gender for a range of benefits, from aggressive recruitment to preference in hiring, in order to reduce discrimination toward members of a group or to alleviate the adverse effects of that discrimination.

disparate impact Significant differences in the effect of a given practice or policy on different racial, ethnic, or other groups (for example, on the proportion of applicants from those groups who are hired), differences that are typically to the disadvantage of a group or groups that have been subject to discrimination.

facially neutral practices Practices governing hiring, admission, promotion, or termination that do not make explicit reference to the race, ethnicity, gender, or other group affiliations of those affected by them.

race-conscious remedies As used in this article, a synonym for affirmative action policies.

racial, ethnic, and gender preferences Policies that confer an advantage in hiring, admission, promotion, or similar decisions on the basis of race, ethnicity, or gender, an advantage that may range from treating membership in a particular group as a slight "plus" factor to applying different minimum standards to people of different groups.

DISCRIMINATION was once a neutral term, referring to the capacity to make distinctions; its valence depended on the appropriateness of the distinctions made. A person was praised for his discrimination in judging character, horses, or wines; he was condemned for making distinctions without any moral or aesthetic difference. In recent decades, however, "discrimination" has become identified with a specific way of distinguishing among people, and its negative valence has become dominant. A person is said to discriminate if she disadvantages others on the basis of their race, ethnicity, or other group membership. The older, neutral sense of the term survives in some grammatical forms; a person may still be praised for *being* discriminating, and for discrimination in making a particular kind of judgment. But she is condemned for discriminating, or for discriminatory acts and practices. To claim that someone discriminates is to subject her to reproach or challenge her for justification; to call discrimination "wrongful" is merely to add emphasis to a morally laden term.

Some claim that there has been a further shift in the

meaning of "discrimination." At the dawn of the civil rights era, they argue, discrimination was a simple concept; now it has become complex. It used to be that a person discriminated only if he deliberately excluded certain people from his factory or school because of their race or other similarly irrelevant characteristics; now, he is said to discriminate if he fails to encourage people from underrepresented groups to apply, if he employs a standardized aptitude test on which members of those groups get disproportionately low scores, or if he fails to modify his entrances, workspaces, job descriptions, training programs, or curricula so that applicants from those groups may more readily compete for scarce openings.

To some, this shift in the meaning of discrimination is disturbing, if not insidious: a bait-and-switch that smuggles in a controversial agenda of redress and reform under a broadly accepted ban on intentional discrimination. To others, the shift in understanding is necessary, reflecting an awareness of how deeply intentional discrimination by individuals has distorted our social practices and institutions, and how, as a result, the harmful effects of intentional discrimination can be perpetuated by actions that do not themselves express hatred or contempt.

I. INTRODUCTION

This article will trace the conflict over the meaning of discrimination through current debates about disparate impact and affirmative action. It will begin by examining the complexities in the supposedly simple concept of intentional discrimination. That concept encompasses a number of overlapping but distinct features, which differ in moral significance: (1) failing to treat people as individuals; (2) failing to judge them on their own merits; (3) taking account of their group membership in ways that disadvantage them; and (4) treating them as moral inferiors by virtue of their group membership. Over the past generation, moral and legal analyses of discrimination have tended to regard the last—the hatred and devaluation of a group—as the core evil in discrimination, to be understood in the context of social practices and institutions that stigmatize and systematically disadvantage the disfavored group.

This emphasis on the social context of individual discrimination has led to two conclusions that are troubling or unacceptable to many people who regard themselves as strongly opposed to discrimination. First, because social practices and institutions come to function independently of the individual attitudes and conduct that originally shaped them, the harmful consequences of intentional discrimination by individuals may be perpetuated by less objectionable acts and practices, including many that are neutral and reasonable on their face. Second, and relatedly, it will sometimes be necessary to adopt policies with the first three features of intentional discrimination in order to eliminate the fourth—the hatred and devaluation of a person because of her group membership. As Justice Blackmun declared in the *Bakke* case, "in order to get beyond racism, we must first take account of race."

The legal regulation of acts and policies with inadvertently disparate impact, and the imposition of "group-conscious" remedies for discrimination, have a common premise: that although discrimination may begin in the hearts of individuals, it does not end there, but is embedded in institutions and social practices. Those institutions and social practices reinforce individual prejudice, ensuring that it will proliferate in a variety of covert and subconscious forms even when it has been publicly renounced. More important, perhaps, they maintain the effects of past prejudice through actions and policies that are not themselves motivated by prejudice. The administrative and judicial responses to discrimination that fall under the rubric of "affirmative action" are designed (albeit not always very well) to modify the institutions and practices that perpetuate the exclusion and disadvantage of stigmatized groups.

As important as it is to recognize the social context and institutional embeddedness of individual discrimination, however, it is also important to maintain the moral distinction between conduct that displays contempt for a group of people and conduct that inadvertently maintains the adverse impact of such contempt. This distinction is obscured when the term "discrimination" is used to cover the latter as well as the former. Unfortunately, that is just what the law does when it treats facially neutral practices with adverse impact on Blacks and women as presumptively discriminatory. And yet the judicial extension of the concept of discrimination has certainly helped to counter the effects of generations of deliberate discrimination. The fact that this practical success has been gained at the cost of so much public confusion and resentment suggests the difficulties of separating the parallel discourses of a moralized law, for which "discrimination" is an evolving term of art, and a legalistic morality, for which "discrimination" has, happily, become a term of opprobrium.

The emerging understanding of the role of institutions in mediating individual discrimination and group disadvantage is particularly controversial as applied to women and people with disabilities, groups defined, unlike racial and ethnic groups, partly in terms of physical characteristics thought to have some effect on major life activities. While there is a broad consensus that women and people with disabilities have often been treated as unworthy of equal concern and respect, there is considerable disagreement about whether it is appropriate to treat them as subordinated "minority" groups. There is also considerable disagreement about whether individual prejudice and its institutional manifestations adequately account for the unfair disadvantage they suffer.

Some writers have located the source of that disadvantage in the norms by which the defining attributes of women and people with disabilities are classified as abnormal, and in the physical structures and social practices that limit their participation. They argue that these norms, structures, and practices embody an unjustifiable bias in favor of the dominant group—men or the "able-bodied." But those who regard this pervasive structural bias as the central problem for women and people with disabilities disagree about whether the concept of discrimination can be enlarged to accommodate it.

II. INTENTIONAL DISCRIMINATION AS AN INDIVIDUAL MORAL OFFENSE

The classic bigot, who refuses to hire, serve, or sell to "those people," might be condemned on several grounds: he fails to judge "those people" by their merit or qualification for the good, service, or activity he withholds; he fails to treat them as individuals; he takes their race, ethnicity, or other group membership into account in denying them that good, service, or activity; and he treats them as moral inferiors because of their group membership.

The first two characterizations are of limited use in identifying the core moral offense. Merit and qualification surely play a role in our understanding of discrimination: we generally do not regard it as discrimination to deny a benefit to someone because he is unqualified for it. Yet "merit" and "qualification" are notoriously vague, elastic terms: many qualities are desirable to an employer or a school, and there are many ways of assessing those qualities, so "merit" and "qualification" often fail to provide clear benchmarks against which to measure discrimination.

Similarly, the second characteristic—the failure to treat the disadvantaged person as an individual—is not adequate to explain the moral offense. Discrimination

does seem to require some kind of adverse generalization: an employer who refused to hire someone because of a specific aversion to him, rather than a general aversion to "people like him," might act irrationally, but she would not, in common parlance, discriminate. Adverse generalization, however, is hardly a sufficient condition for discrimination. An employer who required a minimum grade level or standardized test score for a given job because of its rough correlation with job performance would ordinarily not be said to discriminate against an applicant who lacked that minimum, even if on closer inspection, the applicant would prove to be highly qualified. Although he has failed to treat her as an individual or, arguably, to judge her by her merit, he would be said to discriminate only, and quite controversially, if grade levels or test scores were also correlated with race, ethnicity, or gender.

The third characteristic associated with discrimination—taking account of a person's race, ethnicity, or other group membership in denying a good or service—appears to specify the kind of generalization involved in discrimination. But it raises the obvious and controversial questions of what groups besides racial and ethnic ones can be discriminated against, and of why adverse generalizations involving those groups are particularly objectionable. Some courts and legal scholars have seized on immutability as the critical feature of the attributes that can be subject to discrimination. However annoying or offensive it is to be disadvantaged because of one's "membership" in an accidental or transient group (for example, to be frisked because one happens to be on a crowded subway car just after a gun is fired), this hardly counts as discrimination. On the other hand, certain mutable attributes such as religious affiliation have often been the basis of invidious discrimination.

If not the immutability of membership, what distinguishes the groups that can be subject to discrimination? Two features seem pertinent. First, however vague their boundaries may be, these groups generally have deep social significance: their members are perceived and treated differently in a variety of important respects by the larger society. Second, and relatedly, membership in the group is generally important to the members' self-identity.

But while these features help identify the groups that can be subject to discrimination, they leave open the question of why it is especially objectionable to take account of membership in such groups in denying a benefit or imposing a burden. When we look only at the effects on individual group members, the harm of taking group membership into account is highly contingent. If members of certain groups have been subject to worse treatment in a wide array of circumstances, it adds to the imbalance to disadvantage them on the basis of group membership. That effect will be amplified if members of those groups have a heightened concern about the treatment of other members, or about the fact that the adverse treatment they suffer is based on their membership. But these considerations appear to make the moral appraisal of discrimination depend too heavily on the existing balance of advantage among groups and the varying sensitivities of group members.

A distinct concern is the social cost of taking account of race, ethnicity, and other socially significant groupings in imposing substantial burdens. Precisely because those groupings have been a source of so much injustice and hostility, disadvantaging people on that basis contributes to destructive and often lethal social discord. But groups can be subject to discrimination even if they lack broad social recognition, and even if their mistreatment does not create or exacerbate social discord.

A final concern about taking account of group membership rests on a belief that the tendency to categorize people into "basic kinds" is a deep, recalcitrant, and damaging one. People tend to impose rigid classification schemes on human variation, and they tend to endow the resulting classes with greatly exaggerated diagnostic and predictive value. The use of such categories reflects a deeply ingrained essentialism, which licenses a vast range of generalizations from group membership to important physical, psychological, intellectual, and moral attributes. While they are rarely distinguished, these three concerns—cumulative harm to individuals, social disharmony, and group essentialism—may all contribute to the moral onus of taking group membership into account in imposing burdens or denying benefits.

The fourth characteristic associated with discrimination—the treatment of a person as a moral inferior by virtue of his group membership—can be seen as an aspect of group essentialism. Just as people tend to judge individuals in terms of their "kind," they tend to see kinds as constituting a hierarchy, in which some are superior to others. Such hierarchies are most explicitly developed in caste systems, but they may be present in virtually all social classification schemes. The classic bigot is not just taking account of group membership in refusing to hire, serve, or sell to "those people"; he is treating those people as members of a morally inferior group. While it may be wrong to treat a person as a moral inferior for reasons other than his group membership, it is not discriminatory. And while it may be

discriminatory to take account of a person's group membership without treating him as a moral inferior, such conduct arguably lacks the moral onus of classic bigotry.

Much of the contemporary debate over the meaning of discrimination concerns the comparative importance of the third and fourth features—taking account of group membership in denying a benefit and treating people as moral inferiors by virtue of that membership. The debate centers on the evaluation of actions and policies that display the third but not the fourth feature: that disadvantage people on the basis of their group membership without treating them as moral inferiors. Some writers regard the third feature as the core evil of discrimination, the fourth merely as an aggravating factor; others regard the third without the fourth as injury without insult—a far lesser, more venial form of discrimination.

These conflicts typically surface in two settings: (1) the appraisal of racial preferences and other race-conscious policies that disadvantage some members of the dominant race in order to improve the social prospects of other races seen as oppressed or subordinated, and (2) the appraisal of actions by members of those races that harm or disadvantage members of the dominant race on the basis of race. I will focus on the first setting later in the article. The second setting is important because it suggests the difficulty of judging whether certain actions that disadvantage people on the basis of group membership do in fact treat them as moral inferiors, and because it suggests the importance of social context in making that judgment.

A Black manager who shows a strong preference for Black applicants out of loyalty to "his kind," or from a commitment to reducing the underrepresentation of Blacks in his field, does not thereby treat Whites as moral inferiors, even if he displays an inappropriate or excessive partiality. The character of his policy is less clear-cut if he declines to hire White people on the basis of a group generalization, for example, because he assumes that all or most White people are prejudiced, or because he believes that White employees will enjoy unfair advantages over Black employees once they are in the workforce. While the first generalization is more unfair, and arguably less accurate, than the second, neither displays the kind of contempt and denigration shown by the White manager who refuses to hire Blacks because he believes that most of them are lazy or stupid. To be thought incompetent on the basis of one's race is at least marginally more demeaning than to be stereotyped as prejudiced or overprivileged. Although it is certainly possible for members of a minority group to treat members of the dominant group as moral inferiors, many of the actions by minority group members that are commonly denounced as reverse discrimination may be more aptly characterized as defensive overgeneralization.

Social context affects not only the "message" conveyed by actions that disadvantage people on the basis of their group membership, but also the moral appraisal of actions that clearly do treat the members of a group as moral inferiors. What makes the conduct of the classic bigot particularly reprehensible is that he is actively affirming an oppressive social system. The people that he despises are worse off in significant ways because a range of institutions mirrors his judgment of their inferior worth.

The social context of discrimination is also relevant to the moral appraisal of actions and practices that are *not* discriminatory in either the third or fourth sense above, for example, an employer's good-faith use of a standardized test that is moderately predictive of job performance but has a severely disparate impact on minority applicants. Such actions and practices disadvantage members of subordinated groups without necessarily taking their group membership into account or treating them as moral inferiors. To understand the controversies that have arisen over the moral and legal status of such actions and practices, we need to look more closely at the relationship between individual discrimination and group disadvantage.

III. DISCRIMINATORY INSTITUTIONS AND STIGMATIZED GROUPS: RACIAL DISCRIMINATION AS A PARADIGM

Most contemporary societies have grossly unjust disparities in well-being, however defined, that are highly correlated with membership in ascriptive groups. The worst-off groups are very often those that have been, and continue to be, the most widely despised and the most fully excluded from the political processes by which social benefits are assigned. In the United States, the most despised and excluded group has long been people of African descent. A number of U.S. commentators have seen discrimination in terms of the social and institutional structures that oppress African Americans. They describe a "system of racial oppression" (Wasserstrom); a "caste system" (Fiss); "the social construction of a stigmatized class" (Koppelman). Koppelman, who has developed perhaps the most comprehensive account, identifies three features of group subordination

in a discriminatory system: (1) members of the group are systematically excluded from the processes by which political decisions are made and resources allocated; (2) members of the group are devalued and stigmatized; and (3) members of the group are disadvantaged on almost any index of well-being. The first is a matter of familiar constitutional and legal history, from the "social death" of slavery to the poll tax and at-large representation; the second is illustrated by Dr. Kenneth Clark's influential findings, cited in *Brown v. Board of Education*, on the lasting injuries to the self-esteem of Black children caused by segregation; the third is suggested by the extent to which we can predict the future lives of infants in the maternity ward simply by their skin color.

In late twentieth-century America, the claim that an action or policy discriminates against a group of people typically involves an explicit or implicit comparison to race or ethnicity; it suggests that the members of that group are, or may be, treated like a disfavored racial or ethnic minority. Thus, those who oppose genetic testing by insurers argue that the widespread use of such tests will help create a "biological underclass," a group that is likely to be treated, in the shadow of eugenics, much like other groups that have been regarded as genetically or biologically inferior, from African Americans and Southern European immigrants to people with intellectual and physical disabilities. Opponents of genetic testing recognize obvious differences in membership criteria and membership between the groups targeted by eugenicists and the "group" that is likely to be disadvantaged by genetic testing, mainly people with hidden disabilities and late-onset diseases (and their relatives). Their point is that the latter may, despite these differences, come to be perceived and treated like the former.

We should not expect to find the same constellation of attitudes and social structures in the case of all stigmatized groups in all societies. Widespread hatred and contempt often coexist with economic advantage or privilege, as they have to some extent for overseas Chinese and Indians, medieval Jews, and contemporary Ibos and Tutsis. But although the "places" to which despised minority groups are consigned by the larger society have widely varying economic, social, and political characteristics, it is always a position the larger society holds in contempt.

There is a complex interdependence between a discriminatory system and discrimination by individuals. Such a system could hardly arise without individual prejudice; a regime that did not express hatred or contempt toward disadvantaged groups might be unfair, but it would arguably not be discriminatory. And while individual prejudice could certainly exist outside a discriminatory system, it would be both idiosyncratic and ephemeral. Individuals do not regard groups as morally inferior on a random basis, or feel undifferentiated hostility toward groups other than their own. Rather, their contempt for and devaluation of the members of a group is informed by a social and institutional structure that consigns the group to a particular "place" and endows its members with particular attributes.

That social and intellectual structure also reinforces conscious prejudice by social validation, and it perpetuates both conscious and unconscious prejudice in a variety of less direct ways:

(1). By maintaining social conditions that appear to support prevailing beliefs about the indolence, criminality, promiscuity, and so on, of the subordinated group. In the contemporary United States, racial stereotypes are fed by the concentration of poor Blacks and Hispanics in highly segregated, physically decaying urban areas with chronically high unemployment.

(2). By encouraging those outside the subordinated group to ease the discomfort they feel about its status and treatment by convincing themselves that its members deserve no better.

(3). By giving negative claims about the subordinated group an exaggerated or spurious credibility, by encouraging a very low standard of proof for accepting such claims, and by encouraging their overgeneralization.

(4). By developing an "independent" aversion to qualities or traits associated (but not exclusively) with the subordinated group (e.g., I don't dislike him because he's Jewish, but because he's so calculating) where the source of the aversion is really a dislike for the group, which the aversion serves to rationalize.

We can gauge the extent to which prejudice pervades the attitudes and practices of people who would publicly reject it through experiments, such as those done by HUD and the Urban Institute, that track carefully matched Black/White pairs of housing, loan, or job applicants. Despite being equal on every arguably relevant dimension, Black applicants fare significantly worse. While some small fraction of the real estate agents, loan officers, and employers who reject Black applicants do regard their race as a disqualification or negative factor, it is likely that most do not. They see themselves as evaluating all applicants equally, but their deeply ingrained prejudice operates like a hidden thumb on the scales: they give different weight to the same attributes presented by Black and White applicants, give negative weight to irrelevant attributes found more frequently in Black applicants, or give greater credence to the claims made in support of White applicants.

There has been more sophistication in the detection of these sorts of bias than in their moral appraisal. The persistence of bias in reflex actions and judgments has often been seen as aggravating the offense, as if the biased individual compounded his prejudice with subterfuge or deception. The tendency to condemn unconscious bias as harshly as conscious bias may reflect not only rhetorical excess but also a misleading picture of repression as deliberate concealment—the recalcitrant bigot protecting his prejudices by concealing them—or of the biased subconscious as a homunculus in a white hood, a malevolent intelligence waging a covert campaign of racial oppression.

Although unconscious bias is less reprehensible than conscious bias, it may also be more recalcitrant. Unconscious prejudices are unlikely to give themselves up to sustained inquisition or introspection. On an individual level, they are less easily purged than counteracted (for example, by a deliberate effort to review minority applications in the most favorable light). On a collective level, they may be more effectively remedied by long-term changes in social structure than by exhortations to cease discriminating.

Other harmful effects of a discriminatory system are perpetuated by acts and policies that do not themselves express conscious *or* unconscious prejudice. It is characteristic of such a system to make the perpetuation of group disadvantage the path of least resistance. One obvious way it does so is through the need to accommodate the prejudices of other people. Undoubtedly, many Southern restaurant and hotel owners did not want Blacks in their establishments. But many, perhaps more, barred them largely because they feared the loss of business from White customers. In declining to make such "business necessity" a defense, the 1964 Civil Rights Act prohibited a form of conduct that could not be regarded as intentional discrimination in the fourth sense above—that is, discrimination motivated by racial animus. It also helped to eliminate the "necessity" for such conduct, because all public accommodations fell under the same ban.

The 1964 Civil Rights Act was understood to prohibit another form of exclusion that was not always motivated by racial animus: the use of race in most circumstances as a marker or proxy for other characteristics that *were* a legitimate basis for exclusion. If a restaurant owner could not exclude Blacks because his White customers disliked them, he also could not exclude them because they were more likely to steal from him—even if his statistics were correct, even if he would welcome particular Blacks whom he knew posed no such risk, and even though he could exclude members of other groups, like a particular family, on that basis. The unrestricted use of such generalizations would impose far too great a burden on the innocent, law-abiding members of the stigmatized group. The ban on statistical or proxy discrimination has proven to be far more complicated than the ban on actions that merely accommodate the prejudice of others. But it too reflects an early recognition that in order to dismantle a discriminatory system, the law could not limit its proscription to intentional discrimination based on racial animus.

An even more difficult set of issues is presented by allocative actions and policies that are neutral in appearance and design, but that have the effect of perpetuating the harmful effects of deliberate exclusion. The company that now bases promotion on a seniority that only Whites have been able to acquire because of its prior exclusion of Blacks is perpetuating the effects of its own past discrimination, and it may make little moral difference if it does so intentionally or inadvertently. But a company's responsibility for the disparate impact of certain facially neutral practices is less clear if it has never practiced intentional discrimination (for example, if it has only recently gone into business). Many apparently neutral hiring practices, such as the requirement of a recommendation from a senior employee in a once-discriminatory industry, perpetuate the effects of a regime that excluded Blacks from the social networks in which such contacts are usually made. And even the requirement of a minimum score on a standardized test may perpetuate the adverse effects of an educational system, funded by local property taxes, that has long shortchanged Blacks.

There are obvious moral differences between facially neutral policies that perpetuate the effects of a company's own past discrimination and those that merely perpetuate the effects of industry- or society-wide discrimination. Despite these important differences, courts have largely ignored the distinction between these two kinds of cases in applying the 1964 Civil Rights Act. They have treated the use of facially neutral standards in both kinds of cases as prima facie discrimination and have permitted the continued use of such practices only as a business necessity.

The divergence between legal usage and common-sense moral judgment about what counts as discrimination has significant costs. On the one hand, employers with no history of intentional discrimination are indignant at being held liable for "discrimination" when their conscientious efforts to recruit or promote Blacks fall short of current judicial or administrative guidelines. On the other hand, civil-rights administrators and activists, frustrated by massive institutional inertia, tend to be impatient with pleas of innocent intentions. Ironically, it is the moral consensus forged around the passage of the 1964 Civil Rights Act that makes this conflict over the understanding of "discrimination" so highly charged.

IV. INDIVIDUAL RESPONSIBILITY AND DISCRIMINATORY INSTITUTIONS

As we have seen, the concept of discrimination that has evolved in the past generation, which emphasizes the role of social institutions in mediating individual prejudice and group disadvantage, has focused attention on two issues: (1) the extent that African Americans and other minorities continue to suffer from conscious and unconscious prejudice, and from disadvantages that can be attributed directly or indirectly to past prejudice; (2) the extent that individuals, organizations, and institutions can be expected to change to reduce existing prejudice and the effects of past prejudice. The two issues are closely related, because the fairness of antidiscrimination policies may depend on the magnitude and the recalcitrance of the problem they address. Much of the disagreement about affirmative action concerns the need for remedial policies: opponents tend to see discrimination as a thing of the past, or on its way out, while proponents see it as entrenched and pervasive. But even among those who accept the latter view, there is disagreement about which remedial measures are fair.

Thus, some critics of affirmative action acknowledge the pervasive effects of discrimination but insist that, except to compensate for one's own discrimination, it is not appropriate to take race into account in attempting to eliminate those effects: disadvantaging a White on the basis of race may be less maligning or harmful than disadvantaging a Black, but it is still wrong. Most defenders of racial preferences reject this charge of "reverse discrimination," arguing that there is a basic asymmetry between allocative decisions that disadvantage Blacks and those that disadvantage Whites on the basis of race. In a society where Blacks have always, and Whites have never, been a stigmatized group, policies that disadvantage the latter for the sake of the former may be unfair, placing a large burden on a small number of people, but they do not and perhaps could not express the view that Whites are moral inferiors, unworthy of equal concern and respect. The debate about affirmative action reflects conflicting views of the core evil of discrimination. Defenders regard the core evil as the treatment of people as moral inferiors, and thus regard race-conscious remedies that express no disrespect for the people they disadvantage as potentially acceptable; critics regard the core evil as the imposition of burdens on the basis of race, ethnicity, or other group membership, and thus regard race-conscious remedies as fundamentally immoral.

If there is a fierce debate about the morality of policies that take race into account to undo the effects of past discrimination, there is also a fierce debate about the morality of practices that perpetuate those effects without taking race into account. Some people condemn practices that perpetuate the harmful effects of racial oppression by oversight or self-interest, such as an exclusive reliance on old-boy networks for hiring, almost as harshly as intentional discrimination, especially because such oversight and self-interest often reflect latent bias: we give less weight to the interests of people we see as less worthy of concern and respect. Others see such blanket condemnation as excessive and counterproductive, provoking a fierce backlash precisely because most of the people against whom it is directed regard intentional discrimination as a great evil. Clearly, we need a more nuanced conception of individual responsibility for continuing social injustice, which recognizes the role of neutral acts and practices in perpetuating the effects of intentional discrimination without treating those acts and practices as the moral equivalent of intentional discrimination.

V. DISCRIMINATION AND DIFFERENCE

The effectiveness of discrimination claims in mobilizing public indignation and state intervention, and in exposing the harmful impact of facially neutral policies, has encouraged the application of the concept of discrimination beyond racial, ethnic, and religious groups to groups defined by categorically different criteria: elderly people, women, and people with disabilities. The debate over the applicability of the concept of discrimination to these groups has focused on their social recognition and internal cohesiveness, and the extent to which their members are really treated as moral inferiors by virtue of their group membership.

A. Elderly People

Age discrimination is an interesting case, because the group discriminated against is not a minority in quite the same sense that racial and ethnic groups are. While "the elderly" are almost always (sometimes by definition) a minority of the population at any given time, the vast majority of people will be elderly sooner or later. It might seem that extending the concept of discrimination to the elderly involves the "reification" of a life-stage through which almost all of us pass.

Conflict between specific cohorts, like "baby-boomers" and their parents, certainly contributes to the stigmatization of the age groups to which those cohorts currently belong. But contempt for specific age groups does not require such intergenerational conflict. Many societies have restricted full humanity to the middle range of the human life-span, treating both children and elderly people as intellectually, physically, and morally defective. The denigration of youth and old age has not been based solely on a recognition of the general developmental limitations of the young and the general effects of aging on the elderly. Often, a host of other unattractive moral qualities has been attributed to those age groups. This contempt toward, and devaluation of, children and the elderly has hardly been precluded by the fact that people in their middle years were once children and expect to be adults—people are quite capable of despising what they have been and will become.

B. Women and People with Disabilities

The claim that women and people with disabilities should be seen as "minority" groups subject to widespread discrimination in contemporary American society has been challenged from several directions: not only by those who oppose the "proliferation" of rights and victimized groups, but also by those who doubt that an antidiscrimination analysis can capture the entitlements and grievances of women and people with disabilities.

Some raise questions about the status of women and people with disabilities as stigmatized groups. Although few would deny that American men, and the institutions they dominate, have often had dismissive, condescending attitudes toward women, some find those attitudes fundamentally less malign and virulent than the attitudes of American Whites toward Blacks. And some question whether American men treat women as a distinct group, given the pervasive interconnectedness of their lives. Parallel questions arise about people with disabilities. Although people with certain types of disability, such as limited mental development, have long been regarded as moral inferiors, there is disagreement about whether similar attitudes prevail across the spectrum of physical and mental conditions classified as impairments, and about whether those attitudes are mitigated or exacerbated by the compassion and solicitude many disabilities elicit. The range of those conditions also raises questions about the extent to which people with disabilities are seen, or see themselves, as members of a single stigmatized group.

But even if women or people with disabilities are seen as stigmatized groups, the physical (and mental) differences that demarcate those groups raise difficulties in applying the concept of discrimination. Those differences are at once stigmata—markers for group membership—and attributes with functional significance, which appear relevant to a variety of allocative decisions. At the same time, much of the disadvantage experienced by women and people with disabilities arises from the way those functional differences are treated in the physical and social organization of society. For this reason, an analysis of the disadvantages suffered by women or people with disabilities would be incomplete if it treated the differences demarcating those groups *only* as stigmata, and if it considered only the direct and indirect effects of hatred and contempt toward those groups.

Thus, women, like Blacks, have often protested the disparate impact of facially neutral policies, such as tests of physical strength used by fire and police departments, which are only loosely tailored to the demands of the job. Although the courts have imposed the same standard of business necessity in evaluating tests with disparate impact on women that they have used in evaluating tests with disparate impact on Blacks, the underlying issue is different in one important respect: there is broad (but not universal) agreement that the adverse impact of standardized aptitude tests on Blacks can be attributed to the effects of past discrimination; there is no such agreement about the disparate impact of standardized strength tests on women. Although the average strength of women might well be greater in a more egalitarian society, few believe it would equal the average strength of men.

But this difference should not, or so it is argued, give aid and comfort to those who would exclude women from police and fire departments; it rather suggests that the norms used to evaluate prospective police and firefighters are inherently "gendered," biased in favor of the dominant group. The norm of the qualified firefighter is of a fire*man*; it places a gratuitous premium on the brute physical strength associated with

men. Women who can satisfy that norm are the conspicuous exception, which is why we are so much more inclined to refer to "female firefighters" than to "male" firefighters—the "male" is understood. On this view, the employer's strength standards do not so much perpetuate the effects of past discrimination as embody a fundamentally sexist norm of what a firefighter should be. While the women assessed by that norm have undoubtedly faced conscious prejudice as well, to focus on the latter is to miss the real locus of injustice.

Writers influenced by this feminist approach to sexism have developed a similar analysis of disability. They argue that the physical structures in, and social organization of, most modern societies are designed to accommodate only those who fall within an extremely narrow range of physical and mental variation. The formal neutrality of such practices masks a structural bias against people with disabilities, much as the formal neutrality of seniority and standardized testing have masked the historical oppression of African Americans.

But other writers who share this general understanding of the structural disadvantage faced by people with disabilities doubt that the concept of discrimination, even in its extended form, can adequately accommodate it. Structural bias, they argue, is better seen as a matter of injustice—as a failure to give sufficient weight to the interests of people with disabilities in the physical and social organization of society. While animus toward people with disabilities may help to account for the origins or persistence of grossly unjust arrangements, we cannot ascertain what justice requires merely by eliminating that animus or its effects. What is needed in the case of disabilities is not merely an injunction against discrimination, or the recognition of access rights for people with particular impairments, but a broader theory of distributive justice that would specify how society as a whole should be organized to accommodate impairments. Others, however, doubt whether any account of distributive justice is up to that formidable task, given the difficulties such theories have had in judging distributions of resources among the "able-bodied." Still others suspect that the very idea of distributive justice for people with disabilities involves compensating them for "natural disadvantages," thereby treating their disadvantages as personal rather than social and their needs as "special."

VI. CONCLUSION

Several unresolved issues lie behind contemporary debates about the concept of discrimination. The debate over the moral significance of imposing burdens on the basis of group membership suggests that we have a weak grasp of the relevance of group affiliation, ascribed or chosen, for assessing the treatment of individuals. The debate over the morality of practices with inadvertently disparate impact suggests that we need a far more nuanced account of individual responsibility for maintaining harmful social conditions—not in terms of the actual contribution of specific acts to those conditions, which will often be slight or unknown, but in terms of the agent's degree of complicity with harmful institutions. Finally, the debate over the adequacy of the concept of discrimination for capturing the grievances of women and people with disabilities suggests a broader disagreement about the primacy of individual prejudice and partiality in understanding and evaluating harmful social conditions. The concept of discrimination is likely to remain a subject of contention as long as these issues are unresolved.

Also See the Following Articles

AFFIRMATIVE ACTION • AGEISM • DISABILITY RIGHTS • ETHNOCULTURAL MINORITY GROUPS • HOMOSEXUALITY, SOCIETAL ATTITUDES TOWARD • RACISM • SEXISM

Bibliography

Alexander, L. (1992). What makes wrongful discimination wrong? Biases, preferences, stereotypes, and proxies. *University of Pennsylvania Law Review* **141**, 149–219.

Fiss, O. (1976). Groups and the equal protection clause. *Philosophy & Public Affairs* **5**, 107–177.

Fullinwider, R. (1986). Achieving equal opportunity. In R. K. Fullinwider & C. Mills (Eds.), *The moral foundations of civil rights*. Lanham: Rowman & Littlefield.

Garcia, J. L. A. (1996). The heart of racism. *Journal of Social Philosophy* **27**, 5–45.

Koppelman, A. (1996). *Antidiscrimination law and social equality*. New Haven: Yale University Press.

Lawrence, C. R. (1987). The ego, the id, and equal protection: Reckoning with unconscious racism. *Stanford Law Review* **38**, 317–389.

Lichtenberg, J. (1992). Racism in the head, racism in the world. *Report from the Institute for Philosophy and Public Policy* **12**, 3–5.

MacKinnon, C. A. (1986). Difference and dominance: On sex discrimination. In R. K. Fullinwider & C. Mills (Eds.), *The moral foundations of civil rights*. Lanham: Rowman & Littlefield.

Wasserstrom, R. (1986). One way to understand and defend programs of affirmative action. In R. K. Fullinwider & C. Mills (Eds.), *The moral foundations of civil rights*. Landham: Rowman & Littlefield.

Wendell, S. (1989). Towards a feminist theory of disability. *Hypatia* **4**, 104–124.

DISTRIBUTIVE JUSTICE, THEORIES OF

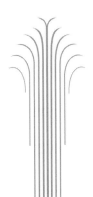

Sirkku Hellsten
University of Helsinki

I. The Paradoxical Nature of the Conception of Justice
II. Politicoeconomical Aspects of Modern Theories of Distributive Justice
III. Categorizing Theories of Justice by the Standards of Distribution
IV. Conclusion

GLOSSARY

atomism The view that things are composed of elementary basic parts. In modern moral and political philosophy, the atomist view is seen to mean that social institutions and political communities are just collections of egoistic and isolated individuals promoting their own benefit and advantage.

collectivism The principle that what applies to a group collectively applies to it as a whole only. Also used as another name for political holism. Usually contrasted with individualism.

deontology The ethical theory that takes duty as the basis of morality, that is, as a view that sees that some acts are morally obligatory regardless of their consequences.

empirical Based on experiment or sense-experience. Empirical knowledge is, for instance, knowledge that we get through experience of the world, and it is not innate.

holism The view that social institutions and certain sorts of events and processes are more than merely the sum of their parts, and thus they can be understood only by examining them as a whole. We cannot, for example, understand the concept of justice by examining what is going on the basis of individual people's actions and intentions, because these can gain significance only by virtue of facts about the whole society.

laissez-faire A doctrine that government should have no control at all over economic matters, therefore, it promotes an economic policy of free competition.

metaphysics A study of the ultimate components of reality, the types of things that exist.

methodological individualism Individualism is a form of atomistic social explanation and is often contrasted with holism. It asserts that the social whole has to be reduced to its parts in order to understand it; that is, social institutions and the principles of justice can be explained by studying the individual members of the societies.

primary goods in John Rawls' welfare liberalism, primary goods include such social goods as rights and liberties, powers and opportunities, income and wealth, and self-respect and liberty, and they are defined as people's needs as citizens, that is, as equally rational and autonomous decision-makers.

teleology The study of aims, purposes, or functions of the universe. Teleological ethics, for its part, asserts that the aim of our actions can be derived from the purpose of human nature, that is, from the realization of our moral capacities.

utility As used by philosophers and economists, utility

means the quantity of value or desirability people's preferences have whether thought of as actual or idealized choices. It is the basic unit of desirability when the values of particular things or actions are compared.

virtue Moral excellence or uprightness; the state of character of a morally worthwhile person; a mean between two extremes. Virtues are often defined as character traits that lead people to a morally good life.

WHAT IS DISTRIBUTIVE JUSTICE? In modern moral, political, and social philosophy the theories of justice are presently divided into three overlapping but still distinguishable spheres. There are (1) theories of political justice or political order, (2) theories of law and punishment, and (3) theories of distributive or social justice. Even if the different spheres of justice are often overlapping, we can say that in this division political justice covers the scope of the other two spheres. Political justice is concerned with the justification of political authority and political order, and it focuses on issues that concern the constitution and legislation of a state. Consequently, the distributional and legal issues are usually included in the conception of political justice. Theories of punishment, for their part, are concerned with the justification of the punishment of those who break the law or disregard generally accepted moral and social norms. Finally, distributive justice focuses on the distributional issues of society's resources; that is, it is concerned with yielding, allotting, assigning, or resigning to the members of society what they need, deserve, or are entitled to. Distributive justice is equated with distributional questions of a society (whether we talk about a particular society or a global community). In this context the terms distributive justice and social justice are, in general, used interchangeably.

This article introduces the main modern Western philosophical theories of distributive justice. Even if certain views may have to be presented through the ideas of particular theorists, the purpose is not to discuss in depth the differences between various theorists, but rather to explain and explore the basic elements, ideas, and terms that are relevant to the contemporary theories of distributive justice. Thus, in order to give the reader an idea of the complexity of the issues involved in the distributional questions, the article gives a general overview of the different features, aspects, and problems that the diverse collection of the theories of distributive justice have.

I. THE PARADOXICAL NATURE OF THE CONCEPTION OF JUSTICE

Questions of justice have always been some of the most fundamental and the most complex questions in our social, political, and moral thinking. On the one hand the questions of justice initiate an abstract philosophical speculation about what is meant by the term justice: what is the just society like? What is the good of a society and what is the good of a human being? What makes governments legitimate, and how can we justify political authority? On the other hand the questions of justice focus our attention on the concrete and practical social problems of our imperfect world. When we define the conception of justice and construct theories of justice, we are not only trying to describe what the perfect world would be like, but we are trying to improve the imperfections of the world we live in. Thus, we also have to ask: how can we justly distribute the social goods and resources? Can it be just that there are poor and starving people living next to those so rich that they have more money and material resources than they can spend in a lifetime? How can we maintain the just balance in rewarding those who work hard and in taking care of those who have no work and who do not contribute to society's public resources? How are we to solve the problems of equality and inequality in distributional issues? (On the conception and definition of justice see also Solomon and Murphy, Eds. (1991). What is justice? *Classic on Contemporary Readings* pp 4–5. Oxford University Press).

Theories of justice are concerned with both the theoretical definition of the word as well as with the normative objectives that guide actual policy-making. On the one hand, they attempt to describe what is meant by the concept of justice and to provide us with an explanation of the concept of justice or, rather, the definition of the word. On the other hand, the theories of justice try to find the means to strive for a more just and harmonious society and are thus concerned with the social and political issues that are related to the maintenance or the return of social harmony. This means that they also try in a prescriptive sense to develop the kind of concept that—substantively and particularly—justice actually requires in practice. They attempt to provide us with normative guidelines as to what a just society should be like.

This dual sense of the conception of justice makes different theories of justice use the same conception, that is the conception of justice, and it makes these theories agree that there is a need to make our societies more just. Yet, simultaneously, they may profoundly disagree with what it is that the realization of a just society would demand from us, because it is extremely difficult to find a definition for justice that is simultaneously sufficiently general to command a broad consensus and sufficiently specific as to permit its useful application. However, even if the theories of justice may disagree as to how we can best reach a just society, in general they seem to agree that the essential element of distributive justice is some variation on the theme of allotting or yielding to each their own.

To make matters more complicated, the conception of justice also points in two different directions. The ideal society and the practical measures to be taken in order to reach this ideal can at a theoretical level be divided into corrective and distributive elements that either stretch backward or forward. The corrective element of distributive justice essentially looks backward. It is an individualistic ideal of securing for all individuals their presumed rewards and entitlements by ordering punishments or redistributing social resources and thus correcting the prevalent injustices. This notion of justice requires empirical preparatory research into the conduct and background of all of the various persons and institutions concerned, and into their several and consequent deserts and entitlements. The *egalitarian collectivist ideal* of imposing equality of outcome, for its part, is forward-looking. Since Aristotle (384–322 B.C.) distributive justice has been distinguished from corrective justice. Corrective (sometimes also called retributive) justice is concerned with who ought to get what social goods, and with punishment for offenses commited. (On the dual nature of the conception of justice see also Anthony Flew (1979), *A dictionary of philosophy*. (Revised 2nd ed.), p. 188, New York: St. Martin's Press.)

This starting point leads modern theories of justice easily into a debate in which the promoters of different theories discuss the problems of justice on very different levels. In such a situation no consistent solution can be found to this dispute. Hence, often the real issue of the dispute is not so much the contents of the conception of justice, but rather fundamental disagreements, usually of a methodological nature. For instance *Robert Nozick's* (b. 1938) procedural redistributive "entitlement theory" is a backward-looking theory of a just society, whereas *John Rawls's* (b. 1921) more egalitarian view on justice as fairness is essentially forward-looking. Because these theories have incommensurable methodological premises, their suggestions about the practical political measures that are to be taken cannot directly be compared with each

other either—and one cannot be simply considered to be better than the other.

Theories of justice, and particularly those of distributive justice, always reflect, at least partly, the social, political, and economic environment they were born in. Consequently, the meaning and the substantial structure of the conception of justice changes over time. Particularly during the last couple of centuries, the emphasis on questions of justice has shifted from an analysis of justice *tout court* to that of distributive or social justice. One reason for this is that modern social and economic development has made it evident that individual justice, that is justice between wrongdoer and victim, is today seen to be a form of justice that is too incomplete and inadequate. The development of the welfare state, which in itself can be considered an application of the notion of distributive and social justice, has shifted the emphasis from the classical Aristotelian view based on individual morality, to a more impersonal view based on right procedure—from acting subject to the object that is acted on. This means that whereas the classical conception of justice focused on the just man, the person who is to act justly, the modern view focuses on more general demands of just treatment and the concept of a citizen to whom just treatment is due. Simultaneously, the method that is used to derive the principles of distributive justice has changed its emphasis from a holistic viewpoint toward the more atomistic viewpoint of methodological individualism, that rejects virtue ethics and instead uses the idea of the social contract as its method of justification of the principles of justice.

II. POLITICOECONOMIC ASPECTS OF MODERN THEORIES OF DISTRIBUTIVE JUSTICE

The concept of distributive justice is usually defined as meaning the fairness of distribution of redistribution of social and material goods, including liberties, rights, and entitlements. There seems to be general agreement that distributive justice is related to the distribution of social goods and material resources, and that these should be distributed according to what one deserves or needs. However, there is wide disagreement on the content and meaning of "desert" or "need." Thus, different theories of justice promote very different views on distributional issues. According to their politicoeconomical views and their normative conclusions, modern theories of distributive justice are traditionally divided into three categories based on the ideological background assumptions. These categories are:

A. The *egalitarian* theories of distributive justice, which can be further divided for instance into "minimum egalitarianism," "welfare egalitarianism," and "socialist egalitarianism."
B. The *utilitarian* theories of distributive justice, which are sometimes called "welfarism" or "welfarist consequentialism."
C. The *liberal* theories of distributive justice, which are further divided into "welfare liberalism" and "libertarianism," and sometimes also described as "neoliberalism."

These categories of theories of distributive justice often overlap, and their politicoeconomic views are closely linked with each other. Many of the theories of distributive justice have been created as criticism of the already-existing theories or of prevailing social practices. Thus, in order to understand the fundamental features of a particular theory, it is often essential to be familiar with the main features of some other theories that have preceded it as well as the social situation it in which it was originated. Thus, when introducing some of the central features of a particular theory it may often be necessary to refer to other theoretical formulations and politicoeconomic views that have, in one way or another, inspired these approaches. This means that in order to understand socialist egalitarianism or Marxism, we have to first understand the central features of capitalism and the problems of the market economy; in order to grasp the central aspects of contemporary libertarianism, we have to know the main problems of socialist egalitarianism; in order to understand the main focus of welfare liberal reasoning, we have to have an idea of what is meant by the utilitarian and the libertarian views of distributive issues; and in order better to understand the communitarian view of the justification of the distributional issues, we have to be at least somewhat familiar with both Aristotle's conception of justice as well as with Rawls's welfare liberalism.

A. Egalitarianism

The egalitarian concept of distributive justice promotes the view that people are equal and are entitled to equal rights and equal treatment in society. Egalitarianism emphasizes the ideal that all political distribution should be done according to people's equal worth. In principle this means that all citizens of a state should be accorded the same rights, privileges, social services, and material resources. There are, however, conflicting interpretations of what is really meant by *equality* and what the commitment to equality requires in practice. This means that even if the egalitarian conception of distributive justice is in general seen to promote left-wing politics and state socialism, nonsocialist theories may also present certain egalitarian features. For instance, conservative right-wing libertarians see that John Rawls's welfare liberalism, which promotes the equality of opportunity, is an egalitarian form of a liberal conception of distributive justice. The main difference is that the socialist view emphasizes the equal distribution of material resources and liberal egalitarianism emphasizes the equal distribution of political rights and basic social services. Thus, in order to clarify the central features of egalitarianism we should first make a distinction between the three major stands of egalitarianism:

1. Egalitarianism can mean that all *political rights* should be the same for all adult human beings. In terms of access to politics, suffrage, and equality before the law, social class, religion, ethnicity, or other criterion should not be allowed to produce inequality. This is the *minimum definition of egalitariansim,* and this part of it is accepted, at least in theory and often also in practice, in most Western democracies, and also some other types of states. It is also promoted by most of the liberal rights-based theories.

2. Egalitarianism may also be held to involve *equality of opportunity*, which implies that regardless of the socioeconomic situation into which someone is born, one should have the same chance as everybody else to develop one's talents and to acquire the same qualifications that others have. When individuals then, for instance, apply for jobs, their cases will be considered entirely on the basis of such talents and qualifications, and will not depend on their social status or on other random factors that they cannot themselves influence. Realizing this kind of egalitarianism requires, at the very least, an education and a social-welfare system that will train and will provide for the less-advantaged so that they can really compete on equal terms with those from more favorable social backgrounds. Politically, this could be seen as the philosophical justification for a social democracy, which allows some state involvement in distributional affairs. In practice, states try to achieve this situation by the application of a mixed economy, that is, partly capitalist and partly nationalized and planned, with high taxes and extensive welfare services. Philosophically or theoretically, for instance,

Rawls's welfare liberalism can be interpreted as giving a justification for this sort of *welfare egalitarianism*. Even if no modern state can be said to actually have achieved the goal of equality of opportunity, most of the modern welfare states have adopted this, at least in principle, as their ideal.

3. The most extreme version of egalitarianism is *socialist egalitarianism*, which would require not only equality of opportunity, but actual equality in material welfare and perhaps, at least in theory, also in political weight. Most Communist states accepted this socialist egalitarianism as the final aim, at least in principle. At its simplest, the core meaning of the socialist conception of distributive justice is its promotion of a politicoeconomic system where the state controls, either through planning or more directly, and may legally own the basic means of production and the distribution and redistribution of material and social resources. By its ownership of these resources the state controls industrial, agricultural, and other plants in order to produce what is needed by society, without regard to what may be most profitable to produce. The goal of the socialist theory of distributive justice is to produce an egalitarian society, one in which all are cared for by society, with no place for poverty and with no need for relief from poverty by private charity. The principles of socialist distribution are summarized in a famous dictum of Karl Marx (1818–1883): "From each according to his ability, to each according to his need."

Socialism or socialist egalitarianism, as a politicoeconomic theory, has gone though many variations, and dating its exact origin is impossible. Modern socialism stemmed from the industrial revolution. It arose as a reaction to capitalism after the development of extensive industrial private property in a society based on contractual rather than on semifeudal status relations. The general feature of the modern socialist view of distributive justice is that it sees the abolition of private ownership of property as essential, because the control of property is the very definition of a class system. Man takes his essence from labor in pursuit of material ends, and the control of material resources creates upper and lower classes and it gives the upper class control over politics, including the construction of ideologies and a social consciousness. According to socialism there are implacable economic rules that ultimately determine economic development. These economic laws make it inevitable that, ultimately, capitalist society will collapse because of its own inherent contradictions; then Communism will emerge. When summarized, the three tenets of the modern socialist theory of distributive justice are: (1) that economic matters ultimately control political and cultural phenomena; (2) that abolition of private property is necessary to ensure equality and an end to exploitation; (3) that the road to such a Communist society must come about through the proletariat and its leaders, with the development of a revolutionary consciousness. However, the essential ideas of material equality and the demands for common property can be also found in earlier views on distributive justice such as those found in Plato's (c.428–347 B.C.) *Republic*, and in the works of the such earlier social reformers as Fourier (1772–1837) and Saint-Simon (1760–1825).

1. The Problem of Egalitarianism

The problem of egalitarianism, and particularly socialist egalitarianism, is that such total equality in distribution of social and material goods, as suggested by it, is not regarded as possible, either theoretically or in practice. The practical difficulties of a fully equal distribution of material resources within one country or even just one city would be immense; to distribute equally among all the citizens would be logistically very difficult. Even if the socialist egalitarians were to settle for the idea that the equal distribution of material resources could be accomplished, for instance, by giving equal wages to everybody, there would still be problems. And only short-lived equality would be achieved by an equal distribution of wealth in this way. Different people tend to use their money in many different ways; the clever, the deceitful, and the strong would quickly acquire the wealth of those who are weaker, more gullible, or ignorant. Some people would squander their money, others might save it. Some might gamble their property away as soon as they got it, others might steal or cheat to increase their shares. The only way of maintaining anything like an equal ditribution of wealth and material resources would be by the forceful intervention of coercive authority. This would no doubt involve intrusion into people's private lives and would limit their freedom to do what they want to do. Thus, it is argued that equal distribution of material welfare, social services, and money is not only an unattainable but is also an undesirable goal in political reality. First, because such a sitution of total equality could only be attained by the extensive loss of liberty and, second, because it would be economically inefficient because it would provide no material incentives that reward effort. Empirical proof for this is evidenced from the states in Communist socialism that accepted the socialist egalitarianism as their ideal but failed tragically in realizing it.

B. Utilitarian Conception of Distributive Justice

At is core *utilitarianism* is the moral, social, and political theory that presents a simple equation between the good and happiness or pleasure. It claims that whatever measures, polity, choice, or decision we make, we judge our actions in terms of their consequences, whether these consequences are defined in terms of happiness, absence of pain and suffering, preferences, or "utility." The term utility does not refer merely to the usefulness of a particular thing, but rather means the quantity of value or desirability some things have in the utilitarian calculation. Generally, the aim of the utilitarian calculation is the greatest happiness of the greatest number.

We can distinguish three different features of utilitarianism:

1. Consequentialism: the rightness of actions—and more generally of the choice of all control variables (e.g., acts, rules, motives)—must be judged entirely by the goodness of the consequent state of affairs.
2. Welfarism: the goodness of states of affairs must be judged entirely by the goodness of the set of individual utilities in the respective state of affairs.
3. Sum-ranking: the goodness of any set of individual utilities must be judged entirely by their sum total.

Utilitarianism can then be discussed in two different roles: on the one hand as a theory of personal morality, and on the other hand as a theory of public choice, or of the criteria that are applicable to public policy. In this context utilitarianism is considered almost exclusively from the latter point of view, or as a theory of the correct way to assess or assign value to states of affairs that claims that the correct basis of assessment is welfare, satisfaction, or people getting what they prefer. The utilitarian tradition of Jeremy Bentham (1748–1832), James Mill (1773–1836), and John Stuart Mill (1806–1873), the maximization of social utility of all individuals, was made the basic criterion of morality and of the justification of public policies. What these classical utilitarians saw as social utility would now be the social welfare function of modern welfare economics. There have been many adjustments and refinements to the basic utilitarian theory over the years. Some of the most well-known contributors to the utilitarian theory of distributive justice include Henry Sidgwick (1838–1900), G. E. Moore 1873–1958), R. B. Brant, R. M. Hare (1919–), and John C. Harsanyi.

Modern utilitarian theories of distributive justice often present a particular form of utilitarianism called "welfarism" or "welfarist consequentialism." This requires the simple addition of individual welfares or utilities to assess the consequences, a property that is sometimes called sum-ranking. Sum-ranking, for its part, is a principle commonly used in economics, in which actions are judged entirely in terms of consequences, and consequences in terms of the welfare level of the worst-off person. The utilitarian calculation is seen to offer not merely a descriptive way of answering questions of the form, "How is society really going?" but also a prescriptive criterion of public action. It therefore must assume a public agent, some supreme body that chooses general states of affairs for the society as a whole: an ideal formulation of public rationality. In utilitarian theory this public rationality is usually described as an ideal of the "fully rational observer" who can calculate all the consequences of all our actions. There is also a utilitarian calculation that is based on the expected or foreseeable consequences and thus does not assume that all actual consequences were to be known. (On the utilitarian conception of justice and its criticism see Amartya Sen and Bernard Williams, *Utilitarianism and beyond.*)

The aim of utilitarianism is to escape, as much as possible, from reliance on any source of moral authority, whether this authority is religion, another metaphysic, or whether it appeals to such abstractions as "natural law." Although is not always explicated, nearly all parties and governments in the Western world tend to operate according to utilitarian reasoning. Most of economic theory, the whole of welfare economics, and many of the theoretical models of justification for democracy appear to be based, at least partly, on utilitarian views. Policy analysis, especially as developed by civil servants and academic specialists in the 1960s, is also based on utility calculus. And until recently the prevailing theories of law and jurisprudence were mainly derived from utilitarianism. Only after the 1970s did non-Marxist political theories begin to develop nonutilitarian general political philosophies and theories of distributive justice. It is also worth noting that even the new liberal approaches that were created as critical alternatives to utilitarian approach to distributive issues, such John Rawls's welfare liberalism and Robert Nozick's libertarianism, are, at least partly, based on a return to the classic liberal social contract tradition, which had clear utilitarian features built into its very structure. Mainly this is the tradition that started from John Locke (1632–1704) and developed to liberal utilitarianism by John Stuart Mill (1806–1073). In a modern secular society that has left behind the intellectual view of "scientific socialism," and that attempts to operate with minimal coercion in a more-or-less democratic manner, it seems to have been very difficult to find a serious alternative to an appeal to rational self interest, which is what also utilitarianism amounts to. (A summary in the utilitarian approach of political and economic decision making is to be found in Robertson, David (1985), *The Penguin dictionary of politics* (pp 328–339), Middlesex: Penguin Books.)

1. The Problems of Utilitarianism

There are three more obvious criticisms presented against utilitarianism. First, there is the practical difficulty of its application. It is extremely difficult to measure utility or happiness and to compare the utility or happiness of different people in different circumstances. How can we accurately assess the amount of utility or happiness that is likely to be yielded by particular actions, general rules, or distributional policies? A person's experience, the information one has, circumstances, and personal capabilities affect what one actually desires or what makes one happy. Should, for instance, those living in luxury with gourmet tastes receive more than those who live in more modest or even in poor circumstances with "cheap" tastes? Second, a utilitarian account of distributive justice is often criticized for its unfairness. The happiness of the majority may best be served by the sacrifice of some innocent party (i.e., for instance by sacrificing an individual in the name of the maintenance of social harmony) or by some manifestly unjust institution, such as slavery. And third, the utilitarian view of justice is seen to be too one-sided when it analyzes morality and justice entirely through actions and their consequences. When utilitarian reasoning is applied to practical politicoeconomic issues, it leaves individuals as mere rational and egoistic maximizers of their own utility, preferences, interests, or happiness. This makes the questions of justice an automatic rational calculation, and it ignores other moral intentions or motives, such as personal integrity and honesty.

C. Liberal Conception of Distributive Justice

A liberal conception of justice is, in general, seen as a rival or alternative view to both the socialist and the utilitarian conceptions of justice. However, despite the fact that liberals themselves are critical of both the socialist and the utilitarian approaches toward distribu-

tion in their own theoretical constructions, liberals have adopted, either explicitly or implicitly, some of the same features that appear to present a form of egalitarianism or that have some consequentialist elements in them. On the other hand a liberal conception of justice itself presents a collection of diverse views on distributional and other political issues. By its politicoeconomic agenda liberal theory is divided into two quite different approaches: welfare liberalism and libertarianism. Both of these approaches are liberal at the core because they promote liberal values of freedom and "natural" individual rights, particularly the right to property. Politically and economically, however, they present very divergent and even incommensurable views. When it comes to the practical measures that are needed to realize the liberal values of freedom and equality, they further almost opposite measures.

1. Welfare-Liberal Theory

For welfare liberals such as John Rawls, Will Kymlicka, and Ronald Dworkin, fairness, or a right to basic welfare and a right to equal opportunity, is the ultimate political ideal. Thus, welfare liberalism advocates *positive freedom* with more government intervention, especially when this is thought necessary to achieve what is valued by contemporary welfare liberals: for freeing people from ignorance and misery, or for solving other social problems, such as poverty. Today, welfare liberalism is sometimes used merely to politically designate any left-wing position, and it is said to be close to social democracy. In its promotion of equality of opportunity the welfare-liberal view clearly has some egalitarian features in it.

A welfare-liberal view on the distributional issues is most fully presented by John Rawls in *A Theory of Justice* (1971) and in *Political Liberalism* (1993). We now examine the main features of the welfare-liberal view of the distribution of social resources. Rawls's welfare-liberal theory was an attack on the prevailing utilitarian theories of social justice. It tried to reestablish some form of Natural Rights arguments that claimed that there are some values we all hold as absolute, such as the right to liberty and a right to equality. Rawls wanted to replace the utilitarian cost-accounting methodology with a more absolute form of argumentation. In order to do this he introduces a modernized form of the traditional social contract that can be used as a simple test to see whether a political or social institution is fair or not. When the contracting parties select the principles of justice in the "original position," they are not in a state of nature, but the parties are presented as rational and reasonable people. However, because "justice as fairness" emphasizes blindness to random differences between individuals, the bargaining advantages that inevitably arise within the background institution of any society (from cumulative social, historical, and natural tendencies) have to be eliminated. Thus, the parties of selection are subject to certain constraints on their motivation and knowledge. Though self-interested, these rational and reasonable agents are also disinterested in the other's interests and they are concerned only with their share of the primary social goods (such as rights and liberties, powers and opportunities, income and wealth, and self-respect and liberty). People in the original position operate behind "a veil of ignorance," which prevents them from knowing their natural characteristic and endowments, their social or economic position in society, their values or personal goals, or the historical period they are born into. The point then is that if you do not know whether you are to be slave or ruler, man or woman, of the twentieth or the twenty-first century, you could not opt for "unfair" rules, lest you end up on the wrong side of the bargain. Given these conditions Rawls believes that two principles will be selected: the first, which guarantees equal liberty, and the second, "the difference principle," which permits inequalities in other goods if they help the least-advantaged. The difference principle also then requires that those with various natural talents must be harnessed to benefit the least-advantaged.

There are several important critiques presented against the welfare-liberal view. First, Rawls's theoretical formulation of a welfare-liberal conception of justice is seen to be too abstract. In reality there are no such rational agents as the fictive social-contract method of justification describes. People are more or less tied to their social environment and to their existing social ties. In its attempt to be impartial and morally neutral, the welfare-liberal view may actually end up promoting inequality in practice by disregarding the actual relations of dependence and interdependence. Consequently, the problem of Rawls's distributive principles of the primary goods is that by assuming that justice as fairness means "difference blindness" it ends up assuming that people are quite similar, or indeed are each other's clones. In reality, however people are diverse in various ways, and they need different amounts of (different) goods to maintain the same level of well-being. Variations related to sex, age, genetic endowment, and many other features give us unequal powers to build freedom in our lives even when we have the same bundle of goods. Hence, equality in holding Rawl-

sian primary goods can go hand-in-hand with serious inequalities in actual freedom enjoyed by different persons.

Second, welfare-liberal theory also fails to explain what motivates us to adopt these two principles of justice. Why should people who are not in the original position believe it important that those subject to its stringent constraints happen to choose certain principles? Why should their choice "justify" our adopting these two principles of justice?

2. Libertarian Theory

Even as recently as the 1960s libertarianism or neoliberalism was somewhat of a fringe politicoeconomic theory that held extreme versions of liberal capitalist beliefs. Lately there has been a considerable upsurge in interest in libertarian thinking in some quarters, especially in the United States and in the United Kingdom, but also in some other modern Western welfare democracies. This is due to, first, the failure of state socialism, and second, the bankruptcy of most other non-Marxist political theories in the postwar world that have resulted in the political and economic crisis of the modern welfare democracies. The central feature of the libertarian view on distributive justice is that it is totally individualist. It rejects any idea that societies, states, or collectives of any form can be the bearers of rights or can owe duties. Social collectives are legitimate only insofar as they are voluntary aggregations of individuals, and not just because they may, as a matter of fact, make most or all their individual members betters off. Consequently, libertarian political theory is semianarchist in that it regards as legitimate only the very minimal state power that is necessary to uphold the prior existing rights, particularly the property rights, of the individual citizens. The essence of the libertarian approach is laissez-faire economics and a deep distrust of government intervention that would put social and legal constraints on individual freedom. Libertarianism, then, promotes *negative freedom* and sees that political liberty and the freedom of the markets are the most important things in society. Thus, restrictive laws, taxes, welfare, state economic control, and so on, should be eliminated or minimized. The libertarian theory holds that all individual human beings have a certain sort of natural rights, which are indefeasible. The prime natural right is the right to property. These natural rights cannot be given up, and they may not be taken away in the interest of the collective. Unlike in welfare liberal theory the state may not intervene to balance the rights and to ensure, for example, that someone who is starving is given welfare payments by breaching the property rights of another.

Hence, the libertarian view is politically farthest from socialist egalitarianism in distributional issues. Libertarians are individualists who see that different people deserve different amounts of financial rewards for the jobs that they do, and for the contribution that they make to society. They can argue that industrial and commercial proprietors deserve their wealth and affluence because of their relatively greater contribution to the city or the nation. After all, they make it possible for other people to work and to increase the general economic well-being of the whole geographic area or country in which they operate. On the other hand the higher wages are seen to be needed as an incentive for getting the important jobs done efficiently. No one capable of doing a difficult or a hard job, which may also require long training or an expensive education, would be willing to take one without the incentive of higher pay and a more prestigious social status. Thus, in the libertarian view the utilitarian features (although they are not usually explicated as such) come out when they justify inequality by appealing to the greater overall benefits to society that are seen to outweigh the costs of social inequality. Without big businesses, industrial production, and specialists there might be much less to go around for everyone. Libertarians believe then that gross inequalities in wealth between individuals are acceptable, and that everyone is mainly responsible for his or her own fate. Libertarians see that it is the attempt to distribute money and wealth equally that violates the equal rights of individuals, particularly the right to own property. According to libertarians this violation of the individual's right is always morally wrong because rights always trump any other considerations.

The theoretical formulation of contemporary libertarian political ideas has occurred as a criticism of the welfare-liberal theories of justice, as in Robert Nozick's *Anarchy, State, and Utopia* (1974), which heavily criticized Rawls's welfare-liberal political and economic ideas, for instance the idea that all goods that either exist already or are yet to be produced are the collective property of the social contractors, to be distributed among themselves at their absolute collective discretion. Nozick insists, first, that economic goods are not "manna from heaven," but instead usually are subject to prior claims of possession. Second he insists that we are all individually entitled to possess whatever we either have acquired without injustice, or will so acquire in the future. This also includes the products of our personal talents. This view emphasizes the Lockean classical liberal view of "self-ownership" that sees that individuals are entitled to whatever they produce by their own labor. According to Nozick when an individual has a right to property, this can come about in two ways: one may have legitimately acquired that property in the first place as an original act, or one may have had it transferred to him by a legitimate process from someone else who had a legitimate entitlement. As long as any distribution of property is covered by such rules, then the distribution is just, however inegalitarian it may be. Views such as Rawls's welfare liberalism, which concentrates on the justice of an "end state," that is, a particular distribution of property rights that seems valid in itself, miss the point that actual distribution arises from historical processes that give people entitlement, and justice inheres in the justice of the entitlement chain, not in the consequences of the momentary distribution. Nozick's libertarian enthusiasm for the free-market economy is also present, for instance, in the works of David Gauthier, F.A. van Hayek, and Milton Friedman, who all would like to return to the classical liberalism's historic concern to enhance for individuals the pliability and subtleness of life in regard to the constraints of social institutions, cultural traditions, and norms.

3. The Problems of Libertarianism

Libertarian right-based theory usually views the natural right to property as preceding political life and not being the product of the state. However, it fails to state where these rights come from. Thus, by natural rights libertarians do not mean legal rights, although such rights may coincide with legal rights in a just society: legal rights are those laid down by government or the appropriate authority. Natural rights, for their part, are rights that can be derived from "natural law," and ideally they should guide the formation of legislation and laws. But it is uncertain what the "natural law" is that gives people these property rights.

Second, it is argued that the contractarian conception of justice (thus, up to a certain degree this criticism is valid also with the welfare-liberal view) is based on the idea that sees justice as reciprocity, and thus ignores the social needs and rights of those who cannot fully contribute to the production of the social goods. This would leave the disabled, the old, the ill, and other marginal groups justifiably outside the scope of justice. The politicoeconomic problem of libertarianism is then that it leaves those who are the worst off in the hands of private charity and at the mercy of other people. However, because it is based on the idea that human beings are egoistic and think only of their own benefit, it does not encourage private morality or altruism. In practice libertarian policies then create broad social inequalities that tend to divide society between the rich and the poor. In this society there is a danger that the social harmony cannot be maintained and that the tension between these classes will turn into crime and violence.

III. CATEGORIZING THEORIES OF JUSTICE BY THE STANDARDS OF DISTRIBUTION

The politicoeconomic division does not succeed in covering all the central aspects of the theories of distributive justice. It leaves aside particularly the contemporary methodological discussion on the foundations of justice. Thus, it is justifiable to present another categorization that is achieved by dividing the theories of distributive justice by the standards these theories use as the basis of the distribution of social goods and material resources. (This is a division that was first presented by Thomas A. Spragens, Jr., in his article "The Antinomies of Social Justice," in *The Review of Politics* Vol. 55, Spring 1993, No. 2, but is further developed and discussed here.)

If we divide theories of distributive justice by the standard of distribution we arrive at three different categories. These are:

A. Hegemonic. Defending a single determining standard, such as needs for Marx, rights for Rawls, and entitlements for Nozick.
B. Skeptical. Finding that any standards for distributive justice are radically indeterminate if not meaningless, and thus the only proper way to distribute social goods is to rely on a rational decision-making strategy—the means and the practical outcome of this strategy vary depending on the circumstances. Such a protoutilitarian theorist as Hume, a utilitarian such as Harsanyi, and libertarians like Gauthier and Hayek would fit in this category.
C. Pluralistic. Claiming that we can disqualify all but a handful of standards but that we cannot definitely adjudicate among these, and thus we should rather focus on determining what it is that we want to realize with the just distribution. For example, human flourishing in Aristotle, autonomy and ideal citizenship in Michael Walzer, and human capabilities in Martha Nussbaum and Amartya Sen.

A. Hegemonic Theories of Distributive Justice

The hegemonic approaches to the questions of distributive justice define a single standard for the distribution of social goods and resources. In this hegemonic category we could then place such otherwise diverse liberal thinkers as Rawls, who uses the concept of individual rights, and Nozick, who uses entitlements as such a standard. These adherents of the hegemonic approach believe that it is in fact possible to ascertain a single substantive standard of social justice that is rationally persuasive. They believe that their conception of distributive justice should be capable of universal acceptance—by, at least, all rational people of good will. If the principles of justice are derived from eternal ideas, or from the demands of pure reason as is in the case with the social contract theory, or from the inevitabilities of a rational cosmos, one might attribute to them a legitimate hegemony over any contrary notions. In very different ways, the Marxist distribution according to need can therefore also be pressed with hegemonic force.

B. Skeptical Theories of Distributive Justice

Diametrically opposed to hegemonic theorists of distributive justice are the skeptics. The skeptical theories of distributive justice see that attempts to find any standards for distributive justice are radically indeterminate, if not meaningless. Thus, the only proper way to distribute social goods is to rely on a rational decision-making strategy—the means and the practical outcome of this strategy vary depending on the circumstances. In this category we could place at least the utilitarian calculus and even some of the most radical libertarian views.

For instance, the utilitarians theory expressly denies, at least in its earlier versions, any ordering, moral or otherwise, of the sources of pleasure as the highest good. Except for the distribution principles, "each man should count as one, and none for more than one," utilitarianism allows no other moral or political criteria of decision but the rational calculation. Utilitarians argue that, at least in principle, it ought to be possible directly to quantify and sum the positive and negative consequences in terms of pleasure or utility. Policymaking for society, as much as private moral decision-making for an individual, would then become essentially an automatic process. The skeptical approach denies the very possibility of a universal conception of social justice. For skeptics justice is merely a word, an illusory and artificial moral concept, customarily deployed in a hypocritical fashion to give a cover of fraudulent legitimacy to acts that are in fact based on pure self-interest. No matter how this is concealed or disguised in a theory the idea of justice in practice always receives a definition that coincides with the interests of the strongest party in society. Thus, the utilitarian theorists could be seen as skeptics who displace distributive justice with prudential calculation. Different outcomes are produced under this heading, depending upon the interpretation given to "utility." An example of this approach can, for instance, be found in the social philosophy of David Hume. As Hume notes, the abstract meaning of justice is "to each to his due." However, Hume argues, it is social convention that determines what shall be "due" to particular individuals. No transcendent criterion antedates the legal and conventional determination of this standard. What determines the content of social justice, then are the overriding general interests of society, and, in Hume's account, these general interests center upon peace and security. Thus, rules of social justice are conventions of property distribution that civil societies create and enforce in pursuit of their happiness and tranquillity. (See Spragens, 1993, pp. 196–197).

On the other hand some of the libertarian theories, such as those of von Hayek and Gauthier, may be said to deploy a similar skepticism about social justice to different effect: the libertarian insistence that every individual has his or her own goals and his or her own standard of justice. These goals and standards differ. The goals are legitimate expressions of individual preference, and the standards are, presumably, the product of sincere belief. No one is entitled to determine for others what their goals should be, and no one seems to be able to gain universal acquiescence in his or her particular conception of justice. We must choose, then, between tyranny and laissez-faire: either one party gains the power to impose his or her particular standards upon unwilling and unbelieving subjects, or each individual conception should be permitted to retain sovereignty over his or her own resources. Fidelity to market outcomes, it is concluded, provides the most perfect embodiment of the latter, nontyrannical alternative. (See Spragens, 1993, p. 196).

C. Pluralistic Theories of Distributive Justice

The pluralistic theories claim that we can disqualify all but a handful of standards, but that we cannot definitely adjudicate among these and thus we should rather focus on determining what it is that we want to realize with the just distribution. Thus, in order to choose the right procedure or right standards of distribution we have to know first what is the goal that we want to realize by just distribution. The pluralist position begins then by contesting both the hegemonic and skeptical claims. The pluralist approach to distributive justice finds unpersuasive the hegemonic-theories claim that a single substantive account for social justice can be demonstrated to enjoy superiority over all others. The pluralist approach also denies the skeptic's conclusion that a potentially infinite number of conceptions of justice can be generated—corresponding to a potentially infinite multiplicity of human interests—none of which may be deemed better than any other. Instead, in this view, theories of justice may be analytically reduced to a small finite set. Not one of this small finite group of conceptions of social justice can achieve a clear priority over the others. Each of them rests upon persuasive considerations adduced from rationally defensible moral principles. As a group, however, they exhaust the field of persuasive theories: no other theories are extant that can compare in logical or moral force. Hence, it is not appropriate, with the skeptic, to identify conceptions of justice with mere tastes, preferences, or simple interests.

Historically, we could say that the pluralistic tradition starts with Aristotle, with his criticism of Plato's hegemonic totalitarian socialism (not yet named in those terms). Aristotle developed an economic formulation of distributive justice that was close to that of modern social democracy. However, rather than trying to define the fair procedure of distribution, he focused on the goal of the distribution, that is, to the good that is to be realized by this distribution. Aristotle's theory was pluralistic in two senses. Aristotle not only saw that the goods should be distributed in consideration of how they realize human flourishing, but, as already mentioned, he also noted that there were two different spheres of justice to begin with: the distributive, or the forward-looking one, and the corrective, or the backward-looking one.

The modern pluralistic theories present very different views, but all of them tend to have their roots in an Aristotelian approach to distribution and in the instrumental value of social goods and material wealth. The similarity between Aristotelian and contemporary views is that they all base the standards of distribution on the ends that are to be realized. The difference, however, is that the contemporary view starts with redefinition of the concept of equality, whereas Aristotle started with the definition of "the good life." *The commu-*

nitarian view to distributive justice has been most fully explicated by Michael Walzer in his *Spheres of Justice* (1983), where he claims that each social good determines its own criterion of just distribution. Walzer's account is also pluralistic in a second sense, particularly when applied in practice. Walzer claims tht many different kinds of social goods (and evils) whose distribution is a matter of justice have their own particular criterion of distribution. For instance, the criteria used to determine who should get public honors cannot be the same as the criteria used to determine who should get medical care. He, however, does not provide any underlying principles that stand behind all of these distributive criteria, no core idea that might explain why honors are to be distributed in one way and medical care in another. Despite the fact that Walzer deliberately rejects the search for any fundamental principles of justice, he nonetheless wants to make one general claim about societies that respect distributive pluralism of the kind just outlined. The ultimate goal of distribution is to realize individual autonomy and ideal citizenship. This can be done only by creating a "complex equality" among the members of society. Complex equality occurs when different people get ahead in each of the various spheres of distribution, but because they are unable to convert their advantages from one sphere into another, none is able to dominate the rest.

Complex equality in this sense can be understood as an idea of equal citizenship. Complex equality is not a fundamental principle in the way in which equality, need, desert, or inalienable rights have served in the hegemonic theories. Complex equality cannot generate spheres of distribution, but it is better understood as an ethically important byproduct that, according to Walzer, appears in liberal societies when the autonomy of each distributive sphere is maintained. Walzer then follows the Aristotelian idea that the meaning of each social good determines its criterion of just distribution. Once we know what we have to allocate, Walzer argues, we also know how we should allocate—to whom and by what means. In the case of medical care, for instance, the distributive criterion is need; in the case of money and commodities, it is free exchange in the market, in the case of education, it is equality at the basic level and a capacity to benefit at a higher level: If there is disagreement about the distributive criteria, this must reflect disagreement about the nature of the good itself, so once we have settled the latter issue, the distributive question will resolve itself. Once we can establish for instance what medical care really means to us, we shall know by what methods and criteria it ought to be allocated among potential claimants.

The capability approach, for its part, was developed by Martha Nussbaum and Amartya Sen (it should be noted here that despite their emphasis on human capabilities, their separate approaches have different starting points). The capability approach attempts to replace the idea of a quantitative standard of living by quality of life. It defends the moral appropriateness of the concepts of functioning and capability in contrast to such alternative concepts as commodity and utility. The capability approach therefore heavily criticizes utilitarianism, libertarianism, and Rawlsian deontological liberalism. It attempts to build a distributive theory of justice that takes the goal of the distribution into account, that is, it sets the aims prior to the means. Following the Aristotelian view and Marxist criticism of capitalism, the capability approach sees that most of the modern views of justice, particularly the liberal ones, are based on "commodity fetishism," which gives intrinsic value to material goods and prosperity instead of the actual well-being of individuals. This means that material goods and commodities are valued as intrinsically good and thus the mere means are transformed to ends. The capability approach emphasizes that material goods and commodities are not good in themselves but are good only by virtue of their relationship to—and what they do for—human beings. It considers them to be mere means to well-being rather than having intrinsic value. Thus, we should ask, "what can goods do for people" or rather "what people can do with these goods," rather than seeing them as the end in themselves. Nussbaum and Sen also claim that modern views of justice disregard variations among individuals, and they ignore the fact that the same commodity has very different value for diverse people in different circumstances. It is evident that very different types of clothing promote our basic functioning in Africa than at the North Pole, or that a disadvantaged and incapable person gets less from primary goods than many other people. The capability approach suggests, therefore, that instead of focusing on the mechanically equal procedure of distributing individual rights, other primary goods, and commodities, we should look for the final goal of this distribution, that is, human well-being. According to the capability approach, this well-being can be defined in the form of human "capabilities" and "functionings," or "doings" and "beings." If we asked which things are so important that we will not count a life as a human life without them, we would end up agreeing with a list of the capabilities that make life worth living. The object of distributive justice is the enhancement of these valuable and valued capabilities that reflect an individual's actual freedom to choose between alternative lives (i.e., functioning combinations). The capability approach is introduced, for instance, in the works of Nussbaum, (1993), *Human Functioning and Social Justice*; in "Defense of Aristotelian Essentialism" (*Political Theory*, Vol. 20, No. 2, pp. 202–246); and in Sen (1992, *Inequality Reexamined*, Oxford: Clarendon Press).

To summarize, the three fundamental features of the pluralistic theories follow. First, the pluralistic theories create a view that rejects the idea of some universal fundamental principle or example that is believed to be behind all the more concrete beliefs and judgments that we express when we say that this or that action or practice is a fair or just one. This view is developed in conscious opposition to the hegemonic approaches, and it is radically pluralist in nature. There are no universal laws of justice or single standards of justice. Instead, we must see justice as the creation of a particular political community at a particular time, and the account we give must be given from within such a community. Because there is no single standard that can be used to distribute social goods, it is the goal of the just distribution of social goods that ultimately determines their distribution. This teleological nature of the pluralistic account seems to require that there is either a metaphysical or at least a conceptual link between the meaning of the goods and their principle of distribution. Hence, if someone proposed to distribute the goods in another way, this would, in the most literal sense, mean that he or she has failed to understand what the good in question really is. Thus, in the pluralistic theories, the meaning of the good and its criterion of just distribution really are tightly interlocked.

The second feature that the pluralistic theories of distributive justice have in common is their attempt to redefine and clarify the vague conception of equality. Rather than seeing equality as having intrinsic value, it is seen as a means to further ends. According to pluralistic accounts, equality as "blindness to difference" does not take into account the differences between people—the differences in their actual needs. The pluralist view sees that the theories based on ideal rationality present a "view from nowhere," which has no connection to reality and to the real problems and injustices of our world. A pluralistic approach involves the claim that justice needs more than abstract principles, and it needs to pay more attention to interpersonal and cultural differences rather than to merely ignore or disregard them.

It follows, then, that the third feature that these accounts share is their attempt to find a method of justification that does not argue from abstract principles but rather from meaning that is grounded in everyday social experience. This more empirical method is defended as a means that brings the theories of distributive justice closer to everyday politics and to the life of people, and that takes real injustices into account.

The problem of the pluralistic account lies in its vagueness and its ambiguity. For instance, it is difficult to define what is actually meant by valuable capabilities, and how the relevant capabilities can be distinguished from the irrelevant ones. It is also unclear how else, apart from merely following our intuition, we can know what kind of distribution different goods require. And finally, it seems that the emphasis on cultural and other differences between people may easily lead the pluralistic approach toward cultural relativity or conventionality, despite its teleological aspects.

IV. CONCLUSION

The categorical division presented here is not exhaustive and it does not attempt to cover all the central aspects of the theories of distributive justice. However, the purpose is to introduce the different types of theories and to emphasize the complexity of the issues of distributive justice. The modern distributive theories of justice, such as socialist egalitarianism, utilitarianism, or liberalism lately have been criticized for their abstractness and their failure to take into account the personal differences, local circumstances, and social ties that all affect our ability to enjoy our share of social goods. Thus, besides the traditional policoeconomic division of the theories of distributive justice, there is a renewed interest in developing theories of justice that focus on the goals of just distribution rather than on procedures that are merely right. These pluralistic theories attempt to replace abstract philosophical analysis and speculation with more empirical methodological views of the problems of distributive justice. In general, comparisons between different theories of distributive justice are very difficult. The theories themselves are often methodologically incommensurable, but they still overlap politically. The difficulty of a direct comparison between different theories is then due to their methodological incompatibility rather than to the economic or political views they present.

Also See the Following Articles

CONSEQUENTIALISM AND DEONTOLOGY • EGOISM AND ALTRUISM • THEORIES OF JUSTICE: RAWLS • UTILITARIANISM • VIRTUE ETHICS

Bibliography

Barry, B. (1989). *Theories of justice*. Berkeley and Los Angeles: University of California Press.

Crocker, D. (1992). Functioning and capability. The foundations of Sen's and Nussbaum's development ethic. *Political Theory,* **20**(4), 584–612.

Flew, A. (1985). The Concept, and Conceptions, of Justice. *Journal of Applied Philosophy,* **2**(2), 191–196.

Kymlicka, W. (1990). *Contemporary political philosophy*. Oxford and New York: Clarendon Press.

Miller, D., & Walzer, M. (Eds.). (1995). *Pluralism, justice and equality*. Oxford: Oxford University Press.

Sen, A., & Williams, B. (Eds.). (1982). *Utilitarianism and beyond*. Cambridge: Cambridge University Press.

Solomon, R., & Murphy, M. (Eds.). (1990). *What is justice? Classic on contemporary readings*. New York and Oxford: Oxford University Press.

DIVORCE

Bernard Baumrin
City University of New York

GLOSSARY

constructive desertion An established concept of desertion holding that if one person by physical or mental abuse makes it impossible for the other to live with the former, it is the former, the abuser, who is deserting and not the one forced to leave.

desertion A form of fault, where one party leaves (the home or the person). The other party then has (or should have) the opportunity formally to end the marriage. The deserting party is at fault.

divorce The legally sanctioned termination of a legally valid marriage.

separation agreement An agreement that stipulates property division, patterns of behavior, and issues of custody and maintenance of children and joint marital property.

DIVORCE, of course, is entirely parasitic on marriage. It is not only the case that one cannot have the former without the latter, but nearly always the very possibility of obtaining a divorce is embedded in the conceptualization of marriage employed when the marriage is actualized. A divorce is the legally sanctioned termination of a legally valid marriage. Marriage itself, as is well known, is not conceptually transparent. The standard case, qualifications aside, of a man and a woman joining together to form a family unit is mimicked by homosexual unions styling themselves as "marriages," with the distinct possibility that states will sanction such unions, and also by betrothals of underage individuals to each other and to persons of age. One should look at standard cases and ideal cases of marriage before examining standard and ideal cases of divorce, and one should understand the ingenuity that humankind has devoted to creating variations on the marriage theme.

I. MARRIAGE

The "ideal" case of marriage is one in which two adult (e.g., over 18 years of age) persons (one male and one female) voluntarily undertake to join together to form a union, a socially single entity, like a corporation or a partnership where, among other things, sexual exclusivity is assumed for both, and mutual ownership of the union's property and offspring is likewise assumed. No sooner said then exceptions spring to mind: one woman, several husbands; one man, several wives; "open" marriages where sexual exclusivity is not assumed (and may not be practiced); underage spouses; and property only in men, or only in women, or, for

that matter, resting with the father (or the mother) of one, depending on the social variation that has become traditional in a particular society. No feature of marriage is by itself absolutely essential so that one can say that without it there can be no marriage. The essential features are socially determined for a given society by the recognition that unions are accorded in that society. Indeed the Nuer of Africa are said to have a social system that permits unmarried women to marry dead men to legitimize children that they have had with other men.

One can argue that some unions are morally superior to others, and undoubtedly within certain societies or social groups, these arguments will be given significant attention. Arguments for monogamy will be received with interest where monogamy is the received practice, and arguments for polygamy where the practice is polygamy. It is unlikely that social practices will be changed by argument—rather, they are likely to be changed by actions. Just as women in Islamic societies may move (however gingerly) toward monogamy, just so people may move toward homosexual unions, calling them marriages, or to irregular (common law) unions and call them whatever one wishes.

To understand marriage, one must look at the law of the land within which the marriage will exist—perhaps no more can be hoped. So, where the state recognizes only male–female licensed unions as marriages, so in such places there are by definition no nonstandard marriages that are other than illicit, whether bigamous, same-sex, polygamous, or with the underaged. They may be marriages but not legal marriages. States that permit one or more of the above also permit ideal marriages, so we may take the ideal marriage as our jumping off point and treat nonideal marriages for the purpose of divorce analogously.

An ideal marriage involves at least the following properties: (1) a male and a female, (2) voluntarily agreeing to (3) a state-licensed or socially sanctioned union, and (4) publicly recognized or practiced. Whether the union is to be (5) life-long, (6) include sexual exclusivity, and (7) encumber property in special ways is inessential, however ubiquitous these features may be. They are, of course, crucial to the conceptualization and process of divorce. Whatever the society includes in its understanding of the marriage union is what is to be severed by the divorce. Properties (2)–(4) automatically end with divorce, but (5)–(7) may not. Yet more problematic is the status of children born to a licit union who, for one reason or another, one might wish to delegitimize. Here, in this area, only the laws of the society matter. If the law permits it (on a certain

showing), then a judge may delegitimize, but if it does not, the question never comes up; it is extrajudicial. In the Judeo-Christian tradition there is a rebuttable presumption of legitimacy for offspring born during a legitimized union. Courts are very reluctant to delegitimize offspring of a regular union, but it can happen and has happened. In some societies, particularly matrilineal or polyandrous ones, delegitimization is impossible.

Divorce, then, is the severing of the union marriage created. Still, before we look at divorce itself, we need to understand what kind of marriage we are seeking to dissolve. There are three main varieties, even in western culture. These are sacramental, contractual, and common law marriages. The first, usually created or administered by a religious personage, creates a union before god(s). Whether the state also requires such unions to be licensed is irrelevant; the characteristics of the union are determined by the religious context within which they occur. Contractual marriages (usually licensed, but not necessarily) take their form from the details of the agreement and what the state imputes to those holding themselves as married. Common law marriage is imputed to those who cohabit, in order to protect offspring and the (possibly weaker) spouse. States prefer these unions to be regularized (e.g., by licenses) because of the evident problem of bigamy which looms largest here since each cohabitor may go on to repeat the behavior with others. Palimony actions have their root in common law marriage, where each party may quite legitimately claim that there was (or that there was not) a marriage.

II. DIVORCE

Understanding, then, that the marriage in question might be any one of the three types, we may look to the question of dissolution by the operation of law—divorce. Common law marriage (whether or not legally recognized) raises the usual questions associated with divorce even though there will be no formal divorce if there is no legal recognition of the union.

Sacramental unions may be divorceable or undivorceable—that rests uniquely with the religion within which they occur. The state (particularly in multicultural or cosmopolitan societies) may permit divorce of persons sacramentally joined in an indissoluble union, much to the dismay of the practicing religious community. The state aside, the religion itself may provide for divorce; i.e., permit it in special or extraordinary circumstances. For example, a man may be

permitted to divorce a barren woman (regardless of whose fault), and a woman may divorce a man who seeks to become a celibate priest, is missing in battle, is gone 7 (or 10 or 2) years, or has become hopelessly insane. The difference between a divorce in these and other circumstances and an annulment is that the latter recreates the status of the parties as if the marriage had never occurred, and even though it cannot restore virginity, annulment can create illegitimacy, since the mother of the offspring was in theory never married to the father.

If some state (say Persia) legally permits divorce (for sacramental unions as well as contractual unions), then the law of divorce takes over the basic disposition of the rights and property of the parties. The law also specifies, in some cases in some detail, what it takes for the state to grant a divorce. States are generally opposed to automatic or even easy divorce because experience has shown that easy divorce often leads to women and their offspring becoming, in whole or in part, wards of the state. Hume in fact held in his essay "Of Polygamy and Divorces" that states should never permit divorce. He thinks that it is both immoral and a great social evil. Likewise Kant, for very different reasons, also argued for a blanket prohibition of divorce. A great deal of the law of divorce is concerned with preventing women and children becoming state dependents. Thus the grounds upon which one may seek a divorce—a state-sanctioned end to a voluntary union— are usually construed narrowly. There are the obvious grounds—infertility, adultery, incompetence, insanity, and desertion—each of which needs to be adequately proved, and then there are the less obvious ones—abuse (physical and mental) and incompatibility. The softening up of the rather negative view of divorce in modern western society stems in part from the extraordinary lengths that people went to prove they were entitled to a divorce under whatever legal system they were under, and in part from the combination of a falling birthrate and rising longevity. When "till death do us part" meant 15–20 years, divorce looked more self-indulgent than it does when the married period becomes routinely 30–50 years. Moreover, and surprisingly, a key element in the reason to marry—to provide financial security for women—eroded rapidly after WWII in western culture. Security becomes less an issue when women can enter the workforce and earn an adequate living on their own, and this has been facilitated by the wide availability of birth control devices which permit smaller and smaller families. To divorce a woman with five or so children is really no different than desertion (if made easy), while to do so if there are one or two (or even none)

is not, particularly if they are now themselves adults, off to university, or merely out of school.

It is, surely, not difficult to imagine that legally sanctioned marriage was initially embraced to provide security to pregnant and child-rearing mothers. Marriage serves as a socially enforceable tie. Security (not love) is still, in most of the world's societies, thought to be the primary reason a woman marries. Of course it is nice if it is to someone one loves, but failing that, some marriage is much better than no marriage. That is increasingly not true in advanced industrial societies. No marriage may be preferable to a bad or even a so-so one.

But, if even part of the purpose of a marriage is security, then a socially permitted divorce must provide as much as possible for that security as well, or else one party to the bargain, a voluntary union, may be being involuntarily divested of precisely what was originally bargained for—hence the other party is or would be unjustly enriched. Note that most of the problems associated with divorce would disappear if both parties had to consent to the divorce—so surely would a very great number of divorces disappear.

III. JUST ALLOCATIONS

Divorce, like any other termination of a contractual agreement, must provide for the termination either by the terms of the original agreement or by the operation of law. The parties, in contemplation of the possibly temporary nature of their alliance, may provide explicit terms (as in a collateral prenuptial agreement before the marriage occurs or in a postnuptial agreement after the marriage, or subsequent written modifications of either) for what will happen should the alliance end. The parties then divorcing may look to implement the specific terms of the operative agreement. The only legal issues will be whether the agreement was made under duress, or by one under age or incompetent and the like, or whether it flies in the face of some settled social policy as when it might seem after the fact to delegitimize otherwise legitimate children. Then the courts will not uphold the agreement, or at least those parts of the agreement which are so flawed. Some ethical issues will remain, as whether the agreement justly compensates each party, from the joint wherewithal, for their participation. The courts do not need to look at the ethical issues where there is a *valid* pre- or postnuptial agreement.

In the absence of such an agreement, the terms of a divorce must rest in the allocation of rights and responsibilities in accordance either with the terms of a *valid* separation agreement between the parties or with the operation of law (which itself will vary from society to society and even from social class to social class within a society). What will be a just allocation in one society (or social class) may be viewed as transparently unjust in another.

Before analyzing the problem of just allocations of a divorce, we should review the critical elements already discussed. These are that marriage is an agreement (if voluntary) whose terms are socially determined, unless modified by other agreements, prenuptial or postnuptial. Agreements, taken broadly, are mutual promises, so the law of contract and the ethics of promise keeping and promise breaking are involved. A principal point of undertaking marriage is security, usually, though not necessarily, for the woman, and usually, though not necessarily, for the offspring of the union. The state has an interest in protecting the weaker parties, particularly the children, and to prevent becoming the caretaker of those abandoned. The property of the spouses is jointly owned—at least the property accrued during the marriage, though arguably all property that comes (or will come) to the parties is joint property because in marrying one may very well do so banking on expectations which will accrue jointly after the union. Unless specific provisions of a voluntary agreement or the operation of law modify these expectations, they belong to the parties as a union or alliance and not to them as individuals.

This concept of joint ownership of the assets of a union is particularly difficult for men to accommodate themselves to. Generally, and in some societies nearly always, the men are the asset creators and conservators, particularly of money, real estate, financial instruments, and business interests. Men look at these assets that they have generated as their own; indeed in many societies they even perceive their women and their children as owned as well. Locke also subscribed to the view that men owned their children. Such conceptualizations prevent men from being at ease with the notion that some rather large fraction (perhaps even half!) of everything accumulated during a marriage belongs to the wife, soon to be disposed of. This conceptual problem is, and has been, the principal sticking point in divorce settlements even in the west. In many eastern societies the concept is rare. This disparity would be a fruitful area for philosophical investigation. Philosophers in the western tradition, on the whole, have no conceptual problem with equal distribution and, implicitly, would consider substantially unequal distribution basically unjust. But were this view adumbrated by philosophers

(the *prima facie* validity of near equal distributions) it would implicitly condemn other cultural patterns as immoral. This outcome raises the possibility that any proposal supporting equal or near equal entitlements would be looked at as merely a western cultural artifact.

The intertwining in divorce of moral, legal, religious, cultural, emotional, and psychological issues forms an almost impenetrable knot. The legal decision to grant or withhold a divorce (even when clear) does not really resolve the other issues satisfactorily.

Where marriages are created or recognized by the state, the state, usually through a court, recognizes (or decrees) a divorce, freeing the parties to remarry. The court evaluates the property interests of the parties and determines the allocation of the joint or marital property (in line with the social patterns and expectations of the society within which the court operates). Statutes, however, may predetermine various distribution patterns: e.g., community property, a 50/50 allocation; equitable distribution, allocation proportionate to the contribution of each party; and dower or dowry, an older pattern that guarantees the divorced woman a fixed amount or a fixed percentage of the marital or common property usually, though not necessarily, on her husband's death. In English (and hence American) common law this was one-third. This outcome was rare because until recently divorce was rare or in some places even nonexistent. A state may have no policy that protects women's property interests beyond providing alimony and/or child support, and it may not even provide for these elementary modes of security. The financially weaker party, usually the wife, may find herself immediately in financial difficulty as a function of an inadequate property settlement and no or sparse income prospects—especially if she is still child rearing or has no job skills beyond homemaking. While this state of affairs may be regrettable, it is often the only outcome since there may be very little joint wherewithal to begin with, and the husband's income may be inadequate to support even one home, much less two.

The parties themselves can negotiate the terms of their divorce by means of an agreement prior to a divorce, usually styled as a "separation agreement" which may stipulate property division, patterns of behavior, and issues of custody and maintenance of children and joint marital property. Where a pre- or postnuptial agreement already exists, its terms may already control any prospective divorce. Such agreements control so long as the parties voluntarily agreed, and, even though the agreements might be immoral, the courts will accept them and enforce them, so long as there are no illegal provisions.

The principal philosophic problems center around the idea of a just division of property and a just or moral division of responsibility for and custody of minor children. Both problem areas have to be viewed in both nonsocietal and societal terms. Analyses that *overlook* societal differences will appear very much like monotheistic theology appears to polytheistic and nontheistic cultures—at best, interesting irrelevant exercises, and at worst, cultural imperialism. Analyses occurring *within* a social context will, besides being ungeneralizable, have the appearance of ad hoc justifications of existing immoral practices. Western analytic philosophy is best suited to the former, but will appear, as much of this brief essay will already have appeared, to be idiosyncratic to a specific kind of society at a specific point in its development. Were we to produce a full-blown theory of ideal divorce, it might fit no present state pattern of divorce or at best just a very few.

IV. IDEAL DIVORCE

Ideal divorce concepts are easy to come by—they abound in the western press and in popular literature. The parties decide they do not wish to live together anymore (or at least one so decides). They draw up a separation agreement (probably with the help of professionals) that both parties are willing to agree to. This agreement sets out the following terms:

1. When the marriage will end, and when the separation will be official
2. What property each gets (or retains), and the relevant mechanisms for liquidation, division, and delivery
3. Who is to have custody of the children
4. Who is to support whom after the divorce, for how much, and for how long
5. Who is to support the child(ren), for how much, and for how long
6. Who is to have what responsibilities, and to whom, and when, and for how long; this particularly involves: (a) visitation for the noncustodial parent, (b) terms of joint custody, if that has been agreed to, and (c) occupancy and responsibility for the marital home if it is to be retained after the divorce
7. Such other terms and conditions that are relevant to the particular parties, including care of aging extended family members, adult children, and mutual business interests

An ideal separation agreement should dispose explicitly of each party's rights and responsibilities, unambiguously, and be one such that, emotions or psychological issues aside, each party (or any similarly situated person) will be willing to agree to and live by. I set aside emotions and psychological issues, because these may lead either party to hang on to the marriage, regardless of the justness of the agreement, or either party may wish to punish the other for wrongs done or imagined, and for pain inflicted during the marriage. No objectively adequate agreement can lay such issues to rest and there can be no ideal separation or divorce in such circumstances. In such cases, surely the majority, compromise is called for. Vindication and revenge should be avoided as much as is possible in order to make the rest of each party's life as satisfactory as possible.

The classic solution, prohibition of divorce, is the least satisfactory, and the next worst is the idea that the wronged party is to gain the largest share of the rights (e.g., the marital assets or custody of minor children). There are probably really no thoroughly innocent wronged parties involved. The most frequent wrongs that lead to divorce—adultery, boredom, and physical or mental abuse—do not occur in emotional or psychological vacuums. Each spouse is partly responsible for getting the couple to where they are. Other causes which lead to the desire to divorce are more functional and the blame more theoretical, i.e., related to the vow to cohabit forever rather than to what one party has done specifically to the other. Some couples are simply not suited to each other and the sooner they sever the inappropriate knot they have tied the better for both. Some mature, deepen, or age at different rates so that what might have appeared a reasonable long-term relationship becomes a patently unreasonable and increasingly unsatisfactory one. Some people are unsuited for the role of parent and cannot properly make the transition despite the desire to do so. In some, when health, physical or mental, is lost or the infirmities of age accrue, the marriage loses its reasons to be and ceases to gratify at least one party, and one may reasonably argue that only one life need be sacrificed because of any of the preceding circumstances rather than two (or perhaps more, if young children are involved). What needs to be clearly kept in view in these relatively faultless cases is that divorce does not cure the evil, it simply ends the relationship, and the parties, *as much as is humanly possible,* should make provision for each other.

Further on I will discuss the role of fault in divorce, but first let me turn to the condition introduced above—*as much as is humanly possible.* This is a way of capturing the justice condition of a divorce settlement. The concept of an ideal divorce includes the idea that as people both parties are equal. In societies and social groups where this equality is not recognized, ideal divorce is unlikely, and probably impossible. To respect the equality condition also requires a sensitivity to individual differences, rather than a merely mechanical 50/50 division of rights, responsibilities, and property. Some things, for example, children and houses, cannot be equally divided. Further, women are often rendered socially dysfunctional by marriage, particularly prolonged marriages involving child rearing and homemaking. In some societies once a woman has wed she is no longer marriageable again in that society. That a woman should get reasonable compensation for her now narrowed possibilities does not imply that her former husband spend his life supporting his now divorced spouse just as or nearly as she was when they were married.

What is just in large measure depends on what is reasonable given the means and resources of the individuals. If the joint means of the parties is inadequate for one comfortable household it cannot properly be divided to create the means for two adequate households. Both parties will be worse off. Working out the details of a reasonable division of property, rights, and responsibilities, including custody arrangements for minor children, is what should have the name of equitable distribution—that is, distribution in accordance with some notion of merit or desert. This concept has great promise but, because its implementation cannot be mechanical, it requires case by case application of the idea of meritorious division, not moral merit or the desert of revenge, but what will go furthest in dividing to further the interests of all the parties and leave each principal with some reward for the special efforts they have previously made or talents that are theirs alone.

In places where the idea of gender equality is foreign or rare, equitable distribution is not on the conceptual horizon; only where it is recognized that marital property is joint property and marital rights and responsibilities are joint can the idea of meritorious (or equitable) division develop the richness and ease of application to make it the prime vehicle for healthy, satisfactory, and emotionally acceptable divorces.

It should be clear that the present entry is advocating a position that justice recommends, but a position which is not widely practiced and one which would be considered quite revolutionary to most of the present population of the world. It is revolutionary because it not only holds that women have property rights (as well as custodial rights) in the property accrued by a couple during their marriage but, with respect to that property, they have equal claims. The idea being advanced is that departures from equal division require special justification. The rule of thumb should be, in the absence of a signed (pre- or postnuptial) agreement, the property accumulated by married persons during the period of their marriage is jointly and equally owned by them. Special circumstances might be employed to vary the result; e.g., if a spouse is absent for a considerable time and is making no contribution to the marital wherewithal, that might serve as a good reason to reduce the absent party's interest.

If a divorce is difficult or impossible to obtain then there is a sense in which the parties are not voluntarily increasing their joint property and one might wish to divide the property more along the lines of who put in the greater share should be rewarded with the greater share. This, of course, is the root idea underlying the theory of equitable distribution. But one should be looking more at the amount and quality of the effort and talent invested than at the actual wealth accumulated. Measuring variation from equal sharing is difficult but not impossible, and is desirable if a just division is to be made when the parties' input is vastly different. There is no philosophically sound reason to hold that a man (or a woman) when entering into a marital pact owns all he or she now has and all that will accrue; nor is there a compelling reason to measure each party's input only in monetarily expressible terms. It seems more reasonable to hold as a baseline concept that the parties hold and will hold equal shares in their joint wealth unless and until they sever their marital ties.

The baseline concept that each party holds an *equal share* of the common wherewithal appeals to the notion of justness as equality or fairness. Throughout the foregoing discussion I have suggested that this mechanical formula is inadequate (though relatively easy to apply). Equitable distribution, distribution according to desert or merit, while difficult to determine, appeals to a different conception of justice and one which is always, or very nearly so, inconsistent with equality or fairness. We can characterize the two patterns of entitlements as follows: in *common property* everything accruing to the spouses belongs to them equally, and if a division is to be made it is to be divided equally or as equally as possible. In *equitable property* each is entitled to a share proportional to the value of their investment. The investment need not be thought of only in monetary terms, though normally the payout will be made by a largely monetary division. Plainly, in equitable distribution, there will be no way of determining entitlement shares on other than a case by case basis, nor will the person who made the larger, or, indeed, the only, cash contribution be necessarily entitled even to half of the marital wherewithal. Distributive shares will very much depend on who did what for how long and under what conditions.

No doubt one whose ideal of justice is equality will perceive injustice in anything but an equal distribution. Similarly, one whose ideal of justness crucially involves desert will be put out by an equal distribution. In actual cases divorce settlements tend to fudge the distinction between the two patterns of distribution. Rarely, if ever, is homemaking valued above bread winning on an hourly basis so that the nonemployed spouse gets a larger share of the joint wherewithal, but clearly this should happen in a significant number of cases. In the United States, generally speaking, in equitable distribution jurisdictions women never get 50% of the joint property.

Even though these two patterns of division of marital property are inconsistent with one another, each, by itself, can lay claim to being a just division. Divisions that cannot be seen as a version of one or the other are *prima facie* unjust, and should be rejected by courts (and avoided by legislators). In this regard the recommendation that a state adopt either pattern can be viewed as a bit of cultural imperialism. There can be, however, no compromise philosophically on the equality of status that men and women share. It is not long ago, for example, in England and in the United States that women could not hold property in their own names and supervise their own financial lives. This is still true in many of the world's communities. Wherever women still stand to lose financially by marriage there is considerable room for moral progress.

The same rule of thumb, equal sharing, should be applied to the thorny issue of custody of minor children. Ideally this issue should be decided by the parties in some predivorce agreement. However, this is often not possible because of the emotional investment that parties place in their children. When the fractious issues related to fault are laid aside, the determining factor for an intervening third party (like a judge) should be what is optimal for the children in the circumstances, given the reality that what is best for them is unlikely to be an available alternative.

Interestingly, philosophers (who rarely discuss such issues) have held widely divergent views on who has the superior right to custody. For example, both Locke and Filmer thought that fathers owned their offspring, and Hobbes (writing before Filmer's *Patriarcha* was published in 1680 and before Locke wrote) thought it was clear that mothers should have custody (primarily on the ground that one could always be surer that the

children were indeed the mother's). Such rigid rules no longer seem appropriate. What seems more reasonable, given the extraordinary emotional stake that is involved, is that on the whole the children should be primarily with the parent that can provide the most suitable environment for the children. In some cases that may mean that one or more of the children will go with the father and one or more of the children with the mother, and of course there should be no initial bias that mothers are to be preferred to fathers (as in Locke's time there seems to have been such a bias in favor of fathers). Justice is served by having the parties start out with equal claims, and the final determination should rest entirely with the particular circumstances of the case.

V. FAULT

I turn now to the concept of fault and its consequences for divorce. Briefly, I already said that probably no party is a thoroughly wronged innocent. But, of course, one might be thought to be very much more blameworthy than the other. There are four areas of behavior that can be isolated, and blameworthiness aside, we need also address the question of whether or to what extent fault should play any role in divorce. If, for instance, divorce is freely available to either party (regardless of the reason) then fault, if it is to play any role, affects only the divorce settlement. If it is not freely available but requires that one party allege and prove something (e.g., adultery, insanity, or barrenness), then fault goes to the essence of the possibility of divorce, but might arguably have nothing to do with the settlement.

The four areas are vow breaking, incompatibility, desertion, and becoming another. First, and best known, are the varieties of vow breaking, of which the most salient is the very desire itself to terminate the marriage. The parties undertook to live together in sickness, and for worse, until death. One party is now terminating these undertakings. This, even in the absence of any specific act(s) of betrayal, is a moral fault: promise breaking of the most solemn vow one ever makes to another human being. From this point of view every person who seeks a divorce is immoral, whether they are the wronged or wronging party. Frequently infidelity is alleged as the ground for a divorce, and the wronged party is thought entitled to have one. But clearly adultery, at least in sacramental marriages, should not be grounds because the wronged party undertook to forgive (or at least overlook) when the wronged party vowed "for better or worse till death do us part." The adulterer is, of course, immoral, for he or she is already a vow breaker, but this does not license the wronged party to break a vow that clearly encompassed the wrong in question. So when the law permits divorce on the grounds of adultery, or any other specific act of immorality, it permits the wronged party to do something equally immoral, namely, break their solemn vow to endure. One might imagine that the vow is already modified by the statutory ground for divorce, but this is incorrect. A mere contract for marriage, followed by a license, might reasonably be thought to be conditioned by its nullifying ground, but a vow contemplates no nullifying ground—they are irrelevant to the boundless scope of the vow. In this regard sacramental unions are more serious undertakings than either licensed contractual marriages or common law unions.

Second, incompatibility, or whatever other name one might employ to designate mutual unsuitability, names the fact that people often can not get along with each other, and to marry each other is not the obvious solution. When they have already married and then find this out the quicker they part the better. Unfortunately the laws, or offspring, may make this difficult, or even impossible. Here the fault comes from marrying in haste, or without sufficiently serious investigation into the nature of the other person. Both defects are frequent with the young and, of course, it is the young who do most of the marrying. Is anyone really to blame for the resulting mismatch? Probably not, or at least not much. But prolonging the marriage seems the least desirable outcome. Hopefully in such cases both parties will want to end the relationship amicably, causing the least damage possible. Legal systems should readily accommodate themselves to faultless mutually voluntary divorce—sometimes incorrectly styled "no-fault divorce." Strictly speaking, "no-fault divorce" is simply the right to obtain a divorce without alleging fault in the other party. Such a right enables one to obtain a divorce even when the other party opposes it.

Desertion, as a third form of fault, is pretty straightforward. If one party leaves (the home or the person) then the one who remains has (and should have) the opportunity formally to end the marriage so that he or she can, perhaps, start a new separate life. The deserting party is clearly at fault, having broken the vow, but also is not entitled to any of the marital property or custody of the children. And just as clearly, if they left with most of the marriage's wherewithal they have stolen at least some of the deserted party's wealth. What conceptually complicates desertion is that one party may create a "living hell" for the other or the minor children and drive the other out or away. If they leave are they deserting? A famous Australian case from the late 1940s, *Lang v. Lang* (1948; A.L. 1953), established the concept of constructive desertion. The point of constructive desertion is that if one spouse by physical or mental abuse makes it impossible for the other to live with the former, it is the former, the abuser, who is deserting and not the one forced to leave. So the one who leaves in such circumstances retains whatever rights one had. The fault is with the abuser, not the abused, who should not further suffer for taking the rational way out. Of course, the deserted (abused) spouse is entitled to a divorce, and surely not less than half the marital assets and custody of minor children and the marital home, just as much as if the abusing spouse had left for points unknown.

Finally I come to "becoming another," which contains elements of the preceding. Sometimes people simply grow apart; they deepen differently, they age or mature at different rates, they become infirm or alcoholic, etc. Together the couple are not just an older version of who they started out as—they are, or at least one is, different people, seemingly still now bound by the vows of a distant long-forgotten youth. The vows of course last till death, but is this different person still to be bound by them? This raises the issues familiar in philosophy in the problem of personal identity. The law of contract does not recognize the concept of becoming another, nor could it, but the law of divorce could. First, because these older people could have become incompatible, and second, in a sense, though not an obvious one, one spouse is deserting or already has deserted the other (at least psychologically). But while there will be blame for vow breaking, should one leave or seek a divorce there is no real fault here. One becomes what one becomes slowly, often choicelessly, and not fully cognizant of what one is giving up or where one is going. When we get there, for example, as an alcoholic, priest, or homosexual, we are not what we were nor will we ever be again.

The changes need not be so dramatic. A person may simply have, for example, ceased being, or have become, a socialist or a Christian. In short, the person one married is gone, replaced in some cases by an unacceptable impostor—physically the same, though older, but intellectually hugely different; so different it would be like living with an unpalatable stranger to continue to cohabit. Such change it has seemed to many justifies divorce very much more so than any single ground, and the fault, were one to continue to analyze with such an intellectually dull tool, is in both parties—the one who has stood still surely as much as the one who vaulted ahead.

The outcome of this analysis is that there is no relevant concept of fault that should play a role in either the justification or the prevention of divorce. It should be enough that either party wants it. So long as the rights and responsibilities of the parties are justly allocated, no bar should be made or penalty exacted for having been in the wrong. Such concepts need play no serious part in divorce; relationships change, deteriorate, and collapse. Divorce simply brings them to their proper end.

Also See the Following Articles

CHILDREN'S RIGHTS • FAMILY, THE • PERSONAL RELATIONSHIPS

Bibliography

Becker, G. S. (1991). *A treatise on the family*. Cambridge, MA: Harvard Univ. Press.

Elster, J. (1989). *Solomonic judgments*. New York: Cambridge Univ. Press.

Glendon, M. A. (1989). *The transformation of family law: State, law and family in the United States and western Europe*. Chicago: Univ. of Chicago Press.

Jacob, H. (1988). *Silent revolution: The transformation of divorce law in the United States*. Chicago: Univ. of Chicago Press.

Phillips, R. (1989). *Putting asunder: A history of divorce in western society*. New York: Cambridge Univ. Press.

Stone, L. (1990). *Road to divorce: England 1530–1967*. Oxford: Oxford Univ. Press.

Trainer, B. T. (1992). The state, marriage and divorce. *Journal of Applied Philosophy, 9*(2).

Weitzman, L. J. (1985). *The divorce revolution: The unexpected social and economic consequences of divorce for women and children*. New York: Free Press.

DO-NOT-RESUSCITATE DECISIONS

Johannes J. M. van Delden
Utrecht University

I. Morally Relevant Facts
II. Ethical Aspects of DNR
III. Conclusion

GLOSSARY

cardiopulmonary resuscitation A treatment for acute failure of circulation and/or respiration, and of which at least chest compressions and/or breathing form a part, without which death is certain.

competence A task-specific threshold concept that addresses the decision-making process. Someone is competent when she is able to appreciate the nature of the situation so as to reach a decision adequately.

do-not-resuscitate (DNR) decision An explicit, anticipatory decision not to attempt cardiopulmonary resuscitation when a patient sustains a heart and/or breathing arrest.

do-not-resuscitate policy A total of formalized agreements on the level of a unit or on the level of an institute concerning the resuscitation of patients.

do-not-resuscitate protocol A written DNR policy.

futile Describing treatment from which no positive effect may be expected or for which a consensus exists among physicians that the chances of such an effect are too small.

therapeutic privilege An exception to the rule of informed consent, based on the judgment that to disclose the information would be potentially harmful to a patient in a way that outweighs possible benefits.

THE FIGHT AGAINST AN UNTIMELY DEATH is an element of medical science which comes to the fore especially with cardiopulmonary resuscitation. A successful cardiopulmonary resuscitation constitutes a victory over death. Hence modern resuscitation techniques are considered one of the breakthroughs which advanced medical science has offered humanity. The importance of resuscitation is reinforced by the fact that everyone eventually dies. For everyone there is the moment when heartbeat and/or respiration fails. Thus all humanity is a possible candidate for resuscitation.

However, resuscitation has its drawbacks. Resuscitation is more often than not unsuccessful, and practicing it involves some technical violence. When the resuscitation attempt is not successful, then the process of dying may have been severely disturbed with no compensatory positive effects attributed to the intervention. Moreover, death need not be fought with all possible force for all people. In short, sometimes it is better not to resuscitate at all. When not to resuscitate is the subject of the present contribution.

One problem is the fact that the decision to start resuscitation needs to be taken quickly. Hence the question, "should this patient be resuscitated or not?" must be answered when there is time to think it over. When this kind of decision-making process leads to the decision not to intervene, a do-not-resuscitate decision (DNR decision) has been taken. Only decisions taken before a possible arrest are looked upon as DNR decisions. A decision to stop a resuscitation attempt already in progress is not covered by this definition. This matter derives its moral importance from the fact that by making a DNR decision, one takes the responsibility that the decision may shorten a patient's life.

The objective of this contribution is to describe some morally relevant facts, to give a normative analysis of the reasons not to resuscitate, and to offer some considerations with which to formulate a DNR policy. The focus is on hospitals, because this is where DNR decisions are most often made. Some mention of nursing homes will also be made, however.

I. MORALLY RELEVANT FACTS

A. Cardiopulmonary Resuscitation

1. What It Is

Cardiopulmonary resuscitation (CPR) is a treatment for the acute failure of circulation and/or respiration. Although it is often looked upon as another example of high-tech modern medicine, its roots are much older, probably as old as the human being. The present method of resuscitation, however, was developed in the 1950s, when the scientific basis for rescue breathing with the mouth-to-mouth technique and for closed chest compressions was provided. Even today the provision of an open *airway*, the performance of rescue *breathing*, and the restoration of *circulation* by means of chest compressions form the ABC of the first phase of CPR, called basic life support (American Heart Association, 1992. J. Am. Med. Assoc. **268**, 2171–2295). In health care institutions, be it hospitals or nursing homes, this will often be done by the nursing staff.

The second phase of CPR is called advanced cardiac life support. In this phase adjunctive equipment and special techniques are used for establishing and maintaining effective ventilation and circulation. This includes electrocardiographic monitoring of the cardiac rhythm, establishing an intravenous access, drug therapy, and intubation. Also, defibrillation by electroshocks may be necessary. Advanced life support is provided by special resuscitation teams.

2. The Results

The results of cardiopulmonary resuscitation in hospitals have been described in a considerable number of studies. The comparability of these studies is limited, however, for reasons of study design and definitions. With these limitations in mind, it can be calculated that on average resuscitation is initially successful—that is, heartbeat is restored—in 38% of the cases. As many patients die later on, the chance of discharge from hospital is much smaller, to wit, 14% on average (H. Tunstall-Pedoe *et al.*, 1992. *Br. Med. J.* **304**, 1347–1351). One may expect these percentages to rise with the increasing number of do-not-resuscitate of (DNR) decisions because only patients with good chances of success are resuscitated. Factors determining the success rate include the underlying illness of the patient, the type of rhythm disorder with which the arrest began (fibrillation versus asystole), and the time between cardiac arrest and start of resuscitation.

Not all of these aspects are known at the moment a DNR decision is considered, but the patient's condition is. Roughly, it is possible to distinguish between cardiac patients (where resuscitation is relatively successful) and patients with an advanced, progressive, ultimately lethal illness (where resuscitation attempts are mostly without success). It has been shown that patients in the following situations have extremely low chances of survival (meaning almost zero percent) to hospital discharge (D. J. Murphy and T. E. Finucane, 1993. *Arch. Intern. Med.* **153**, 1641–1643):

— Metastatic cancer (patient bedfast)
— End-stage liver disease (advanced cirrhosis)
— HIV infection (after two or more episodes of pneumocystis carinii pneumonia)
— Coma patients, not awake after 48 hr
— Patients with multiple organ failure without improvement after 3 days in intensive care
— Unsuccessful out-of-hospital CPR

Whether age alone has predictive value has long been an unsettled matter. According to some studies it does, while others have seemed to prove that it does not. However, combination of the results of several studies shows that persons over 70 years of age do have a smaller chance of survival to discharge (relative risk 1.4). Nevertheless, old age alone does not preclude a successful resuscitation (Tunstall-Pedoe *et al.*, 1992).

It is not only the chance of survival that influences the decision of whether or not to resuscitate—the quality of life after successful resuscitation is also a morally relevant fact. This quality is to a large extent influenced by the neurological condition of the patient. In spite of this, not many studies describe this factor. The study of Longstreth does, however. He found that one out of five patients who initially survive the resuscitation but who die before discharge from hospital regain consciousness. A number of neurologic disorders occur with one-third of the surviving patients (A. S. Jaffe and W. M. Landau, 1993. *Neurology* **43**, 2173–2178; W. T. Longstreth *et al.*, 1983. *Ann. Intern. Med.* **98**, 588–592). These disorders range from memory deficits to persistent vegetative state.

The quality of life after resuscitation may also, at least temporarily, be influenced by complications due to resuscitation. Skin burns, broken ribs, and stomach injuries may result from CPR, even when properly performed. Incidences range from 21 to 65% of resuscitations. Although the American Heart Association correctly observes that fear of complications should not prevent one from providing CPR (AHA, 1992), these complications are part of an analysis of the burdens and benefits of CPR.

B. Do-Not-Resuscitate Decisions

1. Incidence

During the 1960s cardiopulmonary resuscitation developed from a "treatment" for unexpected cardiac death to a technique which was always tried when a patient was found pulseless and/or without breathing. Soon, however, the inappropriateness of this policy was recognized. In 1974 the American Heart Association stated that the purpose of CPR was the prevention of sudden unexpected death and that CPR was not indicated in cases of terminal irreversible illness. This made it necessary to decide when to use CPR and when not to. Thus do-not-resuscitate decisions came into being. They can be defined as explicit, anticipatory decisions not to attempt cardiopulmonary resuscitation when a patient sustains a heart and/or breathing arrest.

The number of DNR decisions has been increasing since those days and continues to do so. The Netherlands probably had the first nationwide study of DNR decisions (J. J. M. van Delden *et al.*, 1993. *J. Med. Ethics* **19**, 200–205). All interviewed specialists, regardless of specialty, had at some time made a DNR decision. In most cases (96%) they had done so at least once during the past year. It was estimated that 90,800 DNR decisions were made in hospitals in 1990. This amounts to 6% of hospital admissions. Of all in-hospital deaths (the total being 53,500 per year) 61% were preceded by a DNR decision. In acute deaths there is no time to make anticipating decisions. When these cases were ignored, 80% of patients died with a DNR decision. With 90,800 DNR decisions per year and 32,000 deaths preceded by DNR, 65% of DNR patients left the hospital alive.

The Dutch percentage of admissions in which a DNR decision is made (6%) is higher than that given by American studies in the 1980s. Then it was usually reported that a DNR decision was made for 3–4% of all hospitalized patients (B. Lo *et al.*, 1985. *Arch. Intern. Med.* **145**, 1115–1117; C. J. Stolman *et al.*, 1989. *Arch. Intern. Med.* **149**, 1851–1856). More recent American investigators reported incidences of 9–12%. The percentage of deaths preceded by a DNR decision is reported to be 62–70% in the United States (Stolman, 1989). This coincides with the Dutch figure (61%). DNR decisions thus clearly form an intrinsic part of daily medical practice in hospitals on both sides of the Atlantic Ocean.

2. Different Interpretations

One of the problems with DNR decisions is that doctors (and nurses) interpret them differently. In spite of the fact that the scope of the decision in almost all definitions is limited to resuscitation, a DNR decision often leads to other limitations of medical treatment. In one study DNR decisions de facto led to limitations in the use of artificial respiration, ICU admission, blood transfusions, antibiotics, and even analgesics. In another study the author found that some form of treatment was withdrawn for 28% of patients for whom a DNR decision had been made (S. E. Bedell *et al.*, 1986. *J. Am. Med. Assoc.* **256**, 233–237). And yet another reported that nurses are significantly less likely to perform a variety of monitoring modalities and interventions for patients with DNR decisions.

Some comments need to be made at this point. Generally speaking, two situations have to be distinguished. On the one hand the mere fact that a DNR decision is made might lead a doctor to assume that other care needs to be limited as well. This type of reasoning endangers the efficacy of any DNR policy, since other doctors, in response, might become reluctant to make DNR decisions out of fear of stigmatizing their patients.

On the other hand the circumstances that justified the DNR decision might also form the reason for other nontreatment decisions (NTD). If these NTDs are discussed with the patient or his surrogate and have a sound medical (and ethical) basis, there is no need to condemn them. In short, DNR decisions are compatible with maximum medical care (short of CPR), but may also be accompanied by other NTDs. This is especially true because DNR decisions seem to mark a change in the chances attributed to a patient. When the hope for recovery lessens, a DNR decision is often the first of a series of NTDs.

3. Slow Codes and Partial Codes

Another problem arises when doctors use slow codes. Slow codes are named after the fact that in hospitals the resuscitation team is warned by dialing a certain code. They are sometimes part of a official DNR policy, but more often will live an unofficial life. In case of a slow code, the resuscitation team is supposed to "run slowly" to the patient. By doing so they create a situation in which resuscitation will certainly fail. Thus, slow codes really are "show codes": the purpose is to appear to provide CPR while not actually doing so. These codes are therefore not morally (nor medically) defensible.

Slow codes are to be distinguished from partial codes in which resuscitative efforts are explicitly limited. It may be very well defensible to decide only to resuscitate when ventricular fibrillation occurs, because the patient resuscitated for this kind of rhythm disorder has a relatively good prognosis. Partial codes, however, may also be used to deceive, and in that case are as objectionable as slow codes.

II. ETHICAL ASPECTS OF DNR

A. Why Bother?

Why should doctors think about the appropriateness of CPR and record DNR decisions in medical charts? Why do they not "simply" resuscitate everyone with an arrest? After all, if the patient lives, a life is saved, and if she dies, the outcome would be the same as without resuscitation. What, then, is the benefit of DNR decisions?

The purpose of thinking about whether or not to use CPR is to prevent a pointless reduction of the quality of dying. Quality of dying is defined as the quality of life at the end of life. An unsuccessful resuscitation attempt disturbs the process of dying while adding nothing. All treatments that are greatly appreciated as tools for saving a life become violent and intrusive techniques if they are used without a chance of success. The loss involved when CPR fails is not the death of the patient, but the damage to the quality of the last part of life.

Although the reason mentioned above seems to be the most important one, other reasons for thinking about CPR can be given. In some cases patients themselves will not want to fight death at all costs. Moreover, in certain circumstances CPR may not be a wise or just use of limited medical resources. In some Dutch nursing homes, for instance, the management (working with a fixed budget) preferred extra nursing staff over resuscitation facilities, arguing that the emphasis should be on care instead of a (high-tech) cure. Finally, medical and nursing staff will get demoralized by too many unsuccessful resuscitations. That is why it is sometimes better not to resuscitate at all and always good to determine the appropriateness of CPR.

B. Who Decides?

1. Involvement of the Patient

If DNR decisions are (sometimes) justified, then who is to make the decision? In this section the following "candidates" are considered: the patient and the physician. In some circumstances the patient may be represented by someone else. This will be discussed in Section C.

In health care it is of supreme importance to respect patients as autonomous people. Therefore, the same requirements stand for CPR as for any other treatment: it may only be performed after obtaining informed consent from the patients. And the same goes for deciding not to resuscitate. This latter point needs more justification, because doctors normally are not required to seek consent for everything they do not do. But if they plan to withhold a treatment that a patient may reasonably expect to get, as is the case with CPR, they should discuss this, generally speaking, with the patient involved.

But let us see what actually happens. Are patients involved in the decision-making process and do they want to be? In the Netherlands the decision not to resuscitate was discussed with the patient in 14% of all cases (van Delden *et al.*, 1993). These patients constituted 32% of all competent patients with DNR, which means that 68% of competent patients were not involved in the DNR decision.

One study found a similar practice of infrequent discussions with patients in Sweden. This contrasts rather sharply with the United States, where a large majority (77–98%) of competent patients are involved in the decision (Bedell, 1986; Lo, 1985; Stolman, 1989).

Patients themselves have been shown to want to participate in deciding about CPR in a number of studies. One of these contains the interesting observation that patients would rather be informed about their situation (e.g., prognosis) than decide themselves. It is not without value to mention at this point that the way in which the information is given is very influential. It would need a very self-assured patient to answer in the affirmative the question, Do you really want us to do all the heroics and pound on your chest and maybe break your bones?

One of the reasons for not involving a patient may be the concern of the doctor that the patient cannot cope with discussing CPR. In that case the physician invokes the therapeutic privilege. In the Dutch study this was done quite often (van Delden *et al.*, 1993). There were 60 cases (30% of total) in which the DNR decision was not discussed with a competent patient. In 35 of these the physician stated in one way or another that this discussion would be too burdensome for the patient, thus invoking the therapeutic privilege. In 10 cases of these the respondent added that for this reason it was his policy never to talk about DNR decisions with a patient.

In accordance with the views of many ethicists (e.g., T. L. Beauchamp and J. F. Childress, 1994. *Principles of Biomedical Ethics,* 4th ed. Oxford Univ. Press, New York) one should reject such a practice. It seems to be a relic of paternalistic behavior in medicine that no longer fits the present day views on the physician–patient relationship. One fears that discussing DNR is rather too burdensome for the physician instead of for the patient. One should plead, therefore, for a strict interpretation of the therapeutic privilege. Moreover, empirical evidence indicates that negative effects such as anxiety materialize less often than physicians tend to think.

At the beginning of this subsection it was stated that patients should be involved in the DNR decision. We saw that quite often they are not, and also that this happens for the wrong reasons. It seems, therefore, that medical practice, in this respect, still has to catch up with moral theory.

2. Decisions by Physicians

One reason for not involving a patient may be the thought that resuscitation is futile. Often it is understood that nontreatment decisions based on the futility of treatment are the sole responsibility of the physician; this means that in those cases the patient does not have to be involved in the decision.

Hence, the "futile" judgment does two things: first, it implies that a certain treatment should not be carried out, and second it implies that (only) the doctor decides, because she is the expert. "Futility" has the air of the objectivity of scientific evidence. This is what provides the justification for not involving the patient: his opinion cannot change the facts. Leaving aside the philosophical question of whether such objective truths exist at all, the test for any definition of futility is the reasonableness of the combination of the two implications.

What, then, is the definition of futility? For this, two aspects should be distinguished: one concerns the effectiveness of the treatment and the other the proportionality (burden/benefit ratio) of it. Applying the test just specified, one is tempted to conclude that determining the effectiveness of resuscitation is a medical judgment whereas determining the proportionality in the individual case is not, that is, not solely. However, the matter is a little bit more complicated.

Firstly, determining the effectiveness of resuscitation is not free of value judgments. Describing effectiveness, one uses certain end points; in the case of CPR these are, for instance, restoration of cardiac rhythm, 24-h survival, survival to discharge, and long-term survival. The choice for one of these is based on values. It is common to describe success rates of CPR in terms of survival to hospital discharge, for instance. This implies that the time before discharge has less value.

Secondly, if only treatments with 0% chance of success were considered futile, there would hardly be any futile treatments in medicine. Mostly, one uses a cutoff point below which one considers the treatment futile. The choice of this cutoff point is precisely that, a choice. Still, as long as these choices are shared among peers and as long as they are made on a population level, determining effectiveness should be left to the physician(s!).

The assessment of the burden/benefit ratio on the individual level, however, is incomplete without the patient's perception of both the burdens and the benefits. Determining the proportionality of CPR in the individual case is therefore a matter for discussion between doctor and patient.

This is not to say that doctors are not entitled to opinions. It is only that opinions should not be "medicalized." Doctors are good judges of what a patient may be advised to choose, but it must be advice only, not a decision the patient is not even aware of. This is of course supported by the nowdays common adherence to the principle of autonomy. However, one should warn against an atomistic view on autonomy. It is only by shared decision making, not by leaving patients alone with the decision, that the mutual trust between patient and physician is strengthened.

C. Deciding in the Case of Incompetent Patients

In spite of DNR policies seeking an early discussion with the patient, it is inevitable that sometimes a physician has to decide about resuscitating an incompetent patient. It is beyond the scope of this contribution to discuss at length the rules of decision making in these circumstances, but the main lines may be described.

In accordance with what was previously said, a physician may unilaterally make a DNR decision if resuscitation is futile. The patient's opinion is not decisive in these circumstances, and the fact that the opinion is unknowable, due to the state of incompetence, does not influence the decision-making process.

However, when disproportionality forms the basis for a DNR decision, the opinion of the incompetent patient is deeply missed. There are several ways to compensate for this; none of them, however, are completely satisfactory. These compensatory strategies all aim at constructing an autonomous wish of the now incompetent patient.

The most important strategy is to look for written evidence of the patient's opinion. If she, before becoming incompetent, made up an advance directive, one usually accepts this as a substitute for the actual wish. In spite of the apparent strength of this substitute (no need to guess, it is all written down!), there are at least two problems with advance directives.

Because of the fact that the patient at the time of writing the directive does not know what is to come, she will use broad terms to cover different situations. Thus the specificity decreases and one will be able to ask, Is this what she really meant? The second problem concerns the continuity of the wish. People tend to accommodate new circumstances—they learn to live with them. Therefore, a now incompetent patient might have changed her opinion on the once fictitious but now actual circumstances. Unfortunately, we are not able to hear this new opinion because of the incompetence. Of course this is all a thought experiment; many incompetent patients are beyond opinions. Nevertheless this experiment teaches us that we can ask a second question: Would she still think of it in the same way?

One could argue, of course, that one need not worry about this second question, because the person who wrote the advance directive consciously took the "risk" of living (while incompetent) with a nonactual wish. Such a strategy would be very practical, but would not take away the moral problem.

In the absence of advance directives one could ask relatives whether they know of relevant utterances of the patient. If such statements exist, they may be very helpful in determining the right course of action. Nevertheless a third problem is added to the two mentioned above: it is not certain that the patient, when saying what she said, meant to give directives for deciding in case of incompetence.

If no relevant utterances are known, a values history might help; if the patient has always lived by certain values (religious or nonreligious), these should be re-flected in the decision. The regulating power of the value history itself will not be very large; some interpretation will be necessary before the general value fits the specific circumstance.

Beyond this not even a shadow of an autonomous wish can be constructed. Then one has to rely on a best-interests judgment. These should be made by the physician and the relatives of the patient together. Their task is to place themselves in the patient's place and decide from her perspective. This amounts to Hare's role-reversal, but with only the patient's preferences counting (R. M. Hare, 1981. *Moral Thinking*. Clarendon Press, Oxford). It should be stressed that, however difficult, the decision has to be faced because avoiding it will imply a decision in favor of CPR by default.

D. DNR Policy

1. Introduction

The core of a DNR policy is outlined in the previous section. Here the pros and cons of formal policy and some aspects of executing a DNR policy are discussed. In this contribution a DNR policy is understood to mean a total of formalized agreements on the level of a unit or on the level of an institute concerning the resuscitation of patients. A DNR policy can be laid down in a written protocol, but that is not an absolute requirement.

For a DNR policy to function well, one would need to settle the following issues:

— The type of policy
— The exception and the rule
— When to initiate a discussion on CPR
— The meaning of a DNR decision for other caregivers
— How to record the decision
— Evaluating the decision

Not all of these are equally morally laden. How and where to record the DNR decision, for instance, is morally neutral and contingent upon local customs. Hence this matter will not be discussed at length here. The same goes more or less for the way and frequency with which a DNR decision is evaluated.

This does not mean, however, that those issues are completely void of morals. One could argue that rules form an expression of certain values. With respect to DNR decisions the following virtues are considered relevant: careful attention to technical knowledge and skills; respect for the patient; honesty, sincerity, and faith; patience, modesty, and stamina; benevolence, compassion, and humanity; and an open attitude and a readiness to give an account of one's decisions. Especially the latter are important when settling the procedural aspects of a DNR policy. It could be stated, therefore, that rules for recording and evaluating DNR should reflect these virtues.

2. Pros and Cons

In 1976 the first DNR protocols were published. Since then they have become widespread, at least in the United States. This development was partly triggered by positions taken in influential government reports and by the fact that the Joint Commission on Accreditation of Healthcare Organizations made a DNR policy a prerequisite for accreditation. In the Netherlands, DNR policies nowadays come into use more and more.

Several arguments against protocols as such have been put forward:

— They are formulated in general terms and hence are not useful in individual cases
— They may justify wrong decisions
— They weaken professional autonomy
— Values behind protocols remain hidden and need not be shared

On the other hand, many endorse protocols because

— They improve the quality of decision making
— They can help control the costs of health care
— They form an instrument for providing insight into medical decisions

Balancing these arguments need not be an entirely theoretical matter. Many studies have reported a positive effect of protocols, in the sense that decisions were made more openly and more explicitly and that they were recorded more often. Also, implementing a DNR protocol appeared to help create an atmosphere in which pointless efforts to postpone death were no longer undertaken. One study showed that CPR rates and days on ventilatory support decreased after implementing a DNR policy.

Apart from (but of course underlined by) these empirical data, it can be argued that protocols on balance should be judged positively. As long as they are not interpreted as fixed rules but more as guidelines, professional autonomy remains intact. This would also imply that one would need someone to adjust the guidelines to the specific circumstances, and this could help prevent wrong decisions. In short, guidelines may enhance the quality of decision making without obfuscating responsibilities.

3. Types of Protocols

There are mainly two types of DNR protocols. There are protocols in which a dichotomy is used, CPR or DNR, and those in which the DNR decision is part of one or several "care categories." In this latter case other NTDs are part of the protocol. A famous example is the protocol described in 1976 by a committee of the Massachusetts General Hospital:

— Class A, maximal therapeutic effort
— Class B, maximal therapeutic effort but with daily evaluation because probability of survival is low
— Class C, selective limitation of therapeutic measures
— Class D, all therapy can be discontinued

In some protocols one of the care categories consists of a combination of certain measures that are to be withheld. "No CPR and no ICU" is a well-known example. Such combinations are mostly unfortunate. There is no compelling reason why patients who are not to be resuscitated could never benefit from ICU admittance.

Protocols with several classes have the advantage of preventing wide interpretations of DNR decisions (see Section I.B.2) by being explicit about other NTDs. In general three classes would seem to suffice. Class 1 would imply maximal therapeutic effort, and class 3 maximal palliative care (comfort measuers only). In between these two, there would be an unspecified class in which treatments which are to be withheld (including CPR) are to be mentioned.

4. The Exception and the Rule

In theory one could choose as a baseline either one of the following rules: "resuscitate always, unless a DNR decision exists," or "never resuscitate, unless it is specified that CPR is allowed." In general, both in the United States and in the Netherlands, the first rule is used in hospitals. In Dutch nursing homes the opposite appears to be the rule.

There are several reasons for appointing CPR the rule and DNR the exception. First of all, losing time while figuring out whether or not to resuscitate a patient with an arrest lessens her chance of survival. Therefore it has to be absolutely clear what to do in case of an emergency. Of course this is not an argument for CPR as the rule because clarity can also be achieved with DNR as the rule. The problem, however, is that there will always be patients in a hospital for whom a decision (clarity) has not yet been made. When such a patient arrests, a resuscitation should be started promptly. That is only achieved by adopting CPR as the rule.

The stand that a resuscitation should be started promptly is not based on medical information only. Behind this is the position that resuscitating once too often is preferable to arbitrarily forgoing CPR in a patient who might benefit from it or want it, because one has to err on the side of life. By doing so, one shows respect for life.

Not only should CPR be the rule, it is also desirable that DNR remain the exception. A presumption in favor of treatment implies that a DNR decision can be made only after careful scrutiny and justification.

Others argue, however, that since CPR has such low chances of success and is such an invasive kind of treatment, the principle of the integrity of the human body demands that doctors resuscitate only after informed consent (in advance, of course) of the patient.

The balancing of these arguments is highly influenced by the weight one attributes to the principle of respect for life (some would say sanctity of life) and to the integrity of the body. Nevertheless, even when one chooses CPR as the rule (as is done in this *article*), the counterargument is strong enough to stimulate early decision making.

5. When to Initiate a Discussion on CPR

The previous section ended with the conclusion that one should not hesitate in raising the issue of whether or not CPR would be desirable. But what is the ideal timing for this?

Some would say as early as possible. The American Heart Association, for instance, suggests discussing CPR with every adult patient admitted to the hospital or with their surrogates (AHA, 1992). The drawback of this policy in a hospital setting is that in the many cases where cardiopulmonary arrest is highly unlikely, this discussion will seem misplaced. In case of admission to a nursing home, however, this is certainly the policy of choice, since nursing home residents are more at risk for serious illnesses that may involve the necessity of resuscitation.

Others (such as the American Medical Association) plead for a policy of discussing CPR "only" with patients at risk for cardiopulmonary arrest. The latter policy runs the risk of losing the patient as a partner in the discussion. Typically, the possibility of cardiopulmonary arrest becomes clear as a patient's condition deteriorates; at that point the patient often is no longer competent. Moreover, by discussing CPR only with sicker patients, one reinforces the belief that such discussion signifies a bleak prognosis.

The choice for one of these policies will depend to a large extent on the *couleur locale*. In the Netherlands, for instance, a policy of always discussing CPR upon admission would meet with strong resistance both from patients and from physicians. In the United States the Patient Self-Determination Act may have created a climate in which such discussions are understood better. Thus the consequences of a policy differ with the setting. It should be stressed, however, that whatever policy one chooses, a DNR decision has to be considered at a moment where the course of the illness still allows consultation of the patient.

6. The Meaning of a DNR Decision for Other Caregivers

A DNR decision should be binding for other caregivers within the same institute. If such a decision could easily be ignored it might as well not exist. This means that also the physician on call, who has probably not been involved in the decision-making process, should go along with the decision. Objections should lead to a discussion with the attending physician, not to ignoring a DNR decision.

The same goes for surgeons and anesthesiologists. The argument has been put forward that since anesthesia implies a calculated risk for an arrest, a DNR decision should be ignored during anesthesia. This would mean asking the specialists involved to work with their hands tied. Although one can see this problem, disregarding all DNR decisions categorically would be the wrong solution. If the risk of an arrest is really increased during a certain procedure (this goes for procedures other than surgery as well), this should be treated as a relevant piece of information to be discussed with the patient in advance.

When the patient is discharged from the hospital and no changes in the reasons underlying a DNR decision have occurred, then the decision and the arguments involved have to be reported to the physician who continues the treatment. This is often forgotten, at least in the Netherlands.

III. CONCLUSION

Since in hospitals it is common practice to resuscitate any patient with a cardiac and/or breathing arrest, these phenomena are part of the final, common pathway to death, and resuscitation in itself is a rather violent treatment, thinking about whether or not to resuscitate is very appropriate. Moreover, because do-not-resuscitate decisions are made in advance, when no emergency exists (yet), one has time to weigh burdens and benefits. This makes DNR decisions a paradigm case for describing and regulating the decision-making process in non-treatment decisions.

Also See the Following Articles

AUTONOMY • DEATH, MEDICAL ASPECTS OF • INFORMED CONSENT • MEDICAL CODES AND OATHS

Bibliography

Asplund, K., and Britton, M. (1990). Do-not-resuscitate orders in Swedish medical wards. *J. Intern. Med.,* **228,** 139–145.

Davila, F. (1996). The impact of do not resuscitate and patient care category policies on CPR and ventilator support rates. *Arch. Intern. Med.* **156,** 405–408.

DeBard, M. L. (1981). Cardiopulmonary resuscitation: Analysis of six years' experience and review of the literature. *Ann. Emerg. Med.* **10,** 408–416.

Ebell, M. H. (1992). Prearrest predictors of survival following in-hospital cardiopulmonary resuscitation: A meta-analysis. *J. Fam. Pract.* **34**(5), 551–558.

Elam, J. O., Brow, E. S., and Elder, J. D. (1954). Artificial respiration by mouth-to-mask method. A study of the respiratory gas exchange of paralyzed patients ventilated by operator's expired air. *N. Engl. J. Med.* **250,** 749.

Gleeson, K., and Wise S. (1990). The do-not-resuscitate order. Still too little too late. *Arch. Intern. Med.,* **150,** 1057–1060.

Henneman, E. A., Baird, B., Bellamy, P. E., Faber, L. L., and Oye, R. K. (1994). Effect of do not resuscitate orders on the nursing care of critically ill patients. *Am. J. Crit. Care,* **3,** 467–472.

Jayes, R. L., Zimmerman, J. E., Wagner, D. P., Draper, E. A., and Knaus, W. A. (1993). Do not resuscitate orders in intensive care units. Current practices and recent changes. *JAMA,* **270,** 2213–2217.

Jonsson, P. V., McNamee, M., and Campion, E. W. (1988). The "do not resuscitate" order. A profile of its changing use. *Arch. Intern. Med.* **148,** 2373–2375.

Kouwenhoven, W. B., Jude, J. R., and Knickerbocker, G. G. (1960). Closed chest massage. JAMA (1986). **173,** 1064–1067.

Lipton, H. L. (1986). Do-not-resuscitate decisions in a community hospital. JAMA, **256,** 1164–1169.

McGracth, R. B. (1987). In-house cardiopulmonary resuscitation—After a quarter of a century. *Ann. Emerg. Med.* **16,** 1365–1368.

Safar, P., Escarraga, L. A., and Elam, J. O. (1958). A comparison of mouth-to-mouth and mouth-to-airway methods of artificial respiration with the chest-pressure arm-lift methods. *N. Engl. J. Med.* **258,** 671.

Stolman, C. J., Gregory, J. J., Dunn, D., and Ripley, B. (1989). Evaluation of the do not resuscitate orders at a community hospital. *Arch. Intern. Med.* **149,** 1851–1856.

Strull, W. M., Lo, B., and Charles, G. (1984). Do patients want to participate in medical decision making? *J. Am. Med. Assoc.* **252,** 2990–2994.

Uhlmann, R. F., Cassel, C. K., and McDonald, W. J. (1984). Some treatment withholding implications of no code orders in an academic hospital. *Crit. Care Med.* **12,** 879–881.

Uhlmann, R. F., McDonald, W. J., and Inui, T. S. (1984). Epidemiology of no-code orders in an academic hospital. *West. J. Med.* **140,** 114–116.

van Delden, J. J. M. (1993). "Deciding Not to Resuscitate" (in Dutch). Van Gorcum, Assen.

van der Maas, P. J., van Delden, J. J. M., and Pijnenborg, L. (1992). "Euthanasia and Other Medical Decisions Concerning the End of Life." Elsevier, Amsterdam.

Varon, J., and Sternbach, G. L. (1991). Cardiopulmonary resuscitation: Lessons from the past. *J. Emerg. Med.* **9,** 503–507.

Wenger, N. S., Pearson, M. L., Desmond, K. A., *et al.* (1995). Epidemiology of do not resuscitate orders. *Arch. Intern. Med.* **155,** 2056–2062.

DRUGS: MORAL AND LEGAL ISSUES

Douglas N. Husak
Rutgers University

GLOSSARY

consequentialist Any theory that assesses the moral status of an act by reference to its effects.

Controlled Substances Act The 1970 statute that created the current basis for most federal and state regulation of drugs.

drug Any substance other than food which by its chemical nature effects the structure or function of the living organism.

Harrison Narcotics Act The 1914 statute that first subjected narcotics to federal controls.

Marijuana Tax Act The 1937 statute that first subjected marijuana to federal controls.

nonconsequentialist Describing any theory that assesses the moral status of an act by reference to something other than its effects.

paternalism A rationale that purports to justify coercion in order to protect the person coerced.

recreational use Use designed to increase the pleasure or euphoria of the user.

THE MORAL AND LEGAL ISSUES OF DRUG USE are organized around 10 related but distinct questions that need to be addressed in any comprehensive examination of this subject. Rather than beginning by separating drugs into different categories, this entry discusses some of the important moral issues that arise in the use of drugs generally, and how these issues affect drug laws and policies.

I. WHAT ARE DRUGS? IS THE QUESTION IMPORTANT?

An account of the moral and legal issues surrounding drug use should describe the parameters of the inquiry by addressing the prior question of what a drug is—and whether an adequate definition is needed. A definition would be helpful in deciding whether alcohol and tobacco are within the scope of the discussion. Unfortunately, no single characterization of drugs is used in each discipline; different conceptions are employed for different purposes. Perhaps the most frequently cited definition in the medical profession is "any substance other than food which by its chemical nature affects the structure or function of the living organism." This definition does not refer to the legal status of a substance; a substance need not be regulated by law in order for it to be categorized as a drug. For this reason, this definition departs from ordinary language. Speakers of English do not tend to classify a substance as a drug unless its use is illegal. A minority of the public believe that alcohol and nicotine qualify as drugs, whereas an overwhelming majority agree that heroin and cocaine are drugs. Despite this tension with everyday speech, the foregoing medical definition of drugs is useful. Part of the objective of a moral analysis of drug use is to help decide whether existing attitudes, laws, and policies are sensible. If arguments about the moral status of drug use cannot be applied to legal substances because they are not defined as drugs, a moral analysis is deprived of its critical potential, and hard questions are resolved by definitional fiat.

Still, the foregoing definition is problematic for three reasons. First, it is not always easy to say when an effect on structure or function is due to the *chemical* nature of a substance. A person who swallows a bullet undergoes a structural change by chemical processes. Does the bullet thereby become a drug? Second, the definition presupposes some baseline from which judgments are made about whether the structure or function of an organism has been affected. Is this baseline statistical, normative, or some combination of the two? Does a substance that blocks ultraviolet radiation qualify as a drug because it decreases the probability that an average person will contract skin cancer? Finally, this definition precludes the possibility that a food can be a drug. Applications of this definition require a clear conception of the nature of foods. Some substances, such as herbs, seem to share characteristics of both foods *and* drugs.

One might hope that legislation regulating drug use would have succeeded in clarifying the concept of a drug. Surprisingly, statutes provide no such clarification. Statutory definitions might be sought in two places—the Controlled Substances Act, or the Food, Drug, and Cosmetic Act. The former Act creates the authority to regulate "drugs or controlled substances." "Substance" is undefined, and a substance is "controlled" if the Act regulates it. Anything the statute regulates becomes a controlled substance. Thus the question of whether a substance is or is not a drug is irrelevant to the issue of whether that substance is eligible for regulation under the terms of the Controlled Substances Act.

The Food, Drug, and Cosmetic Act includes a complicated definition of drugs. Basically, the definition identifies drugs as "substances recognized in the official *United States Pharmacopeia*," "substances intended for use in the diagnosis, cure, mitigation, treatment, or prevention of disease in man or animals," or "substances (other than food) intended to affect the structure or any function of the body of man or other animals." The first of these disjuncts simply defers to the expertise of persons with authority to include or to delete a substance from the *Pharmcopeia*. No insight is provided as to how these experts make their decisions. In fact, political rather than pharmacological considerations often influence these determinations. Tobacco was removed from the *Pharmcopeia* in order to persuade legislators from tobacco-producing states to support passage of the Food and Drug Act.

The latter two disjuncts of this definition identify drugs by a peculiar reference to intentions. Substances qualify as drugs if they are *intended* to have a given use or effect. The statute does not identify the person(s) whose intentions are relevant. In any event, this reference to intentions produces some curious results. Two substances can be identical in both their molecular structure and their effects on the body, yet one but not the other can satisfy this definition and thereby qualify as a drug.

This state of confusion and uncertainty about what constitutes a drug may seem intolerable. Classifying a substance as a drug has extraordinary significance to the public; presumably there must be some reasonably clear criteria of what a drug is so that these labels might be challenged. On the other hand, a precise definition may not be needed in order to make progress in preparing a moral and legal analysis of drug use. Why would anyone think it is crucial to decide, for example, whether an herb is a food or a drug? Perhaps the standards that should be applied to assess the morality or legality of the use of drugs should be no different from those that should be applied to assess the morality or legality of the use of substances that are not drugs. If these standards apply indifferently to both drugs and nondrugs, an analysis of moral and legal issues need not await a more precise definition. One of the most important preliminary questions an analysis must address is whether drugs are *sui generis* and special, so that the moral and legal principles that apply to their use are somehow fundamentally different and inapplicable to the use of substances that are not drugs.

II. THE PURPOSE FOR WHICH A DRUG IS USED

A few substances—such as LSD and heroin—are popularly believed to be wrongful to use in any circumstances. For many drugs, however, such sweeping judgments are not made. Attempts to decide whether most drugs are good or bad are like attempts to decide whether fires are good or bad: it depends on the purposes for which they are used. Drugs are used for a wide variety of purposes, and reasonable moral and legal judgments about drug use must be sensitive to these several purposes. A taxonomy of different purposes must be devised, so that the contrast between legitimate and illegitimate drug use can be developed. Perhaps the most important distinctions are between religious, medicinal, and recreational drug use. Since the exercise of religious expression is widely believed to be a fundamental right, the use of drugs in ceremonial contexts, such as the use of wine in Christian sacraments, is almost never subjected to criticim. Some (but not all) states allow peyote to be consumed for religious purposes. Similarly, the use of drugs by medical practitioners who act in good faith to treat disease and illness seldom gives rise to serious moral controversies. Doctors are given wide (but hardly unlimited) freedom to prescribe the drugs they believe to be most effective in treating disease and illness. But the use of drugs for recreational purposes—that is, to increases pleasure and euphoria—is frequently condemned in the strongest moral and legal terms.

If moral criticism is reserved largely for recreational drug use, it becomes crucial to decide whether a given use is recreational. Unfortunately, the foregoing purposes cannot be distinguished so clearly. The ingestion of a drug to alleviate depression, or to combat fatigue and boredom, is not easily classified as recreational or medicinal. Persons who drink caffeine in order to remain alert are not obviously using the drug to treat a medical condition. And if drug addiction itself should be regarded as a disease, the use of a substance to alleviate the symptoms of that disease should be evaluated differently from the use of that same substance by nonaddicts. To complicate matters still further, many drug users maintain that illicit substances contribute to creativity and psychic development. The use of a drug to enhance enlightenment or to expand consciousness may or may not give rise to the same moral and legal concerns as the use of that drug to "get high." These purposes for using drugs raise somewhat different issues from paradigm cases of recreational use. Still, the particular purpose that is consistently identified as morally problematic is the use of a drug to create pleasure or euphoria. In most contexts, this purpose is easily recognized.

Thus the question of whether a given drug is "legal" or "illegal" is greatly oversimplified. A given drug may be legal when used for some purposes, but illegal when used for other purposes. This conclusion is plausible in the moral realm as well. Whatever moral judgment might be made about the use of opium to enhance sexual enjoyment, for example, the use of that same drug under medical supervision to alleviate the pain of a terminally ill cancer patient is clearly an altogether different matter. The Controlled Substances Act makes the content of legal judgments responsive to the objective or purpose of the user by placing various substances on five distinct statutory schedules. This placement affects such matters as manufacturing quotas, import restrictions, dispensing limits, and criminal penalties for unlawful trafficking. Use per se is not proscribed; the Act effectively prohibits use by prohibiting possession. The criteria by which substances are assigned to their respective schedules are somewhat obscure and have given rise to litigation. Some substances, such as marijuana and heroin, are placed on Schedule I, and are thought to have "no accepted medical use." Other substances, such as cocaine and amphetamine-like stimulants, are placed on Schedule II, and are thought to have "a currently accepted medical use" but, like Schedule I substances, to have a "high potential for abuse."

III. RECENT HISTORY OF DRUG LAWS AND POLICIES

In the early part of the 20th century, a few states began to restrict the purchase and use of cocaine, marijuana, and the opiates. Millions of Americans consumed drugs in widely available tonics and patent medicines. Perhaps 200,000 Americans, many of whom were middle and upper-class southern Whites, were addicts at the end of the 19th century.

Federal controls began in 1914, when Congress passed the Harrison Narcotics Act. This Act was designed to bring domestic traffic in narcotics under a federally supported licensing system by requiring the registration of sellers and dispensers of opiates or cocaine. Soon thereafter, the Supreme Court held that physicians could not prescribe narcotics to their addicted patients. Addiction was quickly transformed from a medical problem to a criminal justice problem. The early part of the 20th century included a temperance movement that culminated in a Constitutional Amendment to prohibit the manufacture, sale, or transportation (but not the possession or use) of alcohol. The repeal of alcohol prohibition in 1933 led few Americans to demand a return to the time when narcotics were unregulated. In 1937, Congress effectively added marijuana to the list of illicit substances by passage of the Marijuana Tax Act. In 1970, Congress supplanted previous statutory schemes for prohibiting drugs by enacting the Comprehensive Drug Abuse Prevention and Control Act, popularly known as the Controlled Substances Act. The great majority of states model their drug prohibitions after this Act, although the details of their regulatory schemes vary from one jurisdiction to another.

IV. THE LEGAL ENFORCEMENT OF MORAL JUDGEMENTS

Two normative questions about recreational drug use must be distinguished. First, what moral judgments should be made about recreational drug use itself? Second, what laws about recreational drug use are justifiable? These issues are almost certainly related. The supposition that recreational drug use is morally impermissible is probably a necessary condition for the justification of criminal prohibitions. Unless someone were prepared to morally condemn the recreational use of a given drug, it is hard to see why he would favor criminal laws against the use of that drug, or seek to deter its use through criminal punishment. But the converse relation is much less straightforward. Even commentators who express moral reservations about the use of a given drug frequently conclude that criminal prohibitions are unjustified.

These commentators provide a number of reasons against using the criminal law to enforce moral judgments about recreational drug use. Many researchers have concluded that drug proscriptions are ineffective and/or counterproductive. Attempts to curtail recreational drug use in a free society have not been especially successful. No proposed measures to further reduce either supply or demand seem realistic. As long as there is a desire for drugs among the public, and a strong economic incentive to produce and distribute them, the effectiveness of legislation to combat drug use is bound to be limited. Despite several years of waging a "drug war" that has consumed countless millions of dollars in law enforcement, illicit drug use continues unabated. Perhaps these efforts are doomed to failure; the use of psychoactive substances to alter consciousness is pervasive in human history. The very scale of the phenomenon of illicit drug use is daunting; over 70 million living Americans have violated drug laws, including a majority of those born between 1950 and 1970.

In adddition, efforts to punish drug users have pro-

duced many negative consequences that a number of commentators—such as Ethan Nadelmann—believe to be worse than the effects of drugs themselves. As proved to be the case in the era of alcohol prohibition, current proscriptions of drugs such as marijuana and heroin provide lucrative opportunities for organized crime. Some addicts resort to predatory offenses to gain money to buy illicit drugs—which are expensive not so much because they cost more to produce than alcohol or tobacco, but because they are illegal. Law enforcement has been corrupted by the drug trade, and drug laws have been selectively enforced—often to the detriment of minorities. The criminal justice system has been overwhelmed by drug offenders, diverting resources from other important concerns. Physicians are unable or unwilling to use widely abused drugs for legitimate medical purposes. Disrespect and mistrust of law are widespread. Drug users have died or become ill after ingesting impure and contaminated substances. The international consequences of America's drug war are deeply troubling. Persons punished for drug offenses suffer the most from drug prohibitions. The war on drugs has made criminals of millions of Americans whose behavior is otherwise lawful. Families have been torn apart because young parents are sent to jail for drug offenses. In assessing the negative social effects of drugs, it is imperative to distinguish the bad effects of drugs per se from the bad effects of drug prohibitions. Clearly, a great many of the negative social consequences attributed to drugs are more plausibly attributed to the enforcement of drug prohibitions.

V. WHAT MORAL PREDICATES SHOULD BE APPLIED TO DRUG USE?

Various negative judgments might be made about recreational drug use. Only some of these negative judgments are moral in nature. Recreational drug use might be foolish, stupid, unhealthy, irrational, and the like. But these judgments do not clearly amount to moral condemnation, and probably cannot be invoked to justify criminal prohibitions. Of course, the line between moral and nonmoral criticism is elusive, and different philosophers have drawn it in different places. But it is important to emphasize that the recreational use of drugs need not be encouraged or recommended if moral judgments against drug use cannot be defended. Morality permits persons to make less than ideal choices.

The most familiar *moral* predicate that might be applied is that some or all recreational drug use is *wrong-*

ful. If this predicate were appropriate to apply, recreational drug users would be eligible for condemnation and censure. But negative moral predicates other than wrongfulness might be applied to some or all recreational drug use. Some philosophers believe that the question, "What kind of person should I be?" merits more attention than it has received from moral theorists, most of whom have sought to evaluate conduct rather than character. The prospects for defending a negative moral evaluation of recreational drug use seem more promising within an ethics of virtue. Perhaps the truly virtuous person abstains from recreational drug use altogether. Or perhaps her recreational drug use is moderate, and she avoids a degree of intoxication that interferes with her cognitive and volitional capacities. Of course, an account of human excellence must be provided in order to support these judgments. Theorists can be expected to disagree about the extent to which virtuous persons pursue pleasure. But if these judgments were defensible, persons who use drugs for recreational purposes—at least to excess—would be lacking in human excellence. They would fall short of an ideal to which all persons should aspire.

The distinction between the judgment that recreational drug use is morally wrongful and the judgment that such use indicates a character defect or lack of virtue is important for purposes of addressing the preceding question about the enforcement of moral judgments. Virtue-based judgments are not ordinarily thought to provide a rationale for legal policies, and certainly not for criminal prohibitions. Many kinds of conduct are contrary to plausible conceptions of human excellence—such as failing to study in school—but neither are nor ought to be eligible for punishment by law. The criminal sanction is typically thought to establish a floor below which persons are not permitted to fall, rather than a ceiling to which persons are exhorted to aspire.

VI. CONSEQUENTIALIST AND NONCONSEQUENTIALIST CONSIDERATIONS

The justification of criminal punishment probably depends on the judgment that recreational drug use is morally wrongful. Perhaps this widespread attitude about recreational drug use is little more than an indefensible prejudice that will eventually be changed. But how might one attempt to support this moral judgment? Two very different kinds of answers might be given.

First, the alleged wrongfulness may inhere in the mere act of taking a drug for recreational purposes, quite apart from any effects the drug may cause. Second, the alleged wrongfulness may inhere in the effects caused by the drug.

For two reasons, the nonconsequentialist alternative is problematic. If recreational drug use were alleged to be inherently wrongful, the difficulty of defining drugs would assume critical importance. The question of whether a given substance qualifies as a drug would become crucial. Moreover, this nonconsequentialist alternative would be hard-pressed to explain how or why the wrongfulness of using a given drug for recreational purposes could be greater than the wrongfulness of using some other drug. The most plausible reason to suppose that the use of crack is more objectionable than the use of caffeine, for example, depends on the different effects these drugs produce. If the effects of different drugs were thought to be irrelevant to the content of moral judgments about their recreational use, all drugs would appear to be equally objectionable.

Thus the consequentialist alternative, which locates the alleged wrongfulness of recreationsl drug use in its effects, seems to be more plausible. This alternative need assign no special status to drugs relative to other substances. Presumably, if two different substances were to produce identical effects, any moral or legal judgments that apply to the recreational use of the first substance should apply with comparable force to the second. Since each existing drug produces somewhat different effects, consequentialist accounts provide a basis to maintain that the use of some drugs might be worse than the use of other drugs, while the use of still other drugs might be altogether unobjectionable.

Consequentialist defenses, however, encounter difficulties of their own. If the effects of using a drug were indistinguishable from the effects of an activity that did not involve the use of a drug, consequentialists would assign the same evaluation to both acts. Some theorists believe that the same altered states of consciousness produced by recreational drug use can be created by such activities as meditation, physical exertion, prayer, or fasting. If they are correct, these activities are just as wrongful as drug use—a conclusion that few are likely to accept, and no one would endeavor to enforce by criminal legislation. Presumably, consequentialists block this conclusion by denying the possibility that such activities as long-distance running *can* produce the same effects as wrongful acts of recreational drug use. But the question remains open.

Despite this difficulty, consequentialists are correct to locate the alleged moral wrongfulness of the recreational use of some or all drugs in their negative effects. Call these negative consequences *harms*. The harms in virtue of which recreational drug use is thought to be wrongful might befall either or both of two parties. First, these harms might be suffered by the user herself. Second, these harms might be suffered by persons other than the user. The first alternative might be described as *paternalistic*. According to a paternalistic rationale, drug use is wrongful because it is harmful to the very persons who use drugs. The second alternative is *nonpaternalistic;* drug use is wrongful because it is harmful to persons other than those who use drugs. Of course, a theorist can combine these alternatives.

Claims that given activities are wrongful on paternalistic grounds are notoriously difficult to assess. Some commentators believe that *no* activity is morally wrongful in virtue of its effects on the persons who engage in it. Suppose a person squanders his talents, fails to develop his potential, lives a very unhealthy lifestyle, and even decides to commit suicide. Such a person might behave stupidly, irrationally, or nonvirtuously, but never wrongfully, as long as only the effects of his behavior on himself are concerned. Other commentators, however, see no reason to withhold moral condemnation of activities that harm the persons who engage in them. Again, the contrast between *moral* and *nonmoral* judgments must be developed in order to assess whether or in what circumstances the impact of irrational and unhealthy choices on oneself becomes eligible for *moral* criticism.

If the alleged wrongfulness of recreational drug use is a function of its consequences on users themselves, are these effects wrongful because of their quantity or their quality? Suppose, for example, that drug use is deemed to be wrongful because it is unhealthy. Of course, much behavior that is seldom condemned, such as eating junk foods or failing to exercise, is unhealthy as well. An attempt to differentiate drug use from these other unhealthy activities might take two forms. First, the difference may be one of degree. Drug use is wrongful because it is *more* unhealthy, perhaps by an order of magnitude, than these other activities. A defense of this alternative requires empirical evidence about the extent of harm suffered by drug users relative to that suffered by persons who engage in these other activities. Boxing, for example, is probably more harmful than the use of any existing recreational drug. Of course, some drugs are much more harmful than others. By many accounts, tobacco appears to be the most lethal substance, shortening the life expectancy of one quarter of the persons who use it by 10 to 15 years.

Alternatively, the alleged wrongfulness of recreational drug use may be a function of its qualitative effects on users. Perhaps moral condemnation is appropriate because the nature of the harms produced by recreational drug use is sufficiently different in kind from those harms produced by other unhealthy recreational activities. A defense of this alternative requires an account of how the harms suffered by drug users are qualitatively unlike the harms suffered by persons who harm themselves without using drugs. The most promising such qualitative differences cite the faculties that drugs affect. Perhaps those drugs that affect reasoning processes and the brain are morally worse than those drugs and other activities that harm organs like the liver and lungs. This point is explored more fully in the subsequent discussion of addiction.

Paternalism aside, the claim that a given activity is wrongful because it is harmful *to others* is more familiar and less controversial. But the difficulty in condemning recreational drug use under a "harm-to-others" rationale is formidable. Unlike a paradigm case of behavior that is wrongful because it is invariably harmful to others—an act of murder or robbery, for example— each token of recreational drug use need *not* actually harm another. Almost certainly there is no existing drug that causes users to harm others on each and every occasion in which it is consumed. It is hard to see, for example, how a curious adult who experiments with PCP on a single instance in the privacy of her home need be thought to be harming anyone (except perhaps herself). If her activity is to be condemned on the ground that it is harmful to others, the basis for this conclusion must be that her experimentation creates an unacceptable *risk* of harm to others. Arguments that condemn recreational drug use as wrongful on this basis must be evaluated by whatever criteria are applied to assess the moral status of risky behavior. These criteria are enormously controversial.

Perhaps the use of some or all drugs for recreational purposes can be shown to be wrongful because of the unjustifiable risk of harm that such use poses to others. But a defense of this judgment must overcome several obstacles. First, much recreational behavior that does not involve drugs and does not warrant moral or legal condemnation exposes other persons to substantial risks as well. Criteria must be developed to determine whether the risk of harm to others is *unacceptable*. Presumably, the distinction between acceptable and unacceptable risks of harm to others depends primarily on the *extent* of the risk that is created. The issue of whether the use of a drug creates substantial risks of harm to others must be decided drug by drug; the causal linkage between the use of a given drug and the risk of harm to others must be established through careful empirical study. By some estimates, for example, second-hand tobacco smoke causes approximately 18,000 deaths a year. Comparable figures for illicit drugs are difficult to obtain. Here, as elsewhere, the effects of a drug itself must be distinguished from the effects that are produced by criminal proscriptions of that drug.

Moreover, any criteria to distinguish acceptable from unacceptable risks must identify those effects on others that qualify as harms, as opposed to those effects on others that merely produce disutility or are disliked. A person may be unhappy that his friend or neighbor devotes so much time to his hobby or interest, but it is unlikely that his neighbor thereby *harms* him. According to the account of harm defended by Joel Feinberg, a harm requires the violation of a right. If so, many of the socially undesirable consequences frequently attributed to recreational drug use—decreased productivity and reduced levels of motivation in workers, for example—cannot plausibly be described as *harms* to others unless someone has a *right* that workers be highly productive and motivated. Theorists may be unwilling to accept the general claim that others possess these rights.

Adequate criteria to distinguish acceptable from unacceptable risks must also include some determination of the extent to which the activity is valuable or important. Persons subject others to substantial risks of harm simply by driving their cars to the beach, but these risks are typically thought to be justifiable because of the importance of fast and convenient travel. If the euphoria of recreational drug use is dismissed as trivial and unimportant, any risks that such use might pose to others are far more likely to be deemed unjustifiable. But there is little consensus about the value and significance of recreational activities in general—and thus about recreational drug use in particular.

VII. ADDICTION AND AUTONOMY

The judgment that some acts of recreational drug use are wrongful may be based on the claim that some drugs are addictive. How might the supposition that some drugs are addictive support the judgment that recreational use of that drug is morally impermissible? Perhaps the most plausible response is that the phenomenon of addiction is important to an assessment of the moral status of drug use because of the threat that addiction might pose to the autonomy of the user. Persons are generally free to make foolish and unhealthy choices—unless there is some reason to believe that

these choices are nonautonomous. The repeated use of addictive substances might undermine the capacity for autonomous choice that would otherwise protect the agent from interference. Some philosphers have argued that the freedom to use addictive drugs should be infringed in order to protect the agent's capacity for autonomous choice. Evaluating this argument is among the most difficult tasks in an assessment of the moral status of recreational drug use.

Attempts to understand the relationship between addiction and autonomy are doubly problematic. The concept of addiction is far from clear. Only some of the several conceptions of addiction support the judgment that addiction undermines the capacity for autonomous choice. Moreover, moral philosophers have defended radically different conceptions of moral autonomy. Not all such conceptions support the judgment that the use of addictive substances undermines the capacity for autonomous choice.

First, a conception of addiction is required. According to some broad conceptions, virtually *any* activity can be addictive. Persons are said to be "workaholics," "sexaholics," or "chocaholics." No conception so broad is likely to be helpful for the purpose at hand. If the use of a recreational drug is to be condemned because of its addictive properties, and these addictive properties are shared by a great many other activities, no reason has been given to believe that drugs pose a special threat to the autonomy of agents. How might the addictive nature of drugs be different from the (supposed) addictive nature of other unwise and unhealthy activities that are thought to be morally permissible? How might this difference support the conclusion that the use of addictive substances poses a threat to autonomy, unlike the performance of these other activities?

Perhaps no good answer to this question can be given. Many of the criteria of addiction *are* shared by activities that do not involve drugs. Addiction is generally understood to include a craving or psychological compulsion. Addicts typically gain a tolerance for a substance, so that increasingly greater amounts are required to produce the same effect. Addicts usually attach an extraordinarily high priority to the use of a substance relative to other activities that are important to them. Addicts frequently admit to an inability to stop using a substance, despite attempts to do so. But it is unclear how any of these characteristics of addiction might pose a special threat to the capacity for autonomous choice, since the same characteristics apply to many other activities as well. For present purposes, perhaps the most important property of drug addiction is that addicts suffer painful and unpleasant withdrawal symptoms when they stop using the substance to which they are addicted. Resumption of drug use alleviates these symptoms. Presumably this characteristic of drug addiction is not shared by other activities like the playing of video games. Persons "addicted" to video games do not experience painful withdrawal symptoms when these games become unavailable. But persons seemingly suffer painful withdrawal symptoms when love relationships are ended. Again, the distinctive nature of *drug* addiction remains elusive.

If the use of drugs to prevent or to alleviate the severity of withdrawal symptoms is to be regarded as nonautonomous, a conception of autonomy is required to defend this judgment. Some moral and political philosophers equate autonomy with liberty, others with rationality, and still others with freedom of the will. A demonstration of the alleged incompatibility between addictive drug use and the preservation of moral autonomy must proceed differently for each of these conceptions. Consider, for example, the particular conception of autonomy developed by Gerald Dworkin. He construes autonomy as a second-order capacity of persons to reflect critically upon their first-order preferences and desires, and the capacity to accept or to attempt to change these in light of higher-order preferences. The use of some drugs might be destructive of autonomy as so conceived because addiction might prevent persons from bringing their first-order desires into conformity with their higher-order preferences. In other words, someone may desire to use drugs, but prefer that he not desire to use drugs. If he is unable to change his first-order desire to use drugs, his drug use would be categorized as nonautonomous.

Why might someone be unable to change his desire to use drugs in light of his higher-order preference not to use drugs? An addict who tries to bring his first-order desires into conformity with his second-order preference may be unable to succeed because the pain of withdrawal is too severe to bear. If the pain of choosing not to perform an act is sufficiently great, persons are said to have "no choice" but to perform that act. Thus the addict who uses drugs to avoid withdrawal pains might be thought to have "no choice." In other words, his drug use is nonautonomous.

The foregoing argument provides some reason to conclude that the use of addictive substances might present a special threat to autonomy and thereby render drug use morally wrongful. But a number of qualifications are needed. First, many drug users may experience no tension whatsoever between their first- and second-order desires: they want to use drugs, and they want to want to use drugs. Moreover, many users of even the most addictive drugs do not exhibit all or most of the symptoms of addiction. Only some regular users of heroin ever become addicts. Empirical studies that indicate the possibility of casual, nonaddictive use of addictive drugs demonstrate that more is involved in undermining the capacity for autonomous choice than the persistent use of an addictive substance. In addition, in any sensible conception of addiction, not all illicit drugs are addictive. Many commentators condemn the use of some substances—such as LSD—even though they satisfy few if any of the criteria of addiction. In particular, persons who stop using these substances do not experience painful withdrawal symptoms. If the use of such drugs is wrongful, some altogether different basis for this judgment must be found. Finally, many drugs that are unquestionably addictive—such as nicotine—are less likely to be included among those examples of drugs that undermine the capacity for autonomous choice. Perhaps attitudes about nicotine are ripe for reexamination. Or perhaps judgments about the destructive effect of addictive substances on autonomous choice must be rethought.

In any event, it seems highly unlikely that the recreational use of all addictive substances that create withdrawal symptoms could be thought to undermine autonomy and justify moral condemnation. The cessation of the use of substances such as caffeine frequently gives rise to unpleasant withdrawal symptoms, but no one supposes that caffeine addicts have wrongfully impaired their precious capacity for autonomous choice. Why not? Presumably, withdrawal symptoms must exceed a given threshold of severity before addicts who use that substance to avoid these symptoms can be said to act nonautonomously. Caffeine withdrawal is not sufficiently severe to warrant the conclusion that drinkers of coffee have "no choice" but to persist. If so, it becomes crucial to determine how severe the withdrawal symptoms of any given drug must be before one should infer that the use of that drug to alleviate those symptoms is nonautonomous. Empirical evidence is required to show whether the withdrawal symptoms of existing addictive drugs exceed that threshold of severity. Does alcohol qualify? How does the withdrawal from crack compare with the severity of withdrawal from the use of tobacco products? Do any or all opiates satisfy the test? Lines are exceedingly difficult to draw here. But such lines must be drawn by persons who suppose that the use of addictive drugs is morally wrongful because they undermine the capacity for autonomous choice.

VIII. DEGREES OF WRONGFULNESS

If drug use is morally wrongful, just *how* wrongful is it? This question has special significance for gauging the appropriate response of law in general and the criminal law in particular. Surely the degree to which wrongdoers deserve blame should be a function of the extent to which their conduct is wrongful. This claim supports the principle of proportionality in sentencing law, according to which the severity of the punishment should be a function of the seriousness of the crime. In order to apply this principle in either morality or law, ordinal rankings of the moral wrongfulness of conduct and of the seriousness of crime are required. For what reasons might an act of recreational drug use be more or less wrongful than other wrongful acts, such as breaking a promise, committing a burglary, or killing a police officer?

Unfortunately, few theories have made systematic attempts to assess the relative wrongfulness of conduct, or the relative seriousness of crime. Judgments about recreational drug use underscore the need for such a theory. For example, many persons condemn the use of hallucinogens in very strong moral terms. The criminal law has responded by imposing punishments of a degree of severity typically reserved for the most violent offenders. The Supreme Court has upheld a sentence of life imprisonment for the offense of cocaine possession. How might such severe punishments be justified? Perhaps recreational drug use *is* extraordinarily wrongful, comparable in seriousness to such wrongful acts as armed robbery or rape. More plausibly, however, the severity of punishment is thought to be necessary to create an adequate deterrent. In light of the private, consensual nature of most drug offenses, violators are very difficult to apprehend and convict. Offenders are warranted in believing that they will evade prosecution. According to some utilitarian conceptions, the degree of punishment should be increased to the extent that offenders are difficult to detect. The severity of these sanctions calls into question the legitimacy of exemplary punishments. It is one thing to believe that recreational drug use merits moral censure, and quite another to think that the degree of condemnation and punishment that is frequently applied is proportionate to the degree to which such activity is wrongful.

IX. SPECIAL CIRCUMSTANCES

How might whatever moral judgments apply to recreational drug use in "normal circumstances" differ when these circumstances are special or unusual? The immediate difficulty, of course, is to identify what might make a circumstance "special" to support a different moral judgment than is typically applied. Note the circumstances in which many persons, including legislators, condemn behavior that is not generally proscribed at all, or increase the punishment of behavior that is usually punished less severely. Alcohol and nicotine provide helpful illustrations. Adults are permitted to consume alcohol, but are not permitted to drive or to fly airplanes while drinking. Adults are permitted to smoke tobacco, but are not permitted to do so in confined public spaces. These judgments are sensible. What is their basis? Presumably, these exceptions acknowledge the circumstances in which the use of some substances may pose a special risk of harm to others. Drugs that dull reflexes or impair judgment are not to be consumed when persons operate vehicles that, even under the best of conditions, create substantial risks of harm to others. Drugs that are smoked in cigarettes or pipes and thereby force others to breathe unhealthy air are condemned on similar grounds.

At least two questions are raised by attempts to make moral judgments about recreational drugs sensitive to the circumstances in which these drugs are used. First, what are the circumstances in which otherwise permissible drug use becomes impermissible, and how should the criminal law respond to these circumstances? Pregnancy provides an example in which reasonable minds may differ about whether legal policy should mirror moral judgment. Suppose that the use of a given drug increases the risk of harm to developing fetuses. If so, the use of that drug by pregnant women is morally problematic relative to the use of that drug by others. Should the law therefore punish pregnant women for what would otherwise be permissible, or increase the punishment for what would otherwise be a less serious offense? Commentators who argue that drug laws are often counterproductive insist that matters are seldom so simple. Would not the threat of such sanctions discourage pregnant drug users from seeking health care? If so, these sanctions are objectionable on the ground that they do more harm than good.

Second, are there cases in which the use of a substance should be condemned altogether, and proscribed without exception, because there are so many circumstances in which the use of that drug is especially risky? In other words, do the exceptions ever swallow the rule? Most commentators resist a blanket prohibition of the recreational use of such drugs as alcohol and tobacco, and reserve their moral condemnation for the special circumstances in which they believe such use is objectionable. But most people endorse a blanket prohibition of the recreational use of such drugs as cocaine and heroin, apparently believing that the circumstances in which such use is objectionable are so numerous that no recreational use should be permitted at all. A principled distinction between drugs that are permissible for recreational purposes generally but impermissible in special circumstances and drugs that are impermissible for recreational purposes altogether is very difficult to draw.

Clearly the most "special" circumstance is that of adolescent use. So much antidrug rhetoric invokes adolescents that no moral or legal perspective on drug use that hopes to be responsive to public concerns can afford to ignore its impact on the drug use of minors. Even those commentators who urge a fundamental rethinking of moral attitudes and legal policies about recreational drug use call for severe punishments of adults who distribute drugs to underage users.

Many laws are designed to offer special protection to adolescents. For example, statutes frequently impose greater punishments on persons who dispense a controlled substance within a given distance of a school. States enhance the punishment of drug distribution to persons under 18. The employment of minors in a drug distribution scheme is often punishable under separate laws.

Why does recreational drug use by adolescents pose particular concerns? Two kinds of answers might be given. First, the use of a given drug may be more harmful when consumed by an adolescent than when consumed by an adult. This determination must be made drug by drug. Second, adolescents may be incompetent to assume the risks that an activity will harm them, even if these risks are comparable in quantity and quality to those assumed by adults. Addictive drugs create a special problem in this context. If persons who are not yet fully autonomous begin to use an addictive substance, they are likely to become addicted before becoming sufficiently mature to make a rational and informed decision about whether to undertake that risk. Many commentators have expressed conerns about the age at which users of nicotine first became addicted.

Do the dangers of adolescent drug use ever provide a good reason to prohibit the use of a drug altogether? Adults who use drugs may set a bad example for adolescents and thereby encourage them to experiment. Such arguments play a prominent role in debates about why present policy toward illicit substances should be continued, although few contemporary theorists are prepared to claim that they provide good reason to proscribe the adult use of tobacco and alcohol. The

argument that a drug should not be used by adults because of the impact that such availability will have on adolescents is made almost exclusively about drugs that are already illicit.

X. ISSUES RELATED TO USE

How do whatever moral and legal judgments are made about recreational drug use pertain to activities related to but distinct from use? Presumably, whatever moral or legal judgments apply to drug use would also apply to drug possession. The freedom (or the lack of freedom) to use a drug seemingly entails the freedom to possess (or not to possess) quantities of that drug for personal use. These judgments would also apply to the production of drugs for personal use. The freedom to use a drug seemingly entails the freedom to produce quantities of that drug for oneself. But the moral status of other activities related to use is more problematic. The moral freedom to use a drug does not entail a comparable freedom to import, sell, or distribute that drug to others; the moral and legal status of these latter activities must be assessed on their own merits. Independent judgments must also be made about the commercial advertising of that drug. Perhaps a vice model is morally and legally appropriate for the recreational use of some or all drugs. Recreational drug use and possession and production for personal use would be allowed, but distribution, mass production, and advertising would be proscribed. Or perhaps most or all drugs should be regulated much like tobacco and alcohol. Drug reformers have said more about the difficulties with our present policy than about the details of a preferable alternative.

Also See the Following Articles

CONSEQUENTIALISM AND DEONTOLOGY • PSYCHOPHARMACOLOGY AND DRUG MARKET

Bibliography

Dworkin, G. (1988). "The Theory and Practice of Autonomy." Cambridge Univ. Press, Cambridge.
Feinberg, J. (1984). "Harm to Others." Oxford Univ. Press, London.
Feinberg, J. (1986). *Harm to Self.* Oxford Univ. Press, London.
Goodin, R. (1992). "No Smoking." Univ. of Chicago Press, Chicago.
Husak, D. (1992). "Drugs and Rights." Cambridge Univ. Press, Cambridge.
Nadelmann, E. (1980). Drug prohibition in the United States: Costs, consequences, and alternatives. *Science* **245**, 939–947.
Richards, D. (1982). "Sex, Drugs, Death and the Law." Rowman & Littlefield, Totowa, NJ.

ISBN 0-12-227066-5

90038